**TENTH EDITION**

# Psychology Applied to Modern Life

## ADJUSTMENT IN THE 21ST CENTURY

**WAYNE WEITEN**
University of Nevada, Las Vegas

**DANA S. DUNN**
Moravian College

**ELIZABETH YOST HAMMER**
Xavier University of Louisiana

**WADSWORTH**
CENGAGE Learning™

Australia • Brazil • Japan • Korea • Mexico • Singapore • Spain • United Kingdom • United States

**Psychology Applied to Modern Life: Adjustment in the 21st Century, Tenth Edition**
Wayne Weiten, Dana S. Dunn, and Elizabeth Yost Hammer

Senior Publisher: Linda Schreiber-Ganster

Executive Editor: Jon-David Hague

Senior Developmental Editor: Kristin Makarewycz

Assistant Editor: Paige Leeds

Editorial Assistant: Sheli DeNola

Media Editor: Lauren Keyes

Marketing Manager: Liz Rhoden

Marketing Assistant: Anna Anderson

Executive Marketing Communications Manager: Talia Wise

Senior Content Project Manager: Pat Waldo

Design Director: Rob Hugel

Art Director: Vernon Boes

Print Buyer: Karen Hunt

Rights Acquisitions Specialist: Don Schlotman

Production Service: Joan Keyes, Dovetail Publishing Services

Text Designer: Liz Harasymczuk

Photo Researcher: Sarah Evertson/Image Quest

Text Researcher: Sue C. Howard

Copy Editor: Jackie Estrada

Proofreader: Mary Falcon

Illustrator: Carol Zuber-Mallison

Cover Designer: Cheryl Carrington

Cover Image: Peter McArthur; inset sky images: Getty Images

Compositor: MPS Content Services

For product information and technology assistance, contact us at **Cengage Learning Customer & Sales Support, 1-800-354-9706.**

For permission to use material from this text or product, submit all requests online at **www.cengage.com/permissions**. Further permissions questions can be e-mailed to **permissionrequest@cengage.com**

Library of Congress Control Number: 2010931646

Student Edition:

ISBN-13: 978-1-111-18663-0

ISBN-10: 1-111-18663-4

Loose-leaf Edition:

ISBN-13: 978-1-111-29798-5

ISBN-10: 1-111-29798-3

**Wadsworth**
20 Davis Drive
Belmont, CA 94002-3098
USA

Cengage Learning is a leading provider of customized learning solutions with office locations around the globe, including Singapore, the United Kingdom, Australia, Mexico, Brazil, and Japan. Locate your local office at **www.cengage.com/global**

Cengage Learning products are represented in Canada by Nelson Education, Ltd.

To learn more about Wadsworth, visit **www.cengage.com/Wadsworth**

Purchase any of our products at your local college store or at our preferred online store **www.CengageBrain.com**

Printed in the United States of America
2 3 4 5 6 7 14 13 12 11

# About the Authors

**WAYNE WEITEN** is a graduate of Bradley University and received his Ph.D. in social psychology from the University of Illinois, Chicago in 1981. He currently teaches at the University of Nevada, Las Vegas. He has received distinguished teaching awards from Division Two of the American Psychological Association (APA) and from the College of DuPage, where he taught until 1991. He is a Fellow of Divisions 1 and 2 of the American Psychological Association. In 1991, he helped chair the APA National Conference on Enhancing the Quality of Undergraduate Education in Psychology and in 1996–1997 he served as President of the Society for the Teaching of Psychology. Weiten has conducted research on a wide range of topics, including educational measurement, jury decision-making, attribution theory, stress, and cerebral specialization. His recent interests have included pressure as a form of stress and the technology of textbooks. He is also the author of *Psychology: Themes & Variations* (Wadsworth, 2010) and the creator of an educational CD-ROM titled *PsykTrek: A Multimedia Introduction to Psychology*.

**DANA S. DUNN** earned his B.A. in psychology from Carnegie Mellon and received his PhD in social psychology from the University of Virginia. He is currently professor of psychology and Director of the Learning in Common Curriculum at Moravian College in Bethlehem, PA. He chaired the Psychology Department at Moravian for six years. A Fellow of the American Psychological Association (APA) and the Association for Psychological Science (APS), Dunn served as President of the Society for the Teaching of Psychology in 2010. A frequent speaker at national and regional disciplinary conferences, Dunn has written numerous articles, chapters, and book reviews concerning his areas of research interest: the teaching of psychology, social psychology, rehabilitation psychology, and educational assessment. He is the author or editor of 13 books, including the *The Practical Researcher* (2010), *Research Methods for Social Psychology* (2009), and *A Short Guide to Writing about Psychology* (2011).

**ELIZABETH YOST HAMMER** earned her B.S. in psychology from Troy State University and received her Ph.D. in social psychology from the Tulane University. She is currently Kellogg Professor in Teaching in the Psychology Department and director of the Center for the Advancement of Teaching at Xavier University of Louisiana in New Orleans. She is a Fellow of Division Two of the American Psychological Association (APA) and is a past President of Psi Chi, the National Honor Society in Psychology. Recently, she was elected as treasurer for the Society for the Teaching of Psychology. She is passionate about teaching and has published on collaborative learning, service learning, the application of social psychological theories to the classroom, and mentoring students. After her experience with Hurricane Katrina, she developed a Psychology of Disasters course.

# To the Instructor

Many students enter adjustment courses with great expectations. They've ambled through their local bookstores, and in the "Psychology" section they've seen numerous self-help books that offer highly touted recipes for achieving happiness for a mere $12.95. After paying far more money to enroll in a college course that deals with the same issues as the self-help books, many students expect a revelatory experience. However, the majority of us with professional training in psychology or counseling take a rather dim view of self-help books and the pop psychology they represent. Psychologists tend to see this literature as oversimplified, intellectually dishonest, and opportunistic and often summarily dismiss the pop psychology that so many students have embraced. Instructors try to supplant pop psychology with more sophisticated academic psychology, which is more complex and less accessible.

In this textbook, we have tried to come to grips with this problem of differing expectations between student and teacher. Our goal has been to produce a comprehensive, serious, research-oriented treatment of the topic of adjustment that also acknowledges the existence of popular psychology and looks critically at its contributions. Our approach involves the following:

● In Chapter 1 we confront the phenomenon of popular self-help books. We try to take the student beneath the seductive surface of such books and analyze some of their typical flaws. Our goal is to make the student a more critical consumer of this type of literature.

● While encouraging a more critical attitude toward self-help books, we do not suggest that they should all be dismissed. Instead, we acknowledge that some of them offer authentic insights. With this in mind, we highlight some of the better books in Recommended Reading boxes sprinkled throughout the text. These recommended books tie in with the adjacent topical coverage and show the student the interface between academic and popular psychology. Additional Recommended Reading boxes can be found in the Weiten Psychology CourseMate (www.cengagebrain.com/shop/ISBN/1111186634).

● We try to provide the student with a better appreciation of the merits of the empirical approach. This effort to clarify the role of research, which is rare for an adjustment text, appears in the first chapter.

● Recognizing that adjustment students want to leave the course with concrete, personally useful information, we end each chapter with an application section. The Applications are "how to" discussions that address everyday problems. While they focus on issues that are relevant to the content of the particular chapter, they contain more explicit advice than the text proper.

In summary, we have tried to make this book both challenging and applied. We hope that our approach will help students better appreciate the value of scientific psychology.

## Philosophy

A certain philosophy is inherent in any systematic treatment of the topic of adjustment. Our philosophy can be summarized as follows:

● We believe that an adjustment text should be a resource book for students. We have tried to design this book so that it encourages and facilitates the pursuit of additional information on adjustment-related topics. It should serve as a point of departure for more learning.

● We believe in theoretical eclecticism. This book will not indoctrinate your students along the lines of any single theoretical orientation. The psychodynamic, behavioral, and humanistic schools of thought are all treated with respect, as are cognitive, biological, evolutionary, and other perspectives.

● We believe that effective adjustment requires taking charge of one's own life. Throughout the book we try to promote the notion that active coping efforts are generally superior to passivity and complacency.

## Changes in the Tenth Edition

One of the exciting things about psychology is that it is not a stagnant discipline. It continues to progress at what seems a faster and faster pace. A good textbook must evolve with the discipline. Although the professors and students who used the earlier editions of this book did not clamor for change, we have made countless content changes to keep up with new developments in psychology—adding and deleting some topics, condensing and reorganizing others, and updating everything (there are about 1,400 new references). A brief overview of some of these changes, listed chapter-by-chapter, can be found on pages viii–xii following this preface.

The most significant change in this edition is the addition of an entirely new chapter devoted to the topic of positive psychology. Although we have had coverage of positive psychology sprinkled throughout the text since this movement surfaced around the turn of the 21st century (most of which remains throughout the book), we feel that the area of positive psychology has matured to the point where it merits a full chapter of its own (Chapter 16). The focus and themes of positive psychology seem highly relevant to the issues discussed in the Adjustment course. We are confident that our greatly expanded coverage of positive psychology will resonate with today's students.

The addition of the new chapter on positive psychology prompted us to reexamine the overall organization of *Psychology Applied to Modern Life*. After some reflection, we decided to shuffle the order of the chapters a bit. We moved the chapter on health psychology (formerly Chapter 14) to follow on the heels of the chapters on stress and coping, so it is now Chapter 5. Similarly, we moved the chapter on sexuality (formerly Chapter 13) so that it follows related chapters on love and intimate relationships, making it Chapter 12. In light of this juggling, 11 of the 15 previously existing chapters have new chapter numbers. We think this reorganization groups related chapters together more effectively. That said, we write our chapters to be largely self-contained so that you can assign them in virtually any order you like.

Yet another significant change is that we have taken the *Personal Explorations Workbook* that has accompanied many previous editions of this text as a separate ancillary and incorporated the vast majority of it into the text itself. You will find the workbook at the very back of this text, after the references and the indexes. Putting it at the end allowed us to print it on special, perforated paper, so you will have the option of having students complete workbook exercises and tear them out for submission as homework. We think the inclusion of the workbook in the text will make it easier to use.

We have also added a new appendix that focuses on the timely issue of sustainability. It explains how sustainability depends on changes in individuals' behavior more than any other single factor. It focuses on the cognitive and behavioral processes that tend to impede environmentally responsible behavior, as well as the alterations in behavior that will be necessary to sustain the world's natural resources for future generations.

## Writing Style

This book has been written with the student in mind. We have tried to integrate the technical jargon of our discipline into a relatively informal and down-to-earth writing style. We use concrete examples extensively to clarify complex concepts and to help maintain student interest. Although we now have three authors, the original author of this book (Wayne Weiten) continues to do the final rewrite of all 16 chapters to ensure stylistic consistency.

## Features

This text contains a number of features intended to stimulate interest and enhance students' learning. These special features include Applications, Recommended Reading boxes, Web Links, Practice Tests, a didactic illustration program, and cartoons.

## Applications

The Applications should be of special interest to most students. They are tied to chapter content in a way that should show students how practical applications emerge out of theory and research. Although some of the material covered in these sections shows up frequently in adjustment texts, much of it is unique. Some of the Applications include the following:

- Understanding Intimate Violence
- Improving Academic Performance
- Understanding Eating Disorders
- Getting Ahead in the Job Game
- Building Self-Esteem
- Enhancing Sexual Relationships
- Understanding Mixed-Sex Communication

## Recommended Reading Boxes

Recognizing students' interest in self-help books, we have sifted through hundreds of them to identify some that may be especially useful. These books are featured in boxes that briefly review some of the higher-quality books. These Recommended Reading boxes are placed where they are germane to the material being covered in the text. Some of the recommended books are well known, while others are obscure. Although we make it clear that we don't endorse every idea in every book, we think they all have something worthwhile to offer. This feature replaces the conventional suggested readings lists that usually appear at the ends of chapters, where they are almost universally ignored by students.

## Web Links

The Internet is rapidly altering the landscape of modern life, and students clearly need help dealing with the information explosion in cyberspace. To assist them, we recruited web expert Vincent Hevern (Le Moyne College) to evaluate hundreds of psychology- and adjustment-related sites and to come up with some recommendations that appear to provide reasonably accurate, balanced, and empirically sound information. Short descriptions of these recommended websites are dispersed throughout the chapters, adjacent to related topical coverage. Because URLs change frequently, we have not included the URLs for the Web Links in the book. If your students are interested in visiting these sites, we recommend that they do so through the Weiten Psychology CourseMate at www.cengagebrain.com/shop/ISBN/1111186634. Links to all the recommended websites are maintained there. Of course, students can also use search engines such as Google to locate the recommended websites.

## Practice Tests

Each chapter ends with a ten-item multiple-choice Practice Test that should give students a fairly realistic assessment of their mastery of that chapter and valuable practice in taking the type of test that many of them will face in the classroom (if the instructor uses the Test Bank). This feature grew out of some research on students' use of textbook pedagogical devices (see Weiten, Guadagno, & Beck, 1996). This research indicated that students pay scant attention to some standard pedagogical devices. When students were grilled to gain a better understanding of this perplexing finding, it quickly became apparent that students are pragmatic about pedagogy. Essentially, their refrain was, "We want study aids that will help us pass the next test." With this mandate in mind, we added the Practice Tests. They should be very realistic, as many of the items came from the Test Banks for previous editions (these items do not appear in the Test Bank for the current edition). Additional practice tests can be found in the Weiten Psychology CourseMate at www.cengagebrain.com/shop/ISBN/1111186634.

## Didactic Illustration Program

The illustration program is once again in full color, and many new figures have been added along with extensive redrawing of many graphics. Although the illustrations are intended to make the book attractive and to help maintain student interest, they are not merely decorative: They have been carefully selected and crafted for their didactic value to enhance the educational goals of the text.

## Cartoons

A little comic relief usually helps keep a student interested, so we've sprinkled numerous cartoons throughout the book. Like the figures, most of these have been chosen to reinforce ideas in the text.

## Personal Explorations Workbook

As mentioned earlier, the *Personal Explorations Workbook* can be found in the very back of the text. It contains experiential exercises for each text chapter, designed to help your students achieve personal insights. For each chapter, we have included one *Self-Assessment* exercise and one *Self-Reflection* exercise. The self-assessments are psychological tests or scales that your students can take and score for themselves. The self-reflections consist of questions intended to help students think about themselves in relation to issues raised in the text. These exercises can be invaluable homework assignments. To facilitate assigning them as homework, we have printed the workbook section on perforated paper, so students can tear out the relevant pages and turn them in to their instructors. In addition to providing easy-to-use homework assignments, many of these exercises can be used in class to stimulate lively discussion.

## Learning Aids

A number of learning aids have been incorporated into the text to help the reader digest the wealth of material:

- The *outline* at the beginning of each chapter provides the student with a preview and overview of what will be covered.
- *Headings* are used extensively to keep material well organized.
- To help alert your students to key points, *learning objectives* are distributed throughout the chapters, after the level-1 headings.
- *Key terms* are identified with **blue italicized boldface** type to indicate that these are important vocabulary items that are part of psychology's technical language.
- An *integrated running glossary* provides an on-the-spot definition of each key term as it is introduced in the text. These formal definitions are printed in **blue boldface** type.
- An *alphabetical glossary* is found in the back of the book, as key terms are usually defined in the integrated running glossary only when they are first introduced.
- *Italics* are used liberally throughout the text to emphasize important points.
- A *chapter review* is found at the end of each chapter. Each review includes a concise but thorough summary of the chapter's key ideas, a list of the key terms that were introduced in the chapter, and a list of important theorists and researchers who were discussed in the chapter.

## Supplementary Materials

A complete teaching/learning package has been developed to supplement *Psychology Applied to Modern Life*. These supplementary materials have been carefully coordinated to provide effective support for the text.

### Instructor's Manual

The *Instructor's Manual*, revised by Lenore Frigo of Shasta College, is available as a convenient aid for your educational endeavors. It provides a thorough overview of each chapter and includes a wealth of suggestions for lecture topics, class demonstrations, exercises, and discussion questions, organized around the content of each chapter in the text.

### Test Bank

The *Test Bank*, revised by Joan Thomas-Spiegel of Los Angeles Harbor College, contains an extensive collection of multiple-choice questions for objective tests, all closely tied to the learning objectives found in the text chapters. We're confident that you will find this to be a dependable and usable test bank.

## PowerLecture® with JoinIn® and ExamView®

This one-stop lecture and class preparation tool makes it easy for you to assemble, edit, publish, and present custom lectures for your course, using Microsoft® PowerPoint®. It includes text-specific lecture outlines and art from the text on PowerPoint® slides (written by Elizabeth Garner of Tallahassee Community College), along with video clips and other integrated media. The CD-ROM also contains the full Instructor's Manual and Test Bank in Microsoft® Word® format. Preloaded with all of the questions in the *Test Bank,* ExamView® allows you to create, deliver, and customize tests and study guides (both print and online) in minutes. Exam-View® offers both a Quick Test Wizard and an Online Test Wizard that guides you step by step through the process of creating tests, while its unique "what you see is what you get" capability allows you to see the test you are creating onscreen exactly as it will print or display online. JoinIn allows instructors to pose book-specific questions and display students' responses, in conjunction with the clicker hardware and student response system of your choice.

## Study Guide

The *Study Guide,* written by William Addison of Eastern Illinois University, is designed to help students master the information contained in the text. It contains a programmed review of learning objectives, quiz boxes, and a self-test for each chapter. Your students should find it helpful in their study efforts.

## Culture and Modern Life

*Culture and Modern Life* is a small paperback intended to help your students appreciate how cultural factors moderate psychological processes and how the viewpoint of one's own culture can distort one's interpretation of the behavior of people from other cultures. Written by David Matsumoto (San Francisco State University), a leading authority on cross-cultural psychology, this supplementary book should greatly enhance your students' understanding of how culture can influence adjustment. *Culture and Modern Life* can be ordered shrinkwrapped with the text.

## Critical Thinking Exercises

We have developed a set of critical thinking exercises that can be found in the Weiten Psychology CourseMate at www.cengagebrain.com/shop/ISBN/1111186634. Written by Jeffry Ricker (Scottsdale Community College), these exercises are intended to introduce students to specific critical thinking skills, such as recognizing extraneous variables, sampling bias, and fallacies in reasoning. The exercises also challenge students to apply these skills to adjustment-related topics on a chapter-by-chapter basis.

## Highlights of Content Changes in the Tenth Edition

To help professors who have used this book over many editions, we are providing an overview of the content changes in the current edition. The following list is not exhaustive, but it should alert faculty to most of the major changes in the book.

### Chapter 1 Adjusting to Modern Life

New coverage of the tragic sweat lodge deaths that occurred during James Ray's self-realization seminar in Sedona in 2009

New *Living in Today's World* box on adjustment implications of the recent economic meltdown

Added discussion of how self-help books may fuel increased narcissism

New example of naturalistic observation research on the innate basis of facial expressions of emotion

New example of case study research focusing on investigation of suicide victims

New example of survey research profiling cross-cultural study of gender differences in desire for sexual variety

New coverage of associations between culture and happiness

Discussion of marriage and happiness now emphasizes the role of relationship satisfaction rather than marriage per se

New *Recommended Reading* box profiling Daniel Gilbert's *Stumbling on Happiness* (2006)

Revised discussion of the factors that underlie effective reading of textbooks

New discussion of how effective text marking can enhance students' reading

New research on the testing effect, the finding that testing on material enhances retention

New data on how distributed practice can enhance retention of information

### Chapter 2 Theories of Personality

Revised figure providing more detailed information on the five-factor model of personality traits

Expanded description of the Big Five traits

New discussion of how the Big Five traits are predictive of important life outcomes, such as occupational attainment and mortality

Addition of sublimation to the roster of defense mechanisms covered

New discussion in critique of behavioral theories that includes their fragmented approach to personality

New *Recommended Reading* box features Sam Gosling's *Snoop: What Your Stuff Says About You* (2008)

New evaluation of Eysenck's theory regarding the roots of introversion

Includes coverage of Zuckerman's description of sensation seeking as a personality trait

New discussion of the influence of sensation seeking on sports and entertainment preferences and intimate relationships

New discussion of the relations between sensation seeking and various risk-taking behaviors

New *Living in Today's World* box on escalating narcissism among American college students

Streamlined discussion of terror management theory

New information on the trend toward conducting more personality testing over the Internet

Added coverage of recent concerns about personality testing via the Internet

## Chapter 3 Stress and Its Effects

New transition into everyday nature of stress

New figure on the frequency of various types of daily hassles

New discussion of negative affect, perceived control, and personality as buffers against the effects of daily hassles

Expanded discussion of community violence as a source of environmental stress

Expanded coverage of cultural influences on stress, including new research on diverse samples

Added discussion of anticipatory stressors

New data suggesting that stress leads to overreliance on habitual actions

New discussion of indirect exposure to trauma (e.g., through television) and "virtual" PTSD

*Living in Today's World* box restructured around traumatic events in the 21st century

Discussion of how risky behaviors may contribute to the relations between stress and physical health

New discussion of potential negative aspects of social networks

Discussion of the debate regarding the drawbacks of unrealistic optimism

*Monitoring Your Stress* Application moved to the Personal Explorations Workbook (which now appears in the back of the text) as a self-assessment

New Application on self-modification and self-control (formerly the Application for Chapter 4)

## Chapter 4 Coping Processes

New figure reporting data on the worst cities for road rage

New discussion of factors that make aggressive responses to frustration more likely

New brain-imaging (fMRI) research on effects of virtual (video game) violence

Expanded discussion of the fallout of self-blame

Emphasis shifted from terrorism to traumatic events in general in the *Living in Today's World* box

Added research on rumination in the *Living in Today's World* box

New research on different types of humor and the relationship of each to well-being

New evidence on the mechanisms through which humor promotes wellness

New research on culture and the tendency to seek social support

New discussion of coping strategies directly related to emotional intelligence

New study of the stress-reduction benefits of meditation on mental health workers in New Orleans after Hurricane Katrina

New Application section on coping with loss covering attitudes about death and the process of dying

New Application coverage of research on bereavement and grieving

## Chapter 5 Psychology and Physical Health

Updated material on women and heart disease

New figure on cardiovascular mortality rates for men and women in the United States

Clear distinctions drawn between anger and hostility as links to cardiovascular problems

New material on heart reactivity as a coronary predictor among African Americans

Broadened discussion of emotion and heart disease, including suppressing emotion and rumination

Updated discussion of recent evidence associating psychosocial stress factors with cancer

New material on stress and the onset of the common cold

Concept of unrealistic optimism introduced in discussion of risk taking and health behavior

Updated material on the causes, incidence, and consequences of smoking

New figure categorizing the types of drinkers in the United States

Additional material on alcohol and traffic accidents

New section on gastric banding and bypass surgery in the weight loss section

New example of an HIV prevention program based on people's expectations

Updated discussion of individuals' sick roles in which illness is ignored in order to not jeopardize work

## Chapter 6 The Self

New material on identity motives underlying desired and feared possible selves

Discussion of self-discrepant thoughts as a risk factor for suicidal ideation

Broadened coverage of self-affirmation in response to information that threatens the self-concept

Intriguing new research on the N-effect and social comparison, in which more available competitors reduce the motivation to compete

New discussion of culture-as-situated cognition linked to individualist and collectivist perspectives

New evidence that low self-esteem is an independent risk factor for depressive symptoms from young adulthood to old age

Addition of self-evaluation—domain specific self-esteem—as a third way to construe self-esteem

Discussion of a recent study on cultural differences in parenting styles, in which permissive parenting in Spain was found to be somewhat more effective than authoritative parenting

Broader discussion of self-esteem differences between men and women based on recent meta-analytic results

Additional details on self-handicapping and gender

Discussion of new findings concerning self-regulation, ego-depletion, and self-control

## Chapter 7 Social Thinking and Social Influence

Discussion of multiracial identities as example of appearance as an influence on person perception processes

New example of how emotion is more often attributed to women's personalities than to men's

Expanded discussion of the confirmation bias, including its importance in law enforcement and medical decision making

New examples of possible self-fulfilling prophecies in daily life: the "storm and stress" of adolescence and reactions to popular trends

New discussion of the potential impact of outgroup homogeneity effect on eyewitness identification

Added discussion of how people use subtypes to explain individuals who do not conform to their stereotypes

Broader discussion of research on the attractiveness stereotype

Exploration of self-control over prejudiced thought by reviewing an experiment in which glucose consumption promotes reduced bias

A new *Living in Today's World* box on stereotype threat and the "Obama effect"

New ageism-related example of how stereotypes can be triggered unconsciously and influence subsequent behavior

New research in which people high in social dominance orientation were found to be more charitable to a minority group after being exposed to morally praiseworthy behavior

New study of the contact hypothesis and prejudice between white and black college roommates

New discussion of how people often believe others are conformists but they themselves are not, despite showing the same conformity

## Chapter 8 Interpersonal Communication

New opening vignette illustrating an example of paralanguage

Discussion of how people interpret communications they receive through their own frame of reference

New material on how communication is selective, systemic, unique, and follows a process

New *Living in Today's World* box on maintaining privacy in the digital age

New research indicating that older individuals are less likely to recall angry facial expressions than younger people

More detailed discussion concerning when eye contact is likely to be maintained or broken

Discussion of a new study suggesting that a five-second touch from one person to another can convey a specific emotion

Added comparison of daily "white" lies with more serious lies

Discussion of the promise of brain-imaging technology for lie detection purposes

New section regarding what kinds of information people do or do not disclose to others

New discussion of the significance of disclosure styles for intimate relationships

Broader discussion of communication apprehension, academic success, and listening skills

Addition of tactic of "ambushing" to the discussion of barriers to effective communication

Comparison of Japanese and American negotiation styles, with accompanying figure

New discussion of how being gracious can be a way to reduce conflict

## Chapter 9 Friendship and Love

New discussion about how proximity affects attraction

Revised coverage of the role of physical appearance in relation to gender and whether one is interested in a short-term or long-term relationship

New data from a 2005 BBC Internet survey on important traits in a partner

Revised section on what makes someone attractive, organized around Cunningham's four categories

New figure on the top surgical cosmetic procedures

Updated section on playing hard to get, including new findings

New research on the benefits of friendship

New section on friendship repair rituals

New section on low levels of satisfaction as a factor in romantic breakups

New section describing Duck's model of processes involved in relationship dissolution

New *Living in Today's World* box on forming close relationships online

New figure on the reported uses of social networking sites

New *Recommended Reading* box on *Loneliness* by Cacioppo & Patrick (2008)

## Chapter 10 Marriage and Intimate Relationships

New section on cultural influences on marriage

Added cross-cultural perspective in the discussion of polygamy

New longitudinal study on the link between parents' conflict resolution patterns and their children's marital adjustment

Recent research on positive emotional expression as a predictor of later marital adjustment

New section on stressful events as related to marital adjustment

New mention of the potential benefits of caregiving roles in the family life cycle

New research showing that maternal employment does not produce "sleeper effects" on children

Expanded discussion of the significance of communication difficulties in marital relationships

Added discussion of the potential for positive effects from parental divorce

Updated discussion of the effects of divorce

New figure depicting a seven-stage model of stepfamily development

Revised section on gay couples, with new material on sexual prejudice and gay marriage

Added figure showing 2008 Gallup poll data on attitudes toward homosexuality

## Chapter 11 Gender and Behavior

Added 2010 meta-analysis of almost 500,000 participants, finding only small gender differences in mathematical abilities

Added 2009 meta-analysis of 115 studies that examined gender differences in specific domains of self-esteem, including a new figure summarizing results

New study demonstrating that playing action video games may contribute to gender differences in mental rotation skills

Added analysis of 200 best-selling and award-winning children's books that examined gender stereotyping

Added content analysis of gender stereotyping comparing the major U.S. networks to an African American cable network (BET)

New evidence on the role of TV in fostering gender stereotypes

New discussion of the precariousness of manhood as opposed to womanhood

Revised discussion of the ability-achievement gap in women

Revised coverage of economic discrimination suffered by women

New research demonstrating that women who break traditional gender roles in male-dominated organizations are the most likely to be targets of sexual harassment

New analysis of the contemporary relevance of Bem's sex role inventory

Major revision of the Application section downplaying Tannen's model of gender communication

Added section on speaking styles in the Application

## Chapter 12 Development and Expression of Sexuality

New material on physical changes in the transition to adolescence

Inclusion of intersex/hermaphroditism

New section on religion as a psychosocial influence on sexual identity development, including discussion of abstinence pledges

Inclusion of a content analysis of the sexual content of over 2,000 television programs

Expanded description of research on rap music and sexuality

Inclusion of Salvin-Williams's (2009) components of sexual orientation

Added section on the relationship between attributions for, and attitudes about, sexual orientation, including racial differences

Section on sexual identity development changed to focus on disclosing one's sexual orientation and the coming out process

Inclusion of theories of submission fantasies

Added description of 2009 experimental study on the benefits of kissing

Inclusion of new research on vibrator use

Revised material on sex outside committed relationships

Expanded discussion of "hooking up" and additional material on "friend-with-benefits"

Expanded section on sex in late adulthood

New material on individual, interpersonal, and societal reasons individuals engage in unprotected sex

Added mention of the "down low" syndrome

New study of sex therapists' beliefs about the optimal length of intercourse

New material on sexual activities reported by heterosexual couples

## Chapter 13 Careers and Work

New opening vignette discussing work as a defining element in most people's lives

Data on daily routines and the time they require, highlighting the enormous amount of time dedicated to work

Discussion of the importance of emotional/interpersonal intelligence in the world of work

Two new entries in the list of essential information regarding occupations

More nuanced discussion of the links between educational attainment, GPA, and successful job performance

New material concerning Holland's person-environment fit model

Updated information concerning Super's developmental model of career choice

Discussion of "telecommuting" as a means for interfacing with the office while working at home

Introduction of job sharing as new trend in the workplace

New figure showing common stressors as more likely to be work-related in older as opposed to younger adults

Expanded discussion of how the unpredictability of the economy can be source of stress

New figure listing common symptoms of burnout among workers

Review of additional consequences of sexual harassment, including lower work satisfaction, possible symptoms of posttraumatic stress, and lowered organizational commitment

New data linking how many hours women work to their marital satisfaction

## Chapter 14 Psychological Disorders

New discussion of the influence of stigmatizing labels on the mentally ill

New coverage of the debate about categorical versus dimensional approaches to describing disorders

Added discussion of the controversy about adding everyday problems to the diagnostic system

New coverage of the socioeconomic costs of mental illness

Streamlined coverage of the prevalence of psychological disorders

New discussion of Öhman and Mineka's notion of an evolved module for fear learning in relation to the acquisition of phobias

Expanded discussion of gender differences in depression

New section on the association between mood disorders and suicide

Revised discussion of the role of rumination in depressive and other disorders

Revised discussion of the course and outcome of schizophrenic disorders

New coverage of predictors associated with a favorable prognosis for schizophrenia

Reports new data linking marijuana use to increased vulnerability to schizophrenia

Condensed discussion of brain abnormalities and schizophrenia

New emphasis on the elevated mortality associated with eating disorders

## Chapter 15 Psychotherapy

New research on the proportion of individuals seeking therapy who do not meet the criteria for a mental disorder

New data on the extent to which psychiatrists rely on drug treatments to the exclusion of other interventions

Coverage of new findings on the efficacy of psychodynamic therapies

Added section on innovative insight therapies inspired by the positive psychology movement

Streamlined discussion of therapy and the recovered memories controversy

Discussion of how antidepressant medications are not as effective for bipolar patients (in comparison to patients with unipolar depression)

New coverage of serotonin-norepinephrine reuptake inhibitors

Updated coverage of whether antidepressants elevate suicide risk in adolescents

New graphic clarifies the association between suicidal risk and initiating therapy (medication or other treatments)

New *Living in Today's World* box on brain stimulation therapies of TMS and DBS

New graphic illustrating how direct brain stimulation works

New figure showing the distribution of psychologists' theoretical approaches to therapy

Elaborated discussion of eclecticism in the practice of therapy

New evidence on ethnic disparities in mental health care

New discussion on the impact of poverty on psychotherapy

New information on the importance of a strong therapeutic alliance and the value of adapting treatments for ethnic minority clients

## Chapter 16 Positive Psychology

Everything is new.

# Acknowledgments

This book has been an enormous undertaking, and we want to express our gratitude to the innumerable people who have influenced its evolution. To begin with, we must cite the contribution of our students who have taken the adjustment course. It is trite to say that they have been a continuing inspiration—but they have.

We also want to express our appreciation for the time and effort invested by the authors of various ancillary books and materials: Vinny Hevern (Le Moyne College), Bill Addison (Eastern Illinois University), Britain Scott (University of St. Thomas), Susan Koger (Willamette University), Jeffry Ricker (Scottsdale Community College), David Matsumoto (San Francisco State University), Lenore Frigo (Shasta College), Elizabeth Garner (Tallahassee Community College), and Joan Thomas-Spiegel (Los Angeles Harbor College). In spite of tight schedules, they all did commendable work.

The quality of a textbook depends greatly on the quality of the prepublication reviews by psychology professors around the country. The reviewers listed on pages xiv–xv have contributed to the development of this book by providing constructive reviews of various portions of the manuscript in this or earlier editions. We are grateful to all of them.

We would also like to thank Jon-David Hague, who has served as editor of this edition. He has done a wonderful job following in the footsteps of Claire Verduin, Eileen Murphy, Edith Beard Brady, and Michele Sordi, to whom we remain indebted. We are also grateful to Jackie Estrada, for an excellent job of copyediting and indexing; Joan Keyes, who performed superbly as our production editor; Liz Harasymczuk, who created the new design; Sarah Evertson, who provided outstanding photo research; and Carol Zuber-Mallison, who created excellent new graphics. Others who have made significant contributions to this project include Pat Waldo (project manager), Kristin Makarewycz and Angela Kao (developmental editors), Paige Leeds (ancillaries editor), Elisabeth Rhoden (marketing), Kelly Miller (editorial assistant), Lauren Keyes (media editor), and Vernon Boes (art director).

In addition, Wayne Weiten would like to thank his wife, Beth Traylor, who has been a steady source of emotional support despite the demands of her medical career, and his son, T. J., who adds a wealth of laughter to his dad's life. Dana Dunn thanks his wife, Sarah, and his children, Jake and Hannah, for their usual support during the writing process. He also thanks two students, Amanda Kostalis and Blake Ritchey, for doing library research, as well as his colleague, Bob Brill, for recommending new references. Dana is also grateful to Wayne and Elizabeth for their camaraderie as authors and friends. Elizabeth Yost Hammer would like to thank Elliott Hammer—her constant source of inspiration, encouragement, and support—for far too much to list here. She is especially grateful to Alycia K. Boutté, Adrienne Glover, Patrick M. Jackson, Whitney Danielle Miller, and Nelanhta K. Riley for their outstanding research assistance. Finally, she is grateful to Bart Everson for challenging her, to Janice Florent for celebrating with her, and to Olivia Crum for getting her out the door. Finally, she wishes to thank Wayne Weiten for inviting her to be part of this project.

*Wayne Weiten*
*Dana S. Dunn*
*Elizabeth Yost Hammer*

# Reviewers

David Ackerman
*Rhodes College*

David W. Alfano
*Community College of Rhode Island*

Jeff Banks
*Pepperdine University*

David Baskind
*Delta College*

Marsha K. Beauchamp
*Mt. San Antonio College*

Robert Biswas-Diener
*Portland State University (USA)/*
*Centre for Applied Positive*
*Psychology*

John R. Blakemore
*Monterey Peninsula College*

Barbara A. Boccaccio
*Tunxis Community College*

Paul Bowers
*Grayson County College*

Amara Brook
*Santa Clara University*

Tamara L. Brown
*University of Kentucky*

George Bryant
*East Texas State University*

James F. Calhoun
*University of Georgia*

Robert Cameron
*Fairmont State College*

David Campbell
*Humboldt State University*

Bernardo J. Carducci
*Indiana University, Southeast*

Richard Cavasina
*California University of*
*Pennsylvania*

M. K. Clampit
*Bentley College*

Meg Clark
*California State Polytechnic*
*University–Pomona*

Stephen S. Coccia
*Orange County Community*
*College*

William C. Compton
*Middle Tennessee State University*

Dennis Coon
*Santa Barbara City College*

Katherine A. Couch
*Eastern Oklahoma State College*

Tori Crews
*American River College*

Salvatore Cullari
*Lebenon Valley College*

Kenneth S. Davidson
*Wayne State University*

Lugenia Dixon
*Bainbridge College*

Jean Egan
*Asnuntuck Community College*

Ron Evans
*Washburn University*

Richard Furhere
*University of Wisconsin–Eau Claire*

R. Kirkland Gable
*California Lutheran University*

Laura Gaudet
*Chadron State College*

Lee Gills
*Georgia College*

Chris Goode
*Georgia State University*

Lawrence Grebstein
*University of Rhode Island*

Bryan Gros
*Louisiana State University*

Kyle Max Hancock
*Utah State University*

Barbara Hansen Lemme
*College of DuPage*

Robert Helm
*Oklahoma State University*

Barbara Herman
*Gainesville College*

Jeanne L. Higbee
*University of Minnesota*

Robert Higgins
*Central Missouri State University*

Clara E. Hill
*University of Maryland*

Michael Hirt
*Kent State University*

Fred J. Hitti
*Monroe Community College*

William M. Hooper
*Clayton College and State University*

Joseph Horvat
*Weber State University*

Kathy Howard
*Harding University*

Teresa A. Hutchens
*University of Tennessee–Knoxville*

Howard Ingle
*Salt Lake Community College*

Brian Jensen
*Columbia College*

Jerry Jensen
*Minneapolis Community &*
*Technical College*

Walter Jones
*College of DuPage*

Wayne Joose
*Calvin College*

Bradley Karlin
*Texas A&M University*

Margaret Karolyi
*University of Akron*

Lambros Karris
*Husson College*

Martha Kuehn
*Central Lakes College*

Susan Kupisch
*Austin Peay State University*

Robert Lawyer
*Delgado Community College*

Jimi Leopold
*Tarleton State University*

Harold List
*Massachusetts Bay Community*
*College*

Corliss A. Littlefield
*Morgan Community College*

Louis A. Martone
*Miami Dade Community College*

Richard Maslow
*San Joaquin Delta College*

Sherri McCarthy
*Northern Arizona Community College*

William T. McReynolds
*University of Tampa*

Fred Medway
*University of South Carolina–*
*Columbia*

Fredrick Meeker
*California State Polytechnic*
*University–Pomona*

Mitchell Metzger
*Pennsylvania State University–*
*Shenago Campus*

John Moritsugu
*Pacific Lutheran University*

Jeanne O'Kon
*Tallahassee Community College*

Gary Oliver
*College of DuPage*

William Penrod
*Middle Tennessee State University*

Joseph Philbrick
*California State Polytechnic*
*University–Pomona*

Barbara M. Powell
*Eastern Illinois University*

James Prochaska
*University of Rhode Island*

Megan Benoit Ratcliff
*University of Georgia*

Bob Riesenberg
*Whatcom Community College*

Katherine Elaine Royal
*Middle Tennessee State University*

Joan Royce
*Riverside Community College*

Joan Rykiel
*Ocean County College*

John Sample
*Slippery Rock University*

Thomas K. Savill
*Metropolitan State College of Denver*

Patricia Sawyer
*Middlesex Community College*

Carol Schachat
*De Anza College*

Norman R. Schultz
*Clemson University*

Dale Simmons
*Oregon State University*

Sangeeta Singg
*Angelo State University*

Krishna Stilianos
*Oakland Community College*

Valerie Smead
*Western Illinois University*

Dolores K. Sutter
*Tarrant County College–Northeast*

Karl Swain
*Community College of Southern Nevada*

Diane Teske
*Penn State Harrisburg*

Kenneth L. Thompson
*Central Missouri State University*

Joanne Viney
*University of Illinois Urbana/Champaign*

Davis L. Watson
*University of Hawaii*

Deborah S. Weber
*University of Akron*

Clair Wiederholt
*Madison Area Technical College*

J. Oscar Williams
*Diablo Valley College*

Raymond Wolf
*Moraine Park Technical College*

Raymond Wolfe
*State University of New York at Geneseo*

Michael Wolff
*Southwestern Oklahoma State University*

Madeline E. Wright
*Houston Community College*

Norbet Yager
*Henry Ford Community College*

# BRIEF CONTENTS

# CONTENTS

## CHAPTER 1  *Adjusting to Modern Life*  1

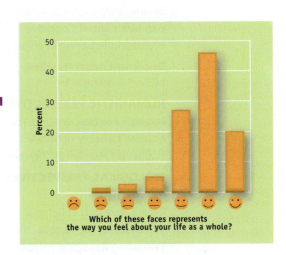

Which of these faces represents the way you feel about your life as a whole?

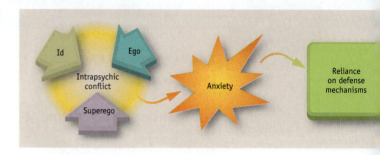

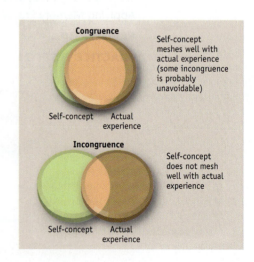

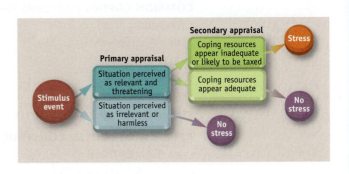

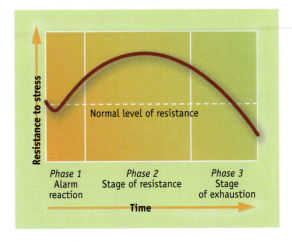

# CHAPTER 4  *Coping Processes*  104

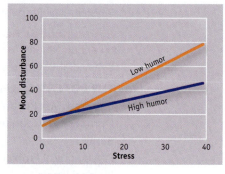

# CHAPTER 5  *Psychology and Physical Health*  138

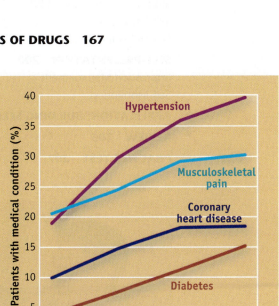

# CHAPTER 6 *The Self* 176

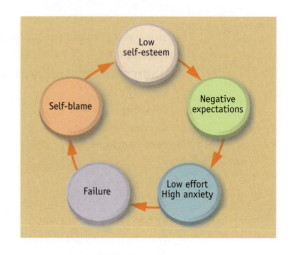

© David Young-Wolff/PhotoEdit

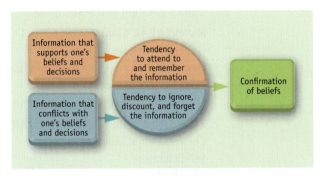

## CHAPTER 8  *Interpersonal Communication*  240

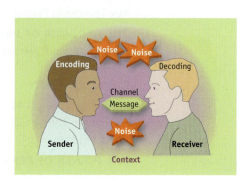

© Yellow Dog Productions/Getty Images/The Image Bank

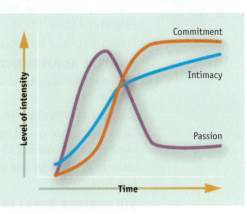

© John Lund/Annabelle Breakey/Blend Images/Corbis

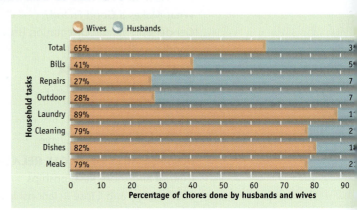

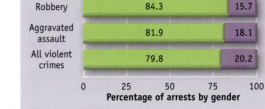

| Type of offense | Males | | Females |
|---|---|---|---|
| Rape/ sexual assault | 97.0 | | 3.0 |
| Robbery | 84.3 | | 15.7 |
| Aggravated assault | 81.9 | | 18.1 |
| All violent crimes | 79.8 | | 20.2 |

Percentage of arrests by gender

© Guy Cali/Corbis

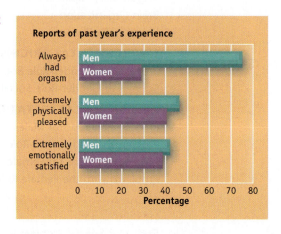

© Tony DiMaio/iPhoto/newscom

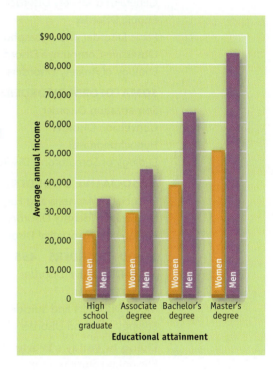

© John Gress/Reuters/Landov

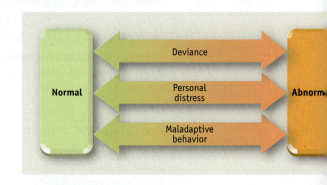

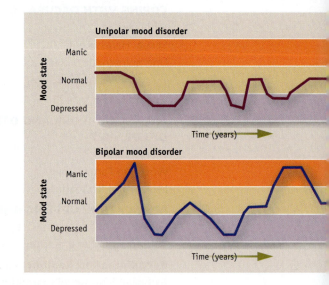

# CHAPTER 15  *Psychotherapy*  476

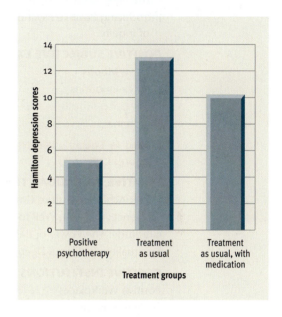

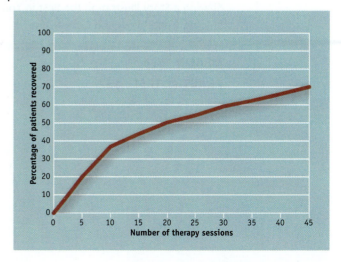

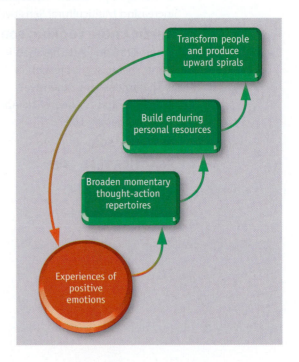

# To the Student

In most college courses students spend more time with their textbooks than with their professors. Given this reality, it helps if you like your textbook. Making textbooks likable, however, is a tricky proposition. By its very nature, a textbook must introduce a great many new concepts, ideas, and theories. If it doesn't, it isn't much of a textbook, and instructors won't choose to use it—so you'll never see it anyway. Consequently, we have tried to make this book as likable as possible without compromising the academic content that your instructor demands. Thus, we have tried to make the book lively, informal, engaging, well organized, easy to read, practical, and occasionally humorous. Before you plunge into Chapter 1, let us explain some of the key features that can help you get the most out of the book.

## Learning Aids

Mastering the content of this text involves digesting a great deal of information. To facilitate this learning process, we've incorporated a number of instructional aids into the book.

● *Outlines* at the beginning of each chapter provide you with both a preview and an overview of what will be covered. Think of the outlines as road maps, and bear in mind that it's easier to reach a destination if you know where you're going.

● *Headings* are used extensively to keep material well organized.

● To help alert you to key points, *learning objectives* are found throughout the chapters, immediately after the level-1 headings.

● *Key terms* are identified with **blue italicized boldface** type to indicate that these are important vocabulary items that are part of psychology's technical language.

● An *integrated running glossary* provides an on-the-spot definition of each key term as it's introduced in the text. These formal definitions are printed in **blue boldface** type. It is often difficult for students to adapt to the jargon used by scientific disciplines. However, learning this terminology is an essential part of your educational experience. The integrated running glossary is meant to make this learning process as painless as possible.

● An *alphabetical glossary* is provided in the back of the book, as key terms are usually defined in the running glossary only when they are first introduced. If you run into a technical term that was introduced in an earlier chapter and you can't remember its meaning, you can look it up in the alphabetical glossary instead of backtracking to find the place where it first appeared.

● *Italics* are used liberally throughout the book to emphasize important points.

● A *chapter review* near the end of each chapter includes a thorough summary of the chapter and lists key terms and important theorists, with page references. Reading over these review materials can help ensure that you've digested the key points in the chapter.

● Each chapter ends with a ten-item *practice test* that should give you a realistic assessment of your mastery of that chapter and valuable practice taking multiple-choice tests that will probably be representative of what you will see in class (if your instructor uses the test bank designed for this book).

## Recommended Reading Boxes

This text should function as a resource book. To facilitate this goal, particularly interesting self-help books on various topics are highlighted in boxes within the chapters. Each box provides a brief description of the book. We do not agree with everything in these recommended books, but all of them are potentially useful or intriguing. The main purpose of this feature is to introduce you to some of the better self-help books that are available. You can find additional Recommended Readings in the Weiten Psychology CourseMate at www.cengagebrain.com/shop/ISBN/1111186634.

## Web Links

To help make this book a rich resource guide, we have included Web Links, which are recommended websites that can provide you with additional information on adjustment-related topics. The recommended sites were selected by Vincent Hevern, the former Internet editor for the Society for the Teaching of Psychology. Professor Hevern sought out sites that are interesting, that are relevant to adjustment, and that provide accurate, empirically sound information. As with the Recommended Reading boxes, we cannot say that we agree with everything posted on these web pages, but we think they have some real value. The Web Links are dispersed throughout the chapters, adjacent to related topical coverage. Because URLs change frequently, we have not included the URLs for the Web Links in the book. If you are interested in visiting these sites, we recommend that you do so through the Weiten Psychology CourseMate at www.cengagebrain.com/shop/ISBN/1111186634. Links to all the recommended websites are maintained there. Of course, you can also use a search engine, such as Google, to locate the recommended websites.

## Personal Explorations Workbook

The *Personal Explorations Workbook,* which can be found in the very back of the text, contains interesting, thought-provoking experiential exercises for each chapter. These exercises are designed to help you achieve personal insights. The *Self-Assessment* exercises are psychological tests or scales that you can take, so you can see how you score on various traits discussed in the text. The *Self-Reflection* exercises consist of questions intended to help you think about issues in your personal life in relation to concepts and ideas discussed in the text. Many students find these exercises to be quite interesting, even fun. Hence, we encourage you to use the *Personal Explorations Workbook.*

## Study Guide

The *Study Guide* that accompanies this text, written by William Addison of Eastern Illinois University, is an excellent resource designed to assist you in mastering the information contained in the book. It includes a wealth of review exercises to help you organize information and a self-test for assessing your mastery. You should be able to purchase it at your college bookstore or you can order it online at cengagebrain.com.

## A Concluding Note

We sincerely hope that you find this book enjoyable. If you have any comments or advice that might help us improve the next edition, please write to us in care of the publisher, Cengage Learning, 20 Davis Drive, Belmont, CA 94002. There is a form in the back of the book that you can use to provide us with feedback. Finally, let us wish you good luck. We hope you enjoy your course and learn a great deal.

*Wayne Weiten*
*Dana S. Dunn*
*Elizabeth Yost Hammer*

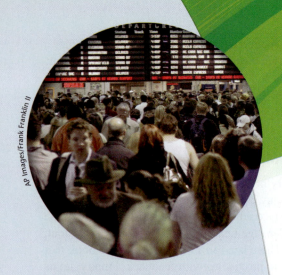

AP Images/Frank Franklin II

# Adjusting to Modern Life

The immense Boeing 747 lumbers into position to accept its human cargo. The passengers make their way on board. In a tower a few hundred yards away, air traffic controllers diligently monitor radar screens, radio transmissions, and digital readouts of weather information. At the reservation desk in the airport terminal, clerks punch up the appropriate ticket information on their computers and quickly process the steady stream of passengers. Mounted on the wall are video screens displaying up-to-the-minute information on flight arrivals, departures, and delays. Back in the cockpit of the plane, the flight crew calmly scans the complex array of dials, meters, and lights to assess the aircraft's readiness for flight. In a few minutes, the airplane will slice into the cloudy, snow-laden skies above Chicago. In a little over three hours its passengers will be transported from the piercing cold of a Chicago winter to the balmy beaches of the Bahamas. Another everyday triumph for technology will have taken place.

# The Paradox of Progress

## LEARNING OBJECTIVES

- Describe three examples of the paradox of progress.
- Explain what is meant by the paradox of progress and how theorists have explained it.

We are the children of technology. We take for granted such impressive feats as transporting 300 people over 1500 miles in a matter of hours. After all, we live in a time of unparalleled progress. Our modern Western society has made extraordinary strides in transportation, energy, communication, agriculture, and medicine. Yet despite our technological progress, social problems and personal difficulties seem more prevalent and more prominent than ever before. This paradox is evident in many aspects of contemporary life, as seen in the following examples.

**Point.** *Modern technology has provided us with countless time-saving devices.* Automobiles, telephones, vacuum cleaners, dishwashers, photocopiers, and personal computers all save time. Today, cell phones with headsets allow people to talk to friends or colleagues and battle rush hour at the same time. In a matter of seconds a personal computer can perform calculations that would take months if done by hand.

**Counterpoint.** *Nonetheless, most of us complain about not having enough time.* Our schedules overflow with appointments, commitments, and plans. Surveys suggest that a majority of people subjectively feel that they have less and less time for themselves. Time has become such a precious commodity, one national survey found that 51% of the adult respondents would rather have more time than more money (Weil & Rosen, 1997). Part of the problem is that in our modern society, work follows people home. Thus, Peter Whybrow (2005) comments, "Citizens find themselves tethered to their jobs around the clock by the same nomadic tools—cell phones, pagers, wireless e-mail—that were heralded first as instruments of liberation" (p. 158). To deal with this time crunch, more and more people are cutting back on their sleep as they attempt to juggle work, family, and household responsibilities, leading noted sleep researcher William Dement to comment that "most Americans no longer know what it feels like to be fully alert" (Toufexis, 1990, p. 79). Sleep experts assert that American society suffers from an epidemic of sleep deprivation (Walsh, Dement, & Dinges, 2005). Unfortunately, research indicates that chronic sleep loss can have significant negative effects on individuals' daytime functioning, as well as their mental and physical health (Dinges, Rogers, & Baynard, 2005).

**Point.** *The range of life choices available to people in modern societies has increased exponentially in recent decades.* For example, Barry Schwartz (2004) describes how a simple visit to a local supermarket can require a consumer to choose from 285 varieties of cookies, 61 suntan lotions, 150 lipsticks, and 175 salad dressings. Although increased choice is most tangible in the realm of consumer goods and services, Schwartz argues that it also extends into more significant domains of life. Today, people tend to have unprecedented opportunities to make choices about how they will be educated (e.g., vastly more flexible college curricula are available, not to mention online delivery systems), how and where they will work (e.g., telecommuting presents employees with all sorts of new choices about how to accomplish their work), how their intimate relationships will unfold (e.g., people have increased freedom to delay marriage, cohabit, not have children, and so forth), and even how they will look (advances in plastic surgery have made personal appearance a matter of choice).

**Counterpoint.** *Although increased choice sounds attractive, Schwartz (2004) argues that the overabundance of choices in modern life has unexpected costs.* He argues that people routinely make errors even when choosing among a handful of alternatives and that errors become much more likely when decisions become more complex. And he explains how having more alternatives increases the potential for rumination, postdecision regret, and anticipated regret. Ultimately, he argues, the malaise associated with choice overload undermines individuals' happiness and contributes to depression. Consistent with this analysis, studies have found that the incidence of depressive disorders has increased over the last 50 years (Kessler, 2002). Average anxiety levels have also gone up substantially in recent decades (Twenge, 2000). It is hard to say whether choice overload is the chief culprit underlying these trends, but it is clear that increased freedom of choice has not resulted in enhanced tranquillity or improved mental health.

**Point.** *Modern technology has gradually provided us with unprecedented control over the world around us.* Advances in agriculture have dramatically increased food production, and biotechnology advocates claim that genetically modified crops will make our food supply more reliable that ever before. Elaborate water

Barry Schwartz argues that people in modern societies suffer from choice overload. He maintains that the endless choices people are presented with lead them to waste countless hours weighing trivial decisions and ruminating about whether their decisions were optimal.

supply systems, made up of hundreds of miles of canals, tunnels, and pipelines, along with dams, reservoirs, and pumping stations, permit massive metropolitan areas to grow in inhospitable deserts. Thanks to progress in medicine, doctors can reattach severed limbs, use lasers to correct microscopic defects in the eye, and even replace the human heart.

**Counterpoint.** *Unfortunately, modern technology has also had a devastating negative impact on our environment.* It has contributed to global warming, destruction of the ozone layer, deforestation, exhaustion of much of the world's fisheries, widespread air and water pollution, and extensive exposure of plants and animals to toxic chemicals. Many experts worry that in a few generations the earth's resources will be too depleted to sustain an adequate quality of life (Winter, 2004). To most people, these crises sound like technical problems that call for technological answers, but they are also behavioral problems in that they are fueled by overconsumption and waste (Koger & Scott, 2011). In North America and Europe, the crucial problem is excessive consumption of the world's natural resources. As Kitzes et al. (2008) put it, "If everyone in the world had an ecological footprint equivalent to that of the typical North American or Western European, global society would overshoot the planet's biocapacity three to five fold" (p. 468).

All these apparent contradictions reflect the same theme: *The technological advances of the past century, impressive though they may be, have not led to perceptible improvement in our collective health and happiness.* Indeed, many social critics argue that the quality of our lives and our sense of personal fulfillment have declined rather than increased. This is the paradox of progress.

What is the cause of this paradox? Many explanations have been offered. Erich Fromm (1963, 1981) has argued that the progress we value so much has scrambled our value systems and undermined our traditional sources of emotional security, such as family, community, and religion. Alvin Toffler (1970, 1980) attributes our collective alienation and distress to our being overwhelmed by rapidly accelerating cultural change. Robert Kegan (1994) maintains that the mental demands of modern life have become so complex, confusing, and contradictory that most of us are "in over our heads." Tim Kasser (2002) speculates that excessive materialism weakens the social ties that bind us, stokes the fires of insecurity, and undermines our collective sense of well-being. Micki McGee (2005) suggests that modern changes in gender roles, diminished job stability, and other social trends have fostered an obsession with self-improvement that ultimately undermines many individuals' sense of security and their satisfaction with their identity. According to McGee, our "makeover culture," nourishes the belief that we can all reinvent ourselves as needed, but this assumption can create tremendous pressures on people that "foster rather than quell their anxieties" (p. 17).

Whatever the explanation, many theorists, working from varied perspectives, agree that *the basic challenge of modern life has become the search for meaning, a sense of direction, and a personal philosophy* (Dolby, 2005; Emmons, 2003; Naylor, Willimon, & Naylor, 1994; Sagiv, Roccas, & Hazan, 2004). This search involves struggling with such problems as forming a solid sense of identity, arriving at a coherent set of values, and developing a clear vision of a future that realistically promises fulfillment. Centuries ago, problems of this kind were probably much simpler. As we'll see in the next section, today it appears that many of us are foundering in a sea of confusion.

# Hard Times: Adjustment in an Era of Economic Distress

The fall of 2008 brought the worst economic meltdown since the Great Depression. The subprime mortgage crisis led to countless fore-closures and a precipitous decline in housing values. The entire banking industry teetered on the brink of collapse, and even after a massive government bailout, it remained highly dys-functional, as individuals and businesses were unable to secure loans. The banking gridlock and the rapid decline of consumer confidence undermined most sectors of the economy, leading to soaring unemployment. As David von Drehle (2009) put it in a *Time* magazine article, "Consumers have stopped spending, factories have stopped operating, employers have stopped hiring— and home values continue to fall. For millions of people the margin between getting by and getting buried is becoming as thin and as bloody as a razor blade."

As you might anticipate, research clearly shows that economic hardships are a huge source of stress for individuals and their families. Few events are more stressful than watching one's retirement accounts shrivel up, losing one's job, or, worse yet, losing one's home to foreclosure. A recent study of people going through foreclosure found that 29% were burdened by medical bills they could not afford, 58% had to skip meals due to lack of money, 47% suffered from minor to major depression, and a substantial portion had increased their smoking or drinking since their foreclosure (Pollack & Lynch, 2009). Other research has shown that pro-longed economic setbacks typically send families into a downward emotional spiral marked by anxiety, depres-sion, anger, alienation, and marital conflict (Conger & Donnellan, 2007). The stress on parents often spills over to affect their children, who act out and struggle in school. Another line of research, looking at the effects of unemployment and underemployment, has shown that these afflictions are associated with anxiety, depres-sion, hostility, paranoia, pessimism, helplessness, social isolation, and a host of physical maladies (McKee-Ryan et al., 2005; Probst & Sears, 2009). And unemployment and foreclosures tend to hit minorities and low-income groups disproportionately, thus deepening existing income disparities (Pollack & Lynch, 2009).

The popular press has placed most of the blame for the economic crisis on greedy bankers, sleazy Wall Street investors, and short-sighted government regula-tors. All of these culprits surely deserve an enormous amount of blame, but some critics have noted that the regular folks from Main Street America also contributed in substantial ways to the economic debacle by buying houses they could not really afford, maxing out their credit cards on luxury goods, and reducing their saving to historically low levels (Anderson, 2009). In his book *The Culture of Excess* J. R. Slosar (2009) argues that we live in a world that nurtures a sense of entitlement to material goods, emphasizes immediate gratification, and fails to instill self-discipline. He attributes the current economic disaster to a cultural milieu that fosters self-indulgence, overconsumption, and excessive risk taking. In a similar vein, Peter Whybrow (2009) asserts that "the debt-fueled consumptive frenzy that has gripped the American psyche for the past few decades was a night-mare in the making—a seductive, twisted, and com-mercially conjured version of the American dream that now threatens our environmental, individual, and civic health" (p. B11) Characterizing the American public as addicted to materialism, Whybrow notes that "shopping became the national pastime, and at all levels of society we hungered for more—more money, more power, more food, more stuff" (p. B13). Ironically, even in good times, materialism does not seem to foster well-being. In his book *The High Price of Materialism,* Tim Kasser (2002) summarizes research showing that people who are especially concerned with money and possessions tend to report lower levels of happiness than others.

Clearly, the current economic downturn will present monumental adjustment challenges for millions upon millions of people. There aren't any simple solutions for coping with severe economic distress. No one can wave a magic wand and make it go away. But sound knowl-edge about the dynamics of stress, coping, and adjust-ment can be helpful. In the chapters that lie ahead you will find many insights and suggestions that may help a little here and a little there in reducing the impact of stress and promoting resilience.

# The Search for Direction

### LEARNING OBJECTIVES

- Provide some examples of people's search for direction.
- Describe four problems that are common in popular self-help books.
- Summarize advice about what to look for in quality self-help books.
- Summarize the philosophy underlying this textbook.

We live in a time of unparalleled social and technological mutation. According to a number of social critics, the kaleidoscope of change that we see around us creates feelings of anxiety and uncertainty, which we try to alleviate by searching for a sense of direction. This search, which sometimes goes awry, manifests itself in many ways.

For example, we could discuss how hundreds of thousands of Americans have invested large sums of money to enroll in "self-realization" programs such as Scientology, Silva Mind Control, John Gray's Mars and Venus relationship seminars, and Tony Robbins's Life Mastery seminars. These programs typically promise to provide profound enlightenment and quickly turn one's life around. Many participants claim that the programs have revolutionized their lives. However, most experts characterize such programs as intellectually bankrupt, and book and magazine exposés reveal them as simply lucrative money-making schemes (Behar, 1991; Pressman, 1993). In a particularly scathing analysis of these programs, Steve Salerno (2005) outlines the enormous financial benefits reaped by their inventors, such as Tony Robbins ($80 million in annual income), Dr. Phil ($20 million in annual income), and John Gray ($50,000 per speech). In his critique, Salerno also attacks the hypocrisy and inflated credentials of many leading self-help gurus. For example, he asserts that John Gray's doctorate came from a nonaccredited correspondence college; that Dr. Phil has a history of alleged marital infidelity and that some of his video segments are contrived to a degree that would make Jerry Springer proud; and that Dr. Laura is "a critic of premarital and extramarital sex who's indulged in both" (p. 44). More than anything else, the enormous success of these self-help gurus and self-realization programs demonstrates just how desperate some people are for a sense of direction and purpose in their lives.

For the most part, self-realization programs are harmless scams that appear to give some participants an illusory sense of purpose or a temporary boost in self-confidence. But in some cases they probably lead people down ill-advised pathways that prove harmful. The ultimate example of the potential for harm unfolded in October 2009 in Sedona, Arizona, where 3 people died and 18 others were hospitalized, many with serious injuries, after participating in a "spiritual warrior" retreat that required them to spend hours in a makeshift sweat lodge (Harris & Wagner, 2009; Whelan, 2009). The retreat was run by James Ray, a recently popular self-help guru whose web site promises to teach people "how to trigger your Unconscious Mind to automatically increase your level of wealth and fulfillment," and to "accelerate the releasing of your limitations and push yourself past your self-imposed and conditioned borders." Ray, who has authored inspirational books (Ray, 1999, 2005) and appeared on TV shows such as *Oprah* and *Larry King Live,* has built a $9-million-a-year self-help empire. The 50 to 60 people who participated in his ill-fated retreat paid over $9,000 apiece for the privilege. After spending 36 hours fasting in the desert on a "vision quest,"

The tarp-covered sweat lodge in Sedona that proved to be a death trap for three participants in an endurance challenge can be seen here. James Ray, the self-help guru who organized the event, was arrested in February 2010 and charged with three counts of manslaughter.

they were led into a tarp-covered sweat lodge for an endurance challenge that was supposed to show them that they could gain confidence by conquering physical discomfort (Kraft, 2009). Unfortunately, the sweat lodge turned out to be poorly ventilated and overheated, so that within an hour people began vomiting, gasping for air, and collapsing. Undaunted, Ray, urged his followers to persevere, telling them that the vomiting was good for them and saying "you have to go through this barrier" (Doughtery, 2009). No one was physically forced to stay (and a few did leave), but Ray was an intimidating presence who strongly exhorted everyone to remain, so they could prove that they were stronger than their bodies. Tragically, he pushed their bodies too far; by the end of the ceremony many of the participants were seriously ill. Yet, according to one account, "At the conclusion, seemingly unaware of the bodies of the unconscious lying around him, Ray emerged triumphantly, witnesses said, pumping his fist because he had passed his own endurance test" (Whelan, 2009).

Some of the aftermath of this event has also proven revealing. Consistent with Salerno's (2005) assertion that it really is all about the money, Ray provided a *partial* refund to the family of Kirby Brown, a participant who *died* in the sweat lodge (Martinez, 2009). And the reactions of some of Ray's followers after the sweat lodge tragedy have been illuminating. You might think, after inadvertently, but recklessly leading people "over a cliff," Ray might be discredited in the eyes of his followers. But think again. Reporters working on this horrific story had no trouble finding Ray advocates who continued to enthusiastically champion his vision for self-improvement (Kraft, 2009). As one supporter put it, "He sets up the stage for people to change their lives" (Doughtery, 2009). In the wake of the Sedona fiasco, this unwavering faith in Ray's teachings is a remarkable testimonial to the enormous persuasive power of the charismatic leaders who promote self-realization programs.

We could also discuss how a number of unorthodox religious groups—commonly called *cults*—have attracted countless converts who voluntarily embrace a life of regimentation, obedience, and zealous ideology. It is difficult to get good data, but one study suggested that more than 2 million young adults are involved with cults in the United States (Robinson, Frye, & Bradley, 1997). Most of these cults flourish in obscurity, unless bizarre incidents—such as the 1997 mass suicide of the Heaven's Gate cult near San Diego—attract public attention. It is widely believed that cults use brainwashing and mind control to seduce lonely outsiders (Richardson & Introvigne, 2001), but in reality converts are a diverse array of normal people who are swayed by ordinary—albeit sophisticated—social influence strategies (Baron, 2000; Singer, 2003; Zimbardo, 2002). According to Philip Zimbardo (1992), people join cults because these groups appear to provide simple solutions to complex problems, a sense of purpose, and a structured lifestyle that reduces feelings of uncertainty. Hunter (1998) emphasizes how alienation, identity confusion, and weak community ties make some people particularly vulnerable to seduction by cults.

And, if you would like a mundane, everyday example of people's search for direction, you need look no farther than your radio, where you will find that the hottest nationally syndicated personality is "Dr. Laura," who doles out advice to millions of listeners. Even though only seven or eight people get through to her during each show, an astonishing 75,000 people call each day to seek her unique brand of blunt, outspoken, judgmental advice. Dr. Laura, who is not a psychologist or psychiatrist (her doctorate is in physiology), analyzes callers' problems in more of a moral than psychological framework. Unlike most therapists, she preaches to her audience about how they ought to lead their lives. In many instances she is insulting to her callers, models intolerance, and provides questionable advice (Epstein, 2001). In an editorial in *Psychology Today,* Robert Epstein (2001) concludes that "no legitimate mental health professional would ever give the kind of hateful, divisive advice that Schlessinger doles out daily" (p. 5). Yet, the remarkable popularity of her highly prescriptive advice demonstrates once again that many people are eager for guidance and direction.

There are many manifestations of our search for a sense of direction, including the astonishing popularity of "Dr. Laura."

THIS MODERN WORLD by TOM TOMORROW

Copyright © 2000. Used by permission. tomtomorrow@ix.netcom.com

lion-a-year industry (McGee, 2005). This fascination with self-improvement is nothing new. For decades American readers have displayed a voracious appetite for self-help books such as *I'm OK—You're OK* (Harris, 1967), *Your Erroneous Zones* (Dyer, 1976), *The Seven Habits of Highly Effective People* (Covey, 1989), *Men Are from Mars, Women Are from Venus* (Gray, 1992), *Ageless Body, Timeless Mind* (Chopra, 1993), *Don't Sweat the Small Stuff . . . and It's All Small Stuff* (Carlson, 1997), *The Purpose Driven Life* (Warren, 2002), *The Secret* (Byrne, 2006), and *Become a Better You: Seven Keys to Improving Your Life Everyday* (Osteen, 2009).

With their simple recipes for achieving happiness, these books have generally not been timid about promising to change the quality of the reader's life. Unfortunately, merely reading a book is not likely to turn your life around. If only it were that easy! If only someone could hand you a book that would solve all your problems! If the consumption of these literary narcotics were even remotely as helpful as their publishers claim, we would be a nation of serene, happy, well-adjusted people. It is clear, however, that serenity is not the dominant national mood. Quite the contrary, as already noted, in recent decades Americans' average anxiety level has moved upward (Twenge, 2000), and the prevalence of depression has increased as well (Kessler, 2002). The multitude of self-help books that crowd bookstore shelves represent just one more symptom of our collective distress and our search for the elusive secret of happiness.

Although we might choose to examine any of these examples of people's search for a sense of direction, we will reserve our in-depth analysis for a manifestation of this search that is even more germane to our focus on everyday adjustment: the spectacular success of best-selling "self-help" books.

## Self-Help Books

Americans spend roughly $650 million annually on "self-help books" that offer do-it-yourself treatments for common personal problems (Arkowitz & Lilienfeld, 2006). If you include self-help audiotapes, CDs, DVDs, software, Internet sites, lectures, seminars, and life coaching, self-improvement appears to be a $2.5 bil-

### The Value of Self-Help Books

It is somewhat unfair to lump all self-help books together for a critique, because they vary widely in quality (Fried & Schultis, 1995; Norcross et al., 2003). Surveys exploring psychotherapists' opinions of self-help books suggest that there are some excellent books that offer authentic insights and sound advice (Starker, 1990, 1992). Many therapists encourage their patients to read carefully selected self-help books (Campbell & Smith, 2003). A few books have even been tested in clinical trials with favorable results (Floyd, 2003; Gregory et al., 2004), although the studies have often had methodological weaknesses

**WEB LINK 1.1   Psychological Self-Help**

Clinical psychologist and professor Clayton E. Tucker-Ladd has spent some 25 years exploring how individuals can help themselves deal with personal issues and problems from a psychological perspective. Here he has assembled an online 12-chapter book, grounded in up-to-date research, that complements this textbook extremely well.
**Note: The URLs (addresses) for the Web Links can be found on the CourseMate for this text (www.cengagebrain.com/shop/ISBN/1111186634), or you can find them using a search engine such as Google.**

© AP Images/Stephen Chernin

**The newest rage in self-help books is _The Secret,_ written by Australian Rhonda Byrne, shown here at a Time magazine gala publicizing the magazine's selection of the 100 most influential people in the world. Byrne's (2006) book, DVD, and CDs have been flying off the shelves of American bookstores. The marketing campaign for the book has been absolutely brilliant (who can resist the opportunity to learn the secret to life?). What is Byrne's captivating thesis? The former television producer asserts that "your current thoughts are creating your future life. What you think about the most or focus on the most will appear as your life" (p. 25). In other words, just think more about earning that "A" in Biochemistry, losing weight, or taking that expensive vacation, and events will go your way (no need to study, exercise, or save money). Characterized by psychologist John Norcross as "pseudoscientific, psychospiritual babble," (Adler, 2007), _The Secret_ provides a remarkable demonstration of how seductive self-help books can be.**

(Arkowitz & Lilienfeld, 2006). Thus, it would be foolish to dismiss all these books as shallow drivel. In fact, some of the better self-help books are highlighted in the Recommended Reading boxes that appear throughout this text. Unfortunately, however, the gems are easily lost in the mountains of rubbish. A great many self-help books offer little of real value to the reader. Generally, they suffer from four fundamental shortcomings.

First, they are dominated by "psychobabble." The term _psychobabble,_ coined by R. D. Rosen (1977), seems appropriate to describe the "hip" but hopelessly vague language used in many of these books. Statements such as "It's beautiful if you're unhappy," "You've got to get in touch with yourself," "You have to be up front," "You gotta be you 'cause you're you," and "You need a real high-energy experience" are typical examples of this language. At best, such terminology is ill-defined; at worst, it is meaningless. Clarity is sacrificed in favor of a hip jargon that prevents, rather than enhances, effective communication.

A second problem is that self-help books tend to place more emphasis on sales than on scientific soundness. The advice offered in these books is far too rarely based on solid, scientific research (Ellis, 1993; Paul, 2001; Rosen, 1987, 1993). Instead, the ideas are frequently based on the authors' intuitive analyses, which may be highly speculative. Even when books are based on well-researched therapeutic programs, interventions that are effective in clinical settings with professional supervision may not be effective when self-administered without professional guidance (Rosen, Glasgow, & Moore, 2003). Moreover, even when responsible authors provide scientifically valid advice and are careful not to mislead their readers, sales-hungry publishers routinely slap outrageous, irresponsible promises on the books' covers, often to the dismay of the authors (Rosen et al., 2003).

The third shortcoming is that self-help books don't usually provide explicit directions about how to change your behavior. These books tend to be smoothly written and "touchingly human" in tone. They often strike responsive chords in the reader by aptly describing a common problem that many of us experience. The reader says, "Yes, that's me!" Unfortunately, when the book focuses on how to deal with the problem, it usually provides only a vague distillation of simple common sense, which could be covered in 2 rather than 200 pages. These books often fall back on inspirational cheerleading in the absence of sound, explicit advice.

Fourth, many of these books encourage a remarkably self-centered, narcissistic approach to life (Justman, 2005). **_Narcissism_ is a personality trait marked by an inflated sense of importance, a need for attention and admiration, a sense of entitlement, and a tendency to exploit others.** The term is based on the Greek myth of Narcissus, an attractive young man in search of love who sees himself reflected in water and falls in love with his own image. Although there are plenty of exceptions, the basic message in many self-help books is "Do whatever you feel like doing, and don't worry about the consequences for other people." According to McGee (2005), this mentality began to creep into books in the 1970s, as "bald proposals that one ought to 'look out for # 1' or 'win through intimidation' marked a new ruthlessness in the self-help landscape" (p. 50). This "me first" philosophy emphasizes

## DOONESBURY

self-admiration, one's entitlement to special treatment, and an exploitive approach to interpersonal relationships. Interestingly, research suggests that narcissism levels have increased among recent generations of college students (Twenge & Campbell, 2009; Twenge et al., 2008; see Chapter 2). It is hard to say how much popular self-help books have fueled this rise in narcissism, but surely they have contributed (the most widely used measure of narcissism is included in the *Personal Explorations Workbook* in the back of this text).

### What to Look for in Self-Help Books

Because self-help books vary so widely in quality, it seems a good idea to provide you with some guidelines about what to look for in seeking genuinely helpful books. The following thoughts give you some criteria for judging books of this type.

**1.** Clarity in communication is essential. Advice won't do you much good if you can't understand it. Try to avoid drowning in the murky depths of psychobabble.

**2.** This may sound backward, but look for books that do not promise too much in the way of immediate change. The truly useful books tend to be appropriately cautious in their promises and realistic about the challenge of altering your behavior. As Arkowitz and Lilienfeld (2006, p. 79) put it, "Be wary of books that make promises that they obviously cannot keep, such as curing a phobia in five minutes or fixing a failing marriage in a week."

**3.** Try to check out the credentials of the author or authors. Book jackets will often exaggerate the expertise of authors, but these days a quick Internet search can often yield more objective biographical information and perhaps some perceptive reviews of the book.

**4.** Try to select books that mention, at least briefly, the theoretical or research basis for the pro-

gram they advocate. It is understandable that you may not be interested in a detailed summary of research that supports a particular piece of advice. However, you should be interested in whether the advice is based on published research, widely accepted theory, anecdotal evidence, clinical interactions with patients, or pure speculation by the author. Books that are based on more than personal anecdotes and speculation should have a list of references in the back (or at the end of each chapter).

**5.** Look for books that provide detailed, explicit directions about how to alter your behavior. Generally, these directions represent the crucial core of the book. If they are inadequate in detail, you have been short-changed.

**6.** More often than not, books that focus on a particular kind of problem, such as overeating, loneliness, or marital difficulties, deliver more than those that promise to cure all of life's problems with a few simple ideas. Books that cover everything are usually superficial and disappointing. Books that devote a great deal of thought to a particular topic tend to be written by authors with genuine expertise on that topic. Such books are more likely to pay off for you.

### The Approach of This Textbook

Clearly, in spite of our impressive technological progress, we are a people beset by a great variety of personal problems. Living in our complex, modern society is a formidable challenge. This book is about that challenge. It is about you. It is about life. Specifically, it summarizes for you the scientific research on human behavior that appears relevant to the challenge of living effectively in contemporary society. It draws primarily, but not exclusively, from the science we call psychology.

This text deals with the same kinds of problems addressed by self-help books, self-realization programs,

and Dr. Laura: anxiety, stress, interpersonal relationships, frustration, loneliness, depression, self-control. However, it makes no boldly seductive promises about solving your personal problems, turning your life around, or helping you achieve tranquillity. Such promises simply aren't realistic. Psychologists have long recognized that changing a person's behavior is a difficult challenge, fraught with frustration and failure (Seligman, 1994). Troubled individuals sometimes spend years in therapy without resolving their problems.

This reality does not mean that you should be pessimistic about your potential for personal growth. You most certainly can change your behavior. Moreover, you can often change it on your own without consulting a professional psychologist. We would not be writing this text if we did not believe it could be beneficial to our readers. But it is important that you have realistic expectations. Reading this book will not be a revelatory experience. No mysterious secrets are about to be unveiled. All this book can do is give you some useful information and point you in some potentially beneficial directions. The rest is up to you.

In view of our criticisms of self-realization programs and self-help books, it seems essential that we explicitly lay out the philosophy that underlies the writing of this text. The following statements summarize the assumptions and goals of this book.

**1.** *This text is based on the premise that accurate knowledge about the principles of psychology can be of value to you in everyday life.* It has been said that knowledge is power. Greater awareness of why people behave as they do should help you in interacting with others as well as in trying to understand yourself.

**2.** *This text attempts to foster a critical attitude about psychological issues and to enhance your critical thinking skills.* Information is important, but people also need to develop effective strategies for evaluating information. Critical thinking involves subjecting ideas to systematic, skeptical scrutiny. Critical thinkers ask tough questions, such as: What exactly is being asserted? What assumptions underlie this assertion? What evidence or reasoning supports this assertion? Are there alternative explanations? Some general guidelines for thinking critically are outlined in **Figure 1.1** on the next page. We have already attempted to illustrate the importance of a critical attitude in our evaluation of self-help books, and we'll continue to model critical thinking strategies throughout the text.

**3.** *This text should open doors.* The coverage in this book is broad; we tackle many topics. Therefore, in some places it may lack the depth or detail that you would like. However, you should think of it as a resource book that can introduce you to other books or techniques or therapies, which you can then pursue on your own.

**Figure 1.1**

**Guidelines for thinking critically.** Critical thinking should not be equated with criticism; it's not a matter of learning how to tear down others' ideas. Rather, critical thinkers carefully subject others' ideas—and their own—to careful, systematic, objective evaluation. The guidelines shown here, taken from Wade and Tavris (1990), provide a succinct overview of what it means to think critically.

Source: From Wade, C., & Tavris, C. (1990). *Learning to think critically: A handbook to accompany psychology.* New York: Harper & Row. Copyright © 1989 by Harper & Row Publishers, Inc. Reproduced by permission of Pearson Education, Inc.

## Guidelines for Thinking Critically

**1 Ask questions; be willing to wonder.** To think critically you must be willing to think creatively—that is, to be curious about the puzzles of human behavior, to wonder why people act the way they do, and to question conventional explanations and examine new ones.

**2 Define the problem.** Identify the issues involved in clear and concrete terms, rather than vague generalities such as "happiness," "potential," or "meaningfulness." What does meaningfulness mean, exactly?

**3 Examine the evidence.** Consider the nature of the evidence that supports all aspects of the problem under examination. Is it reliable? valid? Is it someone's personal assertion or speculation? Does the evidence come from one or two narrow studies, or from repeated research?

**4 Analyze biases and assumptions—your own and those of others.** What prejudices, deeply held values, and other personal biases do you bring to your evaluation of a problem? Are you willing to consider evidence that contradicts your beliefs? Be sure you can identify the bias of others, in order to evaluate their arguments as well.

**5 Avoid emotional reasoning** ("If I feel this way, it must be true"). Remember that everyone holds convictions and ideas about how the world should operate and that your opponents are as serious about their convictions as you are about yours. Feelings are important, but they should not substitute for careful appraisal of arguments and evidence.

**6 Don't oversimplify.** Look beyond the obvious. Reject simplistic, either-or thinking. Look for logical contradictions in arguments. Be wary of "arguments by anecdote."

**7 Consider other interpretations.** Before you leap to conclusions, think about other explanations. Be especially careful about assertions of cause and effect.

**8 Tolerate uncertainty.** This may be the hardest step in becoming a critical thinker, for it requires the ability to accept some guiding ideas and beliefs—yet the willingness to give them up when evidence and experience contradict them.

---

**4.** *This text assumes that the key to effective adjustment is to take charge of your own life.* If you are dissatisfied with some aspect of your life, it does no good to sit around and mope about it. You have to take an active role in attempting to improve the quality of your life. Doing so may involve learning a new skill or pursuing a particular kind of help. In any case, it is generally best to meet problems head-on rather than trying to avoid them.

**WEB LINK 1.3  Foundation for Critical Thinking**

How can students best develop those skills that go beyond merely acquiring information to actively weighing and judging information? The many resources of the Foundation for Critical Thinking at Sonoma State University are directed primarily toward teachers at every level to help them develop their students' critical thinking abilities.

# The Psychology of Adjustment

### LEARNING OBJECTIVES

● Describe the two key facets of psychology.
● Explain the concept of adjustment.

Now that we have spelled out our approach in writing this text, it is time to turn to the task of introducing you to some basic concepts. In this section, we'll discuss the nature of psychology and the concept of adjustment.

## What Is Psychology?

**Psychology** is the science that studies behavior and the physiological and mental processes that underlie it, and it is the profession that applies the accumulated knowledge of this science to practical problems. Psychology leads a complex dual existence

as both a *science* and a *profession.* Let's examine the science first. Psychology is an area of scientific study, much like biology or physics. Whereas biology focuses on life processes and physics focuses on matter and energy, psychology focuses on *behavior* and *related mental and physiological processes.*

**Behavior** is any overt (observable) response or activity by an organism. Psychology does *not* confine itself to the study of human behavior. Many psychologists believe that the principles of behavior are much the same for all animals, including humans. As a result, these psychologists often prefer to study animals—

mainly because they can exert more control over the factors influencing the animals' behavior.

Psychology is also interested in the mental processes—the thoughts, feelings, and wishes—that accompany behavior. Mental processes are more difficult to study than behavior because they are private and not directly observable. However, they exert critical influence over human behavior, so psychologists have strived to improve their ability to "look inside the mind."

Finally, psychology includes the study of the physiological processes that underlie behavior. Thus, some psychologists try to figure out how bodily processes such as neural impulses, hormonal secretions, and genetic coding regulate behavior.

Practically speaking, all this means that psychologists study a great variety of phenomena. Psychologists are interested in maze running in rats, salivation in dogs, and brain functioning in cats, as well as visual perception in humans, play in children, and social interaction in adults.

As you probably know, psychology is not all pure science. It has a highly practical side, represented by the many psychologists who provide a variety of professional services to the public. Although the profession of psychology is quite prominent today, this aspect of psychology was actually slow to develop. Until the 1950s psychologists were found almost exclusively in the halls of academia, teaching and doing research. However, the demands of World War II in the 1940s stimulated rapid growth in psychology's first professional specialty—clinical psychology. **Clinical psychology is the branch of psychology concerned with the diagnosis and treatment of psychological problems and disorders.** During World War II, a multitude of academic psychologists were pressed into service as clinicians to screen military recruits and treat soldiers suffering from trauma. Many found their clinical work interesting and returned from the war to set up training programs to meet the continued high demand for clinical services. Soon, about half of the new PhDs in psychology were specializing in clinical work. Psychology had come of age as a profession.

## What Is Adjustment?

We have used the term *adjustment* several times without clarifying its exact meaning. The concept of adjustment was originally borrowed from biology. It was modeled after the biological term *adaptation,* which refers to efforts by a species to adjust to changes in its environment. Just as a field mouse has to adapt to an unusually brutal winter, a person has to adjust to changes in circumstances such as a new job, a financial setback, or the loss of a loved one. Thus, **adjustment refers to the psychological processes through which people manage or cope with the demands and challenges of everyday life.**

The demands of everyday life are diverse, so in studying the process of adjustment we will encounter a broad variety of topics. In our early chapters we discuss general issues, such as how personality affects people's patterns of adjustment, how individuals are affected by stress, and how they use coping strategies to deal with stress. From there we move on to chapters that examine adjustment in an interpersonal context. We discuss topics such as prejudice, persuasion, social conflict, behavior in groups, friendship, love, marriage, divorce, gender roles, career development, and sexuality. Finally, toward the end of the book we discuss how the process of adjustment influences a person's psychological health, look at how psychological disorders can be treated, and delve into the newly developing domain of positive psychology. As you can see, the study of adjustment enters into nearly every corner of people's lives, and we'll be discussing a diverse array of issues and topics. Before we begin considering these topics in earnest, however, we need to take a closer look at psychology's approach to investigating behavior—the scientific method.

# The Scientific Approach to Behavior

### LEARNING OBJECTIVES

- Explain the nature of empiricism.
- Explain two advantages of the scientific approach to understanding behavior.
- Describe the experimental method, distinguishing between independent and dependent variables and between experimental and control groups.

- Distinguish between positive and negative correlation, and explain what the size of a correlation coefficient means.
- Describe three correlational research methods.
- Compare the advantages and disadvantages of experimental versus correlational research.

We all expend a great deal of effort in trying to understand our own behavior as well as the behavior of others. We wonder about any number of behavioral questions: Why am I so anxious when I interact with new people? Why is Sam always trying to be the center of attention at the office? Why does Juanita cheat on her wonderful husband? Are extraverts happier than introverts? Is depression more common during the Christmas holidays?

Given that psychologists' principal goal is to explain behavior, how are their efforts different from everyone else's? The key difference is that psychology is a *science,* committed to *empiricism.*

## The Commitment to Empiricism

*Empiricism* **is the premise that knowledge should be acquired through observation.** When we say that scientific psychology is empirical, we mean that its conclusions are based on systematic observation rather than on reasoning, speculation, traditional beliefs, or common sense. Scientists are not content with having ideas that sound plausible; they must conduct research to *test* their ideas. Whereas our everyday speculations are informal, unsystematic, and highly subjective, scientists' investigations are formal, systematic, and objective.

In these investigations, scientists formulate testable hypotheses, gather data (make observations) relevant to their hypotheses, use statistics to analyze these data, and report their results to the public and other scientists, typically by publishing their findings in a technical journal. The process of publishing scientific studies allows other experts to evaluate and critique new research findings.

## Advantages of the Scientific Approach

Science is certainly not the only method that can be used to draw conclusions about behavior. We can also turn to logic, casual observation, and good old-fashioned common sense. Because the scientific method often requires painstaking effort, it seems reasonable to ask: What exactly are the advantages of the empirical approach?

The scientific approach offers two major advantages. The first is its clarity and precision. Commonsense notions about behavior tend to be vague and ambiguous. Consider the old truism "Spare the rod and spoil the child." What does this generalization about childrearing amount to? How severely should children be punished if parents are not to "spare the rod"? How do parents assess whether a child qualifies as "spoiled"? Such statements can have different meanings to different people. When people disagree about this assertion, it may be because they are talking about entirely different things. In contrast, the empirical approach requires that scientists specify *exactly* what they are talking about when they formulate hypotheses (the ideas they want to test). This clarity and precision enhance communication about important ideas.

The second advantage offered by the scientific approach is its relative intolerance of error. Scientists subject their ideas to empirical tests. They also scrutinize one another's findings with a critical eye. They demand objective data and thorough documentation before they accept ideas. When the findings of two studies conflict, they try to figure out why the studies reached different conclusions, usually by conducting additional research.

In contrast, common sense and casual observation often tolerate contradictory generalizations, such as "Opposites attract" and "Birds of a feather flock together." Furthermore, commonsense analyses involve little effort to verify ideas or detect errors, so that many myths about behavior come to be widely believed.

All this is not to say that science has a copyright on truth. However, the scientific approach does tend to yield more accurate and dependable information than casual analyses and armchair speculation. Knowledge of empirical data can thus provide a useful benchmark against which to judge claims and information from other kinds of sources.

Now that we have an overview of how the scientific enterprise works, we can look at some of the specific research methods that psychologists depend on most. The two main types of research methods in psychology are *experimental* and *correlational.* We discuss them separately because there is an important distinction between them.

## Experimental Research: Looking for Causes

Does misery love company? This question intrigued social psychologist Stanley Schachter. When people feel anxious, do they want to be left alone, or do they prefer to have others around? Schachter's hypothesis was that increases in anxiety would cause increases in the desire to be with others, which psychologists call the *need for affiliation.* To test this hypothesis, Schachter (1959) designed a clever experiment. **The *experiment* is a research method in which the investigator manipulates one (independent) variable under carefully controlled conditions and observes whether any changes occur in a second (dependent) variable as a result.** Psychologists depend on this method more than any other.

### Independent and Dependent Variables
An experiment is designed to find out whether changes in one variable (let's call it $x$) cause changes in another variable (let's call it $y$). To put it more concisely, we want to know how $x$ affects $y$. In this formulation, we refer to $x$ as the independent variable, and we call $y$ the dependent variable. **An *independent variable* is a condition or event that an experimenter varies in order to see its impact on another variable.** The independent variable is the variable that the experimenter controls or manipulates. It is hypothesized to have some effect on the dependent variable. The experiment is conducted to verify this effect. **The *dependent variable* is the variable that is thought to be affected by the manipulations of the independent variable.** In psychology studies, the dependent variable usually is a measurement of some aspect of the subjects' behavior.

In Schachter's experiment, *the independent variable was the participants' anxiety level,* which he manipulated in the following way. Subjects assembled in his laboratory were told by a Dr. Zilstein that they would be participating in a study on the physiological effects of electric shock and that they would receive a series of shocks. Half of the participants were warned that the shocks would be very painful. They made up the *high-anxiety* group. The other half of the participants, assigned to the *low-anxiety* group, were told that the shocks would be mild and painless. These procedures were simply intended to evoke different levels of anxiety. In reality, no one was actually shocked at any time. Instead, the experimenter indicated that there would be a delay while he prepared the shock apparatus for use. The participants were asked whether they would prefer to wait alone or in the company of others. *This measure of the subjects' desire to affiliate with others was the dependent variable.*

### Experimental and Control Groups

To conduct an experiment, an investigator typically assembles two groups of participants who are treated differently in regard to the independent variable. We call these groups the experimental and control groups. **The *experimental group* consists of the subjects who receive some special treatment in regard to the independent variable. The *control group* consists of similar subjects who do not receive the special treatment given to the experimental group.**

Let's return to the Schachter study to illustrate. In this study, the participants in the high-anxiety condition were the experimental group. They received a special treatment designed to create an unusually high level of anxiety. The participants in the low-anxiety condition were the control group.

It is crucial that the experimental and control groups be similar except for the different treatment they receive in regard to the independent variable. This stipulation brings us to the logic that underlies the experimental method. If the two groups are alike in all respects *except for the variation created by the manipulation of the independent variable*, then any differences between the two groups on the dependent variable *must be due to this manipulation of the independent variable.* In this way researchers isolate the effect of the independent variable on the dependent variable. In his experiment, Schachter isolated the impact of anxiety on need for affiliation. What did he find? As predicted, he found that increased anxiety led to increased affiliation. The percentage of people who wanted to wait with others was nearly twice as high in the high-anxiety group as in the low-anxiety group.

The logic of the experimental method rests heavily on the assumption that the experimental and control groups are alike in all important matters except for their different treatment with regard to the independent variable. Any other differences between the two groups cloud the situation and make it difficult to draw solid conclusions about the relationship between the independent variable and the dependent variable. To summarize our discussion of the experimental method, **Figure 1.2** provides an overview of the various elements in an experiment, using Schachter's study as an example.

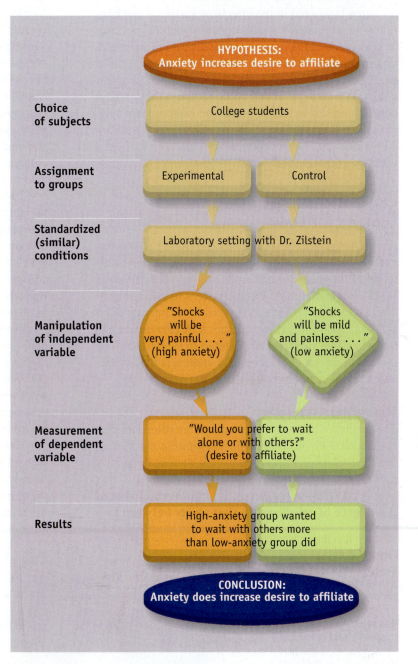

**Figure 1.2**

**The basic elements of an experiment.** This diagram provides an overview of the key features of the experimental method, as illustrated by Schachter's study of anxiety and affiliation. The logic of the experiment rests on treating the experimental and control groups alike except for the manipulation of the independent variable.

## Advantages and Disadvantages

The experiment is a powerful research method. Its principal advantage is that it allows scientists to draw conclusions about cause-and-effect relationships between variables. Researchers can draw these conclusions about causation because the precise control available in the experiment permits them to isolate the relationship between the independent variable and the dependent variable. No other research method can duplicate this advantage.

For all its power, however, the experimental method has its limitations. One disadvantage is that researchers are often interested in the effects of variables that cannot be manipulated (as independent variables) because of ethical concerns or practical realities. For example, you might want to know whether being brought up in an urban area as opposed to a rural area affects people's values. A true experiment would require you to assign similar families to live in urban and rural areas, which obviously is impossible to do. To explore this question, you would have to use correlational research methods, which we turn to next.

## Correlational Research: Looking for Links

As we just noted, in some cases psychologists cannot exert experimental control over the variables they want to study. In such situations, all a researcher can do is make systematic observations to see whether a link or association exists between the variables of interest. Such an association is called a correlation. **A *correlation* exists when two variables are related to each other.** The definitive aspect of correlational studies is that the researchers cannot control the variables under study.

### Measuring Correlation

The results of correlational research are often summarized with a statistic called the *correlation coefficient.* We'll be referring to this widely used statistic frequently as we discuss studies throughout the remainder of this text. **A *correlation coefficient* is a numerical index of the degree of relationship that exists between two**

**WEB LINK 1.4** **Research Methods Tutorials**

Bill Trochim's classes in research and program design at Cornell University have assembled tutorial guides for undergraduate and graduate students for more than 50 topics at this subpage of the Web Center for Social Research Methods. Students new to research design may find these tutorials particularly helpful.

**variables.** A correlation coefficient indicates (1) how strongly related two variables are and (2) the direction (positive or negative) of the relationship.

Two kinds of relationships can be described by a correlation. A *positive* correlation indicates that two variables co-vary in the same direction. This means that high scores on variable *x* are associated with high scores on variable *y* and that low scores on variable *x* are associated with low scores on variable *y*. For example, there is a positive correlation between high school grade point average (GPA) and subsequent college GPA. That is, people who do well in high school tend to do well in college, and those who perform poorly in high school tend to perform poorly in college (see **Figure 1.3**).

In contrast, a *negative* correlation indicates that two variables co-vary in the opposite direction. This means that people who score high on variable *x* tend to score low on variable *y,* whereas those who score low on *x* tend to score high on *y*. For example, in most college courses, there is a negative correlation between how frequently a student is absent and how well the student performs on exams. Students who have a high number of absences tend to earn low exam scores, while students who have a low number of absences tend to get higher exam scores (see **Figure 1.3**).

While the positive or negative sign indicates whether an association is direct or inverse, the *size* of the coefficient indicates the *strength* of the association between two variables. A correlation coefficient can vary between 0 and +1.00 (if positive) or between 0 and −1.00 (if negative). A coefficient near zero tells us there is no relationship between the variables. The closer the correlation is to either −1.00 or +1.00, the stronger the relationship. Thus, a correlation of +.90 represents

**Figure 1.3**

**Positive and negative correlations.** Variables are positively correlated if they tend to increase and decrease together and are negatively correlated if one variable tends to increase when the other decreases. Hence, the terms *positive correlation* and *negative correlation* refer to the *direction* of the relationship between two variables.

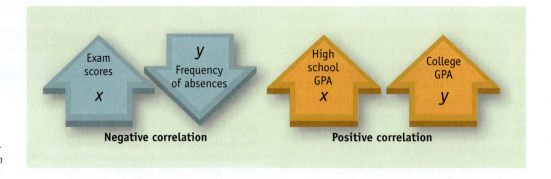

a stronger tendency for variables to be associated than a correlation of +.40 does (see **Figure 1.4**). Likewise, a correlation of −.75 represents a stronger relationship than a correlation of −.45. Keep in mind that the *strength* of a correlation depends only on the size of the coefficient. The positive or negative sign simply shows whether the correlation is direct or inverse. Therefore, a correlation of −.60 reflects a stronger relationship than a correlation of +.30.

Correlational research methods comprise a number of approaches, including naturalistic observation, case studies, and surveys. Let's examine each of these to see how researchers use them to detect associations between variables.

In a creative application of naturalistic observation, Matsumoto and Willingham (2009) shot photos of the award ceremonies for congenitally blind and sighted athletes to gain insight into whether facial expressions of emotion are innate.

© Bob Willingham/bob@twoj.org

### Naturalistic Observation

In *naturalistic observation* **a researcher engages in careful observation of behavior without intervening directly with the subjects.** This type of research is called *naturalistic* because behavior is allowed to unfold naturally (without interference) in its natural environment—that is, the setting in which it would normally occur.

As an example, consider a recent study by Matsumoto and Willingham (2009), which sought to determine whether the facial expressions that go with spontaneous emotions are largely innate. A variety of theorists have suggested that emotional facial expressions are universal across cultures and biologically built-in by-products of evolutionary forces (Eibl-Ebesfeldt, 1975; Izard, 1994). Yet it has proven difficult to clearly demonstrate that emotional facial expressions are not influenced by learning. However, Matsumoto and Willingham came up with an ingenious

way to investigate the issue using naturalistic observation: they compared the facial expressions of congenitally blind athletes with sighted athletes. Learning could not be a source of influence on the facial expressions of congenitally blind individuals, so if the blind athletes' facial expressions turned out to be indistinguishable from those of sighted athletes, this finding would provide definitive evidence on the matter. Thus, Matsumoto and Willingham carefully photographed the facial expressions of congenitally blind judo athletes in the Paralympic Games and of sighted judo athletes in the Olympic Games, just after they had won or lost their crucial final matches (for gold, silver, or bronze medals). The photos were shot right after each match decision was announced and during the medal ceremonies right after the athletes received their medals. The athletes' expressions were evaluated using an elaborate coding system that has been used in countless studies of facial expressions. The analysis of thousands of photos of numerous athletes from 23 countries

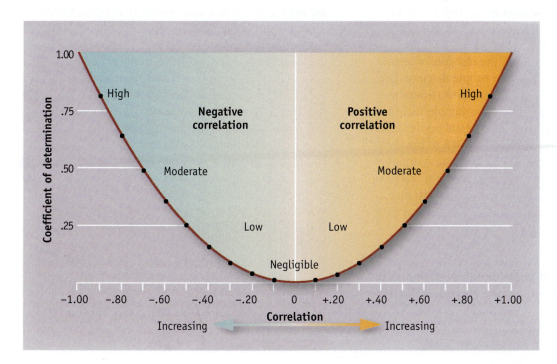

**Figure 1.4**

**Interpreting correlation coefficients.** The magnitude of a correlation coefficient indicates the strength of the relationship between two variables. The closer a correlation is to either +1.00 or −1.00, the stronger the relationship between the variables. The square of a correlation, which is called the *coefficient of determination,* is an index of a correlation's strength and predictive power. This graph shows how the coefficient of determination and predictive power goes up as the magnitude of a correlation increases.

yielded clear results: the facial expressions of sighted and blind athletes were indistinguishable. These findings provide strong support the hypothesis that the facial expressions that go with emotions are wired into the human brain.

## Case Studies

**A *case study* is an in-depth investigation of an individual subject.** Psychologists typically assemble case studies in clinical settings where an effort is being made to diagnose and treat some psychological problem. To achieve an understanding of an individual, a clinician may use a variety of procedures, including interviewing the person, interviewing others who know the individual, direct observation, examination of records, and psychological testing. Usually, a single case study does not provide much basis for deriving general laws of behavior. If researchers have a number of case studies available, however, they can look for threads of consistency among them, and they may be able to draw some general conclusions.

This was the strategy used by a research team in Finland that wanted to explore the psychological characteristics of people who take their own lives (Henriksson et al., 1993; Isometsa et al., 1995). Their sample consisted of all the known suicides in Finland for an entire year. The investigators conducted thorough interviews with the families of the suicide victims and with the health care professionals who had treated them. The researchers also examined the suicide victims' medical, psychiatric, and social agency records, as well as relevant police investigations and forensic reports. Comprehensive case reports were then assembled for each person who committed suicide. These case studies revealed that in 93% of the suicides the victim suffered from a significant psychological disorder (Henriksson et al., 1993). The most common diagnoses, by a large margin, were depression and alcohol dependence. In 571 cases, victims had a health care appointment during the last four weeks of their lives, but only 22% of these people discussed the possibility of suicide during their final visit (Isometsa et al., 1995). Even more surprising, the sample included 100 people who saw a health professional on the same day they killed themselves, yet only 21% of these individuals raised the issue of suicide. The investigators concluded that mental illness is a contributing factor in virtually all completed suicides and that the vast majority of suicidal people do not spontaneously reveal their intentions to health care professionals.

## Surveys

***Surveys* are structured questionnaires designed to solicit information about specific aspects of participants' behavior.** They are sometimes used to measure dependent variables in experiments, but they are mainly used in correlational research. Surveys are commonly used to gather data on people's attitudes and on aspects of behavior that are difficult to observe directly (marital interactions, for instance).

As an example, consider a study by David Schmitt and colleagues (2003) that set out to determine whether gender differences in desire for sexual variety transcend culture. Previous research in the United States had found a significant gender gap in the number of sex partners people reported they would like to have over the course of their lives (Buss & Schmitt, 1993). To find out whether these differences would replicate in other cultures, Schmitt and his associates surveyed 16,288 people from 6 continents, 13 islands, and 52 nations. Their survey, which was translated into a variety of languages, asked participants how many sexual partners they ideally would like to have over time periods ranging from 1 month to 30 years. In the statistical analysis, the data from the 52 nations was grouped into 10 world regions. **Figure 1.5** shows the mean number of sex partners desired over the next 30 years for men and women in the 10 world regions. As you can see, in all 10 regions men reported that they were interested in having substantially more sex partners than women did. The authors conclude that sex differences in the desire for sexual variety "are cross-culturally universal," and they go on to discuss the possible evolutionary significance of this gender gap (see Chapter 9).

## Advantages and Disadvantages

Correlational research methods give psychologists a way to explore questions that they could not examine with experimental procedures. Consider the study of whether gender differences in desire for sexual variety transcend culture. Obviously, investigators cannot manipulate the variables of gender or what culture people are raised in. No one can randomly assign subjects to different cultural backgrounds. But correlational methods allowed Schmitt and his colleagues (2003) to gather useful information on culture, gender, and interest in sexual variety. Thus, *correlational research broadens the scope of phenomena that psychologists can study.*

Unfortunately, correlational methods have one major disadvantage. The investigator does not have the opportunity to control events in a way to isolate cause and effect. *Consequently, correlational research cannot demonstrate conclusively that two variables are*

**WEB LINK 1.5   American Psychological Association (APA)**

As the largest professional organization of psychologists, the APA frequently publicizes research findings related to many of the topics discussed in this textbook. A small sampling of the topics covered at this site would include aging, anxiety, eating disorders, parenting, sexuality, shyness, stress, suicide, therapy, and workplace issues.

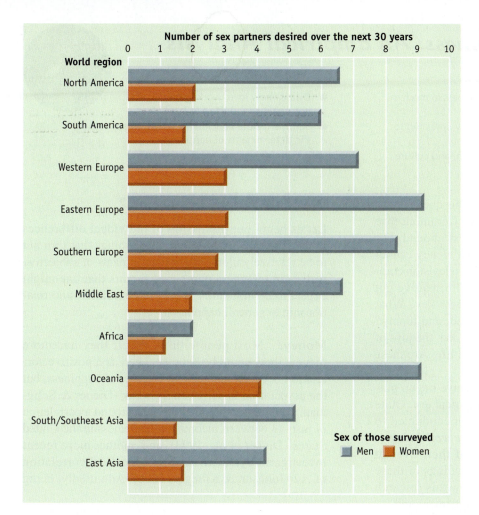

**Number of sex partners desired over the next 30 years**

**Figure 1.5**
**Survey data on the gender gap in desire for a variety of sexual partners.** Schmitt et al. (2003) gathered cross-cultural data on gender disparities in the number of sex partners desired by people. Survey respondents were asked about how many sexual partners they ideally would like to have in the next 30 years. As evolutionary theorists would predict, males reported that they would like to have more sexual partners in all ten world regions examined.

Source: Schmitt, D. P., and 118 Members of the International Sexuality Description Project. (2003). Universal sex differences in the desire for sexual variety: Tests from 52 nations, 6 continents, and 13 islands. *Journal of Personality and Social Psychology, 85,* 85–104. Copyright © 2003 by the American Psychological Association. Reprinted by permission of the authors.

*causally related.* The crux of the problem is that correlation is no assurance of causation.

When we find that variables *x* and *y* are correlated, we can safely conclude only that *x* and *y* are related. We do not know *how x* and *y* are related. We do not know whether *x* causes *y,* whether *y* causes *x,* or whether both are caused by a third variable. For example, survey studies show a positive correlation between relationship satisfaction and sexual satisfaction (Christopher & Sprecher, 2000; Schwartz & Young, 2009). Although it's clear that good sex and a healthy intimate relationship go hand in hand, it's hard to tell what's

causing what. We don't know whether healthy relationships promote good sex or whether good sex promotes healthy relationships. Moreover, we can't rule out the possibility that both are caused by a third variable. Perhaps sexual satisfaction and relationship satisfaction are both caused by compatibility in values. The plausible causal relationships in this case are diagrammed for you in **Figure 1.6**, which illustrates the "third-variable problem" in interpreting correlations. This problem occurs often in correlational research. Indeed, it will surface in the next section, where we review the empirical research on the determinants of happiness.

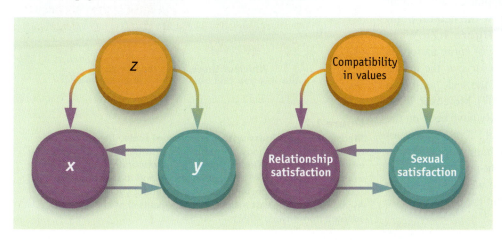

**Figure 1.6**
**Possible causal relations between correlated variables.** When two variables are correlated, there are several possible explanations. It could be that *x* causes *y,* that *y* causes *x,* or that a third variable, *z,* causes changes in both *x* and *y.* As the correlation between relationship satisfaction and sexual satisfaction illustrates, the correlation itself does not provide the answer. This conundrum is sometimes referred to as the "third variable problem."

# The Roots of Happiness: An Empirical Analysis

**LEARNING OBJECTIVES**

- Discuss the prevalence of reported happiness in modern society.
- List the various factors that are surprisingly unrelated to happiness.
- Explain how health, social activity, religion, and culture are related to happiness.
- Discuss how love, work, genetics, and personality are related to happiness.
- Summarize the conclusions drawn about the determinants of happiness.

What exactly makes a person happy? This question has been the subject of much speculation. Commonsense hypotheses about the roots of happiness abound. For example, you have no doubt heard that money cannot buy happiness. But do you believe it? A television commercial says, "If you've got your health, you've got just about everything." Is health indeed the key? What if you're healthy but poor, unemployed, and lonely? We often hear about the joys of parenthood, the joys of youth, and the joys of the simple, rural life. Are these the factors that promote happiness?

In recent years, social scientists have begun putting these and other hypotheses to empirical test. Quite a number of survey studies have been conducted to explore the determinants of *subjective well-being—* **individuals' personal assessments of their overall happiness or life satisfaction.** The findings of these studies are quite interesting. We review this research because it is central to the topic of adjustment and because it illustrates the value of collecting data and putting ideas to an empirical test. As you will see, many commonsense notions about happiness appear to be inaccurate.

The first of these is the apparently widespread assumption that most people are relatively unhappy. Writers, social scientists, and the general public seem to believe that people around the world are predominantly dissatisfied, yet empirical surveys consistently find that the vast majority of respondents—even those who are poor or disabled—characterize themselves as fairly happy (Diener & Diener, 1996). When people are asked to rate their happiness, only a small minority place themselves below the neutral point on the various scales used (see **Figure 1.7**). When the average subjective well-being of entire nations is computed, based on almost 1000 surveys, the means cluster toward the positive end of the scale, as shown in **Figure 1.8** (Tov & Diener, 2007). Moreover, these national happiness scores generally have been on the rise since the 1980s (Inglehart et al., 2008). That's not to say that everyone is equally happy. Researchers have found substantial and thought-provoking disparities among people in subjective well-being, which we will analyze momentarily. But the overall picture seems rosier than anticipated.

## What Isn't Very Important?

Let us begin our discussion of individual differences in happiness by highlighting those things that turn out to be relatively unimportant determinants of subjective well-being. Quite a number of factors that one might expect to be influential appear to bear little or no relationship to general happiness.

**Money.** Most people think that if they had more money, they would be happier. There *is* a positive correlation between income and feelings of happiness, but the association is surprisingly weak (Diener & Seligman, 2004). For example, one study found a correlation of just .13 between income and happiness in the United States (Diener et al., 1993), and another more recent investigation yielded an almost identical correlation of .12 (Johnson & Krueger, 2006). Admittedly, being

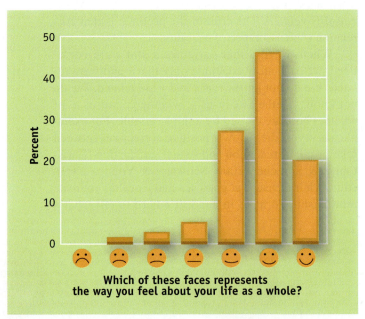

**Figure 1.7**

**Measuring happiness with a nonverbal scale.** Researchers have used a variety of methods to estimate the distribution of happiness. For example, in one study in the United States, respondents were asked to examine the seven facial expressions shown and to select the one that "comes closest to expressing how you feel about your life as a whole." As you can see, the vast majority of participants chose happy faces. (Data adapted from Myers, 1992)

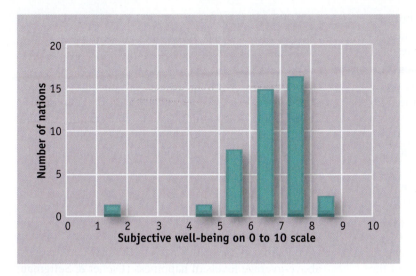

**Figure 1.8**

**The subjective well-being of nations.** Veenhoven (1993) combined the results of almost 1000 surveys to calculate the average subjective well-being reported by representative samples from 43 nations. The mean happiness scores clearly pile up at the positive end of the distribution, with only two scores falling below the neutral point of 5. (Data adapted from Diener and Diener, 1996)

very poor can make people unhappy, but once people ascend above the poverty level, there is little relation between income and happiness. On the average, even very wealthy people are only marginally happier than those in the middle classes. One reason for this weak association is that a disconnect seems to exist between actual income and how people feel about their financial situation. Recent research (Johnson & Krueger, 2006) suggests that the correlation between actual wealth and

people's subjective perceptions of whether they have enough money to meet their needs is surprisingly modest (around .30).

Another problem with money is that in this era of voracious consumption, rising income contributes to escalating material desires (Frey & Stutzer, 2002; Kasser et al., 2004). When these growing material desires outstrip what people can afford, dissatisfaction is likely (Solberg et al., 2002). Thus, complaints about not having enough money are routine even among people who earn hefty six-figure incomes. Interestingly, there is some evidence that people who place an especially strong emphasis on the pursuit of wealth and materialistic goals tend to be somewhat less happy than others (Kasser, 2002; Van Boven, 2005). Perhaps they are so focused on financial success that they derive less satisfaction from other aspects of their lives (Nickerson et al, 2003). Consistent with this view, a study (Kahneman et al., 2006) found that higher income was associated with working longer hours and allocating fewer hours to leisure pursuits (see **Figure 1.9**). Insofar as money does foster happiness, it appears to do so by reducing the negative impact of life's setbacks, allowing wealthier people to feel like they have a little more control over their lives (Johnson & Krueger, 2006; Smith et al., 2005).

**Age.** Age and happiness are consistently found to be unrelated (Lykken, 1999). Age accounts for

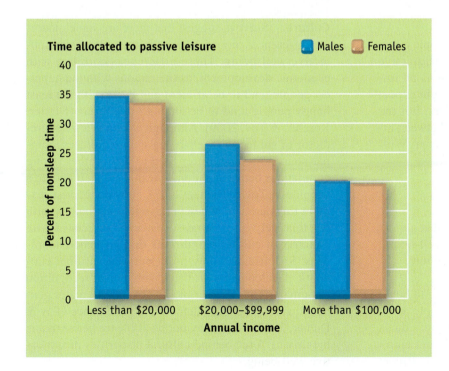

**Figure 1.9**

**Income and leisure.** In an influential study of happiness, Nobel laureate Daniel Kahneman and his colleagues (2006) attempted to shed light on why the association between income and subjective well-being is so weak. One of their key findings was that as income goes up, the time devoted to work increases, and hence, the time left for leisure declines. This graph shows the percentage of nonsleep time devoted to passive leisure activities for three levels of income.

less than 1% of the variation in people's happiness (Inglehart, 1990; Myers & Diener, 1997). The key factors influencing subjective well-being may shift some as people grow older—work becomes less important, health more so—but people's average level of happiness tends to remain remarkably stable over the life span.

**Gender.** Women are treated for depressive disorders about twice as often as men (Nolen-Hoeksema, 2002; see Chapter 14), so one might expect that women are less happy on the average. And Lykken (1999) notes that "men still tend to have better jobs than women do, and get higher pay for the same jobs . . . but they report well-being levels as high as those of men" (p. 181). Thus, like age, gender accounts for less than 1% of the variation in people's subjective well-being (Myers, 1992).

**Parenthood.** Children can be a tremendous source of joy and fulfillment, but they can also be a tremendous source of headaches and hassles. Compared to childless couples, parents worry more and experience more marital problems (Argyle, 1987). Apparently, the good and bad aspects of parenthood balance each other out, because the evidence indicates that people who have children are neither more nor less happy than people without children (Argyle, 2001).

**Intelligence.** Intelligence is a highly valued trait in modern society, but researchers have not found an association between IQ scores and happiness (Diener, Kesebir, & Tov, 2009). Educational attainment also appears to be unrelated to life satisfaction (Ross & Van Willigen, 1997).

**Physical attractiveness.** Good-looking people enjoy a variety of advantages in comparison to unattractive people. Given that physical attractiveness is an important resource in Western society, we might expect attractive people to be happier than others, but the available data indicate that the correlation between attractiveness and happiness is negligible (Diener, Wolsic, & Fujita, 1995).

## What Is Somewhat Important?

Research has identified four facets of life that appear to have a moderate impact on subjective well-being: health, social activity, religious belief, and culture.

**Health.** Good physical health would seem to be an essential requirement for happiness, but people adapt to health problems. Research reveals that individuals who develop serious, disabling health conditions aren't as unhappy as one might guess (Myers, 1992; Riis et

al., 2005). Good health may not, by itself, produce happiness, because people tend to take good health for granted. Such considerations may help explain why researchers find only a moderate positive correlation (average = .32) between health status and subjective well-being (Argyle, 1999). While health may promote happiness to a moderate degree, happiness may also foster better health, as recent research has found a positive correlation between happiness and longevity (Veenhoven, 2008).

**Social activity.** Humans are social animals, and people's interpersonal relations *do* appear to contribute to their happiness. People who are satisfied with their friendship networks and who are socially active report above-average levels of happiness (Diener & Seligman, 2004; Myers, 1999). And people who score as exceptionally happy tend to report greater satisfaction with their social relations than others (Diener & Seligman, 2002).

**Religion.** The link between religiosity and subjective well-being is modest, but a number of surveys suggest that people with heartfelt religious convictions are more likely to be happy than people who characterize themselves as nonreligious (Abdel-Khalek, 2006; Myers, 2008). Researchers aren't sure how religious faith fosters happiness, but Myers (1992) offers some interesting conjectures. Among other things, he discusses how religion can give people a sense of purpose and meaning in their lives, help them accept their setbacks gracefully, connect them to a caring, supportive community, and comfort them by putting their ultimate mortality in perspective.

**Culture.** Surveys suggest that there are some moderate differences among nations in mean levels of subjective well-being. These differences correlate with economic development, as the nations with the happiest people tend to be affluent and those with the least happy people tend to be among the poorest (Diener, Kesebir, & Tov, 2009). Although wealth is a weak predictor of subjective well-being *within* cultures, comparisons *between* cultures tend to yield rather strong correlations between nations' wealth and their people's happiness (Tov & Diener, 2007). How do theorists explain this paradox? They believe that national wealth is a relatively easy-to-measure marker associated with a matrix of cultural conditions that influence happiness. Specifically, they point out that nations' economic development correlates with greater recognition of human rights, greater income equality, greater gender equality, and more democratic governance (Tov & Diener, 2007). So, it may not be affluence per se that is the driving force behind cultural disparities in subjective well-being.

Research on the correlates of happiness suggests that two key ingredients of happiness are a rewarding work life and satisfaction in intimate relationships.

## What Is Very Important?

The list of factors that turn out to be very important ingredients of happiness is surprisingly short. Only a few variables are strongly related to overall happiness.

**Love, marriage, and relationship satisfaction.** Romantic relationships can be stressful, but people consistently rate being in love as one of the most critical ingredients of happiness (Myers, 1999). Furthermore, although people complain a lot about their marriages, the evidence indicates that marital status is a key correlate of happiness. Among both men and women, married people are happier than people who are single or divorced (see **Figure 1.10**; Myers & Diener, 1995), and this disparity holds around the world in widely different cultures (Diener et al., 2000). And among married people, marital satisfaction predicts personal well-being (Proulx, Helms, & Buehler, 2007).

The research in this area generally has used marital status as a crude but easily measured marker of relationship satisfaction. In all likelihood, it is relationship satisfaction that fosters happiness. In other words, one does not have to be married to be happy. Relationship satisfaction probably has the same association with happiness in cohabiting heterosexual couples and gay couples.

**Work.** Given the way people often complain about their jobs, we might not expect work to be a key source of happiness, but it is. Although less critical than relationship satisfaction, job satisfaction is strongly associated with general happiness (Judge & Klinger, 2008; Warr, 1999). Studies also show that unemployment has strong negative effects on subjective well-being (Lucas et al., 2004). It is difficult to sort out whether job satisfaction causes happiness or vice versa, but evidence suggests that causation flows both ways (Argyle, 2001).

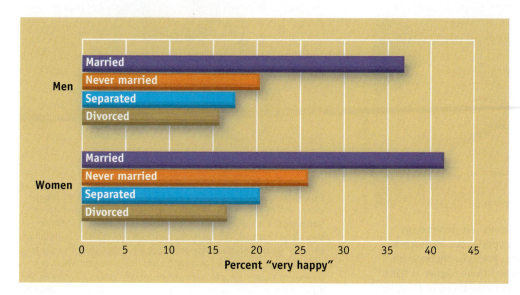

### Figure 1.10

**Happiness and marital status.** This graph shows the percentage of adults characterizing themselves as "very happy" as a function of marital status. Among both women and men, happiness shows up more in those who are married as opposed to those who are separated, who are divorced, or who have never married. These data and many other findings suggest that relationship satisfaction is a key ingredient of happiness.

Source: Adapted from Myers, D. G. (1999). Close relationships and quality of life (Fig. 19.1). In D. Kahneman, E. Diener, & N. Schwarz (Eds.), *Well-being: The foundations of hedonic psychology*, New York: Russell Sage Foundation. Copyright © 1999 Russell Sage Foundation, 112 East 64th St., NY, NY 10065. Reprinted with permission.

**Genetics and personality.** The best predictor of individuals' future happiness is their past happiness (Lucas & Diener, 2008). Some people seem destined to be happy and others unhappy, regardless of their triumphs or setbacks. The limited influence of life events was highlighted in a fascinating study that found only modest differences in overall happiness between recent lottery winners and recent accident victims who became quadriplegics (Brickman, Coates, & Janoff-Bulman, 1978). Investigators were amazed that extremely fortuitous and horrible events like these didn't have a dramatic impact on happiness. Actually, *several* lines of evidence suggest that happiness does not depend on external circumstances—buying a nice house, getting promoted—as much as on internal factors, such as one's outlook on life (Lykken & Tellegen, 1996; Lyubomirsky, Sheldon, & Schkade, 2005).

With this reality in mind, researchers have investigated whether there might be a hereditary basis for variations in happiness. These studies suggest that people's genetic predispositions account for a substantial portion of the variance in happiness, perhaps as much as 50% (Lyubomirsky et al., 2005; Stubbe et al., 2005). How can one's genes influence one's happiness? Presumably, by shaping one's temperament and personality, which are known to be highly heritable (Weiss, Bates,

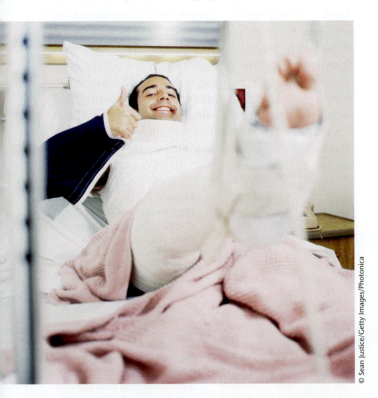

© Sean Justice/Getty Images/Photonica

**Research shows that happiness does not depend on people's positive and negative experiences as much as one would expect. Some people, presumably because of their personality, seem destined to be happy in spite of major setbacks, and others seem destined to cling to unhappiness even though their lives seem reasonably pleasant.**

& Luciano, 2008). Hence, researchers have begun to look for links between personality and subjective well-being, and they have found some relatively strong correlations. For example, *extraversion* is one of the better predictors of happiness (Lucas & Diener, 2008). People who are outgoing, upbeat, and sociable tend to be happier than others. Additional personality correlates of happiness include conscientiousness, agreeableness, self-esteem, and optimism (Lucas, 2008; Lyubomirsky, Tkach, & DiMatteo, 2006).

## Conclusions

We must be cautious in drawing inferences about the causes of happiness, because most of the available data are correlational (see **Figure 1.11**). Nonetheless, the empirical evidence suggests that many popular beliefs about the sources of happiness are unfounded. The data also demonstrate that happiness is shaped by a complex constellation of variables. Despite this complexity, however, a number of worthwhile insights about human adjustment can be gleaned from research on the correlates of subjective well-being.

First, research on happiness demonstrates that the determinants of subjective well-being are precisely that: subjective. *Objective realities are not as important as subjective feelings.* In other words, your health, your wealth, your job, and your age are not as influential as how you *feel* about your health, wealth, job, and age (Schwarz & Strack, 1999).

Second, *when it comes to happiness, everything is relative* (Argyle, 1999; Hagerty, 2000). In other words,

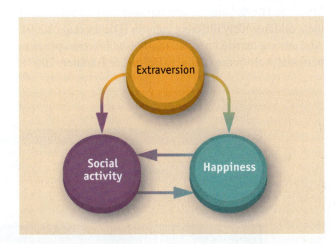

**Figure 1.11**

**Possible causal relations among the correlates of happiness.** Although we have considerable data on the correlates of happiness, it is difficult to untangle the possible causal relationships. For example, we know that a moderate positive correlation exists between social activity and happiness, but we can't say for sure whether high social activity causes happiness or whether happiness causes people to be more socially active. Moreover, in light of the finding that a third variable—extraversion—correlates with both variables, we have to consider the possibility that extraversion causes both greater social activity and greater happiness.

you evaluate what you have relative to what the people around you have. Thus, people who are wealthy assess what they have by comparing themselves to their wealthy friends and neighbors. This is one reason for the low correlation between wealth and happiness. You might have a lovely home, but if it sits next to a neighbor's palatial mansion, it might be a source of more dissatisfaction than happiness. People's evaluations are also made relative to their *expectations*. Research suggests that bad outcomes feel worse when unexpected than when expected, while good outcomes feel better when unexpected than when expected (Shepperd & McNulty, 2002). Thus, the same objective event, such as a pay raise of $2000 annually, may generate positive feelings in someone who wasn't expecting a raise and negative feelings in someone expecting a much larger increase.

Third, *research on happiness has shown that people are surprisingly bad at predicting what will make them happy.* We assume that we know what is best for us. But research on **affective forecasting—efforts to predict one's emotional reactions to future events—**suggests otherwise (Gilbert, 2006; Hsee & Hastie, 2005; Wilson & Gilbert, 2005). People routinely overestimate the pleasure that they will derive from buying an expensive automobile, taking an exotic vacation, earning an important promotion, moving to a beautiful coastal city, or building their dream home (see the Recommended Reading Box and Chapter 6 for more on affective forecasting). Likewise, people tend to overestimate the misery and regret that they will experience if they have a romantic breakup, don't get into the college they want, fail to get a promotion, or develop a serious illness. Thus, the roadmap to happiness is less clearly marked than widely assumed.

Fourth, *research on subjective well-being indicates that people often adapt to their circumstances.* This adaptation effect is one reason that an increase in income doesn't necessarily bring an increase in happiness. Thus, **hedonic adaptation occurs when the mental scale that people use to judge the pleasantness-unpleasantness of their experiences shifts so that their neutral point, or baseline for comparison, is changed** (*hedonic* means related to pleasure). Unfortunately, when people's experiences improve, hedonic adaptation may *sometimes* put them on a *hedonic treadmill*—their baseline moves upward, so that the improvements yield no real benefits (Kahneman, 1999). However, when people have to grapple with major setbacks, hedonic adaptation probably helps protect their mental and physical health. For example, people who are sent to prison and people who develop debilitating diseases are not as unhappy as one might assume, because they adapt to their changed situations and evaluate events from a new perspective (Frederick & Loewenstein, 1999).

That's not to say that hedonic adaptation in the face of life's difficulties is inevitable or complete (Lucas,

## Recommended READING

### Stumbling on Happiness
by Daniel Gilbert (HarperCollins, 2006)

Do you think you know what will make you happy? Think again. If you read this book, you won't be nearly so confident about what will provide you with pleasure in the years to come. Daniel Gilbert is a Harvard psychologist who has pioneered research on *affective forecasting*—people's tendency to predict their emotional reactions to future events. This research shows that people tend to be reasonably accurate in anticipating whether events will generate positive or negative emotions, but they often are way off the mark in predicting the intensity and duration of their emotional reactions. Why are people's predictions of their emotional reactions surprisingly inaccurate? A number of factors can contribute. One consideration is that people often assume they will spend a lot of time dwelling on a setback or relishing a triumph, but in reality a variety of other events and concerns will compete for their attention. Another consideration is that most people do not fully appreciate just how effective humans tend to be in rationalizing, discounting, and overlooking their failures and mistakes. People exhibit several cognitive biases that help them insulate themselves from the emotional fallout of life's difficulties. But they do not factor this peculiar "talent" into the picture when making predictions about their emotional reactions to setbacks. In this wide-ranging book, Gilbert ventures far beyond the work on affective forecasting, profiling research on a host of related topics (especially peculiarities in decision making), but the central theme is that people's expectations about what will bring them happiness are surprisingly inaccurate. As you may have already gathered, this is not a self-help book per se. But it makes for fascinating reading that has some important implications for the never-ending pursuit of happiness. Although he describes a great deal of research, Gilbert's writing is so accessible, engaging, and humorous it never feels like a review of research.

*Go to the Psychology CourseMate for Weiten at* **www.cengagebrain.com/shop/ISBN/1111186634** *for descriptions of other recommended books.*

2007). Evidence suggests that people adapt more slowly to negative events than to positive ones (Larsen & Prizmic, 2008). Thus, even years later, people who suffer major setbacks, such as the death of a spouse or a serious illness, often are not as happy as they were before the setback, but generally they are not nearly as unhappy as they or others would have predicted (Diener & Oishi, 2005). The downside to the concept of hedonic adaptation is that it suggests that there is nothing people can do to increase their happiness. Fortunately, recent research on the hedonic treadmill is not as pessimistic as earlier research (Diener, Lucas, & Scollon, 2006). Although, this research has provided additional evidence that the hedonic treadmill is a genuine and common phenomenon, it has also shown that people vary considerably in the degree to which they experience hedonic adaptation and that enduring increases in individuals' set points for happiness can be achieved.

We turn next to an example of how psychological research can be applied to everyday problems. In our first application section, we will review research evidence related to the challenge of being a successful student.

# Improving Academic Performance

### LEARNING OBJECTIVES

- List three steps for developing sound study habits.
- Discuss some strategies for improving reading comprehension.
- Summarize advice on how to get more out of lectures.
- Summarize how memory is influenced by practice, organization, and depth of processing.
- Describe several mnemonic devices that can aid memory.

*Answer the following "true" or "false."*

___ **1.** If you have a professor who delivers chaotic, hard-to-follow lectures, there is little point in attending class.

___ **2.** Cramming the night before an exam is an efficient way to study.

___ **3.** In taking lecture notes, you should try to be a "human tape recorder" (that is, take down everything exactly as said by your professor).

___ **4.** Outlining reading assignments is a waste of time.

As you will soon learn, all of these statements are false. If you answered them all correctly, you may already have acquired the kinds of skills and habits that lead to academic success. If so, however, you are not typical. Today, a huge number of students enter college with remarkably poor study skills and habits—and it's not entirely their fault. The U.S. educational system generally does not provide much in the way of formal instruction on good study techniques. So, in this first Application, we'll start with the basics and try to remedy this deficiency to some extent by sharing some insights that psychology can provide on how to improve your academic performance. We will discuss how to promote better study habits, how to enhance reading efforts, how to get more out of lectures, and how to make your memory more effective.

## Developing Sound Study Habits

Effective study is crucial to success in college. You may run into a few classmates who boast about getting good grades without studying, but you can be sure that if they perform well on exams, they study. Students who claim otherwise simply want to be viewed as extremely bright rather than as studious.

Learning can be immensely gratifying, but studying usually involves hard work. The first step toward effective study habits is to face this reality. You don't have to feel guilty if you don't look forward to studying. Most students don't. Once you accept the premise that studying doesn't come naturally, it should be clear that you need to set up an organized program to promote adequate study. Such a program should include the following three considerations (Siebert & Karr, 2003).

**Set up a schedule for studying.** Research on the differences between successful and unsuccessful college students suggests that successful students monitor and regulate their use of time more effectively (Allgood et al., 2000). If you wait until the urge to study hits you, you may still be waiting when the exam rolls around. Thus, it is important to allocate

**WEB LINK 1.6  Sites to Promote Academic Success**

This site provides links to a number of other sites that provide advice on a diverse array of study-related topics, such as time management, effective note taking, memory-improvement strategies, and test-taking skills. Developed by Linda Walsh, a psychology professor at the University of Northern Iowa, it is an invaluable resource for students seeking to improve their chances of academic success.

definite times to study. Review your time obligations (work, housekeeping, and so on) and figure out in advance when you can study. In allotting certain times to studying, keep in mind that you need to be wide awake and alert. Be realistic, too, about how long you can study at one time before you wear down from fatigue. Allow time for study breaks; they can revive sagging concentration.

It's important to write down your study schedule. Doing so serves as a reminder and increases your commitment to the schedule. As shown in **Figure 1.12**, you should begin by setting up a general schedule for the quarter or semester. Then, at the beginning of each week, plan the specific assignments that you intend to work on during each study session. This approach should help you avoid cramming for exams at the last minute. Cramming is an ineffective study strategy for most students (L. A. Wong, 2006). It will strain your memorization capabilities, can tax your energy level, and may stoke the fires of test anxiety.

In planning your weekly schedule, try to avoid the tendency to put off working on major tasks such as term papers and reports. Time management experts such as Alan Lakein (1996) point out that many of us tend to tackle simple, routine tasks first, saving larger tasks for later, when we supposedly will have more time. This common tendency leads many of us to delay working on major assignments until it's too late to do a good job. You can avoid this trap by breaking major assignments into smaller component tasks that you schedule individually.

Although some students downplay the importance of study efforts, the reality is that effective study habits are crucial to academic success.

**Find a place to study where you can concentrate.** Where you study is also important. The key is to find a place where distractions are likely to be minimal. Most people cannot study effectively while watching TV, listening to loud music, or overhearing conversations. Don't depend on willpower to carry you through these distractions. It's much easier to plan ahead and avoid the distractions altogether. Some learning theorists believe that it is wise to set up one or two specific places used solely for study (Hettich, 1998).

**Reward your studying.** One of the reasons it is so difficult to motivate oneself to study regularly is that the payoffs for studying often lie in the distant future. The ultimate reward, a degree, may be years away. Even shorter-term rewards, such as an A in the course, may be weeks or months off. To combat this problem, it helps to give yourself immediate rewards for studying. It is easier to motivate yourself to study if you reward yourself with a tangible payoff, such as a snack, TV show, or phone call to a friend, when you finish. Thus, you should set realistic study goals and then reward yourself when you meet them. This systematic manipulation of rewards involves harnessing the principles of *behavior modification*, which are described in some detail in the Chapter 3 Application.

## Improving Your Reading

Much of your study time is spent reading and absorbing information. The keys to improving reading comprehension are to preview reading assignments section by section, work hard to actively process the meaning of the information, strive to identify the key ideas of each paragraph, and carefully review these key ideas after each section. Modern

|  | Mon | Tues | Wed | Thurs | Fri | Sat | Sun |
|---|---|---|---|---|---|---|---|
| 8 A.M. |  |  |  |  |  | Work |  |
| 9 A.M. | History | Study | History | Study | History | Work |  |
| 10 A.M. | Psych |  | Psych |  | Psych | Work |  |
| 11 A.M. | Study | French | Study | French | Study | Work |  |
| Noon | Math | Study | Math | Study | Math | Work | Study |
| 1 P.M. |  |  |  |  |  |  | Study |
| 2 P.M. | Study |  | Study |  | Study |  | Study |
| 3 P.M. | Study | English | Study | English | Study |  | Study |
| 4 P.M. |  |  |  |  |  |  |  |
| 5 P.M. |  |  |  |  |  |  |  |
| 6 P.M. | Work | Study | Work |  |  |  | Study |
| 7 P.M. | Work | Study | Work |  |  |  | Study |
| 8 P.M. | Work | Study | Work |  |  |  | Study |
| 9 P.M. | Work | Study | Work |  |  |  | Study |
| 10 P.M. | Work |  | Work |  |  |  |  |

**Figure 1.12**

**Example of an activity schedule.** One student's general activity schedule for a semester is shown here. Each week the student fills in the specific assignments to work on during the upcoming study sessions.

textbooks often contain a variety of learning aids that you can use to improve your reading. If a book provides a chapter outline, chapter summary, or learning objectives, don't ignore them. They can help you recognize the important points in the chapter. A lot of effort and thought go into formulating these and other textbook learning aids. It is wise to take advantage of them.

Another important issue related to textbook reading is whether and how to mark up one's reading assignments. Many students deceive themselves into thinking that they are studying by running a marker through a few sentences here and there in their text. If they do so without thoughtful selectivity, they are simply turning a textbook into a coloring book. This reality probably explains why some professors are skeptical about the value of highlighting textbooks. Nonetheless, research suggests that highlighting textbook material *is* a useful strategy—if students are reasonably effective in focusing on the main ideas in the material and if they subsequently review what they have highlighted (Caverly, Orlando, & Mullen, 2000).

When executed effectively, highlighting can foster active reading, improve reading comprehension, and reduce the amount of material that one has to review later (Van Blerkom, 2006). The key to effective text marking is to identify (and highlight) only the main ideas, key supporting details, and technical terms (Daiek & Anter, 2004). Most textbooks are carefully crafted such that every paragraph has a purpose for being there. Try to find the sentence or two that best captures the purpose of each paragraph. Text marking is a delicate balancing act. If you highlight too little of the content, you are not identifying enough of the key ideas. But if you highlight too much of the content, you are not going to succeed in condensing what you have to review to a manageable size.

## Getting More out of Lectures

Although lectures are sometimes boring and tedious, it is a simple fact that poor class attendance is associated with poor grades. For example, Lindgren (1969) found that absences from class were much more common among "unsuccessful" students (grade average of C− or below) than among "successful" students (grade average of B or above), as shown in **Figure 1.13**. Even when you have an instructor who delivers hard-to-follow lectures from which you learn virtually nothing, it is still important to go to class. If nothing else, you'll get a feel for how the instructor thinks. Doing so can help you anticipate the content of exams and respond in the manner your professor expects.

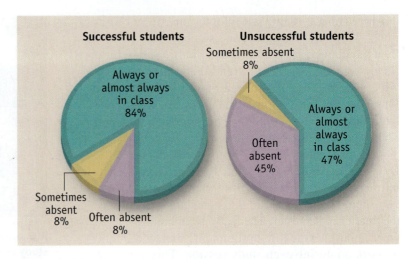

**Figure 1.13**

**Successful and unsuccessful students' class attendance.** Lindgren (1969) found that attendance was much better among successful students than unsuccessful students.

Fortunately, most lectures are reasonably coherent. Studies indicate that attentive note taking *is* associated with enhanced learning and performance in college classes (Titsworth & Kiewra, 2004; Williams & Eggert, 2002). However, research also shows that many students' lecture notes are surprisingly incomplete, with the average student often recording less than 40% of the crucial ideas in a lecture (Armbruster, 2000). Thus, the key to getting more out of lectures is to stay motivated, stay attentive, and expend the effort to make your notes as complete as possible. Books on study skills (Longman & Atkinson, 2005; McWhorter, 2007) offer a number of suggestions on how to take good-quality lecture notes. These suggestions include:

● *Use active listening procedures.* With active listening, you focus full attention on the speaker. Try to anticipate what's coming and search for deeper meanings. Pay attention to nonverbal signals that may serve to further clarify the lecturer's intent or meaning.

● *Prepare for lectures by reading ahead on the scheduled subject in your text.* Then you have less information to digest that is brand new. This strategy is especially important when course material is complex and difficult.

● *Write down lecturers' thoughts in your own words.* Don't try to be a human tape recorder. Translating the lecture into your own words forces you to organize the ideas in a way that makes sense to you.

● *Look for subtle and not-so-subtle clues about what the instructor considers to be important.* These clues may range from simply repeating main points to saying things like "You'll run into this again."

● *Ask questions during lectures.* Doing so keeps you actively involved and allows you to clarify points you may have misunderstood. Many students are more

bashful about asking questions than they should be. They don't realize that most professors welcome questions.

## Applying Memory Principles

Scientific investigation of memory processes dates back to 1885, when Hermann Ebbinghaus published a series of insightful studies. Since then, psychologists have discovered a number of principles about memory that are relevant to helping you improve your study skills.

### Engage in Adequate Practice

Practice makes perfect, or so you've heard. In reality, practice is not likely to guarantee perfection, but repeatedly reviewing information usually leads to improved retention. Studies show that retention improves with increased rehearsal (Greene, 1992). Continued rehearsal may also pay off by improving your *understanding* of assigned material (Bromage & Mayer, 1986). Evidence suggests that it even pays to overlearn material (Driskell, Willis, & Copper, 1992). **Overlearning** *is continued* **rehearsal of material after you have first appeared to master it.** In one study, after participants mastered a list of nouns (they recited the list without error), Krueger (1929) required them to continue rehearsing for 50% or 100% more trials (repetitions). Measuring

retention at intervals of up to 28 days, Kreuger found that overlearning led to better recall of the list. Modern studies have also shown that overlearning can enhance performance on an exam that occurs within a week, although the evidence on its long-term benefits (months later) is inconsistent (Peladeau, Forget, & Gagne, 2003; Rohrer et al., 2005).

Although the benefits of practice are well known, people have a curious tendency to overestimate their knowledge of a topic and how well they will perform on a subsequent memory test of this knowledge (Koriat & Bjork, 2005). That's why it is a good idea to informally test yourself on information that you think you have mastered before confronting a real test. In addition to checking your mastery, recent research suggests that testing actually enhances retention, a phenomenon dubbed the *testing effect* (Karpicke & Roediger, 2008; Roediger & Karpicke, 2006a). Studies have shown that taking a test on material increases performance on a subsequent test even more than studying for an equal amount of time (see **Figure 1.14** on the next page). Interestingly, the testing effect is observed on both closed-book and open-book exams (Agarwal et al., 2008), and the favorable effects of testing are enhanced if participants are provided feedback on their test performance (Butler & Roediger, 2008). Why is testing so

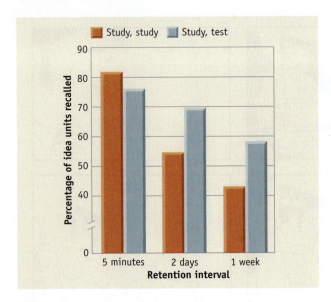

**Figure 1.14**
**The testing effect.** In one study by Roediger and Karpicke (2006b), participants studied a brief prose passage for 7 minutes. Then, some of them studied it again for 7 minutes while others took a 7-minute test on the material. In the second phase of the study, subjects took another test on the material after either 5 minutes, 2 days, or 1 week. There wasn't much of a performance gap when subjects were tested over a 5-minute retention interval, but the testing group showed a significant advantage in recall when the retention interval was extended to 2 days or 1 week.

Source: Roediger, III, H. L., & Karpicke, J. D. (2006). Test-enhanced learning: Taking memory tests improves long-term retention. *Psychological Science, 17*(3), 249–255. Copyright © 2006 Blackwell Publishing. Reprinted by permission of Sage Publications.

beneficial? Theorists are not sure yet, but the key may be that testing forces students to engage in deeper processing of the material (Roediger & Karpicke, 2006b). In any event, self-testing appears to be an excellent memory tool, which suggests that it would be prudent to take the Practice Tests in this text or additional tests available on the website for the book.

**Figure 1.15**
**Effects of massed versus distributed practice on retention.** In a review of over 300 experiments on massed versus distributed practice, Cepeda et al. (2006) examined the importance of the retention interval. As you can see, spaced practice was superior to massed practice at all retention intervals, but the gap widened at longer intervals. These findings suggest that distributed practice is especially advantageous when you need or want to remember material over the long haul. (Based on data from Cepeda et al., 2006)

## Use Distributed Practice

Let's assume that you are going to study 9 hours for an exam. Is it better to "cram" all of your study into one 9-hour period (massed practice) or distribute it among, say, three 3-hour periods on successive days (distributed practice)? The evidence indicates that retention tends to be greater after distributed practice than massed practice (Rohrer & Taylor, 2006; Seabrook, Brown, & Solity, 2005). Moreover, a recent review of over 300 experiments (Cepeda et al., 2006) showed that the longer the retention interval between studying and testing, the bigger the advantage for massed practice, as shown in **Figure 1.15**. The same review concluded that the longer the retention interval, the longer the optimal "break" between practice trials. When an upcoming test is more than two days away, the optimal interval between practice periods appears to be around 24 hours. The superiority of distributed practice over massed practice provides another reason why cramming is an ill-advised approach to studying for exams.

## Organize Information

Retention tends to be greater when information is well organized (Einstein & McDaniel, 2004). Hierarchical organization is particularly helpful when it is applicable (Tigner, 1999). Thus, it may be a good idea to *outline* reading assignments for school. Consistent with this reasoning, there is some empirical evidence that outlining material from textbooks can enhance retention of the material (McDaniel, Waddill, & Shakesby, 1996).

## Emphasize Deep Processing

One line of research suggests that how *often* you go over material is less critical than the *depth* of processing that you engage in (Craik & Tulving, 1975). Thus, if you expect to remember what you read, you have to

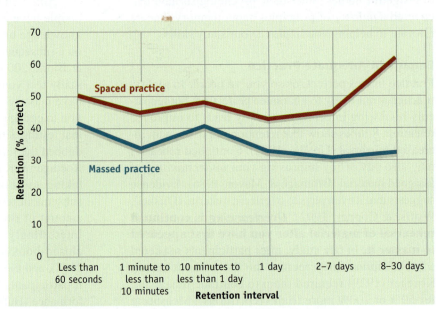

wrestle fully with its meaning (Einstein & McDaniel, 2004). Many students could probably benefit if they spent less time on rote repetition and devoted more effort to actually paying attention to and analyzing the meaning of their reading assignments. In particular, it is useful to make material *personally* meaningful. When you read your textbooks, try to relate information to your own life and experience. For example, if you're reading in your psychology text about the personality trait of assertiveness, you can think about which people you know who are particularly assertive and why you would characterize them as being that way.

## Use Mnemonic Devices

Of course, it's not always easy to make something personally meaningful. When you study chemistry, you may have a hard time relating to polymers at a personal level. This problem has led to the development of many **mnemonic devices, or strategies for enhancing memory,** that are designed to make abstract material more meaningful.

**Acrostics and acronyms.** *Acrostics* are phrases (or poems) in which the first letter of each word (or line) functions as a cue to help you recall the abstract words that begin with the same letter. For instance, you may remember the order of musical notes with the saying "Every good boy does fine" (or "deserves favor"). A variation on acrostics is the *acronym*—a word formed out of the first letters of a series of words. Students memorizing the order of colors in the light spectrum often store the name "Roy G. Biv" to remember red, orange, yellow, green, blue, indigo, and violet. Acrostics and acronyms that individuals create for themselves can be effective memory tools (Hermann, Raybeck, & Greenberg, 2002).

**Rhymes.** Another verbal mnemonic that people often rely on is rhyming. You've probably repeated, "I before E except after C" thousands of times. Perhaps you also remember the number of days in each month with the old standby, "Thirty days hath September . . ." Rhyming something to remember it is an old and useful trick.

**Link method.** The *link method* involves forming a mental image of items to be remembered in a

way that links them together. For instance, suppose that you are going to stop at the drugstore on the way home and you need to remember to pick up a news magazine, shaving cream, film, and pens. To remember these items, you might visualize a public figure likely to be in the magazine shaving with a pen while being photographed. Some researchers suggest that the more bizarre the images, the better they will be remembered (Iaccino, 1996; Worthen, 1997).

**Method of loci.** The *method of loci* involves taking an imaginary walk along a familiar path where you have associated images of items you want to remember with certain locations. The first step is to commit to memory a series of loci, or places along a path. Usually these loci are specific locations in your home or neighborhood. Then envision each thing you want to remember in one of these locations. Try to form distinctive, vivid images. When you need to remember the items, imagine yourself walking along the path. The various loci on your path should serve as retrieval cues for the images that you formed (see **Figure 1.16**). The method of loci assures that items are remembered in their correct order because the order is determined by the sequence of locations along the pathway. Empirical studies have supported the value of this method for memorizing lists (Massen & Vaterrodt-Plünnecke, 2006; Moe & De Beni, 2004).

### Figure 1.16

**The method of loci.** In this example from Bower (1970), a person about to go shopping pairs items to be remembered with familiar places (loci) arranged in a natural sequence: (1) hot dogs/driveway; (2) cat food/garage; (3) tomatoes/front door; (4) bananas/coat closet; (5) whiskey/kitchen sink. As the last panel shows, the shopper recalls the items by mentally touring the loci associated with them.

Source: Adapted from Bower, G. H. (1970). Analysis of a mnemonic device. *American Scientist, 58,* 496–499. Copyright © 1970 by Scientific Research Society. Reprinted by permission.

### The Paradox of Progress

● Although our modern era has seen great technological progress, personal problems have not diminished. In spite of many time-saving devices, people tend to have less free time. The life choices available to people have increased greatly, but Schwartz argues that choice overload undermines individuals' happiness.

● Although we have unprecedented control over the world around us, we seem to create as many problems as we solve. Thus, many theorists argue that technological progress has brought new, and possibly more difficult, adjustment problems.

### The Search for Direction

● According to many theorists, the basic challenge of modern life has become the search for a sense of direction and meaning. This search has many manifestations, including the appeal of self-realization programs, religious cults, and media "therapists" such as Dr. Laura.

● The enormous popularity of self-help books is an interesting manifestation of people's struggle to find a sense of direction. Some self-help books offer worthwhile advice, but most are dominated by psychobabble and are not based on scientific research. Many also lack explicit advice on how to change behavior and some encourage a self-centered, narcissistic approach to interpersonal interactions.

● Although this text deals with many of the same issues as self-realization programs, self-help books, and other types of pop psychology, its philosophy and approach are quite different. This text is based on the premise that accurate knowledge about the principles of psychology can be of value in everyday life.

### The Psychology of Adjustment

● Psychology is both a science and a profession that focuses on behavior and related mental and physiological processes. Adjustment is a broad area of study in psychology concerned with how people adapt effectively or ineffectively to the demands and pressures of everyday life.

### The Scientific Approach to Behavior

● The scientific approach to understanding behavior is empirical. Psychologists base their conclusions on formal, systematic, objective tests of their hypotheses, rather than reasoning, speculation, or common sense. The scientific approach is advantageous in that it puts a premium on clarity and has little tolerance for error.

● Experimental research involves manipulating an independent variable to discover its effects on a dependent variable. The experimenter usually does so by comparing experimental and control groups, which must be alike except for the variation created by the manipulation of the independent variable. Experiments permit conclusions about cause-effect relationships between variables, but this method isn't usable for the study of many questions.

● Psychologists conduct correlational research when they are unable to exert control over the variables they want to study. The correlation coefficient is a numerical index of the degree of relationship between two variables. Correlational research methods include naturalistic observation, case studies, and surveys. Correlational research facilitates the investigation of many issues that are not open to experimental study, but it cannot demonstrate that two variables are causally related.

### The Roots of Happiness: An Empirical Analysis

● A scientific analysis of happiness reveals that many common-sense notions about the roots of happiness appear to be incorrect, including the notion that most people are unhappy. Factors such as money, age, gender, parenthood, intelligence, and attractiveness are not correlated with subjective well-being.

● Physical health, social relationships, religious faith, and culture appear to have a modest impact on feelings of happiness. The only factors that are clearly and strongly related to happiness are love and marriage, work satisfaction, and personality, which probably reflects the influence of heredity.

● Happiness is a relative concept mediated by people's highly subjective assessments of their lives. Research on affective forecasting shows that people are surprisingly bad at predicting what will make them happy. Individuals adapt to both positive and negative events in their lives, which creates a hedonic treadmill effect.

### Application: Improving Academic Performance

● To foster sound study habits, you should devise a written study schedule and reward yourself for following it. You should also try to find places for studying that are relatively free of distractions.

● You should use active reading techniques to select the most important ideas from the material you read. Highlighting textbook material *is* a useful strategy—if students are reasonably effective in focusing on the main ideas in the material and if they subsequently review what they have highlighted. Good note taking can help you get more out of lectures. It's important to use active listening techniques and to record lecturers' ideas in your own words.

● Rehearsal, even when it involves overlearning, facilitates retention. The process of being tested on material seems to enhance retention of that material. Distributed practice and deeper processing tend to improve memory. Evidence also suggests that organization facilitates retention, so outlining reading assignments can be valuable.

● Meaningfulness can be enhanced through the use of mnemonic devices such as acrostics and acronyms. The link method and the method of loci are mnemonic devices that depend on the value of visual imagery.

## KEY TERMS

Adjustment   p. 11
Affective forecasting   p. 23
Behavior   p. 10
Case study   p. 16
Clinical psychology   p. 11
Control group   p. 13
Correlation   p. 14
Correlation coefficient   p. 14
Dependent variable   p. 12
Empiricism   p. 12
Experiment   p. 12
Experimental group   p. 13
Hedonic adaptation   p. 23
Independent variable   p. 12
Mnemonic devices   p. 29
Narcissism   p. 7
Naturalistic observation   p. 15
Overlearning   p. 27
Psychology   p. 10
Subjective well-being   p. 18
Surveys   p. 16

## QUESTIONS

1. Technological advances have not led to perceptible improvement in our collective health and happiness. This statement defines
   a. escape from freedom.
   b. the point/counterpoint phenomenon.
   c. modern society.
   d. the paradox of progress.

2. Barry Schwartz (2004) argues that
   a. life choices have increased dramatically in modern society.
   b. the abundance of life choices has unexpected costs.
   c. an overabundance of choices increases the potential for rumination and postdecision regret.
   d. all of the above are true.

3. Which of the following is *not* offered in the text as a criticism of self-help books?
   a. They are infrequently based on solid research.
   b. Most don't provide explicit directions for changing behavior.
   c. The topics they cover are often quite narrow.
   d. Many are dominated by psychobabble.

4. The adaptation of animals when environments change is similar to _____ in humans.
   a. orientation          c. evolution
   b. assimilation        d. adjustment

5. An experiment is a research method in which the investigator manipulates the _____ variable and observes whether changes occur in a (an) _____ variable as a result.
   a. independent; dependent
   b. control; experimental
   c. experimental; control
   d. dependent; independent

6. A researcher wants to determine whether a certain diet causes children to learn better in school. In the study, the independent variable is
   a. the type of diet.
   b. a measure of learning performance.
   c. the age or grade level of the children.
   d. the intelligence level of the children.

7. A psychologist collected background information about a psychopathic killer, talked to him and people who knew him, and gave him psychological tests. Which research method was she using?
   a. case study
   b. naturalistic observation
   c. survey
   d. experiment

8. The principal advantage of experimental research is that
   a. it has a scientific basis and is therefore convincing to people.
   b. experiments replicate real-life situations.
   c. an experiment can be designed for any research problem.
   d. it allows the researcher to draw cause-and-effect conclusions.

9. Research has shown that which of the following is moderately correlated with happiness?
   a. income
   b. intelligence
   c. parenthood
   d. social activity

10. A good reason for taking notes in your own words, rather than verbatim, is that
    a. most lecturers are quite wordy.
    b. "translating" on the spot is good mental exercise.
    c. it reduces the likelihood that you'll later engage in plagiarism.
    d. it forces you to assimilate the information in a way that makes sense to you.

## ANSWERS

1. d Page 1
2. d Page 1
3. c Pages 7–8
4. d Page 11
5. a Page 12
6. a Pages 12–13
7. a Page 16
8. d Page 14
9. d Pages 19–20
10. d Page 26

## Personal Explorations Workbook

Go to the *Personal Explorations Workbook* in the back of your textbook for exercises that can enhance your self-understanding in relation to issues raised in this chapter. **Exercise 1.1** *Self-Assessment:* Narcissistic Personality Inventory. **Exercise 1.2** *Self-Reflection:* What Are Your Study Habits Like?

Access an interactive eBook, chapter-specific interactive learning tools, including Personal Explorations, Recommended Readings, Critical Thinking Exercises, flashcards, quizzes, videos and more in your Psychology CourseMate, available at **www.cengagebrain.com/ shop/ISBN/1111186634**.

# CHAPTER 2

# Theories of Personality

Imagine that you are hurtling upward in an elevator with three other persons when suddenly a power blackout brings the elevator to a halt 45 stories above the ground. Your three companions might adjust to this predicament differently. One might crack jokes to relieve tension. Another might make ominous predictions that "we'll never get out of here." The third might calmly think about how to escape from the elevator. These varied ways of coping with the same stressful situation occur because each person has a different personality. Personality differences significantly influence people's patterns of adjustment. Thus, theories intended to explain personality can contribute to our effort to understand adjustment processes.

In this chapter, we introduce you to various theories that attempt to explain the structure and development of personality. Our review of personality theory will also serve to acquaint you with four major theoretical perspectives in psychology: the psychodynamic, behavioral, humanistic, and biological perspectives. These theoretical approaches are conceptual models that help explain behavior. Familiarity with them will help you understand many of the ideas that you will encounter in this book, as well as in other books about psychology.

# The Nature of Personality

**LEARNING OBJECTIVES**

- Explain the concepts of personality and traits.
- Describe the Big Five personality traits.
- Discuss how the Big Five traits are related to important life outcomes.

To discuss theories of personality effectively, we need to digress momentarily to come up with a definition of personality and to discuss the concept of personality traits.

## What Is Personality?

What does it mean if you say that a friend has an optimistic personality? Your statement suggests that the person has a fairly *consistent tendency* to behave in a cheerful, hopeful, enthusiastic way, looking at the bright side of things, across a wide variety of situations. In a similar vein, if you note that a friend has an "outgoing" personality, you mean that she or he consistently behaves in a friendly, open, and extraverted manner in a variety of circumstances. Although no one is entirely consistent in his or her behavior, this quality of *consistency across situations* lies at the core of the concept of personality.

*Distinctiveness* is also central to the concept of personality. Everyone has traits seen in other people, but each individual has her or his own distinctive *set* of personality traits. Each person is unique. Thus, as illustrated by our elevator scenario, the concept of personality helps explain why people don't all act alike in the same situation.

In summary, we use the idea of personality to explain (1) the stability in a person's behavior over time and across situations (consistency) and (2) the behavioral differences among people reacting to the same situation (distinctiveness). We can combine these ideas into the following definition: *personality* **refers to an individual's unique constellation of consistent behavioral traits.** Let's look more closely at the concept of traits.

## What Are Personality Traits?

We all make remarks like "Melanie is very *shrewd*" or "*Doug is too timid* to succeed in that job" or "I wish I could be as *self-assured* as Antonio." When we attempt to describe an individual's personality, we usually do so in terms of specific aspects of personality, called traits. **A *personality trait* is a durable disposition to behave in a particular way in a variety of situations.** Adjectives such as *honest, dependable, moody, impulsive, suspicious, anxious, excitable, domineering,* and *friendly* describe dispositions that represent personality traits.

Most trait theories of personality assume that some traits are more basic than others. According to this notion, a small number of fundamental traits determine other, more superficial traits. For example, a person's tendency to be impulsive, restless, irritable, boisterous, and impatient might all derive from a more basic tendency to be excitable.

A number of psychologists have taken on the challenge of identifying the basic traits that form the core of personality. For example, Raymond Cattell (1950, 1966, 1990) used the statistical procedure of *factor analysis* to reduce a list of 171 personality traits compiled by Gordon Allport (1937) to just 16 basic dimensions of personality. In *factor analysis,* **correlations among many variables are analyzed to identify closely related clusters of variables.** If the measurements of a number of variables (in this case, personality traits) correlate highly with one another, the assumption is that a single factor is influencing all of them. Factor analysis is used to identify these hidden factors. Based on his factor analytic work, Cattell concluded that an individual's personality can be described completely by measuring just 16 traits. The 16 crucial traits are listed in **Figure 2.22**, which can be found in the Application, where we discuss a personality test that Cattell designed to assess these traits.

## The Five-Factor Model of Personality

In recent years, Robert McCrae and Paul Costa (1987, 1997, 2003, 2008a, 2008b) have used factor analysis to arrive at an even simpler, five-factor model of personality. They argue that the vast majority of personality traits derive from just five higher-order traits that have come to be known as the "Big Five": extraversion, neuroticism, openness to experience, agreeableness, and conscientiousness (see **Figure 2.1** on the next page). Let's take a closer look at these traits:

1. *Extraversion.* People who score high in extraversion are characterized as outgoing, sociable, upbeat, friendly, assertive, and gregarious. Referred to as *positive emotionality* in some trait models, extraversion has been studied extensively in research for many decades

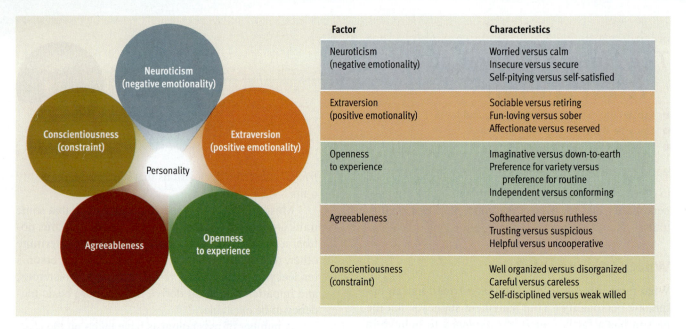

| Factor | Characteristics |
|---|---|
| Neuroticism (negative emotionality) | Worried versus calm<br>Insecure versus secure<br>Self-pitying versus self-satisfied |
| Extraversion (positive emotionality) | Sociable versus retiring<br>Fun-loving versus sober<br>Affectionate versus reserved |
| Openness to experience | Imaginative versus down-to-earth<br>Preference for variety versus preference for routine<br>Independent versus conforming |
| Agreeableness | Softhearted versus ruthless<br>Trusting versus suspicious<br>Helpful versus uncooperative |
| Conscientiousness (constraint) | Well organized versus disorganized<br>Careful versus careless<br>Self-disciplined versus weak willed |

**Figure 2.1**

**The five-factor model of personality.** Trait models attempt to break down personality into its basic dimensions. McCrae and Costa (1987, 1997, 2003) maintain that personality can be described adequately with the five higher-order traits identified here, widely known as the Big Five traits.

Source: Trait descriptions from McCrae, R. R., & Costa, P. T. (1986). Clinical assessment can benefit from recent advances in personality psychology. *American Psychologist, 41,* 1001–1003.

(Watson & Clark, 1997). Extraverts tend to be happier than others (Fleeson, Malanos, & Achille, 2002). They also have a more positive outlook on life and are motivated to pursue social contact, intimacy, and interdependence (Wilt & Revelle, 2009).

**2.** *Neuroticism.* People who score high in neuroticism tend to be anxious, hostile, self-conscious, insecure, and vulnerable. Like extraversion, this trait has been the subject of thousands of studies. In some trait models it is called *negative emotionality.* Those who score high in neuroticism tend to overreact more in response to stress than others (Mroczek & Almeida, 2004). They also tend to exhibit more impulsiveness and emotional instability than others (Widiger, 2009).

**3.** *Openness to experience.* Openness is associated with curiosity, flexibility, vivid fantasy, imaginativeness, artistic sensitivity, and unconventional attitudes. People who are high in openness tend to be tolerant of ambiguity and have less need for closure on issues than others (McCrae & Sutin, 2009). McCrae (1996) maintains that the importance of this trait has been underestimated. Citing evidence that openness fosters liberalism, he argues that this trait is the key determinant of people's political attitudes and ideology. For example, evidence suggests that people high in openness tend to exhibit less prejudice against minorities than others (Flynn, 2005).

**4.** *Agreeableness.* Those who score high in agreeableness tend to be sympathetic, trusting, cooperative, modest, and straightforward. People who score at the

opposite end of this personality dimension are characterized as suspicious, antagonistic, and aggressive. Agreeableness is associated with constructive approaches to conflict resolution (Jensen-Campbell & Graziano, 2001) and with empathy and helping behavior (Graziano & Tobin, 2009).

**5.** *Conscientiousness.* Conscientious people tend to be diligent, disciplined, well organized, punctual, and dependable. Referred to as *constraint* in some trait models, conscientiousness is associated with strong self-discipline and the ability to regulate oneself effectively (Roberts et al., 2009). Studies have also shown that conscientiousness fosters dependability in the workplace (Lund et al., 2007).

Research shows that the Big Five traits are predictive of specific aspects of behavior, as one would expect (McCrae & Costa, 2008a; Paunonen, 2003). For example, extraversion correlates positively with popularity and dating a greater variety of people; conscientiousness correlates with greater honesty, higher job performance ratings, and relatively low alcohol consumption; openness to experience is associated with playing a musical instrument; and agreeableness correlates with honesty.

Correlations have also been found between the Big Five traits and quite a variety of important life outcomes (Ozer & Benet-Martinez, 2006). For instance, higher grades (GPA) in both high school and college are associated with higher conscientiousness, primarily because conscientious students work harder (Noftle & Robins,

2007). Several of the Big Five traits are associated with occupational attainment (career success). Extraversion and conscientiousness are positive predictors of occupational attainment, whereas neuroticism is a negative predictor (Roberts, Caspi, & Moffitt, 2003). The likelihood of divorce can also be predicted by personality traits, as neuroticism elevates the probability of divorce, whereas agreeableness and conscientiousness reduce it (Roberts et al., 2007). Finally, and perhaps most important, two of the Big Five traits are related to health and mortality over the course of the life span. Neuroticism is associated with an elevated prevalence of virtually all of the major mental disorders not to mention a number of physical illnesses (Widiger, 2009), whereas conscientiousness is correlated with the experience of less illness and with reduced mortality (Goodwin & Friedman, 2006; Martin, Friedman, & Schwartz, 2007). It is not hard to figure out why this is the case, as conscientiousness is inversely related to just about every health-impairing behavior you can think of, including drinking, excessive eating, smoking, drug use, lack of exercise, and various risky practices, while it promotes adherence to medical advice (Roberts et al., 2009). Thus, conscientious people live longer than others.

McCrae and Costa maintain that personality can be described adequately by measuring the five basic traits they've identified. Their bold claim has been supported in many studies by other researchers, and the five-factor model has become the dominant conception of personality structure in contemporary psychology (John, Naumann, & Soto, 2008; McCrae, 2005). These traits have been characterized as the "latitude and longitude" along which personality should be mapped (Ozer & Reise, 1994, p. 361).

However, some theorists maintain that more than five traits are necessary to account for most of the variation seen in human personality (Boyle, 2008; De Raad, 2009). The debate about how many dimensions are necessary to describe personality is likely to continue for many years to come. As you'll see throughout the chapter, the study of personality is an area in psychology that has a long history of "dueling theories." We'll begin our tour of these theories by examining the influential work of Sigmund Freud and his followers.

# Psychodynamic Perspectives

### LEARNING OBJECTIVES

- Describe Freud's three components of personality and how they are distributed across levels of awareness.
- Explain the importance of sexual and aggressive conflicts in Freud's theory.
- Describe eight defense mechanisms identified by Freud.
- Outline Freud's stages of psychosexual development and their theorized relations to adult personality.
- Summarize Jung's views on the unconscious.
- Summarize Adler's views on key issues relating to personality.
- Evaluate the strengths and weaknesses of psychodynamic theories of personality.

**Psychodynamic theories include all the diverse theories descended from the work of Sigmund Freud that focus on unconscious mental forces.** Freud inspired many brilliant scholars who followed in his intellectual footsteps. Some of these followers simply refined and updated Freud's theory. Others veered off in new directions and established independent, albeit related, schools of thought. Today, the psychodynamic umbrella covers a large collection of related theories. In this section, we'll examine Freud's ideas in some detail and then take a brief look at the work of two of his most significant followers, Carl Jung and Alfred Adler.

## Freud's Psychoanalytic Theory

Born in 1856, Sigmund Freud grew up in a middle-class Jewish home in Vienna, Austria. He showed an early interest in intellectual pursuits and became an intense, hardworking young man. He dreamed of achieving fame by making an important discovery. His determination was such that in medical school he dissected 400 male eels to prove for the first time that they had testes. His work with eels did not make him famous. However, his later work with people made him one of the most influential and controversial figures of modern times.

Freud was a physician specializing in neurology when he began his medical practice in Vienna near the end of the 19th century. Like other neurologists in his era, he often treated people troubled by nervous problems such as irrational fears, obsessions, and anxieties. Eventually

**Sigmund Freud**

he devoted himself to the treatment of mental disorders using an innovative procedure he developed, called *psychoanalysis,* that required lengthy verbal interactions in which Freud probed deeply into patients' lives. Decades of experience with his patients provided much of the inspiration for Freud's theory of personality.

National Library of Medicine

Freud's psychoanalytic theory was based on decades of clinical work. He treated a great many patients in the consulting room pictured here. The room contains numerous artifacts from other cultures—and the original psychoanalytic couch.

Although Freud's theory gradually gained prominence, most of Freud's contemporaries were uncomfortable with it, for at least three reasons. First, he argued that unconscious forces govern human behavior. This idea was disturbing because it suggested that people are not masters of their own minds. Second, he claimed that childhood experiences strongly determine adult personality. This notion distressed many, because it suggested that people are not masters of their own destinies. Third, he said that individuals' personalities are shaped by how they cope with their sexual urges. This assertion offended the conservative, Victorian values of his time. Thus, Freud endured a great deal of criticism, condemnation, and outright ridicule, even after his work began to attract more favorable attention. What were these ideas that generated so much controversy?

### Structure of Personality

Freud (1901, 1920) divided personality structure into three components: the id, the ego, and the superego. He saw a person's behavior as the outcome of interactions among these three components.

**The *id* is the primitive, instinctive component of personality that operates according to the pleasure principle.** Freud referred to the id as the reservoir of

**WEB LINK 2.1   Sigmund Freud Museum, Vienna, Austria**

This online museum, in both English and German versions, offers a detailed chronology of Freud's life and explanations of the most important concepts of psychoanalysis. The highlights, though, are the rich audiovisual resources, including online photos, amateur movie clips, and voice recordings of Freud.

psychic energy. By this he meant that the id houses the raw biological urges (to eat, sleep, defecate, copulate, and so on) that energize human behavior. The id operates according to the *pleasure principle,* which demands immediate gratification of its urges. The id engages in *primary process thinking,* which is primitive, illogical, irrational, and fantasy oriented.

**The *ego* is the decision-making component of personality that operates according to the reality principle.** The ego mediates between the id, with its forceful desires for immediate satisfaction, and the external social world, with its expectations and norms regarding suitable behavior. The ego considers social realities—society's norms, etiquette, rules, and customs—in deciding how to behave. The ego is guided by the *reality principle,* which seeks to delay gratification of the id's urges until appropriate outlets and situations can be found. In short, to stay out of trouble, the ego often works to tame the unbridled desires of the id. As Freud put it, the ego is "like a man on horseback, who has to hold in check the superior strength of the horse" (Freud, 1923, p. 15).

In the long run, the ego wants to maximize gratification, just like the id. However, the ego engages in *secondary process thinking,* which is relatively rational, realistic, and oriented toward problem solving. Thus, the ego strives to avoid negative consequences from society and its representatives (for example, punishment by parents or teachers) by behaving "properly." It also attempts to achieve long-range goals that sometimes require putting off gratification.

While the ego concerns itself with practical realities, **the *superego* is the moral component of personality that incorporates social standards about what represents right and wrong.** Throughout their lives, but especially during childhood, individuals receive training about what is good and bad behavior. Eventually they internalize many of these social norms, meaning that they truly *accept* certain moral principles, then *they* put pressure on *themselves* to live up to these standards. The superego emerges out of the ego at around 3 to 5 years of age. In some people, the superego can become irrationally demanding in its striving for moral perfection. Such people are plagued by excessive guilt.

According to Freud, the id, ego, and superego are distributed across three levels of awareness. He contrasted the unconscious with the conscious and preconscious (see **Figure 2.2**). **The *conscious* consists of whatever one is aware of at a particular point in time.** For example, at this moment your conscious may include the current train of thought in this text and a dim awareness in the back of your mind that your eyes are getting tired and you're beginning to get hungry. **The *preconscious* contains material just beneath the sur-**

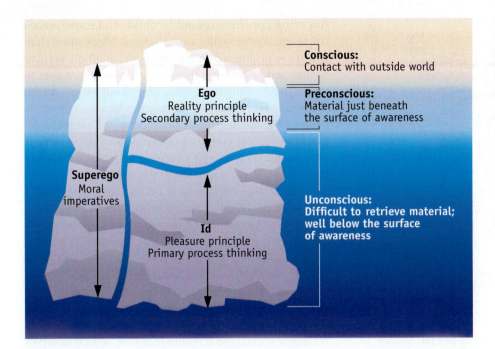

**Figure 2.2**

**Freud's model of personality structure.** Freud theorized that people have three levels of awareness: the conscious, the preconscious, and the unconscious. To dramatize the size of the unconscious, it has often been compared to the portion of an iceberg that lies beneath the water's surface. Freud also divided personality structure into three components—id, ego, and superego—that operate according to different principles and exhibit different modes of thinking. In Freud's model, the id is entirely unconscious, but the ego and superego operate at all three levels of awareness.

Labels in figure:

**Conscious:** Contact with outside world

**Preconscious:** Material just beneath the surface of awareness

**Ego** Reality principle Secondary process thinking

**Superego** Moral imperatives

**Unconscious:** Difficult to retrieve material; well below the surface of awareness

**Id** Pleasure principle Primary process thinking

face of awareness that can be easily retrieved. Examples might include your middle name, what you had for supper last night, or an argument you had with a friend yesterday. The *unconscious* contains thoughts, memories, and desires that are well below the surface of conscious awareness but that nonetheless exert great influence on one's behavior. Examples of material that might be found in your unconscious would include a forgotten trauma from childhood or hidden feelings of hostility toward a parent.

## Conflict and Defense Mechanisms

Freud assumed that behavior is the outcome of an ongoing series of internal conflicts. Battles among the id, ego, and superego are routine. Why? Because the id wants to gratify its urges immediately, but the norms of civilized society frequently dictate otherwise. For example, your id might feel an urge to clobber a co-worker who constantly irritates you. However, society frowns on such behavior, so your ego would try to hold this urge in check, and you would find yourself in a conflict. You may be experiencing conflict at this very moment. In Freudian terms, your id may be secretly urging you to abandon reading this chapter so you can watch television or go online. Your ego may be weighing this appealing option against your society-induced need to excel in school (or at least pass your courses).

Freud believed that conflicts dominate people's lives. He asserted that individuals career from one conflict to another. The following scenario provides a fanciful illustration of how the three components of personality interact to create constant conflicts.

*Imagine your alarm clock ringing obnoxiously as you lurch across the bed to shut it off. It's 7 a.m. and time to*

*get up for your history class. However, your id (operating according to the pleasure principle) urges you to return to the immediate gratification of additional sleep. Your ego (operating according to the reality principle) points out that you really must go to class since you haven't been able to decipher the stupid textbook on your own. Your id (in its typical unrealistic fashion) smugly assures you that you will get the A that you need. It suggests lying back to dream about how impressed your roommate will be. Just as you're relaxing, your superego jumps into the fray. It tries to make you feel guilty about the tuition your parents paid for the class that you're about to skip. You haven't even gotten out of bed yet—and there is already a pitched battle in your psyche.*

*Let's say your ego wins the battle. You pull yourself out of bed and head for class. On the way, you pass a donut shop and your id clamors for cinnamon rolls. Your ego reminds you that you're gaining weight and that you are supposed to be on a diet. Your id wins this time. After you've attended your history lecture, your ego reminds you that you need to do some library research for a paper in philosophy. However, your id insists on returning to your apartment to watch some sitcom reruns. It's only midmorning—and already you have been through a series of internal conflicts.*

Freud believed that conflicts centering on sexual and aggressive impulses are especially likely to have far-reaching consequences. Why did he emphasize sex and aggression? Two reasons were prominent in his thinking. First, Freud thought that sex and aggression are subject to more complex and ambiguous social controls than other basic motives. The norms governing sexual and aggressive behavior are subtle, and people often get mixed messages about what is appropriate.

"ALL I WANT FROM THEM IS A SIMPLE MAJORITY ON THINGS."

Thus, he believed that these two drives are the source of much confusion.

Second, Freud noted that the sexual and aggressive drives are thwarted more regularly than other basic biological urges. Think about it: If you get hungry or thirsty, you can simply head for a nearby convenience store or a drinking fountain. But if a department store clerk infuriates you, you aren't likely to slug the clerk, because that isn't socially acceptable. Likewise, when you see an attractive person who inspires lustful urges, you don't normally walk up and propose a tryst in a nearby broom closet. There is nothing comparable to convenience stores or drinking fountains for the satisfaction of sexual and aggressive urges. Thus, Freud gave great importance to these needs because social norms dictate that they be routinely frustrated.

Most psychic conflicts are trivial and are quickly resolved one way or the other. Occasionally, however, a conflict will linger for days, months, and even years, creating internal tension. Indeed, Freud believed that

lingering conflicts rooted in childhood experiences cause most personality disturbances. More often than not, these prolonged and troublesome conflicts involve sexual and aggressive impulses that society wants to tame. These conflicts are often played out entirely in the unconscious. Although you may not be aware of these unconscious battles, they can produce *anxiety* that slips to the surface of conscious awareness. This anxiety is attributable to your ego worrying about the id getting out of control and doing something terrible.

The arousal of anxiety is a crucial event in Freud's theory of personality functioning (see **Figure 2.3**). Anxiety is distressing, so people try to rid themselves of this unpleasant emotion any way they can. This effort to ward off anxiety often involves the use of defense mechanisms. ***Defense mechanisms* are largely unconscious reactions that protect a person from painful emotions such as anxiety and guilt.** Typically, they are mental maneuvers that work through self-deception. A common example is *rationalization,* **which involves creating false but plausible excuses to justify unacceptable behavior.** You would be rationalizing if, after cheating someone in a business transaction, you tried to reduce your guilt by explaining that "everyone does it."

Characterized as "the flagship in the psychoanalytic fleet of defense mechanisms" (Paulhus, Fridhandler, & Hayes, 1997, p. 545), repression is the most basic and widely used defense mechanism. ***Repression* involves keeping distressing thoughts and feelings buried in the unconscious.** People tend to repress desires that make them feel guilty, conflicts that make them anxious, and memories that are painful. Repression is "motivated forgetting." If you forget a dental appointment or the name of someone you don't like, repression may be at work.

Self-deception can also be seen in the mechanisms of projection and displacement. ***Projection* involves attributing one's own thoughts, feelings, or motives to another.** For example, if your lust for a co-worker

**Figure 2.3**

**Freud's model of personality dynamics.** According to Freud, unconscious conflicts between the id, ego, and superego sometimes lead to anxiety. This discomfort may lead to the use of defense mechanisms, which may temporarily relieve anxiety.

makes you feel guilty, you might attribute any latent sexual tension between the two of you to the *other person's* desire to seduce you. ***Displacement* involves diverting emotional feelings (usually anger) from their original source to a substitute target.** If your boss gives you a hard time at work and you come home and slam the door, yell at your dog, and lash out at your spouse, you are displacing your anger onto irrelevant targets. Unfortunately, social constraints often force people to hold back their anger until they end up expressing it toward the people they love the most.

Other prominent defense mechanisms include reaction formation, regression, and identification. ***Reaction formation* involves behaving in a way that is exactly the opposite of one's true feelings.** Guilt about sexual desires often leads to reaction formation. Freud theorized that many males who ridicule homosexuals are defending against their own latent homosexual impulses. The telltale sign of reaction formation is the exaggerated quality of the opposite behavior (such as trying to be ultra-nice in order to mask feelings of hostility).

***Regression* involves a reversion to immature patterns of behavior.** When anxious about their self-worth, some adults respond with childish boasting and bragging (as opposed to subtle efforts to impress others). For example, a fired executive having difficulty finding a new job might start making ridiculous statements about his incomparable talents and achievements. Such bragging is regressive when it is marked by massive exaggerations that anyone can see through.

***Identification* involves bolstering self-esteem by forming an imaginary or real alliance with some person or group.** For example, youngsters often shore up precarious feelings of self-worth by identifying with rock stars, movie stars, or famous athletes. Adults may join exclusive country clubs or civic organizations with which they identify.

Finally, Freud described the defense of *sublimation,* **which occurs when unconscious, unacceptable impulses are channeled into socially acceptable, perhaps even admirable, behaviors.** For example, intense aggressive impulses might be rechanneled by taking up boxing or football. Freud believed that many creative endeavors, such as painting, poetry, and sculpture, were sublimations of sexual urges. For instance, he argued that Leonardo da Vinci's painting of Madonna figures was a sublimation of his longing for intimacy with his mother (Freud, 1910). By definition, sublimation is regarded as a relatively healthy defense mechanism.

Additional examples of the defense mechanisms we've described can be found in **Figure 2.4**. If you see defensive maneuvers that you have used, you shouldn't be surprised. According to Freud, everyone uses defense mechanisms to some extent. They become problematic only when a person depends on them excessively. The seeds for psychological disorders are sown when defenses lead to wholesale distortion of reality.

### Development: Psychosexual Stages

Freud made the startling assertion that the foundation of an individual's personality is laid down by the tender age of 5! To shed light on the crucial early years, he formulated a stage theory of development that emphasized how young children deal with their immature, but powerful, sexual urges (he used the term "sexual" in a

| Defense Mechanisms, with Examples | |
|---|---|
| **Definition** | **Example** |
| *Repression* involves keeping distressing thoughts and feelings buried in the unconscious. | A traumatized soldier has no recollection of the details of a close brush with death. |
| *Projection* involves attributing one's own thoughts, feelings, or motives to another person. | A woman who dislikes her boss thinks she likes her boss but feels that the boss doesn't like her. |
| *Displacement* involves diverting emotional feelings (usually anger) from their original source to a substitute target. | After a parental scolding, a young girl takes her anger out on her little brother. |
| *Reaction formation* involves behaving in a way that is exactly the opposite of one's true feelings. | A parent who unconsciously resents a child spoils the child with outlandish gifts. |
| *Regression* involves a reversion to immature patterns of behavior. | An adult has a temper tantrum when he doesn't get his way. |
| *Rationalization* involves the creation of false but plausible excuses to justify unacceptable behavior. | A student watches TV instead of studying, saying that "additional study wouldn't do any good anyway." |
| *Identification* involves bolstering self-esteem by forming an imaginary or real alliance with some person or group. | An insecure young man joins a fraternity to boost his self-esteem. |
| *Sublimation* involves channeling unconscious, unacceptable impulses into socially acceptable or admirable activities. | A person obsessed with sex becomes a sex therapist and helps others with their sexual problems. |

**Figure 2.4**

**Defense mechanisms.** According to Freud, people use a variety of defense mechanisms to protect themselves from painful emotions. Definitions of eight commonly used defense mechanisms are shown on the left, along with examples of each on the right.

**Figure 2.5**
**Freud's stages of psychosexual development.** Freud theorized that people evolve through the series of psychosexual stages summarized here. The manner in which certain key tasks and experiences are handled during each stage is thought to leave a lasting imprint on one's adult personality.

| Freud's Stages of Psychosexual Development | | | |
|---|---|---|---|
| **Stage** | **Approximate ages** | **Erotic focus** | **Key tasks and experiences** |
| Oral | 0–1 | Mouth (sucking, biting) | Weaning (from breast or bottle) |
| Anal | 2–3 | Anus (expelling or retaining feces) | Toilet training |
| Phallic | 4–5 | Genitals (masturbating) | Identifying with adult role models; coping with Oedipal crisis |
| Latency | 6–12 | None (sexually repressed) | Expanding social contacts |
| Genital | Puberty onward | Genitals (being sexually intimate) | Establishing intimate relationships; contributing to society through working |

general way to refer to many urges for physical pleasure, not just the urge to copulate). According to Freud, these sexual urges shift in focus as children progress from one stage to another. Indeed, the names for the stages (oral, anal, genital, and so on) are based on where children are focusing their erotic energy at the time. Thus, *psychosexual stages* are developmental periods with a characteristic sexual focus that leave their mark on adult personality.

Freud theorized that each psychosexual stage has its own unique developmental challenges or tasks, as outlined in **Figure 2.5**. The way these challenges are handled supposedly shapes personality. The notion of *fixation* plays an important role in this process. *Fixation is a failure to move forward from one stage to another as expected.* Essentially, the child's development stalls for a while. Fixation is caused by *excessive gratification* of needs at a particular stage or by *exces-*

*sive frustration* of those needs. Either way, fixations left over from childhood affect adult personality. Generally, fixation leads to an overemphasis on the psychosexual needs that were prominent during the fixated stage.

Freud described a series of five psychosexual stages. Let's examine some of the major features of each stage.

**Oral stage.** During this stage, which usually encompasses the first year of life, the main source of erotic stimulation is the mouth (in biting, sucking, chewing, and so on). How caretakers handle the child's feeding experiences is supposed to be crucial to subsequent development. Freud attributed considerable importance to the manner in which the child is weaned from the breast or the bottle. According to Freud, fixation at the oral stage could form the basis for obsessive eating or smoking later in life (among many other things).

According to Freudian theory, a child's feeding experiences are crucial to later development. Fixation at the oral stage could lead to an overemphasis on, for example, smoking or eating in adulthood.

**Anal stage.** In their second year, children supposedly get their erotic pleasure from their bowel movements, through either the expulsion or retention of feces. The crucial event at this time is toilet training, which represents society's first systematic effort to regulate the child's biological urges. Severely punitive toilet training is thought to lead to a variety of possible outcomes. For example, excessive punishment might produce a latent feeling of hostility toward the "trainer," who usually is the mother. This hostility might generalize to women in general. Another possibility is that heavy reliance on punitive measures might lead to an association between genital concerns and the anxiety that the punishment arouses. This genital anxiety from severe toilet training could evolve into anxiety about sexual activities later in life.

**Phallic stage.** Around age 4, the genitals become the focus for the child's erotic energy, largely through self-stimulation. During this pivotal stage, the *Oedipal complex* emerges. Little boys develop an erotically tinged preference for their mother. They also feel hostility toward their father, whom they view as a competitor for mom's affection. Little girls develop a special attachment to their father. At about the same time, they learn that their genitals are very different from those of little boys, and they supposedly develop *penis envy*. According to Freud, girls feel hostile toward their mother because they blame her for their anatomical "deficiency."

To summarize, in **the *Oedipal complex* children manifest erotically tinged desires for their other-sex parent, accompanied by feelings of hostility toward their same-sex parent.** The name for this syndrome was taken from the Greek myth of Oedipus, who was separated from his parents at birth. Not knowing the identity of his real parents, he inadvertently killed his father and married his mother.

According to Freud, the way parents and children deal with the sexual and aggressive conflicts inherent in the Oedipal complex is of paramount importance. The child has to resolve the dilemma by giving up the sexual longings for the other-sex parent and the hostility toward the same-sex parent. Healthy psychosexual development is supposed to hinge on the resolution of the Oedipal conflict. Why? Because continued hostile relations with the same-sex parent may prevent the child from identifying adequately with that parent. Without such identification, Freudian theory predicts that many aspects of the child's development won't progress as they should.

**Latency and genital stages.** Freud believed that from age 6 through puberty, the child's sexuality is suppressed—it becomes "latent." Important events during this *latency stage* center on expanding social contacts beyond the family. With the advent of puberty, the child evolves into the *genital stage*. Sexual urges reappear and focus on the genitals once again. At this point the sexual energy is normally channeled toward peers of the other sex, rather than toward oneself, as in the phallic stage.

In arguing that the early years shape personality, Freud did not mean that personality development comes to an abrupt halt in middle childhood. However, he did believe that the foundation for one's adult personality is solidly entrenched by this time. He maintained that future developments are rooted in early, formative experiences and that significant conflicts in later years are replays of crises from childhood.

In fact, Freud believed that unconscious sexual conflicts rooted in childhood experiences cause most personality disturbances. His steadfast belief in the psychosexual origins of psychological disorders eventually led to bitter theoretical disputes with two of his most brilliant colleagues: Carl Jung and Alfred Adler. Jung and Adler both argued that Freud overemphasized sexuality. Freud summarily rejected their ideas, and the other two theorists felt compelled to go their own way, developing their own psychodynamic theories of personality.

## Jung's Analytical Psychology

© Bettmann/Corbis

**Carl Jung**

Swiss psychiatrist Carl Jung called his new approach *analytical psychology* to differentiate it from Freud's psychoanalytic theory. Like Freud, Jung (1921, 1933) emphasized the unconscious determinants of personality. However, he proposed that the unconscious consists of two layers. The first layer, called the *personal unconscious,* is essentially the same as Freud's version of the unconscious. The personal unconscious houses material from one's life that is not within one's conscious awareness because it has been repressed or forgotten. In addition, Jung theorized the existence of a deeper layer he called the collective unconscious. **The *collective unconscious* is a storehouse of latent memory traces inherited from people's ancestral past that is shared with the entire human**

**WEB LINK 2.2  C. G. Jung, Analytical Psychology, and Culture**

Synchronicity, archetypes, collective unconscious, introversion, extraversion—these and many other important concepts arising from analytical psychology and Jung's tremendously influential theorizing are examined at this comprehensive site.

**race.** Jung called these ancestral memories *archetypes*. They are not memories of actual, personal experiences. Instead, *archetypes* **are emotionally charged images and thought forms that have universal meaning.** These archetypal images and ideas show up frequently in dreams and are often manifested in a culture's use of symbols in art, literature, and religion. Jung felt that an understanding of archetypal symbols helped him make sense of his patients' dreams. Doing so was of great concern to him because he depended extensively on dream analysis in his treatment of patients.

Jung's unusual ideas about the collective unconscious had little impact on the mainstream of thinking in psychology. Their influence was felt more in other fields, such as anthropology, philosophy, art, and religious studies. However, many of Jung's other ideas *have* been incorporated into the mainstream of psychology. For instance, Jung was the first to describe the personality dimension of extraversion-introversion, which eventually became central to most trait theories of personality.

## Adler's Individual Psychology

© Bettmann/Corbis

**Alfred Adler**

Alfred Adler was a charter member of Freud's inner circle—the Vienna Psychoanalytic Society. However, he soon began to develop his own theory of personality, which he christened *individual psychology*. Adler (1917, 1927) argued that the foremost human drive is not sexuality, but a *striving for superiority.* Adler viewed striving for superiority as a universal drive to adapt, improve oneself, and master life's challenges. He noted that young children understandably feel weak and helpless in comparison to more competent older children and adults. These early inferiority feelings supposedly motivate individuals to acquire new skills and develop new talents.

Adler asserted that everyone has to work to overcome some feelings of inferiority. *Compensation* **involves efforts to overcome imagined or real inferiorities by developing one's abilities.** Adler believed that compensation is entirely normal. However, in some people inferiority feelings can become excessive, resulting in what is widely known today as an *inferiority complex*—exaggerated feelings of weakness and inadequacy. Adler thought that either parental pampering or parental neglect (or actual physical handicaps) could cause an

inferiority problem. Thus, he agreed with Freud on the importance of early childhood, although he focused on different aspects of parent-child relations.

Adler explained personality disturbances by noting that an inferiority complex can distort the normal process of striving for superiority (see **Figure 2.6**). He maintained that some people engage in *overcompensation* in order to conceal, even from themselves, their feelings of inferiority. Instead of working to master life's challenges, people with an inferiority complex work to achieve status, gain power over others, and acquire the trappings of success (fancy clothes, impressive cars, or whatever looks important to them). They

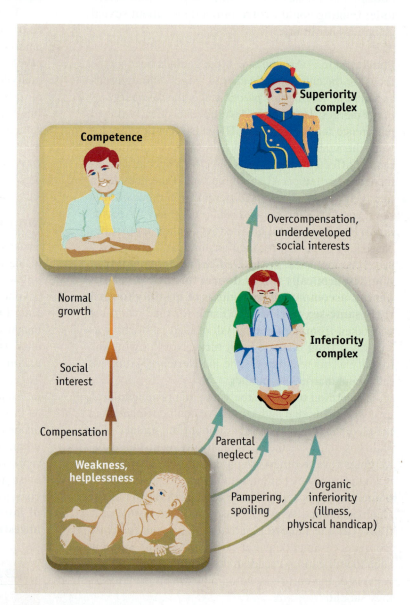

### Figure 2.6

**Adler's view of personality development.** Like Freud, Adler believed that early childhood experiences exert momentous influence over adult personality. However, he focused on children's social interactions rather than on their grappling with their sexuality. According to Adler, the roots of personality disturbances typically lie in excessive parental neglect or pampering, which can lead to overcompensation.

tend to flaunt their success in an effort to cover up their underlying inferiority complex. The problem is that such people engage in unconscious self-deception, worrying more about *appearances* than *reality*.

Adler's theory stressed the social context of personality development (Hoffman, 1994). For instance, it was Adler who first focused attention on the possible importance of *birth order* as a factor governing personality. His theory stimulated hundreds of studies on the effects of birth order, but these studies generally failed to support his hypotheses (Ernst & Angst, 1983; Harris, 2000). More recently, Frank Sulloway (1995, 1996) has revived interest in the relationship between birth order and personality, but the research findings have continued to be rather inconsistent (Harris, 2000; Rohde et al., 2003; Skinner, 2003).

## Evaluating Psychodynamic Perspectives

The psychodynamic approach has given us a number of far-reaching theories of personality. These theories yielded some bold new insights for their time. Psychodynamic theory and research have demonstrated that (1) unconscious forces can influence behavior, (2) internal conflict often plays a key role in generating psychological distress, (3) early childhood experiences can exert considerable influence over adult personality, and (4) people do rely on defense mechanisms to reduce their experience of unpleasant emotions (Bornstein, 2003; Solms, 2004; Westen, 1998; Westen, Gabbard, & Ortigo, 2008).

In a more negative vein, psychodynamic formulations have been criticized on several grounds, including the following (Crews, 2006; Fine, 1990; Kramer, 2006; Macmillan, 1991; Torrey, 1992):

**1.** *Poor testability.* Scientific investigations require testable hypotheses. Psychodynamic ideas have often been too vague to permit a clear scientific test. Concepts such as the superego, the preconscious, and collective unconscious are difficult to measure.

**2.** *Inadequate evidence.* The empirical evidence on psychodynamic theories has often been characterized as inadequate. The approach depends too much on case studies, in which it is easy for clinicians to see what they expect to see based on their theory. Reexaminations of Freud's own clinical work suggest that he sometimes distorted his patients' case histories to mesh with his theory (Esterson, 1993, 2001; Sulloway, 1991) and that a substantial disparity existed between Freud's writings and his actual therapeutic methods (Lynn & Vaillant, 1998). Insofar as researchers have accumulated evidence on psychodynamic theories, it has provided only modest support for the central hypotheses (Fisher & Greenberg, 1996; Westen, Gabbard, & Ortigo, 2008).

**3.** *Sexism.* Many critics have argued that psychodynamic theories harbor a bias against women. Freud believed that females' penis envy made them feel inferior to males. He also thought that females tended to develop weaker superegos and to be more prone to neurosis than males. He dismissed female patients' reports of sexual molestation during childhood as mere fantasies. Admittedly, sexism isn't unique to Freudian theories, and the sex bias in modern psychodynamic theories has been reduced considerably. But the psychodynamic approach has generally provided a rather male-centered viewpoint (Lerman, 1986; Person, 1990).

It's easy to ridicule Freud for concepts such as penis envy and to point to ideas that have turned out to be wrong. Remember, though, that Freud, Jung, and Adler began to fashion their theories over a century ago. It is not entirely fair to compare these theories to other models that are only a few decades old. That's like asking the Wright brothers to race a supersonic jet. Freud and his psychodynamic colleagues deserve great credit for breaking new ground. Standing at a distance a century later, we have to be impressed by the extraordinary impact that psychodynamic theory has had on modern thought. No other theoretical perspective in psychology has been as influential, except for the one we turn to next—behaviorism.

# Behavioral Perspectives

### LEARNING OBJECTIVES

- Describe Pavlov's classical conditioning and its contribution to understanding personality.
- Discuss how Skinner's principles of operant conditioning can be applied to personality development.
- Describe Bandura's social cognitive theory and his concept of self-efficacy.
- Evaluate the strengths and weaknesses of behavioral theories of personality.

**Behaviorism is a theoretical orientation based on the premise that scientific psychology should study observable behavior.** Behaviorism has been a major school of thought in psychology since 1913, when John B. Watson published an influential article. Watson argued that psychology should abandon its earlier focus on the mind and mental processes and focus exclusively on overt behavior. He contended that psychology could not study mental processes in a scientific manner because these processes are private and not accessible to outside observation.

In completely rejecting mental processes as a suitable subject for scientific study, Watson took an extreme position that is no longer dominant among modern behaviorists. Nonetheless, his influence was enormous, as psychology changed its primary focus from the study of the mind to the study of behavior.

The behaviorists have shown little interest in internal personality structures such as Freud's id, ego, and superego, because such structures can't be observed. They prefer to think in terms of "response tendencies," which *can* be observed. Thus, most behaviorists view an individual's personality as a *collection of response tendencies that are tied to various stimulus situations.* A specific situation may be associated with a number of response tendencies that vary in strength, depending on an individual's past experience (see **Figure 2.7**).

Although behaviorists have shown relatively little interest in personality structure, they have focused extensively on personality *development.* They explain development the same way they explain everything else—through learning. Specifically, they focus on how children's response tendencies are shaped through classical conditioning, operant conditioning, and observational learning. Let's look at these processes.

## Pavlov's Classical Conditioning

Do you go weak in the knees when you get a note at work that tells you to go see your boss? Do you get anxious when you're around important people? When you're driving, does your heart skip a beat at the sight of a police car—even when you're driving under the speed limit? If so, you probably acquired these common responses through classical conditioning. **Classical conditioning is a type of learning in which a neutral stimulus acquires the capacity to evoke a response that was originally evoked by another stimulus.** This process was first described back in 1903 by Ivan Pavlov.

© Bettmann/Corbis

**Ivan Pavlov**

Pavlov was a prominent Russian physiologist who did Nobel Prize–winning research on digestion. He was a dedicated scientist who was obsessed with his research. Legend has it that Pavlov severely reprimanded an assistant who was late for an experiment because he was trying to avoid street fighting in the midst of the Russian Revolution. The assistant defended his tardiness, saying, "But Professor, there's a revolution going on, with shooting in the streets!" Pavlov supposedly replied, "Next time there's a revolution, get up earlier!" (Fancher, 1979; Gantt, 1975).

### The Conditioned Reflex

Pavlov (1906) was studying digestive processes in dogs when he discovered that the dogs could be trained to salivate in response to the sound of a tone. What was so significant about a dog salivating when a tone was rung? The key was that the tone started out as a *neutral* stimulus; that is, originally it did not produce the response of salivation (after all, why should it?). However, Pavlov managed to change that by pairing the tone with a stimulus (meat powder) that did produce the salivation response. Through this process, the tone acquired the capacity to trigger the response of salivation. What Pavlov had demonstrated was *how learned reflexes are acquired.*

At this point we need to introduce the special vocabulary of classical conditioning (see **Figure 2.8**). In Pavlov's experiment the bond between the meat powder and salivation was a natural association that was not created through conditioning. In unconditioned bonds, **the *unconditioned stimulus (UCS)* is a stimulus that evokes an unconditioned response without previous conditioning. The *unconditioned response (UCR)* is an unlearned reaction to an unconditioned stimulus that occurs without previous conditioning.**

**Figure 2.7**

**A behavioral view of personality.** Behaviorists devote little attention to the structure of personality because it is unobservable, but they implicitly view personality as an individual's collection of response tendencies. A possible hierarchy of response tendencies for a specific stimulus situation is shown here. In the behavioral view, personality is made up of countless response hierarchies for various situations.

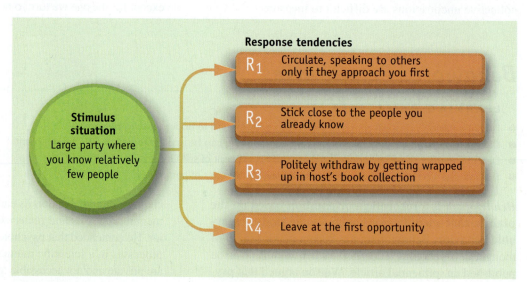

**Response tendencies**

Stimulus situation
Large party where you know relatively few people

R₁ Circulate, speaking to others only if they approach you first

R₂ Stick close to the people you already know

R₃ Politely withdraw by getting wrapped up in host's book collection

R₄ Leave at the first opportunity

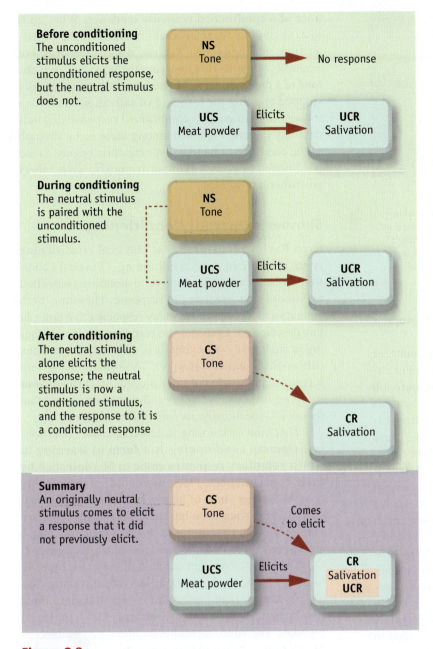

**Before conditioning**
The unconditioned stimulus elicits the unconditioned response, but the neutral stimulus does not.

NS Tone → No response

UCS Meat powder — Elicits → UCR Salivation

**During conditioning**
The neutral stimulus is paired with the unconditioned stimulus.

NS Tone

UCS Meat powder — Elicits → UCR Salivation

**After conditioning**
The neutral stimulus alone elicits the response; the neutral stimulus is now a conditioned stimulus, and the response to it is a conditioned response

CS Tone

CR Salivation

**Summary**
An originally neutral stimulus comes to elicit a response that it did not previously elicit.

CS Tone — Comes to elicit → CR Salivation

UCS Meat powder — Elicits → CR Salivation UCR

**Figure 2.8**
**The process of classical conditioning.** The sequence of events in classical conditioning is outlined here. As we encounter new examples of classical conditioning throughout the book, you will see diagrams like that shown in the fourth panel, which summarizes the process.

In contrast, the link between the tone and salivation was established through conditioning. In conditioned bonds, **the *conditioned stimulus (CS)* is a previously neutral stimulus that has acquired the capacity to evoke a conditioned response through conditioning. The *conditioned response (CR)* is a learned reaction to a conditioned stimulus that occurs because of previous conditioning.** Note that the unconditioned response and conditioned response often involve the same behavior (although there may be subtle differences). In Pavlov's initial demonstration, salivation was an unconditioned response when evoked by the UCS (meat

powder) and a conditioned response when evoked by the CS (the tone). The procedures involved in classical conditioning are outlined in **Figure 2.8**.

Pavlov's discovery came to be called the *conditioned reflex*. Classically conditioned responses are viewed as reflexes because most of them are relatively involuntary. Responses that are a product of classical conditioning are said to be *elicited*. This word is meant to convey the idea that these responses are triggered automatically.

## Classical Conditioning in Everyday Life

What is the role of classical conditioning in shaping personality in everyday life? Among other things, it contributes to the acquisition of emotional responses, such as anxieties, fears, and phobias (Antony & McCabe, 2003; Mineka & Zinbarg, 2006). This is a relatively small but important class of responses, as maladaptive emotional reactions underlie many adjustment problems. For example, one middle-aged woman reported being troubled by a bridge phobia so severe that she couldn't drive on interstate highways because of all the viaducts she would have to cross. She was able to pinpoint the source of her phobia. Back in her childhood, whenever her family would drive to visit her grandmother, they had to cross a little-used, rickety, dilapidated bridge out in the countryside. Her father, in a misguided attempt at humor, made a major production out of these crossings. He would stop short of the bridge and carry on about the enormous danger of the crossing. Obviously, he thought the bridge was safe or he wouldn't have driven across it. However, the naive young girl was terrified by her father's scare tactics, and the bridge became a conditioned stimulus eliciting great fear (see **Figure 2.9** on the next page). Unfortunately, the fear spilled over to all bridges, and 40 years later she was still carrying the burden of this phobia. Although a number of processes can cause phobias, it is clear that

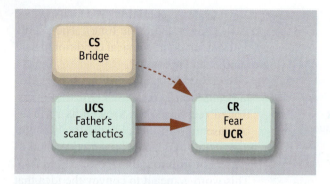

**Figure 2.9**

**Classical conditioning of a phobia.** Many emotional responses that would otherwise be puzzling can be explained as a result of classical conditioning. In the case of one woman's bridge phobia, the fear originally elicited by her father's scare tactics became a conditioned response to the stimulus of bridges.

classical conditioning is responsible for many people's irrational fears.

Classical conditioning also appears to account for more realistic and moderate anxiety responses. For example, imagine a news reporter in a high-pressure job where he consistently gets negative feedback about his work from his bosses. The negative comments from his supervisors function as a UCS eliciting anxiety. These reprimands are paired with the noise and sight of the newsroom, so that the newsroom becomes a CS triggering anxiety, even when his supervisors are absent (see **Figure 2.10**). Our poor reporter might even reach a point at which the mere *thought* of the newsroom elicits anxiety when he is elsewhere.

Fortunately, not every frightening experience leaves a conditioned fear in its wake. A variety of factors influence whether a conditioned response is acquired in a particular situation. Furthermore, a newly formed stimulus-response bond does not necessarily last indefinitely. The right circumstances can lead to *extinction*—**the gradual weakening and disappear-**

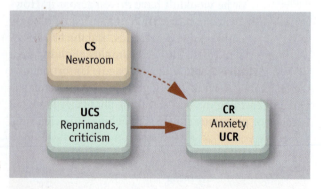

**Figure 2.10**

**Classical conditioning of anxiety.** A stimulus (in this case, a newsroom) that is frequently paired with anxiety-arousing events (reprimands and criticism) may come to elicit anxiety by itself, through classical conditioning.

**ance of a conditioned response tendency.** What leads to extinction in classical conditioning? It is the consistent presentation of the CS *alone,* without the UCS. For example, when Pavlov consistently presented *only* the tone to a previously conditioned dog, the tone gradually stopped eliciting the response of salivation. How long it takes to extinguish a conditioned response depends on many factors. Foremost among them is the strength of the conditioned bond when extinction begins. Some conditioned responses extinguish quickly, while others are difficult to weaken.

## Skinner's Operant Conditioning

Even Pavlov recognized that classical conditioning is not the only form of conditioning. Classical conditioning best explains reflexive responding controlled by stimuli that *precede* the response. However, both animals and humans make many responses that don't fit this description. Consider the response you are engaging in right now—studying. It is definitely not a reflex (life might be easier if it were). The stimuli that govern it (exams and grades) do not precede it. Instead, your studying response is mainly influenced by events that follow it—specifically, its *consequences.*

This kind of learning is called *operant conditioning. Operant conditioning* **is a form of learning in which voluntary responses come to be controlled by their consequences.** Operant conditioning probably governs a larger share of human behavior than classical conditioning, since most human responses are voluntary rather than reflexive. Because they are voluntary, operant responses are said to be *emitted* rather than *elicited.*

The study of operant conditioning was led by B. F. Skinner (1953, 1974, 1990), a Harvard University psychologist who spent most of his career studying simple responses made by laboratory rats and pigeons. The fundamental principle of operant conditioning is uncommonly simple. Skinner demonstrated that *organisms tend to repeat those responses that are followed by favorable consequences, and they tend not to repeat those responses that are followed by neutral or unfavorable consequences.* In Skinner's scheme, favorable, neutral, and unfavorable consequences involve reinforcement, extinction, and punishment, respectively. We'll look at each of these concepts in turn.

B. F. Skinner

### The Power of Reinforcement

According to Skinner, reinforcement can occur in two ways, which he called *positive reinforcement* and *negative reinforcement. Positive reinforcement* **occurs when a response is strengthened (increases in frequency) because it is followed by the arrival of a**

**(presumably) pleasant stimulus.** Positive reinforcement is roughly synonymous with the concept of reward. Notice, however, that reinforcement is defined *after the fact,* in terms of its effect on behavior. Why? Because reinforcement is subjective. Something that serves as a reinforcer for one person may not function as a reinforcer for another. For example, peer approval is a potent reinforcer for most people, but not all.

Positive reinforcement motivates much of everyday behavior. You study hard because good grades are likely to follow as a result. You go to work because this behavior produces paychecks. Perhaps you work extra hard in the hope of winning a promotion or a pay raise. In each of these examples, certain responses occur because they have led to positive outcomes in the past.

Positive reinforcement influences personality development in a straightforward way. Responses followed by pleasant outcomes are strengthened and tend to become habitual patterns of behavior. For example, a youngster might clown around in class and gain appreciative comments and smiles from schoolmates. This social approval will probably reinforce clowning-around behavior (see **Figure 2.11**). If such behavior is reinforced with some regularity, it will gradually become an integral element of the youth's personality. Similarly, whether or not a youngster develops traits such as independence, assertiveness, or selfishness depends on whether the child is reinforced for such behaviors by parents and by other influential persons.

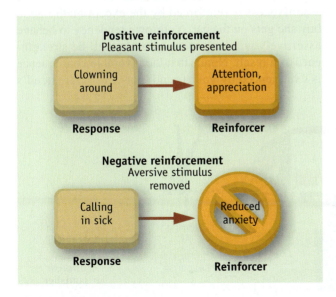

**Figure 2.11**

**Positive and negative reinforcement in operant conditioning.** Positive reinforcement occurs when a response is followed by a favorable outcome, so that the response is strengthened. In negative reinforcement, the removal (symbolized here by the "No" sign) of an aversive stimulus serves as a reinforcer. Negative reinforcement produces the same result as positive reinforcement: The person's tendency to emit the reinforced response is strengthened (the response becomes more frequent).

***Negative reinforcement* occurs when a response is strengthened (increases in frequency) because it is followed by the removal of a (presumably) unpleasant stimulus.** Don't let the word *negative* here confuse you. Negative reinforcement *is* reinforcement. Like positive reinforcement, it strengthens a response. However, this strengthening occurs because the response gets rid of an aversive stimulus. Consider a few examples: You rush home in the winter to get out of the cold. You clean your house to get rid of a mess. Parents give in to their child's begging to halt his whining.

Negative reinforcement plays a major role in the development of avoidance tendencies. As you may have noticed, many people tend to avoid facing up to awkward situations and sticky personal problems. This personality trait typically develops because avoidance behavior gets rid of anxiety and is therefore negatively reinforced. Recall our imaginary newspaper reporter whose work environment (the newsroom) elicits anxiety (as a result of classical conditioning). He might notice that on days when he calls in sick, his anxiety evaporates, so this response is gradually strengthened—through negative reinforcement (shown in **Figure 2.11**). If his avoidance behavior continues to be successful in reducing his anxiety, it might carry over into other areas of his life and become a central aspect of his personality.

## Extinction and Punishment

Like the effects of classical conditioning, the effects of operant conditioning may not last forever. In both types of conditioning, *extinction* refers to the gradual weakening and disappearance of a response. In operant conditioning, extinction begins when a previously reinforced response stops producing positive consequences. As extinction progresses, the response typically becomes less and less frequent and eventually disappears.

Thus, the response tendencies that make up one's personality are not necessarily permanent. For example, the youngster who found that his classmates reinforced clowning around in grade school might find that his attempts at comedy earn nothing but indifferent stares in high school. This termination of reinforcement would probably lead to the gradual extinction of the clowning-around behavior. How quickly an operant response extinguishes depends on many factors in the person's earlier reinforcement history.

Some responses may be weakened by punishment. In Skinner's scheme, ***punishment* occurs when a response is weakened (decreases in frequency) because it is followed by the arrival of a (presumably) unpleasant stimulus.** The concept of punishment in operant conditioning confuses many students on two counts. First, it is often mixed up with negative reinforcement because both involve aversive (unpleasant) stimuli.

Please note, however, that they are altogether different events with opposite outcomes! In negative reinforcement, a response leads to the removal of something aversive, and this response is strengthened. In punishment, a response leads to the arrival of something aversive, and this response tends to be weakened.

The second source of confusion involves the tendency to view punishment as only a disciplinary procedure used by parents, teachers, and other authority figures. In the operant model, punishment occurs whenever a response leads to negative consequences. Defined in this way, the concept goes far beyond actions such as parents spanking children or teachers handing out detentions. For example, if you wear a new outfit and your friends make fun of it and hurt your feelings, your behavior has been punished, and your tendency to wear this clothing will decline. Similarly, if you go to a restaurant and have a horrible meal, in Skinner's terminology your response has led to punishment, and you are unlikely to return.

The impact of punishment on personality development is just the opposite of reinforcement. Generally speaking, those patterns of behavior that lead to punishing (that is, negative) consequences tend to be weakened. For instance, if your impulsive decisions always backfire, your tendency to be impulsive should decline.

According to Skinner (1987), conditioning in humans operates much as it does in the rats and pigeons that he has studied in his laboratory. Hence, he assumes that conditioning strengthens and weakens people's response tendencies "mechanically"—that is, without their conscious participation. Like John Watson (1913) before him, Skinner asserted that we can explain behavior without being concerned about individuals' mental processes.

Skinner's ideas continue to be influential, but his mechanical view of conditioning has not gone unchallenged by other behaviorists. Theorists such as Albert Bandura have developed somewhat different behavioral models in which cognition plays a role. *Cognition* is another name for the thought processes that behaviorists have traditionally shown little interest in.

## Bandura's Social Cognitive Theory

Albert Bandura is one of several theorists who have added a cognitive flavor to behaviorism since the 1960s. Bandura (1977), Walter Mischel (1973), and Julian Rotter (1982) take issue with Skinner's view. They point out that humans obviously are conscious, thinking, feeling beings. Moreover, these theorists argue

that in neglecting cognitive processes, Skinner ignores the most distinctive and important feature of human behavior. Bandura and like-minded theorists originally called their modified brand of behaviorism *social learning theory*. Today, Bandura refers to his model as *social cognitive theory*.

*Courtesy Albert Bandura*

**Albert Bandura**

Bandura (1986, 1999b, 2006) agrees with the basic thrust of behaviorism in that he believes that personality is largely shaped through learning. However, he contends that conditioning is not a mechanical process in which people are passive participants. Instead, he maintains that individuals actively seek out and process information about their environment in order to maximize their favorable outcomes.

### Observational Learning

Bandura's foremost theoretical contribution has been his description of observational learning. *Observational learning* **occurs when an organism's responding is influenced by the observation of others, who are called models.** Bandura does not view observational learning as entirely separate from classical and operant conditioning. Instead, he asserts that both classical and operant conditioning can take place indirectly when one person observes another's conditioning (see **Figure 2.12**).

To illustrate, suppose you observe a friend behaving assertively with a car salesman. Let's say that her assertiveness is reinforced by the exceptionally good buy she gets on the car. Your own tendency to behave assertively with salespeople might well be strengthened as a result. Notice that the favorable consequence is experienced by your friend, not you. Your friend's

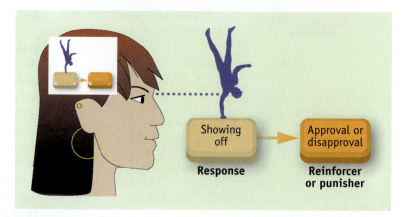

**Figure 2.12**
**Observational learning.** In observational learning, an observer attends to and stores a mental representation of a model's behavior (for example, showing off) and its consequences (such as approval or disapproval from others). According to social cognitive theory, many of our characteristic responses are acquired through observation of others' behavior.

tendency to bargain assertively should be reinforced directly. But your tendency to bargain assertively may also be strengthened indirectly.

The theories of Skinner and Pavlov make no allowance for this type of indirect learning. After all, observational learning requires that you pay *attention* to your friend's behavior, that you *understand* its consequences, and that you store this *information* in *memory*. Obviously, attention, understanding, information, and memory involve cognition, which behaviorists used to ignore.

As social cognitive theory has been refined, it has become apparent that some role models tend to be more influential than others (Bandura, 1986). Both children and adults tend to imitate people they like or respect more so than people they don't. People are also especially prone to imitate the behavior of those they consider attractive or powerful (such as celebrities). In addition, imitation is more likely when individuals see similarity between the model and themselves. Thus, children imitate same-sex role models somewhat more than other-sex models. Finally, as noted before, people are more likely to copy a model if they see the model's behavior leading to positive outcomes.

### Self-Efficacy

Bandura (1993, 1997, 2004) believes that *self-efficacy* is a crucial element of personality. **Self-efficacy is one's belief about one's ability to perform behaviors that should lead to expected outcomes.** When a person's self-efficacy is high, he or she feels confident in executing the responses necessary to earn reinforcers. When self-efficacy is low, the individual worries that the necessary responses may be beyond her or his abilities. Perceptions of self-efficacy are subjective and specific to different kinds of tasks. For instance, you might feel extremely confident about your ability to handle difficult social situations but doubtful about your ability to handle academic challenges.

Perceptions of self-efficacy can influence which challenges people tackle and how well they perform. Studies have found that feelings of greater self-efficacy are associated with reduced procrastination (Steel, 2007); greater success in giving up smoking (Boudreaux et al., 1998); greater adherence to an exercise regimen (Rimal, 2001); more-effective weight-loss efforts (Linde et al., 2006); better outcomes in substance abuse treatment (Bandura, 1999a); more success in coping with medical rehabilitation (Waldrop et al., 2001); better self-care among diabetics (Williams & Bond, 2002); reduced disability from problems with chronic pain (Hadjistavropoulos et al., 2007); greater persistence and effort in academic pursuits (Zimmerman, 1995); higher levels of academic performance (Chemers, Hu, & Garcia, 2001); reduced vulnerability to anxiety and depression in childhood (Muris, 2002); less jealousy in romantic relationships (Hu, Zhang, & Li, 2005); enhanced performance in athletic competition (Kane et al., 1996); greater receptiveness to technological training (Christoph, Schoenfeld, & Tansky, 1998); greater success in searching for a new job (Saks, 2006); higher work-related performance (Stajkovic & Luthans, 1998); reduced strain from occupational stress (Grau, Salanova, Peiro, 2001); and greater resistance to stress (Jex et al., 2001), among many other things.

### Evaluating Behavioral Perspectives

Behavioral theories are firmly rooted in empirical research rather than clinical intuition. Pavlov's model has shed light on how conditioning can account for people's sometimes troublesome emotional responses. Skinner's work has demonstrated how personality is shaped by the consequences of behavior. Bandura's social cognitive theory has shown how people's observations mold their characteristic behavior.

According to Bandura, people acquire a diverse array of responses from role models through observational learning.

Behaviorists, in particular Walter Mischel (1973, 1990), have also provided the most thorough account of why people are only moderately consistent in their behavior. For example, a person who is shy in one context might be quite outgoing in another. Other models of personality largely ignore this inconsistency. The behaviorists have shown that it occurs because people behave in ways they think will lead to reinforcement in the situation at hand. In other words, situational factors are important determinants of behavior. Thus, a major contribution of the behavioral perspective has been its demonstration that personality factors and situational factors jointly and interactively shape behavior (Fleeson, 2004; Roberts & Pomerantz, 2004)

Of course, each theoretical approach has its shortcomings, and the behavioral approach is no exception. Major lines of criticism include the following (Liebert & Liebert, 1998; Pervin & John, 2001):

**1.** *Dilution of the behavioral approach.* The behaviorists used to be criticized because they neglected cognitive processes, which clearly are important factors in human behavior. The rise of social cognitive theory blunted this criticism. However, social cognitive theory undermines the foundation on which behaviorism was built—the idea that psychologists should study only observable behavior. Thus, some critics complain that behavioral theories aren't very behavioral anymore.

**2.** *Overdependence on animal research.* Many principles in behavioral theories were discovered through research on animals. Some critics, especially humanistic theorists, argue that behaviorists depend too much on animal research and that they indiscriminately generalize from the behavior of animals to the behavior of humans.

**3.** *Fragmentation of personality.* Behaviorists have also been criticized for providing a fragmented view of personality. The behavioral approach carves personality up into stimulus-response associations. There are no unifying structural concepts (such as Freud's ego) that tie these pieces together. Humanistic theorists, whom we shall cover next, have been particularly vocal in criticizing this piecemeal analysis of personality.

## Recommended READING

### Snoop: What Your Stuff Says About You
by Sam Gosling (Basic Books, 2008)

You may have heard someone comment that a particular house or specific room "has personality." This metaphor is usually intended to convey that the house or room is unusual or distinctive. But personality researcher Sam Gosling points out that people proactively choose and shape their environments, raising the possibility that rooms could *literally* have personality—the personality of their occupants. For example, people who choose formal or informal furniture or conventional versus unconventional decorating convey something about who they are, as do people who display an Amy Winehouse poster or photos of their travels. In places where they dwell, people also leave a *behavioral residue*—remnants of their activities, such as books, magazines, computer printouts, drawings, musical instruments, snacks, and discarded beer cans. Cognizant of these realities, Sam Gosling and his colleagues set out to determine just how much observers, or "snoops," can infer about an individual's personality based on visiting the person's office or bedroom. In a series of studies they demonstrated that much can be learned about persons from the places in which they dwell. Much of this research has centered around the five-factor model of personality. In these studies, observers visit individuals' personal spaces and estimate how the people shape up on the Big Five traits. These estimates are then compared to actual assessments of the target persons on the Big Five traits. It turns out that bedrooms yield more reliable information than offices, but both can be revealing. This book provides a charming, easy-to-understand overview of Gosling's research on how one can draw astute inferences about individuals' personality from their personal spaces, their musical tastes, and their personal websites. In addition to reviewing his own studies, Gosling profiles the work of several other psychologists who have investigated how people often provide subtle clues about the inner workings of their personality. The result is a thought-provoking overview of an entirely new approach to examining the repercussions of personality.

*Go to the Psychology CourseMate for Weiten at* **www.cengagebrain.com/shop/ISBN/1111186634** *for descriptions of other recommended books.*

# Humanistic Perspectives

Humanistic theory emerged in the 1950s as something of a backlash against the behavioral and psychodynamic theories (Cassel, 2000; DeCarvalho, 1991). The principal charge hurled at these two models was that they were dehumanizing. Freudian theory was criticized for its belief that primitive, animalistic drives dominate behavior. Behaviorism was criticized for its preoccupation with animal research. Critics argued that both schools view people as helpless pawns controlled by their environment and their past, with little capacity for self-direction. Many of these critics blended into a loose alliance that came to be known as "humanism" because of its exclusive interest in human behavior. **Humanism is a theoretical orientation that emphasizes the unique qualities of humans, especially their free will and their potential for personal growth.** Humanistic psychologists do not believe that we can learn anything of significance about the human condition from animal research.

Humanistic theorists take an optimistic view of human nature. In contrast to most psychodynamic and behavioral theorists, humanistic theorists believe that (1) human nature includes an innate drive toward personal growth, (2) individuals have the freedom to chart their courses of action and are not pawns of their environment, and (3) humans are largely conscious and rational beings who are not dominated by unconscious, irrational needs and conflicts. Humanistic theorists also maintain that one's subjective view of the world is more important than objective reality (P. T. P Wong, 2006). According to this notion, if you *think* you are homely, or bright, or sociable, that belief will influence your behavior more than the actual realities of how homely, bright, or sociable you are.

The humanistic approach clearly provides a different perspective on personality than either the psychodynamic or behavioral approach. In this section we'll review the ideas of the two most influential humanistic theorists, Carl Rogers and Abraham Maslow.

## Rogers's Person-Centered Theory

Carl Rogers (1951, 1961, 1980) was one of the founders of the human potential movement, which emphasizes personal growth through sensitivity training, encounter groups, and other exercises intended to help people get in touch with their true selves. Working at the University of Chicago in the 1940s, Rogers devised a major new approach to psychotherapy. Like Freud, Rogers based his personality theory on his extensive therapeutic interactions with many clients. Because of his emphasis on a person's subjective point of view, Rogers called his approach a *person-centered theory*.

**Carl Rogers**

*Carl Rogers Memorial Library*

### The Self and Its Development

Rogers viewed personality structure in terms of just one construct. He called this construct the *self*, although it is more widely known today as the *self-concept*. **A self-concept is a collection of beliefs about one's own nature, unique qualities, and typical behavior.** Your self-concept is your mental picture of yourself. It is a collection of self-perceptions. For example, a self-concept might include such beliefs as "I am easygoing" or "I am pretty" or "I am hardworking."

Rogers stressed the subjective nature of the self-concept. Your self-concept may not be entirely consistent with your actual experiences. To put it more bluntly, your self-concept may be inaccurate. Most people are prone to distort their experiences to some extent to promote a relatively favorable self-concept. For example, you may believe that you are quite bright academically, but your grade transcript might suggest otherwise. Rogers used the term *incongruence* **to refer to the disparity between one's self-concept and one's actual experience.** In contrast, if a person's self-concept is reasonably accurate, it is said to be *congruent* with reality. Everyone experiences *some* incongruence; the crucial issue is how much (see **Figure 2.13** on the next page). Rogers maintained that a great deal of incongruence undermines a person's psychological well-being.

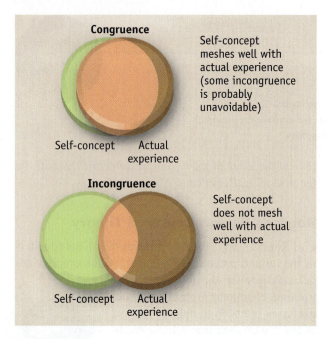

**Congruence**

Self-concept meshes well with actual experience (some incongruence is probably unavoidable)

Self-concept    Actual experience

**Incongruence**

Self-concept does not mesh well with actual experience

Self-concept    Actual experience

**Figure 2.13**

**Rogers's view of personality structure.** In Rogers's model, the self-concept is the only important structural construct. However, Rogers acknowledged that one's self-concept may not jell with the realities of one's actual experience—a condition called incongruence. Different people have varied amounts of incongruence between their self-concept and reality.

In terms of personality development, Rogers was concerned with how childhood experiences promote congruence or incongruence. According to Rogers, everyone has a strong need for affection, love, and acceptance from others. Early in life, parents provide most of this affection. Rogers maintained that some parents make their affection *conditional.* That is, they make it depend on the child's behaving well and living up to expectations. When parental love seems conditional, children often distort and block out of their memory

*"Just remember, son, it doesn't matter whether you win or lose—unless you want Daddy's love."*

those experiences that make them feel unworthy of love. At the other end of the spectrum, Rogers asserted that some parents make their affection *unconditional.* Their children have less need to block out unworthy experiences because they have been assured that they are worthy of affection no matter what they do.

Rogers believed that unconditional love from parents fosters congruence and that conditional love fosters incongruence. He further theorized that individuals who grow up believing that affection from others (besides their parents) is conditional go on to distort more and more of their experiences to feel worthy of acceptance from a wider and wider array of people, making the incongruence grow.

### Anxiety and Defense

According to Rogers, experiences that threaten people's personal views of themselves are the principal cause of troublesome anxiety. The more inaccurate your self-concept, the more likely you are to have experiences that clash with your self-perceptions. Thus, people with highly incongruent self-concepts are especially likely to be plagued by recurrent anxiety (see **Figure 2.14**).

To ward off this anxiety, such people often behave defensively. That is, they ignore, deny, and twist reality to protect their self-concept. Consider a young woman who, like most of us, considers herself a "nice person." Let us suppose that in reality she is rather conceited and selfish, and she gets feedback from both boyfriends and girlfriends that she is a "self-centered, snotty brat." How might she react to protect her self-concept? She might ignore or block out those occasions when she behaves selfishly and then deny the accusations by her friends that she is self-centered. She might also attribute her girlfriends' negative comments to their jealousy of her good looks and blame the boyfriends' negative remarks on their disappointment because she won't get more serious with them. Meanwhile, she might start doing some kind of charity work to show everyone (including herself) that she really is a nice person. As you can see, people often go to great lengths to defend their self-concept.

Rogers's theory can explain defensive behavior and personality disturbances, but he also emphasized the importance of psychological health. Rogers held that psychological health is rooted in a congruent self-concept. In turn, congruence is rooted in a sense of personal worth, which stems from a childhood saturated with unconditional affection from parents and others. These themes are similar to those emphasized by the other major humanistic theorist, Abraham Maslow.

### Maslow's Theory of Self-Actualization

Abraham Maslow grew up in Brooklyn and spent much of his career at Brandeis University, where he provided crucial leadership for the fledgling humanistic

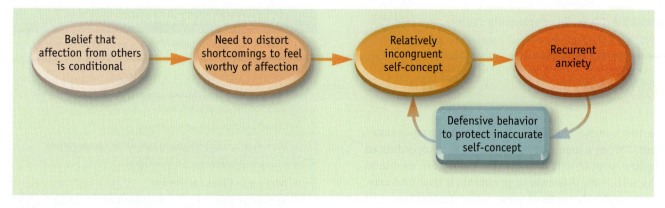

**Figure 2.14**

**Rogers's view of personality development and dynamics.** Rogers's theory of development posits that conditional love leads to a need to distort experiences, which fosters an incongruent self-concept. Incongruence makes one prone to recurrent anxiety, which triggers defensive behavior, which fuels more incongruence.

movement. Like Rogers, Maslow (1968, 1970) argued that psychology should take a greater interest in the nature of the healthy personality, instead of dwelling on the causes of disorders. "To oversimplify the matter somewhat," he said, "it is as if Freud supplied to us the sick half of psychology and we must now fill it out with the healthy half" (Maslow, 1968, p. 5). Maslow's key contributions were his analysis of how motives are organized hierarchically and his description of the healthy personality.

Courtesy Abraham Maslow

**Abraham Maslow**

### Hierarchy of Needs

Maslow proposed that human motives are organized into a *hierarchy of needs*—a systematic arrangement of needs, according to priority, in which basic needs **must be met before less basic needs are aroused.** This hierarchical arrangement is usually portrayed as a pyramid (see **Figure 2.15**). The needs toward the bottom of the pyramid, such as physiological or security needs, are the most basic. Higher levels in the pyramid consist of progressively less basic needs. When a person manages to satisfy a level of needs reasonably well (complete satisfaction is not necessary), *this satisfaction activates needs at the next level.*

Like Rogers, Maslow argued that humans have an innate drive toward personal growth—that is, evolution toward a higher state of being. Thus, he described the needs in the uppermost reaches of his hierarchy as *growth needs.* These include the needs for knowledge, understanding, order, and aesthetic beauty. Foremost among the growth needs is the *need for self-actualization,* **which is the need to fulfill one's potential;** it is the highest need in Maslow's motivational hierarchy.

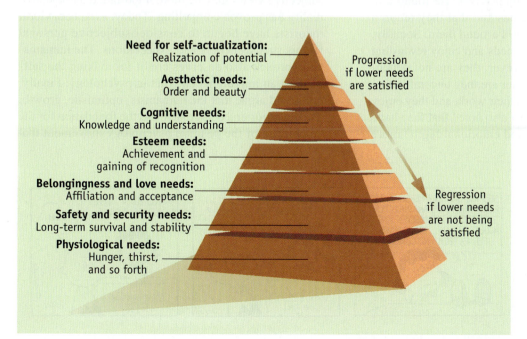

**Figure 2.15**

**Maslow's hierarchy of needs.** According to Maslow, human needs are arranged in a hierarchy, and individuals must satisfy their basic needs first, before progressing to higher needs. In the diagram, higher levels in the pyramid represent progressively less basic needs. People progress upward in the hierarchy when lower needs are satisfied reasonably well, but they may regress back to lower levels if basic needs cease to be satisfied.

Maslow summarized this concept with a simple statement: "What a man *can* be, he *must* be." According to Maslow, people will be frustrated if they are unable to fully utilize their talents or pursue their true interests. For example, if you have great musical talent but must work as an accountant, or if you have scholarly interests but must work as a sales clerk, your need for self-actualization will be thwarted.

### The Healthy Personality

Because of his interest in self-actualization, Maslow set out to discover the nature of the healthy personality. He tried to identify people of exceptional mental health so that he could investigate their characteristics. In one case, he used psychological tests and interviews to sort out the healthiest 1 percent of a sizable population of college students. He also studied admired historical figures (such as Thomas Jefferson and psychologist-philosopher William James) and personal acquaintances characterized by superior adjustment. Over a period of years, he accumulated his case histories and gradually sketched, in broad strokes, a picture of ideal psychological health.

Maslow called people with exceptionally healthy personalities *self-actualizing persons* because of their commitment to continued personal growth. He identified various traits characteristic of self-actualizing people, which are listed in **Figure 2.16**. In brief, Maslow found that self-actualizers are accurately tuned in to reality and are at peace with themselves. He found that they are open and spontaneous and that they retain a fresh appreciation of the world around them. Socially, they are sensitive to others' needs and enjoy rewarding interpersonal relations. However, they are not dependent on others for approval, nor are they uncomfortable with solitude. They thrive on their work, and they enjoy their sense of humor. Maslow also noted that they have "peak experiences" (profound emotional highs) more

| **Characteristics of Self-Actualizing People** |
|---|
| • Clear, efficient perception of reality and comfortable relations with it |
| • Spontaneity, simplicity, and naturalness |
| • Problem centering (having something outside themselves they "must" do as a mission) |
| • Detachment and need for privacy |
| • Autonomy, independence of culture and environment |
| • Continued freshness of appreciation |
| • Mystical and peak experiences |
| • Feelings of kinship and identification with the human race |
| • Strong friendships, but limited in number |
| • Democratic character structure |
| • Ethical discrimination between means and ends, between good and evil |
| • Philosophical, unhostile sense of humor |
| • Balance between polarities in personality |

**Figure 2.16**

**Characteristics of self-actualizing people.** Humanistic theorists emphasize psychological health instead of maladjustment. Maslow's sketch of the self-actualizing person provides a provocative picture of the healthy personality.

often than others. Finally, he found that they strike a nice balance between many polarities in personality, in that they can be both childlike and mature, rational and intuitive, conforming and rebellious.

## Evaluating Humanistic Perspectives

The humanists added a refreshing perspective to the study of personality. Their argument that a person's subjective views may be more important than objective reality has proven compelling. Today, even behavioral theorists have begun to consider subjective personal factors such as beliefs and expectations. The humanistic approach also deserves credit for making the self-concept an important construct in psychology. Finally, one could argue that the humanists' optimistic, growth, and health-oriented approach laid the foundation for the emergence of the positive psychology movement that

PEANUTS © United Feature Syndicate, Inc.

is increasingly influential in contemporary psychology (Sheldon & Kasser, 2001b; Taylor, 2001).

Of course, there is a negative side to the balance sheet as well. Critics have identified some weaknesses in the humanistic approach to personality, including the following (Burger, 2008; P. T. P. Wong, 2006):

**1.** *Poor testability.* Like psychodynamic theorists, the humanists have been criticized for proposing hypotheses that are difficult to put to a scientific test. Humanistic concepts such as personal growth and self-actualization are difficult to define and measure.

**2.** *Unrealistic view of human nature.* Critics also charge that the humanists have been overly optimistic in their assumptions about human nature and unrealistic in their descriptions of the healthy personality. For instance, Maslow's self-actualizing people sound *perfect*. In reality, Maslow had a hard time finding self-actualizing persons. When he searched among the living, the results were so disappointing that he turned to the study of historical figures. Thus, humanistic portraits of psychological health are perhaps a bit unrealistic.

**3.** *Inadequate evidence.* Humanistic theories are based primarily on discerning but uncontrolled observations in clinical settings. Case studies can be valuable in generating ideas, but they are ill-suited for building a solid database. More experimental research is needed to catch up with the theorizing in the humanistic camp. This situation is precisely the opposite of the one you'll encounter in the next section, on biological perspectives, where more theorizing is needed to catch up with the research.

# Biological Perspectives

### LEARNING OBJECTIVES

- Describe Eysenck's views on personality structure and development.
- Summarize recent twin studies that support the idea that personality is largely inherited.
- Summarize evolutionary analyses of why certain personality traits appear to be important.
- Evaluate the strengths and weaknesses of biological theories of personality.

*Like many identical twins reared apart, Jim Lewis and Jim Springer found they had been leading eerily similar lives. Separated four weeks after birth in 1940, the Jim twins grew up 45 miles apart in Ohio and were reunited in 1979. Eventually, they discovered that both drove the same model blue Chevrolet, chain-smoked Salems, chewed their fingernails, and owned dogs named Toy. Each had spent a good deal of time vacationing at the same three-block strip of beach in Florida. More important, when tested for such personality traits as flexibility, self-control, and sociability, the twins responded almost exactly alike. (Leo, 1987, p. 63)*

So began a *Time* magazine summary of a major twin study conducted at the University of Minnesota, where investigators have been exploring the hereditary roots of personality. The research team has managed to locate and complete testing on 44 rare pairs of identical twins separated early in life. Not all the twin pairs have been as similar as Jim Lewis and Jim Springer, but many of the parallels have been uncanny (Lykken et al., 1992). Identical twins Oskar Stohr and Jack Yufe were separated soon after birth. Oskar was sent to a Nazi-run school in Czechoslovakia, while Jack was raised in a Jewish home on a Caribbean island. When they were reunited for the first time during middle age, they both showed up wearing similar mustaches, haircuts, shirts, and wire-rimmed glasses. A pair of previously separated

© Michael Nichols/Magnum Photos

**Is personality largely inherited? The story of these identical twins would certainly suggest so. Although they were reared apart from 4 weeks after their birth, Jim Lewis (left) and Jim Springer (right) exhibit remarkable correspondence in personality. Some of the similarities in their lives—such as the benches built around trees in their yards—seem uncanny.**

female twins both arrived at the Minneapolis airport wearing seven rings on their fingers. One had a son named Richard Andrew, and the other had a son named Andrew Richard!

Could personality be largely inherited? These anecdotal reports of striking resemblances between identical twins reared apart certainly raise this possibility. In this section we'll discuss Hans Eysenck's theory, which emphasizes the influence of heredity, and look at behavioral genetics and evolutionary perspectives on personality.

## Eysenck's Theory

Hans Eysenck was born in Germany but fled to London during the era of Nazi rule. He went on to become one of Britain's most prominent psychologists. According to Eysenck (1967), "Personality is determined to a large extent by a person's genes" (p. 20). How is heredity linked to personality in Eysenck's model? In part, through conditioning concepts borrowed from behavioral theory. Eysenck (1967, 1982, 1991) theorizes that some people can be conditioned more readily than others because of inherited differences in their physiological functioning (specifically, their level of arousal). These variations in "conditionability" are assumed to influence the personality traits that people acquire through conditioning.

Courtesy Hans Eysenck, photo by Mark Gerson

**Hans Eysenck**

Eysenck views personality structure as a hierarchy of traits. Numerous superficial traits are derived from a smaller number of more basic traits, which are derived from a handful of fundamental higher-order traits, as shown in **Figure 2.17**. Eysenck has shown a special interest in explaining variations in *extraversion-introversion,* the trait dimension first described years earlier by Carl Jung. He has proposed that introverts tend to have higher levels of physiological arousal than extraverts. This higher arousal purportedly motivates them to avoid social situations that will further elevate their arousal and makes them more easily conditioned than extraverts. According to Eysenck, people who condition easily acquire more conditioned inhibitions than others. These inhibitions, coupled with their relatively high arousal, make them more bashful, tentative, and uneasy in social situations. This social discomfort leads them to turn inward. Hence, they become introverted.

Is there any research to support Eysenck's explanation of the origins of introversion? Yes, but the evidence is rather inconsistent. Many studies *have* found that introverts tend to exhibit higher levels of arousal or greater reactivity to sensory stimuli than extraverts, but quite a few studies have also failed to find the predicted differences (de Geus & Neumann, 2008; Stelmack & Rammsayer, 2008). Part of the problem is that the concept of physiological arousal and reactivity has turned out to be much more multifaceted and difficult to measure than Eysenck originally anticipated.

## Recent Research in Behavioral Genetics

Recent twin studies have provided impressive support for Eysenck's hypothesis that personality is largely inherited. **In *twin studies* researchers assess hereditary influence by comparing the resemblance of identical**

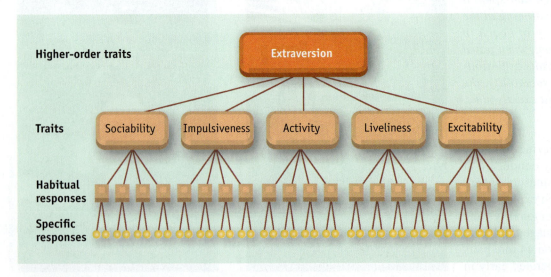

## Figure 2.17

**Eysenck's model of personality structure.** Eysenck describes personality structure as a hierarchy of traits. In this scheme, a few higher-order traits (such as extraversion) determine a host of lower-order traits (such as sociability), which determine one's habitual responses (such as going to lots of parties).

Source: From Eysenck, H. J. (1967). *The biological basis of personality,* p. 36. Springfield, IL: Charles C. Thomas. Courtesy of Charles C. Thomas.

**twins and fraternal twins on a trait.** The logic underlying this comparison is as follows. *Identical twins* emerge from one egg that splits, so that their genetic makeup is exactly the same (100% overlap). *Fraternal twins* result when two eggs are fertilized simultaneously; their genetic overlap is only 50%. Both types of twins *usually* grow up in the same home, at the same time, exposed to the same relatives, neighbors, peers, teachers, events, and so forth. Thus, both kinds of twins normally develop under similar environmental conditions, but identical twins share more genetic kinship. Hence, if sets of identical twins exhibit more personality resemblance than sets of fraternal twins, this greater similarity is probably attributable to heredity rather than to environment. The results of twin studies can be used to estimate the heritability of personality traits and other characteristics. **A *heritability ratio* is an estimate of the proportion of trait variability in a population that is determined by variations in genetic inheritance.** Heritability can be estimated for any trait. For example, the heritability of height is estimated to be around 90% (Plomin, 1994), whereas the heritability of intelligence appears to be about 50%–70% (Petrill, 2005; Plomin & Spinath, 2004).

The accumulating evidence from twin studies suggests that heredity exerts considerable influence over many personality traits (Livesley, Jang, & Vernon, 2003; Rowe & van den Oord, 2005). For instance, in research on the Big Five personality traits, identical twins have been found to be much more similar than fraternal twins on all five traits (Plomin et al., 2008). Some skeptics still wonder whether identical twins might exhibit more personality resemblance than fraternal twins because they are raised more similarly. In other words, they wonder whether environmental factors (rather than heredity) could be responsible for identical twins'

**WEB LINK 2.6   Great Ideas in Personality**

At this site, personality psychologist G. Scott Acton demonstrates that scientific research programs in personality generate broad and compelling ideas about what it is to be a human being. He charts the contours of 12 research perspectives, including behaviorism, behavioral genetics, and sociobiology, and supports them with extensive links to published and online resources associated with each perspective.

greater similarity. This nagging question can be answered only by studying identical twins who have been reared apart. Which is why the twin study at the University of Minnesota has been so important.

The Minnesota study (Tellegen et al., 1988) was the first to administer the same personality test to identical and fraternal twins reared together as well as apart. Most of the twins reared apart were separated quite early in life (median age of 2.5 months) and remained separated for a long time (median period of almost 34 years). Nonetheless, on all three of the higher-order traits examined, the identical twins reared apart displayed more personality resemblance than fraternal twins reared together. Based on the pattern of correlations observed, the researchers estimated that the heritability of personality is around 50%. Another large-scale twin study of the Big Five traits conducted in Germany and Poland yielded similar conclusions (Riemann, Angleitner, & Strelau, 1997). The heritability estimates based on the data from this study, which are shown in **Figure 2.18**, are in the same range as the estimates from the Minnesota study. Overall, five decades of research on the determinants of the Big Five traits suggests that the heritability of each trait is in the vicinity of 50% (Krueger & Johnson, 2008).

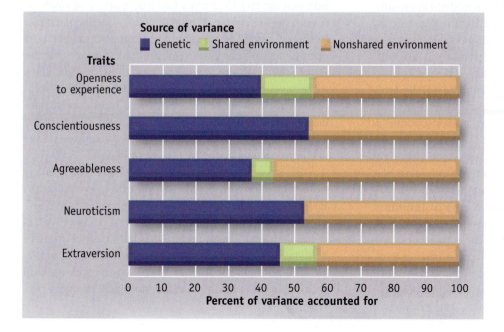

**Figure 2.18**

**Heritability and environmental variance for the Big Five traits.** Based on the twin study data of Riemann et al. (1997), Plomin and Caspi (1999) estimated the heritability of each of the Big Five traits. The data also allowed them to estimate the amount of variance on each trait attributable to shared environment and nonshared environment. As you can see, the heritability estimates hovered in the vicinity of 40 percent, with two exceeding 50 percent. As in other studies, the influence of shared environment was very modest.

Source: Based on Plomin, R., & Caspi, A. (1999). Behavioral genetics and personality. In L. A. Pervin & O. P. John (Eds.), *Handbook of personality: Theory and research.* New York: The Guilford Press. Adapted by permission.

## The Evolutionary Approach to Personality

In the realm of biological approaches to personality, the most recent development has been the emergence of an evolutionary perspective. Evolutionary psychologists assert that the patterns of behavior seen in a species are products of evolution in the same way that anatomical characteristics are. *Evolutionary psychology* **examines behavioral processes in terms of their adaptive value for members of a species over the course of many generations.** The basic premise of evolutionary psychology is that natural selection favors behaviors that enhance organisms' reproductive success—that is, passing on genes to the next generation. Evolutionary theorists assert that personality has a biological basis because natural selection has favored certain personality traits over the course of human history (Figueredo et al., 2005, 2009). Thus, evolutionary analyses of personality focus on how various traits—and the ability to recognize these traits in others—may have contributed to reproductive fitness in ancestral human populations.

For example, David Buss (1991, 1995, 1997) has argued that the Big Five personality traits stand out as important dimensions of personality across a variety of cultures because those traits have had significant adaptive implications. Buss points out that humans have historically depended heavily on groups, which afford protection from predators or enemies, opportunities for sharing food, and a diverse array of other benefits. In the context of these group interactions, people have had to make difficult but crucial judgments about the characteristics of others, asking such questions as: Who will make a good member of my coalition? Who can I depend on when in need? Who will share their resources? Thus, Buss (1995) argues, "Those individuals able to accurately discern and act upon these individual differences likely enjoyed a considerable reproductive advantage" (p. 22). According to Buss, the Big Five emerge as fundamental dimensions of personality because humans have evolved special sensitivity to variations in the ability to bond with others (extraversion), the willingness to cooperate and collaborate (agreeableness), the tendency to be reliable and ethical (conscientiousness), the capacity to be an innovative problem solver (openness to experience), and the ability to handle stress (low neuroticism). In a nutshell, Buss argues that the Big Five reflect the most salient features of others' adaptive behavior over the course of evolutionary history.

Daniel Nettle (2006) takes this line of thinking one step further, asserting that the traits themselves (as opposed to the ability to recognize them in others) are products of evolution that were adaptive in ancestral environments. For example, he discusses how extraversion could have promoted mating success, how neuroticism could have fueled competitiveness and avoidance

of dangers, how agreeableness could have fostered the effective building of coalitions, and so forth. Nettle also discusses how each of the Big Five traits may have had adaptive costs (extraversion, for example, is associated with risky behavior) as well as benefits. Thus, he argues that evolutionary analyses of personality need to weigh the *trade-offs* between the adaptive advantages and disadvantages of the Big Five traits.

## Evaluating Biological Perspectives

Recent research in behavioral genetics has provided convincing evidence that biological factors help shape personality. Evolutionary theorists have developed thought-provoking hypotheses about how natural selection may have sculpted the basic architecture of personality. Nonetheless, we must take note of some weaknesses in biological approaches to personality:

1. *Problems with estimates of hereditary influence.* Efforts to carve personality into genetic and environmental components with statistics are ultimately artificial. The effects of heredity and environment are twisted together in complicated interactions that can't be separated cleanly (Funder, 2001; Rutter, 2007; Sternberg, Grigorenko, & Kidd, 2005). Although heritability ratios sound precise, they are estimates based on a complicated chain of inferences that are subject to debate.

2. *Hindsight bias in evolutionary theory.* **Hindsight bias—the common tendency to mold one's interpretation of the past to fit how events actually turned out**—presents thorny problems for evolutionary theorists, who generally work backward from known outcomes to reason out how adaptive pressures in humans' ancestral past may have led to those outcomes (Cornell, 1997). Evolutionary theorists' assertion that the Big Five traits had major adaptive implications over the course of human history seems plausible, but what would have happened if other traits, such as dominance or sensation seeking, had shown up in the Big Five? With the luxury of hindsight, evolutionary theorists surely could have constructed plausible explanations for how these traits promoted reproductive success in the distant past. Thus, some critics have argued that evolutionary explanations are post hoc, speculative accounts contaminated by hindsight bias.

3. *Lack of adequate theory.* At present there is no comprehensive biological theory of personality. Eysenck's model does not provide a systematic overview of how biological factors govern personality development (and it was never intended to). Evolutionary analyses of personality are even more limited in scope. Additional theoretical work is needed to catch up with recent empirical findings on the biological basis for personality.

# Contemporary Empirical Approaches to Personality

**LEARNING OBJECTIVES**

- Describe the personality trait of sensation seeking.
- Summarize some of the correlates of high sensation seeking.
- Explain the chief concepts and hypotheses of terror management theory.
- Describe how reminders of death influence people's behavior.

So far, our coverage has been devoted to grand, panoramic theories of personality. In this section we'll examine some contemporary empirical approaches that are narrower in scope. In modern personality research programs, investigators typically attempt to describe and measure an important personality trait, shed light on its development, and ascertain its relationship to other traits and behaviors. To get a sense of this kind of research, we'll take a look at research on a trait called *sensation seeking*. We'll also look at an influential new approach called *terror management theory* that focuses on personality dynamics rather than personality traits.

## Sensation Seeking: Life in the Fast Lane

Perhaps you have friends who prefer "life in the fast lane." If so, they're probably high in the personality trait of sensation seeking. *Sensation seeking* **is a generalized preference for high or low levels of sensory stimulation.** People who are high in sensation seeking prefer a high level of stimulation. They're always looking for new and exhilarating experiences. People who are low in sensation seeking prefer more modest levels of stimulation. They tend to choose tranquillity over excitement. Sensation seeking was first described by Marvin Zuckerman (1971, 1979), a biologically oriented theorist influenced by Hans Eysenck's views. Zuckerman (1991, 1996, 2008) believes that there is a strong genetic predisposition to high or low sensation seeking.

Sensation-seeking tendencies are measured by Zuckerman's (1984, 1996) Sensation Seeking Scale. Sensation seeking is distributed along a continuum, and many people fall in the middle. Factor analyses indicate that the personality trait of sensation seeking consists of four related components (Arnaut, 2006; Zuckerman, 1994): (1) thrill and adventure seeking, (2) attraction to unusual experiences, (3) lack of inhibitions, and (4) easy susceptibility to boredom.

High sensation seekers' zest for action influences the types of sports and entertainment they find intriguing. In regard to sports they are much more likely to be drawn to high-risk activities such as mountain climbing, sky diving, and hang gliding, whereas low sensation seekers are more likely to get involved in golf, swimming, or baseball (Arnaut, 2006). In the realm of entertainment, high sensation seekers tend to prefer violent movies, horror movies, and fast-paced action-adventure flicks, whereas low sensation seekers are more likely to enjoy musical and romantic movies (Zuckerman, 2006).

According to Zuckerman, incompatibility in sensation seeking places a strain on intimate relationships. He theorizes that persons very high and very low in sensation seeking may have difficulty understanding and relating to each other, not to mention finding mutually enjoyable activities. These considerations may explain why spouses tend to be more similar in sensation seeking than most other personality traits (Bratko & Butkovic, 2003). One advantage for those who are high in sensation seeking is that they are relatively tolerant of stress. They find many types of potentially stressful events to be less threatening and anxiety arousing than others (Arnaut, 2006).

© SB Photography/Alamy

People who are high in sensation seeking ardently pursue experiences that are arousing and exhilarating, such as whitewater rafting and other extreme sports.

## Is There a Rising Epidemic of Narcissism?

As we noted in Chapter 1, *narcissism* is a personality trait marked by an inflated sense of importance, a need for attention and admiration, a sense of entitlement, and a tendency to exploit others. The term is drawn from the Greek myth of Narcissus, which is about an attractive young man's search for love. In the mythical tale he eventually sees his reflection in water, falls in love with his own image, and gazes at it until he dies, thus illustrating the perils of excessive self-love. The concept of narcissism was originally popularized over a century ago by pioneering sex researcher Havelock Ellis (1898) and by Sigmund Freud (1914). Psychoanalytic writings characterized narcissists as having grandiose, but shaky, self-concepts that require extensive defensive manuevers to protect illusory feelings of superiority (Rhodewalt & Peterson, 2009). Of course, these inflated self-concepts were assumed to be rooted in a childhood history of troubled relationships.

The syndrome of narcissism was not widely discussed outside of psychoanalytic circles until 1980 when the American Psychiatric Association published a massive revision of its diagnostic system that describes various psychological disorders (see Chapter 14). The revised diagnostic system included a new condition called *narcissistic personality disorder (NPD)*. Among other things, the key symptoms of this new disorder included (1) a grandiose sense of importance, (2) preoccupation with fantasies of unlimited power and success, (3) constant need for attention, (4) difficulty dealing with criticism, (5) a sense of entitlement, and (6) interpersonal exploitiveness. NPD is viewed as an extreme, pathological manifestation of narcissism that is seen in only a small number (3%–5%) of people.

The formal description of NPD inspired some researchers to start investigating lesser, nonpathological manifestations of narcissim in the general population. This research led to the development of scales intended to assess narcissism as a normal personality trait. Of these scales, the Narcissistic Personality Inventory (NPI), developed by Robert Raskin and colleagues (Raskin & Hall, 1979, 1981; Raskin & Terry, 1988), has become the most widely used measure of narcissism (see Exercise 1.1 in the *Personal Explorations Workbook* in the back of this text). The NPI has been used in hundreds of studies.

Based on a variety of social trends, Jean Twenge and colleagues (2008) suspected that narcissism might be increasing in recent generations. To test this hypothesis they gathered data from 85 studies dating back to the 1980s in which American college students had been given the NPI. As you can see in **Figure 2.19**, their analysis revealed that NPI scores have been rising, going from a mean of about 15.5 in the 1980s to almost 17.5 in 2005–2006. Consistent with this trend, other research has found that the prevalence of narcissistic personality disorder has also been increasing in recent generations (Stinson et al., 2008).

Based on this research Jean Twenge and W. Keith Campbell (2009) have written a popular book, *The Narcissism Epidemic,* that outlines the possible ramifications of escalating narcissism. In their book, they argue that rising narcissism has fueled an obsessive concern about being physically attractive in young people, leading to unhealthy dieting, overuse of cosmetic surgery, and steroid-fueled body building. They also assert that narcissists' "me first" attitude has led to increased materialism and overconsumption of the earth's resources, thereby contributing to the current environmental crisis and economic meltdown. They go on to discuss how narcissism can foster aggressive, abusive, antisocial behavior, how it can corrode healthy intimate relationships, and how it can undermine the diligence and loyalty of employees in the workplace. They also discuss how the "look at me" mentality seen on Internet sites such as MySpace, Facebook, and YouTube reflects the increase in narcissism in contemporary society.

Is the situation as dire as Twenge and Campbell (2009) suggest? Well, their analyses are fascinating and well thought out, but attributing everything from global warming to laziness at work to a 2-point increase in narcissism seems like a bit of a stretch. That said, their evidence that narcissism is on the rise seems convincing and the trend is a legitimate source of concern.

---

More than anything else, sensation seeking is associated with elevated risk-taking behavior. High sensation seekers are more likely than others to engage in high-risk sexual practices, such as unprotected sex and sleeping with many partners (Hoyle, Fejfar, & Miller, 2000; Zuckerman, 2007); health-impairing habits, such as smoking, excessive drinking, and recreational drug use (Zuckerman, 2008), reckless driving (Jonah, 1997; Zuckerman, 2009) and gambling (McDaniel & Zuckerman, 2003). Thus, high sensation seeking may be more maladaptive than adaptive.

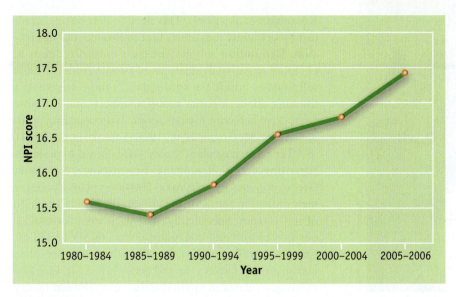

**Figure 2.19**

**Increased narcissism among American college students.** This graph shows how mean scores on the Narcissistic Personality Inventory (NPI) have escalated in samples of college students since the early 1980s. As you can see, the data suggest that NPI scores have increased steadily in recent decades.

Source: Based on Twenge, J. M., Konrath, S., Foster, J. D., Campbell, W. K., & Bushman B. J. (2008). Egos inflating over time: A cross-temporal meta-analysis of the Narcissistic Personality Inventory. *Journal of Personality, 76*, 875–901.

## Terror Management Theory

*Terror management theory* emerged as an influential perspective in the 1990s. Although the theory borrows from Freudian and evolutionary formulations, it provides its own unique analysis of the human condition. Developed by Sheldon Solomon, Jeff Greenberg, and Tom Pyszczynski (1991, 2004b), this fresh perspective is currently generating a huge volume of research.

One of the chief goals of terror management theory is to explain why people need self-esteem (Solomon, Greenberg, & Pyszczynski, 1991). The theory begins with the assumption that humans share an evolutionary heritage with other animals that includes an instinctive drive for self-preservation. However, unlike other animals, humans have evolved complex cognitive abilities that permit self-awareness and contemplation of the future. These cognitive capacities make humans keenly aware that life can be snuffed out unpredictably at any time. The collision between humans' self-preservation instinct and their awareness of the inevitability of death creates the potential for experiencing anxiety, alarm, and terror when people think about their mortality (see **Figure 2.20**).

How do humans deal with this potential for terror? According to terror management theory, "What saves us is culture. Cultures provide ways to view the world—worldviews—that 'solve' the existential crisis engendered by the awareness of death" (Pyszczynski, Solomon, & Greenberg, 2003b, p. 16). Cultural worldviews diminish anxiety by providing answers to universal questions such as "Why am I here?" and "What is the meaning of life?" Cultures create stories, traditions, and institutions that give their members a sense of being part of an enduring legacy through their contributions to their families, tribes, schools, churches, professions, and so forth. Thus, faith in a cultural worldview can give people a sense of order, meaning, and context that can soothe their fear of death.

Where does self-esteem fit into the picture? Self-esteem is viewed as a sense of personal worth that depends on one's confidence in the validity of one's cultural worldview and the belief that one is living up to the standards prescribed by that worldview. Hence, self-esteem buffers people from the profound anxiety associated with the awareness that they are transient animals destined to die. In other words, self-esteem serves a *terror management* function (refer to **Figure 2.20**).

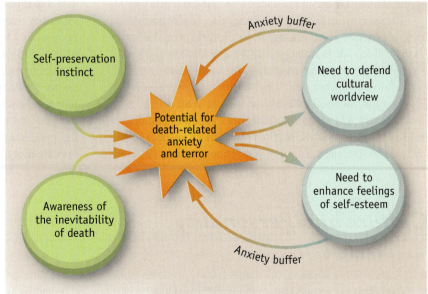

**Figure 2.20**

**Overview of terror management theory.** This graphic maps out the relations among the key concepts proposed by terror management theory. The theory asserts that humans' unique awareness of the inevitability of death fosters a need to defend one's cultural worldview and one's self-esteem, which serve to protect one from mortality-related anxiety.

Terror management theory has been applied to a remarkably wide range of phenomena. For example, it has even been used to explain conspicuous consumption.

The notion that self-esteem functions as an *anxiety buffer* has been supported by numerous studies (Pyszczynski et al., 2004). In many of these experiments, researchers have manipulated what they call *mortality salience* (the degree to which subjects' mortality is prominent in their minds), usually by asking participants to briefly think about their own future death. Consistent with the anxiety buffer hypothesis, reminding people of their mortality leads subjects to engage in a variety of behaviors that are likely to bolster their self-esteem, thus reducing anxiety (see Chapter 6 for more on the terror management function of self-esteem).

Increasing mortality salience also leads people to work harder at defending their cultural worldview (Arndt, Cook, & Routledge, 2004). For instance, after briefly pondering their mortality, research participants (1) hand out harsher penalties to moral transgressors, (2) respond more negatively to people who criticize their country, (3) give larger rewards to people who uphold cultural standards, and (4) show more respect for cultural icons, such as a flag (Greenberg et al., 1990;

Rosenblatt et al., 1989). This need to defend one's cultural worldview may even fuel prejudice and aggression. Reminding subjects of their mortality leads to (1) more negative evaluations of people from different religious or ethnic backgrounds, (2) more stereotypic thinking about minority group members, and (3) more aggressive behavior toward people with opposing political views (McGregor et al., 1998; Schimel et al., 1999).

Terror management theory yields novel hypotheses regarding many phenomena. For instance, Solomon, Greenberg, and Pyszczynski (2004a) explain excessive materialism in terms of the anxiety-buffering function of self-esteem. Specifically, they argue that "conspicuous possession and consumption are thinly veiled efforts to assert that one is special and therefore more than just an animal fated to die and decay" (p. 134). One fascinating study even applied terror management theory to the political process. Cohen et al. (2004) found that mortality salience increases subjects' preference for "charismatic" candidates who articulate a grand vision that makes people feel like they are part of an important movement of lasting significance.

At first glance, a theory that explains everything from prejudice to compulsive shopping in terms of death anxiety may seem highly implausible. After all, most people do not appear to walk around all day obsessing about the possibility of their death. The architects of terror management theory are well aware of this reality. They explain that the defensive reactions uncovered in their research generally occur when death anxiety surfaces on the fringes of conscious awareness and that these reactions are automatic and subconscious (Pyszczynski, Greenberg, & Solomon, 1999). They also assert that people experience far more reminders of their mortality than most of us appreciate. They point out that people may be reminded of their mortality by a variety of everyday events, such as driving by a cemetery or funeral home, reading about an auto accident, visiting a doctor's office, hearing about a celebrity's heart attack, learning about alarming medical research, skipping over the obituaries in the newspaper, and so forth. Thus, the processes discussed by terror management theory may be more commonplace that one might guess.

# *Culture and Personality*

## LEARNING OBJECTIVES

- Discuss whether the five-factor model has any relevance in non-Western cultures.
- Explain how researchers have found both cross-cultural similarities and disparities in personality.
- Summarize recent research on the accuracy of perceptions of national character.

Are there connections between culture and personality? The investigation of this question dates back to the 1930s and 1940s, when researchers set out to identify various cultures' *modal personality* (Kardiner & Linton, 1945) or *national character* (Kluckhohn & Murray, 1948). These investigations sought to describe the *prototype* or *typical* personality in various cultures. For example, Ruth Benedict (1934) concluded that American Pueblo Indians were sober, orderly, conventional, and cooperative. Largely guided by Freud's psychoanalytic theory, this line of research generated interest for a couple of decades but ultimately met with little success (Bock, 2000; Draguns, 2009; LeVine, 2001). Part of the problem may have been the rather culture-bound, Eurocentric nature of Freudian theory, but the crux of the problem was that it was unrealistic to expect to find a single, dominant personality profile in each culture (Benet-Martinez & Oishi, 2008).

Studies of the links between culture and personality dwindled to almost nothing for many decades. However, in recent decades psychology has become more interested in cultural factors, sparking a renaissance in culture-personality research. This research has sought to determine whether Western personality constructs are relevant to other cultures and whether cultural differences can be seen in the strength of specific personality traits. These studies have found evidence of both continuity and variability across cultures.

For the most part, continuity has been apparent in cross-cultural comparisons of the *trait structure* of personality. When English language personality scales have been translated and administered in other cultures, the predicted dimensions of personality have emerged from the factor analyses (Chiu, Kim, & Wan, 2008). For example, when scales that tap the Big Five personality traits have been administered and subjected to factor analysis in other cultures, the usual five traits have typically emerged (Katigbak et al., 2002; McCrae & Costa, 2008b). Thus, research tentatively suggests that the basic dimensions of personality trait structure may be universal.

On the other hand, some cross-cultural variability is seen when researchers compare the average trait scores of samples from various cultural groups. For example, in a study comparing 51 cultures, McCrae et al. (2005) found that Brazilians scored relatively high in neuroticism, Australians in extraversion, Germans in openness to experience, Czechs in agreeableness, and Malaysians in conscientiousness, to give but a handful of examples. These findings should be viewed as very preliminary, as a variety of methodological problems make it difficult to ensure that samples from different cultures are comparable (Heine, Buchtel, & Norenzayan, 2008). Nonetheless, the findings suggest that genuine cultural differences may exist in some personality traits. That said, the observed cultural disparities in average trait scores were modest in size.

The availability of the data from the McCrae et al. (2005) study allowed Terracciano et al. (2005) to revisit the concept of *national character*. Terracciano and his colleagues asked subjects from many cultures to describe the *typical* member of *their* culture on rating forms guided by the five-factor model. Generally, subjects displayed substantial agreement on these ratings of what was typical for their culture. The averaged ratings, which served as the measures of each culture's national character, were then correlated with the actual mean trait scores for various cultures compiled in the McCrae et al. (2005) study. The results were definitive—the vast majority of the correlations were extremely low and often even negative. In other words, there was little or no relationship between perceptions of national character and actual trait scores for various cultures (see **Figure 2.21**). People's beliefs about national character, which often fuel cultural prejudices, turned out to be profoundly inaccurate stereotypes (McCrae & Terracciano, 2006).

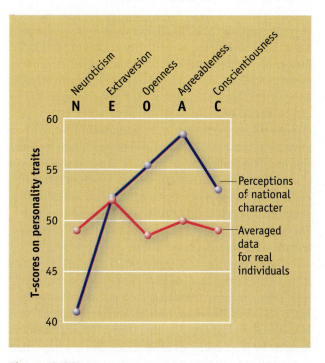

**Figure 2.21**

**An example of inaccurate perceptions of national character.** Terracciano et al. (2005) found that perceptions of national character (the prototype or typical personality for a particular culture) are largely inaccurate. The data shown here for one culture—Canadians—illustrates this inaccuracy. Mean scores on the Big Five traits for a sample of real individuals from Canada are graphed in red. Averaged perceptions of national character for Canadians are graphed in blue. The discrepancy between perception and reality is obvious. Terracciano et al. found similar disparities between views of national character and actual trait scores for a majority of the cultues they studied. (Adapted from McCrae & Terracciano, 2005)

# Assessing Your Personality

### LEARNING OBJECTIVES

● Explain the concepts of standardization, test norms, reliability, and validity.
● Discuss the value and the limitations of self-report inventories.
● Discuss the value and limitations of projective tests.
● Analyze the emerging role of the Internet in personality testing.

*Answer the following "true" or "false."*

___ **1.** Responses to personality tests are subject to unconscious distortion.

___ **2.** The results of personality tests are often misunderstood.

___ **3.** Personality test scores should be interpreted with caution.

___ **4.** Personality tests may be quite useful in helping people to learn more about themselves.

If you answered "true" to all four questions, you earned a perfect score. Yes, personality tests are subject to distortion. Admittedly, test results are often misunderstood, and they should be interpreted cautiously. In spite of these problems, however, psychological tests can be very useful.

We all engage in efforts to size up our own personality as well as that of others. When you think to yourself that "this salesman is untrustworthy," or when you remark to a friend that "Howard is too timid and submissive," you are making personality assessments. In a sense, then, personality assessment is part of daily life. However, psychological tests provide much more systematic assessments than casual observations do.

The value of psychological tests lies in their ability to help people form a realistic picture of their personal qualities. Thus, we have included a variety of personality tests in the *Personal Explorations Workbook* that can be found in the back of this text. We hope that you may gain some insights by responding to these scales. But it's important to understand the logic and limitations of such tests. To facilitate your use of these and other tests, this Application discusses some of the basics of psychological testing.

## Key Concepts in Psychological Testing

A *psychological test* **is a standardized measure of a sample of a person's behavior.** Psychological tests are measurement instruments. They are used to measure abilities, aptitudes, and personality traits.

Note that your responses to a psychological test represent a *sample* of your behavior. This fact should alert you to one of the key limitations of psychological tests: It's always possible that a particular behav-

ior sample is not representative of your characteristic behavior. We all have our bad days. A stomachache, a fight with a friend, a problem with your car—all might affect your responses to a particular test on a particular day. Because of the limitations of the sampling process, test scores should always be interpreted *cautiously.* Most psychological tests are sound measurement devices, but test results should not be viewed as the "final word" on one's personality and abilities because of the everpresent sampling problem.

Most psychological tests can be placed in one of two broad categories: (1) mental ability tests, and (2) personality tests. *Mental ability tests,* such as intelligence tests, aptitude tests, and achievement tests, often serve as gateways to schooling, training programs, and jobs. *Personality* tests measure various aspects of personality, including motives, interests, values, and attitudes. Many psychologists prefer to call these tests personality *scales,* since the questions do not have right and wrong answers as do those on tests of mental abilities.

### Standardization and Norms

Both personality scales and tests of mental abilities are *standardized* measures of behavior. **Standardization refers to the uniform procedures used to administer and score a test.** All subjects get the same instructions, the same questions, the same time limits, and so on, so that their scores can be compared meaningfully.

The standardization of a test's scoring system includes the development of test norms. **Test norms provide information about where a score on a psychological test ranks in relation to other scores on that test.** Why do we need test norms? Because in psychological testing, everything is relative. Psychological tests tell you how you score *relative to other people.* They tell you, for instance, that you are average in impulsiveness, or slightly above average in assertiveness, or far below average in anxiety. These interpretations are derived from the test norms.

### Reliability and Validity

Any kind of measuring device, whether it's a tire gauge, a stopwatch, or a psychological test, should be reasonably consistent. That is, repeated measurements should yield reasonably similar results. To appreciate the importance of reliability, think about how you would react if a tire pressure gauge gave you several very different readings for the same tire. You would probably conclude that the gauge was broken and toss it into the garbage, because you know that consistency in measurement is essential to accuracy.

*Reliability* **refers to the measurement consistency of a test.** A reliable test is one that yields similar results upon repetition of the test (see **Figure 2.22**). Like most other types of measuring devices, psychological tests are not perfectly reliable. They usually do not yield the exact same score when repeated. A certain amount of inconsistency is unavoidable because human behavior is variable. Personality tests tend to have lower reliability than mental ability tests because daily fluctuations in mood influence how people respond to such tests.

Even if a test is quite reliable, we still need to be concerned about its validity. *Validity* **refers to the ability of a test to measure what it was designed to measure.** If we develop a new test of assertiveness, we have to provide some evidence that it really measures assertiveness. Validity can be demonstrated in a variety of ways. Most of them involve correlating scores on a test with other measures of the same trait, or with related traits.

## Self-Report Inventories

The vast majority of personality tests are self-report inventories. *Self-report inventories* **are personality scales that ask individuals to answer a series of questions about their characteristic behavior.** When you respond to a self-report personality scale, you endorse statements as true or false as applied to you, you indicate how often you behave in a particular way, or you rate yourself with respect to certain qualities. For example, on the Minnesota Multiphasic Personality

Inventory, people respond "true," "false," or "cannot say" to 567 statements such as the following:

*I get a fair deal from most people.*
*I have the time of my life at parties.*
*I am glad that I am alive.*
*Several people are following me everywhere.*

The logic underlying this approach is simple: Who knows you better than you do? Who has known you longer? Who has more access to your private feelings?

The entire range of personality traits can be measured with self-report inventories. Some scales measure just one trait dimension, such as the Sensation Seeking Scale (SSS), which you can take in your *Personal Explorations Workbook*. Others simultaneously assess a multitude of traits. The Sixteen Personality Factor Questionnaire (16PF), developed by Raymond Cattell and his colleagues (Cattell, Eber, & Tatsuoka, 1970), is a representative example of a multitrait inventory. The 16PF is a 187-item scale that measures 16 basic dimensions of personality, called source traits, which are shown in **Figure 2.23** on the next page. The current, fifth edition of this test continues to enjoy widespread useage (Cattell & Mead, 2008).

As we noted earlier, some theorists believe that only five trait dimensions are required to provide a full

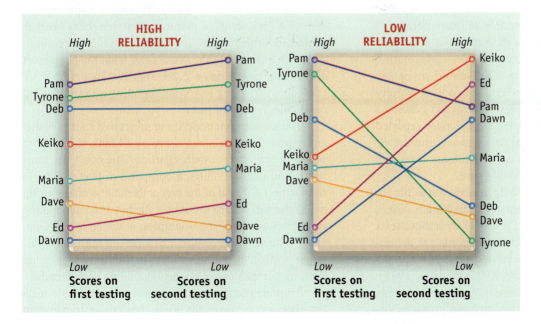

**Figure 2.22**
**Test reliability.** Subjects' scores on the first administration of an assertiveness test are represented on the left, and their scores on a second administration (a few weeks later) are represented on the right. If subjects obtain similar scores on both administrations, the test measures assertiveness consistently and is said to have high reliability. If subjects get very different scores when they take the assertiveness test a second time, the test is said to have low reliability.

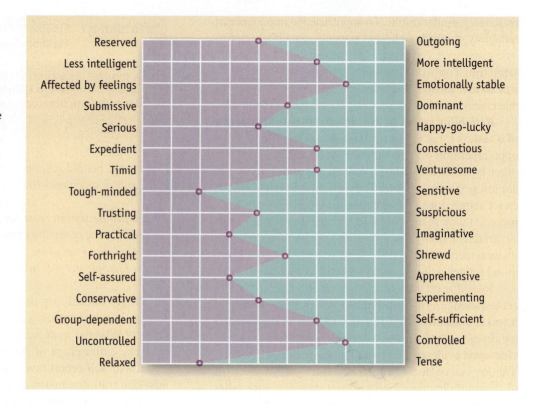

**Figure 2.23**

**The Sixteen Personality Factor Questionnaire (16PF).** Cattell's 16PF is designed to assess 16 basic dimensions of personality. The pairs of traits listed across from each other in the figure define the 16 factors measured by this self-report inventory. The profile shown is the average profile seen among a group of airline pilots who took the test.

Source: Adapted from Cattell, R. B. (1973, July). Personality pinned down. *Psychology Today*, 40–46. Reprinted by permission of Psychology Today Magazine. Copyright © 1973 Sussex Publishers, Inc.

| Reserved | Outgoing |
| Less intelligent | More intelligent |
| Affected by feelings | Emotionally stable |
| Submissive | Dominant |
| Serious | Happy-go-lucky |
| Expedient | Conscientious |
| Timid | Venturesome |
| Tough-minded | Sensitive |
| Trusting | Suspicious |
| Practical | Imaginative |
| Forthright | Shrewd |
| Self-assured | Apprehensive |
| Conservative | Experimenting |
| Group-dependent | Self-sufficient |
| Uncontrolled | Controlled |
| Relaxed | Tense |

description of personality. The five-factor model led to the creation of the NEO Personality Inventory. Developed by Paul Costa and Robert McCrae (1985, 1992), the NEO Inventory is designed to measure the Big Five traits: neuroticism, extraversion, openness to experience, agreeableness, and conscientiousness. The NEO Inventory is widely used in research and clinical work, and updated revisions of the scale have been released (Costa & McCrae, 2008; McCrae & Costa, 2004, 2007).

To appreciate the strengths of self-report inventories, consider how else you might assess your personality. For instance, how assertive are you? You probably have some vague idea, but can you accurately estimate how your assertiveness compares to other people's? To do that, you need a great deal of comparative information about others' usual behavior—information that all of us lack. In contrast, a self-report inventory inquires about your typical behavior in a wide variety of circumstances requiring assertiveness and generates an exact comparison with the typical behavior reported by many other respondents for the same circumstances. Thus, self-report inventories are much more thorough and precise than casual observations are.

However, these tests are only as accurate as the information that the test-takers provide (Ben-Porath, 2003). Deliberate deception can be a problem with these tests (Rees & Metcalfe, 2003), and some people are unconsciously influenced by the social desirability or acceptability of the statements (Kline, 1995; Paulhus, 1991). Without realizing it, they endorse only those statements that make them look good. This problem provides an-

other reason why personality test results should always be regarded as suggestive rather than definitive.

## Projective Tests

Projective tests, which all take a rather indirect approach to the assessment of personality, are used extensively in clinical work. *Projective tests* **ask people to respond to vague, ambiguous stimuli in ways that may reveal the respondents' needs, feelings, and personality traits.** The Rorschach test, for example, consists of a series of ten inkblots. Respondents are asked to describe what they see in the inkblots. In the Thematic Apperception Test (TAT), a series of pictures of simple scenes is presented to subjects who are asked to tell stories about what is happening in the scenes and what the characters are feeling (see **Figure 2.24**). For instance, one TAT card shows a young boy contemplating a violin resting on a table in front of him.

The assumption underlying projective testing is that ambiguous materials can serve as a blank screen onto which people project their characteristic concerns, conflicts, and desires. Thus, a competitive person who is shown the TAT card of the boy at the table with the violin might concoct a story about how the boy is contemplating an upcoming musical competition at which he hopes to excel. The same card shown to a person high in impulsiveness might elicit a story about how the boy is planning to sneak out the door to go dirt-bike riding with friends.

Proponents of projective tests assert that the tests have two unique strengths. First, they are not transparent

**Figure 2.24**
**The Thematic Apperception Test (TAT).** In taking the TAT, a respondent is asked to tell stories about scenes such as this one. The themes apparent in each story can be scored to provide insight about the respondent's personality.

Source: From Murray. H. A. (1971). *Thematic Apperception Test.* Cambridge, MA: Harvard University Press. Copyright © 1943 by The President and Fellows of Harvard College, Copyright © 1971 by Henry A. Murray. Reprinted by permission of the publisher.

to subjects. That is, the subject doesn't know how the test provides information to the tester. Hence, it may be difficult for people to engage in intentional deception (Groth-Marnat, 1997). Second, the indirect approach used in these tests may make them especially sensitive to unconscious, latent features of personality.

Unfortunately, the scientific evidence on projective measures is unimpressive (Garb, Florio, & Grove, 1998; Hunsley, Lee, & Wood, 2003). In a thorough review of the relevant research, Lillienfeld, Wood, and Garb (2000) conclude that projective tests tend to be plagued by inconsistent scoring, low reliability, inadequate test norms, cultural bias, and poor validity estimates. They also assert that, contrary to advocates' claims, projective tests are susceptible to some types of intentional deception (primarily, faking poor mental health). Based on their analysis, Lillienfeld and his colleagues argue that projective tests should be referred to as projective "techniques" or "instruments" rather than tests because

"most of these techniques as used in daily clinical practice do not fulfill the traditional criteria for psychological tests" (p. 29). In spite of these problems, projective tests continue to be used by many clinicians. Although the questionable scientific status of these techniques is a very real problem, their continued popularity suggests that they yield subjective information that many clinicians find useful (Viglione & Rivera, 2003).

## Personality Testing on the Internet

The emergence of the Internet has had a considerable impact on the process of personality assessment. Self-report inventories are increasingly being administered over the Internet by researchers, clinicians, and companies (Naglieri et al., 2004). Most of the widely used personality scales are available in an online format. The advantages of online testing are substantial (Buchanan, 2007). Tests can be completed quickly, with reduced labor costs, and the data flow directly into interpretive software. Online testing also allows test administrators to collect additional data that would not be available from a traditional paper-and-pencil test. For instance, they can track answer changing and how long respondents ponder specific questions. Online testing also allows clinicians to deliver assessment services to rural clients who do not have access to local psychologists (Barak & Buchanan, 2004). Given all these advantages, Buchanan (2007, p. 450) notes that "it is easy to imagine a future where virtually all testing is conducted online."

Are there any disadvantages to online personality assessment? Well, there are issues that merit concern, but they appear to be manageable. The item content of some tests is closely guarded, so security is an issue for them (Naglieri et al., 2004). And when personality tests are used for hiring purposes, verifying the identity of the respondent is important. The chief theoretical issue is whether tests delivered online yield results that are equivalent to what is found when the same tests are administered in a paper-and-pencil format. For the most part, research suggests that online tests are equivalent to their offline counterparts, but this issue should be checked empirically whenever a specific test is migrated to an online format (Buchanan, 2007; Epstein & Klinkenberg, 2001). Overall, though, the future of online personality testing appears bright. That said, consumers should remember that the Internet is utterly unregulated, so you can find an abundance of pop psychology tests online that have no scientific or empirical basis (Naglieri et al., 2004).

## KEY IDEAS

### The Nature of Personality

● The concept of personality explains the consistency in individuals' behavior over time and situations while also explaining their distinctiveness. Some theorists suggest that the complexity of personality can be reduced to just five basic traits: extraversion, neuroticism, openness to experience, agreeableness, and conscientiousness.

### Psychodynamic Perspectives

● Freud's psychoanalytic theory emphasizes the importance of the unconscious. Freud described personality structure in terms of three components (id, ego, and superego), operating at three levels of awareness, that are involved in internal conflicts, which generate anxiety.

● According to Freud, people often ward off anxiety and other unpleasant emotions with defense mechanisms, which work through self-deception. Freud described five psychosexual stages that children undergo in their personality development.

● Jung's analytical psychology stresses the importance of the collective unconscious. Adler's individual psychology emphasizes how people strive for superiority to compensate for feelings of inferiority.

### Behavioral Perspectives

● Behavioral theories view personality as a collection of response tendencies shaped through learning. Pavlov's classical conditioning can explain how people acquire emotional responses.

● Skinner's model of operant conditioning shows how consequences such as reinforcement, extinction, and punishment shape behavior. Bandura's social cognitive theory shows how people can be conditioned indirectly through observation.

### Humanistic Perspectives

● Rogers focused on the self-concept as the critical aspect of personality. He maintained that incongruence between one's self-concept and reality creates anxiety and leads to defensive behavior.

● Maslow theorized that needs are arranged hierarchically. He asserted that psychological health depends on fulfilling the need for self-actualization.

### Biological Perspectives

● Eysenck believes that inherited individual differences in physiological functioning affect conditioning and thus influence personality. Behavioral genetics research suggests that the heritability of each of the Big Five traits is around 50%. Evolutionary psychologists maintain that natural selection has favored the emergence of the Big Five traits.

### Contemporary Empirical Approaches to Personality

● Sensation seeking is a generalized preference for high or low levels of sensory stimulation. Above all else, high sensation seeking is associated with increased risk-taking behavior.

● Terror management theory proposes that self-esteem and faith in a cultural worldview shield people from the profound anxiety associated with their mortality. Consistent with this analysis, increasing mortality salience leads people to make efforts to bolster their self-esteem and defend their worldviews.

### Culture and Personality

● Research suggests that the basic trait structure of personality may be much the same across cultures, as the Big Five traits usually emerge in cross-cultural studies. Cultural variations have been found in average trait scores on the Big Five traits, but the differences are modest. People's perceptions of national character appear to be remarkably inaccurate.

### Application: Assessing Your Personality

● Test norms indicate what represents a high or low score. Psychological tests should produce consistent results upon retesting, a quality called reliability. Validity refers to the degree to which a test measures what it was designed to measure.

● Self-report inventories, such as the 16PF and NEO Personality Inventory, can provide a better snapshot of personality than casual observations can, but they are vulnerable to deception and social desirability bias.

● Projective tests, such as the Rorschach and TAT, assume that people's responses to ambiguous stimuli reveal something about their personality. Projective tests' reliability and validity appear to be disturbingly low.

● Self-report inventories are increasingly being administered over the Internet. The advantages of online testing are substantial, although there are concerns about security and test equivalence.

## KEY TERMS

Archetypes   p. 42
Behaviorism   p. 43
Classical conditioning   p. 44
Collective unconscious   p. 41
Compensation   p. 42
Conditioned response (CR)   p. 45
Conditioned stimulus (CS)   p. 45
Conscious   p. 36
Defense mechanisms   p. 38
Displacement   p. 39
Ego   p. 36
Evolutionary psychology   p. 58
Extinction   p. 46
Factor analysis   p. 33
Fixation   p. 40
Heritability ratio   p. 57
Hierarchy of needs   p. 53
Hindsight bias   p. 58
Humanism   p. 51
Id   p. 36
Identification   p. 39
Incongruence   p. 51
Need for self-actualization   p. 53
Negative reinforcement   p. 47
Observational learning   p. 48
Oedipal complex   p. 41
Operant conditioning   p. 46
Personality   p. 33
Personality trait   p. 33
Positive reinforcement   p. 46
Preconscious   p. 36
Projection   p. 38
Projective tests   p. 66
Psychodynamic theories   p. 35
Psychological test   p. 64
Psychosexual stages   p. 40
Punishment   p. 47
Rationalization   p. 38
Reaction formation   p. 39
Regression   p. 39
Reliability   p. 65
Repression   p. 38
Self-concept   p. 51
Self-efficacy   p. 49
Self-report inventories   p. 65
Sensation seeking   p. 59
Standardization   p. 64
Sublimation   p. 39
Superego   p. 36
Test norms   p. 64
Twin studies   p. 56
Unconditioned response (UCR)   p. 44
Unconditioned stimulus (UCS)   p. 44
Unconscious   p. 37
Validity   p. 65

## KEY PEOPLE

Alfred Adler   pp. 42–43
Albert Bandura   pp. 48–49
Hans Eysenck   p. 56
Sigmund Freud   pp. 35–41
Carl Jung   pp. 41–42
Abraham Maslow   pp. 52–54
Ivan Pavlov   pp. 44–45
Carl Rogers   pp. 51–52
B. F. Skinner   pp. 46–48

# CHAPTER 2 PRACTICE TEST

## QUESTIONS

1. Which of the following is *not* included in McCrae and Costa's five-factor model of personality?
   a. neuroticism
   b. extraversion
   c. conscientiousness
   d. authoritarianism

2. You're feeling guilty after your third bowl of ice cream. You tell yourself it's all right because yesterday you skipped lunch. Which defense mechanism is at work?
   a. conceptualization
   b. displacement
   c. rationalization
   d. identification

3. According to Adler, _____ is a universal drive to adapt, improve oneself, and master life's challenges.
   a. compensation
   b. striving for superiority
   c. avoiding inferiority
   d. social interest

4. The strengthening of a response tendency by virtue of the fact that the response leads to the removal of an unpleasant stimulus is
   a. positive reinforcement.
   b. negative reinforcement.
   c. primary reinforcement.
   d. punishment.

5. Self-efficacy is
   a. the ability to fulfill one's potential.
   b. one's belief about one's ability to perform behaviors that should lead to expected outcomes.
   c. a durable disposition to behave in a particular way in a variety of situations.
   d. a collection of beliefs about one's nature, unique qualities, and typical behavior.

6. According to Rogers, disparity between one's self-concept and actual experience is referred to as
   a. a delusional system.
   b. dissonance.
   c. conflict.
   d. incongruence.

7. According to Maslow, which of the following is *not* characteristic of self-actualizing persons?
   a. accurate perception of reality
   b. being open and spontaneous
   c. being uncomfortable with solitude
   d. sensitivity to others' needs

8. If identical twins exhibit more personality resemblance than fraternal twins, it's probably due mostly to
   a. similar treatment from parents.
   b. their greater genetic overlap.
   c. their strong identification with each other.
   d. others' expectations that they should be similar.

9. Research on terror management theory has shown that increased mortality salience leads to all of the following except:
   a. increased striving for self-esteem.
   b. more stereotypic thinking about minorities.
   c. more aggressive behavior toward people with opposing views.
   d. reduced respect for cultural icons.

10. In psychological testing, consistency of results over repeated measurements refers to
    a. standardization.
    b. validity.
    c. statistical significance.
    d. reliability.

## ANSWERS

1. d Pages 33–34
2. c Pages 38–39
3. b Page 42
4. b Page 47
5. b Page 49
6. d Pages 51–52
7. c Page 54
8. b Pages 56–57
9. d Pages 61–62
10. d Page 65

## Personal Explorations Workbook

Go to the *Personal Explorations Workbook* in the back of your textbook for exercises that can enhance your self-understanding in relation to issues raised in this chapter. **Exercise 2.1** *Self-Assessment:* Sensation Seeking Scale. **Exercise 2.2** *Self-Reflection:* Who Are You?

## CourseMate

Access an interactive eBook, chapter-specific interactive learning tools, including Personal Explorations, Recommended Readings, Critical Thinking Exercises, flashcards, quizzes, videos and more in your Psychology CourseMate, available at **www.cengagebrain.com/shop/ISBN/1111186634**.

# CHAPTER 3

# *Stress and Its Effects*

You're in your car headed home from school. Traffic is barely moving. You groan as radio report indicates that the traffic jam is only going to get worse. Another motorist nearly takes off your fender trying to cut into your lane. Your pulse quickens as you shout insults at the driver, who cannot even hear you. Your stomach knots up as you think about the term paper that you have to work on tonight. If you don't finish the paper soon, you won't be able to find any time to study for your math test, not to mention your biology quiz. Suddenly you remember that you promised the person you're dating that the two of you would get together tonight. There's no way. Another fight looms on the horizon. Your classmate asks how you feel about the tuition increase the college announced yesterday. You've been trying not to think about it. You're already in debt. Your parents are bugging you about changing schools, but you don't want to leave your friends. Your heartbeat quickens as you contemplate the debate you'll have to wage with your parents. You feel wired with tension as you realize that the stress in your life never seems to let up.

As this example shows, many circumstances can create stress in people's lives. Stress comes in all sorts of packages: large and small, pretty and ugly, simple and complex. All too often, the package is a surprise. In this chapter, we analyze the nature of stress, outline the major types of stress, and discuss how people respond to stressful events at several levels.

In a sense, stress is what a course on adjustment is all about. Recall from Chapter 1 that adjustment essentially deals with how people manage to cope with various demands and pressures. These demands and pressures represent the core of stressful experience. Thus, the central theme in a course such as this is: How do people adjust to stress, and how might they adjust more effectively?

# The Nature of Stress

## LEARNING OBJECTIVES

● Describe the nature of stress and discuss how common it is.
● Distinguish between primary and secondary appraisal of stress.
● Summarize the evidence on ambient stress.
● Explain how culture and ethnicity are related to stress.

Over the years, the term *stress* has been used in different ways by different theorists. Some have viewed stress as a *stimulus* event that presents difficult demands (a divorce, for instance), while others have viewed stress as the *response* of physiological arousal elicited by a troublesome event (Cooper & Dewe, 2004). However, the emerging consensus among contemporary researchers is that stress is neither a stimulus nor a response but a special stimulus-response transaction in which one feels threatened or experiences loss or harm (Carver, 2007; McEwen, 2000). Hence, we will define **stress as any circumstances that threaten or are perceived to threaten one's well-being and thereby tax one's coping abilities.** The threat may be to one's immediate physical safety, long-range security, self-esteem, reputation, or peace of mind. Stress is a complex concept—so let's dig a little deeper.

## Stress Is an Everyday Event

Stress is a part of everyday life. So much so that the term *stress* has become part of our colloquial speech. It is a noun (*We have stress*). It is an adjective (*He has a stressful job*). It is an adverb (*She acts stressed*). And it is a verb (*Writing a paper stresses me*). Indeed, a recent poll by the American Psychological Association (2007) shows that, for many of us, stress levels are high and are on the rise. One-third of Americans surveyed reported "living with extreme stress," and nearly half believed that their stress had "increased over the past 5 years." It seems that being "stressed out" has become a hallmark of modern life.

Undeniably, stress is associated with overwhelming, traumatic crises such as hijackings, floods, earthquakes, and nuclear accidents. Studies conducted in the aftermath of such disasters typically find elevated rates of psychological problems and physical illness in the affected communities (Raphael & Dobson, 2000; van Griensven et al., 2007; Weisler, Barbee, & Townsend, 2007). However, these infrequent events represent the tip of the iceberg. Many everyday events, such as waiting in line, having car trouble, misplacing your keys, and staring at bills you can't pay, are also stressful. Of course, major and minor stressors are not entirely independent. A major stressful event, such as going through a divorce, can trigger a cascade of minor stressors, such as looking for an attorney, taking on new household responsibilities, and so forth (Pillow, Zautra, & Sandler, 1996).

You might guess that minor stressors would produce minor effects, but that isn't necessarily true. Research shows that routine hassles may have significant negative effects on a person's mental and physical health (Delongis, Folkman, & Lazarus, 1988; Klumb & Baltes, 2004; Sher, 2003). In fact, researchers found that scores on a scale measuring daily hassles were more strongly related to participants' mental health than the scores on a scale measuring major life events were (Kanner et al., 1981). Why would minor hassles be more strongly related to mental health than major stressful events? Many theorists believe that stressful events can have a *cumulative* or *additive* impact (Seta, Seta, & McElroy, 2002). In other words, stress can add up. Routine stresses at home, at

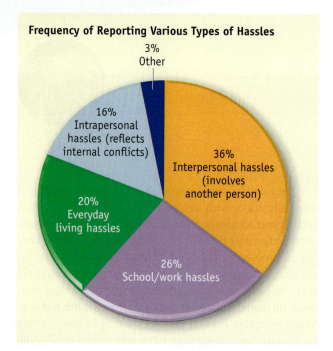

**Frequency of Reporting Various Types of Hassles**

3%
Other

16%
Intrapersonal hassles (reflects internal conflicts)

36%
Interpersonal hassles (involves another person)

20%
Everyday living hassles

26%
School/work hassles

**Figure 3.1**

**Frequency of reporting different types of hassles.** One hundred and sixty-four undergraduate students generated a list of over 800 hassles when asked to list the major hassles in their lives. The investigators were able to sort most of these hassles into four broad categories. The percentage of hassles falling into each category is shown in this pie chart. (Based on McIntyre, Korn, & Matsuo, 2008)

school, and at work might be fairly benign individually, but collectively they can create great strain. Whatever the reason, it is evident that daily hassles make important contributions to psychological distress (Serido, Almeida, & Wethington, 2004). **Figure 3.1** shows the frequency of some categories of commonly reported hassles.

Not everyone becomes overwhelmed by stress from daily hassles. As we'll see later in this chapter, certain personal characteristics such as resilience and optimism can buffer the distressing effects of daily hassles (Lai, 2009; Pinquart, 2009). Research indicates that hassles that evoke strong negative emotions are the ones most related to stress (McIntyre, Korn, & Matsuo, 2008). And perceiving a situation as threatening elicits negative emotions (Schneider, 2008). Therefore, individual perceptions are important in how people experience stress (Monroe & Slavich, 2007).

## Stress Lies in the Eye of the Beholder

The experience of feeling threatened depends on what events you notice

and how you choose to interpret or appraise them (Monroe & Kelley, 1995). Events that are stressful for one person may be routine for another. For example, many people find flying in an airplane somewhat stressful, but frequent fliers may not even raise an eyebrow. Some people enjoy the excitement of going out on a date with someone new; others find the uncertainty terrifying.

In discussing appraisals of stress, Richard Lazarus and Susan Folkman (1984) distinguish between primary and secondary appraisal (see **Figure 3.2**). *Primary appraisal* **is an initial evaluation of whether an event is (1) irrelevant to you, (2) relevant but not threatening, or (3) stressful.** When you view an event as stressful, you are likely to make a *secondary appraisal,* **which is an evaluation of your coping resources and options for dealing with the stress.** For instance, your primary appraisal would determine whether you saw an upcoming job interview as stressful. Your secondary appraisal would determine how stressful the interview appeared, in light of your ability to deal with the event.

*Courtesy Richard Lazarus*

**Richard Lazarus**

It should come as no surprise that people's appraisals about stressful events alter the impact of the events themselves (Daniels, Hartley, & Travers, 2006). Recent research has demonstrated that negative interpretations of events are often associated with increased distress surrounding these events (Boelen, van den Bout & van den Hout, 2003). In fact, when studying a sample of children after the 9/11 terrorist attacks, Lengua and her colleagues (2006) found that children's appraisals of the event predicted their stress symptoms as much as factors such as their coping style or pre-attack stress loads.

People are rarely objective in their appraisals of potentially stressful events. A classic study of hospitalized

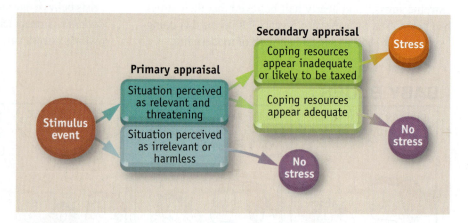

**Figure 3.2**

**Primary and secondary appraisal of stress.** *Primary appraisal* is an initial evaluation of whether an event is (1) irrelevant to you, (2) relevant but not threatening, or (3) stressful. When you view an event as stressful, you are likely to make a *secondary appraisal,* which is an evaluation of your coping resources and options for dealing with the stress. (Based on Lazarus & Folkman, 1994)

patients awaiting surgery showed only a slight correlation between the objective seriousness of a person's upcoming surgery and the amount of fear the person experienced (Janis, 1958). Clearly, some people are more prone to feel threatened by life's difficulties than are others. A number of studies have shown that anxious, neurotic people are more likely to make threat appraisals as well as to report more stress than people with less anxiety (Cooper & Bright, 2001; Schneider, 2004). Thus, stress lies in the eye (actually, the mind) of the beholder, and people's appraisals of stressful events are highly subjective.

## Stress May Be Embedded in the Environment

Although the perception of stress is a highly personal matter, many kinds of stress come from the environmental circumstances that individuals share with others. *Ambient stress consists of chronic environmental conditions that, although not urgent, are negatively valued and place adaptive demands on people.* Features of the environment such as excessive noise, traffic, and pollution can threaten well-being and leave their mark on mental and physical health. For example, investigators have found an association between chronic exposure to high levels of noise and elevated blood pressure among children attending school near Los Angeles International Airport (Cohen et al., 1980). Similarly, studies of children living near Munich International Airport (Evans, Hygge, & Bullinger, 1995; Hygge, Evans, & Bullinger, 2002) have found elevated stress hormones, reading and memory deficits, and poor task persistence in samples of schoolchildren (see **Figure 3.3**).

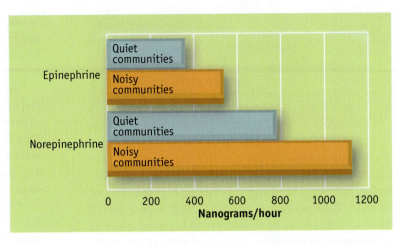

### Figure 3.3

**Excessive noise and stress hormones.** Evans, Hygge, and Bullinger (1995) compared children from noisy areas near Munich International Airport with similar children from quiet neighborhoods in Munich. They found elevated levels of two hormones (epinephrine and norepinephrine) associated with stress reactions in the children exposed to the high noise of the airport.

Source: Adapted with permission from Evans, G. W., Hygge, S., & Bullinger, M. (1995). Chronic noise and psychological stress. *Psychological Science, 6,* 333–338, Figure 3.2.

Crowding is a major source of environmental stress. Temporary experiences of crowding, such as being packed into a passenger train for a crowded commute, can be stressful (Evans & Wener, 2007). However, most of the research on crowding has focused on the effects of residential density. Generally, studies suggest an association between high density and increased physiological arousal, psychological distress, and social withdrawal (Evans, 2001; Evans & Stecker, 2004). Siddiqui and Pandey (2003) found crowding to be one of the most critical stressors for urban residents in Northern India, indicating that this is an important issue that goes well beyond Western cities.

Psychologists have also explored the repercussions of living in areas that are at risk for disaster. For instance,

**Stress can be caused by environmental circumstances such as pollution, excessive noise, crowding, traffic jams, and urban decay.**

studies suggest that people who live near nuclear power plants, hazardous waste sites, waste incinerators, or polluting industrial facilities experience higher levels of distress (Downey & van Willigen, 2005; Lima, 2004). Similarly, residents in an area prone to earthquakes or hurricanes may experience increased stress (Carr, 2000; Dougall & Baum, 2000).

Finally, investigators have examined urban poverty and violence as a source of environmental stress. There is considerable evidence that exposure to community violence, whether as a victim or as a witness, is associated with anxiety, depression, anger, and aggression among urban youth (Margolin & Gordis, 2004; Scarpa & Haden, 2006; Thompson & Massat, 2005). Although it's clear that exposure to violence and emotional problems are linked, researchers are still exploring the mechanisms underlying this connection. One such mechanism is the stress associated with the experience of community violence (Overstreet, 2000). Children who report recent exposure to traumatic events show increased stress hormones (Bevans, Cerbone, & Overstreet, 2008).

## Stress Is Influenced by Culture

Although certain types of events (such as the loss of a loved one) are probably viewed as stressful in virtually all human societies, cultures vary greatly in the predominant forms of stress their people experience. Obviously, the challenges of daily living encountered in modern, Western cities like Montreal or Philadelphia are quite different from the day-to-day difficulties experienced in indigenous societies in Africa or South America. Indeed, culture sets the context in which people experience and appraise stress (Chun, Moos, & Cronkite, 2006). The potential importance of culture is illustrated by the substantial body of evidence that *cultural change*—such as increased modernization and urbanization and shifting values and customs—has been a major source of stress in many societies around the world (Dessler, 2000). In some cases, a specific cultural group may be exposed to pervasive stress that is unique to that group (Berry & Ataca, 2000). For example, the ethnic cleansing of Albanians in Kosovo in 1999 and the devastating and widespread destruction from the tsunami in Indonesia and regions of Southeast Asia in 2004 were extraordinary forms of stress distinctive to these societies. Our discussion of stress largely focuses on the types of stressors confronted in everyday life in contemporary, Western society, but you should be aware that life in our society is not necessarily representative of life around the world.

Moreover, even within the modern, Western world, disparities can be found in the constellation of stressors experienced by specific cultural groups (Mino, Profit, & Pierce, 2000). In recent years, social scientists have explored the effects of ethnicity-related sources of stress experienced by African Americans, Hispanic Americans, Asian Americans, and other minority groups (Contrada et al., 2000; Williams & Mohammed, 2007), and they have documented that racial discrimination negatively affects mental health and well-being (Ong, Fuller-Rowell, & Burrow, 2009). Although overt racial discrimination in America has declined in recent decades, covert expressions of ethnic prejudice continue to be commonplace (Dovidio & Gaertner, 1999). For example, in one study of 520 African Americans, 96% of the respondents reported experiencing some type of racial discrimination in the most recent year—and 95% of these subjects indicated that they found this discrimination to be stressful (Klonoff & Landrine, 1999).

Everyday discrimination can take many forms, including verbal insults (ethnic slurs), negative evaluations, avoidance, denial of equal treatment, and threats of aggression. Feldman-Barrett and Swim (1998) emphasize that these acts of discrimination are often subtle and ambiguous ( e.g., "The clerk seemed to be ignoring me"). Hence, minority group members may experience stress not only from explicit discrimination but also from the subjective perception of discrimination in ambiguous situations (Williams & Mohammed, 2007). In one study, Black participants showed cognitive impairment following ambiguous (but not blatant) prejudice, apparently as a result of grappling with the uncertainty (Salvatore & Shelton, 2007). In fact, perceived discrimination has been linked to greater psychological distress, higher levels of depression, and decreased well-being for a variety of minority groups including sexual minorities (Lewis et al., 2006; Moradi & Risco, 2006; Swim, Johnston, & Pearson, 2009).

For immigrants, **acculturation, or changing to adapt to a new culture**, is a major source of stress related to reduced well-being (Moradi & Risco, 2006; Ying & Han, 2006). This pattern holds even for children (Suarez-Morales & Lopez, 2009). Studies show that the discrepancy between what individuals *expect* before immigrating and what they actually *experience* once they do immigrate is related to the amount of acculturation stress they report (Negy, Schwartz, & Reig-Ferrer, 2009). It seems likely that the extra layers of stress experienced by minority group members takes its toll. Scientists are still exploring the degree to which ethnicity-related stress may have detrimental effects on individuals' mental and physical health.

# Major Sources of Stress

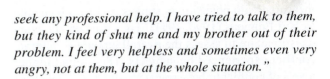

### LEARNING OBJECTIVES

- Distinguish between acute, chronic, and anticipatory stressors.
- Describe frustration as a source of stress.
- Outline the three types of internal conflict, and discuss typical reactions to conflicts.
- Analyze evidence on life change as a source of stress.
- Discuss evidence on pressure as a source of stress.

An enormous variety of events can be stressful for one person or another. To achieve a better understanding of stress, theorists have tried to analyze the nature of stressful events and divide them into subtypes. One sensible distinction involves differentiating between *acute stressors* and *chronic stressors* (Dougall & Baum, 2001). **Acute stressors are threatening events that have a relatively short duration and a clear endpoint.** Examples would include having a difficult encounter with a belligerent drunk, waiting for the results of a medical test, or having your home threatened by severe flooding. **Chronic stressors are threatening events that have a relatively long duration and no readily apparent time limit.** Examples would include persistent financial strains produced by huge credit card debts, ongoing pressures from a hostile boss at work, or the demands of caring for a sick family member over a period of years. Of course, this distinction is far from perfect. It is hard to decide where to draw the line between a short-lived versus lengthy stressor, and even brief stressors can have long-lasting effects.

Robert Sapolsky, a leading authority on stress, points out another type of stressor that is unique to humans. **Anticipatory stressors are upcoming or future events that are perceived to be threatening.** That is, we anticipate the impact of the event even though it has not happened yet. We may have increased anxiety or worry about break-ups that might never occur, bad grades we may never receive, or hurricanes that will never make landfall. The problem with anticipatory stress is that it can affect us psychologically and physically just as strongly as actual stressors do (Sapolsky, 2004). However we classify them (acute, chronic, or anticipatory), stressors come from all aspects of our lives. Let's take a look at four major sources of stress: frustration, internal conflict, change, and pressure. As you read about each of them, you'll surely recognize some familiar adversaries.

Robert Sapolsky

Linda A. Cicero/Stanford News Service

## Frustration

*"It has been very frustrating to watch the rapid deterioration of my parents' relationship. Over the last year or two they have argued constantly and have refused to seek any professional help. I have tried to talk to them, but they kind of shut me and my brother out of their problem. I feel very helpless and sometimes even very angry, not at them, but at the whole situation."*

This scenario illustrates frustration. As psychologists use the term, *frustration* **occurs in any situation in which the pursuit of some goal is thwarted.** In essence, you experience frustration when you want something and you can't have it. Everyone has to deal with frustration virtually every day. Traffic jams, long daily commutes, and annoying drivers, for instance, are a routine source of frustration that can elicit anger and increase levels of stress (Evans & Wener, 2006; Hennessy & Wiesenthal, 1999). Frustration often leads to aggression; even artificially induced frustration in a laboratory setting can lead to increased aggression from participants (Verona & Curtin, 2006). Some frustrations, such as *failures* and *losses,* can be sources of significant stress. Fortunately, most frustrations are brief and insignificant. You may be quite upset when you go to the auto shop to pick up your car and find that it hasn't been fixed as promised. However, a few days later you'll probably have your precious car back, and all will be forgotten.

More often than not, frustration appears to be the culprit at work when people feel troubled by environmental stress (Graig, 1993). Excessive noise, heat, pollution, and crowding are most likely stressful because they frustrate the desire for quiet, a comfortable body temperature, clean air, and adequate privacy. Frustration also plays a role in the aggressive behaviors associated with "road rage" (Wickens, Wiesenthal, & Rippey, 2005). Interestingly, frustration in the workplace often results in burnout (Lewandowski, 2003), a specific effect of stress that we will discuss later in this chapter.

## Internal Conflict

*"Should I or shouldn't I? I became engaged at Christmas. My fiancé surprised me with a ring. I knew if I refused the ring he would be terribly hurt and our relationship would suffer. However, I don't really know whether or not I want to marry him. On the other hand, I don't want to lose him either."*

Like frustration, internal conflict is an unavoidable feature of everyday life. That perplexing question "Should I or shouldn't I?" comes up countless times on a daily basis. *Internal conflict* **occurs when two or more incompatible motivations or behavioral impulses compete for expression.** As we discussed in Chapter 2, Sigmund Freud proposed over a century ago that internal conflicts generate considerable psychological distress. This link between conflict and distress was measured with precision in studies by Laura King and Robert Emmons (1990, 1991). They used an elaborate questionnaire to assess the overall amount of internal conflict experienced by subjects. They found higher levels of conflict to be associated with higher levels of psychological distress.

Conflicts come in three types, which were originally described by Kurt Lewin (1935) and investigated extensively by Neal Miller (1944, 1959). These types—approach-approach, avoidance-avoidance, and approach-avoidance—are diagrammed in **Figure 3.4**.

Courtesy Neal Miller

**Neal Miller**

In an *approach-approach conflict* **a choice must be made between two attractive goals.** The problem, of course, is that you can choose just one of the two goals. For example, you have a free afternoon; should you play tennis or go to the movies? You're out for a meal; do you want to order the pizza or the spaghetti? You can't afford both; should you buy the blue sweater or the gray jacket? Among the three kinds of conflict, the approach-approach type tends to be the least stressful. People don't usually stagger out of restaurants, exhausted by the stress of choosing which of several appealing entrees to eat. In approach-approach conflicts you typically have a reasonably happy ending, whichever way you decide to go. Nonetheless, approach-approach conflicts centering on important issues may sometimes be troublesome. If you are torn between two appealing college majors or two attractive job offers, you may find the decision-making process quite stressful.

In an *avoidance-avoidance conflict* **a choice must be made between two unattractive goals.** Forced to choose between two repelling alternatives, you are, as the expression goes, "caught between a rock and a hard place." For example, let's say you have painful backaches. Should you submit to surgery that you dread, or should you continue to live with the pain? Or you might need to decide between staying in a unsatisfying relationship or being alone. Obviously, avoidance-avoidance conflicts are most unpleasant and highly stressful. Typically, people keep delaying their decision as long as possible, hoping that they will somehow be able to escape the conflict situation. For example, you might delay surgery in the hope that your backaches will disappear on their own.

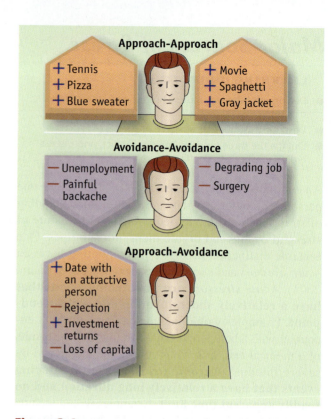

**Figure 3.4**

**Types of conflict.** Psychologists have identified three basic types of conflict. In approach-approach and avoidance-avoidance conflicts, the person is torn between two goals. In an approach-avoidance conflict only one goal is under consideration, but it has both positive and negative aspects.

In an *approach-avoidance conflict* **a choice must be made about whether to pursue a single goal that has both attractive and unattractive aspects.** For instance, imagine that you're offered a job promotion that will mean a large increase in pay. The catch is that you will have to move to a city that you hate. Approach-avoidance conflicts are common, and they can be highly stressful. Any time you have to take a risk to pursue some desirable outcome, you are likely to find yourself in an approach-avoidance conflict. Should you risk rejection by asking out that attractive person in class? Should you risk your savings by investing in a new business that could fail? Approach-avoidance conflicts often produce *vacillation*. That is, people go back and forth, beset by indecision that can create stress. Fortunately we are equipped to focus on the positive aspects of our decision once it has been made (Brehm, 1956).

## Change

*"After graduation, I landed my dream job and moved to another state. For the first time, I am living alone, far away from my friends and family. My biggest stress is getting used to my new life. Everything is different. I am learning how to do my new job, trying to make friends,*

BLONDIE

Panel 1: "ARE YOU ENJOYING YOUR SUMMER VACATION SO FAR?" "ACTUALLY, IT'S KIND OF STRESSFUL"

Panel 2: "STRESSFUL?" "YEAH"

Panel 3: "I DON'T KNOW WHETHER TO WASTE TIME AT THE BEACH, OR WASTE TIME AT THE MALL"

BLONDIE © 2001 KING FEATURES SYNDICATE

*and navigating my way around my new city. I love my job and my new location, but I am having difficulties dealing with all these changes at once."*

Life changes may represent a key type of stress. **Life changes are any noticeable alterations in one's living circumstances that require readjustment.** Research on life change began when Thomas Holmes, Richard Rahe, and their colleagues set out to explore the relation between stressful life events and physical illness (Holmes & Rahe, 1967; Rahe & Arthur, 1978). They interviewed thousands of tuberculosis patients to find out what kinds of events preceded the onset of their disease. Surprisingly, the frequently cited events were not uniformly negative. The list included plenty of aversive events, as expected, but patients also mentioned many seemingly positive events, such as getting married, having a baby, or getting promoted.

Why would positive events, such as moving to a nicer home, produce stress? According to Holmes and Rahe, it is because they produce *change.* Their thesis is that disruptions of daily routines are stressful. According to their theory, changes in personal relationships, changes at work, changes in finances, and so forth can be stressful even when the changes are welcomed.

Based on this analysis, Holmes and Rahe (1967) developed the Social Readjustment Rating Scale (SRRS) to measure life change as a form of stress. The scale assigns numerical values to 43 major life events that are supposed to reflect the magnitude of the readjustment required by each change (see **Figure 3.5** on the next page). In responding to the scale, respondents are asked to indicate how often they experienced any of these 43 events during a certain time period (typically, the past year). The person then adds up the numbers associated with each event checked. This sum is an index of the amount of change-related stress the person has recently experienced.

The SRRS and similar scales have been used in thousands of studies by researchers all over the world.

Overall, these studies have shown that people with higher scores on the SRRS tend to be more vulnerable to many kinds of physical illness—and many types of psychological problems as well (Lynch et al., 2005; Rahe et al., 2000; Scully, Tosi, & Banning, 2000). These results have attracted a great deal of attention, and the SRRS has been reprinted in many newspapers and popular magazines. The attendant publicity has led to the widespread conclusion that life change is inherently stressful.

However, experts have criticized this research, citing problems with the methods used and raising questions about the meaning of the findings (Cooper & Dewe, 2007; Jones & Kinman, 2001; Monroe & McQuaid, 1994). These experts have argued that the SRRS does not measure *change* exclusively. The list of life changes on the SRRS is dominated by events that are clearly negative or undesirable (marital separation, fired at work, and so on). These negative events probably generate great frustration. So even though the scale contains some positive events, it could be that frustration (generated by negative events), rather than change, creates most of the stress assessed by the scale.

To investigate this possibility, researchers came up with ways to take into account the desirability and undesirability of respondents' life changes. Participants were asked to indicate the desirability of the events that they checked off on the SRRS and similar scales. The findings in these studies clearly indicated that life change is *not* the crucial dimension measured by the SRRS and that in fact undesirable or negative life events cause much of the stress tapped by the scale (McLean & Link, 1994; Turner & Wheaton, 1995).

Should we discard the notion that change is stressful? Not entirely. Other lines of research, independent of work with the SRRS, support the hypothesis that change is an important form of stress. For instance, researchers have found associations between geographic mobility and impaired mental and physical health that presumably reflect the impact

## Social Readjustment Rating Scale

| Life event | Mean value | Life event | Mean value |
|---|---|---|---|
| Death of a spouse | 100 | Son or daughter leaving home | 29 |
| Divorce | 73 | Trouble with in-laws | 29 |
| Marital separation | 65 | Outstanding personal achievement | 28 |
| Jail term | 63 | Spouse begins or stops work | 26 |
| Death of close family member | 63 | Begin or end school | 26 |
| Personal injury or illness | 53 | Change in living conditions | 25 |
| Marriage | 50 | Revision of personal habits | 24 |
| Fired at work | 47 | Trouble with boss | 23 |
| Marital reconciliation | 45 | Change in work hours or conditions | 20 |
| Retirement | 45 | Change in residence | 20 |
| Change in health of family member | 44 | Change in school | 20 |
| Pregnancy | 40 | Change in recreation | 19 |
| Sex difficulties | 39 | Change in church activities | 19 |
| Gain of a new family member | 39 | Change in social activities | 18 |
| Business readjustment | 39 | Loan for lesser purchase (car, TV, etc.) | 17 |
| Change in financial state | 38 | Change in sleeping habits | 16 |
| Death of a close friend | 37 | Change in number of family get-togethers | 15 |
| Change to a different line of work | 36 | Change in eating habits | 15 |
| Change in number of arguments with spouse | 35 | Vacation | 13 |
| Mortgage or loan for major purchase | 31 | Christmas | 12 |
| Foreclosure of mortgage or loan | 30 | Minor violations of the law | 11 |
| Change in responsibilities at work | 29 | | |

**Figure 3.5**

**Social Readjustment Rating Scale (SRRS).** Devised by Holmes and Rahe (1967), this scale is designed to measure the change-related stress in one's life. The numbers on the right are supposed to reflect the average amount of stress (readjustment) produced by each event. Respondents check off the events that have occurred to them recently and add up the associated numbers to arrive at their stress scores.

Source: Adapted from Holmes, T. H., & Rahe, R. H. (1967). The social readjustment rating scale. *Journal of Psychosomatic Research, 11*(12), 213–218. Copyright © 1967 with permission from Elsevier.

of change (Brett, 1980; Shuval, 1993). A study by Brown and McGill (1989) suggests that desirable life changes may be stressful for some people but not for others. More research is needed, but it is quite plausible that change constitutes a major type of stress in people's lives. However, we have little reason to believe that change is *inherently* or *inevitably stressful.* Some life changes may be quite challenging, while others may be quite benign.

**WEB LINK 3.2   Psychological Self-Tools: Anxiety and Worry**

The Mental Help Net website exists "to promote mental health and wellness education and advocacy." Basically, this site provides a comprehensive online self-help book with a discussion of the nature of stress and its relationship to psychological and physical disorders.

## Pressure

*"My father questioned me at dinner about some things I did not want to talk about. I know he doesn't want to hear my answers, at least not the truth. My father told me when I was little that I was his favorite because I was 'pretty near perfect' and I've spent my life trying to keep that up, even though it's obviously not true. Recently, he has begun to realize this and it's made our relationship very strained and painful."*

At one time or another, most of us have probably remarked that we were "under pressure." What does that expression mean? ***Pressure* involves expectations or demands that one behave in a certain way.** Pressure can be divided into two subtypes: the pressure to *perform* and the pressure to *conform.* You are under pressure to perform when you are expected to execute tasks and responsibilities quickly, efficiently, and successfully.

For example, salespeople are usually under pressure to move lots of merchandise. Professors at research institutions are often under pressure to publish in prestigious journals. Comedians are under pressure to be amusing. Pressures to conform to others' expectations are also common. Businessmen are expected to wear suits and ties. Suburban homeowners are expected to keep their lawns manicured. Teenagers are expected to adhere to their parents' values and rules.

Although widely discussed by the general public, the concept of pressure has received scant attention from researchers. However, one scale has been developed to measure pressure as a form of life stress (Weiten, 1988). Studies with this scale have found a strong relationship between pressure and a variety of psychological symptoms and problems (Weiten, 1988, 1998). In fact, pressure has turned out to be more strongly related to measures of mental health than the SRRS and other established measures of stress (see **Figure 3.6**). Academic pressures, common for students worldwide, are related to increased anxiety and depression and affect student motivation and concentration (Andrews & Hejdenberg, 2007). Recent research suggests that stress resulting from academic pressure may actually impede academic performance and lead to problematic escape behaviors such as drinking (Kaplan, Liu, & Kaplan, 2005; Kieffer, Cronin, & Gawet, 2006).

We tend to think of pressure as something imposed from outside forces. However, studies of high school and college students find that pressure is often self-imposed (Kouzma & Kennedy, 2004; Misra & Castillo, 2004). For example, you might sign up for

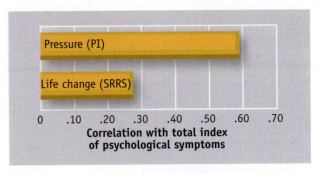

**Figure 3.6**

**Pressure and psychological symptoms.** A comparison of pressure and life change as sources of stress suggests that pressure may be more strongly related to mental health than change is. In one study, Weiten (1988) found a correlation of .59 between scores on the Pressure Inventory (PI) and symptoms of psychological distress. In the same sample, the correlation between SRRS scores and psychological symptoms was only .28.

extra classes to get through school quickly. Or you might actively seek additional leadership positions to impress your family. Self-imposed stress doesn't stop when you complete your education. People frequently put pressure on themselves to rapidly climb the corporate ladder or to be perfect parents. Even the pressure that modern people put on themselves to maintain a proper work-family balance can serve as a source of stress (Grzywacz & Butler, 2007; Quick, Henley, & Quick, 2004). In sum, because individuals might create stress by embracing unrealistic expectations for themselves, they might have more control over our stress than they realize.

Pressure comes in two varieties: pressure to perform and pressure to conform. For example, workers on assembly lines are often expected to maintain high productivity with few mistakes (performance pressure), while suburban homeowners are typically expected to maintain well-groomed exteriors (conformity pressure).

# Responding to Stress

## LEARNING OBJECTIVES

- List three categories of negative emotions commonly elicited by stress.
- Discuss the role of positive emotions in the stress process.
- Explain the effects of emotional arousal on coping efforts, and describe the inverted-U hypothesis.
- Describe the fight-or-flight response, and contrast it with the tend-and-befriend response.
- Identify the three stages of the general adaptation syndrome.
- Distinguish between the two major pathways along which the brain sends signals to the endocrine system in response to stress.
- Clarify the concept of coping.

The human response to stress is complex and multidimensional. Stress affects people on several levels. Consider again the chapter's opening scenario, in which you're driving home in heavy traffic, thinking about overdue papers, relationship conflicts, tuition increases, and parental pressures. Let's look at some of the reactions we mentioned. When you groan in reaction to the traffic report, you're experiencing an *emotional response* to stress—in this case, annoyance and anger. When your pulse quickens and your stomach knots up, you're exhibiting *physiological responses* to stress. When you shout insults at another driver, your verbal aggression is a *behavioral response* to the stress at hand. Thus, we can analyze people's reactions to stress at three levels: (1) their emotional responses, (2) their physiological responses, and (3) their behavioral responses. **Figure 3.7** depicts these three levels of response.

## Emotional Responses

Emotion is an elusive concept. Psychologists debate how to define emotion, and many conflicting theories purport to explain emotion. However, everybody has had extensive personal experience with emotions. Everyone has a good idea of what it means to be anxious, elated, gloomy, jealous, disgusted, excited, guilty, or nervous. So rather than pursue the technical debates about emotion, we'll rely on your familiarity with the concept and simply note that *emotions* **are powerful, largely uncontrollable feelings, accompanied by physiological changes.** When people are under stress, they often react emotionally. More often than not, stress tends to elicit unpleasant emotions (Lazarus, 1993). In studying one of the most severe disasters of modern times, the Indian Ocean tsunami of 2004, researchers found that almost 84% of survivors showed signs of severe emotional distress, including depression and anxiety (Souza et al., 2007). Emotional responses to stress seem to transcend time and culture. Recently, a historical researcher, examining texts from 2100–2000 B.C., found evidence that core negative emotional reactions to trauma have not really changed over the millennia (Ben-Ezra, 2004).

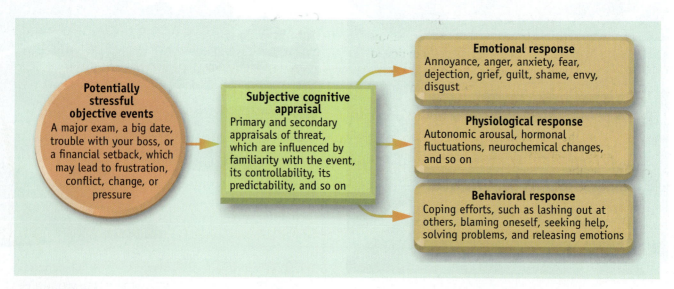

**Figure 3.7**

**The multidimensional response to stress.** A potentially stressful event, such as a major exam, will elicit a subjective, cognitive appraisal of how threatening the event is. If the event is viewed with alarm, the stress may trigger emotional, physiological, and behavioral reactions. The human response to stress is multidimensional.

The huge earthquake in Haiti in January of 2010 produced overwhelming trauma for countless people. Individuals experiencing severe stress have emotional, physiological, and behavioral reactions. Emotional responses to extreme stress (such as grief, anxiety, and fear) appear to transcend culture.

© Damon Winter/The New York Times/Redux Pictures

## Negative Emotions

There are no simple one-to-one connections between certain *types* of stressful events and particular emotions, but researchers have begun to uncover some strong links between specific *cognitive reactions to stress* and specific emotions (Lazarus, 2006; Smith & Lazarus, 1993). For example, self-blame tends to lead to guilt, helplessness to sadness, and so forth. Although stressful events can evoke many negative emotions, some are certainly more likely than others. According to Richard Lazarus (1993), common negative emotional responses to stress include the following:

• *Annoyance, anger, and rage.* Stress often produces feelings of anger ranging in intensity from mild annoyance to uncontrollable rage. As previously mentioned, frustration is particularly likely to generate anger.

• *Apprehension, anxiety, and fear.* Stress probably evokes anxiety and fear more frequently than any other emotions. As we saw in Chapter 2, Freudian theory has long recognized the link between conflict and anxiety. However, anxiety can also be elicited by the pressure to perform, the threat of impending frustration, or the uncertainty associated with change.

**WEB LINK 3.3    American Psychological Association: Stress**

The American Psychological Association is the largest professional organization for psychologists. This website presents up-to-date coverage of stress research, including recent press releases and psychological research in the news. This site provides a peek into stress research currently being published.

• *Dejection, sadness, and grief.* Sometimes stress—especially frustration—simply brings one down. Routine setbacks, such as traffic tickets and poor grades, often produce feelings of dejection. More profound setbacks, such as deaths and divorces, typically leave one grief-stricken.

Of course, the above list is not exhaustive. In his insightful analyses of stress-emotion relations, Richard Lazarus (1991, 1993) mentions five other negative emotions that often figure prominently in reactions to stress: guilt, shame, envy, jealousy, and disgust.

## Positive Emotions

Although investigators have tended to focus heavily on the connection between stress and negative emotions, research by Susan Folkman (1997, 2008) has shown that positive emotions also occur during periods of stress. This finding may seem counterintuitive, but researchers have found that people experience a diverse array of pleasant emotions even while enduring the most dire of circumstances. Consider, for example, the results of a five-year study of coping patterns in 253 caregiving partners of men with AIDS (Folkman et al., 1997). Surprisingly, over the course of the study the caregivers reported experiencing positive emotions about as often as they experienced negative ones—except during the time immediately surrounding the death of their partners.

Similar findings have been observed in some other studies of serious stress that made an effort to look for

Courtesy Susan Folkman

**Susan Folkman**

positive emotions. The most interesting was a study that examined subjects' emotional functioning early in 2001 and then again in the weeks following the 9/11 terrorist attacks in the United States (Fredrickson et al., 2003). Like most U.S. citizens, these subjects reported many negative emotions in the aftermath of 9/11, including anger, sadness, and fear. However, within this "dense cloud of anguish," positive emotions also emerged. For example, people felt gratitude for the safety of their loved ones, many took stock and counted their blessings, and quite a few reported renewed love for their friends and family. Fredrickson et al. (2003) also found that the frequency of pleasant emotions correlated positively with a measure of subjects' resilience, whereas unpleasant emotions correlated negatively with resilience (see **Figure 3.8**). Based on their analyses, the researchers concluded that "positive emotions in the aftermath of crises buffer resilient people against depression and fuel thriving" (p. 365). Similar results were found for survivors of the 2001 El Salvador earthquake (Vazquez et al., 2005). Thus, contrary to common sense, positive emotions do *not* vanish during times of severe stress. Moreover, these positive emotions appear to play a key role in helping people bounce back from the negative emotions associated with stress (Ong et al., 2006; Tugade & Fredrickson, 2004).

Simply put, positive emotions can contribute to building social, intellectual, and physical resources that can be helpful in dealing with stress and allow one to experience flourishing mental health (Fredrickson, 1998, 2001; Fredrickson & Losada, 2005). In fact, the benefits of positive emotions are so strong that Fredrickson (2006) argues that people should "cultivate positive emotions in themselves and in those around them as means to achieving psychological growth and improved psychological and physical well-being over time" (p. 85). Chapter 16 discusses positive emotions in more detail.

## Effects of Emotional Arousal

Emotional responses are a natural and normal part of life. Even unpleasant emotions serve important purposes. Like physical pain, painful emotions can serve as warnings that one needs to take action. However, strong emotional arousal can also hamper efforts to cope with stress. For example, research has found that high emotional arousal can sometimes interfere with attention and memory retrieval and can impair judgment and decision making (Janis, 1993; Mandler, 1993).

The well-known problem of *test anxiety* illustrates how emotional arousal can hurt performance. Often students who score poorly on an exam will nonetheless insist that they know the material. Many of them are probably telling the truth. Several researchers have found a negative correlation between test-related anxiety and exam performance. That is, students who display high test anxiety tend to score low on exams (Bin Kassim, Hanafi, & Hancock, 2008; Hancock, 2001). Test anxiety can interfere with test taking in several ways, but one critical consideration appears to be the disruption of attention to the test (Keough et al., 2004). Many test-anxious students waste too much time worrying about how they're doing and wondering whether others are having similar problems. In addition, there is evidence that test anxiety may deplete one's capacity for self-control, increasing the likelihood of poor performance (Oaten & Cheng, 2005). In other words, once distracted, test-anxious students might not have the self-control to get themselves back on course. This tendency is related to a concept called *ego depletion* that we will discuss in Chapter 6.

Although emotional arousal may hurt coping efforts, this isn't *necessarily* the case. The *inverted-U hypothesis* predicts that task performance should improve with increased emotional arousal—up to a point, after which further increases in arousal become disruptive and performance deteriorates (Anderson, 1990; Mandler, 1993). This idea is referred to as the inverted-U hypothesis because plotting performance as a function of arousal results in graphs that approximate an upside-down U (see **Figure 3.9**). In these graphs, the level of arousal at which performance peaks is characterized as the *optimal level of arousal* for a task.

This optimal level of arousal appears to depend in part on the complexity of the task at hand. The

| Correlation Between Resilience and the Frequency of Selected Emotions in the Aftermath of 9/11 | |
| --- | --- |
| **Specific emotions** | **Correlation with resilience** |
| **Negative emotions** | |
| Angry/irritated/annoyed | −.44* |
| Sad/downhearted/unhappy | −.29* |
| Scared/fearful/afraid | −.19 |
| Disgust/distaste/revulsion | −.09 |
| **Positive emotions** | |
| Grateful/appreciative/thankful | .13 |
| Glad/happy/joyful | .52* |
| Hopeful/optimistic/encouraged | .40* |
| Content/serene/peaceful | .47* |
| *Statistically significant | |

**Figure 3.8**

**Positive and negative emotions as correlates of resilience.**
Fredrickson et al. (2003) asked subjects to rate the frequency with which they experienced 20 different emotions in the aftermath of 9/11. The frequency ratings for specific emotions were then correlated with a measure of participants' resiliency. Representative results (for 8 of the 20 emotions studied) are shown here. As you can see, the frequency of pleasant emotions correlated positively with resilience, whereas the opposite was true for negative emotions.

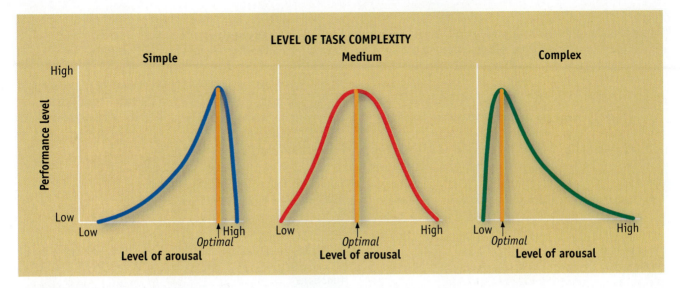

**Figure 3.9**

**Arousal and performance.** Graphs of the relationship between emotional arousal and task performance tend to resemble an inverted U, as increased arousal is associated with improved performance up to a point, after which higher arousal leads to poorer performance. The optimal level of arousal for a task depends on the complexity of the task. On complex tasks, a relatively low level of arousal tends to be optimal. On simple tasks, however, performance may peak at a much higher level of arousal.

conventional wisdom is that *as tasks become more complex, the optimal level of arousal (for peak performance) tends to decrease.* This relationship is depicted in **Figure 3.9**. As you can see, a fairly high level of arousal should be optimal on simple tasks (such as driving eight hours to help a friend in a crisis). However, performance should peak at a lower level of arousal on complex tasks (such as making a major decision in which you have to weigh many factors).

The research evidence on the inverted-U hypothesis is inconsistent and subject to varied interpretations (Neiss, 1988, 1990). The original formulation of this hypothesis was more related to animal learning than to human performance in stressful situations (Hancock & Ganey, 2003). Hence, it may be risky to generalize this principle to the complexities of everyday coping efforts. However, scientists argue that the theory should be refined rather than discarded (Landers, 2007; Muse, Harris, & Field, 2003). The inverted-U hypothesis provides a plausible model of how emotional arousal could have either beneficial or disruptive effects on coping, depending on the nature of the stressful demands.

## Physiological Responses

As we have seen, stress frequently elicits strong emotional responses. These responses bring about important physiological changes. Even in cases of moderate stress, you may notice that your heart has started beating faster, you have begun to breathe harder, and you are perspiring more than usual. How does all this (and much more) happen? Let's see.

### The "Fight-or-Flight" Response

Even though he did not refer to it as stress, Walter Cannon (1929, 1932) was a pioneer in stress research with his work on the fight-or-flight response. **The *fight-or-flight response* is a physiological reaction to threat that mobilizes an organism for attacking (fight) or fleeing (flight) an enemy.** For instance, you see a threatening figure and your heart rate increases, blood pressure rises, respiration increases, digestion slows—all things that prepare you to act and that are evolutionarily advantageous (Sapolsky, 2004). These responses occur in the body's autonomic nervous system. **The *autonomic nervous system (ANS)* is made up of the nerves that connect to the heart, blood vessels, smooth muscles, and glands.** As its name hints, the autonomic nervous system is somewhat *autonomous.* That is, it controls involuntary, visceral functions that people don't normally think about, such as heart rate, digestion, and perspiration.

The autonomic nervous system can be broken into two divisions (see **Figure 3.10** on the next page). The *parasympathetic division* of the ANS generally conserves bodily resources. For instance, it slows heart rate and promotes digestion to help the body save and store energy. The fight-or-flight response is mediated by the *sympathetic division* of the autonomic nervous system, which mobilizes bodily resources for emergencies. In one experiment, Cannon studied the fight-or-flight response in cats by confronting them with dogs. Among other things, he noticed an immediate acceleration in breathing and heart rate and a reduction in digestive processes.

Shelley Taylor and her colleagues (2000) have questioned whether the fight-or-flight model applies

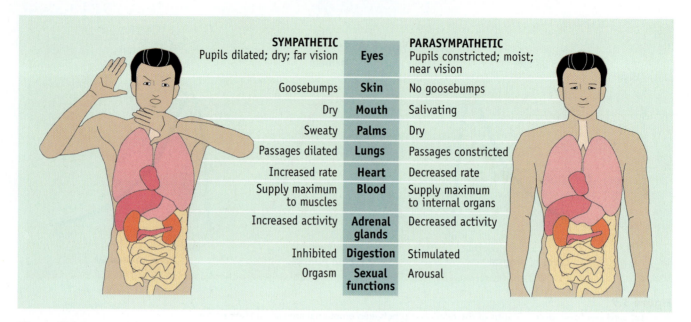

| SYMPATHETIC | | PARASYMPATHETIC |
|---|---|---|
| Pupils dilated; dry; far vision | **Eyes** | Pupils constricted; moist; near vision |
| Goosebumps | **Skin** | No goosebumps |
| Dry | **Mouth** | Salivating |
| Sweaty | **Palms** | Dry |
| Passages dilated | **Lungs** | Passages constricted |
| Increased rate | **Heart** | Decreased rate |
| Supply maximum to muscles | **Blood** | Supply maximum to internal organs |
| Increased activity | **Adrenal glands** | Decreased activity |
| Inhibited | **Digestion** | Stimulated |
| Orgasm | **Sexual functions** | Arousal |

**Figure 3.10**

**The autonomic nervous system (ANS).** The ANS is composed of the nerves that connect to the heart, blood vessels, smooth muscles, and glands. The ANS is subdivided into the *sympathetic division,* which mobilizes bodily resources in times of need, and the *parasympathetic division,* which conserves bodily resources. Some of the key functions controlled by each division of the ANS are summarized in the center of the diagram.

equally well to both males and females. They note that in most species females have more responsibility for the care of young offspring than males do. Using an evolutionary perspective, they argue that this disparity may make fighting and fleeing less adaptive for females, as both responses may endanger offspring and thus reduce the likelihood of an animal passing on its genes. Taylor and colleagues maintain that evolutionary processes have fostered more of a "tend and befriend" response to stress in females. According to this analysis, in reacting to stress females allocate more effort to the care of offspring and to seeking help and support. Consistent with this theory, David and Lyons-Ruth (2005) found gender differences in how infants respond to threat. Specifically, when frightened, female infants showed more approach behaviors toward their mothers than male infants did. Taylor speculates that the hormone oxytocin signals the need for affiliation in females in times of social distress. More research is needed to evaluate this provocative analysis. Even though they hypothesize some gender differences in responses to stress, Taylor and her colleagues are quick to note that the "basic neuroendocrine core of stress responses" is largely the same for males and females.

Our physiological responses to stress are part of the fight-or-flight syndrome seen in many species. In a sense, this automatic reaction is a leftover from our evolutionary past. It is clearly an adaptive response for many animals, as the threat of predators often requires a swift response of fighting or fleeing (picture the gazelle escaping from the lion on the Discovery Channel). Likewise,

the fight-or-flight response probably was adaptive among ancestral humans who routinely had to deal with acute stressors involving threats to their physical safety. But in our modern world, the fight-or-flight response may be less adaptive for human functioning than it was thousands of generations ago (Neese & Young, 2000). Most modern stressors cannot be handled simply through fight or flight. Work pressures, marital problems, and financial difficulties require far more complex responses. Moreover, these chronic stressors often continue for lengthy periods of time, so that the fight-or-flight response leaves one in a state of enduring physiological arousal. Concern about the effects of prolonged physical arousal was first voiced by Hans Selye, a Canadian scientist who conducted extensive research on stress.

**The General Adaptation Syndrome**

The concept of stress was popularized in both scientific and lay circles by Hans Selye (1936, 1956, 1982). Although born in Vienna, Selye spent his entire professional career at McGill University in Montreal, Canada. Beginning in the 1930s, Selye exposed laboratory animals to a diverse array of unpleasant stimuli (heat, cold, pain, mild shock, restraint, and so on). The patterns of physiological arousal he observed in the animals were largely the same, regardless of which unpleasant stimulus elicited them. Thus, Selye concluded that stress reactions are *nonspecific.* In other words, they do not vary according to the specific type of circumstances encountered. Initially, Selye wasn't sure what to call this nonspecific response to a variety of noxious agents. In the 1940s, he decided to call it *stress,* and his influential writings gradually helped make the word part of our everyday vocabulary (Cooper & Dewe, 2004).

Hans Selye
© Bettmann/Corbis

To capture the general pattern all species exhibit when responding to stress, Selye (1956, 1974) formulated a seminal theory called the general adaptation syndrome (see **Figure 3.11**). The *general adaptation syndrome* is a model of the body's stress response, consisting of three stages: alarm, resistance, and exhaustion. In the first stage of the general adaptation syndrome, an *alarm reaction* occurs when an organism recognizes the existence of a threat (whether a lion, a mugger, or a big deadline). Physiological arousal increases as the body musters its resources to combat the challenge. Selye's alarm reaction is essentially the fight-or-flight response originally described by Cannon.

However, Selye took his investigation of stress a couple of steps further by exposing laboratory animals to *prolonged stress,* similar to the chronic stress often endured by humans. If stress continues, the organism may progress to the second phase of the general adaptation syndrome, called the *stage of resistance.* During this phase, physiological changes stabilize as coping efforts get under way. Typically, physiological arousal continues to be higher than normal, although it may level off somewhat as the organism becomes accustomed to the threat.

If the stress continues over a substantial period of time, the organism may enter the third stage, called the *stage of exhaustion.* According to Selye, the body's re-

sources for fighting stress are limited. If the stress cannot be overcome, the body's resources may be depleted, and physiological arousal will decrease. Eventually, the individual may collapse from exhaustion. During this phase, the organism's resistance declines. This reduced resistance may lead to what Selye called "diseases of adaptation," such as ulcers or high blood pressure.

Selye's theory and research forged a link between stress and physical illness. He showed how prolonged physiological arousal that is meant to be adaptive could lead to diseases. His theory has been criticized because it ignores individual differences in the appraisal of stress (Lazarus & Folkman, 1984), and his belief that stress reactions are nonspecific remains the subject of debate (Kemeny, 2003; McCarty & Pacak, 2000). However, his model provided guidance for generations of researchers who worked out the details of how stress reverberates throughout the body. Let's look at some of those details.

### Brain-Body Pathways

When you experience stress, your brain sends signals to the endocrine system along two major pathways (Clow, 2001; Dallman, Bhatnagar, & Viau, 2000; Felker & Hubbard, 1998). The *endocrine system* consists of glands that secrete chemicals called hormones into the bloodstream. The major endocrine glands, such as the pituitary, pineal, thyroid, and adrenal glands, are shown in **Figure 3.12** on the next page.

The *hypothalamus,* a small structure near the base of the brain, appears to initiate action along both pathways. The first pathway (shown on the right in **Figure 3.13**) is routed through the autonomic nervous system. The hypothalamus activates the sympathetic division of the ANS. A key part of this activation involves stimulating the central part of the *adrenal glands* (the adrenal medulla) to release large amounts of *catecholamines* into the bloodstream. These hormones radiate throughout your body, producing many important physiological changes. The net result of catecholamine elevation is that your body is mobilized for action (Lundberg, 2000). Heart rate and blood flow increase, pumping more blood to your brain and muscles. Respiration and oxygen consumption speed up, facilitating alertness. Digestive processes are inhibited to conserve your energy. The pupils of your eyes dilate, increasing visual sensitivity.

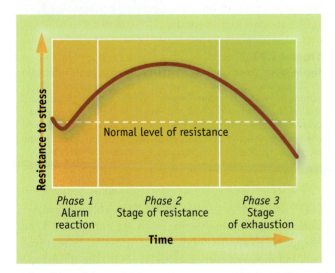

**Figure 3.11**

**The general adaptation syndrome.** According to Selye, the physiological response to stress can be broken into three phases. During the first phase, the body mobilizes its resources for resistance after a brief initial shock. In the second phase, resistance levels off and eventually begins to decline. If the third phase of the general adaptation syndrome is reached, resistance is depleted, leading to health problems and exhaustion.

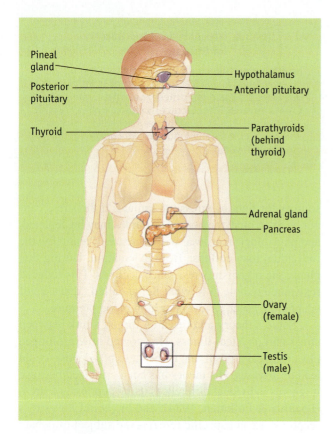

**Figure 3.12**

**The endocrine system.** The endocrine glands secrete hormones into the bloodstream. The locations of the principal endocrine glands are shown here. The hormones released by these glands regulate a variety of physical functions and play a key role in the physiological response to stress.

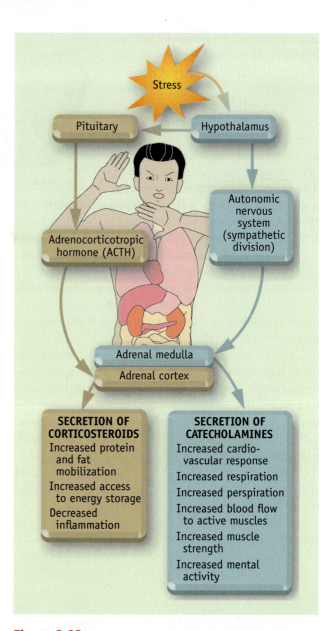

**Figure 3.13**

**Brain-body pathways in stress.** In times of stress, the brain sends signals along two pathways. The pathway through the autonomic nervous system (shown in blue on the right) controls the release of catecholamine hormones that help mobilize the body for action. The pathway through the pituitary gland and the endocrine system (shown in brown on the left) controls the release of corticosteroid hormones that increase energy and ward off tissue inflammation.

The second pathway (shown on the left in **Figure 3.13**) involves more direct communication between the brain and the endocrine system. The hypothalamus sends signals to the so-called master gland of the endocrine system, the *pituitary gland.* The pituitary secretes a hormone (ACTH) that stimulates the outer part of the adrenal glands (the adrenal cortex) to release another important set of hormones—*corticosteroids.* These hormones play an important role in the response to stress (de Kloet, Joels, & Holsboer, 2005). They stimulate the release of chemicals that help increase your energy and help inhibit tissue inflammation in case of injury (Munck, 2000). *Cortisol* is a type of corticosteroid that is often used as a physiological indicator of stress in humans. In fact, many of the studies discussed in this chapter used cortisol as a measure of subjects' response to stress.

Stress can also produce other physiological changes that we are just beginning to understand. The most critical changes occur in the immune system. Your immune system provides you with resistance to infections. However, evidence indicates that stress can suppress certain aspects of the multifaceted immune response, reducing its overall effectiveness in repelling invasions by infectious agents (Chiappelli & Hodgson, 2000; Kemeny,

2007, McEwen & Lasley, 2007). The exact mechanisms underlying immune suppression are complicated, but it appears likely that both sets of stress hormones (catecholamines and corticosteroids) contribute (Dantzer & Mormede, 1995). In any case, it is becoming clear that physiological responses to stress extend into every corner of the body. Moreover, some of these responses may persist long after a stressful event has ended (Esterling et al., 1994). As you will see, these physiological reactions can have an impact on both mental and physical health.

## Behavioral Responses

Although people respond to stress at several levels, their behavior is the crucial dimension of these reactions. Emotional and physiological responses to stress—which are often undesirable—tend to be largely automatic. However, dealing effectively with stress at the behavioral level may shut down these potentially harmful emotional and physiological reactions.

Most behavioral responses to stress involve coping. ***Coping* refers to active efforts to master, reduce, or tolerate the demands created by stress.** Notice that this definition is neutral as to whether coping efforts are healthy or maladaptive. The popular use of the term often implies that coping is inherently healthy. When we say that someone "coped with her problems," we imply that she handled them effectively.

In reality, coping responses may be either healthy or unhealthy (Kleinke, 2007; Moos & Schaefer, 1993). For example, if you were flunking a history course at midterm, you might cope with this stress by (1) increasing your study efforts, (2) seeking help from a tutor, (3) blaming your professor for your poor grade, or (4) giving up on the class. Clearly, the first two coping responses would more likely lead to a positive outcome than would the second two.

People cope with stress in a variety of ways. Because of the complexity and importance of coping processes, we devote all of the next chapter to ways of coping. At this point, it is sufficient to note that coping strategies help determine whether stress has any positive or negative effects on an individual. In the next section, you'll see what some of those effects can be as we discuss the possible outcomes of people's struggles with stress.

# *The Potential Effects of Stress*

### LEARNING OBJECTIVES

- Explain the phenomenon of choking under pressure.
- Summarize evidence regarding how stress can affect cognitive functioning.
- Identify the symptoms and causes of burnout.
- Assess the potential impact of stress on psychological health.

- Discuss the prevalence, symptoms, and causes of posttraumatic stress disorder.
- Discuss the effects of stress on physical health.
- Articulate three ways in which stress might lead to beneficial effects.

People struggle with stressors every day, most of which come and go without leaving any enduring imprint. However, when stress is severe or when demands pile up, stress may have long-lasting effects. These effects, often called "adaptational outcomes," are relatively long-lasting (though not necessarily permanent) consequences of exposure to stress. **Figure 3.14** lists some of the common effects of trauma. Although stress can have beneficial effects, research has focused mainly on possible negative outcomes, so you'll find our coverage slanted in that direction. Note that we will discuss *reducing* the effects of stress in the next chapter.

| Selected Effects of Trauma | |
| --- | --- |
| **Function** | **Effect** |
| Cognitive processes | Impaired |
| Emotional expression | Suppressed |
| Memory for prior stressors | Increased |
| Ruminations on trauma | Increased |
| Vulnerability to gastric ulcers | Increased |
| Vulnerability to inflammatory bowel disease | Increased |

**Figure 3.14**

**The effects of trauma on psychological and physical functioning.** Scientists have discovered many negative effects of experiencing extreme stress. This table presents only a limited set of ways that the experience of trauma can affect us psychologically and physically.

Source: Adapted from Overmier, J. B., & Murison, R. (2005). Trauma and resulting sensitization effects are modulated by psychological factors. *Psychoneuroendocrinology, 30*(10), 965–973, Table 2. Copyright 2005, with permission from Elsevier.

## Impaired Task Performance

Frequently, stress takes its toll on the ability to perform effectively on a task at hand. For instance, Roy Baumeister (1984) theorized that pressure to perform often makes people self-conscious and that this elevated self-consciousness disrupts their attention, thereby interfering with performance. He theorizes that attention may be distorted in two ways. First, elevated self-consciousness may divert attention from the demands of the task, creating distractions. Second, on well-learned tasks that should be executed almost automatically, the self-conscious person may focus *too* much attention on the task. Thus, the person thinks too much about what he or she is doing.

Baumeister (1984) found support for his theory in a series of laboratory experiments in which he manipulated the pressure to perform on a simple perceptual-motor task. His theory also garnered some support in a pair of studies of the past performance of professional sports teams in championship contests (Baumeister, 1995; Baumeister & Steinhilber, 1984). These findings were particularly impressive in that gifted professional athletes are probably less likely to choke under pressure than virtually any other sample one might assemble. Perhaps to reach that level, athletes must thrive under pressure and therefore simply don't feel performance pressure the way that we assume they do (Wallace, Baumeister, & Vohs, 2005). Laboratory research on "normal" subjects is more pertinent to the issue, and it suggests that choking under pressure is fairly common (Butler & Baumeister, 1998; Lewis & Linder, 1997).

Choking isn't the only impairment of task performance related to stress. Recent research on rats has found that chronic stress might actually affect the brain in a way that leads to an overreliance on habits, even when the habits are no longer advantageous (Dias-

Ferreira et al., 2009). Although habitual actions take less energy and effort, which might be beneficial during times of stress, they can keep one from adapting to changing circumstances and thus result in impairments in one's performance.

## Disruption of Cognitive Functioning

The effects of stress on task performance often result from disruptions in thinking or in cognitive functioning. In a study of stress and decision-making, Keinan (1987) measured participants' attention under stressful and nonstressful conditions and found that stress disrupted two specific aspects of attention. First, it increased participants' tendency to jump to a conclusion too quickly without considering all their options. Second, it increased their tendency to do an unsystematic, poorly organized review of their available options. Brandes et al. (2002) examined trauma survivors within days of their experience and found that those with severe stress levels had poorer attention than those with few distress symptoms. Brandes speculates that poor attention might play an important role in actually shaping one's memory for a traumatic event.

The results of some studies also suggest that stress can have detrimental effects on certain aspects of memory functioning (Kellogg, Hopko, & Ashcraft, 1999; Shors, 2004). In order to affect memory, stressors do not have to be major; even minor day-to-day or anticipatory stressors can have a negative impact (Lindau, Almkvist, & Mohammed, 2007; Neupert et al., 2006). Recent evidence suggests that stress can reduce the efficiency of the "working memory" system that allows people to juggle information on the spot (Beilock et al., 2004; Markman, Maddox, & Worthy, 2006). Thus, under stressful situations, people may not be able to process, manipulate, or integrate new information as effectively as normal. Ironically, simply being in a situation where you need cognitive resources the most (studying for a final exam, traveling in a foreign country) can produce this cognitive-sapping stress effect. Researchers note, however, that stress has a complicated relationship with memory in that short-term, mild-to-moderate stressors can actually enhance memory, especially for emotional aspects of events (Buchanan & Tranel, 2008; Sapolsky, 2004).

## Burnout

Burnout is an overused buzzword that means different things to different people. Nonetheless, a few researchers have described burnout in a systematic way that has facilitated scientific study of the syndrome (Maslach & Leiter, 1997, 2007; Pines, 1993). **Burnout is a syndrome involving physical and emotional exhaustion, cynicism, and a lowered sense of self-efficacy that is attributable to work-related stress.** Exhaustion, which is central to burnout, includes chronic fatigue, weakness, and low energy. Cynicism is manifested in highly negative attitudes toward oneself, one's work, and life in general. Reduced self-efficacy involves declining feelings of competence at work that give way to feelings of hopelessness and helplessness.

What causes burnout? According to Maslach and Leiter (2007), "Burnout is a cumulative stress reaction to ongoing occupational stressors" (p. 368). The conventional wisdom is that burnout occurs because of some flaw or weakness within the person, but Christina Maslach (2003) asserts that "the research case is much stronger for the contrasting argument that burnout is more a function of the situation than of the person" (p. 191). Factors in the workplace that appear to promote burnout include work overload, interpersonal conflicts at work, lack of control over responsibilities and outcomes, and inadequate recognition for one's work (see **Figure 3.15**). Physical conditions such as noise, light, and temperature can also contribute to workplace stress, as can night and rotating shift work (Lundberg, 2007; Sulsky & Smith, 2007). As you might expect, burnout is associated with increased absenteeism and reduced productivity, as well as increased vulnerability to a variety of health problems (Grossi et al., 2003; Maslach & Leiter, 2007).

## Psychological Problems and Disorders

On the basis of clinical impressions, psychologists have long suspected that chronic stress might contribute to many types of psychological problems and mental disorders. Since the late 1960s, advances in the measurement of stress have allowed researchers to verify these suspicions in empirical studies. In the domain of common psychological problems, studies indicate that stress may contribute to poor academic performance (Akgun & Ciarrochi, 2003), insomnia and other sleep disturbances (Akerstedt et al., 2007; Vgontzas, Bixler, & Kales, 2000), sexual difficulties (Lemack, Uzzo, & Poppas, 1998; Slowinski, 2007), alcohol abuse (Colder, 2001; Edwards et al., 2006), and drug abuse (Goeders, 2004). Stress is also associated with increases in negative mood (Schneiders et al., 2006).

Beyond these everyday problems, research reveals that stress often contributes to the onset of full-fledged psychological disorders, including depression (Monroe & Reid, 2009; Rehm, Wagner, & Ivens-Tyndal, 2001), schizophrenia (McGlashan & Hoffman, 2000), anxiety disorders (Falsetti & Ballenger, 1998), and eating disorders (Cooper, 1995; Loth et al., 2008).

Extremely stressful, traumatic incidents can leave a lasting imprint on victims' psychological functioning. *Posttraumatic stress disorder (PTSD)* **involves enduring psychological disturbance attributed to the experience of a major traumatic event.** Researchers began to appreciate the frequency and severity of posttraumatic stress disorder after the Vietnam war ended in 1975 and a great many psychologically scarred veterans returned home. These veterans displayed a diverse array of psychological problems and symptoms that in many cases lingered much longer than expected. Studies suggest that nearly a half million Vietnam veterans were still suffering from PTSD over a decade after the end of the war (Schlenger et al., 1992). PTSD did not become an official psychological diagnosis until 1980, and since that time researchers have studied the disorder extensively to better understand the long-term impact of exposure to trauma (Yehuda, 2003). Currently, PTSD is being examined in military returnees from the Afghanistan and Iraq wars. Similar to Vietnam veterans, these

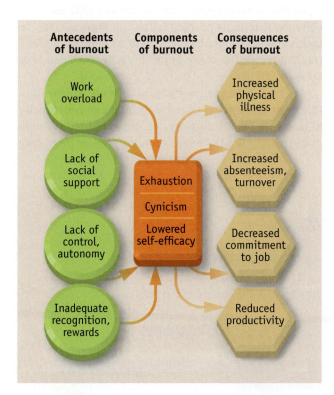

## Figure 3.15
**The antecedents, components, and consequences of burnout.** Christina Maslach and Michael Leiter have developed a systematic model of burnout that specifies its antecedents, components, and consequences. The antecedents on the left in the diagram are the stressful features of the work environment that cause burnout. The burnout syndrome itself consists of the three components shown in the center of the diagram. Some of the unfortunate results of burnout are listed on the right. (Based on Leiter & Maslach, 2007)

**WEB LINK 3.5    National Center for PTSD**

Maintained by the U.S. Department of Veterans Affairs, this site is devoted to the understanding and treatment of posttraumatic stress disorder. The site has materials for both professionals and the public and includes a wealth of new postings related to the psychological consequences of terrorism.

Major disasters, such as Hurricane Katrina, which devastated New Orleans and the Gulf Coast region, are just one of about a half-dozen types of calamitous events that can lead to posttraumatic stress disorders.

AP Images/Ben Sklar

U.S. troops are showing elevated rates of PTSD upon returning home (Friedman, 2006).

Although posttraumatic stress disorder is widely associated with the experiences of veterans, it is seen in response to other cases of traumatic stress as well, and it appears to be much more common than originally believed. Research suggests that approximately 9% of people have suffered from PTSD at some point in their lives, and it is twice as common in women as compared to men (Feeny, Stines, & Foa, 2007). PTSD is seen in children as well as adults, and children's symptoms often show up in their play or drawings (La Greca, 2007). In some instances, PTSD does not surface until many months or years after a person's exposure to severe stress (Holen, 2007).

What types of stress besides combat are severe enough to produce PTSD? The syndrome is frequently seen after a rape, a serious automobile accident, a robbery or assault, or the witnessing of someone's death (Koren, Arnon, & Klein, 1999; Stein et al., 1997b). Studies indicate that PTSD is also common in the wake of major disasters, such as floods, hurricanes, earthquakes, fires, and so forth (Koopman, Classen, & Spiegel, 1994; Vernberg et al., 1996). Unfortunately, research by Stein et al. (1997b) suggests that the various types of traumatic events that can cause PTSD are more common than most people realize (see **Figure 3.16**). In fact, experts speculate that 50% of us will encounter a traumatic event at some point in our lives (Yehuda & Wong, 2007).

Recently, some psychologists have argued that traumatic events don't need to be experienced directly to lead to PTSD. Exposure can occur indirectly, such as by witnessing the event on television or providing

**Figure 3.16**

**The prevalence of traumatic events.** We tend to think that traumatic events are relatively unusual and infrequent, but research by Stein et al. (1997b) suggests otherwise. When they interviewed over 1000 people in Winnipeg, they found that 74.2% of the women and 81.3% of the men reported having experienced at least one highly traumatic event. The percentage of respondents reporting specific types of traumatic events are summarized in this graph.

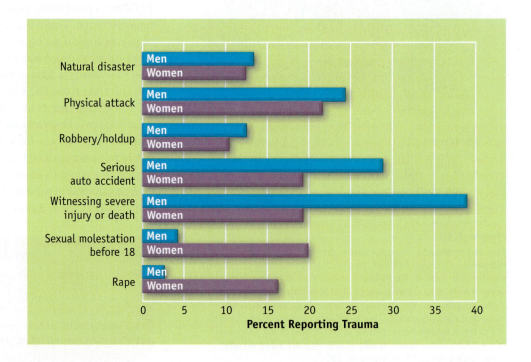

psychological services to survivors. Some recent evidence surrounding 9/11 supports this perspective (Marshall et al., 2007). For example, Zimering and colleagues (2006) found that relief workers (including social workers, psychologists, and clergy members) who were indirectly exposed to the disaster through survivors' narratives showed elevated rates of PTSD. These researchers argue that our understanding of PTSD needs to be broadened to include traumas that are not personally experienced. Other researchers take exception to this notion of "virtual PTSD," arguing that, because viewing television or counseling someone is a voluntary act under one's control, that person does not become a "victim" of the event. Therefore, the person can't develop PTSD. With regard to television viewing, perhaps those who repeatedly and purposefully expose themselves to traumatic images have pathological preoccupations that could account "for both the amount of viewing and the symptoms of distress reported" (McNally & Breslau, 2008, p. 282).

What are the symptoms of posttraumatic stress disorder? Common symptoms include reexperiencing the traumatic event in the form of nightmares and flashbacks, emotional numbing, alienation, problems in social relations, and elevated arousal, anxiety, and guilt (Flannery, 1999; Shalev, 2001). PTSD is also associated with an elevated risk for substance abuse, depression, and anxiety disorders, as well as a great variety of physical health problems (Brady, Back, & Coffey, 2004; Yehuda & Wong, 2007). The frequency and severity of posttraumatic symptoms usually decline gradually over time, but in many cases the symptoms never completely disappear. Neuroscientific evidence is mounting that PTSD is associated with alterations in the structure and function of the brain, and that these changes build up with exposure to multiple traumatic events (Kolassa & Elbert, 2007).

Although PTSD is fairly common in the wake of traumatic events, the vast majority of people who experience such events do *not* develop PTSD (Bonanno et al., 2006; Ozer & Weiss, 2004). Thus, a current focus of research is to determine what factors make certain people more (or less) susceptible than others to the ravages of severe stress (Bonanno, 2004). According to McKeever and Huff (2003), this vulnerability probably depends on complex interactions among a number of biological and environmental factors. One key predictor that emerged in a recent review of the relevant research is the *intensity of one's reaction at the time of the traumatic event* (Ozer et al., 2003). Individuals who have especially intense emotional reactions during or immediately after the traumatic event go on to show elevated vulnerability to PTSD. Vulnerability seems to be greatest among people whose reactions are so intense that they report *dissociative experiences* (such as a sense

that things are not real, that time is stretching out, or that one is watching oneself in a movie).

## Physical Illness

Stress can also have an impact on one's physical health. The idea that stress can contribute to physical ailments is not entirely new. Evidence that stress can cause physical illness began to accumulate back in the 1930s. By the 1950s, the concept of psychosomatic disease was widely accepted. ***Psychosomatic diseases* were defined as genuine physical ailments thought to be caused in part by stress and other psychological factors.** The classic psychosomatic illnesses were high blood pressure, peptic ulcers, asthma, skin disorders such as eczema and hives, and migraine and tension headaches (Kaplan, 1989; Rogers, Fricchione, & Reich, 1999). Please note, these diseases were not regarded as *imagined* physical ailments. The term *psychosomatic* has often been misused to refer to physical ailments that are "all in one's head," but that is an entirely different syndrome (see Chapter 14). Rather, psychosomatic diseases were viewed as authentic organic maladies that were heavily stress related.

Since the 1970s, the concept of psychosomatic disease has gradually fallen into disuse because research has shown that stress can contribute to the development of a diverse array of other diseases previously believed to be purely physiological in origin. Although there is room for debate on some specific diseases, stress may influence the onset and course of heart disease, stroke, gastrointestinal disorders, tuberculosis, multiple sclerosis, arthritis, diabetes, leukemia, cancer, various types of infectious disease, and probably many other types of illnesses (Brummett et al., 2004; Critelli & Ee, 1996; Dougall & Baum, 2001; Murison & Milde, 2007). Thus, it has become apparent that there is nothing unique about the psychosomatic diseases that requires a special category. Chapter 5 goes into greater detail, but suffice it to say that modern evidence continues to demonstrate that the classic psychosomatic diseases are influenced by stress, but so are numerous other diseases (Jones & Bright, 2007; Levenson et al., 1999).

Of course, stress is only one of many factors that may contribute to the development of physical illness. Some of the physical effects of stress might be

Miller (2007) points out that "recent social, political, and environmental factors have had a profound impact on the health and well-being of the global population" (p. 890). He points to wars, famine, school-based violence, climate change, and natural disasters, all recent events as well as on-going threats. Given these trends, it is obvious that "psychology has an essential role to play in this new millennium" (p. 895). In light of these unpleasant facts, what can psychological research tell us about how people respond to traumatic events? Lazarus (2007) argued that one's appraisal of stressful events exert enormous influence over one's emotional reaction to them.

There is a rich literature on reactions to traumatic events, including major disasters (such as earthquakes and floods) and personal traumas (such as automobile accidents and armed robberies). Based on this research, common reactions to such events include the following (Danieli, Engdahl, & Schlenger, 2004; Flannery, 1999; Foa et al., 2001; Wilson, Drozdek, & Turkovic, 2006):

**Fear and anxiety.** Anxiety is a normal response to threatening events. Many people find that certain cues associated with a traumatic event repeatedly trigger their anxiety.

**Reexperiencing the trauma.** Many people are troubled by unwanted thoughts of the traumatic event that they are unable to control. Some experience flashbacks in which they vividly relive the traumatic moments. Nightmares about traumatic experiences are also common.

**Increased arousal.** In the aftermath of traumatic events people tend to feel jumpy, jittery, and physically on edge. This physiological arousal may make sleep difficult.

**Avoidance.** Many people try to avoid situations or cues that remind them of their trauma. People also tend to suppress painful thoughts and feelings. This coping strategy sometimes results in feelings of emotional numbness.

**Anger and irritability.** Anger is a normal response to the perceived injustice of disastrous events. Coupled with increased arousal, this anger makes many people highly irritable. Ironically, some people get angry with themselves about their irritability.

**Grief and depression.** In the wake of traumatic events, people often experience sadness, despair, and hopelessness. Future plans that once were important seem trivial. Activities that were once enjoyable seem empty. People understandably grieve for what they have lost.

**Shame and guilt.** It is not uncommon for survivors of trauma to experience feelings of shame or guilt. This is especially likely if people feel that their behavior was somehow responsible for the traumatic event. As you might imagine, these feelings of self-blame are usually irrational.

**Increased sense of vulnerability.** Traumatic events often lead to negative changes in one's view of the world. People come to believe that the world is a dangerous place and that others cannot be trusted. One's sense of self-efficacy may be undermined by feelings of helplessness, vulnerability, and the perception that events are uncontrollable.

**Positive emotions.** Traumatic events can elicit positive emotions such as gratitude or compassion. These responses tend to be associated with posttraumatic growth (see page 93).

These reactions are normal short-term responses to traumatic events. Experiencing such reactions does not mean that you are weak or that you are "losing it." For most people these reactions usually dissipate within one to three months, although others may recover more slowly. If negative reactions such as these persist indefinitely and interfere with one's social, occupational, or family functioning, a diagnosis of *posttraumatic stress disorder* may be applicable (see page 89). If your reactions to a traumatic event are especially severe, persistent, and disabling, it may be wise to seek professional help.

---

exacerbated by the risky behaviors in which people are more likely to engage when stressed (Friedman & Silver, 2007). For example, stress appears to be related to increases in substance abuse, including problematic drinking (McCreary & Sadava, 1998; Veenstra et al., 2007), chronic marijuana use (Preston, 2006), and cigarette smoking (Wills, 1986). Obviously, these behaviors come with their own health hazards. Add stress to the

mix and one becomes even more vulnerable to disease and illness.

## Positive Effects

The effects of stress are not entirely negative. Recent years have brought increased interest in positive aspects of the stress process, including favorable outcomes that

DILBERT © Scott Adams/Dist. by United Feature Syndicate, Inc.

follow in the wake of stress (Folkman & Moskowitz, 2000). To some extent, the new focus on the possible benefits of stress reflects a new emphasis on "positive psychology." Some influential theorists have argued that the field of psychology has historically devoted too much attention to pathology, weakness, and damage and how to heal suffering (Seligman, 2003). This approach has yielded valuable insights and progress, but it has also resulted in an unfortunate neglect of the forces that make life worth living. The positive psychology movement seeks to shift the field's focus away from negative experiences. This movement is so relevant that we devote all of Chapter 16 to it. For now, know that advocates of positive psychology argue for increased research on well-being, contentment, hope, courage, perseverance, nurturance, tolerance, and other human strengths and virtues (Aspinwall & Staudinger, 2003; Peterson & Seligman, 2004). One of these strengths is resilience in the face of stress. The beneficial effects of stress may prove more difficult to pinpoint than the harmful effects because they may be more subtle. However, there appear to be at least three ways in which stress can have positive effects.

First, stress can promote positive psychological change, or what Tedeschi and Calhoun (1996) call *post-traumatic growth*. Experiences of posttraumatic growth are now well documented, and it appears that this phenomenon is evident in people facing a variety of stressful circumstances, including bereavement, cancer, sexual assault, and combat (Tedeschi & Calhoun, 2004). Stressful events sometimes force people to develop new skills, reevaluate priorities, learn new insights, and acquire new strengths. In other words, the adaptation process initiated by stress may lead to personal changes for

the better. For example, a breakup with a boyfriend or a girlfriend may lead individuals to change aspects of their behavior that they find unsatisfactory. Helgeson, Reynolds, and Tomich (2006) found that experiences of posttraumatic growth are related to lower levels of depression and enhanced well-being. Ironically, these experiences are also related to increased intrusive thoughts about the stressful event. They note that these thoughts do not necessarily indicate distress. It could be that people are cognitively working through the stressful event and that it is in this process that the growth happens.

Second, stressful events help satisfy the need for stimulation and challenge. Studies suggest that most people prefer an intermediate level of stimulation and challenge in their lives (Sutherland, 2000). Although we think of stress in terms of stimulus overload, underload can be stressful as well (Goldberger, 1993). Thus, most people would experience a suffocating level of boredom if they lived a stress-free existence. In a sense, then, stress fulfills a basic need of the human organism.

Third, today's stress can inoculate and psychologically prepare individuals so that they are less affected by tomorrow's stress. Some studies suggest that exposure to stress can increase stress tolerance—as long as the stress isn't overwhelming (Meichenbaum, 1993). Further, by dealing with a stressful event people will be better prepared for subsequent stress (Janoff-Bulman, 2004). Thus, a woman who has previously endured business setbacks may be much better prepared than most people to deal with a bank foreclosure on her home. In light of the negative effects that stress can have, improved stress tolerance is a desirable goal. We'll look next at the factors that influence the ability to tolerate stress.

# Factors Influencing Stress Tolerance

### LEARNING OBJECTIVES

- Explain how social support moderates the impact of stress.
- Describe hardiness and how it influences stress tolerance.
- Clarify how optimism is related to stress tolerance.
- Describe the potential problem of unrealistic optimism.

Some people seem to be able to withstand the ravages of stress better than others (Holahan & Moos, 1990, 1994). Why? Because a number of *moderator variables* can soften the impact of stress on physical and mental health. To shed light on differences in how well people tolerate stress, we'll look at a number of key moderator variables, including social support, hardiness, and optimism. As you'll see, these factors influence people's emotional, physical, and behavioral responses to stress. These complexities are diagrammed in **Figure 3.17**, which builds on **Figure 3.7** to provide a more complete

overview of the factors involved in individual reactions to stress.

## Social Support

Friends may be good for your health! This startling conclusion emerges from studies on social support as a moderator of stress. *Social support* refers to various types of aid and succor provided by members of one's social networks. Over the last two decades, a vast body of literature has found evidence that social

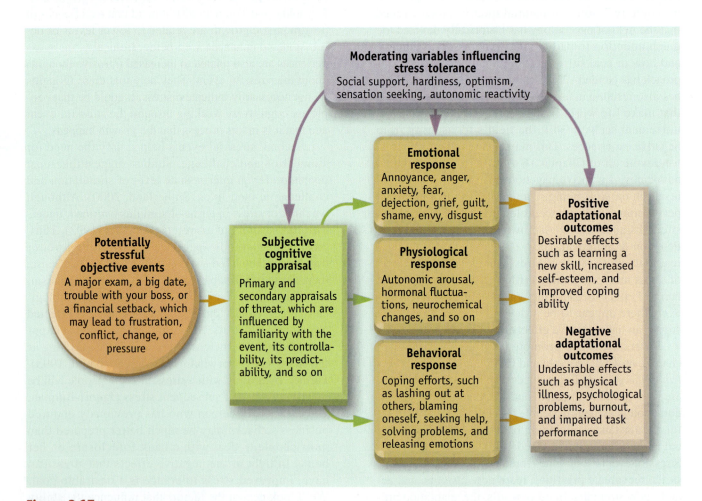

**Figure 3.17**

**Overview of the stress process.** This diagram builds on **Figure 3.7** (the multidimensional response to stress) to provide a more complete overview of the factors involved in stress. This diagram adds the potential effects of stress (seen on the far right) by listing some of the positive and negative adaptational outcomes that may result from stress. It also completes the picture by showing moderating variables (seen at the top) that can influence the effects of stress (including some variables not covered in the chapter).

The availability of social support is a key factor influencing stress tolerance. Decades of research have shown that social support reduces the negative effects of stress and has positive effects of its own.

support is favorably related to physical health (Taylor, 2007; Wills & Fegan, 2001). For example, Jemmott and Magloire (1988) examined the effect of social support on immune response in a group of students going through the stress of final exams. They found that students who reported stronger social support had higher levels of an antibody that plays a key role in warding off respiratory infections. Positive correlations between high social support and greater immune functioning have been observed in quite a number of studies with diverse samples (Kennedy, 2007; Uchino, Cacioppo, & Kiecolt-Glaser, 1996).

Social support seems to be good medicine for the mind as well as the body, as most studies also find an association between social support and mental health (Davis, Morris, & Kraus, 1998; Sarason, Pierce, & Sarason, 1994). It appears that social support serves as a protective buffer during times of high stress, reducing the negative impact of stressful events—and that social support has its own positive effects on health, which may be apparent even when people aren't under great stress (Peirce et al., 1996; Wills & Fegan, 2001). In the

workplace, social support has been shown to reduce the prevalence of burnout (Greenglass, 2007). With regard to more severe stress, social support appears to be a key factor in reducing the likelihood of PTSD among Vietnam veterans (King et al., 1998) and increasing the likelihood of posttraumatic growth (Prati & Pietrantoni, 2009).

The mechanisms underlying the connection between social support and wellness have been the subject of considerable debate (Hobfoll & Vaux, 1993). A variety of mechanisms may be at work. Among other things, social support could promote wellness by making appraisals of stressful events more benign, dampening the intensity of physiological reactions to stress, reducing health-impairing behaviors such as smoking and drinking, encouraging preventive behaviors such as regular exercise and medical checkups, and fostering more constructive coping efforts (Taylor, 2007; Wills & Fegan, 2001).

Recent studies suggest that *providing* social support to others can also have both psychological benefits (less depression and perceived stress) and physical benefits (lower blood pressure) (Brown et al., 2003; Piferi & Lawler, 2006). Another study found that the personality trait of sociability (being friendly and agreeable), which certainly helps people build supportive social networks, is independently associated with reduced susceptibility to infectious disease (Cohen et al., 2003). Yet another study has demonstrated that many pet owners view their pets as sources of support in their lives, with resultant health benefits (Allen, Blascovich, & Mendes, 2002). Thus, it appears that there are many aspects of social support that have some bearing on individuals' wellness.

Although the benefits outweigh the costs, social support networks have their drawbacks. It is only recently that researchers have begun to examine some of the negative aspects of social support (conflict, role strain, additional responsibilities, dependency), a research area that bears watching in the near future (Antonucci, Lansford, & Ajrouch, 2007).

## Hardiness

Another line of research indicates that an attribute called *hardiness* may moderate the impact of stressful events. Suzanne (Kobasa) Ouellette reasoned that if stress affects some people less than others, some people must be *hardier* than others. Hence, she set out to determine what factors might be the key to these differences in hardiness.

Kobasa (1979) used a modified version of the Holmes and Rahe (1967) stress scale (SRRS) to measure the amount of stress experienced by a group of executives. As in most

**Suzanne Ouellette**

other studies, she found a modest correlation between stress and the incidence of physical illness. However, she carried her investigation one step further than previous studies. She compared the high-stress executives who exhibited the expected high incidence of illness against the high-stress executives who stayed healthy. She administered a battery of psychological tests and found that the hardier executives "were more committed, felt more in control, and had bigger appetites for challenge" (Kobasa, 1984, p. 70). These traits have also shown up in many other studies of hardiness (Maddi, 2002, 2006, 2007; Ouellette, 1993).

Thus, *hardiness* **is a disposition marked by commitment, challenge, and control that is purportedly associated with strong stress resistance.** Hardiness may reduce the effects of stress by altering stress appraisals or fostering more active coping (Crowley, Hayslip, & Hobdy, 2003; Maddi, 2006, 2007; Maddi & Hightower, 1999). The benefits of hardiness showed up in a study of Vietnam veterans, which found that higher hardiness was related to a lower likelihood of developing posttraumatic stress disorders (King et al., 1998). In fact, research shows that hardiness is a good predictor of success in high stress occupations such as the military (Bartone et al., 2008). Fortunately, it appears that hardiness can be learned, and it often comes from strong social support and encouragement from those around us (Maddi, 2007). Although the research on hardiness is promising, debate continues about how to measure hardiness and about its key elements (Klag & Bradley, 2004; Oullette & DiPlacido, 2001; Younkin & Betz, 1996).

## Optimism

Everyone knows someone whose glass is always half full, who sees the world through rose-colored glasses, who is an optimist. *Optimism* **is a general tendency to expect good outcomes.** Pioneering research in this area by Michael Scheier and Charles Carver (1985) found a correlation between optimism as measured by the Life Orientation Test (see **Figure 3.18**) and relatively good physical health in a sample of college students. In studies that focused on surgical patients, optimism was found to be associated with a faster recovery and better postsurgery adjustment (Scheier et al., 1989; Shelby et al., 2008). Additionally, optimism is associated with more effective immune functioning (Segerstrom et al., 1998, 2007). More recently, optimism was inversely related to PTSD symptoms for college students who knew a victim of the 9/11 terrorist attacks (Ai, Santangelo, & Cascio, 2006). Over 20 years of research has consistently shown that optimism is associated with better mental and physical health (Carver & Scheier, 2005; Scheier & Carver, 2007; Scheier, Carver, & Bridges, 2001).

### Measuring Optimism

In the following spaces, mark how much you agree with each of the items, using the following scale:

**4** = strongly agree
**3** = agree
**2** = neutral
**1** = disagree
**0** = strongly disagree

_____ **1.** In uncertain times, I usually expect the best.

_____ **2.** It's easy for me to relax.

_____ **3.** If something can go wrong for me, it will.

_____ **4.** I always look on the bright side of things.

_____ **5.** I'm always optimistic about my future.

_____ **6.** I enjoy my friends a lot.

_____ **7.** It's important for me to keep busy.

_____ **8.** I hardly ever expect things to go my way.

_____ **9.** Things never work out the way I want them to.

_____ **10.** I don't get upset too easily.

_____ **11.** I'm a believer in the idea that "every cloud has a silver lining."

_____ **12.** I rarely count on good things happening to me.

**Scoring**

Cross out and ignore the responses you entered for items 2, 6, 7, and 10, which are "filler" items. For items 3, 8, 9, and 12, you need to reverse the numbers you entered. If you entered a 4, change it to 0. If you entered a 3, change it to 1. If you entered a 2, leave it unchanged. If you entered a 1, change it to 3. If you entered a 0, change it to 4. Now add up the numbers for items 1, 3, 4, 5, 8, 9, 11, 12, using the new numbers for the reversed items. This sum is your score on the Life Orientation Test. For college students, approximate norms are as follows: High score (25–32), intermediate score (18–24), low score (0–17).

**Figure 3.18**

**The Life Orientation Test (LOT).** The personality trait of optimism, which appears to foster resilience in the face of stress, can be measured by the Life Orientation Test (LOT) developed by Scheier and Carver (1985). Follow the instructions for this scale to obtain an estimate of your own optimism. High and low scores are based on scoring three-fifths of a standard deviation above or below the mean.

Source: Adapted from Scheier, M. F., & Carver, C. S. (1985). Optimism, coping, and health: Assessment and implications of generalized outcome expectancies. *Health Psychology, 4,* 219–247. Copyright 1985 by Informa Medical and Pharmaceutical Science - Journals. Reproduced with permission of Informa Medical and Pharmaceutical Science - Journals in the formats textbook and extranet posting via Copyright Clearance Center.

In a related line of research, Christopher Peterson and Martin Seligman have studied how people explain bad events (personal setbacks, mishaps, disappointments, and such). These researchers identified a *pessimistic explanatory style,* in which people tend to blame setbacks on their own personal shortcomings, versus an *optimistic explanatory style,* which leads people to attribute setbacks to temporary situational factors. In two retrospective studies of people born many decades ago, they found an association between this optimistic explanatory style and relatively good health (Peterson,

Seligman, & Vaillant, 1988; Sepahvand, Guilani, & Zamani, 2007) and increased longevity (Peterson et al., 1998). Many other studies have linked the optimistic explanatory style to superior physical health (Peterson & Bossio, 2001), as well as higher academic achievement, increased job productivity, enhanced athletic performance, and higher marital satisfaction (Gillham et al., 2001) (see Chapter 6 for more on the ramifications of an optimistic versus pessimistic explanatory style).

Why does optimism promote a variety of desirable outcomes? Above all else, research suggests that optimists cope with stress in more adaptive ways than pessimists (Aspinwall, Richter, & Hoffman, 2001; Carver & Scheier, 2002; Chang, 1996). Optimists are more likely to engage in action-oriented, problem-focused, carefully planned coping and are more willing than pessimists to seek social support. Optimism is also related to constructs of hardiness and posttraumatic growth (Prati & Pietrantoni, 2009; Wise & Rosqvist, 2006). By comparison, pessimists are more likely to deal with stress by avoiding it, giving up, or engaging in denial. In a recent study of college students, a pessimistic explanatory style

was linked to more thoughts of suicide following a traumatic event (Hirsch et al., 2009). We will be discussing specific types of coping styles in the next chapter.

Even with all these benefits, psychologists are currently debating whether or not optimism is always beneficial (Armor, Massey, & Sackett, 2008; Carver & Scheier, 2005). What about times when a rosy outlook is inaccurate and unrealistic? Does it really benefit an employee to be optimistic about that promotion if there isn't much chance she'll get it? Additionally, being optimistic can lead to risky behaviors if one holds an "it-can't-happen-to-me" attitude. Research has demonstrated that women with an optimistic bias toward their risk for breast cancer are less likely to go in for screening (Clarke at al., 2000). And optimistic smokers are more likely to endorse myths such as "all lung cancer is cured" and "there is no risk of lung cancer if you only smoke for a few years" (Dillard et al., 2006). Gillham and Reivich (2007) argue that, when it comes to optimism, what is most adaptive is some sort of middle ground where one displays "optimism that is closely tied to the strength of wisdom" (p. 320).

## APPLICATION

# Reducing Stress Through Self-Control

### LEARNING OBJECTIVES

- Explain why traits cannot be target behaviors in self-modification programs.
- Identify the three kinds of information you should pursue in gathering your baseline data.
- Discuss how to use reinforcement to increase the strength of a response.

- Explain how to use reinforcement, control of antecedents, and punishment to decrease the strength of a response.
- Analyze issues related to fine-tuning and ending a self-modification program.

*Answer the following "yes" or "no."*

___ **1.** Do you have a hard time passing up food, even when you're not hungry?

___ **2.** Do you wish you studied more often?

___ **3.** Would you like to cut down on your smoking or drinking?

___ **4.** Do you experience difficulty in getting yourself to exercise regularly?

___ **5.** Do you wish you had more willpower?

It is clear that a sense of control is important to one's appraisal and experience of stress (Steptoe, 2007). As you have learned, control is one of the major components of hardiness (Maddi, 2007). If you answered "yes" to any of the questions above, you have struggled with the challenge of self-control. This Application discusses how you can use the techniques of behavior modification to improve your self-control. If you stop to think

about it, self-control—or rather a lack of it—underlies many of the stressors that people struggle with in everyday life.

***Behavior modification* is a systematic approach to changing behavior through the application of the principles of conditioning.** Advocates of behavior modification assume that behavior is a product of learning, conditioning, and environmental control. They further assume that *what is learned can be unlearned*. Thus, they set out to "recondition" people to produce more desirable patterns of behavior. The technology of behavior modification has been applied with great success in schools, businesses, hospitals, factories, child-care facilities, prisons, and mental health centers (Goodall, 1972; Kazdin, 1982, 2001; Rachman, 1992). Behavior modification techniques have been used to treat a variety of issues including attention disorders (Pelham, 2001) and childhood obesity (Berry et al., 2004).

Smoking is just one of the many types of maladaptive habits that can be reduced or eliminated through self-modification techniques.

Think back to the sources of stress. Many of these sources can be reduced through self-control. For instance, one can start exercising to reduce the frustration of poor fitness, or stop procrastinating to reduce pressure in a course. Behavior modification techniques have proven particularly valuable in efforts to improve self-control. Our discussion will borrow liberally from an excellent book on self-modification by David Watson and Roland Tharp (2007). We will discuss five steps in the process of self-modification, which are outlined in **Figure 3.19**.

## Specifying Your Target Behavior

The first step in a self-modification program is to specify the target behavior(s) that you want to change. Behavior modification can only be applied to a clearly defined response, yet many people have difficulty pinpointing the behavior they hope to alter. They tend to describe their problems in terms of unobservable personality *traits* rather than overt behaviors. For example, asked what behavior he would like to change, a man might say, "I'm too irritable." That may be true, but it is of little help in designing a self-modification program. To identify target responses, you need to think about past behavior or closely observe future behavior and list specific *examples* of responses that lead to the trait description. For instance, the man who regards himself as "too irritable" might identify two overly frequent responses, such as arguing with his wife and snapping at his children. These are specific behaviors for which he could design a self-modification program.

## Gathering Baseline Data

The second step in behavior modification is to gather baseline data. You need to systematically observe your target behavior for a period of time (usually a week or two) be-

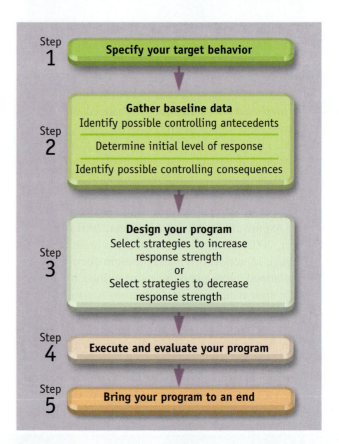

**Figure 3.19**

**Steps in a self-modification program.** This flowchart provides an overview of the steps necessary to execute a self-modification program.

fore you work out the details of your program. In gathering your baseline data, you need to monitor three things.

First, you need to determine the initial response level of your target behavior. After all, you can't tell whether your program is working effectively unless you have a baseline for comparison. In most cases, you would simply keep track of how often the target response occurs in a certain time interval. Thus, you might count the daily frequency of snapping at your children, smoking cigarettes, or biting your fingernails. If studying is your target behavior, you will probably monitor hours of study. If you want to modify your eating, you will probably keep track of how many calories you consume. Whatever the unit of measurement, *it is crucial to gather accurate data*. You should keep permanent written records, preferably in the form of some type of chart or graph (see **Figure 3.20**).

Second, you need to monitor the antecedents of your target behavior. **Antecedents are events that typically precede the target response.** Often these events play a major role in evoking your target behavior. For example, if your target is overeating, you might discover that the bulk of your overeating occurs late in the evening while you watch TV. If you can pinpoint this kind of antecedent-response connection, you may be able to design your program to circumvent or break the link.

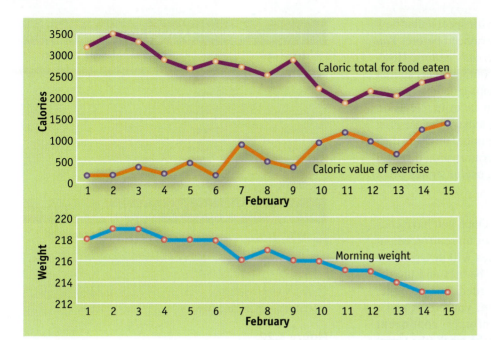

**Figure 3.20**

**Example of record keeping in a self-modification program for losing weight.** Graphic records are ideal for tracking progress in behavior modification efforts.

Third, you need to monitor the typical consequences of your target behavior. Try to identify the reinforcers that are maintaining an undesirable target behavior or the unfavorable outcomes that are suppressing a desirable target behavior. In trying to identify reinforcers, remember that avoidance behavior is usually maintained by negative reinforcement (see Chapter 2). That is, the payoff for avoidance is usually the removal of something aversive, such as anxiety or a threat to self-esteem. You should also take into account the fact that a response may not be reinforced every time, as most behavior is maintained by intermittent reinforcement.

## Designing Your Program

Once you have selected a target behavior and gathered adequate baseline data, it is time to plan your intervention program. Generally speaking, your program will be designed either to increase or to decrease the frequency of a target response.

### Increasing Response Strength

Efforts to increase the frequency of a target response depend largely on the use of positive reinforcement. In other words, you reward yourself for behaving properly. Although the basic strategy is quite simple, doing it skillfully involves a number of considerations.

**Selecting a reinforcer.**  To use positive reinforcement, you need to find a reward that will be effective for you. Reinforcement is subjective—what is reinforcing for one person may not be reinforcing for another. **Figure 3.21** lists questions you can ask yourself to help you determine your personal reinforcers. Be sure to be realistic and choose a reinforcer that is really available to you.

### What Are Your Reinforcers?

1. What will be the rewards of achieving your goal?
2. What kind of praise do you like to receive, from yourself and others?
3. What kinds of things do you like to have?
4. What are your major interests?
5. What are your hobbies?
6. What people do you like to be with?
7. What do you like to do with those people?
8. What do you do for fun?
9. What do you do to relax?
10. What do you do to get away from it all?
11. What makes you feel good?
12. What would be a nice present to receive?
13. What kinds of things are important to you?
14. What would you buy if you had an extra $20? $50? $100?
15. On what do you spend your money each week?
16. What behaviors do you perform every day? (Don't overlook the obvious or commonplace.)
17. Are there any behaviors you usually perform instead of the target behavior?
18. What would you hate to lose?
19. Of the things you do every day, which would you hate to give up?
20. What are your favorite daydreams and fantasies?
21. What are the most relaxing scenes you can imagine?

**Figure 3.21**

**Selecting a reinforcer.** The questions listed here may help you to identify your personal reinforcers.

Source: From Watson, D. L., & Tharp, R. G. (1993). *Self-directed behavior: Self-modification for personal adjustment* (4th ed., pp. 213–214). Pacific Grove, CA: Brooks/Cole. Copyright © 1972, 1977, 1981, 1985, 1993 by Brooks/Cole Publishing Company.

You don't have to come up with spectacular new reinforcers that you've never experienced before. *You can use reinforcers that you are already getting.* However, you have to restructure the contingencies so that you get them only if you behave appropriately. For example, if you normally watch your favorite television show on Thursday nights, you might make this viewing contingent on studying a certain number of hours during the week. Making yourself earn rewards that you used to take for granted is often a useful strategy in a self-modification program.

**Arranging the contingencies.**   Once you have chosen your reinforcer, you have to set up reinforcement contingencies. These contingencies will describe the exact behavioral goals that must be met and the reinforcement that may then be awarded. For example, in a program to increase exercise, you might make spending $40 on clothes (the reinforcer) contingent on having jogged 15 miles during the week (the target behavior).

Try to set behavioral goals that are both challenging and realistic. You want your goals to be challenging so that they lead to improvement in your behavior. However, setting unrealistically high goals—a common mistake in self-modification—often leads to unnecessary discouragement.

You also need to be concerned about doling out too much reinforcement. If reinforcement is too easy to get, you may become *satiated*, and the reinforcer may lose its motivational power. One way to avoid the satiation problem is to put yourself on a token economy. A *token economy* **is a system for doling out symbolic reinforcers that are exchanged later for a variety of genuine reinforcers.** Thus, you might develop a point system for exercise behavior, accumulating points that can be spent on clothes, movies, restaurant meals, and so forth. You can also use a token economy to reinforce a variety of related target behaviors, as opposed to a single, specific response. The token economy in **Figure 3.22**, for instance, is set up to strengthen three different, though related, responses (jogging, tennis, and sit-ups).

**Shaping.**   In some cases, you may want to reinforce a target response that you are not currently capable of making, such as speaking in front of a large group or jogging ten miles a day. This situation calls for *shaping,* **which is accomplished by reinforcing closer and closer approximations of the desired response.** Thus, you might start jogging two miles a day and add a half-mile each week until you reach your goal. In shaping your behavior, you should set up a schedule spelling out how and when your target behaviors and reinforcement contingencies should change. Generally, it is a good idea to move forward gradually.

| Responses Earning Tokens | | |
| --- | --- | --- |
| **Response** | **Amount** | **Number of Tokens** |
| Jogging | 1/2 mile | 4 |
| Jogging | 1 mile | 8 |
| Jogging | 2 miles | 16 |
| Tennis | 1 hour | 4 |
| Tennis | 2 hours | 8 |
| Sit-ups | 25 | 1 |
| Sit-ups | 50 | 2 |

| Redemption Value of Tokens | |
| --- | --- |
| **Reinforcer** | **Tokens required** |
| Purchase one compact disc of your choice | 30 |
| Go to movie | 50 |
| Go to nice restaurant | 100 |
| Take special weekend trip | 500 |

**Figure 3.22**
**Example of a token economy to reinforce exercise.** This token economy was set up to strengthen three types of exercise behavior. The person can exchange tokens for four types of reinforcers.

## Decreasing Response Strength

Let's turn now to the challenge of reducing the frequency of an undesirable response. You can go about this task in a number of ways. Your principal options are reinforcement, control of antecedents, and punishment.

**Reinforcement.**   Reinforcers can be used in an indirect way to decrease the frequency of a response. This may sound paradoxical, since you have learned that reinforcement strengthens a response. The trick lies in how you define the target behavior. For example, in the case of overeating you might define your target behavior as eating more than 1600 calories a day (a response that you want to decrease) or, alternatively as eating less than 1600 calories a day (a response that you want to increase). If you choose the latter definition, you can reinforce yourself whenever you eat less than 1600 calories in a day which ultimately decreases your overeating.

**Control of antecedents.**   A worthwhile strategy for decreasing the occurrence of an undesirable response may be to identify its antecedents and avoid exposure to them. This strategy is especially useful when you are trying to decrease the frequency of a consummatory response, such as smoking or eating. In the case of overeating, for instance, the easiest way to resist temptation is to avoid having to face it. Thus, you might stay away from enticing restaurants, minimize time spent in your kitchen, shop for groceries just after eating (when willpower is higher), and avoid purchasing favorite foods.

**Punishment.** The strategy of decreasing unwanted behavior by punishing yourself for that behavior is an obvious option that people tend to overuse. The biggest problem with punishment in a self-modification effort is the difficulty in following through and punishing oneself. If you're going to use punishment, keep two guidelines in mind. First, do not use punishment alone. Use it in conjunction with positive reinforcement. If you set up a program in which you can earn only negative consequences, you probably won't stick to it. Second, use a relatively mild punishment so that you will actually be able to administer it to yourself. Nurnberger and Zimmerman (1970) developed a creative method of self-punishment. They had subjects write out a check to an organization they hated (for instance, the campaign of a political candidate whom they despised). The check was held by a third party who mailed it if subjects failed to meet their behavioral goals. Such a punishment is relatively harmless, but it can serve as a strong source of motivation.

## Executing and Evaluating Your Program

Once you have designed your program, the next step is to put it to work by enforcing the contingencies that you have carefully planned. During this period, you need to continue to accurately record the frequency of your target behavior so you can evaluate your progress. The success of your program depends on your not "cheating." The most common form of cheating is to reward yourself when you have not actually earned it.

You can do two things to increase the likelihood that you will comply with your program. One is to make up a *behavioral contract*—**a written agreement outlining a promise to adhere to the contingencies of a behavior modification program** (see **Figure 3.23**). The formality of signing such a contract in front of friends or family seems to make many people take their program more seriously. You can further reduce the likelihood of cheating by having someone other than yourself dole out the reinforcers and punishments.

Behavior modification programs often require some fine-tuning. So don't be surprised if you need to make a few adjustments. Several flaws are especially common in designing self-modification programs. Among those that you should look out for are (1) depending on a weak reinforcer, (2) permitting lengthy delays between appropriate behavior and delivery of reinforcers, and (3) trying to do too much too quickly by setting unrealistic goals. Often, a small revision or two can turn a failing program around and make it a success.

## Ending Your Program

Ending you program involves setting terminal goals such as reaching a certain weight, studying with a certain regularity, or going without cigarettes for a certain length of time. Often, it is a good idea to phase out your program by planning a gradual reduction in the frequency or potency of your reinforcement for appropriate behavior.

If your program is successful, it may fade away without a conscious decision on your part. Often, new, improved patterns of behavior such as eating right, exercising, or studying diligently become self-maintaining. Whether you end your program intentionally or not, you should always be prepared to reinstitute the program if you find yourself slipping back to your old patterns of behavior. Ironically, it can be the very stress we are trying to reduce that drives use back into old, unhealthy habits.

---

I, _____, do hereby agree to initiate my self-change strategy as of (date) _____ and to continue it for a minimum period of _____ weeks—that is, until (date) _____.

My specific self-change strategy is to _____
_____
_____

I will do my best to execute this strategy to my utmost ability and to evaluate its effectiveness only after it has been honestly tried for the specified period of time.

Optional Self-Reward Clause: For every _____ day(s) that I successfully comply with my self-change contract, I will reward myself with _____
_____

In addition, at the end of my minimum period of personal experimentation, I will reward myself for having persisted in my self-change efforts. My reward at that time will be _____
_____

I hereby request that the witnesses who have signed below support me in my self-change efforts and encourage my compliance with the specifics of this contract. Their cooperation and encouragement throughout the project will be appreciated.

Signed _____

Date _____

Witness: _____

Witness: _____

**Figure 3.23**
**A behavioral contract.** Behavior modification experts recommend the use of a formal, written contract similar to that shown here to increase commitment to one's self-modification program.

### The Nature of Stress

● Stress involves transactions with the environment that are perceived to be threatening. Stress is a common, everyday event, and even routine hassles can be problematic. To a large degree, stress lies in the eye of the beholder. According to Lazarus and Folkman, primary appraisal determines whether events appear threatening, while secondary appraisal assesses whether one has the resources to cope with challenges. How one appraises an event can alter the impact of the event.

● Some of the stress that people experience comes from their environment. Examples of environmental stimuli that can be stressful include excessive noise, crowding, urban decay, and community violence. Stress can vary with culture. Within Western culture, ethnicity and discrimination can be a source of stress in a variety of ways.

### Major Sources of Stress

● Stress can be acute, chronic, or anticipatory. Major sources of stress include frustration, internal conflict, change, and pressure. Frustration occurs when an obstacle prevents one from attaining some goal. There are three principal types of conflict: approach-approach, avoidance-avoidance, and approach-avoidance.

● A large number of studies with the SRRS suggest that change is stressful. Although that may be true, it is now clear that the SRRS is a measure of general stress rather than just change-related stress. Pressure (to perform and to conform) also appears to be stressful. Often this pressure is self-imposed.

### Responding to Stress

● Emotional reactions to stress typically involve anger, fear, or sadness. However, people also experience positive emotions while under stress and these positive emotions may promote resilience. Emotional arousal may interfere with coping. As tasks get more complex, the optimal level of arousal declines.

● Physiological arousal in response to stress was originally called the fight-or-flight response by Cannon. Taylor has proposed an alternative response ("tend and befriend") that might be more applicable to females. Selye's general adaptation syndrome describes three stages in the physiological reaction to stress: alarm, resistance, and exhaustion. Diseases of adaptation may appear during the stage of exhaustion.

● In response to stress, the brain sends signals along two major pathways to the endocrine system. Actions along these paths release two sets of hormones into the bloodstream, catecholamines and corticosteroids. Stress can also lead to suppression of the immune response.

● Behavioral responses to stress involve coping, which may be healthy or maladaptive. If people cope effectively with stress, they can short-circuit potentially harmful emotional and physical responses.

### The Potential Effects of Stress

● Common negative effects of stress include impaired task performance, disruption of attention and other cognitive processes, and pervasive emotional exhaustion known as burnout. Other effects include a host of everyday psychological problems, full-fledged psychological disorders including posttraumatic stress disorder, and varied types of physical illnesses.

● However, stress can also have positive effects. Stress fulfills a basic human need for challenge and can lead to personal growth and self-improvement. Stress can also have an inoculation effect, preparing us for the next stressful event.

### Factors Influencing Stress Tolerance

● People differ in how much stress they can tolerate without experiencing ill effects. A person's social support can be a key consideration in buffering the effects of stress. The personality factors associated with hardiness—commitment, challenge, and control—may increase stress tolerance. People high in optimism also have advantages in coping with stress, although unrealistic optimism can be problematic.

### Application: Reducing Stress Through Self-Control

● In behavior modification, the principles of learning are used to change behavior directly. Behavior modification techniques can be used to increase one's self-control. The first step in self-modification is to specify the overt target behavior to be increased or decreased.

● The second step is to gather baseline data about the initial rate of the target response and identify any typical antecedents and consequences associated with the behavior. The third step is to design a program. If you are trying to increase the strength of a response, you'll depend on positive reinforcement. A number of strategies can be used to decrease the strength of a response, including reinforcement, control of antecedents, and punishment.

● The fourth step is to execute and evaluate the program. Self-modification programs often require some fine-tuning. The final step is to determine how and when you will phase out your program.

Acculturation   p. 74
Acute stressors   p. 75
Ambient stress   p. 73
Antecedents   p. 98
Anticipatory stressors   p. 75
Approach-approach conflict   p. 76
Approach-avoidance conflict   p. 76
Autonomic nervous system (ANS)   p. 83
Avoidance-avoidance conflict   p. 76
Behavioral contract   p. 101
Behavior modification   p. 97
Burnout   p. 88
Chronic stressors   p. 75
Coping   p. 87
Emotions   p. 80
Endocrine system   p. 85
Fight-or-flight response   p. 83
Frustration   p. 75
General adaptation syndrome   p. 85
Hardiness   p. 96
Internal conflict   p. 76
Life changes   p. 77
Optimism   p. 96
Posttraumatic stress disorder (PTSD)   p. 89
Pressure   p. 78
Primary appraisal   p. 72
Psychosomatic diseases   p. 91
Secondary appraisal   p. 72
Shaping   p. 100
Social support   p. 94
Stress   p. 71
Token economy   p. 100

Susan Folkman   p. 81
Thomas Holmes and Richard Rahe   p. 77
Suzanne (Kobasa) Ouellette   pp. 95–96
Richard Lazarus   p. 72
Neal Miller   p. 76
Robert Sapolsky   p. 75
Hans Selye   pp. 84–85
Shelley Taylor   pp. 83–84

## QUESTIONS

1. Secondary appraisal refers to:
   a. second thoughts about what to do in a stressful situation.
   b. second thoughts about whether an event is genuinely threatening.
   c. initial evaluation of an event's relevance, threat, and stressfulness.
   d. evaluation of coping resources and options for dealing with a stressful event.

2. Don just completed writing a 10-page report. When he went to save it, the computer crashed and he lost all his work. What type of stress is Don experiencing?
   a. frustration
   b. conflict
   c. life change
   d. pressure

3. Betty is having a hard time deciding whether she should buy a coat. On the one hand, it is a name brand coat on sale for a great price. On the other hand, it is an ugly mold-green color. Betty is experiencing what type of conflict?
   a. approach-approach
   b. avoidance-avoidance
   c. approach-avoidance
   d. life change

4. The optimal level of arousal for a task appears to depend in part on:
   a. one's position on the optimism/pessimism scale.
   b. how much physiological change an event stimulates.
   c. the complexity of the task at hand.
   d. how imminent a stressful event is.

5. The fight-or-flight response is mediated by the:
   a. sympathetic division of the autonomic nervous system.
   b. sympathetic division of the endocrine system.
   c. visceral division of the peripheral nervous system.
   d. parasympathetic division of the autonomic nervous system.

6. Selye exposed lab animals to various stressors and found that:
   a. each type of stress caused a particular physiological response.
   b. each type of animal responded to stress differently.
   c. patterns of physiological arousal were similar, regardless of the type of stress.
   d. patterns of physiological arousal were different, even when stressors were similar.

7. Salvador works as an art director at an advertising agency. His boss overloads him with responsibility but never gives him any credit for all his hard work. He feels worn down, disillusioned, and helpless at work. Salvador is probably experiencing:
   a. an alarm reaction.
   b. burnout.
   c. posttraumatic stress disorder.
   d. a psychosomatic disorder.

8. Stress can _____ the functioning of the immune system.
   a. stimulate
   b. destroy
   c. suppress
   d. enhance

9. Joan has a personal disposition marked by commitment, challenge, and control. She appears to be stress tolerant. This disposition is referred to as:
   a. hardiness.
   b. optimism.
   c. courage.
   d. conscientiousness.

10. A system providing for symbolic reinforcers is called a(n):
    a. extinction system.
    b. token economy.
    c. endocrine system.
    d. symbolic reinforcement system.

## ANSWERS

1. d  Page 72
2. a  Page 75
3. c  Page 76
4. c  Pages 82–83
5. a  Pages 83–84
6. c  Pages 84–85
7. b  Pages 88–89
8. c  Page 86
9. a  Pages 95–96
10. b  Page 100

## Personal Explorations Workbook

Go to the *Personal Explorations Workbook* in the back of your textbook for exercises that can enhance your self-understanding in relation to issues raised in this chapter. **Exercise 3.1** *Self-Assessment: The Life Experience Survey (LES).* **Exercise 3.2** *Self-Reflection: Stress—How Do You Control It?*

CourseMate

Access an interactive eBook, chapter-specific interactive learning tools, including Personal Explorations, Recommended Readings, Critical Thinking Exercises, flashcards, quizzes, videos and more in your Psychology CourseMate, available at **www.cengagebrain.com/shop/ISBN/1111186634**.

© Martin Ruegner/Getty Images/Photographer's Choice

# CHAPTER 4

# Coping Processes

*"I have begun to believe that I have intellectually and emotionally outgrown my husband. However, I'm not really sure what this means or what I should do. Maybe this feeling is normal and I should ignore it and continue my present relationship. This seems to be the safest route. Maybe I should seek a lover while continuing with my husband. Then again, maybe I should start anew and hope for a beautiful ending with or without a better mate."*

The woman quoted above is in the throes of a thorny conflict. Although it is hard to tell just how much emotional turmoil she is experiencing, it's clear that she is under substantial stress. What should she do? Is it psychologically healthy to remain in an emotionally hollow marriage? Is seeking a secret lover a reasonable way to cope with this unfortunate situation? Should she just strike out on her own and let the chips fall where they may? These questions have no simple answers. As you'll soon see, decisions about how to cope with life's difficulties can be incredibly complex.

In the previous chapter we discussed the nature of stress and its effects. We learned that stress can be a challenging, exciting stimulus to personal growth. However, we also saw that stress can prove damaging to people's psychological and physical health because it often triggers physiological responses that may be harmful. Controlling the effects of stress depends on the behavioral responses people make to stressful situations. Thus, a person's mental and physical health depends, in part, on his or her ability to *cope* effectively with stress.

This chapter focuses on how people cope with stress. We begin with a general discussion of the concept of coping. Then we review some common coping patterns that tend to have relatively little value. After discussing these ill-advised coping techniques, we offer an overview of what it means to engage in healthier, "constructive" coping. The remainder of the chapter expands on the specifics of constructive coping. We hope our discussion provides you with some new ideas about how to deal with the stresses of modern life.

# The Concept of Coping

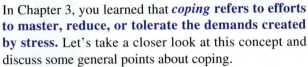

**LEARNING OBJECTIVES**

- Describe the variety of coping strategies that people use.
- Discuss the role of flexibility in coping.

In Chapter 3, you learned that *coping* **refers to efforts to master, reduce, or tolerate the demands created by stress.** Let's take a closer look at this concept and discuss some general points about coping.

*People cope with stress in many ways.* A number of researchers have attempted to identify and classify the various coping techniques that people use in dealing with stress. Their work reveals quite a variety of coping strategies. In fact, one review of the literature found over 400 distinct coping techniques (Skinner et al., 2003). To simplify things, Carver, Scheier, and Weintraub (1989) found that they could sort their participants' coping tactics into 14 categories, which are listed in **Figure 4.1**. Thus, in grappling with stress, people select their coping tactics from a large and varied menu of options.

*It is most adaptive to use a variety of coping strategies.* Even with a large menu of coping tactics to choose from, most people come to rely on some strategies more than others (Carver & Scheier, 1994; Shiota, 2006). However, Cheng (2001, 2003) has argued that flexibility in coping is more desirable than consistently relying on the same strategy. The ability to show coping flexibility and use multiple coping strategies has been related to increased resilience and decreased distress during stressful events (Lam & McBride-Chang, 2007;

Roussi et al., 2007). Cheng and Cheung (2005) identified a key difference between individuals with high and low coping flexibility. Flexible copers can differentiate among stressful events in terms of controllability and impact, which is important information to know when choosing a coping strategy. Indeed, the ability to select a particular coping strategy to deal with a specific adversity helps people avoid becoming stuck in a rut with a problematic strategy (Carbonell, Reinherz, & Beardslee, 2005). Although everyone has an individual style of coping with life's difficulties, this need for flexibility may explain why people's coping strategies show only moderate stability across varied situations (Schwartz et al., 1999).

*Coping strategies vary in their adaptive value.* In everyday terms, when we say that someone "coped with her problems," we imply that she handled them effectively. In reality, however, all strategies are not created equal. Coping processes range from the helpful to the counterproductive (Carver et al., 1989; Vaillant, 2000). For example, coping with the disappointment of not getting a good grade by plotting to sabotage your professor's computer would clearly be a problematic way of coping. Hence, we distinguish between coping patterns that tend to be helpful and those that tend to

| Types of Coping Strategies | |
| --- | --- |
| **Coping strategy** | **Example** |
| Active coping | I take additional action to try to get rid of the problem. |
| Planning | I come up with a strategy about what to do. |
| Suppression of competing activities | I put aside other activities in order to concentrate on this. |
| Restraint coping | I force myself to wait for the right time to do something. |
| Seeking social support for instrumental reasons | I ask people who have had similar experiences what they did. |
| Seeking social support for emotional reasons | I talk to someone about how I feel. |
| Positive reinterpretation and growth | I look for the good in what is happening. |
| Acceptance | I learn to live with it. |
| Turning to religion | I seek God's help. |
| Focus on and venting of emotions | I get upset and let my emotions out. |
| Denial | I refuse to believe that it has happened. |
| Behavioral disengagement | I give up the attempt to get what I want. |
| Mental disengagement | I turn to work or other substitute activities to take my mind off things. |
| Alcohol-drug disengagement | I drink alcohol or take drugs in order to think about it less. |

**Figure 4.1**

**Classifying coping strategies.** Carver, Scheier, and Weintraub (1989) sorted their participants' coping responses into 14 categories. The categories are listed here, along with a representative example from each category. As you can see, people use quite a variety of coping strategies.

Source: From Carver, C. S., Scheier, M. F., & Weintraub, J. K. (1989). Assessing coping strategies: A theoretically based approach. *Journal of Personality and Social Psychology, 56*(2), 267–283. Copyright 1989 by the American Psychological Association. Reprinted by permission of the authors.

be maladaptive. Bear in mind, however, that our generalizations about the adaptive value of various coping strategies are based on trends or tendencies identified by researchers. Unlike what many self-help books and talk show hosts would have you believe, no coping strategy can guarantee a successful outcome. Furthermore, the adaptive value of a coping technique depends on the exact nature of the situation. As you'll see in the next section, even ill-advised coping strategies may have adaptive value in some instances.

# Common Coping Patterns of Limited Value

### LEARNING OBJECTIVES

- Analyze the adaptive value of giving up as a response to stress.
- Describe the adaptive value of aggression as a response to stress, including the research on media violence as catharsis.
- Evaluate the adaptive value of indulging yourself as a response to stress.

- Discuss the adaptive value of negative self-talk as a response to stress.
- Explain how defense mechanisms work.
- Evaluate the adaptive value of defense mechanisms, including recent work on healthy illusions.

*"Recently, after an engagement of 22 months, my fiancée told me that she was in love with someone else and that we were through. I've been a wreck ever since. I can't study because I keep thinking about her. I think constantly about what I did wrong in the relationship and why I wasn't good enough for her. Getting drunk is the only way I can get her off my mind. Lately, I've been getting plastered about five or six nights a week. My grades are really hurting, but I'm not sure that I care."*

This young man is going through a difficult time and does not appear to be handling it very well. He's blaming himself for the breakup with his fiancée. He's turning to alcohol to dull the pain that he feels, and it sounds like he may be giving up on school. These coping responses aren't particularly unusual in such situations, but they're only going to make his problems worse.

In this section, we'll examine some relatively common coping patterns that tend to be less than optimal. Specifically, we'll discuss giving up, aggression, self-indulgence, self-blame, and defense mechanisms. Some of these coping tactics may be helpful in certain circumstances, but more often than not, they are counterproductive.

## Giving Up

When confronted with stress, people sometimes simply give up and withdraw from the battle. This response of apathy and inaction tends to be associated with the emotional reactions of sadness and dejection. Martin Seligman (1974, 1992) has developed a model of this giving-up syndrome that sheds light on its causes. In Seligman's original research, animals were subjected to electric shocks that they could not escape. The animals were then given an opportunity to learn a response that would allow them to escape the shock. However, many of the animals became so apathetic and listless that they didn't even try to learn the escape response. When researchers made similar manipulations with *human* subjects using inescapable noise (rather than shock) as the stressor, they observed parallel results (Hiroto & Seligman, 1975). This syndrome is referred to as learned helplessness. **Learned helplessness is passive behavior produced by exposure to unavoidable aversive events.** Unfortunately, this tendency to give up may be transferred to situations in which one is not really helpless. Hence, some people routinely respond to stress with fatalism and resignation, passively accepting setbacks that might be dealt with effectively. In adolescents, learned helplessness is associated with disengagement in academics and an increase in depression (Maatta, Nurmi, & Stattin, 2007). Interestingly, Evans and Stecker (2004) argue that environmental stressors, such as excessive noise, crowding, and traffic (see Chapter 3), often produce a syndrome that resembles learned helplessness.

Seligman originally viewed learned helplessness as a product of conditioning. However, research with human participants has led Seligman and his colleagues to revise their theory. Their current model proposes that people's *cognitive interpretation* of aversive events determines whether they develop learned helplessness. Specifically, helplessness seems to occur when individuals come to believe that events are beyond their control. This belief is particularly likely to emerge in people who exhibit a pessimistic explanatory style. Among other things, such people tend to attribute setbacks to personal inadequacies instead of situational factors (Abramson, Seligman, & Teasdale, 1978; Seligman, 1990). As discussed in Chapter 3, this explanatory style is associated with poorer physical health and increased depression and anxiety (Wise & Rosqvist, 2006).

Overall, giving up is not a highly regarded method of coping. Carver and his colleagues (1989, 1993) have studied this coping strategy, which they refer to as *behavioral disengagement*, and found that it is associated with increased rather than decreased distress. A recent study of college students after the September 11 terrorist attacks supports this assertion, finding that behavioral disengagement was associated with increased anxiety shortly after the attack, even for those indirectly affected (Liverant, Hafmann, & Litz, 2004). However, giving up could be adaptive in some instances. For example, if you are thrown into a job that you are not equipped to handle, it might be better to quit rather than face constant pressure and diminishing self-esteem. Research has demonstrated that withdrawing effort from unattainable goals can be an effective coping strategy, associated with a reduction in anxiety and depression and better self-reported health (Kraaij et al., 2008; Wrosch et al., 2007). There is something to be said for recognizing one's limitations, avoiding unrealistic goals, and minimizing self-imposed stress.

## Acting Aggressively

*A young man, aged 17, cautiously edged his car into traffic on the Corona Expressway in Los Angeles. His slow speed apparently irritated the men in a pickup truck behind him. Unfortunately, he angered the wrong men—they shot him to death. During that same weekend there were six other roadside shootings in the Los Angeles area; all of them triggered by minor incidents or "fender benders." Frustrated motorists are attacking each other more and more frequently, especially on the overburdened highways of Los Angeles.*

Lashing out at others with verbal aggression tends to be an ineffective coping tactic that often backfires, creating additional stress.

These tragic incidents of highway violence—so-called "road rage"—exemplify maladaptive ways in which drivers cope with the stress, anxiety, and hostility experienced while driving. These incidents have unfortunately become common enough that some professionals are calling for road rage to become an official psychiatric diagnosis (Ayar, 2006). The U.S. cities with the most (and least) reports of road rage are listed in **Figure 4.2**. Road rage vividly illustrates that people often respond to stressful events by acting aggressively. *Aggression is any behavior intended to hurt someone, either physically or verbally.* Snarls, curses, and insults are much more common than shootings or fistfights, but aggression of any kind can be problematic.

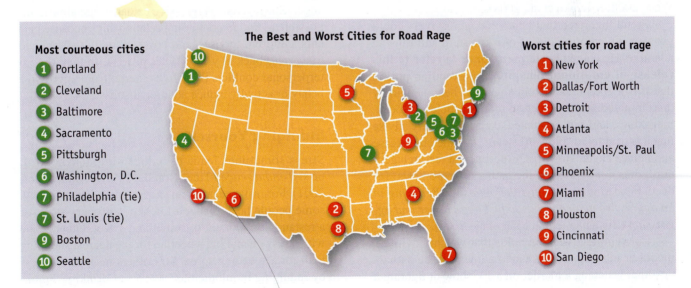

### The Best and Worst Cities for Road Rage

**Most courteous cities**
1. Portland
2. Cleveland
3. Baltimore
4. Sacramento
5. Pittsburgh
6. Washington, D.C.
7. Philadelphia (tie)
7. St. Louis (tie)
9. Boston
10. Seattle

**Worst cities for road rage**
1. New York
2. Dallas/Fort Worth
3. Detroit
4. Atlanta
5. Minneapolis/St. Paul
6. Phoenix
7. Miami
8. Houston
9. Cincinnati
10. San Diego

### Figure 4.2

**Road rage survey.** In 2009, AutoVantage, a national auto club, conducted its annual road rage survey. For the first time in four years, New York was listed higher than Miami as the city with the most road rage. When asked to identify the major causes of road rage, survey participants commonly listed bad driving, traffic problems, stress, and frustration.

Source: From Affinion Group. (2009, June 16). *AutoVantage road rage survey reveals best, worst cities* [Press release]. Retrieved from http://www.affiniongroupmedia.com/themes/site_themes/affinionassets/releases/autovantage/Road_Rage_09/media/National_Rls.pdf.

As you learned in Chapter 3, frustration is a major source of stress. Many years ago, a team of psychologists (Dollard et al., 1939) proposed the *frustration-aggression hypothesis,* which held that aggression is always due to frustration. Decades of research eventually showed that there isn't an inevitable link between frustration and aggression, but this research also supported the basic idea that frustration *does* frequently elicit aggression (Berkowitz, 1989).

People often lash out aggressively at others who had nothing to do with their frustration, especially when they can't vent their anger at the real source of their frustration. Thus, you'll probably suppress your anger rather than lash out verbally at a police officer who gives you a speeding ticket. Twenty minutes later, however, you might be downright brutal in rebuking a waiter who is slow in serving your lunch. As we discussed in Chapter 2, Sigmund Freud noticed this diversion of anger to a substitute target long ago; he called it *displacement.* Unfortunately, research suggests that when someone is provoked, displaced aggression is a common response (Hoobler & Brass, 2006; Marcus-Newhall et al., 2000).

Aggressive responses to frustration are more likely if the person ruminates about being provoked (Bushman et al., 2005), if he or she has a depleted capacity for self-control (DeWall et al., 2007), or if alcohol is involved (Aviles et al., 2005; Denson et al., 2008). Feelings of security and anonymity in one's personal space also influence aggressive tendencies. For instance, aggressive driving behaviors are more common among those who report a territorial attachment to their cars and those who feel anonymous or detached in their cars because of locked doors or tinted windows (Conkle & West, 2008; Szlemko et al., 2008).

Freud theorized that behaving aggressively could get pent-up emotion out of one's system and thus be adaptive. He coined the term **catharsis to refer to this release of emotional tension.** The Freudian notion that it is a good idea to vent anger has become widely disseminated and accepted in modern society. Books, magazines, and self-appointed experts routinely advise that it is healthy to "blow off steam" and thereby release and reduce anger. However, experimental research generally has *not* supported the catharsis hypothesis. Indeed, *most studies find just the opposite: Behaving in an aggressive manner tends to fuel more anger and aggression* (Bushman, 2002; Lohr et al., 2007).

Conventional wisdom holds that watching violent media or playing violent video games can be cathartic—that watching a murder on a TV show or fighting a fictional character in a game can release pent-up anger and hostility. However, the research evidence strongly suggests that this is simply not true. Craig Anderson and Brad Bushman (2001) conducted a groundbreaking review of the research on violent video games and found that playing these games was related to increased

aggression, physiological arousal, and aggressive thoughts and to decreased prosocial behavior. In fact, they found that the relationship between media violence and aggressive behavior was almost as strong as the relationship between smoking and cancer (Bushman & Anderson, 2001; see **Figure 4.3**). Exposure to media violence not only desensitizes people to violent acts, it also encourages aggressive self-views and automatic aggressive responses (Bartholow, Bushman, & Sestir, 2006; Uhlmann & Swanson, 2004) and increases feelings of hostility (Arriaga et al., 2006).

Experimental studies using a variety of violent media, diverse laboratory conditions, and many kinds of participants continue to find convergent evidence that video games and other forms of violent media do not provide cathartic effects; rather, they increase aggressive tendencies (Anderson, 2004). Today we have sophisticated equipment to study the activity of the brain (for example, functional magnetic resonance imaging). Preliminary research using brain-imaging procedures indicates that although people are aware that video game violence is fantasy, the brain reacts to it as if it is real. Thus, "engaging in virtual violence could impact neural systems in a manner comparable with engaging in actual violence" (Carnagey, Anderson, & Bartholow, 2007, p. 181).

Is there an up side to anger and aggression? Some argue that feeling anger can be beneficial when one is about to engage in a confrontational task (Tamir, 2009). However, as a coping strategy, acting aggressively has little value. Carol Tavris (1982, 1989) points out that aggressive behavior usually backfires because it elicits aggressive responses from others that generate more anger. She asserts, "Aggressive catharses are almost impossible to find in continuing relationships because parents, children, spouses, and bosses usually feel obliged to aggress back at you" (1982, p. 131). In fact, the interpersonal conflicts that often emerge from aggressive behavior actually induce additional stress.

## Indulging Yourself

Stress sometimes leads to reduced impulse control, or *self-indulgence* (Tice, Bratslavsky, & Baumeister, 2001). For instance, after an exceptionally stressful day, some people head for their kitchen, a grocery store, or a restaurant in pursuit of something sweet. Others cope with stress by making a beeline for the nearest shopping mall for a spending spree. Still others respond to stress by indulging in injudicious patterns of drinking, smoking, gambling, and drug use.

Moos and Billings (1982) identified *developing alternative rewards* as a common response to stress. It makes sense that when things are going poorly in one area of your life, you may try to compensate by pursuing substitute forms of satisfaction. Thus, it is not

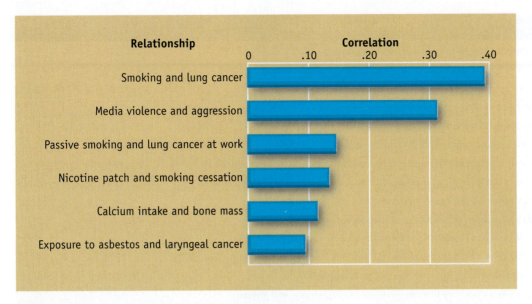

**Figure 4.3**

**Comparison of the relationship between media violence and aggression to other correlations.** Many studies have found a correlation between exposure to media violence and aggression. However, some critics have argued that the correlation is too weak to have any practical significance in the real world. In a rebuttal of this criticism, Bushman and Anderson (2001) note that the average correlation in studies of media violence and aggression is .31. They argue that this association is almost as strong as the correlation between smoking and the probability of developing lung cancer, which is viewed as relevant to real-world issues and notably stronger than a variety of other correlations shown here that are assumed to have practical importance.

Source: Adapted from Bushman, B. J., & Anderson, C. A. (2001). Media violence and the American public. *American Psychologist, 56*(6–7), 477–489. (Figure 2). Copyright © 2001 American Psychological Association. Reprinted by permission of the publisher and authors.

surprising that there is evidence of stress-induced eating (Barker, Williams, & Galambos, 2006; Wardle & Gibson, 2007), smoking (McClernon & Gilbert, 2007), gambling (Ricketts & Macaskill, 2003; Wood & Griffiths, 2007), and alcohol and drug use (Goeders, 2004; Spada & Wells, 2006). In fact, Ng and Jeffery (2003) speculate that the general relationship between stress and poor physical health might be attributable in part to these unhealthy behaviors.

A more recent manifestation of this coping strategy is the tendency to immerse oneself in the online world of the Internet. Kimberly Young (1998) has described a syndrome called *Internet addiction,* **which consists of spending an inordinate amount of time on the Internet and inability to control online use** (see **Figure 4.4** on the next page). People who exhibit this syndrome tend to feel anxious, depressed, or empty when they are not online (Kandell, 1998). Their Internet use is so excessive, it begins to interfere with their functioning at work, at school, or at home, leading victims to start concealing the extent of their dependence on the Internet. Some people exhibit pathological Internet use

CATHY © Cathy Guisewite Reprinted with permission of UNIVERSAL UCLICK. All rights reserved.

## Internet Addiction Test

To assess your level of addiction, answer the following questions using this scale:

1 = Not at all     2 = Rarely     3 = Occasionally     4 = Often     5 = Always

| Question | 1 | 2 | 3 | 4 | 5 |
|---|---|---|---|---|---|
| 1. How often do you find that you stay online longer than you intended? | 1 | 2 | 3 | 4✗ | 5 |
| 2. How often do you neglect household chores to spend more time online? | 1 | 2 | 3 | 4✗ | 5 |
| 3. How often do you prefer the excitement of the Internet to intimacy with your partner? | 1 | 2 | 3✗ | 4 | 5 |
| 4. How often do you form new relationships with fellow online users? | 1 | 2 | 3 | 4✗ | 5 |
| 5. How often do others in your life complain to you about the amount of time you spend online? | 1 | 2 | 3 | 4✗ | 5 |
| 6. How often do your grades or school work suffer because of the amount of time you spend online? | 1 | 2✗ | 3 | 4 | 5 |
| 7. How often do you check your e-mail before something else that you need to do? | 1 | 2 | 3 | 4✗ | 5 |
| 8. How often does your job performance or productivity suffer because of the Internet? | 1✗ | 2 | 3 | 4 | 5 |
| 9. How often do you become defensive or secretive when anyone asks you what you do online? | 1 | 2 | 3 | 4 | 5✗ |
| 10. How often do you block out disturbing thoughts about your life with soothing thoughts of the Internet? | 1 | 2✗ | 3 | 4 | 5 |
| 11. How often do you find yourself anticipating when you will go online again? | 1 | 2✗ | 3 | 4 | 5 |
| 12. How often do you fear that life without the Internet would be boring, empty, and joyless? | 1 | 2 | 3✗ | 4 | 5 |
| 13. How often do you snap, yell, or act annoyed if someone bothers you while you are online? | 1 | 2 | 3 | 4✗ | 5 |
| 14. How often do you lose sleep due to late-night log-ins? | 1 | 2 | 3 | 4✗ | 5 |
| 15. How often do you feel preoccupied with the Internet when off-line, or fantasize about being online? | 1 | 2✗ | 3 | 4 | 5 |
| 16. How often do you find yourself saying "just a few more minutes" when online? | 1 | 2 | 3✗ | 4 | 5 |
| 17. How often do you try to cut down the amount of time you spend online and fail? | 1 | 2 | 3 | 4✗ | 5 |
| 18. How often do you try to hide how long you've been online? | 1✗ | 2 | 3 | 4 | 5 |
| 19. How often do you choose to spend more time online over going out with others? | 1 | 2✗ | 3 | 4 | 5 |
| 20. How often do you feel depressed, moody, or nervous when you are off-line, which goes away once you are back online? | 1✗ | 2 | 3 | 4 | 5 |

After you've answered all the questions, add the numbers you selected for each response to obtain a final score. The higher your score, the greater your level of addiction and the problems your Internet usage causes. Here's a general scale to help measure your score.

**20–39 points:** You are an average online user. You may surf the Web a bit too long at times, but you have control over your usage.

**40–69 points:** You are experiencing frequent problems because of the Internet. You should consider their full impact on your life.

**70–100 points:** Your Internet usage is causing significant problems in your life. You need to address them now.

**Figure 4.4**

**Measuring addiction to the Internet.** The questions on Young's (1998) Internet Addiction Test highlight the traits that make up this syndrome. You can check to see whether you exhibit any signs of Internet addiction by responding to the items and computing your score.

Source: From Young, K. S. (1998). *Caught in the Net: How to recognize the signs of Internet addiction—and a winning strategy for recovery.* New York: John Wiley. Copyright © 1998 John Wiley & Sons, Inc. This material is used by permission of John Wiley & Sons, Inc

for one particular purpose, such as online sex or online gaming, whereas others exhibit a general, global pattern of Internet addiction (Davis, 2001). It is difficult to estimate the prevalence of Internet addiction, but the syndrome does *not* appear to be rare (Greenfield, 1999; Morahan-Martin & Schumacher, 2000). Research suggests that Internet addiction is not limited to shy, male computer whizzes, as one might expect (Young, 1998). Nor is it a strictly Western phenomenon; rates appear to be higher in China than in the U.S. (Zhang, Amos, & McDowell, 2008). Although not all psychologists agree about whether excessive Internet surfing should be classified as an *addiction* (Goldsmith & Shapira, 2006; Yellowlees & Marks, 2007), it is clear that this coping strategy can result in a disruption of time, ultimately increasing one's stress levels (Chou, Condron, & Belland, 2005).

There is nothing inherently maladaptive about indulging oneself as a way of coping with life's stresses. If a hot fudge sundae, some new clothes, or chatting online can calm your nerves after a major setback, who can argue? In fact, connecting with online social support has been shown to reduce stress and anxiety (Leung, 2007). However, if a person consistently responds to stress with excessive self-indulgence, obvious problems are likely to develop. Stress-induced eating is typically unhealthy (one rarely craves broccoli or grapefruit after a hard day) and may result in poor nutrition or obesity. Excesses in drinking and drug use may endanger one's health and affect work or relationship quality.

Experts disagree about whether excessive Internet use should be characterized as an addiction, but the inability to control online use appears to be an increasingly common syndrome.

Additionally, these indulgences can cause emotional ambivalence as immediate pleasure gives way to regret, guilt, or embarrassment (Ramanathan & Williams, 2007). Given the risks associated with self-indulgence, it has rather marginal adaptive value.

## Blaming Yourself

In a postgame interview after a tough defeat, a prominent football coach was brutally critical of himself. He said that he had been outcoached, that he had made poor decisions, and that his game plan was faulty. He almost eagerly assumed all the blame for the loss himself. In reality, he had taken some reasonable risks that didn't go his way and had suffered the effects of poor execution by his players. Looking at it objectively, the loss was attributable to the collective failures of 50 or so players and coaches. However, the coach's unrealistically negative self-evaluation was a fairly typical response to frustration. When confronted by stress (especially frustration and pressure), people often become highly self-critical.

The tendency to engage in "negative self-talk" in response to stress has been noted by a number of influential theorists. As we will discuss in greater detail later in this chapter, Albert Ellis (1973, 1987) calls this phenomenon "catastrophic thinking" and focuses on how it is rooted in irrational assumptions. Aaron Beck (1976, 1987) analyzes negative self-talk into specific tendencies. Among other things, he asserts that people often (1) unreasonably attribute their failures to personal shortcomings, (2) focus on negative feedback from others while ignoring favorable feedback, and (3) make unduly pessimistic projections about the future. Thus, if you performed poorly on an exam, you might respond to this stress by blaming it on your woeful stupidity,

dismissing a classmate's comment that the test was unfair, and hysterically predicting that you will flunk out of school.

According to Ellis, catastrophic thinking causes, aggravates, and perpetuates emotional reactions to stress that are often problematic. Along even more serious lines, researchers have found that self-blame is associated with increased distress and depression for individuals who have experienced a variety of traumas such as sexual assault, war, and natural disasters (Frazier, Mortensen, & Steward, 2005, Jeney-Gammon et al., 1993; Kraaij & Garnefski, 2006). For victims of sexual assault specifically, self-blame is associated with heightened PTSD symptoms and greater feelings of shame (Ullman et al., 2007; Vidal & Petrak, 2007). Likewise, blaming oneself is related to increased depression and anxiety for those dealing with serious health issues (Anson & Ponsford, 2006; Kraaij, Garnefski, & Vlietstra, 2008). Although being realistic and recognizing one's weaknesses has value, especially when one is engaging in problem solving, Ellis and Beck agree that self-blame as a coping strategy can be enormously counterproductive. We cover Ellis's advice on more constructive thinking later in this chapter, and we discuss Beck's recommendations for more effective coping in our chapter on psychotherapy (Chapter 15).

## Using Defensive Coping

Defensive coping is a common response to stress. We noted in Chapter 2 that the concept of defense mechanisms was originally developed by Sigmund Freud. Though rooted in the psychoanalytic tradition, this concept has gained acceptance from psychologists of most persuasions (Cramer, 2000). Building on Freud's initial insights, modern psychologists have broadened the scope of the concept and added to Freud's list of defense mechanisms.

### The Nature of Defense Mechanisms

*Defense mechanisms* **are largely unconscious reactions that protect a person from unpleasant emotions such as anxiety and guilt.** A number of coping strategies fit this definition. For example, Laughlin

**WEB LINK 4.1**   **American Self-Help Clearinghouse Sourcebook**

This online clearinghouse provides contact information for hundreds of self-help groups and organizations across the United States. For individuals trying to cope with specific problems or challenging life situations, one of these groups may be particularly helpful with focused advice and suggestions.

| Mechanism | Example |
|---|---|
| *Denial of reality.* Protecting oneself from unpleasant reality by refusing to perceive or face it. | A smoker concludes that the evidence linking cigarette use to health problems is scientifically worthless. |
| *Fantasy.* Gratifying frustrated desires by imaginary achievements. | A socially inept and inhibited young man imagines himself chosen by a group of women to provide them with sexual satisfaction. |
| *Intellectualization (isolation).* Cutting off emotion from hurtful situations or separating incompatible attitudes in logic-tight compartments. | A prisoner on death row awaiting execution resists appeal on his behalf and coldly insists that the letter of the law be followed. |
| *Undoing.* Atoning for or trying to magically dispel unacceptable desires or acts. | A woman who feels guilty about insulting her co-worker excessively praises her after each insult. |
| *Overcompensation.* Covering up felt weaknesses by emphasizing some desirable characteristic, or making up for frustration in one area by overgratification in another. | A dangerously overweight woman goes on eating binges when she feels neglected by her husband. |

**Figure 4.5**

**Additional defense mechanisms.** Like the seven defense mechanisms described in the discussion of Freudian theory in Chapter 2 (see **Figure 2.4**), these five defenses are frequently used in people's efforts to cope with stress.

Source: Adapted from Carson, R. C., Butcher, J. N., & Coleman, J. C. (1988). *Abnormal psychology and modern life*. Glenview, IL: Scott, Foresman. © 1988 Pearson Education, Inc. Reproduced by permission of Pearson Education, Inc.

(1979) lists 49 different defenses. In our discussion of Freud's theory in Chapter 2, we described seven common defenses. **Figure 4.5** introduces another five defenses that people use with some regularity. Although widely discussed in the popular press, defense mechanisms are often misunderstood. We will use a question-answer format to elaborate on the nature of defense mechanisms in the hopes of clearing up any misconceptions.

**What do defense mechanisms defend against?**
Above all else, defense mechanisms shield the individual from the *emotional discomfort* elicited by stress.

Their main purpose is to ward off unwelcome emotions or to reduce their intensity. Foremost among the emotions guarded against is anxiety. People are especially defensive when the anxiety is the result of some threat to their self-esteem. They also use defenses to prevent dangerous feelings of anger from exploding into acts of aggression. Guilt and dejection are two other emotions that people often try to evade through defensive maneuvers.

**How do they work?** Defense mechanisms work through *self-deception*. They accomplish their goals by distorting reality so it does not appear so threaten-

ing (Aldwin, 2007). Let's say you're doing poorly in school and are in danger of flunking out. Initially, you might use *denial* to block awareness of the possibility that you could fail. This tactic might temporarily fend off feelings of anxiety. If it becomes difficult to deny the obvious, you might resort to *fantasy*, daydreaming about how you will salvage adequate grades by getting spectacular scores on the upcoming final exams, when the objective fact is that you are hopelessly behind in your studies. Thus, defense mechanisms work their magic by bending reality in self-serving ways (Bowins, 2004).

**Are they conscious or unconscious?** Mainstream Freudian theory originally assumed that defenses operate entirely at an unconscious level. However, the concept of defense mechanisms has been broadened to include maneuvers that people may have some awareness of. Thus, defense mechanisms operate at varying levels of awareness and can be conscious or unconscious (Erdelyi, 2001).

**Are they normal?** Definitely. Most people use defense mechanisms on a fairly regular basis (Thobaben, 2005). They are entirely normal patterns of coping. The notion that only neurotic people use defense mechanisms is inaccurate.

### Can Defense Mechanisms Ever Be Healthy?

This is a critical and complicated question. More often than not, the answer is no. In fact, defensive coping has been linked to increased negative affect, depression, and suicide risk (Hovanesian, Isakov, & Cervellione, 2009; Steiner et al., 2007). Generally, defense mechanisms are poor ways of coping for a number of reasons. First, defensive coping is an avoidance strategy, and avoidance rarely provides a genuine solution to our problems. In fact, Holahan and his colleagues (2005) found that avoidance coping is associated with increased chronic and acute life stressors as well as increased depressive symptoms. Second, defenses such as denial, fantasy, and projection represent "wishful thinking," which is likely to accomplish little. In a study of how students coped with the stress of taking the Medical College Admissions Test (MCAT), Bolger (1990) found that students who engaged in a lot of wishful thinking experienced greater increases in anxiety than other students as the exam approached. Third, a defensive coping style has been related to poor health, in part because it often leads people to delay facing up to their problems (Weinberger, 1990). For example, if you were to block out obvious warning signs of cancer or diabetes and failed to obtain needed

medical care, your defensive behavior could be fatal. Although illusions may protect us from anxiety in the short term, they can create serious problems in the long term.

Most theorists used to regard accurate contact with reality as the hallmark of sound mental health (Jahoda, 1958; Jourard & Landsman, 1980). However, Shelley Taylor and Jonathon Brown (1988, 1994) have reviewed several lines of evidence suggesting that defensive "illusions" may be adaptive for mental health and well-being. First, they note that "normal" (that is, nondepressed) people tend to have overly favorable self-images. In contrast, depressed people exhibit less favorable—but more realistic—self-concepts. Second, normal participants overestimate the degree to which they control chance events. In comparison, depressed participants are less prone to this illusion of control. Third, normal individuals are more likely than their depressed counterparts to display unrealistic optimism in making projections about the future.

Courtesy Shelley Taylor

**Shelley Taylor**

A variety of other studies have also provided support for the hypothesis that positive illusions promote well-being and positive health outcomes (Segerstrom & Roach, 2008). For example, studies of individuals diagnosed with AIDS show that those with unrealistically optimistic expectations of the likely course of their disease actually experience a less rapid course of illness (Reed et al., 1999). In a laboratory study, Taylor et al. (2003) found that participants who tended to exhibit positive illusions showed lower cardiovascular responses to stress, quicker cardiovascular recovery from stress, and lower levels of a key stress hormone. Further, a study of retirees found that those who held an exaggerated youthful bias reported higher self-esteem, better perceived health, and less boredom than those who held an accurate perception of their age (Gana, Alaphilippe, & Bailly, 2004).

As you might guess, critics have expressed considerable skepticism about the idea that illusions are adaptive. For example, Colvin and Block (1994) make an eloquent case for the traditional view that accuracy and realism are healthy. Moreover, they report data showing that overly favorable self-ratings are correlated with maladaptive personality traits (Colvin, Block, & Funder, 1995). One possible resolution to this debate is Roy Baumeister's (1989) theory that it's all a matter of degree and that there is an "optimal margin of illusion." According to Baumeister, extreme self-deception is maladaptive, but small illusions may often be beneficial.

# The Nature of Constructive Coping

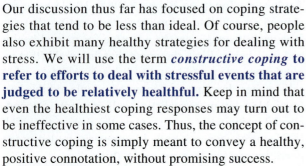

- Describe the nature of constructive coping.
- Distinguish among the three categories of constructive coping.

Our discussion thus far has focused on coping strategies that tend to be less than ideal. Of course, people also exhibit many healthy strategies for dealing with stress. We will use the term ***constructive coping* to refer to efforts to deal with stressful events that are judged to be relatively healthful.** Keep in mind that even the healthiest coping responses may turn out to be ineffective in some cases. Thus, the concept of constructive coping is simply meant to convey a healthy, positive connotation, without promising success.

What makes a coping strategy constructive? Frankly, in labeling certain coping responses constructive or healthy, psychologists are making value judgments. It's a gray area in which opinions will vary to some extent. Nonetheless, some consensus emerges from the burgeoning research on coping and stress management. Key themes in this literature include the following (Kleinke, 2007):

**1.** Constructive coping involves confronting problems directly. It is task relevant and action oriented. It involves a conscious effort to rationally evaluate your options in an effort to solve your problems.

**2.** Constructive coping takes effort. Using these strategies to reduce stress is an active process that involves planning.

**3.** Constructive coping is based on reasonably realistic appraisals of your stress and coping resources.

A little self-deception may sometimes be adaptive, but excessive self-deception and highly unrealistic negative thinking are not.

**4.** Constructive coping involves learning to recognize and manage potentially disruptive emotional reactions to stress.

**5.** Constructive coping involves learning to exert some control over potentially harmful or destructive habitual behaviors. It requires the acquisition of some behavioral self-control.

These points should give you a general idea of what we mean by constructive coping. They will guide our discourse in the remainder of this chapter as we discuss how to cope more effectively with stress. To organize our discussion, we will use a classification scheme proposed by Moos and Billings (1982) to divide constructive coping techniques into three broad categories: *appraisal-focused coping* (aimed at changing one's interpretation of stressful events), *problem-focused coping* (aimed at altering the stressful situation itself), and *emotion-focused coping* (aimed at managing potential emotional distress). **Figure 4.6** shows common coping strategies that fall under each category. It is important to note that many strategies could fall under more than one category. For instance, one could seek social support for practical purposes (problem-focused) or emotional purposes (emotion-focused).

**Figure 4.6**

**Overview of constructive coping tactics.** Coping tactics can be organized in several ways, but we will use the classification scheme shown here, which consists of three categories: appraisal-focused strategies, problem-focused strategies, and emotion-focused strategies. The list of coping tactics in each category is not exhaustive. Most, but not all, of the listed strategies are discussed in our coverage of constructive coping.

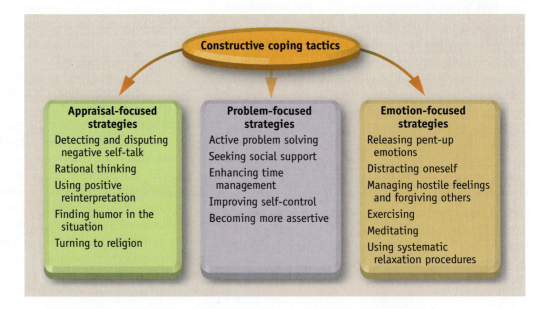

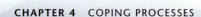

# Appraisal-Focused Constructive Coping

### LEARNING OBJECTIVES

- Explain Ellis's analysis of the causes of maladaptive emotions.
- Identify some assumptions that contribute to catastrophic thinking.
- Describe some ways to reduce catastrophic thinking.
- Discuss the merits of humor in coping with stress, including the work on different types of humor.
- Assess positive reinterpretation as a coping strategy.

As we've seen, the experience of stress depends on how one interprets or appraises threatening events. People often underestimate the importance of the appraisal phase in the stress process. They fail to appreciate the highly subjective feelings that color the perception of threat to one's well-being. A useful way to deal with stress is to alter your appraisal of threatening events. In this section, we'll examine Albert Ellis's ideas about reappraisal and discuss the value of using humor and positive reinterpretation to cope with stress.

## Ellis's Rational Thinking

Albert Ellis (1977, 1985, 1996, 2001a, 2001b) was a prominent and influential theorist who died in 2007 at the age of 93. He believed that people could short-circuit their emotional reactions to stress by altering their appraisals of stressful events. Ellis's insights about stress appraisal are the foundation for his widely used system of therapy. **Rational-emotive behavior therapy** is an **approach to therapy that focuses on altering clients' patterns of irrational thinking to reduce maladaptive emotions and behavior.**

Ellis maintained that *you feel the way you think*. He argued that problematic emotional reactions are caused by negative self-talk, which, as we mentioned earlier, he called catastrophic thinking. *Catastrophic thinking involves unrealistic appraisals of stress that exaggerate the magnitude of one's problems.* Ellis used a simple A-B-C sequence to explain his ideas (see **Figure 4.7**):

**Albert Ellis**

*Courtesy Albert Ellis Institute*

**A.** *Activating event.* The A in Ellis's system stands for the activating event that produces the stress. The activating event may be any potentially stressful transaction. Examples might include an automobile accident, the cancellation of a date, a delay while waiting in line

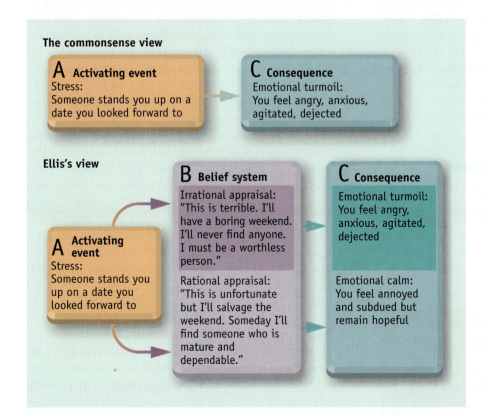

**The commonsense view**

**A Activating event**
Stress:
Someone stands you up on a date you looked forward to

**C Consequence**
Emotional turmoil:
You feel angry, anxious, agitated, dejected

**Ellis's view**

**A Activating event**
Stress:
Someone stands you up on a date you looked forward to

**B Belief system**
Irrational appraisal:
"This is terrible. I'll have a boring weekend. I'll never find anyone. I must be a worthless person."

Rational appraisal:
"This is unfortunate but I'll salvage the weekend. Someday I'll find someone who is mature and dependable."

**C Consequence**
Emotional turmoil:
You feel angry, anxious, agitated, dejected

Emotional calm:
You feel annoyed and subdued but remain hopeful

**Figure 4.7**
**Albert Ellis's A-B-C model of emotional reactions.** Most people are prone to attribute their negative emotional reactions (C) directly to stressful events (A). However, Ellis argues that emotional reactions are really caused by the way individuals think about these events (B).

at the bank, or a failure to get a promotion you were expecting.

**B.** *Belief system.* B stands for your belief about the event. This represents your appraisal of the stress. According to Ellis, people often view minor setbacks as disasters, engaging in catastrophic thinking: "How awful this is. I can't stand it!" "Things never turn out fairly for me." "I'll be in this line forever." "I'll never get promoted."

**C.** *Consequence.* C stands for the consequence of your negative thinking. When your appraisals of stressful events are highly negative, the consequence tends to be emotional distress. Thus, you feel angry, outraged, anxious, panic stricken, disgusted, or dejected.

Ellis asserts that most people do not understand the importance of phase B in this three-stage sequence. They unwittingly believe that the activating event (A) *causes* the consequent emotional turmoil (C). However, Ellis maintains that A does *not* cause C. It only appears to do so. Instead, Ellis asserts that B causes C. Emotional distress is actually caused by one's catastrophic thinking in appraising stressful events.

According to Ellis, it is common for people to turn inconvenience into disaster and make "mountains out of molehills." For instance, imagine that someone stands you up on a date that you were eagerly looking forward to. You might think, "Oh, this is terrible. I'm going to have another boring weekend. People always mistreat me. I'll never find anyone to fall in love with. I must be an ugly, worthless person." Ellis would argue that such thoughts are irrational. He would point out that it does not follow logically from being stood up that you (1) must have a lousy weekend, (2) will never fall in love, or (3) are a worthless person. Thinking this way does nothing but increase distress. Indeed, research indicates that the tendency toward catastrophic thinking is a risk factor for developing posttraumatic stress disorder (see Chapter 3) (Bryant & Guthrie, 2005).

## The Roots of Catastrophic Thinking

Ellis (1994, 1995, 2004) theorized that unrealistic appraisals of stress are derived from the irrational assumptions that people hold. He maintained that if you scrutinize your catastrophic thinking, you will find that your reasoning is based on an unreasonable premise, such as "I must have approval from everyone" or "I must per-

form well in all endeavors." These faulty assumptions, which most people hold unconsciously, generate catastrophic thinking and emotional turmoil. To facilitate emotional self-control, it is important to learn to spot irrational assumptions and the unhealthy patterns of thought that they generate. Here are four particularly common irrational assumptions:

**1.** *I must have love and affection from certain people.* Everyone wants to be liked and loved. There is nothing wrong with that. However, many people foolishly believe that they should be liked by everyone they come into contact with. If you stop to think about it, that's clearly unrealistic. Once individuals fall in love, they tend to believe that their future happiness depends absolutely on the continuation of that one, special relationship. They believe that if their current love relationship were to end, they would never again be able to achieve a comparable one. This is an unrealistic view of the future. Such views make the person anxious during a relationship and severely depressed if it comes to an end.

**2.** *I must perform well in all endeavors.* We live in a highly competitive society. We are taught that victory brings happiness. Consequently, we feel that we must always win. For example, many athletes are never satisfied unless they perform at their best level. However, by definition, their best level is not their typical level, and they set themselves up for inevitable frustration.

**3.** *Other people should always behave competently and be considerate of me.* People are often angered by others' stupidity and selfishness. For example, you may become outraged when a mechanic fails to fix your car properly or when a salesperson treats you rudely. It would be nice if others were always competent and considerate, but you know better—they are not! Yet many people go through life unrealistically expecting others' efficiency and kindness in every situation.

**4.** *Events should always go the way I like.* Some people simply won't tolerate any kind of setback. They assume that things should always go their way. For example, some commuters become tense and angry each time they get stuck in rush-hour traffic. They seem to believe that they are entitled to coast home easily every day, even though they know that rush hour rarely is a breeze. Such expectations are clearly unrealistic and doomed to be violated. Yet few people recognize the obvious irrationality of the assumption that underlies their anger unless it is pointed out to them.

## Reducing Catastrophic Thinking

How can you reduce your unrealistic appraisals of stress? Ellis asserts that you must learn (1) how to detect catastrophic thinking and (2) how to dispute the irrational assumptions that cause it. Detection involves acquiring the ability to spot unrealistic pessimism and

**WEB LINK 4.2  The Albert Ellis Institute**

Albert Ellis developed rational-emotive behavior therapy in the mid-1950s as an effective alternative to psychoanalytically inspired treatment approaches. This site demonstrates the growth of Ellis's approach over the subsequent decades.

Some traumatic events, whether natural (such as earthquakes or flu epidemics) or human-made (such as war or financial meltdowns) can provoke psychological instability in an entire population. Unfortunately, a normal feature of human mental processing makes it difficult to accurately process the actual threat implied by these events. However, being aware of this cognitive tendency can help people to be more rational in their thinking. To introduce you to this cognitive tendency, consider the following problem:

*Various causes of death are paired up below. For each pairing, decide which is the more likely cause of death.*

*Asthma or tornadoes?*

*Syphilis or botulism (food poisoning)?*

*Tuberculosis or floods?*

Would you believe that the first choice in each pair causes at least 18 times as many deaths as the second choice? If your guesses were wrong, don't feel bad. Most people tend to greatly overestimate the likelihood of dramatic and vivid—but infrequent—events that receive heavy media coverage. Thus, the number of fatalities caused by tornadoes, floods, and food poisonings is usually overestimated (Slovic, Fischhoff, & Lichtenstein, 1982), whereas fatalities caused by asthma and other run-of-the-mill diseases tend to be underestimated. This tendency to overestimate the improbable reflects the operation of the *availability heuristic,* which involves basing the estimated probability of an event on the ease with which relevant instances come to mind.

Relying on the availability heuristic is a normal cognitive tendency. However, to the extent that certain events occur infrequently but are easily available in memory, your estimates will be biased. Instances of hurricanes, tornadoes, and terrorists attacks are readily available in memory because these events receive a great deal of media attention. The result is that people tend to greatly exaggerate the likelihood that they might be a victim of such adverse events, and such overestimates fuel fear. Ironically, experiencing fear results in greater perceptions of being at risk (Keller, Siegrist, & Gutscher, 2006), which then makes one feel more fear—creating a vicious cycle of anxiety and alarm.

Often this cycle can result in *rumination,* repetitively focusing on one's distress, including its cause and consequences. Rumination has been linked to a number of negative outcomes, such as depression, negative thinking, impaired problem solving, and disrupted social support (Nolen-Hoeksema, Wisco, & Lyubomirsky, 2008). Excessive rumination has also been associated with decreases in positive emotional expression and poorer physical health (Ciarrochi & Scott, 2006; Watkins, 2008).

Admittedly, no one knows what the future might bring. However, it is wise to be mindful of the natural tendency to overestimate the likelihood that you might be affected by a traumatic event. Thinking more rationally about the probability of being victimized can reduce people's collective sense of alarm.

wild exaggeration in your thinking. Examine your self-talk closely. Ask yourself why you're getting upset. Force yourself to verbalize your concerns, covertly or out loud. Look for key words that often show up in catastrophic thinking, such as *should, ought, always, never,* and *must.*

Disputing your irrational assumptions requires subjecting your entire reasoning process to scrutiny. Try to root out the assumptions from which your conclusions are derived. Most people are unaware of their assumptions. Once these thoughts are unearthed, their irrationality may be quite obvious. If your assumptions seem reasonable, ask yourself whether your conclusions follow logically. Try to replace your catastrophic thinking with more low-key, rational analyses. These strategies should help you to redefine stressful situations in ways that are less threatening. Challenging your assumptions

isn't the only appraisal-based coping strategy; another way to defuse such situations is to turn to humor.

## Humor as a Stress Reducer

In a New Orleans suburb in the aftermath of Hurricane Katrina, "the grimy residue of receded floodwater covered the blue Chevrolet pickup parked outside a shattered two-story house, but the offer spray-painted on the vehicle in white overflowed with enthusiasm: 'For Sale. Like New. Runs Great'" (Associated Press, 2005). Obviously, the hurricane didn't destroy this victim's sense of humor. When the going gets tough, finding some humor in the situation is not uncommon and is usually beneficial. In a study of coping styles, McCrae (1984) found that 40% of his participants reported using humor to deal with stress.

© Radhika Chalasani/Getty Images

**People often turn to humor to help themselves cope during difficult times, as this photo taken in the aftermath of Hurricane Katrina illustrates. Research suggests that humor can help reduce the negative impact of stressful events.**

Empirical evidence showing that humor moderates the impact of stress has been accumulating over the last 25 years (Lefcourt, 2001, 2005). For instance, in one influential study, Martin and Lefcourt (1983) found that a good sense of humor functioned as a buffer to lessen the negative impact of stress on mood. Some of their results are presented in **Figure 4.8**, which shows how mood disturbance increased as stress went up in two groups of participants—those who were high or low in their use of humor. Notice how high-humor participants were less affected by stress than were their low-humor counterparts. Similar findings have been observed in other studies (Abel, 1998; Martin, 1996). Further, there is increasing evidence that humor is associated with enhanced immune functioning (Godfrey, 2004; Lefcourt, 2005).

It appears that some types of humor are more effective than others in reducing stress. Chen and Martin (2007) found that humor that is affiliative (used to engage or amuse others) or self-enhancing (maintaining a humorous perspective in the face of adversity) is related to better mental health. In contrast, coping through humor that is self-defeating (used at one's own expense) or aggressive (criticizing or ridiculing others) is related to poorer mental health. Likewise, using a lot of self-defeating humor and very little self-enhancing or affiliative humor is associated with increased depression (Frewen et al., 2008).

How does humor help reduce the effects of stress and promote wellness? Several explanations have been proposed (see **Figure 4.9**). One possibility is that humor affects appraisals of stressful events (Abel, 2002). Jokes can help people put a less-threatening spin on their trials and tribulations. Kuiper, Martin,

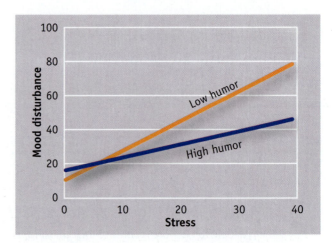

**Figure 4.8**

**Humor and coping.** Martin and Lefcourt (1983) related stress to mood disturbance in participants who were either high or low in their use of humor. Increased stress led to smaller increases in mood disturbance in the high-humor group, suggesting that humor has some value in efforts to cope with stress.

Source: Adapted from Martin, R. A., & Lefcourt, H. M. (1983). Sense of humor as a moderator of the relation between stressors and moods. *Journal of Personality and Social Psychology, 45* (6), 1313–1324. Copyright © 1983 by the American Psychological Association. Adapted by permission.

and Olinger (1993) demonstrated that students who used coping humor were able to appraise a stressful exam as a positive challenge, which in turn lowered their perceived stress levels. Another possibility is that humor increases the experience of positive emotions (Martin, 2002). In a study of laughter in the workplace, participants who practiced laughing 15 minutes a day for three weeks showed significant increases in positive emotions, even

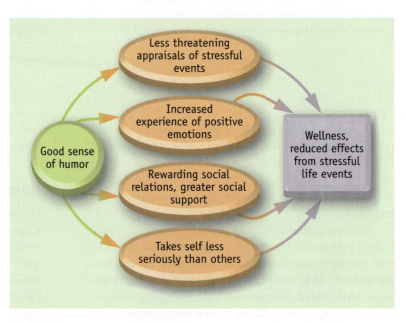

**Figure 4.9**

**Possible explanations for the link between humor and wellness.** Research suggests that a good sense of humor buffers the effects of stress and promotes wellness. Four hypothesized explanations for the link between humor and wellness are outlined in the middle column of this diagram. As you can see, humor may have a variety of beneficial effects.

90 days after the study was over (Beckman, Regier, & Young, 2007). As we discussed in Chapter 3, positive emotions can help people bounce back from stressful events (Tugade & Fredrickson, 2004). A study comparing types of constructive coping found that strategies that increased positive emotions were most strongly associated with well-being (Shiota, 2006).

Another hypothesis is that a good sense of humor buffers the effects of stress by facilitating positive social interactions, which promote social support (Martin, 2002). In a study of Vietnam prisoners of war, Henman (2001) found that using humor to build connections "contributed to the survival and resilience of these men" (p. 83). Finally, Lefcourt and colleagues (1995) argue that high-humor people may benefit from not taking themselves as seriously as low-humor people do. As they put it, "If persons do not regard themselves too seriously and do not have an inflated sense of self-importance, then defeats, embarrassments, and even tragedies should have less pervasive emotional consequences for them" (p. 375). Thus, humor is a rather versatile coping strategy that may have many benefits.

## Positive Reinterpretation

When you are feeling overwhelmed by life's difficulties, you might try the commonsense strategy of recognizing that "things could be worse." No matter how terrible your problems seem, you probably know someone who has even bigger troubles. That is not to say that you should derive satisfaction from others' misfortune, but rather that comparing your own plight with others' even tougher struggles can help you put your problems in perspective. Research suggests that this strategy of making positive comparisons with others is a common coping mechanism that can result in improved mood and self-esteem (Wills & Sandy, 2001). Moreover, this strategy does not depend on knowing others who are clearly worse off. You can simply imagine yourself in

a similar situation with an even worse outcome (example: two broken legs after a horseback-riding accident instead of just one). One healthy aspect of positive reinterpretation is that it can facilitate calming reappraisals of stress without the necessity of distorting reality. Over time this perspective can decrease the stress of the situation (Aldwin, 2007).

Another way to engage in positive reinterpretation is to search for something good in a bad experience. Distressing though they may be, many setbacks have positive elements. After experiencing divorces, illnesses, layoffs, and the like, many people remark that "I came out of the experience better than I went in,"

or "I grew as a person." Studies of victims of natural disasters, heart attacks, and bereavement have found an association between this type of *benefit finding* under duress and relatively sound psychological and physical health (Nolen-Hoeksema & Davis, 2005; Lechner, Tennen & Affleck, 2009). Further, benefit finding is associated with actual personal growth following adversity (Linley & Joseph, 2004). Of course, the positive aspects of a personal setback may be easy to see after the stressful event is behind you. The challenge is to recognize these positive aspects while you are still struggling with the setback, so that it becomes less stressful.

# Problem-Focused Constructive Coping

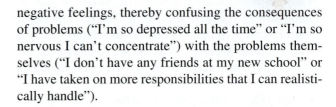

### LEARNING OBJECTIVES

- List and describe four steps in systematic problem solving.
- Discuss the adaptive value of seeking help as a coping strategy.
- Describe cultural differences in seeking social support.

- Explain five common causes of wasted time.
- Identify the causes and consequences of procrastination.
- Summarize advice on managing time effectively.

Problem-focused coping includes efforts to remedy or conquer the stress-producing problem itself. This type of coping is associated with positive outcomes such as emotional growth in times of stress (Karlsen, Dybdahl, & Vitterso, 2006). In this section, we'll discuss systematic problem solving, the importance of seeking help, and effective time management.

## Using Systematic Problem Solving

In dealing with life's problems, the most obvious (and often most effective) course of action is to tackle them head-on. In fact, problem solving has been linked to better psychological adjustment, lower levels of depression, reduced alcohol use, and fewer health complaints (Heppner & Lee, 2005). Obviously, people vary in their problem-solving skills. However, evidence suggests that these skills can be enhanced through training (Heppner & Lee, 2002, 2005). With this thought in mind, we will sketch a general outline of how to engage in more systematic problem solving. The plan described here is a synthesis of observations by various experts, especially Mahoney (1979), Miller (1978), and Chang and Kelly (1993).

### Clarify the Problem

You can't tackle a problem if you're not sure what the problem is. Therefore, the first step in any systematic problem-solving effort is to clarify the nature of the problem. Sometimes the problem will be all too obvious. At other times the source of trouble may be quite difficult to pin down. In any case, you need to arrive at a specific concrete definition of your problem.

Two common tendencies typically hinder people's efforts to get a clear picture of their problems. First, they often describe their problems in vague generalities ("My life isn't going anywhere" or "I never have enough time"). Second, they tend to focus too much on

negative feelings, thereby confusing the consequences of problems ("I'm so depressed all the time" or "I'm so nervous I can't concentrate") with the problems themselves ("I don't have any friends at my new school" or "I have taken on more responsibilities that I can realistically handle").

### Generate Alternative Courses of Action

The second step in systematic problem solving is to generate alternative courses of action. Notice that we did not call these alternative *solutions*. Many problems do not have a readily available solution that will completely resolve the problem. If you think in terms of searching for complete solutions, you may prevent yourself from considering many worthwhile courses of action. Instead, it is more realistic to search for alternatives that may produce some kind of improvement in your situation.

Besides avoiding the tendency to insist on solutions, you need to avoid the temptation to go with the first alternative that comes to mind. Many people are a little trigger-happy. They thoughtlessly try to follow through on the first response that occurs to them. Various lines of evidence suggest that it is wiser to engage in brainstorming about a problem. **Brainstorming is generating as many ideas as possible while withholding criticism and evaluation.** In other words, you generate alternatives without paying any attention to their apparent practicality. This approach facilitates creative expression of ideas and can lead to more alternative courses of action from which to choose.

### Evaluate Your Alternatives and Select a Course of Action

Once you generate as many alternatives as you can, you need to start evaluating the possibilities. There are no simple criteria for judging the relative merits of your alternatives. However, you will probably want to address three general issues. First, ask yourself whether each alternative is realistic. In other words, what is the probability that you can successfully execute the intended course of action? Try to think of any obstacles you may have failed to anticipate. In making this assessment, it is important to try to avoid both foolish optimism and unnecessary pessimism.

Second, consider any costs or risks associated with each alternative. The "solution" to a problem can be worse than the problem itself. Assuming you can successfully implement your intended course of action, what are the possible negative consequences? Third, compare the desirability of the probable outcomes of each alternative. In making your decision, you have to ask yourself "What is important to me? Which outcomes do I value the most?" Through careful evaluation you can select the best course of action.

### Take Action While Maintaining Flexibility

You can plan your course of action as thoughtfully and intentionally as possible, but no plan works if you don't follow through and implement it. In so doing, try to maintain flexibility. Do not get locked into a particular plan. Few choices are truly irreversible. You need to monitor results closely and be willing to revise your strategy.

In evaluating your course of action, try to avoid the simplistic success/failure dichotomy. You should simply look for improvement of any kind. If your plan doesn't work out too well, consider whether it was undermined by any circumstances that you could not have anticipated. Finally, remember that you can learn from your failures. Even if things did not work out, you may now have new information that will facilitate a new attack on the problem.

### Seeking Help

In Chapter 3, we saw that social support can be a powerful force that helps buffer the deleterious effects of stress and has positive effects of its own (Taylor, 2007; Wills & Fegan, 2001). In trying to tackle problems directly, it pays to keep in mind the value of seeking aid from friends, family, co-workers, and neighbors. So far, we have discussed social support as if it were a stable, external resource available to different people in varying degrees. In reality, social support fluctuates over time and evolves out of our interactions with oth-

ers (Newcomb, 1990). Some people have more support than others because they have personal characteristics that attract more support or because they make more effort to seek support.

Interestingly, cultural factors, often overlooked by researchers, seem to play an important role in what individuals see as problems and how they solve them (Heppner, 2008). This is especially true with regard to who seeks social support. Taylor and colleagues (2004) found that Asians and Asian Americans are less likely to seek social support in times of stress than are European Americans. When examined closely, this difference appears to be rooted in cultural concerns about relationships. That is, individuals from cultures high in collectivism (see Chapter 6) don't want to risk straining relationships or disrupting group harmony by calling on others for help in times of stress (Kim et al., 2006; Taylor, 2004). When using social support for coping, Asian Americans tend to benefit more from support that does not involve disclosure of personal distress—that is, support that doesn't emotionally burden the other person (Kim, Sherman, & Taylor, 2008). Of course, broad *similarities* exist in how people from different cultures react to stress. For example, individuals from both collectivistic and individualistic cultures view receiving comfort as an effective coping strategy. There appear to be cultural differences, however, in actively *seeking* that help (Mortenson, 2006). Given that social support is such an important resource, researchers will no doubt continue to examine it within a cultural context.

### Using Time More Effectively

Do you constantly feel that you have too much to do and too little time in which to do it? Do you feel overwhelmed by your responsibilities at work, at school, and at home? Do you feel like you're always rushing around, trying to meet an impossible schedule? If you answered yes to some of these questions, you're struggling with time pressure, a huge source of stress in modern life. You can estimate how well you manage time by responding to the brief questionnaire in **Figure 4.10** on the next page. If the results suggest that your time is out of your control, you may be able to make your life less stressful by learning sound time-management strategies.

R. Alec Mackenzie (1997), a prominent time-management researcher, points out that time is a nonrenewable resource. It can't be stockpiled like money, food, or other precious resources. You can't turn back the clock. Furthermore, everyone, whether rich or poor, gets an equal share of time—24 hours per day, 7 days a week. Although time is our most equitably distributed resource, some people spend it much more wisely than others. Let's look at some of the ways in which people let time slip through their fingers without accomplishing much.

> **WEB LINK 4.3  Mind Tools**
> This site offers practical techniques to help people deal with the world more efficiently and effectively. It houses useful information on several of the topics discussed in this chapter, including stress management, time management, and effective problem solving.

## How Well Do You Manage Your Time?

Listed below are ten statements that reflect generally accepted principles of good time management. Answer these items by circling the response most characteristic of how you perform your job. Please be honest. No one will know your answers except you.

1. Each day I set aside a small amount of time for planning and thinking about my job.
   0. Almost never  1. Sometimes  2. Often  3. Almost always

2. I set specific, written goals and put deadlines on them.
   0. Almost never  1. Sometimes  2. Often  3. Almost always

3. I make a daily "to do list," arrange items in order of importance, and try to get the important items done as soon as possible.
   0. Almost never  1. Sometimes  2. Often  3. Almost always

4. I am aware of the 80/20 rule and use it in doing my job. (The 80/20 rule states that 80 percent of your effectiveness will generally come from achieving only 20 percent of your goals.)
   0. Almost never  1. Sometimes  2. Often  3. Almost always

5. I keep a loose schedule to allow for crises and the unexpected.
   0. Almost never  1. Sometimes  2. Often  3. Almost always

6. I delegate everything I can to others.
   0. Almost never  1. Sometimes  2. Often  3. Almost always

7. I try to handle each piece of paper only once.
   0. Almost never  1. Sometimes  2. Often  3. Almost always

8. I eat a light lunch so I don't get sleepy in the afternoon.
   0. Almost never  1. Sometimes  2. Often  3. Almost always

9. I make an active effort to keep common interruptions (visitors, meetings, telephone calls) from continually disrupting my work day.
   0. Almost never  1. Sometimes  2. Often  3. Almost always

10. I am able to say no to others' requests for my time that would prevent my completing important tasks.
    0. Almost never  1. Sometimes  2. Often  3. Almost always

To get your score, give yourself

3 points for each "almost always"
2 points for each "often"
1 point for each "sometimes"
0 points for each "almost never"

Add up your points to get your total score.

If you scored

| | |
|---|---|
| 0–15 | Better give some thought to managing your time. |
| 15–20 | You're doing OK, but there's room for improvement. |
| 20–25 | Very good. |
| 25–30 | You cheated! |

### Figure 4.10

**Assessing your time management.** The brief questionnaire shown here is designed to evaluate the quality of one's time management. Although it is geared more for working adults than college students, it should allow you to get a rough handle on how well you manage your time.

Source: From Le Boeuf, M. (1980, February). Managing time means managing yourself. *Business Horizons Magazine*, p. 45. Copyright © by the Foundation for the School of Business at Indiana University. Used with permission.

## The Causes of Wasted Time

When people complain about "wasted time," they're usually upset because they haven't accomplished what they really wanted to do with their time. Wasted time is time devoted to unnecessary, unimportant, or unenjoyable activities. There are many reasons we waste time on such activities.

**Inability to set or stick to priorities.** Time consultant Alan Lakein (1996) emphasizes that it's often tempting to deal with routine, trivial tasks ahead of larger and more difficult tasks. Thus, students (or professors for that matter) working on a major paper often check Facebook, fold the laundry, or reorganize their desk instead of concentrating on the paper. Why? Routine tasks are easy, and working on them allows people to rationalize their avoidance of more important tasks. Unfortunately, many of us spend too much time on trivial pursuits, leaving our more important tasks undone.

**Inability to say no.** Other people are constantly making demands on our time. They want us to exchange gossip in the hallway, go out to dinner on Friday night, cover their hours at work, help with a project, listen to their sales pitch on the phone, join a committee, or coach Little League. Clearly, we can't do everything that everyone wants us to. However, some people just can't say no to others' requests for their time. Such people end up fulfilling others' priorities instead of their own. Thus, McDougle (1987) concludes, "Perhaps the most successful way to prevent yourself from wasting time is by saying *no*" (p. 112).

**Inability to delegate responsibility.** Some tasks should be delegated to others—assistants, subordinates, fellow committee members, partners, spouses, children, and so on. However, many people have difficulty delegating work to others. Barriers to delegation include unwillingness to give up any control, lack of confidence in subordinates, fear of being disliked, the need to feel needed, and the attitude that "I can do it better myself" (Mitchell, 1987). The problem, of course, is that people who can't delegate waste a lot of time on trivial work or others' work.

**Inability to throw things away.** Some people are pack rats who can't throw anything into the wastebasket. Their desks are cluttered with piles of mail, newspapers, magazines, reports, and books. Their filing cabinets overflow with old class notes or ancient memos. At home, their kitchen drawers bulge with rarely used utensils and their closets bulge with old clothes that are never worn. Pack rats lose time looking for things that have disappeared among all the chaos and end up reshuffling the same paper, rereading the

For many people, an inability to throw things away is a key factor promoting wasted time.

same mail, resorting the same files, and so on. According to Mackenzie (1997), they would be better off if they made more use of their wastebaskets.

**Inability to accept anything less than perfection.** High standards are admirable, but some people have difficulty finishing projects because they expect them to be flawless. They can't let go. They dwell on minor problems and keep making microscopic changes in their papers, projects, and proposals. They are caught in what Emanuel (1987) calls the "paralysis of perfection." They end up spinning their wheels, redoing the same work over and over instead of moving on to the next task. Perfectionism can be troublesome in many ways. In a review of the literature on perfectionism, Leonard and Harvey (2008) report that it has been linked to depression, anxiety, job stress, substance abuse, eating disorders, interpersonal conflict, and procrastination, which we turn to next.

### The Problem of Procrastination

*Procrastination* is the tendency to delay tackling tasks until the last minute. Almost everyone procrastinates on occasion. For example, 70%–90% of college students procrastinate before beginning academic assignments (Knaus, 2000). However, research suggests that about 20% of adults are chronic procrastinators (Ferrari, 2001). Not just a U.S. phenomenon, this trend appears to apply to a number of cultures (Ferrari et al., 2007). Procrastination is more likely when people have to work on aversive tasks or when they are worried about their performance being evaluated (Milgram, Marshevsky, & Sadeh, 1995; Senecal, Lavoie, & Koestner, 1997).

Why do people procrastinate? In a review of the literature Steel (2007) found that procrastination was strongly related to low self-efficacy, low conscientiousness, lack of self-control, poor organization, low achievement motivation, and high distractibility. The type of irrational thinking described by Albert Ellis also seems to foster procrastination (Bridges & Roig, 1997), as does a strong fear of failure (Lay, 1992) and excessive perfectionism (Flett, Hewitt, & Martin, 1995).

Other factors besides personality can affect procrastination. Schraw and colleagues (2007) identified six general principles related to academic procrastination, including these three:

**1.** *Desire to minimize time on a task.* As you know, the modern student is busy—studying, working, socializing, and maintaining a personal life. Time is at a premium. Sometimes delaying as much academic work as possible seems to be a way to safeguard some personal time. As one student reported, "The truth is, I just don't have time *not* to procrastinate. If I did everything the way it could be done, I wouldn't have a life" (Schraw et al., 2007, p. 21).

**2.** *Desire to optimize efficiency.* Procrastination can be viewed as allowing one to be optimally efficient, concentrating academic work into focused time frames. Students reported that being pressed for time means that there is less opportunity for busywork, boredom, or false starts.

**3.** *Close proximity to reward.* Schraw et al. (2007) found that students often procrastinate because they are rewarded for it. By putting off academic work until the last minute, students not only get more immediate feedback (the grade), but they also get a sudden release of stress. In this way, procrastination is similar to other thrill-seeking behaviors.

Although these principles seem reasonable and many people rationalize their delaying tactics by claiming that "I work best under pressure" (Ferrari, 1992; Lay, 1995), the empirical evidence suggests otherwise. Studies show that procrastination tends to have a negative impact on the quality of task performance (Ferrari, Johnson, & McCown, 1995; Tice & Baumeister, 1997). In fact, Britton and Tesser (1991) found that time management was a better predictor of college GPA than SAT scores! Procrastinators may often underestimate how much time will be required to complete a task effectively, or they experience unforeseen delays and then run out of time because they didn't allow any "cushion." Another consideration is that waiting until the last minute may make a task more stressful—and while the release of this built-up stress might be exciting, performance often declines under conditions of high stress (as we saw in Chapter 3). Moreover, work quality may not be the only thing that suffers when people procrastinate. Studies indicate that as a deadline looms, procrastinators tend to experience elevated anxiety and increased health problems (Lay et al., 1989; Tice & Baumeister, 1997).

People who struggle with procrastination often impose deadlines and penalties on themselves. This practice can be helpful, but self-imposed deadlines are not as effective as externally imposed ones (Ariely & Wertenbroch, 2002). Let's discuss some effective ways to manage your time.

## Time-Management Techniques

Individuals vary in their time perspectives. Some people are *future oriented*, able to see the consequences of immediate behavior for future goals, whereas others are *present oriented*, focused on immediate events and not worried about consequences. These orientations influence how they manage their time and meet their time-related commitments. Future-oriented individuals, for example, are less likely to procrastinate and are more reliable in meeting their commitments (Harber, Zimbardo, & Boyd, 2003). Regardless of orientation, most people could benefit from more effectively managing their time.

What's the key to better time management? Most people assume that it's increased *efficiency*—that is, learning to perform tasks more quickly. Improved efficiency may help a little, but time-management experts maintain that efficiency is overrated. They emphasize that the key to better time management is increased *effectiveness*—that is, learning to allocate time to your most important tasks. This distinction is captured by a widely quoted slogan in the time-management literature: "Efficiency is doing the job right, while effectiveness is doing the right job." Here are some suggestions for using your time more effectively (based on Lakein, 1996; Mackenzie, 1997; Morgenstern, 2000):

1. *Monitor your use of time.* The first step toward better time management is to monitor your use of time to see where it all goes (Douglass & Douglass, 1993). Doing so requires keeping a written record of your activities, similar to that shown in **Figure 4.11**. At the end of each week, you should analyze how your time was allocated. Based on your personal roles and responsibilities, create categories of time use such as studying, child care, housework, commuting, working at the office, working at home, going online, eating, and sleeping. For each day, add up the hours devoted to each category. Record this information on a summary sheet like that in **Figure 4.12**. Two weeks of record-keeping should allow you to draw some conclusions about where your time goes. Your records will help you make informed decisions about reallocating your time. When you begin your time-management program, these records will also give you a baseline for comparison, so that you can see whether your program is working.

2. *Clarify your goals.* You can't wisely allocate your time unless you decide what you want to accomplish. Lakein (1996) suggests that you ask yourself, "What are my lifetime goals?" Write down all the goals that you can think of, even relatively frivolous things like going deep-sea fishing or becoming a wine expert. Some of your goals will be in conflict. For instance, you can't become a vice-president at your company in Wichita and still move to the West Coast. Thus, the tough part comes next. You have to wrestle with your goal conflicts. Figure out which goals are most important to you, and order them in terms of priority. These priorities should guide you as you plan your activities on a daily, weekly, and monthly basis.

3. *Plan your activities using a schedule.* People resist planning because it takes time, but in the long run planning saves time. Thorough planning is essential to effective time management (McGee-Cooper & Trammell, 1994). At the beginning of each week, you should make a list of short-term goals. This list should be translated into daily "to do" lists of planned activities. To avoid the tendency to put off larger projects, break them into smaller, manageable components, and set deadlines for completing the components. Your planned activities should be allocated to various time slots on a written schedule. Schedule your most important activities into the time periods when you tend to be most energetic and productive.

4. *Protect your prime time.* The best-laid plans can quickly go awry because of interruptions. There isn't any foolproof way to eliminate interruptions, but you may be able to shift most of them into certain time slots while protecting your most productive time. The trick is to announce to your family, friends, and co-workers that you're blocking off certain periods of "quiet time" when visitors and phone calls will be turned away. Of course, you also have to block off periods of "available time" when you're ready to deal with everyone's problems.

5. *Increase your efficiency.* Although efficiency is not the key to better time management, it's not irrelevant. Time-management experts do offer some suggestions for improving efficiency, including the following (Klassen, 1987; Schilit, 1987):

- *Handle paper once.* When e-mails, letters, reports, and such cross your desk, they should not be stashed away to be read again and again before you deal with them. Most paperwork can and should be dealt with immediately.
- *Tackle one task at a time.* Jumping from one problem to another is inefficient. As much as possible, stick with a task until it's done. In scheduling your activities, try to allow enough time to complete tasks.
- *Group similar tasks together.* It's a good idea to bunch up small tasks that are similar. This strategy is

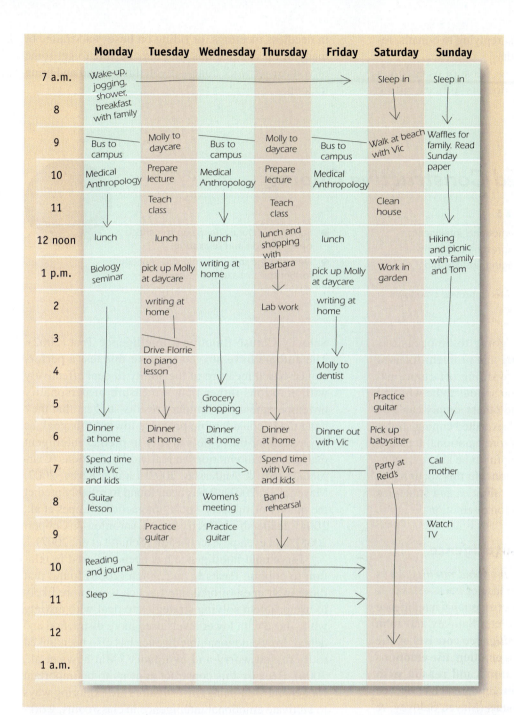

**Figure 4.11**

**Example of a time log.** Experts recommend keeping a detailed record of how you use your time if you are to improve your time management. This example shows the kind of recordkeeping that should be done.

| | Monday | Tuesday | Wednesday | Thursday | Friday | Saturday | Sunday |
|---|---|---|---|---|---|---|---|
| 7 a.m. | Wake-up, jogging, shower, breakfast with family → | | | | | Sleep in | Sleep in |
| 8 | | | | | | | |
| 9 | Bus to campus | Molly to daycare | Bus to campus | Molly to daycare | Bus to campus | Walk at beach with Vic | Waffles for family. Read Sunday paper |
| 10 | Medical Anthropology | Prepare lecture | Medical Anthropology | Prepare lecture | Medical Anthropology | | |
| 11 | | Teach class | | Teach class | | Clean house | |
| 12 noon | lunch | lunch | lunch | lunch and shopping with Barbara | lunch | | Hiking and picnic with family and Tom |
| 1 p.m. | Biology seminar | pick up Molly at daycare | writing at home | | pick up Molly at daycare | Work in garden | |
| 2 | | writing at home | | Lab work | writing at home | | |
| 3 | | | | | | | |
| 4 | | Drive Florrie to piano lesson | | | Molly to dentist | | |
| 5 | | | Grocery shopping | | | Practice guitar | |
| 6 | Dinner at home | Dinner at home | Dinner at home | Dinner at home | Dinner out with Vic | Pick up babysitter | |
| 7 | Spend time with Vic and kids → | | Spend time with Vic and kids | | | Party at Reid's | Call mother |
| 8 | Guitar lesson | | Women's meeting | Band rehearsal | | | |
| 9 | | Practice guitar | Practice guitar | | | | Watch TV |
| 10 | Reading and journal → | | | | | | |
| 11 | Sleep → | | | | | | |
| 12 | | | | | | | |
| 1 a.m. | | | | | | | |

**Time Use Summary Form**

| Activity | Mon. | Tues. | Wed. | Thurs. | Fri. | Sat. | Sun. | Total | % |
|---|---|---|---|---|---|---|---|---|---|
| 1. Sleeping | 8 | 6 | 8 | 6 | 8 | 7 | 9 | 52 | 31 |
| 2. Eating | 2 | 2 | 3 | 2 | 3 | 2 | 3 | 17 | 10 |
| 3. Commuting | 2 | 2 | 2 | 2 | 2 | 0 | 0 | 10 | 6 |
| 4. Housework | 0 | 1 | 0 | 3 | 0 | 0 | 2 | 6 | 4 |
| 5. In class | 4 | 2 | 4 | 2 | 4 | 0 | 0 | 16 | 9 |
| 6. Part-time job | 0 | 5 | 0 | 5 | 0 | 3 | 0 | 13 | 8 |
| 7. Studying | 3 | 2 | 4 | 2 | 0 | 4 | 5 | 20 | 12 |
| 8. Relaxing | 5 | 4 | 3 | 2 | 7 | 8 | 5 | 34 | 20 |
| 9. | | | | | | | | | |
| 10. | | | | | | | | | |

**Figure 4.12**

**Time use summary.** To analyze where your time goes, you need to review your time log and create a weekly time use summary, like the one shown here. The exact categories to be listed on the left depend on your circumstances and responsibilities.

useful when you're paying bills, replying to e-mails, returning phone calls, and so forth.

● *Make use of your downtime.* Most of us endure a lot of "downtime," waiting in doctors' offices, sitting in needless meetings, or riding on buses and trains. In many of these situations, you may be able to get some of your easier work done—if you think ahead and bring it along.

# Emotion-Focused Constructive Coping

### LEARNING OBJECTIVES

● Clarify the nature and value of emotional intelligence.
● Analyze the adaptive value of expressing emotions.
● Discuss the importance of managing hostility and forgiving others' transgressions.
● Understand how exercise can foster improved emotional functioning.

● Summarize the evidence on the effects of meditation and relaxation.
● Describe the requirements and procedure for Benson's relaxation response.

Let's be realistic: There are going to be occasions when appraisal-focused coping and problem-focused coping are not successful in warding off emotional turmoil. Some problems are too serious to be whittled down much by reappraisal, and others simply can't be "solved." Moreover, even well-executed coping strategies may take time to work before emotional tensions begin to subside. Thus, it is helpful to be able to recognize and modulate one's emotions. In this section, we will discuss a variety of coping abilities and strategies that relate mainly to the regulation of emotions.

## Enhancing Emotional Intelligence

According to some theorists, *emotional intelligence* is the key to being resilient in the face of stress (Slaski & Cartwright, 2003). The concept of emotional intelligence was originally formulated by Peter Salovey and John Mayer (1990). **Emotional intelligence consists of the ability to perceive and express emotion, use emotions to facilitate thought, understand and reason with emotion, and regulate emotion.** Emotional intelligence includes four essential components (Mayer, Salovey, & Caruso, 2008; Salovey, Mayer, & Caruso, 2002, 2005). First, people need to be able to accurately perceive emotions in themselves and in others and to have the ability to express their own emotions effectively. Second, people need to be aware of how their emotions shape their thinking, decision making, and coping with stress. Third, people need to be able to understand and analyze their emotions, which may often be complex and contradictory. Fourth, people need to be able to regulate their emotions so that they can dampen negative emotions and make effective use of positive emotions.

Researchers have developed several tests to measure the concept of emotional intelligence. The test that has the strongest empirical foundation is the Mayer-Salovey-Caruso Emotional Intelligence Test (2002). The authors have strived to make this test a performance-based measure of the ability to deal effectively with emotions rather than a measure of personality or temperament. Preliminary results suggest that they have made considerable progress toward this goal, as evidenced by the scale's ability to predict intelligent management of emotions in real-world situations (Ciarrochi, Dean, & Anderson, 2002; Lam & Kirby, 2002; Mayer et al., 2001). It has been found to reliably predict the quality of subjects' social interactions (Lopes et al., 2004), leadership effectiveness (Antoniou & Cooper, 2005), and even physical health (Schutte et al., 2007).

Emotional intelligence has been explored in relation to coping. Pashang and Singh (2008) found that those high in emotional intelligence were more likely to use problem solving strategies to deal with anxiety while those with lower levels used more distraction and denial. Low emotional intelligence has also been linked to increased worry and avoidance (Matthews et al., 2006). Because this construct appears to be important for general well-being, investigators are exploring ways to cultivate emotional intelligence in classrooms, workplaces, and counseling settings. One study found that positive emotional expression can lead to an increase in emotional intelligence (Wing, Schutte, & Byrne, 2006). That leads us to our next topic.

## Expressing Emotions

Try as you might to redefine or resolve stressful situations, you no doubt still go through times when you feel wired with stress-induced tension. When this happens, there's merit in the commonsense notion that you should try to release the emotions welling up inside. Why? Because the physiological arousal that accompanies emotions can become problematic. For example, research

## Recommended READING

### Emotional Intelligence: Why It Can Matter More Than IQ

by Daniel Goleman (Bantam Books, 2006)

It's great to see a book like this make the bestseller lists. It is a serious, scholarly, yet readable analysis of how emotional functioning is important in everyday life. Daniel Goleman is both a psychologist and a journalist who writes about the behavioral sciences for the *New York Times*. In this book, he synthesizes the research of many investigators as he argues that emotional intelligence may be more important to success than high IQ. The concept of emotional intelligence, as originally developed by Peter Salovey and John Mayer (1990), languished in relative obscurity until Goleman's book attracted attention. He views emotional intelligence more broadly than Salovey and Mayer, who focused primarily on people's ability to access, monitor, and express their own emotions and to interpret and understand others' emotions. Goleman includes all of their ingredients but adds social poise and skill, strong motivation and persistence, and some desirable personality traits, such as optimism and conscientiousness. One can argue that Goleman's concept of emotional intelligence is too much of a hodgepodge of traits to be measureable or meaningful, but his broad view yields a wide-ranging book that discusses innumerable examples of how social finesse and emotional sensitivity can foster career success, marital satisfaction, and physical and mental health. In the course of this analysis, Goleman discusses research on a diverse array of topics in an exceptionally lucid manner.

*Go to the Psychology CourseMate for Weiten at* **www.cengagebrain.com/shop/ISBN/1111186634** *for descriptions of other recommended books.*

© Tim Macpherson/cultura/Corbis

**In times of stress, seeking support from one's friends is a very useful coping strategy. Releasing pent-up emotions by talking about one's difficulties appears to be a particularly beneficial coping mechanism.**

suggests that people who inhibit the expression of anger and other emotions are somewhat more likely than other people to have elevated blood pressure (Jorgensen et al., 1996). Moreover, research suggests that efforts to actively suppress emotions result in increased stress and autonomic arousal (Butler et al., 2003; Gross, 2001). Please note that such findings do not mean you should act aggressively (a coping strategy of limited value discussed earlier in the chapter). Instead, we are focusing on appropriate, healthy expression of emotions.

James Pennebaker and his colleagues have shown that emotional expression through talking or writing about traumatic events can have beneficial effects. For example, in one study of college students, half the subjects were asked to write three essays about their dif-ficulties in adjusting to college. The other half wrote three essays about superficial topics. The participants who wrote about their personal problems and traumas enjoyed better health in the following months than the other subjects did (Pennebaker, Colder, & Sharp, 1990). Additionally, emotional disclosure, or "opening up," is associated with improved mood, more positive self-perceptions, fewer visits to physicians, and enhanced immune functioning (Hemenover, 2003; Niederhoffer & Pennebaker, 2005; Smyth & Pennebaker, 2001). It has even been linked to improved academic performance for college students (Lumley & Provenzano, 2003). Smyth and Pennebaker (1999) assert that "when people put their emotional upheavals into words, their physical and mental health seems to improve markedly." They conclude that "the act of disclosure itself is a powerful therapeutic agent" (p. 70). Indeed, written emotional disclosure is effective in reducing anxiety and depression in psychotherapy patients (Graf, Gaudiano, & Geller, 2008).

The research on emotional disclosure indicates that both writing and talking about important personal issues can be beneficial (Smyth & Pennebaker, 2001). Thus, if you can find a good listener, it may be wise to let your secret fears, misgivings, and suspicions spill out in a candid conversation. Of course, confiding in others about one's problems can be awkward and difficult. Therein lies the beauty and appeal of the writing approach, which can be kept private. **Figure 4.13** on the next page summarizes some guidelines for writing about personal issues and trauma that should make this coping strategy more effective.

## Guidelines for Writing About Emotional Experiences

- Find a location where there will be no disturbances (from others, the phone, etc.).

- Set aside about 30 minutes each day: 20 minutes for writing, with a few minutes afterward to compose yourself if necessary.

- Write for three or four days, usually consecutively.

- Explore your deepest thoughts and feelings about any experiences or topics that are weighing heavily upon you.

- Explore how this topic is related to a variety of issues in your life: your childhood, your relationships, who you are, who you would like to be, and so forth.

- Write continuously, without regard for spelling or grammar.

- Remember that the writing is for you, not someone else.

### Figure 4.13

**Using writing about emotional experiences as a coping strategy.** Many studies have shown that writing about traumatic experiences and sensitive issues can have beneficial effects on mental and physical health. These guidelines can help you to use this coping strategy.

Source: From Smyth, J. M. & Pennebaker, J. W. (1999). Sharing one's story. In C. R. Snyder (Ed.), *Coping: The psychology of what works.* New York: Oxford. Copyright © 1999 by Oxford University Press. Reprinted by permission.

## Managing Hostility and Forgiving Others

Scientists have compiled quite a bit of evidence that hostility is related to increased risk for heart attacks and other types of illness (Williams, 2001; see Chapter 5). So how can individuals effectively regulate negative emotions that include anger and hostility? The goal of hostility management is not merely to suppress the overt expression of hostility that may continue to seethe beneath the surface, but to actually reduce the frequency and intensity of one's hostile feelings. The first step toward this goal is to learn to quickly recognize one's anger. A variety of strategies can be used to decrease hostility, including reinterpretation of annoying events, distraction, and the kind of rational self-talk advocated by Ellis (Williams & Williams, 1993). Efforts to increase empathy and tolerance can also contribute to hostility management, as can forgiveness, which has become the focus of a contemporary line of research in psychology.

People tend to experience hostility and other negative emotions when they feel "wronged"—that is, when they believe that the actions of another person were harmful, immoral, or unjust. People's natural inclination is either to seek revenge or to avoid further contact with the offender (McCullough & Witvliet, 2005). Although there is debate among researchers about the exact definition (Lawler-Row et al., 2007; Macaskill, 2005), *forgiveness* **involves counteracting the natural tendencies to seek vengeance or avoid an offender, thereby releasing this** **person from further liability for his or her transgression.** Research suggests that forgiving is an effective emotion-focused coping strategy that is associated with better adjustment and well-being (McCullough & Witvliet, 2002; Worthington et al., 2007). For example, in one study of divorced or permanently separated women, the extent to which the women had forgiven their former husbands was positively related to several measures of well-being and was inversely related to measures of anxiety and depression (McCollough, 2001). In another study, when participants were instructed to think actively about a grudge they had nursed and to think about forgiving it, the forgiving thoughts were associated with more positive emotions and reduced physiological arousal (Witvliet, Ludwig, & Vander Laan, 2001). Forgiveness not only decreases one's own psychological distress, it also increases one's empathy and positive regard for the offending person (Macaskill, Maltby, & Day, 2002; Williamson & Gonzales, 2007).

In contrast, research shows that vengefulness is correlated with more rumination and negative emotion and with lower levels of life satisfaction (McCullough et al.,

In September 1994, Reg and Maggie Green were vacationing in Italy when their seven-year-old son, Nicholas, was shot and killed during a highway robbery. In an act of foregiveness that stunned Europe, the Greens chose to donate their son's organs, which went to seven Italians. The Greens, shown here five years after the incident, have weathered their horrific loss better than most, perhaps in part because of their willingness to forgive.

2001). Further, researchers have identified certain personality characteristics such as narcissistic entitlement as barriers to forgiveness (Exline et al., 2004). Although there is more work to be done in this area, findings to date suggest that it may be healthy for people to learn to forgive others more readily.

## Exercising

Another healthy way to deal with overwhelming emotions is to engage in physical exercise. In fact, one study found that people who participated in a two-month program of regular exercise showed an increase in emotional control and a decrease in emotional distress (Oaten & Cheng, 2006). Even 20-minute sessions of regular aerobic exercise can lead to improved psychological health (Rendi et al., 2008). Exercise is an ideal coping strategy because it provides multiple benefits: an outlet for frustration, a distraction from the stressor, and benefits to physical and psychological health (Sapolsky, 2004). Regular exercise is related to decreases in depression, anxiety, and hostility, as well as increases in self-esteem and energy (Puetz, O'Connor, & Dishman, 2006; Spencer, 1990).

On the whole, it is well documented that physical activity promotes overall mental and physical health (Edwards, 2006; Saxena et al., 2005). For instance, in a longitudinal study of long-term breast cancer survivors, increased physical activity following diagnosis predicted a higher quality of life and improved physical health, even 10 years after the diagnosis (Kendall et al. 2005). Likewise, psychiatric patients showed significant increases in psychological well-being after an 8- to 12-week voluntary exercise intervention (Tetlie et al., 2008). Of course these findings must be interpreted with caution. Although it appears likely that exercise increases quality of life, it could be that those with a higher quality of life are more likely to exercise (de Geus & Stubbe, 2007). Even with this caveat, however, exercise is an effective coping strategy. In fact, psychologists are starting to wonder if exercise should be a routine mental health intervention (Berk, 2007; Cynkar, 2007).

Sapolosky (2004) asserts that to get maximal benefits from physical exercise, you should consider three rules. First, you must *want* to exercise. Forcing yourself to do something you don't want to do, even if that something is good for you, can be stressful in and of itself. Second, you should engage in aerobic exercise (such as jogging, swimming, or bicycling) because most of the positive effects come from this type of exercise. Third, you should exercise on a regular basis. Of course, regular exercise requires discipline and self-control. One of the main predictors of exercise maintenance is self-efficacy, a belief that you can do it (Sullum, Clark, & King, 2000). If you are not currently as physically active as you would like, perhaps you could use the self-modification techniques covered in the Application section at the end of Chapter 3 to improve your exercise habits. Advice on devising an effective exercise program can also be found in Chapter 5.

As with other types of exercise, there is mounting evidence that practicing yoga has psychological benefits (Novotney, 2009). Yoga is a specific kind of exercise that typically includes meditation and relaxation, issues we consider next.

## Using Meditation and Relaxation

Recent years have seen an increased interest in meditation as a method for modulating negative emotions caused by stress. *Meditation* **refers to a family of mental exercises in which a conscious attempt is made to focus attention in a nonanalytical way.** There are many approaches to meditation. In the United States, the most widely practiced approaches are those associated with yoga, Zen, and transcendental meditation (TM). Relaxation is one of the benefits of meditation, although meditation isn't the only way to achieve relaxation.

Advocates of meditation claim that it can improve learning, energy level, work productivity, physical health, mental health, and general happiness while reducing tension and anxiety caused by stress (Andresen, 2000; Shapiro, Schwartz, & Santerre, 2005). These are not exactly humble claims. Let's examine the scientific evidence on meditation.

What are the immediate *physical* effects of going into a meditative state? Most studies find decreases in participants' heart rate, respiration rate, oxygen consumption, and carbon dioxide elimination (Whitehouse, Orne, & Orne, 2007). Taken together, these physical changes suggest that meditation can lead to a potentially beneficial physiological state characterized by relaxation and suppression of arousal (Carrington, 1993; Fenwick, 1987; Travis, 2001).

What about the long-term *psychological* benefits that have been claimed for meditation? Research suggests that meditation may have some value in reducing the effects of stress (Anderson et al., 1999; Winzelberg & Luskin, 1999). In particular, regular meditation is associated with lower levels of some stress hormones (Infante et al., 2001). Research also suggests that meditation can improve mental health while reducing

**WEB LINK 4.4** **Stress Management and Emotional Wellness Links**

This website functions as a gateway to several other sites that may be relevant to the subject of coping with stress. Included are links to sites that deal with humor, relaxation, meditation, increasing social support, crisis intervention, and stress management for college students.

anxiety and drug abuse (Alexander et al., 1994). Other studies report that meditation may have beneficial effects on blood pressure (Barnes, Treiber, & Davis, 2001), self-esteem (Emavardhana & Tori, 1997), mood and one's sense of control (Easterlin & Cardena, 1999), happiness (Smith, Compton, & West, 1995), and overall physical health and well-being (Reibel et al., 2001). Waelde and colleagues (2008) studied a meditation intervention in mental health workers in New Orleans following Hurricane Katrina. Their participants attended a four-hour meditation workshop that included instructions on guided practice, breathing, mantra repetition, and letting go of intrusive thoughts. Then they practiced meditation at home six days a week for eight weeks. The results showed that the meditation intervention led to reductions in PTSD symptoms and anxiety, and these improvements were positively correlated with the amount of daily meditation practiced.

At first glance these results are impressive, but they need to be viewed with some caution. Critics wonder whether placebo effects, sampling bias, and other methodological problems may contribute to some of the reported benefits of meditation (Bishop, 2002; Shapiro et al., 2005). In addition, at least some of these beneficial effects may be just as attainable through other mental focusing procedures, such as systematic relaxation (Shapiro, 1984; Smith, 1975).

Indeed, ample evidence suggests that relaxation procedures can soothe emotional turmoil and reduce stress-induced physiological arousal (Lehrer & Woolfolk, 1984, 1993; Smyth et al., 2001). And a recent controlled experiment comparing meditation and relaxation found that they decreased distress and increased posi-

tive moods equally well (Jain et al., 2007). There are a number of worthwhile approaches to achieving beneficial relaxation. We'll discuss one approach that is so simple that virtually anyone can learn to use it.

After studying various approaches to meditation, Herbert Benson, a Harvard Medical School cardiologist, concluded that elaborate religious rituals and beliefs are not necessary for someone to profit from meditation. He also concluded that what makes meditation beneficial is the relaxation it induces. After "demystifying" meditation, Benson (1975) set out to devise a simple, nonreligious procedure that could provide similar benefits. He calls his procedure the "relaxation response." According to Benson, four factors are critical to effective practice of the relaxation response:

**1.** *A quiet environment.* It is easiest to induce a relaxation response in a distraction-free environment. After you become skilled at the relaxation response, you may be able to accomplish it in a crowded subway. Initially, however, you should practice it in a quiet, calm place.

**2.** *A mental device.* To shift attention inward and keep it there, you need to focus it on a constant stimulus, such as a sound or word that you recite over and over. You may also choose to gaze fixedly at a bland object, such as a vase. Whatever the case, you need to focus your attention on something.

**3.** *A passive attitude.* It is important not to get upset when your attention strays to distracting thoughts. You must realize that such distractions are inevitable. Whenever your mind wanders from your focus, calmly redirect attention to your mental device.

**4.** *A comfortable position.* Reasonable body comfort is essential to avoid a major source of potential distraction. Simply sitting up straight works well for most people. Some people can practice the relaxation response lying down, but for most people such a position is too conducive to sleep.

Benson's deceptively simple procedure for inducing the relaxation response is described in **Figure 4.14**. For full benefit, it should be practiced daily.

Now that we have looked at numerous constructive coping tactics, in the following Application we turn to one of the most stress-inducing life events that we all have to cope with at some point in time: death and dying.

"I'm learning how to relax, doctor —
but I want to relax *better* and *faster*!
I want to be on the cutting edge of relaxation!"

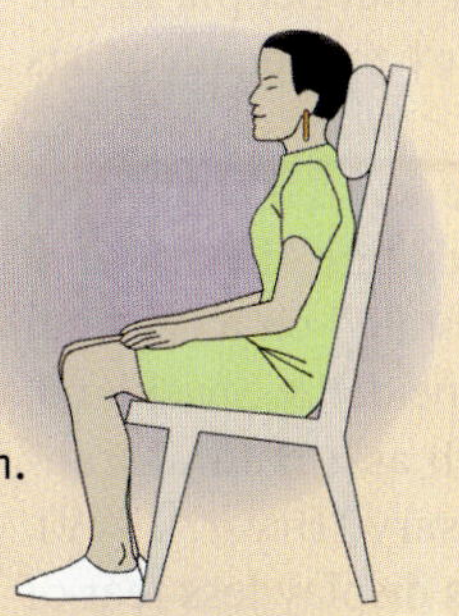

1  Sit quietly in a comfortable position.

2  Close your eyes.

3  Deeply relax all your muscles, beginning at your feet and progressing up to your face. Keep them relaxed.

4  Breathe through your nose. Become aware of your breathing. As you breathe out, say the word "one" silently to yourself. For example, breathe in . . . out "one"; in . . . out "one"; and so forth. Breathe easily and naturally.

5  Continue for 10 to 20 minutes. You may open your eyes to check the time, but do not use an alarm. When you finish, sit quietly for several minutes, at first with your eyes closed and later with your eyes opened. Do not stand up for a few minutes.

6  Do not worry about whether you are successful in achieving a deep level of relaxation. Maintain a passive attitude and permit relaxation to occur at its own pace. When distracting thoughts occur, try to ignore them by not dwelling on them, and return to repeating "one." With practice, the response should come with little effort. Practice the technique once or twice daily but not within two hours after any meal, since digestive processes seem to interfere with the elicitation of the relaxation response.

**Figure 4.14**

**Benson's relaxation response.** The relaxation procedure advocated by Herbert Benson is a simple one that should be practiced daily.

Source: From Benson, H., & Klipper, M. Z. (1975, 1988). *The relaxation response.* New York: Morrow. Copyright © 1975 by William Morrow & Co. Reprinted by permission of HarperCollins Publishers.

# APPLICATION

## Coping with Loss

### LEARNING OBJECTIVES

- Discuss cultural and individual attitudes about death, including death anxiety.
- Describe Kübler-Ross's five stages of dying and research findings about the dying process.
- Analyze cultural variations in mourning practices, and discuss the grieving process.
- Discuss various types of loss and what helps people cope with bereavement.

*Answer "yes" or "no" to the following questions (based on a scale by Conte, Weiner, & Plutchik, 1982).*

____ 1. Do you worry about dying?

____ 2. Does it bother you that you may die before you have done everything you wanted to do?

____ 3. Do you worry that dying may be very painful?

____ 4. Do you worry that those you care about may not remember you after your death?

____ 5. Are you worried about not knowing what to expect after death?

If you answered yes to the majority of these questions you likely experience high anxiety around the issue of death and dying. Life is indeed a journey and death is the ultimate destination. Dealing with the deaths of close friends and loved ones is an increasingly frequent adjustment problem as people move through adulthood. Moreover, the final challenge of life is to confront one's own death. Educating yourself about death and dying can help you cope with the grieving process.

### Attitudes About Death

Because death is a taboo topic in modern Western society, the most common strategy for coping with it is *avoidance.* There is abundant evidence of Americans' inability to confront death comfortably. People often use euphemisms such as "passed away" to avoid even the word itself. To minimize exposure to the specter of death, we sometimes unnecessarily quarantine dying people in hospitals and nursing homes. Professionals take custody of the body at death and manage funeral arrangements for families. These are all manifestations of what Kastenbaum (2001) calls a **death system—the collection of rituals and procedures used by a culture to handle death.** Death systems vary from culture to culture. Ours happens to be rather negative and evasive. Some scholars even argue that people in our culture use defensive coping to deny that death exists (Becker, 1997).

Negativism and avoidance are *not* universal features of death systems. In Mexican culture, death is discussed frequently and is even celebrated on a national feast day, the Day of the Dead (DeSpelder & Strickland, 1983). Also, the Amish view death as a natural transition rather than a dreaded adversary (Bryer, 1979). Thus, some cultures and subcultures display less fear of death than others do.

Stressors induce feelings of anxiety and, when it come to death, this anxiety can be especially powerful. **Death anxiety is the fear and apprehension about one's own death.** In Chapter 2, we noted that terror management theory asserts that death anxiety stems from the conflict between humans' instinct for self-preservation and their awareness of the inevitability of death. According to terror management theory, cultures provide traditions and institutions to help people deal with death anxiety. In support of the theory, adults who have a strong faith in a higher force or being have lower death anxiety (Cicirelli, 1999, 2002). Having a well-formulated personal philosophy of death, rather than having a particular religious affiliation, is associated with lower death anxiety. For instance, one study found that both devout Christians and confirmed atheists were less anxious about death than those with ambivalent religious views (Moore, 1992). Also, individuals who haven't accomplished all that they had hoped are more likely to fear death, as are those who are anxious and depressed (Neimeyer & Van Brunt, 1995).

## The Process of Dying

Pioneering research on the experience of dying was conducted by Elisabeth Kübler-Ross (1969, 1970) during the 1960s. At first, her project met with immense resistance. Fellow physicians at the hospital where she worked were initially unresponsive to her requests to interview dying patients. Gradually, however, it became apparent that many such patients were enthusiastic about the discussions. They were frustrated by the

© Ken Ross

**Elisabeth Kübler-Ross**

"conspiracy of silence" that surrounds death and were relieved to get things out in the open. Eventually, Kübler-Ross interviewed over 200 terminally ill patients and developed a model of the process of dying. According to her model, people evolve through a series of five stages as they confront their own death:

*Stage 1: Denial.* Denial, shock, and disbelief are the first reactions to being informed of a serious, life-terminating illness. According to Kübler-Ross, few patients maintain this stance to the end.

*Stage 2: Anger.* After denial, the patient often becomes nasty, demanding, difficult, and hostile. Asking and resolving the question "Why me?" can help the patient reduce resentment.

*Stage 3: Bargaining.* In this stage the patient wants more time and asks for favors to postpone death. The bargaining may be carried out with the physician or, more frequently, with God.

*Stage 4: Depression.* Depression is a signal that the acceptance process has really begun. Kübler-Ross has referred to this stage as "preparatory grief"—the sadness of anticipating an impending loss.

*Stage 5: Acceptance.* The person who achieves acceptance has taken care of unfinished business. The patient has stopped fighting the inevitable and is now ready to die. He or she will want to be with close family members, usually a spouse or partner and children; dying children want to be with their parents. Although patients desire the presence of someone warm, caring, and accepting at this time, verbal communication may be totally unnecessary.

Although Kübler-Ross asserted that people do not necessarily progress through these five stages in lock-step sequence, her use of the term "stages" implies otherwise. Thus, it is not surprising that her theory has been criticized on this confusing point (Kastenbaum, 1999). Instead of progressing though a common, five-stage process, dying people seem to show "a jumble of conflicting or alternating reactions running the gamut from denial to acceptance, with tremendous variation affected by age, sex, race, ethnic group, social setting, and personality" (Butler & Lewis, 1982, p. 370). Nonetheless, Kübler-Ross greatly improved our understanding of the process of dying and stimulated research that continues to add to our knowledge.

## Bereavement and Grieving

When a friend, spouse, or relative dies, individuals must cope with **bereavement, or the painful loss of a loved**

**WEB LINK 4.5    The End of Life: Exploring Death in America**

Since late 1997, National Public Radio (NPR) has regularly aired a range of programs relating to dying and death as experienced in American culture. This companion website at NPR offers not only printed and audio transcripts of each program but many bibliographical and organizational resources as well.

**one through death.** The death of someone close typically brings forth the painful and complex emotions of *grief. Mourning* **refers to the formal practices of an individual and a community in response to a death.** Many cultural and religious rituals help survivors adjust to and cope with their loss.

## Cultural Variations

Considerable variation exists among and within cultures with regard to grieving. In the U.S. and Western European countries, the bereaved are typically encouraged to break their emotional ties with the deceased relatively quickly and to return to their regular routines. In Asian, African, and Hispanic cultures, the bereaved are encouraged to maintain emotional ties to their dead loved ones (Bonanno, 1998). Almost all Japanese homes have altars dedicated to family ancestors, and family members routinely talk to the deceased and offer them food. Regardless of the particular form that mourning takes, all such rituals are designed to make death meaningful and to help the bereaved cope with the pain and disruption of death.

## The Grieving Process

Grief is a natural response to loss. Common emotional responses include shock, sadness, guilt, anger, and fear. Although everyone grieves differently, John Bowlby (1980) characterized grieving as a four-stage process:

*Stage 1: Numbness.* In this initial phase, survivors are typically dazed and confused. They may experience physical reactions such as nausea or tightness in the chest or throat. This phase may last several days or, in cases when death has been unexpected, several weeks.

*Stage 2: Yearning.* Here, survivors try to recover the lost person. Individuals may report that they see the deceased and may wander as if they are searching for the loved one. They often feel frustration, anger, and guilt. In addition, they may experience intense feelings of sadness and may cry and sob uncontrollably. They may also suffer loss of appetite and insomnia.

*Stage 3: Disorganization and despair.* Searching for the loved one ceases as the loss is accepted as real. However, accepting the loss brings feelings of helplessness, despair, and depression. Survivors often

Grief is a natural response to loss that commonly includes shock, sadness, and guilt. Here troops mourn their fellow soldiers killed in the 2009 Fort Hood shooting.

experience extreme fatigue and a need to sleep much more than usual.

*Stage 4: Reorganization.* Individuals are able to resume their normal routines at home and at work. Depression lifts, regular sleeping habits return, and energy increases. Thoughts of the loved one may bring sadness, but these feelings are no longer overwhelming.

Although Bowlby's model is certainly plausible, research suggests that most grief reactions do not follow this straightforward path (Wortman & Boerner, 2007; Wortman, Wolff, & Bonanno, 2004). Just as people react differently to the experience of their own impending deaths, they also show variable responses to bereavement. For instance, one study examined the patterns of change in depression in a sample of older adults prior to a spouse's death and at 6 and 18 months after spousal loss (Bonanno et al., 2002). By measuring depression both before and after a spouse's death, researchers could separate preloss depression from loss-induced depression. Participants' grief reactions could be categorized into various patterns. *Absent grief* is characterized by low levels of depression before and after the spouse's death. In *chronic grief*, depression exists before and after the spouse's death. *Common grief* is characterized by an increase in depression shortly after the spouse's death and a decrease in depression over time. When you examine **Figure 4.15**, you may be surprised to find that common grief is *not* the most frequent pattern. In fact, absent grief occurs much more frequently; almost half of the participants follow this pattern.

Other research examines grief reactions as time passes. The bulk of available studies track grief in the first year or years following the death of a spouse, and

**WEB LINK 4.6  Mental Health America: Coping with Bereavement**

This site includes information on seeking treatment and support groups for dealing with grief. This site may be particularly helpful for those who are dealing with loss.

many are aimed at examining who is resilient versus being at risk for psychological distress (Boerner, Wortman, & Bonanno, 2005). A recent study involved a national, representative sample of widowed people whose spouses had been dead for many years (Carnelley et al., 2006). Even after 20 years, many widowed people reported thinking about their spouse every week or so and spoke about the person about once a month. Feelings of distress were found to dissipate after the first decade following the death, and most people did report being upset when recalling their loved one.

## Coping with Various Types of Loss

It is important to note that many types of loss can cause grief. The death of a loved one, a miscarriage, the death of a pet, loss of health, and a relationship breakup are just a few life events that can cause one to grieve. The research we have been discussing looked only at the experiences of widows and widowers. The researchers would probably have obtained quite different findings if the subjects had been parents who had lost a child, the most difficult type of death adults must cope with (Stillion, 1995). One study compared the grief reactions of 255 middle-aged women who had experienced the death of a spouse, a parent, or a child in the two

**Figure 4.15**

**Five reactions to spousal loss.** Researchers gathered data on 205 older individuals prior to spousal loss and 6 months and 18 months following spousal loss. As you can see, 90% of the participants exhibited one of the five bereavement patterns shown in the figure. Contrary to popular belief, "absent grief" or the "resilient pattern" was the most frequently experienced reaction, while "common grief" occurred relatively infrequently. Traditional views of grief hold that the "common grief" reaction is the only healthy response to loss, but numerous studies contradict that view. (Adapted from Bonanno et al., 2002)

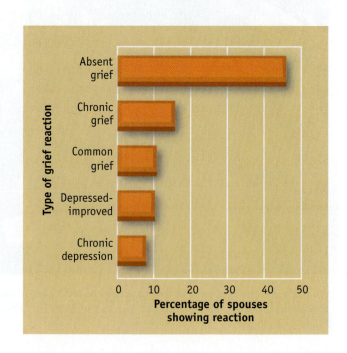

The 2004 Southeast Asian tsunami disaster was a rare and dramatic example of bereavement overload, the devastating experience of having to cope with several or more deaths at the same time.

years preceding the study (Leahy, 1993). As you might expect, mothers who had lost children had the highest levels of depression. And women whose husbands had died were significantly more depressed than women who had lost a parent.

A particularly difficult bereavement situation occurs when a child or an adolescent loses a parent to death. In these cases, grieving typically involves frequent crying, angry outbursts, trouble concentrating at school, and sleep problems. These symptoms may last from several months to a year (Silverman & Worden, 1992). It is important for adults to take the time to talk with grieving children. In particular, children need to be assured that the parent did not leave out of anger and that the remaining parent will not disappear (Furman, 1984).

*Bereavement overload* occurs when individuals experience several deaths at the same time or in close succession. For example, when the 2008 Sichuan earthquake devastated that region in China, tens of thousands of individuals died, many of whom were children. On a less dramatic scale, other groups who are likely to suffer bereavement overload include members of the gay community, who have lost lovers and friends to AIDS, and the elderly, who must deal with the loss of spouses, friends, and siblings because of advancing years.

The following points summarize advice that mental health professionals offer on coping with grief:

**1.** *Seek support while you are grieving.* Of course the presence of friends and family can't substitute for a loved one who has died (Stroebe et al., 1996). But to cope with loss, people need the sympathy and support of family and friends. There are also support groups for the bereaved that one can locate via local hospitals, hospices, or funeral homes.

**2.** *Care for your own emotional needs while grieving.* Be aware of your emotional state and allow yourself the time and space to grieve. To deal with painful feelings, utilize emotion-focused constructive coping techniques such as written emotional expression, relaxation, and physical activity. Recognize and avoid coping strategies that have limited value for you.

**3.** *Care for your own physical needs while grieving.* Pay special attention to your diet and sleep patterns. Taking care of yourself physically can pay off psychologically.

**4.** *Be aware and plan for grief triggers.* Anniversaries, holidays, and special locations can ignite one's feelings of grief. Recognizing this situation and planning ahead can help one deal with these difficult feelings.

## KEY IDEAS

### The Concept of Coping

● Coping involves behavioral efforts to master, reduce, or tolerate the demands created by stress. People cope with stress in many ways, but most have specific styles of coping. Coping strategies vary in their adaptive value, and flexibility is important when choosing a strategy.

### Common Coping Patterns of Limited Value

● Giving up, possibly best understood in terms of learned helplessness, is a common coping pattern that tends to be of limited value. Another is engaging in aggressive behavior. Frequently caused by frustration, aggression tends to be counterproductive because it often creates new sources of stress.

● Indulging oneself is a common coping strategy that is not inherently unhealthy, but it is frequently taken to excess and thus becomes maladaptive. Internet addiction is a relatively new form of self-indulgence. Blaming yourself with negative self-talk is associated with depression.

● Defensive coping is common and may involve any of a number of defense mechanisms. However, the adaptive value of defensive coping tends to be less than optimal. Although some illusions may be healthful, extreme forms of self-deception are maladaptive.

### The Nature of Constructive Coping

● Constructive coping involves efforts to deal with stress that are judged as relatively healthful. Constructive coping is rational, realistic, and action oriented. It takes effort and involves managing emotions.

### Appraisal-Focused Constructive Coping

● Appraisal-focused constructive coping depends on altering appraisals of threatening events. Ellis maintains that catastrophic thinking causes problematic emotional reactions. He asserts that catastrophic thinking can be reduced by digging out the irrational assumptions that cause it.

● Evidence indicates that the use of humor can reduce the negative effects of stress through a variety of mechanisms. Positive reinterpretation and benefit finding are also valuable strategies for dealing with some types of stress.

### Problem-Focused Constructive Coping

● Systematic problem solving can be facilitated by following a four-step process: (1) clarify the problem, (2) generate alternative courses of action, (3) evaluate your alternatives and select a course of action, and (4) take action while maintaining flexibility.

● A problem-focused coping tactic with potential value is seeking social support. There appear to be cultural differences regarding who seeks social support.

● Improving time management can also aid problem-focused coping. Effective time management doesn't depend on increased efficiency so much as on setting priorities and allocating time wisely. There are many causes of wasted time.

● It is helpful to avoid the common tendency to procrastinate on aversive tasks. Engaging in sound time-management techniques can reduce time-related stress.

### Emotion-Focused Constructive Coping

● Emotional intelligence may help people to be more resilient in the face of stress. Inhibition of emotions appears to be associated with increased health problems. Thus, it appears that appropriate emotional expression is adaptive. Research shows that writing about traumatic events or sensitive issues is associated with enhanced wellness.

● Research suggests that it is wise for people to learn how to manage their feelings of hostility. New evidence also suggests that forgiving people for their offenses is healthier than nursing grudges.

● Exercise is a healthy way to deal with emotional distress. Physical activity provides an outlet for frustration, can distract one from the stress, and is related to improved physical and mental health.

● Meditation can be helpful in soothing emotional turmoil. Meditation is associated with lower levels of stress hormones, improved mental health, and other indicators of wellness. Systematic relaxation procedures, such as Benson's relaxation response, can be effective in reducing troublesome emotional arousal.

### Application: Coping with Loss

● Attitudes about death vary from one culture to another. Attitudes in Western culture are characterized by negativism, avoidance, and fear.

● Kübler-Ross's research on the process of dying indicated that individuals progress through a sequence of five stages. Later research has called into question the idea that people's reactions to dying follow such a straightforward path.

● A wide variation exists between and within cultures regarding how death is acknowledged. Research has revealed a variety of patterns of grieving, calling into question traditional views of the process of mourning.

● Various kinds of loss cause grief. In dealing with bereavement, people should seek social support, recognize and care for their emotional and physical needs, and be aware of circumstances that might trigger their grief.

## KEY TERMS

| | |
|---|---|
| Aggression  p. 107 | Emotional intelligence |
| Bereavement  p. 132 | p. 126 |
| Brainstorming  p. 120 | Forgiveness  p. 128 |
| Catastrophic thinking  p. 115 | Internet addiction  p. 109 |
| Catharsis  p. 108 | Learned helplessness  p. 106 |
| Constructive coping  p. 114 | Meditation  p. 129 |
| Coping  p. 105 | Mourning  p. 133 |
| Death anxiety  p. 132 | Procrastination  p. 123 |
| Death system  p. 131 | Rational-emotive behavior |
| Defense mechanisms  p. 111 | therapy  p. 115 |

## KEY PEOPLE

| | |
|---|---|
| Herbert Benson  p. 130 | Elisabeth Kübler-Ross  p. 132 |
| John Bowlby  pp. 133–134 | James Pennebaker |
| Albert Ellis  pp. 115–117 | pp. 127–128 |
| Sigmund Freud  pp. 108, 111–113 | Martin Seligman  p. 106 |
| | Shelley Taylor  p. 113 |

## QUESTIONS

1. Who of the following is most likely to cope with stress effectively?
   a. David, who consistently relies on the same coping strategy for daily hassles.
   b. Tania, who is flexible in her coping strategies depending on the situation.
   c. Ricardo, who relies on catharsis to "blow off steam."
   d. Suzie, who engages in defensive coping when the going gets tough.

2. Which of the following assertions is *not* supported by research on the cathartic effects of media violence?
   a. Playing violent video games releases pent-up hostility.
   b. Playing violent video games is related to decreased prosocial behavior.
   c. Exposure to media violence desensitizes individuals to violent acts.
   d. Exposure to media violence encourages aggressive responses.

3. Richard feels sure that he failed his calculus exam and that he will have to retake the course. He is very upset. When he gets home, he orders a jumbo-size pizza and drinks two six-packs of beer. Richard's behavior illustrates which of the following coping strategies?
   a. catastrophic thinking
   b. defensive coping
   c. self-indulgence
   d. positive reinterpretation

4. Defense mechanisms involve the use of _____ to guard against negative _____.
   a. self-deception, behaviors
   b. self-deception, emotions
   c. self-denial, behaviors
   d. self-denial, emotions

5. Taylor and Brown found that "normal" people's self-images tend to be _____; depressed people's tend to be _____.
   a. accurate, inaccurate
   b. less favorable, more favorable
   c. overly favorable, more realistic
   d. more realistic, overly favorable

6. According to Albert Ellis, people's emotional reactions to life events result mainly from:
   a. their arousal level at the time.
   b. their beliefs about events.
   c. congruence between events and expectations.
   d. the consequences following events.

7. Which of the following is *not* listed in your text as a cause of wasted time?
   a. inability to set priorities
   b. inability to work diligently
   c. inability to delegate responsibility
   d. inability to throw things away

8. Wanda works at a software firm. Today her boss unfairly blamed her for the fact that a new program is way behind schedule. The unjustified public criticism really had an impact on Wanda. Later that evening, she went for a long run to get her anger under control. Wanda is engaging in which category of coping?
   a. self-focused coping
   b. appraisal-focused coping
   c. problem-focused coping
   d. emotion-focused coping

9. Research by James Pennebaker and his colleagues suggests that wellness is promoted by:
   a. depending on more mature defense mechanisms.
   b. strong self-criticism.
   c. writing about one's traumatic experiences.
   d. inhibiting the expression of anger.

10. Less anxiety about death is found among those who:
    a. feel they haven't accomplished all that they had hoped.
    b. have a particular religious affiliation.
    c. have ambivalent religious views.
    d. have a well-formulated philosophy of death.

## ANSWERS

| | | | |
|---|---|---|---|
| 1. b Page 105 | 6. b Page 116 | | |
| 2. a Page 108 | 7. b Pages 122–123 | | |
| 3. c Page 108 | 8. d Page 129 | | |
| 4. b Page 112 | 9. c Page 127 | | |
| 5. c Page 113 | 10. d Page 132 | | |

## Personal Explorations Workbook

Go to the *Personal Explorations Workbook* in the back of your textbook for exercises that can enhance your self-understanding in relation to issues raised in this chapter. **Exercise 4.1** *Self-Assessment:* Barnes-Vulcano Rationality Test. **Exercise 4.2** *Self-Reflection:* Analyzing Coping Strategies.

## CourseMate

Access an interactive eBook, chapter-specific interactive learning tools, including Personal Explorations, Recommended Readings, Critical Thinking Exercises, flashcards, quizzes, videos and more in your Psychology CourseMate, available at **www.cengagebrain.com/shop/ISBN/1111186634**.

© Tim Tadder/Corbis

# Psychology and Physical Health

Janet is a fairly typical student. She carries a full course load, works a part-time job, and plans to pursue a challenging career in nursing. She hopes to work in a hospital for a few years before enrolling in graduate school. Right now, however, her life is regulated by work: homework, her job, and more school-related work in the wards of the teaching hospital where she learns the science and practice of nursing. In a typical semester, Janet feels under control for the first few weeks, but then her work piles up: tests, papers, reading, appointments, labs, and so on. She feels anxious and stressed. Instead of getting eight full hours of sleep, she often does with much less. Fast food becomes a familiar and necessary comfort—she doesn't have time to prepare, let alone eat, healthy and well-balanced meals. Her regular exercise routine often gives way to other time commitments; she can't jog or get to the gym as much as she'd like. On the rare occasion she does take a break, it tends to involve watching television, catching up with friends on Facebook, or texting with her boyfriend, who attends another school. By the end of the term, she is anxious, stressed, tired, and run down. In fact, she usually celebrates the end of the semester by getting sick and ending up in bed for a few days instead of having relaxing times with her friends and family. And then this unfortunate cycle repeats itself the next semester.

Are you at all like Janet? How often do you become ill in a typical semester? Do you begin strong and healthy but feel worn out and frayed by the end? If you are like many students, your lifestyle has a close connection to your health and well-being. In the past few decades, research has demonstrated quite clearly that health is affected by social and psychological factors as well as biological ones. In other words, health is affected not just by germs or viruses but also by the choices people make and the lives they lead.

This chapter focuses on the fact that more than any other time in history, people's health is more likely to be compromised by *chronic diseases*—conditions that develop across many years—rather than by *contagious diseases*, those caused by specific infectious agents (such as measles, flu, or tuberculosis—see **Figure 5.1**). Moreover, lifestyle and stress play a much larger role in the development of chronic diseases than they do in contagious diseases. Today, the three leading chronic

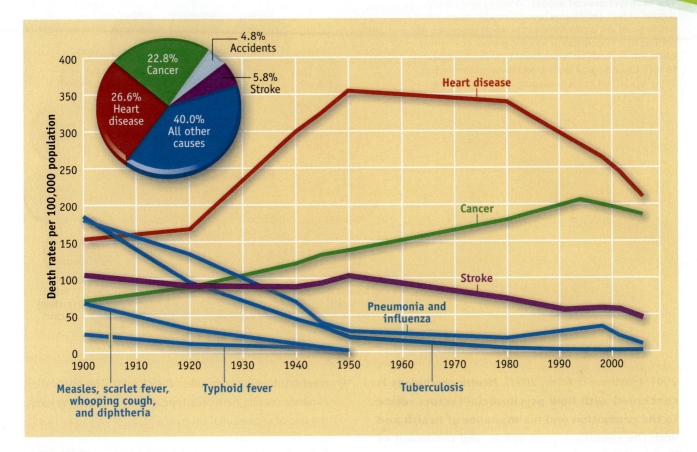

**Figure 5.1**

**Changing patterns of illness.**
Trends in the death rates for various diseases during the 20th century reveal that contagious diseases (shown in blue) declined as a threat to health. However, the death rates for stress-related chronic diseases (shown in red) remained quite high. The pie chart (inset), which depicts the percentage of deaths caused by most of the leading killers today, shows the results of these trends: Three chronic diseases (heart disease, cancer, and stroke) account for almost 55% of all deaths. (Source: Based on data from *National Vital Statistics Reports,* 2008, Vol. 56, No. 10.)

diseases (heart disease, cancer, and stroke) account for almost 60% of all deaths in the United States, and these mortality statistics reveal only the tip of the iceberg. Psychological and social factors also contribute to many other, less serious maladies, such as headaches, insomnia, backaches, skin disorders, asthma, and ulcers.

In light of these trends, it is not surprising that the way we think about illness is changing. Traditionally, illness has been thought of as a purely biological phenomenon produced by an infectious agent or some internal physical breakdown in the body. However, the shifting patterns of disease and new findings relating stress to physical illness have rocked the foundation of this biological model. In its place a new model has gradually emerged (Leventhal, Musumeci, & Leventhal, 2006; Schneiderman, 2004; Suls & Rothman, 2004). The **biopsychosocial model holds that physical illness**

**is caused by a complex interaction of biological, psychological, and sociocultural factors.** This model does not suggest that biological factors are unimportant. Rather, it simply asserts that biological factors operate in a psychosocial context that can also be highly influential. Medical and psychological professionals who adhere to the biopsychosocial model attend to additional factors, including cultural values (Landrine & Klonoff, 2001), that can affect the ways individuals think about and deal with chronic illness, especially where interactions with health care providers and adherence to treatments are concerned (Sperry, 2006). **Figure 5.2** on the next page illustrates how the three factors in the biopsychosocial model affect one another and, in turn, health.

The growing recognition that psychological factors influence physical health led to the development of a new specialty within psychology (Baum, Revenson, & Singer,

## Figure 5.2

**The biopsychosocial model.** Whether one's health is good or bad, the biopsychosocial model assumes that health is not just attributable to biological processes. According to this increasingly influential view, one's physical health depends on interactions between biological factors, psychological factors, and social system factors. Some key factors in each category are depicted here.

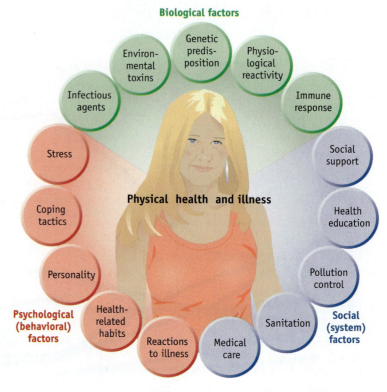

Biological factors

Infectious agents · Environmental toxins · Genetic predisposition · Physiological reactivity · Immune response

Stress · Coping tactics · Personality · Health-related habits · Reactions to illness

Psychological (behavioral) factors

Physical health and illness

Social support · Health education · Pollution control · Sanitation · Medical care

Social (system) factors

---

2001; Friedman & Adler, 2007). **Health psychology is concerned with how psychosocial factors relate to the promotion and maintenance of health and with the causation, prevention, and treatment of illness.** This specialty is relatively young, having emerged in the late 1970s (Baum, Perry, & Tarbell, 2004). In this chapter we focus on the rapidly growing domain of health psychology. The chapter's first section analyzes the link between stress and illness. The second section examines common health-impairing habits, such as smoking and overeating. The third section discusses how people's

reactions to illness can affect their health. The Application expands on one particular type of health-impairing habit: the use of recreational drugs.

> **WEB LINK 5.1  healthfinder**
>
> Through the U.S. Department of Health and Human Services, the government has opened an ambitious online gateway to consumer-oriented information about health in all its aspects. Annotated descriptions are available for all resources identified in no-cost searches of this database.

# Stress, Personality, and Illness

### LEARNING OBJECTIVES

- Describe the Type A personality, and discuss evidence regarding its most toxic element.
- Understand possible explanations for the link between hostility and heart disease.
- Summarize evidence relating emotional reactions and depression to heart disease.

- Discuss the evidence linking stress and personality to cancer.
- Summarize evidence linking stress to a variety of diseases and immune functioning.
- Evaluate the strength of the relationship between stress and illness.

What does it mean to say that personality can affect wellness? A guiding assumption is that a person's characteristic demeanor can influence his or her physical health. As noted in Chapter 2, personality is made up of the unique grouping of behavioral traits that a person exhibits consistently across situations. Thus, an individual who is chronically grumpy, often hostile toward others, and routinely

frustrated is more likely to develop an illness and perhaps even to die earlier than someone who is emotionally open, who is friendly, and who leads a balanced life (Friedman, 2007; Smith, 2006). Of course, the link between personality and disease is somewhat more complex but nonetheless real. We begin with a look at heart disease, far and away the leading cause of death in North America.

## Personality, Emotions, and Heart Disease

Heart disease accounts for nearly 27% of the deaths in the United States every year. **Coronary heart disease results from a reduction in blood flow through the coronary arteries, which supply the heart with blood.** This type of heart disease causes about 90% of heart-related deaths. Atherosclerosis is the principal cause of coronary disease (Giannoglou et al., 2008). **Atherosclerosis is a gradual narrowing of the coronary arteries,** usually caused by a buildup of fatty deposits and other debris on the inner walls (see **Figure 5.3**). Atherosclerosis progresses slowly over many years. Narrowed coronary arteries may eventually lead to situations in which the heart is temporarily deprived of adequate blood flow, causing a condition known as *myocardial ischemia*. This ischemia may be accompanied by brief chest pain, called *angina*. If a coronary artery is blocked completely (by a blood clot, for instance), the abrupt interruption of blood flow can produce a full-fledged heart attack, or *myocardial infarction*. Established risk factors for coronary disease include smoking, diabetes, high cholesterol levels, and high blood pressure (Greenland et al., 2003; Khot et al., 2003). Smoking and diabetes are somewhat stronger risk factors for women than for men (Stoney, 2003).

Contrary to public perception, cardiovascular diseases kill women just as much as men (Liewer et al., 2008) but these diseases tend to emerge in women about 10 years later than in men (Stoney, 2003). Interestingly, when women reach menopause—usually around age 50—they have a higher risk of heart disease than men (Mattar et al., 2008).

Recently, attention has shifted to the possibility that inflammation may contribute to atherosclerosis and elevated coronary risk (Hackam & Anand, 2003; Pilote et al., 2007). Evidence is mounting that inflammation plays a key role in the initiation and progression of atherosclerosis, as well as the acute complications that trigger heart attacks (Abi-Saleh et al., 2008; Albert et al., 2002; Libby, Ridker, & Maseri, 2002). The presence of stress and depression, too, can be related to inflammation (Miller & Blackwell, 2006). Fortunately, researchers have found a marker—levels of C-reactive protein (CRP) in the blood—that may help physicians estimate individuals' coronary risk more accurately than was possible previously (Ridker,

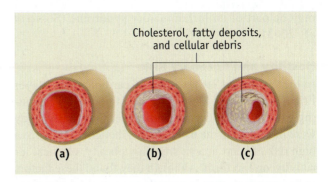

**Figure 5.3**
**Atherosclerosis.** Atherosclerosis, a narrowing of the coronary arteries, is the principal cause of coronary disease. **(a)** A normal artery. **(b)** Fatty deposits, cholesterol, and cellular debris on the walls of the artery have narrowed the path for blood flow. **(c)** Advanced atherosclerosis. In this situation, a blood clot might suddenly block the flow of blood through the artery.

2001). **Figure 5.4** shows how combined levels of CRP and cholesterol appear to be related to coronary risk. CRP levels are also predictive of the development of high blood pressure, which suggests that hypertension

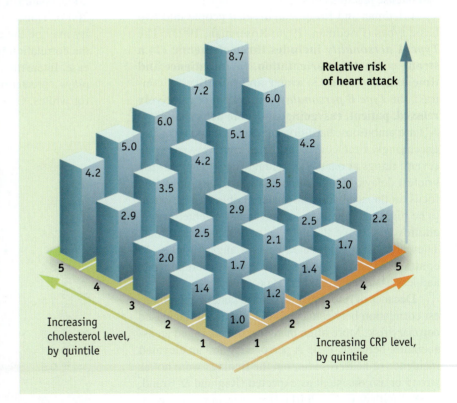

**Figure 5.4**
**The relationship of cholesterol and inflammation to coronary risk.** Levels of C-reactive protein (CRP) in the blood appear to be a useful index of the inflammation that contributes to atherosclerosis (Ridker, 2001). This graph shows how increasing CRP levels and increasing cholesterol levels combine to elevate cardiovascular risk (for a heart attack or stroke). The relative risks shown are for successive quintiles on each measure (each quintile represents one-fifth of the sample, ordered from those who scored lowest to those who scored highest). The relative risks are in relation to those who fall in the lowest quintile on both measures.

Source: Adapted from Ridker, P. M. (2001). High sensitivity C-reactive protein: Potential adjunct for global risk assessment in primary prevention of cardiovascular disease. *Circulation, 103,* 1813–1818. Copyright © 2001 American Heart Association. Adapted by permission of the publisher Lippincott Williams & Wilkins and the author.

may be part of an inflammatory syndrome (Sesso et al., 2003).

## Hostility and Coronary Risk

In the 1960s and 1970s a pair of cardiologists, Meyer Friedman and Ray Rosenman (1974), were investigating the causes of coronary disease. Originally, they were interested in the usual factors thought to produce a high risk of heart attack: smoking, obesity, physical inactivity, and so forth. Although they found these factors to be important, they eventually recognized that a piece of the puzzle was missing. Many people who smoked constantly, got little exercise, and were severely overweight still managed to avoid the ravages of heart disease. Meanwhile, others who seemed to be in much better shape with regard to these risk factors experienced the misfortune of a heart attack. What was their explanation for these perplexing findings? Stress! Specifically, they identified an apparent connection between coronary risk and a pattern of behavior they called the *Type A personality,* which involves self-imposed stress and intense reactions to stress.

Friedman and Rosenman divided people into two basic types (Friedman, 1996; Rosenman, 1993). The **Type A personality includes three elements: (1) a strong competitive orientation, (2) impatience and time urgency, and (3) anger and hostility.** In contrast, the **Type B personality is marked by relatively relaxed, patient, easygoing, amicable behavior.** Type A's are ambitious, hard-driving perfectionists who are exceedingly time conscious. They routinely try to do several things at once. They fidget frantically over the briefest delays, are concerned with numbers, and often focus on the acquisition of material objects. They tend to be highly competitive, achievement-oriented workaholics who drive themselves with many deadlines. They are easily aggravated and get angry quickly. In contrast, Type B's are less hurried, less competitive, and less easily angered than Type A's.

Decades of research uncovered a tantalizingly modest correlation between Type A behavior and increased coronary risk. More often than not, studies found an association between Type A personality and an elevated incidence of heart disease, but the findings were not as strong or as consistent as expected (Ragland & Brand, 1988; Smith & Gallo, 2001). However, in recent years, researchers have found a stronger link between personality and coronary risk by focusing on a specific component of the Type A personality: anger and hostility (Myrtek, 2007; Rozanski, Blumenthal, & Kaplan, 1999). *Hostility* **refers to a persistent negative attitude marked by cynical, mistrusting thoughts, feelings of anger, and overtly aggressive actions.** In fact, an early researcher interested in hostility argued that individuals who use anger as a response for dealing with interpersonal problems were at an elevated risk for heart

disease (Williams, 1989). For example, in one study of almost 13,000 men and women who had no prior history of heart disease (Williams et al., 2000), investigators found an elevated incidence of heart attacks among participants who exhibited an angry temperament. The participants, who were followed for a median period of 4.5 years, were classified as being low (37.1%), moderate (55.2%), or high (7.7%) in anger. Among participants with normal blood pressure, the high-anger subjects experienced almost three times as many coronary events as the low-anger subjects (see **Figure 5.5**). In another study, CT scans were used to look for signs of atherosclerosis in a sample of 374 men and women whose cynical hostility had been assessed a decade earlier when they were 18 to 30 years old (Irabarren et al., 2000). Participants with above-average hostility scores were twice as likely to exhibit atherosclerosis as participants with below-average hostility scores.

Many other studies have also found an association between hostility and various aspects of cardiovascular disease (Eaker et al., 2004; Nelson, Franks, & Brose, 2005; Niaura et al., 2002), including CRP levels (Suarez, 2004). Thus, recent research trends suggest that hostility may be the crucial toxic element that accounts for the correlation between Type A behavior and heart disease. Interestingly, there is some evidence that hostility plays a greater role in cardiovascular risk for blacks than for whites. One recent study using a sample of healthy

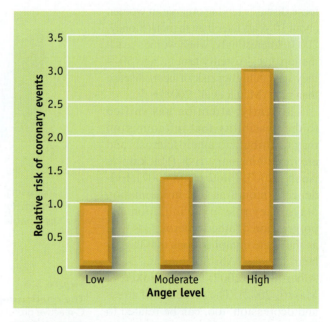

## Figure 5.5

**Anger and coronary risk.** Working with a large sample of healthy men and women who were followed for a median of 4.5 years, Williams et al. (2000) found an association between trait anger and the likelihood of a coronary event. Among subjects who manifested normal blood pressure at the beginning of the study, a moderate anger level was associated with a 36% increase in coronary attacks, and a high level of anger nearly tripled participants' risk for coronary disease.

Research suggests that excessive anger and hostility are associated with an increased risk for various types of heart disease.

© Siephoto/Radius Images/Masterfile

participants found that younger African Americans who exhibited high hostility showed a greater elevation in cardiovascular risk factors than a similar group of young white adults (Cooper & Waldstein, 2004).

Why are anger and hostility associated with coronary risk? First, let's be clear about some distinctions between these two responses. Anger is an unpleasant emotion that is accompanied by physiological arousal, whereas hostility involves a social component—a negative attitude toward others (Suls & Bunde, 2005). No one can avoid experiencing anger in their lives, however, which means it may be less of a risk factor in the development of heart disease. The manner in which individuals deal with their anger, though, may be quite consequential, creating a link to hostility toward others. Research has uncovered a number of possible explanations linking anger and hostility (see **Figure 5.6**). First, anger-prone individuals appear to exhibit greater physi-

ological reactivity than those lower in hostility (Smith & Gallo, 1999; Suarez et al., 1998). The frequent ups and downs in heart rate and blood pressure may create wear and tear in their cardiovascular systems. Such reactivity is especially high among African Americans (Merritt et al., 2004; Suarez et al., 2004). One explanation for this finding is emotional reactions to experiences of discrimination (Clark, 2003; Lepore et al., 2006).

Second, hostile people probably create additional stress for themselves (Smith, 2006; Smith & Gallo, 2001; Smith, Glazer, & Ruiz, 2004). For example, their quick anger may provoke many arguments and conflicts with others. Consistent with this line of thinking, Smith and colleagues (1988) found that subjects high in hostility reported more hassles, more negative life events, more marital conflict, and more work-related stress than subjects who were lower in hostility.

Third, thanks to their antagonistic ways of relating to others, hostile individuals tend to have less social support than others (Brummett et al., 2001; Chen, Gilligan, & Coups, 2005; Smith, 2003). Women who perceive little or no social support at home or at work are at greater risk for mortality resulting from a heart attack than other women (Kawachi et al., 1994). Living alone following a cardiac event actually increases a person's risk for a subsequent heart attack. Williams (1996), for example, found that single people or those who had no close friend with whom they could disclose private thoughts and concerns were three times more likely to die in a five-year period after their original heart attack than those who had either a spouse or a close friend. Thus, individuals with larger social networks tend to cope better, perhaps because they are more likely to have help getting to and from rehabilitation appointments (Molloy et al., 2008). As we noted

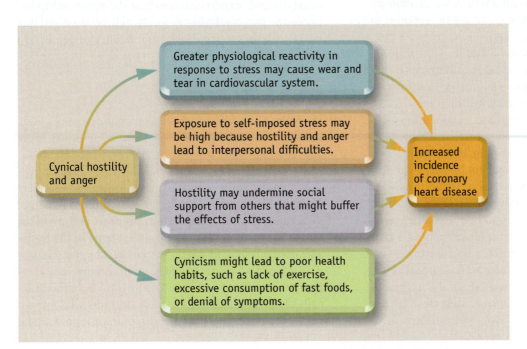

**Figure 5.6**

**Mechanisms that may link hostility and anger to heart disease.** Explanations for the apparent link between cynical hostility and heart disease are many and varied. Four widely discussed possibilities are summarized in the middle column of this diagram.

in Chapter 3, research suggests that social support may be an important coping resource that promotes health and buffers the effects of stress (Wills & Fegan, 2001). Moreover, research indicates that low social support may be an independent risk factor for coronary disease (Krantz & McCeny, 2002; Rozanski, Blumenthal, & Kaplan, 1999).

Fourth, perhaps because of their cynicism, people high in anger and hostility seem to exhibit a higher prevalence of poor health habits that may contribute to the development of cardiovascular disease. For example, people high in hostility are more likely to smoke, drink alcohol and coffee, and be overweight than others (Everson et al., 1997; Siegler et al., 1992; Watkins, Ward, & Southard, 1992). One reason this matters is that physical fitness mediates cardiac reactivity: People who stay in good physical shape have lower reactivity than those in poor shape (Wright et al., 2007).

## Emotional Reactions and Heart Disease

Although work on personality risk factors has dominated research on how psychological functioning contributes to heart disease, recent studies suggest that emotional reactions may also be critical. *One line of research has supported the hypothesis that transient mental stress and the resulting emotions that people experience can tax the heart.* Laboratory experiments with cardiology patients have shown that brief periods of mental stress can trigger acute symptoms of heart disease, such as myocardial ischemia and angina (Gottdiener et al., 1994). Overall, the evidence suggests that mental stress can elicit ischemia in about 30%–70% of patients with ongoing heart problems (Kop, Gottdiener, & Krantz, 2001). Moreover, research indicates that these patients have a higher risk for heart attack than the cardiology patients who do not manifest ischemia in response to mental stress (Krantz et al., 2000).

Related research considers the impact of holding back or suppressing emotions, particularly anger. Ironically, perhaps, keeping negative emotions to oneself is potentially more harmful than expressing anger toward others (Harburg et al., 2003; Jorgensen & Kolodziej, 2007). A related form of suppressed emotion is *rumination*—engaging in repetitive and negative thinking about some event. Going over and over the incident heightens negative feelings as well as depression (Hogan & Linden, 2004). Over time, this relentless mental "stewing" can become a negative coping strategy that actually increases people's risk for cardiac problems. Learning to recognize one's impending emotional state, as when one becomes angry, but then expressing the emotion as calmly and rationally as possible may be a healthier response (Siegman, 1994).

## Depression and Heart Disease

Another line of research has recently implicated depression as a major risk factor for heart disease. *Depressive disorders,* which are characterized by persistent feelings of sadness and despair, are a fairly common form of psychological disorder (see Chapter 14). Over the years, many studies have found elevated rates of depression among patients suffering from heart disease, but most theorists have explained this correlation by asserting that being diagnosed with heart disease makes people depressed. However, studies conducted in the last decade or so have suggested that the causal relations may also flow in the opposite direction—*that the emotional dysfunction of depression may cause heart disease* (Goldston & Baillie, 2008; Thomas, Kalaria, & O'Brien, 2004). For example, Pratt and colleagues (1996) examined a large sample of people 13 years after they were screened for depression. They found that participants who had been depressed at the time of the original study were four times more likely than others to experience a heart attack during the intervening 13 years. Because the participants' depressive disorders preceded their heart attacks, one cannot argue that their heart disease caused their depression. In some supporting research, damage to the arteries of the heart has been found among depressed teens (Tomfohr, Martin, & Miller, 2008).

Overall, studies have found that depression roughly doubles one's chances of developing heart disease (Lett et al., 2004; Rudisch & Nemeroff, 2003). Moreover, depression also appears to influence how heart disease progresses, as it is associated with a worse prognosis among cardiology patients (Glassman et al., 2003), including increased mortality rates within six months of the first cardiac episode (Blumenthal, 2008). Although the new emphasis is on how depression contributes to heart disease, experts caution that the relationship between the two conditions is surely bidirectional and that heart disease also increases vulnerability to depression (Sayers, 2004).

## Stress and Cancer

If one single word can strike terror into most people's hearts, it is probably *cancer*. People generally view cancer as the most sinister, tragic, frightening, and unbearable of diseases. In reality, cancer is actually a *collection* of over 200 related diseases that vary in their characteristics and amenability to treatment (Nezu et al., 2003). **Cancer refers to malignant cell growth, which may occur in many organ systems in the body.** The core problem in cancer is that cells begin to reproduce in a rapid, disorganized fashion. As this reproduction process lurches out of control, the teeming new cells clump together to form tumors. If this wild growth continues unabated, the spreading tumors cause tissue damage and begin to interfere with normal functioning in the affected organ systems.

It is widely believed by the general public that stress and personality play major roles in the development of cancer (McKenna et al., 1999). However, the research linking psychological factors to the *onset* of cancer is extremely weak. For example, one prospective study of twins found that extraversion and neuroticism (two of the Big Five personality traits; see Chapter 2) were unrelated to increased risk of cancer (Hansen et al., 2005). However, a few retrospective studies found evidence that high stress precedes the development of cancer (Cohen, Kunkel, & Levenson, 1998; Katz & Epstein, 2005). More recently, a careful meta-analysis of 165 independent studies revealed unequivocally that stress-related psychosocial variables are associated with cancer (Chida et al., 2008). The study demonstrated that stress predicted higher rates of the disease in initially healthy populations, lower survival rates among individuals diagnosed with cancer, and higher cancer mortality in general. Naturally, stress can also encourage people to engage in unhealthy behaviors that can increase the disease's progress (Carlson et al., 2007). Note that these results are suggestive but are by no means definitive. Stress is related to but is not necessarily causally linked to cancer; thus, the debate continues (Reiche, Nunes, & Morimoto, 2004; Tez & Tez, 2008)

Although efforts to link psychological factors to the onset of cancer have produced equivocal findings, more convincing evidence has shown that stress and personality influence the *course* of the disease. The onset of cancer frequently sets off a chain reaction of stressful events (Andersen, Golden-Kreutz, & DiLillo, 2001). Patients typically have to grapple with fear of the unknown; difficult and aversive treatment regimens; nausea, fatigue, and other treatment side effects; interruptions in intimate relationships; career disruptions; job discrimination; and financial worries. Moreover, depression can become a problem among cancer patients during active treatment (Reich, Lesur, & Perdrizet-Chevallier, 2009). Such stressors may often contribute to the progress of the disease, perhaps by impairing certain aspects of immune system functioning (Andersen, Kiecolt-Glaser, & Glaser, 1994). The impact of all this stress may depend in part on one's personality. Research suggests that mortality rates are somewhat higher among patients who respond with depression, repressive coping, and other negative emotions (Friedman, 1991). In contrast, prospects appear to be better for patients who can maintain their emotional stability and enthusiasm.

## Stress and Other Diseases

The development of questionnaires to measure life stress has allowed researchers to look for correlations between stress and a variety of diseases. Among infectious diseases, stress has been clearly implicated in development of the common cold (Cohen, 2005; Cohen et al., 1998). The typical research paradigm is to intentionally inoculate healthy volunteers with cold viruses, keep them under quarantine (in separate hotel rooms), and then observe who does or does not come down with a cold. People reporting higher levels of stress are more likely to become ill. Interestingly, people who are social and agreeable are at lower risk of getting a cold after exposure to a virus (Cohen et al., 2003).

What about more chronic diseases? Zautra and Smith (2001) found an association between life stress and the course of rheumatoid arthritis (see also, Davis et al., 2008; Fifield et al., 2004). Another study found an association between stressful life events and the emergence of lower back pain (Lampe et al., 1998). Other researchers have connected stress to the occurrence of asthmatic reactions (Chen & Miller, 2007; Ritz et al., 2000) and periodontal disease (Marcenes & Sheiham, 1992). Studies have also found an association between high stress and flareups of irritable bowel syndrome (Blanchard & Keefer, 2003) and peptic ulcers (Levenstein, 2002).

These are just a handful of representative examples of research relating stress to physical diseases. **Figure 5.7** provides a longer list of health problems that have been linked to stress. Many of these stress-illness connections are based on tentative or inconsistent findings, but the sheer length and diversity of the list is remarkable. Why should stress increase the risk for so many kinds of illness? A partial answer may lie in immune functioning.

## Stress and Immune Functioning

The apparent link between stress and many types of illness probably reflects the fact that stress can undermine the body's immune functioning. **The *immune response* is the body's defensive reaction to invasion by bacteria, viral agents, or other foreign substances.** The human immune response works to protect the body from many forms of disease. Immune reactions are remarkably complex and multifaceted (Chiappelli & Liu, 2000). Hence, there are a great many ways to measure immune function in an organism, and these multiple measures can sometimes produce conflicting, confusing results in research.

Nonetheless, a wealth of studies indicate that experimentally induced stress can impair immune functioning *in animals* (Moynihan & Ader, 1996). That is, stressors such as crowding, shock, food restriction, and

### Health Problems That May Be Linked to Stress

| Health Problem | Representative evidence |
| --- | --- |
| Common cold | Mohren et al. (2005) |
| Ulcers | Levenstein (2002) |
| Asthma | Lehrer et al. (2002) |
| Migraine headaches | Ramadan (2000) |
| Premenstrual distress | Stanton et al. (2002) |
| Vaginal infections | Williams & Deffenbacher (1983) |
| Herpes virus | Padgett & Sheridan (2000) |
| Skin disorders | Arnold (2000) |
| Rheumatoid arthritis | Keefe et al. (2002) |
| Chronic back pain | Lampe et al. (1998) |
| Diabetes | Landel-Graham, Yount, & Rudnicki (2003) |
| Complications of pregnancy | Dunkel-Schetter et al. (2001) |
| Hyperthyroidism | Yang, Liu, & Zang (2000) |
| Hemophilia | Buxton et al. (1981) |
| Stroke | Harmsen et al. (1990) |
| Appendicitis | Creed (1989) |
| Multiple sclerosis | Grant et al. (1989) |
| Periodontal disease | Marcenes & Sheiham (1992) |
| Hypertension | O'Callahan, Andrews, & Krantz (2003) |
| Cancer | Holland & Lewis (1993) |
| Coronary heart disease | Orth-Gomer et al. (2000) |
| AIDS | Ironson et al. (2000) |
| Inflammatory bowel disease | Searle & Bennett (2001) |
| Epileptic seizures | Kelly & Schramke (2000) |

**Figure 5.7**

**Stress and healh problems.** The onset or progress of the health problems listed here *may* be affected by stress. Although the evidence is fragmentary in many instances, it's alarming to see the number and diversity of problems on this list.

restraint reduce various aspects of immune reactivity in laboratory animals (Chiappelli & Hodgson, 2000). Of course, stress can affect animal immune function in natural settings, as well (Nelson & Demas, 2004).

Studies by Janice Kiecolt-Glaser and her colleagues have also related stress to suppressed immune activity *in humans* (Kiecolt-Glaser & Glaser, 1995). In one study, medical students provided researchers with blood samples so that their immune response could be assessed at various points (Kiecolt-Glaser et al., 1984). The students provided the baseline sample a month before final exams and contributed the "high-stress" sample on the first day of their finals. The subjects also responded to the Social Readjustment Rating Scale (SRRS; see Chapter 3) as a measure of recent stress. Reduced levels of immune activity were found during the extremely stressful finals week. Reduced immune activity was also correlated with higher scores on the SRRS.

Chronic illnesses have a negative impact on immune function (Nelson et al., 2008) and the presence of stress renders people's abilities to deal with these illnesses even worse (Fang et al., 2008). In a thorough review of 30 years of research on stress and immunity, Segerstrom and Miller (2004) conclude that chronic stress can reduce both *cellular immune responses* (which attack intracellular pathogens, such as viruses) and *humoral immune responses* (which attack extracellular pathogens, such as bacteria). They also report that the *duration* of a stressful event is a key factor determining its impact on immune function. Long-lasting stressors, such as caring for a seriously ill spouse or enduring unemployment for months, are associated with greater immune suppression than relatively brief stressors (Cohen et al., 1998).

Underscoring the importance of the link between stress and immune function, a recent study found evidence that chronic stress may produce *premature aging of immune system cells* (Epel et al., 2004). The study revealed that women who were dealing with heavy, long-term stress (caring for a child with a serious, chronic illness, such as cerebral palsy) had immune system cells that appeared to be a decade older than their chronological age, perhaps shedding light for the first time on why people under severe stress often look old and haggard. Unfortunately, evidence suggests that in the face of stress, people's immune systems do not fight off illness as well as they grow older (Graham, Christian, & Kiecolt-Glaser, 2006; Kiecolt-Glaser & Glaser, 2001). To summarize, scientists have assembled impressive evidence that stress can temporarily suppress human immune functioning, which can make people more vulnerable to infectious disease agents.

## Conclusions

A wealth of evidence suggests that stress influences physical health. However, virtually all of the relevant research is correlational, so it cannot demonstrate conclusively that stress *causes* illness (Smith & Gallo, 2001; Watson & Pennebaker, 1989). The association between stress and illness could be due to a third variable. Perhaps some aspect of personality or some type of physiological predisposition makes people overly prone to interpret events as stressful *and* overly prone to interpret unpleasant physical sensations as symptoms of illness (see **Figure 5.8**). Moreover, critics of this research note that many of the studies used research designs that may have inflated the apparent link between stress and illness (Schwarzer & Schulz, 2003; Turner & Wheaton, 1995). Alternatively, stress may simply alter health-related behaviors, increasing the incidence of "bad habits"—more smoking, drinking alcohol, using illegal drugs, sleeping less—all of which increase people's risk for diseases and disrupt their immunity (Segerstrom & Miller, 2004).

Despite methodological problems favoring inflated correlations, the research in this area consistently indicates that the *strength* of the relationship between stress and health is modest. The correlations typically fall in the .20s and .30s (Cohen, Kessler, & Gordon, 1995). Clearly, stress is not an irresistible force that produces inevitable effects on health. Actually, this fact should come as no surprise. As we saw in Chapter 3, some people handle stress better than others. Furthermore, stress is only one actor on a crowded stage. A complex network of biopsychosocial factors influence health, including genetic endowment, exposure to infectious agents and environmental toxins, and the choices people make in daily life. In the next section we look at some of these factors as we examine health-impairing habits and lifestyles.

Janice
Kiecolt-Glaser

Courtesy Janice Kiecolt-Glaser

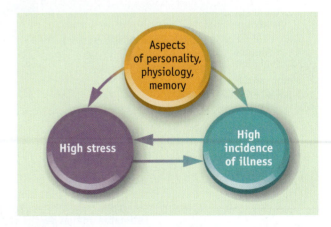

**Figure 5.8**

**The stress/illness correlation.** Based on the evidence as a whole, most health psychologists would probably accept the assertion that stress often contributes to the causation of illness. However, some critics argue that the stress-illness correlation could reflect other causal processes. One or more aspects of personality, physiology, or memory might contribute to the correlation between high stress and a high incidence of illness. (See Chapter 3 for additional discussion of this complex issue.)

**WEB LINK 5.2  Centers for Disease Control and Prevention (CDC)**

The CDC is the federal agency charged with monitoring and responding to serious threats to the nation's health as well as taking steps to prevent illness. This site's "Health Information from A to Z" offers the public in-depth medical explanations of many health problems both common (flu, allergies) and unusual (fetal alcohol syndrome, meningitis).

# Habits, Lifestyles, and Health

## LEARNING OBJECTIVES

- Identify some reasons that people develop health-impairing habits.
- Discuss the health effects of smoking and the dynamics of giving up smoking.
- Summarize data on patterns of alcohol use and the health risks and social costs of drinking.
- Discuss the health risks and determinants of obesity.
- Outline the key elements in effective weight-loss efforts.

- Provide examples of links between nutrition and health, and outline three general goals to foster sound nutrition.
- Assess the benefits and risks of exercise.
- List four guidelines for embarking on an effective exercise program.
- Describe AIDS, and summarize evidence on the transmission of the HIV virus.

Some people seem determined to dig an early grave for themselves. They do precisely those things they have been warned are particularly bad for their health. For example, some people drink heavily even though they know they're corroding their liver. Others eat all the wrong foods even though they know they're increasing their risk for a heart attack. Unfortunately, health-impairing habits contribute to far more deaths than most people realize. In a recent analysis of the causes of death in the United States, Mokdad and colleagues (2004) estimate that unhealthy behaviors are responsible for about half of all deaths each year. The habits that account for the most premature mortality, by far, are smoking and poor diet/physical inactivity (see **Figure 5.9**). Other leading behavioral causes of death include alcohol consumption, unsafe driving, sexually transmitted diseases, and illicit drug use.

It may seem puzzling that people behave in self-destructive ways. Why do they do it? Several factors are involved. First, many health-impairing habits creep up on people slowly. For instance, drug use may grow imperceptibly over years, or exercise habits may decline ever so gradually. Second, many health-impairing habits involve activities that are quite pleasant at the time. Actions such as eating favorite foods, smoking cigarettes, and getting "high" are potent reinforcing events. Third, the risks associated with most health-impairing habits are chronic diseases such as cancer that usually take 10, 20, or 30 years to develop. It is relatively easy to ignore risks that lie in the distant future.

Fourth, it appears that *people have a tendency to underestimate the risks associated with their own health-impairing habits* while viewing the risks associated with others' self-destructive behaviors much more accurately (Weinstein, 2003; Weinstein & Klein, 1996). In other words, most people are aware of the dangers associated with certain habits, but they often engage in *denial* when

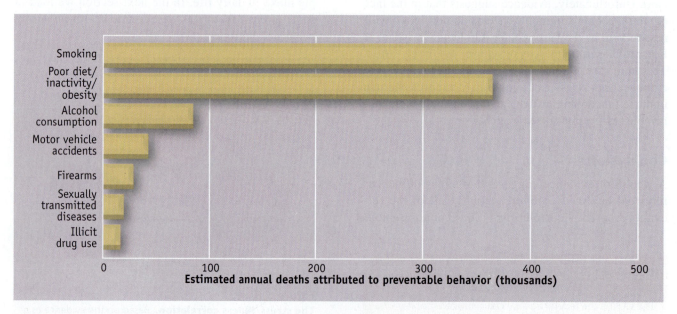

**Figure 5.9**

**Mortality due to health-impairing behaviors.** Synthesizing data from many sources, Mokdad and colleagues (2004) estimated the number of annual deaths in the United States attributable to various health-impairing behaviors in an article published in *The Journal of the American Medical Association.* As you can see, their calculations suggest that smoking and obesity are the leading causes of preventable mortality. However, their mortality estimate for obesity has proven controversial and is the subject of some debate (some experts argue that their estimate is too high).

it is time to apply this information to themselves. Thus, some people exhibit *unrealistic optimism* **wherein they are aware that certain health-related behaviors are dangerous, but they erroneously view those dangers as risks for others rather than themselves.** In effect, they say to themselves "bad things may well happen to other people, but not to me" (Gold, 2008; Klein & Weinstein, 1997). Of course, we have already learned that, in general, optimism is a beneficial personality trait (see Chapter 3). However, in the context of taking health risks and engaging in unwise behavior, unrealistic optimism may prevent people from taking appropriate precautions to protect their physical and mental well-being.

Yet another problem is that people are exposed to so much conflicting information about what's healthy and what isn't. It seems like every week a report in the media claims that yesterday's standard health advice has been contradicted by new research. This apparent inconsistency confuses people and undermines their motivation to pursue healthy habits. Sometimes it seems that health and happiness are more a matter of luck than anything else. In reality, the actions individuals take and the self-control they exercise can matter a great deal.

In this section we discuss how health is affected by smoking, drinking, overeating and obesity, poor nutrition, and lack of exercise. We also look at behavioral factors that relate to AIDS. The health risks of recreational drug use are covered in the Application.

## Smoking

Why do people smoke? Smokers claim that cigarettes elevate their mood, suppress hunger pangs (which they believe helps them stay thin), and enhances alertness and attention. The percentage of people who smoke has declined noticeably since the mid-1960s (see **Figure 5.10** on the next page). Nonetheless, about 24% of adult men and 18% of adult women in the United States continue to smoke regularly. Smoking among college-aged students has dropped from close to 30% to just under 20% (Harris, Schwartz, & Thompson, 2008; Thompson et al., 2007; Wechsler et al., 2001). Unfortunately, smoking is all-too-common in many other countries.

### Health Effects

Accumulating evidence clearly shows that smokers face a much greater risk of premature death than nonsmokers. For example, the average smoker has an estimated life expectancy *13–14 years shorter* than that of a similar nonsmoker (Schmitz & Delaune, 2005). The overall risk is positively correlated with the number of cigarettes smoked and their tar and nicotine content. Cigar smoking, which has increased dramatically in recent years, elevates health risks almost as much as cigarette smoking (Baker et al., 2000).

Why are mortality rates higher for smokers? In the first place, tobacco contains around 500 chemicals

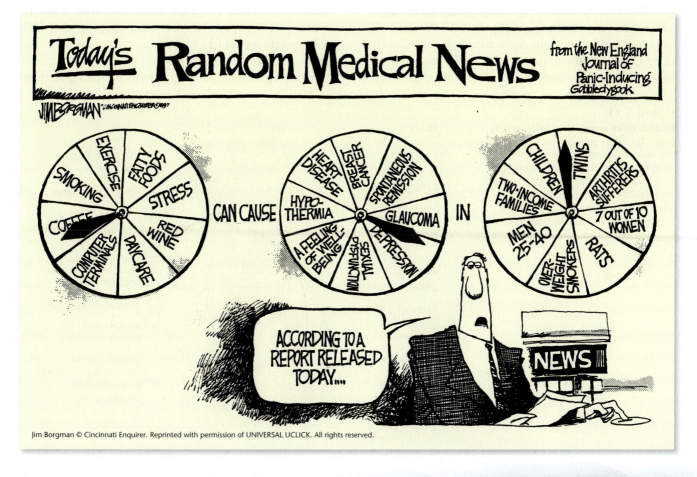

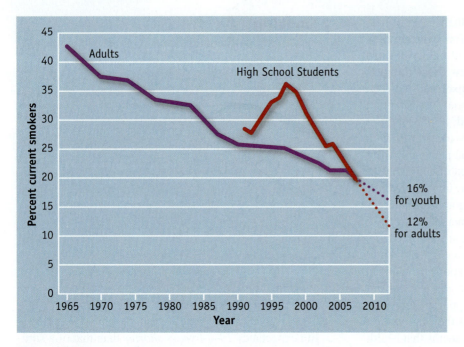

## Figure 5.10

**The prevalence of smoking in the United States.** This graph shows how the percentage of U.S. adults who smoke has declined steadily since the mid-1960s. It also shows how smoking among high school aged students, which rose in the early 1990s and then peaked between 1995 and 1996, has also declined. Although considerable progress has been made, smoking still accounts for about 435,000 premature deaths each year. (Data from Centers for Disease Control)

to succumb to cardiovascular disease as nonsmokers are. Smokers also have an elevated risk for oral, bladder, and kidney cancer, as well as cancers of the larynx, esophagus, and pancreas; for atherosclerosis, hypertension, stroke, and other cardiovascular diseases; and for bronchitis, emphysema, and other pulmonary diseases (U.S. Department of Health and Human Services, 2004). Most smokers know about the risks associated with tobacco use, but they tend to underestimate the actual risks as applied to themselves (Ayanian & Cleary, 1999) at the same time they overestimate the likelihood they can quit smoking when they want to (Weinstein, Slovic, & Gibson, 2004).

### Giving Up Smoking

Studies show that if people can give up smoking, their health risks decline reasonably quickly (Kenfield et al., 2008; Williams et al., 2002). Five years after people stop smoking, their health risk is already noticeably lower than that for people who continue to smoke. The health risks for people who give up tobacco continue to decline until they reach a normal level after about 15 years (see **Figure 5.12**). Evidence suggests that 70% of smokers would like to quit, but they are reluctant to give up a major source of pleasure and they worry about craving cigarettes, gaining weight, becoming anxious

and the smoke emanating from it holds another 4000 chemicals (Dube & Green, 1982). Smoking increases the likelihood of developing a surprisingly large range of diseases, as you can see in **Figure 5.11** (Schmitz & Delaune, 2005; Woloshin, Schwartz, & Welch, 2002). Lung cancer and heart disease kill the largest number of smokers; in fact, smokers are almost twice as likely

## Figure 5.11

**Health risks associated with smoking.** This figure provides an overview of the various diseases that are more common among smokers than nonsmokers. As you can see, tobacco elevates one's vulnerability to a remarkably diverse array of diseases, including the three leading causes of death in the modern world—heart attack, cancer, and stroke.

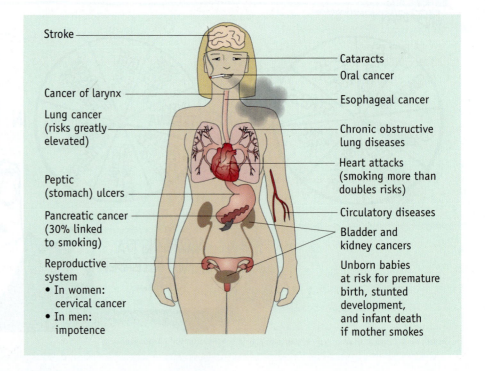

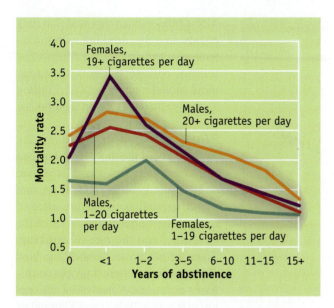

**Figure 5.12**

**Quitting smoking and mortality.** Research suggests that various types of health risks associated with smoking decline gradually after people give up tobacco. The data shown here, from the 1990 U.S. Surgeon General's report on smoking, illustrate the overall effects on mortality rates. The mortality rates on the vertical axis show how much death rates are elevated among smokers and ex-smokers in comparison to nonsmokers. For example, a mortality rate of 3.0 would mean that smokers' death rate was triple that of nonsmokers. (Data from U.S. Department of Health and Human Services, 1990)

and irritable, and feeling less able to cope with stress (Grunberg, Faraday, & Rahman, 2001). Smoking is a difficult habit to drop. In one study comparing dependence on drugs, alcohol, and smoking, individuals reported that giving up cigarettes would be the greatest challenge (Kozlowski et al., 1989).

Research shows that long-term success rates for efforts to quit smoking are in the vicinity of only 25% (Cohen et al., 1989). Light smokers are somewhat more successful at quitting than heavy smokers (but see Schachter, 1982). Discouragingly, people who enroll in formal smoking cessation programs are only slightly more successful than people who try to quit on their own (Swan, Hudman, & Khroyan, 2003). In fact, it is estimated that the vast majority of people who successfully give up smoking quit on their own, without professional help (Niaura & Abrams, 2002).

In recent years attention has focused on the potential value of *nicotine substitutes,* which can be delivered

*"There's no shooting—we just make you keep smoking."*

via gum, pills like Chantix, skin patches, nasal sprays, or inhalers. The rationale for nicotine substitutes is that insofar as nicotine is addictive, using a substitute might be helpful during the period when the person is trying to give up cigarettes. Do these substitutes work? They do help (Stead et al., 2008). Controlled studies have demonstrated that nicotine substitutes increase long-term rates of quitting in comparison to placebos (Swan, Hudman, & Khroyan, 2003). However, the increases are modest and the success rates are still discouragingly low. Nicotine substitutes are not a magic bullet or a substitute for a firm determination to quit. The various methods of nicotine delivery seem to be roughly equal in effectiveness, but combining a couple of methods appears to increase the chances of quitting successfully (Schmitz & Delaune, 2005).

## Drinking

Alcohol rivals tobacco as one of the leading causes of health problems in North America. Alcohol encompasses a variety of beverages containing ethyl alcohol, such as beers, wines, and distilled spirits. The concentration of alcohol in these drinks varies from about 4% in most beers up to 40% in 80-proof liquor (or more in higher-proof liquors). Survey data indicate that about half of adults in the United States drink. As **Figure 5.13** on the next page shows, per capita consumption of alcohol in the United States declined in the 1980s and 1990s, but this decrease followed decades of steady growth, and alcohol consumption remains relatively high, although certainly not the highest in the world. **Figure 5.14** shows the percentage of adults in the United States who are regular, infrequent, or former drinkers.

Drinking is particularly prevalent on college campuses. When researchers from the Harvard School of Public Health surveyed nearly 11,000 undergraduates at 119 schools, they found that 81% of the students drank (Wechsler et al., 2002). Moreover, 49% of the men and

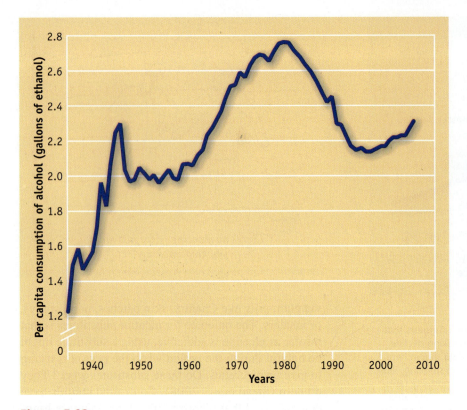

**Figure 5.13**

**Drinking in America.** Drinking in the United States, as indexed by per capita consumption (average consumed per person per year) of ethanol in gallons, rose steadily through most of the 20th century, although notable declines occurred during the 1980s and 1990s. (Data from National Institute on Alcohol Abuse and Alcoholism and U.S. Department of Health and Human Services)

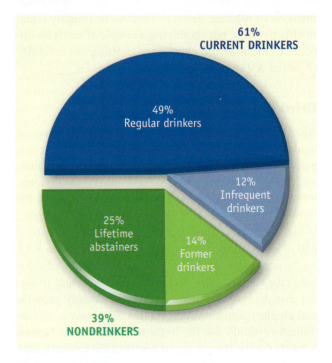

**Figure 5.14**

**Types of Adult Drinkers in the United States.** Just over 60% of adults in the United States categorize themselves as current drinkers. About one-quarter of all adults are lifelong abstainers.

Source: Adapted from *Healthy United States, 2007* (Table 68), 2007, by National Center for Health Statistics, Hyattsville, MD; U.S. Government Printing Office.

41% of the women reported that they engage in binge drinking with the intention of getting drunk. Perhaps most telling, college students spend far more money on alcohol ($5.5 billion annually) than they do on their books.

## Why Do People Drink?

The effects of alcohol are influenced by the user's experience, relative size and weight, gender, motivation, and mood, as well as by the presence of food in the stomach, the proof of the beverage, and the rate of drinking. Thus, we see great variability in how alcohol affects different people on different occasions. Nonetheless, the central effect is a "Who cares?" brand of euphoria that temporarily boosts self-esteem as one's problems melt away. Negative emotions such as tension, worry, anxiety, and depression are dulled, and inhibitions may be loosened (Johnson & Ait-Daoud, 2005). Thus, when first-year college students are asked why they drink, they say it's to relax, to feel less tense in social situations, to keep friends company, and to forget their problems. Of course, many other factors are also at work (Wood, Vinson, & Sher, 2001). Families and peer groups often encourage alcohol use. Drinking is a widely endorsed and encouraged social ritual in our culture. Its central role is readily apparent if you think about all the alcohol consumed at weddings, reunions, sports events, holiday parties, and so forth. Moreover, the alcohol industry spends hundreds of millions of dollars on advertising to convince us that drinking is cool, sexy, sophisticated, and harmless.

**Overindulging in alcohol is particularly widespread among college students.**

© Sean Murphy/Getty Images/Stone

## Short-Term Risks and Problems

Alcohol has a variety of side effects, including some that can be very problematic. To begin with, we have that infamous source of regret, the "hangover," which may include headaches, dizziness, nausea, and vomiting. In the constellation of alcohol's risks, however, hangovers are downright trivial. For instance, life-threatening overdoses are more common than most people realize. Although it's possible to overdose with alcohol alone, a more common problem is overdosing on combinations of alcohol and sedative or narcotic drugs.

In substantial amounts, alcohol has a decidedly negative effect on intellectual functioning and perceptual-motor coordination. The resulting combination of tainted judgment, slowed reaction time, and reduced coordination can be deadly when people attempt to drive after drinking (Gmel & Rehm, 2003). Depending on one's body weight, it may take only a few drinks for driving to be impaired. It's estimated that alcohol contributes to 40% of all automobile fatalities in the United States (Yi et al., 2006). Drunk driving is a major social problem and the leading cause of death in young adults. Don't assume, however, that fatal accidents are perpetrated exclusively by problem drinkers. In reality, half of the people involved in car crashes are not problem drinkers (Voas et al., 2006). Alcohol is also implicated in many other types of accidents. Victims test positive for alcohol in 38% of fire fatalities, 49% of drownings, and 63% of fatal falls (Smith, Branas, & Miller, 1999).

With their inhibitions released, some drinkers become argumentative and prone to aggression. In the Harvard survey of undergraduates from 119 schools, 29% of the students who did *not* engage in binge drinking reported that they had been insulted or humiliated by a drunken student, 19% had experienced serious arguments, 9% had been pushed, hit, or assaulted, and 19.5% had been the target of unwanted sexual advances (Wechsler et al., 2002). Worse yet, alcohol appears to contribute to about 90% of student rapes and 95% of violent crime on campus. In society at large, alcohol is associated with a variety of violent crimes, including murder, assault, child abuse, and intimate partner violence (Foran & O'Leary, 2008; Wood et al., 2001), as well as suicide attempts and suicidal ideation (Schaffer, Jeglic, & Stanley, 2008).

The phrase "associated with" can also be interpreted literally: A recent study suggests that people become more aggressive when primed to think about alcohol and aggression in the absence of actual consumption (Bartholow & Heinze, 2006). In other words, people's perceptions about alcohol can matter as much as their consumption. Finally, other research finds that forced sexual encounters are more likely to occur among people who have been drinking (whether as perpetrator or victim) than not imbibing (Testa, Vazile-Tamsen, & Livingston, 2004).

## Long-Term Health Effects

Alcohol's long-term health risks are mostly (but not exclusively) associated with chronic, heavy consumption of alcohol. Estimates of the number of people at risk vary considerably. According to Schuckit (2000) approximately 5%–10% of American men and women engage in chronic alcohol abuse and another 10% of men and 3%–5% of women probably suffer from *alcohol dependence,* or *alcoholism.* **Alcohol dependence (alcoholism) is a chronic, progressive disorder marked by a growing compulsion to drink and impaired control over drinking that eventually interferes with health and social behavior.** Whether alcoholism is best viewed as a disease or as a self-control problem is the source of considerable debate, but experts have reached a reasonable consensus about the warning signs of alcoholism. These signs include preoccupation with alcohol, drinking to relieve uncomfortable feelings, gulping drinks, clandestine drinking, and the other indicators listed in **Figure 5.15**.

| Warning Signs of Problem Drinking or Alcoholism |
| --- |
| 1. Gulping drinks. |
| 2. Drinking to modify uncomfortable feelings. |
| 3. Personality or behavioral changes after drinking. |
| 4. Getting drunk frequently. |
| 5. Experiencing "blackouts"—not being able to remember what happened while drinking. |
| 6. Frequent accidents or illness as a result of drinking. |
| 7. Priming—preparing yourself with alcohol before a social gathering at which alcohol is going to be served. |
| 8. Not wanting to talk about the negative consequences of drinking (avoidance). |
| 9. Preoccupation with alcohol. |
| 10. Focusing social situations around alcohol. |
| 11. Sneaking drinks or clandestine drinking. |

**Figure 5.15**

**Detecting a drinking problem.** Facing the reality that one has a problem with alcohol is always difficult. This list of the chief warning signs associated with problem drinking is intended to help with this process.

Source: Adapted from Edlin, G., & Golanty, E. (1992). *Health and wellness.* Boston: Jones & Bartlett. Copyright © 1992 Jones & Bartlett Publishers, Inc. Reprinted with permission.

Alcoholism and problem drinking are associated with an elevated risk for a wide range of serious health problems, which are summarized in **Figure 5.16** (Mack, Franklin, & Frances, 2003; Moak & Anton, 1999). Although there is some thought-provoking evidence that moderate drinking may reduce one's risk for coronary disease (Chick, 1998; Mukamal et al., 2003; Klatsky, 2008), it is clear that heavy drinking increases the risk for heart disease, hypertension, and stroke. Excessive drinking is also correlated with an elevated risk for various types of cancer, including oral, stomach, pancreatic, colon, and rectal cancer. Moreover, serious drinking problems can lead to cirrhosis of the liver, malnutrition, pregnancy complications, brain damage, and neurological disorders. Finally, alcoholism can produce severe psychotic states, characterized by delirium, disorientation, and hallucinations.

## Overeating

Obesity is a common health problem. The criteria for obesity vary considerably. One simple, intermediate criterion is to classify people as obese if their weight exceeds their ideal body weight by 20%. If this criterion is used, 31% of men and 35% of women in the United States qualify as obese (Brownell & Wadden, 2000), and this problem is projected to persist well into the middle of the twenty-first century (National Center for Health Statistics, 2006). This is an immediate and growing problem: For instance, as recently as the 1980s, only 13 percent of adult Americans were considered to be obese (Ogden, Carroll, & Flegal, 2008).

Many experts prefer to assess obesity in terms of *body mass index (BMI)—weight (in kilograms) divided by height (in meters) squared ($kg/m^2$).* This increasingly used index of weight controls for variations in height. A BMI of 25.0–29.9 is typically regarded as overweight, and a BMI over 30 is considered obese (Björntorp, 2002). Although American culture seems to be obsessed with slimness, recent surveys show surprisingly sharp increases in the incidence of obesity (Corsica & Perri, 2003). If a BMI over 25 is used as the cutoff, almost two-thirds of American adults are struggling with weight problems (Sarwer, Foster, & Wadden, 2004). Moreover, they have plenty of company from their children, as weight problems among children and adolescents have increased 15%–22% in recent decades (West, Harvey-Berino, & Raczynski, 2004).

Obesity is similar to smoking in that it exerts a relatively subtle impact on health that is easy for many people to ignore. Nevertheless, the long-range effects can be quite dangerous; obesity is a significant health problem that elevates one's mortality risk (Allison et al., 1999; Bender et al., 1999). In fact, obesity is probably responsible for the early deaths of well over a quarter of a million people in North America each year (DeAngelis, 2004). Overweight people are more vulnerable than others to heart disease, diabetes, hypertension, respiratory problems, gallbladder disease, stroke, arthritis, some cancers, muscle and joint pain, and back problems (Manson, Skerrett, & Willet, 2002; Pi-Sunyer, 2002). For example, **Figure 5.17** shows how the prevalence of diabetes, hypertension, coronary

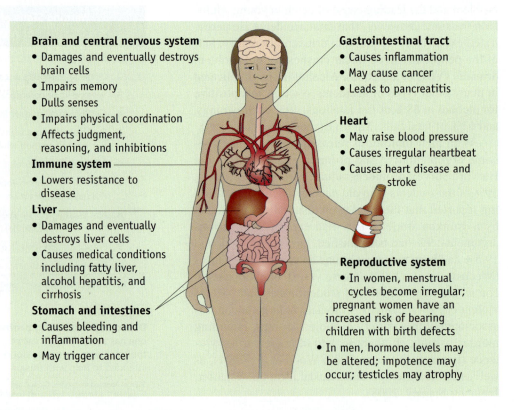

**Figure 5.16**

**Health risks associated with drinking.** This figure provides an overview of the various diseases more common among drinkers than abstainers. As you can see, alcohol elevates one's vulnerability to a remarkably diverse array of diseases.

**Brain and central nervous system**
- Damages and eventually destroys brain cells
- Impairs memory
- Dulls senses
- Impairs physical coordination
- Affects judgment, reasoning, and inhibitions

**Immune system**
- Lowers resistance to disease

**Liver**
- Damages and eventually destroys liver cells
- Causes medical conditions including fatty liver, alcohol hepatitis, and cirrhosis

**Stomach and intestines**
- Causes bleeding and inflammation
- May trigger cancer

**Gastrointestinal tract**
- Causes inflammation
- May cause cancer
- Leads to pancreatitis

**Heart**
- May raise blood pressure
- Causes irregular heartbeat
- Causes heart disease and stroke

**Reproductive system**
- In women, menstrual cycles become irregular; pregnant women have an increased risk of bearing children with birth defects
- In men, hormone levels may be altered; impotence may occur; testicles may atrophy

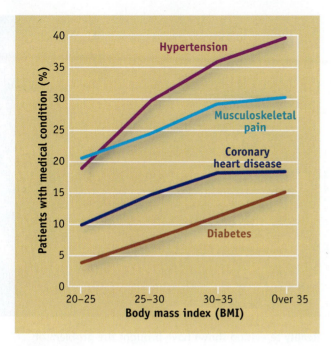

**Figure 5.17**

**Weight and the prevalence of various diseases.** This graph shows how obesity, as indexed by BMI, is related to the prevalence of four common types of illness. The prevalence of diabetes, heart disease, muscle pain, and hypertension increases as BMI goes up. Clearly, obesity is a significant health risk. (Data from Brownell & Wadden, 2000)

disease, and musculoskeletal pain are elevated as BMI increases.

Evolution-oriented researchers have a plausible explanation for the dramatic increase in the prevalence of obesity (Pinel, Assanand, & Lehman, 2000). They point out that over the course of history, most animals and humans have lived in environments in which there was fierce competition for limited, unreliable food resources and starvation was a very real threat. As a result, warm-blooded, foraging animals evolved a propensity to consume more food than immediately necessary when the opportunity presented itself, because food might not be available later. Excess calories were stored in the body to prepare for food shortages, and having extra fat on the body was actually considered to be an appealing quality (Nelson & Morrison, 2005). This approach to eating remains adaptive for most species of animals that continue to struggle with the ebb and flow of unpredictable food supplies. However, in today's modern, industrialized societies, the vast majority of humans live in environments that provide an abundant, reliable supply of tasty, high-calorie food. In these environments, humans' evolved tendency to overeat when food is plentiful leads most people down a pathway of chronic, excessive food consumption. Most people in food-replete environments tend to overeat in relation to their physiological needs, but because of variations in genetics, metabolism, and other factors only some become overweight.

## Determinants of Obesity

A few decades ago it was widely believed that obesity was a function of personality. Obesity was thought to occur mostly in depressed, anxious, compulsive people who overeat to deal with their negative emotions or in individuals who are lazy and undisciplined. However, research eventually showed that there is no such thing as an "obese personality" (Rodin, Schank, & Striegel-Moore, 1989). Instead, research indicated that a complex network of interacting factors—biological, social, and psychological— determine whether people develop weight problems (Berthoud & Morrison, 2008).

**Heredity.** Chief among the factors contributing to obesity is *genetic predisposition* (Bouchard, 2002). In one influential study, adults raised by foster parents were compared with their biological parents in regard to body mass index (Stunkard et al., 1986). The investigators found that the adoptees resembled their biological parents much more than their adoptive parents. In a subsequent *twin study,* Stunkard and associates (1990) found that identical twins reared apart were far more similar in body mass index than fraternal twins reared together (see Chapter 2 for a discussion of the logic underlying twin studies). Based on a study of over 4000 twins, Allison and colleagues (1994) estimate that genetic factors account for 61% of the variation in weight among men and 73% of the variation among women. These genetic factors probably explain why some people can eat constantly without gaining weight whereas other people grow chubby eating far less. Thus, it appears that some people inherit a genetic vulnerability to obesity (Cope, Fernández, & Allison, 2004).

**Excessive eating and inadequate exercise.** The bottom line for overweight people is that their energy intake from food consumption chronically exceeds their energy expenditure from physical activities and resting metabolic processes. In other words, they eat too much in relation to their level of exercise (Wing & Polley, 2001). In modern America, the tendency to eat too much and to exercise too little is easy to understand (Henderson & Brownell, 2004). Tasty, caloric, high-fat foods are readily available nearly everywhere, not just in restaurants and grocery stores but in shopping malls, airports, gas stations, schools, and workplaces. And when people eat out, they tend to eat larger meals and consume more high-fat food than they would at home (French, Harnack, & Jeffery, 2000). Unfortunately, the increased availability of highly caloric food in America has been paralleled by declining physical activity. Both Americans (Pereira et al., 2005) and people in developing countries (Finkelstein, Ruhm, & Kosa, 2005) eat too much fast food and then spend inordinate amounts of time watching television, playing video games, or surfing the Internet. Many people's private lives as well as their work lives promote sedentary comfort, so that many of the activities they engage in daily are more mental than physical. People work and play less with their bodies than past generations, and a number of labor-saving devices improve today's quality of life while reducing the rate at which people obtain "natural" exercise that burns off calories.

**Set point.**   People who lose weight on a diet have a rather strong (and depressing) tendency to gain back all the weight they lose. The reverse is also true: People who have to work to put weight on often have trouble keeping it on (Leibel, Rosenbaum, & Hirsch, 1995). According to Richard Keesey (1995), these observations suggest that each body may have a *set point,* or a natural point of stability in body weight. ***Set-point theory* proposes that the body monitors fat-cell levels to keep them (and weight) fairly stable.** When fat stores slip below a crucial set point, the body supposedly begins to compensate for this change (Keesey, 1993). This compensation apparently leads to increased hunger and decreased metabolism (Horvath, 2005). Studies have raised some doubts about various details of set-point theory, leading some researchers to propose an alternative called *settling-point theory* (Pinel et al., 2000). ***Settling-point theory* proposes that weight tends to drift around the level at which the constellation of factors that determine food consumption and energy expenditure achieve an equilibrium.** According to this view, weight tends to remain stable as long as there are no durable changes in any of the factors that influence it (e.g., diet, exercise or the lack thereof, stress, sleep). Settling-point theory casts a much wider net than set-point theory, which attributes weight stability to specific physiological processes. Another difference is that set-point theory asserts that an obese person's body will initiate processes that actively defend an excessive weight, whereas settling-point theory suggests that if an obese person makes long-term changes in eating or exercise, that person's settling point will drift downward without active resistance. Thus, settling-point theory is a little more encouraging to those who hope to lose weight.

## Losing Weight

Whether out of concern about their health or just old-fashioned vanity, an ever-increasing number of people are trying to lose weight. One study found that at any given time, about 21% of men and 39% of women are dieting (Hill, 2002), and a subsequent survey yielded similar percentages by gender (Kruger, Galuska, Serdula, & Jones, 2004). Research has provided some good news for those who need to lose weight. Studies have demonstrated that relatively modest weight reductions can significantly diminish many of the health risks as-

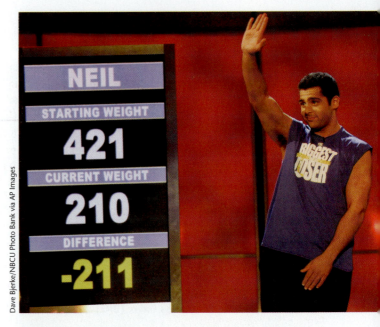

Reality television shows have brought the problem of obesity and the challenge of sustaining weight loss to the public's attention.

sociated with obesity. For example, a 10% weight loss is associated with reduced risks (Jeffery et al., 2000). Thus, the traditional objective of obesity treatment—reducing to one's ideal weight—has been replaced by more modest and realistic goals (Sarwer et al., 2004).

While many factors may contribute to obesity, there is only one way to lose weight. Individuals must change their ratio of energy intake (food consumption) to energy output (physical activities). To be quite specific, to lose one pound a person needs to burn up 3,500 more calories than he or she consumes. Those wanting to shed pounds have three options in trying to change their ratio of energy input to energy output: (1) sharply reduce food consumption, (2) sharply increase exercise output, or (3) simultaneously decrease food intake and step up exercise output in more moderate ways. Dieting alone is unlikely to be sufficient to lose weight and to maintain the loss (Jeffery et al., 2004). Virtually all experts recommend the third option. Simply put, exercise is an essential ingredient of an effective weight-loss regimen (Brownell, 1995; Manson et al., 2004). Exercise seems especially important for *maintaining* reduced weight, as it is the single best predictor of long-term weight loss (Curioni & Lourenco, 2005; Wing & Polley, 2001). Moreover, exercise can yield many other benefits, which we will discuss momentarily.

Some people opt for surgery to reduce their weight, an increasingly popular choice for weight control (Smoot et al., 2006). This option is generally reserved for individuals who are seriously obese or who possess other weight problems that warrant drastic action to cause weight loss quickly. One popular form of surgery

essentially shrinks the size of the stomach by placing what is known as a gastric band around it. Another surgical option is a gastric bypass, in which food is re-routed around the bulk of the stomach and a portion of the intestines (Buchwald et al., 2004). Both procedures involve risks and are life-altering; patients must usually take food supplements while carefully watching their food consumption for the rest of their lives (Tucker, Szomstetin, & Rosenthal, 2007).

Finally, self-modification techniques (see the Chapter 3 Application) can be helpful in achieving gradual weight loss. Indeed, behavior modification procedures represent the cornerstone of most reputable, professional weight-loss programs. Overall, the evidence on weight-loss programs suggests that they are moderately successful in the short term (the first 6 months), but in the long run the vast majority of people regain most of the weight that they lose (Jeffery et al., 2000).

## Poor Nutrition

*Nutrition* **is a collection of processes (mainly food consumption) through which an organism utilizes the materials (nutrients) required for survival and growth.** The term also refers to the *study* of these processes. Unfortunately, most of us don't study nutrition very much. Moreover, the cunning mass marketing of nutritionally worthless foods makes maintaining sound nutritional habits more and more difficult.

### Nutrition and Health

We are what we eat. Evidence is accumulating that patterns of nutrition influence susceptibility to a variety of diseases and health problems. For example, in a study of over 42,000 women, investigators found an association between a measure of overall diet quality and mortality. Women who reported poorer quality diets had elevated mortality rates (Kant et al., 2000). What are the specific links between diet and health? In addition

to the problems associated with obesity, other possible connections between eating patterns and health include the following:

**1.** Heavy consumption of foods that elevate serum cholesterol level (eggs, cheeses, butter, shellfish, sausage, and the like) appears to increase the risk of cardiovascular disease (Stamler et al., 2000; see **Figure 5.18** on the next page). Eating habits are only one of several factors that influence serum cholesterol level, but they do make an important contribution.

**2.** Vulnerability to cardiovascular diseases may also be influenced by other dietary factors. For example, low-fiber diets may increase the likelihood of coronary disease (Timm & Slavin, 2008) and high intake of red and processed meats, sweets, potatoes, and refined grains is associated with increased cardiovascular risk (Hu & Willett, 2002). Recent research indicates that the omega 3 fatty acids found in fish and fish oils offer some protection against coronary disease (Din, Newby, & Flapan, 2004).

**3.** High salt intake is thought to be a contributing factor in the development of hypertension (Havas,

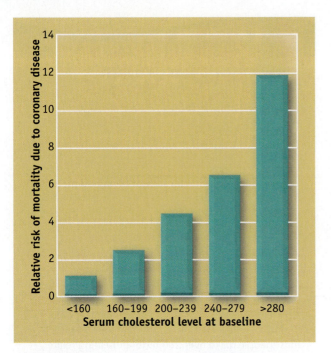

**Figure 5.18**

**The link between cholesterol and coronary risk.** In a review of several major studies, Stamler et al. (2000) summarize crucial evidence on the association between cholesterol levels and the prevalence of cardiovascular disease. This graph is based on a sample of over 11,000 men who were 18 to 39 at the beginning of the study (1967–1973) when their serum cholesterol level was measured. The data shown here depict participants' relative risk for coronary heart disease during the ensuing 25 years as a function of their initial cholesterol level.

Dickinson, & Wilson, 2007), although there is still some debate about its exact role.

4. High caffeine consumption may elevate one's risk for hypertension (James, 2004) and for coronary disease (Happonen, Voutilainen, Salonen, 2004), although the negative effects of caffeine appear relatively modest.

5. High-fat diets have been implicated as possible contributors to cardiovascular disease (Melanson, 2007) and to some forms of cancer, especially prostate cancer (Rose, 1997), colon and rectal cancer (Shike, 1999), and breast cancer (Wynder et al., 1997). Some studies also suggest that high-fiber diets may reduce one's risk for for breast cancer, colon cancer, and diabetes (Timm & Slavin, 2008).

**WEB LINK 5.5   Go Ask Alice!**

One of the longest standing and most popular sources of frank information on the Net has been *Alice!* from Columbia University's Health Education Program. Geared especially to the needs of undergraduate students, *Alice!* offers direct answers to questions about relationships, sexuality and sexual health, fitness and nutrition, alcohol and drug consumption, emotional health, and general health.

Of course, nutritional habits interact with other factors—genetics, exercise, environment, and so on—to determine whether someone will develop a particular disease. Nonetheless, the examples just described indicate that eating habits can influence physical health.

### The Basis for Poor Nutrition

Our nutritional shortcomings are the result of ignorance and poor motivation. Americans are remarkably naive about the basic principles of nutrition. Schools tend to provide little education in this area, and most people are not highly motivated to make sure their food consumption is nutritionally sound. Instead, people approach eating very casually, guided not by nutritional needs but by convenience, palatability, and clever advertising.

For most people, then, the first steps toward improved nutrition involve changing attitudes and acquiring information. First and foremost, individuals need to recognize the importance of nutrition and commit themselves to making a real effort to regulate their eating patterns. Second, they should try to acquire a basic education in nutritional principles.

### Nutritional Goals

The most healthful approach to nutrition is to follow well-moderated patterns of food consumption that ensure nutritional adequacy while limiting the intake of certain substances that can be counterproductive. Here are some general guidelines for achieving these goals:

1. *Consume a balanced variety of foods.* Food is made up of a variety of components, six of which are essential to your physical well-being. These six *essential nutrients* are proteins, fats, carbohydrates, vitamins, minerals, and fiber. Proteins, fats, and carbohydrates supply the body with its energy. Vitamins and minerals help release that energy and serve other important functions as well. Fiber provides roughage that facilitates digestion. Educational efforts to promote adequate intake of all essential nutrients have generally suggested that people should be guided by the classic food pyramid published by the U.S. Department of Agriculture (see **Figure 5.19**). Although the food pyramid remains a useful benchmark, it has been subjected to considerable criticism and hotly debated revisions (Norton, 2004). The principal problem with the food pyramid is its failure to distinguish between different types of fat, different forms of carbohydrates, and different sources of protein (Willett & Stampfer, 2003). For example, the current thinking is that monounsaturated and polyunsaturated fats are healthy, whereas saturated fats should be consumed sparingly. A revised food pyramid, which takes distinctions such as these into consideration, is shown in **Figure 5.20**.

Fats (naturally occurring and added)
Sugars (added)

Fats, oils, and sweets
**Use sparingly**

Milk, yogurt, and cheese
**2–3 servings**

Meat, poultry, fish, eggs, dry beans, and nuts
**2–3 servings**

Vegetable group
**3–5 servings**

Fruit group
**2–4 servings**

Breads, cereal, rice, and pasta group
**6–11 servings**

**Figure 5.19**

**The food guide pyramid.** The food pyramid, endorsed in 1992 by the U.S. Department of Agriculture, is intended to provide a simple and easy guide to nutritionally balanced eating. It identifies key categories of food and makes recommendations about how many daily servings one should have in each category. As your text explains, it has been subjected to considerable criticism.

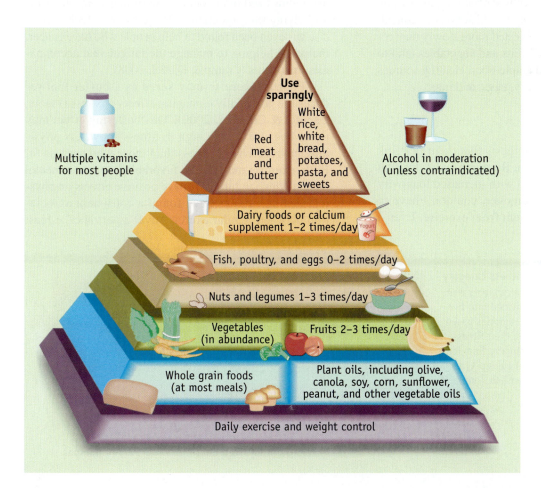

Multiple vitamins for most people

**Use sparingly**
White rice, white bread, potatoes, pasta, and sweets
Red meat and butter

Alcohol in moderation (unless contraindicated)

Dairy foods or calcium supplement 1–2 times/day

Fish, poultry, and eggs 0–2 times/day

Nuts and legumes 1–3 times/day

Vegetables (in abundance)

Fruits 2–3 times/day

Whole grain foods (at most meals)

Plant oils, including olive, canola, soy, corn, sunflower, peanut, and other vegetable oils

Daily exercise and weight control

**Figure 5.20**

**The healthy eating pyramid.** This alternative food pyramid was developed by Walter Willett and colleagues at the Harvard Medical School. It corrects a variety of flaws that were apparent in the USDA food pyramid and incorporates recent scientific findings on healthy versus unhealthy fats and carbohydrates.

Source: Adapted from Willett, W. C. (2001). *Eat, drink, and be healthy: The Harvard Medical School guide to healthy eating.* New York: Free Press. Copyright © 2001, 2006 by the President and Fellows at Harvard College. Adapted with permission of Simon & Schuster, Inc.

**2.** *Avoid excessive consumption of saturated fats, cholesterol, refined-grain carbohydrates, sugar, and salt.* These commodities are all overrepresented in the typical American diet. It is particularly prudent to limit the intake of saturated fats by eating less beef, pork, ham, hot dogs, sausage, lunch meats, whole milk, and fried foods. Consumption of many of these foods should also be limited in order to reduce cholesterol intake, which influences vulnerability to heart disease. In particular, beef, pork, lamb, sausage, cheese, butter, and eggs are high in cholesterol. Refined-grain carbohydrates, such as white bread, pasta, and white rice, are problematic because they increase glucose levels in the blood too quickly. Refined (processed) sugar is believed to be grossly overconsumed. Hence, people should limit their dependence on soft drinks, chocolate, candy, pastries, and high-sugar cereals. Finally, many people should cut down on their salt intake. Doing so may require more than simply ignoring the salt shaker or passing up the potato chips, since many prepackaged foods are loaded with salt.

**3.** *Increase consumption of polyunsaturated fats, whole-grain carbohydrates, natural sugars, and foods with fiber.* To substitute polyunsaturated fats for saturated ones, people can eat more fish, chicken, turkey, and veal; trim fat off meats more thoroughly; use skim (nonfat) milk; and switch to vegetable oils that are high in polyunsaturated fats. Healthy carbohydrates include whole-grain foods such as whole wheat bread, oatmeal, and brown rice, which are digested more slowly than refined-grain carbohydrates. Fruits and vegetables tend to provide natural sugars and ample fiber. Healthy sources of protein include fish, poultry, eggs, and nuts.

## Lack of Exercise

A great deal of evidence suggests that there is a link between exercise and health. Research indicates that regular exercise is associated with increased longevity (Lee & Skerrett, 2001). Moreover, you don't have to be a dedicated athlete to benefit from exercise. Even a moderate level of reasonably regular physical activity is associated with lower mortality rates (Richardson et al., 2004; see **Figure 5.21**). Unfortunately, physical fitness appears to be declining in the United States. Only 25% of American adults get an adequate amount of regular exercise (Dubbert et al., 2004).

### Benefits and Risks of Exercise

Exercise is correlated with greater longevity because it promotes a diverse array of specific benefits. First, an appropriate exercise program can enhance cardiovascular fitness and thereby reduce one's susceptibility to cardiovascular problems (Caspersen et al., 1991; Schlicht, Kanning, & Bös, 2007). Fitness is associated with reduced risk for coronary disease, stroke, and hypertension (Blair, Cheng, & Holder, 2001; Lee et al., 2001). Second, regular physical activity can contribute to the avoidance of obesity (Corsica & Perri, 2003; Hill & Wyatt, 2005; Jakicic & Otto, 2005). Hence, fitness may indirectly reduce one's risk for a variety of obesity-related health problems, including diabetes, respiratory difficulties, arthritis, and back pain. Third, some studies suggest that physical fitness is also associated with a decreased risk for colon cancer and for breast and reproductive cancer in women (Thune & Furberg, 2001). The apparent link between exercise and reduced cancer risk has been a pleasant surprise for scientists, who are now scrambling to replicate the findings and figure out the physiological mechanisms underlying this association (Rogers et al., 2008). Exercise has even been found to help people who have cancer, including helping to manage the fatigue that accompanies treatments (Cramp & Daniel, 2008).

Fourth, exercise may serve as a buffer that reduces the potentially damaging effects of stress (Plante, Caputo, & Chizmar, 2000). This buffering effect may occur because people high in fitness show less physiological reactivity to stress than those who are less fit. Fifth, exercise may have a favorable impact on mental health, which in turn may have positive effects on physical health. Studies have found a consistent association between regular exercise over a period of at least

**Figure 5.21**

**Physical fitness and mortality.** Blair et al. (1989) studied death rates among men and women who exhibited low, medium, or high fitness. Even medium fitness was associated with lower mortality rates in both genders. The investigators note that one could achieve this level of fitness by taking a brisk half-hour walk each day.

**Fitness category**
Participants were divided into five categories based on their fitness, ranging from least fit (group 1) to most fit (group 5).

Regular exercise has many physical and psychological benefits that promote increased longevity.

**WEB LINK 5.6  About.Com: Health and Fitness**

About.com is a commercial endeavor enlisting subject experts to edit topic-specific directories with annotated links and other information resources. More than 60 directories related to topics of health and fitness—including alcoholism, substance abuse, and smoking cessation—are now available at About.com.

in one's mood, self-esteem, and work efficiency, as well as reductions in tension and anxiety (Dunn, Trivedi, & O'Neal, 2001; Hays, 1999; Sonstroem, 1997).

## Devising an Exercise Program

Putting together a good exercise program is difficult for many people. Exercise is time consuming, and if you're out of shape, your initial attempts may be painful, aversive, and discouraging. People who do not get enough exercise cite lack of time, lack of convenience, and lack of enjoyment as the reasons (Jakicic & Gallagher, 2002). To circumvent these problems, it is wise to heed the following advice (Greenberg, 2002; Jakicic & Gallagher, 2002; Phillips et al., 2001):

1. *Look for an activity that you will find enjoyable.* You have a great many physical activities to choose from (see **Figure 5.22**). Shop around for one that you find intrinsically enjoyable. Doing so will make it much easier for you to follow through and exercise regularly.

eight weeks and reduced depression (Phillips, Kiernan, & King, 2001), which is important given the evidence that depression is correlated with increased vulnerability to heart disease. Sixth, successful participation in an exercise program can produce desirable personality changes that may promote physical wellness. Research suggests that fitness training can lead to improvements

| How Beneficial Is Your Favorite Sport? | | | | | | | | | | | | | |
|---|---|---|---|---|---|---|---|---|---|---|---|---|---|
| **Physical fitness** | **Jogging** | **Bicycling** | **Swimming** | **Skating (ice or roller)** | **Handball/ Squash** | **Skiing— Nordic** | **Skiing— Alpine** | **Basketball** | **Tennis** | **Calisthenics** | **Walking** | **Golf** | **Softball** | **Bowling** |
| Cardiorespiratory endurance (stamina) | 21 | 19 | 21 | 18 | 19 | 19 | 16 | 19 | 16 | 10 | 13 | 8 | 6 | 5 |
| Muscular endurance | 20 | 18 | 20 | 17 | 18 | 19 | 18 | 17 | 16 | 13 | 14 | 8 | 8 | 5 |
| Muscular strength | 17 | 16 | 14 | 15 | 15 | 15 | 15 | 15 | 14 | 16 | 11 | 9 | 7 | 5 |
| Flexibility | 9 | 9 | 15 | 13 | 16 | 14 | 14 | 13 | 14 | 19 | 7 | 9 | 9 | 7 |
| Balance | 17 | 18 | 12 | 20 | 17 | 16 | 21 | 16 | 16 | 15 | 8 | 8 | 7 | 6 |
| **General well-being** | | | | | | | | | | | | | | |
| Weight control | 21 | 20 | 15 | 17 | 19 | 17 | 15 | 19 | 16 | 12 | 13 | 6 | 7 | 5 |
| Muscle definition | 14 | 15 | 14 | 14 | 11 | 12 | 14 | 13 | 13 | 18 | 11 | 6 | 5 | 5 |
| Digestion | 13 | 12 | 13 | 11 | 13 | 12 | 9 | 10 | 12 | 11 | 11 | 7 | 8 | 7 |
| Sleep | 16 | 15 | 16 | 15 | 12 | 15 | 12 | 12 | 11 | 12 | 14 | 6 | 7 | 6 |
| **Total** | **148** | **142** | **140** | **140** | **140** | **139** | **134** | **134** | **128** | **126** | **102** | **67** | **64** | **51** |

**Figure 5.22**

**A scorecard on the benefits of 14 sports and exercises.** Here is a summary of how seven experts rated the value of 14 sports activities (the highest rating possible on any one item was 21). The ratings were based on vigorous participation four times per week.

Source: Adapted from Conrad, C. C. (1976, May). How different sports rate in promoting physical fitness. *Medical Times,* p. 45. Copyright 1976 by Romaine Pierson Publishers. Reprinted by permission.

**2.** *Exercise regularly without overdoing it.* Sporadic exercise will not improve your fitness. At the other extreme, an overzealous approach can lead to frustration, not to mention injury. If you experience injuries, avoid the common tendency to ignore them. Consult your physician to see whether continuing your exercise program is advisable. One study found that people are more likely to stick to an exercise regimen consisting of more frequent workouts of moderate intensity than a regimen of less frequent but more intense workouts (Perri et al., 2002).

**3.** *Increase the amount of time you exercise gradually.* Don't rush it. Start slowly and build up, as any amount of exercise is apt to be better than no exercise. For example, healthy people between the ages of 18 and 65 should do some moderate physical activity for half an hour, five days a week (or vigorous exercise three times a week for 20 minutes) (Haskell et al., 2007). When you think about it, 20 or 30 minutes is not that much time—you just need to build it into your schedule.

**4.** *Reinforce yourself for your participation.* To offset the inconvenience or pain that may be associated with exercise, it is a good idea to reinforce yourself for your participation. The behavior modification procedures discussed in Chapter 3 can be helpful in devising a viable exercise program.

**5.** *It's never too late to begin an exercise regimen.* Be forewarned: The number of people who engage in regular exercise declines with age (Phillips et al., 2001). Yet even modest regular exercise has pronounced health benefits, as has been shown in studies with participants well into their 70s, 80s, and 90s (Fiatrone et al., 1993; Raloff, 1996). As they age, people may believe that health declines are not only natural but inevitable (O'Brien & Vertinsky, 1991). A better and more apt belief is this one: Use it or lose it.

## Behavior and AIDS

At present, some of the most problematic links between behavior and health may be those related to AIDS, a pandemic, or worldwide epidemic. AIDS stands for **acquired immune deficiency syndrome, a disorder in which the immune system is gradually weakened and eventually disabled by the human immunodeficiency virus (HIV).** Being infected with the HIV virus is *not* equivalent to having AIDS. AIDS is the final stage of the HIV infection process, typically manifested about 7–10 years after the original infection (Carey & Vanable, 2003). With the onset of AIDS, one is left virtually defenseless against a number of opportunistic infectious agents. The symptoms of AIDS vary widely depending on the specific constellation of diseases that one develops (Cunningham & Selwyn, 2005). Unfortunately, the worldwide prevalence of this deadly disease continues to increase at an alarming rate, especially in certain re-

gions of Africa (De Cock & Janssen, 2002; UNAIDS, 2005).

Prior to 1996–1997, the average length of survival for people after the onset of the AIDS syndrome was about 18 to 24 months. Encouraging advances in the treatment of AIDS with drug regimens referred to as *highly active antiretroviral therapy* hold out promise for *substantially* longer survival (Anthony & Bell, 2008; Hammer et al., 2006; Sande & Ronald, 2004). But these drugs are being rushed into service and their long-term efficacy is yet to be determined. Medical experts are concerned that the general public has gotten the impression that these treatments have transformed AIDS from a fatal disease to a manageable one, which is a premature conclusion. HIV strains are evolving, and many have developed resistance to the currently available antiretroviral drugs (Trachtenberg & Sande, 2002). Moreover, many patients do not respond well to the new drugs, which often have adverse side effects (Beusterien et al., 2008; Hammer et al., 2006). Another daunting problem is that these expensive new drugs remain largely unavailable in developing nations, which have not seen progress in treatment. In some African nations the impact of AIDS has reduced life expectancy to levels not seen for hundreds of years. In Botswana, for instance, projections suggest that life expectancy has declined from 66 to 33 years (Carey & Vanable, 2003).

### Transmission

The HIV virus is transmitted through person-to-person contact involving the exchange of bodily fluids, primarily semen and blood. The two principal modes of transmission in the United States have been sexual contact and the sharing of needles by intravenous (IV) drug users. In the United States, sexual transmission has occurred primarily among gay and bisexual men, but heterosexual transmission has increased in recent years (Catania et al., 2001; Centers for Disease Control, 2006). In the world as a whole, infection through heterosexual relations has been more common from the beginning. In heterosexual relations, male-to-female transmission is estimated to be about eight times more likely than female-to-male transmission (Ickovics, Thayaparan, & Ethier, 2001). Although the HIV virus can be found in the tears and saliva of infected individuals, the concentrations are low, and there is no evidence that the infection can be spread through casual contact. Even most forms of noncasual contact, including kissing, hugging, and sharing food with infected individuals, appear safe (Kalichman, 1995).

### Misconceptions

Misconceptions about AIDS are widespread. Ironically, the people who hold these misconceptions fall into two polarized camps. On the one hand, a great many people have unrealistic fears that AIDS can be readily transmitted through casual contact with infected individuals. These people worry unnecessarily about contracting AIDS from a handshake, a sneeze, or an eating utensil. They tend to be paranoid about interacting with homosexuals, thus fueling discrimination against gays. Some people also believe that it is dangerous to donate blood when, in fact, blood donors are at no risk whatsoever.

On the other hand, many young heterosexuals who are sexually active with a variety of partners foolishly downplay their risk for HIV, naively assuming that they are safe as long as they avoid IV drug use and sexual relations with gay or bisexual men. They greatly underestimate the probability that their sexual partners may have previously used IV drugs or had unprotected sex with an infected individual. They don't understand, for instance, that most bisexual men do not disclose their bisexuality to their female partners (Kalichman et al., 1998). Also, because AIDS is usually accompanied by discernible symptoms, many young people believe that prospective sexual partners who carry the HIV virus will exhibit telltale signs of illness. However, as we have already noted, having AIDS and being infected with HIV are not the same thing, and HIV carriers often remain healthy and symptom-free for many years after they are infected. Indeed, one study screened over 5000 men for HIV and found that 77% of those who were found to be HIV-positive were previously unaware of their infection (MacKellar et al., 2005). In sum, many myths about AIDS persist, despite extensive efforts to educate the public about this complex and controversial disease. **Figure 5.23** contains a short quiz to test your knowledge of the facts about AIDS.

**Prevention**

The behavioral changes that minimize the risk of developing AIDS are fairly straightforward, although making the changes is often easier said than done (Coates & Collins, 1998). In all groups, the more sexual partners a person has, the higher the risk that he or she will be exposed to the HIV virus. Thus, people can reduce their risk by having sexual contacts with fewer partners and by using condoms to control the exchange of semen. It is also important to curtail certain sexual practices (in particular, anal sex) that increase the probability of semen/blood mixing. The 1980s and early 1990s saw considerable progress toward wider use of safe sex practices and the evolution of prevention strategies (Wolitski, Henny, & Lyles, 2006), but new cohorts of young people appear to be much less concerned about the risk of HIV infection than the generation that witnessed the original emergence of AIDS (Jaffe,

---

### AIDS Risk Knowledge Test

Answer the following "true" or "false."

| | | |
|---|---|---|
| T | F | **1.** The AIDS virus cannot be spread through kissing. |
| T | F | **2.** A person can get the AIDS virus by sharing kitchens and bathrooms with someone who has AIDS. |
| T | F | **3.** Men can give the AIDS virus to women. |
| T | F | **4.** The AIDS virus attacks the body's ability to fight off diseases. |
| T | F | **5.** You can get the AIDS virus by someone sneezing, like a cold or the flu. |
| T | F | **6.** You can get AIDS by touching a person with AIDS. |
| T | F | **7.** Women can give the AIDS virus to men. |
| T | F | **8.** A person who got the AIDS virus from shooting up drugs cannot give the virus to someone by having sex. |
| T | F | **9.** A pregnant woman can give the AIDS virus to her unborn baby. |
| T | F | **10.** Most types of birth control also protect against getting the AIDS virus. |
| T | F | **11.** Condoms make intercourse completely safe. |
| T | F | **12.** Oral sex is safe if partners "do not swallow." |
| T | F | **13.** A person must have many different sexual partners to be at risk for AIDS. |
| T | F | **14.** It is more important to take precautions against AIDS in large cities than in small cities. |
| T | F | **15.** A positive result on the AIDS virus antibody test often occurs for people who do not even have the virus. |
| T | F | **16.** Only receptive (passive) anal intercourse transmits the AIDS virus. |
| T | F | **17.** Donating blood carries no AIDS risk for the donor. |
| T | F | **18.** Most people who have the AIDS virus look quite ill. |

Answers: 1. T  2. F  3. T  4. T  5. F  6. F  7. T  8. F  9. T  10. F  11. F  12. F  13. F  14. F  15. F  16. F  17. T  18. F

**Figure 5.23**

**A quiz on knowledge of AIDS.**
Because misconceptions about AIDS abound, it may be wise to take this brief quiz to test your knowledge.

Source: Adapted from Kalichman, S. C. (1995). *Understanding AIDS: A guide for mental health professionals.* Washington, DC: American Psychological Association. Copyright © 1995 by the American Psychological Association. Adapted with permission of the author.

Valdiserri, & De Cock, 2007). In particular, experts are concerned that recent advances in treatment may lead to more casual attitudes about risky sexual practices, a development that would not bode well for public health efforts to slow the spread of AIDS (Cabaj, 2006; Crepaz, Hart, & Marks, 2004; Kalichman et al., 2007; van Kesteren et al., 2007). This false sense of security among young adults may have dire consequences in the long run unless they adopt prevention practices and an attitude of vigilance. Indeed, by the year 2015, fully half of all cases of HIV/AIDS in the United States are projected to be among adults who are 50 and older (Centers for Disease Control, 2006).

There is some good news, however. Some interventions aimed at educating people about the risks of contracting HIV actually work. One recent study showed that people's expectations matter. If they anticipated learning something useful by reading educational brochures, chances increased that people would watch an educational video, which enhanced the likelihood they would take part in a subsequent counseling session on ways to reduce sexual risks (Albarćin et al., 2008).

# Reactions to Illness

## LEARNING OBJECTIVES

- Summarize evidence on patterns of treatment-seeking behavior.
- Explain the appeal of the "sick role."
- Identify the factors that tend to undermine doctor-patient communication, and discuss how to improve it.
- Discuss the prevalence of nonadherence to medical advice and its causes.

So far we have emphasized the psychosocial aspects of maintaining health and minimizing the risk of illness. Health is also affected by how individuals respond to physical symptoms and illnesses. Some people engage in denial and ignore early-warning signs of developing diseases. Others engage in active coping efforts to conquer their diseases. In this section, we discuss the decision to seek medical treatment, the sick role, communication with health providers, and compliance with medical advice.

## The Decision to Seek Treatment

Have you ever experienced nausea, diarrhea, stiffness, headaches, cramps, chest pains, or sinus problems? Of course you have; everyone experiences some of these problems periodically. However, whether you view these sensations as *symptoms* is a matter of individual interpretation, and the level of symptoms is what prompts people to seek medical advice (Ringström et al., 2007). When two persons experience the same unpleasant sensations, one may shrug them off as a nuisance, while the other may rush to a physician (Leventhal, Cameron, & Leventhal, 2005; Martin & Leventhal, 2004). Studies suggest that those who are relatively high in anxiety and neuroticism tend to report more symptoms of illness than others do (Feldman et al., 1999). Those who are extremely attentive to bodily sensations and health concerns also report more symptoms than the average person (Barsky, 1988). When feeling ill, women report more symptoms and higher distress than men do (Koopmans & Lamers, 2007).

Variations in the perception of symptoms help explain why people vary so much in their readiness to seek medical treatment (Cameron, Leventhal, & Leventhal, 1993). Generally, people are more likely to seek medical care when their symptoms are unfamiliar, appear to be serious, last longer than expected, or disrupt their work or social activities (Bernard & Krupat, 1994; Martin et al., 2003). Social class matters, too. Higher socioeconomic groups report having fewer symptoms and better health, but when sickness occurs, member of these groups are more likely to seek medical care than lower-income people are (Grzywacz et al., 2004).

Another key consideration is how friends and family react to the symptoms. Medical consultation is much more likely when friends and family view symptoms as serious and encourage the person to seek medical care, although nagging a person about seeking care can sometimes backfire (Martin et al., 2003). Gender also influences decisions to seek treatment, as women are much more likely than men to utilize medical services (Bertakis et al., 2000; Galdas, Cheater, & Marshall, 2005). Finally, age matters: Young children (age 5 and under) and older adults (late middle age and beyond) are more likely to utilize health services (U.S. Department of Health and Human Services, 1995). These facts should not be surprising, especially in the case of young children, who often experience frequent illnesses and vaccinations and have parents or caregivers who take them for frequent checkups.

The process of seeking medical treatment can be divided into three stages of active, complex problem solving (Martin et al., 2003). First, people have to decide that their physical sensations *are* symptoms—that they are indicative of illness. Second, they have to decide that their apparent illness warrants medical attention. Third, they

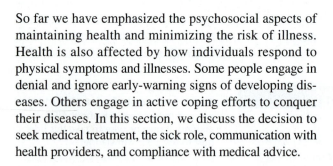

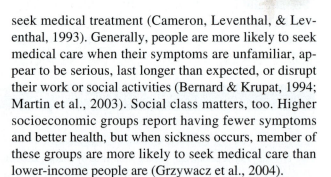

have to go to the trouble to make the actual arrangements for medical care, which can be complicated and time consuming. The task of checking insurance coverage, finding an appropriate doctor, negotiating an appointment, arranging to get off work or take care of children, and so forth can be a huge series of hassles.

Small wonder then, that the biggest problem in regard to treatment seeking is the tendency of many people to delay the pursuit of needed professional consultation. Delays can be important, because early diagnosis and quick intervention can facilitate more effective treatment of many health problems. Unfortunately, procrastination is the norm even when people are faced with a medical emergency, such as a heart attack (Martin & Leventhal, 2004).

## The Sick Role

Although many people tend to delay medical consultations, some people are actually eager to seek medical care. Given this reality, it is not surprising that up to 60% of patients' visits to their primary care physicians appear to have little medical basis (Ellington & Wiebe, 1999). Many of the people who are quick to solicit medical assistance probably have learned that there are potential benefits in adopting the "sick role" (Hamilton, Deemer, & Janata, 2003; Lubkin, 1990). For instance, the sick role absolves people from responsibility for their incapacity and can be used to exempt them from many of their normal duties and obligations (Segall, 1997). Fewer demands are placed on sick people, who can often be selective in deciding which demands to ignore. Illness can provide a convenient, face-saving excuse for one's failures (Wolinsky, 1988). Sick people may also find themselves receiving lots of attention (affection, concern, sympathy) from friends and relatives. This positive attention can be rewarding and can encourage the maintenance of symptoms (Walker, Claar, & Garber, 2002).

Of course, there are also some people who refuse to play the sick role under any circumstances. That is, they may well be sick but they are nonetheless determined to continue their normal routines. People who worry that they could lose their job, for example, will go to work even if they are ill (Bloor, 2005). So will people who feel dedicated to their job, as will those who have good rapport with their co-workers (Biron et al., 2006).

## Communicating with Health Providers

When people seek help from physicians and other health care providers, many factors can undermine effective communication. A large portion of medical patients leave their doctors' offices not understanding what they have been told and what they are supposed to

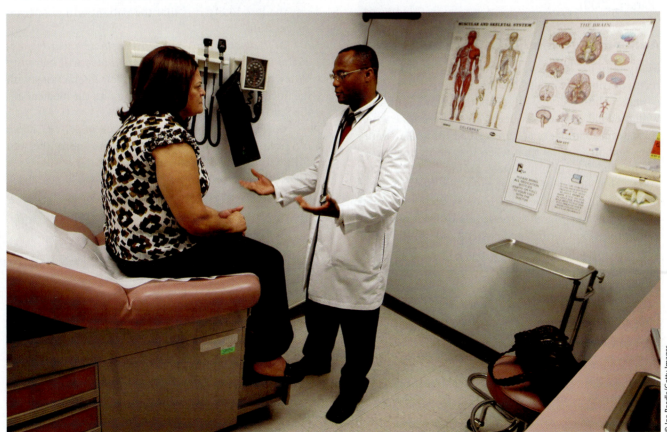

**Communication between health care providers and patients tends to be far from optimal for a variety of reasons.**

© Joe Raedle/Getty Images

Public Relations

REACTIONS TO ILLNESS    **165**

do (Johnson & Carlson, 2004). This situation is unfortunate, because good communication is a crucial requirement for sound medical decisions, informed choices about treatment, and appropriate follow-through by patients (Buckman, 2002; Gambone, Reiter, & DiMatteo, 1994).

There are many barriers to effective provider-patient communication (Beisecker, 1990; DiMatteo, 1997). Economic realities dictate that medical visits be generally quite brief, allowing little time for discussion. Illness and pain are subjective matters that may be difficult to describe. Many providers use too much medical jargon and overestimate their patients' understanding of technical terms. Some providers are uncomfortable being questioned and discourage their patients' information seeking. Patients who are upset and worried about their illness may simply forget to report some symptoms or to ask questions they meant to ask. Other patients are evasive about their real concerns because they fear a serious diagnosis. Many patients are reluctant to challenge doctors' authority and are too passive in their interactions with providers. Doctors and nurses often believe their explanations are clear; however, patient misunderstanding can be a common phenomenon, one posing particular problems for individuals whose instructions regarding diagnosis, treatment, and medication are complex (Parker, 2000).

## Adherence to Medical Advice

Many patients fail to adhere to the instructions they receive from physicians and other health care professionals. The evidence suggests that noncompliance with medical advice may occur 30% of the time when short-term treatments are prescribed for acute conditions and 50% of the time when long-term treatments are needed for chronic illness (Johnson & Carlson, 2004). Nonadherence takes many forms. Patients may fail to begin a treatment regimen, stop the regimen early, reduce or increase the levels of treatment that were prescribed, or be inconsistent and unreliable in following treatment procedures (Clifford, Barber, &

Horn, 2008; Dunbar-Jacob & Schlenk, 2001). Nonadherence is a major problem that has been linked to increased sickness, treatment failures, and higher mortality (Christensen & Johnson, 2002; DiMatteo et al., 2002). Moreover, nonadherence wastes expensive medical visits and medications and increases hospital admissions, leading to enormous economic costs. Robin DiMatteo (2004), a leading authority on compliance, speculates that in the United States alone, nonadherence may be a $300 billion a year drain on the health care system.

Here are some considerations that influence the likelihood of adherence (Dunbar-Jacob & Schlenk, 2001; Johnson & Carlson, 2004):

1. *Frequently, noncompliance is due to patients simply forgetting instructions or failing to understand the instructions as given.* Medical professionals often forget that what seems obvious and simple to them may be obscure and complicated to many of their patients.

2. *Another key factor is how aversive or difficult the treatments are.* If the prescribed regimen is unpleasant, compliance will tend to decrease. For example, adherence is reduced when prescribed medications have many severe side effects. And the more that following instructions interferes with routine behavior, the less likely it is that the patient will cooperate successfully.

3. *If a patient has a negative attitude toward a physician, the probability of noncompliance will increase.* When patients are unhappy with their interactions with the doctor, they're more likely to ignore the medical advice provided.

4. *Treatment adherence can be improved when physicians do follow-ups.* Patients are more likely to follow prescribed treatments if their doctors pay attention to them after the diagnosis has been made (Llorca, 2008).

Courtesy M. Robin DiMatteo

**Robin DiMatteo**

In response to the noncompliance problem, researchers have investigated many methods of increasing patients' adherence to medical advice. Interventions have included simplifying instructions, providing more rationale for instructions, reducing the complexity of treatment regimens, helping patients with emotional distress that undermines adherence, and training patients in the use of behavior modification strategies. All of these interventions can improve adherence, although their effects tend to be modest (Christensen & Johnson, 2002; Roter et al., 1998).

# Understanding the Effects of Drugs

**LEARNING OBJECTIVES**

● Explain the concepts of drug tolerance, physical and psychological dependence, and overdose.
● Summarize the main effects and risks of narcotics and sedatives.
● Describe the main effects and risks of stimulant drugs and hallucinogens.
● Outline the main effects and risks of marijuana and ecstasy (MDMA).

*Answer the following "true" or "false."*

___ **1.** Smoking marijuana can make men impotent and sterile.

___ **2.** Overdoses caused by cocaine are relatively rare.

___ **3.** It is well documented that LSD causes chromosome damage.

___ **4.** Hallucinogens are addictive.

___ **5.** Ecstasy is a relatively harmless drug.

As you will learn in this Application, all of these statements are false. If you answered all of them accurately, you may already be well informed about drugs. If not, you *should* be. Intelligent decisions about drugs require an understanding of their effects and risks.

This Application focuses on the use of drugs for their pleasurable effects, commonly referred to as *drug abuse* or *recreational drug use*. Drug abuse reaches into every corner of our society and is a problematic health-impairing habit. Although small declines appear to have occurred in the overall abuse of drugs in recent years, survey data show that illicit drug use

has mostly been increasing since the 1960s (Winick & Norman, 2005).

Recreational drug use involves personal, moral, political, and legal, as well as occasionally religious, issues that are not matters for science to resolve. However, the more knowledgeable you are about drugs, the more informed your decisions and opinions about them will be. Accordingly, this Application is intended to provide you with nonjudgmental, realistic coverage of issues related to recreational drug use. We begin by reviewing key drug-related concepts and then examine the effects and risks of six types of widely abused drugs: narcotics, sedatives, stimulants, hallucinogens, marijuana, and ecstasy (MDMA).

**WEB LINK 5.8   National Institute on Drug Abuse (NIDA)**

This government-sponsored site houses a great deal of information on the medical consequences of abusing various drugs. It also is an resource for statistics on trends in drug abuse.

**Recreational drug users come from all ages and all walks of life.**

© image100/Alamy Images

## Drug-Related Concepts

The principal types of recreational drugs are described in **Figure 5.24**. This table lists representative drugs in each of the five categories and indicates how the drugs are taken, their principal medical uses, their desired effects, and their common side effects.

Most drugs produce tolerance effects. *Tolerance is a progressive decrease in a person's responsiveness to a drug with continued use.* Tolerance effects usually lead people to consume larger and larger doses of a drug to attain the effects they desire. Tolerance builds more rapidly to some drugs than to others. The first column in **Figure 5.25** (which lists the risks associated with drug abuse) indicates whether various categories of drugs tend to produce rapid or gradual tolerance.

In evaluating the potential problems associated with the use of specific drugs, a key consideration is the likelihood of either physical or psychological dependence. Although both forms of drug dependence have a physiological basis (Di Chiara, 1999; Self, 1998), important differences exist between the two syndromes. *Physical dependence exists when a person must continue to take a drug to avoid withdrawal illness (which occurs when drug use is terminated).* The symptoms of *withdrawal illness* (also called *abstinence syndrome*) vary depending on the drug. Withdrawal from heroin and barbiturates can produce fever, chills, tremors, convulsions, seizures, vomiting, cramps, diarrhea, and severe aches and pains. The agony of withdrawal from these drugs virtually compels addicts to continue using them. Withdrawal from stimulants leads to a different and somewhat milder syndrome dominated by fatigue, apathy, irritability, depression, and disorientation.

*Psychological dependence exists when a person must continue to take a drug to satisfy intense mental and emotional craving for it.* Psychological dependence is more subtle than physical dependence, as it is not marked by a clear withdrawal reaction. However, psychological dependence can create a powerful, overwhelming need for a drug. The two types of dependence often coexist—that is, many people manifest both psychological and physical dependence on a specific drug. Both types of dependence are established gradually with repeated use of a drug. However, specific drugs vary greatly in their potential for creating dependence. The second and third col-

## Comparison of Major Categories of Abused Drugs

| Drugs | Methods of administration | Principal medical uses | Desired effects | Short-term side effects |
|---|---|---|---|---|
| **Narcotics** (opiates) Morphine Heroin | Injected, smoked, oral | Pain relief | Euphoria, relaxation, anxiety reduction, pain relief | Lethargy, drowsiness, nausea, impaired coordination, impaired mental functioning, constipation |
| **Sedatives** Barbiturates (e.g., Seconal) Nonbarbiturates (e.g., Quaalude) | Oral, injected | Sleeping pill, anticonvulsant | Euphoria, relaxation, anxiety reduction, reduced inhibitions | Lethargy, drowsiness, severely impaired coordination, impaired mental functioning, emotional swings, dejection |
| **Stimulants** Amphetamines Cocaine | Oral, sniffed, injected, freebased, smoked | Treatment of hyperactivity and narcolepsy; local anesthetic (cocaine only) | Elation, excitement, increased alertness, increased energy, reduced fatigue | Increased blood pressure and heart rate, increased talkativeness, restlessness, irritability, insomnia, reduced appetite, increased sweating and urination, anxiety, paranoia, increased aggressiveness, panic |
| **Hallucinogens** LSD Mescaline Psilocybin | Oral | | Increased sensory awareness, euphoria, altered perceptions, hallucinations, insightful experiences | Dilated pupils, nausea, emotional swings, paranoia, jumbled thought processes, impaired judgment, anxiety, panic reaction |
| **Cannabis** Marijuana Hashish THC | Smoked, oral | Treatment of glaucoma; other uses under study | Mild euphoria, relaxation, altered perceptions, enhanced awareness | Bloodshot eyes, dry mouth, reduced memory, sluggish motor coordination, sluggish mental functioning, anxiety |

**Figure 5.24**

**Major categories of abused drugs.** This chart summarizes the methods of ingestion, chief medical uses, and principal effects of five major types of recreational drugs. Alcohol is covered in the main body of the chapter. (Based on Julien, 2008; Levinthal, 2008; Lowinson, et al., 2005)

| Risks Associated with Major Categories of Abused Drugs | | | | |
|---|---|---|---|---|
| Drugs | Tolerance | Risk of physical dependence | Risk of psychological dependence | Fatal overdose potential |
| Narcotics (opiates) | Rapid | High | High | High |
| Sedatives | Rapid | High | High | High |
| Stimulants | Rapid | Moderate | High | Moderate to high |
| Hallucinogens | Gradual | None | Very low | Very low |
| Cannabis | Gradual | None | Low to moderate | Very low |

**Figure 5.25**

**Specific risks for various categories of drugs.** This chart shows the estimated risk potential for tolerance, dependence, and overdose for the five major categories of drugs discussed in this Application.

umns in **Figure 5.25** provide estimates of the risk of each kind of dependence for the drugs covered in our discussion.

An *overdose* is an excessive dose of a drug that can seriously threaten one's life. Any drug can be fatal if a person takes enough of it, but some drugs carry more risk of overdose than others. In **Figure 5.25**, column 4 estimates the risk of accidentally consuming a lethal overdose of various drugs. Drugs that are central nervous system (CNS) depressants—narcotics and sedatives—carry the greatest risk of overdose. It's important to understand that the effects of these drugs are additive. Many overdoses involve lethal *combinations* of CNS depressants. What happens when people overdose on these drugs? Their respiratory system usually grinds to a halt, producing coma, brain damage, and death within a brief period. In contrast, fatal overdoses with CNS stimulants (cocaine and amphetamines) usually involve a heart attack, stroke, or cortical seizure.

Now that our basic vocabulary is spelled out, we can begin to examine the effects and risks of major recreational drugs. Of course, we'll be describing the *typical* effects of each drug. Please bear in mind that the effects of any drug depend on the user's age, body weight, physiology, personality, mood, expectations, and previous experience with the drug. The dose and potency of the drug, the method of administration, and the setting in which the drug is taken also influence its effects (Leavitt, 1995). Our coverage is based largely on comprehensive books by Julien (2008), Levinthal (2008), and Lowinson and colleagues (2005), but we cite additional sources when discussing specific studies or controversial points.

## Narcotics

*Narcotics* (or opiates) are drugs derived from opium that are capable of relieving pain. In government regulations, the term *narcotic* is used in a haphazard way to refer to a variety of drugs besides opiates. The most widely abused opiates are heroin, morphine, and a rela-

tively new painkiller called Oxycontin. However, less potent opiates, such as codeine, Demerol, and Vicodin, are also subject to misuse.

### Effects

The most significant narcotics problem in modern, Western society is the use of heroin. Most users inject this drug intravenously with a hypodermic needle. The main effect is an overwhelming sense of euphoria. This "Who cares?" feeling makes the heroin high an attractive escape from reality. Common side effects include nausea, lethargy, drowsiness, constipation, and slowed respiration.

### Risks

Narcotics carry a high risk for both *psychological and physical dependence* (Knapp, Ciraulo, & Jaffe, 2005). It is estimated that there are about 600,000 heroin addicts in the United States (Winick & Norman, 2005). Although heroin withdrawal usually isn't life threatening, it can be terribly unpleasant, so that "junkies" have a desperate need to continue their drug use. Once dependence is entrenched, users tend to develop a *drug-centered lifestyle* that revolves around the need to procure more heroin. This lifestyle occurs because the drug is expensive and available only through highly undependable black market channels. Obviously, it is difficult to lead a productive life if one's existence is dominated by a desperate need to "score" heroin. The inordinate cost of the drug forces many junkies to resort to criminal activities to support their habit. Heroin use in the U.S. has leveled off since the 1990s (Johnston et al., 2007, 2008). Still, heroin is blamed for over 4,000 deaths annually in the United States, so *overdose* is a very real danger. Opiates are additive with other CNS depressants, and most narcotic overdoses occur in combination with the use of sedatives or alcohol. Junkies also risk *contracting infectious disease* because they often share hypodermic needles and tend to be sloppy about sterilizing them. The most common of these diseases used to be hepatitis, but in recent years AIDS has been transmitted at an alarming rate through the population of intravenous drug users (Des Jarlais, Hagan, & Friedman, 2005).

## Sedatives

*Sedatives* **are sleep-inducing drugs that tend to decrease central nervous system and behavioral activity.** In street jargon, they are often called "downers." Over the years, the most widely abused sedatives have been the barbiturates, which are compounds derived from barbituric acid. However, barbiturates have gradually become medically obsolete and diminished in availability, so sedative abusers have had to turn to drugs in the benzodiazepine family, such as Valium (Wesson et al., 2005).

### Effects

People abusing sedatives generally consume larger doses than are prescribed for medical purposes. These overly large doses have a euphoric effect similar to that produced by drinking large amounts of alcohol (Wesson et al., 2005). Feelings of tension, anxiety, and depression are temporarily replaced by a relaxed, pleasant state of intoxication, in which inhibitions may be loosened. Sedatives carry a truckload of dangerous side effects. Motor coordination suffers badly, producing slurred speech and a staggering walk, among other things. Intellectual functioning also becomes sluggish, and judgment is impaired. One's emotional tone may become unstable, with feelings of dejection often intruding on the intended euphoric mood.

### Risks

Sedatives have the potential to produce *both psychological and physical dependence.* They are also among the leading causes of *overdoses* in the United States because of their additive interactions with other CNS depressants (especially alcohol) and because of the degree to which they impair judgment. In their drug-induced haze, sedative abusers are likely to take doses they would ordinarily recognize as dangerous. Sedative users also elevate their risk for *accidental injuries* because these drugs can have significant effects on motor coordination.

## Stimulants

Whereas sedatives slow people's metabolic rate (Julien, 2008), stimulants create a feeling of alertness. *Stimulants* **are drugs that tend to increase central nervous system and behavioral activity.** They range from mild, widely available forms, such as caffeine and nicotine, to stronger, carefully regulated stimulants, such as cocaine and amphetamines ("speed"). Here we focus on the latter two drugs.

Cocaine, an organic substance extracted from the coca shrub, is usually consumed as a crystalline powder that is snorted through the nasal cavities, although it can be consumed orally or intravenously. "Crack" is a processed variant of cocaine, consisting of little chips of cocaine that are usually smoked. Smoking crack tends to be more dangerous than snorting cocaine powder because smoking leads to a more rapid absorption of the drug into the bloodstream and more concentrated delivery of cocaine to the brain. That said, all the forms of cocaine and all the routes of administration can deliver highly toxic amounts of the drug to the brain (Repetto & Gold, 2005).

Synthesized in a pharmaceutical laboratory, amphetamines are usually consumed orally. However, speed is also sold as a crystalline powder (called "crank" or "crystal meth") that may be snorted or injected intravenously. A smokable form of methamphetamine, called "ice," is seen in some regions.

### Effects

Amphetamines and cocaine have almost indistinguishable effects, except that cocaine produces a very brief high (20–30 minutes unless more is taken), while a speed high can last many hours (Gold, Miller, & Jonas, 1992). Stimulants produce a euphoria very different from that created by narcotics or sedatives. They produce a buoyant, elated, enthusiastic, energetic, "I can conquer the world!" feeling accompanied by increased alertness. Common side effects include increased blood pressure, muscle tension, sweating, and restlessness. Some users experience unpleasant feelings of irritability, anxiety, and paranoia.

### Risks

Stimulants can cause physical dependence, but the physical distress caused by stimulant withdrawal is mild compared to that caused by narcotic or sedative withdrawal. Psychological dependence on stimulants is a more common problem. Cocaine can create an exceptionally *powerful psychological dependence* that compels the user to pursue the drug with a fervor normally seen only when physical dependence exists (Gold & Jacobs, 2005).

Both cocaine and amphetamines can suppress appetite and disrupt sleep. Thus, heavy use of stimulants may lead to poor eating, poor sleeping, and ultimately, a *deterioration in physical health.* Furthermore, stimulant use increases one's risk for stroke, heart attack, and other forms of cardiovascular disease, and crack smoking is associated with a host of respiratory problems (Gourevitch & Arnsten, 2005; Weaver & Schnoll, 1999). Heavy stimulant use occasionally leads to the onset of a severe psychological disorder called *amphetamine* or *cocaine psychosis* (depending on the drug involved), which is dominated by intense paranoia (King & Ellinwood, 2005). All of the risks associated with stimulant use increase when more potent forms of the drugs (crack and ice) are used. Overdoses on stimulants used to be relatively infrequent (Kalant & Kalant, 1979). However, in recent years, *cocaine overdoses have increased sharply* as more people experiment with more dangerous modes of ingestion.

## Hallucinogens

*Hallucinogens* **are a diverse group of drugs that have powerful effects on mental and emotional functioning, marked most prominently by distortions in sensory and perceptual experience.** The principal hallucinogens are LSD, mescaline, and psilocybin, which have similar effects, although they vary in potency. Mescaline comes from the peyote plant, psilocybin comes from a particular type of mushroom, and LSD is a synthetic drug. Common street names for hallucinogens include "acid," "mushrooms," "fry," and "blotter."

### Effects

Hallucinogens intensify and distort perception in ways that are difficult to describe, and they temporarily impair intellectual functioning as thought processes become meteoric and jumbled. These drugs can produce awesome feelings of euphoria that sometimes include an almost mystical sense of "oneness" with the human race. This is why they have been used in religious ceremonies in various cultures. Unfortunately, at the other end of the emotional spectrum, they can also produce nightmarish feelings of anxiety, fear, and paranoia, commonly called a "bad trip."

### Risks

There is no potential for physical dependence on hallucinogens, and no deaths attributable to overdose are known to have occurred. Psychological dependence has been reported but appears to be rare. Research reports that LSD increases chromosome breakage were based on poor methodology (Dishotsky et al., 1971). However, like most drugs, hallucinogens may be harmful to a fetus if taken by a pregnant woman.

Although the dangers of hallucinogens have probably been exaggerated in the popular press, there are some significant risks (Pechnick & Ungerleider, 2005). Emotion is highly volatile with these drugs, so users can never be sure that they won't experience *acute panic* from a terrifying bad trip. Generally, this disorientation subsides within a few hours, leaving no permanent emotional scars. However, in such a severe state of disorientation, *accidents and suicide* are possible. *Flashbacks* are vivid hallucinogenic experiences occurring long after the original drug ingestion. They do not appear to be a common problem, but repetitious flashbacks have proved troublesome for some individuals. In a small minority of users, hallucinogens may contribute to the emergence of a *variety of psychological disorders* (psychoses, depressive reactions, paranoid states) that may be partially attributable to the drug (Pechnick & Ungerleider, 2005).

## Marijuana

*Cannabis* **is the hemp plant from which marijuana, hashish, and THC are derived.** Marijuana (often called "pot," "weed," "reefer," or "grass") is a mixture of dried leaves, flowers, stems, and seeds taken from the plant, while hashish comes from the plant's resin. THC, the active chemical ingredient in cannabis, can be synthesized for research purposes (for example, to give to animals).

### Effects

When smoked, cannabis has an almost immediate impact that may last several hours. The effects of the drug vary greatly, depending on the user's expectations and experience with it, the drug's potency, and the amount smoked. The drug has subtle effects on emotion, perception, and cognition (Grinspoon, Bakalar, & Russo, 2005). Emotionally, the drug tends to create a mild, relaxed state of euphoria. Perceptually, it enhances the impact of incoming stimulation, thus making music sound better, food taste better, and so on. Cannabis tends to produce a slight impairment in cognitive functioning (especially short-term memory) and perceptual-motor coordination while the user is high. However, there are huge variations among users.

### Risks

Overdose and physical dependence are not problems with marijuana, but as with any other drug that produces pleasant feelings, it has the potential to produce *psychological dependence* (Grinspoon, Bakalar, & Russo, 2005). Marijuana can also cause *transient problems with anxiety and depression* in some people. Of greater concern is recent research which has suggested that marijuana use during adolescence *may help to precipitate schizophrenia* in young people who have a genetic vulnerability to the disorder (Compton, Goulding, & Walker, 2007; Degenhardt & Hall, 2006; see Chapter 14). Studies also suggest that cannabis may have a more *negative effect on driving* than has been widely believed (Ramaekers, Robbe, & O'Hanlon, 2000). Indeed, people often make riskier decisions under the influence of marijuana (Lane et al., 2005), which may account for its link to increased risk for injuries (Kalant, 2004). Like tobacco smoke, marijuana smoke carries carcinogens and impurities into the lungs, thus increasing one's chances for *respiratory and pulmonary diseases, and probably lung cancer* (Kalant, 2004; Stephens, 1999). However, the evidence on other widely publicized risks remains controversial. Here is a brief overview of the evidence on some of these controversies:

● *Does marijuana reduce one's immune response?* Research with animals clearly demonstrates that cannabis can suppress various aspects of immune system responding (Cabral & Pettit, 1998). However, infectious diseases do not *appear* to be more common among marijuana smokers than among nonsmokers. Thus, it is unclear whether marijuana increases susceptibility to infectious diseases in humans (Bredt et al., 2002; Klein, Friedman, & Specter, 1998).

● *Does marijuana lead to impotence and sterility in men?* Research with humans has yielded weak, inconsistent, and reversible effects on testosterone and sperm levels (Brown & Dobs, 2002). At present, the evidence suggests that marijuana has little lasting impact on male smokers' fertility or sexual functioning (Grinspoon, Bakalar, & Russo, 2005).

● *Does marijuana have long-term negative effects on cognitive functioning?* Some studies using elaborate and precise assessments of cognitive functioning *have* found an association between chronic, heavy marijuana use and measureable impairments in attention and memory (see **Figure 5.26**) that show up when users are not high (Ehrenreich et al., 1999; Solowij et al., 2002). However, the cognitive deficits that have been observed are modest and certainly not disabling, and one study found that the deficits vanished after a month of marijuana abstinence (Pope, Gruber, & Yurgelun-Todd, 2001; Pope et al., 2001).

## Ecstasy (MDMA)

A relatively recent drug controversy in Western society centers on MDMA, better known as "ecstasy." MDMA was originally formulated in 1912 but was not widely used in the United States until the 1990s, when it became popular in the context of "raves" and dance clubs (Millman & Beeder, 1994). This compound is related to both amphetamines and hallucinogens, especially mescaline. It produces a high that typically lasts a few hours or more. Users report that they feel warm, friendly, euphoric, sensual, insightful, and empathetic, yet alert and energetic. Problematic side effects include increased blood pressure, muscle tension, sweating, blurred vision, insomnia, and transient anxiety.

Empirical research on ecstasy is still in its infancy, so assertions about its risks and dangers must be tentative and provisional. Data on adverse effects are also complicated by the fact that the vast majority of MDMA

**Figure 5.26**

**Chronic cannabis use and cognitive performance.** Solowij and associates (2002) administered a battery of neuropsychological tests to 51 long-term cannabis users who had smoked marijuana regularly for an average of 24 years; 51 short-term cannabis users who had smoked marijuana regularly for an average of 10 years; and 33 control subjects who had little or no history of cannabis use. The cannabis users were required to abstain from smoking marijuana for a minimum of 12 hours prior to their testing. The study found evidence suggestive of subtle cognitive impairments among the long-term cannabis users on many of the tests. The graph shown here depicts the results observed for overall performance on the Rey Auditory Verbal Learning Test, which measures several aspects of memory functioning.

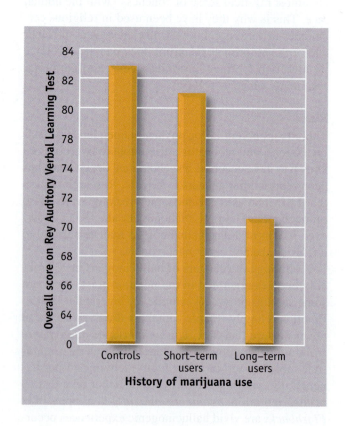

users ingest it in conjunction with many other drugs (Hammersley et al., 1999; Pedersen & Skrondal, 1999). There is some evidence that it creates problems regarding maintaining normal body temperature and the immune system (Connor, 2004). Yet another complicating factor is that MDMA often contains potentially harmful impurities, contaminants, and toxic by-products introduced during its illicit manufacture (Grob & Poland, 2005).

MDMA does not appear to be especially addictive, but psychological dependence can clearly become a problem for some people. MDMA has been implicated in cases of stroke and heart attack, seizures, heat stroke, and liver damage, but its exact contribution is hard to gauge given all the other drugs that MDMA users typically consume (Burgess, O'Donohoe, & Gill, 2000; Grob & Poland, 2005). Chronic, heavy use of ecstasy appears to be associated with sleep disorders, depression, and elevated anxiety and hostility (Morgan, 2000). Moreover, studies of former MDMA users suggest that ecstasy may have subtle, long-term effects on cognitive functioning (Medina, Shear, & Corcoran, 2005; Parrott, 2000). Quite a few studies have found memory deficits in former users (Bhattachary & Powell, 2001; Zakzanis & Young, 2001). Other studies have found decreased performance on laboratory tasks requiring attention and learning (Gouzoulis-Mayfrank et al., 2000). Thus, although more research is needed, there are many reasons to be concerned about the possible effects of ecstasy.

MDMA, better known as "ecstasy," surged in popularity in the 1990s in the context of "raves" and dance clubs. Although many people view MDMA as a relatively harmless drug, recent research suggests otherwise.

## KEY IDEAS

### Stress, Personality, and Illness

● The biopsychosocial model holds that physical health is influenced by a complex network of biological, psychological, and sociocultural factors. Stress is one of the psychological factors that can affect physical health. In particular, cynical hostility has been implicated as a contributing cause of coronary heart disease. A number of mechanisms may contribute to this connection.

● Emotional reactions may also influence susceptibility to heart disease. Recent research has suggested that transient mental stress and the negative emotions that result may tax the heart. Yet another line of research has identified the emotional dysfunction of depression as a risk factor for heart disease.

● The connection between psychological factors and the onset of cancer is not well documented, but stress and personality do appear to influence the course of the disease. Researchers have found associations between stress and the onset of a variety of other diseases. Stress may play a role in a variety of diseases because it can temporarily suppress immune functioning. While there's little doubt that stress can contribute to the development of physical illness, the link between stress and illness is modest.

### Habits, Lifestyles and Health

● People commonly engage in health-impairing habits and lifestyles. These habits creep up slowly, and their risks are easy to ignore because the dangers often lie in the distant future.

● Smokers have much higher mortality rates than nonsmokers because they are more vulnerable to a variety of diseases. Giving up smoking can reduce one's health risks, but doing so is difficult and relapse rates are high.

● Drinking rivals smoking as a source of health problems. In the short term, drinking can impair driving, cause various types of accidents, and increase the likelihood of aggressive interactions or reckless sexual behavior. In the long term, chronic, excessive alcohol consumption increases one's risk for numerous health problems, including cirrhosis of the liver, heart disease, hypertension, stroke, and cancer.

● Obesity elevates one's risk for many health problems. Body weight is influenced by genetic endowment, eating and exercise habits, and perhaps set point or settling point. Weight loss is best accomplished by decreasing caloric consumption while increasing exercise.

● Poor nutritional habits have been linked to many health problems, including cardiovascular diseases and some types of cancer, although some of the links are tentative. One's health can best be served by following balanced food consumption patterns while limiting the intake of saturated fats, cholesterol, refined carbohydrates, sugar, and salt.

● Lack of exercise is associated with elevated mortality rates. Regular exercise can reduce one's risk for cardiovascular disease, cancer, and obesity-related diseases; buffer the effects of stress; and lead to desirable personality changes.

● Although misconceptions abound, HIV is transmitted almost exclusively by sexual contact and the sharing of needles by intravenous drug users. One's risk for HIV infection can be reduced by avoiding IV drug use, having fewer sexual partners, using condoms, and curtailing certain sexual practices.

### Reactions to Illness

● Variations in seeking treatment are influenced by the severity, duration, and disruptiveness of one's symptoms and by the reactions of friends and family. The biggest problem is the tendency of many people to delay needed medical treatment. At the other extreme, a minority of people learn to like the sick role because it earns them attention and allows them to avoid stress.

● Good communication is crucial to effective health services, but many factors undermine communication between patients and health providers, such as short visits, overuse of medical jargon, and patients' reluctance to ask questions.

● Noncompliance with medical advice is a major problem, which appears to occur 30%–50% of the time. The likelihood of nonadherence is greater when instructions are difficult to understand, when recommendations are difficult to follow, and when patients are unhappy with their doctor.

### Application: Understanding the Effects of Drugs

● Recreational drugs vary in their potential for tolerance effects, psychological dependence, physical dependence, and overdose. The risks associated with narcotics use include both types of dependence, overdose, and the acquisition of infectious diseases.

● Sedatives can also produce both types of dependence, are subject to overdoses, and elevate the user's risk for accidental injuries. Stimulant use can lead to psychological dependence, overdose, psychosis, and a deterioration in physical health. Cocaine overdoses have increased greatly in recent years.

● Hallucinogens can in some cases contribute to accidents, suicides, and psychological disorders, and they can cause flashbacks. The risks of marijuana use include psychological dependence, impaired driving, transient problems with anxiety and depression, and respiratory and pulmonary diseases. Recent studies suggest that marijuana use may have some long-term negative effects on cognitive processes.

● More research is needed, but it appears that the use of ecstasy (MDMA) may contribute to a variety of acute and chronic physical maladies. MDMA may also have subtle, negative effects on cognitive functioning.

## KEY TERMS

Acquired immune deficiency syndrome (AIDS)  p. 162
Alcohol dependence  p. 153
Alcoholism  p. 153
Atherosclerosis  p. 141
Biopsychosocial model  p. 139
Body mass index (BMI)  p. 154
Cancer  p. 144
Cannabis  p. 171
Coronary heart disease  p. 141
Hallucinogens  p. 171
Health psychology  p. 140
Hostility  p. 142
Immune response  pp. 146
Narcotics  p. 169
Nutrition  p. 157
Overdose  p. 169
Physical dependence  p. 168
Psychological dependence  p. 168
Sedatives  p. 170
Set-point theory  p. 156
Settling-point theory  p. 156
Stimulants  p. 170
Tolerance  p. 168
Type A personality  p. 142
Type B personality  p. 142
Unrealistic optimism  p. 149

## KEY PEOPLE

Robin DiMatteo  p. 166
Meyer Friedman and Ray Rosenman  p. 142
Janice Kiecolt-Glaser  pp. 146–147

## QUESTIONS

1. The greatest threats to health in our society today are:
   a. environmental toxins.
   b. accidents.
   c. chronic diseases.
   d. contagious diseases caused by specific infectious agents.

2. Which of the following is *not* associated with elevated coronary risk?
   a. cynical hostility
   b. strong emotional reactions to transient mental stress
   c. obsessive-compulsive disorder
   d. depression

3. Why do people tend to act in self-destructive ways?
   a. because many health-impairing habits creep up on them
   b. because many health-impairing habits involve activities that are quite pleasant at the time
   c. because the risks tend to lie in the distant future
   d. all of the above

4. Some short-term risks of alcohol consumption include all but which of the following?
   a. hangovers and life-threatening overdoses in combination with other drugs
   b. poor perceptual coordination and driving drunk
   c. increased aggressiveness and argumentativeness
   d. transient anxiety from endorphin-induced flashbacks

5. Twin studies and other behavioral genetics research suggest that:
   a. genetic factors have little impact on people's weight.
   b. heredity has scant influence on BMI but does influence weight.
   c. heredity accounts for 60% or more of the variation in weight.
   d. heredity is responsible for severe, morbid obesity but has little influence over the weight of normal people.

6. Which of the following has *not* been found to be a mode of transmission for AIDS?
   a. sexual contact among homosexual men
   b. the sharing of needles by intravenous drug users
   c. sexual contact among heterosexuals
   d. sharing food

7. Regarding the seeking of medical treatment, the biggest problem is:
   a. the tendency of many people to delay seeking treatment.
   b. the tendency of many people to rush too quickly for medical care for minor problems.
   c. not having enough doctors to cover peoples' needs.
   d. the tendency of people in higher socioeconomic categories to exaggerate their symptoms.

8. In which of the following cases are people most likely to follow the instructions they receive from health care professionals?
   a. when the instructions are complex and punctuated with impressive medical jargon
   b. when they do not fully understand the instructions but still feel the need to do something
   c. when they like and understand the health care professional
   d. all of the above

9. Which of the following risks is *not* typically associated with narcotics use?
   a. overdose
   b. infectious disease
   c. physical dependence
   d. flashbacks

10. The use of sedatives may result in personal injury because they:
    a. cause motor coordination to deteriorate.
    b. enhance motor coordination too much, making people overconfident about their abilities.
    c. suppress pain warnings of physical harm.
    d. trigger hallucinations such as flying.

## ANSWERS

1. c   Pages 138–139
2. c   Pages 141–144
3. d   Pages 148–149
4. d   Page 153
5. c   Page 155
6. d   Pages 162–163
7. a   Page 165
8. c   Page 166
9. d   Pages 169–170
10. a   Page 170

## Personal Explorations Workbook

Go to the *Personal Explorations Workbook* in the back of your textbook for exercises that can enhance your self-understanding in relation to issues raised in this chapter. **Exercise 5.1** *Self-Assessment:* Chronic Self-Destructiveness Scale. **Exercise 5.2** *Self-Reflection:* How Do Your Health Habits Rate?

## CourseMate

Access an interactive eBook, chapter-specific interactive learning tools, including Personal Explorations, Recommended Readings, Critical Thinking Exercises, flashcards, quizzes, videos and more in your Psychology CourseMate, available at **www.cengagebrain.com/shop/ISBN/1111186634**.

© didi/Getty Images/amana-images

# CHAPTER 6

# The Self

At last you are in college and on your own, away from home. You are a little nervous but excited about your new life and its challenges. Today is your first official day of college and psychology is your first class. You arrive early. You take a seat near the front of the lecture hall and immediately feel conspicuous. You don't know anyone in the class; in fact, you suddenly realize you don't know anyone at the university except for your roommate, who is still more or less a stranger. Many students seem to know one another. They are laughing, talking, and catching up while you just sit there, quiet and alone. They seem friendly, so why won't they talk to you? Should you speak to them first? Are you dressed okay—what about your hair? You begin to question yourself: Will you ever make any friends in this class or at the university? Oh, here comes the professor. She seems nice enough, but you wonder what she expects. Will this class be difficult? Well, you do plan to work hard and study a lot, but how will psychology help you in the future? Perhaps you should be taking a more practical class, maybe accounting, which will lead right to a career. Wait a minute: What if the professor calls on you in front of all these strangers who already know each other? Will you sound intelligent or look foolish? As the professor begins to take the class roll, your mind is racing. You feel tense and your stomach gets a little queasy as she gets closer in the alphabet to your name.

This scenario illustrates the process of self-perception and the effects it can have on emotion, motivation, and goal setting. People engage in this sort of self-reflection constantly, especially when they are trying to understand the causes of their own behavior.

In this chapter, we highlight the self and its important role in adjustment. We begin by looking at two major components of the self: self-concept and self-esteem. Then we review some key principles of the self-perception process. Next, we turn to the important topic of self-regulation. Finally, we focus on how people present themselves to others. In this chapter's Application, we offer some suggestions for building self-esteem.

# Self-Concept

## LEARNING OBJECTIVES

- Identify some key aspects of the self-concept.
- Cite two types of self-discrepancies, and describe their effects.
- Describe two ways of coping with self-discrepancies.
- Discuss important factors that help form the self-concept.
- Understand how individualism and collectivism influence the self-concept.

If you were asked to describe yourself, what would you say? You'd probably start off with some physical attributes such as "I'm tall," "I'm of average weight," or "I'm blonde." Soon you'd move on to psychological characteristics: "I'm friendly," "I'm honest," "I'm reasonably intelligent," and so forth. People usually identify whatever makes them unique in a particular situation. These distinctive qualities fit into their self-definitions. American schoolchildren, for example, define themselves by highlighting how they are different from their classmates (McGuire & Pawader-Singer, 1978). You probably do the same thing. How did you develop these beliefs about yourself? Have your self-views changed over time? Read on.

## The Nature of the Self-Concept

Although we usually talk about the self-concept as a single entity, it is actually a multifaceted structure (Mischel & Morf, 2003). That is, the *self-concept* **is an organized collection of beliefs about the self.** These beliefs, also called *self-schemas*, shape social perception (Green & Sedikides, 2001), are developed from past experience, and are concerned with one's personality traits, abilities, physical features, values, goals, and social roles (Campbell, Assanand, & DiPaula, 2000). People have self-schemas on dimensions that are important to them, including both strengths and weaknesses. **Figure 6.1** depicts the self-concepts of two hypothetical individuals.

Each self-schema is characterized by relatively distinct thoughts and feelings. For instance, you might have considerable information about your social skills and feel quite self-assured about them but have limited information and less confidence about your physical skills. Current thinking is that only a portion of the total self-concept operates at any one time. The self-concept that is accessible at any given moment has been termed the *working self-concept* by Hazel Markus, a leading researcher in this area (Markus & Wurf, 1987). Our self-concept is apt to be "relational," that is, one's sense of self is based on the current as well as past relationships one has with significant others in one's life, such as friends, family, and romantic partners (Andersen & Chen, 2002).

Hazel Markus

Stanford University News Service, photo by L. A. Cicero

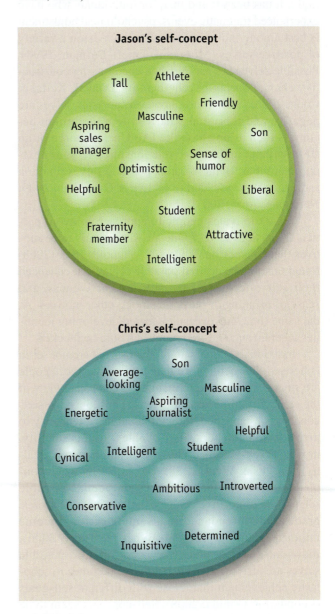

**FIGURE 6.1**

**The self-concept and self-schemas.** The self-concept is composed of various self-schemas, or beliefs about the self. Jason and Chris have different self-concepts in part because they have different self-schemas.

Beliefs about the self influence not only current behavior but also future behavior. ***Possible selves*** **are one's conceptions about the kind of person one might become in the future** (Erikson, 2007; Markus & Nurius, 1986). If you have narrowed your career choices to personnel manager and psychologist, they would represent two possible selves in the career realm. Possible selves are developed from past experiences, current behavior, and future expectations. They make people attentive to goal-related information and role models and mindful of the need to practice goal-related skills. As such, they help individuals not only to envision desired future goals but also to achieve them (Cross & Markus, 1991; Hock, Deshler, & Schumaker, 2006). Interestingly, it has been found that, for individuals who have experienced traumatic events, psychological adjustment is best among those who are able to envision a variety of positive selves (Morgan & Janoff-Bulman, 1994). Possible selves are useful when encouraging constructive change during psychotherapy (Dunkel, Kelts, & Coon, 2006). Sometimes, however, possible selves are negative and represent what you fear you might become—such as an alcoholic like Uncle George or an adult without an intimate relationship like your next-door neighbor. In these cases, possible selves function as images to be avoided (e.g., Lee & Oyserman, 2009; Norman & Aron, 2003).

What motivates people to approach or avoid particular possible selves? One answer appears to be motives that enhance one's identity. Vignoles et al. (2008) found that people desired possible selves that enhanced their self-esteem, self-perceived effectiveness, and sense of meaning or purpose, among other motives. At the same time, however, they feared developing identities wherein such desired motives would be blocked.

Individuals' beliefs about themselves are not set in concrete—but neither are they easily changed. People are strongly motivated to maintain a consistent view of the self across time and situations. Thus, once the self-concept is established, the individual has a tendency to preserve and defend it. In the context of this stability, however, self-beliefs do have a certain dynamic quality (Markus & Wurf, 1987). For example, when coupled with educational strategies, "academic possible selves" led to positive changes in planning, test scores, grades, and attendance in a sample of low-income minority youth (Oyserman, Bybee, & Terry, 2006). Individuals with academic or career-oriented possible selves are also more persistent when it comes to scholastic achievement than those with different self-goals (Leondari & Gonida, 2008). Self-concepts seem to be most susceptible to change when people shift from an important and familiar social setting to an unfamiliar one, such as when they go off to college or to a new city for their first "real" job. This flexibility clearly underscores the social foundations of the self-concept.

**WEB LINK 6.1   Research Sources: Concepts of Person and Self**

Over the past century psychologists, philosophers, and many others have wondered what is meant by terms like "person" and "self." Professor Shaun Gallagher of the University of Central Florida's Philosophy and Cognitive Science Department provides visitors with a variety of resources to explore these concepts.

## Self-Discrepancies

Some people perceive themselves pretty much the way they'd like to see themselves. Others experience a gap between what they actually see and what they'd like to see. For example, Nathan describes his actual self as "shy" but his ideal self as "outgoing." According to E. Tory Higgins (1987), individuals have several organized self-perceptions: an *actual self* (qualities you believe you *actually* possess), an *ideal self* (characteristics you would *like* to have), and an *ought self* (traits you believe you *should* possess). The ideal and ought selves serve as personal standards or self-guides that direct behavior. ***Self-discrepancy*** **consists of a mismatch between the self-perceptions that make up the actual self, ideal self, and ought self.** These self-discrepancies are measureable and have consequences for how people think, feel, and act (Hardin & Lakin, 2009).

### Self-Discrepancies and Their Effects

The differences among one's actual, ideal, and ought selves influence how one feels about oneself and can create some particular emotional vulnerabilities (Higgins, 1999). According to Higgins, when people live up to their personal standards (ideal or ought selves), they experience high self-esteem; when they don't meet their own expectations, their self-esteem suffers (Moretti & Higgins, 1990). In addition, he says, certain types of self-discrepancies are associated with specific emotions (see **Figure 6.2**). One type of self-discrepancy occurs when the *actual* self is at odds with the *ideal* self. Such instances trigger *dejection-related* emotions (sadness, disappointment). As actual-ideal discrepancies outnumber actual-ideal congruencies, sadness increases and cheerfulness decreases (Higgins, Shah, & Friedman, 1997). Consider Tiffany's situation: She knows that she's attractive, but she is also overweight and would like to be thinner. Self-discrepancy theory predicts that she would feel dissatisfied and dejected. Interestingly, research has shown an association between discrepant actual/ideal views of body shape and eating disorders (Sawdon, Cooper, & Seabrook, 2007; Strauman et al., 1991).

Self-discrepant thoughts may trigger more powerful feelings than just dissatisfaction or dejection. Some recent research demonstrates a link between two types of actual-ideal self-discrepancies and suicidal thoughts

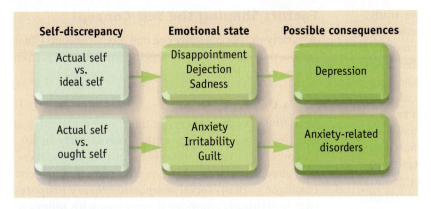

## FIGURE 6.2

**Types of self-discrepancies, their effects on emotional states, and possible consequences.** According to E. Tory Higgins (1989), discrepancies between actual and ideal selves produce disappointment and sadness, whereas discrepancies between actual and ought selves result in irritability and guilt. Such self-discrepancies can make individuals vulnerable to more serious psychological problems, such as depression and anxiety-related disorders.

(Cornette et al., 2009). A sample of college students completed a self-discrepancy scale and measures of depression, hopelessness, and suicidal ideation (thinking about suicide but not necessarily acting on it). Current actual-ideal and actual-ideal-future self-discrepancies were linked to levels of hopelessness, which in turn contributed to depression and suicidal ideation. The researchers suggest that when self-discrepancies act as a form of negative self-evaluation, these perceptions can heighten a person's risk for engaging in suicidal thinking.

A second type of discrepancy involves a mismatch between *actual* and *ought* selves. Let's say you don't stay in touch with your grandparents as often as you feel you should. According to Higgins, actual/ought self-discrepancies produce *agitation-related* emotions (irritability, anxiety, and guilt). As actual-ought discrepancies outnumber actual-ought congruencies, anxiety increases and calm emotions decrease (Higgins, Shah, & Friedman, 1997). Extreme discrepancies of this type can result in anxiety-related psychological disorders.

Everyone experiences self-discrepancies, yet most people manage to feel reasonably good about themselves. How is this possible? Three factors seem to be important: the amount of discrepancy you experience, your awareness of the discrepancy, and whether the discrepancy is actually important to you (Higgins, 1999). Thus, a pre-med major who gets a C in calculus will probably feel a lot worse than an English major who gets a C in the course.

### Coping with Self-Discrepancies

Can individuals do anything to blunt the negative emotions and blows to self-esteem associated with self-discrepancies? Yes! For one thing, people can *change their behavior* to bring it more in line with their ideal or ought selves. For instance, if your ideal self is a person who gets above-average grades and your actual self just

got a D on a test, you can study more effectively for the next test to improve your grade. But what about the times you can't match your ideal standards? Perhaps you had your heart set on being on the varsity tennis team but didn't make the cut. One way to ease the discomfort associated with such discrepancies is to bring your ideal self a bit more in line with your actual abilities. You may not achieve your ideal self right away, if ever, but by behaving in ways that are consistent with that self, you will get closer to it and be more content (Haidt, 2006; Wilson, 2002). Alternatively, subtle encouragement to consider ways to approach an ideal self (perhaps a constructive, friendly suggestion from a friend or a teacher) is apt to raise your spirits in a positive way (Shah & Higgins, 2001).

Another, less positive, approach is to *blunt your self-awareness,* or how much you focus on what you like or dislike about yourself, your self-perceived strengths and shortcomings, and so on. You can do so by avoiding situations that increase your self-awareness—if you don't want to appear to be shy, don't attend a party where you expect to spend a miserable evening talking to yourself. If your weight is bothering you, you might stay off the scale or avoid shopping for new clothes (as well as gazing into full-length mirrors).

Some people use alcohol to blunt self-awareness. In one study, college students were put into either a high or a low self-awareness group based on test scores (Hull & Young, 1983). Then both groups were given a brief version of an intelligence test as well as false feedback on their test performance. Half of the high self-awareness group were told that they had done quite well on the test and the other half were told that they had done quite

**When people don't live up to their personal standards, self-esteem suffers, and some turn to alcohol to blunt their awareness of the discrepancy.**

poorly. Next, supposedly as part of a separate study, these participants were asked to taste and evaluate various wines for 15 minutes. The experimenters predicted that the high self-awareness participants who had been told that they had done poorly on the IQ test would drink more than the other groups, and this is precisely what the study found (see **Figure 6.3**). Those who couldn't escape negative information about themselves drank more alcohol to reduce their self-awareness. Similarly, in the real world it has been found that alcoholics who have high self-awareness and who experience negative or painful life events relapse more quickly and completely (Hull, Young, & Jouriles, 1986).

Heightened self-awareness doesn't always make people focus on self-discrepancies and negative aspects of the self. If that were true, most people would feel a lot worse about themselves than they actually do. As you recall, self-concepts are made up of numerous self-beliefs—many of them positive, some negative. Because individuals have a need to feel good about themselves, they tend to focus on their positive features rather than their "warts" (Tesser, 2001; Tesser, Wood, & Stapel, 2005). In fact, when a person's self-concept is threatened (a job interview doesn't go well), the individual can recover by affirming competence in an unrelated domain (focusing on extraordinary talent as a salsa dancer) (Aronson, Cohen, & Nail, 1999; Steele, 1988; Steele, Spencer & Lynch, 1993). Alternatively, people can also affirm their self-identities by focusing on the important values they believe in, which in turn can help them reflect on larger life issues that matter more than self-related setbacks (Wakslak & Trope, 2009). In fact, an easy way to engage in self-affirmation (while also reducing defensiveness in the face of uncomfortable feedback) is to write about values that are important to you (Crocker, Niiya, & Mischkowski, 2008).

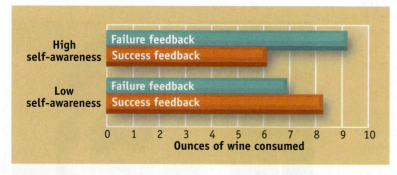

**FIGURE 6.3**

**Self-awareness and alcohol consumption.** Individuals who were high in self-awareness drank significantly more wine in a 15-minute period if they believed they had performed poorly on an IQ test than did any other group. This finding shows how people sometimes try to blunt self-awareness to cope with self-discrepancies.

Source: From Hull, J. G., & Young, R. D. (1983), Self-consciousness, self-esteem, and success-failure as determinants of alcohol consumption in male social drinkers. *Journal of Personality and Social Psychology, 44*, 1097–1109. Copyright © 1983 American Psychological Association. Reprinted by permission of the author.

## Factors Shaping the Self-Concept

A variety of sources influence one's self-concept. Chief among them are one's own observations, feedback from others, and cultural values.

### One's Own Observations

Individuals begin observing their own behavior and drawing conclusions about themselves early in life. Children will make statements about who is the tallest, who can run fastest, or who can swing the highest. Leon Festinger's (1954) *social comparison theory* **proposes that individuals compare themselves with others in order to assess their abilities and opinions.** People compare themselves to others to determine how attractive they are, how they did on the history exam, how their social skills stack up, and so forth. In short, social comparisons can be ego enhancing (Helgeson & Michelson, 1995), especially when comparing oneself to a close friend or peer. The direction of social comparison appears to matter, however, as less self-positivity is generated when one is asked to compare a friend or a peer with oneself (Pahl, Etser, & White, 2009).

Although Festinger's original theory claimed that people engage in social comparison for the purpose of accurately assessing their abilities, research suggests that they also engage in social comparison to improve their skills and to maintain their self-image (Wheeler & Suls, 2005; Wood & Wilson, 2003). Sometimes social comparison is self-focused, such as when a successful professional woman compares her "current self" to the passive, withdrawn "past self" of high school (Ross & Wilson, 2002; Wilson & Ross, 2000). Generally, however, people compare themselves against others with particular qualities. **A *reference group* is a set of people who are used as a gauge in making social comparisons.** People choose their reference groups strategically. For example, if you want to know how you did on your first test in social psychology (ability appraisal), your reference group would likely be the entire class. In terms of acquiring accurate self-knowledge about your performance, this sort of comparison is a good one if you are confident your classmates are similar to you (Wheeler, Koestner, & Driver, 1982). Thus, people use others, even complete strangers (Mussweiler, Rütter, & Epstude, 2004), as social benchmarks for comparison (Mussweiler & Rütter, 2003; Mussweiler & Strack, 2000).

What happens when people compare themselves to others who are better or worse off than them? For instance, if you want to improve your tennis game (skill development), your reference group should be limited to superior players, whose skills give you a goal to pursue. Such *upward social comparisons* can motivate you and direct your future efforts (Blanton et al., 1999). On the other hand, if your self-esteem needs bolstering, you will probably make a *downward social comparison,* looking to those whom you perceive to be worse off, thereby enabling you to feel better about yourself (Aspinwall & Taylor, 1993; Lockwood, 2002). We'll have more to say about downward social comparison a little later in the chapter.

People's observations of their own behavior are not entirely objective. The general tendency is to distort reality in a positive direction (see **Figure 6.4**). In other words, most people tend to evaluate themselves in a more positive light than they really merit (Taylor & Brown, 1988, 1994). The strength of this tendency was highlighted in a large survey of high school seniors conducted as part of the SAT (Myers, 1980). By definition, 50% of students must be "above average" and 50% "below average" on specific questions. However, 100% of the respondents saw themselves as above average

in "ability to get along with others." And 25% of the respondents thought that they belonged in the top 1%! This better-than-average effect seems to be a common phenomenon (Kuyper & Dijkstra, 2009).

In some academic situations, however, social comparisons may be reduced by circumstantial information. Garcia and Tor (2009) introduced what they call the "N-effect," in which the number of recognized or known competitors (or N, which refers to their number) appears to reduce the motivation to compete, a result of making particular social comparisons. One study found that some individuals completing an easy quiz did so much faster if they believed they were competing against 10 rather than 100 other people. Another study revealed that social comparisons become less important to individuals as N rises. And what about SAT scores? Garcia and Tor also found evidence suggesting that SAT scores drop as the average number of test takers increases at the testing site. Think about the N-effect with respect to your own academic achievement behavior:

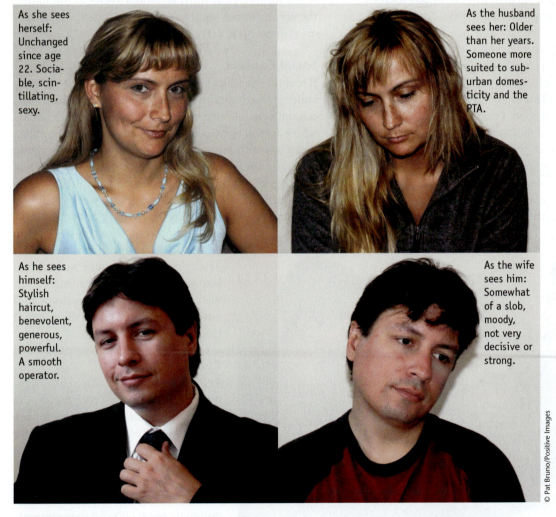

As she sees herself: Unchanged since age 22. Sociable, scintillating, sexy.

As the husband sees her: Older than her years. Someone more suited to suburban domesticity and the PTA.

As he sees himself: Stylish haircut, benevolent, generous, powerful. A smooth operator.

As the wife sees him: Somewhat of a slob, moody, not very decisive or strong.

© Pat Bruno/Positive Images

**FIGURE 6.4**

**Distortions in self-images.** How people see themselves may be different from how others see them. These pictures and text illustrate the subjective quality of self-concept and people's perception of others. Generally, self-images tend to be distorted in a positive direction.

Do smaller classes encourage you to be more competitive than larger ones?

## Feedback from Others

Individuals' self-concept is shaped significantly by the feedback they get from important people in their lives. Early on, parents and other family members play a dominant role. Parents give their children a great deal of direct feedback, saying such things as "We're so proud of you" or "If you just tried harder, you could do a lot better in math." Most people, especially when young, take this sort of feedback to heart. Thus, it comes as no surprise that studies find a link between parents' views of a child and the child's self-concept (Berne & Savary, 1993; Burhans & Dweck, 1995). There is even stronger evidence for a relationship between children's *perceptions* of their parents' attitudes toward them and their own self-views (Felson, 1989, 1992).

Teachers, Little League coaches, Scout leaders, classmates, and friends also provide feedback during childhood. In later childhood and adolescence, parents and classmates are particularly important sources of feedback and support (Harter, 2003). Later in life, feedback from close friends and marriage partners assumes importance. In fact, there is evidence that a close partner's support and affirmation can bring the loved one's actual self-views and behavior more in line with his or her ideal self (Drigotas et al., 1999). For this situation to happen, the partner needs to hold views of the loved one that match the target person's ideal self and behave in ways to bring out the best in the person. If the target person's behavior can closely match the ideal self, then self-views can move nearer to the ideal self. Researchers have labeled this process the *Michelangelo phenomenon* to reflect the partner's role in "sculpting" into reality the ideal self of a loved one.

Keep in mind that people filter feedback from others through their existing self-perceptions. That is, individuals don't see themselves exactly as others see them but rather as they *believe* others see them (Baumeister & Twenge, 2003; Tice & Wallace, 2003). Thus, feedback from others usually reinforces people's self-views. When feedback about the self conflicts with a person's central self-conceptions, he or she is quite capable of selectively forgetting it; yet the person can recall it when motivated toward self-improvement, including the way he or she regulates close relationships with others (Green et al., 2009).

## Social Context

Receiving feedback from others reveals that the self-concept does not develop in isolation. Of course, it's not only people that matter; so do the social contexts where interactions occur. Think about it: You're much more boisterous (and less self-conscious) when you are out with friends at a dance or a diner than when you are sitting in class. Social context effects how people think and feel about others, as well, including the impressions they may knowingly convey to others in different situations (Carlson & Furr, 2009). In office settings, for example, a superior will act and feel like a leader with subordinates but will quickly change demeanor and outlook in the presence of an equal (Moskowitz, 1994).

## Cultural Values

Self-concept is also shaped by cultural values. Among other things, the society in which one is reared defines what is desirable and undesirable in personality and behavior. For example, American culture puts a high premium on individuality, competitive success, strength, and skill. When individuals meet cultural expectations, they feel good about themselves and experience increases in self-esteem (Cross & Gore, 2003).

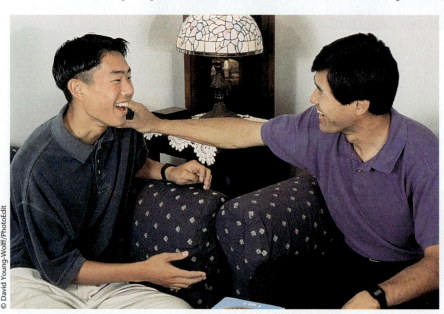

© David Young-Wolff/PhotoEdit

**Whether positive or negative, feedback from others plays an important role in shaping a youngster's self-concept.**

Cross-cultural studies suggest that different cultures shape different conceptions of the self (Cross & Markus, 1999; Cross & Gore, 2003). One important way cultures differ is on the dimension of individualism versus collectivism (Hofstede, 1983; Triandis, 1989, 2001). *Individualism involves putting personal goals ahead of group goals and defining one's identity in terms of personal attributes rather than group memberships.* In contrast, *collectivism involves putting group goals ahead of personal goals and defining one's identity in terms of the groups one belongs to* (such as one's family, tribe, work group, social class, caste, and so on). Although it's tempting to think of these perspectives in either-or terms, it is more appropriate to view them as points along a continuum that can be assessed (Fischer et al., 2009). Thus, it is more accurate to say that certain cultures are more or less individualistic (or collectivist) than others rather than seeing them as either one or the other.

Here is a clever but telling example illustrating the difference between individualist and collectivist cultures when simple choice is concerned. American students and Indian students selected a pen from a group composed of one blue pen and four red ones. American students consistently picked the singular blue pen, while the Indian students always chose the common red pen (Nicholson, 2006; see also, Connor Snibe & Markus, 2005; Stephens, Markus, & Townsend, 2007). In Western culture, we need to remember that "agency," or how people express their sense of power or influence in the social world, is not always found in other cultures or cultural contexts (Markus & Kitayama, 2004). In a follow-up study, once the students made their choice, some were told "Actually, you can't have that pen. Here, take this one instead." All students were then told to try their new pen, either the one "chosen" for them or the one "given" to them, and to rate it. The Americans preferred the pens they originally chose, thus devaluing the pen they were "given." How did the Indian students react? They showed no preference for either the pen they freely chose or the one given to them. Individualistic cultures promote freedom and choice, and people who live in these cultures do not like to have either threatened.

A variety of factors influence societies' tendencies to cherish individualism or collectivism. Among other things, increases in a culture's affluence, education, urbanization, and social mobility tend to foster more individualism (Triandis, 1994, 1995). Many contemporary societies are in transition, but generally speaking North American and Western European cultures tend to be individualistic, whereas Asian, African, and Latin American cultures tend to be collectivist (Hofstede, 1980, 1983).

Individuals reared in individualistic cultures usually have an *independent view of the self,* perceiving themselves as unique, self-contained, and distinct from others. In contrast, individuals reared in collectivist cultures typically have an *interdependent view of the self.* They see themselves as inextricably connected to others and believe that harmonious relationships with others are of utmost importance. Thus, in describing herself, a person living in an individualistic culture might say, "I am kind," whereas someone in a collectivist culture might respond, "My family thinks I am kind" (Triandis, 2001). **Figure 6.5** depicts the self-conceptions of individuals from these contrasting cultures.

Of course, how and when people adopt an individualistic or a collectivist orientation often depends on the situation in which they find themselves. In fact, when the requirements of a task fit one's cultural mindset, easier tasks are completed more quickly and more demanding tasks are finished with greater accuracy (Oyserman et al., 2009). In one study, Korean speakers were asked to circle either singular (individualist group) or plural (collectivist group) pronouns in a paragraph written in Korean. Subsequently, each group saw a picture with

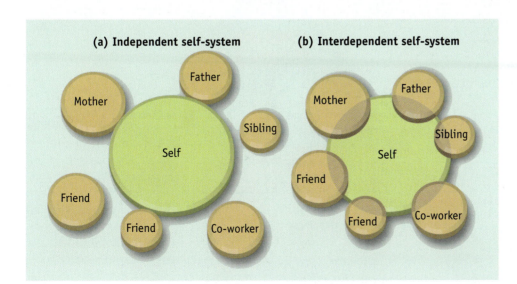

**FIGURE 6.5**

**Independent and interdependent views of the self.** **(a)** Individuals in cultures that support an independent view perceive the self as clearly separated from significant others. **(b)** Individuals in cultures that support an interdependent view perceive the self as inextricably connected to others.

Source: Adapted from Markus, H. R., & Kitayama, S. (1991). Culture and the self: Implications for cognition, emotion, and motivation. *Psychological Review, 98,* 224–253. Copyright © 1991 American Psychological Association. Adapted by permission of the publisher and author.

28 objects in it (e.g., car, anchor, sun) for 90 seconds. Afterward, they listed or drew as many of the objects as they could recall. As expected, those in the collectivist group correctly recalled more objects than those in the individualist group, presumably because the former were primed to think about the individual objects and how they related to one another in the display. Oyserman and her colleagues refer to this as an example of culture-as-situated-cognition.

Researchers have noted parallels between the self-views promoted by individualistic and collectivist cultures and the self-views of some groups. For example, women usually have more interdependent self-views

than men (Cross & Madson, 1997). But don't take this finding to mean that men are less social than women; rather, it means that men and women get their social needs met in different ways (Baumeister & Sommer, 1997). Thus women are usually involved in close relationships involving intimate friends and family members (*relational* interdependence), while men tend to interact in social groups such as clubs and sports teams (*collective* interdependence) (Gabriel & Gardner, 1999). These gender differences in self-views may explain other observed gender differences, such as women being more likely than men to share their feelings and thoughts with others.

# Self-Esteem

### LEARNING OBJECTIVES

- Clarify the implications of self-concept confusion and self-esteem instability.
- Understand how high and low self-esteem are related to adjustment.
- Distinguish between high self-esteem and narcissism, and discuss narcissism and aggression.
- Discuss some key influences in the development of self-esteem.
- Summarize the findings on ethnicity and gender regarding self-esteem.

One of the functions of the self-concept is to evaluate the self; the result of this self-evaluation is termed *self-esteem*. **Self-esteem refers to one's overall assessment of one's worth as a person.** Do you think of yourself in primarily positive or negative terms? Self-esteem is a global self-evaluation that blends many specific evaluations about one's adequacy as a student, an athlete, a

worker, a spouse, a parent, or whatever is personally relevant. **Figure 6.6** shows how specific elements of the self-concept may contribute to self-esteem. If you feel basically good about yourself, you probably have high self-esteem.

People with high self-esteem are confident, taking credit for their successes in various ways (Blaine &

**FIGURE 6.6**

**The structure of self-esteem.** Self-esteem is a global evaluation that combines assessments of various aspects of one's self-concept, each of which is built up from many specific behaviors and experiences. (Adapted from Shavelson, Hubner, & Stanton, 1976)

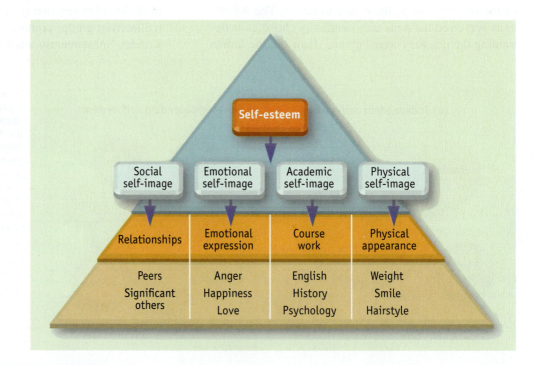

FIGURE 6.7

## The Rosenberg (1965) Self-Esteem Scale

Using the scale below, indicate your agreement with each of the following statements.

| 1 | 2 | 3 | 4 |
|---|---|---|---|
| Strongly disagree | Disagree | Agree | Strongly agree |

___ 1. I feel that I am a person of worth, at least on an equal basis with others.

___ 2. I feel that I have a number of good qualities.

___ 3. All in all, I am inclined to feel that I am a failure.

___ 4. I am able to do things as well as most other people.

___ 5. I feel I do not have much to be proud of.

___ 6. I take a positive attitude toward myself.

___ 7. On the whole, I am satisfied with myself.

___ 8. I wish I could have more respect for myself.

___ 9. I certainly feel useless at times.

___ 10. At times I think I am no good at all.

To calculate your score, first reverse the scoring for the five negatively worded items (3, 5, 8, 9, and 10) as follows: 1 = 4, 2 = 3, 3 = 2, 4 = 1. Then, sum your scores across the 10 items. Your total score should fall between 10 and 40. A higher score indicates higher self-esteem.

**FIGURE 6.7**

**A popular measure of self-esteem: Rosenberg Self-Esteem Scale.** The scale shown here is a widely used research instrument that taps respondents' feelings of general self-esteem.

Source: Adapted from Rosenberg, M. (1965). *Society and the adolescent self-image*. Princeton, NJ: Princeton University Press. Copyright © by Princeton University Press. http://www.bsos.umd.edu/socy/grad/socpsy_rosenberg.html

Crocker, 1993) while seeking venues for demonstrating their skills (Baumeister, 1998). Compared to individuals with low self-esteem, they are also relatively sure of who they are (Campbell, 1990). In reality, the self-views of people with low self-esteem are not more negative; rather, they are more confused and tentative (Campbell, 1990; Campbell & Lavallee, 1993). In other words, their self-concepts seem to be less clear, less complete, more self-contradictory, and more susceptible to short-term fluctuations than the self-views of high-self-esteem individuals. According to Roy Baumeister (1998), an eminent researcher on the self, this "self-concept confusion" means that individuals with low self-esteem simply don't know themselves well enough to strongly endorse many personal attributes on self-esteem tests, which results in lower self-esteem scores.

Although self-concept confusion may resolve itself over time if people learn who they truly are, there is compelling evidence that low self-esteem is a challenge at all phases of the adult lifespan. Recent longitudinal research reveals that low self-esteem is found to be a consistent risk factor for depressive symptoms among people aged 18 to 88 (Orth et al., 2009a). Further, low self-esteem's link to people's risk for depression is independent of other factors, such as stressful life events (Orth et al., 2009b).

Self-esteem can be construed in two primary ways: as a trait or a state. *Trait self-*esteem refers to the ongoing sense of confidence people possess regarding their abilities (athletic, assertive) and characteristics (friendliness, helpfulness). People's traits tend to stay with them and to remain constant; if one has high or low self-esteem in childhood, chances are one will have a similar level

Courtesy Roy Baumeister

**Roy Baumeister**

as an adult (Block & Robins, 1993; Trzesniewski, Donnellan, & Robins, 2003). **Figure 6.7** presents a basic self-report measure often used in research when self-esteem is studied as a trait. In contrast, *state self-esteem* is dynamic and changeable, referring to how individuals feel about themselves in the moment (Heatherton & Polivy, 1991). Feedback from others, self-observation, one's point in the lifespan, moods, a temporary financial setback, even the loss of one's alma mater's team (Hirt et al., 1992)—all can lower one's current sense of self-worth. Those whose self-esteem fluctuates in response to daily experiences are highly sensitive to interactions and events that have potential relevance to their self-worth, and they may even mistakenly view irrelevant events as having significance (Kernis & Goldman, 2002). They always feel their self-worth is on the line.

There is a third way to construe self-esteem: as domain specific (Brown & Marshall, 2006). When self-esteem is linked to a particular area of one's life, it is best described as composed of one's self-evaluations. Thus, people may think of themselves as athletic (i.e., trait self-esteem), and feel good after winning a round of golf (i.e., state self-esteem), but when asked, they may not feel very good about their running speed when playing tennis (i.e., self-evaluation within a domain).

Investigating self-esteem is challenging for several reasons. For one thing, obtaining accurate measures of self-esteem is difficult. The problem is that researchers tend to rely on self-reports from subjects, which obviously may be biased. As you've seen, most individuals typically hold unrealistically positive views about themselves; moreover, some people may choose not to disclose their actual self-esteem on a questionnaire. (What about you? Did you answer the questions in **Figure 6.7** truthfully and without any self-enhancing biases? How can you be sure?) Second, in probing self-esteem it is often quite difficult to separate cause from effect. Thousands of correlational studies report that high and low self-esteem are associated with various behavioral characteristics. For instance, you saw in Chapter 1 that self-esteem is a correlate of happiness. However, it is hard to tell whether high self-esteem causes happiness or vice versa. You should keep this problem in pinpointing causation in mind as we zoom in on this fascinating topic.

## The Importance of Self-Esteem

Popular wisdom holds that self-esteem is the key to practically all positive outcomes in life. In fact, its actual benefits are much fewer—but, we hasten to add, not unimportant (Krueger, Vohs, & Baumeister, 2009; Swann, Chang-Schneider, & McClarty, 2007). A comprehensive review of research examined the purported and actual advantages of self-esteem (Baumeister et al., 2003). Let's look at the findings that relate to self-esteem and adjustment.

### Self-Esteem and Adjustment

The clearest advantages of self-esteem are in the *emotional sphere.* Namely, self-esteem is strongly and consistently related to happiness. In fact, Baumeister and his colleagues are persuaded that high self-esteem actually leads to greater happiness, although they acknowledge that research has not clearly established the direction of causation. On the other side, low self-esteem is more likely than high self-esteem to lead to depression.

In the area of *achievement,* high self-esteem has not been shown to be a reliable cause of good academic performance (Forsyth et al., 2007). In fact, it may actually be the (weak) result of doing well in school. Baumeister and his colleagues speculate that other factors may underlie both self-esteem and academic performance. Regarding job performance, the results are mixed. Some studies find that high self-esteem is linked to better performance, but others find no difference. And it may be that occupational success leads to high self-esteem.

In the *interpersonal realm,* Baumeister and his colleagues report that people with high self-esteem claim to be more likable and attractive, to have better relationships, and to make better impressions on others than people with low self-esteem do. Interestingly, these advantages seem to exist mainly in the minds of the beholders, because objective data (ratings of peers) do not support these views. In fact, Mark Leary's *sociometer theory* suggests that self-esteem is actually a subjective measure of one's interpersonal popularity and success (Leary, 2004; Leary & Baumeister, 2000; Leary et al., 1995). Regarding romantic relationships, those with low self-esteem are more likely to distrust their partners' expressions of love and support and to worry about rejection compared to high-self-esteem individuals. Still there is no evidence that self-esteem (high or low) is related to how quickly relationships end. When it comes to working in groups, high-self-esteem people are more likely to speak up and to criticize the group's approach. And they are perceived as contributing more to groups.

What about self-esteem and *coping,* a key aspect of adjustment? Individuals with low self-esteem *and* a self-blaming attributional style are definitely at a disadvantage here. For one thing, they become more demoralized after a failure than those with high self-esteem do. For them, failure contributes to depression and undermines their motivation to do better the next time. By contrast, individuals with high self-esteem persist longer in the face of failure. Second, as can be seen in **Figure 6.8**, individuals with low self-esteem often have negative expectations about their performance (in a social situation, at a job interview, on a test). Because self-esteem affects expectations, it operates in a self-perpetuating fashion. As a result, they feel anxious and may not prepare for the challenge. Then, if they blame themselves when they do poorly, they feel depressed and deliver one more blow to their already battered self-esteem. Of course, this cycle also works (in the opposite way) for those with high self-esteem. In either case, the important point is that self-esteem can affect not only the present, but also the future.

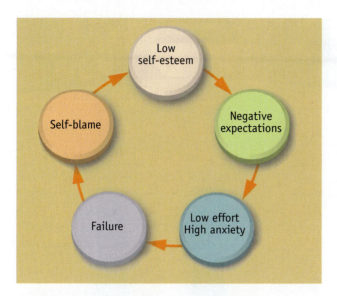

**FIGURE 6.8**

**The vicious circle of low self-esteem and poor performance.** Low self-esteem is associated with low or negative expectations about performance. These low expectations often result in inadequate preparation and high anxiety, which heighten the likelihood of poor performance. Unsuccessful performance triggers self-blame, which feeds back to lower self-esteem.

Source: Adapted from Brehm, S. S., & Kassin, S. M. (1993). *Social psychology*. Boston: Houghton Mifflin. Copyright © 1993 by Houghton Mifflin Company. Adapted with permission.

## High Self-Esteem Versus Narcissism

Although feeling good about oneself is desirable, problems arise when people's self-views are inflated and unrealistic. Indeed, high self-esteem may not be all it's cracked up to be (Crocker & Park, 2004). As we noted in Chapters 1 and 2, narcissism is the tendency to regard oneself as grandiosely self-important. Narcissistic individuals passionately want to think well of themselves and are highly sensitive to criticism (Twenge & Campbell, 2003). They are preoccupied with fantasies of success, believe that they deserve special treatment, and react aggressively when they experience threats to their self-views (ego threats). Those with fragile (unstable) self-esteem also respond in this manner (Kernis, 2003a, 2003b). On the other hand, individuals whose positive self-appraisals are secure or realistic are not so susceptible to ego threats and are less likely to resort to hostility and aggression in the face of them. Note that narcissists' aggression must be provoked; without provocation, they are no more likely to aggress than non-narcissists (Baumeister, Bushman, & Campbell, 2000; Twenge & Campbell, 2003).

Baumeister and his colleagues speculate that narcissists who experience ego threats have an elevated propensity to engage in aggression such as partner abuse, rape, gang violence, individual and group

hate crimes, and political terrorism (Baumeister, 1999; Baumeister, Smart, & Boden, 1996; Bushman et al., 2003). Is there any evidence to support this idea? In a series of studies, researchers gave participants the opportunity to aggress against someone who had either insulted or praised an essay they had written (Bushman & Baumeister, 1998). The narcissistic participants reacted to their "insulters" with exceptionally high levels of aggression (see **Figure 6.9**). Another study compared male prisoners and college men on narcissism and self-esteem. Violent offenders scored significantly higher in narcissism, but their self-esteem scores were similar to those of the college men (Bushman & Baumeister, 2002).

These findings have important practical implications (Baumeister, Smart, & Bolden, 1996). Most rehabilitation programs for spousal abusers, delinquents, and criminals are based on the faulty belief that these individuals suffer from low self-esteem. So far, there is little empirical evidence that low self-esteem leads to either direct (e.g., hitting someone) or indirect (e.g., giving someone a negative evaluation) aggression (Bushman et al., 2009). Indeed, current research suggests that efforts to boost (already inflated) self-esteem are misguided; a better approach is to help such individuals develop more self-control and more realistic views of themselves.

## The Development of Self-Esteem

Although people's sense of self-worth emerges in early childhood, individual differences in self-esteem begin to stand out in middle childhood and remain across the lifespan (Harter, 2006). The typical pattern found involves high self-esteem in childhood, an observed fall in adolescence (especially among girls), a

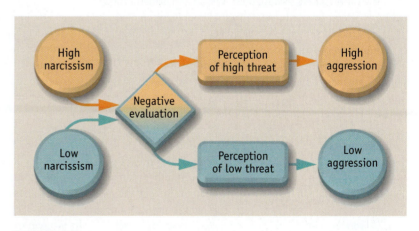

**FIGURE 6.9**

**The path from narcissism to aggression.** Individuals who score high on narcissism perceive negative evaluations by others to be extremely threatening. This experience of ego threat triggers strong hostile feelings and aggressive behavior toward the evaluator in retaliation for the perceived criticism. Low scorers are less likely to perceive negative evaluations as threatening and, therefore, behave much less aggressively toward evaluators. (Adapted from Bushman & Baumeister, 1998).

Is life reducible to a 7-point rating scale ranging from "unhappy" to "happy," where higher numbers reflect a greater degree of real or expected happiness? Let's take a moment so that you can imagine what your future will be like and, more important, allow you to use this hypothetical scale to rate how you will feel about particular events that occur within it. Here goes:

How happy will you be once you start your first job or move to one you really want?

How happy will you be once you own your own home?

How will you feel once the current semester or quarter is over?

Of course, even if you view your future as being a very bright one, some clouds may appear. Consider these:

How will you feel if you lose a job because the company downsizes you?

How will you feel once your next vacation comes to an end?

How will you feel if you end up renting for several years before you buy a home?

These sorts of questions reflect commonplace situations that trigger emotional reactions everyday.

Sometimes we feel sad, other times we are quite happy—and just as important perhaps, at least where making decisions or plans for the future is concerned, is anticipating how we expect to feel when the time comes. Recently, social psychologists have become interested in the issue of emotional accuracy: How well do people predict their future feelings in response to good and bad events? As noted in Chapter 1, this process is known as *affective forecasting* (Gilbert, Driver-Linn, & Wilson, 2002; Wilson & Gilbert, 2003; 2005). Wilson and Gilbert (2005) have demonstrated repeatedly that people mispredict how much pleasure or displeasure they will feel once future events come to pass. The challenge people face is not the valence—or direction—of their feelings. Individuals are reasonably good at judging what makes them happy or unhappy. Instead, the problem is the *intensity* and the *duration* of positive or negative feelings.

One source of bias in affective forecasting is the *impact bias*, which occurs when people misjudge the eventual intensity and duration of their emotional response to some future event. In this case, they over- rather than underestimate their feelings. Here's an example many readers can relate to: where they live on campus. Dunn, Wilson, & Gilbert (2003) asked college students to estimate how happy or unhappy they would be a year after being assigned to a desirable or an undesirable dormitory. As shown in **Figure 6.10**, the students expected that where they ended up living would have a fairly substantial impact on their overall levels of happiness. As you can see, however, a year after moving into the desired or

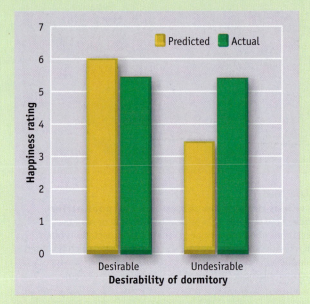

## FIGURE 6.10

**Biased impact: Students' predicted versus actual levels of happiness a year after being assigned to a desirable or undesirable dormitory.** Using a 7-point scale (where 1 = unhappy and 7 = happy), college students predicted how happy they would be a year later if they were randomly assigned to live in a desirable or an undesirable dormitory. Students anticipated that their dorm assignment would have a pronounced positive or negative impact on their overall happiness (yellow bars); however a year later, those who ended up living in undesirable housing versus the desirable dorms showed nearly identical levels of happiness (green bars).

Source: Wilson, T. D., & Gilbert, D. T. (2005). Affective forecasting: Knowing what to want. *Current Directions in Psychological Science*, 14, 131–134, Fig. 1. Copyright © 2006 Blackwell Publishing. Reprinted by permission of Sage Publications.

less desired housing, self-reported happiness was virtually identical (see **Figure 6.10**). In other words, people often overestimate the emotional impact of a single event because of what researchers call *focalism*, the tendency to overemphasize how much one will think about an event in the future while also underestimating how other events will compete for one's thoughts and feelings (Schkade & Kahneman, 1998; Wilson et al., 2000).

Dorm life may not seem to be a very dramatic backdrop for adventures in affective forecasting, but other, more consequential life events have been studied. Research has found that people overestimate how unhappy they will be a couple months after a romance ends; women miscalculate their level of unhappiness on getting unwanted results from a pregnancy test; and untenured college faculty misjudge how unhappy they will be five years after being turned down for tenure (Loewenstein, O'Donoghue, & Rabin, 2003; Mellers & McGraw, 2001; Wilson & Gilbert, 2003). Thus, impact bias and focalism can distort expectations great and small.

gradual return and rise in adulthood, and a precipitous decline once more during old age (Robins & Trzesniewski, 2005). Because the foundations of self-esteem are laid early in life (Harter, 2003), psychologists have focused much of their attention on the role of parenting in self-esteem development. Indeed, there is ample evidence that parental involvement, acceptance, support, and exposure to clearly defined limits have marked influence on children's self-esteem (Felson, 1989; Harter, 1998).

Two major dimensions underlie parenting behavior: acceptance and control (Maccoby & Martin, 1983). Diana Baumrind (1967, 1971, 1978) identified four distinct parenting styles as interactions between these two dimensions (see **Figure 6.11**). *Authoritative parenting* uses high emotional support and firm, but reasonable limits (high acceptance, high control). *Authoritarian parenting* entails low emotional support with rigid limits (low acceptance, high control). *Permissive parenting* uses high emotional support with few limits (high acceptance, low control), and *neglectful parenting* involves low emotional support and few limits (low acceptance, low control). Baumrind and others have found correlations between these parenting styles and children's traits and behaviors, including self-esteem (Furnham & Cheng, 2000; Maccoby & Martin, 1983). Authoritative parenting is associated with the highest self-esteem scores, and this finding generally holds true across different ethnic groups (Wissink, Dekovic, & Meijer, 2006). One recent study conducted in Spain, however, found that permissive parenting was sometimes better than authoritative parenting, but that both styles yielded better outcomes than the authoritarian or neglectful styles (García & Gracia, 2009). In this study, permissive parenting was characterized as indulgent—that is, as lenient and understanding. Usually, authoritarian parenting, permis-

Parents, teachers, coaches, and other adults play a key role in shaping self-esteem.

sive parenting, and neglectful parenting are second, third, and fourth in line. These results suggest that cultural differences and traditions may have some bearing on the benefits of one parenting style over another. In any case, all of these studies were correlational, so keep in mind they don't demonstrate that parenting style *causes* high or low self-esteem.

## Ethnicity, Gender, and Self-Esteem

Because prejudice and discrimination are still pervasive in the United States, people commonly assume that members of minority groups have lower self-esteem than members of the majority group. Research both supports and contradicts this assumption. On the one hand, the self-esteem of Asians, Hispanics, and Native Americans is lower than that of whites, although the differences are small (Twenge & Crocker, 2002). On the other hand, the self-esteem of blacks is higher than that of whites (Gray-Little & Hafdahl, 2000; Twenge & Crocker, 2002). Adding gender to the mix complicates the picture even more. White males have higher self-esteem than white females, but minority males have lower self-esteem than minority females (Twenge & Crocker, 2002).

Thus, ethnicity and gender interact in complex ways in self-esteem. The role of cultural differences in the self-concept may provide some insight here. Recall

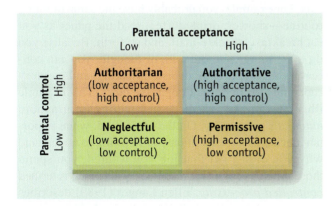

**FIGURE 6.11**

**Baumrind's parenting styles.** Four parenting styles result from the interactions of parental acceptance and parental control, as theorized by Diana Baumrind.

Source: Adapted from Baumrind, D. (1971). Current patterns of parental authority [Monograph]. *Developmental Psychology, 4*(1, Pt. 2), 1–103. Copyright © 1971 American Psychological Association. Adapted by permission of the publisher and author.

our earlier discussion of individualism and collectivism. Note that differences on this dimension are found not only between nations but also within a given country. And here's another fact: High individualism is associated with high self-esteem. What's interesting here is that the pattern of ethnic differences in individualism closely mirrors the pattern of ethnic differences in self-esteem (Twenge & Crocker, 2002). That is, blacks score higher than whites, whites do not differ significantly from Hispanics, and Hispanics score higher than Asian Americans. Thus, the ethnic differences in self-esteem are likely rooted in how the different groups view themselves, based on cultural messages.

Although females are not a minority group, they resemble ethnic minorities in that they tend to have lower status and less power than males. The popular press abounds with reports of low self-esteem in adolescent girls and women (Orenstein, 1994; Pipher, 1994). Is there any empirical basis for this assertion? One recent meta-analysis of 115 studies found that men had higher domain-specific self-esteem for physical appearance, athleticism, personal self (self-evaluation of personality independent of body or relationships to others), and self-satisfaction (happiness with self), while women

did so in the domains of behavioral conduct (socially acceptable actions) and moral-ethical self-esteem (Gentile et al., 2009). Interestingly, the difference in self-esteem for physical appearance only appeared after 1980 and was largest among adult participants. The reason, Gentile and colleagues speculate, is increased media focus on how people look. Interestingly, men and women did not differ in their self-esteem levels for academic ability, social acceptance, family, or affect (emotional well-being).

In an earlier and more extensive meta-analysis, researchers examined gender differences in self-esteem by statistically summarizing the results of several hundred studies (with respondents ranging from 7 to 60 years of age) as well as the data from three nationally representative surveys of adolescents and young adults (Kling et al., 1999). In both analyses, males scored higher on self-esteem than females, although the differences were small for the most part. The largest difference occurred in the 15- to 18-year-old age group. Also, white girls have lower self-esteem than minority girls do. The fact that white girls tend to have more negative body images than minority girls may be a factor in their lower self-esteem (Twenge & Crocker, 2002).

# Basic Principles of Self-Perception

### LEARNING OBJECTIVES

- Distinguish between automatic and controlled processing.
- Define self-attributions, and identify the key dimensions of attributions.
- Explain how optimistic and pessimistic explanatory styles are related to adjustment.
- Identify four motives that guide self-understanding.
- Explain how downward comparisons and the self-serving bias can promote positive feelings about the self.
- Discuss how basking in reflected glory and self-handicapping contribute to self-enhancement.

Now that you're familiar with some of the major aspects of the self, let's consider how people construct and maintain a coherent and positive view of the self. First we look at the basic cognitive processes involved and then at the fascinating area of self-attributions. Then we move on to discussions of explanatory style and the key motives guiding self-understanding, with a special emphasis on self-enhancement techniques.

## Cognitive Processes

People are faced with an inordinate number of decisions on a daily basis. How do they keep from being overwhelmed? The key lies in how people process information. According to Shelley Taylor (1981a), people are "cognitive misers." In this model, cognitive resources (attention, memory, and so forth) are limited, so the mind works to "hoard" them by taking cognitive short-

cuts. For example, you probably have the same morning routine—shower, drink coffee, read the paper as you eat breakfast, check e-mail, and so forth. Because you do these things without a lot of thought, you can conserve your attentional, decision-making, and memory capacities for important cognitive tasks. This example illustrates the default mode of handling information: *automatic processing*. On the other hand, when important decisions arise or when you're trying to understand why you didn't get that job you wanted, you spend those precious cognitive resources. This mode is termed *controlled processing*. Ellen Langer (1989) describes these two states as *mindlessness* and *mindfulness*, respectively. Mindfulness promotes cognitive flexibility, which in turn can lead to self-acceptance (Carson & Langer, 2006) and well-being (Langer, 2002, 2009) In contrast, mindlessness leads to rigid thinking where details and important distinctions are lost.

Another way that cognitive resources are protected is through *selective attention,* with high priority given to information pertaining to the self (Bargh, 1997). An example of this tendency is a phenomenon known as the "cocktail party effect"—the ability to pick out the mention of your name in a roomful of chattering people (Moray, 1959; Wood & Cowan, 1995).

Another principle of self-cognition is that people strive to understand themselves. One way they do so, as you saw in our discussion of social comparison theory, is to compare themselves with others (Wood & Wilson, 2003). Yet another is to engage in attributional thinking, our next topic.

## Self-Attributions

Let's say that you win a critical match for your school's tennis team. To what do you attribute your success? Is your new practice schedule starting to pay off? Did you have the home court advantage? Perhaps your opponent was playing with a minor injury? This example from everyday life illustrates the nature of the self-attribution process. *Self-attributions* **are inferences that people draw about the causes of their own behavior.** People routinely make attributions to make sense out of their experiences (Malle, 2006). These attributions involve inferences that ultimately represent guesswork on each person's part.

Fritz Heider (1958) was the first to assert that people tend to locate the cause of a behavior either within a person, attributing it to personal factors, or outside of a person, attributing it to environmental factors. He thus established one of the crucial dimensions along which attributions are made: internal versus external. The other two dimensions are stable-unstable and controllable-uncontrollable. Let's discuss these different types of attributions in greater detail.

**Internal or external.**    Elaborating on Heider's insight, various theorists have agreed that explanations of behavior and events can be categorized as internal or external attributions (Jones & Davis, 1965; Kelley, 1967; Weiner, 1974, 2006). *Internal attributions* **ascribe the causes of behavior to personal dispositions, traits, abilities, and feelings.** *External attributions* **ascribe the causes of behavior to situational demands and environmental constraints.** For example, if you credit your poor statistics grade to your failure to prepare adequately for the test or to getting overly anxious during the test, you are making internal attributions. An external attribution could be that the course is simply too hard, that the teacher is unfair, or that the book is incomprehensible.

Whether one's self-attributions are internal or external can have a tremendous impact on one's personal adjustment. Studies suggest that people who attribute their setbacks to internal, personal causes while discounting external, situational explanations may be more prone to depression than people who display opposite tendencies (Riso et al., 2003).

**Stable or unstable.**    A second dimension people use in making causal attributions is the stability of the causes underlying behavior (Weiner, 1986, 1994). A stable cause is one that is more or less permanent and unlikely to change over time. A sense of humor and intelligence are *stable internal* causes of behavior. *Stable external* causes of behavior include such things as laws and rules (speed limits, no smoking areas). Unstable causes of behavior are variable or subject to change. *Unstable internal* causes of behavior include such things as mood (good or bad) and motivation (strong or weak). *Unstable external* causes could be the weather and the presence or absence of other people. According to Bernard Weiner (1986, 1994), the stable-unstable dimension in attribution cuts across the internal-external dimension, creating four types of attributions for success and failure, as shown in **Figure 6.12**.

Let's apply Weiner's model to a concrete event. Imagine that you are contemplating why you just landed the job you wanted. You might credit your situation to internal factors that are stable (excellent ability) or unstable (hard work on your eye-catching résumé). Or you might attribute the outcome to external factors that are stable (lack of top-flight competition) or unstable (luck). If you didn't get the job, your explanations would fall in the same four categories: internal-stable

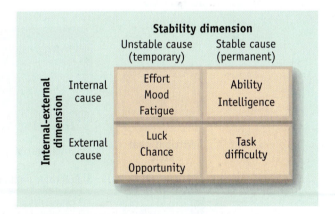

**FIGURE 6.12**
**Key dimensions of attributional thinking.** Weiner's model assumes that people's explanations for success and failure emphasize internal versus external causes and stable versus unstable causes. For example, if you attribute an outcome to great effort or to lack of effort, you are citing causes that lie within the person. Since effort can vary over time, the causal factors at work are unstable. Other examples of causal factors that fit into each of the four cells in Weiner's model are shown in the diagram.

Source: From Weiner, B., Frieze, I., Kukla, A., Reed, L. & Rosenbaum, R. M. (1972). Perceiving the causes of success and failure. In E. E. Jones, D. E. Kanuouse, H. H. Kelly, R. E. Nisbett, S. Valins, & B. Weiner (Eds.), *Perceiving causes of behavior.* Morristown, NJ: General Learning Press. Reprinted by permission of the author.

(lack of ability), internal-unstable (inadequate effort on your résumé), external-stable (too much competition in your field), and external-unstable (bad luck).

**Controllable or uncontrollable.** A third dimension in the attribution process acknowledges the fact that sometimes events are under one's control and sometimes they are not (Weiner, 1986, 1994). For example, the amount of effort you expend on a task is typically perceived as something under your control, whereas an aptitude for music is viewed as something you are born with (beyond your control). Controllability can vary with each of the other two factors.

These three dimensions appear to be the central ones in the attribution process. Research has documented that self-attributions are motivational, guiding one toward or away from possible courses of action. Thus, one's self-beliefs can influence future expectations (success or failure) and emotions (pride, hopelessness, guilt), and these expectations and emotions can combine to influence subsequent performance (Weiner, 1986, 1994, 2006). Self-attributions, then, play a key role in one's feelings, motivational state, and behavior.

## Explanatory Style

Julio and Josh are freshmen who have just struck out trying to get their first college dates. After this disappointment, they reflect on the possible reasons for it. Julio speculates that his approach was too subtle. Look-

ing back, he realizes that he wasn't very direct because he was nervous about asking the woman out. When she didn't reply, he didn't follow up for fear that she didn't really want to go out with him. On further reflection, he reasons that she probably didn't respond because she wasn't sure of his intentions. He vows to be more direct the next time. Josh, on the other hand, mopes, "I'll never have a relationship. I'm a total loser." On the basis of these comments, who do you think is likely to get a date in the future? If you guessed Julio, you are probably correct. Let's see why.

According to Martin Seligman (1991), people tend to exhibit, to varying degrees, an *optimistic explanatory style* or a *pessimistic explanatory style* (see **Figure 6.13**). As we saw in Chapter 3, **explanatory style refers to the tendency to use similar causal attributions for a wide variety of events in one's life.** The person with an optimistic explanatory style usually attributes setbacks to external, unstable, and specific factors (Peterson & Steen, 2009). A person who failed to get a desired job, for example, might attribute this misfortune to factors in the interview situation ("The room was really hot," "The questions were slanted") rather than to personal shortcomings. This style can be psychologically protective (Wise & Rosqvist, 2006), helping people to discount their setbacks and thus maintain a favorable self-image (Gordon, 2008). It also helps people bounce back from failure. One study found that optimistic students had more confidence and performed better than pessimistic students after a sports failure (Martin-Krumm et al., 2003).

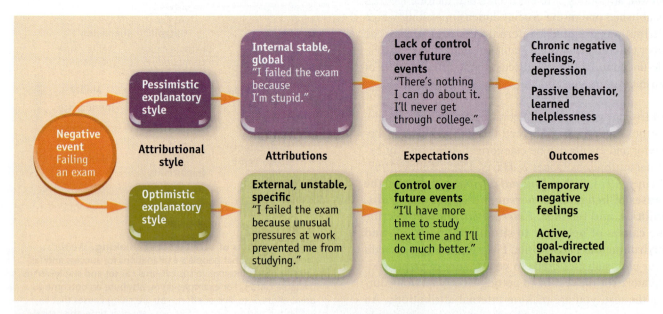

**FIGURE 6.13**

**The effects of attributional style on expectations, emotions, and behavior.** The pessimistic explanatory style is seen in the top row of boxes. This attributional style, which attributes setbacks to internal, stable, and global causes, tends to result in an expectation of lack of control over future events, depressed feelings, and passive behavior. A more adaptive, optimistic attributional style is shown in the bottom row of boxes.

In contrast, people with a pessimistic explanatory style tend to attribute their setbacks to internal, stable, and global (or pervasive) factors. These attributions make them feel bad about themselves and doubtful about their ability to handle challenges in the future. As noted in Chapter 4, such a style can foster passive behavior and make people more vulnerable to *learned helplessness* and depression (Peterson, Maier, & Seligman, 1993), especially when they expect that things won't work out in their favor (Peterson & Vaidya, 2001). Of more concern is some suggestive evidence from a longitudinal sample of people that "catastrophizing"—attributing negative events to global causes—predicted accidental and violent deaths (Peterson et al., 1998). Luckily, cognitive-behavioral therapy appears to be effective at helping individuals who are at risk for depression (Seligman, Schulman, & Tryon, 2007) as well as encouraging depressed individuals to change their pessimistic explanatory style (Seligman et al., 1999).

## Motives Guiding Self-Understanding

Whether people evaluate themselves by social comparisons, attributional thinking, or other means, they are highly motivated to pursue self-understanding. In seeking self-understanding, people are driven by four major motives: assessment, verification, improvement, and enhancement (Biernat & Billings, 2001; Sedikides & Strube, 1997).

### Self-Assessment

The *self-assessment motive* is reflected in people's desire for truthful information about themselves (Trope, 1983, 1986). The problem is straightforward: Individuals don't know themselves all that well (Dunning, 2006). Unfortunately, many self-assessments are quite flawed; the only good news is that people are typically unaware of this fact (Dunning, Heath, & Suls, 2004), presumably because evaluating one's own abilities is a formidable challenge (Carter & Dunning, 2008). Still, there is some hope. Individuals do seek accurate feedback about many types of information, including their personal qualities, abilities, physical features, and so forth. It's obvious why people look for accurate information. After all, it helps them set realistic goals and behave in appropriate ways (Oettingen & Gollwitzer, 2001). Still, the bald truth is not always welcome. Accordingly, people are also motivated by other concerns.

### Self-Verification

The *self-verification motive* drives people toward information that matches what they already believe about themselves, whether it is positive or negative (North & Swann, 2009a). This tendency to strive for a consistent self-image ensures that individuals' self-concepts are relatively stable. Individuals maintain consistent self-perceptions in a number of subtle ways and are often unaware of doing so (Schlenker & Pontari, 2000). For example, people maintain consistency between their past and present behavior by erasing past memories that conflict with present ones. To illustrate, people who were once shy and who later became outgoing have been shown to recall memories about themselves that indicate that they perceive themselves as always having been outgoing (Ross & Conway, 1986).

Another way people maintain self-consistency is by seeking out feedback and situations that will confirm their existing self-perceptions and avoiding potentially disconfirming situations or feedback. Thus, self-verification processes are not only adaptive, they have other positive qualities, as well (North & Swann, 2009b). According to William Swann's *self-verification theory,* **people prefer to receive feedback from others that is consistent with their own self-views.** Thus, people with positive self-concepts should prefer positive feedback from others and those with negative self-concepts should prefer negative feedback. Research usually finds this situation to be the case (Swann, Rentfrow, & Guinn, 2003). In one study, college men were divided into positive and negative self-concept groups based on test scores. They were then asked to choose a partner for a subsequent 2- to 3-hour interaction. Participants were led to believe that one of the prospective partners held views of him that were consistent with his self-view and that the other held views of him that were inconsistent with his self-view. As predicted, subjects with positive self-views preferred partners who viewed them positively, whereas those with negative self-views chose partners who viewed them negatively (Swann, Stein-Seroussi, & Geisler, 1992). Among depressed persons, the persistent self-views predicted by self-verification processes may account for treatment setbacks or ongoing dysphoria (Petit & Joiner, 2006).

### Self-Improvement

What is your current self-improvement project? To study more? To get more exercise? When people seek to better themselves, often after a failure or some other setback, the *self-improvement motive* comes into play (Kurman, 2006). In trying to improve, individuals typically look to successful others for inspiration (Collins, 1996). Advertisers of personal care products (tooth whiteners, exercise machines, and so forth) tap into this motive by showing before-and-after photographs of individuals who have used the products.

### Self-Enhancement

Finally, people are motivated by the *self-enhancement motive.* **Self-enhancement is the tendency to maintain positive feelings about oneself.** Psychologically, self-enhancement can appear in at least four ways: as an observed response or behavior, a process, a personality trait, or an underlying motive (Sedikides & Gregg, 2008). One example of self-enhancement is the tendency to hold flattering views of one's personal qualities, a tendency termed the *better-than-average effect* (Alicke, 1985; Buckingham & Alicke, 2002). You've already seen an example of this effect in our earlier report that 100% of students who took the SAT rated themselves above average in the ability to get along with others—a mathematical impossibility. Students can take perverse pleasure in knowing that faculty also succumb to this bias: 94% of them regard their teaching as above average (Cross, 1977)!

A second example of self-enhancement concerns *illusions of control* (Langer, 1975), in which people overestimate their degree of control over outcomes. Thus, individuals who pick their own "lucky" numbers on lottery tickets falsely believe that they can influence the outcome of such random events, an act and inference that makes them feel good (Dunn & Wilson, 1990). A third form of self-enhancement is the tendency to have *unrealistic optimism about future events* (Weinstein, 1980). For example, most people believe that they will have a brighter future and experience fewer negative events than others (Helweg-Larsen & Shepperd, 2001), especially where health and safety are concerned (Weinstein, 1982).

## Methods of Self-Enhancement

The powerful self-enhancement motive drives individuals to seek positive (and reject negative) information about themselves. Let's examine four cognitive strategies people commonly use in this process.

### Downward Comparisons

We've already mentioned that people routinely compare themselves to others as a means of learning more about themselves (social comparison). However, once a threat to self-esteem enters the picture, people often adjust their strategy and choose to compare themselves with those who are worse off than they are (Wood, 1989). **Downward social comparison is a defensive tendency to compare oneself with someone whose troubles are more serious than one's own.** Why do people change strategies under threat? Because they need to feel better, often doing so by connecting to the experience of others (Wayment & O'Mara, 2008). Research shows that downward social comparisons are associated with increases in both mood and self-esteem (Reis, Gerrard, & Gibbons, 1993).

If you have ever been in a serious traffic accident in which your car was "totaled," you probably reassured yourself by reflecting on the fact that at least no one was seriously injured. Similarly, people with chronic illnesses may compare themselves with those who have life-threatening diseases.

### Self-Serving Bias

Suppose that you and three other individuals apply for a part-time job in the parks and recreation department and you are selected for the position. How do you explain your success? Chances are, you tell yourself that you were hired because you were the most qualified for the job. But how do the other three people interpret their negative outcome? Do they tell themselves that you got the job because you were the most able? Unlikely! Instead, they probably attribute their loss to "bad luck" or to not having had time to prepare for the interview. These different explanations for success and failure reflect **the *self-serving bias*, or the tendency to attribute one's successes to personal factors and one's failures to situational factors** (Miller and Ross, 1975; Shepherd et al., 2008). One explanation for the self-serving bias is that unbiased self-judgments require a high degree of self-control, which is usually overridden by one's automatic drive toward self-enhancement (Krusemark, Campbell, & Clementz, 2008).

For example, in one experiment, two strangers jointly took a test. They then received bogus success or failure feedback about their test performance and were asked to assign responsibility for the test results. Successful participants claimed credit, but those who failed blamed their partners (Campbell et al., 2000). Still, people don't always rush to take credit. In another experiment in the just-cited study, participants were actual friends. In this case, participants shared responsibility for both successful and unsuccessful outcomes. Thus, friendship places limits on the self-serving bias.

Although the self-serving bias has been documented in a variety of cultures (Fletcher & Ward 1988), it seems to be particularly prevalent in individualistic, Western societies, where the emphasis on competition and high self-esteem motivates people to try to impress others, as well as themselves. In contrast, Japanese subjects exhibit a *self-effacing bias* in explaining successes (Akimoto & Sanbonmatsu, 1999; Markus & Kitayama, 1991), as they tend to attribute their successes to the help they receive from others or to the ease of the task, while downplaying the importance of their ability. When they fail, Japanese subjects tend to be more self-critical than subjects from individualistic cultures (Heine & Renshaw, 2002). They are more likely to accept responsibility for their failures and to use their setbacks as an impetus for self-improvement (Heine et al., 2001). When Japanese students' apprehension at being evaluated is reduced, however, they make more internal attributions for success than failure (Kudo, 2003). Studies have also failed to find the usual self-serving bias in Nepalese and Chinese samples (Lee & Seligman, 1997; Smith & Bond, 1999).

## PEANUTS

PEANUTS © United Feature Syndicate, Inc.

### Basking in Reflected Glory

When your favorite sports team won the national championship last year, did you make a point of wearing the team cap? And when Ben, your best friend, won that special award, do you remember how often you told others the good news about him? If you played a role in someone's success, it's understandable that you would want to share in the recognition; however, people often want to share recognition even when they are on the sidelines of an outstanding achievement. **Basking in reflected glory is the tendency to enhance one's image by publicly announcing one's association with those who are successful.**

Robert Cialdini and his colleagues (1976) studied this phenomenon on college campuses with nationally ranked football teams. The researchers predicted that, when asked how their team had fared in a recent football game, students would be more likely to say, "We won" (in other words, to bask in reflected glory, or to "BIRG"—pronounced with a soft "g") when the home team had been successful than to respond "We lost" when it had been defeated. Indeed, the researchers found that students were more likely to BIRG when their team won than when it lost. Also, subjects who believed that they had just failed a bogus test were more likely to use the words "We won" than those who believed they had performed well. BIRGing has also been found in the text of soccer fan magazines (Bernache-Assollant, Lacassagne, & Braddock, 2007).

A related self-enhancement strategy is "CORFing," or *cutting off reflected failure*. Because self-esteem is partly tied to an individual's associations with others, people often protect their self-esteem by distancing themselves from those who are unsuccessful (Boen, Van-Beselaere, & Feys, 2002; Cialdini et al., 1976). Thus, if your cousin is arrested for drunk driving, you may tell others that you don't really know him very well. Interestingly, BIRGing and CORFing are apparently not limited to the United States or to public settings. For example, websites of Belgian and Dutch soccer teams receive significantly more "surfers" after the teams win matches (BIRGing) than when they lose (CORFing) (Boen, VanBeselaere, & Feys, 2002).

### Self-Handicapping

When people fail at an important task, they need to save face. In such instances, individuals can usually come up with a face-saving excuse ("I had a terrible stomachache"). Curiously,

People frequently claim association with others who are successful (basking in the reflected glory) to maintain positive feelings about the self.

© GDT/Stone/Getty Images

some people actually behave in a way that sets them up to fail so that they have a readymade excuse for failure, should it occur. *Self-handicapping* **is the tendency to sabotage one's performance to provide an excuse for possible failure.** For example, when a big test is looming, they put off studying until the last minute or go out drinking the night before the test. If, as is likely, they don't do well on the exam, they explain their poor performance by saying they didn't prepare. (After all, wouldn't you rather have others believe that your poor performance is due to inadequate preparation rather than to lack of ability?) Lack of effort is often indicative of self-handicapping; however, one recent study demonstrated that sometimes exerting too much effort—ironically, an active behavioral strategy—can reveal it, too. A group of men were led to believe that *too much* practice could hurt their future performance on a task. Within the group, those who scored high on a trait measure of self-handicapping were found to practice more compared to those low on this trait. Ironically, by overpreparing to ensure a poor performance, the high self-handicappers were able to save face—they could readily attribute their failure to their overpractice rather than a lack of skill, which is a more psychologically threatening explanation (Smith, Hardy, and Arkin, 2009). People use a variety of other tactics for handicapping their performance: alcohol, drugs, procrastination, a bad mood, a distracting stimulus, anxiety, depression, and being overcommitted (Baumeister, 1998).

Self-handicapping should not be confused with *defensive pessimism,* a trait causing some people to mentally identify the worst possible outcome and to then subsequently work hard to make sure it never occurs (Norem, 1989, 2002, 2008; Norem & Smith, 2006). (Take the quiz in **Figure 6.14** to learn whether you are a defensive pessimist.) Although the two constructs appear similar, defensive pessimists are motivated to avoid bad outcomes, whereas self-handicappers undermine their own efforts (Elliot & Church, 2003; Martin et al., 2003). Imagine working on a huge end-of-term project for a class—one that will make or break your final course grade. Optimists cope with anxiety by anticipating they will do their best. Defensive pessimists will expect the worst and then get right to work, ending up pleasantly surprised when they do well. People engaging in self-handicapping, however, might procrastinate or do any number of things that, as we will see, can undermine their successful completion of the project.

Self-handicapping seems like a "win-win" strategy: If you fail, you have a face-saving excuse ready, and if you happen to succeed, you can claim that you are unusually gifted! However, it probably has not escaped your attention that self-handicapping is highly risky. By giving yourself an attributional "out" in case of failure, your self-defeating behavior will likely result in poor performance (Zuckerman, Kieffer, & Knee, 1998). Moreover,

## Recommended READING

### The Positive Power of Negative Thinking: Using Defensive Pessimism to Harness Anxiety and Perform at Your Peak
by Julie Norem (Basic Books, 2002)

Can negative thoughts, such as fear of failing or performing poorly, ever be a good thing? Perhaps a little anxiety can help rather than harm. Surprisingly, social-personality psychologist Julie Norem of Wellesley College argues that some negative self-views can actually galvanize one's resolve and lead to success. How so? Imagine the benefits of "defensive pessimism" by envisioning worst case scenarios prior to undertaking a difficult or challenging task and then working hard to avoid them. Once you identify the demons and dangers blocking you from your goal, you can plan a strategy for moving forward. Setting expectations at low or even moderate levels can lead to large emotional dividends if you end up outperforming your beginning benchmarks. If nothing else, defensive pessimism is a compelling antidote to unrealistic optimism or maladaptive self-strategies, such as denial, procrastination, or self-handicapping.

*Go to the Psychology CourseMate for Weiten at* **www.cengagebrain.com/shop/ISBN/1111186634** *for descriptions of other recommended books.*

while self-handicapping may save you from negative self-attributions about your ability, it does not prevent others from making different negative attributions about you. Others may perceive you as lazy, inclined to drink too much, or highly anxious, depending on the means you use to self-handicap, perceptions that are sometimes accurate (Zuckerman & Tsai, 2005). Consequently, this self-enhancement tactic has serious drawbacks.

Potentially, anyone can engage in self-handicapping behavior (surely, you have come up with an excuse or two when things did not go your way), but research suggests that men self-handicap more than women, possibly because the latter place more importance on displaying effort (McCrea et al., 2008). High-status individuals are also prone to use self-handicapping as a social strategy (Lucas & Lovaglia, 2005). Why? Self-handicapping is likely to occur when self-esteem is threatened. Thus, high-status individuals will be more motivated to preserve their level of self-worth than people of a lower status. Interestingly, when gender is controlled, race and ethnicity matter somewhat: European Americans self-handicap more than non-European Americans (Lucas & Lovaglia, 2005), as do narcissists, who tend to be arrogant or conceited (Rhodelwalt, Tragakis, & Finnerty, 2006).

## Defensive Pessimism Questionnaire

Using this scale, rate your agreement with the following statements.

| 1 | 2 | 3 | 4 | 5 | 6 | 7 |
|---|---|---|---|---|---|---|
| Not at All True of Me | | | | | | Very True of Me |

___ I often start out expecting the worst, even though I will probably do okay.

___ I worry about how things will turn out.

___ I carefully consider all possible outcomes.

___ I often worry that I won't be able to carry through my intentions.

___ I spend lots of time imagining what could go wrong.

___ I imagine how I would feel if things went badly.

___ I try to picture how I could fix things if something went wrong.

___ I'm careful not to become overconfident in these situations.

___ I spend a lot of time planning when one of these situations is coming up.

___ I imagine how things would feel if things went well.

___ In these situations, sometimes I worry more about looking like a fool than doing really well.

___ Considering what can go wrong helps me to prepare.

To figure out where you stand, add your scores for all the questions. Possible scores range from 12 to 84, and higher scores indicate a stronger tendency to use defensive pessimism. If you score above 50, you would qualify as a defensive pessimist in Norem's studies. Scores falling below 30 indicate optimism (for more on the use of this questionnaire, please see Norem [2001]).

**FIGURE 6.14**

**The Defensive Pessimism Questionnaire.** Think of a situation where you want to do your best. It may be related to work, your social life, or to any of your goals. When you answer the following questions, think about how you prepare for that kind of situation. Rate how true each statement is for you. Directions for determining your score on the scale are provided following the questions.

Source: Adapted from Norem, J. K. (2001). *The positive power of negative thinking: Using defensive pessimism to manage anxiety and perform at your peak.* New York: Basic Books. Copyright © 2002 by Julie K. Norem. Reprinted by permission of Basic Books, a member of Perseus Book Group.

# Self-Regulation

### LEARNING OBJECTIVES

- Define self-regulation, and explain the ego-depletion model of self-regulation.
- Explain why self-efficacy is important to psychological adjustment.
- Discuss how individuals develop self-efficacy.
- Describe the three categories of self-defeating behavior.

"Should I have that hot fudge sundae or not?" "I guess I'd better get started on that English paper." "Would I better off checking Facebook one more time or going to bed?" People are constantly trying to resist impulses and make themselves do things they don't really want to do. **Self-regulation is the process of directing and controlling one's behavior.** Clearly, the ability to manage and direct what you think, how you feel, and how you behave is tied to your success at work, your relationships, and your mental and physical health (Baumeister & Vohs, 2003, 2007; Vohs, Baumeister, & Tice, 2008). Being able to forgo immediate gratification (studying instead of partying) and focus one's behavior toward important, longer-range goals (graduating and getting a good job) is of paramount importance if one is to be successful in life.

It's possible that people have a limited amount of self-control resources. If you tax these resources resisting temptation in a given situation, you may have a hard time resisting the next temptation or persisting at a new task. As a result, self-control can have a cost (Baumeister & Alquist, 2009). At least that's the idea behind the *ego depletion model of self-regulation* (Baumeister et al., 1998). To investigate this hypothesis, researchers asked college students to participate in a study of taste perception (the study was actually on self-control) (Baumeister et al., 1998). Some participants were asked to eat two or three radishes in 5 minutes but not to touch the chocolate candy and chocolate chip cookies that were nearby. Others were asked to eat some candy or some cookies but were told not to eat any of the nearby radishes. A control group didn't participate in this part of the study. Then all subjects were asked to solve what were, unbeknownst-to-them, unsolvable puzzles while they supposedly waited for another part of the study. Researchers measured the subjects' self-control by the amount of time they persisted at the puzzles and the number of attempts they made. According to the ego depletion model, the radish eaters would use more self-control resources (resisting the chocolate) than the chocolate eaters (resisting the radishes) or the subjects in the no-food control group.

Thus, this group should have the fewest self-control resources left to use for persisting at a difficult task. As you can see in **Figure 6.15**, the radish eaters gave up sooner and made fewer attempts on the puzzles than the chocolate eaters or the control group. One of the reasons people rely so often on habit and automatic processing is to conserve these important self-control resources (Baumeister, Muraven, & Tice, 2000). By not doing so, people can inadvertently undermine their own positive qualities. For example, ego depletion has been found to make people less helpful to strangers but not, fortunately, family members (DeWall et al., 2008). Being asked to make too many choices or decisions can also reduce people's self-control (Vohs et al., 2008).

Self-regulation seems to develop early and remain relatively stable. One study reported that 4-year-olds who were better at delaying gratification did better in terms of both academic performance and social competence some ten years later (Mischel, Shoda, & Peake, 1988; Shoda, Mischel, & Peake, 1990). Recent evidence suggests that self-regulation is malleable and can be strengthened like a muscle, which means that with regular "exercise," people can become less vulnerable to ego depletion effects (Baumeister et al., 2006). Being in a good mood (Tice et al., 2007) and ingesting sugar, which fuels energy (Gailliot et al., 2007), can restore people's self-control. In the next section, we examine self-efficacy, a key aspect of self-regulation, and then discuss self-defeating behavior, a case of self-control failure.

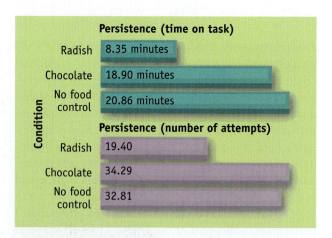

**FIGURE 6.15**

**Persistence on unsolvable puzzles.** Participants who were instructed to eat radishes and not to eat chocolate treats used more self-control resources than participants who were instructed to eat the chocolate and not touch the radishes or participants in the no-food control group. Because the radish eaters had relatively few self-control resources remaining to help them persist at a difficult task (unsolvable puzzles), they persisted for the shortest time and made the fewest attempts to solve the puzzles compared to the other two groups. (Adapted from Baumeister et al., 1998)

## Self-Efficacy

As explained in Chapter 2, *self-efficacy* **refers to one's belief about one's ability to perform behaviors that should lead to expected outcomes.** Self-efficacy represents people's conviction that they can achieve specific goals. According to Albert Bandura (1997, 2000), efficacy beliefs vary according to the person's skills. You may have high self-efficacy when it comes to making friends but low self-efficacy when it comes to speaking in front of a group. However, simply having a skill doesn't guarantee that you will be able to put it into practice. Like the Little Engine That Could, you must also *believe* that you are capable of doing so ("I *think* I can, I *think* I can . . ."). In other words, self-efficacy is concerned not with the skills you have, but with your *beliefs about what you can do* with these skills.

**Albert Bandura**

### Correlates of Self-Efficacy

A number of studies have shown that self-efficacy affects individuals' commitments to goals, their performance on tasks, and their persistence toward goals in the face of obstacles (Maddux & Gosselin, 2003). Self-efficacy is related to health promotion (Bandura, 2004), academic success (Caprara et al., 2008; Schunk, 2003), career choice (Betz & Klein, 1996), job performance (Stajkovic & Luthans, 1998), and coping with unemployment (Creed, Lehman, & Hood, 2009). Because of the importance of self-efficacy in psychological adjustment (Bandura, 2008), it is worth keeping in mind that self-efficacy is learned and can be changed. Research shows that increasing self-efficacy is an effective way to improve health (losing weight, stopping smoking) (Maddux & Gosselin, 2003) and to treat a variety of psychological problems, including test anxiety (Smith, 1989), fear of computer use (Wilfong, 2006), phobias (Williams, 1995), fear of sexual assault (Ozer & Bandura, 1990), eating disorders (Goodrick et al., 1999), and substance abuse (DiClemente, Fairhurst, & Piotrowski, 1995), including marijuana dependence (Lozano, Stephens, & Roffman, 2006).

### Developing Self-Efficacy

Self-efficacy is obviously a valuable quality. How does one acquire it? Bandura (1997, 2000) identifies four sources of self-efficacy: mastery experiences, vicarious experiences, persuasion/encouragement, and interpretation of emotional arousal.

1. *Mastery experiences.* The most effective path to self-efficacy is through mastering new skills. Sometimes new skills come easily—learning how to use the copy machine in the library, for instance. Some things

© JGI/Blend Images/Corbis

*Ironically, difficulties and failures can ultimately contribute to the development of a strong sense of self-efficacy. Self-efficacy tends to improve when youngsters learn to persist through difficulties and overcome failures.*

are harder to master, such as learning how to drive a stick-shift in a standard transmission car or how to play the piano. In acquiring more difficult skills, people usually make mistakes. If they persist through failure experiences to eventual success, they learn the lesson of self-efficacy: I *can* do it!

**2.** *Vicarious experiences.* Another way to improve self-efficacy is by watching others perform a skill you want to learn. It's important that you choose a model who is competent at the task, and it helps if the model is similar to you (in age, gender, and ethnicity). For example, if you're shy about speaking up for yourself, observing someone who is good at doing so can help you develop the confidence to do it yourself.

**3.** *Persuasion and encouragement.* Although it is less effective than the first two approaches, a third way to develop self-efficacy is through the encouragement of others. For example, if you're having a hard time asking someone for a date, a friend's encouragement might give you just the push you need.

**4.** *Interpretation of emotional arousal.* The physiological responses that accompany feelings and one's interpretations of these responses are another source of self-efficacy. Let's say you're sitting in class waiting for your professor to distribute an exam. You notice that your palms are moist, your stomach feels a little queasy,

and your heart is pounding. If you attribute these behaviors to fear, you can temporarily dampen your self-efficacy, thus decreasing your chances of doing well. Alternatively, if you attribute your sweaty palms and racing heart to the arousal everyone needs to perform well, you may be able to boost your self-efficacy and increase your chances of doing well. Of course, self-regulation doesn't always succeed. That's the case in self-defeating behavior, our next topic.

### Self-Defeating Behavior

People typically act in their own self-interest. But sometimes they knowingly do things that are bad for them—such as smoking, having unprotected sex, and completing important assignments at the last minute. *Self-defeating behaviors* **are seemingly intentional actions that thwart a person's self-interest.** According to Roy Baumeister (1997; Baumeister & Scher, 1988), there are three categories of intentional self-defeating behaviors: deliberate self-destruction, tradeoffs, and counterproductive strategies. The key difference among these three behaviors lies in how intentional they are. As you can see in **Figure 6.16**, attempts at deliberate self-destruction involve the most intent; counterproductive strategies are the least intentional, and tradeoffs fall in between.

In *deliberate self-destruction,* people want to harm themselves and choose courses of action that will forseeably lead to that result. Although this type of behavior may occur in individuals with psychological disorders, deliberate self-destruction appears to be infrequent in normal populations.

In *tradeoffs,* people foresee the possibility of harming themselves but accept it as a necessary accompaniment to achieving a desirable goal. Overeating, smoking, and drinking to excess are examples that come readily to mind. Other examples include procrastinating (putting off tasks feels good in the short

| Three Categories of Self-Defeating Behavior | | |
| --- | --- | --- |
| **Type of self-defeating behavior** | **Harm foreseen?** | **Harm desired?** |
| Deliberate self-destruction | Yes | Yes |
| Tradeoffs | Yes | No |
| Counterproductive strategies | No | No |

### FIGURE 6.16

**Three categories of self-defeating behavior.** Roy Baumeister and Steven Scher (1988) distinguished three categories of self-defeating behaviors, based on how intentional the behaviors are. Intentionality is determined by two factors: an individual's awareness that a behavior could bring possible harm and an individual's desire to harm himself or herself. Deliberate self-destruction is the most intentional, followed by tradeoffs, then counterproductive strategies.

run, but the struggle to meet looming deadlines results in poor performance and increased stress and illness), failing to follow prescribed health care advice (it's easier to slack off now, but doing so leads to future problems), shyness (avoiding social situations protects against anxiety but makes loneliness more likely), and self-handicapping (getting drunk before an exam explains poor performance but increases the chances of failure). People engage in tradeoffs because they bring immediate, positive, and reliable outcomes, not because they want to hurt themselves in the short or the long run.

In *counterproductive strategies,* a person pursues a desirable outcome but misguidedly uses an approach that is bound to fail. Of course, you can't always know in advance if a strategy will pay off. Thus, people must *habitually* use this strategy for it to qualify as self-defeating. For example, some people tend to persist in unproductive endeavors, such as pursuing an unreachable career goal or an unrequited love. People persist in these behaviors because they erroneously believe they'll be successful, not because they are intent on self-defeat.

To conclude, although most people engage in self-defeating behavior at some time, there is little evidence that they deliberately try to harm themselves or to fail at a task. Instead, self-defeating behavior appears to be the result of people's distorted judgments or strong desires to escape from immediate, painful feelings (Twenge et al., 2002).

© Marc Vaughn/Masterfile

**Self-defeating behaviors come in many forms with many underlying motivations. Overeating is a matter of *trade-offs*. People realize that excessive eating may be harmful in the long run, but it is enjoyable at the time.**

# Self-Presentation

### LEARNING OBJECTIVES

- Explain why and when individuals engage in impression management.
- Cite some strategies people use to make positive impressions on others.
- Understand how high self-monitors are different from low self-monitors.

Whereas your self-concept involves how you see yourself, your public self involves how you want others to see you. **A *public self* is an image presented to others in social interactions.** This presentation of a public self may sound deceitful, but it is perfectly normal, and everyone does it (Schlenker, 2003). Many self-presentations (ritual greetings, for example) take place automatically and without awareness. But when it really counts (job interviews, for example), people consciously strive to make the best possible impression so they are perceived favorably.

Typically, individuals have a number of public selves that are tied to certain situations and certain people. For instance, you may have one public self for your parents and another for your peers. You may have still others for your teachers, your boss, your co-workers, and so forth. Also, people differ in the degree of overlap or congruence among their various public selves (see **Figure 6.17**). Does it matter whether you perceive yourself to be essentially the same person in different situations? It seems so. People who see themselves as being similar across different social roles (with friends, at work, at school, with parents, with romantic partners) are better adjusted than those who perceive less integration in their self-views across these roles (Donahue et al., 1993; Lutz & Ross, 2003; but see Baird, Le, & Lucas, 2006).

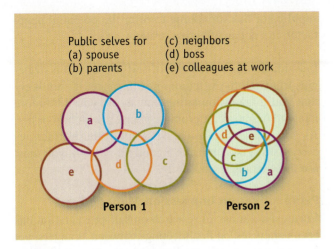

Public selves for
(a) spouse
(b) parents
(c) neighbors
(d) boss
(e) colleagues at work

Person 1

Person 2

**FIGURE 6.17**

**Public selves and adjustment.** Person 1 has divergent public selves with relatively little overlap among them. Person 2, whose public selves are more congruent with each other, is likely to be better adjusted than Person 1.

## Impression Management

Interestingly, people think others notice and evaluate them more than is the actual case (Gilovich, Kruger, & Medvec, 2002). This common tendency is aptly termed *the spotlight effect*. In a related phenomenon, the *guilty by association effect*, people erroneously assume their social standing suffers due to embarrassing actions or blunders perpetrated by those they associate with ("My friend is making me look bad!") (Fortune & Newby-Clark, 2008). These two self-focused responses remind us that people normally strive to make a positive impression on others to be liked, respected, hired, and so forth (Baumeister & Twenge, 2003). The sociologist Erving Goffman (1959) used the term *face* to describe the idealized image of ourselves we try to create in the minds of others. **Impression management refers to usually conscious efforts by people to influence how others think of them.** To see impression management in operation, let's look at a study of behavior in simulated job interviews (von Baeyer, Sherk, & Zanna, 1981). In this study, female job applicants were led to believe that the man who would interview them held either traditional, chauvinistic views of women or just the opposite. The researchers found that applicants who expected a chauvinist presented themselves in a more traditionally feminine manner than subjects in the other condition. Their self-presentation efforts extended to both their appearance (they wore more makeup) and their communication style (they talked less and gave more traditional answers to a question about marriage and children). In a job interview, people are particularly attentive to making a good impression, but impression management also operates in everyday interactions, although individuals may be less aware of it (Schlenker, 2003). Let's look at some common impression management strategies.

**WEB LINK 6.3  Impression Management**

This short article at TheFreeDictionary.com explains impression management and provides a number of links to other articles on related issues.

## Impression Management Strategies

One reason people engage in impression management is to claim a particular identity (Baumeister, 1998). Thus, you select a type of dress, hairstyle, and manner of speech to present a certain image of yourself. Tattoos and body piercings also create a specific image. A second motive for impression management is to gain liking and approval from others—by editing what you say about yourself and by using various nonverbal cues such as smiles, gestures, and eye contact. Because self-presentation is practiced so often, people usually do it automatically. At other times, however, impression management may be used intentionally—to get a job, a date, a promotion, and so forth. Some common self-presentation strategies include ingratiation, self-promotion, exemplification, intimidation, and supplication (Jones, 1990). To this list, we add a rarely recognized strategy, negative acknowledgment:

**1.** *Ingratiation.* Of all the self-presentation strategies, ingratiation is the most fundamental and most frequently used. **Ingratiation is behaving in ways to make oneself likable to others.** For example, *giving compliments* is effective, as long as you are sincere (people dislike insincerity and can often detect it). One study found that waitresses could increase their tips simply by praising the food choices of customers as they ordered (Seiter, 2007). *Doing favors for others* is also a common tactic, as long as your gestures aren't so spectacular they leave others feeling indebted (Gordon, 1996). Other ingratiation tactics include *expressing liking for others* and *going along with others* (to get others to like you, it helps to do the things that they want to do).

**2.** *Self-promotion.* The motive behind self-promotion is earning respect. You do so by playing up your strong points so you will be perceived as competent. For instance, in a job interview, you might find ways to mention that you earned high honors at school and that you were president of the student body and a member of the soccer team. To keep from coming across as a braggart, you shouldn't go overboard with self-promotion. For this reason, false modesty ("Oh, thanks, but it was nothing special") often works well.

**3.** *Exemplification.* Because most people try to project an honest image, you have to demonstrate exemplary behavior to claim special credit for integrity or character. Occupations fraught with danger, such as those in the military or law enforcement, provide obvious opportunities to exemplify moral virtue or to demonstrate courage. A less dramatic, but still effective, strategy is to behave consistently according to high ethical standards—as long as you don't come across as self-righteous. Also, your words and deeds need to match unless you want to be labeled a hypocrite.

**4.** *Negative acknowledgment.* Can confessing you've made a relatively minor error motivate people to like you a bit more? Ward and Brenner (2006) found that making negative acknowledgments—candidly admitting to possessing some negative quality—triggered positive responses. In one study, when a hypothetical college student divulged that his high school record was by no means an outstanding one, his grades were judged more favorably than when he did not comment on his academic history. Perhaps negative acknowledgment leads people to see one as honest. As long as the quality does not define the person, admitting that one is not perfect and that everyone makes small mistakes may sometimes be an advantage.

**5.** *Intimidation.* This strategy sends the message, "Don't mess with me." Intimidation usually works only in nonvoluntary relationships—for instance, when it's hard for workers to find another employer or for an economically dependent spouse to leave a relationship. Obvious intimidation tactics include threats and the withholding of valuable resources (salary increases, promotions, sex). A more subtle tactic is emotional intimidation—holding over a person's head the threat of an aggressive outburst if you don't get your way. The other self-presentation strategies work by creating a favorable impression; intimidation usually generates dislike. Nonetheless, it can work.

**6.** *Supplication.* This is usually the tactic of last resort. To get favors from others, individuals try to present themselves as weak and dependent—as in the song, "Ain't Too Proud to Beg." Students may plead or break into tears in an instructor's office in an attempt to get a grade changed. Because of the social norm to help those in need, supplication may work; however, unless the

supplicator has something to offer the potential benefactor, it's not an effective strategy.

Individuals tailor their use of self-presentation strategies to match the situation. For instance, it's unlikely that you'd try intimidating your boss; you'd be more likely to ingratiate or promote yourself with him or her. As you can see in **Figure 6.18**, all of these strategies carry risks. Thus, to make a good impression, you must use these strategies skillfully.

## Perspectives on Impression Management

Curiously, almost all research on self-presentation has been conducted on first meetings between strangers, yet the vast majority of actual social interactions take place between people who already know each other. Noting the gap between reality and research, Dianne Tice and her colleagues (1995) investigated whether self-presentation varied in these two situations. They found that people strive to make positive impressions when they interact with strangers but shift toward modesty and neutral self-presentations when they are with friends. Why the difference? Because strangers don't know you, you want to give them positive information so they'll form a good impression of you. Besides, strangers have no way of knowing whether you are bending the truth. On the other hand, your friends already know your positive qualities. Thus, belaboring them is unnecessary and may make you seem immodest. Likewise, your friends know you well enough to know whether you are grandstanding, so you don't bother. The best approach to managing impressions may be a balanced one. Robinson, Johnson, and Shields (1995) found that people who presented themselves using a mix of self-promoting and self-deprecating comments were viewed as more genuine and likeable than those who relied exclusively on either type of descriptions.

How good are people at discerning the results of their impression management attempts? As we noted earlier, individuals are much better judges of how

| Strategic Self-Presentation Strategies | | | |
|---|---|---|---|
| **Presentation Strategy** | **Impression Sought** | **Emotion to Be Aroused in Target** | **Negative Impressions Risked** |
| Ingratiation | Likable | Affection | Boot-licker, conformist |
| Self-promotion | Competent | Respect | Conceited, defensive |
| Exemplification | Morally superior | Guilt | Hypocrite, sanctimonious |
| Intimidation | Dangerous | Fear | Blusterer, ineffectual |
| Supplication | Helpless | Obligation | Undeserving, lazy |

**FIGURE 6.18**

**Strategic self-presentation strategies.** Individuals rely on a variety of self-presentation strategies to present a certain image of themselves to others. Five strategies described by Jones (1990) are compared here. A sixth strategy (negative acknowledgment) is also discussed in the text. To avoid the risks associated with the strategies, it's important to use the tactics skillfully.

Source: Based on Jones, E. E. (1990). *Interpersonal perception.* New York: W. H. Freeman & Company, p. 198.

people, in general, view them than they are of how specific persons evaluate them.

## Self-Monitoring

According to Mark Snyder (1979, 1986; Gangestad & Snyder, 2000), people vary in their awareness of how they are perceived by others. *Self-monitoring* **refers to the degree to which people attend to and control the impressions they make on others.** People who are high self-monitors seem to be very sensitive to their impact on others. Low self-monitors, on the other hand, are less concerned about impression management and behave more spontaneously.

**Mark Snyder**

Courtesy Mark Snyder

Compared to low self-monitors, high self-monitors want to make a favorable impression and try to tailor their actions accordingly; they are skilled at deciphering what others want to see. In fact, high self-monitors

manage their social relations well, earning status from others by offering them aid while avoiding asking for assistance themselves (Flynn et al., 2006). Because they are able to control their emotions and deliberately regulate nonverbal signals, they are talented at self-presentation (Gangestad & Snyder, 2000). In contrast, low self-monitors are more likely to express their true beliefs or, possibly, to try to convey the impression that they are sincere and genuine individuals.

As you might infer, these two personality types view themselves differently (Gangestad & Snyder, 2000). Low self-monitors see themselves as having strong principles and behaving in line with them, whereas high self-monitors perceive themselves as flexible and pragmatic. Because high self-monitors don't see a necessary connection between their private beliefs and their public actions, they aren't troubled by discrepancies between beliefs and behavior.

In the upcoming Application, we redirect our attention to the critical issue of self-esteem and outline seven steps for boosting it.

## APPLICATION

# Building Self-Esteem

### LEARNING OBJECTIVES
- Explain when it is inadvisable to increase one's self-esteem and why this is so.
- List seven ways to build self-esteem.

*Answer the following "yes" or "no."*

____ **1.** I worry that others don't like me.

____ **2.** I have very little confidence in my abilities.

____ **3.** I often feel awkward in social situations and just don't know how to take charge.

____ **4.** I have difficulty accepting praise or flattery.

____ **5.** I have a hard time bouncing back from failure experiences.

If you answered "yes" to most of these questions, you may suffer from low self-esteem. As we noted earlier, people with low self-esteem are less happy and more prone to depression, become demoralized after failures, and are anxious in relationships. Moreover, even people with high global self-esteem may have pockets of low self-esteem. For example, you may feel great about your "social self" but not so good about your "academic self." Thus, this Application can be useful to many people.

We have one caveat, however: It is possible for self-esteem to be too high—recall our earlier discus-

sion about narcissism, ego threats, and violence. Better adjustment is associated with realistically high (and stable) self-esteem. Thus, our suggestions are directed to those whose self-esteem could use a legitimate boost, not to those whose self-esteem is already inflated. The latter group can benefit from developing more realistic self-views.

As you saw in our discussion of self-efficacy, there is ample evidence that efforts at self-improvement can pay off by boosting self-esteem. Following are seven guidelines for building self-esteem. These suggestions are distilled from the advice of many experts, including

**WEB LINK 6.4   National Association for Self-Esteem**

This site is dedicated to fostering self-esteem. It explains the nature of self-esteem, permits browsers to estimate their self-esteem, discusses parenting and self-esteem, and provides links to other relevant websites.

Baumeister et al. (2003), Ellis (1989), McKay and Fanning (2000), Rogers (1977), and Zimbardo (1990).

## 1. Recognize That You Control Your Self-Image

The first thing you must do is recognize that *you* ultimately control how you see yourself. You *do* have the power to change your self-image. True, we have discussed at length how feedback from others influences your self-concept. Yes, social comparison theory suggests that people need such feedback and that it would be unwise to ignore it completely. However, the final choice about whether to accept or reject such feedback rests with you. Your self-image resides in your mind and is a product of your thinking. Although others may influence your self-concept, you are the final authority.

## 2. Learn More About Yourself

People with low self-esteem don't seem to know themselves in as much detail as those with high self-esteem. Accordingly, to boost your self-esteem, you need to take stock of yourself. To do so, review what you know about your physical appearance, personality characteristics, relations with others, school and job performance, intellectual functioning, and sexuality. By thinking through each area, you may discover that you're fuzzy about certain aspects of yourself. To get a clearer picture, pay careful attention to your thoughts, feelings, and behavior and utilize feedback from others.

## 3. Don't Let Others Set Your Goals

A common trap that many people fall into is letting others set the standards by which they evaluate themselves. Others are constantly telling you that you should do this or you ought to do that. Thus, you hear that you "should study accounting" or "ought to lose weight." Most of this advice is well intentioned and may contain good ideas. Still, it is important that you make your *own* decisions about what you will do and what you will believe in. Think about the source of and basis for your personal goals and standards. Do they really represent ideals that *you* value? Or are they beliefs that you have passively accepted from others without thinking?

## 4. Recognize Unrealistic Goals

Even if you truly value certain ideals and sincerely want to achieve certain goals, another question remains: Are your goals realistic? Many people demand too much of themselves. They want to always perform at their best, which is obviously impossible. For instance, you may have a burning desire to achieve national acclaim as an actress. However, the odds against such an achievement are enormous. It is important to recognize this reality so that you do not condemn yourself to failure. Some overly demanding people pervert the social comparison process by always comparing themselves against the *best* rather than against similar others. They assess their looks by comparing themselves with famous models, and they judge their finances by compar-

If you like singing star Taylor Swift, that's fine, but she is not a sensible benchmark for evaluating your attractiveness or success. Some people distort the social comparison process.

© Kevin Winter/Getty Images

## FRANK & ERNEST

ing themselves with the wealthiest people they know. Such comparisons are unrealistic and almost inevitably undermine self-esteem.

### 5. Modify Negative Self-Talk

How you think about your life influences how you see yourself (and vice versa). People who are low in self-esteem tend to engage in various counterproductive modes of thinking. For example, when they succeed, they may attribute their success to good luck, and when they fail, they may blame themselves. Quite to the contrary, you should take credit for your successes and consider the possibility that your failures may not be your fault. As discussed in Chapter 4, Albert Ellis has pointed out that people often think irrationally and draw unwarranted negative conclusions about themselves. If someone breaks off a romantic relationship with you, do you think, "He doesn't love me. I must be a worthless, unlovable person?" The conclusion that you are a "worthless person" does *not* follow logically from the fact of the breakup. Such irrational thinking and negative self-talk breed poor self-esteem. Recognize the destructive potential of negative self-talk and bring it to a halt.

### 6. Emphasize Your Strengths

This advice may seem trite, but it has some merit. People with low self-esteem often derive little satisfaction from their accomplishments and virtues. They pay little heed to their good qualities while talking constantly about their defeats and frailties. The fact is that everyone has strengths and weaknesses. You should accept those personal shortcomings that you are powerless to change and work on those that are changeable, without becoming obsessed about it. At the same time, you should embrace your strengths and learn to appreciate them.

### 7. Approach Others with a Positive Outlook

Some people with low self-esteem try to cut others down to their (subjective) size through constant criticism. This fault finding and negative approach does not go over well. Instead, it leads to tension, antagonism, and rejection. This rejection lowers self-esteem still further (see **Figure 6.19**). You can boost your esteem-building efforts by recognizing and reversing this self-defeating tendency. Cultivate the habit of maintaining a positive, supportive outlook when you approach people. Doing so will promote rewarding interactions and help you earn others' acceptance. There is probably nothing that enhances self-esteem more than acceptance and genuine affection from others.

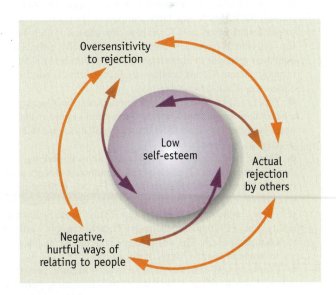

**FIGURE 6.19**

**The vicious circle of low self-esteem and rejection.** A negative self-image can make expectations of rejection a self-fulfilling prophecy, because people with low self-esteem tend to approach others in negative, hurtful ways. Real or imagined rejections lower self-esteem still further, creating a vicious circle.

## KEY IDEAS

### Self-Concept

● The self-concept is composed of a number of beliefs about what one is like, and it is not easily changed. It governs both present and future behavior. Discrepancies between one's ideal self and one's actual or ought self can produce negative emotions and lowered self-esteem. To cope with these negative states, individuals may bring their behavior in line with their ideal selves or blunt their awareness of self-discrepancies.

● The self-concept is shaped by several factors, including individuals' observations of their own behavior, which often involve social comparisons with others. Self-observations tend to be biased in a positive direction. In addition, feedback from others shapes the self-concept; this information is also filtered to some extent. Cultural guidelines also affect the way people see themselves. Members of individualistic cultures usually have an independent view of the self, whereas those in collectivist cultures often have an interdependent view of the self.

### Self-Esteem

● Self-esteem is a person's global evaluation of his or her worth. Like the self-concept, it tends to be stable, but it can fluctuate in response to daily ups and downs.

● Compared to those with high self-esteem, individuals with low self-esteem are less happy, are more likely to be depressed, are more prone to giving up after failure, and are less trusting of others.

● Narcissistic individuals are prone to aggression when their self-esteem is threatened. Self-esteem develops through interactions with significant others. Self-esteem, ethnicity, and gender interact in complex ways.

### Basic Principles of Self-Perception

● To avoid being overwhelmed with information, people tend to use automatic processing, but for important decisions, they shift to controlled processing. To explain the causes of their behavior, individuals make self-attributions. Generally, people attribute their behavior to internal or external factors and to stable or unstable factors. Controllability-uncontrollability is another key dimension of self-attributions.

● People tend to use either an optimistic explanatory style or a pessimistic explanatory style to understand various events that occur in their lives, and these attributional styles are related to psychological adjustment.

● People are guided by four distinct motives in seeking to understand themselves. The self-assessment motive directs people toward accurate feedback about the self. The self-verification motive drives people toward information that matches their current self-views, even though doing so may involve some distortion of reality. The self-improvement motive underlies people's attempts to better themselves. The self-enhancement motive enables people to maintain positive views of themselves.

● Common self-enhancement strategies include downward comparisons to others whose problems are more serious than one's own, attributing successes to personal factors and failures to external factors (the self-serving bias), basking in the reflected glory of others who are successful, and sabotaging one's performance to provide an excuse for possible failure (self-handicapping).

### Self-Regulation

● Self-regulation involves setting goals and directing behavior to meet those goals. Engaging in self-control can temporarily deplete what appears to be a limited underlying resource. A key aspect of self-regulation is self-efficacy—an individual's belief that he or she can achieve specific goals. Self-efficacy plays a key role in adjustment and can be learned through mastery experiences, vicarious experiences, persuasion, and positive interpretations of emotional arousal.

● Sometimes normal people knowingly do things that are bad for them. These self-defeating actions fall into three categories: deliberate self-destruction, tradeoffs, and counterproductive strategies.

### Self-Presentation

● Public selves are the various images that individuals project to others. Generally, people try to manage the impressions they make by using a variety of strategies, including ingratiation, self-promotion, negative acknowledgment, exemplification, intimidation, and supplication. High self-monitors pay more attention to the impressions they make on others and tend to be more concerned about making favorable impressions than low self-monitors are.

### Application: Building Self-Esteem

● The seven building blocks to higher self-esteem are (1) recognize that you control your self-image, (2) learn more about yourself, (3) don't let others set your goals, (4) recognize unrealistic goals, (5) modify negative self-talk, (6) emphasize your strengths, and (7) approach others with a positive outlook.

## KEY TERMS

Basking in reflected glory p. 195
Collectivism p. 183
Downward social comparison p. 194
Explanatory style p. 192
External attributions p. 191
Impression management p. 201
Individualism p. 183
Ingratiation p. 201
Internal attributions p. 191
Possible selves p. 178
Public self p. 200
Reference group p. 180
Self-attributions p. 191

Self-concept p. 177
Self-defeating behaviors p. 199
Self-discrepancy p. 178
Self-efficacy p. 198
Self-enhancement p. 193
Self-esteem p. 184
Self-handicapping p. 196
Self-monitoring p. 203
Self-regulation p. 197
Self-serving bias p. 194
Self-verification theory p. 193
Social comparison theory p. 180

## KEY PEOPLE

Albert Bandura pp. 198–199
Roy Baumeister pp. 185–187
Hazel Markus pp. 177–178
Mark Snyder p. 203

## QUESTIONS

1. Which of the following statements about the self-concept is false?
   a. It is composed of one dominant belief about the self.
   b. It is composed of many self-beliefs.
   c. It is relatively stable over time.
   d. It influences present as well as future behavior.

2. Mismatches between one's actual and ought selves result in lower self-esteem and:
   a. dejection-related feelings.
   b. agitation-related feelings.
   c. feelings of self-enhancement.
   d. no particular feelings.

3. A person reared in a collectivist culture is likely to have a(n) _____ self-view, whereas a person reared in an individualistic culture is likely to have a(n) _____ self-view.
   a. self-discrepant; self-consistent
   b. self-consistent; self-discrepant
   c. independent; interdependent
   d. interdependent; independent

4. Low self-esteem is associated with:
   a. happiness.
   b. high trust of others.
   c. self-concept confusion.
   d. recovering after failure experiences.

5. Aggression in response to self-esteem threats is more likely to occur in people who are:
   a. high in self-esteem.
   b. low in self-esteem.
   c. narcissistic.
   d. self-defeating.

6. Which of the following is *not* a basic principle of self-perception?
   a. People are "cognitive spenders."
   b. People's explanatory style is related to adjustment.
   c. People want to receive information that is consistent with their self-views.
   d. People want to maintain positive feelings about the self.

7. Keisha is upset when a textbook is stolen, but she feels better after she hears that a classmate's book bag, including her cell phone and wallet, was stolen. This is an example of:
   a. the self-serving bias.
   b. basking in reflected glory.
   c. downward comparison.
   d. self-handicapping.

8. Which of the following statements about self-efficacy is true?
   a. It can be developed by persevering through failure until one achieves success.
   b. It is something that one is born with.
   c. It essentially is the same as self-esteem.
   d. It refers to conscious efforts to make a certain impression on others.

9. The self-presentation strategy of ingratiation involves trying to make others:
   a. respect you.
   b. fear you.
   c. feel sorry for you.
   d. like you.

10. Which of the following will *not* help you build higher self-esteem?
    a. minimizing negative self-talk
    b. comparing yourself with those who are the best in a given area
    c. working to improve yourself
    d. approaching others with positive expectations

## ANSWERS

1. a Page 177
2. b Page 179
3. d Pages 183–184
4. c Page 185
5. c Page 187
6. a Pages 190–194
7. c Page 194
8. a Pages 198–199
9. d Page 201
10. b Pages 203–205

## Personal Explorations Workbook

Go to the *Personal Explorations Workbook* in the back of your textbook for exercises that can enhance your self-understanding in relation to issues raised in this chapter. **Exercise 6.1** *Self-Assessment:* Self-Monitoring Scale. **Exercise 6.2** *Self-Reflection:* How Does Your Self-Concept Compare to Your Self-Ideal?

## CourseMate

Access an interactive eBook, chapter-specific interactive learning tools, including Personal Explorations, Recommended Readings, Critical Thinking Exercises, flashcards, quizzes, videos and more in your Psychology CourseMate, available at **www.cengagebrain.com/shop/ISBN/1111186634**.

© Blend Images/ColorBlind Images/Getty Images

# Social Thinking and Social Influence

You have a new boss at work. Your old boss was let go because of poor performance. The new boss looks very serious. He always wears a white shirt and a conservative tie, and he rarely smiles. Unlike your old boss, who was friendly and joked around a lot, this fellow is very reserved. He rarely even says hello to you when your paths cross in the halls or out in the parking lot. You wonder whether he doesn't like you or happens to treat everyone that way. Maybe he's just driven by his work. You resolve to ask around the office to see how he acts with your co-workers. You do know that he fired a woman who worked a few doors down the hall. You're not sure why; she seemed nice, always smiling and saying hello. She sure looked like a hard worker. Maybe he thought she was too friendly? The new boss is also not much older than you—in fact, he might be your age. What if he thinks you are not working hard enough? Maybe he feels you should have advanced further in the company, or that you are too nice? Could he be thinking about firing you?

This situation illustrates the process of person perception in everyday life. Everyone asks and answers "why" questions about the people around them. Individuals constantly form impressions to try to make sense of the people they encounter, not only to understand them but also to predict how they will behave. This chapter explores how people form impressions of others, as well as how and why such judgments can be incorrect. Our consideration of *social cognition* (how people think about people, as well as themselves) then broadens to examine the problems posed by prejudice. We then look at how others try to influence one's beliefs and behavior. To do so, we explore the power of persuasive messages and the social pressures to conform and obey. As you will learn, social thinking and social influence play important roles in personal adjustment.

# Forming Impressions of Others

- Cite the five sources of information people use to form impressions of others.
- Understand the key differences between snap judgments and systematic judgments.
- Define attributions, and explain when people are likely to make them.

- Describe two expectancies that can distort observer's perceptions.
- Recognize four important cognitive distortions and how they operate.
- Identify some ways in which perceptions of others are efficient, selective, and consistent.

Do you recall the first time you met your roommate? She seemed friendly but a little shy, and perhaps a bit on the neat side, so much so that you wondered whether you two would get along. You like things less structured; not messy, but decidedly lived-in or comfortable. You were worried that you'd have to change your ways, straightening up your space all the time. Happily, once you got to know her better, she warmed up to you and your clutter—now you are close friends. As people interact with others, they constantly engage in *person perception,* **the process of forming impressions of others.** Because impression formation is usually such an automatic process, people are unaware that it is taking place. Nonetheless, the process is a complex one, involving perceivers, their social networks, and those who are perceived (Smith & Collins, 2009; Waggoner, Smith, & Collins, 2009). Let's review some of its essential aspects.

## Key Sources of Information

Because you can't read other people's minds, you are dependent on *observations* of others to determine what they are like. In forming impressions of others, people rely on five key sources of observational information: appearance, verbal behavior, actions, nonverbal messages, and situational cues.

1. *Appearance.* Despite the admonition "You can't judge a book by its cover," people frequently do exactly that. Physical features such as height, weight, skin color, race, and hair color are some of the cues used to "read" other people. Regardless of their accuracy, beliefs about physical features are used to form impressions of others (Hellström & Tekle, 1994). For example, Americans learn to associate the wearing of eyeglasses with studiousness. Styles of dress, clothing or jewelry that designate religious beliefs, body piercings, and tattoos also provide clues about others. Failing to dress appropriately for a job interview can reduce the chances of being hired (Turner-Bowker, 2001).

Consider the impact of race as a case of appearance. Multiracial identities are anticipated to expand dramatically in the next 100 years, a fact that will pose a problem for perceivers who are used to deciding quickly whether someone is of their own or another race. Interestingly, where memory is concerned, research suggests that multiracial individuals are remembered less well than those whose race is the same as (*ingroup*) or distinctly different from (*outgroup*) that of perceivers (Pauker et al., 2009). Generally, a same-race bias accounts for whether people are recalled. Thus, one experiment found that racially ambiguous faces were recalled less accurately than own-race faces (Pauker et al., 2009). A second study by the same research team found that memory for biracial faces can be enhanced if the perceivers are motivated to see such faces as part of the ingroup.

2. *Verbal behavior.* Another obvious source of information about others is what they say. People form impressions based on what and how much others self-disclose, how often they give advice and ask questions, and how judgmental they are (Berry et al., 1997; Tardy & Dindia, 2006). If Tanisha speaks negatively about most of the people she knows, you will probably conclude that she is a critical person.

3. *Actions.* Because people don't always tell the truth, you have to rely on their behavior to provide insights about them. For instance, when you learn that Wade volunteers five hours a week at the local homeless shelter, you are likely to infer that he is a caring person. In impression formation, actions speak louder than words.

4. *Nonverbal messages.* As discussed in Chapter 8, a key source of information about others is nonverbal communication: facial expressions, eye contact, body language, and gestures (DePaulo & Friedman, 1998; Ekman, 2007; Knapp & Hall, 2006). These nonverbal cues provide information about people's emotional states and dispositions. For example, in our culture a bright smile and steady eye contact signal friendliness and openness. Also, because people know that verbal behavior is easily manipulated, they often rely on nonverbal cues to determine the truth of what others say (Frank & Ekman, 1997).

5. *Situations.* The setting in which behavior occurs provides crucial information about how to interpret a person's behavior (Cooper & Withey, 2009; Reis, 2008;

In forming impressions of others, people rely on cues such as appearance, actions, and verbal and nonverbal messages, as well as the nature of the situation.

Trope & Gaunt, 2003). For instance, without situational cues (such as being at a wedding versus a funeral), it would be hard to know whether a person crying was happy or sad.

When it comes to drawing inferences about people, one bad piece of information can outweigh or undo a collection of positive characteristics. Social psychological research repeatedly demonstrates that the presence of a trait perceived to be negative ("untrustworthy") can have more influence on forming impressions than

several positive qualities ("warm," "open," "friendly," "clever") (Skowronski & Carlston, 1989; Vonk, 1993). When an immoral act is performed, other good or virtuous behaviors cannot undo the damage to people's perceptions of the offender's character (Riskey & Birnbaum, 1974). In fact, a single bad deed can eliminate a good reputation, but one good deed cannot redeem an otherwise bad standing in the eyes of others (Skowronski & Carlston, 1992). Thus, in the realm of perception *bad impressions tend to be stronger than good ones* (Baumeister et al., 2001).

## Snap Judgments Versus Systematic Judgments

In their interactions with others, people are bombarded with more information than they can possibly handle. To avoid being overwhelmed, they rely on alternative ways to process information. *Snap judgments* about others are those made quickly and based on only a few bits of information and preconceived notions. Thus, they may not be particularly accurate. Nevertheless, people can get by with superficial assessments of others quite often. As Susan Fiske (2004) puts it, "Good-enough accuracy in forming impressions allows us to navigate our social seas and not collide or run aground too often" (p. 132). Often, interactions with others are so fleeting or inconsequential that it makes little difference that such judgments are imprecise.

Susan Fiske

On the other hand, when it comes to selecting a friend, a mate, or an employee, it's essential that impressions be as accurate as possible. Thus, it's not surprising that people are motivated to take more care in these assessments. In forming impressions of those who can affect their welfare and happiness, people make *systematic judgments* rather than snap decisions (see **Figure 7.1**).

**FIGURE 7.1**

**The process of person perception.** In forming impressions of others, perceivers rely on various sources of observational information. When it's important to form accurate impressions of others, people are motivated to make systematic judgments, including attributions. When accuracy isn't a priority, people make snap judgments about others.

Source: Adapted from Brehm, S. S., & Kassin, S. M. (1993) *Social psychology*. Boston: Houghton Mifflin. Copyright © 1993 by Houghton Mifflin Company. Adapted with permission.

That is, they take the time to observe the person in a variety of situations and to compare that person's behavior with that of others in similar situations.

In assessing what a significant individual is like, people are particularly interested in learning why the person behaves in a certain way. This deeper level of understanding is vital if one is to make accurate predictions about the person's future behavior. How do people make such decisions? What information do they consider? To determine the cause of others' behavior, people engage in the process of causal attribution.

## Attributions

As we have noted in earlier chapters, *attributions* **are inferences that people draw about the causes of their own behavior, others' behavior, and events.** In Chapter 6, we focused on self-attributions. Here, we'll apply attribution theory to the behavior of *other people*. For example, suppose that your boss bawls you out for doing a sloppy job on an insignificant project. To what do you attribute this tongue lashing? Was your work really that bad? Is your boss just in a grouchy mood? Is your boss under too much pressure?

In Chapter 6, we noted that attributions have three key dimensions: internal versus external, stable versus unstable, and controllable versus uncontrollable (Jones & Davis, 1965; Kelley, 1950; Weiner, 1974). For this discussion, we focus only on the internal/external dimension (Heider, 1958). When people ascribe the causes of someone's behavior to personal dispositions, traits, abilities, or feelings, they are making *internal* attributions. When they impute the causes of their behavior to situational demands and environmental constraints, they are making *external* attributions. For example, if a friend's business fails, you might attribute the failure to your friend's lack of business skills (an internal factor) or to negative trends in the economy (an external factor).

The types of attributions people make about others can have a tremendous impact on everyday social interactions. Consider the judgments people make about the nature of others' emotional experiences or reactions, for example. People often assume that women are the more emotional gender when, in fact, they are no more emotional than men except where outward displays of emotion are concerned (DeAngelis, 2001; Kring & Gordon, 1998; see Chapter 11). This bias can color the conclusions observers make about the emotional experiences of men and women in similar circumstances. In two experiments, participants were given either situational ("was having a rough day") or dispositional ("so emotional") information as the cause of expressions in a series of photographs of male and female faces (Barrett & Bliss-Moreau, 2009). Even when the information was attributed to situational sources, the women's expressions were more likely to be characterized as being

due to their personalities. These findings may explain why men, but not women, are often give an attributional "pass" when they show too much feeling in front of others (Mendoza-Denton, Parker, & O'Connor, 2008).

Obviously, people don't make attributions about every person they meet. Research suggests that people are relatively selective in this process (Jones, 1990; Malle, 2004; Malle & Knobe, 1997). It seems that people are most likely to make attributions (1) when others behave in unexpected or negative ways, (2) when events are personally relevant, and (3) when they are suspicious about another person's motives. For example, if Serena laughs loudly at the local student hangout, no one bats an eye. But if she does so in the middle of a serious lecture, it raises eyebrows and generates speculation about why she behaved this way.

Some aspects of the attribution process are logical (Trope & Gaunt, 2003). Nonetheless, research also shows that the process of person perception is sometimes illogical and unsystematic, as in the case of snap judgments. Other sources of error also creep into the process, a topic we take up next.

## Perceiver Expectations

Remember Evan, that bully from the fourth grade? He made your life miserable—constantly looking for opportunities to poke fun at you and beat you up. Now when you meet someone named Evan, your initial reaction is negative, and it takes a while to warm up to him (Andersen & Chen, 2002). Why? Your negative past experiences with an Evan have led you to expect the worst, whether or not it's warranted (Andersen, Reznik, & Manzella, 1996). This is just one example of how *perceiver expectations* can influence the perception of others (de Calvo & Reich, 2009). Let's look at two of the principles governing perceiver expectations: confirmation bias and self-fulfilling prophecy.

### Confirmation Bias

Shortly after you begin interacting with someone, you start forming hypotheses about what the person is like. In turn, these hypotheses can influence your behavior toward that person in such a way as to confirm your expectations. Thus, if on your first encounter with Xavier he has a camera around his neck, you will probably hypothesize that he has an interest in photography and

**WEB LINK 7.1  Social Psychology Network**
Wesleyan University social psychologist Scott Plous offers a broad collection of more than 5,000 web links related to all aspects of social and general psychology, including how people understand and influence each other interpersonally.

DILBERT

DILBERT, I'D LIKE YOU TO MEET BEN, OUR NEWEST FAST-TRACK MANAGER.

HI

BEN HAS NO REAL EXPERIENCE BUT HE'S VERY TALL, SO WE KNOW HE'LL GO FAR.

I ALSO HAVE EXECUTIVE STYLE HAIR.

WE THINK IT WILL TURN SILVER.

DILBERT © Scott Adams/Dist. by United Feature Syndicate, Inc.

question him selectively about his shutterbug activities. You might also neglect to ask more wide-ranging questions that would give you a more accurate picture of him. *Confirmation bias* **is the tendency to seek information that supports one's beliefs while not pursuing disconfirming information.**

Confirmation bias is a well-documented phenomenon (Dougherty, Turban, & Callendar, 1994; Nickerson, 1998; Snyder & Swann, 1978). It occurs in casual social interactions as well as in job interviews and in courtrooms, where the interviewer or attorney may ask leading questions (Fiske & Taylor, 1991). Law enforcement officers, for example, should be careful to evaluate evidence without any preconceived notion of a suspect's guilt or innocence (Lilienfeld & Landfield, 2008). Confirmation bias can also affect medical professionals when, for example, patient symptoms are ambiguous. Trying to make sense of such ambiguity in the absence of clear indicators can lead doctors to make inaccurate diagnoses. In one study, for example, doctors listened to identical sounds in two lungs, but those who had already and unknowingly made an incorrect diagnosis of the problem "heard" a difference, thereby demonstrating a confirmation bias (Tschan et al., 2009). When it comes to forming first impressions of others, the principle is not so much that "seeing is believing" but rather that "believing is seeing" (see **Figure 7.2**), and some people may be more susceptible to displaying confirmation biases than others (Rassin, 2008). In other words, some people's personalities may predispose them to focus on facts that fit their theories instead of weighing all of the available information more critically.

Confirmation bias also occurs because individuals selectively recall facts to fit their views of others. In one experiment

(Cohen, 1981), participants watched a videotape of a woman engaging in a variety of activities, including listening to classical music, drinking beer, and watching TV. Half of them were told that the woman was a waitress and the other half were told that she was a librarian. When asked to recall the woman's actions on the videotape, participants tended to remember activities consistent with their stereotypes of waitresses and librarians. Thus, those who thought that the woman was a waitress recalled her drinking beer; those who thought she was a librarian recalled her listening to classical music.

Can a confirmation bias be used to characterize perceptions of group behaviors as well as individual actions? Apparently so. A recent study considered whether confirmation bias is linked to the pervasive belief in a sexual double standard, namely that men are rewarded for sexual activity while women are derogated for it (Marks & Fraley, 2006). Think about it: In our culture, isn't promiscuity sometimes praised (or at least

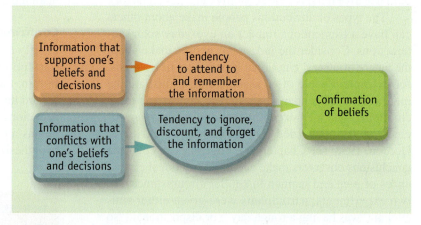

**FIGURE 7.2**

**Confirmation bias.** Confirmation bias is a two-pronged process in which people seek and remember information that supports their beliefs while discounting and forgetting information that is inconsistent with their beliefs. This common cognitive slant often distorts the process of person perception, leading to inaccurate impressions of people.

ignored) when men engage in it? However, women run the risk of losing their reputations if they become known to have a variety of sexual partners. Participants in the study by Marks and Fraley (2006) read brief accounts about either a target male or female that contained an equal number of positive and negative observations about the individual's sexual behavior. Despite perceived advances in sexual equality and living in a society that is increasingly open minded about sexual behavior, people were more likely to recall information that "confirmed" the double standard (pro-male, anti-female) than contradicted it. In other words, "boys will be boys" and they can get away with promiscuity, but women cannot without sullying their reputations.

## Self-Fulfilling Prophecies

Sometimes a perceiver's expectations can actually change another person's behavior. **A *self-fulfilling prophecy* occurs when expectations about a person cause him or her to behave in ways that confirm the expectations.** This term was originally coined by sociologist Robert Merton (1948) to explain such phenomena as "runs" on banks that occurred during the Depression. That is, when unfounded rumors would circulate that a bank couldn't cover its deposits, people would rush to the bank and withdraw their funds, thereby draining the deposits from the bank and making real what was initially untrue.

**Figure 7.3** depicts the three steps in the self-fulfilling prophecy. First, the perceiver has an initial impression of someone. (A teacher believes that Jennifer is highly intelligent.) Then the perceiver behaves toward the target person in line with his or her expectations. (He asks her interesting questions and praises her answers.) The third step occurs when the target person adjusts his or her behavior to the perceiver's actions, which confirms the perceiver's hypothesis about the target person. (Jennifer performs well in class.) Note that both individuals are unaware that this process is operating. Also note that because perceivers are unaware of their expectations and of the effect they can have on others, they mistakenly attribute the target person's behavior to an internal cause (Jennifer is smart), rather than an external one (their own expectations).

The best-known experiments on the self-fulfilling prophecy have been conducted in classroom settings, looking at the effect of teachers' expectations on students' academic performance (Rosenthal, 1985; see also, Rosenthal, 2002). A review of 400 studies of this phenomenon over a period of 30 years reported that teacher expectations significantly influenced student performance in 36% of the experiments. When found in the classroom, however, the effect tends to be relatively small, and its broader impact remains unclear (Jussim & Harber, 2005). In a related vein, perhaps the "storm and stress" of early adolescence, particularly teen rebellion

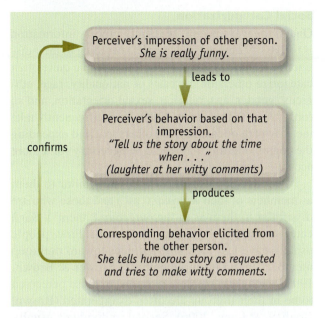

## FIGURE 7.3

**The three steps of the self-fulfilling prophecy.** Through a three-step process, your expectations about a person can cause that person to behave in ways that confirm those expectations. First, you form an impression of someone. Second, you behave toward that person in a way that is consistent with your impression. Third, the person exhibits the behavior that you encourage, which confirms your initial impression.

Source: Adapted from Smith, E. R., & Mackie, D. M. (1995). *Social psychology*. New York: Worth, p. 103. Copyright © 1995 Worth Publishing. Reprinted with permission.

and risk taking, and the predictable parental reactions to both, are sometimes expectation-based (Buchanan & Hughes, 2009). When both teens and parents anticipate tension and alienation, for example, they may look for, instigate, or see other behaviors as fitting their respective perceptions.

The self-fulfilling prophecy also operates with adults and in noneducational settings such as the military, factories and businesses, courtrooms, and physicians' offices (Ambady et al., 2002; Halverson et al., 1997; Kierein & Gold, 2000; Rosenthal, 2003). Trends in popular culture, such as the perceived popularity of unknown bands, may also serve as self-fulfilling prophecies (Salganik & Watts, 2008). If the rate of downloads for a song by a new musical group suddenly increases, for example, the band's perceived standing and reputation may grow, if only for a short time, as other listeners "follow the herd." Perhaps these sorts of self-fulfilling prophecies explain the short-term success and rapid falls of "one hit wonders."

## Cognitive Distortions

Another source of error in person perception comes from distortions in the minds of perceivers. These errors in judgment are most likely to occur when a perceiver is in a hurry, is distracted, or is not motivated to pay careful attention to another person.

## Social Categorization

One of the ways people efficiently process information is to classify objects (and people) according to their distinctive features (Fiske, 1998). Thus, people quite often categorize others on the basis of nationality, race, ethnicity, gender, age, religion, sexual orientation, and so forth (Crisp & Hewstone, 2006). People frequently take the easy path of categorizing others to avoid expending the cognitive effort that would be necessary for a more accurate impression.

People categorize those who are similar to them as members of their *ingroup* ("us") and those who are dissimilar to them as in the *outgroup* ("them"). Such categorizing has three important results. First, people usually have less favorable attitudes toward outgroup members than ingroup members (Brewer & Brown, 1998), such that empathic reactions to those perceived to be in their ingroup are often exaggerated (Brown, Bradley, & Lang, 2006). Second, individuals usually see outgroup members as being much more alike than they really are, whereas they see members of their ingroup as unique individuals (Oakes, 2001). In other words, people frequently explain the behavior of outgroup members on the basis of the characteristic that sets them apart ("Those *Nerdians* are *all* drunks"), but attribute the same behavior by an ingroup member to individual personality traits ("*Brett* is a heavy drinker"). This phenomenon is termed the *outgroup homogeneity effect* (Linville & Jones, 1980).

A third result of categorizing is that it heightens the visibility of outgroup members when there are only a few of them within a larger group. In other words, minority group status in a group makes more salient the quality that distinguishes the person—ethnicity, gender, whatever. When people are perceived as being unique or distinctive, they are also seen as having more influence in a group, and their good and bad qualities are given extra weight (Crocker & McGraw, 1984). Significantly, distinctiveness—some quality that makes one person stand out from others—can also trigger stereotyping.

Finally, based on their proclivity to categorize, people are even likely to see outgroup members as looking more like each other than they actually do. Various studies clearly show that eyewitnesses are better at identifying people of their own race than recognizing people who belong to a different racial group (Devine & Malpass, 1985; Meissner & Brigham, 2001). The exception to this rule is when outgroup members are angry (Ackerman, Zuroff, & Moskowitz, 2006). Under such conditions, angry outgroup members are much easier to identify than angry ingroup members, a result suggesting that the human mind carefully tracks strangers who may pose a threat.

## Stereotypes

*Stereotypes* **are widely held beliefs that people have certain characteristics because of their membership in a particular group.** For example, many people assume that Jews are shrewd and ambitious, that African Americans have special athletic and musical abilities, and that Muslims are religious fanatics. Although a kernel of truth may underlie some stereotypes, it should be readily apparent that not all Jews, African Americans, Muslims, and so forth behave alike. If you take the time to think about it, you will recognize that there is enormous diversity in behavior within any group.

What happens when we meet someone who is an exception to our stereotype, say, an accountant who is not quiet and reserved but, instead, rather boisterous and outgoing? Instead of adjusting or broadening our stereotype, we are likely to categorize such an exception as a misfit or a *subtype* (Altermatt & DeWall, 2003; Richards & Hewstone, 2001). Subtypes are categories people rely on for understanding people who do not fit their general stereotypes. Earlier in this chapter we noted that women are erroneously thought of as being much more emotional than men. Imagine you endorse this stereotypic view but have a good woman friend who rarely displays any emotions, whether positive or negative. As her behavior neither conforms to, nor confirms, your prevailing stereotype, you store information and thoughts about her in a subtype reserved for "unemotional women."

The most prevalent stereotypes in America are those based on gender, age, and ethnicity (Fiske, 1993). Gender stereotypes, although in transition, remain pervasive. For example, in a study of gender stereotypes in 30 countries, males were typically characterized as adventurous, powerful, and independent, while females were characterized as sentimental, submissive, and superstitious (Williams & Best, 1982, 1990). Because of their wide-ranging significance, we cover gender stereotypes in detail in Chapter 11.

Stereotypes may also be based on physical appearance. In particular, there is plenty of evidence that physically attractive people are believed to have desirable personality traits. This widespread perception is termed the *"what-is-beautiful-is-good" stereotype* (Dion, Berscheid, & Walster, 1972). Specifically, beautiful people are usually viewed as happier, more socially competent, more assertive, better adjusted, and more intellectually competent than those who are less attractive (Eagly et al., 1991; Jackson, Hunter, & Hodge,

**WEB LINK 7.2   Social Cognition Paper Archive and Information Center**

Eliot R. Smith at Indiana University maintains a popular site that includes information about papers (abstracts, mostly) and people in the field of social cognition. The site also provides extensive links to the wider social psychological research community.

1995). This attractiveness stereotype is not exclusively Western, but it can vary somewhat in other cultures. Koreans, for example, consider honesty and concern for others to be extremely important, and they tend to believe that attractive others will score above average on these traits (Wheeler & Kim, 1997). Yet most such perceptions have little basis in fact.

Attractive people *do* have an advantage in the social arena. Attractive children, for example, tend to be perceived as more popular than less attractive ones; sad to say, their teachers like them better, too (Clifford & Walster, 1973; Dion, 1973; Dion, Berscheid, & Walster, 1972). Is there a long-term consequence? Well, good-looking adults have better social skills, are more popular, are less socially anxious (especially about interactions with the other gender), are less lonely, and are more sexually experienced (Feingold, 1992b). However, they are not any different from others in intelligence, happiness, mental health, or self-esteem (Feingold, 1992b; Langlois et al., 2000). Thus, attractive people are perceived in a more favorable light than is actually justified. Unfortunately, the positive biases toward attractive people also operate in reverse. Hence, unattractive people are unjustifiably seen as less well adjusted and less intellectually competent than others. Most Americans believe that good looks are an advantage in everyday life (see **Figure 7.4**).

How does the attractiveness stereotype affect most people, including you and me? First, the bad news: Highly attractive people end up with one another (all else being equal, a perfect "10" might marry a "9," for example, but is unlikely to pair off with a "4" or a "5"). If there is any solace we can take, it's this: Most of us pair up with people who match our own level of attractiveness. Thus, we are likely to date those who match

our own level of attractiveness (Berscheid et al., 1971). In fact, the correlation between lovers' respective levels of attractiveness is fairly robust (Feingold, 1988). Interestingly, close to the same level of association in rated appearance is found between male friends. Thus, we may not realize it, but the attractiveness stereotype can have profound effects in our lives.

Stereotypes can be spontaneously triggered when people encounter members of commonly stereotyped groups—even in those who are not prejudiced (Devine, 1989; Dunning & Sherman, 1997). Worse still, racially based stereotypes can cause regrettable—and potentially dangerous—split-second decisions in which people see a weapon that isn't actually there (Payne, 2006). Stereotypes can exist outside a person's awareness (Bodenhausen, Macrae, & Hugenberg, 2003; Dasgupta, 2009; Greenwald & Banaji, 1995). Because stereotyping is automatic, some psychologists are pessimistic about being able to control it (Bargh, 1999); others take a more optimistic view (Uleman et al., 1996). For example, a recent study found less automatic race bias when men and women of different races (except blacks) were surreptitiously induced to smile while looking at photographs of blacks (Ito et al., 2006). If people put forth effort to respond in a friendly and open manner to individuals who are different from them on some important dimension (race, sexual orientation), perhaps the positive behaviors will lead to a reduction in automatic biases when reacting to others.

One conclusion from such studies is that exerting some degree of self-control is a way to reduce prejudice. Maintaining such self-control can actually be a challenge, however, as research suggests that exerting self-control depletes available energy, which means a drop in blood sugar or glucose (Gailliot, 2008). Could the tendency to stereotype be reduced if perceivers ingested sugar, which would replenish energy and promote more self-control? In a study by Gailliot and colleagues (2009), participants drank lemonade that contained either sugar or Splenda (a no-calorie sugar substitute) and then engaged in an impression formation task. Those who consumed sugar used fewer stereotypes when writing an essay about a gay man than those in the control (no-sugar) condition did. Further, persons high in prejudice in the glucose group offered fewer derogatory statements in their essays than did the high-prejudice individuals in the control group. Thus, under some circumstances, people may be able to override the predilection to stereotype.

Why do stereotypes persist? For one thing, they are functional (Quinn, Macrae, & Bodenhausen, 2003). Recall that people are "cognitive misers." Because they are deluged with much more information than they can process, the tendency is to reduce complexity to simplicity (Bodenhausen & Macrae, 1994). But, as we noted earlier, the tradeoff for simplification is inaccuracy.

| Poll Question | "Fairly important" or "Very important" answers | | | |
|---|---|---|---|---|
| | Year | Men | Women | Total |
| "How important do you think a person's physical attractiveness is in our society today in terms of his or her happiness, social life, and ability to get ahead?" | 1990 | 82% | 85% | 84% |
| | 1999 | 76% | 76% | 76% |

**Most Americans Believe Good Looks Are an Advantage**

**FIGURE 7.4**

**Physical attractiveness as a social advantage.** A Gallup poll reported that a large majority of men and women believe that physical attractiveness is an advantage when it comes to happiness, social life, and the ability to get ahead. It is clear that most people continue to believe that good looks are advantageous.

Source: Data from Newport, F. (1999, September 15), *Americans agree that being attractive is a plus in American society.* Retrieved June 10, 2001 from http://gallup.com/poll/releases/pr990915.

Stereotypes also endure because of confirmation bias. Thus, when individuals encounter members of groups that they view with prejudice, they are likely to see what they expect to see. The self-fulfilling prophecy is a third reason stereotypes persist: Beliefs about another person may actually elicit the anticipated behavior and thus confirm biased expectations.

## The Fundamental Attribution Error

When explaining the causes of others' behavior, people invoke personal attributions and discount the importance of situational factors. Although this tendency is not universal (Choi, Nisbett, & Norenzayan, 1999; Miyamoto & Kitayama, 2002), it is strong enough that Lee Ross (1977) called it the "*fundamental* attribution error." **The *fundamental attribution error* refers to the tendency to explain other people's behavior as the result of personal, rather than situational, factors.**

This tendency (sometimes termed *correspondence bias;* Jones, 1990) differs from stereotyping in that inferences are based on actual behavior. Nonetheless, those inferences may still be inaccurate. If Jeremy leaves class early, you may be correct in inferring that he is inconsiderate, but he might also have had a previously scheduled job interview. Thus, a person's behavior at a given time may or may not reflect his or her personality or character—but observers tend to assume that it does. The situations people encounter can have profound effects on their behavior, often overpowering the influence of their dispositions—they just don't realize it (Ross & Ward, 1996).

What's behind this tendency to discount situational influences on people's behavior? Once again, the culprit is people's tendency to be cognitive misers. It seems that making attributions is a two-step process (Gilbert & Malone, 1995). As you can see in **Figure 7.5**, in the first step, which occurs automatically, observers make an internal attribution because they are focusing on the person rather than the situation. (At your bank, if you observe the man ahead of you yell at the teller, you might infer that he is a hostile person.) In the second step, observers weigh the impact of the situation on the target person's behavior and adjust their inference. (If you overhear the customer claim this is the third time in three weeks that the bank has made the same error in his account, you're likely to temper your initial judgment about his hostile tendencies.)

The first step in the attribution process occurs spontaneously, but the second step requires cognitive effort and attention. Thus, it is easy to stop after step one—especially if one is in a hurry or distracted. Failure to take the effortful second step can result in the fundamental attribution error. However, when people are motivated to form accurate impressions of others (Webster, 1993) or when they are suspicious about another's motives (Fein, 1996), they do expend the effort to complete the second step. In these cases, they are more likely to make accurate attributions. Some evidence suggests that these two steps may be related to different types of brain activity (Lieberman et al., 2004). Unfortunately, much of the time people are busy with their work and social lives, which severely limits opportunities for attributional corrections while interpreting the intentions and behavior of others (Geeraert et al., 2004; Gilbert, 2002). Only when people are forced or seriously motivated to do a thorough analysis of possible causes

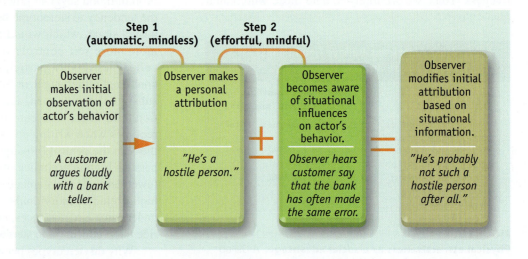

**FIGURE 7.5**

**Explaining the fundamental attribution error.** People automatically take the first step in the attribution process (making a personal attribution). However, they often fail to take the second step (considering the possible influence of situational factors on a person's behavior), because that requires extra effort. The failure to consider situational factors causes observers to exaggerate the role of personal factors in behavior—that is, they make the fundamental attribution error. (Adapted from Brehm, Kassin, & Fein, 2002)

for the behavior of another or others can they reduce the impact of the fundamental attribution error (e.g., Stalder, 2009).

Cultural values seem to promote different attributional errors. In *individualistic* cultures, where independence is valued, it is assumed that individuals are responsible for their actions. In *collectivist* societies, conformity and obedience to group norms are valued, so it is assumed that an individual's behavior reflects adherence to group expectations (see Chapter 6). Some experts speculate that different styles of thinking underlie cultural differences in attributional styles (Nisbett & Miyamoto, 2005; Nisbett et al., 2001). They suggest that the Western mentality is *analytical* (attention is focused on an object, and causality is ascribed to it), whereas the East Asian mentality is *holistic* (attention is focused on the field surrounding an object, and causality is understood to reside in the relationship between the object and its field) (Masuda & Nisbett, 2006; Miyamoto, Nisbett, & Masuda, 2006). Consistent with both of these views, researchers have found that Americans explain others' behavior in terms of internal attributions more often than Hindus do (Miller, 1984), Chinese (Chua, Leu, & Nisbett, 2005; Morris & Peng, 1994), Japanese (Weisz, Rothbaum, & Blackburn, 1984), or Koreans (Choi et al., 2003; Norenzayan, Choi, & Nisbett, 2002).

### Defensive Attribution

Observers are especially likely to make internal attributions in trying to explain the calamities and tragedies that befall other people. When a woman is abused by a boyfriend or husband, for example, people frequently blame the victim by remarking how stupid she is to stay with the man, rather than condemning the aggressor for his behavior (Summers & Feldman, 1984). Similarly, rape victims are often judged to have "asked for it" (Abrams et al., 2003).

*Defensive attribution* **is a tendency to blame victims for their misfortune, so that one feels less likely to be victimized in a similar way.** Blaming victims for their calamities also helps people maintain their belief that they live in a "just world" where people get what they deserve and deserve what they get (Hafer & Bègue, 2005; Haynes & Olson, 2006; Lerner, 1980, 1998). Acknowledging that the world is not just—that unfortunate events can happen as a result of chance factors—would mean having to admit the frightening possibility that the catastrophes that happen to others could also happen to oneself (Lambert, Burroughs, & Nguyen, 1999), especially when the victim is perceived to be like oneself (Correia, Vala, & Aguiar, 2007). Defensive attributions are a self-protective, but irrational, strategy that allows people to avoid such unnerving thoughts and helps them feel in control of their lives (Hafer, 2000; Lipkus, Dalbert, & Siegler, 1996). Unfortunately, when victims are blamed for their setbacks, people unfairly attribute

A common example of defensive attribution is the tendency to blame the homeless for their plight.

undesirable traits to them, such as incompetence, foolishness, and laziness.

## Key Themes in Person Perception

The process of person perception—how people mentally construe each others' behavior—is a complex one (Trope & Gaunt, 2003). Nonetheless, we can detect three recurrent themes in this process: efficiency, selectivity, and consistency.

### Efficiency

In forming impressions of others, people prefer to exert no more cognitive effort or time than is necessary. Thus, much social information is processed automatically and effortlessly. According to Susan Fiske (1993), people are like government bureaucrats, who "only bother to gather information on a 'need to know' basis" (p. 175). Efficiency has two important advantages: People can make judgments quickly, and it keeps things simple. The big disadvantage is that snap judgments are error-prone. Still, on balance, efficiency works pretty well as an operating principle.

### Selectivity

The old saying that "people see what they expect to see" has been confirmed repeatedly by social scientists. In a classic study, Harold Kelley (1950) showed how a person is preceded by his or her reputation. Students in a class at the Massachusetts Institute of Technology were told that a new lecturer would be speaking to them that day. Before the instructor arrived, the students were given a short description of him, with one important variation. Half the students were led to expect a "warm" person, while the other half were led to expect a "cold" one (see **Figure 7.6** on the next page). All the participants were exposed to exactly the same 20 minutes of lecture and interaction with the new instructor. However, those who were led to expect a warm person rated the instructor as significantly more considerate, sociable, humorous, good-natured, informal, and humane than those who anticipated a cold person.

Mr. Blank is a graduate student in the Department of Economics and Social Science here at M.I.T. He has had three semesters of teaching experience in psychology at another college. This is his first semester teaching Ec. 70. He is 26 years old, a veteran, and married. People who know him consider him to be a rather **cold** person, industrious, critical, practical, and determined.

Mr. Blank is a graduate student in the Department of Economics and Social Science here at M.I.T. He has had three semesters of teaching experience in psychology at another college. This is his first semester teaching Ec. 70. He is 26 years old, a veteran, and married. People who know him consider him to be a very **warm** person, industrious, critical, practical, and determined.

**FIGURE 7.6**

**Descriptions of the guest lecturer in Kelley's (1950) study.** These two descriptions, provided to two groups of students before the lecturer spoke, differ by only an adjective. But this seemingly small difference caused the two groups to form different perceptions of the lecturer.

## Consistency

How many times did your parents remind you to be on your best behavior when you were meeting someone for the first time? As it turns out, they were onto something! Considerable research supports the idea that first impressions are powerful (Asch, 1956; Belmore, 1987). **A *primacy effect* occurs when initial information carries more weight than subsequent information.** We risk being labeled a hypocrite, for example, if we say one thing and then do another (such as claiming to have an open mind and then make a cutting, judgmental remark about someone) rather than the reverse (Barden, Rucker, & Petty, 2005). Initial negative impressions may be especially hard to change (Mellers, Richards, & Birnbaum, 1992). Thus, getting off on the wrong foot may be particularly damaging. As noted earlier in this chapter, negative information can outweigh positive factors; bad can indeed be stronger than good. Only if people are motivated to form an accurate impression and are not tired will they be less likely to lock in their initial impressions (Webster, Richter, & Kruglanski, 1996).

Why are primacy effects so potent? Because people find comfort in cognitive *consistency;* cognitions that contradict each other tend to create tension and discomfort. This principle applies to people's perceptions of others. Hence, once people believe that they have formed an accurate picture of someone, they tend to tune out or discount subsequent information that seems to contradict that picture (Belmore, 1987). It is not impossible to override an initial impression, but the built-in preference for consistency makes it more difficult than most people realize.

To conclude, although the process of person perception is highly subjective, people are relatively accurate perceivers of others (Fiske, 1998). Even when misperceptions occur, they are often harmless. However, there clearly are occasions when such inaccuracies are problematic. This is certainly true in the case of prejudice, which we consider next.

# The Problem of Prejudice

## LEARNING OBJECTIVES

● Explain how "old-fashioned" and modern discrimination differ.
● Understand how authoritarianism and cognitive distortions can contribute to prejudice.
● Clarify how intergroup competition and threats to social identity can foster prejudice.
● Describe the operation of several strategies for reducing prejudice.

Let's begin our discussion by clarifying a couple of terms that are often confused. ***Prejudice* is a negative attitude toward members of a group;** *discrimination* **involves behaving differently, usually unfairly, toward the members of a group.** Prejudice and discrimination do tend to go together, but that is not always the case (see **Figure 7.7**). One classic social psychology study found almost no discriminatory behavior aimed at a Chinese couple traveling around the country with a white professor in the 1930s. Before making the trips, the professor anticipated that they would encounter some prejudice about where they could stay or dine, but they were only declined service a few times. When the professor wrote to all the establishments they vis-

ited months later to ask whether Chinese guests were welcome, however, the majority of the responses were, in fact, prejudiced and rather uninviting, showing that, attitudes don't always predict behavior (LaPiere, 1934). Why can people respond in discriminatory ways sometimes but not always? It is possible that a restaurant owner would be prejudiced against Chicanos and yet treat them like anyone else because he needed their business. This is an example of prejudice without discrimination. Although it is probably less common, discrimination without prejudice may also occur. For example, an executive who has favorable attitudes toward blacks may not hire them because he thinks his boss would be upset.

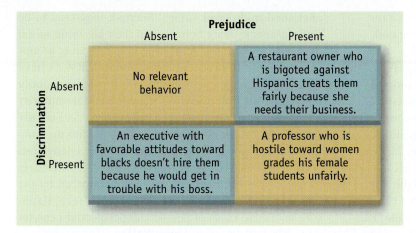

**FIGURE 7.7**

**Prejudice and discrimination.** Prejudice and discrimination are highly correlated, but they don't necessarily go hand in hand. As the examples in the blue cells show, prejudice can exist without discrimination and discrimination without prejudice.

Sometimes, too, prejudices and stereotypes can be triggered without conscious awareness (Wittenbrink & Schwartz, 2007) and can have consequences for behavior. For example, in one study, college students were given a sentence completion task in which half of them received a word list containing words stereotypically associated with elderly people (wrinkle, gray, Florida). Once the idea of old age was surreptitiously "primed" in their thoughts, these same college students were later found to take 13% longer to walk to an elevator than a control group that received a neutral word list (Bargh, Chen, & Burrows, 1996).

## "Old-Fashioned" Versus Modern Discrimination

Over the past 40 years, prejudice and discrimination against minority groups have diminished in the United States. Racial segregation is no longer legal, and discrimination based on race, ethnicity, gender, and religion is much less common than it was in the 1950s and 1960s. Thus, the good news is that overt, or *"old-fashioned," discrimination* against minority groups has declined. The bad news is that a more subtle form of prejudice and discrimination has emerged (Dovidio & Gaertner, 1996; Gaertner & Dovidio, 1986). That is, people may privately harbor racist or sexist attitudes but express them only when they feel such views are

justified or when it's safe to do so. This new phenomenon has been termed *modern discrimination* (also called "modern racism"). Modern discrimination is also operating when people endorse equality as an abstract principle but oppose concrete programs intended to promote equality on the grounds that discrimination against minority groups no longer exists (Wright & Taylor, 2003). As an example, in **Figure 7.8**, you can see the kinds of items used to measure old-fashioned and modern sexism.

While modern racists do not wish to return to the days of segregation, they also feel that minority groups should not push too fast for advancement or receive special treatment by the government. Individuals who endorse statements that favor "modern" discrimination are much more likely to vote against a black political candidate, to oppose school busing and affirmative action, and to favor tax laws that benefit whites at the expense of blacks, compared to those who do not endorse such views (Murrell et al., 1994).

One important trend in the study of prejudice is the recognition that most white people consider the possibility that they might hold racist views to be very

### Items Related to Old-Fashioned Sexism

1. Women are generally not as smart as men.

2. It is more important to encourage boys than to encourage girls to participate in athletics.

### Items Related to Modern Sexism

1. Discrimination against women is no longer a problem in the United States.

2. Over the past few years, the government and news media have been showing more concern about the treatment of women than is warranted by women's actual experiences.

**Scoring:** Possible responses to the statements range from "strongly agree" to "strongly disagree." Individuals who moderately or strongly agree with the above items reflect old-fashioned or modern sexism, respectively.

**FIGURE 7.8**

**Measuring old-fashioned and modern sexism.** Research shows similarities between old-fashioned and modern beliefs about both racism and sexism. Janet Swim and colleagues (1995) have developed a scale to measure the presence of both old-fashioned and modern sexism. Four items from the 13-item scale are shown here. Old-fashioned sexism is characterized by endorsement of traditional gender roles and acceptance of stereotypes that portray females as less competent than males. In contrast, subtle, modern sexism is characterized by denial of continued discrimination and rejection of policies intended to help women.

Source: From Swim, J. K., Aikin, K. J., Hall, W. S., & Hunter, B. A. (1995). Sexism and racism: Old-fashioned and modern prejudices. *Journal of Personality and Social Psychology, 68,* 199–214. Copyright © 1995 American Psychological Association. Adapted by permission of the publisher and the author.

upsetting; indeed, they are conflicted about it. As a result, they avoid acting in any way that might be construed as racist by others or even by themselves. The upshot is that well-intentioned whites can engage in *aversive racism,* an indirect, subtle, ambiguous form of racism that occurs when their conscious endorsement of egalitarian ideals is in conflict with unconscious, negative reactions to minority group members (Dovidio & Gaertner, 2004; Dovidio, Gaertner, & Pearson, 2005; Dovidio et al., 2009). An aversive racist might act in a racist manner when a nonracist excuse is available ("I interviewed several qualified blacks for the job but I had to hire the best candidate, who happened to be white"). Fortunately, researchers are seeking ways to combat such unintended but real bias toward others (Gaertner & Dovidio, 2005). When people cannot reconcile the conflict between their expressed attitudes and how they act, for example, their prejudice decreases (Son Hing, Li, & Zanna, 2002).

## Causes of Prejudice

Prejudice is obviously a complex issue and has multiple causes. Although we can't thoroughly examine all of the causes of prejudice, we'll examine some of the major psychological and social factors that contribute to this vexing problem.

### Authoritarianism

In some of the earliest research on prejudice, Robert Adorno and his colleagues (1950) identified the *authoritarian personality,* a personality type characterized by prejudice toward *any* group perceived to be different from oneself. Subsequent research found serious methodological weaknesses in the study, calling into question the validity of the personality type.

Over the past 50 years, both the definition and measurement of authoritarianism have evolved (Dion, 2003). The construct is now termed *right-wing authoritarianism* (RWA) (Altemeyer, 1988a, 1988b), and it is characterized by authoritarian submission (exaggerated deference to those in power), authoritarian aggression (hostility toward targets sanctioned by authorities), and conventionalism (strong adherence to values endorsed by authorities). Because authoritarians tend to support established authority, RWA is more commonly found among political conservatives than among political liberals (who are more likely to challenge the status quo). RWA has even been linked to the Big Five personality traits (recall Chapter 2) in that authoritarian individuals tend to score low on openness to experience and conscientiousness (Sibley & Duckitt, 2008).

What causes RWAs to be prejudiced? According to Robert Altemeyer (1998), there are two key factors. First, they organize their social world into ingroups and outgroups, and they view outgroups as threatening their

cherished traditional values. Second, they tend to be self-righteous: They believe that they are more moral than others, and they feel justified in derogating groups that authority figures define as immoral. RWAs have typically been reared in highly religious and socially homogeneous groups, with little exposure to minority groups and unconventional behavior. They feel unduly threatened by social change—a fear picked up from their parents who believe that "the world is a dangerous and hostile place" (Altemeyer, 1988b, p. 38). Altemeyer also notes that fearful attitudes are reinforced by the mass media's emphasis on crime and violence. Exposure to diverse kinds of people and perspectives can reduce RWA (Peterson & Lane, 2001).

Authoritarian behavior has been linked with other types of personalities. Recently, a related personality type, *social dominance orientation* (SDO), has received much research attention (Kahn et al., 2009; Sidanius & Pratto, 1999; Son Hing, Bobocel, & Zanna, 2007). People high in SDO prefer inequality among social groups, believing in a hierarchy where some are destined to dominate others, such as men over women, majorities over minorities, or heterosexuals over homosexuals (Pratto et al., 1994). Those low in SDO are less likely to think in terms of a social pecking order where society's "haves" should control what happens to the "have nots." **Figure 7.9** illustrates some sample items from a scale designed to assess SDO.

Can socially dominant feelings like those held by members of a majority race toward minority-group members be reduced? Although changing someone's personality is quite a challenge, there is some evidence that exposing those who believe in inequality between groups to morally worthy behavior can make them

| Sample Items from the Social Dominance Orientation Scale |
| --- |
| Some groups of people are simply inferior to other groups. |
| It's okay if some groups have more of a chance in life than others. |
| If certain groups stayed in their place, we would have fewer problems. |
| It's probably a good thing that certain groups are at the top and other groups are at the bottom. |
| Sometimes other groups must be kept in their place. |

**FIGURE 7.9**

**A preference for social hierarchies.** Social dominance orientation (SDO) refers to a person's preference for maintaining inequality among groups (based on race, gender, religion, social class) in society, so that some groups dominate the others. These five sample items are from the longer 16-item SDO questionnaire. Responses are scored on a 9-point scale ranging from "very negative" to "very positive."

Source: From Pratto, F., Sidanius, J., Stallworth, L. M., & Malle, B. F. (1994). Social dominance orientation: A personality variable predicting social and political attitudes. *Journal of Personality and Social Psychology, 67,* 741–763. Copyright © 1994 American Psychological Association. Adapted by permission of the publisher and the author.

more open minded, if only for a short time. Freeman et al. (2009) elicited feelings of warmth and admiration in participants by having them watch a film clip of actors committing morally good deeds. Later, even individuals high in group-based dominance, a component of SDO, were more likely to donate money to a black-oriented charity compared to those in a control group.

## Cognitive Distortions and Expectations

Much of prejudice is rooted in automatic cognitive processes that operate without conscious intent (Wright & Taylor, 2003). As you recall, *social categorization* predisposes people to divide the social world into ingroups and outgroups. This distinction can trigger negativity toward outgroup members.

Perhaps no factor plays a larger role in prejudice than *stereotyping* (Schneider, 2004). Many people subscribe to derogatory stereotypes of various ethnic groups. Although racial stereotypes have declined over the last 50 years, they're not entirely a thing of the past (Dovidio et al., 2003). Racial profiling, in which law enforcement officers stop motorists, pedestrians, or airline passengers solely on the basis of skin color, is a case in point. Similarly, the events of September 11, 2001 caused some Americans to view all Muslims and Arabs as potential terrorists (Hendricks et al., 2007).

This clever poster, sponsored by the American Civil Liberties Union, focuses a spotlight on the sensitive issue of racial profiling. Racial profiling, which is a manifestation of modern racism, reflects the influence of stereotyping. The phenomenon of racial profiling shows how simple, often automatic, cognitive distortions can have unfortunate consequences in everyday life.

**Which man looks guilty?** If you picked the man on the right, you're wrong.

Wrong for judging people based on the color of their skin. Because if you

look closely, you'll see they're the same man. Unfortunately, racial stereo-

typing like this happens every day. On America's highways, police stop drivers

based on their skin color rather than for the way they are driving. For example,

in Florida 80% of those stopped and searched were black and Hispanic,

while they constituted only 5% of all drivers. These humiliating and illegal

searches are violations of the Constitution and must be fought. Help us defend

your rights. Support the ACLU. www.aclu.org **american civil liberties union**

Our discussion in this chapter has focused on stereotypes that are directed at others—that is, how each person relies on simplified beliefs associating groups of people with particular traits. What happens when individuals are the target of a stereotype used by other people to characterize the group they belong to? Is the stereotype ignored, or does the person internalize its impact?

Consider African Americans, for example. One pernicious stereotype is that African American students perform poorly on standardized tests compared to, say, white students. Claude Steele (1992, 1997) of Columbia University suggests that while socioeconomic disadvantages can serve as an explanatory factor for the underperformance of blacks relative to whites on such tests, there may be other legitimate reasons, including feelings of vulnerability in educational contexts. How so? Steele suggests that the availability and awareness of derogatory stereotypes connected to various stigmatized groups, including blacks, leads to *stereotype vulnerability*, otherwise known as stereotype threat. Feelings of stereotype vulnerability can undermine group members' performance on standardized tests, as well as other measures of academic achievement.

In one study by Steele and Aronson (1995), for example, black and white college students who scored well above average in academic ability were recruited (their comparable academic backgrounds ruled out cultural disadvantage as a factor in the research). All participants were asked to take a challenging 30-minute test of verbal ability composed of items drawn from the Graduate Record Exam (GRE). In one condition, stereotype vulnerability was made salient: The test was described as being an excellent index of a person's general verbal ability. In the other condition, the test was described as a means for researchers to analyze people's problem-solving strategies (thus, not as a measure of intellectual ability). What did Steele and Aronson find? When the African American students' stereotype vulnerability was not emphasized, the performances of black and white students did not differ (see the bars on the left side of **Figure 7.10**). Yet when the same test was presented in a way that increased stereotype threat, the black students scored significantly lower than the white test takers (see the two bars on the right side of **Figure 7.10**).

The impact of stereotype threat has been replicated numerous times (Cadinu et al., 2005; Croizet et al., 2004; Shapiro & Neuberg, 2007). Steele and his colleagues have demonstrated that stereotype threat can influence the performance of a variety of groups, not just minorities, suggesting its applicability to a variety of behavioral phenomena. Thus, for example, women have been shown to be vulnerable to stereotype threat concerning the belief that men perform better on math-related tasks (Spencer, Steele, & Quinn, 1999; Stone & McWhinnie, 2008). In turn, white men have been found

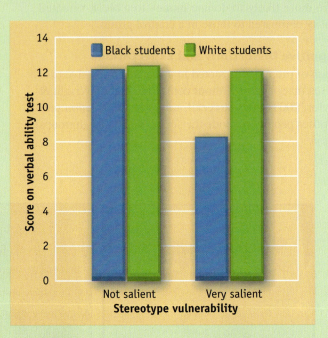

**FIGURE 7.10**
**Stereotype vulnerability and test performance.**
Steele and Aronson (1995) compared the performances of African American and white students of equal ability on a 30-item verbal ability test constructed from difficult GRE questions. When the black students' stereotype vulnerability was not obvious, their performance did not differ from that of the white students; but when the threat of stereotype vulnerability was raised, the African American students performed significantly worse than the white students.

Source: Adapted from Steele, C. M., & Aronson, J. (1995). Stereotype threat and the intellectual test performance of African Americans. *Journal of Personality and Social Psychology, 69,* 797–811. Copyright © 1995 by the American Psychological Association. Reprinted by permission of the author.

to be "threatened" by the stereotype that men of Asian descent are superior when it comes to doing well at mathematics (Aronson et al., 1999).

More recently, some researchers have argued that the election of Barack Obama as the first African American president of the United States has had a beneficial influence on African-Americans' academic accomplishments (Marx, Ko, & Friedman, 2009). Specifically, the "Obama effect" was used to explain an increase in black Americans' on-line exam performance in a quasi-experiment held at four intervals in the summer and fall leading up to and after the 2008 election. Awareness of Obama as a real-world role model was shown to counter the normal impact of stereotype threat by dramatically reducing its incidence in a nationwide random sample of black and white adults. However, a subsequent experiment designed to test the Obama effect failed to confirm the previous findings (Aronson et al., 2009). Clearly, more research needs to be conducted to determine the viability of the Obama effect.

People are more likely to make the *fundamental attribution error* when evaluating targets of prejudice (Hewstone, 1990; Levy, Stroessner, & Dweck, 1998). Thomas Pettigrew (2001) suggests that perceiving negative characteristics as being dispositional (personality based) and due to group membership is the *ultimate attribution error*. Thus, when people take note of ethnic neighborhoods dominated by crime and poverty, they blame these problems on the residents (they're lazy and ignorant) and downplay or ignore situationally based explanations (job discrimination, poor police service, and so on). The old saying, "They should pull themselves up by their own bootstraps" is a blanket dismissal of how situational factors may make it especially difficult for minorities to achieve upward mobility. Similarly, in trying to understand why individuals in some countries hold negative views of the United States, many Americans depict such people as "crazy" or "evil" rather than looking at possible situational causes, such as the negative effects of American foreign policy on their countries or the negative portrayal of the United States in their media.

*Defensive attributions,* in which people unfairly blame victims of adversity to reassure themselves that the same thing won't happen to them, can also contribute to prejudice. For example, individuals who claim that people who contract AIDS deserve it may be trying to reassure themselves that they won't suffer a similar fate.

Expectations can also foster and maintain prejudice. You already know that once people have formed impressions, they are invested in maintaining them. For instance, people note and recall behavior that confirms their stereotypes better than information that is inconsistent with their beliefs (Bodenhausen, 1988). Also, when an outgroup member's behavior contradicts a stereotype, people often "explain away" such behavior to leave their stereotype intact (Ickes et al., 1982). Unfortunately, the fact that social thinking is automatic, selective, and consistent means that people usually see what they expect to see when they look through prejudiced eyes, even when viewing objective presentations from media sources (Vallone, Ross, & Lepper, 1985).

## Competition Between Groups

Back in 1954, Muzafer Sherif and his colleagues conducted a now-classic study at Robbers' Cave State Park in Oklahoma to look at competition and prejudice (Sherif et al., 1961). In this study, 11-year-old white boys were invited, with parental permission, to attend a three-week summer camp. What the boys didn't know was that they were participants in an experiment. The boys were randomly assigned to one of two groups; at camp, they went directly to their assigned campsites and had no knowledge of the other group's presence. During the first week, the boys got to know members of their own group through typical camp activities (hiking, swimming, and camping out); each group also chose a name (the Rattlers and the Eagles).

In the second week, the Rattlers and Eagles were introduced to each other through intergroup competitions. Events included a football game, a treasure hunt, and a tug of war, with medals, trophies, and other desirable prizes for the winning team. Almost immediately after competitive games were introduced, hostile feelings erupted between the two groups and quickly escalated to highly aggressive behavior: Food fights broke out in the mess hall, cabins were ransacked, and group flags were burned. This classic study and more recent research (Schopler & Insko, 1992) suggest that groups often respond more negatively to competition than individuals do.

This experimental demonstration of the effects of competition on prejudice is often mirrored in the real world. For example, disputes over territory often provoke antagonism, as is the case in the former Yugoslavia and in the Israeli-Palestinian conflict. The lack of jobs or other important resources can also create competition between social groups. Still, competition does not always breed prejudice. In fact, the *perception* of threats to one's ingroup (loss of status, for example) is much more likely to cause hostility between groups than actual threats to the ingroup are (Brown et al., 2001; Dovidio et al., 2003). Unfortunately, such perceptions are quite

AP Images/Jeff Roberson

In 2008, the election of our nation's first African American President, Barack Obama, provided minority youth with an important role model. Whether there really is an Obama Effect, however, continues to be debated within the social science community.

common, because ingroup members usually assume that outgroup members are competitive and will try to thwart the ingroup's success (Fiske & Ruscher, 1993). To conclude, there is ample evidence that conflict over actual and perceived scarcity of resources can prejudice individuals toward outgroup members.

## Threats to Social Identity

Although group membership provides individuals with a sense of identity and pride, it can also foster prejudice and discrimination, as we just noted. Members' individual psychologies become merged with group and even societal processes (Turner & Reynolds, 2004). To explore a different facet of this idea, we turn to *social identity theory,* developed by Henri Tajfel (1982) and John Turner (1987). According to this theory, self-esteem is partly determined by one's *social identity,* or collective self, which is tied to one's group memberships (nationality, religion, gender, major, occupation, political party affiliation, and so forth) (Luhtanen & Crocker, 1992; Sidanius, Van Laar, & Levin, 2004). Whereas your personal self-esteem is elevated by individual accomplishments (you got an A on a history exam), your collective self-esteem is boosted when an ingroup is successful (your team wins the football game, your country wins a war). Likewise, your self-esteem can be threatened on both the personal level (you didn't get called for that job interview) and the collective level (your football team loses the championship game, your country is defeated in a war).

Threats to both personal and social identity motivate individuals to restore self-esteem, but threats to social identity are more likely to provoke responses that foster prejudice and discrimination (Crocker & Luhtanen, 1990). When collective self-esteem is threatened, individuals react in two key ways to bolster it. The most common response is to show *ingroup favoritism*—for example, tapping an ingroup member for a job opening or rating the performance of an ingroup member higher than that of an outgroup member (Branscombe et al., 1993; Stroebe, Lodewijkx, & Spears, 2005). In fact, when individuals become wrapped up in identifying with a group, they respond to group criticism as if it were a critique of the self (McCoy & Major, 2003). The second way to deal with threats to social identity is to engage in *outgroup derogation*—in other words, to "trash" outgroups that are perceived as threatening. This latter tactic is especially likely to be used by individuals who identify strongly with an ingroup (Perreault & Bourhis, 1999). **Figure 7.11** depicts the various elements of social identity theory.

Significantly, it is "ingroup love," not "outgroup hate" that underlies most discrimination (Brewer,

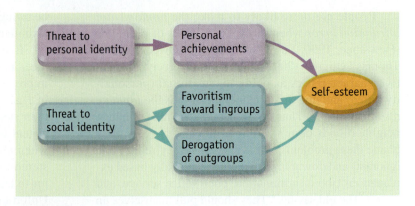

### FIGURE 7.11

**Social identity theory.** According to Tajfel (1982) and Turner (1987), individuals have both a personal identity (based on a unique sense of self) and a social identity (based on group memberships). When social identity is threatened, people are motivated to restore self-esteem by either showing favoritism to ingroup members or derogating outgroup members. These tactics contribute to prejudice and discrimination.

Source: Adapted from Brehm, S. S., & Kassin, S. M. (1993). *Social psychology.* Boston: Houghton Mifflin. Copyright © 1993 by Houghton Mifflin Company. Adapted with permission.

1999). In other words, ingroups reward their own members and withhold rewards from outgroups, rather than deliberately blocking outgroups from desired resources (Fiske, 2002). And here's the final rub: Ingroup favoritism is often subtle and can be triggered by arbitrary and inconsequential factors, such as shared musical tastes (Lonsdale & North, 2009).

## Reducing Prejudice

For decades, psychologists have searched for ways to reduce prejudice. Such a complicated problem requires solutions on a number of levels. Let's look at a few interventions that have been shown to help.

### Cognitive Strategies

Because stereotypes are part of the social air that people breathe, practically everyone learns stereotypes about various groups. This means that stereotyped thinking about others becomes a mindless habit—even for individuals who have been taught to be tolerant of those who are different from themselves (Devine, 1989; Fiske, 2002).

Although it's true that stereotypes kick in automatically, unintentionally, and unconsciously, individuals *can* override them—with some cognitive effort (Fiske, 2002). Thus, if you meet someone who speaks with an accent, your initial, automatic reaction might be negative. However, if you believe that prejudice is wrong and if you are aware that you are stereotyping, you can intentionally inhibit such thoughts. According to Patricia Devine's (1989) model of prejudice reduction, this process requires an intentional shift from *automatic processing* to *controlled processing*—or from *mindlessness* to *mindfulness,* in Ellen Langer's terms (see

Chapters 6 and 16). Thus, you can reduce prejudice if you are motivated to pay careful attention to what and how you think.

## Intergroup Contact

Let's return to the Robbers' Cave study. When we left them, the Rattlers and Eagles were engaged in food fights and flag burning. Understandably, the experimenters were eager to restore peace. First, they tried speaking with each group, talking up the other group's good points and minimizing their differences. They also made the Eagles and the Rattlers sit together at meals and "fun" events like movies. Unfortunately, these tactics fell flat.

Next, the experimenters designed intergroup activities based on the principle of *superordinate goals*—goals that require two or more groups to work together to achieve mutual ends. For example, each boy had to contribute in some way (building a fire, preparing the food) on a cookout so that all could eat. After the boys had participated in a variety of such activities, the hostility between the two groups was much reduced. In fact, at the end of the three-week camping period, the Eagles and the Rattlers voted to ride the same bus back home. Cooperating to reach common goals, then, can reduce conflict (Bay-Hinitz, Peterson, & Quilitch, 1994)

Researchers have identified four necessary ingredients in the recipe for reducing intergroup hostility (Brewer & Brown, 1998). First, groups must *work together for a common goal*—merely bringing hostile groups into contact is not an effective way to reduce intergroup antagonism and may in fact worsen it. Second, cooperative efforts must have *successful outcomes*—if groups fail at a cooperative task, they are likely to blame each other for the failure. Third, group members must have the opportunity to establish *meaningful connections* with one another and not merely go through the motions of interacting. The fourth factor of *equal status contact* requires bringing together members of different groups in ways that ensure that everyone has equal status. A large meta-analysis demonstrated clear support for intergroup contact that meets these conditions as a means of reducing prejudice (Pettigrew & Tropp, 2000, 2006).

What about the contact hypothesis in collegiate life? Shook and Fazio (2008) conducted a field experiment in which white college students were randomly assigned to share a dorm room with a white or a black roommate. Although students in the interracial situation did report less satisfaction with their roommates than those with same-race assignments, there was an important positive outcome of contact in this housing experiment. Those students living in the interracial rooms were found to be less prejudiced across time compared to those with same-race living arrangements.

# *The Power of Persuasion*

### LEARNING OBJECTIVES

- Cite the key elements in the persuasion process.
- Describe several source factors that influence persuasion.
- Discuss the evidence on one-sided versus two-sided messages and the value of arousing fear or positive feelings in persuasion.

- Identify several receiver factors that influence persuasion.
- Explain how the two cognitive routes to persuasion operate.

Every day you are bombarded by attempts to alter your attitudes through persuasion. You may not even be out of bed before you start hearing radio advertisements that are meant to persuade you to buy specific toothpastes, cell phones, and athletic shoes. When you watch the morning news, you hear statements from numerous government officials, all of which have been carefully crafted to shape your opinions. On your way to school, you see billboards showing attractive models draped over cars in the hopes that they can induce positive feelings that will transfer to the vehicles. Walking to class, a friend tries to get you to vote for his candidate for student body president. "Does it ever let up?" you wonder.

When it comes to persuasion, the answer is "no." As Anthony Pratkanis and Elliot Aronson (2000) note, Americans live in the "age of propaganda." In light of

this reality, let's examine some of the factors that determine whether persuasion works.

*Persuasion* **involves the communication of arguments and information intended to change another person's attitudes.** What are attitudes? For the purposes of our discussion, we'll define *attitudes* **as beliefs and feelings about people, objects, and ideas.** Let's look more closely at two of the terms in this definition. We use the term *beliefs* to mean thoughts and judgments about people, objects, and ideas. For example, you may *believe* that equal pay for equal work is a fair policy or that capital punishment is not an effective deterrent to crime. The "feeling" component of attitudes refers to the positivity and negativity of one's feelings about an issue as well as how strongly one feels about it. For example, you may *strongly favor* equal pay for equal work but only *mildly disagree* with the idea that capital punishment reduces the crime rate. Psychologists assume that attitudes predict behavior (Albarraci, Johnson, & Zanna, 2005; Petty & Fazio, 2008)—if you are favorably disposed toward some new product, you are likely to buy it; if not, you won't (Eagly & Chaiken, 1998). Of course, there is more to the persuasion side of the attitude-behavior relation: Read on.

## Elements of the Persuasion Process

The process of persuasion or attitude change (Crano & Prislin, 2008) includes four basic elements (see **Figure 7.12**). The *source* **is the person who sends a communication, and the** *receiver* **is the person to whom the message is sent.** Thus, if you watched a presidential address on TV, the president would be the source, and you and millions of other viewers would be the receivers in this persuasive effort. **The** *message* **is the information transmitted by the source; the** *channel* **is the medium through which the message is sent.** In examining communication channels, investigators have often compared face-to-face interaction against appeals sent via mass media (such as television and radio). Although the research on communication channels is interesting, we'll confine our discussion to source, message, and receiver variables.

### Source Factors

Persuasion tends to be more successful when the source has high *credibility* (Petty, Wegener, & Fabrigar, 1997). Two subfactors make a communicator credible: expertise and trustworthiness (Hovland & Weiss, 1951). People try to convey their *expertise* by mentioning their degrees, their training, and their experience, or by showing an impressive grasp of the issue at hand (Wood

& Kallgren, 1988). As to *trustworthiness,* whom would you believe if you were told that your state needs to reduce corporate taxes to stimulate its economy—the president of a huge corporation in your state or an economics professor from out of state? Probably the latter. Trustworthiness is undermined when a source, such as the corporation president, appears to have something to gain. In contrast, trustworthiness is enhanced when people appear to argue against their own interests (Petty et al., 2001). This effect explains why salespeople often make remarks like "Frankly, my snowblower isn't the best and they have a better brand down the street if you're willing to spend a bit more . . ."

*Likability* is a second major source factor and includes a number of subfactors (Petty et al., 1997). A key consideration is a person's *physical attractiveness* (Petty et al., 1997). For example, one researcher found that attractive students were more successful than less attractive students in obtaining signatures for a petition (Chaiken, 1979). People also respond better to sources who are *similar* to them in ways that are relevant to the issue at hand (Mackie, Worth, & Asuncion, 1990). Thus, politicians stress the values they and their constituents hold in common.

Source variables are used to great effect in advertising. Many companies spend a fortune to obtain a spokesperson such as George Foreman, who combines trustworthiness, likability, and a knack for connecting with the average person. Companies quickly abandon spokespersons whose likability declines. For example, many companies cancelled endorsement contracts with basketball star Kobe Bryant and golf legend Tiger Woods after they were implicated in tawdry sexual affairs. Thus, source variables are extremely important factors in persuasion.

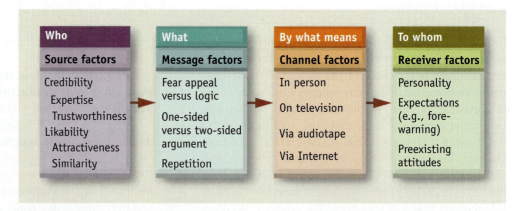

**FIGURE 7.12**
**Overview of the persuasion process.** The process of persuasion essentially boils down to *who* (the source) communicates *what* (the message) *by what means* (the channel) *to whom* (the receiver). Thus, four sets of variables influence the process of persuasion: source, message, channel, and receiver factors. The diagram lists some of the more important factors in each category (including some that are not discussed in the text because of space limitations).

Advertisers frequently employ well-liked celebrities such as Catherine Zeta-Jones to pitch their products, hoping that the positive feelings of the audience toward the source will transfer to the product.

## Message Factors

Imagine that you are going to advocate the selection of a high-profile entertainer as the speaker at your commencement ceremony. In preparing your argument, you ponder the most effective way to structure your message. On the one hand, you're convinced that having a well-known entertainer on campus would be popular with students and would boost the image of your university in the community and among alumni. Still, you realize that this performer would cost a lot and that some people believe that an entertainer is not an appropriate commencement speaker. Should you present a *one-sided argument* that ignores the possible problems? Or should you present a *two-sided argument* that acknowledges concern about the problems and then downplays them?

In general, two-sided arguments seem to be more effective (Crowley & Hoyer, 1994). In fact, just mentioning that there are two sides to an issue can increase your credibility with an audience (Jones & Brehm, 1970). One-sided messages work only when your audience is uneducated about the issue or when they already favor your point of view.

Persuaders also use emotional appeals to shift attitudes. Insurance companies show scenes of homes on fire to arouse fear. Antismoking campaigns emphasize the threat of cancer. Deodorant ads prey on the fear of embarrassment. Does *fear arousal* work? Yes, studies involving a wide range of issues (nuclear policy, auto safety, and dental hygiene among others) have shown that the arousal of fear often increases persuasion (Perloff, 1993). And fear appeals are influential if people feel susceptible to the threat (De Hoog et al., 2007). However, there are limiting conditions (Rogers & Prentice-Dunn, 1997). Fear appeals are most likely to work when your listeners already agree with you (Keller, 1999) or view the dire consequences that you describe as exceedingly unpleasant, as fairly probable if they don't take your advice, and as avoidable if they do (Das, deWit, & Stroebe, 2003). If you induce strong fear in your audience without providing a workable solution to the problem (such as a surefire stop-smoking or weight-loss program), you may make your audience defensive, causing them to tune you out (Petty & Wegener, 1998).

Generating *positive feelings* is also an effective way to persuade people. Familiar examples of such tactics include the use of music and physically attractive actors in TV commercials, the use of laugh tracks in TV programs, and the practice of wining and dining prospective customers. People attend better to humorous messages than sober ones (Duncan & Nelson, 1985); later, they may recall that something was funny but forget what it was about (Cantor & Venus, 1980). Shortly after the 2001 terrorist attacks on America, you probably noticed that patriotic themes and images in ads increased dramatically. Producing positive feelings to win people over *can* be effective—provided they don't care too much about the issue. If people do care about the topic, it takes more than good feelings to move them. For example, one study showed that the use of music in TV commercials was effective in persuading viewers, but only when the message concerned a trivial topic (Park & Young, 1986).

## Receiver Factors

What about the receiver of the persuasive message? Are some people easier to persuade than others? Yes, but the answer is complicated. For instance, receptivity to a message can sometimes depend on people's *moods:* optimistic people process uplifting messages better than pessimists, who are drawn to counter-attitudinal communications, or those opposing their current views (Wegener & Petty, 1994). Other people want to think deeply about issues, having a so-called **need for cognition, the tendency to seek out and enjoy effortful thought, problem-solving activities, and in-depth analysis**. Such people, who truly relish intellectual give-and-take as well as debate, are more likely to be convinced by high-quality arguments than those who prefer more superficial analyses (Cacioppo et al., 1996). Moreover, they are more likely to be motivated to process complex messages more carefully (See et al., 2009).

Transient factors also matter in receptivity to persuasive messages. *Forewarning* the receiver about a persuasive effort and a receiver's initial position on an issue, for instance, seem to be more influential than a receiver's personality. When you shop for a new TV or a car, you expect salespeople to work at persuading you. To some extent, this forewarning reduces the impact of their arguments (Petty & Wegener, 1998). When receivers are forewarned about a persuasion attempt on a personally important topic, it is harder to persuade them than when they are not forewarned (Wood & Quinn, 2003). But when they are told to expect a persuasive message on an unimportant topic, their attitudes shift in the direction of the persuasive appeal even before it occurs—to avoid appearing gullible! Thus, the old saying, "To be forewarned is to be forearmed" is often true.

Understandably, receivers are harder to persuade when they encounter a position that is incompatible with their existing beliefs. In general, people display a *disconfirmation bias* in evaluating such arguments (Edwards & Smith, 1996). Also, people from different cultures respond to different themes in persuasive messages. In one study, participants from an individualistic culture (the United States) preferred magazine ads that stressed the theme of uniqueness, while those from a collectivist culture (Korea) preferred ads that stressed conformity (Kim & Markus, 1999).

## The Whys of Persuasion

*Why* do people change their attitudes in response to persuasive messages? Thanks to the work of Richard Petty and John Cacioppo (1986), psychologists have a good understanding of the cognitive processes that underlie attitude change.

**Richard Petty**

**John Cacioppo**

According to the *elaboration likelihood model,* an individual's thoughts about a persuasive message (rather than the actual message itself) will determine whether attitude change will occur (Benoit & Benoit, 2008; Petty & Cacioppo, 1986; Petty et al., 2005). As we have noted, sometimes people make quick, sloppy decisions (automatic processing, mindlessness, snap judgments), whereas at other times they process information carefully (controlled processing, mindfulness, systematic judgments). Sometimes people choose to think, others times they choose not to. These processes also operate in persuasion, with messages sometimes persuading receivers through a *peripheral* route and sometimes through a *central* route.

When people are distracted, tired, or uninterested in a persuasive message, they fail to key in on the true merits of the product or issue. They do process information, but not mindfully. Being in a happy mood can produce the same effect (Sinclair, Mark, & Clore, 1994). Surprisingly, even when people do not carefully evaluate a message, attitude change can occur (Petty & Cacioppo, 1990). What happens is that the receiver is persuaded by cues that are peripheral to the message—thus the term *peripheral route* (see **Figure 7.13**). Just because you're not mindfully analyzing a TV commercial for a new fruit drink doesn't mean that you're totally tuned out. You may not be paying attention to the substance of the commercial, but you are aware of superficial aspects of the ad—you like the music, your favorite basketball player is pitching the product, and boy, that beach scene sure looks nice.

Although persuasion usually occurs via the peripheral route, senders can also use another route to

**FIGURE 7.13**

**The peripheral and central routes to persuasion.** Persuasion can occur via two different routes. The central route, which results in high elaboration, tends to produce longer-lasting attitude change and stronger attitudes than the peripheral route.

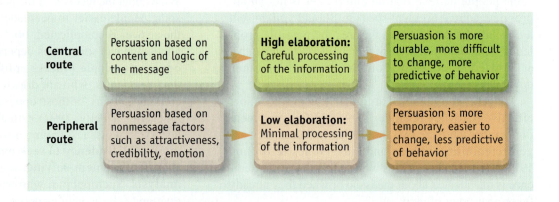

| Central route | Persuasion based on content and logic of the message | **High elaboration:** Careful processing of the information | Persuasion is more durable, more difficult to change, more predictive of behavior |
| Peripheral route | Persuasion based on nonmessage factors such as attractiveness, credibility, emotion | **Low elaboration:** Minimal processing of the information | Persuasion is more temporary, easier to change, less predictive of behavior |

attitude change—the *central route* (see **Figure 7.13**). In this case, receivers process persuasive messages mindfully, by thinking about the logic and merits of the pertinent (or central) arguments. In other words, the receiver cognitively *elaborates* on the persuasive message—hence, the name of the model—and messages that receive greater and deeper processing are more resistant to persuasion (Blankenship & Wegener, 2008). If people have a favorable reaction to their thoughtful evaluation of a message, positive attitude change occurs; an unfavorable reaction results in negative attitude change.

For the central route to override the peripheral route, two requirements must be met. First, receivers must be *motivated* to process the persuasive message carefully. Motivation is triggered when people are interested in the issue, find it personally relevant, have a high need for cognition, and have time and energy to think about it carefully. For example, if your university is considering changing its grading system, you will probably make a point of thinking carefully about the various options and their implications. Second, receivers must have the *ability* to grasp the message—that is, the message must be comprehensible, and individuals must be capable of understanding it. If people are distracted, tired, or find the message uninteresting or irrelevant, they will not pay careful attention to it, and superficial cues will become salient.

Ultimately, the two routes to persuasion are not equally effective. Attitudes formed via the central route are longer lasting and more resistant to challenge than those formed via the peripheral route (Petty & Wegener, 1998). They are also better predictors of a person's behavior (Petty, Priester, & Wegener, 1994).

To conclude, although we can't stem the tide of persuasive messages bombarding you every day, we hope we've alerted you to the need to be a vigilant recipient of persuasion attempts. Of course, persuasion is not the *only* method through which people try to influence you, as you'll see in the next section.

Political candidates use music, flags, and slogans to persuade via the peripheral route; when they present their views on an issue, they are going for the central route.

*© David McNew/Getty Images*

## Recommended READING

### Influence: Science and Practice
by Robert B. Cialdini (Collins, 2007)

Cialdini, a social psychologist, has conducted extensive research on a host of social influence tactics (see the Application). As you might expect, Cialdini's book is based on his studies and his review of other scientific research on the topic. However, what makes his book unique is that he went far beyond laboratory research in his effort to better understand the ins and outs of social influence. For three years, he immersed himself in the real world of influence artists, becoming a "spy of sorts." As he puts it, "When I wanted to learn about the compliance tactics of encyclopedia (or vacuum cleaner, or portrait photography, or dance lessons) sales organizations, I would answer a newspaper ad for sales trainees and have them teach me their methods. Using similar but not identical approaches, I was able to penetrate advertising, public relations, and fundraising agencies to examine their techniques" (from the preface). The result is an insightful book that bolsters scientific data with anecdotal accounts of how influence artists ply their trade. Familiarity with their strategies can help you avoid being an easy mark, or "patsy."

*Go to the Psychology CourseMate for Weiten at* **www.cengagebrain.com/shop/ISBN/1111186634** *for descriptions of other recommended books.*

# The Power of Social Pressure

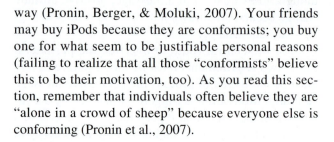

**LEARNING OBJECTIVES**

- Summarize what Asch discovered about conformity.
- Distinguish between normative and informational influences on conformity.
- Identify some conformity pressures in everyday life and how people can resist them.
- Describe Milgram's research on obedience to authority.
- Cite an important factor in resisting inappropriate demands of authority figures.

In the previous section, we showed you how others attempt to change your *attitudes*. Now you'll see how others attempt to change your *behavior*—by trying to get you to agree to their requests and demands.

## Conformity and Compliance Pressures

If you extol the talent of popular singer Taylor Swift or keep a well-manicured lawn, are you exhibiting conformity? According to social psychologists, it depends on whether your behavior is freely chosen or the result of group pressure. *Conformity* **occurs when people yield to real or imagined social pressure.** For example, if you like Taylor Swift because you truly enjoy her music, that's not conformity. However, if you like her because it's "cool" and your friends would question your taste if you didn't, then you're conforming. Similarly, if you maintain a well-groomed lawn just to avoid complaints from your neighbors, you're yielding to social pressure. In short, people are apt to explain the behavior of others as conforming but not think of their own actions this

way (Pronin, Berger, & Moluki, 2007). Your friends may buy iPods because they are conformists; you buy one for what seem to be justifiable personal reasons (failing to realize that all those "conformists" believe this to be their motivation, too). As you read this section, remember that individuals often believe they are "alone in a crowd of sheep" because everyone else is conforming (Pronin et al., 2007).

### The Dynamics of Conformity

To introduce this topic, we'll re-create a classic experiment devised by Solomon Asch (1955). The participants are male undergraduates recruited for a study of visual perception. A group of seven participants are shown a large card with a vertical line on it and asked to indicate which of three lines on a second card matches the original "standard line" in length (see **Figure 7.14**). All seven participants are given a turn at the task, and each announces his choice to the group. The subject in the sixth chair doesn't know it, but everyone else in the group is an accomplice of the experimenter.

The accomplices give accurate responses on the first two trials. On the third trial, line 2 clearly is the correct response, but the first five participants all say that line 3 matches the standard line. The genuine subject can't believe his ears. Over the course of the experiment, the accomplices all give the same incorrect response on 12 out of 18 trials. Asch wanted to see how the subject would respond in these situations. The line judgments are easy and unambiguous. Without group pressure, people make matching errors less than 1% of the time. So, if the subject consistently agrees with the accomplices, he isn't making honest mistakes—he is conforming. Will the subject stick to his guns, or will he go along with the group? Asch (1955) found that the men conformed (made mistakes) on 37% of the 12 trials. The subjects varied considerably in their tendency to conform, however. Of the 50 participants, 13

Conformity is far more common than most people appreciate. We all conform to social expectations in an endless variety of ways. There is nothing inherently good or bad about conforming to social pressures; it all depends on the situation. However, it is prudent to be aware of how social expectations can sometimes have a profound influence on our behavior.

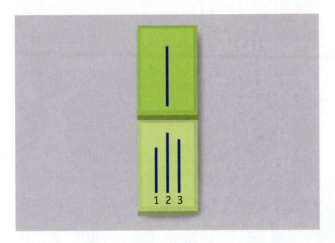

**FIGURE 7.14**

**Stimuli used in Asch's conformity studies.** Subjects were asked to match a standard line (top) with one of three other lines displayed on another card (bottom). The task was easy—until experimental accomplices started responding with obviously incorrect answers, creating a situation in which Asch evaluated subjects' conformity.

Source: Adapted from illustration on p. 35 by Sarah Love in Asch, S. (1955, November). Opinions and social pressure. *Scientific American, 193*(5), 31–35. Copyright © 1955 by Scientific American, Inc.

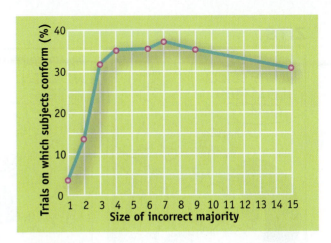

**FIGURE 7.15**

**Conformity and group size.** This graph shows the percentage of trials on which participants conformed as a function of the number of individuals with an opposing view. Asch found that conformity became more frequent as group size increased, up to about 7 persons, and then leveled off.

Source: Adapted from illustration on p. 32 by Sarah Love in Asch, S. (1955, November). Opinions and social pressure. *Scientific American,193*(5), 31–35. Copyright © 1955 by Scientific American, Inc.

never caved in to the group, while 14 conformed on more than half the trials. One could argue that the results show that people confronting a unanimous majority generally tend to *resist* the pressure to conform, but given how clear and easy the line judgments were, most social scientists viewed the findings as a dramatic demonstration of humans' propensity to conform.

In subsequent studies, Asch (1956) determined that group size and group unanimity are key determinants of conformity. To examine group size, Asch repeated his procedure with groups that included 1 to 15 accomplices. Little conformity was seen when a subject was pitted against just one accomplice. Conformity increased rapidly as group size went from 2 to 4, peaked at a group size of 7, and then leveled off (see **Figure 7.15**). Thus, Asch concluded that as group size increases, conformity increases—up to a point. Significantly, Asch found that group size made little difference if just one accomplice "broke" with the others, wrecking their unanimous agreement. The presence of another dissenter lowered conformity to about one-quarter of its peak, even when the dissenter made inaccurate judgments that happened to conflict with the majority view. Apparently, the participants just needed to hear a second person question the accuracy of the group's perplexing responses. Recent research suggests that when individuals have a high need for uniqueness—that is, when they feel indistinguishable from others and are motivated to reestablish a sense of individuality—they can resist majority pressures to conform (Imhoff & Erb, 2009).

## Conformity Versus Compliance

Did the conforming participants in Asch's study really change their beliefs in response to social pressure, or did they just pretend to change them? Subsequent studies asked participants to make their responses privately, instead of publicly (Deutsch & Gerard, 1955; Insko et al., 1985). Conformity declined dramatically when participants wrote down their responses. Thus, it is likely that Asch's participants did not really change their beliefs. Based on this evidence, theorists concluded that Asch's experiments evoked a particular type of conformity, called compliance. *Compliance* **occurs when people yield to social pressure in their public behavior, even though their private beliefs have not changed.** For example, many people comply with modest group pressure daily—they "dress up" for work by wearing suits, ties, dresses, and so on—when they would prefer to wear more casual clothing.

## The Whys of Conformity

People often conform or comply because they are afraid of being criticized or rejected. *Normative influence* **operates when people conform to social norms for fear of negative social consequences.** Compliance often results from subtle, implied pressure. For example, for fear of making a negative impression, you may remove your eyebrow ring for a job interview. However, compliance also occurs in response to explicit rules, requests, and commands. Thus, you'll probably follow your boss's instructions even when you think they're lousy ideas.

ZITS © 2006 ZITS Partnership, King Features Syndicate

People are also likely to conform when they are uncertain how to behave (Cialdini, 2001; Sherif, 1936). Thus, if you're at a nice restaurant and don't know which fork to use, you may watch others to see what they're doing. *Informational influence* **operates when people look to others for how to behave in ambiguous situations.** In situations like this, using others as a source of information about appropriate behavior is a good thing. But relying on others to know how to behave in unfamiliar situations can sometimes be problematic, as you'll see shortly.

### Resisting Conformity Pressures

Sometimes conforming is just harmless fun—such as participating in Internet-generated "flash mobs." At other times, people conform on relatively trivial matters—such as dressing up for a nice restaurant. In this case, conformity and compliance minimize the confusion and anxiety people experience in unfamiliar situations. However, when individuals feel pressured to conform to antisocial norms, tragic consequences may result. Negative examples of "going along with the crowd" include drinking more than one knows one should because others say, "C'mon, have just one more" and driving at someone's urging when under the influence of alcohol or drugs. Other instances include refusing to socialize with someone simply because the person isn't liked by one's social group and failing to come to another's defense when it might make one unpopular.

The above examples all concern normative influence, but pressure can come from informational influence as well. A useful example concerns a paradox called **the** *bystander effect*—**the tendency for individuals to be less likely to provide help when others are present than when they are alone.** Numerous studies have confirmed that people are less helpful in emergency situations when others are around (Latané and Nida, 1981; Levine et al., 1994). This effect even shows up on the Internet, when members of different-sized

chat groups receive requests for assistance (Markey, 2000). Thankfully, the bystander effect is less likely to occur when the need for help is very clear (Fischer, Greitemeyer, & Pollozek, 2006).

What accounts for the bystander effect? A number of factors are at work, and conformity is one of them. The bystander effect is most likely to occur in *ambiguous situations,* because people look around to see whether others are acting as if there's an emergency (Harrison & Wells, 1991). If everyone hesitates, this inaction (informational influence) suggests that help isn't needed. So the next time you witness what you think might be an emergency, don't automatically give in to the informational influence of inaction.

To resist conformity pressures, we offer these suggestions: First, make an effort to pay more attention to the social forces operating on you. Second, if you find yourself in a situation where others are pressuring you, try to identify someone in the group whose views match yours. Recall that just one dissenter in Asch's groups significantly reduced conformity pressures. And, if you know in advance that you're heading into this kind of situation, consider inviting a friend with similar views to go along.

## Pressure from Authority Figures

*Obedience* **is a form of compliance that occurs when people follow direct commands, usually from someone in a position of authority.** In itself, obedience isn't good or bad; it depends on what one is being told to do. For example, if the fire alarm goes off in your classroom building and your instructor "orders" you to leave, obedience is a good idea. On the other hand, if your boss asks you to engage in an unethical or illegal act, *disobedience* is probably in order.

### The Dynamics of Obedience

Like many other people after World War II, social psychologist Stanley Milgram was troubled by how readily the citizens of Germany had followed the orders of dictator Adolf Hitler, even when the orders required morally repugnant actions, such as the slaughter of millions of Jews, as well as Russians, Poles, Gypsies, and homosexuals (Blass, 2004). This observation was Milgram's motivation to study the dynamics of obedience. Milgram's (1963) participants were a diverse collection of 40 men from the local community who volunteered for a study on the effects of punishment on learning. When they arrived at the lab, they drew slips of paper from a hat to get their assignments. The drawing was rigged so that the subject always became the "teacher" and an experimental accomplice (a likable 47-year-old accountant) became the "learner."

**Stanley Milgram**

The teacher watched while the learner was strapped into a chair and electrodes were attached to his arms (to be used to deliver shocks whenever he made a mistake on the task). The subject was then taken to an adjoining room that housed the shock generator that he would control in his role as the teacher. Although the apparatus looked and sounded realistic, it was a fake, and the learner was never shocked. The experimenter played the role of the authority figure who told the teacher what to do and who answered any questions that arose.

The experiment was designed such that the learner would make many mistakes, and the teacher was in-

**WEB LINK 7.4   Stanley Milgram**

This site provides a wealth of accurate information about the work of Stanley Milgram, arguably one of the most controversial and creative social psychologists in the field's history. The site is maintained by Thomas Blass, a psychology professor at the University of Maryland (Baltimore County), who has published many articles and books on the life and work of Milgram.

structed to increase the shock level after each wrong answer. At 300 volts, the learner began to pound on the wall between the two rooms in protest and soon stopped responding to the teacher's questions. From this point forward, participants frequently turned to the experimenter for guidance. Whenever they did so, the experimenter (authority figure) firmly stated that the teacher should continue to give stronger and stronger shocks to the now-silent learner. Milgram wanted to know the maximum shock the teacher was willing to administer before refusing to cooperate.

As **Figure 7.16** shows, 65% of the subjects administered all 30 levels of shock. Although they tended to obey the experimenter, many participants voiced and displayed considerable distress about harming the learner. They protested, groaned, bit their lips, trembled, and broke into a sweat—but they continued administering the shocks. Based on these findings, Milgram concluded that obedience to authority was even more common than he or others had anticipated. A recent

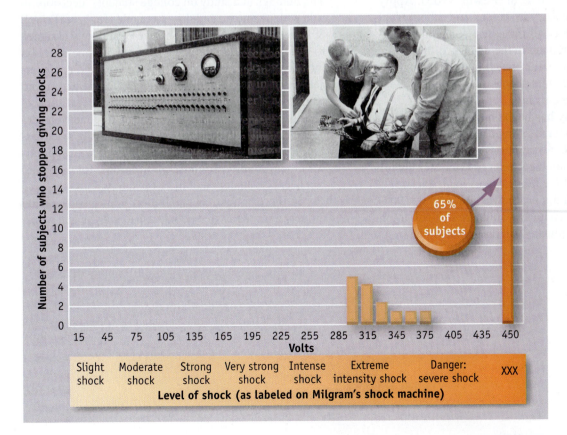

**FIGURE 7.16**
**Milgram's (1963) experiment on obedience.** The photos show the fake shock generator and the "learner" being connected to the shock generator during an experimental session. The results of the study are summarized in the bar graph. The vast majority of subjects (65%) delivered the entire series of shocks to the learner.

Photos copyright © 1965 by Stanley Milgram. From the film *Obedience,* distributed by The Pennsylvania State University. Reprinted by permission of Alexandra Milgram.

replication by Burger (2009) suggests Milgram's conclusion still stands: Although participants were stopped at the 150 volt level for ethical reasons, 70% continued to shock the learner despite hearing cries of anguish (Milgram found that 80% of his participants continued to shock after 150 volts).

## The Causes of Obedience

After his initial demonstration, Milgram (1974) tried about 20 variations on his experimental procedure, looking for factors that influenced participants' obedience. For instance, he studied female participants to look at gender differences in obedience (he found no evidence of such differences). In another condition, two confederates played the role of teachers who defied the experimenter's demands to continue, one at 150 volts and one at 210 volts. In this condition, only 10% of the subjects shocked at the maximum level.

What caused the obedient behavior observed by Milgram? First, the demands on the participants (to shock the learner) escalated gradually so that very strong shocks were demanded only after the participant was well into the experiment. Second, participants were told that the authority figure, not the teacher, was responsible if anything happened to the learner. Third, subjects evaluated their actions in terms of how well they lived up to the authority figure's expectations, not by their harmful effects on the victim. Taken together, these findings suggest that human behavior is determined not so much by the *kind of person* one is as by the *kind of situation* one is in (Lewin, 1935). Applying this insight to Nazi war crimes and other atrocities, Milgram made a chilling assertion: Inhuman and evil visions may originate in the disturbed mind of an authority figure like Hitler, but it is only through the obedient actions of normal people that such ideas can be turned into frightening reality.

Milgram's study has been consistently replicated for many years, in diverse settings, with a variety of participants and procedural variations (Blass, 1999, 2000; Burger, 2009). Overall, the weight of evidence supports Milgram's results. Of course, critics have questioned the ethics of Milgram's procedure (Baumrind, 1964). Today, at most universities it would be difficult to obtain permission to replicate Milgram's study—an ironic epitaph for what may be psychology's best-known experiment.

**WEB LINK 7.5  Stanford Prison Experiment**

The Stanford Prison Simulation is one of psychology's most renowned studies. Like Milgram's study of obedience, Phil Zimbardo's study provided a dramatic demonstration of the power of situational factors and how they can promote conformity and obedience. The site includes a slideshow explaining the study in depth. Also included are reflections on the study 30 years after it was conducted and recent writings by Zimbardo that analyze the Abu Ghraib prison scandal.

## To Obey or Not to Obey?

The findings of obedience research confront us with the chilling fact that most people can be coerced into engaging in actions that violate their morals and values. Perhaps you've heard of the 1968 My Lai incident, an American "crime of obedience," in which U.S. military forces killed 400–500 Vietnamese women, children, and elderly men (Kelman & Hamilton, 1989). The Abu Ghraib prison scandal in Iraq is a more recent reminder that strong social pressures can produce morally repugnant behavior (Fiske, Harris, & Cuddy, 2004).

In keeping with Milgram's finding that participants in the condition with two disobedient confederates found it easier to defy authority, it seems that social support plays a critical role in disobedient behavior. The findings of a study on college students' decisions to ride with an intoxicated driver are relevant here (Powell & Drucker, 1997). Participants were randomly assigned to one of four conditions: (1) driver with one beer, (2) intoxicated driver, (3) intoxicated driver and confederate who enters the car, and (4) intoxicated driver and confederate who refuses to enter the car. Participants consistently chose to enter the car in all conditions except when the confederate refused. Especially when disobedience involves risk, aligning oneself with supportive others (family, friends, labor unions, for example) can decrease anxiety and increase safety.

In the Application, we'll alert you to some social influence strategies that people use to get you and others to agree to their requests.

# Seeing Through Compliance Tactics

### LEARNING OBJECTIVES

- Describe two compliance strategies based on the principles of consistency.
- Recognize some compliance strategies based on the principle of reciprocity.
- Discuss how the principle of scarcity can increase a person's desire for something.

*Which of the following statements is true?*

___ **1.** It's a good idea to ask for a small favor before soliciting the larger favor that you really want.

___ **2.** It's a good idea to ask for a large favor before soliciting the smaller favor that you really want.

Would you believe that *both* of these conflicting statements are true? Although the two approaches work for different reasons, both can be effective ways to get people to do what you want. It pays to understand these and other social influence strategies because advertisers, salespeople, and fundraisers (not to mention friends and neighbors) use them frequently to influence people's behavior. So you can see the relevance of these strategies to your own life, we've grouped them by the principles that make them work. Much of our discussion is based on the work of Robert Cialdini (2007), a social psychologist who spent years observing social influence tactics used by compliance professionals. His book, *Influence: Science and Practice,* is an excellent and entertaining discussion of social influence principles in action.

*Courtesy Robert Cialdini*

**Robert Cialdini**

## The Consistency Principle

Once people agree to something, they tend to stick with their initial commitment (Cialdini, 2007). This tendency to prefer consistency in one's behavior is used to gain compliance in two ways. Both involve a person getting another individual to commit to an initial request and then changing the terms of the agreement to the requestor's advantage. Because people often stay with their initial commitments, the target will likely agree to the revised proposal, even though it may not be to his or her benefit.

### The Foot-in-the-Door Technique

Door-to-door salespeople have long recognized the importance of gaining a *little* cooperation from sales targets (getting a "foot in the door") before hitting them with the real sales pitch. **The *foot-in-the-door* (FITD)** **technique involves getting people to agree to a small request to increase the chances that they will agree to a larger request later** (see **Figure 7.17a** on the next page). This technique is widely used. For example, groups seeking donations often ask people to simply sign a petition first. Salespeople routinely ask individuals to try a product with "no obligations" before they launch their hard sell. In a similar vein, a wife might ask her husband to get her a cup of coffee, and when he gets up to fetch it say, "While you're up, would you fix me a peanut butter sandwich?"

The FITD technique was first investigated by Jonathon Freedman and his colleagues. In one study (Freedman & Fraser, 1966), the large request involved telephoning homemakers to ask whether a team of six men doing consumer research could come into their home to classify all their household products. Imagine six strangers trampling through your home, pulling everything out of your closets and cupboards, and you can understand why only 22% of the subjects in the control group agreed to this outlandish request. Subjects in the experimental group were contacted three days before the unreasonable request was made and were asked to answer a few questions about the soaps used in their home. When the large request was made three days later, 53% of the experimental group complied with that request.

Of course, no strategy works all the time. A review of research reported that the FITD tactic increases compliance rates, on the average, about 13% (Burger, 1999). The technique may be ineffective if the second request follows too quickly on the heels of the first one (Chartrand, Pinckert, & Burger, 1999), if the initial request is too trivial to register, or if the second request is so large it is unreasonable (Burger, 1999). When this influence technique does work, however, it can be used in socially beneficial ways, such as increasing people's willingness to consider organ donation (Fabian, 2002) or to enhance teen participation rates in smoking cessation programs (Bloom, McBride, & Pollack, 2006).

Why does this strategy work? The best explanation is rooted in Daryl Bem's *self-perception theory* or the idea that people sometimes infer their attitudes by observing their own behavior (Burger & Caldwell, 2003;

**FIGURE 7.17**

**The foot-in-the-door and door-in-the-face techniques.** These two influence techniques are essentially the reverse of each other, but both can work. **(a)** In the foot-in-the-door technique, you begin with a small request and work up to a larger one. **(b)** In the door-in-the-face technique, you begin with a large request and work down to a smaller one.

Burger & Guadagno, 2003). When Joe agrees to sign a petition, he infers that he is a helpful person. So when he is confronted with a second, larger request to collect petition signatures, "helpful person" comes to mind, and Joe complies with the request.

**The Lowball Technique**

A second commitment-based strategy is the *lowball technique,* **which involves getting someone to commit to an attractive proposition before its hidden costs are revealed.** The name for this technique derives from a common practice in automobile sales, in which a customer is offered a terrific bargain on a car. The bargain price gets the customer to commit to buying, but soon after, the dealer starts revealing some hidden costs. Typically, the customer discovers that options expected to be included in the original price are actually going to cost extra. Once they have committed to buying a car, most customers are unlikely to cancel the deal. Car dealers aren't the only ones who use this technique. For instance, a friend might ask if you want to spend a week with him at his charming lakeside cabin. After you accept this seemingly generous offer, he may add, "Of course, there's a little work to do. We need to paint the doors, repair the pier, and . . ." You might think that people would become angry and back out of a deal once its hidden costs are revealed. Sometimes this

does happen, but lowballing is a surprisingly effective strategy (Burger & Cornelius, 2003).

**The Reciprocity Principle**

Most people have been socialized to believe in the *reciprocity principle*—**the rule that one should pay back in kind what one receives from others.** Charities frequently make use of this principle. Groups seeking donations for the disabled, the homeless, and so forth routinely send "free" address labels, key rings, and other small gifts with their pleas for donations. The belief that people should reciprocate others' kindness is a powerful norm; thus, people often feel obliged to reciprocate by making a donation in return for the gift. According to Cialdini (2007), the reciprocity norm is so powerful that it often works even when (1) the gift is uninvited, (2) the gift comes from someone you dislike, or (3) the

**WEB LINK 7.6   Influence at Work**

This website, by researchers Robert Cialdini and Kelton Rhodes, offers an intriguing set of pages that explore a wide variety of social influence phenomena: persuasion, propaganda, brainwashing, and the tactics of various types of cults.

gift results in an uneven exchange. Let's review some basic influence tactics that take advantage of our belief in reciprocity.

### The Door-in-the-Face Technique

The door-in-the-face technique reverses the sequence of requests used with the foot-in-the-door technique. **The door-in-the-face (DITF) technique involves making a large request that is likely to be turned down in order to increase the chances that people will agree to a smaller request later** (see **Figure 7.17b**). The name for this strategy is derived from the expectation that the initial request will be quickly rejected. For example, a wife who wants to coax her frugal husband into agreeing to buy a $30,000 sports car might begin by proposing that they purchase a $40,000 sports car. By the time he has talked his wife out of the more expensive car, the $30,000 price tag may look quite reasonable to him. For the DITF to work, there must be no delay between the two requests (O'Keefe & Hale, 2001). Interestingly, the effect has been shown to increase solicited donations online and in the absence of face-to-face interaction (Gueguen, 2003).

### Other Reciprocity-Based Techniques

Salespeople who distribute free samples to prospective customers are also using the reciprocity principle. Cialdini (2007) describes the procedures used by the Amway Corporation, which sells such household products as detergent, floor wax, and insect spray. Amway's door-to-door salespeople give homemakers many bottles of their products for a "free trial." When they return a few days later, most of the homemakers feel obligated to buy some of the products.

The reciprocity norm is meant to promote fair exchanges in social interactions. However, when people manipulate the reciprocity rule, they usually give something of minimal value in the hopes of getting far more in return. For example, a person selling large computer systems may treat a potential customer at an exclusive restaurant in an effort to close a deal worth hundreds of thousands of dollars.

### The Scarcity Principle

It's no secret that telling people they can't have something only makes them want it more. According to Cialdini (2007), this principle derives from two sources. First, people have learned that items that are hard to get are of better quality than items that are easy to get. From there, they often assume, erroneously, that anything that is scarce must be good. Second, when people's choices (of products, services, romantic partners, job candidates) are constrained in some way, they often want what they can't have even more (Brehm & Brehm,

1981; Williams et al., 1993). The psychological term for this is *reactance* (Brehm, 1966).

Companies and advertisers frequently use the scarcity principle to drive up the demand for their products. Thus, you constantly see ads that scream "limited supply available," "for a limited time only," "while they last," and "time is running out." Perhaps the scarcity principle accounts for the reason so many antique and "vintage" items on eBay generate so much interest and auction dollars.

In summary, people use a variety of methods to coax compliance from one another. Despite the fact that many of these influence techniques are more or less dishonest, they're still widely used. There is no way to completely avoid being hoodwinked by influence strategies, and sometimes individuals may be more susceptible to such influence, as appears to be the case when someone feels ostracized and wants to get back in the good graces of a group (Carter-Sowell, Chen, & Williams, 2008). However, being alert to these techniques can reduce the likelihood that you'll be a victim of influence artists. As we noted in our discussion of persuasion, "to be forewarned is to be forearmed."

Advertisers often try to artificially create scarcity to make their products seem more desirable.

## KEY IDEAS

### Forming Impressions of Others

● In forming impressions of other people, individuals rely on appearance, verbal behavior, actions, nonverbal messages, and situational cues. Individuals usually make snap judgments about others unless accurate impressions are important. To explain the causes of other people's behavior, individuals make attributions (either internal or external).

● People often try to confirm their expectations about what others are like, which can result in biased impressions. Self-fulfilling prophecies can actually change a target person's behavior in the direction of a perceiver's expectations.

● Categorization of people into ingroups and outgroups can slant social perceptions. Stereotypes, which are widely held beliefs about the typical characteristics of various groups, can distort one's perceptions of others. When people make the fundamental attribution error they discount situational factors and explain others' behavior in terms of internal attributions. Defensive attribution often leads people to blame victims for their misfortunes. The process of person perception is characterized by the themes of efficiency, selectivity, and consistency.

### The Problem of Prejudice

● Prejudice is a particularly unfortunate outcome of the tendency to view others inaccurately. Blatant ("old-fashioned") discrimination occurs relatively infrequently today, but subtle expressions of prejudice and discrimination ("modern discrimination," aversive racism) have become more common.

● Common causes of prejudice include right-wing authoritarianism, a strong social dominance orientation, cognitive distortions due to stereotyping and attributional errors, actual competition between groups, and threats to one's social identity. Strategies for reducing prejudice are rooted in social thinking and collaborative intergroup contact.

### The Power of Persuasion

● The success of persuasive efforts depends on several factors. A source of persuasion who is expert, trustworthy, likable, physically attractive, and similar to the receiver tends to be relatively effective. Although there are some limitations, two-sided arguments, arousal of fear, and generation of positive feelings are effective elements in persuasive messages. Persuasion is undermined when receivers are forewarned or have beliefs that are incompatible with the position being advocated.

● Persuasion takes place via two processes. The central route to persuasion requires a receiver to be motivated to process persuasive messages carefully (elaboration). A favorable reaction to such an evaluation will result in positive attitude change. When a receiver is unmotivated or unable to process persuasive messages carefully, persuasion may take place via the peripheral route (on the basis of simple cues such as a catchy tune). Persuasion undertaken via the central route tends to have more enduring effects on attitudes.

### The Power of Social Pressure

● Asch found that subjects often conform to the group, even when the group reports inaccurate judgments. Asch's experiments may have produced public compliance while subjects' private beliefs remained unchanged. Both normative and informational influence can produce conformity. Being mindful of social pressures and getting support from others with similar views are ways to resist conformity pressures.

● In Milgram's landmark study of obedience to authority, subjects showed a remarkable tendency to follow orders to shock an innocent stranger. Milgram's findings highlight the influence of situational pressures on behavior. Although people often obey authority figures, sometimes they are disobedient, usually because they have social support.

### Application: Seeing Through Compliance Tactics

● Although they work for different reasons, all compliance tactics have the same goal: getting people to agree to requests. The foot-in-the-door and the lowball technique are based on the fact that people prefer consistency in their behavior.

● The door-in-the-face technique and the tactic of offering "giveaway" items are manipulations of the principle of reciprocity, the rule that one should pay back in kind what one receives from others. When advertisers suggest that products are in short supply, they are taking advantage of the scarcity principle. Understanding these strategies can make you less vulnerable to manipulation.

## KEY TERMS

Attitudes   p. 225
Attributions   p. 211
Bystander effect   p. 232
Channel   p. 226
Compliance   p. 231
Confirmation bias   p. 212
Conformity   p. 230
Defensive attribution   p. 217
Discrimination   p. 218
Door-in-the-face technique   p. 237
Elaboration likelihood model   p. 228
Foot-in-the-door technique   p. 235
Fundamental attribution error   p. 216
Informational influence   p. 232
Lowball technique   p. 236
Message   p. 226
Need for cognition   p. 227
Normative influence   p. 231
Obedience   p. 232
Person perception   p. 209
Persuasion   p. 225
Prejudice   p. 218
Primacy effect   p. 218
Receiver   p. 226
Reciprocity principle   p. 236
Self-fulfilling prophecy   p. 213
Source   p. 226
Stereotypes   p. 214

## KEY PEOPLE

Solomon Asch   pp. 230–231
Robert Cialdini   pp. 229, 235–237
Susan Fiske   pp. 210, 217
Stanley Milgram   pp. 232–234
Richard Petty and John Cacioppo   pp. 228–229
Muzafer Sherif   pp. 223, 225

## QUESTIONS

1. Inferences that people draw about the causes of events, their own behavior, and others' behavior are called:
   a. snap judgments.
   b. self-fulfilling prophecies.
   c. attributions.
   d. attitudes.

2. Which of the following is *not* a potential source of cognitive distortion in perception?
   a. categorizing
   b. the bystander effect
   c. stereotypes
   d. defensive attribution

3. Which of the following is *not* a theme in person perception?
   a. efficiency
   b. selectivity
   c. consistency
   d. mindfulness

4. "Old-fashioned" discrimination is _____; modern discrimination is _____.
   a. blatant; subtle
   b. legal; illegal
   c. common; rare
   d. race-based; gender-based

5. Which of the following is a cause of prejudice?
   a. mindfulness
   b. right-wing authoritarianism
   c. the fundamental attribution error
   d. activities based on superordinate goals

6. Receivers who are forewarned that someone will try to persuade them will most likely:
   a. be very open to persuasion.
   b. listen intently but openly argue with the speaker.
   c. be more resistant to persuasion.
   d. heckle the persuader.

7. Compared to attitudes formed via the peripheral route, those formed via the central route:
   a. operate subliminally.
   b. are more enduring and harder to change.
   c. last only a short time.
   d. are poor predictors of behavior.

8. When people change their outward behavior but not their private beliefs, _____ is operating.
   a. conformity
   b. persuasion
   c. obedience
   d. compliance

9. The results of Milgram's (1963) study imply that:
   a. situational factors can exert tremendous influence over behavior.
   b. in the real world, most people resist pressures to act in harmful ways.
   c. most people are willing to give obviously wrong answers on rigged perceptual tasks.
   d. disobedience is far more common than obedience.

10. When charities send prospective donors free address labels and the like, which of the following social influence principles are they manipulating?
    a. the consistency principle
    b. the scarcity principle
    c. the reciprocity principle
    d. the foot-in-the-door principle

## ANSWERS

| | | |
|---|---|---|
| 1. c Page 211 | 2. b Pages 213–217 | 3. d Pages 217–218 |
| 4. a Pages 219–220 | 5. b Pages 220–224 | 6. c Page 228 |
| 7. b Pages 228–229 | 8. d Page 231 | 9. a Page 234 |
| 10. c Pages 236–237 | | |

## Personal Explorations Workbook

Go to the *Personal Explorations Workbook* in the back of your text-book for exercises that can enhance your self-understanding in relation to issues raised in this chapter. **Exercise 7.1** *Self-Assessment:* Argumentativeness Scale. **Exercise 7.2** *Self-Reflection:* Can You Identify Your Prejudicial Stereotypes?

## CourseMate

Access an interactive eBook, chapter-specific interactive learning tools, including Personal Explorations, Recommended Readings, Critical Thinking Exercises, flashcards, quizzes, videos and more in your Psychology CourseMate, available at **www.cengagebrain.com/ shop/ISBN/1111186634**.

Masterfile (Royalty-Free Div.)

# Interpersonal Communication

Veronica, a high school senior, is getting ready for the prom. Her date, Javier, is waiting downstairs. As she fixes her hair, checks her makeup for what is probably the tenth time in the last hour, and smoothes the front of her new and costly dress, her 13-year-old sister, Amy, wanders into the room. As Veronica looks at her own reflection in a full-length mirror, she hears Amy snort, "*Nice* dress. Really *nice*." Amy's voice brims with the sort of sarcasm that is refined in middle-school hallways, but it is enough to shake Veronica's confidence. "What do you mean? What's wrong with this dress? It's beautiful—isn't it?" she says quickly, worry creeping into her voice. "*Oh, that* dress," grins Amy. "Why there's *not* a thing wrong with it, I am *so* sure Javier will just *love* it." While making that last statement Amy rolls her eyes. A shouting match ensues. Veronica's mother intervenes, telling Veronica she "must have misunderstood—Amy would never make fun of such a nice dress."

Minutes later, her confidence still a bit rattled, Veronica descends the stairs, wondering if it is too late to put on something else—maybe the dress she wore to the junior-senior dance last year? Would anyone remember she wore it before? Would Javier? A moment later, she hears Javier say, "Wow—that is a *really* nice dress. You look terrific, even amazing." Thoughts of changing dresses flee her mind as quickly as they arrived. She smiles at Javier and says, "Thanks, Javier, I think it's a nice dress, too." A memorable night begins.

Sometimes it's not so much what people say that matters but how they say it. The same word—like the word "nice"—can drip with sarcasm (as Amy demonstrated) or sincerity (as Javier showed us). Learning to manage the interpersonal communication in daily life is an important way to deal with people and to interpret their intentions accurately.

Communication skills are highly relevant to adjustment because they can be critical to happiness and success in life. In this chapter, we begin with an overview of the communication process and then turn to the important topic of nonverbal communication. Next, we discuss ways to communicate more effectively and examine common communication problems. Finally, we look at interpersonal conflict, including constructive ways to deal with it. In the Application, we consider ways to develop an assertive communication style.

# The Process of Interpersonal Communication

- Describe various aspects of the communication process.
- List several important differences between face-to-face and computer-mediated communication.
- Discuss how interpersonal communication is important to adjustment.

*Communication* can be defined as the process of sending and receiving messages that have meaning. Your personal thoughts have meaning, of course, but when you "talk to yourself," you are engaging in *intra*personal communication. In this chapter, we will focus on *inter*personal communication—the transmission of meaning between two or more people. For the most part, we'll concentrate on two-person interactions.

We define **interpersonal communication as an interactional process in which one person sends a message to another.** Note several points about this definition. First, for communication to qualify as *interpersonal,* at least two people must be involved. Second, interpersonal communication is a *process.* By this, we simply mean that it usually involves a series of actions: Kelli talks/Jason listens, Jason responds/Kelli listens, and so on. Third, this process is *interactional.* Effective communication is not a one-way street: Both participants send as well as receive information when they're interacting. Communicators also interpret and create messages by reflecting on their own experiences. People with similar backgrounds are apt to understand each other better (at least initially) than individuals with different frames of reference (Schramm, 1955). A key implication of these facts is that you need to pay attention to both *speaking* and *listening* if you want to be an effective communicator, just as you should learn to ask focused questions to clarify the meaning or intent of the communications you receive.

## Components and Features of the Communication Process

Let's take a look at the essential components of the interpersonal communication process. The key elements (most of which were introduced in Chapter 7) are (1) the sender, (2) the receiver, (3) the message, (4) the channel through which the message is sent, (5) noise or interference, and (6) the context in which the message is communicated. As we describe these components, refer to **Figure 8.1** to see how they work together.

The *sender* **is the person who initiates the message.** In a typical two-way conversation, both people serve as senders (as well as receivers). Keep in mind that each person brings a unique set of expectations and understandings to each communication situation.

The *receiver* **is the person to whom the message is targeted.**

The *message* **refers to the information or meaning that is transmitted from the sender to the receiver.** The message is the *content* of the communication— that is, the ideas and feelings conveyed to another person. Two important cognitive processes underlie the transmission of messages: Speakers *encode* or transform their ideas and feelings into symbols and organize them into a message; receivers *decode* or translate a speaker's message into their own ideas and feelings (see **Figure 8.1**). Generally, fluent speakers of a language are unaware of these processes. If you've ever learned a new language, however, you have consciously experienced encoding (groping for the right word to express an idea) and decoding (trying to discover a word's meaning by how it is used).

The primary means of sending messages is language, but people also communicate to others non-verbally, through the facial expressions, gestures, and vocal inflections used to supplement (and sometimes entirely change) the meaning of verbal messages. For example, when you say, "Thanks a lot," your inflection can convey either sincere gratitude or heavy sarcasm.

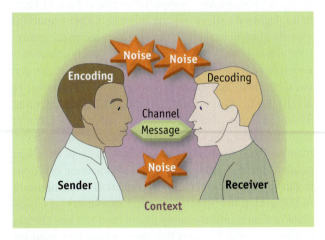

**FIGURE 8.1**

**A model of interpersonal communication.** Interpersonal communication involves six elements: the sender, the receiver, the message, the channel through which the message is transmitted, distorting noise, and the context in which the message is sent. In conversations, both participants function as sender and receiver.

The *channel* refers to the sensory means through which the message reaches the receiver. Typically, people receive information from multiple channels simultaneously. They not only hear what the other person says, they also see the person's facial expressions, observe his or her gestures, experience eye contact, and sometimes feel the person's touch. Note that the messages in the various channels may be consistent or inconsistent with each other, making their interpretation more or less difficult. Sometimes sound is the only channel available for receiving information—when you talk on the telephone, for instance. Through sound, people hear both the literal content of messages and vocal inflections. In computer-mediated communication (e-mail, chat rooms, and so on), only the visual channel is called into play, as individuals communicate in writing.

Whenever two people interact, miscommunication can occur. *Noise* refers to any stimulus that interferes with accurately expressing or understanding a message. Sources of noise include environmental factors (street traffic, loud music, computer spam or pop-ups, crowded rooms), physical factors (poor hearing, poor vision), and physiological factors (hunger, headaches, medications). Noise can also have semantic origins (Verderber, Verderber, & Berryman-Fink, 2008). For instance, profanity, ethnic slurs, or sexist language can cause a listener to disregard the larger message. In addition, psychological factors such as defensiveness and anxiety can contribute to noise, as we'll see later in the chapter.

All social communication occurs in and is influenced by a *context,* the environment in which communication takes place. Context includes the *physical environment* such as location, time of day, and noise level and how a conversation takes place: face-to-face, in a telephone call, or via the Internet. Other important aspects of context include the nature of the participants' *relationship* (work associates, friends, family), their *history* (previous interactions), their current *mood* (happy, stressed), and their *cultural backgrounds* (Verderber et al., 2008). Culture is especially important in the United States because of the varieties of subcultures, many with different rules of communication. The Recommended Reading *Multicultural Manners* is an excellent guide to the cultural variety in communication practices in our diverse nation. Cultural context is also important in the global marketplace, as the marketers of Coca-Cola in China unfortunately discovered too late (Petras & Petras, 1993). It seems that the symbols they used for the brand name translated to something like "Bite the wax tadpole" in Chinese!

Most person-to-person communications are characterized by common features. For example, you are probably not interested in engaging in intimate or pri-

## Recommended READING

### Multicultural Manners: New Rules of Etiquette for a Changing Society
by Norine Dresser (John Wiley & Sons, 2005)

This interesting book seeks to help Americans interact more comfortably and effectively as the nation becomes increasingly ethnically diverse. Written with humor, the book covers a wealth of practical issues that arise in a variety of settings: business, social, educational, and medical. The majority of the book addresses issues and situations that can result in miscommunication: body language, childrearing practices, classroom behavior, gift giving, male/female relations, verbal expressions, and so on. Each chapter includes real-life incidents of miscommunication, explanations of what happened in the situation, and verbal and behavioral guidelines for avoiding such problems. In two smaller sections of the book, Dresser explores the diversity in rules for holidays and worship (to help people feel comfortable when they visit unfamiliar places of worship) as well as multicultural health practices (some of which are benign, others of which are dangerous). Examples involve African Americans, Native Americans, Caribbean Islanders, Asians, Latinos, and recently arriving groups of immigrants. The author also provides information about the practices of a number of diverse religious groups.

*Go to the Psychology CourseMate for Weiten at* **www.cengagebrain.com/shop/ISBN/1111186634** *for descriptions of other recommended books.*

vate exchanges with everyone you meet. Instead, you are *selective* in initiating or responding to communications. Communications between people are not isolated events; rather, they have a *systemic* quality because of time, situation, social class, education, culture, personal histories, and other influences that are beyond individuals' control but that nonetheless affect how they interact with each other. Communications within a given relationship (such as those between you and a close friend) are also *unique*, possessing special patterns, vocabulary, even rhythms (Nicholson, 2006). When you become close to a given person, you may establish particular roles and rules for how you interact with each other that are distinct from the roles or rules used in your other relationships (Dainton, 2006; Duck, 2006). Finally, communications are said to be *processual*—that is, part of a continuous and evolving process that becomes more personal as people interact with greater frequency. More to the point, people's past communications affect their present and future communications (Wood, 2006) because they cannot edit or "unsay" sent messages.

## Technology and Interpersonal Communication

The recent explosion in electronic and wireless communication technology has revolutionized our notions of interpersonal communication. Today, communication via e-mail, mailing lists, text messaging, "tweets," Facebook, blogs and vlogs, chat rooms, and videoconferencing must be considered along with face-to-face interactions. *Electronically mediated communication is interpersonal communication that takes place via technology* (cell phones, computers, and hand-held devices). Even a new type of slang ("netlingo") has developed to facilitate quick and easy communication for use in text messaging, e-mail messages, and chat rooms (Ellis, 2006). **Figure 8.2** provides some examples of this slang.

Cell phones have both advantages and disadvantages. On the positive side, they are a convenient way to keep in touch with others, provide a sense of security, and can summon aid in an emergency. On the down side, they tie people to their jobs, can disrupt classrooms and public events, and bring private conversations into public places. Who hasn't been forced to listen to someone yelling his or her personal business into a cell phone in

**WEB LINK 8.1   NetLingo**

This unusual site is the place to go to stay abreast of the latest terms related to cyberspace and technology. Visitors will find an Internet Dictionary containing thousands of technology terms and guides to the meaning of hundreds of text messaging acronyms as well as various emoticons (or smileys). Among the site's "Top 50" lists is one titled "Top 50 Internet Acronyms Every Parent Needs to Know."

a public place? By now, most people are familiar with the basic rules of etiquette for cell phone use in public: (1) turn off your phone (or put it on "vibrate" mode) when the ringing will disturb others, (2) keep your calls short, and (3) make and receive calls unobtrusively or out of earshot from others.

In the area of computer-mediated communication, e-mail is by far the most widely used application, but

### Examples of Netlingo

| Acronymn | Meaning |
| --- | --- |
| B4N or BFN | Bye For Now |
| CYM | Check Your Mail |
| GTG | Got To Go |
| IDK | I Don't Know |
| LOL | Laughing Out Loud |
| NBD | No Big Deal |
| PAL | Parents Are Listening |
| RUOK | Are You OK? |
| TY | Thank You |
| WKEWL | Way Cool |
| DGT | Don't Go There |
| F2F | Face to Face |
| LDR | Long Distance Relationship |
| SAPFU | Surpassing All Previous Foul Ups |
| ZZZ | Sleeping, Bored, Tired |

**FIGURE 8.2**

**Cyberspace slang.** A new type of slang has developed that allows quick and easy communication in e-mail messages, text messages, and chat rooms. Here you can see some frequently used text messaging acronyms and their meanings. These acronyms are variously termed netlingo, techspeak, or e-talk. Although netlingo is obviously useful for cybercommunication, its use in more formal settings (school, work) is problematic. (Information from NetLingo.com)

© John Lund/Paula Zacharias/photolibrary/Blend Images

**Cell phone etiquette in public places calls for turning off your phone or putting it on vibrate mode, keeping your voice low, and making your calls short.**

Do you take part in any social networking site (SNS), such as Facebook or MySpace? If you are a typical college student or a young adult, there is a good chance you have posted a profile of yourself on one of these popular Internet destinations. The primary benefit of any SNS is being able to present yourself virtually to other people who may already know you, remember you from a (shared) past (high school, for example), or want to connect with you ("friend you," in Internet parlance) because of some common interest. Most online profiles contain all kinds of personal or private information, everything from your favorite books, movies, or food to your political, social, and even religious beliefs. In effect, an SNS allows you to express yourself and to develop relationships with others who share similar attitudes, beliefs, interests, backgrounds, or whatever the dimension in question might be.

Is there any drawback or down side to taking part in an SNS? There can be if you do not take appropriate steps to maintain your online privacy. Why should privacy be a concern? Simply put, you never know who is reading your profile or what they are doing with the information you have shared (Lewis, Kaufman, & Christakis, 2008). Surely, you are already aware that you should be careful what financial information (such as PIN numbers) you share online and know that interfacing with a website is never a good idea unless you know it is a secure one (LaRose & Rifon, 2007). But what about the information you post on your SNS? Should you worry about that?

Possibly yes. Consider the fact that Facebook has over 70 million active users (Facebook, 2008). To presume that all of those users are well intentioned seems somewhat foolhardy. There is also ample evidence that the content of student postings has been used to raid student parties (Hass, 2006) and to keep individuals from getting jobs (Finder, 2006). In short, private information is not always so private. Think for a moment: Is your SNS profile set so that it cannot be read, accessed, or searched by nonfriends (strangers)? Or can anyone see your personal pages?

Based on their analyses of an SNS dataset composed of user profiles, Lewis et al. (2008) claim that students are likely to act to maintain their online privacy based on two factors: social influence and personal incentives. Where social influence is concerned, students follow the lead of those close to them, thus, they are likely to keep their profiles private if their roomates and friends do so. Perhaps not surprisingly, women are more likely to maintain private profiles than men are.

What about those "personal incentives"? Interestingly, people with private profiles are online with greater regularity than those with public profiles. Within their dataset, Lewis et al. (2008) found that people who maintain their privacy are also likely to have more esoteric tastes in music, books, and movies compared to those whose pages are public. So, maintaining privacy is not only wise from a security perspective, it may also represent a way to demonstrate one's sociocultural tastes (albeit to friends rather than strangers).

chat rooms are also popular, especially among teens and those in their early and middle 20s (Nie & Erbring, 2002). As we have noted, face-to-face communication relies on the spoken word, while Internet communication depends on the written word. You can see other important differences in **Figure 8.3**. The absence of nonverbal cues in computer-mediated communication means that you need to take special care that the other person understands your intended meaning. Thus, you should choose your words carefully, provide clarifying details, and describe your feelings, if necessary. It's also a good idea to review what you have written before you send it! The lack of nonverbal cues and the anonymous nature of computer-mediated communication also have important implications for relationship development (Bargh & McKenna, 2004), an issue we take up in Chapter 9.

## Communication and Adjustment

Before we plunge further into the topic of interpersonal communication, let's take a moment to emphasize its significance. Communication with others—friends, lovers, parents, spouses, children, employers, workers—is such an essential and commonplace aspect of everyday life that it's hard to overstate its role in adjustment. Many of life's gratifications (and frustrations and heartaches, as well) hinge on one's ability to communicate effectively with others. Numerous studies have shown that good communication can enhance satisfaction in relationships (Cordova, Gee, & Warren, 2005; Egeci & Gençöz, 2006) and that poor communication ranks high as a cause of breakups among both straight and gay couples (Kurdek, 1994, 1998).

## Face-to-Face versus Electronic Communication

| Dimension | Face-to-Face | Internet |
|---|---|---|
| *Physical distance* | People need to be in the same place at the same time to meet. | People can meet and develop a relationship with someone thousands of miles away. |
| *Anonymity* | One can't be anonymous in real-life interactions. | People take greater risks in disclosing personal information than they otherwise do. Thus, feelings of intimacy can develop more quickly. |
| *Richness of communication* | People have access to nonverbal cues such as facial expressions and tone of voice to detect nuances in meaning or deception. | In cyberspace, these cues are absent, making social and status cues, such as gender, age, social class, race, and ethnicity less discernible. |
| *Visual cues* | Physical appearance and visual cues play a big role in attraction in face-to-face relationships. | These cues are generally absent on the Internet (although people can exchange photographs online). |
| *Time* | Two people have to connect at the same time. | Although instant messaging and chat room conversations take place in real time, there is no need for an immediate response, so time becomes relatively unimportant. On the Internet, you can take as long as you like to craft a response so you can more completely explain yourself. |

**FIGURE 8.3**

**Differences between face-to-face and electronically mediated communication.**
Electronically mediated communication applications (cell phone text messaging, e-mail, chat rooms, news groups, and so forth) have dramatically changed the ways people interact and develop relationships. These two types of communication differ from each other in five important ways. (Adapted from Bargh & McKenna, 2004; Boase & Wellman, 2006; Verderber & Verderber, 2004)

# Nonverbal Communication

### LEARNING OBJECTIVES

- List five general principles of nonverbal communication.
- Discuss the determinants and significance of personal space.
- Understand what can be discerned from facial cues and eye contact.
- Describe the roles of body movement, posture, and gestures in communication.
- Summarize the research findings on touching and paralanguage.
- Recognize the difficulty in detecting deception and clarify the nonverbal cues linked to deception.
- Assess the significance of nonverbal sensitivity in interpersonal interactions.

You're standing at the bar in your favorite hangout, gazing across a dimly lit room filled with people drinking, dancing, and talking. You signal to the bartender that you'd like another drink. Your companion comments on the loudness of the music, and you nod your head in agreement. You spot an attractive stranger across the bar; your eyes meet for a moment and you smile. In a matter of seconds, you have sent three messages without uttering a syllable. To put it another way, you have just sent three *nonverbal* messages. **Nonverbal communication is the transmission of meaning from one person to another through means or symbols other than words.** Communication at the nonverbal level takes place through a variety of behaviors: interpersonal distance, facial expression, eye contact, body posture and movement, gestures, physical touch, and tone of voice (e.g., Mehrabian, 2008).

Clearly, a great deal of information is exchanged through nonverbal channels—more than most people realize. You can significantly enhance your communication skills by learning more about this important aspect of communication.

## General Principles

Let's begin by examining some general principles of nonverbal communication.

**1.** *Nonverbal communication conveys emotions.* People can communicate their feelings without saying a word—for example, "a look that kills." Nonverbal demonstrations of positive feelings include sitting or standing close to those you care for, touching them often, and looking at them frequently. Still, nonverbal signals on their own are not the precise indicators of emotional states that they were once believed to be (Samovar, Porter, & McDaniel, 2007), so you should be cautious in making inferences.

**2.** *Nonverbal communication is multichanneled.* Nonverbal communication typically involves simultaneous messages sent through a number of channels. For instance, information may be transmitted through gestures, facial expressions, eye contact, and vocal tone at the same time. In contrast, verbal communication is limited to a single channel: speech. If you have ever tried to follow two people speaking at once, you understand how difficult it is to process multiple inputs of information. This means that many nonverbal transmissions can sail by the receiver unnoticed.

**3.** *Nonverbal communication is ambiguous.* A shrug or a raised eyebrow can mean different things to different people. Moreover, receivers may have difficulty determining whether nonverbal messages are being sent intentionally. Although some popular books on body language imply otherwise, few nonverbal signals carry universally accepted meanings, even within the same culture. Thus, nonverbal cues are informative, but they are most reliable when accompanied by verbal messages and embedded in a familiar cultural and social context (Samovar et al., 2007).

**4.** *Nonverbal communication may contradict verbal messages.* How often have you seen people proclaim "I'm not angry" even though their bodies shout that they are positively furious? When confronted with such an inconsistency, which message should you believe? Because of their greater spontaneity, you're probably better off heeding the nonverbal signs. Research shows that when someone is instructed to tell a lie, deception is most readily detected through nonverbal signals (DePaulo, LeMay, & Epstein, 1991; Sporer & Schwandt, 2007).

**5.** *Nonverbal communication is culture-bound.* Like language, nonverbal signals are different in different cultures (Andersen et al., 2002; Samovar et al., 2007; Weisbuch & Amady, 2008). Sometimes cultural differences can be quite dramatic. For example, in Tibet people greet their friends by sticking out their tongues (Ekman, 1975).

In a 2008 vice presidential candidate debate against Joe Biden, Sarah Palin used a wink to try to create rapport with the audience; it worked on some people but not others. Politicians often learn the hard way that the public can easily misinterpret their nonverbal gestures.

## Elements of Nonverbal Communication

Nonverbal signals can provide a great deal of information in interpersonal interactions. As we discuss specific nonverbal behaviors, we will focus on what they communicate about interpersonal attraction and social status.

### Personal Space

*Proxemics* **is the study of people's use of interpersonal space.** *Personal space* **is a zone of space surrounding a person that is felt to "belong" to that person.** Personal space is like an invisible bubble you carry around with you in your social interactions. The size of this mobile zone is related to your cultural background, social status, personality, age, and gender.

The amount of interpersonal distance people prefer depends on the nature of the relationship and the situation (E. T. Hall, 2008; J. A. Hall, 1990). The appropriate distance between people is also regulated by social norms and varies by culture (J. A. Hall, 1990; Samovar et al., 2007). For instance, people of Northern European heritage tend to engage in less physical contact and keep a greater distance between themselves than people of Latin or Middle Eastern heritage. The United States is usually characterized as a medium-contact culture, but there is a lot of variability among ethnic groups. The situation matters, too: Consider how much distance from others people desire when they are using an ATM. Those waiting behind you in line know that you want your privacy in order to preserve the personal information you enter into the machine during a transaction (Li & Li, 2007). They, in turn, expect the same courtesy.

Anthropologist Edward T. Hall (1966) has described four interpersonal distance zones that are appropriate for middle-class encounters in American culture (see **Figure 8.4**). The general rule is that the more you like someone, the more comfortable you feel being physically close to that person. Of course, there are obvious exceptions, such as in crowded subways and elevators, but these situations are often experienced as stressful. Women seem to have smaller personal-space zones than men do (Holland et al., 2004). When talking, women sit or stand closer together than men do.

Personal distance can also convey information about status. People generally stand farther away from high-status communication partners versus partners of lower power (Holland et al., 2004). Moreover, it is the prerogative of the more powerful person in an interaction to set the "proper" distance (Henley, 1986). One study in Japan found that female subordinates kept male superiors at the greatest distance as compared to male or female peers (Aono, 2003).

Invasions of personal space usually produce discomfort and stimulate attempts to restore your privacy zone. To illustrate, if someone stands too close, you may back up. Or, if a stranger sits down at "your" table

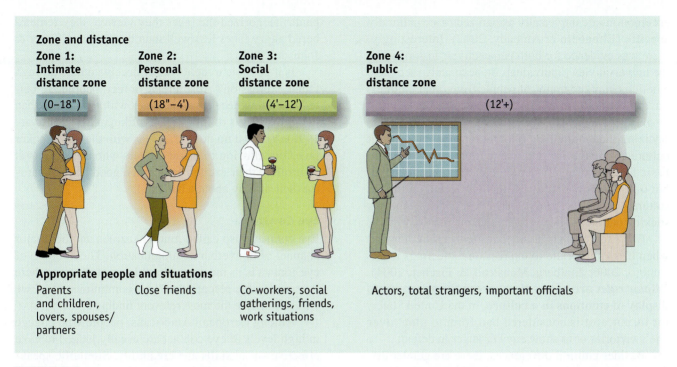

**FIGURE 8.4**

**Interpersonal distance zones.** According to Edward Hall (1966), people like to keep a certain amount of distance between themselves and others. The distance that makes one feel comfortable depends on whom one is interacting with and the nature of the situation.

in the library and forces you to share it, you may reorient your body away from the intruder, place a barrier (for example, a stack of books) between you and the invader, or move to a different table. Invasions of personal space rarely go unnoticed, and they usually elicit a variety of reactions.

## Facial Expression

More than anything else, facial expressions convey emotions (Hess & Thibault, 2009; Horstmann, 2003). Paul Ekman and Wallace Friesen have identified six distinctive facial expressions that correspond with six

basic emotions: anger, disgust, fear, happiness, sadness, and surprise (Ekman, 1994; Ekman & Friesen, 1984). Early research involving participants from many countries supported the idea that these six emotions are universally recognized (Ekman, 1972). In such studies, researchers showed photographs depicting different emotions to subjects from a variety of Western and non-Western cultures and asked them to match the photographs with an emotion. Some representative results from this research are depicted in **Figure 8.5**.

A more recent meta-analysis of 97 studies (based on studies in over 40 countries) looked at whether these

**FIGURE 8.5**

**Facial expressions and emotions.** Ekman and Friesen (1984) found that people in highly disparate cultures showed fair agreement on the emotions portrayed in these photos. This consensus across cultures suggests that the facial expressions associated with certain emotions may have a biological basis.

Photos from *Unmasking the Face*, © 1975 by Paul Ekman, photographs courtesy of Paul Ekman

| Country | Emotion displayed | | | |
| | Fear | Disgust | Happiness | Anger |
|---|---|---|---|---|
| | Agreement in judging photos (%) | | | |
| United States | 85 | 92 | 97 | 67 |
| Brazil | 67 | 97 | 95 | 90 |
| Chile | 68 | 92 | 95 | 94 |
| Argentina | 54 | 92 | 98 | 90 |
| Japan | 66 | 90 | 100 | 90 |
| New Guinea | 54 | 44 | 82 | 50 |

six emotions are universally recognized or are culturally specific (Elfenbein & Ambady, 2002). Interestingly, there was evidence for both perspectives. In support of the universal view, individuals do accurately recognize emotions in photographs of people from other cultures. Favoring cultural specificity, there was evidence of an "ingroup advantage." Thus, observers are better at recognizing the emotions in photographs from their own cultural groups than from other cultural groups. A few basic facial expressions are universally recognizable, but other emotional expressions vary from culture to culture—as we noted in the earlier example of Tibetans sticking out their tongues to greet their friends.

Each society has rules that govern whether and when it is appropriate to express one's feelings (Matsumoto, 2006; Zaalberg, Manstead, & Fischer, 2004). *Display rules* **are norms that govern the appropriate display of emotions in a culture.** In the United States, for instance, it is considered bad form to gloat over one's victories or to show envy or anger in defeat.

Besides cultural differences, there are gender differences in facial expression (LaFrance, Hecht, & Paluck, 2003). For example, men typically show less facial expression than women do, a finding linked to social pressures for males to inhibit such displays (Kilmartin, 2007). Also, as you might expect, people high in self-monitoring (see Chapter 6) are better than low self-monitors at managing their facial expressions (Gangestad & Snyder, 2000).

What about decoding the emotion displayed on faces? There is some evidence that age matters. In one study on facial identification and memory, it was found that when compared to younger people, older individuals were less able to identify angry expressions on either young or older faces. Moreover, once the older partici-

pants categorized the faces they viewed, they remembered angry faces less well than happy ones (Ebner & Johnson, 2009).

Is it possible to deliberately deceive others through facial expression? Absolutely. In fact, people are better at sending deceptive messages with their faces than with other areas of their bodies (Ekman & O'Sullivan, 1991). You are no doubt familiar with the term "poker face," an allusion to poker players who are experts at controlling their excitement about a good hand of cards (or their dismay about a bad one).

### Eye Contact

Eye contact (also called mutual gaze) is another major channel of nonverbal communication. The duration of eye contact is its most meaningful aspect. Because there is considerable research on "eye communication," we will summarize the most relevant findings.

Among European Americans, people who engage in high levels of eye contact are usually judged to have effective social skills and credibility. Similarly, speakers, interviewers, and experimenters receive higher ratings of competence when they maintain high rather than low eye contact with their audience. As a rule, people engage in more eye contact when they're listening than when they're talking (Bavelas, Coates, & Johnson, 2002). Where listening is concerned, mutual gaze can even promote music appreciation: More eye contact between a musician and audience actually leads to greater levels of enjoyment of the musical performance (Antonietti, Cocomazzi, & Iannello, 2009).

Yet there may be times when some types of communication either enhance or reduce eye contact. For example, researchers have long speculated that people are more likely to make eye contact with others when making sincere statements. Conversely, psychologists assumed that speakers making sarcastic or derisive comments become gaze averse— that is, they are more likely to break eye contact with listeners. A controlled study using speaker-listener pairs confirmed these expectations (Williams, Burns, & Harmon, 2009).

Gaze also communicates the *intensity* (but not the positivity or negativity) of feelings. For example, couples who say they are in love spend more time gazing at each other than other couples do (Patterson, 1988). Also, maintaining moderate (versus constant or no) eye contact with others typically generates positive feelings in them. When women make eye contact with men, a longer gaze can generate the latter's interest, sustaining it when smiling is part of the interaction (Guéguen et al., 2008).

In a negative interpersonal context, a steady gaze becomes a stare that causes most people to feel uncomfortable (Kleinke, 1986).

Display rules require unsuccessful contestants in beauty pageants to suppress the display of resentful, envious, or angry feelings.

The eyes can be used to convey either very positive or very negative feelings.

Moreover, like threat displays among nonhuman primates such as baboons and rhesus monkeys, a stare can convey aggressive intent (Henley, 1986). Thus, if you want to avoid road rage incidents, avoid making eye contact with hostile motorists. People also communicate by *reducing* eye contact with others. Unpleasant interactions, embarrassing situations, or invasions of personal space usually trigger this behavior (Kleinke, 1986). Indeed, in the absence of verbal or contextual information, such looking away can communicate fear; in effect, people sometimes "point" to danger with their eyes (Hadjikhani et al., 2008).

Culture strongly affects patterns of eye contact (Samovar et al., 2007). For example, Americans should be sensitive to the fact that direct eye contact is perceived as an insult in Mexico, Latin America, Japan, and Africa, and in some Native American tribes. By contrast, people from Arab countries look directly into the eyes of their conversational partners for longer periods than Americans are used to.

In the United States, gender and racial differences have been found in eye contact. For instance, women tend to gaze at others more than men do (Briton & Hall, 1995). However, the patterning of eye contact also reflects status, and gender and status are often confounded. Higher-status individuals look at the other person more when speaking than when listening, while lower-status people behave just the opposite. Women usually show the lower-status visual pattern because they are typically accorded lower status

than men. As you can see in **Figure 8.6**, when women are in high-power positions, they show the high-status visual pattern to the same extent that men do (Dovidio et al., 1988). African Americans use more continuous eye contact than European Americans when speaking, but less

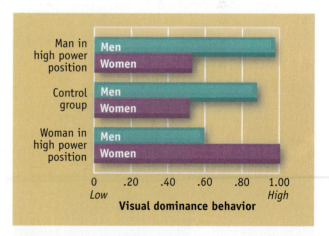

**FIGURE 8.6**

**Visual dominance, status, and gender.** Women typically show low visual dominance (see control condition) because they are usually accorded lower status than men (Dovidio et al. 1988). However, when researchers placed women in a high-power position and measured their visual behavior, women showed the high visual dominance pattern and men showed the low visual dominance pattern. When men were placed in the high-power position, the visual dominance patterns reversed. Thus, visual dominance seems to be more a function of status than of gender.

when listening (Samovar & Porter, 2004). Misunderstandings can arise if gaze behaviors that are intended to convey interest and respect are interpreted as being disrespectful or dishonest.

## Body Language

Body movements—those of the head, trunk, hands, legs, and feet—also provide nonverbal avenues of communication. **Kinesics is the study of communication through body movements.** By noting a person's body movements, observers may be able to tell an individual's level of tension or relaxation. For instance, frequent touching or scratching suggests nervousness (Harrigan et al., 1991).

*Posture* also conveys information. Leaning back with arms or legs arranged in an asymmetrical or "open" position conveys a feeling of relaxation. Posture can also indicate someone's attitude toward you (McKay, Davis, & Fanning, 1995). A body leaning toward you typically indicates interest and a positive attitude. Conversely, a body angled away from you or crossed arms may indicate a negative attitude or defensiveness.

Posture can also convey status differences. Generally, a higher-status person will look more relaxed. By contrast, a lower-status person will tend to exhibit a more rigid body posture, often sitting up straight with feet together, flat on the floor, and arms close to the body (a "closed" position) (J. A. Hall, 1984; Vrugt & Luyerink, 2000). Again, status and gender differences are frequently parallel. That is, men are more likely to exhibit the high-status "open" posture and women the lower-status "closed" posture (Cashdan, 1998).

People use *hand gestures* to describe and emphasize the words they speak, as well as to persuade (Maricchiolo et al., 2009). You might point to give directions or slam your fist on a desk to emphasize an assertion. To convey "no," you can extend the index finger of your dominant hand and wave it back and forth from left to right. Children know that when adults slide their right index finger up and down their left index finger, it means "shame on you." As travelers frequently discover, the meaning of gestures is not universal (Samovar et al., 2007). For instance, a circle made with the thumb and forefinger means that everything is "OK" to an American, but it is considered an obscene gesture in some countries.

## Touch

Touch takes many forms and can express a variety of meanings, including support, consolation, and sexual intimacy. Touch can also convey messages of status and power (Hall, 2006a; Hall, Coats, & Smith-LeBeau, 2005). In the United States, people typically "touch downward"—i.e., higher-status individuals are freer to touch subordinates than vice versa (Henley & Freeman, 1995). Higher-status people who touch others while making requests ("I'm conducting a survey—will you answer some questions for me?") actually increase compliance rates (Guéguen, 2002). How people interpret the possible messages communicated by touch depends on the age and gender of the individuals involved, the setting in which the touching takes place, and the relationship between the toucher and recipient, among other things (Major, Schmidlin, & Williams, 1990).

The potential force of body language can be seen in these photos showing Lyndon Baines Johnson, who was the U. S. Senate majority leader at the time (1957), working over a fellow senator (Theodore Green). The status difference between Johnson and his colleague is obvious and the way Johnson leans into Green is a clear attempt at intimidation.

**Hand gestures can be louder than words: A waving index finger can mean "no, no, no" and one index finger sliding up and down the other says "shame on you."**

There are also gender differences related to status and touch: Adult women use touch to convey closeness or intimacy, whereas men use touch as a means to control or indicate their power in social situations (DiBaise & Gunnoe, 2004; Hall, 2006a; Jhally & Katz, 2001). Finally, there are strong norms about *where* on the body people are allowed to touch friends. These norms are quite different for same-gender as opposed to cross-gender interactions, as can be seen in **Figure 8.7**.

Other findings about touching behavior have come from an observational study of 4,500 pairs of Bostonians interacting in a variety of public places, such as shopping malls, hotel lobbies, and subway stations (Hall & Veccia, 1990, 1991). For one thing, female-female pairs touched each other significantly more than male-male pairs. Second, in younger pairs men touched women more, but in older pairs the pattern was reversed. Comparable age changes were not found for same-gender pairs.

More recently, a simple but provocative study found that a five-second touch from one person to another can often convey a specific emotion (Hertenstein, Holmes et al., 2009). Undergraduate research recruits were to touch or be touched by a stranger. Touchers were instructed to convey one of eight specific emotions via their fingers: sympathy, love, gratitude, anger, disgust, sadness, fear, or happiness. Touchers made

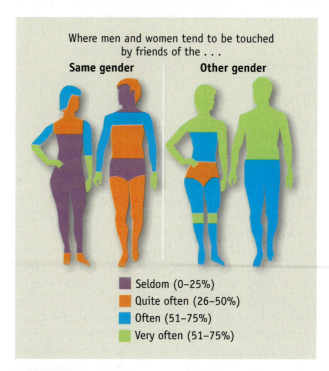

**FIGURE 8.7**

**Where friends touch each other.** Social norms govern where friends tend to touch each other. As these figures show, the patterns of touching are different in same-gender as opposed to cross-gender interactions.

Source: Adapted from Marsh, P. (Ed.). (1988). *Eye to eye: How people interact.* Topsfield, MA: Salem House. Copyright © 1988 by Andromeda Oxford Ltd. Reprinted by permission of HarperCollins, Publishers, Inc. and Andromeda Oxford Ltd.

contact by selecting the face, head, arms, hands, shoulders, trunk, or back. Those receiving were blindfolded so as not to know the sex of the touchers. Afterward, recipients reviewed a list of the eight emotions and were told to choose the one they believed was conveyed by the touch. Strikingly, judgments of emotional accuracy ranged between 50% and 78% (if they had simply guessed about the emotion linked to each touch, average precision would be around 12.5%). One tentative conclusion is that intimate interactions—those in which people touch others they know very well—can convey as much emotion as facial expressions.

## Paralanguage

The term *paralanguage* refers to *how* something is said rather than to *what* is said. Thus, **paralanguage includes all vocal cues other than the content of the verbal message itself**. Cues to paralanguage include grunts, sighs, murmurs, gasps and other vocal sounds. It can also entail how loudly or softly people speak, how fast they talk, and the pitch, rhythm, and quality (such as accent, pronunciation, sentence complexity) of their speech. Each of these vocal characteristics can affect the message being transmitted.

Variations in vocal emphasis can give the same set of words very different meanings. Consider the sentence "I really enjoyed myself." By varying the word that is accented, you can speak this sentence in three ways, each suggesting a different meaning:

- *I* really enjoyed myself! (Even though others may not have had a good time, I did.)
- I *really* enjoyed myself! (My enjoyment was exceptional.)
- I really *enjoyed* myself! (Much to my surprise, I had a great time.)

As you can see from these examples, you can actually reverse the literal meaning of a verbal message by how you say it (such as with sarcasm). The vignette that opens this chapter also illustrates how paralanguage can change the meaning of words.

Aspects of vocalization can also communicate emotions (Banse & Scherer, 1996). For example, rapid speech may mean that a person is happy, frightened, or nervous. Slower speech might be used when people are uncertain or when they want to emphasize a point. Loud vocalization often signals anger. A relatively high pitch may indicate anxiety. Slow speech, low volume, and low pitch are often associated with sadness. Thus, vocal quality provides another window on someone's true feelings. Keep in mind, however, that it is easy to assign meanings to voice quality that aren't valid, such as associating a deep voice with masculinity and maturity and a high, breathy voice with femininity and youth.

In cyberspace communication, e-mailers use various substitutes for the paralanguage cues used in spoken communication. For instance, capital letters are used for emphasis ("I had a GREAT vacation"); however, using capital letters throughout a message is viewed as shouting and considered rude behavior. Using *emoticons* (punctuation marks arranged to indicate the writer's emotions) has also become a common practice; thus, :-) indicates a smile and :-( indicates a frown. Other common emoticons are shown in **Figure 8.8**.

## Detecting Deception

Like it or not, lying is a part of everyday life (DePaulo, 2004; DePaulo et al., 2003). People typically tell one to two lies a day (DePaulo et al., 1997). Most of these everyday lies are inconsequential "white lies," such as claiming to be better than one actually is or lying to avoid hurting someone's feelings. Of course, people tell more serious lies, too. When they do, such lies are used to gain some advantage—that is, to get what they

**FIGURE 8.8**

**Conveying emotion in cyberspace by using emoticons.** People sometimes complain that online communication, chiefly e-mail or text messaging, does not allow recipients to read senders' emotional states. Emoticons, or punctuation marks and some letters joined to convey emotion visually, can fill in this digital age gap in interpersonal communication. (Source: Wikipedia entry "List of Emoticons" on June 24, 2009.)

want or to obtain something they feel entitled to, such as gaining credit for an idea (DePaulo et al., 2004). People tell serious lies, too, when they want to avoid conflict or to protect or even harm other people.

Courtesy Bella DePaulo

**Bella DePaulo**

Is it possible to catch people in a lie? Yes, but it's difficult—even for experts (Bond & DePaulo, 2006). Some studies have found that professionals whose work involves detecting lies (police officers, FBI agents, and psychiatrists, for example) are more accurate judges of liars than nonexperts are (Ekman, O'Sullivan, & Frank, 1999). Still, even these individuals have accuracy rates around 57%—not much better than chance (50%). Moreover, recent meta-analyses found no significant differences in the accuracy rates of experts and nonexperts (Bond & DePaulo, 2006, 2008; Ekman, 2009). Regardless, people overestimate their ability to detect liars (DePaulo et al., 1997).

The popular stereotypes about how liars give themselves away don't necessarily correspond to the actual clues related to dishonesty. For example, observers tend to focus on the face (the least revealing channel) and to ignore more useful information (Burgoon, 1994). In **Figure 8.9**, you can review the research findings on the nonverbal behaviors actually associated with deception (based on DePaulo, Stone, & Lassiter, 1985). By comparing the second and third columns in the figure, you can see which cues are actually associated with decep-

tion and which are erroneously linked with it. Contrary to popular belief, lying is *not* associated with slow talking, long pauses before speaking, excessive shifting of posture, reduced smiling, or lack of eye contact. A meta-analysis of over 300 studies generally supported these findings, concluding that liars say less, tell less-compelling stories, make a more negative impression, are more tense, and include less unusual content in their stories than truth tellers do (DePaulo et al., 2003).

So, how *do* liars give themselves away? As you may have noted in **Figure 8.9**, many of the clues "leak" from nonverbal channels, because speakers have a harder time controlling these channels (DePaulo & Friedman, 1998; Ekman and Friesen, 1974). For example, liars may blink less than usual while telling a lie because of cognitive demand (Leal & Vrij, 2008). Eye blinks then accelerate once the lie has been told. Vocal cues include speaking with a higher pitch, giving relatively short answers, and excessive hesitations. Visual cues include dilation of the pupils. It's also helpful to look for inconsistencies between facial expressions and lower body movements. For example, a friendly smile accompanied by a nervous shuffling of feet could signal deception.

Bella DePaulo (1994), a noted researcher in this area, isn't too optimistic about the prospects of teaching people to spot lies, because the cues are usually subtle. If she's correct, perhaps *machines* can do better. **The polygraph is a device that records fluctuations in physiological arousal as a person answers questions.**

| Nonverbal Cues and Deceptions | | |
|---|---|---|
| **Kind of cue** | **Are cues associated with actual deception?** | **Are cues believed to be a sign of deception?** |
| **Vocal cues** | | |
| Speech hesitations | YES: Liars hesitate more | YES |
| Voice pitch | YES: Liars speak with higher pitch | YES |
| Speech errors (stutters, stammers) | YES: Liars make more errors | YES |
| Speech latency (pause before starting to speak or answer) | NO | YES: People think liars pause more |
| Speech rate | NO | YES: People think liars talk slower |
| Response length | YES: Liars give shorter answers | NO |
| **Visual cues** | | |
| Pupil dilation | YES: Liars show more dilation | (No research data) |
| Adapters (self-directed gestures) | YES: Liars touch themselves more | NO |
| Blinking | YES: Liars blink less | (No research data) |
| Postural shifts | NO | YES: People think liars shift more |
| Smile | NO | YES: People think liars smile less |
| Gaze (eye contact) | NO | YES: People think liars engage in less eye contact |

**FIGURE 8.9**

**Detecting deception from nonverbal behaviors.** This chart summarizes evidence on which nonverbal cues are *actually* associated with deception and which are *believed* to be a sign of deception, based on a research review by DePaulo, Stone, and Lassiter (1985).

Although called a "lie detector," it's really an emotion detector. The polygraph monitors key indicators of autonomic arousal such as heart rate, blood pressure, respiration rate, and perspiration, or galvanic skin response (GSR). The assumption is that when people lie, they experience emotion that produces noticeable changes in these physiological indicators (see **Figure 8.10**).

Polygraph experts claim that lie detector tests are 85%–90% accurate and that there is research support for the validity of polygraph testing (Honts, Raskin, & Kircher, 2002). These claims are clearly not supported by the evidence. Methodologically sound research on this question is surprisingly sparse (largely because the research is difficult to do), and the limited evidence available is not very impressive (Branaman & Gallagher, 2005; Fiedler, Schmid, & Stahl, 2002; Iacono, 2009). One problem is that when people respond to incriminating questions, they may experience emotional arousal even when they are telling the truth. Thus, polygraph tests often lead to accusations against the innocent. Another problem is that some people can lie without experiencing physiological arousal. Thus, because of high error rates, polygraph results are not admitted as evidence in most types of courtrooms (Iacono, 2008). Yet, many companies require prospective and current employees to take lie detector tests to weed out thieves. Obviously, it would be extremely useful to have a test or a machine that could easily and accurately detect deception. Thus, researchers continue to search for such a device.

One promising method is the use of brain-imaging procedures for detecting lies. Such tools enable researchers to create computer images of brain structures and to assess changes, such as blood flow, during thought tasks. Some preliminary evidence is that, under highly controlled conditions, brain-imaging technology can separate liars from those who are telling the truth with a higher degree of success than the conventional polygraph (Simpson, 2008). Drawbacks include the practicality of implementing such technology, the costs involved, and ethical issues surrounding the ability to peer inside people's heads.

To summarize, deception is potentially detectable, but the nonverbal behaviors that accompany lying are subtle and difficult to spot.

## The Significance of Nonverbal Communication

Good nonverbal communication skills are associated with good social adjustment and with relationship satisfaction (Schachner, Shaver, & Mikulincer, 2005). Experts give particular attention to *nonverbal sensitivity*—**the ability to accurately encode (express) and decode (understand) nonverbal cues.** Nonverbal sensitivity is related to social and academic competence even in children (Hubbard & Coie, 1994; Izard et al., 2001).

In a study of college students' romantic relationships, nonverbal sensitivity was correlated with relationship well-being (Carton, Kessler, & Pape, 1999). And it's been found that spouses with poor nonverbal communication skills are more dissatisfied with their marriages (Noller, 1987). Since these are correlational studies, we can't tell whether nonverbal insensitivity leads to marital dissatisfaction or whether unhappy

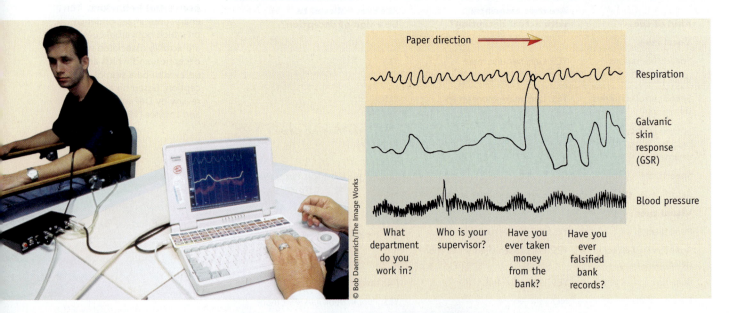

© Bob Daemmrich/The Image Works

**FIGURE 8.10**

**The polygraph measures emotional reactions.** A lie detector measures the physiological arousal that most people experience when they tell a lie. After using nonthreatening questions to establish a baseline, a polygraph examiner looks for signs of arousal (such as the sharp change in GSR shown here) on incriminating questions.

relationships cause couples to make less effort at communicating. Both possibilities probably play a role. And nonverbal insensitivity and dissatifaction can set up a vicious cycle that spirals downward (Miller, Perlman, and Brehm, 2007).

What about sensitivity for decoding and responding to facial expressions of emotion? The facial expression for fear has long been considered a trigger for prosocial behavior; when someone looks fearful, others should respond with help. A series of experiments found that people who identified fear more accurately than others were more likely to offer some form of aid, such as donating money or time for some cause (Marsh, Kozak, & Ambady, 2007). Moreover, recognizing such nonverbal cues of fear proved to be a better predictor of helping behavior than gender, mood state, or empathy.

Generally, women are better encoders and decoders of nondeceptive messages than men (Hall, 1998, 2006b). It is not that women are innately better at these skills or that they have lower status than men, but rather that women are more motivated than men to exert effort at these skills (Hall, Coats, & LeBeau, 2005; Hall & Matsumoto, 2004). The good news is that men (and women) who are willing to use some effort can improve their nonverbal communication skills—and enjoy happier and more satisfying relationships.

# Toward More Effective Communication

## LEARNING OBJECTIVES

● Identify five steps involved in making small talk.
● Explain how self-disclosure is important to adjustment.
● Understand the role of self-disclosure in relationship development.

● Analyze cultural and gender differences in self-disclosure.
● Cite four points good listeners need to keep in mind.

If you are like most people, you probably overestimate how effectively you communicate with others (Keysar & Henly, 2002). In this section, we turn to some practical issues that will help you become a more effective communicator with your family, friends, romantic partner, and co-workers. We'll review conversational skills, self-disclosure, and effective listening.

## Conversational Skills

When it comes to meeting strangers, some people launch right into a conversation, while others break into a cold sweat as their minds go completely blank. If you fall into the second category, don't despair! The art of conversation is actually based on conversational *skills*. And these skills can be learned. To get you started, we'll offer a few general principles, gleaned primarily from *Messages: The Communication Skills Book* by McKay and associates (1995). If you want to explore this topic in greater depth, their book is an excellent source of practical advice.

First, follow the Golden Rule: Give to others what you would like to receive from them. In other words, give others your attention and respect and let them know that you like them. Second, focus on the other person instead of yourself. Concentrate on what the person is saying, rather than on how you look, what you're going to say next, or winning the argument. Third, as we have noted, use nonverbal cues to communicate your interest in the other person. Like you, others also find it easier to interact with a person who signals friendliness. A welcoming smile can make a big difference in initial contacts.

Now, how do you actually get the conversational ball rolling? Psychologist Bernardo Carducci (1999) suggests five steps for making successful small talk. We'll use his template and fill in with additional suggestions:

**1.** *Indicate that you are open to conversation by commenting on your surroundings.* ("This line sure is slow.") Of course, you can begin with other topics, too, but you should be careful about your opening line. In one study, participants viewed videotapes of a man or a woman approaching an other-gender stranger and initiating a conversation using a cute/flippant, an innocuous, or a direct opening line (Kleinke, Meeker, & Staneski, 1986). The preferred openers were either innocuous ("Where are you from?") or direct ("Hi, I'm a little embarrassed about this, but I'd like to get to know you"). In contrast, the least preferred openers were of the cute/flippant variety ("Hi, I'm easy—are you?"). Because cute lines often backfire, your best bet is probably the conventional approach.

2. *Introduce yourself.* You don't have to be an extravert to behave like one in an unfamiliar situation. If no one is saying anything, why not make the first move by extending your hand, looking the person in the eye, and introducing yourself. Do this early in the conversation and use specifics to give the other person information to help find common ground ("I'm Adam Weaver. I'm a psychology major at the university").

3. *Select a topic others can relate to.* Keep an eye out for similarities and differences between you and your conversational partner (McKay et al., 1995). Look for things you have in common—a tattoo, a class, a hometown—and build a conversation around that ("I heard a great band last night"). Alternatively, work off your differences ("How did you get interested in science fiction? I'm a mystery fan myself").

4. *Keep the conversational ball rolling.* You can keep things going by elaborating on your initial topic ("After the band finished, a bunch of us walked to the new coffeehouse and tried their death-by-chocolate dessert special"). Alternatively, you can introduce a related topic or start a new one.

5. *Make a smooth exit.* Politely end the conversation ("Well, I've got to be going. I enjoyed talking with you"). When you see the person again, be sure to give a friendly smile and a wave. You need not become friends in order to be friendly.

After you've learned a little about another person, you may want to move the relationship to a deeper level. This is where self-disclosure comes into play, the topic we address next.

## Self-Disclosure

***Self-disclosure* is the act of sharing information about yourself with another person.** In other words, self-disclosure involves opening up about yourself to others. The information you share doesn't have to be a deep, dark secret, but it may be. Conversations with strangers and acquaintances typically start with superficial self-disclosure—your opinion of the TV show you saw last night or your views on who will win the World Series. Typically, only when people have come to like and trust each other do they begin to share private information—such as self-consciousness about one's weight, or jealousy of one's brother (Greene, Derlega, & Mathews, 2006). **Figure 8.11** illustrates how self-disclosure varies according to type of relationship.

In discussing self-disclosure, we focus on verbal communication—how disclosers and recipients decide to share information with each other (Ignatius & Kokkonen, 2007). But keep in mind that *non*verbal communication plays an equally important role in self-disclosure (Laurenceau & Kleinman, 2006). For example, you have already seen how nonverbal cues can support or completely change the meaning of the words they accompany. Also, nonverbal behaviors can determine whether interactions have positive, neutral, or negative outcomes. Thus, if you tell a friend about a distressing experience and she signals her concern via sympathtic nonverbal cues (eye contact, leaning forward, intent facial expression), your feelings about the interaction will be positive. But if she conveys a lack of interest (looking around the room, bored facial expression), you will walk away with negative feelings.

Self-disclosure is critically important to adjustment for several reasons. First, sharing fears and problems (as well as good news) with others who are trustworthy and supportive plays a key role in mental health (Greene et al., 2006). Recall from Chapter 4 that sharing your feelings can reduce stress. And after mutual self-disclosures, people experience a boost in positive feelings (Vittengl

Cartoon DAVE © 1993 Dave Miller. Reprinted with permission of the artist. All rights reserved.

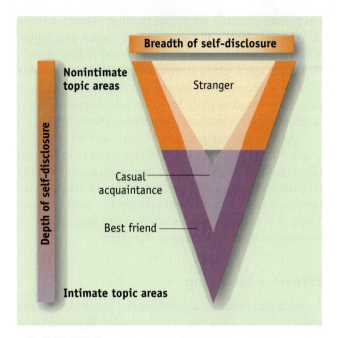

**FIGURE 8.11**

**Breadth and depth of self-disclosure.** Breadth of self-disclosure refers to how many topics one opens up about; depth refers to how far one goes in revealing private information. Both the breadth and depth of one's disclosures are greater with best friends as opposed to casual acquaintances or strangers. (Adapted from Altman & Taylor, 1973)

& Holt, 2000). Second, self-disclosure is a way to build relationships with friends and co-workers (Tardy & Dindia, 2006). Third, emotional (but not factual) self-disclosures lead to feelings of closeness, as long as disclosers feel that listeners are understanding and accepting (Laurenceau & Kleinman 2006; Reis & Shaver, 1988). And, as you saw in Chapter 1, having close relationships is an important ingredient of happiness. Fourth, self-disclosure in romantic relationships correlates positively with relationship satisfaction (Greene et al., 2006). More specifically, *equity* in self-disclosure, rather than high self-disclosure, may be the critical factor that helps couples avoid stress (Bowers, Metts, & Duncanson, 1985).

## Self-Disclosure: What People Tell and Don't Tell Others About Themselves

What sorts of information do people share about themselves with others? What do they hold back? One common thing all people do is recount stories about themselves. The emotional content of these narrative experiences may determine what they share and what we keep to themselves. Three studies on self-disclosure and narrative identity found some intriguing results (Pasupathi, McLean, & Weeks, 2009). While individuals may disclose some emotional events, they are less likely to do so if the events are social transgressions. For example, consider a common indiscretion such as shoplifting. A first-year college student who once acted on a youth-

ful dare may be ashamed to tell her new roommate and potential friend about the experience. In addition, when an event is memorable (such as the death of a beloved grandparent in a hospice), even if the emotion surrounding the event is negative, disclosure is likely to occur. But, when an event is important but distant in time (such as a parental divorce during one's childhood), more negative feelings and less positive emotions regarding it predict a decreased likelihood of disclosure.

### Self-Disclosure and Relationship Development

Earlier, we noted that self-disclosure leads to feelings of intimacy. Actually, the process is a little more complicated than that. Research suggests that only certain types of disclosures lead to feelings of closeness (Laurenceau, Barrett, & Rovine, 2005). For instance, emotional-evaluative self-disclosures (how you feel about your sister, for instance) do, but factual-descriptive self-disclosures (that you have three siblings, for example) do not. Moreover, for intimacy to develop in a relationship, a discloser must feel understood and cared for (Lin & Huang, 2006; Reis & Patrick, 1996). In other words, self-disclosure alone doesn't lead to intimacy—how listeners respond matters, too (Maisel, Gable, & Strachman, 2008). Interestingly, people seem to feel strongly that their expressions of values and what they care about reveal a great deal to others about themselves. However, such self-disclosure is not necessarily viewed as revealing by observers (Pronin, Fleming, & Steffel, 2008).

Self-disclosure varies over the course of relationships. At the beginning of a relationship, high levels of mutual disclosure prevail (Taylor & Altman, 1987). Once a relationship is well established, the level of disclosure tapers off, although responsiveness remains high (Reis & Patrick, 1996). Also, in established relationships people are less likely to reciprocate disclosures in the same conversation. Thus, when a lover or a good friend reveals private information, you frequently respond with words of sympathy and understanding rather than a similar disclosure. This movement away from equal exchanges of self-disclosure appears to be based on twin needs that emerge as intimate relationships develop: (1) the need for connection (via openness) and (2) the need for autonomy (via privacy) (Planalp, Fitness, & Fehr, 2006). By reciprocating support (versus information), individuals can strengthen relationships while maintaining a sense of privacy. In fact, successfully balancing these contradictory needs seems to be an important factor in relationship satisfaction (Finkenauer & Hazam, 2000).

When relationships are in distress, self-disclosure patterns change. For example, one or both individuals may decrease the breadth and depth of their self-disclosures, indicating that they are emotionally withdrawing (Baxter, 1988).

## Culture, Gender, and Self-Disclosure

Americans generally assume that personal sharing is essential to close friendships and happy romantic partnerships. This view is consistent with an individualistic culture that emphasizes the individual and the expression of each person's unique feelings and experiences. In collectivist cultures such as China and Japan, people are open about their group memberships and status because these factors guide social interactions; however, sharing personal information is reserved for established relationships (Samovar et al., 2007).

In the United States, it has been found that females tend to be more openly self-disclosing than males, although the disparity seems smaller than once believed (Fehr, 2004). This gender difference is strongest in *same-gender* friendships, with female friends sharing more personal information than male friends (Reis, 1998; Wright, 2006). In *other-gender* relationships, self-disclosure is more equal, although men with traditional gender-role attitudes are less likely to self-disclose, because they view sharing personal information as a sign of weakness. Also, women share more personal information and feelings, whereas men share more nonpersonal information, both in conversations and in e-mail messages (Boneva, Kraut, & Frohlich, 2001; Kilmartin, 2007).

What about the disclosure styles of men and women in more intimate relationships? One theory argues that such intimate interactions are best fostered by a combination of self-disclosure and empathic responding—that is, being a compassionate listener and supportive partner (Reis & Shaver, 1988). Men and women appear to differ in the emphasis placed on these two behaviors. A recent study found that men's degree of disclosure and empathic responding predicted their own feelings of closeness and confidence in the relationship. Women's feelings of intimacy, however, were more likely to be based on their male partner's degree of disclosure and empathic responding (Mitchell et al., 2008).

Gender disparities in self-disclosure are attributed to socialization. In American culture, most men are taught to conceal tender emotions and feelings of vulnerability, especially from other men (Athenstaedt, Haas, & Schwab, 2004; Kilmartin, 2007). But differ-

ent gender patterns are found in other countries (Reis & Wheeler, 1991). For example, in Jordan and Japan, where early intimacy between male and female friends is discouraged, close contacts between same-gender friends is encouraged. Japanese college students have also been found to score lower on self-disclosure measures that their American counterparts (Kito, 2005).

And, in the early stages of other-gender relationships, American men often disclose more than women (Derlega et al., 1985). This finding is consistent with the traditional expectations that males should initiate relationships and females should encourage males to talk. Thus, it is an oversimplification to say that American women are always more open than men.

## Effective Listening

Listening and hearing are two distinct processes that are often confused. *Hearing* is a physiological process that occurs when sound waves come into contact with our eardrums. In contrast, **listening is a mindful activity and complex process that requires one to select and to organize information, interpret and respond to communications, and recall what one has heard.** Listening well is an active skill, one that even has devoted following (visit the website of the International Listening Association).

Effective listening is a vastly underappreciated skill. There's a lot of truth in the old saying, "We have two ears and only one mouth, so we should listen more than we speak." Because listeners process speech much more rapidly than people speak (between 500 and 1,000 words per minute versus 125–175 words per minute), it's easy for them to become bored, distracted, and inattentive (Hanna, Suggett, & Radtke, 2008). Fatigue and preoccupation with one's own thoughts are other factors that interfere with effective listening.

To be a good listener, you need to keep four points in mind. First, *signal your interest in the speaker by using nonverbal cues.* Face the speaker squarely and lean toward him or her (rather than slouching or leaning back in a chair). This posture shows that you are interested in what the other person has to say. Try not to cross your arms and legs, as this posture can signal defensiveness. Maintaining eye contact with the speaker also conveys your attentiveness. (You know how annoying it is to talk with someone whose eyes are roaming around the room.) Communicate your feelings about what the speaker is saying by nodding your head or raising your eyebrows.

Second, *hear the other person out before you respond.* Listeners often tune out or interrupt a conversational partner when (1) they know someone well (because they believe that they already know what the speaker will say), (2) a speaker has mannerisms listeners find frustrating (stuttering, mumbling, speaking in

---

**WEB LINK 8.3   Cross-Cultural Communication Strategies**

Citizens of the 21st century are challenged to communicate sensitively with individuals from other cultural groups both within the United States and around the world. This site, maintained by the Conflict Research Consortium at the University of Colorado, provides commentaries by experts on a variety of intercultural communication settings.

© Yellow Dog Productions/Getty Images/The Image Bank

**Being a good listener is an essential skill that contributes to success in relationships and on the job.**

a monotone), and (3) a speaker discusses ideas (abortion, politics) that generate strong feelings or uses terms (*welfare cheat, redneck*) that push "hot buttons." Although it is challenging not to tune out a speaker or lob an insult in these situations, you'll be better able to formulate an appropriate response if you allow the speaker to complete his or her thought.

Third, *engage in active listening* (Verderber et al., 2008). Pay attention to what the speaker is saying and mindfully process the information. Active listening also involves the skills of clarifying and paraphrasing. Inevitably, a speaker will skip over an essential point or say something that is confusing. When this happens, you need to ask for clarification. "Was Bill her boyfriend or

her brother?" Clarifying ensures that you have an accurate picture of the message and also tells the speaker that you are interested. Paraphrasing takes clarifying another step. To paraphrase means to state concisely what you believe the speaker said. You might say, "Let me see if I've got this right . . ." or "Do you mean . . .?" It's obviously silly to paraphrase every single thing the speaker says; you need to paraphrase only when the speaker says something important. Paraphrasing has a number of benefits: It reassures the speaker that you are "with" him or her, it derails misinterpretations, and it keeps you focused on the conversation.

Paraphrasing can take several forms (Verderber et al., 2008). In *content paraphrasing,* you focus on the literal meaning of the message. In *feelings paraphrasing,* you focus on the emotions connected to the content of the message. If your friend declares, "I just can't believe he showed up at the party with my old girlfriend!," a feelings paraphrase is obviously in order ("You were really hurt by that").

To develop your skill at paraphrasing, try practicing it with a friend. Have the friend tell you about something. Your job is to paraphrase from time to time to be sure that you really understand what your friend is trying to communicate. After each paraphrase, your friend can tell you whether he or she agrees with your interpretation. Don't be surprised if you have to rephrase several times. Keep trying until you get it right. You may discover that paraphrasing is harder than you think!

Finally, *pay attention to the other person's nonverbal signals.* Listeners use a speaker's words to get the "objective" meaning of a message, but they rely on nonverbal cues for the emotional and interpersonal meanings of a message. Your knowledge of body language, tone of voice, and other nonverbal cues can give you deeper understanding of what others are communicating. Remember that these cues are available not only when the other person is speaking but also when you are talking. If you often get signals that your listener is drifting away, you might be going overboard on irrelevant details or, perhaps, hogging the conversation. The antidote is active listening.

Most people are inadequate listeners because they are unaware of the elements of effective listening—information you now have. Also, effective listening hinges largely on your attitude. If you're willing to work at it, you can become a good listener fairly quickly.

*"Of course I'm listening. I'm in a heightened state of alert."*

© Leo Cullum/The New Yorker Collection/www.cartoonbank.com

# Communication Problems

**LEARNING OBJECTIVES**

● Discuss some common responses to communication apprehension.
● Identify four barriers to effective communication.

In this section, we focus on two problems that can interfere with effective communication: anxiety and communication barriers.

## Communication Apprehension

It's the first day of your child psychology class and you have just learned that 30-minute oral presentations are a course requirement. Do you welcome this requirement as an opportunity to polish your public speaking skills or, panic-stricken, do you race to the nearest computer station to drop the class? If you opted for the latter, you may suffer from *communication apprehension,* **or anxiety caused by having to talk with others.** Some people experience communication apprehension in all speaking situations (including one-on-one encounters), but most people who have the problem notice it only when they have to speak before groups. Communication apprehension is a concern for students as well as teachers because it can adversely affect general academic success as well as performance related to public speaking requirements in the classroom (Bourhis, Allen, & Bauman, 2006). Interestingly, greater confidence in one's communication skills is positively associated with better listening skills. However, more-confident people apparently have a more difficult time extracting emotional content from communications than those who are less certain of themselves (Clark, 1989). The explanation may be that less-certain individuals review emotional communications with greater care.

Bodily experiences associated with communication apprehension can range from "butterflies" in the stomach to cold hands, dry mouth, and a racing heart rate. These physiological effects are stress-induced "fight or flight" responses of the autonomic nervous system (see Chapter 3). The physiological responses themselves aren't the root of communication apprehension; rather, the problem lies in the speaker's *interpretation* of these bodily responses. That is, high scorers on measures of communication apprehension frequently interpret the bodily changes they experience in public speaking situations as indications of fear. In contrast, low scorers often chalk up these reactions to the normal excitement in such a situation (Richmond & McCroskey, 1995).

Researchers have identified four responses to communication apprehension (Richmond & McCroskey, 1995). The most common is *avoidance,* or choosing not to participate when confronted with a voluntary communication opportunity. If people believe that speaking will make them uncomfortable, they will typically avoid the experience. *Withdrawal* occurs when people unexpectedly find themselves trapped in a communication situation they can't escape. Here they may clam up entirely or say as little as possible. *Disruption* refers to the inability to make fluent oral presentations or to engage in appropriate verbal or nonverbal behavior. Of course, inadequate communication skills can produce this same behavioral effect, and it isn't always possible for the average person to identify the actual cause of the problem. *Overcommunication* is a relatively unusual response to high communication apprehension, but it does occur. An example would be someone who attempts to dominate social situations by talking nonstop. Although such individuals are seen as poor communicators, they are not usually perceived as having communication apprehension. That's because we expect to see this problem only in those who talk very little. Of course, overcommunication may be caused by other factors as well.

Obviously, avoidance and withdrawal tactics are merely short-term strategies for coping with communication apprehension (Richmond & McCroskey, 1995). Because it is unlikely that you can go though life without having to speak in front of a group, it is important to learn to cope with this stressful event rather than avoid it time and again. Allowing the problem to get out of hand can result in self-limiting behavior, such as refusing a job promotion that entails public speaking. People with high communication apprehension are likely to have difficulties in relationships, at work, and at school (Richmond & McCroskey, 1995).

Happily, there are effective ways to reduce speech anxiety. With the technique of visualization, for example, you picture yourself successfully going through

**WEB LINK 8.4  Effective Presentations**

Students often tell teachers that they are terrified of making a presentation in front of a class. Professor Jeff Radel (University of Kansas Medical Center) has crafted an excellent set of guides to show the best ways of communicating by means of oral presentations, visual materials, and posters.

all of the steps involved in preparing for and making a presentation. Research shows that people who practice visualization have less anxiety and fewer negative thoughts when they actually speak compared to pre-visualization levels (Ayres, Hopf, & Ayres, 1994; but see Ayres, 2005). Both *positive reinterpretation* (see Chapter 4) and *systematic desensitization* (Chapter 15) are also highly effective methods for dealing with this problem.

## Barriers to Effective Communication

Earlier in the chapter, we discussed noise and its disruptive effects on interpersonal communication. Now we want to check out some psychological factors that contribute to noise. These barriers to effective communication can reside in the sender, in the receiver, or sometimes in both. Common obstacles include defensiveness, ambushing, motivational distortion, and self-preoccupation.

### Defensiveness

Perhaps the most basic barrier to effective communication is *defensiveness*—**an excessive concern with protecting oneself from being hurt**. People usually react defensively when they feel threatened, such as when they believe that others are evaluating them or trying to control or manipulate them. Defensiveness is also triggered when others act in a superior manner. Thus, those who flaunt their status, wealth, brilliance, or power often put receivers on the defensive. Dogmatic people who project "I'm always right" also breed defensiveness. A threat need not be real to elicit defensive behavior. If you persuade yourself that Brandon won't like you, your interactions with him will probably not be very positive. And, if the self-fulfilling prophecy kicks in, you may produce the negative reaction you fear. Strive to cultivate a communication style that minimizes defensiveness in others. At the same time, keep in mind that you don't have complete control over others' perceptions and reactions.

### Ambushing

Some listeners are really just looking for the opportunity to attack a presenter. Although the person who is about to attack—we might label such people verbal "bushwhackers"—is really listening carefully and intently to what is being said, his or her purpose in doing so is simply to assail or harass the speaker (Wood, 2010). Understanding, discussing, or having an otherwise thoughtful exchange of ideas and opinions is not the point. People who engage in ambushing almost always arouse defensiveness from others, especially in those whom they attack. Sadly, ambushing can be an effective barrier to communication because few people relish being hassled or bullied in front of others.

### Motivational Distortion

In Chapter 7, we discussed distortions and expectancies in person perception. These same processes operate in communication. That is, motivational distortion occurs when people hear what they want to hear instead of what is actually being said. Each person has a unique frame of reference—certain attitudes, values, and expectations—that can influence what he or she hears. Information that contradicts an individual's own views often produces emotional distress. One way people avoid such unpleasant feelings is to engage in *selective attention,* or actively choosing to attend to information that supports their beliefs and ignoring information that contradicts them. Similarly, an individual may read unintended meanings into statements or jump to erroneous conclusions. This tendency to distort information occurs most often when people are discussing issues they feel strongly about, such as politics, racism, sexism, homosexuality, or abortion.

### Self-Preoccupation

Who hasn't experienced the frustration of trying to communicate with someone who is so self-focused as to make two-way conversation impossible? Self-preoccupied people are engaging in what is called *pseudolistening,* or pretending to listen while their minds are occupied with other topics that have captured their attention (O'Keefe, 2002). These annoying individuals seem to talk to hear themselves talk. If you try to slip in a word about *your* problems, they cut you off by proclaiming, "That's nothing. Listen to what happened to me!" Further, self-preoccupied people are poor listeners. When someone else is talking, they're mentally rehearsing their next comments. Because they are self-focused, these individuals are usually oblivious to their negative impact on others. Self-preoccupied people arouse negative reactions in others for several reasons. First, their remarks are usually so self-serving (seeking to impress, to gain unwarranted sympathy, and so on) that others find the remarks offensive. Another problem is that they consistently take up more than their fair share of conversation time. After a "conversation" with such a person, listeners feel ignored. No wonder people try to avoid these individuals if they can. If they can't, they usually respond only minimally to end the conversation quickly. Needless to say, you risk alienating others if you ignore the norm that conversations should involve a mutual sharing of information.

# Interpersonal Conflict

## LEARNING OBJECTIVES

- Assess the pros and cons of avoiding versus facing conflict.
- Recognize five personal styles of dealing with interpersonal conflict.
- Articulate eight tips for coping effectively with interpersonal conflict.

People do not have to be enemies to be in conflict, and being in conflict does not make people enemies. *Interpersonal conflict* **exists whenever two or more people disagree.** By this definition, conflict occurs between friends and lovers as well as between competitors and enemies. Interpersonal conflict is present anytime people have disparate views, opposing perspectives, incompatible goals, and a desire to try to address and resolve their differences (Wilmot & Hocker, 2006). The discord may be caused by a simple misunderstanding, or it may be a product of incompatible goals, values, attitudes, or beliefs. Because conflict is an unavoidable aspect of interactions, knowing how to deal constructively with it is essential. Many studies report associations between effective conflict management and relationship satisfaction (Gill, Christensen, & Fincham, 1999; Kline et al., 2006).

## Beliefs About Conflict

Many people assume that any kind of conflict is bad and that it should be suppressed if at all possible. In reality, conflict is neither inherently bad nor inherently good. It is a natural phenomenon that may lead to

either good or bad outcomes, depending on how people deal with it. When people see conflict as negative, they tend to avoid dealing with it. Of course, sometimes avoiding conflict can be good. If a relationship or an issue is of little importance to you, or if you believe that the costs of confrontation are too high (your boss might fire you), avoidance might be the best way to handle a conflict. Also, cultures differ in how conflict should be handled. Collectivist cultures (such as China and Japan) often avoid conflict, whereas individualistic cultures tend to encourage direct confrontations (Samovar et al., 2007; Zhang, Harwood, & Hummert, 2005). In individualistic cultures, the consequences of avoiding conflict depend on the nature of the relationship. When relationships and issues are important, avoiding conflict is generally counterproductive. For one thing, it can lead to a self-perpetuating cycle (see **Figure 8.12**).

Let's consider an example of a cultural difference—a comparison of Japanese and American styles of negotiation, a situation where conflict may arise (McDaniel & Quasha, 2000; Weiss, 1987). Japanese values urge those involved in negotiations to seek ways to

Disagreements are a fact of everyday life, so effective communicators need to learn how to deal with them constructively.

© Radius Images/Alamy

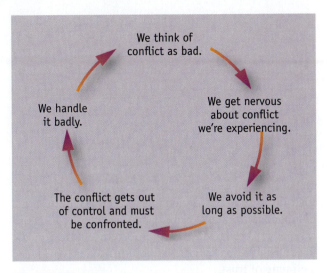

**FIGURE 8.12**

**The conflict avoidance cycle.** Avoiding conflict can lead to a self-perpetuating cycle: (1) People think of conflict as bad, (2) they get nervous about a conflict they are experiencing, (3) they avoid the conflict as long as possible, (4) the conflict gets out of control and must be confronted, and (5) they handle the confrontation badly. In turn, this negative experience sets the stage for avoiding conflict the next time—usually with the same negative outcome. (Adapted from Lulofs, 1994)

avoid conflict. In contrast, American values encourage a bit of competition as well as assertiveness (see **Figure 8.13**). As you review the figure's content, imagine you were involved in delicate negotiations regarding some business transaction: Which cultural style for dealing with conflict would you prefer?

When dealt with openly and constructively, interpersonal conflict can lead to a variety of valuable outcomes (Clark & Grote, 2003). Among other things, constructive confrontation may (1) bring problems out into the open where they can be solved, (2) put an end to chronic sources of discontent in a relationship, and (3) lead to new insights through the airing of divergent views.

## Styles of Managing Conflict

How do you react to conflict? Most people have a habitual way or personal style of dealing with dissension. Studies have consistently revealed five distinct patterns of dealing with conflict: avoiding/withdrawing, accommodating, competing/forcing, compromising, and collaborating (Lulofs & Cahn, 2000). Two dimensions underlie these different styles: interest in satisfying one's own concerns and interest in satisfying others' concerns (Rahim & Magner, 1995). You can see the location of these five styles on these two dimensions in **Figure 8.14** on the next page. As you read about these styles, try to determine where you fit.

● *Avoiding/withdrawing* (low concern for self and others). Some people simply find conflict extremely distasteful. When a conflict emerges, the avoider will change the subject, deflect discussion with humor, make a hasty exit, or pretend to be preoccupied with something else. Usually, people who prefer this style hope that ignoring a problem will make it go away. For minor problems, this tactic is often a good one—there's no need to react to every little annoyance. For bigger conflicts, avoiding/withdrawing is not a good strategy; it usually just delays the inevitable clash. A particular problem occurs when an avoider has greater power in a relationship (parent, supervisor, romantic partner). This situation prevents the less powerful person from airing his or her concerns and breeds frustration and resentment. Of course, in some cases it is good to postpone a discussion, especially if one or both individuals are tired or rushed or need time to cool off. Postponing qualifies as avoiding only if the promised discussion never takes place.

● *Accommodating* (low concern for self, high concern for others). Like the avoider, the accommodator feels uncomfortable with conflict. However, instead of

| Japanese and American Styles of Negotiation | |
|---|---|
| **American style** | **Japanese style** |
| Overstate your initial position to establish a strong image. | Understate your initial position or state it vaguely to allow the other side to state their position. |
| Keep your bottom line secret from the other person to preserve your power and gain the most. | Find informal ways to let the other person know your bottom line to move agreement forward without directly confronting the other with your bottom line. |
| Where there are differences, assert your position and attempt to win the other's assent. | Look for areas of agreement and focus talk on them. |
| Be adversarial. | Avoid confrontation or explicit disagreement. |
| Work to win all you can. | Work to make sure that neither you nor the other person fails. |
| Push to reach decisions as rapidly as possible. | Plan to spend a long time discussing issues before even moving toward a decision. |

**FIGURE 8.13**

**Navigating conflict by negotiation through cultural values.** Different cultures have different ways of navigating conflicts and reaching agreements. Visitors to other cultures, particularly those from the business world, risk ruining deals or possible partnerships if they fail to interpret their colleagues correctly. Here are some examples of how Japanese and Americans differ in their typical style of negotiation.

Source: Adapted from Wood, J. T. (2010). *Interpersonal communication: Everyday encounters* (6th ed.). Boston, MA: Wadsworth (p. 232), based on McDaniel & Quasha (2000) and Weiss (1987).

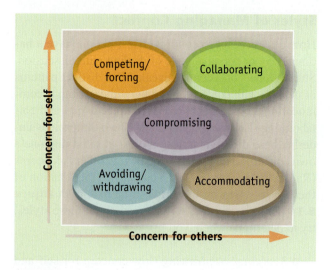

**FIGURE 8.14**

**Five styles of handling interpersonal conflict.** In dealing with discord, individuals typically prefer one of five styles. The two dimensions of *concern for self* and *concern for others* underlie each of the five styles.

ignoring the disagreement, this person brings the conflict to a quick end by giving in easily. People who are overly concerned about acceptance and approval from others commonly use this strategy of surrender. Habitual accommodating is a poor way of dealing with conflict because it does not generate creative thinking and effective solutions. Moreover, feelings of resentment (on both sides) may develop because the accommodator often likes to play the role of a martyr. Of course, when you don't have strong preferences (for instance, where to eat out), occasional accommodating is perfectly appropriate. Also, in some cultures (such as Japan), it is the preferred style of dealing with conflict (Samovar et al., 2007).

● *Competing/forcing* (high concern for self, low concern for others). The competitor turns every conflict into a black-and-white, win-or-lose situation. Competitors will do virtually anything to emerge victorious from confrontations; thus, they can be deceitful and aggressive—including using verbal attacks and physical threats. They rigidly adhere to one position and will use threats and coercion to force the other party to submit. This style is undesirable because, like accommodation, it fails to generate creative solutions to problems. Moreover, this approach is especially likely to lead to post-conflict tension, resentment, and hostility.

● *Compromising* (moderate concern for self and others). Compromising is a pragmatic approach to conflict that acknowledges the divergent needs of both parties. Compromisers are willing to negotiate and to meet the other person halfway. With this approach, each person gives up something so both can have partial satisfaction. Because both parties gain some satisfaction, compromising is a fairly constructive approach to conflict, especially when the issue is moderately important.

● *Collaborating* (high concern for self and others). Whereas compromising simply entails "splitting the difference" between positions, collaborating involves a sincere effort to find a solution that will optimally satisfy both parties. In this approach, conflict is viewed as a mutual problem to be solved as effectively as possible. Collaborating thus encourages openness and honesty. It also stresses the importance of criticizing the other person's *ideas* in a disagreement rather than the other *person*. To collaborate, you have to work on clarifying differences and similarities in positions so that you can build on the similarities. Generally, this is the most productive approach for dealing with conflict. Instead of resulting in a postconflict residue of tension and resentment, collaborating tends to produce a climate of trust.

## Dealing Constructively with Conflict

As you have seen, the most effective approach to conflict management is collaborating. To help you implement such an approach, we will offer some specific suggestions. But, before we get down to specifics, there are a few principles to keep in mind (Alberti & Emmons, 2001; Verderber et al., 2007). First, in a conflict situation, try to give the other person the benefit of the doubt; don't automatically assume that those who disagree with you are ignorant or mean-spirited. Show respect for their position, and do your best to empathize with, and fully understand, their frame of reference. Second, approach the other person as an equal. If you have a higher status or more power (parent, supervisor), try to set this difference aside. Third, define the conflict as a mutual problem to be solved cooperatively, rather than as a win-lose proposition. Fourth, choose a mutually acceptable time to sit down and work on resolving the conflict. It is not always best to tackle the conflict when and where it first arises. Finally, communicate your flexibility and willingness to modify your position.

Here are some explicit guidelines for dealing effectively with interpersonal conflict (Alberti & Emmons, 2001; Verderber et al., 2007):

● *Make communication honest and open.* Don't withhold information or misrepresent your position. Avoid deceit and manipulation.

**WEB LINK 8.5   The Conflict Resolution Information Source**

This excellent resource on conflict management is provided by the University of Colorado's Conflict Research Consortium. The site is actually a gateway to a huge variety of resources on conflict management and is easy to navigate.

- *Use specific behaviors to describe another person's annoying habits rather than general statements about their personality.* You'll probably get further with your roommate if you say something like, "Please throw your clothes in the hamper" rather than "You're such an inconsiderate slob." Remarks about specific actions are less threatening and are less likely to be taken personally. They also clarify what you hope will change.

- *Avoid "loaded" words.* Certain words are "loaded" in the sense that they tend to trigger negative emotional reactions in listeners. For example, you can discuss politics without using terms such as "right-winger" and "knee-jerk liberal."

- *Try using grace.* The word "grace" refers to honoring the needs of others by putting aside one's own desires (Wood, 2010). Graceful acts occur when one person shows kindness that is likely never to be repaid; indeed, the person doesn't expect to receive any compensation in return. Perhaps you and your roommate agreed to split chores. She fails to live up to her part of the agreement one week, presumably because she has an inordinate amount of schoolwork to do. Instead of instigating a conflict, you do her chores and say nothing about it. Your gracious act helps her and at the same time avoids creating a conflict; in a sense, you are helping yourself as well.

- *Use a positive approach and help the other person save face.* Saying "I love it when we cook dinner together" will go over better than "You never help with dinner, and I resent it." Similarly, you can increase your chances of having a request accepted if you say, "I really-

ize that you are very busy, but I'd really appreciate it if you would look at my paper again. I've marked the places I'd like you to reconsider."

- *Limit complaints to recent behavior and to the current situation.* Dredging up past grievances only rekindles old resentments and distracts you from the current problem. And avoid saying things like "You *always* say you're too busy" or "You *never* do your fair share of the housework." Such categorical statements are bound to put the other person on the defensive.

- *Assume responsibility for your own feelings and preferences.* Rather than "*You* make me mad," say "*I* am angry." Or, try "I'd appreciate it if you'd water the garden" instead of "Do you think the garden needs watering?"

- *Use an assertive (as opposed to submissive or aggressive) communication style.* This approach will make it easier to head off and deal constructively with conflict situations. In the upcoming Application, we elaborate on *assertive communication* and its usefulness in a wide variety of interpersonal communication situations, such as making acquaintances, developing relationships, and resolving conflicts.

We'll close this section with some food for thought. Think of relationships as having a "bank account" (Notarius & Markman, 1993). People make both deposits to (kindnesses, compliments) and withdrawals from (negative interactions, hostile comments) these accounts. Happy couples know that to avoid being overdrawn, it's important to make frequent deposits to offset the unavoidable withdrawals (Kline, et al., 2006)

# APPLICATION

## *Developing an Assertive Communication Style*

### LEARNING OBJECTIVES

- Distinguish among assertive, submissive, and aggressive communication.
- List five steps that lead to more assertive communication.

*Answer the following questions "yes" or "no."*

____ 1. When someone asks you for an unreasonable favor, is it difficult to say no?

____ 2. Do you feel timid about returning flawed merchandise?

____ 3. Do you have a hard time requesting even small favors from others?

____ 4. When a group is hotly debating an issue, are you shy about speaking up?

____ 5. When a salesperson pressures you to buy something you don't want, is it hard for you to resist?

If you answered "yes" to several of these questions, you may need to increase your assertiveness. Many people have a hard time being assertive; however, this problem is more common among females because they are socialized to be more submissive than males—to "be nice." Consequently, assertiveness training is especially popular among women. Men, too, find assertiveness training helpful, both because some have been socialized to be passive and because others want to learn to be less aggressive and more assertive. In this Application we elaborate on the differences between assertive, submissive, and aggressive behavior and discuss some procedures for increasing assertiveness.

Keep in mind that the views here reflect an individualistic perspective. Other cultures may have different perspectives on submissiveness, assertiveness, and aggressiveness (Samovar et al., 2007). For instance, some Native American tribes disdain both assertiveness and aggression. Similarly, such collectivist societies as China, Japan, Thailand, and the Philippines place a high value on interpersonal harmony. By contrast, Israelis and members of the Jewish culture tend to have a more confrontational interactional style in which vigorous debate is expected. Within the United States, African Americans tend to have a somewhat more assertive style than European Americans (Houston, 2004; Orbuch & Veroff, 2002).

## The Nature of Assertiveness

*Assertiveness* **involves acting in one's own best interests by expressing one's thoughts and feelings directly and honestly.** Essentially, assertiveness involves standing up for your rights when someone else is about to infringe on them. To be assertive is to speak out rather than pull your punches.

The nature of assertive communication can best be clarified by contrasting it with other types of communication. *Submissive communication* is deferential, as it involves giving in to others on points of possible contention. Submissive people often let others take advantage of them. Typically, their biggest problem is that they cannot say no to unreasonable requests. A common example is the college student who can't tell her roommate not to borrow her clothes. Submissive people also have difficulty voicing disagreement with others and making requests themselves. In traditional trait terminology, they are timid.

Although the roots of submissiveness have not been investigated fully, they appear to lie in excessive concern about gaining the social approval of others. However, the strategy of "not making waves" is more likely to garner others' contempt than their approval. Moreover, individuals who use this style often feel bad about themselves (for being "pushovers") and resentful of those whom they allow to take advantage of them. These feelings often lead the submissive individual to try to punish the other person by withdrawing, sulking, or crying (Bower & Bower, 1991, 2004). These manipulative attempts to get one's own way are sometimes referred to as "passive aggression" or "indirect aggression."

At the other end of the spectrum, *aggressive communication* focuses on saying and getting what one wants at the expense of others' feelings and rights. With assertive behavior, however, one strives to respect others' rights and defend one's own. The problem in real life is that assertive and aggressive behaviors *may* overlap. When someone is about to infringe on their rights, people often lash out at the other party (aggression) while defending their rights (assertion). The challenge, then, is to be firm and assertive without becoming aggressive. Advocates of assertive communication argue that it is much more adaptive than either submissive or aggressive communication (Alberti & Emmons, 2001; Bower & Bower, 1991, 2004). They maintain that submissive behavior leads to poor self-esteem, self-denial, emotional suppression, and strained interpersonal relationships. Conversely, aggressive communication

## KUDZU

© Tribune Media Services, Inc. All Rights Reserved. Reprinted with permission.

tends to promote guilt, alienation, and disharmony. In contrast, assertive behavior is said to foster high self-esteem, satisfactory interpersonal relationships, and effective conflict management. Here are three different ways to express the same desire:

*Aggressive:* "I want Chinese food tonight, so that is what we are going to eat. End of story."

*Assertive:* "I feel like having Chinese food tonight—do you?"

*Submissive:* "It's okay with me if we don't have Chinese food tonight; whatever you feel like having is fine with me."

The essential point with assertiveness is that you are able to state what you want clearly and directly. Being able to do so makes you feel good about yourself and will usually make others feel good about you, too. And, although being assertive doesn't guarantee your chances for getting what you want, it certainly enhances them.

## Steps in Assertiveness Training

Numerous assertiveness training programs are available in book form, on CDs or DVDs, or through seminars. Most of the programs are behavioral and emphasize gradual improvement and reinforcement of appropriate behavior. Here we summarize the key steps in assertiveness training.

### 1. Understand What Assertive Communication Is

To produce assertive behavior, you need to understand what it looks and sounds like. Thus, most programs begin by clarifying the nature of assertive communication. Assertiveness trainers often ask clients to imagine situations calling for assertiveness and compare hypothetical submissive (or passive), assertive, and aggressive responses. Let's consider one such comparison. In this example, a woman in assertiveness training is asking her roommate to cooperate in cleaning their apartment once a week. The roommate, who is uninterested in the problem, is listening to music when the conversation begins. In this example, the roommate is playing the role of the antagonist—called a "downer" in the following scripts (excerpted from Bower & Bower, 2004, pp. 8, 9, 11).

### The Passive Scene

**SHE:** *Uh, I was wondering if you would be willing to take time to decide about the housecleaning.*

**DOWNER:** *(listening to the music) Not now, I'm busy.*

**SHE:** *Oh, okay.*

### The Aggressive Scene

**SHE:** *Listen, I've had it with you not even talking about cleaning this damn apartment. Are you going to help me?*

**DOWNER:** *(listening to the music) Not now, I'm busy.*

**SHE:** *Why can't you look at me when you turn me down? You don't give a damn about the housework or me! You only care about yourself!*

**DOWNER:** *That's not true.*

**SHE:** *You never pay any attention to the apartment or to me. I have to do everything around here!*

**DOWNER:** *Oh, shut up! You're just neurotic about cleaning all the time. Who are you, my mother? Can't I relax with my stereo for a few minutes without you pestering me? This was my apartment first, you know!*

### The Assertive Scene

**SHE:** *I know housework isn't the most fascinating subject, but it needs to be done. Let's plan when we'll do it.*

**DOWNER:** *(listening to music) Oh, c'mon—not now! I'm busy.*

**SHE:** *This won't take long. I feel that if we have a schedule, it will be easier to keep up with the chores.*

**DOWNER:** *I'm not sure I'll have time for all of them.*

**SHE:** *I've already drawn up a couple of rotating schedules for housework, so that each week we have an equal division of tasks. Will you look at them? I'd like to hear your decisions about them, say, tonight after supper?*

**DOWNER:** *[indignantly] I have to look at these now?*

**SHE:** *Is there some other time that's better for you?*

**DOWNER:** *Oh, I don't know.*

**SHE:** *Well, then let's discuss plans after supper for 15 minutes. Is that agreed?*

**DOWNER:** *I guess so.*

**SHE:** *Good! It won't take long, and I'll feel relieved when we have a schedule in place.*

A helpful way to distinguish among the three types of communication is in terms of how people deal with their own rights and the rights of others. Submissive people sacrifice their own rights. Aggressive people tend to ignore the rights of others. Assertive people consider both their own rights *and* the rights of others.

As we have noted, the nonverbal aspect of communication is extremely important. To ensure that your assertive words have impact, it is important to back them up with congruent nonverbal messages. Thus, you'll come across as more assertive if you face the person you're talking with, look directly at him or her, and maintain eye contact, rather than looking away from the other person, fidgeting, slouching, and shuffling your feet (Bower &

Bower, 1991, 2004). You'll find some additional guidelines for behaving assertively in **Figure 8.15**.

## 2. Monitor Your Assertive Communication

Most people's assertiveness varies from one situation to another. In other words, they may be assertive in some social contexts and timid in others. Consequently, once you understand the nature of assertive communication, you should monitor yourself and identify when you are nonassertive. In particular, you should figure out *who* intimidates you, on *what topics,* and in *which situations.*

## 3. Observe a Model's Assertive Communication

Once you have identified the situations in which you are nonassertive, think of someone who communicates assertively in those situations and observe that person's behavior closely. In other words, find someone to model yourself after. This is an easy way to learn how to behave assertively in situations crucial to you. Your observations should also allow you to see how rewarding assertive communication can be, which should strengthen your assertive tendencies. If an assertive model isn't available, you can adapt the relevant scenarios in most self-help books on assertiveness.

### FIGURE 8.15

**Guidelines for assertive behavior.** Gordon and Sharon Bower (1991, 2004) outline a four-step program intended to help readers create successful assertive scripts for themselves. The four steps are (1) *describe* the unwanted behavior from another person (called your "Downer") that is troubling you, (2) *express* your feelings about the behavior to the other person, (3) *specify* the changes needed, and (4) try to provide rewarding *consequences* for the change. Using this framework, the table shown here provides some useful dos and don'ts for achieving effective assertive behavior.

Source: Adapted from Bower, S. A., & Bower, G. H. (1991). *Asserting yourself: A practical guide for positive change* (2nd ed.). Reading, MA: Addison-Wesley. Copyright © 2004 by Sharon Anthony Bower and Gordon H. Bower. Reprinted by permission of Da Capo Press, a member of the Perseus Books Group.

| Rules for Assertive Scripts | |
|---|---|
| **Do** | **Don't** |
| **Describe** | |
| Describe the other person's behavior objectively. | Describe your emotional reaction to it. |
| Use concrete terms. | Use abstract, vague terms. |
| Describe a specified time, place, and frequency of the action. | Generalize for "all time." |
| Describe the action, not the "motive." | Guess at your Downer's motives or goals. |
| **Express** | |
| Express your feelings. | Deny your feelings. |
| Express them calmly. | Unleash emotional outbursts. |
| State feelings in a positive manner, as relating to a goal to be achieved. | State feelings negatively, making Downer attack. |
| Direct yourself to the specific offending behavior, not to the whole person. | Attack the entire character of the person. |
| **Specify** | |
| Ask explicitly for change in your Downer's behavior. | Merely imply that you'd like a change. |
| Request a small change. | Ask for too large a change. |
| Request only one or two changes at one time. | Ask for too many changes. |
| Specify the concrete actions you want to see stopped and those you want to see performed. | Ask for changes in nebulous traits or qualities. |
| Take account of whether your Downer can meet your request without suffering large losses. | Ignore your Downer's needs or ask only for your satisfaction. |
| Specify (if appropriate) what behavior you are willing to change to make the agreement. | Consider that only your Downer has to change. |
| **Consequences** | |
| Make the consequences explicit. | Be ashamed to talk about rewards and penalties. |
| Give a positive reward for change in the desired direction. | Give only punishments for lack of change. |
| Select something that is desirable and reinforcing to your Downer. | Select something that only you might find rewarding. |
| Select a reward that is big enough to maintain the behavior change. | Offer a reward you can't or won't deliver. |
| Select a punishment of a magnitude that "fits the crime" of refusing to change behavior. | Make exaggerated threats. |
| Select a punishment that you are actually willing to carry out. | Use unrealistic threats or self-defeating punishment. |

## Assertive Responses to Some Common Putdowns

| Nature of remark | Put-down sentence | Suggested assertive reply |
|---|---|---|
| Nagging about details | "Haven't you done this yet?" | "No, when did you want it done?" (Answer without hedging, and follow up with a question.) |
| Prying | "I know I maybe shouldn't ask, but . . ." | "If I don't want to answer, I'll let you know." (Indicate that you won't make yourself uncomfortable just to please this person.) |
| Putting you on the spot socially | "Are you busy Tuesday?" | "What do you have in mind?" (Answer the question with a question.) |
| Pigeonholing you | "That's a woman for you!" | "That's one woman, not *all* women." (Disagree—assert your individuality.) |
| Using insulting labels for your behavior | "That's a dumb way to . . ." | "I'll decide what to call my behavior." (Refuse to accept the label.) |
| Basing predictions on an amateur personality analysis | "You'll have a hard time. You're too shy." | "In what ways do you think I'm too shy?" (Ask for clarification of the analysis.) |

**FIGURE 8.16**

**Assertive responses to common put-downs.** Having some assertive replies at the ready can increase your confidence in difficult social interactions.

Source: Adapted from Bower, S. A., & Bower, G. H. (1991). *Asserting yourself: A practical guide for positive change* (2nd ed.). Reading, MA: Addison-Wesley. Copyright © 2004 by Sharon Anthony Bower and Gordon H. Bower. Reprinted by permission of Da Capo Press, a member of the Perseus Books Group.

### 4. Practice Assertive Communication

The key to achieving assertive communication is to practice it and work toward gradual improvement. Your practice can take several forms. In *covert rehearsal,* you imagine a situation requiring assertion and the dialogue that you would engage in. In *role playing,* you ask a friend or therapist to play the role of an antagonist. Then practice communicating assertively in this artificial situation.

Eventually, of course, you want to transfer your assertiveness skills to real-life situations. Most experts recommend that you use *shaping* to increase your assertive communication gradually. As we discussed in the Chapter 3 Application, shaping involves rewarding yourself for making closer and closer approximations of a desired behavior. For example, in the early stages of your behavior-change program, your goal might be to make at least one assertive comment every day, while toward the end you might be striving to make at least eight such comments a day. Obviously, in designing a shaping program, it is important to set realistic goals for yourself.

### 5. Adopt an Assertive Attitude

Most assertiveness training programs have a behavioral orientation and focus on specific responses for specific situations (see **Figure 8.16**). However, it's obvious that real-life situations only rarely match those portrayed in books. Thus, some experts maintain that acquiring a repertoire of verbal responses for certain situations is not as important as developing a new attitude that you're not going to let people push you around (or let yourself push others around, if you're the aggressive type) (Alberti & Emmons, 2001). Although most programs don't talk explicitly about attitudes, they do appear to instill a new attitude indirectly. A change in attitude is probably crucial to achieving flexible, assertive behavior.

### The Process of Interpersonal Communication

● Interpersonal communication is the interactional process that occurs when one person sends a message to another. Communication takes place when a sender transmits a message to a receiver either verbally or nonverbally. The widespread use of electronic communication devices has raised new issues in interpersonal communication. Although people often take it for granted, effective communication contributes to their adjustment in school, in relationships, and at work.

### Nonverbal Communication

● Nonverbal communication conveys emotions, above all. It tends to be more spontaneous than verbal communication, and it is more ambiguous. Sometimes it contradicts what is communicated verbally. It is often multichanneled and, like language, is culturally bound.

● The amount of personal space that people prefer depends on culture, gender, social status, and situational factors. Facial expressions can convey a great deal of information about people's emotions. Variations in eye contact can influence nonverbal communication in a host of ways.

● Body postures can hint at interest in communication, and they often reflect status differences. Touch can communicate support, consolation, intimacy, status, and power. Paralanguage refers to *how* something is said rather than *what* is said.

● Certain nonverbal cues are associated with deception, but many of these cues do not correspond to popular beliefs about how liars give themselves away. Discrepancies between facial expressions and other nonverbal signals may suggest dishonesty. The vocal and visual cues associated with lying are so subtle, however, that the detection of deception is difficult. Machines used to detect deception (polygraphs) are not particularly accurate.

● Nonverbal communication, particularly nonverbal sensitivity, plays an important role in adjustment, especially in the quality of interpersonal relationships. Women are typically more nonverbally sensitive than men because they exert more effort at it.

### Toward More Effective Communication

● To be an effective communicator, it's important to develop good conversational skills, including knowing how to make small talk with strangers.

● Self-disclosure—opening up to others—is associated with good mental health, happiness, and satisfying relationships. The emotional content of an experience may determine whether individuals will share it with others or keep it to themselves.

● Self-disclosure can foster emotional intimacy in relationships. Emotional-evaluative self-disclosures lead to feelings of closeness, but factual-descriptive disclosures do not. The level of self-disclosure varies over the course of relationships. Cultures vary in their preferred level of self-disclosure. American women tend to disclose more than men, but this disparity is not as large as it once was. Effective listening is an essential aspect of interpersonal communication.

### Communication Problems

● A number of problems can arise that interfere with effective communication. Individuals who become overly anxious when they talk with others suffer from communication apprehension. This difficulty can cause problems in relationships and in work and educational settings. Sometimes communication can produce negative interpersonal outcomes. Barriers to effective communication include defensiveness, ambushing, motivational distortion, and self-preoccupation.

### Interpersonal Conflict

● Dealing constructively with interpersonal conflict is an important aspect of effective communication. Individualistic cultures tend to encourage direct confrontations, whereas collectivist cultures often avoid them. Nonetheless, many Americans have negative attitudes about conflict.

● In dealing with conflict, most people have a preferred style: avoiding/withdrawing, accommodating, competing, compromising, or collaborating. This last style is the most effective in managing conflict.

### Application: Developing an Assertive Communication Style

● Assertiveness enables individuals to stand up for themselves while respecting the rights of others. To become more assertive, individuals need to understand what assertive communication is, monitor assertive communication, observe a model's assertive communication, practice being assertive, and adopt an assertive attitude.

Assertiveness   p. 266
Channel   p. 242
Communication apprehension
  p. 260
Context   p. 242
Defensiveness   p. 261
Display rules   p. 248
Electronically mediated
  communication   p. 243
Interpersonal communication
  p. 241
Interpersonal conflict   p. 262
Kinesics   p. 250

Listening   p. 258
Message   p. 241
Noise   p. 242
Nonverbal communication
  p. 245
Nonverbal sensitivity   p. 254
Paralanguage   p. 252
Personal space   p. 246
Polygraph   p. 253
Proxemics   p. 246
Receiver   p. 241
Self-disclosure   p. 256
Sender   p. 241

Bella DePaulo   pp. 252–253
Paul Ekman and Wallace
  Friesen   p. 247

Edward T. Hall   pp. 246–247

## QUESTIONS

1. Which of the following is *not* a component of the inter-personal communication process?
   a. the sender
   b. the receiver
   c. the channel
   d. the monitor

2. Research shows that individuals from a variety of cultures:
   a. agree on the facial expressions that correspond with all emotions.
   b. agree on the facial expressions that correspond with 15 basic emotions.
   c. agree on the facial expressions that correspond with 6 basic emotions.
   d. do not agree on the facial expressions that correspond with any emotions.

3. Which of the following is *not* an aspect of nonverbal communication?
   a. facial expressions
   b. homogamy
   c. posture
   d. gestures

4. According to research, which of the following cues is associated with dishonesty?
   a. speaking with a higher-than-normal pitch
   b. speaking slowly
   c. giving relatively long answers to questions
   d. lack of eye contact

5. With regard to self-disclosure in romantic relationships, it is best to:
   a. share a lot about yourself when you first meet someone.
   b. share very little about yourself for a long time.
   c. seek equity in disclosure with a partner.
   d. give no personal information on a first encounter, but share a lot the next time.

6. Paraphrasing is an important aspect of:
   a. nonverbal communication.
   b. active listening.
   c. communication apprehension.
   d. assertiveness.

7. When people hear what they want to hear instead of what is actually said, _____ is operating.
   a. assertiveness
   b. self-preoccupation
   c. motivational distortion
   d. active listening

8. The conflict style that reflects low concern for self and low concern for others is:
   a. competing/forcing.
   b. compromising.
   c. accommodating.
   d. avoiding/withdrawing.

9. Generally, the most productive style for managing conflict is:
   a. collaboration.
   b. compromise.
   c. accommodation.
   d. avoidance.

10. Expressing your thoughts directly and honestly without trampling on other people is a description of which communication style?
    a. aggressive
    b. empathic
    c. submissive
    d. assertive

## ANSWERS

| | |
|---|---|
| 1. d Pages 241–242 | 6. b Page 259 |
| 2. c Pages 247–248 | 7. c Page 261 |
| 3. b Pages 246–252 | 8. d Page 263 |
| 4. a Page 253 | 9. a Page 264 |
| 5. c Page 257 | 10. d Pages 266–267 |

## Personal Explorations Workbook

Go to the *Personal Explorations Workbook* in the back of your textbook for exercises that can enhance your self-understanding in relation to issues raised in this chapter. **Exercise 8.1** *Self-Assessment:* Opener Scale. **Exercise 8.2** *Self-Reflection:* How Do You Feel About Self-Disclosure?

### CourseMate

Access an interactive eBook, chapter-specific interactive learning tools, including Personal Explorations, Recommended Readings, Critical Thinking Exercises, flashcards, quizzes, videos and more in your Psychology CourseMate, available at **www.cengagebrain.com/shop/ISBN/1111186634**.

© Koki Iino/Getty Images

# Friendship and Love

Antonio was so keyed up, he tossed and turned all night. When morning finally arrived, he was elated. In less than two hours, he would be meeting Sonia for coffee! In his first class that morning, thoughts and images of Sonia constantly distracted him from the lecture. When class was finally over, he had to force himself not to walk too fast to the Student Union, where they had agreed to meet. Sound familiar? Chances are that you recognize Antonio's behavior as that of someone falling in love.

Friendship and love play a major role in psychological adjustment. Recall from Chapter 1 that the strongest predictor of happiness, after personality, is social connectedness. Conversely, social isolation is associated with poor physical and mental health and antisocial behavior (Baumeister & Leary, 1995; Smith, McPherson, & Smith-Lovin, 2009). We begin this chapter by defining close relationships. Next, we consider why people are attracted to each other and why they stay in or leave relationships. Then we probe more deeply into friendship and romantic love and discuss the issues of how culture and the Internet influence relationships. Finally, in the Application section, we focus on the painful problem of loneliness and how to overcome it.

# The Ingredients of Close Relationships

### LEARNING OBJECTIVES

- Describe typical characteristics of close relationships.
- Explain the paradox of close relationships.

Typically, *close relationships* **are those that are important, interdependent, and long lasting.** In other words, people in close relationships spend a lot of time and energy maintaining the relationship, and what one person says and does affects the other. Close relationships are characterized by partners who are irreplaceable, whereas as in casual social relationships (such as between store clerk and customer), partners can be interchangeable (Livesay & Duck, 2009).

Close relationships come in many forms, from family relationships, friendships, and work relationships to romantic relationships and marriages. When college students were asked to identify the person to whom they felt closest, 47% named a romantic partner, 36% listed a friend, 14% mentioned a family member, and 3% named another individual such as a co-worker (Berscheid, Snyder, & Omoto, 1989). Regardless of the type of relationship, humans are social animals and close relationships are central to our lives (Perlman, 2007).

As you are aware, close relationships can arouse intense feelings—both positive (passion, concern, caring) and negative (rage, jealousy, despair). This phenomenon is termed the *paradox of close relationships* (Perlman, 2007; Rook & Pietromonaco, 1987). Close relationships are related to some of the best aspects of life (well-being, happiness, health), but they do have a dark side (abuse, deception, break-ups). This paradox makes friendship and love perennial interests for poets, philosophers, and psychologists alike. Let's examine the first stage of relationships: initial attraction.

**WEB LINK 9.1  The Unabridged Student Counseling Virtual Pamphlet Collection**

This site includes links to online information for the problems and issues faced by students. The section on relationships provides advice on a diverse array of topics, including getting along with a roommate, online dating, fighting fair, preventing violence, and dealing with loneliness.

# Initial Attraction and Relationship Development

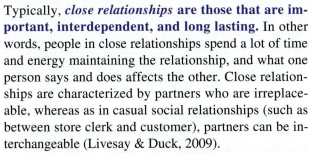

### LEARNING OBJECTIVES

- Discuss the roles of proximity and familiarity in initial attraction.
- Clarify the findings on the role of physical attractiveness in initial attraction.
- Understand the role of reciprocal liking and similarity in getting acquainted.
- Outline some commonly used relationship maintenance strategies, and explain what is meant by "minding" relationships.
- Summarize interdependence theory, and explain how rewards, costs, and investments influence relationship satisfaction and commitment.

*Attraction* is the initial desire to form a relationship. Individuals use a multitude of factors to assess another person's appeal as a mate or a friend. Furthermore, because attraction is a two-way street, intricate interactions occur among variables. To simplify this complex issue, we divide our coverage into four segments. First, we review the factors that operate in initial encounters. Then we consider elements that come into play as relationships begin to develop. Next, we review what's involved in maintaining relationships. Finally, we look at what influences people to stay in or get out of relationships.

Our review of research in this section pertains to both friendships and romantic relationships. In some cases, a particular factor (such as physical attractiveness) may play a more influential role in love than in friendship, or vice versa. However, all the factors discussed in this section enter into both types of relationships. These factors also operate in the same way in both straight and gay friendships and romantic relationships (Peplau & Fingerhut, 2007). But we should note that homosexuals face three unique dating challenges (Peplau & Spaulding, 2003): They have a smaller pool of potential partners; they are often under pressure to conceal their sexual orientation; and they have limited ways to meet prospective partners. Also, fears of hostility may cause them to guard their self-disclosures to acquaintances and friends.

## Initial Encounters

Sometimes initial encounters begin dramatically with two strangers' eyes locking across a room. More often, two people become aware of their mutual interest, usually triggered by each other's looks and early conversations. What draws two strangers together as either friends or lovers? Three factors stand out: proximity, familiarity, and physical attractiveness.

### Proximity

Attraction usually depends on proximity: People have to be in the same place at the same time. *Proximity* refers to geographic, residential, and other forms of spatial closeness. Of course, proximity is not an issue in cyberspace interactions (Fehr, 2008). But in everyday life people become attracted to, and acquainted with, someone who lives, works, shops, or plays nearby. Proximity effects may seem self-evident, but it is sobering to realize that your friendships and love interests are often shaped by seating charts, apartment availability, shift assignments, and office locations (Berscheid & Reis, 1998).

The importance of proximity was apparent in a study of Maryland state police trainees (Segal, 1974). At the training academy, both dormitory rooms and classroom seats were assigned on the basis of alphabetical order. Six months after their arrival, participants were asked to name their three closest friends among the group of trainees. The trainees whose last names were closer together in the alphabet were much more likely to be friends than trainees whose names were widely separated in the alphabet.

How does proximity increase attraction? Goodfriend (2009) asserts that first, people who are near each other are more likely to get acquainted and find out their similarities. Second, individuals who live or work close by may be seen as more convenient and less costly (in terms of time and energy) than those farther away. Finally, people might develop attraction just because someone in close proximity becomes familiar to them.

### Familiarity

You probably walk the same route to your classes several times a week. As the term progresses, you begin to recognize some familiar faces on your route. Have you also found yourself nodding or smiling at these people? If so, you've experienced the *mere exposure effect,* **or an increase in positive feelings toward a novel stimulus (person) based on frequent exposure to it** (Zajonc, 1968). Note that the positive feelings arise just

on the basis of seeing someone frequently—not because of any interaction.

The implications of the mere exposure effect on initial attraction should be obvious. Generally, the more familiar someone is, the more you will like him or her (Le, 2009). And greater liking increases the probability that you will strike up a conversation and, possibly, develop a relationship with the person. There is, however, an important exception to the familiarity principle: If your initial reaction to someone is negative, increased exposure will only intensify your dislike (Swap, 1977). Of course, people can be attracted to total strangers, so familiarity isn't the only factor involved in initial attraction (Fitness, Fletcher, & Overall, 2007).

### Physical Attractiveness

Physical attractiveness plays a major role in initial face-to-face encounters (Neff, 2009; Peretti & Abplanalp, 2004). In other words, most people pay no mind to clichés such as "Beauty is only skin deep" and "You can't judge a book by its cover." Among American college students, physical attractiveness in a dating partner has increased in importance over the past 50 years—for both sexes, but especially for men (Buss et al., 2001). As you might expect, the importance of physical appearance is different for a future spouse or life partner, than for casual relationships. For a marriage partner, both male and female college students ranked the traits of honesty and trustworthiness most highly (Regan & Berscheid, 1997). For a sexual partner, both men and women ranked "attractive appearance" the highest. Good looks play a role in friendships as well (Fehr, 2009). People, especially males, prefer attractiveness in their same- and other-gender friends (Aboud & Mendelson, 1996; Fehr, 2000).

Do gays and straights differ in the importance they place on the physical attractiveness of prospective dating partners? It seems not (Peplau & Spaulding, 2000). In fact, researchers often find gender rather than sexual orientation to be the more important factor in partner preferences. For example, in the wording of gay and straight personal advertisements in newspapers, both heterosexual and homosexual men are more likely to request physically attractive partners than are heterosexual or homosexual women (Bailey et al., 1997; Deaux & Hanna, 1984). There are, however, a few meaningful sexual orientation differences. Lippa (2007) found that heterosexuals valued religion, fondness for children, and parenting abilities more than homosexuals did.

The emphasis on beauty may not be quite as great as the evidence reviewed thus far suggests. In a cross-cultural study conducted in 37 countries on the characteristics commonly sought in a mate, Buss (1989) found that personal qualities, such as kindness and intelligence, were ranked higher by both genders than physical attractiveness was. Similarly, a 1997 survey

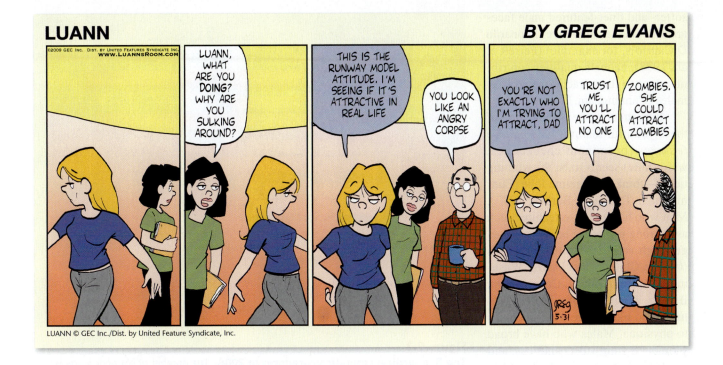

LUANN © GEC Inc./Dist. by United Feature Syndicate, Inc.

of American college students' most preferred qualities in a mate reported that both men and women ranked "mutual attraction/love," "dependable character," and "emotional stability/maturity" as their highest priorities (Buss et al., 2001). "Good looks" was ranked only 8th by men and 13th by women (out of 18 total qualities). More recently, in a 2005 Internet survey of over 200,000 participants, intelligence, humor, honesty, and kindness were ranked as the most important traits in a partner, with good looks coming in fifth. However, when results were separated by gender, attractiveness was still ranked higher by men than women (Lippa, 2007). **Figure 9.1** summarizes these findings. Keep in mind that verbal reports don't always predict people's actual priorities and behavior, and some people might not be aware of what actually attracts them (Sprecher & Felmlee, 2008).

**What makes someone attractive?** Although people can hold different views about what makes a person attractive, they tend to agree on the key elements of good looks. Researchers who study attractiveness focus almost exclusively on facial features and physique. Both aspects are important in perceived attractiveness, but an unattractive body is seen as a greater liability than an unattractive face (Alicke, Smith, & Klotz, 1986). Males, whether gay or straight, place more emphasis on body build and physical attractiveness than females do (Franzoi & Kern, 2009).

Michael Cunningham (2009a), a pioneer in this area of research, identified four categories of qualities that cause someone to be seen as more or less attractive: neonate (baby-face) qualities, mature features,

expressiveness, and grooming. Even across different ethnic groups and countries, there seems to be strong agreement on attractive facial features (Cunningham et al., 1995; Langlois et al., 2000). Women who have *neonate qualities* such as large eyes, a small nose, and full lips get high ratings (Jones, 1995). Although

| Ranking | Men | Women |
|---------|-----|-------|
| 1 | Intelligence | Humor |
| 2 | *Good looks* | Intelligence |
| 3 | Humor | Honesty |
| 4 | Honesty | Kindness |
| 5 | *Attractive face* | Values |
| 6 | Kindness | Communication skills |
| 7 | Values | Dependability |
| 8 | Communication skills | *Good looks* |
| 9 | Dependability | *Attractive face* |
| 10 | Age | Ambition |

**Important Traits in Romantic Partners**

**Figure 9.1**
**Rank order of traits chosen by men and women as one of their most important traits in a partner.** In a 2005 international Internet survey of over 200,000 participants (including heterosexuals and homosexuals, men and women), Lippa (2007) found that intelligence, humor, honesty, kindness, and good looks were ranked (in that order) as the most important traits in a partner for all participants. However, when the findings were separated by gender, good looks were still ranked higher by men than women.

Source: Adapted from Lippa, R. A. (2007). The preferred traits of mates in a cross-national study of heterosexual and homosexual men and women: An examination of biological and cultural influences. *Archives of Sexual Behavior, 36*(2), 193–208.

softer- and finer-featured male faces are also rated as attractive (Leonardo DiCaprio's, for example) (Perrett et al., 1998), neonate qualities contribute more to the attractiveness of females (Cunningham, 2009a).

In particular, the combination of these youthful features with *mature features* (prominent cheekbones, wide smile) seems to be the winning ticket—think of Angelina Jolie (Cunningham, Druen, & Barbee, 1997). Men who have mature features such as a strong jaw and a broad forehead get high ratings on attractiveness (George Clooney and Denzel Washington come to mind) (Cunningham, Barbee, & Pike, 1990). Mature features also play a role when it comes to physique. Males who have broad shoulders, slim waists and legs, and small buttocks receive high attractiveness ratings (Singh, 1995). In recent years, the ideal body shape for males has become more muscular (Martins, Tiggeman, & Kirkbride, 2007). Tall men are also considered attractive (Lynn & Shurgot, 1984). Women of average weight with an "hourglass" figure and medium-sized breasts are rated high in attractiveness (Franzoi & Herzog, 1987; Singh, 1993). African American men and women prefer a larger body type than European American men and women do (Jackson & McGill, 1996; Rosenfeld et al., 1999). Nonetheless, being considerably overweight is viewed very negatively in the United States, despite the increasing incidence of obesity (Hebl & Mannix, 2003).

*Expressive traits*, such as a large smile and high set eyebrows, are also related to perceptions of attractiveness (Cunningham, 2009a). A broad smile is seen as more attractive, perhaps because it can indicate friendliness, and high-set eyebrows could be seen as a sign of interest and agreeableness. *Grooming qualities* are characteristics people use to enhance their other physical qualities, such as cosmetics, hairstyle, clothing, and accessories (Cunningham, 2009). Individuals will go to great lengths to enhance their physical attractiveness, as demonstrated by the increased rate of cosmetic surgery, especially among younger people. Between 2003 and 2004, the number of cosmetic surgeries performed on Americans 18 and younger increased by a whopping 48% (Springen, 2004). In 2008, over 10.2 million cosmetic procedures were performed (see **Figure 9.2**), with breast augmentations and liposuction being the top two (American Society for Aesthetic Plastic Sur-

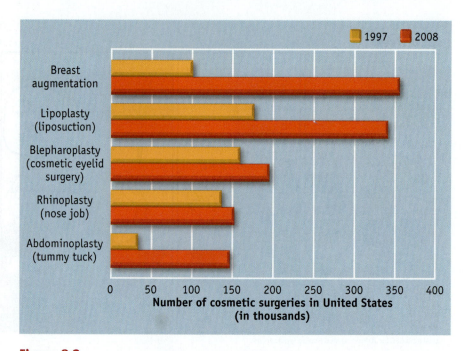

**Figure 9.2**

**Top five surgical cosmetic procedures in 2008.** The number of cosmetic surgeries performed annually is on the rise. In 2008, over 10.2 million cosmetic procedures were performed.

Source: Retrieved December 23, 2009 from the American Society for Aesthetic Plastic Surgery, 2008, http://www.surgery.org/media/statistics.

gery, 2008). The popularity of television shows such as *Extreme Makeover* no doubt account for some of the interest in these procedures (Nabi, 2009).

Currently in the United States, thinness receives heightened emphasis, especially for girls and women. Many studies show that repeated exposure to media portrayals of the thin ideal are associated with body dissatisfaction (Groesz, Levine, & Murnen, 2002; Stice, Spangler, & Agras, 2001). Thus, it is not surprising that high school girls underestimate the body size that boys find attractive (Paxton, et al., 2005). High school girls also believe that other girls have thinner bodies and that the ideal body shape is smaller than their own (Sanderson et al., 2008). Also, many college women perceive themselves to be heavier than they actually are and wish to be thinner (Vartanian, Giant, & Passino, 2001). This emphasis on thinness likely lies behind the high incidence of eating disorders among European American, Asian American, and Hispanic adolescent girls (Halpern et al., 1999). Not surprisingly, women who associate positive attributes with being underweight have a higher incidence of eating disorders (Ahern, Bennett, & Hetherington, 2008). Mexican American women who are oriented toward Anglo American culture are significantly more likely to have eating disorders than those oriented toward Mexican culture, illustrating the role of acculturation (Cachelin et al., 2006). Eating disorders are less common among African American females, likely because the ideal physique for this group is larger than that for European American females (Polivy & Herman, 2002).

Gay males also live in a subculture that emphasizes physical appearance. A study that experimentally induced self-objectification (wearing a swimsuit versus a turtleneck sweater) showed that gay males felt more body shame, had more body dissatisfaction, and ate less when given the opportunity than straight males did (Martins et al., 2007). Although gay men show greater dissatisfaction with their overall body, studies indicate that they are most dissatisfied with their body hair and muscularity (Martins, Tiggemann, & Churchett, 2008). On average, both gay and heterosexual men desire to be thinner and more muscular, and this dissatisfaction increases with age (Tiggemann, Martins, & Kirkbride, 2007). As American culture increasingly objectifies male bodies, and as men feel greater pressure to meet the ideals of the male body shape, appearance may become more central to men's self-concept, leading to greater body dissatisfaction and more eating disorders in this group (Martins et al., 2007). We explore the important issue of eating disorders in the Chapter 14 Application.

**Matching up on looks.**   Thankfully, people can enjoy rewarding social lives without being spectacularly good-looking. In the process of dating and mating, people apparently take into consideration their own level of attractiveness. **The *matching hypothesis* proposes that people of similar levels of physical attractiveness gravitate toward each other.** This hypothesis is supported by findings that both dating and married het-

According to the matching hypothesis, people tend to wind up with someone similar to themselves in attractiveness. However, other factors, such as personality, intelligence, and social status, also influence attraction.

erosexual couples tend to be similar in physical attractiveness (Feingold, 1988; Hatfield & Sprecher, 2009). That is, individuals tend to partner with others who are "in their same league." There is some debate, however, about whether people match up by their own choice (Aron, 1988; Kalick & Hamilton, 1986). Some theorists believe that individuals mostly pursue highly attractive partners and that their matching is the result of social forces beyond their control, such as rejection by more attractive others. Another theory maintains that physical attractiveness is a resource that partners bring to the relationship and, in general, partners want to maintain an equitable balance (Hatfield & Sprecher, 2009).

**Attractiveness and resource exchange.**   Although the matching hypothesis is often at work, physical attractiveness can be viewed as a resource that partners can exchange in relationships (Mathes & Kozak, 2008). A number of studies have shown that, in heterosexual dating, males "trade" occupational status for youth and physical attractiveness in females, and vice versa (Fletcher, Overall, & Friesen, 2006; Fletcher et al., 2004). This finding also holds true in many other cultures. Men in most countries rate physical attractiveness in a prospective mate as more important than women do, whereas women rate "good financial prospects" and "ambitious and industrious" as more important characteristics than men do (Buss, 1989). In reviewing the content of personal ads in newspapers and magazines, Wiederman (1993) reported that female advertisers sought financial resources in prospective partners 11 times more often than the men did.

Evolutionary social psychologists such as David Buss (1988) believe that these findings on age, status, and physical attractiveness reflect gender differences in inherited reproductive strategies that have been sculpted over thousands of generations by natural selection. Their thinking has been guided by *parental investment theory,* **which maintains that a species' mating patterns depend on what each sex has to invest—in the way of time, energy, and survival risk—to produce and nurture offspring.** According to this model, members of the gender that makes the smaller investment will compete with each other for mating opportunities with the gender that makes the larger investment, and the gender with the larger investment will tend to be more discriminating in selecting its partners (Webster, 2009).

How does this analysis apply to humans? Like many mammalian species, human males are required to invest little in the production of offspring beyond the act of copulation, so their reproductive potential is maximized by mating with as many females

David Buss

BIZARRO

ONE SECOND BEFORE THE BLIND DATE

BIZARRO © 2000 Dan Piraro. King Features Syndicate

© John Lund/Annabelle Breakey/Blend Images/photolibrary

**Although most couples are similar in age and attractiveness, sometimes men exchange occupational status or wealth for physical attractiveness in women, and vice versa.**

as possible. Also, males should prefer young and attractive females because these qualities are assumed to signal fertility, which should increase the chances of conception and passing genes on to the next generation. The situation for females is quite different. Females have to invest nine months in pregnancy, and our female ancestors typically had to devote at least several additional years to nourishing offspring through breastfeeding. These realities limit the number of offspring women can produce, regardless of how many males they mate with. Hence, females have little or no incentive for mating with many males. Instead, females can optimize their reproductive potential by selectively mating with reliable

partners who have greater material resources (Buss, 1994; Schmitt, 2008). These preferences should increase the likelihood that a male partner will be committed to a long-term relationship and will be able to support the woman and their children, thus ensuring that her genes will be passed on (see **Figure 9.3**).

Are there alternatives to the evolutionary explanation for patterns of mate selection and resource exchange in heterosexual relationships? Yes, sociocultural models can also provide plausible explanations that center on traditional gender-role socialization and men's greater economic power (Li & Tausczik, 2009; Sprecher, Sullivan, & Hatfield, 1994). Some theorists argue

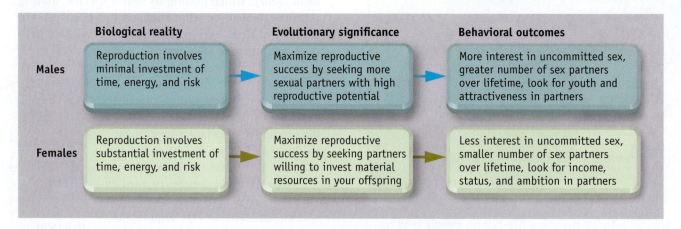

| | Biological reality | Evolutionary significance | Behavioral outcomes |
|---|---|---|---|
| **Males** | Reproduction involves minimal investment of time, energy, and risk | Maximize reproductive success by seeking more sexual partners with high reproductive potential | More interest in uncommitted sex, greater number of sex partners over lifetime, look for youth and attractiveness in partners |
| **Females** | Reproduction involves substantial investment of time, energy, and risk | Maximize reproductive success by seeking partners willing to invest material resources in your offspring | Less interest in uncommitted sex, smaller number of sex partners over lifetime, look for income, status, and ambition in partners |

**Figure 9.3**

**Parental investment theory and mating preferences.** Parental investment theory suggests that basic differences between males and females in parental investment have great adaptive significance and lead to gender differences in mating propensities and preferences, as outlined here.

that women have learned to value men's economic clout because their own economic potential has been severely limited in virtually all cultures by a long history of discrimination. Consistent with this hypothesis, it is women in countries with limited educational and career opportunities for females who show the strongest preferences for men with high incomes (Eagly & Wood, 1999). Moreover, when women's economic power increases, so does their preference for a physically attractive mate (Gangestad, 1993). Now that we have explored initial attraction, let's consider the factors that are important as individuals get to know one another.

## Getting Acquainted

After several initial encounters, people typically begin the dance of getting to know each other. Is it possible to predict which budding relationships will flower and which will die on the vine? We'll examine two factors that can keep the ball rolling: reciprocal liking and perceived similarity.

### Reciprocal Liking

An old adage advises, "If you want to *have* a friend, *be* a friend." This suggestion captures the idea of the reciprocity principle in relationships. **Reciprocal liking refers to liking those who show that they like you.** Many studies show that if you believe another person likes you, you will like him or her (Aron, Fisher, & Strong, 2006; Berscheid & Walster, 1978). Think about it. You respond positively when others sincerely flatter you, do favors for you, and use nonverbal behavior to signal their interest in you (eye contact, leaning forward). These interactions are enjoyable, validating, and positively reinforcing (Smith & Caprariello, 2009). As such, you usually reciprocate such behavior.

You can see a self-fulfilling prophecy at work here. If you believe that someone likes you, you behave in a friendly manner toward that person. Your behavior encourages him or her to respond positively, which confirms your initial expectation. A study by Rebecca Curtis and Kim Miller (1986) showed self-fulfilling prophecy in action. College students who were strangers were divided into pairs for a 5-minute "get acquainted" conversation. Afterward, one member of each pair was led to believe that the other student either did or didn't like him or her. Then the pairs met again and talked about current events for 10 minutes. Raters, blind to the experimental condition of the participants, listened to tape recordings of the 10-minute interactions and rated the participants on a number of behaviors. As predicted, the participants who believed that they were liked were rated as disclosing more about themselves, behaving more warmly, disagreeing less, and having a more positive tone of voice and general attitude than those who believed that they were disliked (see **Figure 9.4**).

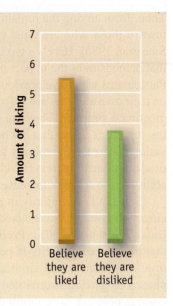

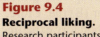

**Figure 9.4**
**Reciprocal liking.** Research participants were led to believe that their research partners either did or did not like them. The participants who believed that their partners liked them liked their partners more than the participants who believed that their partners did not like them. These results illustrate how reciprocity and self-fulfilling prophecy can influence attraction to others. (Adapted from Curtis & Miller, 1986)

The common strategy of "playing hard to get" (non-reciprocity) is at odds with the reciprocity principle. The thought behind this tactic is that people should not reciprocate prematurely lest they be seen as desperate or unselective (Cupach & Spitzberg, 2008). Eastwick and colleagues (2007) assert that "not all reciprocity is created equal," it's best when it's exclusive. They found that romantic desires directed at one person are viewed positively, but not when they are directed toward many individuals. In general, however, you should probably avoid playing hard to get. People are usually turned off by others who reject them (Wright & Contrada, 1986).

### Similarity

Do "birds of a feather flock together," or do "opposites attract"? Research offers far more support for the first adage than the second (Surra et al., 2006). Despite the increasing diversity in the United States, similarity continues to play a key role in attraction (Macionis, 1997), and the similarity principle operates in both friendships and romantic relationships regardless of sexual orientation (Morry, 2007, 2009; Peplau & Fingerhut, 2006). In a longitudinal study of best friends, researchers found that similarity among friends in 1983 actually predicted their closeness in 2002—19 years later (Ledbetter, Griffin, & Sparks, 2007). We've already explored similarity in physical attractiveness (the matching hypothesis). Now, let's consider other similarities to contribute to attraction.

Heterosexual married and dating couples tend to be similar in *demographic characteristics* (such as age, race, religion, socioeconomic status, and education), *physical attractiveness, intelligence,* and *attitudes* (Kalmijn, 1998; Watson et al., 2004). According to Donn Byrne's two-stage model, people first "sort" for dissimilarity, avoiding those who appear to be different.

Then, from among the remaining group, they gravitate toward those who are most similar (Byrne, Clore, & Smeaton, 1986). Here's a typical laboratory experiment that demonstrates the impact of similarity on attraction: Participants who have previously provided information on their own attitudes are led to believe that they will be meeting a stranger. They are given information about the stranger's views that has been manipulated to show various degrees of similarity to their own views. As attitude similarity increases, subjects' ratings of the likability of the stranger increase.

Support for similarity in *personality* as a factor in attraction is weaker and mixed (Klohnen & Luo, 2003; Luo & Klohnen, 2005). Preliminary results indicate that perceived similarity in personality might be more important than actual similarity, at least in the early phases of getting acquainted (Selfhout et al., 2009). Once people are in committed relationships, however, similarity in personality is associated with relationship satisfaction (Gonzaga, Campos, & Bradbury, 2007; Luo & Klohnen, 2005).

What is the appeal of similarity? For one thing, you assume that a similar person will probably like you (Condon & Crano, 1988). Second, when others share your beliefs, you feel validated (Byrne & Clore, 1970). Finally, people who are similar are more likely to react to situations in the same way, thus reducing the chances for conflicts and stress (Gonzaga, 2009).

## Established Relationships

Over time, some acquaintanceships evolve into established relationships. Individuals mutually determine the desired level of intimacy they want in a relationship, whether friendship or romantic. For some, not all relationships need to be highly intimate to be satisfying. For others, intimacy is an essential ingredient of relationship satisfaction. In either case, if they are to continue, close relationships need to be maintained.

### Maintenance of Ongoing Relationships

*Relationship maintenance* **involves the actions and activities used to sustain the desired quality of a relationship.** In **Figure 9.5**, you can see a list of commonly used relationship maintenance behaviors. Often, these behaviors occur spontaneously (calling to check in, eating meals together); at other times, behaviors are more intentional and require more planning (traveling to visit family and friends) (Canary & Stafford, 2001). When coding the content of e-mails for long-distance romantic partners, Johnson and colleagues (2008) found that the most common categories were assurances, openness, and positivity, in that order. Obviously, strategies vary depending on the nature of a relationship (familial, friendship, romantic) and its stage of development (new, developing, mature). For example, married cou-

| Relationship Maintenance Strategies | |
|---|---|
| **Strategy** | **Behavioral example** |
| Positivity | Try to act nice and cheerful |
| Openness | Encourage him/her to disclose thoughts and feelings to me |
| Assurances | Stress my commitment to him/her |
| Social networking | Show that I am willing to do things with his/her friends and family |
| Task sharing | Help equally with tasks that need to be done |
| Joint activities | Spend time hanging out |
| Mediated communication | Use e-mail to keep in touch |
| Avoidance | Respect each other's privacy and need to be alone |
| Antisocial behaviors | Act rude to him/her |
| Humor | Call him/her by a funny nickname |
| No flirting | Do not encourage overly familiar behavior (relevant in cross-gender friendships) |

**Figure 9.5**
**Relationship maintenance strategies.** College students were asked to describe how they maintained three different personal relationships over a college term. Their responses were grouped into 11 categories. You can see that, ironically, some people behave negatively in an attempt to enhance relationships. Openness was the most commonly nominated strategy. (Adapted from Canary & Stafford, 1994)

ples engage in more assurances and social networking than dating partners do (Stafford & Canary, 1991). Both spontaneous and intentional maintenance activities are correlated with relationship satisfaction and commitment (Canary & Dainton, 2006). Of the behaviors in **Figure 9.5**, the best predictors of marital satisfaction are positivity, assurances, and sharing tasks (Canary, Stafford, & Semic, 2002). Also, when the frequency of one partner's maintenance activities is in line with the other's expectations or when maintenance contributions are equitable, relationship satisfaction is higher (Dainton, 2000; Stafford & Canary, 2006). Gay and lesbian couples generally use the same maintenance behaviors as heterosexual couples (Hass & Stafford, 1998).

Another approach to relationship maintenance is the use of "minding" (Harvey & Omarzu, 1997; Omarzu, 2009). *Minding* is an active and ongoing process of continuing mutual self-disclosure and maintaining relationship-enhancing beliefs and attributions about one's partner. This model asserts that a high level of minding is associated with satisfying and intimate long-term relationships, and vice versa. To elaborate, a high degree of minding involves using good listening skills, having detailed knowledge about your partner's opinions, making generally positive attributions for your partner's behaviors, expressing feelings of trust and commitment, recognizing your partner's support and effort, and having an optimistic view of the future of the relationship. By contrast, a low degree of minding is characterized by a lack of interest in your partner's self-disclosures, generally negative attributions for your partner's behavior, dwelling on your partner's faults, and a pessimistic view of the future of the relationship. As you can see, this model has a strong cognitive flavor. Although Harvey and Omarzu focus on committed romantic relationships, they suggest that their model likely applies to family and friendship relationships as well (Omarzu, 2009).

## Relationship Satisfaction and Commitment

How do you gauge your satisfaction in a relationship? What determines whether you will stay in or get out of a relationship? *Interdependence* or *social exchange theory* postulates that interpersonal relationships are governed by perceptions of the rewards and costs exchanged in interactions. Basically, this model predicts that interactions between acquaintances, friends, and lovers will continue as long as the participants feel that the benefits they derive from the relationship are reasonable in comparison to the costs of being in the relationship. Harold Kelley and John Thibaut's interdependence theory (Kelley & Thibaut, 1978; Thibaut & Kelley, 1959) is based on B. F. Skinner's principle of reinforcement, which assumes that people try to maximize their rewards in life and minimize their costs (see Chapter 2).

Rewards include such things as emotional support, status, and sexual gratification (in romantic relationships); costs are such things as the time and energy that a relationship requires, emotional conflicts, and the inability to engage in other rewarding activities be-

cause of relationship obligations. According to interdependence theory, people assess a relationship by its *outcome*—their subjective perception of the rewards of the relationship minus its costs (see **Figure 9.6**).

Individuals assess their *satisfaction* with a relationship by comparing the relationship outcomes (rewards minus costs) to their subjective expectations. **A comparison level is a personal standard of what constitutes an acceptable balance of rewards and costs in a relationship.** It is based on the outcomes you have experienced in previous relationships and the outcomes you have seen others experience in their relationships. Your comparison level may also be influenced by your exposure to fictional relationships, such as those you have read about or seen on television. Consistent with the predictions of exchange theory, research shows that relationship satisfaction is higher when rewards are perceived to be high and costs are viewed as relatively low.

To understand the role of *commitment* in relationships, we need to consider two additional factors. The first is the **comparison level for alternatives, or one's estimation of the available outcomes from alternative relationships.** In using this standard, individuals assess their current relationship outcomes in

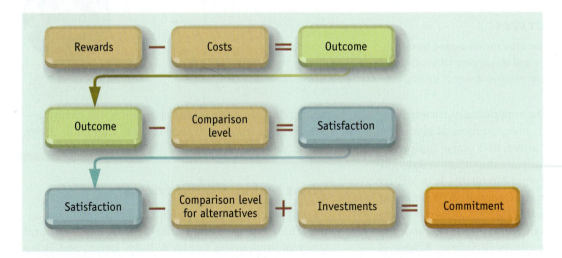

### Figure 9.6

**The key elements of social exchange theory and their effects on a relationship.** According to social exchange theory, relationship *outcome* is determined by the rewards minus the costs of a relationship. Relationship *satisfaction* is based on the outcome matched against comparison level (expectations). *Commitment* to a relationship is determined by one's satisfaction minus one's comparison level for alternatives plus one's investments in the relationship.

Source: Adapted from Brehm, S. S., & Kassin, S, M. (1993). *Social psychology.* Boston: Houghton Mifflin. Copyright © 1993 by Houghton Mifflin Company. Adapted with permission.

comparison to the potential outcomes of other similar relationships that may be available to them. This principle helps explain why many unsatisfying relationships are not terminated until another love interest actually appears. It also explains why someone might leave a seemingly happy relationship, if that person's expectations and standards were not being met. The second factor that figures in relationship commitment is *investments, or things that people contribute to a relationship that they can't get back if the relationship ends.* Investments include past costs (time, money) that they can never recover if the relationship fails. Understandably, putting investments into a relationship strengthens one's commitment to it.

**Figure 9.6** demonstrates how interdependence theory works. If both members of a couple feel that they are getting a lot out of the relationship (lots of strokes, high status) compared to its costs (a few arguments, occasionally giving up preferred activities), they will probably perceive the relationship as satisfactory and will keep it going. However, if either one begins to feel that the ratio of rewards to costs is falling below his or her comparison level, dissatisfaction is likely to occur. The dissatisfied person may attempt to alter the balance of costs and rewards or try to ease out of the relationship. The likelihood of ending the relationship depends on the number of important investments a person has in the relationship and whether the person believes that an alternative relationship is available that could yield greater satisfaction.

Research generally supports interdependence theory and its extensions (Le & Agnew, 2003; Sabatelli, 2009). Social exchange principles seem to operate in a similar fashion regardless of a couple's sexual orientation (Peplau & Fingerhut, 2007). However, many people resist the idea that close relationships operate according to an economic model. Much of this resistance probably comes from discomfort with the idea that self-interest plays such an important role in the maintenance of relationships. Resistance may also stem from doubts about how well social exchange principles apply to close relationships. In fact, there is some empirical support for this position (Harvey & Wenzel, 2006). Margaret Clark and Judson Mills (1993) distinguish between *exchange relationships* (with strangers, acquaintances, co-workers) and *communal relationships* (with close friends, lovers, family members). Research suggests that in exchange relationships, the usual principles of social exchange dominate, but in communal relationships these principles seem to be applied differently (Morrow, 2009). For example, in communal relationships, rewards are usually given freely, without any expectation of prompt reciprocation (Clark & Mills, 1993). Also, individuals pay more attention to the needs of a partner in a communal relationship than in an exchange relationship. In other words, you use a need-based norm with people who are close to you and help them without calculating whether and when they will reward you in kind (Clark & Grote, 2003).

# Friendship

## LEARNING OBJECTIVES
- Summarize the research on what makes a good friend.
- Describe some key gender and sexual orientation differences in friendships.
- Explain the friendship repair ritual as a way of dealing with conflict in friendships.

It's hard to overestimate the importance of friends. They give help in times of need, advice in times of confusion, consolation in times of failure, and praise in times of achievement. Friends clearly are important to individuals' adjustment. In fact, friendship quality is predictive of overall happiness (Demir, Ozdemir, & Weitekamp, 2006, Demir & Weitekamp, 2007). College students with strong friendships are more optimistic and deal better with stressful life events (Brissette, Scheir, & Carver, 2002). Intimate and stable friendships are associated with less stress in adulthood and less troublesome behavior among teens (Hartup & Stevens, 1999). Same-gender friendships between women are linked to positive mental and physical health (Knickmeyer, Sexton, & Nishimura, 2002). Also, developing friendships with people who are different from oneself—in

terms of ethnicity or sexual orientation, for example—can break down prejudices (Herek & Capitanio, 1996; Levin, van Laar, & Sidanius, 2003).

## What Makes a Good Friend?

Exactly what makes someone a good friend? One approach to this question comes from a cross-cultural study of students in England, Italy, Japan, and Hong Kong (Argyle & Henderson, 1984). Notably, in this diverse sample, there was enough agreement on how friends should conduct themselves to identify six informal rules governing friendships. As **Figure 9.7** shows, the common thread running through these rules seems to be providing emotional and social support to friends.

| The Rules of Friendship |
| --- |
| Share news of success with a friend |
| Show emotional support |
| Volunteer help in time of need |
| Strive to make a friend happy when in each other's company |
| Trust and confide in each other |
| Stand up for a friend in his or her absence |

**Figure 9.7**
**Vital behaviors in friendship.** A cross-cultural inquiry into the behaviors that are vital to friendship identified these six rules of friendship. (Adapted from Argyle & Henderson, 1984)

We can also look at the common themes that underlie friendships of all ages in order to understand the nature of friendship. Researchers have identified three such themes (de Vries, 1996). The first involves the emotional dimension of friendship (self-disclosure, expressing affection and support, and so forth). A second theme concerns the communal nature of friendship (participating in or supporting each other in mutually shared activities). The third dimension entails sociability and compatibility (friends are sources of fun and recreation). These studies and others show that the most important element of friendship is emotional support (Collins & Madsen, 2006).

## Gender and Sexual Orientation Issues

Men's and women's same-gender friendships have a lot in common (Wright, 2006); both sexes value intimacy, self-disclosure, and trust (Winstead, 2009). However, some interesting differences appear to be rooted in traditional gender roles and socialization. In the United States, women's friendships are more often emotionally based, whereas men's tend to be activity based. Although some researchers have challenged this characterization (Walker, 1994), the current belief is that men's friendships are typically based on shared interests and doing things together, whereas women's friendships more often focus on talking—usually about personal matters (Fehr, 1996, 2004).

We can also compare American men's and women's friendships on *preferred topics* of conversation. Women are far more likely than men to discuss personal problems, people, relationships, and feelings (Fehr, 2004). Men, on the other hand, are much more likely to talk about sports, work, vehicles, and computers than personal concerns. E-mail communications also reflect this gender difference (Colley & Todd, 2002). So whose friendships are more intimate, men's or women's? Currently, there is controversy over this question. The most widely accepted view is that women's friendships are closer and more satisfying because they involve more self-disclosure (Fehr, 2004; Reis, 1998).

What short-circuits intimate connections between men? Several factors stand out for American men (Bank & Hansford, 2000; Kilmartin, 2007). First, men are socialized to be self-sufficient, which inhibits self-disclosure. Second, homophobia, which is stronger in males than females, is a barrier to intimacy among males and contributes to inconsistent and often ambiguous standards for emotional expression and intimacy between men (Nardi, 2007). Third, traditional gender-role expectations encourage men to see each other as competitors. Why reveal weaknesses to someone who might take advantage of you? Studies indicate that interpersonal competition is highest in male-male friendships (Singleton & Vacca, 2007).

The boundaries between the friendship and romantic or sexual relationships of gay men and lesbians appear to be more complex than those of heterosexuals (Diamond & Dubé, 2002; Peplau & Fingerhut, 2007). Many intimate relationships among lesbians begin as friendships and progress to romance and then to a sexual relationship (Diamond, 2007; Peplau & Spaulding, 2003). Obviously, discerning and negotiating these shifts can be difficult. Also, both lesbians and gay men are much more likely than heterosexuals to maintain social contacts with former sexual partners (Solomon, Rothblum, & Balsam, 2004). One possible explanation for this phenomenon is the small size of some gay and lesbian social networks (Peplau & Fingerhut, 2007). Also, compared to heterosexual couples, gay and lesbian couples have less support from families and societal institutions (Kurdek, 2005). So, maintaining close connections with friends and creating "safe spaces" through these connections is especially important (Goode-Cross & Good, 2008).

## Conflict in Friendships

Friends, especially long-term ones, are bound to experience conflicts. As with other types of relationships, conflicts can result from incompatible goals, mismatched expectations, or changes in individuals' interests over time. If the conflicts are great enough, they can result in the friendship ending. Alternatively, individuals can engage in behavior to preserve the relationship. Cahn (2009) describes three steps in friendship repair rituals. First, there is a *reproach*, in which the offended party acknowledges the problem and asks the offender for an explanation. Second, the offender offers a *remedy* by taking responsibility and offering a justification, a concession, an apology, or a combination of these three. Finally in the *acknowledgment* stage the offended party acknowledges the remedy and the friendships progresses. Of course at any point, either party can call off the ritual and dissolve the friendship. Ultimately, conflict is a reality in all relationships, whether platonic or romantic (Reis, Snyder, & Roberts, 2009).

# Romantic Love

### LEARNING OBJECTIVES

- Clarify the research findings on the experience of love in gay and straight couples.
- Identify some gender differences regarding love.
- Distinguish among passion, intimacy, and commitment, and explain Sternberg's eight types of love.
- Understand adult attachment styles, including their correlates and stability.

- Discuss the course of romantic love over time.
- Explain why relationships fail.
- Identify the processes that couples go through as they dissolve a relationship.
- Describe what couples can do to help relationships last.

Wander through a bookstore and you'll see an overwhelming array of titles such as *Men Who Can't Love, Women Who Love Too Much,* and *Getting the Love You Want.* Turn on your radio and you'll hear the refrains of "All You Need Is Love," "My Love," and "I Will Always Love You." Although there are other forms of love, such as parental love and platonic love, these books and songs are all about *romantic love,* a subject of consuming interest for almost everyone.

Love is difficult to define, difficult to measure, and frequently difficult to understand. Nonetheless, psychologists have conducted thousands of studies and developed a number of interesting theories on love and romantic relationships.

## Sexual Orientation and Love

*Sexual orientation* **refers to a person's preference for emotional and sexual relationships with individuals of the same gender, the other gender, or either gender.** *Heterosexuals* seek emotional-sexual relationships with members of the other gender. *Homosexuals* seek emotional-sexual relationships with members of the same gender. *Bisexuals* seek emotional-sexual relationships with members of both genders. In recent years, the terms *gay* and *straight* have become widely used to refer to homosexuals and heterosexuals, respectively. *Gay* can refer to homosexuals of either gender, but most homosexual women prefer to call themselves *lesbians.* Chapter 12 goes into more details regarding sexual orientation.

Many studies of romantic love and relationships suffer from **heterosexism, or the assumption that all individuals and relationships are heterosexual.** For instance, most questionnaires on romantic love and romantic relationships fail to ask participants about their sexual orientation. Thus, when data are analyzed, there is no way to know whether subjects are referring to same- or other-gender romantic partners. Assuming that their subjects are all heterosexuals, some researchers proceed to describe their findings without any mention of homosexuals. Because most people identify themselves as heterosexual, heterosexism in research isn't likely to distort conclusions about heterosexuals;

however, it renders homosexual relationships invisible. Further, research on same-sex relationships tends to focus on white, middle class Americans (Peplau & Ghavami, 2009). Consequently, psychologists don't know as much about the range of homosexual relationships as they would like to. Researchers are now devoting much more attention to these issues.

We discuss gay and lesbian committed relationships more in Chapter 10, so we will just touch on the basics here. We *do* know that homosexual romances and

The experience of romantic love seems to be the same regardless of a person's sexual orientation.

relationships are essentially the same as those of heterosexuals. Both groups experience romantic and passionate love and make commitments to relationships (Kurdek, 1994, 1998; Peplau & Ghavami, 2009). Both heterosexual and homosexual couples hold similar values about relationships, report similar levels of relationship satisfaction, perceive their relationships to be loving and satisfying, and say they want their partners to have characteristics similar to theirs (Peplau & Fingerhut, 2007). When relationship differences are found, they are much more likely to be rooted in gender than in sexual orientation, as we'll see next.

## Gender Differences

Stereotypes hold that women are more romantic than men. Nonetheless, research suggests just the opposite—that men are the more romantic gender (Dion & Dion, 1988). For example, men hold more romantic beliefs ("Love lasts forever" or "There is one perfect love in the world for everyone") (Peplau, Hill, & Rubin, 1993). In addition, men fall in love more easily than women, whereas women fall out of love more easily than men (Hill, Rubin, & Peplau, 1976; Rubin, Peplau, & Hill, 1981).

In contrast, women are more likely to report physical symptoms associated with being in love—for instance, feeling as though they are "floating on a cloud" (Peplau & Gordon, 1985)—and they are somewhat more likely to verbalize and display tender emotions (Dindia & Allen, 1992). We should note, however, that most of the differences are small, and there is more similarity than disparity in men's and women's conceptions of love (Aron, Fisher, & Strong, 2009; Fehr, 2008). It appears that the notion that men and women are from different relational planets is somewhat of an exaggeration.

## Theories of Love

Can the experience of love be broken down into certain key components? How are romantic love relationships similar to other types of close relationships? These are the kinds of questions that two current theories of love address.

### Triangular Theory of Love

Robert Sternberg's (1986, 1988, 2006) *triangular theory of love* posits that all love experiences are made up of three components: intimacy, passion, and commitment. Each of the components is represented as a point of a triangle, from which the theory derives its name (see **Figure 9.8**).

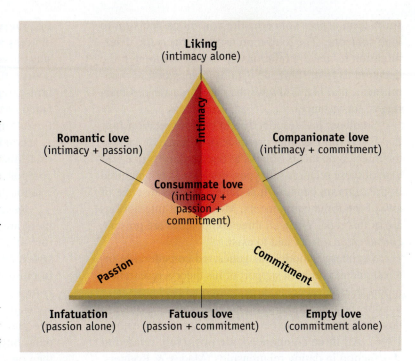

**Figure 9.8**

**Sternberg's triangular theory of love.** According to Robert Sternberg (1986), love includes three components: intimacy, passion, and commitment. These components are portrayed here as points on a triangle. The possible combinations of these three components yield the seven types of relationships mapped out here. The absence of all three components is called nonlove, which is not shown in the diagram.

Source: From Sternberg, R. J. (1986). A triangular theory of love. *Psychological Review, 93,* 119–135. Copyright © 1986 by the American Psychological Association. Reprinted by permission of the author.

***Intimacy* refers to warmth, closeness, and sharing in a relationship.** Signs of intimacy include giving and receiving emotional support, valuing the loved one, wanting to promote the welfare of the loved one, and sharing one's self and one's possessions with another. Self-disclosure is necessary to achieve and maintain feelings of intimacy in a relationship, whether platonic or romantic.

***Passion* refers to the intense feelings (both positive and negative) experienced in love relationships, including sexual desire.** Passion is related to drives that lead to romance, physical attraction, and sexual consummation. Although sexual needs may be dominant in many close relationships, other needs also figure in the experience of passion, including the needs for nurturance, self-esteem, dominance, submission, and self-actualization. For example, self-esteem is threatened when someone experiences jealousy. Passion obviously figures most prominently in romantic relationships.

***Commitment* involves the decision and intent to maintain a relationship in spite of the difficulties and costs that may arise.** According to Sternberg, commitment has both short-term and long-term aspects. The

**Robert Sternberg**

Courtesy of Robert Sternberg

short-term aspect concerns the conscious decision to love someone. The long-term aspect reflects the determination to make a relationship endure. Although the decision to love someone usually comes before commitment, that is not always the case (in arranged marriages, for instance).

Sternberg has described eight types of relationships that can result from the presence or absence of each of the three components of love, as depicted in **Figure 9.8**. One of these relationship types, nonlove, is not pictured in the diagram because it is defined as the absence of any of the three components. Most casual interactions are of this type. When all three components are present, *consummate love* is said to exist.

Sternberg's model has generated considerable interest and research. In support of his theory, researchers report that Sternberg's three components characterize not only how people think about love in general but also how they personally experience love (Aron & Westbay, 1996). All three components are positively related to satisfaction in dating relationships (Madey & Rodgers, 2009). Also, measures of commitment and intimacy were found to be among the best predictors of whether dating couples continued their relationships (Hendrick, Hendrick, & Adler, 1988). Another study looked at changes in passion, intimacy, and commitment scores over time (Lemieux & Hale, 2002). Participants aged 18 to 75 were classified as casually dating, exclusively dating, engaged, or married. Passion and intimacy scores were lower for casual daters, higher for engaged participants, and lower for married subjects, while commitment scores increased from casually dating participants to married participants. In a cross-cultural study of Chinese and American heterosexual couples in their 20s, questionnaires were used to measure intimacy, passion, and commitment (Gao, 2001). Scores on these three components of love increased as relationships became more serious. Although there were no significant differences between the two groups on intimacy and commitment scores, Americans scored significantly higher on the passion scale than the Chinese did.

The triangular theory alone doesn't fully capture the complexity of love. It seems that how people bond with others plays a role. Madey and Rodgers (2009) found that attachment style predicts intimacy and commitment levels, each of which predict satisfaction. To see why that might be the case, let's turn our attention to attachment theory.

## Romantic Love as Attachment

In a groundbreaking theory of love, Cindy Hazan and Phillip Shaver (1987) asserted that romantic love can be conceptualized as an attachment process, with similarities to the bond between infants and their caregivers. According to these theorists, adult romantic love and infant attachment share a number of features: intense

fascination with the other person, distress at separation, and efforts to stay close and spend time together. Of course, there are also differences: Infant-caregiver relationships are one-sided, whereas caregiving in romantic relationships works both ways. A second difference is that romantic relationships usually have a sexual component, whereas infant-caregiver relationships do not.

Cindy Hazan

*Bill Warren/Ithaca Journal*

Researchers who study attachment are keenly interested in the nature and development of ***attachment styles*, or typical ways of interacting in close relationships.** Their interest is fueled by the belief that attachment styles develop during the first year of life and strongly influence individuals' interpersonal interactions from then on.

Phillip Shaver

*Courtesy of UC Davis News Service*

**Infant attachment.** Hazan and Shaver's ideas build on earlier work in attachment theory by John Bowlby (1980) and Mary Ainsworth (Ainsworth et al., 1978). Based on actual observations of infants and their primary caregivers, they identified three attachment styles. Over half of infants develop a *secure attachment style*. However, other infants develop insecure attachments. Some infants are very anxious when separated from their caretaker and show resistance at reunion, a response characterized as an *anxious-ambivalent attachment style*. A third group of infants never connect very well with their caretaker and are classified in the *avoidant attachment style*. How do attachments in infancy develop? As you can see in **Figure 9.9**, three parenting styles have been identified as likely determinants of attachment quality. A *warm/responsive* approach seems to promote secure attachments, whereas a *cold/rejecting* style is associated with avoidant attachments. An *ambivalent/inconsistent* style seems to result in anxious-ambivalent attachments.

**Adult attachment.** What do these attachment styles look like in adulthood? To answer this question, we'll summarize the findings of a number of studies (Mickelson, Kessler, & Shaver, 1997; Shaver & Hazan, 1993). You can also see capsule summaries of adult attachment styles in **Figure 9.9.**

● *Secure adults* (about 55% of participants). These people trust others, find it easy to get close to them, and are comfortable with mutual dependence. They rarely worry about being abandoned by their partner. Secure adults have the longest-lasting relationships and the fewest divorces. They describe their parents as behaving warmly toward them and toward each other.

● *Avoidant adults* (about 25% of participants). These individuals both fear and feel uncomfortable about getting close to others. They are reluctant to trust others and prefer to maintain emotional distance from others. They have the lowest incidence of positive relationship experiences of the three groups. Avoidant adults describe their parents as less warm than secure adults do and see their mothers as cold and rejecting.

● *Anxious-ambivalent adults* (about 20% of participants). These adults are obsessive and preoccupied with their relationships. They want more relationship closeness than their partners do and suffer extreme feelings of jealousy, based on fears of abandonment. Their relationships have the shortest duration of the three groups. Ambivalent adults describe their relationship with their parents as less warm than secure adults do and feel that their parents had unhappy marriages.

Cross-cultural studies in Australia and Israel have confirmed that people are distributed across the three attachment styles with similar percentages in those countries (Feeney & Noller, 1990; Mikulincer, Florian, & Tolmacz, 1990). Also, males and females are distributed similarly across the three styles, and the proportions of gay men and lesbians in the different attachment styles match those of straight men and women (Ridge & Feeney, 1998).

The latest thinking assumes that attachment style is determined by where people fall on two continuous dimensions (Brennanet, Clark, & Shaver, 1998; Mikulincer, 2006). *Attachment anxiety* reflects how much a person worries that a partner will not be available when needed. This fear of abandonment stems, in part, from a person's doubts about his or her lovability. *Attachment avoidance* reflects the degree to which a person

| Parent's caregiving style | Infant attachment | Adult attachment style |
|---|---|---|
| **Warm/responsive—** She/he was generally warm and responsive; she/he was good at knowing when to be supportive and when to let me operate on my own; our relationship was always comfortable, and I have no major reservations or complaints about it. | **Secure attachment—** An infant-caregiver bond in which the child welcomes contact with a close companion and uses this person as a secure base from which to explore the environment. | **Secure—**I find it relatively easy to get close to others and am comfortable depending on them and having them depend on me. I don't often worry about being abandoned or about someone getting too close to me. |
| **Cold/rejecting—**She/he was fairly cold and distant, or rejecting, not very responsive; I wasn't her/his highest priority, her/his concerns were often elsewhere; it's possible that she/he would just as soon not have had me. | **Avoidant attachment—** An insecure infant-caregiver bond, characterized by little separation protest and a tendency for the child to avoid or ignore the caregiver. | **Avoidant—**I am somewhat uncomfortable being close to others; I find it difficult to trust them, difficult to allow myself to depend on them. I am nervous when anyone gets too close, and often love partners want me to be more intimate than I feel comfortable being. |
| **Ambivalent/ inconsistent—** She/he was noticeably inconsistent in her/his reactions to me, sometimes warm and sometimes not; she/he had her/his own agenda, which sometimes got in the way of her/his receptiveness and responsiveness to my needs; she/he definitely loved me but didn't always show it in the best way. | **Anxious/ambivalent attachment—**An insecure infant-caregiver bond, characterized by strong separation protest and a tendency of the child to resist contact initiated by the caregiver, particularly after a separation. | **Anxious/ambivalent—** I find that others are reluctant to get as close as I would like. I often worry that my partner doesn't really love me or won't want to stay with me. I want to merge completely with another person, and this desire sometimes scares people away. |

**Figure 9.9**

**Infant attachment and romantic relationships.** According to Hazan and Shaver (1987), romantic relationships in adulthood are similar in form to attachment patterns in infancy, which are determined in part by parental caregiving styles. The theorized relationships between parental styles, attachment patterns, and intimate relations are outlined here. Hazan and Shaver's (1987) study sparked a flurry of follow-up research, which has largely supported the basic premises of their groundbreaking theory, although the links between infant experiences and close relationships in adulthood appear to be somewhat more complex than those portrayed here. (Based on Hazan and Shaver, 1986, 1987; Shaffer, 1989)

distrusts a partner's goodwill and has tendencies to maintain emotional and behavioral distance from a partner. People's scores on these two dimensions as measured by self-report data yield four attachment styles: secure, preoccupied (anxious-ambivalent), avoidant-dismissing, and avoidant-fearful (Bartholomew & Horowitz, 1991; Brennan et al., 1998). You are already familiar with the secure style, and "preoccupied" is just a different label for the anxious-ambivalent style. The dismissing and fearful styles are two variations of the avoidant style.

As you can see in **Figure 9.10,** securely attached individuals (low on both anxiety and avoidance) enjoy close relationships and are not worried that others will leave them. Those in the *preoccupied* category (high on anxiety, low on avoidance) desire closeness with others but fear rejection. Those with an *avoidant-dismissing* style (high on avoidance, low on anxiety) prefer to maintain their distance from others and are not concerned about rejection, while those with an *avoidant-fearful* style (high on both avoidance and anxiety) are uncomfortable being close to others but still worry about rejection. There is evidence that this type of anxiety is at its highest in the early stages of a relationship, before it becomes established (Eastwick & Finkel, 2008)

Although it might appear from **Figure 9.10** that the four attachment styles are distinctly different categories or typologies, that is not the case (Shaver & Mikulincer, 2006). Recall that the two underlying dimensions of anxiety and avoidance are distributed along a continuum (as indicated by the arrows in the figure) from low to high. This means that people are *more or less* anxious

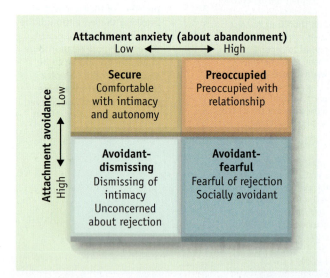

**Figure 9.10**

**Attachment styles and their underlying dimensions.**
Attachment styles are determined by where people fall along two continuous dimensions that range from low to high: attachment avoidance and attachment anxiety (about abandonment). This system yields four attachment styles, which are described here. (Adapted from Brennan, Clark, & Shaver, 1998; Fraley & Shaver, 2000)

(or avoidant) versus totally consumed by anxiety or totally without anxiety. So, as you read about the four attachment styles, keep in mind that they are "convenient labels for sets of anxiety and avoidance scores rather than distinctly different categories that have nothing in common" (Miller, Perlman, & Brehm, 2007).

**Correlates of attachment styles.** The idea of adult attachment styles has stimulated a huge body of research. Among other findings, studies consistently show that securely attached individuals have more committed, satisfying, interdependent, and well-adjusted relationships compared to those who are insecurely attached (Bartholomew, 2009; Mikulincer & Shaver, 2003). Also, having an anxious-ambivalent style is associated with not being in a relationship and with being in relationships of shorter duration, and an avoidant style is associated with shorter relationships (Shaver & Brennan, 1992).

When researchers subject couples to stress in order to study the connection between attachment style and relationship health, the findings generally support attachment theory predictions (Feeney, 2004). That is, securely attached individuals both seek out and provide support under stress. By contrast, avoidant people withdraw from their partners and may become angry either when they are asked for support or when they don't receive the support they want. Anxious individuals become fearful and sometimes exhibit hostility. When discussing conflicts with their partners, anxiously attached individuals report more personal distress and escalate the severity of the conflict (Campbell et al., 2005).

In terms of psychological adjustment, securely attached people typically have better mental health than insecurely attached people (Haggerty, Hilsenroth, & Vala-Stewart, 2009; Meyers & Landsberger, 2002). Individuals who are insecurely attached are more vulnerable to a number of problems, including low self-esteem, low self-confidence, self-consciousness, anger, resentment, anxiety, loneliness, and depression (Cooper et al., 2004; Mikulincer & Shaver, 2003). Finally, attachment patterns exert influence far beyond romantic relationships. For instance, correlations have been found between attachment styles and friendships (Weimer, Kerns, & Oldenburg, 2004), gender roles (Schwartz, Waldo, & Higgins, 2004), health habits (Huntsinger & Luecken, 2004), religious beliefs (Kirkpatrick, 2005), sense of humor (Cann et al., 2008), death anxiety (Shaver & Mikulincer, 2007), and job satisfaction (Schirmer & Lopez, 2001).

**Stability of attachment styles.** A number of studies have demonstrated that early bonding experiences do influence relationship styles later in life. For example, a meta-analysis of longitudinal studies concluded that attachment styles are moderately stable over the first 19 years of life (Fraley, 2002). Also, across adulthood, stability appears to increase to some degree (Fraley & Brumbaugh, 2004). However, despite the relative stability of attachment styles, they are not set in stone. In childhood, changes from secure to insecure attachment are typically related to negative life events (divorce or death of parents, parental substance abuse, maltreatment) (Waters et al., 2000; Weinfield, Sroufe, & Egeland, 2000). Experiences later in life may also lead to shifts in attachment style (Davila & Cobb, 2003; Davila & Sargent, 2003). Consistent support (or lack thereof) from one's partner can either increase or decrease one's attachment anxiety (Bartholomew, 2009; Shaver & Mikulincer, 2008). One study reported that about 30% of individuals had changed their attachment style over a period of four years (Kirkpatrick & Hazan, 1994). In another, a significant number of individuals (aged 26–64 years) in short-term psychotherapy shifted from an insecure to a secure attachment style (Travis et al., 2001). Thus, therapy may be a helpful option for those with attachment difficulties.

## The Course of Romantic Love

Most people find being in love exhilarating and wish the experience could last forever. Must passion fade? Regrettably, the answer to this question seems to be "yes." Consistent with this view, Sternberg's (1986) triangular theory holds that passion peaks early in a relationship and then declines in intensity. In contrast, both intimacy and commitment increase as time progresses, although they develop at different rates (see **Figure 9.11**). Research supports the idea that the intense attraction and arousal one feels for a lover does tend to

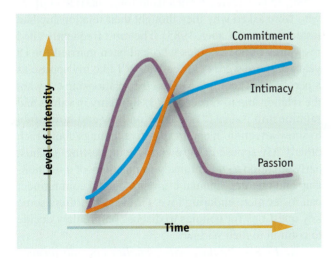

**Figure 9.11**
**The course of love over time.** According to Sternberg (1986), the three components of love typically progress differently over time. He theorizes that passion peaks early in a relationship and then declines. In contrast, intimacy and commitment are thought to build gradually.

subside over time—for both gays and straights (Aron et al., 2006; Kurdek, 2005).

Why does passion fade? It seems that three factors kick into high gear early, then begin to dissipate: fantasy, novelty, and arousal (Miller et al., 2007). At first, love is "blind," so individuals usually develop a fantasy picture of their lover (often a projection of their own needs). However, as time passes, the intrusion of reality undermines this idealized view. Also, the novelty of a new partner fades with increased interactions and knowledge. Finally, people can't exist in a state of heightened physical arousal forever.

Does the decline of passion mean the demise of a relationship? Not necessarily. Some relationships do dissolve when early passion fades. However, many others evolve into different, but deeply satisfying, mixtures of passionate-companionate love. And while passion *does* fade over time, researchers note that passion is typically defined based on the type experienced in new relationships—the type that includes a high obsession component. Acevedo and Aron (2009) found that when you factor out obsession, romantic love (which is both engaging and sexual) does indeed exist in long-term marriages, and it is associated with relationship satisfaction.

### Why Relationships End

The question of why some relationships last while others end is a popular issue in relationship research. Nonetheless, the matter is complex, so easy answers have not been forthcoming. When it comes to break-ups, there are often differences in what people report publicly as the cause, what they actually think is the cause, and what the cause actually is (Powell & Fine, 2009).

If we were to follow seriously dating couples over several years, what proportion of them would split up over that period? If you guessed about half, you'd be right. According to three longitudinal studies (all on heterosexual couples), 58% of dating or engaged college couples broke up over a four-year period (Sprecher, 1994), 51% of "steady or serious" dating couples had split at the end of three years (Kirkpatrick & Davis, 1994), and 45% of dating couples had ended their relationships by the end of two years (Hill, Rubin, & Peplau, 1976). The issue of divorce is discussed in Chapter 10.

Honing in on our key question as to why some relationships stand the test of time and some don't, let's take a closer look at the Boston Couples Study, one of the studies just cited (Hill et al., 1976). Here, 200 couples (predominantly college students in Boston) were followed over two years. To participate, couples had to be "going steady" and believe that they were in love. If couples split, researchers asked them to give their reasons. The results of this and other studies (Buss, 1989; Powell & Fine, 2009; Sprecher, 1994) suggest that five prominent factors contribute to romantic break-ups:

1. *Premature commitment.* Virtually all the reasons for break-ups involved things that could only be known by interacting over time. Hence, it seems that many couples make romantic commitments without taking the time to get to know each other. These individuals may find out later that they don't really like each other or that they have little in common. For these reasons, "whirlwind courtships" are risky. Intimacy needs to be combined with commitment if relationships are to survive. Additionally, perceiving that a partner's commitment is wavering predicts relationships ending, regardless of one's own commitment and satisfaction level (Arriaga et al., 2006).

2. *Ineffective communication and conflict management skills.* All couples have disagreements. Not surprisingly, disagreements increase as couples learn more about each other and become more interdependent (Buss, 1989). Poor conflict management skills are a key factor in relationship distress and can lead to a break-up (Kline et al., 2006). Distressed couples tend to have more negativity in their communication, which can decrease problem solving and increase withdrawal (Cordova & Harp, 2009). As we saw in Chapter 8, the solution to this problem is not to stifle all disagreements, because conflict can be helpful to relationships. The key is to manage conflict constructively.

3. *Becoming bored with the relationship.* Couples who break up rank "boredom with the relationship" high on the list of reasons for splitting. As we have noted, novelty usually fades as people get to know each other, and boredom can set in. Individuals have needs for both novelty and predictability in close relationships (Sprecher, 1994). Balancing the two can be tricky for couples.

4. *Availability of a more attractive relationship.* Whether a deteriorating relationship actually ends depends, in great part, on the availability and awareness of a more attractive alternative (Felmlee, Sprecher, & Bassin, 1990; Miller, 2008). We all know of individuals who remained in unsatisfying relationships only until they met a more appealing prospect. Further, those without desirable alternatives experience more distress during break-ups that those who have desirable alternatives (Simpson, 1987).

5. *Low levels of satisfaction.* All of these factors can contribute to low levels of relationship satisfaction. Becoming dissatisfied in a relationship can erode one's commitment and increase the chances of relationship dissolution. Obviously, many other factors play a role in relationship satisfaction, including one's expectations of a partner, attachment style, and stress level (Powell & Fine, 2009).

## How Relationships End

Sometimes relationships deteriorate to the point where one or both partners decide the relationship should end. Steve Duck and colleagues proposed a model describing six processes that partners go through in relationship dissolution (Duck, 1982; Rollie & Duck, 2006). First, the relationship experiences *breakdown processes,* in which one or both partners become dissatisfied. If this breakdown becomes extreme, either partner might engage in *intrapsychic processes*—ruminating about his or her dissatisfaction, the cost of the relationship, and attractive alternatives. If commitment wavers, the couple will engage in *dyadic processes* by discussing and negotiating the conflict. At this point the relationship can be repaired. However, if partners reach the decision to end their relationship, *social processes* occur as friends and family are alerted to the problem. As the couple moves toward breaking up, *grave dressing processes* occur in which each partner develops a separate account of the break-up for his or her social network. Finally, each partner engages in *resurrection processes* to prepare for his or her new life. This model appears to apply to both romantic relationships and friendships (Norwood & Duck, 2009).

## Helping Relationships Last

Close relationships are important to our health and happiness, so how can we increase the likelihood that they will last? Research supports the following suggestions:

1. *Take plenty of time to get to know the other person before you make a long-term commitment.* Research based on Sternberg's theory found that the best predictors of whether dating couples' relationships would continue were their levels of intimacy and commitment (Hendrick et al., 1988). Regarding intimacy, we have already noted that self-disclosures that lead individuals to feel understood, cared for, and validated are crucial (Green, Derlega, & Matthews, 2006; Reis & Patrick, 1996). Other advice comes from long-married couples who were asked why they thought their relationship had lasted (Lauer & Lauer, 1985). The most frequently cited responses of 351 couples who had been married for 15 years or more were (1) friendship ("I like my spouse as a person"); (2) commitment to the relationship ("I want the relationship to succeed"); (3) similarity in values and relationship issues ("We agree on how and how often to show affection"); and (4) positive feelings about each other ("My spouse has grown more interesting"). Thus, early attention to the intimacy foundations of a relationship and ongoing, mutual efforts to build a commitment can foster more enduring love. **Figure 9.12** offers some key questions for couples to discuss before they decide to commit to their partner.

2. *Emphasize the positive qualities in your partner and relationship.* It is essential to communicate more positive than negative feelings to your partner. Early in a relationship, this is easy to do, but it gets harder as relationships continue. Recall that in well-minded relationships, people explain their partner's behaviors in

**Figure 9.12**

**Key questions for dating couples to discuss before deciding to marry.** To increase their chances for satisfying and long-lasting marriages and partnerships, experts advise dating couples to get to know each other well. Author Susan Piver (2000) has developed a list of 100 essential questions for couples to discuss before they make long-term commitments. The questions cover home, money, work, sex, health and food, family, children, community and friends, and spiritual life. Here is a sample of five questions to consider.

Source: From Piver, S. (2000). *The hard questions: 100 essential questions to ask before you say "I do."* New York: Jeremy P. Tarcher/Putnam.

ways that enhance the relationship (Harvey & Pauwels, 2009). Oddly, married couples generally make more negative and fewer positive statements to their spouse than to strangers, and we presume this situation holds for those in other types of committed relationships as well (Fincham, 2001; Fincham & Beach, 2006). This tendency is more prevalent among distressed than among nondistressed couples (Gottman, 1993). Unfortunately, when one partner engages in this behavior, the other often responds in kind, which can set in motion a pattern of reciprocal negativity that makes things worse. Partners who see the best in each other, even in conflict, are more likely to stay together and experience greater satisfaction (Murray, Holmes, & Griffin, 1996). Similarly, married couples who seek and grant forgiveness have better chances for longer and more satisfying relationships than those who avoid each other or retaliate in kind for a partner's negative behavior (Fincham, 2003). Hence, as the old song advises, it helps to "accentuate the positive."

**3.** *Find ways to bring novelty to long-term relationships.* As romantic partners learn more about each other and develop feelings of intimacy, they also become more predictable to each other. But, too much predictability can translate into loss of interest and, possibly, boredom. Central to relational boredom is the lack of excitement, newness, and motivation (Strong & Harasymchuk, 2009). One way to keep things interesting is to engage in novel activities together (Aron et al., 2000; Baumeister & Bratslavsky, 1999). For example, one study reported that couples who participated in exciting activities together (versus just spending time together) showed increases in relationship satisfaction over a 10-week period (Reissman, Aron, & Bergen, 1993).

**4.** *Develop effective conflict management skills.* Conflicts arise in all relationships, so it's essential to handle them well. For one thing, it's helpful to distinguish between minor annoyances and significant problems. You need to learn to see minor irritations in perspective and recognize how little they matter. With big problems, however, it's usually best to avoid the temptation to sweep them under the rug in the hope that they'll disappear. Important issues rarely vanish on their own, and if you postpone the inevitable discussion, the "sweepings" will have accumulated, making it harder to sort out the various issues. An interaction pattern common to dissatisfied couples is "demand-withdraw" (Eldridge, 2009; Roberts & Krokoff, 1990). Typically, this pattern involves the woman pressing the man to discuss a relationship problem and the man avoiding or withdrawing from the interaction. This pattern is associated with the "closeness versus separateness dilemma," in which one partner wants more intimacy and closeness and the other wants more privacy and independence (Sagrestano, Heavey, & Christensen, 2006). For more specific suggestions on handling conflict, refer to our discussion in Chapter 8.

Engaging in novel activities together, such as traveling to interesting destinations, contributes to long-term relationship satisfaction.

# Perspectives on Close Relationships

- Contrast how people from individualistic cultures and collectivist cultures view love and marriage.
- Clarify how differences between Internet and face-to-face interactions affect relationship development.

Now that we have explored friendships and romantic relationships, let's look at perspectives on close relationships, including how culture shapes people's views of relationships and how the Internet affects relationships.

## Culture and Close Relationships

Cross-cultural research on close relationships is largely limited to romantic relationships, so we'll focus on them. Although it appears that romantic love is experienced in all cultures (Aron, Fisher, & Strong, 2009; Jankowiak & Fischer, 1992), cultures do vary in their emphasis on romantic love as a prerequisite for marriage. Interestingly, love as the basis for marriage goes back only to the 18th century of Western culture (Stone, 1977). According to Elaine Hatfield and Richard Rapson (1993), "Marriage-for-love represents an ultimate expression of individualism" (p. 2). By contrast, marriages arranged by families and other go-betweens remain common in cultures high in collectivism.

Cultural views of love and marriage are linked to both a country's values and its economic health. In one study, researchers asked college students in 11 countries the following question: "If a man (woman) had all the other qualities you desired, would you marry this person if you were not in love with him (her)?" (Levine et al., 1995). Students in countries with more individualistic values and higher standards of living were significantly more likely to answer "no" to the question than were those in countries with more collectivist values and lower standards of living (see **Figure 9.13**). Another

cross-cultural investigation of the meaning of various emotions found that Italians and Americans equated love with happiness, whereas Chinese respondents associated it with sadness and envisioned unrequited love (Shaver, Wu, & Schwartz, 1991).

People from Western societies often hold a simplistic view of collectivist cultures' deemphasis on romantic love and their penchant for arranged marriages, assuming that the modern conception of romantic love as the basis for marriage must result in better marital relationships than collectivist cultures' "antiquated" beliefs and practices (Grearson & Smith, 2009). However, there is little empirical support for this ethnocentric view (Dion & Dion, 1993; Triandis, 1994). Take, for example, a study of couples in India, which found that love grew over the years in arranged marriages, whereas it declined among couples who married for romantic love (Gupta & Singh, 1982). Another study found that Indian couples in arranged marriages living in the United States reported higher marital satisfaction than U.S. couples who married by choice (Madathil & Benshoff, 2008). Further, the expectation that marriage will fill diverse psychological needs places greater pressure on marital relationships in individualistic societies than on those in collectivist cultures; this expectation may be linked to the rapidly escalating divorce rates in these societies (Dion & Dion, 1993). Because cross-cultural research on love is only in its infancy, we can only speculate on these matters. But smug assumptions about the superiority of Western ways are misguided, given our extremely high divorce rates.

Marriages based on romantic love are the norm in Western cultures, whereas arranged marriages prevail in collectivist cultures.

## Cross-Cultural Views on Love and Marriage

"If a man (woman) had all the other qualities you desired, would you marry this person if you were not in love with him (her)?"

| Country | Yes (%) | No (%) | Undecided (%) |
|---|---|---|---|
| Japan | 2.3 | 62.0 | 35.7 |
| United States | 3.5 | 85.9 | 10.6 |
| Brazil | 4.3 | 85.7 | 10.0 |
| Australia | 4.8 | 80.0 | 15.2 |
| Hong Kong | 5.8 | 77.6 | 16.7 |
| England | 7.3 | 83.6 | 9.1 |
| Mexico | 10.2 | 80.5 | 9.3 |
| Philippines | 11.4 | 63.6 | 25.0 |
| Thailand | 18.8 | 33.8 | 47.5 |
| India | 49.0 | 24.0 | 26.9 |
| Pakistan | 50.4 | 39.1 | 10.4 |

**Figure 9.13**

**Culture and views of love.** College students in ten countries and Hong Kong responded to the following question: "If a man (woman) had all the other qualities you desired, would you marry this person if you were not in love with him (her)?" Generally, students in countries with higher standards of living and more individualistic values were significantly less likely to answer "yes" to the question than those in countries with lower standards of living and more collectivist values.

Source: Adapted from Levine, R., Sato, S., Hashimoto, T., & Verma, J. (1995). Love and marriage in eleven cultures. *Journal of Cross-Cultural Psychology 26*(5), pp. 561, 564. Copyright © 1995 by Sage Publications, Inc. Journals. Reproduced with permission of Sage Publications Inc. Journals in the formats Textbook and Other book via Copyright Clearance Center.

## The Internet and Close Relationships

To meet prospective friends and romantic partners, people used to be limited to school, work, and church settings. Then came the "bar scene," personal ads, and speed dating. More recently, the Internet has dramatically expanded opportunities for people to meet and develop relationships through social networking services (Facebook, Twitter), online dating services (eHarmony, Match.com), interactive virtual worlds (Second Life), online multiple player games, chat rooms, and blogs.

Although critics are concerned that Internet relationships are superficial, research suggests that virtual relationships are just as intimate as face-to-face ones and are sometimes even closer (Bargh, McKenna, & Fitzsimons, 2002), for reasons we will discuss shortly. Regardless, many virtual relationships migrate to face-to-face interactions (Boase & Wellman, 2006). When people do decide to move beyond an Internet-based relationship, actual meetings usually take place only after telephone contact. Researchers find that romantic relationships that begin on the Internet seem to be

just as stable over two years as traditional relationships (McKenna, Green, & Gleason, 2002). The Internet has also assumed importance in maintaining established relationships. In a poll of 1,000 Internet users, 94% reported that the Internet made it easier for them to communicate with friends and family who live far away, and 87% said that they use it regularly for that purpose (D'Amico, 1998). **Figure 9.14** depicts the most commonly reported uses of social networking sites. Although some social critics predicted that Internet use would reduce face-to-face interactions, Internet users typically maintain their social involvements while cutting back on TV time (Boase & Wellman, 2006). Additionally, online communication is linked to increased closeness in existing friendships for adolescents (Valkenburg & Peter, 2007). However, playing Internet games and visiting chat rooms are negatively related to the quality of best friendship and romantic relationships (Blais et al., 2008).

Self-disclosure is affected by the differences in face-to-face and Internet communication. Because the Internet is shrouded in the cloak of anonymity, people can take greater risks in online self-disclosure. Thus, feelings of intimacy can develop more quickly (McKenna & Bargh, 2000). Sometimes this experience can set up a false sense of intimacy, which can create uncomfortable feelings if a face-to-face meeting ensues—that is, meeting with a stranger who knows "too much" about you (Hamilton, 1999). Of course, face-to-face meetings can also go smoothly.

Anonymity also allows people to construct a virtual identity. Obviously, this can be a problem if one

## Reported Uses of Social Network Sites by MySpace and Facebook Users

| Use | Percent reporting |
|---|---|
| To keep in touch with old friends | 96 |
| To keep in touch with current friends | 91 |
| To post/look at pictures | 57 |
| To make new friends | 56 |
| To locate old friends | 55 |
| For dating purposes | 8 |

**Figure 9.14**

**How social networking sites are used.** With the help of social networking sites, the Internet has dramatically expanded opportunities for people to meet and develop relationships. When surveyed, the majority of MySpace and Facebook users used their accounts to locate and keep in touch with friends, both old and new. Only a small percentage reported using their accounts for dating purposes.

Source: Adapted from Raacke, J., & Bonds-Raacke, J., (2008). MySpace and Facebook: Applying the uses and gratifications theory in exploring friend-networking sites. *CyberPsychology and Behavior, 11*(2), 169–174. The publisher for this copyrighted material is Mary Ann Liebert, Inc. publishers.

It is becoming increasingly common for the Internet to play a role in social interactions. Critics see these trends as leading to the demise of face-to-face interactions, widespread loneliness and alienation, and millions being lured into dangerous liaisons by unscrupulous people. But research to date generally paints a positive picture of the Internet's impact on people's connections with one another. For example, the web offers a wealth of interaction opportunities for those normally separated because of geography or physical infirmity (McKenna & Bargh, 2000). Also, Internet groups provide a safer venue than "real life" for individuals with social anxiety (Stevens & Morris, 2007) or those with stigmatized identities (for example, transgendered people) to interact. Similarly, Internet groups for those with grave illnesses (cancer, multiple sclerosis, diabetes, AIDS) provide important support and information to their subscribers (Bargh & McKenna, 2004). Research shows that self-disclosure in these support groups is high, and it tends to be reciprocated, especially among female respondents (Barak & Gluck-Ofri, 2007). Of course, the anonymous nature of Internet communication *does* make it easy for dishonest individuals to take advantage of others, so it's smart to be cautious about revealing personal information online.

In a short period of time, the Internet has become an indispensable vehicle for making acquaintances and developing relationships. One survey based on a nationally representative sample of American adults reported that 31% (about 63 million people) knew someone who had used a dating website, and 11% (about 16 million adults) had visited such a site to meet people (Madden & Lenhart, 2006). Among those who used online dating sites, a majority (52%) reported "mostly positive" experiences, although a sizable number (29%) had "mostly negative" experiences. Further, McKenna, Green, and Gleason (2002) reported that 22% of their participants said that they were living with, had become engaged to, or were married to someone they had first met on the Internet. Madden & Lenhart (2006) asked the Internet users who said they were single and looking for a romantic partner to identify how they used the Internet for dating. You can see their responses in **Figure 9.15**.

The differences between Internet and face-to-face communication require psychologists to reexamine the established theories and principles of relationship development that we discuss in this chapter (Bargh & McKenna, 2004). For example, good looks and close physical proximity are powerful factors in initial attraction in the real world. On the Internet, where people form

| Dating-Related Activities Online | |
|---|---|
| **Online activities** | **Single and looking internet users (%)** |
| Flirt with someone | 40 |
| Go to an online dating website | 37 |
| Ask someone out on a date | 28 |
| Find a place offline, like a nightclub or singles event, where you might meet someone to date | 27 |
| Been introduced to a potential date by a third party using e-mail or instant messaging | 21 |
| Participate in an online group where you hope to meet people to date | 19 |
| Search for information about someone you dated in the past | 18 |
| Maintain a long-distance relationship | 18 |
| Search for information about someone you are currently dating or are about to meet for a first date | 17 |
| Break up with someone you are dating | 9 |

**Figure 9.15**

**Dating-related activities online.** Researchers asked Internet users who were single and looking for a romantic partner how they used the Internet (including e-mail and instant messaging) for dating (Madden & Lenhart, 2006). Flirting and going to an online dating website were most frequently mentioned. Most respondents engaged in three or fewer of these activities.

Source: Adapted from Madden & Lenhart (2006). *Online dating.* Retrieved April 29, 2007 from http://www.pewinternet.org/pdfs/PIP_Online_Dating.pdf. (Dating-Related Activities Online table, p. 5) Reprinted by permission of PEW Internet & American Life Project. Washington, D.C.

relationships sight unseen, these factors are irrelevant. In the absence of physical appearance, similarity of interests and values kicks in earlier and assumes more power than it does in face-to-face relationships (McKenna, 2009). Research indicates that the more similar an online friend, the stronger the bond (Mesch & Talmud, 2007). One study found that pairs of strangers who chatted on the Internet liked each other more than if they had talked face-to-face (McKenna et al., 2002). But in another study of pairs randomly assigned to either face-to-face or Internet chat conversations, the face-to-face group felt more satisfied with the experience and felt a higher degree of closeness and self-disclosure with their partners (Mallen, Day, & Green, 2003). Even in long-term friendships, enhanced self-disclosure through e-mails or instant messaging increases feelings of closeness (McKenna, 2009).

Researchers are just beginning to explore this interesting topic. However, with ever-advancing technologies (live video feed, voice chat), we might find that online relationships begin to look more and more like those in the face-to-face world.

*"Your online profile stated that you were tall, dark and handsome. Have you ever considered a career in fiction writing?"*

The Internet is playing a larger and larger role in the formation and maintenance of interpersonal relationships.

person adopts a fictional persona and another assumes that it is authentic and begins to take the relationship seriously. A related concern is truthfulness. In one survey, only 25% of online daters admitted to using deception (Byrm & Lenton, 2001), yet a whopping 86% of participants in an online dating site felt that others misrepresented their physical appearance (Gibbs, Ellison, & Heino, 2006). Some people rationalize lying because it has practical advantages: Men on dating sites who claim to earn high salaries receive more replies than those who say they earn less money (Epstein, 2007). Second, there are semantic misunderstandings: One person's "average" may be another person's "plump." Third, some people "stretch the truth" to work around frustrating constraints imposed by the technological design of dating websites (such as age cutoffs). Finally, creating an accurate online representation of oneself is a complex process: Individuals need to put their best self forward to attract potential dates, but they also need to present themselves authentically—especially if they expect to meet a person face-to-face (Gibbs et al., 2006). One study found that online daters dealt with this tension by constructing profiles that reflected their "ideal self" rather than their "actual self" (Ellison, Heino, & Gibbs, 2006). The most common factors that online daters misrepresent are age, appearance, and marital status (Byrm & Lenton, 2001).

The influence of the Internet goes both ways. While people might misrepresent themselves online, a recent study found that virtual environments can also influence people's own self-perceptions. Researchers found that having a tall and attractive avatar (digital representation) led to more aggressive game performance in undergraduates playing World of Warcraft in a laboratory setting (Yee, Bailenson, & Ducheneaut, 2009).

The Internet has definitely changed the relationship landscape, and not just in the initial stages of relationships. Individuals can use the Internet to sustain contacts, reconnect, and even break up with others. Additional research in this fascinating area will not only provide valuable information about virtual relationships but will also reveal interesting new perspectives on face-to-face relationships.

**WEB LINK 9.3  Online Dating Magazine**

This independent and privately owned online magazine is a source of wide-ranging information about online dating, including reviews of dating services, tips on online safety, tactics used by some dating services to gain members, and advice (from a psychologist) on how to form better social relationships.

# Overcoming Loneliness

## LEARNING OBJECTIVES

- Identify various types of loneliness.
- Discuss the prevalence of loneliness.
- Explain how early experiences and current social trends contribute to loneliness.

- Understand how shyness, poor social skills, and self-defeating attributions contribute to loneliness.
- Summarize the suggestions for conquering loneliness.

*Answer the following "true" or "false."*

____ **1.** Adolescents and young adults are the loneliest age group.

____ **2.** Many people who are lonely are also shy.

____ **3.** The seeds of loneliness are often sown early in life.

____ **4.** Effective social skills can be learned relatively easily.

All of the above are true, as you'll learn shortly. But let's start with a couple of general points. First, being alone doesn't necessarily produce feelings of loneliness. In these fast-paced times, solitude can provide needed down time to recharge your batteries. Also, people need time alone to deepen self-understanding, wrestle with decisions, and contemplate important life issues. Second, people can feel lonely even when surrounded by others (at a party or concert, for instance). It's possible to have a large social network but not feel close to anyone in particular.

## The Nature and Prevalence of Loneliness

**Loneliness occurs when a person has fewer interpersonal relationships than desired or when these relationships are not as satisfying as desired.** Of course, people vary in their needs for social connections. Thus, if you're not distressed by the quantity or quality of your social and emotional ties, you wouldn't be considered lonely.

We can think about loneliness in various ways. One approach is to look at the type of relationship deficit involved (Weiss, 1973). *Emotional loneliness* stems from the absence of an intimate attachment figure. For a child, this figure is typically a parent; for an adult, it is usually a spouse or partner or a best friend. *Social loneliness* results from the lack of a friendship network (typically provided in school, work, or church settings and in community groups). For example, a married couple who move to a new city will experience social loneliness until they make new social connections; however, because they have each other, they should not experience emotional loneliness. On the other hand, a recently divorced person will probably feel emotional loneliness but should not experience social loneliness if work and friendship networks remain intact (which is not always the case).

Emotional loneliness seems to be tied to the absence of a romantic partner in both college students and senior adults (Green et al., 2001). Social loneliness, however, seems to spring from different roots, depending on age. In college students, it's the *quantity* of friendship contacts that counts; among the older group, it's the *quality* of contacts. It's also worth noting that social support can't compensate for emotional loneliness—for example, the presence of friends and family cannot substitute for a loved one who has died (Stroebe et al., 1996). Of course, this is not to say that social support is unimportant. The point is that different types of loneliness require different responses; therefore, you need to pinpoint the exact nature of your social deficits to cope effectively with loneliness.

A second way to look at loneliness is in terms of its duration (Young, 1982). *Transient loneliness* involves brief and sporadic feelings of loneliness, which many people may experience even when their social lives are reasonably adequate. *Transitional loneliness* occurs when people who have had satisfying social relationships in the past become lonely after experiencing a disruption in their social network (the death of a loved one, say, or a divorce or a move). *Chronic loneliness* is a condition that affects people who have been unable to develop a satisfactory interpersonal network over a period of years. Here we focus on chronic loneliness.

How many people are plagued by loneliness? Although we don't have a precise answer to this question, anecdotal evidence suggests that the number is substantial. Telephone hotlines for troubled people report that complaints of loneliness dominate their calls. No doubt some of the popularity of social network sites, instant messaging, and chat rooms can be traced to loneliness.

The prevalence of loneliness in specific age groups actually contradicts stereotypes. For example, many assume that the loneliest age group is the elderly, but this "distinction" actually belongs to adolescents and young adults (Rokach, 2001; Snell & March, 2008). Gay and lesbian adolescents are particularly likely to be lonely

## Recommended READING

### Loneliness: Human Nature and the Need for Social Connection
by John T. Cacioppo and William Patrick
(W. W. Norton & Company, 2008)

John T. Cacioppo is an internationally recognized expert on social and emotional influences on human behavior. With William Patrick he has compiled a readable book summarizing decades of research on one of the most difficult interpersonal problems: loneliness. The first part, "The Lonely Heart," discusses the roots and implications of loneliness in the modern world. In the second part, "From Selfish Genes to Social Beings," the authors use an evolutionary perspective to explore people's need for connectedness. The last part, "Finding Meaning in Connection," offers suggestions for identifying and reducing one's own loneliness. Whether you are lonely or not, this book is an interesting and insightful read.

*Go to the Psychology CourseMate for Weiten at* **www.cengagebrain.com/shop/ISBN/1111186634** *for descriptions of other recommended books.*

**WEB LINK 9.4** **The Science of Loneliness**

This is the companion site for John T. Cacioppo and William Patrick's book *Loneliness: Human Nature and the Need for Social Connection*. It includes summaries of recent research on loneliness, a blog from the authors, and a place for visitors to virtually socialize.

## The Roots of Loneliness

Any event that ruptures the social fabric of a person's life may lead to loneliness, so no one is immune. We'll consider the roles of early experience and social trends.

### Early Experiences

A key problem in chronic loneliness seems to be early negative social behavior that leads to rejection by peers (Asher & Paquette, 2003; Pedersen et al., 2007). Children who are aggressive or withdrawn are likely to suffer peer rejection even in preschool (Ray et al., 1997). What prompts inappropriate social behavior in young children? One factor is an insecure attachment style. One study found that attachment style at the age of only 24 months was predictive of later childhood loneliness (Raikes & Thompson, 2008). Because of difficult early parent-infant interactions, children often develop social behaviors (aggression, aloofness, competitiveness, overdependence) that "invite" rejection by adults and peers (Bartholomew, 1990; Duggan & Brennan, 1994). You can see how a vicious cycle gets set up. A child's inappropriate behavior prompts rejection, which in turn triggers negative expectations about social interactions in the child, which can lead to more negative behavior, and so on. To help break this self-defeating cycle (and head off the loneliness that can result), it is crucial to help children learn appropriate social skills early in life. Without intervention, this vicious cycle can continue and result in chronic loneliness.

### Social Trends

Social isolation appears to be on the rise, according to a study based on national surveys in 1985 and 2004 (McPherson, Smith-Lovin, & Brashears, 2006). Among the troubling findings the researchers reported were that the number of people who said they had no one with whom to discuss important matters almost tripled during this period. Also, in 1985, the average American had three confidants, yet by 2004 that number had dropped to two. Further, 25% of the respondents in 2004 said that they had no one to confide in. It is estimated that in 2010, 29 million people will live alone (Jaffe, 2008).

Some social commentators and social scientists are concerned that recent trends are undermining social connections in our culture (McPherson et al., 2006; Putnam, 1996). Cacioppo and Patrick (2008) discuss

(Westefeld et al., 2001). Another vulnerable group is beginning college students. One study reported that 75% of those in this group experienced loneliness in their first few weeks on campus (Cutrona, 1982). It is likely that frequent changes of schools, jobs, and relationships during adolescence and young adulthood all contribute to the high rates of loneliness for this age group. A second surprising finding is that loneliness decreases with age, at least until the much later years of adulthood when one's friends begin to die (Pinquart & Sörensen, 2001; Schnittker, 2007).

In line with expectations, people who live alone are lonelier than those who live with a partner (Pinquart, 2003). In elderly participants, living alone is associated with cognitive impairments and lower life satisfaction (Gow et al., 2007). Also, divorce often disrupts the relationship between parents and children, especially fathers, and adds to the burden of the divorced person's loneliness (Kaufman & Uhlenberg, 1998). Women are found to be lonelier than men, but only on measures that use words such as "lonely" or "loneliness" (Borys & Perlman, 1985). Thus, it is likely that this apparent gender difference is really men's reluctance to admit to feeling lonely. In fact, when surveying men and women in the Netherlands, researchers found that divorced men are more likely to suffer from emotional loneliness than divorced women are (Dykstra & Fokkema, 2007).

"being lonely in a social world." A number of factors come into play. Parents (especially if they are single) may be so pressed for time that they have little time to cultivate adult relationships. Because of busy schedules, face-to-face interactions at home are reduced as family members eat on the run, on their own, or in front of the TV without meaningful family conversation. While technology makes life easier in some respects and does provide opportunities for developing relationships, it has its down sides. For example, superficial social interactions become prevalent as people order their meals and do their banking at drive-up windows, purchase their groceries via automated checkout stations, and so forth.

## Correlates of Loneliness

For people who are chronically lonely, painful feelings are a fact of life. Three factors that figure prominently in chronic loneliness are shyness, poor social skills, and a self-defeating attributional style. Of course, the link between these factors and loneliness could go either way. Feeling lonely might cause a person to make negative attributions about others, but making negative attributions can also lead to loneliness.

### Shyness

Shyness is commonly associated with loneliness (Jackson et al., 2002). *Shyness* **refers to discomfort, inhibition, and excessive caution in interpersonal relations.** Specifically, shy people tend to (1) be timid about expressing themselves, (2) be overly self-conscious about how others are reacting to them, (3) embarrass

### WEB LINK 9.5   The Shyness Homepage

The Shyness Institute (Portola Valley, CA) offers a "gathering of network resources for people seeking information and services for shyness." The Institute is co-directed by psychologists Lynne Henderson and Philip Zimbardo.

easily, and (4) experience physiological symptoms of their anxiety, such as a racing pulse, blushing, or an upset stomach. In pioneering research on shyness, Philip Zimbardo (1977, 1990) and his associates report that 60% of shy people indicated that their shyness was *situationally specific*. That is, their shyness is triggered only in certain social contexts, such as asking someone for help or interacting with a large group of people (see **Figure 9.16**). Supporting the importance of the situation, one study found that self-reported shyness was related to decreased self-disclosures in an online conversation, but only when a webcam was present. Shyness was not related to self-disclosure when there was no webcam (Brunet & Schmidt, 2007).

### Poor Social Skills

People who suffer from chronic loneliness typically have casual acquaintances rather than close friends, and they date infrequently (Bell, 1991). They spend much of their time in solitary activities such as listening to music or reading (Rubenstein & Shaver, 1982). Often, these individuals are adults who were unable to break out of self-defeating patterns of social behavior

Thanks to automation and online technology, people today are able to take care of many of life's necessities without interacting with other human beings. These reduced opportunities for social interaction help fuel increased loneliness.

© Royalty-Free/Masterfile

## "What Makes You Shy?"

| Sources | Percentage of shy students |
|---|---|
| **Other people** | |
| Strangers | 70 |
| Opposite sex | 64 |
| Authorities by virtue of their knowledge | 55 |
| Authorities by virtue of their role | 40 |
| Relatives | 21 |
| Elderly people | 12 |
| Friends | 11 |
| Children | 10 |
| Parents | 8 |
| **Situations** | |
| Where I am focus of attention—large group (as when giving a speech) | 73 |
| Large groups | 68 |
| Of lower status | 56 |
| Social situations in general | 55 |
| New situations in general | 55 |
| Requiring assertiveness | 54 |
| Where I am being evaluated | 53 |
| Where I am focus of attention—small group | 52 |
| Small social groups | 48 |
| One-to-one different-sex interactions | 48 |
| Of vulnerability (need help) | 48 |
| Small task-oriented groups | 28 |
| One-to-one same-sex interactions | 14 |

**Figure 9.16**

**The situational determinants of shyness.** Zimbardo (1977) asked subjects about the people and circumstances that made them feel shy. The results of his survey showed that shyness depends to a large degree on situational factors.

Source: From Zimbardo, P. (1977). *Shyness: What is it, what to do about it.* Reading, MA: Addison-Wesley. Copyright © 1977 by Philip Zimbardo, Inc.

developed early in life. A variety of problematic social skills are associated with loneliness (Gierveld, van Tilburg, & Dykstra, 2006). A common finding is that lonely people show lower responsiveness to their conversational partners and are more self-focused (Rook, 1998). Similarly, researchers report that lonely people are relatively inhibited and unassertive, speaking less than nonlonely people. They also seem to disclose less about themselves than those who are not lonely. This (often unconscious) tendency has the effect of keeping people at an emotional distance and limits interactions to a relatively superficial level. These interactional problems are based, in part, on heightened fears of rejection (Jackson et al., 2002). It seems that people with "rejection anxiety" believe that their signaled interest is

obvious to others when it is not (Vorauer et al., 2003). Thus, unaware that their signal was invisible, those with rejection anxiety may perceive rejection where none exists. The fact that social skills deficits and peer acceptance are predictive of loneliness isn't simply a Western phenomenon; it has been demonstrated among Japanese and Chinese students as well (Aikawa, Fujita, & Tanaka, 2007; Liu & Wang, 2009).

### Self-Defeating Attributional Style

It's easy to see how repeated rejections can foster negative expectations about social interactions. Thus, lonely people are prone to irrational thinking about their social skills, the probability of their achieving intimacy, the likelihood of being rejected, and so forth. Unfortunately, once people develop these negative ideas, they often behave in ways to confirm their expectations, again setting up a vicious cycle of behavior.

Jeffrey Young (1982) points out that lonely people engage in *negative self-talk* that prevents them from pursuing intimacy in an active and positive manner. He has identified some clusters of ideas that foster loneliness. **Figure 9.17** on the next page gives examples of typical thoughts from six of these clusters of cognitions and the overt behaviors that result. As you can see, several of the cognitions in **Figure 9.17** are stable, internal self-attributions. This tendency to attribute loneliness to stable, internal causes constitutes a self-defeating attributional style (Anderson et al., 1994). That is, lonely people tell themselves that they're lonely because they're basically unlovable individuals. Not only is this a devastating belief, it is also self-defeating because it offers no way to change the situation. Happily, it *is* possible to reduce loneliness, as you'll see.

## Conquering Loneliness

The personal consequences associated with chronic loneliness can be painful and sometimes overwhelming: low self-esteem, hostility, depression, alcoholism, psychosomatic illness, and, possibly, suicide (McWhirter, 1990). Chronic loneliness is also associated with immune system deficits and is a predictor of a number of diseases, including cardiovascular disease and cancer (Hawkley & Cacioppo, 2009; Loving et al., 2006). Although there are no simple solutions to loneliness, there are some effective ones. Let's look at four useful strategies.

One option is to use the Internet to overcome loneliness, although this approach can be a double-edged sword (Cattan, 2009; McKenna & Bargh, 2000). On the plus side, the Internet is an obvious boon to busy people, those with stigmatized social identities, and those who find physical mobility difficult (the infirm and people with serious medical conditions). Moreover, shy people can interact without the anxiety involved in face-to-face

## Figure 9.17

**Patterns of thinking underlying loneliness.** According to Young (1982), negative self-talk contributes to loneliness. Six clusters of irrational thoughts are illustrated here. Each cluster of cognitions leads to certain patterns of behavior (right) that promote loneliness.

Source: From a paper presented at the annual convention of the American Psychological Association, 9/2/79. An expanded version of this paper appears in G. Emery, S. D. Hollan, & R. C. Bedrosian (Eds.) (1981). *New directions in cognitive therapy.* New York: Guilford Press and in L. A. Peplau & D. Perlman (Eds.) (1982). *Loneliness: A sourcebook of current theory, research and therapy.* New York: Wiley. Copyright © 1982 by John Wiley & Sons, Inc. and Jeffrey Young.

### Clusters of Cognitions Typical of Lonely People

| Clusters | Cognitions | Behaviors |
|---|---|---|
| A | 1. I'm undesirable.<br>2. I'm dull and boring. | Avoidance of friendship |
| B | 1. I can't communicate with other people.<br>2. My thoughts and feelings are bottled up inside. | Low self-disclosure |
| C | 1. I'm not a good lover in bed.<br>2. I can't relax, be spontaneous, and enjoy sex. | Avoidance of sexual relationships |
| D | 1. I can't seem to get what I want from this relationship.<br>2. I can't say how I feel, or he/she might leave me. | Lack of assertiveness in relationships |
| E | 1. I won't risk being hurt again.<br>2. I'd screw up any relationship. | Avoidance of potentially intimate relationships |
| F | 1. I don't know how to act in this situation.<br>2. I'll make a fool of myself. | Avoidance of other people |

communication. On the other hand, if lonely people spend a lot of time online, will they devote less time to face-to-face relationships? Will shy individuals develop the self-confidence to pursue relationships offline? Among lonely persons, Internet use is associated with benefits such as reduced loneliness, improved social support, and formation of online friendships (Morahan-Martin & Schumacher, 2003; Shaw, & Gant, 2002). Another study found that Internet training was linked to decreased loneliness, especially social loneliness, in elderly adults (Shapira, Barak, & Gal, 2007; Sum et al., 2008). On the other hand, one study found that lonely individuals more often reported that Internet use caused disturbances in their daily functioning (Morahan-Martin & Schumacher, 2003), raising concerns about Internet addiction (Nalwa & Anand, 2003: Yuen & Lavin, 2004). Clearer answers to these questions await further research.

A second suggestion is to resist the temptation to withdraw from social situations. A study that asked people what they did when they felt lonely found the top responses to be "read" and "listen to music" (Rubenstein & Shaver, 1982). These days, playing computer games and using the Internet are also options. If used occasionally, these activities can be constructive ways of dealing with loneliness. However, as long-term strategies, they do nothing to help a lonely person acquire new "real-world" friends. This situation is particularly relevant to those with an avoidant attachment style. Research indicates that, for first-year college students, involvement in extracurricular activities is related to a lower degree of loneliness (Bohnert, Aikins, & Edidin, 2007). The importance of staying active socially cannot be overemphasized. Recall that proximity is a powerful factor in the development of close relationships. To make friends, you have to be around people.

A third strategy is to break out of the habit of the self-defeating attributional style we just discussed ("I'm lonely because I'm unlovable"). There are other attributions a lonely person could make, and these alternative explanations point to solutions (see **Figure 9.18**). If someone says, "My conversational skills are weak"

## Figure 9.18

**Attributions and loneliness.** Lonely people often have a self-defeating attributional style, in which they attribute their loneliness to stable, internal causes (see upper right quadrant). Learning to make alternative attributions (see other quadrants) can bring to light ways to deal with loneliness and facilitate active coping.

Source: Based on Shaver, P., & Rubenstein, C. (1980). Childhood attachment experience and adult loneliness. In L. Wheeler (Ed.), *Review of personality and social psychology* (Vol.1, pp. 42–73). Thousand Oaks, CA: Sage Publications.

| Internal-external dimension | Stability dimension | |
|---|---|---|
| | Unstable cause (temporary) | Stable cause (permanent) |
| Internal cause | I'm lonely now, but won't be for long. I need to get out and meet some new people. | I'm lonely because I'm unlovable. I'll never be worth loving. |
| External cause | My lover and I just split up. I guess some relationships work and some don't. Maybe I'll be luckier next time. | The people here are cold and unfriendly. It's time to look for a new job. |

(unstable, internal cause), the solution would be: "I'll try to find out how to improve them." Or, if someone thinks, "It always takes time to meet people when you move to a new location" (unstable, external cause), this attribution suggests the solution of trying harder to develop new relationships and giving them time to work. The attribution "I've really searched, but I just can't find enough compatible people at my workplace" (stable, external cause) may lead to the decision, "It's time to look for a new job." As you can see, the last three attributions lead to active modes of coping rather than the passivity fostered by a self-defeating attributional style.

Finally, to thwart loneliness, people need to cultivate their social skills (DiTommaso et al., 2003). You'll find a wealth of information on this important topic in Chapter 8 (Interpersonal Communication). Lonely people, especially, should focus on attending to others' nonverbal signals, deepening the level of their self-disclosure, engaging in active listening, improving their conversational skills, and developing an assertive communication style.

Anyone who feels overwhelmed at the prospect of tackling loneliness on his or her own should consider paying a visit to a counselor or therapist. Dealing with loneliness and shyness usually involves work on two fronts. First, counselors help people improve social skills through *social skills training*. In this program, individuals learn and practice the skills involved in initiating and maintaining relationships. Second, counselors use *cognitive therapy* (see Chapter 15) to help lonely and shy individuals break the habit of automatic negative thoughts and self-defeating attributions. Over a series of sessions, individuals learn to change their negative views of themselves ("I'm boring") and other people ("They're cold and unfriendly"). Both of these approaches have high success rates, and they can pave the way to more positive social interactions that are critical to adjustment.

### The Ingredients of Close Relationships

● Close relationships are those that are important, interdependent, and long-lasting. They include friendships as well as work, family, and romantic relationships. They can elicit both positive and negative emotions.

### Initial Attraction and Relationship Development

● People are initially drawn to others who are nearby, who are seen often, and who are physically attractive. Although physical attractiveness plays a key role in initial attraction, people also seek other desirable characteristics, such as kindness, intelligence, dependable character, and maturity. People often match up on looks, but sometimes men trade status for physical attractiveness in women, and vice versa.

● As people get acquainted, they prefer others who like them and who are similar to them in various ways. Couples tend to be similar in age, race, religion, education, and attitudes.

● Once relationships are established, people engage in various maintenance behaviors and actions to sustain them. Interdependence (social exchange) theory uses principles of reinforcement to predict relationship satisfaction and commitment. How individuals apply social exchange principles depends on whether they are in exchange or communal relationships.

### Friendship

● The key ingredients of friendship are loyalty, emotional support, and letting friends be themselves. Women's same-gender friendships are usually characterized by self-disclosure and intimacy, whereas men's same-gender friendships typically involve doing things together. Some friendship issues are more complex for homosexuals than heterosexuals. Friends must engage in friendship repair if they are dealing with conflict.

### Romantic Love

● Research indicates that the experience of romantic love is the same for heterosexual and homosexual individuals. Contrary to stereotypes, men may be more romantic in some ways than women. In choosing a partner, women are more selective than men.

● Sternberg's triangular theory of love proposes that passion, intimacy, and commitment combine into eight types of love. Hazan and Shaver theorize that love relationships follow the form of attachments in infancy. Researchers subsequently expanded the number of attachment styles from three to four: secure, preoccupied, avoidant-dismissing, and avoidant-fearful. Each style has a characteristic profile. Although attachment styles show stability over time, it is possible for them to change.

● Initially, romantic love is usually characterized by passion, but strong passion appears to fade over time for a number of reasons. In relationships that continue, passionate love evolves into a less intense, more mature form of love.

● The chief causes of relationship failure are the tendency to make premature commitments, ineffective conflict management skills, boredom with the relationship, the availability of a more attractive relationship, and low levels of satisfaction. To help relationships last, couples should take the time to know each other very well, emphasize the positive qualities in their partner and relationship, engage in novel activities together, and develop effective conflict management skills.

### Perspectives on Close Relationships

● People in individualistic cultures believe that romantic love is a prerequisite for marriage, whereas those in collectivist cultures are accustomed to arranged marriages.

● The Internet offers many new vehicles for meeting others and developing relationships. The differences between Internet and face-to-face communication have important implications for established psychological theories and principles of relationship development.

### Application: Overcoming Loneliness

● Loneliness involves discontent with the extent and quality of one's interpersonal network. A surprisingly large number of people in our society are troubled by loneliness. The age groups most affected by loneliness contradict stereotypes.

● The origins of chronic loneliness can often be traced to early negative behavior that triggers rejection by peers and teachers. Social trends may also promote loneliness. Loneliness is associated with shyness, poor social skills, and self-defeating attributions.

● The Internet can be used to overcome loneliness, but it has its drawbacks. The keys to overcoming loneliness include resisting the temptation to withdraw from social situations, avoiding self-defeating attributions, and working on one's social skills.

| | |
|---|---|
| Attachment styles p. 286 | Matching hypothesis p. 277 |
| Close relationships p. 273 | Mere exposure effect p. 274 |
| Commitment p. 285 | Parental investment theory |
| Comparison level p. 281 | p. 277 |
| Comparison level for | Passion p. 285 |
| alternatives p. 281 | Proximity p. 274 |
| Heterosexism p. 284 | Reciprocal liking p. 279 |
| Interdependence theory | Relationship maintenance |
| p. 281 | p. 280 |
| Intimacy p. 285 | Sexual orientation p. 284 |
| Investments p. 282 | Shyness p. 298 |
| Loneliness p. 296 | Social exchange theory p. 281 |

| | |
|---|---|
| David Buss pp. 277–278 | Harold Kelley and John |
| Cindy Hazan and Philip | Thibaut pp. 281–282 |
| Shaver pp. 286–287 | Robert Sternberg |
| | pp. 285–286, 289 |

## QUESTIONS

1. The *mere exposure effect* refers to an increase in positive feelings due to:
   a. seeing someone often.
   b. interacting with someone.
   c. communicating via e-mail.
   d. seeing someone once.

2. Jack and Liz have been dating for two years. They are a good example of the matching hypothesis. This means that they are matched on the basis of:
   a. religion.
   b. personality.
   c. socioeconomic status.
   d. looks.

3. Tracey's personal standard of what constitutes an acceptable balance of rewards and costs in a relationship is termed:
   a. social exchange.
   b. comparison level.
   c. proximity level.
   d. relationship satisfaction.

4. Women's same-gender friendships are typically based on ____; men's are typically based on ____.
   a. shopping together; hunting together
   b. attending sports events; attending sports events
   c. shared activities; intimacy and self-disclosure
   d. intimacy and self-disclosure; shared activities

5. If a researcher fails to determine the sexual orientation of her research participants and reports her findings without any mention of homosexuals, her study suffers from:
   a. homosexism.
   b. social exchange.
   c. heterosexism.
   d. romantic bias.

6. A sociocultural explanation for the finding that women are more selective than men in choosing partners is that women:
   a. have better vision than men.
   b. have less economic power than men.
   c. are less superficial than men.
   d. have to compensate for being more romantic than men.

7. Jenna tends to keep her distance from others and is unconcerned about social rejection. She would be classified in which of the following attachment styles?
   a. secure
   b. preoccupied
   c. avoidant-dismissing
   d. avoidant-fearful

8. Arranged marriages are most common in:
   a. individualistic cultures.
   b. collectivist cultures.
   c. unrequited cultures.
   d. both individualistic and collectivist cultures.

9. Which of the following statements regarding self-disclosure in online communication is accurate?
   a. Because online communication is anonymous, people take fewer risks in online self-disclosure.
   b. Because online communication is anonymous, people take greater risks in online self-disclosure.
   c. Because there is a potential record of one's online communication, people take fewer risks in online self-disclosure.
   d. There is no difference in self-disclosure in online versus face-to-face communication.

10. A self-defeating attributional style associated with loneliness involves attributing loneliness to:
    a. internal, stable factors.
    b. internal, unstable factors.
    c. external, stable factors.
    d. external, unstable factors.

## ANSWERS

1. a Page 274
2. d Page 277
3. b Page 281
4. d Page 283
5. c Page 284
6. b Pages 278–279
7. c Page 288
8. b Page 292
9. b Page 293
10. a Page 299

## Personal Explorations Workbook

Go to the *Personal Explorations Workbook* in the back of your text-book for exercises that can enhance your self-understanding in relation to issues raised in this chapter. **Exercise 9.1** *Self-Assessment:* Social Avoidance and Distress Scale. **Exercise 9.2** *Self-Reflection:* How Do You Relate to Friends?

CourseMate

Access an interactive eBook, chapter-specific interactive learning tools, including Personal Explorations, Recommended Readings, Critical Thinking Exercises, flashcards, quizzes, videos and more in your Psychology CourseMate, available at **www.cengagebrain.com/shop/ISBN/1111186634**.

© Ronnie Kaufman/Getty Images/Blend Images

# Marriage and Intimate Relationships

*"My hands are shaky. I want to call her again but I know it is no good. She'll only yell and scream. It makes me feel lousy. I have work to do but I can't do it. I can't concentrate. I want to call people up, go see them, but I'm afraid they'll see that I'm shaky. I just want to talk. I can't think about anything besides this trouble with Nina. I think I want to cry."—A recently separated man quoted in* Marital Separation *(Weiss, 1975, p. 48)*

This man is describing his feelings a few days after he and his wife broke up. He is still hoping for reconciliation. In the meantime, he feels overwhelmed by anxiety, remorse, and depression. He feels very alone and is scared at the prospect of remaining alone. His emotional distress is so great that he can't think straight or work effectively. His reaction to the loss of an intimate relationship is not all that unusual. Breakups are devastating for most people—a reality that illustrates the enormous importance of intimate relationships in people's lives.

In the previous chapter, we explored the important role of close relationships in personal adjustment. In this chapter we focus on marriage and committed intimate relationships. We discuss why people marry and how they progress toward the selection of a mate. To shed light on marital adjustment, we describe the life cycle of the family, highlighting key vulnerable spots in marital relations and issues related to divorce. We also address alternative relationship lifestyles including gay partnerships, singlehood, and cohabitation. Finally, in the Application we examine the tragic problem of violence in intimate relationships. Let's begin by discussing recent challenges to the traditional concept of marriage.

# Challenges to the Traditional Model of Marriage

## LEARNING OBJECTIVES

● Discuss recent trends relating to the acceptance of singlehood and cohabitation.

● Articulate changing views on the permanence of marriage and gender roles.

● Explain how increased childlessness and the decline of the nuclear family have affected the institution of marriage.

**Marriage is the legally and socially sanctioned union of sexually intimate adults.** Traditionally, the marital relationship has included economic interdependence, common residence, sexual fidelity, and shared responsibility for children. Although the institution of marriage remains popular, it sometimes seems to be under assault from shifting social trends. This assault has prompted many experts to ask whether marriage is in serious trouble (Cherlin, 2004; Lewin, 2004). Although it appears that the institution of marriage will weather the storm, we should note some of the social trends that are shaking up the traditional model of marriage:

**1.** *Increased acceptance of singlehood.* Remaining single is a trend that has been on the rise for several decades (Morris & DePaulo, 2009). In part, this trend reflects longer postponement of marriage than before. **Figure 10.1** shows that the median age at which people marry has been increasing gradually since the mid-1960s. In 2005, the median age of first marriages was 25.8 years for women and 27.1 years for men (U.S. Bureau of the Census, 2006a). Thus, remaining single is becoming a more acceptable lifestyle (DeFrain & Olson, 1999). Furthermore, the negative stereotype of people who remain single—lonely, frustrated, and unchosen—is gradually evaporating.

**2.** *Increased acceptance of cohabitation.* **Cohabitation is living together in a sexually intimate relationship without the legal bonds of marriage.** Negative attitudes toward couples living together have clearly declined (Cherlin, 2004), although many people continue to disapprove of the practice (Thornton & Young-DeMarco, 2001). The prevalence of cohabitation has increased dramatically in recent decades. In fact, recent census figures reveal that married couples are in the minority for the first time, with only 49.7% of households consisting of married couples (Roberts, 2006). Moreover, cohabiting relationships increasingly include children (Smock, 2000; Stanley & Rhoades, 2009), as we discuss more fully later in this chapter.

**3.** *Reduced premium on permanence.* Most people still view marriage as a permanent commitment, but an increasing number of people regard divorce as justifiable if their marriage fails to foster their interests as individuals (Bianchi & Casper, 2000). Accordingly, the social stigma associated with divorce has lessened, and divorce rates have climbed. Some experts estimate that roughly 50% of marriages ultimately end in separation or divorce (Amato, 2004a).

**4.** *Transitions in gender roles.* The women's movement and economic pressures have led to substantial changes in the gender-role expectations of many people entering marriage today (Brewster & Padavic, 2000; Zuo & Tang, 2000). The traditional breadwinner and homemaker roles for the husband and wife are being discarded by many couples, as more and more married women

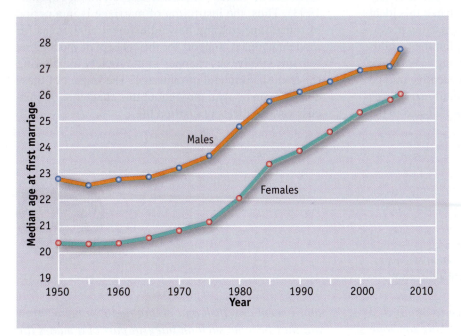

**Figure 10.1**

**Median age at first marriage.** The median age at which people in the United States marry for the first time has been creeping up for both males and females since the mid-1960s. This trend indicates that more people are postponing marriage. (Data from U.S. Bureau of the Census)

enter the workforce (Halpern, 2005; see **Figure 10.2**). Role expectations for husbands and wives are becoming more varied, more flexible, and more ambiguous (Amato et al., 2003). Many people regard this trend as a step in the right direction. However, changing gender roles create new potential for conflict between marital partners (McGraw & Walker, 2004).

**5.** *Increased voluntary childlessness.* In the past two decades, the percentage of women without children has climbed in all age groups as an increasing number of married couples have chosen not to have children or to delay having children (Bulcroft & Teachman, 2004). Researchers speculate that this trend is a result of new career opportunities for women, the tendency to marry at a later age, and changing attitudes (such as a desire for independence or concerns about overpopulation) (Hatch, 2009).

**6.** *Decline of the traditional nuclear family.* Thanks to endless reruns of television shows like *Leave It to Beaver, Happy Days,* and *The Cosby Show,* in the eyes of most American adults the ideal family should consist of a husband and wife married for the first time, rearing two or more children, with the man serving as the sole breadwinner (Coontz, 2000). As McGraw and Walker (2004), put it, "Many people today, both in academic settings and popular culture, continue to idealize the image of the traditional nuclear family—one consisting of a breadwinner father and a homemaker mother . . . Because this ideology remains strong, a dearth of support exists for families that do not conform to the image" (p. 177). In reality, this image was never all that accurate, and today only a small minority of American families are estimated to match this ideal (Coontz, 2000; Halpern, 2005). The increasing prevalence of single-parent households, stepfamilies, childless marriages, unwed parents, and working wives make the traditional nuclear family a highly deceptive mirage that does not reflect the diversity of family structures in America. Interestingly, this change is reflected in the

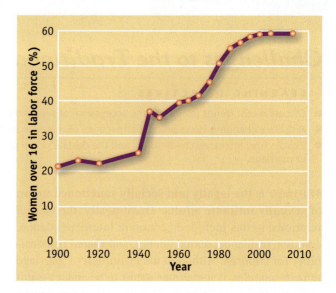

**Figure 10.2**

**Women in the workforce.** The percentage of women in the United States (over age 16) who work outside the home has been rising steadily, although it has leveled off in recent years. (Data from U.S. Bureau of Labor Statistics)

fact that many television shows today depict alternative family structures (for instance, *Two and a Half Men* and *How I Met Your Mother*).

In summary, the norms that mold marital and intimate relationships have been restructured in fundamental ways in recent decades. Traditional values have eroded as people have increasingly embraced more individualistic values (Bianchi & Casper, 2000; Popenoe, 1993). Thus, the institution of marriage is in a period of transition, creating new adjustment challenges for modern couples. Support for the concept of monogamy remains strong, but changes in the society are altering the traditional model of marriage. The impact of these changes can be seen throughout this chapter as we discuss various facets of married life.

# Deciding to Marry

### LEARNING OBJECTIVES

- Describe some cultural influences on marriage.
- Identify several factors influencing the selection of a mate.
- Summarize evidence on predictors of marital success.

*"I'm ashamed of being single, I have to admit it. I have grown to hate the word. The worst thing someone can say is, 'How come you're still not married?' It's like saying, 'What's wrong with you?' I look at women who are frumpy and physically undesirable and they're monochromatic and uninteresting and they*

*don't seem unselfish and giving and I wonder, 'How did they become such an integral part of a man's life that he wanted to marry them and spend his life with them?' I'm envious. They're married and I date."—A woman quoted in* Tales from the Front *(Kavesh & Lavin, 1988, p. 91)*

This woman desperately wants to be married. The intensity of her motivation for marriage may be a bit unusual, but otherwise she is fairly typical. Like most people, she has been socialized to believe that her life isn't complete until she finds a mate. Although alternatives to marriage are more viable than ever, experts project that over 90% of Americans will marry at least once (Cordova & Harp, 2009). Some will do it several times! But why? How does culture influence marriage? How do individuals choose their partners? And what are some predictors of successful marriages? We'll address these questions as we discuss the factors that influence the decision to marry.

## Cultural Influences on Marriage

Modern Western cultures are somewhat unusual in permitting free choice of one's marital partner. Many societies rely on parental arrangements, and often they severely restrict the range of acceptable partners along religious and class lines (Ingoldsby, 1995). Experts estimate that up to 80% of world cultures practice arranged marriage (Pasupathi, 2009). Marriages arranged by families and communities remain common in more collectivist cultures such as India (Gupta, 1992), Japan (Iwao, 1993), China (Xiaohe & Whyte, 1990), and West African countries (Adams, Anderson, & Adonu, 2004). This practice is declining in some societies as a result of Westernization. Still, when people in collectivist societies contemplate marriage, they weigh strongly the impact a relationship will have on their family rather than rely solely on what their heart says (Triandis, 1994). Studies show that attitudes about love in India, Pakistan, Thailand, and West African countries reflect these cultural priorities (Adams et al., 2004; Levine et al., 1995; Medora et al., 2002). Culture is but one influence on marital decisions; let's look at some specific factors that influence one's choice of a mate.

## Selecting a Mate

Mate selection in American culture is a gradual process that begins with dating and moves on to sometimes lengthy periods of courtship. Let's look at some of the factors that influence this important process.

### Monogamy and Polygamy

*Monogamy* **is the practice of having only one spouse at a time.** In our society, monogamous marital relationships are the norm and the law. However, the HBO series *Big Love* has placed *polygamy,* **having more than one spouse at a time,** in the spotlight (Lee, 2006). This show features a fictional suburban, polygamous family. Though many cultures practice polygamy, Westerners typically associate it with the Mormon religion, even though the Mormon Church officially denounced it in the late 19th century (Hatch, 2009; White & White, 2005). Research suggests that polygamy (also called plural marriage) in both well and poorly functioning families is painful for wives. Common ways of dealing with the pain include accepting that this way of life is God's will, allocating household resources equally, and maintaining an attitude of respect for the other wives (Slonim-Nevo & Al-Krenawi, 2006). Polygamy is practiced worldwide in countries such as Algeria, Chad, Kuwait, and Saudi Arabia and in some Islamic groups. Unfortunately, the practice of polygamy tends to be most common in societies where women have little to no independence, access to education, or political power (Cunningham, 2009b).

### Endogamy

*Endogamy* **is the tendency for people to marry within their own social group.** Research demonstrates that people tend to marry others of the same race, religion, ethnic background, and social class (Kalmijn, 1998; McPherson, Smith-Lovin, & Cook, 2001). This behavior is promoted by cultural norms and by the way similarity fosters interpersonal attraction (see Chapter 9). Although endogamy appears to be declining, this decrease has been gradual. For example, in 2000, 6% of all households reported an interracial marriage, with races encompassing black, white, Asian, Native American, and so on (Simmons & O'Connell, 2003). This is up from just 1% in 1970 (Gaines, 2009).

Although some people speculate that interracial relationships carry an extra burden, recent research suggests that there are no differences between interracial couples and same-race couples in terms of relationship quality, conflict patterns, and attachment. In fact, interracial couples tend to report higher relationship satisfaction than others (Troy, Lewis-Smith, & Laurenceau, 2006), especially partners who feel positive about their own race while being accepting of others (Leslie & Letiecq, 2004).

### Homogamy

*Homogamy* **is the tendency for people to marry others who have similar personal characteristics.** Among other things, marital partners tend to be similar in age and education (Fu & Heaton, 2008; Jepsen & Jepsen, 2002), physical attractiveness (Feingold, 1988), attitudes and values (Kilby, 1993; Luo & Klohnen, 2005), marital history (Ono, 2006), and even vulnerability to psychological disorders (Mathews & Reus, 2001). Interestingly, homogamy *is* associated with longer-lasting and more satisfying marital relations (Gaunt, 2006; Gonzaga, 2009). Even in dating relationships, similarity on a variety of characteristics is related to stability and satisfaction (Peretti & Abplanalp, 2004).

People tend to marry others who are similar in race, religion, and social class—a phenomenon called endogamy.

© Michael Newman/PhotoEdit

Deviations from homogamy in age and education do not tend to be symmetrical, as husbands are usually older and better educated than their wives (South, 1991). In fact, men report believing that women with higher income and education levels than themselves will be less likable and less faithful (Greitemeyer, 2006). Cultural norms that discourage women from dating younger men may contribute to a "marriage squeeze" for women. Without the freedom to date younger men, women are likely to find their pool of potential partners dwindling more rapidly than men of similar age do.

### Gender and Mate Selection Preferences

Research reveals that males and females exhibit both similarities and differences in what they look for in a marital partner. Many characteristics, such as physical attractiveness, similarity, emotional stability, dependability, and a pleasant disposition, are rated highly by both sexes (Buss et al., 2001; Peretti & Abplanalp, 2004). Both male and female college students gave high ratings to the traits of honesty and trustworthiness for marriage partners (Regan & Berscheid, 1997). However, a few reliable differences between men's and women's priorities have been found, and these differences appear to be nearly universal across cultures.

As we saw in Chapter 9, women tend to place a higher value than men on potential partners' socioeconomic status, intelligence, ambition, and financial prospects. In contrast, men consistently show more interest than women in potential partners' youthfulness and physical attractiveness (Buss & Kenrick, 1998). Fletcher (2002) asserts that mate selection criteria can be grouped in three major categories: warmth/loyalty, vitality/attractiveness, and status/resources. Compared

to men, women tend to place a greater emphasis on warmth/loyalty and status/resources and less of an emphasis on vitality/attractiveness. This gender difference is greater for long-term as opposed to short-term mate selection (Fletcher et al., 2004). Most theorists explain these gender disparities in terms of evolutionary concepts (Archer, 1996; Buss, 1996; Fletcher, 2002).

### Predictors of Marital Success

Are there any factors that reliably predict marital success? A great deal of research has been devoted to this question. This effort has been plagued by one obvious problem: How do you measure "marital success"? Some researchers have simply compared divorced and intact couples in regard to premarital characteristics. The problem with this strategy is that it only assesses commitment and not satisfaction. Many intact couples obviously do not have happy or successful marriages (Amato, 2007). Other researchers have used elaborate questionnaires to measure couples' marital satisfaction. Unfortunately, these scales also have a number of problems. Among other things, they appear to measure complacency and lack of conflict more than satisfaction (Fowers et al., 1994). Although research shows some thought-provoking correlations between couples' premarital characteristics and marital adjustment, most of the correlations are relatively small. Thus, there are no foolproof predictors of marital success. Nevertheless, here are some of the factors that researchers have looked at.

**Family background.** The marital adjustment of partners is correlated with the marital satisfaction of their parents. People whose parents were divorced are more likely than others to experience divorce themselves (Amato & DeBoer, 2001; Frame, Mattson, & Johnson, 2009). For a number of reasons, there appears to be an intergenerational "divorce cycle" (Wolfinger, 2005). Researchers speculate that this cycle may be due in part to how individuals learn to resolve conflicts. For better or worse, they often learn this from their parents. Whitton and colleagues (2008) found that hostility levels of parents in family interactions predicted the marital hostility levels of their offspring 17 years later. This, in turn, was predictive of marital adjustment, especially for men. The researchers note, however, that other factors, such as the development of insecure attachment styles, might be at play here (Whitton et al., 2008).

**Age.** The ages of the bride and groom are also related to the likelihood of marriage success. Couples who marry young have higher divorce rates (Bramlett & Mosher, 2001), as **Figure 10.3** shows. Perhaps people who marry later have more carefully selected their mate, or are less likely to undergo dramatic personal change that would render them incompatible with their partners. Researchers speculate that as more individuals choose to marry later in life, divorce rates could actually decrease (Teachman, Tedrow, & Hall, 2006).

**Length of courtship.** Longer periods of courtship are associated with a greater probability of marital success (Cate & Lloyd, 1988). Longer courtships may allow couples to evaluate their compatibility more accurately.

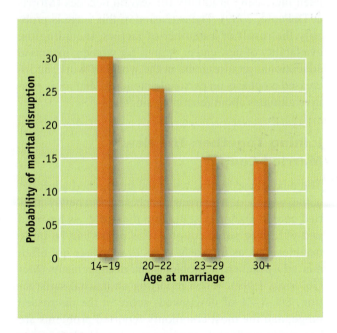

**Figure 10.3**

**Age at marriage and probability of marital disruption in the first five years.** Martin and Bumpass (1989) estimated the likelihood of marital disruption (either divorce or separation) within five years for various groups. The data summarized here show that the probability of marital disruption is substantially higher among those who marry young.

Alternatively, the correlation between courtship length and marital success may exist because people who are cautious about marriage have attitudes and values that promote marital stability.

**Personality.** Generally, studies have found that partners' specific personality traits are not strong predictors of marital success. That said, there are some traits that show modest correlations with marital adjustment. For example, two negative predictors of marital success are perfectionism (Haring, Hewitt, & Flett, 2003) and insecurity (Crowell, Treboux, & Waters, 2002). Recently, researchers have had more success exploring the link between people's underlying emotional dispositions and marital adjustment. They found that intensity of smiling in college yearbooks (an indicator of positive emotional expression) was predictive of a lower likelihood of divorce in later life (Hertenstein et al., 2009). These researchers found similar results when they rated childhood photos of older adults; smiling in photos negatively predicted divorce later in life. While Hertenstein acknowledges that there are other explanations for the link (such as that smiling people might attract more friends and have more social support), he asserts that these results demonstrate the important role of positive emotional dispositions in life.

**Premarital communication.** As you might expect, the degree to which couples get along well during their courtship is predictive of their marital adjustment. The quality of premarital communication appears to be especially crucial. For example, the more that prospective mates are negative, sarcastic, insulting, and unsupportive during courtship, the greater the likelihood of marital distress and divorce (Clements, Stanley, & Markman, 2004). Close relationships that include self-disclosure and acceptance of what is learned through disclosure are likely to be the most satisfying over long periods of time (Harvey & Omarzu, 1999).

Although most research in the area of communication has focused on discussions of conflict, one study found that being understood and validated in conversation is strongly related to satisfaction, even when the conversation is about a positive event (Gable, Gonzaga, & Strachman, 2006). While this research focused on dating couples, Gable and his colleagues speculate that "positive emotional exchanges may serve as a foundation on which stable and satisfying relationships rest" (p. 916). In fact, playfulness and positive emotion in mundane, everyday interactions in couples seem to be emerging as important components in marital adjustment (Driver & Gottman, 2004).

**Stressful Events.** So far we have talked about issues that individual partners bring to a marriage, but these relationships don't exist in a vacuum. Stressful situations surrounding a marriage (unemployment, chronic illness, caregiving for an aging parent) can cause conflict, increase distress, and harm marital stability (Frame et al., 2009). Partners who report higher levels of external stress also report more stress and tension in their close relationships (Bodenmann, Ledermann, & Bradbury, 2007). Research has also found that the stress from work can spill over to affect mood at home, which ultimately can erode a marriage (Lavee & Ben-Ari, 2007). One exception to the stress-distress link is the stress related to becoming new parents, a topic we will talk about in more detail shortly.

# Marital Adjustment Across the Family Life Cycle

## LEARNING OBJECTIVES

- Understand what the family life cycle is.
- Identify factors couples weigh in deciding whether to have children.
- Analyze the dynamics of the transition to parenthood.

- Identify common problems that surface as a family's children reach adolescence.
- Discuss the transitions that occur in the later stages of the family life cycle.

*"Jennifer has taken a lot of time away from us, the time that we normally spend doing things together or talking. It seems like maybe on a weekend when we would normally like to sleep in, or just have lazy sex, Jennifer wakes up and needs to be fed. . . . But I'm sure that will pass as soon as Jennifer gets a little older. We're just going through a phase."—A new mother quoted in* American Couples *(Blumstein & Schwartz, 1983, p. 205)*

"We're just going through a phase." That statement highlights an important point: There are predictable patterns of development for families, just as there are for individuals. These patterns make up the *family life cycle,* **an orderly sequence of developmental stages that families tend to progress through.** The institutions of marriage and family are inevitably intertwined. With the advent of marriage, two persons create an entirely new family. Typically, this new family forms the core of one's life as an adult.

Sociologists have proposed a number of models to describe family development. Our discussion is organized around a six-stage model outlined by Carter and McGoldrick (1988, 1999). **Figure 10.4** provides an overview of their model. It spells out the developmental tasks during each stage of the life cycle for families that eventually have children and remain intact. Admittedly, not all families progress through the family life cycle in an orderly fashion, and some researchers find that marital problems are similar whether a couple are newly married, have young children, or have been married for many years (Miller et al., 2003). Nevertheless, the model does appear to be a useful predictive tool for the marriage experience (Kapinus & Johnson, 2003). Although Carter and McGoldrick have described variations on this basic pattern that are associated with remaining childless or going through a divorce, we will focus primarily on the typical, basic pattern in this section. We will also focus on heterosexual couples in this section.

### Between Families: The Unattached Young Adult

As young adults become independent of their parents, they go through a transitional period during which they are "between families" until they form a new family through marriage. What is interesting about this stage is that more and more people are prolonging it. As we saw in **Figure 10.1,** the median age for marriage has been increasing gradually for several decades (Morris & DePaulo, 2009). The extension of this stage is probably the result of a number of factors, including the availability of new career options for women, increased educational requirements in the world of work, an increased emphasis on personal autonomy, and more positive attitudes about remaining single.

### Joining Together: The Newly Married Couple

The next phase begins when the unattached adult becomes attached. If marriage is chosen, the newly married couple gradually settle into their roles as husband and wife. For some couples, this phase can be quite troublesome, as the early years of marriage are often marred by numerous problems and disagreements (McGoldrick, 1999). When reporting on marital satisfaction, 8%–14% of newlyweds score in the distressed range, and the most commonly reported problems are balancing work and marriage and financial concerns (Schramm et al., 2005). *In general, however, this stage tends to be characterized by great happiness—the proverbial "marital bliss."* Spouses' satisfaction with their relationship tends to be relatively high early in marriage, before the arrival of the first child.

## The Family Life Cycle

| Family life cycle stage | Key developmental task | Additional changes in family status required to proceed developmentally |
|---|---|---|
| **1.** Between families: The unattached young adult | Accepting parent/offspring separation | a. Differentiation of self in relation to family of origin<br>b. Development of intimate peer relationships<br>c. Establishment of self in work |
| **2.** The joining of families through marriage: The newly married couple | Commitment to new system | a. Formation of marital system<br>b. Realignment of relationships with extended families and friends to include spouse |
| **3.** The family with young children | Accepting new members into the system | a. Adjusting marital system to make space for child(ren)<br>b. Taking on parenting roles<br>c. Realignment of relationships with extended family to include parenting and grandparenting roles |
| **4.** The family with adolescents | Increasing flexibility of family boundaries to include children's independence | a. Shifting of parent-child relationships to permit adolescent to move in and out of system<br>b. Refocus on midlife marital and career issues<br>c. Beginning shift toward concerns for older generation |
| **5.** Launching children and moving on | Accepting a multitude of exits from and entries into the family system | a. Renegotiation of marital system as a dyad<br>b. Development of adult-to-adult relationships between grown children and their parents<br>c. Realignment of relationships to include in-laws and grandchildren<br>d. Dealing with disabilities and death of parents (grandparents) |
| **6.** The family in later life | Accepting the shifting of generational roles | a. Maintaining own and/or couple functioning and interests in face of physiological decline; exploration of new familial and social role options<br>b. Support for a more central role for middle generation<br>c. Making room in the system for the wisdom and experience of the elderly; supporting the older generation without over-functioning for them<br>d. Dealing with loss of spouse, siblings, and other peers and preparation for own death; life review and integrations |

**Figure 10.4**

**Stages of the family life cycle.** The family life cycle can be divided into six stages, as shown here (based on Carter & McGoldrick, 1988). The family's key developmental task during each stage is identified in the second column. The third column lists additional developmental tasks at each stage.

This pre-children phase used to be rather short for most newly married couples, as they quickly went about the business of starting a family. Traditionally, couples simply *assumed* that they would proceed to have children. Remaining childless by choice used to be virtually unthinkable for wives, as having a child was viewed as the ultimate fulfillment of womanhood (Ulrich & Weatherall, 2000). This value system meant that women who remained childless often felt incomplete (Morell, 2000) or were viewed by others as selfish (Letherby & Williams, 1999).

In recent decades, however, ambivalence about the prospect of having children has clearly increased (T. W. Smith, 1999), and the percentage of voluntarily childless (often called child-free) couples has roughly doubled since 1980 (Bulcroft & Teachman, 2004). Thus, more and more couples find themselves struggling to *decide* whether to have children. Often, the decision to remain childless occurs after numerous postponements, when the couple finally acknowledge that "the right time" is never going to arrive. Intentions about having children are not as stable over time as one might expect. In one study that followed adult participants over a span of six years, about one-quarter of the respondents changed their plans (Heaton, Jacobson, & Holland, 1999). These subjects were almost evenly split between those who planned to remain childless but subsequently decided they wanted to have children and those who intended to have children but subsequently expressed a preference for remaining child-free.

Couples who choose to remain childless cite the great costs incurred in raising children. In addition to the financial burdens, they mention such costs as giving up educational or career opportunities, loss of time for leisure activities and each other, loss of autonomy, worry about the responsibility associated with child-rearing, and concerns about overpopulation (Bulcroft & Teachman, 2004; Hatch, 2009). Women especially cite career issues as playing a role in their decisions (Park, 2005), and voluntarily childless women tend to have higher incomes and more work experience than other women (Abma & Martinez, 2006).

Although voluntary childlessness is becoming more common, such couples are still in the minority.

Most couples decide to have children, citing the responsibility to procreate, the joy of watching youngsters mature, the sense of purpose that children create, and the satisfaction associated with emotional nurturance and the challenges of childrearing (Cowan & Cowan, 2000; Goetting, 1986). The vast majority of parents rate parenthood as a positive and satisfying experience and report no regret about their choice (Demo, 1992). Similarly, most voluntarily childless couples do not regret their decision (Jeffries & Konnert, 2002).

## Family with Young Children

Although most parents are happy with their decision to have children, the arrival of the first child represents a major transition, and the disruption of routines can be emotionally draining (Belsky, 2009; Carter, 1999). The transition to parenthood tends to have more impact on mothers than fathers (Nomaguchi & Milkie, 2003). The new mother, already physically exhausted by the birth process, is particularly prone to postpartum distress, and about 10%–13% of new moms experience depression within the first 12 weeks after birth (Dennis & Ross, 2005; Formichelli, 2001). Risk factors for developing postpartum depression include past depression, high stress levels, and marital dissatisfaction (O'Hara, 2009). This disorder received increased national attention when the actress Brooke Shields went public with her struggle with postpartum depression after the birth of her daughter in 2003. Issues such as infants' sleep patterns and crying are associated with mothers' depressive symptoms and marital dissatisfaction (Dennis & Ross, 2005; Meijer & van den Wittenboer, 2007).

The transition to parenthood is more difficult when a mother's expectations regarding how much the father will be involved in childcare are not met (Fox, Bruce, & Combs-Orme, 2000). A review of decades of research on parenthood and marital satisfaction found that (1) parents exhibit lower marital satisfaction than comparable nonparents, (2) mothers of infants report the steepest decline in marital satisfaction, and (3) the more children couples have, the lower their marital satisfaction tends to be (Twenge, Campbell, & Foster, 2003).

**WEB LINK 10.1    American Academy of Child and Adolescent Psychiatry (AACAP): Facts for Families**

Many new parents may need help coping with emerging problems in their children. The brochures here (in both English and Spanish) cover a wide range of psychological issues and psychiatric conditions.

Crisis during the transition to first parenthood is not a forgone conclusion, however (Cox et al., 1999). Planning one's pregnancy and having high prepregnancy marital satisfaction buffer against marital declines (Lawrence et al., 2008). Couples with high levels of affection and commitment prior to the first child's birth are likely to maintain a stable level of satisfaction after the child's birth (Shapiro, Gottman, & Carrère, 2000).

AP Images/Susan Walsh

**Actress Brooke Shields, who suffered from postpartum depression after the birth of her daughter, has campaigned for increased awareness of this potentially dangerous illness. She is shown here at a 2007 press conference related to federal legislation that would improve government efforts to detect and treat postpartum depression.**

The key to making this transition less stressful may be to have *realistic expectations* about parental responsibilities (Belsky, 2009; Belsky & Kelly, 1994). Studies find that stress tends to be greatest in new parents who have overestimated the benefits and underestimated the costs of their new role. Reactions to parenthood may also depend on how a couple's marriage is going. Involvement in and satisfaction with parenting tends to be higher when marital quality is higher (Gavin et al., 2002; Rogers & White, 1998). Although children bring their share of trials and tribulations to a marriage, divorce rates are clearly higher for those who remain childless (Shapiro et al., 2000).

## Family with Adolescent Children

Although the adolescent years have long been viewed as a period of great stress and turmoil, research from the past decade has led to the conclusion that adolescence is not as turbulent or difficult as once believed (Steinberg & Levine, 1997). While studies indicate that it is a stressful period for the parents, who overwhelmingly rate adolescence as the most difficult stage of parenting (Gecas & Seff, 1990), problematic parent-teen relationships appear to be the exception rather than the rule (Smetana, 2009).

As adolescent children seek to establish their own identities, parental influence tends to decline while the influence of peer groups tends to increase. Parents tend to retain more influence than peers over important matters, such as educational goals and career plans, but peers gradually gain more influence over less critical matters, such as style of dress and recreational plans (Gecas & Seff, 1990). Thus, conflicts between adolescent children and their parents tend to involve everyday matters such as chores and dress more than substantive issues such as sex and drugs (Barber, 1994). Conflict is particularly likely to surface between adolescents (of both sexes) and their mothers. Adolescents tend to exhibit better adjustment in families in which they are encouraged to participate in decision making but parents ultimately maintain control (Preto, 1999; Smetana, 2009). Parents seem to learn from their experience in dealing with an adolescent child, as they report less conflict with their second adolescent child than their first (Whiteman, McHale, & Crouter, 2003).

In addition to worrying about their adolescent children, middle-aged couples often worry about the care of their aging parents. Adults caught between these conflicting responsibilities have been called the *sandwich generation* (Riley & Bowen, 2005). Based on national survey data from Great Britain and the United States, one-third of women between the ages of 55 and 69 simultaneously provide help to both generations (Grundy & Henretta, 2006). Thanks to increased longevity and decreased family size, today's average married couple has more parents than children, and an increasing number of adults provide care to their aging parents (Starrels et al., 1997). Females tend to assume most of the responsibility for elderly relatives, and it is estimated that in the future women can expect to spend more years caring for their aging parents than for their dependent children (Bromley & Blieszner, 1997). Many theorists are concerned that these multigenerational caregiving responsibilities may prove burdensome and lead to burnout (Fruhauf, 2009). Supporting this concern, one study found that the number of hours spent caring for an aging parent was correlated with wives' psychological distress (Voydanoff & Donnelly, 1999). For women, becoming a caregiver for a parent is associated with declines in happiness, autonomy, and personal growth and increases in financial difficulties later in life (Marks, Lambert, & Choi, 2002; Wakabayashi & Donato, 2006). On the positive side, many caregivers describe the experience as gratifying in that it allowed them to repair or enhance damaged relationships (Fruhauf, 2009). Additionally, these situations allow for increased interaction between children and grandparents (Silverstein & Ruiz, 2009).

## Launching Children into the Adult World

When children begin to reach their twenties, the family has to adapt to a multitude of exits and entries, as children leave and return, sometimes with their own spouses. This period, during which children normally progress from dependence to independence, brings a variety of transitions. In many instances, conflict subsides and parent-child relations become closer and more supportive (Aquilino, 1997).

One might argue that launching children into the adult world tends to be a lengthier and more difficult process today than it once was (Furstenberg, 2001). It is estimated that approximately 40% of young adults will return to live with their parents at some point, typically for one to two years (Aquilino, 2009). The rapidly rising cost of a college education and the shrinking job market have probably led many young adults to linger in their parents' homes. Moreover, crises such as separation, divorce, job loss, and single-parent pregnancy force many children who have ventured out on their own to return to their parents. Young adults who come home after living independently have been characterized as the *boomerang generation* (Mitchell, 2006). Children from intact, two-parent homes are more likely to return than are those with stepparents (Goldscheider & Goldscheider, 1998). Interestingly, young adults have more negative attitudes about returning home than their parents do (Veevers, Gee, & Wister, 1996). Data suggest that living with one's parents during adulthood has a modest negative impact on parent-child relations (White &

Rogers, 1997). Conflicts are particularly likely when returning children have been unsuccessful in moving into autonomous adult roles (Treas & Lawton, 1999).

When parents do manage to get all their children launched into the adult world, they find themselves faced with an "empty nest." This period was formerly thought to be a difficult transition for many parents, especially mothers who were familiar only with the maternal role. In recent decades, however, more women have experience with other roles outside the home and look forward to their "liberation" from childrearing responsibilities. Most parents adjust effectively to the empty nest transition, and the empty nest is associated with improved mood and well-being for most mothers (Dennerstein, Dudley, & Guthrie, 2002). In fact, most parents are more likely to have problems if their children *return* to the once-empty nest, especially if these returns are frequent (Blacker, 1999; Bookwala, 2009). Hence, middle-aged parents who have launched their children into the adult world report more enjoyment of life and higher marital satisfaction than similar-aged parents who still have children at home (White & Edwards, 1990).

## Family in Later Life

Marital satisfaction tends to climb in the postparental period as couples find they have more time to devote attention to each other (Brubaker, 1990). Whether this trend is the result of reduced parental responsibilities, reduced work responsibilities, or other considerations remains unclear (Lee, 1988). Older couples rate children or grandchildren, good memories, and traveling together as the top three sources of pleasure (Levenson, Carstersen, & Gottman, 1993). However, spouses do have to adapt to spending more time with each other and often need to renegotiate role expectations (Walsh, 1999). Of course, age-related considerations that are independent of the relationship, such as the increased likelihood of physical illness, can make the later years stressful. The three most commonly reported problems in late-life marriages are disagreements or disappointments about leisure activities, intimacy, and finances (Henry, Miller, & Giarrusso, 2005). Some gender differences in disappointments are apparent in older couples: Men are more likely to be disappointed about financial matters, whereas women are more likely to be disappointed about personal habits and health matters.

# *Vulnerable Areas in Marital Adjustment*

### LEARNING OBJECTIVES

- Discuss how gaps in role expectations may affect marital adjustment.
- Understand how spouses' work affects their marital satisfaction and their children.
- Clarify how financial issues are related to marital adjustment.
- Summarize evidence on the relationship between communication quality and marital adjustment.

*"When we first got married, the first six months of conflicts were all about getting him to take account of what I had planned for him at home. . . . He would come waltzing in an hour and a half late for dinner, or cancel an evening with friends, because he had to close a deal. . . . We would argue and argue . . . not because I didn't want him to make a living . . . but because I thought he had to be more considerate."—A wife quoted in* American Couples *(Blumstein & Schwartz, 1983, p. 174)*

During courtship, couples tend to focus on pleasurable activities. But once couples are married, they deal with a variety of problems, such as arriving at acceptable role compromises, paying bills, and raising a family. Marital conflict is associated with several negative outcomes for partners and their family members, including increased depression, alcoholism, physical health problems, domestic violence, and divorce (Fincham, 2009). All couples encounter problems, but successful marriages depend on couples' ability to handle their problems. In this section we analyze the major kinds of difficulties that are likely to emerge. Although there are no simple solutions for these problems, it helps to know where you're likely to encounter them.

## Gaps in Role Expectations

When heterosexual individuals marry, they assume new roles—those of husband and wife. Each role comes with certain expectations that the partners hold about how wives and husbands should behave. These expectations may vary greatly from one person to another. Gaps between partners in their role expectations can have a negative effect on couples' marital satisfaction (Lye & Biblarz, 1993). Unfortunately, substantial differences in role expectations seem particularly likely in this era of transition in gender roles, a topic we discuss in depth in Chapter 11.

The traditional role expectations for husbands and wives used to be fairly clear. A husband was supposed to act as the principal breadwinner, make the important decisions, and take care of certain household chores, such as car or yard maintenance. A wife was supposed to raise the children, cook, clean, and follow the leadership of her husband. Spouses had different spheres of influence. The working world was the domain of the husband, the home the domain of the wife. In recent decades, however, the women's movement and other forces of social change have led to new expectations about marital roles. Thus, modern couples need to negotiate and renegotiate role responsibilities throughout the family life cycle (Zvonkovic et al., 1996). Couples in which the husband holds egalitarian attitudes have higher levels of marital happiness than those where the husband holds more traditional attitudes (Frieze & Ciccocioppo, 2009; Kaufman & Taniguchi, 2006).

Women may be especially vulnerable to ambivalence about shifting marital roles. More and more women are aspiring to demanding careers. Yet research shows that husbands' careers continue to take priority over their wives' ambitions (Haas, 1999). It is wives who are expected to interrupt their career to raise young children, stay home when children are sick, and abandon their jobs when husbands' careers require relocation. Moreover, even when both spouses are employed, many husbands maintain traditional role expectations about housework, child care, and decision making. Mothers, whether employed or not, are also more bound to their child's schedule than fathers are (DeCaro & Worthman, 2007).

Although men's contribution to housework has increased noticeably since the 1960s (Calasanti & Harrison-Rexrod, 2009), wives are still doing the bulk of the household chores in America, even when they work outside the home (Coltrane, 2001; Sayer, 2005). For example, research indicates that wives take responsibility for about 65% of total housework (not including child care), while husbands do the remaining 35% (see **Figure 10.5**). Moreover, wives still account for 78% of the essential "core housework" such as cooking, cleaning, and laundry, while men continue to handle more discretionary, traditional "male chores," such as yard or auto maintenance (Bianchi et al., 2000).

Although married women perform the majority of all housework, only about one-third of wives characterize their division of labor as unfair, because most women don't expect a 50–50 split (Coltrane, 2001). This one-third of wives who perceive their division of labor as unfair constitutes a sizable population of women for whom housework is a source of discontent. Research shows that women are more likely to perceive their share of housework as unfair when they have nontraditional attitudes about gender roles and when they work outside the home (Coltrane, 2001). As you might expect, wives who perceive their housework burden to be unfair tend to report lower levels of marital satisfaction

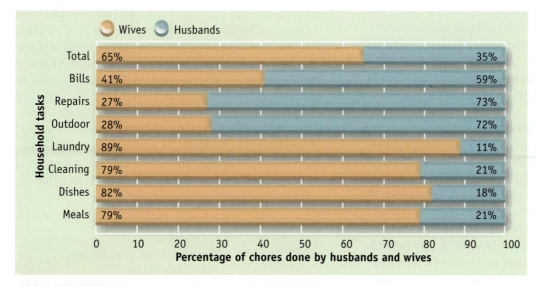

### Figure 10.5

**Division of household labor.** This chart breaks down the proportion of housework done by husbands and wives for specific tasks. The data show that wives continue to do a highly disproportionate share of most household tasks, especially the "core housework" tasks (cooking, cleaning, laundry) that are hard to ignore. Note also that in spite of great changes in modern life, the division of labor in the household still largely meshes with traditional gender roles. (Data from Bianchi et al., 2000)

SALLY FORTH

**THIS ARTICLE SAYS MORE AND MORE MEN ARE PUTTING THEIR FAMILIES AHEAD OF THEIR CAREER ASPIRATIONS.**

**I THINK THAT'S TRUE.**

**AND THAT IN THE PROCESS THEY ARE REDEFINING WHAT IT MEANS TO BE A GOOD HUSBAND AND FATHER.**

**I AGREE.**

**IT GOES ON TO SAY THAT THIS TREND HAS MANY MEN PITCHING IN MORE WITH HOUSEHOLD CHORES AND FINDING THEY ENJOY IT.**

**WHO WROTE THIS GOOFBALL ARTICLE?**

SALLY FORTH © 2002 King Features Syndicate

(Haas, 1999). Interestingly, men who have lived independently for a longer period of time (that is, not with their parents, partners, or in dorms) are more egalitarian in their views about housework and gender than are those who have had less of an independent "bachelorhood" (Pitt & Borland, 2008).

In light of this reality, it is imperative that couples discuss role expectations in depth before marriage. If they discover that their views are divergent, they need to take the potential for problems seriously. Many people casually dismiss gender-role disagreements, thinking they can "straighten out" their partner later on. But assumptions about marital roles, whether traditional or not, may be deeply held and not easily changed.

## Work and Career Issues

The possible interactions between one's occupation and one's marriage are numerous and complex. Although the data on the effect of income and employment on marital stability are inconsistent (Rodrigues, Hall, & Fincham, 2006), individuals' job satisfaction and involvement can affect their own marital satisfaction, their partner's marital satisfaction, and their children's development.

### Work and Marital Adjustment

Many studies have compared the marital adjustment of male-breadwinner versus dual-career couples. The interest in this comparison arises from traditional views that regard men's *lack* of employment, but women's *employment,* as departures from the norm. Typically, these studies simply categorize women as working or nonworking and evaluate couples' marital satisfaction. Most of these studies find little in the way of consistent differences in the marital adjustment of male-breadwinner versus dual-career couples, and there are often some benefits for dual-career couples, such as increased social contacts, self-esteem, and egalitarian attitudes (Haas, 1999; Steil, 2009). Although dual-career couples do face special problems in negotiating career priorities,

child-care arrangements, and other practical matters, their marriage need not be negatively affected.

Other studies have investigated the relationship between spouses' job satisfaction and their marital adjustment. We could speculate that these two variables might be either positively or negatively related. On the one hand, if a spouse is highly committed to a satisfying career, he or she may have less time and energy to devote to marriage and family. On the other hand, the frustration and stress of an unsatisfying job might spill over to contaminate one's marriage.

The research on this question suggests that both scenarios are realistic possibilities (Repetti & Wang, 2009). Both husbands and wives struggle to balance the demands of work and family, and for both, work-family conflict is associated with reduced life satisfaction and quality of marriage (Coursolle & Sweeney, 2009). When pressures at work increase, husbands and wives report more role conflicts and often feel overwhelmed by their multiple commitments (Crouter et al., 1999). Furthermore, studies find that spouses' stress at work can have a substantial negative effect on their marital and family interactions (Perry-Jenkins, Repetti, & Crouter, 2001). For example, after highly stressful days at work, spouses tend to withdraw from family interactions (Crouter & Bumpus, 2001; Repetti & Wang, 2009). The stress associated with working night shifts appears to be especially tough on spouses and families (Presser, 2000), as does the experience of jobs that require travel (Zvonkovic et al., 2005).

**WEB LINK 10.3   National Council on Family Relations (NCFR)**

The National Council on Family Relations has developed a site to reach out to families with practical advice from a cadre of experts on all sorts of family issues. This site includes readable press releases on up-to-date research related to marriage and the family.

Negative work-to-family spillover seems to be more common for mothers than for fathers and is especially problematic when preschool children are involved (Dilworth, 2004; Stevens et al., 2007). Perhaps this difference is due to the fact that even when working, women continue to do more household labor than do men (Sayer, 2005). Work-related demands that increase the likelihood of family conflict and stress include long commutes, bringing work home, and receiving job contacts at home (Voydanoff, 2005). Conversely, family conflict is related to increased work stress for women (Wierda-Boer, Gerris, & Vermulst, 2009).

Although the difficulties involved in juggling work and family roles can be challenging, some theorists have argued that in the long run multiple roles are beneficial to both men and women. Barnett and Hyde (2001) assert that negative effects of stress in one role can be buffered by success and satisfaction in another role. They also note that multiple roles can increase sources of social support and opportunities to experience success. Moreover, when both spouses work outside the home, income tends to be greater, and spouses often find they have more in common. Typically, those who report positive home-work interactions have more positive perceptions of their work and working conditions (Demerouti & Geurts, 2004).

Although many Americans seem to believe that maternal employment is detrimental to children's development, the vast majority of empirical studies have found little evidence that a mother's working is harmful to her children.

## Parents' Work and Children's Development

Another issue of concern has been the potential impact of parents' employment on their children. Virtually all of the research in this area has focused on the effects of mothers' employment outside the home. In 2006, the U.S. Department of Labor reported that 70.9% of mothers with children under the age of 18 were employed. What does the research on maternal employment show? Although many Americans seem to believe that maternal employment is detrimental to children's development, the vast majority of empirical studies have found little evidence that a mother's working is harmful to her children (Gottfried & Gottfried, 2008; Haas, 1999; Perry-Jenkins et al., 2001). For instance, studies generally have not found a link between mothers' employment status and the quality of infant-mother emotional attachment (Etaugh, 1993; NICHD Early Child Care Research Network, 1997) or in children's achievement (Goldberg et al., 2008). In a longitudinal study spanning two decades, early maternal employment showed no "sleeper effects." That is, there were no negative outcomes that showed up later in life, leading researchers to conclude that the adverse outcomes of maternal employment are a "public myth" (Gottfried & Gottfried, 2008, p. 30).

In fact, maternal employment has been shown to have positive effects on children's development in some cases. Recent data from the Canadian National Longitudinal Survey of Children and Youth indicate that maternal employment is related to decreased hyperactivity, lower levels of anxiety, and increased prosocial behavior at age 4 (Nomaguchi, 2006). Further, while maternal employment doesn't eliminate poverty, it does mean that fewer children are raised in poverty (Esping-Anderson, 2007; Lichter & Crowley, 2004). Children brought up in poverty exhibit poorer physical health, reduced mental health, lower academic performance, and increased delinquency in comparison to other children (Seccombe, 2001). However, experts are careful to note that any benefits of maternal employment might also come at the cost of fewer positive interactions between the mother and child (Nomaguchi, 2006).

## Financial Difficulties

Neither financial stability nor wealth can ensure marital satisfaction. However, financial difficulties can cause stress in a marriage. Recall that finances are one of the top concerns for newlyweds (Schramm et al., 2005). Without money, families live in constant dread of financial drains such as illness, layoffs, or broken appliances. Spontaneity in communication may be impaired by an understandable reluctance to talk about financial concerns. Thus, it is not surprising that serious financial worries among couples are associated with increased hostility in husbands, increased depression in wives, and lower marital happiness in both husbands and wives (White & Rogers, 2001). Similarly, husbands' job insecurity is predictive of wives' reports of marital conflict and their thoughts of divorce (Fox & Chancey, 1998). Moreover, evidence consistently demonstrates that the risk of separation and divorce increases as husbands' income declines (Ono, 1998; South & Lloyd, 1995).

Even when financial resources are plentiful, money can be a source of marital strain. Quarrels about how to spend money are common and are potentially damaging at all income levels. For instance, studies have found that perceptions of financial problems (regardless of a family's actual income) are associated with decreased marital satisfaction (Dean, Carroll, & Yang, 2007). Further, newlywed couples who increase their consumer debt spend less time together and argue more about money than those who pay off their debt (Dew, 2008). In a study that examined how happily married couples handled their money in comparison to couples that eventually divorced, Schaninger and Buss (1986) found that the happy couples engaged in more joint decision making on finances. Thus, the best way to avoid troublesome battles over money is probably to engage in extensive planning of expenditures together; that is, *communicate*.

## Inadequate Communication

Effective communication is crucial to the success of a marriage and is consistently associated with increased marital satisfaction (Litzinger & Gordon, 2005; Rogge et al., 2006). Further, the marital communication–satisfaction link seems to be robust across cultures (Rehman & Holtzworth-Munroe, 2007). In a study of couples in the process of divorce, researchers found that communication difficulties were the most frequently cited problem among both husbands and wives (see **Figure 10.6**) (Cleek & Pearson, 1985). Communication is a highly ranked source of conflict for long-term married couples (Levenson, Carstensen, & Gottman, 1993). Spouses' strategies for resolving conflicts may be particularly crucial to marital satisfaction (Crohan, 1992). Because the ability to communicate emotions is associated with better marital adjustment, couples need to feel safe discussing conflict (Cordova, Gee, & Warren, 2005). Research supports the notion that marital adjustment depends not on whether there is conflict (conflict is virtually inevitable) but rather on how conflict is handled when it occurs (Driver et al., 2003).

A number of studies have compared communication patterns in happy and unhappy marriages. This research indicates that unhappily married couples (1) find it difficult to convey positive messages, (2) misunderstand each other more often, (3) are less likely to recognize that they have been misunderstood, (4) use more

### Recommended READING

**Why Marriages Succeed or Fail . . . and How You Can Make Yours Last**

by John Gottman (with Nan Silver) (Simon & Schuster, 1995)

This book is about communication in intimate relationships—a subject that Gottman has studied intensively for over 20 years. A psychology professor at the University of Washington, Gottman is justifiably famous for his landmark research on the prediction of divorce. He has demonstrated that he can predict which couples will divorce with remarkable accuracy, based on careful examination of the couples' communication patterns. According to Gottman, the marriages that last are not those that appear to be free of conflict but those in which couples are able to resolve the conflicts that inevitably arise in intimate relationships. Gottman categorizes couples into three types based on their style of conflict resolution. In *validating marriages,* couples compromise often and work out their disagreements calmly. In *conflict-avoiding marriages,* couples rarely confront their disagreements openly. In *volatile marriages,* couples have frequent and passionate disputes. For all three types, the crucial consideration, according to Gottman, is the relative balance of positive versus negative interactions.

*Why Marriages Succeed or Fail* is an outstanding book loaded with exercises, quizzes, and tips that should help readers improve their marital communication. It is practical and readable, with plenty of case histories to make ideas come alive. Gottman has written other highly practical books on marriage that are worth consulting: *10 Lessons to Transform Your Marriage* (2006), *The Relationship Cure* (2001) and *Baby Makes Three: The Six-Step Plan for Preserving Marital Intimacy and Rekindling Romance After Baby Arrives* (2008).

**Go to the Psychology CourseMate for Weiten at www.cengagebrain.com/shop/ISBN/1111186634 for descriptions of other recommended books.**

frequent, and more intense, negative messages, and (5) often differ in the amount of self-disclosure they prefer in the relationship (Noller & Fitzpatrick, 1990; Noller & Gallois, 1988; Sher & Baucom, 1993). Above all else, unhappy couples tend to get caught up in escalating cycles of conflict from which they cannot escape, whereas happy couples find ways to exit the cycles (Fincham, 2003).

The importance of marital communication was underscored in a widely cited study by John Gottman and his colleagues that attempted to predict the likelihood of divorce in a sample of 52 married couples (Buehlman,

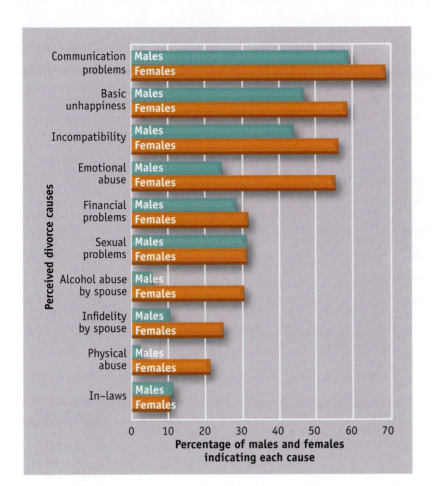

**Figure 10.6**

**Causes of divorce.** When Cleek and Pearson (1985) asked divorcing couples about their perceptions regarding the causes of their divorce, both men and women cited communication difficulties more than any other cause.

Gottman, & Katz, 1992). Each couple provided an oral history of their relationship and a 15-minute sample of their interaction style, during which they discussed two problem areas in their marriage. The investigators rated the spouses on a variety of factors that mostly reflected the subjects' ways of communicating with each other. Based on these ratings, they were able to predict which couples would divorce within three years with 94% accuracy!

Photo by Sharon M. Fentiman

**John Gottman**

Gottman, who is probably the world's foremost authority on marital communication, asserts that conflict and anger are normal in marital interactions and that they are not, in and of themselves, predictive of marital dissolution. Instead, Gottman (1994) identifies four other communication patterns, which he calls the "Four Horsemen of the Apocalypse," that are risk factors for divorce: contempt, criticism, defensiveness, and stonewalling. *Contempt* involves communicating insulting feelings that one's spouse is inferior. *Criticism* involves constantly expressing negative evaluations of one's partner. Criticism typically begins with the word *you* and involves sweeping negative statements. *Defensiveness* refers to responding to contempt and criticism by invalidating, refuting, or denying the partner's statements. This obstructive communication escalates marital conflict. *Stonewalling* is refusing to listen to one's partner, especially the partner's complaints. Gottman eventually added a fifth troublesome communication pattern, *belligerence,* which involves provocative, combative challenges to partners' power and authority (Gottman et al., 1998; Gottman, Gottman, & DeClaire, 2006). Given the importance of good communication, many approaches to marital therapy emphasize the development of better communication skills in partners (Gottman & Gottman, 2008; Gottman et al., 2002).

# Divorce

### LEARNING OBJECTIVES

- Describe the evidence on changing divorce rates.
- Contrast how men and women tend to adjust to divorce.
- Analyze the evidence on the effects of divorce on children.
- Summarize data on the frequency and success of remarriage and the impact of stepfamilies on children.

*"In the ten years that we were married I went from twenty-four to thirty-four and they were a very significant ten years. I started a career, started to succeed, bought my first house, had a child, you know, very significant years. And then all of a sudden, every goddamn thing, I'm back to zero. I have no house. I don't have a child. I don't have a wife. I don't have the same family. My economic position has been shattered. And nothing recoverable. All these goals which I had struggled for, every goddamn one of them, is gone."—A recently divorced man quoted in* Marital Separation *(Weiss, 1975, p. 75)*

**Divorce is the legal dissolution of a marriage.** It tends to be a painful and stressful event for most people, as this bitter quote illustrates. Any of the problems discussed in the previous section might lead a couple to consider divorce. However, people appear to vary in their threshold for divorce, just as they do in their threshold for marriage. Some couples will tolerate a great deal of disappointment and bickering without seriously considering divorce. Other couples are ready to call their attorney as soon as it becomes apparent that their expectations for marital bliss were somewhat unrealistic. Typically, however, divorce is the culmination of a gradual disintegration of the relationship brought about by an accumulation of interrelated problems, which often date back to the beginning of a couple's relationship (Huston, Niehuis, & Smith, 2001).

"We met, fell madly in love, got engaged, had a lovely wedding and honeymoon. Then things turned sour, we grew bitter, separated and divorced. It was quite a busy weekend!"

Copyright 2004 by Randy Glasbergen/www.glasbergen.com

## Divorce Rates

Although relatively accurate statistics are available on divorce rates, it is still difficult to estimate the percentage of marriages that end in divorce. It is clear that divorce rates in the United states increased dramatically between the 1950s and 1980s, but they appear to have stabilized and even declined slightly since then (Teachman, 2009). When divorce rates were at their peak, the most widely cited estimates of future divorce risk were around 50% (Bumpass, Raley, & Sweet, 1995). However, the modest reductions in divorce rates in recent years appear to have lowered the risk of divorce to 40%–45% for today's couples (Bramlett & Mosher, 2001; Whitehead & Popenoe, 2001). The decline in divorce rates is encouraging, but the chances of marital dissolution remain quite high. In 2001, about one in five adults had been divorced (Kreider, 2005). Although most people realize that divorce rates are high, they have a curious tendency to underestimate the likelihood that they will personally experience a divorce. On the average, people peg their probability of divorce at about 10%–11%, which is far below the actual probability for the population as a whole (Fowers et al., 2001).

Divorce rates are higher among blacks than whites or Hispanics, among lower-income couples, among couples who cohabitated, among couples who do not have children, among people who marry at a relatively young age, and among those whose parents divorced (Rodrigues et al., 2006; Teachman, 2009). As **Figure 10.7** shows, the vast majority of divorces occur during the first decade of a marriage (Hiedemann, Suhomlinova, & O'Rand, 1998). What types of marital problems

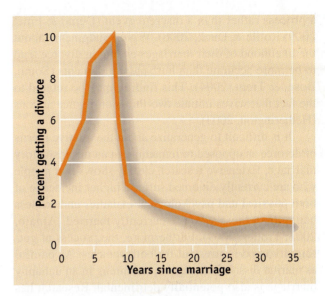

**Figure 10.7**

**Divorce rate as a function of years married.** This graph shows the distribution of divorces in relation to how long couples have been married. As you can see, the vast majority of divorces occur in the early years, with divorce rates peaking between the fifth and tenth years of marriage. (Data from National Center for Health Statistics)

are predictive of divorce? The most frequently cited problems include communication difficulties (not talking; being moody, critical, and easy to anger), infidelity, jealousy, growing apart, foolish spending behavior, and substance abuse problems (Amato & Previti, 2003; Amato & Rogers, 1997).

A wide variety of social trends have probably contributed to increasing divorce rates (Amato et al., 2003; Giddens, 2001; Sabatelli & Ripoll, 2004). The stigma attached to divorce has gradually eroded. Many religious denominations are becoming more tolerant of divorce, and marriage has thus lost some of its sacred quality. The shrinking of families probably makes divorce a more viable possibility. The entry of more women into the workforce has made many wives less financially dependent on the continuation of their marriage. New attitudes emphasizing individual fulfillment seem to have counterbalanced older attitudes that encouraged dissatisfied spouses to suffer in silence. Reflecting all these trends, the legal barriers to divorce have also diminished (Teachmen, 2009).

## Deciding on a Divorce

Divorces are often postponed repeatedly, and they are rarely executed without a great deal of agonizing forethought (Ahrons, 1999). Indecision is common, as roughly two out of five divorce petitions are eventually withdrawn (Donovan & Jackson, 1990). The decision to divorce is usually the outcome of a long series of smaller decisions or relationship stages that may take years to unfold, so divorce should be viewed as

© Matthew McVay/Corbis Saba

The high divorce rate has led to some novel ways of dealing with its worrisome legal aspects. Attorney Robert Nordyke discovered that the drive-up window at his new office—a former savings and loan branch in Salem, Oregon—was perfect for serving legal papers on his clients' spouses.

a process rather than a discrete event (Demo & Fine, 2009; Rollie & Duck, 2006). Wives' judgments about the likelihood of their marriages ending in divorce tend to be more accurate than husbands' judgments (South, Bose, & Trent, 2004). This finding may be related to the fact that wives initiate two-thirds of divorce actions (Hetherington, 2003).

It is difficult to generalize about the relative merits of divorce as opposed to remaining in an unsatisfactory marriage. Extensive research clearly shows that people who are currently divorced suffer a higher incidence of both physical and psychological maladies and are less happy than those who are currently married (Amato, 2001; Trotter, 2009). Furthermore, the process of getting divorced is stressful for both spouses. As painful as marital dissolution may be, remaining in an unhappy marriage is also potentially detrimental. Research has shown that in comparison to divorced individuals, unhappily married people tend to show poorer physical health, lower levels of happiness, less life satisfaction, and lower self-esteem (Hawkins & Booth, 2005; Wickrama et al., 1997). Research shows that divorce can be related to higher rates of autonomy, self-awareness, and job success, especially when individuals have a stable financial situation and a strong social support network (Trotter, 2009). Moreover, like other stressful life events, divorce can lead to personal growth and positive changes in the self (Tashiro, Frazier, & Berman, 2006), so the picture is not entirely negative.

## Adjusting to Divorce

Objectively speaking, divorce appears to be more difficult and disruptive for women than for men, especially in terms of finances (Trotter, 2009; Sayer, 2006). Women are more likely to assume the responsibility of raising the children, whereas men tend to reduce their contact with their children. Within the first year after divorce, half of fathers basically lose contact with their kids (Carter & McGoldrick, 1999). Another key consideration is that divorced women are less likely than their ex-husbands to have adequate income or a satisfying job (Smock, Manning, & Gupta, 1999). For example, one well-designed study found that custodial mothers experienced a 36% percent decrease in their standard of living, whereas noncustodial fathers experienced a 28% *increase* (Bianchi, Subaiya, & Kahn, 1999). The economic consequences of divorce clearly are more severe for women than for men, but in this era of two-income families, many men also experience a noticeable decline in their standard of living after going through a divorce (McManus & DiPrete, 2001).

Although divorce appears to impose greater stress on women than men, researchers do *not* find consistent gender differences in postdivorce adjustment (Amato, 2001). In the aggregate, the magnitude of the negative

**WEB LINK 10.4  Divorce Central**

Divorce Central is one of a number of practical sites that provide information and advice on legal, emotional, and financial issues for individuals contemplating or going through a divorce. Annotated links to the other divorce-related sites can also be found here.

effects of divorce on individuals' psychological and physical well-being seems to be pretty similar for husbands and wives. Among both men and women, high preoccupation with one's ex-spouse is associated with poorer adjustment to divorce (Masheter, 1997). Factors associated with favorable postdivorce adjustment include having higher income, getting remarried, having more positive attitudes about divorce, and being the partner who initiated the divorce (Wang & Amato, 2000). After a divorce, having social relationships, both in terms of one-to-one friendships and being part of a circle of friends, is important to adjustment (Krumrei et al., 2007). Forgiveness of the ex-spouse is also associated with increased well-being and lowered depression (Rye et al., 2004). Interestingly, research shows that the relationship between divorce and adjustment is also influenced by preexisting factors. That is, even before getting married, people who eventually divorce are less happy than people who remain married (Lucas, 2005).

## Effects of Divorce on Children

It's estimated that approximately 30%–40% of all U.S. children will experience divorce by the time they are 16, and approximately 20%–35% of these children will experience significant mental health problems (Hipke, Wolchik, & Sandler, 2008). When couples have children, decisions about divorce must take into account the potential impact on their offspring. Widely publicized research by Judith Wallerstein and her colleagues has painted a rather bleak picture of how di-

*"That's right, Phil. A separation will mean—among other things—watching your own cholesterol."*

© Michael Maslin/The New Yorker Collection/www.cartoonbank.com

vorce affects youngsters (Wallerstein & Blakeslee, 1989; Wallerstein & Lewis, 2004, 2007; Wallerstein, Lewis, & Blakeslee, 2000). This research has followed a sample of 60 divorced couples and their 131 children since 1971. At the 10-year follow-up, almost half of the participants were characterized as "worried, underachieving, self-deprecating, and sometimes angry young men and women" (Wallerstein & Blakeslee, 1989, p. 299). Even *25 years* after their parents' divorce, a majority of subjects were viewed as troubled adults who found it difficult to maintain stable and satisfying intimate relationships (Wallerstein, 2005; Wallerstein & Lewis, 2004). The enduring, long-term effects of divorce reported by Wallerstein were particularly disturbing and generated great interest from the media, resulting in an abundance of TV interviews, magazine articles, and so forth.

**Judith S. Wallerstein**

photo by Kent Marshall © 2010 www.kentmarshall.com

Although the lengthy follow-up in Wallerstein's research is commendable, critics point out that her study suffers from a variety of flaws (Amato, 2003; Cherlin, 1999; Kelly & Emery, 2003). It was based on a small sample of children from a wealthy area in California that clearly was not representative of the population at large. There was no comparison group, and conclusions were based on impressions from clinical interviews, in which it is easy for interviewers to see what they expect to see. Further, critics caution against drawing causal conclusions from correlational data (Gordon, 2005). Coltrane and Adams (2003) also note that Wallerstein is part of a conservative political-religious movement that favors traditional family arrangements and reforms that would make divorces more difficult to obtain. Hence, her conclusions may be shaped in part by a political agenda.

Another complicated issue in assessing the effects of divorce is the choice of who should serve as a baseline for comparison. One can argue that children of divorce should be compared to children from intact homes characterized by persistent marital discord, a group that also shows elevated rates of many types of adjustment problems (Morrison & Coiro, 1999; Papp, Cummings, & Schermerhorn, 2004).

Are Wallerstein's findings consistent with other research? Yes and no. The results of another long-running study by E. Mavis Hetherington (1993, 1999, 2003), which used a larger and more representative sample, a control group, and conventional statistical comparisons, suggest that Wallerstein's conclusions are unduly pessimistic. According to Hetherington, divorce can be traumatic for children, but a substantial majority adjust reasonably well after

**E. Mavis Hetherington**

Courtesy of E. Mavis Hetherington

two to three years, and only about 25% show serious psychological or emotional problems in adulthood (versus 10% in the control group). That is, most children of divorce do not show long-term adjustment problems (Lansford, 2009). Other research has highlighted some positive outcomes of parental divorce for children. These include enhancing personal growth, teaching life management skills, encouraging realistic relationship expectations, and enhancing empathy (Demo & Fine, 2009).

Although Wallerstein's conclusions appear overly negative, *they differ from the results of other research only in degree* (Amato, 2003). After a divorce, many children exhibit depression, anxiety, nightmares, dependency, aggression, withdrawal, distractibility, lowered academic performance, reduced physical health, precocious sexual behavior, and substance abuse (Barber & Demo, 2006; Kelly & Emery, 2003; Knox, 2000). Although these problems dissipate in most children after a few years, divorce can have a lasting impact that extends into adulthood. Experiencing divorce during childhood is a risk factor for many subsequent problems in one's adult years, including maladjustment, marital instability, and reduced occupational attainments (Amato, 1999). Children have more adjustment problems when their parents have a history of particularly bitter, acrimonious conflict (Amato, 2001). Other factors that influence the impact of divorce on children's adjustment include their age, coping resources, and adjustment prior to the divorce (Lansford, 2009; Shelton & Harold, 2007).

So what can we conclude about the effects of divorce on children? Ahrons (2007) cautions that the extensive body of research on divorce suggests a "nuanced picture of divorce, one that defies sound-bite conclusions" (p. 4). Overall, the weight of evidence suggests that divorce tends to have harmful effects on many children but can have beneficial effects for children if their parents' relationship was dominated by conflict (Booth & Amato, 2001). However, the latter assertion is based on the assumption that the parents' divorce brings their bickering to an end. Unfortunately, the conflicts between divorcing spouses often continue for many years after they part ways (Hopper, 2001). This pattern has led to a recent interest in divorce education and intervention programs to ease the transition for families; such efforts still need to be scientifically evaluated (Blaisure & Geasler, 2006). It is also reasonable to conclude that divorces have highly varied effects on children that depend on a complex constellation of interacting factors. As Furstenberg and Kiernan (2001) put it, "Many researchers have become increasingly wary about public discussions of divorce that treat it as an undifferentiated and uniform occurrence resulting in similar outcomes for all children" (p. 446).

# LIVING IN TODAY'S WORLD
## Should the Government Promote Marriage?

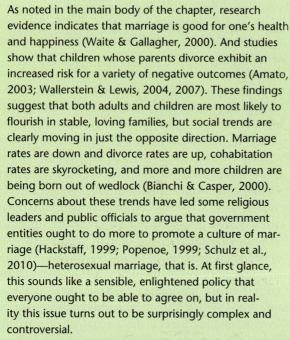

As noted in the main body of the chapter, research evidence indicates that marriage is good for one's health and happiness (Waite & Gallagher, 2000). And studies show that children whose parents divorce exhibit an increased risk for a variety of negative outcomes (Amato, 2003; Wallerstein & Lewis, 2004, 2007). These findings suggest that both adults and children are most likely to flourish in stable, loving families, but social trends are clearly moving in just the opposite direction. Marriage rates are down and divorce rates are up, cohabitation rates are skyrocketing, and more and more children are being born out of wedlock (Bianchi & Casper, 2000). Concerns about these trends have led some religious leaders and public officials to argue that government entities ought to do more to promote a culture of marriage (Hackstaff, 1999; Popenoe, 1999; Schulz et al., 2010)—heterosexual marriage, that is. At first glance, this sounds like a sensible, enlightened policy that everyone ought to be able to agree on, but in reality this issue turns out to be surprisingly complex and controversial.

The pro-marriage movement has been gathering momentum since the early 1990s. The advocates of this movement argue that people today are overly focused on their personal happiness and are unwilling to endure hardship and show loyalty when the going gets rough in a marriage (Fowers, 2000). They also assert that the emergence of no-fault divorce laws since the 1970s has made it too easy to get a divorce. Thus, the pro-marriage advocates campaign for policies that would make divorces more difficult to obtain. For example, several states have enacted *covenant marriage* laws (Rosier & Feld, 2000; Sanchez, 2009). Couples who choose to enter into a covenant marriage agree to complete premarital education programs and pledge to divorce only in response to severe problems (such as spouse abuse or a lengthy prison term), and only after seeking extensive marriage counseling (Adams & Coltrane, 2006; Hawkins et al., 2002). Other advocated reforms have included waiting periods for divorces of up to five years and more demanding legal proceedings for divorces involving children. Some proactive proposals have included mandating high school education programs touting the value of marriage, providing government subsidies for marriage counseling, and requiring couples to complete premarital relationship skills training (Amato, 2004b). Some pro-marriage advocates have also suggested giving married couples preferential treat-ment (over single, divorced, and cohabiting individuals) in regard to government benefits, such as welfare payments and housing subsidies (Murray, 2001).

Critics of the pro-marriage movement raise a variety of objections. First, they question the meaning of the research findings that serve as the rationale for this movement. Although they acknowledge that married people are somewhat healthier and happier than nonmarried adults, they point out that the data are correlational and that no solid evidence exists that being married *causes* this difference (Huston & Melz, 2004). They argue that causation probably runs the other way—that being healthy and happy causes people to have better marital opportunities and greater marital success. Indeed, there is empirical support for this notion (Lyubomirsky, King, & Diener, 2005).

Second, although experiencing divorce can be harmful for children, remaining in a home filled with bitter discord can be just as harmful (Booth & Amato, 2001). Critics express concern that restricting access to divorce could leave some spouses and children stranded in homes riddled with alcoholism, drug abuse, or domestic violence (Gelles, 1996). Third, critics point out that making divorces harder to get just may not be a realistic option in today's society (Coontz, 1997). Although a majority of adults agree—in the abstract—that divorce laws should be tougher, they do not want *their own* personal freedom in this area to be impeded. Consistent with this finding, only around 2% of couples have chosen covenant marriage in the state (Louisiana) that first offered this option and overall divorce rates have not dropped (Allman, 2009). However, preliminary data suggest that those who choose a covenant marriage do appear to have reduced divorced rates (Sanchez, 2009).

Fourth, critics argue that if the government wants to promote marital success, it should focus more on making it *easier to stay married,* as opposed to harder to get a divorce. In particular, they note that divorce rates tend to be high in lower social classes where families could be better strengthened by improving social services (such as child care and job training). Finally, critics maintain that the pro-marriage movement treats the traditional nuclear family as the only legitimate family form and that pro-marriage programs will unfairly discriminate against single parents, divorced persons, cohabiting couples, and gay and lesbian partners (Coltrane, 2001; Scanzoni, 2004).

Although remarried couples tend to have more open communication, the evidence suggests that second marriages are slightly less successful than first marriages, on the average.

## Remarriage and Stepfamilies

Evidence that adequate courtship opportunities exist for the divorced is provided by the statistics on remarriage: Roughly three-quarters of divorced people eventually remarry (Bramlett & Mosher, 2001). The mean length of time between divorce and remarriage is three to four years (Kreider, 2005).

How successful are second marriages? The answer depends on your standard of comparison. Divorce rates *are* higher for second than for first marriages, though the average duration for second marriages is about the same as for first, about eight to nine years (Kreider, 2005; Mason, 1998). However, this statistic may simply indicate that this group of people sees divorce as a reasonable alternative to an unsatisfactory marriage. Nonetheless, studies of marital adjustment suggest that second marriages are slightly less successful than first marriages (Brown & Booth, 1996), especially for women who bring children into the second marriage (Teachman, 2008). Of course, if you consider that in this pool of people *all* the first marriages ran into serious trouble, then the second marriages look rather good by comparison. As with first marriages, communication plays a major role in marital satisfaction for both spouses (Beaudry et al., 2004).

Another major issue related to remarriage is its effect on children.

*Stepfamilies* or *blended families* (where both spouses bring in children from a previous relationship) are an established part of modern life, and adaptation to remarriage can be difficult for children (Bray, 2009). **Figure 10.8** summarizes the developmental stages

| Patterns of Development in Stepfamilies | | |
|---|---|---|
| **Stage** | **Description** | **Example** |
| Stage One: Fantasy | Family has unrealistic, ideal expectations. | I love my new wife, so I'll certainly love her children. |
| Stage Two: Immersion | Real life challenges expectations. | It seems like my husband is closer to his daughter than he is to me. |
| Stage Three: Awareness | Family members attempt to make sense out of the new arrangements. | I understand that my stepchildren are resistant to the new family structure, not because they are bad kids, but because it is hard for them. |
| Stage Four: Mobilization | Family members attempt to negotiate difficulties. | Eating together as a family is important enough to me that I am willing to speak with my husband about it. |
| Stage Five: Action | Family creates strategies to resolve differences. | We will have weekly family meetings to air frustrations. |
| Stage Six: Contact | Positive emotional bonds begin to form. | My stepson and I can resolve this issue by having a heart-to-heart. |
| Stage Seven: Resolution | Norms are established and new family rituals emerge. | My teenage stepdaughter appreciates my perspective on her new boyfriend. |

### Figure 10.8

**Patterns of development in stepfamilies.** Papernow (1993) developed a seven-stage model of the stages through which most stepfamilies pass as they move from fantasy toward resolution.

Source: Adapted from Papernow, P. L. (1993). *Becoming a stepfamily: Patterns of development in remarried families.* San Francisco: Jossey-Bass.

through which most stepfamilies progress. Wallerstein and Lewis (2007) argue that there is an inherent instability in parenting, as parents are caught between their desires to create a new intimate relationship and to maintain their parenting role. Evidence suggests that on the average, interaction in stepfamilies appears to be somewhat less cohesive and warm than interaction in first-marriage families, and stepparent-stepchild relations tend to be more negative and distant than parent-child relations in first marriages (Pasley & Moorefield, 2004), though it is important to note that this doesn't mean that these relationships are necessarily problematic or dysfunctional (Bray, 2009). Stepfamily formation can be a negative experience for children who feel powerless or who undergo dramatic changes in living spaces, rules, and expectations (Stoll et al., 2005).

Taken as a whole, the evidence suggests that children in stepfamilies are a little less well adjusted than children in first marriages and are roughly similar in adjustment to children in single-parent homes (Coleman, Ganong, & Fine, 2001; Sweeney, Wang, & Videon, 2009). In an analysis of 61 studies, Jeynes (2006) found that children in stepfamilies tend to show lower academic achievement and psychological well-being than those from intact or single-parent families. However, the differences between stepfamilies and other types of families in the adjustment of their children tend to be modest. For example, **Figure 10.9** highlights some representative results from one large-scale study (Acock & Demo, 1994).

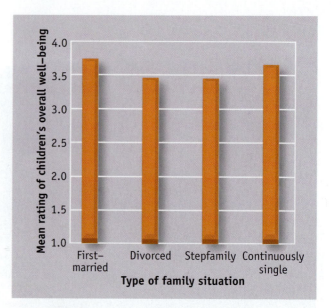

**Figure 10.9**

**Children's adjustment in four types of families.** Acock and Demo (1994) assessed children's adjustment in four types of family structures: first marriages, divorced single-parent homes, stepfamilies, and families in which the mother never married. The comparisons of 2,457 families did turn up some statistically significant differences, as children's overall well-being was highest in intact first marriages. However, as you can see, the differences were rather small, and the authors concluded that "family structure has a modest effect on children's well-being."

# Alternative Relationship Lifestyles

### LEARNING OBJECTIVES

- Discuss contemporary attitudes toward gay couples.
- Compare homosexual and heterosexual couples in regard to the dynamics of their intimate relationships and the adjustment of children.
- Describe stereotypes of single life, and summarize evidence on the adjustment of single people.
- Discuss the prevalence of cohabitation and whether it improves the probability of marital success.

So far we have been discussing the traditional model of marriage, which, as we noted at the beginning of the chapter, has been challenged by a variety of social trends. More and more people are experiencing alternative relationship lifestyles, including gay couples, singles, and partners choosing cohabitation.

## Gay Couples

Up until this point, we have, for purposes of simplicity, focused our attention on *heterosexuals,* those who seek emotional-sexual relationships with members of the other gender. However, we have been ignoring a significant minority group: *homosexual* men and women, who seek committed, emotional-sexual relationships with members of the same gender. (In everyday language, the term *gay* is used to refer to homosexuals of both genders, although many homosexual women prefer the term *lesbian* for themselves.)

Popular stereotypes suggest that gays only rarely get involved in long-term intimate relationships. In reality, most homosexual men, and nearly all homosexual women, prefer stable, long-term relationships, and at any one time roughly 40%–60% of gay males and 45%–80% of lesbians are involved in committed relationships (Kurdek, 2004). Lesbian relationships are generally sexually exclusive. About half of committed male couples have "open" relationships, allowing for the possibility of sexual activity (but not affection) with outsiders.

© Allison Michael Orenstein/Getty Images/Digital Vision

**Despite the common stereotype that homosexuals rarely form long-term relationships, the fact is that they are similar to heterosexual couples in their attitudes and behaviors, and many couples enjoy long-term commitments in marriage-like arrangements.**

## Attitudes Toward Gay Couples

In a 2008 Gallup poll, Americans were equally divided over the morality of homosexual partnerships (Saad, 2008; see **Figure 10.10**). *Homophobia*, also called *sexual prejudice,* is a type of prejudice and discrimination against homosexuals (Herek, 2009b). Unfortunately, sexual prejudice is common, and gay men and lesbians continue to be victims of employment and housing discrimination, not to mention verbal and physical abuse and hate crimes (Herek, 2000; Herek, Cogan, & Gillis,

2002). African Americans, especially men, hold more negative attitudes toward gays than their white counterparts do (Lemelle & Battle, 2004).

With rare exceptions, gay couples cannot choose to legally formalize their unions by getting married; they are therefore denied many economic benefits available to married couples. For example, they can't file joint tax returns, and gay individuals often can't obtain employer-provided health insurance for their partner. Thus, gay and lesbian rights have become a major political issue. Same-gender marriage is now a legal right in states such as Massachusetts, Connecticut, and Vermont, and civil unions and domestic partnerships are legally recognized in other states, such as New Jersey and California. However, during the past decade many states have passed laws prohibiting same-gender marriages, and constitutional amendments banning gay marriage have been introduced in the U.S. Congress. Some argue that allowing gay marriages would erode traditional family values. A study using over a decade of data, however, does not bear this out. This research found no adverse effects on factors such as divorce, abortion rates, or single parenthood as result of allowing (or banning) gay marriage (Langbein & Yost, 2009). The public discussion of gay marriage, as difficult as it is, has highlighted the realities of same-gender couples and their family relationships (Garnets & Kimmel, 2003a).

## Comparisons to Heterosexual Couples

Devoting a separate section to gay couples may seem to imply that the dynamics of their close relationships

**Figure 10.10**

**Attitudes toward homosexual partnerships.** In a 2008 Gallup poll, individuals were asked if they felt certain issues were morally right or morally wrong. As you can see, Americans were equally divided over the morality of homosexual relations (Saad, 2008).

| Attitudes Toward Controversial Topics | | |
|---|---|---|
| Issue | Morally acceptable % | Morally wrong % |
| Divorce | 70 | 22 |
| Gambling | 63 | 32 |
| Death penalty | 62 | 30 |
| Medical research using stem cells obtained from human embryos | 62 | 30 |
| Sex between an unmarried man and woman | 61 | 36 |
| Medical testing on animals | 56 | 38 |
| Having a baby outside of marriage | 55 | 41 |
| Buying and wearing clothing made of animal fur | 54 | 39 |
| Doctor-assisted suicide | 51 | 44 |
| Homosexual relations | 48 | 48 |
| Abortion | 40 | 48 |
| Cloning animals | 33 | 61 |
| Suicide | 15 | 78 |
| Cloning humans | 11 | 85 |
| Polygamy, when one husband has more than one wife at the same time | 8 | 90 |
| Married men and women having an affair | 7 | 91 |

are different from those seen in heterosexual couples. As Garnets and Kimmel (1991) point out, gay relationships "develop within a social context of societal disapproval with an absence of social legitimization and support; families and other social institutions often stigmatize such relationships and there are no prescribed roles and behaviors to structure such relationships" (p. 170). Although gay relationships evolve in a different social context, research has documented that close relationships, gay or heterosexual, function in similar ways (Herek, 2006; Kurdek, 2006). Both types of couples report similar levels of love and commitment in their relationships, similar levels of overall satisfaction with their relationships, and similar levels of sexual satisfaction (Kurdek, 1998; Peplau, 1991; Peplau & Ghavami, 2009). Similarity is also apparent when researchers study what gays and heterosexuals want out of their relationships (Peplau, 1988; see **Figure 10.11**). Furthermore, homosexual and heterosexual couples are similar in terms of the factors that predict relationship satisfaction, the sources of conflict in their relationships, and their patterns of conflict resolution (Kurdek, 2004; Peplau & Ghavami, 2009).

Given the lack of moral, social, legal, and economic support for gay relationships, are gay unions less stable than heterosexual unions? Researchers have not yet been able to collect adequate data on this question, but the limited data available suggest that gay couples'

relationships *are* somewhat briefer and more prone to breakups than heterosexual marriages (Kurdek, 1998; Peplau, 1991). If that's the case, it might be because gay relationships face fewer barriers to dissolution—that is, fewer practical problems that make breakups difficult or costly (Kurdek, 1998; Peplau & Cochran, 1990).

## Gay Parenting

Although research indicates striking similarities between homosexual and heterosexual relationships, basic misconceptions about the nature of gay relationships remain widespread. For example, lesbians and gay men tend to be thought of as individuals rather than as members of families. This thinking reflects a bias that homosexuality and family just don't mesh (Allen & Demo, 1995). In reality, gays are very much involved in families as sons and daughters, as parents and stepparents, and as aunts, uncles, and grandparents (Johnson

### Figure 10.11

**Comparing priorities in intimate relationships.** Peplau (1981) asked heterosexual men and women and homosexual men and women to rate the significance (9 = high importance) of various aspects of their intimate relationships. As you can see, all four groups returned fairly similar ratings. Peplau concluded that gays and heterosexuals largely want the same things out of their relationships.

Source: From Peplau, L. A. (1981, March). What homosexuals want. *Psychology Today, 3,* 28–38. Reprinted with permission from Psychology Today Magazine. Copyright © 1981 Sussex Publishers, Inc.

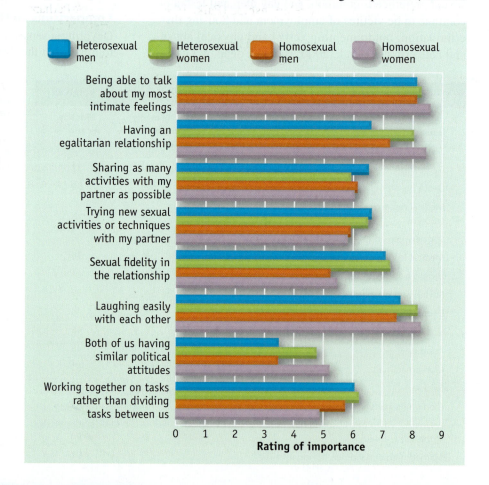

Children reared by gay or lesbian parents do not seem more poorly adjusted than other children. Research indicates that the quality of child-parent interactions is much more important to a child's development than parental sexual orientation.

& Colluci, 1999). According to the 2000 U.S. Census, 33% of female same-gender couples and 22% of male same-gender couples are rearing children. Many of these parental responsibilities are left over from previous marriages, as about 20%–30% of gays have been heterosexually married (Kurdek, 2004). But an increasing number of homosexuals are opting to have children in the context of their gay relationships (Falk, 1994; Gartrell et al., 1999).

What do we know about gays and lesbians as parents? The evidence suggests that gays are similar to their heterosexual counterparts in their approaches to parenting and that their children are similar to the children of heterosexual parents in terms of personal development and peer relations (C. J. Patterson, 2001, 2006, 2009). The overall adjustment of children with gay parents appears similar in quality to that of children of heterosexual parents (Chan et al., 1998; Golombok et al., 2003; Tasker, 2005). Moreover, the vast majority of children of gay parents grow up to identify themselves as heterosexual (Bailey & Dawood, 1998), and some studies suggest that they are no more likely than others to become homosexual (Flaks et al., 1995). In sum, children reared by gay and lesbian parents do not appear to suffer any special ill effects and do not seem noticeably different from other children. Decades of research indicates that the quality of child-parent interactions is much more important to a child's development than parental sexual orientation (Crowl, Ahn, & Baker, 2008; Patterson, 2006, 2009).

## Remaining Single

The pressure to marry is substantial in our society (Berliner, Jacob, & Schwartzberg, 1999). People are socialized to believe that they are not complete until they have found their "other half" and have entered into a partnership for life. And reference is often made to people's "failure" to marry. In spite of this pressure, an increasing proportion of young adults are remaining single (Teachman, Tedrow, & Crowder, 2001), as **Figure 10.12** shows.

Does the greater number of single adults mean that people are turning away from the institution of marriage? Perhaps a little, but for the most part, no. A variety of factors have contributed to the growth of the single population. Much of this growth is a result of the higher median age at which people marry and the increased rate of divorce. The vast majority of single, never-married people *do* hope to marry eventually. In one study of never-married men and women (South, 1993), 87.4% of the 926 respondents ages 19 to 25 agreed with the statement "I would like to get married

**Figure 10.12**

**The proportion of young people who remain single.** This graph shows the percentage of single men and women ages 20–24 and 25–29 in 2008 as compared to 1960 (based on U.S. Census data). The proportion of people remaining single has increased substantially for both sexes, in both age brackets. Single men continue to outnumber single women in these age brackets.

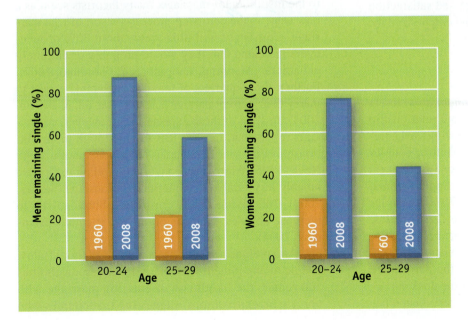

someday," and in a recent study of unmarried parents, most expected to marry (Waller & McLanahan, 2005).

Singles continue to be stigmatized and plagued by two disparate stereotypes (Byrne & Carr, 2005; Morris & DePaulo, 2009). On the one hand, single people are sometimes portrayed as carefree swingers who are too busy enjoying the fruits of promiscuity to shoulder marital responsibilities. On the other hand, they are seen as losers who have not succeeded in snaring a mate, and they may be portrayed as socially inept, maladjusted, frustrated, lonely, and bitter. These stereotypes do a great injustice to the diversity that exists among those who are single. In fact, the negative stereotypes of singles have led some researchers to coin the term *singlism* to capture how single people can be victims of prejudice and discrimination (DePaulo & Morris, 2005, 2006).

Moving beyond stereotypes, what do scientists know about singlehood? It is true that single people exhibit poorer mental and physical health than married people (Joung et al., 1997; Waite, 1995), and they rate themselves as less happy than their married counterparts (Stack & Eshleman, 1998; Waite, 2000). However, we must use caution in interpreting these results; in many studies, "singles" include those who are divorced or widowed, which inflates this finding (Morris & DePaulo, 2009). Furthermore, the differences are modest, and the happiness gap has shrunk, especially among women. The physical health benefits of being married appear to be greater for men than for women (Waite, 2000; Wu & Hart, 2002). But most studies find that single women are more satisfied with their lives and less distressed than comparable single men, and various lines of evidence suggest that women get along without men better than men get along without women (Davies, 1995; Marker, 1996). When interviewing life-long single women between the ages of 65 and 77, Baumbusch (2004) found that these women expressed satisfaction with their decision to remain single and emphasized the importance of their independence.

## Cohabitation

As we noted earlier in the chapter, *cohabitation* refers to living together in a sexually intimate relationship outside of marriage. Recent years have witnessed a tremendous increase in the number of cohabiting couples (see **Figure 10.13**). Although cohabitation is still illegal in five states (Florida, Michigan, Mississippi, Virginia, and West Virginia), it's estimated that 70% of couples live together before marriage (Stanley & Rhoades, 2009). Increasing rates of cohabitation are not unique to the United States and are even higher in many European countries (Kiernan, 2004). However, the percentage of couples living together at any one time does not accurately convey how widespread this phenomenon has

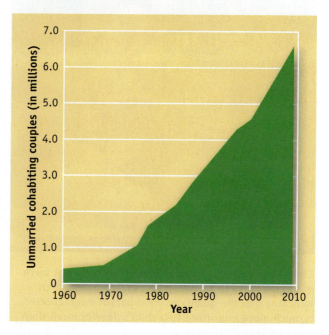

**Figure 10.13**

**Cohabitation in the United States.** The number of unmarried couples living together has been increasing rapidly since 1970 (based on U.S. Census data). This increase shows no signs of leveling off.

become, because cohabiting unions tend to be short (Seltzer, 2004).

Cohabitation tends to conjure up images of college students or other well-educated young couples without children, but these images are misleading. In reality, cohabitation rates have always been higher in the less-educated and lower-income segments of the population (Bumpass & Lu, 2000). Moreover, many cohabiting couples have children: About half of previously married cohabitants and 35% of never-married cohabitants have children in their household (Smock, 2000).

Although many people see cohabitation as a threat to the institution of marriage, many theorists see it as a new stage in the courtship process—a sort of trial marriage. Consistent with this view, about 30% of teenagers indicated that they would probably or definitely cohabitate (Manning, Longmore, & Giordano, 2007). Further, three-quarters of female cohabitants expect to marry their current partner (Lichter, Batson, & Brown, 2004). In spite of these expectations, however, cohabitants report that they are less satisfied with their relationships than married couples (Brown & Booth, 1996; Nock, 1995). Moreover, cohabiting relationships are notably less durable than marital relationships (Seltzer, 2004). Conceiving a child during cohabitation tends to increase couples' chances of staying together (Manning, 2004).

As a prelude to marriage, cohabitation should allow people to experiment with marital-like responsibilities and reduce the likelihood of entering marriage with unrealistic expectations, suggesting that couples who cohabit before they marry should go on to more successful marriages than those who do not. Although this analysis sounds plausible, researchers have *not* found that premarital cohabitation increases the likelihood of subsequent marital success. In fact, studies have consistently found an association between premarital cohabitation and *increased* marital discord and divorce rates (Bumpass & Lu, 2000; Cohan & Kleinbaum, 2002; Teachman, 2003). This association is referred to as the *cohabitation effect,* and it has not decreased as cohabitation becomes more accepted (Stanley & Rhoades, 2009).

What accounts for the cohabitation effect? Many theorists argue that this nontraditional lifestyle has historically attracted a more liberal and less conventional segment of the population with a weak commitment to the institution of marriage and relatively few qualms about getting divorced. This explanation has considerable empirical support (Hall, 1996; Smock, 2000; Stanley, Whitton, & Markman, 2004), but some support also exists for the alternative explanation—that the experience of cohabitation changes people's attitudes, values, or habits in ways that somehow increase their vulnerability to divorce (Kamp Dush, Cohan, & Amato, 2003; Seltzer, 2001).

# APPLICATION

## Understanding Intimate Partner Violence

### LEARNING OBJECTIVES

- Discuss the incidence of partner abuse and the characteristics of batterers.
- Explain why women stay in abusive relationships.

- Discuss the incidence and consequences of date rape.
- Identify factors that contribute to date rape.
- Understand ways to reduce the likelihood of date rape.

*Answer the following statements "true" or "false."*

____ **1.** Most rapes are committed by strangers.

____ **2.** Women are almost never perpetrators of intimate violence.

____ **3.** Most women in abusive relationships are attracted to violent men.

____ **4.** Most men who have witnessed domestic violence as children will batter their intimate partners.

All of the above statements are false, as you will see in this Application, which examines the darker side of intimate relationships. Most people assume they will be safe with those they love and trust. Unfortunately, some people are betrayed by individuals to whom they feel closest. *Intimate partner violence* **is aggression toward those who are in close relationship to the aggressor.** Intimate partner violence takes many forms: psychological, physical, and sexual abuse. Theorists speculate that this type of violence can be categorized as emerging from anger, the need for power, or sadism (Pardue & Arrigo, 2007). Tragically, this violence sometimes ends in homicide. In this Application, we'll focus on two serious social problems: partner abuse and date rape.

### Partner Abuse

Celebrity cases such as those involving Charlie Sheen and Chris Brown have dramatically heightened public awareness of partner violence, particularly wife bat-

tering. *Battering* **encompasses physical abuse, emotional abuse, and sexual abuse of an intimate partner** (Lundberg-Love & Wilkerson, 2006). *Physical abuse* can include kicking, biting, punching, choking, pushing, slapping, hitting with an object, and threatening with or using a weapon. Examples of *emotional abuse* include humiliation, name calling, controlling what the partner does and with whom the partner socializes, refusing to communicate, unreasonably withholding money, and questioning the partner's sanity. *Sexual abuse* is characterized as using sexual behavior to control, manipulate, or demean the other person (Nichols, 2006). Let's explore the research on physical abuse of partners.

### Incidence and Consequences

As with other taboo topics, obtaining accurate estimates of physical abuse is difficult. Research suggests that about 25% of women and 7% of men have been physically assaulted by an intimate partner at some point in their lives (Tjaden & Thoennes, 2000). Women are the perpetrators of intimate partner violence more often than most people realize (Dutton, 2007), but much of wives' aggression appears to be retaliation for abuse, and women tend to inflict less physical damage than men (Johnson, 2000; Swan & Snow, 2006). Women commit one-quarter of spousal murders, so it is an oversimplification to assume that partner abuse involves only male aggression against women. That said, women are the principal victims of severe, dangerous abuse. A woman is the victim in 85% of nonfatal violent crimes

Celebrity cases such as Rihanna's abuse by Chris Brown have dramatically heightened public awareness of intimate partner violence. Sadly, in addition to sustaining physical injuries, victims of partner abuse often suffer from severe anxiety, depression, feelings of helplessness and humiliation, and symptoms of posttraumatic stress disorder.

committed by intimate partners and in 75% of murders by spouses (Rennison & Welchans, 2000). It is inaccurate to assume that intimate violence is seen only in marital relationships—partner abuse is also a significant problem for cohabiting heterosexual couples and for gay couples (Noller, 2009).

The effects of battering reverberate beyond the obvious physical injuries. Victims of partner abuse tend to suffer from severe anxiety, depression, feelings of helplessness and humiliation, stress-induced physical illness, and symptoms of posttraumatic stress disorder (Brewster, 2002; Lundberg-Love & Wilkerson, 2006). They also report higher instances of suicidal ideation (Renner & Markward, 2009). Children who witness marital violence also experience ill effects, such as anxiety, depression, reduced self-esteem, and increased delinquency (Johnson & Ferraro, 2001).

### Characteristics of Batterers

Men who batter women are a diverse group, so a single profile has not emerged (Dixon & Browne, 2003). Some factors associated with an elevated risk for do-

mestic violence include unemployment, drinking and drug problems, a tendency to anger easily, attitudes that condone aggression, and high stress (Stith et al., 2004). Males who were beaten as children or who witnessed their mothers being beaten are more likely to abuse their wives than other men are, although most men who grow up in these difficult circumstances do not become batterers themselves (Stith et al., 2000; Wareham, Boots, & Chavez, 2009). Battering appears to be somewhat more common in families of lower socioeconomic status but, as the celebrity examples illustrate, no social class is immune (Roberts, 2002). Batterers tend to be

**WEB LINK 10.6 Office on Violence Against Women**

This U.S. Department of Justice office was created in 1995 after federal legislation mandated national efforts to reduce domestic violence, sexual assault, and stalking. This site provides a wide variety of legal and social scientific resources in support of this mission.

jealous in relationships, have unrealistic expectations of their partners, blame others for their own problems, and have their feelings hurt easily (Lundberg-Love & Wilkerson, 2006). Other relationship factors that are associated with domestic violence include having frequent disagreements, exhibiting a heated style of dealing with disagreements, and pairing a man holding traditional gender role attitudes with a woman who has nontraditional views of gender roles (DeMaris et al., 2003).

## Why Do Women Stay in Abusive Relationships?

Women leave abusive partners more often than popular stereotypes suggest (Johnson & Ferraro, 2001), but people are still perplexed by the fact that many women remain in abusive relationships that seem horrible and degrading. However, research shows that this phenomenon is not really that perplexing. A number of seemingly compelling reasons explain why many women feel that leaving is not a realistic option, and many of the reasons revolve around fear. Many lack financial independence and fear that they won't be able to survive financially without their partner (Choice & Lamke, 1997; Kim & Gray, 2008). Many simply have no place to go and fear becoming homeless (Browne, 1993a). Many feel guilty and ashamed about their failing relationship and don't want to face disapproval from family and friends, who are likely to fall into the trap of blaming the victim (Barnett & LaViolette, 1993). Above all else, many fear that if they try to leave, they may precipitate more brutal violence and even murder (DeMaris & Swinford, 1996; Grothues & Marmion, 2006). Unfortunately, this fear is not unrealistic, in that many men have shown remarkable persistence in tracking down, stalking, threatening, beating, and killing their ex-partners. Despite the many difficulties of leaving abusive relationships (see **Figure 10.14**), attention is still focused on why women stay rather than on why men batter and on what interventions can prevent women from being brutalized or killed when they do leave (Koss et al., 1994).

## Date Rape

Unfortunately, intimate violence is not limited to marital relations. *Date rape* **refers to forced and unwanted intercourse in the context of dating.** Date rape, a type of acquaintance rape, can occur on a first date, with someone you've dated for a while, or with someone to whom you're engaged. Many people confuse date rape with seduction. Seduction occurs when a woman is persuaded *and agrees* to have sex. Date rape often occurs when seduction fails and the man goes on to have sex with the woman without her consent. The force used in date rape is typically verbal or physical coercion, but sometimes it involves a weapon.

### Incidence and Consequences

It's difficult to estimate how often date rape occurs because the majority of instances go unreported (Frazier, 2009). However, it's much more common than widely

| Perceived Reasons for Returning to Abusive Relationships | |
|---|---|
| **Reasons** | **Mean rating** |
| Give the abuser one more chance | 10.0 |
| Lack of financial resources | 9.1 |
| Emotional dependency on the abuser | 9.0 |
| Lack of housing resources | 8.7 |
| Lack of job opportunities | 7.7 |
| Denial of cycle of violence | 7.6 |
| Lack of support or follow-through by the legal system | 7.6 |
| Lack of child-care resources | 7.1 |
| Lack of transportation | 6.7 |
| Fear that the abuser will find her and do her harm | 6.7 |
| Lack of support from other family members | 6.6 |
| Fear that the abuser will get custody of the children | 5.8 |
| Fear that the abuser will kidnap the children | 5.8 |
| Children miss the absent parent | 5.6 |
| Lack of professional counseling | 5.1 |
| Fear that the abuser will harm the children | 4.6 |

**Figure 10.14**

**Perceived reasons for returning to abusive relationships.** Shelters for battered wives generally report that the majority of their clients return to their partners. In one study (Johnson, Crowley, & Sigler, 1992), workers at ten shelters in Alabama were asked to rate the reasons that women returned to abusive relationships. The most frequently cited reasons are listed here in order of rated importance. As you can see, a variety of factors appear to propel women back into abusive relationships.

Source: From Johnson, I. M., Crowley, J., & Sigler, R. T. (1992). Agency response to domestic violence: Services provided to battered women. In E. C. Viano (Ed.), *Intimate violence: Interdisciplinary perspectives* (pp 191–202, Table on p. 199). Philadelphia: Taylor & Francis. Copyright © 1992 Hemisphere Publishing. Reprinted with permission of Taylor & Francis, Inc.

realized. Research suggests that 13%–30% of women are likely to be victimized by date rape or attempted sexual coercion at some point in their lives (Abbey et al., 2004; Koss & Cook, 1993; Spitzberg, 1999). Further, rape is not limited to the United Sates, but is a global problem. Most people naively assume that the vast majority of rapes are committed by strangers who leap from bushes or dark alleys to surprise their victims. In reality, research indicates that most victims are raped by someone they know (Frazier, 2009) (see **Figure 10.15**).

All rape is traumatic, but it is particularly shattering for a woman to be raped by someone she has trusted. In the aftermath of date rape, women typically experience a variety of emotional reactions, including fear, anger, anxiety, self-blame, and guilt (Kahn & Andrioli Mathie, 1999). Many rape victims suffer from depression, symptoms of posttraumatic stress disorder, and increased risk for suicide (Foa, 1998; Slashinski, Coker, & Davis, 2003; Ullman, 2004). Negative reactions can be exacerbated if the woman's family and friends are not supportive—particularly if family or friends blame the victim for the attack. In addition to the trauma of the rape, women also have to cope with the possibilities of pregnancy and sexually transmitted disease (Golding, 1996). Moreover, if the rape survivor presses charges against her attacker, she may have to deal with difficult legal proceedings, negative publicity, and social stigma.

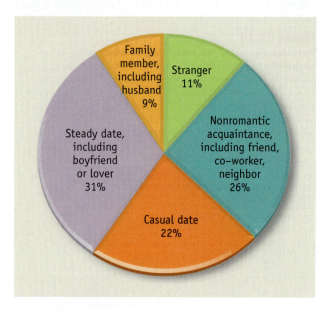

**Figure 10.15**

**Rape victim–offender relationships.** Based on a national survey of 3,187 college women, Mary Koss and her colleagues (1988) identified a sample of 468 women who indicated that they had been a victim of rape and who provided information on their relationship to the offender. Contrary to the prevailing stereotype, only a small minority (11%) had been raped by a stranger. As you can see, over half of rapes occur in the context of dating relationships.

## Contributing Factors

To understand the phenomenon of date rape, it's essential to know something about the factors that contribute to this behavior. It probably comes as no surprise to learn that alcohol contributes to about half of sexually aggressive incidents (Abbey, 2009; Sampson, 2003; Ward & Lundberg-Love, 2006). Alcohol impairs judgment and reduces inhibitions, making men more willing to use force. Drinking also undermines men's ability to interpret ambiguous social cues, making them more likely to overestimate their date's interest in sex. The more intoxicated perpetrators are, the more aggressive they tend to be (Abbey, 2009; Abbey et al., 2003). Alcohol also increases women's vulnerability to sexual coercion. Drinking can cloud women's assessments of their risk and their ability to mount firm resistance or find a way to escape the situation.

So-called "date rape drugs" are also a cause for concern (Pope & Shouldice, 2001; Ward & Lundberg-Love, 2006). Rohypnol ("roofies") and gamma hydroxybutyrate (GHB) are two drugs used to subdue dates. Although these drugs are colorless, odorless, and tasteless, their effects are anything but benign, and they can even be fatal. Victims typically pass out and have no recall of what happened while they were under the influence of the drug. To make it easier to spike a drink, predators typically look for individuals who are already intoxicated.

Gender differences in sexual standards also contribute to date rape. Society still encourages a double standard for males and females. Men are encouraged to have sexual feelings, to act on them, and to "score," whereas women are socialized to be coy about their sexual desires. This double standard can promote sexual aggression by men who come to view dating as a "battle of the sexes" in which they are supposed to persist in their pursuit of sexual conquests (Abbey et al., 2001a; Forbes, Adams-Curtis, & White, 2004; Sampson, 2003). These social norms encourage game playing, so dating partners may not always say what they mean or mean what they say. Whereas the majority of women say "no" and mean it, some women may say "no" to sexual activity when they actually mean "maybe" or "yes." Studies surveying the extent of token resistance among college women report that approximately 38% of them have acted this way (Muehlenhard & McCoy, 1991; Shotland & Hunter, 1995). Unfortunately, this behavior can backfire. For some men, it can cloud the issue of whether a woman has consented to sex (Osman, 2003).

In terms of personal characteristics, males who engage in sexual aggression tend to be relatively impulsive, low in empathy, hostile toward women, and heavy drinkers (Abbey et al., 2001b, 2004). They tend to endorse traditional gender stereotypes about male dominance and to have had more (consensual) sex partners than their age-mates. They also tend to have poor anger management skills (Lundeberg et al., 2004).

### Reducing the Incidence of Date Rape

What can women do to reduce the likelihood of being victimized by date rape? Here are some suggestions: (1) Recognize date rape for what it is: an act of sexual aggression. (2) Become familiar with the characteristics of men who are likely to engage in date rape (see **Figure 10.16**) and be cautious about dating men who exhibit these traits. (3) Beware of excessive alcohol and drug use, which may undermine self-control and self-determination in sexual interactions. (4) When dating someone new, agree to go only to public places and always carry enough money for transportation back home. (5) Communicate feelings and expectations about sex by engaging in appropriate self-disclosure. (6) Finally, be prepared to act *aggressively* if assertive refusals fail to stop unwanted advances.

Although most of us would prefer not to think about this darker side of relationships, intimate violence is a reality we can ill-afford to ignore. It deeply touches the lives of millions of individuals. We can only hope that increased public awareness of intimate violence will help reduce its incidence and its tragic effects.

### Characteristics of Date Rapists

| Sexual entitlement | Power and control | Hostility and anger | Acceptance of interpersonal violence |
| --- | --- | --- | --- |
| Touching women with no regard for their wishes | Interrupting people, especially women | Showing a quick temper | Using threats in displays of anger |
| Sexualizing relationships that are appropriately not sexual | Being a bad loser | Blaming others when things go wrong | Using violence in borderline situations |
| Engaging in conversation that is inappropriately intimate | Exhibiting inappropriate competitiveness | Tending to transform other emotions into anger | Approving observed violence |
| Telling sexual jokes at inappropriate times or places | Using intimidating body language | | Justifying violence |
| Making inappropriate comments about women's bodies, sexuality, and so on | Game playing | | |

**Figure 10.16**

**Date rapists: Warning signs.** According to Rozee, Bateman, and Gilmore (1991), four factors appear to distinguish date rapists: feelings of sexual entitlement, a penchant for exerting power and control, high hostility and anger, and acceptance of interpersonal violence. The presence of more than one of these characteristics is an important warning sign. When sexual entitlement is coupled with any other factor, special heed should be taken.

### Challenges to the Traditional Model of Marriage

● The traditional model of marriage is being challenged by the increasing acceptability of singlehood, the increasing popularity of cohabitation, the reduced premium on permanence, changes in gender roles, the increasing prevalence of voluntary childlessness, and the decline of the traditional nuclear family. Nonetheless, marriage remains quite popular.

### Deciding to Marry

● A multitude of factors, including one's culture, influence an individual's decision to marry. The norm for our society is to select a mate and engage in a monogamous marriage. Mate selection is influenced by endogamy, homogamy, and gender. Women place more emphasis on potential partners' ambition and financial prospects, whereas men are more interested in a partner's youthfulness and physical attractiveness.

● There are some premarital predictors of marital success, such as family background, age, length of courtship, and personality, but the relations are weak. The nature of a couple's premarital communication is a better predictor of marital adjustment. Stressful events surrounding the marriage influence marital stability.

### Marital Adjustment Across the Family Life Cycle

● The family life cycle is an orderly sequence of developmental stages through which families tend to progress. Newly married couples tend to be very happy before the arrival of children. Today more couples are struggling with the decision about whether to have children. The arrival of children is a major transition that is handled best by parents who have realistic expectations about the difficulties inherent in raising a family.

● As children reach adolescence, parents should expect more conflict as their influence declines. They must learn to relate to their children as adults and help launch them into the adult world. Most parents no longer struggle with the empty nest syndrome. Adult children returning home may be more of a problem. Marital satisfaction tends to increase in later life.

### Vulnerable Areas in Marital Adjustment

● Gaps in expectations about marital roles may create marital stress. Disparities in expectations about gender roles and the distribution of housework may be especially common and problematic. Work concerns can clearly spill over to influence marital functioning, but the links between parents' employment and children's adjustment are complex.

● Wealth does not ensure marital happiness, but a lack of money can produce marital problems. Inadequate communication is a commonly reported marital problem and is predictive of divorce.

### Divorce

● Divorce rates have increased dramatically in recent decades, but they appear to be stabilizing. Deciding on a divorce tends to be a gradual process marred by indecision. Unpleasant as divorce may be, the evidence suggests that toughing it out in an unhappy marriage can often be worse.

● Wallerstein's research suggests that divorce tends to have extremely negative effects on children. Hetherington's research suggests that most children recover from divorce after a few years. The effects of divorce on children vary, but negative effects can be long-lasting.

● A substantial majority of divorced people remarry. These second marriages have a somewhat lower probability of success than first marriages. The adjustment of children in stepfamilies appears to be somewhat lower that for other families, but differences are modest.

### Alternative Relationship Lifestyles

● Gay relationships develop in a starkly different social context than marital relationships, and many Americans hold negative attitudes toward gay couples. Nonetheless, most homosexuals desire long-term intimate relationships, and studies have found that heterosexual and homosexual couples are similar in many ways. Children raised by gay parents do not show poorer adjustment than other children.

● An increasing proportion of the young population are remaining single, but this fact does not mean that people are turning away from marriage. Although singles generally have the same adjustment problems as married couples, evidence suggests that singles tend to be somewhat less happy and less healthy.

● The prevalence of cohabitation has increased dramatically. Logically, one might expect cohabitation to facilitate marital success, but research has consistently found an association between cohabitation and marital instability.

### Application: Understanding Intimate Partner Violence

● Research suggests that about 25% of women and 7% of men have been victims of partner abuse. Women are the principal victims of serious, dangerous abuse. Men who batter their partners are diverse, but they tend to anger easily, be jealous, and have unrealistic expectations of their partner. Women stay in abusive relationships for a variety of compelling, practical reasons, including economic realities.

● The majority of rapes are committed by someone the victim knows. Estimates suggest that the chances of a woman being victimized by date rape at some time in her life range from 13% to 30%. Rape is a traumatic experience that has many serious consequences. Alcohol abuse, drug use, and gender-based sexual standards all contribute to date rape. Miscommunication revolving around token resistance is particularly problematic.

| | |
|---|---|
| Battering   p. 331 | Homogamy   p. 307 |
| Cohabitation   p. 305 | Intimate partner violence |
| Date rape   p. 333 | p. 331 |
| Divorce   p. 320 | Marriage   p. 305 |
| Endogamy   p. 307 | Monogamy   p. 307 |
| Family life cycle   p. 310 | Polygamy   p. 307 |

| | |
|---|---|
| John Gottman   pp. 318–320 | Judith Wallerstein |
| E. Mavis Hetherington | pp. 322–323 |
| p. 323 | |

## QUESTIONS

1. Which of the following is *not* one of the social trends that are undermining the traditional model of marriage?
   a. increased acceptance of singlehood
   b. increased voluntary childlessness
   c. increased acceptance of cohabitation
   d. increased premium on permanence in marriage

2. Endogamy refers to:
   a. the tendency to marry within one's social group.
   b. the tendency to marry someone with similar characteristics.
   c. the final marriage in serial monogamy.
   d. norms that promote marriage outside one's social unit.

3. Based on trends in the data, which of the following couples has the greatest likelihood of marital success?
   a. Stephanie and David, whose parents are divorced
   b. Jessica and Carlos, who are both perfectionists
   c. Gwen and Aaron, who had a long courtship
   d. Carla and Turk, who married at a very young age

4. The transition to parenthood tends to be easier when:
   a. the newborn child was not planned for.
   b. the parents have realistic expectations about parenting.
   c. the new parents are relatively young.
   d. the father is not heavily involved in child care.

5. Which of the following characteristics in young children is related to maternal employment?
   a. increased hyperactivity
   b. higher anxiety
   c. decreased cognitive skills
   d. increased prosocial behavior

6. Truc and Hiroshi have plenty of financial resources. In their marriage, arguments about money:
   a. may be common.
   b. don't occur.
   c. are a big problem only if the wife earns more than her husband.
   d. are unrelated to marital satisfaction.

7. The evidence suggests that the negative effects of divorce on former spouses' *psychological* adjustment are:
   a. exaggerated for both sexes.
   b. greater for men than women.
   c. greater for women than men.
   d. about the same for men and women.

8. Which of the following has been supported by research on intimate relationships among gay men and lesbians?
   a. Gay couples rarely experience sexual prejudice.
   b. Gays avoid becoming involved in long-term relationships.
   c. Gays have impoverished family relations.
   d. Gays want the same things out of intimate relationships that heterosexuals want.

9. What is the most probable reason for the increase in the proportion of young people who are single?
   a. loss of faith in the institution of marriage
   b. increased individualism and declining collectivism
   c. the median age at which people get married has increased
   d. an increase in the number of young people unwilling to undertake the financial burdens of marriage and family

10. Research on cohabitation indicates that:
    a. most cohabitants are just not interested in marriage.
    b. most female cohabitants expect to marry their current partner.
    c. cohabitation is declining.
    d. cohabitation experience improves the chances that one's marriage will be successful.

## ANSWERS

1. d  Pages 305–306
2. a  Page 307
3. c  Pages 308–310
4. b  Page 313
5. d  Page 317
6. a  Page 318
7. d  Page 322
8. d  Page 328
9. c  Page 329
10. b  Pages 330–331

## Personal Explorations Workbook

Go to the *Personal Explorations Workbook* in the back of your textbook for exercises that can enhance your self-understanding in relation to issues raised in this chapter. **Exercise 10.1** *Self-Assessment:* Self-Report Jealousy Scale. **Exercise 10.2** *Self-Reflection:* Thinking Through Your Attitudes About Marriage and Cohabitation.

 CourseMate

Access an interactive eBook, chapter-specific interactive learning tools, including Personal Explorations, Recommended Readings, Critical Thinking Exercises, flashcards, quizzes, videos and more in your Psychology CourseMate, available at **www.cengagebrain.com/shop/ISBN/1111186634**.

© Jon Bower China/Alamy

# CHAPTER 11

# *Gender and Behavior*

On January 14, 2005, then-Harvard University President Lawrence H. Summers spoke at a conference of the National Bureau of Economic Research about Harvard's policies regarding diversity. Dr. Summers focused his remarks on the issue of women's underrepresentation in tenured positions in science and engineering at top universities. He offered three broad hypotheses about this gender disparity. The one that attracted the most media attention was what he called a "different availability of aptitude at the high end." While he acknowledged that there are differences in socialization and patterns of discrimination between men and women, he ranked innate gender differences in mathematical and scientific ability as having greater "importance" in explaining the gender disparity. Dr. Summers went on to say, "Because if my reading of the data is right—it's something people can argue about—that there are some systematic differences in variability in different populations . . . My sense is that the unfortunate truth—I would far prefer to believe something else, because it would be easier to address what is surely a serious social problem if something else were true—is that the combination of the [expectations for high powered jobs] and the differing variances probably explains a fair amount of this problem" (Harvard Crimson, 2005).

Summers's remarks on this issue sparked a huge, contentious debate among academics, scientists, and the public. The war of words lingered for months and eventually led to Summers' resignation as president of Harvard. This scenario demonstrates in a highly compelling way that gender research is relevant, important, and frequently controversial. Obviously, psychologists have a lot to offer in this area. In this chapter, we explore some intriguing and controversial questions: Are there genuine behavioral and cognitive differences between males and females? If so, what are their origins? Are traditional gender-role expectations healthy or unhealthy? Why are gender roles in our society changing, and what does the future hold? After addressing those questions, in the Application we explore gender and communication styles.

# Gender Stereotypes

### LEARNING OBJECTIVES

- Distinguish between sex and gender.
- Explain the nature of gender stereotypes and their connection with instrumentality and expressiveness.
- Discuss four important points about gender stereotypes.
- Describe androcentrism.

Let's begin by clarifying some terms. Some scholars prefer to use the term *gender* to refer to male-female differences that are learned and *sex* to designate biologically based differences between males and females. However, as respected authority Janet Shibley Hyde (2004) points out, making this sharp distinction between sex and gender fails to recognize that biology and culture interact. Following this reasoning, we'll use **gender to mean the state of being male or female.** (When we use the term *sex,* we're referring to sexual behavior.) It's important to note that, as *we* use the term, *gender* says nothing about the *causes* of behavior. In other words, if we say that there are gender differences in aggressive behavior, we are simply stating that males and females differ in this area. This behavioral disparity might be caused by biological factors, by environmental factors, or by both. **Figure 11.1** sorts out a number of gender-related terms that we will use in our discussions.

Courtesy of Janet Shibley Hyde

**Janet Shibley Hyde**

Obviously, males and females differ biologically—in their genitals and other aspects of anatomy, and in their physiological functioning. These readily apparent physical disparities between males and females lead people to expect other differences as well. Recall from Chapter 7 that *stereotypes* are widely held beliefs that people possess certain characteristics simply because of their membership in a particular group. Thus, **gender stereotypes are widely shared beliefs about males' and females' abilities, personality traits, and social behavior.** Research indicates that beliefs about the typical attributes characteristic of men and women are widely shared (Desert & Leyens, 2006). For example, a survey of gender stereotypes in 25 countries revealed considerable similarity of views (Williams & Best, 1990; Williams, Satterwhite, & Best, 1999). Because of the widespread gains in educational and occupational attainment by American women since the 1970s, you might expect to find changes in contemporary gender stereotypes for both genders. However, gender stereotypes in this country have remained largely stable since the early 1970s, especially those for men (Diekman & Eagly, 2000; Spence & Buckner, 2000).

Gender stereotypes are too numerous to summarize here. Instead, you can examine **Figure 11.2** on the next page, which lists a number of characteristics people commonly link with femininity and masculinity. Note that the stereotyped attributes for males generally reflect the quality of *instrumentality,* **an orientation toward action and accomplishment,** whereas the stereotypes for females reflect the quality of *expressiveness,* **an orientation toward emotion and relationships** (Eagly, Wood, & Diekman, 2000; Parsons & Bales, 1955).

When it comes to stereotypes, there are some important points to keep in mind. First, despite the general agreement on a number of gender stereotypes,

| Gender-Related Concepts | |
|---|---|
| **Term** | **Definition** |
| Gender | The state of being male or female |
| Gender identity | An individual's perception of himself or herself as male or female |
| Gender stereotypes | Widely held and often inaccurate beliefs about males' and females' abilities, personality traits, and social behavior |
| Gender differences | Actual disparities in behavior between males and females, based on research observations |
| Gender roles | Culturally defined expectations about appropriate behavior for males and females |
| Gender-role identity | A person's identification with the traits regarded as masculine or feminine (one's sense of being masculine or feminine) |
| Sexual orientation | A person's preference for sexual partners of the other gender (heterosexual), the same gender (homosexual), or both genders (bisexual) |

**Figure 11.1**
**Terminology related to gender.** The topic of gender involves many closely related ideas that are easily confused. The gender-related concepts introduced in this chapter are summarized here for easy comparison.

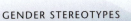

## Elements of Traditional Gender Stereotypes

| Masculine | Feminine |
|-----------|----------|
| Active | Aware of others' feelings |
| Adventurous | Considerate |
| Aggressive | Creative |
| Ambitious | Cries easily |
| Competitive | Devotes self to others |
| Dominant | Emotional |
| Independent | Enjoys art and music |
| Leadership qualities | Excitable in a crisis |
| Likes math and science | Expresses tender feelings |
| Makes decisions easily | Feelings hurt easily |
| Mechanical aptitude | Gentle |
| Not easily influenced | Home oriented |
| Outspoken | Kind |
| Persistent | Likes children |
| Self-confident | Neat |
| Skilled in business | Needs approval |
| Stands up under pressure | Tactful |
| Takes a stand | Understanding |

**Figure 11.2**

**Traditional gender stereotypes.** Gender stereotypes are widely known and relate to many diverse aspects of psychological functioning. This is a partial list of the characteristics that college students associate with a typical man and a typical woman. Gender stereotypes have remained remarkably stable in spite of all the recent changes relating to gender issues in modern societies.

Source: Adapted from Ruble, T. L. (1983). Sex stereotypes: Issues of change in the 70s. *Sex Roles, 9,* 397–402. Copyright © 1983 Plenum Publishing Co. Adapted by permission of Kluwer Academic/Plenum Publishers and the author.

variability also occurs (Best & Thomas, 2004; Williams & Best, 1990). The characteristics in **Figure 11.2** represent the prototypic American male or female: white, middle-class, heterosexual, and Christian. But it is obvious that not everyone fits this set of characteristics. For example, the stereotypes for African American males and females are more similar on the dimensions of competence and expressiveness than those for white American males and females (Kane, 2000). Also, the stereotypes of white and Hispanic women are more positive than those for African American women (Niemann et al., 1994).

A second point about gender stereotypes is that since the 1980s, the boundaries between male and

female stereotypes have become less rigid (Deaux & Lewis, 1983, 1984). Earlier, male and female stereotypes were seen as separate and distinct categories (for example, men are strong and women are weak). Now it seems that people perceive gender as a continuum as opposed to a dichotomy (Beall, Eagly, & Sternberg, 2004).

A third consideration is that the traditional male stereotype is more complimentary than the conventional female stereotype. This fact is related to *androcentrism,* **or the belief that the male is the norm** (Bem, 1993). There is considerable evidence that, in the United States, masculinity is associated with higher overall status and competence (Ridgeway & Bourg, 2004). **Figure 11.3** provides some examples of how androcentrism can be manifested in the workplace. Ironically, this bias is evident even in psychological research on gender. Hegarty and Buechel (2006) examined 388 articles on gender differences from journals published by the American Psychological Association and found evidence of androcentric reporting. Specifically, gender differences were reported in terms of *women* being different, as opposed to men. The implicit assumption, then, is that men are the norm from which women deviate. Look for evidence of this bias as you read about studies in this chapter.

Finally, keep in mind what you learned about stereotypes in Chapter 7: They can bias your perceptions and expectations of others as well as your interactions.

Let's shift from gender stereotypes to what males and females are actually like. Keep in mind that our discussion focuses on modern Western societies; the story may be different in other cultures.

## Androcentrism in the Workplace

| | |
|---|---|
| He's good on details. | She's picky. |
| He follows through. | She doesn't know when to quit. |
| He's assertive. | She's pushy. |
| He stands firm. | She's rigid. |
| He's a man of the world. | She's been around. |
| He's not afraid to say what he thinks. | She's outspoken. |
| He's close-mouthed. | She's secretive. |
| He exercises authority. | She's controlling. |
| He climbed the ladder of success. | She slept her way to the top. |
| He's a stern taskmaster. | She's difficult to work for. |

**Figure 11.3**

**Male bias on the job.** In the world of work, women who exhibit traditional "masculine" characteristics are often perceived negatively. Thus, a man and a woman may display essentially the same behavior but elicit very different reactions.

SIX CHIX

THE THINKER

I GUESS IT JUST DEPENDS ON WHO'S DOING IT.

THE WORRIER

SIX CHIX © Isabella Bannerman, Margaret Shulock, Rina Piccolo, Ann C. Telnaes, Kathryn LeMieux and Stephanie Piro. 2002 KING FEATURES SYNDICATE

# Gender Similarities and Differences

### LEARNING OBJECTIVES

- Explain how meta-analyses have helped researchers who study gender.
- Articulate the gender similarities hypothesis.
- Summarize the research on gender similarities and differences in verbal, mathematical, and spatial abilities.
- Understand the research on gender similarities and differences in personality and social behavior.

- Summarize the research on gender and psychological disorders.
- Clarify the situation regarding overall behavioral similarities and differences between males and females.
- Give two explanations for why gender differences appear larger than they actually are.

Are men more aggressive than women? Do more women than men suffer from depression? Hundreds of studies have attempted to answer these and related questions about gender and behavior. Moreover, new evidence is pouring in constantly, and many researchers report conflicting findings. To add to the confusion, gender differences are not clear cut; they are complex and often subtle. It is an oversimplification, for instance, to say that women are verbal and men are spatial (Spelke, 2005).

Thus, it is an almost overwhelming task to keep up with the research in this area. Thankfully, a statistical technique called meta-analysis helps clarify this body of research (Hyde, 2007b). **Meta-analysis combines the statistical results of many studies of the same question, yielding an estimate of the size and consistency of a variable's effects.** This approach allows a researcher to assess the overall trends across all the previous studies of how gender is related to, say, math abilities or conformity. Meta-analysis has been a great boon to researchers, and quite a few meta-analyses on gender differences have now been conducted.

Janet Shibley Hyde has recently proposed the *gender similarities hypothesis*. Based on the results of over 46 meta-analyses, Hyde (2005, 2007) notes that men and women are similar on most psychological variables

and that most of the time when researchers report a difference, it is quite small. She further asserts that overinflated claims of gender differences have costs associated with them for the workplace and relationships. Critics of this hypothesis argue that Hyde omitted several important variables from her review and that methodological limitations led her to underestimate true gender differences (Davies & Shackelford, 2006; Lippa, 2006). It will be interesting to see where this dispute leads over the next several years.

In addition, there is much debate as to whether gender differences are largely attributable to environmental factors as opposed to biological factors, and there is evidence on both sides of the question (Halpern, 2000; Hyde, Fennema, & Lamon, 1990; Nowell & Hedges, 1998). Before we examine the possible causes of these differences, let's thread our way through the available research in three areas: cognitive abilities, personality traits and social behavior, and psychological disorders.

## Cognitive Abilities

We should first point out that gender differences have *not* been found in *overall* intelligence (Hines, 2007). Of course, this fact shouldn't be surprising, because intelligence tests are intentionally designed to minimize differences between the scores of males and females. But what about gender differences in *specific* cognitive skills? Let's start with verbal abilities.

## Verbal Abilities

Verbal abilities include a number of distinct skills, such as vocabulary, reading, writing, spelling, and grammar abilities. Girls and women generally have the edge in the verbal area, although the gender differences are small (Halpern, 2000; Hyde, 2007; Hyde & Kling, 2001; Weiss et al., 2003). Among the findings worth noting are the facts that girls usually start speaking a little earlier, have larger vocabularies and better reading scores in grade school, and are more verbally fluent (on tests of writing, for instance). Boys seem to fare better on verbal analogies. However, they are three to four times more likely to be stutterers (Skinner & Shelton, 1985) and five to ten times more likely than girls to be dyslexic (Vandenberg, 1987). It is important to remember that while gender differences in verbal abilities generally favor females, these differences are small. The overlap between males and females in verbal abilities is much greater than the gap between them (Weiss et al., 2003).

## Mathematical Abilities

Researchers have also looked at gender differences in *mathematical abilities,* including performing computations and solving word and story problems. Meta-analyses of mathematical abilities show small gender differences favoring males (Hedges & Nowell, 1995; Hyde et al., 1990; Nowell & Hedges, 1998). Interestingly, research shows no such differences in the elementary school years (Aunola et al., 2004). In fact, a recent meta-analysis including almost 500,000 students from over 69 countries found that "on average, males and females differ very little in math achievement," even though males have a more positive attitude toward math (Else-Quest, Hyde, & Linn, 2010, p.125). Further, girls

from countries where gender equality is more prevalent performed highest.

Thus, the current view is that gender differences in mathematical abilities in the general population are essentially nil. However, this conclusion has a few exceptions. In mathematical *problem solving,* boys start to slightly outperform girls when they reach high school. This difference is attributable in part to the fact that boys take more high school math courses (Halpern, 2000). Still, because problem-solving ability is essential for success in scientific courses and careers (arenas currently underpopulated by women), this finding is a concern. Males also outperform females at the high end of the mathematical ability distribution (Dweck, 2007). For instance, when gifted seventh- and eighth-graders take the math subtest of the SAT (to identify mathematically precocious youth), boys outnumber girls 17 to 1 in the group scoring over 700 (Benbow, 1988). Overall, when all students are compared, gender differences in mathematical ability are small but favor males.

## Spatial Abilities

In the cognitive area, the most compelling evidence for gender differences is in *spatial abilities,* which include perceiving and mentally manipulating shapes and figures. Males typically outperform females in most spatial abilities, and gender differences favoring males are consistently found in the ability to perform mental rotations of a figure in three dimensions—a skill important in occupations such as engineering, chemistry, and the building trades (see **Figure 11.4**). This gender gap in the ability to handle mental rotations is relatively large and has been found repeatedly (Halpern, 2000, 2004; Voyer & Hou, 2006), and using creative methods, researchers have demonstrated this difference in infants as young as 5 months old (Moore & Johnson, 2008). However, experience and training can improve mental rotation in both girls and boys (Newcombe, 2007; Sanz de Acedo & Garcia Ganuza, 2003). In fact, playing

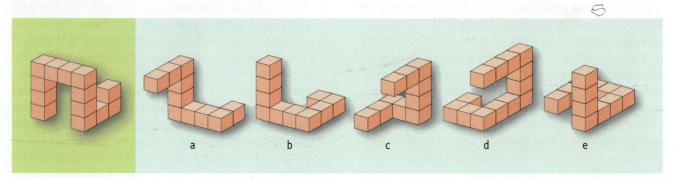

a    b    c    d    e

**Figure 11.4**

**Mental rotation test.** If you mentally rotate the figure on the left, which of the five figures on the right would match it? The answer is "d." This problem illustrates how spatial rotation skills are measured. Researchers have uncovered some interesting gender differences in the ability to mentally rotate figures in space.

Source: Adapted from Shepard, R. N., & Metzler, J. N. (1971). Mental rotation of three-dimensional objects. *Science, 171,* 701–703. Copyright © 1971 by American Association for the Advancement of Science. Adapted by permission of the publisher and author.

action video games has been shown to improve mental rotation skills for both genders (Spence, Feng, & Marshman, 2009). Feng and colleagues (2007) found benefits, especially for women, in rotation skills after only 10 hours of training on an action video game.

## Personality Traits and Social Behavior

Turning to personality and social behavior, let's examine those factors for which gender differences are reasonably well documented.

### Self-Esteem

Females typically score lower than males on tests of self-esteem, but the difference in scores is generally small, and Hyde (2005) argues that this difference has been exaggerated in the popular press. For example, a meta-analysis of several hundred studies that included respondents from 7 to 60 years of age found only a small difference in self-esteem that favored males (Kling et al., 1999). The authors found no support for claims that girls' self-esteem drops dramatically during adolescence (Brody, 1997; Orenstein, 1994). A second meta-analysis also reported only a small overall gender difference favoring males (Major et al., 1999). Other research consistently reports self-esteem differences between white men and women, but findings are mixed for other ethnic groups (Major et al., 1999; Twenge & Crocker, 2002).

Obviously, the findings on self-esteem are complex. To add to the complexity, a recent meta-analysis including 115 studies examined gender differences in specific self-esteem domains (Gentile et al., 2009). As noted in Chapter 6, the researchers found gender differences favoring males with regard to self-esteem domains of physical appearance, athleticism, and self-satisfaction, but differences in behavioral conduct and morality/ethics favored females. There were no gender differences for domains such as academics and social acceptance. **Figure 11.5** summarizes these findings.

### Aggression

*Aggression* **involves behavior that is intended to hurt someone, either physically or verbally** (see Chapter 4). Gender differences in aggression vary depending on the form aggression takes. A summary of cross-cultural meta-analyses reported that males consistently engage in more *physical aggression* than females (Archer, 2005).

| Gender Differences in Specific Self-Esteem Domains | |
|---|---|
| **Specific self-esteem domain** | **Actual finding** |
| Physical appearance | Males higher |
| Athletic | Males higher |
| Academic | No difference |
| Social acceptance | No difference |
| Family | No difference |
| Behavioral conduct | Females higher |
| Self-satisfaction | Males higher |
| Moral-ethical | Females higher |

**Figure 11.5**
**Gender differences in specific self-esteem domains.**
Females typically score lower than males on tests of self-esteem. However, a recent meta-analysis examined gender differences in specific self-esteem domains. As you can see, gender differences in self-esteem are more complex than previously thought.

Source: Adapted from Gentile, B., Grabe, S., Dolan-Pascoe, B., Twenge, J. M., Wells, B. E., & Maitino, A. (2009). Gender differences in domain-specific self-esteem: A meta-analysis. *Review of General Psychology, 13*(1), 34–45. Copyright © 2009 by the American Psychological Association. Adapted with permission.

This difference is evident even in young children (Baillargeon et al., 2007). In the area of *verbal aggression* (insults, threats of harm), the findings are inconsistent (Geen, 1998; Harris, 1996). When it comes to *relational aggression,* such as giving someone the "silent treatment" to get one's way, talking behind another's back, or trying to get others to dislike someone, females are rated higher (Archer, 2005; Coyne, Archer, & Eslea, 2006). Experts believe that the higher rates of relational aggression among girls and women result from the importance that females attach to close relationships (Crick, Casas, & Nelson, 2002).

*Indirect aggression* overlaps to some degree with relational aggression; it involves covert behaviors in which the target is not directly confronted—spreading rumors, for instance. In a study of 8-, 11-, and 15-year-olds from Finland, Israel, Italy, and Poland, researchers looked at gender differences in three types of aggression: physical, verbal, and indirect (Oesterman et al., 1998). Across nations, boys were equally likely to use physical and verbal aggression and less likely to use indirect aggression. Girls most often used indirect aggression, followed by verbal aggression, then physical aggression. Even in controlled laboratory settings where male and female participants are exposed to the same aggression-evoking stimulus, women are more likely than men to aggress indirectly (Giancola et al, 2009; Hess & Hagen, 2006).

However, when you consider extreme forms of aggression, there is no getting around the fact that men commit a grossly disproportionate share of violent crimes. The U.S. Department of Justice (2007) reports that only 7% of all federal inmates are women and, based on self-reports of victims, women make up 14%

of violent offenders. Male youth are an estimated 10 times more likely to commit murder that females (Feder, Levant, & Dean, 2007). Further, the lifetime chances of going to prison are much higher for men (11.3%) than for women (1.8%). **Figure 11.6** shows the stark gender differences in such crimes as assault, armed robbery, rape, and homicide.

### Sexual Attitudes and Behavior

In the sexual domain, meta-analyses have found men to have more permissive attitudes than women about casual, premarital, and extramarital sex (Oliver & Hyde, 1993; Petersen & Hyde, 2010). Again, it's important to note that, in line with the gender similarities hypothesis, most gender differences regarding sexuality are relatively small. However, analyses repeatedly find that males are more sexually active, more likely to use pornography, and more likely to engage in masturbation than females (Hyde & Oliver, 2000; Petersen & Hyde, 2010). In a sample of 168 heterosexual adults, Yost and Zurbriggen (2006) found that for both men and women, the endorsement of casual sex was associated with earlier sexual experiences, a greater number of sexual partners, and more frequent sexual activity. However, for men, this endorsement was also associated with acceptance of rape myths and conservative attitudes toward women, while for women it was associated with sexual fantasies of dominance and lower levels of sexual conservatism.

In a summary of gender differences in sexuality, Letitia Anne Peplau (2003) reported four key differences that hold for both gays and straights. First, men have more interest in sex than women do (they think about sex more often and prefer to have sex more often, for example). Second, the connection between sex and intimacy is more important for women than for men (women typically prefer sex in the context of a relationship). Third, aggression is more often linked to sexuality for men than for women (coercive sex is more likely to be initiated by men). Finally, women's sexuality is more easily shaped by cultural and situational factors (their sexual attitudes are easier to change, for instance).

### Emotional Expression

Conventional wisdom holds that women are more "emotional" than men. Does research support this belief? If by being "emotional," we mean outwardly displaying one's emotions, the answer is yes. A number of studies have found that women express more emotion than men (Ashmore, 1990; Brody & Hall, 1993). Gender differences "favoring" women have been found on such emotions as sadness, disgust, fear, surprise, happiness, and anger. Similarly, women are better than men at recognizing emotions in others based on facial expressions or other nonverbal cues (Hampson, van Anders, & Mullin, 2006).

Do women actually *experience* more emotion? To answer this question, Ann Kring and Albert Gordon (1998) had college students view films selected to evoke sadness, happiness, and fear. The researchers videotaped the participants' facial expressions and asked the subjects to describe their emotional experiences. As expected, they found gender differences in the facial expression of emotion. However, they failed to find any gender differences in *experienced* emotions. Thus, gender differences in emotional functioning may be limited to the outward expression of feelings and could stem from the different rules parents teach their sons and daughters about displaying emotions (DeAngelis, 2001).

### Communication

Popular stereotypes suggest that females are much more talkative than males. In fact, the opposite seems to be true: Men talk more than women (Cameron, 2007; Gleason & Ely, 2002). Men also tend to interrupt women more than women interrupt men, although this difference is small (Eckert & McConnell-Ginet, 2003). Yet when women have more power in work or personal relationships, women interrupt more (Aries, 1998). Thus, this supposed gender difference is probably better seen as a status difference. For more on gender and communication, see this chapter's Application.

### Psychological Disorders

In terms of the *overall* incidence of mental disorders, only minimal gender differences have been found. When researchers assess the prevalence of *specific* disorders, however, they do find some rather consistent gender differences (Klose & Jacobi, 2004; Nolen-Hoeksema & Keita, 2003). Antisocial behavior, alcoholism, and other drug-related disorders are far more prevalent among men than among women. On the other

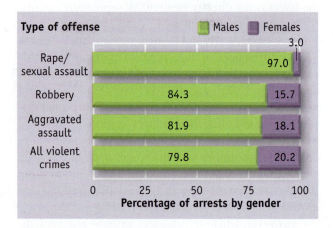

**Figure 11.6**
**Gender differences in violent crimes.** Males are arrested for violent crimes far more often than females, as these statistics show. These data support the findings of laboratory studies indicating that males are more physically aggressive than females. (Data from Bureau of Justice Statistics, 2006)

hand, women are about twice as likely as men to suffer from depression and anxiety disorders (phobias, for example). Even when comparing opposite-sex fraternal twins, females have a higher rate of mood disorders than males (Kendler, Myers, & Prescott, 2005).

Females also show higher rates of eating disorders (see the Chapter 14 Application). In addition, women *attempt* suicide more often than men, but men *complete* suicides (actually kill themselves) more frequently than women (Canetto, 2008; Maris, Berman, & Silverman, 2001). Throughout the lifespan, females are more likely to engage in deliberate self-harm than males (Hawton & Harriss, 2008).

In Chapter 3, we discussed posttraumatic stress disorder (PTSD). In a set of meta-analyses, Tolin and Foa (2006) found that females are more likely than males to develop PTSD, even when the traumatic events are the same. Other researchers attribute this difference to females' typically experiencing trauma at a younger age than males, perceptions of threat and loss, insufficient social support networks, and gender-specific biological reactions to trauma (Olff et al., 2007).

## Putting Gender Differences in Perspective

It pays to be cautious when interpreting gender differences. Although research has uncovered some genuine differences in behavior, remember that these are *group* differences. That is, they tell us nothing about individuals. Essentially, we are comparing the "average man" with the "average woman." Furthermore, as Hyde (2005, 2007b) argues, the differences between these groups are usually relatively small. **Figure 11.7** shows how scores on a trait might be distributed for men and women. Although the group averages are detectably

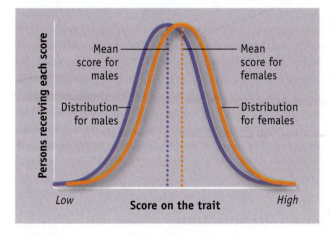

**Figure 11.7**

**The nature of group differences.** Gender differences are group differences that tell us little about individuals because of the great overlap between the groups. For a given trait, one gender may score higher on the average, but there is far more variation within each gender than between the genders.

different, you can see that there is great variability within each group (gender) and huge overlap between the two group distributions. *Ultimately, the similarities between women and men greatly outweigh the differences.* Thus, a gender difference that shows up on the average does not by itself tell us anything about you or any other unique individual.

A second essential point is that gender accounts for only a minute proportion of the differences between individuals. Using complicated statistical procedures, it is possible to gauge the influence of gender (or other factors) on behavior. These tests often show that factors other than gender (for example, the social context in which behavior occurs) are far more important determinants of differences between individuals (Yoder & Kahn, 2003).

Another point to keep in mind is that when gender differences are found, they do not mean that one gender is better than the other (Halpern, 2004). As Diane Halpern (1997) humorously notes, "It is about as meaningful to ask 'Which is the smarter sex?' . . . as it is to ask 'Which has the better genitals?'" (p. 1092). The problem is not with gender differences, but with how these differences are evaluated by the larger society.

Although gender differences in personality and behavior are relatively few in number and small in size, sometimes it seems otherwise. How come? One explanation focuses on gender-based differences in social roles. Alice Eagly's (1987) **social role theory asserts that minor gender differences are exaggerated by the different social roles that males and females occupy.** For example, because women are assigned the role of caregiver, they learn to behave in nurturing ways. Over time, people come to associate such role-related behaviors with individuals of a given gender, not with the roles they play. In other words, people come to see nurturing as a female trait rather than a characteristic that anyone in a nurturing role would demonstrate. This is one way that gender stereotypes develop and persist.

**Alice Eagly**

Another explanation for discrepancies between beliefs and reality is that the differences actually reside in the eye of the beholder, not the beholdee. **Social constructionism asserts that individuals construct their own reality based on societal expectations, conditioning, and self-socialization** (Hyde, 1996; Marecek, 2001). According to social constructionists, people's specific beliefs about gender (as well as their tendency to look for gender differences) are rooted in the "gendered" messages and conditioning that permeate socialization experiences. To better understand these issues, we next explore the role of biological and environmental factors as likely sources of gender differences.

# Biological Origins of Gender Differences

**LEARNING OBJECTIVES**

- Summarize evolutionary explanations for gender differences.
- Review the evidence linking gender differences in cognitive abilities to brain organization.
- Describe the evidence relating hormones to gender differences, both prenatally and after birth.

Are the gender differences that *do* exist biologically built in, or are they acquired through socialization? This is the age-old question of nature versus nurture. The "nature" theorists concentrate on how biological disparities between the genders contribute to differences in behavior. "Nurture" theorists, on the other hand, emphasize the role of learning and environmental influences. Although we will discuss biological and environmental influences separately, keep in mind that most contemporary researchers and theorists in this area recognize that biological and environmental factors interact. Let's first look at three biologically based lines of inquiry on this topic: evolutionary explanations, brain organization, and hormonal influences.

## Evolutionary Explanations

Evolutionary psychologists suggest that gender differences in behavior reflect different natural selection pressures operating on the genders over the course of human history (Archer, 1996; Geary, 2007). That is, natural selection favors behaviors that maximize the chances of passing on genes to the next generation (reproductive success).

To support their assertions, evolutionary psychologists look for gender differences that are consistent across cultures (Kenrick & Trost, 1993, Kenrick, Trost, & Sundie, 2004). Is there consistency across cultures for the better-documented gender differences? Despite some fascinating exceptions, gender differences in cognitive abilities, aggression, and sexual behavior *are* found in many cultures (Beller & Gafni, 1996; Halpern, 2000). According to evolutionary psychologists, these consistent differences have emerged because males and females have been confronted with different adaptive demands. For example, males supposedly are more *sexually active and permissive* because they invest less than females in the process of procreation and can maximize

their reproductive success by seeking many sexual partners (Buss & Kenrick, 1998, Webster, 2009). However, it is important to remember that even in cross-cultural work, there are more differences *within* each gender than *between* the genders, especially when it comes to cognitive abilities (Kenrick et al., 2004).

The gender gap in *aggression* is also explained in terms of reproductive fitness. Because females are more selective about mating than males are, males have to engage in more competition for sexual partners than females do. Greater aggressiveness is thought to be adaptive for males in this competition for sexual access because it should foster social dominance over other males (Kenrick & Trost, 1993). Evolutionary theorists assert that gender differences in *spatial abilities* reflect the division of labor in ancestral hunting-and-gathering societies in which males typically handled the hunting and females the gathering. Males' superiority on most spatial tasks has been attributed to the adaptive demands of hunting (Newcombe, 2007). However, the research offers little actual support for this hypothesis for any species (Jones, Braithwaite, & Healy, 2003).

Evolutionary analyses of gender differences are interesting, but controversial. While it is eminently plausible that evolutionary forces could have led to some divergence between males and females in typical behavior, evolutionary hypotheses are highly speculative and difficult to test empirically (Fausto-Sterling, 1992; Halpern, 2000). In addition, evolutionary theory can be used to claim that the status quo in society is the inevitable outcome of evolutionary forces. Thus, if males have dominant status over females, natural selection must have favored this arrangement. The crux of the problem is that evolutionary analyses can be used to explain almost anything. For instance, if the situation regarding mental rotation were reversed—if females scored higher than males—evolutionary theorists might attribute females' superiority to the adaptive demands of gathering food, weaving baskets, and making clothes—and it would be difficult to prove otherwise.

## Brain Organization

Some theorists propose that male and female brains are organized differently, which might account for gender differences in some gender-specific abilities (Lippa, 2005). As you may know, the human brain is divided into two halves. The ***cerebral hemispheres*** are the

---

**WEB LINK 11.3** **Great Ideas in Personality: Evolutionary Psychology and Sociobiology**

This site includes a major collection of resources supporting and opposing evolutionary psychology and sociobiology—the theory that human behavior is predominantly governed by biological forces, particularly those arising from one's genes.

---

**right and left halves of the cerebrum, which is the convoluted outer layer of the brain.** The cerebrum, the largest and most complicated part of the human brain, is responsible for most complex mental activities. Some evidence suggests that the right and left cerebral hemispheres are specialized to handle different cognitive tasks (Sperry, 1982; Springer & Deutsch, 1998). For example, it appears that the *left hemisphere* is more actively involved in *verbal and mathematical processing,* while the *right hemisphere* is specialized to handle *visual-spatial and other nonverbal processing.*

After these findings on hemispheric specialization surfaced, some researchers began looking for disparities between male and female brain organization as a way to explain the then-observed gender differences in verbal and spatial skills. Some thought-provoking findings have been reported. For instance, males exhibit more cerebral specialization than females (Bryden, 1988; Hines, 1990). In other words, males tend to depend more heavily than females on the left hemisphere in verbal processing and on the right hemisphere in spatial processing. Gender differences have also been found in the size of the **corpus callosum, the band of fibers connecting the two hemispheres of the brain** (Gur & Gur, 2007; Steinmetz et al., 1995). More specifically, some studies suggest that females tend to have a larger corpus callosum. This greater size might allow for better interhemispheric transfer of information, which in turn might underlie the more bilateral organization of female brains (Innocenti, 1994, Lippa, 2005). Thus, some theorists have argued that these differences in brain organization are responsible for gender differences in verbal and spatial ability (Clements et al. 2006; Kimura & Hampson, 1993).

Although this idea is intriguing, there are some important limitations in this line of reasoning. First, studies have not consistently found that males have more specialized brain organization than females (Fausto-Sterling, 1992; Kaiser et al., 2007, 2009), and the finding of a larger corpus callosum in females does not always show up (Hines, 1990). Second, because a significant amount of brain development occurs over the first five to ten years after birth, during which time males and females are socialized differently, it is possible that different life experiences may accumulate to produce slight differences in brain organization (Hood et al., 1987). In other words, the biological factors that supposedly cause gender differences in cognitive functioning may actually reflect the influence of environmental factors. Third, gender accounts for only a small amount of the variance in lateralization; it's more dependent on the type of task (Boles, 2005). Finally, it's important to remember that male and female brains are much more similar than they are different.

Consequently, even though the popular press has often touted the idea that there are "male brains" and

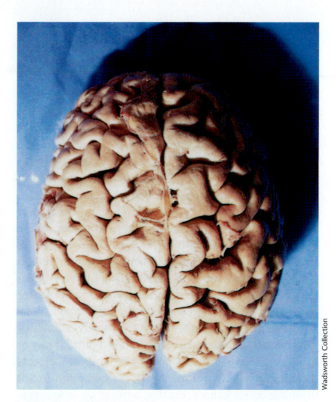

Studies have shown that the brain's cerebral hemispheres, shown here, are somewhat specialized in the kinds of cognitive tasks they handle and that such specialization is more pronounced in males than in females. Whether this difference bears any relation to gender differences in behavior is yet to be determined.

*Wadsworth Collection*

"female brains" that are fundamentally different (Bleier, 1984), the notion that cerebral specialization is linked to gender differences in mental abilities is still under debate. As brain imaging techniques such as MRIs become more sophisticated, the research in this area may advance.

## Hormonal Influences

As we discussed in Chapter 3, *hormones* are chemical substances released into the bloodstream by the endocrine glands. Biological gender is determined by sex chromosomes: An XX pairing produces a female, and an XY pairing produces a male. However, both male and female embryos are essentially the same until about 8 to 12 weeks after conception. Around this time, male and female gonads (sex glands) begin to produce different hormonal secretions. The high level of *androgens* (male hormones such as testosterone) in males and the low level of androgens in females lead to the differentiation of male and female genital organs.

The influence of prenatal hormones on genitalia is clear; however, their influence on behavior is harder to establish and becomes apparent only when something interferes with normal prenatal hormonal secretions (Hines, 2004). Scientists have studied children born to mothers given an androgen-like drug to prevent miscarriage. Two trends have been noted in this research (Collaer & Hines, 1995). First, girls exposed prenatally to abnormally high levels of androgens exhibit more male-typical behavior than other girls do. For example, girls with *congenital adrenal hyperplasia* (elevated levels of androgens) tend to show increased interest in "male" toys, regardless of parental encouragement to play with "female" toys (Pasterski et al., 2005; Servin et al., 2003). Second, boys exposed prenatally to abnormally low levels of androgens exhibit more female-typical behavior than other boys.

These findings suggest that prenatal hormones shape gender differences in humans. But there are a number of problems with this evidence (Basow, 1992; Fausto-Sterling, 1992). First, there is much more and much stronger evidence for females than for males. Second, behavior is always subject to social factors after birth. Third, it's always dangerous to draw conclusions about the general population based on small samples of people who have abnormal conditions. Fourth, most of the endocrine disorders studied have multiple effects (besides altering hormone level) that make it difficult to isolate actual causes. Finally, most of the research is

necessarily correlational, and it is always risky to draw causal conclusions from correlational data.

Postnatally, the hormone testosterone plays an important role in *sexual desire* for both men and women (Bancroft, 2002a). That is, when testosterone is reduced or eliminated, both men and women show decreases in sexual drive. Additionally, high levels of testosterone in men and women correlate with higher rates of *sexual activity* (van Anders, Hamilton, & Watson, 2007). Testosterone has also been linked with higher levels of *aggression* (impulsive and antisocial behavior) in humans, but the picture is complicated because aggressive behavior can produce increases in testosterone (Dabbs, 2000). In fact, a recent study demonstrated that simply interacting with a gun increased testosterone levels in males (Klinesmith, Kasser, & McAndrew, 2006).

The overall evidence suggests that, aside from obvious physical differences, biological factors such as evolution, brain structure, and hormones play a relatively minor role in gender differences. In contrast, efforts to link gender differences to disparities in the way males and females are socialized have proved more fruitful. We consider this perspective next.

# Environmental Origins of Gender Differences

### LEARNING OBJECTIVES

● Define socialization and gender roles, and describe Margaret Mead's findings on the variability of gender roles and their implications.
● Explain how reinforcement and punishment, observational learning, and self-socialization operate in gender-role socialization.
● Describe how parents and peers influence gender-role socialization.
● Understand how schools and the media influence gender-role socialization.

*Socialization* **is the acquisition of the norms and roles expected of people in a particular society.** This process includes all the efforts made by a society to ensure that its members learn to behave in a manner that's considered appropriate. Teaching children about gender roles is an important aspect of the socialization process. *Gender roles* **are cultural expectations about what is appropriate behavior for each gender.** For example, in our culture women have been expected to rear children, cook meals, clean house, and do laundry. On the other hand, men have been expected to be the family breadwinner, do yardwork, and tinker with cars.

Are gender roles in other cultures similar to those seen in our society? Generally, yes—but not necessarily. Despite a fair amount of cross-cultural consistency in gender roles, some dramatic variability occurs as well (Gibbons, 2000). For instance, anthropologist Margaret Mead (1950) conducted a now-classic study of three

tribes in New Guinea. In one tribe, *both* genders followed our masculine role expectations (the Mundugumor); in another, *both* genders approximated our feminine role (the Arapesh). In a third tribe, the male and female roles were roughly the *reverse* of our own (the Tchambuli). Such remarkable discrepancies between cultures existing within 100 miles of one another demonstrate that gender roles are not a matter of biological destiny. Instead, like other roles, gender roles are acquired through socialization.

Keep in mind that gender roles and gender stereotypes are intertwined, each fueling the other. As we noted earlier, Eagly's social role theory suggests that gender differences often occur (and seem bigger than they actually are) because males and females are guided by different role expectations. In the next section, we'll discuss how society teaches individuals about gender roles.

## Processes in Gender-Role Socialization

How do people acquire gender roles? Several key learning processes come into play, including reinforcement and punishment, observational learning, and self-socialization.

### Reinforcement and Punishment

In part, gender roles are shaped by the power of rewards and punishment—the key processes in operant conditioning (see Chapter 2). Parents, teachers, peers, and others often reinforce (usually with tacit approval) "gender-appropriate" behavior (Fagot & Hagan, 1991; Lippa, 2005). For example, a young boy who has hurt himself may be told that "big boys don't cry." If he succeeds in inhibiting his crying, he may get a pat on the back or a warm smile—both powerful reinforcers. Over time, a consistent pattern of such reinforcement will strengthen the boy's tendency to "act like a man" and suppress emotional displays.

Most parents take gender-appropriate behavior for granted and don't go out of their way to reward it. On the other hand, parents are much less tolerant of gender-inappropriate behavior, especially in their sons (Lytton & Romney, 1991; Sandnabba & Ahlberg, 1999). For instance, a 10-year-old boy who enjoys playing with dollhouses will probably elicit strong disapproval. Reactions usually involve ridicule or verbal reprimands rather than physical punishment.

### Observational Learning

Younger children commonly imitate the behavior of a parent or an older sibling. This imitation, or *observational learning,* occurs when a child's behavior is influenced by observing others. These others are called *models.* Parents serve as models for children, as do siblings, teachers, relatives, and others who are important in children's lives. Models are not limited to real people; television, movie, and cartoon characters can also serve as models.

According to *social cognitive theory* (see Chapter 2), young children are more likely to imitate people who are nurturant, powerful, and similar to them (Bussey & Bandura, 1984, 1999, 2004). Children imitate both genders, but most children are prone to imitate same-gender models. Thus, observational learning often leads young girls to play with dolls, dollhouses, and toy stoves. By contrast, young boys are more likely to play with toy trucks, miniature gas stations, and tool kits. Interestingly, same-gender peers may be even more influential models than parents are (Maccoby, 2002).

### Self-Socialization

Children are not merely passive recipients of gender-role socialization. Rather, they play an active role in this process, beginning early in life (Lippa, 2005; Martin, Ruble, & Szkrybalo, 2002). Because society labels people, characteristics, behavior, and activities by gender, children learn that gender is an important social category. For example, they learn that females wear dresses and males don't. Around 2 to 3 years of age, children begin to identify themselves as male or female (Martin et al., 2002). One study found that children start using gender labels as early as 19 months and that using labels is associated with increased gender-typed play (Zosuls et al., 2009). Once children have these labels, they begin to organize the various pieces of gender-relevant information into gender schemas. **Gender schemas are cognitive structures that guide the processing of gender-relevant information.** Basically, gender schemas work like lenses that cause people to view and organize the world in terms of gender (Bem, 1993).

Parents typically reward "gender-appropriate" behavior in their children.

Children learn behaviors appropriate to their gender roles very early in life. According to social learning theory, girls tend to do the sorts of things their mothers do, while boys tend to follow in their fathers' footsteps.

Self-socialization begins when children link the gender schema for their own gender to their self-concept. Once this connection is made, children are motivated to selectively attend to activities and information that are consistent with the schema for their own gender. For example, Terrance knows that he is a boy and also has a "boy" schema that he attaches to himself. Now his self-esteem is dependent on how well he lives up to his boy schema. In this way, children get involved in their own socialization. They are "gender detectives," working diligently to discover the rules that are supposed to govern their behavior (Martin & Ruble, 2004).

## Sources of Gender-Role Socialization

Four major sources of gender-role messages are parents, peers, schools, and the media. Keep in mind that gender-role socialization varies depending on one's culture (Best & Thomas, 2004; Corby, Hodges, & Perry, 2007). For example, black families typically make fewer distinctions between girls and boys compared to white families (Hill, 2002); as a result, gender roles are more flexible for black women (Littlefield, 2003). By contrast, gender roles are relatively rigidly defined in Asian and Hispanic families (Chia et al., 1994; Comas-Diaz, 1987). Asian American families typically encourage subservience in their daughters (Tsai & Uemera, 1988). Also, gender roles are changing, so the generalizations that follow may say more about how *you* were socialized than about how your children will be.

### Parents

Although a meta-analysis of 172 studies of parental socialization practices suggests that parents don't treat girls and boys as differently as one might expect (Lytton & Romney, 1991), there are some important disparities. For one thing, there is a strong tendency for both mothers and fathers to emphasize and encourage *play activities* that are "gender appropriate." For example, studies show that parents encourage boys and girls to play with different types of toys (Wood, Desmarais, & Gugula, 2002). As **Figure 11.8** indicates, gender differences are found in toy preferences, and children as young as preschoolers have a clear definition of girl toys and boy toys (Freeman, 2007). Even in private child-care settings, the toys that are available for children are often gender stereotypic (Chick, Heilman-Houser, & Hunter, 2002). Generally, boys have less leeway to play with "feminine" toys than girls do with "masculine" toys.

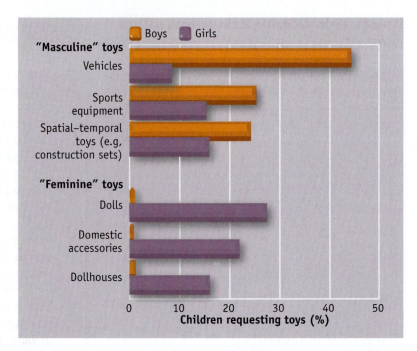

**Figure 11.8**

**Toy preferences and gender.** This graph depicts the percentages of boys and girls asking for various types of toys in letters to Santa Claus (adapted from Richardson & Simpson, 1982). Boys and girls differed substantially in their toy preferences, which probably reflects the effects of gender-role socialization.

Source: Adapted from Richardson, J. G., & Simpson, C. H. (1982). Children, gender and social structure: An analysis of the contents of letters to Santa Claus. *Child Development, 53*, 429–436. Copyright © 1982 by the Society for Research in Child Development, Inc. Reproduced with permission of Blackwell Publishing Ltd.

In addition, the picture books parents buy for their children typically depict characters engaging in gender stereotypic activities (Gooden & Gooden, 2001). An analysis of 200 bestselling and award-winning children's books found nearly twice as many male as female main characters; also, the male characters were more

Boys are under more pressure than girls to behave in gender-appropriate ways. Little boys who show an interest in dolls are likely to be chastised by both parents and peers.

likely to be in the illustrations, and the female characters were more nurturing and less likely to have an occupation (Hamilton et al., 2006). Even books that parents and teachers rate as "nonsexist" portray female characters with stereotypic personalities, chores, and leisure activities (Diekman & Murnen, 2004). Interestingly, this gender bias holds for representations of parents in these books as well. In a content analysis of 200 prominent children's picture books, Anderson and Hamilton (2005) found that fathers were underrepresented and, when they did appear, were withdrawn and ineffectual.

Another way parents emphasize gender is in the assignment of *household chores* (Cunningham, 2001; Lytton & Romney, 1991). Tasks are doled out on the basis of gender stereotypes: Girls usually do laundry and dishes, whereas boys mow the lawn and sweep the garage.

## Peers

Children's preferences for play activities are also highly influenced by peers (Lippa, 2005). Peers form an important network for learning about gender-appropriate and gender-inappropriate behavior. Between the ages of 4 and 6, children tend to separate into same-gender groups, and these preferences appear to be child- rather than adult-driven (Fabes, Hanish, & Martin, 2003). From 6 to about age 12, boys and girls spend much more time with same-gender than other-gender peers. Moreover, according to Eleanor Maccoby (1998, 2002), over time boys' and girls' groups develop different "subcultures" (shared understandings and interests) that strongly shape youngsters' gender-role socialization (Maccoby, 1998, 2002).

Play among same-gender peers takes different forms for boys and girls as well (Maccoby, 1998, 2002). Boys play in larger groups and roam farther away from home, whereas girls prefer smaller groups and stay near the house. In addition, high status in boys' groups tends to be achieved by engaging in dominant behavior (telling others what to do and enforcing orders). In contrast, girls usually express their wishes as suggestions rather than demands. Also, boys engage in rough-and-tumble play much more frequently than girls do (Lippa, 2005).

Because both boys and girls are critical of peers who violate traditional gender norms, they perpetuate stereotypical behavior. Among children ages 3–11, boys are devalued more than girls for dressing like the other gender, whereas girls are evaluated more negatively than boys for playing like the other gender—for instance, loudly and roughly versus quietly and gently (Blakemore, 2003). Further, "gender atypical boys" more often report being a victim of bullying, more loneliness, and greater distress than their "typical" peers (Young & Sweeting, 2004). Associations between negative adjustment and gender atypical behavior, however, appear to be reduced with positive parenting styles (Alanko et al., 2008).

## Schools

The school environment figures importantly in socializing gender roles (Meece & Scantlebury, 2006; Sadker & Sadker, 1994). Children's grade-school *textbooks* have often ignored or stereotyped girls and women (AAUW Educational Foundation, 1992). Traditionally, these books have portrayed males as clever, heroic, and adventurous, whereas females have been shown performing domestic chores. Although the depiction of stereotypical gender roles has declined considerably since the 1970s, researchers still find significant differences in how males and females are portrayed, even in supposedly nonsexist books (Diekman & Murnen, 2004). Many high school and college textbooks also contain gender bias. The most common problems are using generic masculine language ("policeman" versus "police officer" and so forth) and portraying males and females in stereotypic roles. In addition, subtle word choices can reinforce stereotypes, such as passivity in females (for example, women were *given* the right to vote); (Meece & Scantlebury, 2006). Gender bias has even been reported in popular medical textbooks, where relevant gender-specific information is scarce (Dijkstra, Verdonk, & Largro-Janssen, 2008)

Gender bias in schools also shows up in *teachers' treatment of boys and girls.* Preschool and grade-school teachers often reward gender-appropriate behavior in their pupils (Fagot et al., 1985). Teachers also tend to pay greater attention to boys—helping them, praising them, and scolding them more than girls (Beaman, Wheldall, & Kemp, 2006; Sadker & Sadker, 1994). By contrast, girls tend to be less visible in the classroom and to receive less encouragement for academic achievement from teachers. These findings have been replicated in other cultures as well (Best & Thomas, 2004). Overall, these teacher-student interactions reinforce the gender stereotype of male competence and dominance (Meece & Scantlebury, 2006). Even with this bias, however, there is still concern in education today about the "underachieving male" (Beaman et al., 2006).

Gender bias also shows up in *academic and career counseling.* Despite the fact that females obtain higher grades than males (on the average) in all subjects from elementary school through college (Halpern, 2004, 2006), many counselors continue to encourage male students to pursue high-status careers in medicine or engineering while guiding female students toward less prestigious careers (Read, 1991). Stereotypic beliefs that lead to differential treatment by counselors and teachers can facilitate barriers to women's career choices, especially in the areas of science and math (Betz, 2006; Halpern, 2006; Halpern, Bendow et al., 2007).

## The Media

Television is yet another source of gender-role socialization (Luecke-Aleksa et al., 1995). American youngsters spend a lot of time watching TV (see **Figure 11.9**). A recent Nielsen Media Research report (2006) found that TV viewing is at an all time high, with the average household watching 8 hours, 14 minutes of TV per day! A systematic review of the literature indicates that contemporary youth view an average of 1.8–2.8 hours of TV a day, with 28% watching more than 4 hours per day (Marshall, Gorely, & Biddle, 2006). African American children and adolescents spend more time in front of the tube than their white peers (Roberts et al., 1999). Approximately 35% of children are raised in homes where the TV is on "always" or "most of the time," and these children have lower reading ability than their peers (Vandewater et al., 2005). In one study nearly two-thirds of adolescents had a television in their bedroom, and those who did were less likely to engage in healthy behaviors than those without (Barr-Anderson, van den Berg, & Neumark-Sztainer, 2008).

An analysis of male and female characters on prime-time *television programs* showed that the number and variety of roles of female TV characters have increased over the past 30 years but that these shifts lag behind the actual changes in women's lives (Glascock,

**WEB LINK 11.4**  **Center for Screen-Time Awareness**

This site is the home of TV Turnoff Week. It encourages screen-time reduction as "a vital and integral part of all plans that improve health, education and wellness while building stronger families and communities." It includes a thorough set of facts and figures based on recent Neilson Media Research Group reports.

2001; Signorielli & Bacue, 1999). Compared to males, females appear less often, are less likely to be employed (especially in prestigious positions), are more likely to be younger, and are more likely to appear in secondary and comedy roles. As compared to female characters, males are still more likely to demonstrate competence-related behaviors such as reaching a goal, showing ingenuity, and answering questions (Aubrey & Harrison, 2004). In traditional children's adventure *cartoons* (as opposed to educational cartoons), male characters appear more often and engage in more physical aggression, whereas female characters are much more likely to show fear, act romantic, be polite, and act supportive (Leaper et al., 2002).

*Television commercials* are even more gender-stereotyped than TV programs (Furnham & Mak, 1999; Lippa 2005). Women are frequently shown worrying about trivial matters such as laundry and cleaning products, whereas men appear as bold outdoorsmen or energetic sports fans. In a study of gender stereotyping in TV commercials on five continents, researchers reported that, in all the countries studied, men appeared more often than women in both on- and off-screen announcer roles (Furnham & Mak, 1999). In a content analysis of 1,337 prime time commercials from the three major networks, Ganahl and colleagues (2003) found that women were underrepresented in commercials (except for beauty products) and that they often played support roles for men. In another content analysis comparing the major U.S. networks to an African American niche station (Black Entertainment Television—BET), researchers found that the majority of the characters in prime time commercials are male and white, even on BET (Messineo, 2008).

Another manifestation of gender bias is television's inordinate *emphasis on women's physical appearance* (Lauzen & Dozier, 2002). Males on television may or may not be good-looking, but the vast majority of females are young, attractive, and sexy (Signorielli & Bacue, 1999). Overweight female characters are much more likely than male characters to receive negative comments about their weight (Fouts & Burggraf, 1999; Fouts & Vaughan, 2002). As you'll see in the Chapter 14 Application, these cultural expectations have been cited as a cause of the disproportionately high

| Television Viewing Habits | | | |
|---|---|---|---|
| | **Amount of television viewed per day** | | |
| | **≤ 2 hrs** | **3–4 hrs** | **≥ 5 hrs** |
| *Grade* | | | |
| 9th | 49.0 | 32.3 | 18.7 |
| 10th | 53.7 | 31.1 | 15.3 |
| 11th | 62.3 | 26.4 | 11.3 |
| 12th | 66.9 | 24.6 | 8.4 |
| *All females* | *59.0* | *27.5* | *13.5* |
| Black | 25.6 | 37.0 | 37.4 |
| Hispanic | 48.4 | 36.5 | 15.1 |
| White | 69.0 | 24.1 | 6.9 |
| *All males* | *55.5* | *30.3* | *14.2* |
| Black | 27.0 | 32.1 | 40.8 |
| Hispanic | 47.3 | 36.4 | 16.3 |
| White | 62.8 | 29.5 | 7.7 |

### Figure 11.9

**Television viewing habits.** American youngsters spend a lot of time watching TV. This table presents the percentages of high school students who report watching given amounts of television each day.

Source: Adapted from Lowry, R., Wechsler, H., Galuska, D. A., Fulton, J. E., & Kann, L. (2002). Television viewing and its associations with overweight, sedentary lifestyle, and insufficient fruits and vegetables among US high school students: Differences by race, ethnicity, and gender. *Journal of School Health, 72*(10), 413–421. Copyright © 2009, 2002 American School Health Association. Used by permission of John Wiley and Sons.

incidence of eating disorders in females and are related to the development of unhealthy body images (Smolak, 2006).

TV is not the only medium that perpetuates gender stereotypes; gender-role socialization is a multimedia event. Most *video games* push a hypermasculine stereotype featuring search-and-destroy missions, fighter pilot battles, and male sports (Lippa, 2005). Of the few video games directed at girls, the great majority of them are highly stereotypic (shopping and Barbie games). Also, *music videos* frequently portray women as sex objects and men as dominating and aggressive (Sommers-Flanagan, Sommers-Flanagan, & Davis, 1993), and these portrayals appear to influence viewers' gender-role and sexual attitudes (Kalof, 1999; Ward, Hansbrough, & Walker, 2005). As demonstrated in a content analysis of educational software for young children, most software programs had more male than female characters, portrayed males in more stereotypical ways, and focused more on gender-stereotypic ap-

**WEB LINK 11.5  Gender and Race in Media**

The University of Iowa's Communications Studies Program offers a focused guide to the ways in which gender and racial differences are expressed in various media, including a set of materials dealing with gender and advertising.

pearance for females (Sheldon, 2004). Even daily newspaper comics follow these gender-stereotypic patterns (Glascock & Preston-Schreck, 2004).

Do the media actually influence children's views about gender? A meta-analysis reported a link between children's exposure to gender stereotyping in the media and the acquisition of gender-stereotyped beliefs (Oppliger, 2007). Admittedly, this research is correlational, so it is likely that other factors—such as parental values—come into play as well. Nonetheless, once gender stereotypes are learned, they are difficult to change.

# Gender-Role Expectations

### LEARNING OBJECTIVES

- List five elements of the traditional male role, and contrast it with the modern male role.
- Identify three common problems associated with the traditional male role.
- List three major expectations of the female role.
- Identify three common problems associated with the female role.
- Describe two ways in which women are victimized by sexism.

Traditional gender roles are based on several unspoken assumptions: that all members of the same gender have basically the same traits, that the traits of one gender are very different from the traits of the other gender, and that masculine traits are more highly valued. In recent decades, many social critics and theorists in psychology

and other fields have scrutinized gender roles, identifying the essential features and the ramifications of traditional roles. In this section, we review the research and theory in this area and note changes in gender roles over the past 30 to 40 years. We begin with the male role.

## Role Expectations for Males

A number of psychologists have sought to pinpoint the essence of the traditional male role (Brannon, 1976; Levant, 1996, 2003; Pleck, 1995). Many consider *antifemininity* to be the central theme that runs through the male gender role. That is, "real men" shouldn't act in any way that might be perceived as feminine. For example, men should not publicly display vulnerable emotions, should avoid feminine occupations, and should not show obvious interest in relationships—especially homosexual ones. Five key attributes constitute the traditional male role (Brannon, 1976; Jansz, 2000):

1. *Achievement.* To prove their masculinity, men need to beat out other men at work and at sports. Having a high-status job, driving an expensive car, and making lots of money are aspects of this element.

*"Norman won't collaborate."*

© Robert Weber/The New Yorker Collection/www.cartoonbank.com

2. *Aggression.* Men should be tough and fight for what they believe is right. They should aggressively defend themselves and those they love against threats.

3. *Autonomy.* Men should be self-reliant and not admit to being dependent on others.

4. *Sexuality.* Real men are heterosexual and are highly motivated to pursue sexual activities and conquests.

5. *Stoicism.* Men should not share their pain or express their "soft" feelings. They should be cool and calm under pressure.

There is evidence that manhood, as opposed to womanhood, is more precarious (Bosson et al., 2009; Vandello et al, 2008). That is, it is more susceptible to threat and requires social proof and validation. Unfortunately, harmful demonstrations of masculinity such as displays of physical aggression are typical ways of defending one's manhood when this status is threatened (Bosson et al., 2009). This behavior is often at odds with modern gender-role expectations. According to Joseph Pleck (1995), who has written extensively on this issue, in the *traditional male role,* masculinity is validated by individual physical strength, aggressiveness, and emotional inexpressiveness. In the *modern male role,* however, masculinity is validated by economic achievement, organizational power, emotional control (even over anger), and emotional sensitivity and self-expression, but only with women.

Thus, in modern societies, the traditional male role coexists with some new expectations. Some theorists use the plural "masculinities" to describe these variations in the male gender role (Schrock & Schwalbe, 2009; Smiler, 2004). This flux in expectations means that males are experiencing role inconsistencies and pressures to behave in ways that conflict with traditional masculinity: to communicate personal feelings, to nurture children and share in housework, to integrate sexuality with love, and to curb aggression (Levant, 1996, 2003). Some psychologists believe that these pressures have shaken traditional masculine norms sufficiently that many men are experiencing a masculinity crisis and diminished pride in being a man (Levant, 1996, 2003). Brooks (2010) argues that distress over ever-changing gender roles fuels three major problems—violence, substance

abuse, and sexual misconduct—as men channel their distress into these destructive behaviors. The good news is that boys and men are beginning to get more attention from psychological theorists, researchers, and clinicians.

## Problems with the Male Role

It is often assumed that only females suffer from the constricting binds of traditional gender roles. Not so. Increasingly, the costs of the male role are a cause for concern (Levant, 1996; Pleck, 1995). As we examine the relevant research, keep in mind that male gender roles "are not to be regarded as 'given,' neither psychological nor biologically, but rather as socially constructed" (Levant & Richmond, 2007, p. 141). Therefore, many researchers are calling for a closer examination of the influence of culture on gender-role stress (Carter et al., 2005; Wester et al. 2006).

### Pressure to Succeed

Most men are socialized to be highly competitive and are taught that a man's masculinity is measured by the size of his paycheck and job status. As Christopher Kilmartin (2000) notes, "There is always another man who has more money, higher status, a more attractive partner, or a bigger house. The traditional man . . . must constantly work harder and faster" (p. 13).

The majority of men who have internalized the success ethic are unable to fully realize their dreams. This is a particular problem for African American and Hispanic men, who experience more barriers to financial success than European American men do (Biernat & Kobrynowicz, 1997). How does this "failure" affect men? Although many are able to adjust to it, many are not. The men in this latter group are likely to suffer from shame and low self-esteem (Kilmartin, 2000). Men's emphasis on success also makes it more likely that they will spend long hours on the job. This pattern in turn decreases the amount of time families can spend together and increases the amount of time partners spend on housework and child care. A significantly smaller proportion of men between the ages of 18 and 37 are work focused (they want to spend more time with their families) compared to men age 38 and older (Families and Work Institute, 2004).

Gender differences in pressure to succeed might be more perceived than real. When asked about *perceptions,* college students rated the typical man as worrying about achievement more than the typical woman. However, when asked about their *own* worry, females reported more worry about achievement than male students did (Wood et al. 2005). Perhaps this finding reflects men's not wanting to express that they are worrying about anything.

**WEB LINK 11.6  American Men's Studies Association**

This site collects academic resources to advance "the critical study of men and masculinities." It includes links to many other sites and organizations interested in the male experience.

Most men are socialized to be highly competitive and are taught that a man's masculinity is measured by the size of his paycheck and his job status. Experiences such as being laid off can lead to shame and low self-esteem.

## The Emotional Realm

Most young boys are trained to believe that men should be strong, tough, cool, and detached (Brody, 2000; Jansz, 2000). Thus, they learn early to hide vulnerable emotions such as love, joy, and sadness because they believe that such feelings are feminine and imply weakness. Over time, some men become strangers to their own emotional lives (Levant, 1996). With the ex-

ception of anger, men with traditional views of masculinity are more likely to suppress outward emotions and to fear emotions, supposedly because such feelings may lead to a loss of composure (Jakupcak et al., 2003). Keep in mind, however, that some researchers challenge this view (Wong & Rochlen, 2005). As with many gender gaps, differences in emotionality tend to be small, inconsistent, and dependent on the situation. For instance, Robertson and colleagues (2001) found that males who were more traditionally masculine were more emotionally expressive in a structured exercise than when they were simply asked to talk about their emotions.

Males' difficulty with "tender" emotions has serious consequences. First, as we saw in Chapter 3, suppressed emotions can contribute to stress-related disorders. And worse, men are less likely than women to seek social support or help from health professionals (Addis & Mahalik, 2003; Lane & Addis, 2005). Second, men's emotional inexpressiveness can cause problems in their relationships with partners and children. For example, men who endorse traditional masculine norms report lower relationship satisfaction, as do their female partners (Burn & Ward, 2005). Further, children whose fathers are warm, loving, and accepting toward them have higher self-esteem and lower rates of aggression and behavior problems (Rohner & Veneziano, 2001). On a positive note, fathers are increasingly involving themselves with their children. And 30% of fathers report that they take equal or greater responsibility for their children than their working wives do (Bond et al., 2003).

## Sexual Problems

Men often experience sexual problems that derive partly from their gender-role socialization, which gives them a "macho" sexual image to live up to. There are few things that men fear more than a sexual encounter

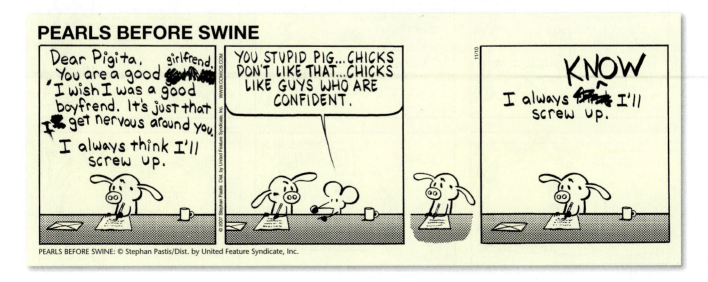

PEARLS BEFORE SWINE: © Stephan Pastis/Dist. by United Feature Syndicate, Inc.

in which they are unable to achieve an erection (Doyle, 1989). Unfortunately, these very fears often *cause* the dysfunction that men dread (see Chapter 12). The upshot is that men's obsession with sexual performance can produce anxiety that may interfere with their sexual responsiveness.

Another problem is that many men learn to confuse feelings of intimacy and sex. In other words, if a man experiences strong feelings of connectedness, he is likely to interpret them as sexual feelings. This confusion has a number of consequences (Kilmartin, 2000). For one thing, sex may be the only way some men can allow themselves to feel intimately connected to another. Thus, men's keen interest in sex may be driven, in part, by strong needs for emotional intimacy that don't get satisfied in other ways. The confusion of intimacy and sex may underlie the tendency for men (compared to women) to perceive eye contact, a compliment, an innocent smile, a friendly remark, or a brush against the arm as a sexual invitation (Kowalski, 1993). Finally, the sexualization of intimate feelings causes inappropriate anxiety when men feel affection for another man, thus promoting *homophobia* or sexual prejudice, *the intense intolerance of homosexuality*. Indeed, endorsement of traditional gender roles and hypermasculinity are both related to negative attitudes toward homosexuality (Parrott et al., 2008; Whitley, 2001).

## Role Expectations for Females

In the past 40 years, the role expectations for American women have undergone dramatic changes, especially with regard to work. Prior to the 1970s, a woman was expected to be a housewife and a stay-at-home mother. Today, there are three major expectations:

**1.** *The marriage mandate.* Remaining single is a trend that has been on the increase for several decades (Morris & DePaulo, 2009); however, there is still a stigma attached to singlehood in a society where marriage is the norm (Gordon, 2003). Most women are socialized to feel incomplete until they find a mate. Women attain adult status when they get married. In the context of marriage, women are expected to be responsible for cooking, cleaning, and other housework.

**2.** *The motherhood mandate.* A major imperative of the female role is to have children. This expectation has been termed the "motherhood mandate" (Rice & Else-Quest, 2006; Russo, 1979). The prevailing ideology of today's motherhood mandate is that women (but not necessarily men) should desire to have children,

DOONESBURY © 1975 G. B. Trudeau. Reprinted with permission of UNIVERSAL UCLICK. All rights reserved.

mothering should be wholly child-centered, and mothers should be self-sacrificing rather than persons who have their own needs and interests (Arendell, 2000; Vandello, 2008).

**3.** *Work outside the home.* Most of today's young women, especially those who are college educated, expect to work outside the home, and they also want a satisfying family life (Family and Work Institute, 2004; Konrad, 2003). As you can see in **Figure 11.10**, the percentage of women in the labor force has been steadily rising over the last 30 years. Yet research shows that husbands' careers continue to take priority over their wives' ambitions (Haas, 1999).

## Problems with the Female Role

Writers in the feminist movement generated some compelling analyses of the problems associated with the pre-1970s traditional role of wife and mother (Friedan, 1964; Millett, 1970). Many criticized the assumption that women, unlike men, did not need an independent identity; it should be sufficient to be Jim Smith's wife and Jason and Robin's mother. Increasingly over the past 40 years, girls and women have been encouraged to develop and use their talents, and work opportunities for women have greatly expanded. Still, there are problems with the female role.

### Diminished Career Aspirations

Despite recent efforts to increase women's opportunities for achievement, young women continue to have lower career aspirations than young men with comparable backgrounds and abilities (Hakim, 2006; Wilgosh, 2001). Also, they are more likely to underestimate their achievement than boys (who overestimate theirs),

**WEB LINK 11.7** **Feminist Majority Foundation**

This site brings together a massive set of resources dealing with issues from a feminist perspective.

especially when estimating performance on "masculine" tasks such as science and math (Eccles, 2001, 2007). This is a problem because science and math are the foundations for many high-paying, high-status careers, and it is often the lack of math background (as opposed to ability) that contributes to the inferior performance of some women (Betz, 2006; Dweck, 2007).

The discrepancy between women's abilities and their level of achievement has been termed the *ability-achievement gap* (Hyde, 1996). The roots of this gap seem to lie in the conflict between achievement and femininity that is built into the traditional female role. The marriage and motherhood mandates fuel women's focus on *heterosexual success*—learning how to attract and interest males as prospective mates. The resulting emphasis on dating and marriage can lead some women away from a challenging career—they worry that they will be seen as unfeminine if they boldly strive for success. Of course, this is not a concern for all women. And, because younger men are more supportive of their wives' working than older men are, this conflict should ease for younger women (Family and Work Institute, 2004).

### Juggling Multiple Roles

Another problem with the female role is that societal institutions have not kept pace with the reality of women's lives, especially if women choose motherhood. Today,

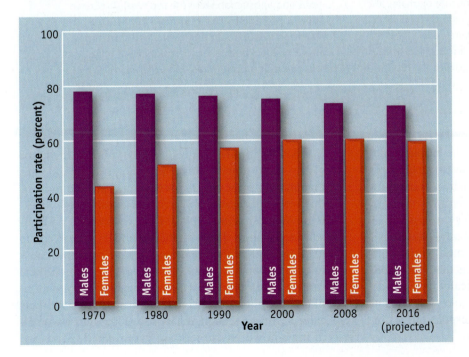

**Figure 11.10**

**Increases in women's workforce participation.** The percentage of women who work outside the home has increased steadily over the past century, especially since 1970, although it appears to be stabilizing at around 60%. (Data from the *Statistical Abstract of the United States*, 2010, Table 575)

# LIVING IN TODAY'S WORLD
## Gender Stereotypes and "Appearance Pressure"

The media, in all their forms, send messages about what is considered attractive for males and females. Images of these gender ideals pervade "women's" and "men's" magazines as well as those that focus on fitness (Vartanian, Giant, & Passino, 2001). Physically attractive men and women dominate television programs and commercials. This pattern is problematic because many of the images are computer enhanced and unrealistic. In an ironic use of the term, "reality" television shows such as *Extreme Makeover* depict real men and women undergoing extensive plastic surgery to improve their lives. The media message for today's women: Thin is "in"; for men: you need "six-pack abs" to be attractive.

Weight is particularly important for women. Typically girls have a greater drive for thinness and are more concerned with dieting than boys (Phares, Steinberg, & Thompson, 2004). For many years, this concern with thinness has existed among white and Asian Americans, but it has been a lesser concern among Hispanics and black Americans (Polivy & Herman, 2002). Unfortunately, some recent evidence suggests that the thin female ideal may be spreading to these two groups as well (Barnett, Keel, & Conoscenti, 2001; Bay-Cheng et al., 2002, but also see Schooler et al. 2004). Failure to live up to these ideals can create body dissatisfaction and lead to eating disorders (Smolak, 2006).

Today, males also seem to be experiencing "appearance pressure." Recent studies show that adolescent boys, college men, and adult males all prefer to be more muscular (Morrison, Morrison, & Hopkins, 2003; Olivardia, Pope, & Phillips, 2000). Pressure on males also appears to be coming from women, who prefer a large torso with narrow waist and hips (Maisey et al., 1999). More men are dieting, working out, and seeking surgery than has been true in the past (Olivardia et al., 2000).

Do televised images of body ideals have any impact on viewers? It seems that they do—negative ones (Grabe, Ward, & Hyde, 2008). For example, in one study, college men and women were exposed to either sexist ads, nonsexist ads, or no ads (Lavine, Sweeney, & Wager, 1999). (The sexist ads portrayed both men and women as sex objects as part of a bogus marketing research study.) The results showed that both the men and women who were exposed to sexist ads had greater body dissatisfaction than students in the other two conditions. Other research has reported similar findings using idealized images of men (Hobza et al., 2007). In a correlational study, the amount of exposure to ideal body images of women on television (based on viewing habits) was measured. Women with a lot of exposure to these ideal images were more likely to prefer a smaller waist and hips and a medium-sized bust for themselves (Harrison, 2003). Even in print media, boys who viewed idealized and objectified images of men's bodies in advertisements showed decreases in self-esteem (Farquhar & Wasylkiw, 2007).

The current social pressures to attain an ideal body shape push many individuals into unhealthy eating behaviors. Experts say that eating disorders are at an all-time high (Gleaves et al., 2000). And some males may turn to dangerous anabolic steroids to build up their muscle mass (Courtenay, 2000). Another response to attractiveness pressure is the increased rate of cosmetic surgeries (Springen, 2004). In 2008, over 10.2 million cosmetic procedures were performed (breast augmentations and liposuction were the top two) (American Society for Aesthetic Plastic Surgery, 2008). Thus, the pressure to live up to an unrealistic, and sometimes unhealthy, ideal body shape is a significant adjustment challenge facing both males and females today.

---

in over 54% of married couples, both the husband and wife work outside the home (U.S. Bureau of the Census, 2006–2008). Yet some workplaces (and many husbands and fathers) still operate as if all women were stay-at-home moms and as if there were no single-parent families. This gap between policies based on outdated assumptions and reality means that women who "want it all" experience burdens and conflicts that most men do not. That's because most men typically have major day-to-day responsibilities in only *one* role: worker. But most women have major day-to-day responsibilities in *three* roles: spouse, parent, and worker.

Although men, and especially younger men, are giving more time to household chores and child care than men in prior generations, women still do most of this work (Calasanti & Harrison-Rexrod, 2009; Family & Work Institute, 2004). One way today's college-educated women deal with these conflicts is to postpone marriage and motherhood (and to have small families) in order to pursue more education or to launch their careers (Hoffnung, 2004). Additionally, they are more likely than men to expect childrearing to disrupt their careers (Singer, Cassin, & Dobson, 2005). Once women in high-powered careers are established, some are temporarily "stepping out" of the workforce to focus on childbearing and rearing their young children (Wallis, 2004). Given the three-role reality of their lives, they trade off the worker role and income for a slower pace and less stress to rear young children. Their strategy: "You can have it all, just not all at the same time" (Wallis, 2004, p. 53).

Of course multiple roles, in themselves, are not inherently problematic. In fact, there is some evidence that multiple roles can be beneficial for mental health, as you'll see in Chapter 13. Rather, the problem stems from the tensions among these roles and the unequal sharing of role responsibilities. Greater participation in household tasks and child care by husbands or others, as well as family-friendly workplaces and subsidized quality child-care programs, would alleviate women's stress in this area. However, this issue is not clear cut. Goldberg and Perry-Jenkins (2004) note that women with traditional gender roles whose husbands did *more* child care after the birth of their first child experienced greater distress. Of course, this might be because women who did *less* child care than they expected experienced greater distress, perhaps because they were not living up to their own gender-role expectations.

### Ambivalence About Sexuality

Like men, women may have sexual problems that stem, in part, from their gender-role socialization. For many women, the problem is difficulty in enjoying sex. Why? For one thing, many girls are still taught to suppress or deny their sexual feelings (Hyde & DeLamater, 2003). For another, they are told that a woman's role in sex is a passive one. In addition, girls are encouraged to focus on romance rather than on gaining sexual experience. As a result, many women feel uncomfortable (guilty, ashamed) with their sexual urges. Indeed, girls associate shame and guilt with sex more than boys do (Cuffee, Hallfors, & Waller, 2007). The experience of menstruation (and its association with blood and pain) and the fear of pregnancy add another dimension of negativity to sex. And females' concerns about sexual exploitation and rape also foster negative emotions. Thus, when it comes to sexuality, women are likely to have ambivalent feelings instead of the largely positive feelings that men have (Hyde, 2004; Tolman, 2002). Unfortunately, this ambivalence is often viewed as sexual "dysfunction" for women, as opposed to an attitude resulting from narrow gender roles and beliefs (Drew, 2003).

### Sexism: A Special Problem for Females

Intimately intertwined with the topic of gender roles is the issue of sexism. **Sexism is discrimination against people on the basis of their gender.** (Using our terminology, the term should be "genderism," but we'll stick with standard terminology for the sake of clarity.) Sexism usually refers to discrimination by men against women. However, sometimes *women* discriminate against other women and sometimes *men* are the victims of gender-based discrimination. In this section, we'll discuss two specific problems: economic discrimination and aggression toward women.

### Economic Discrimination

Women are victimized by two forms of economic discrimination: differential access to jobs and differential treatment once on the job. Concerning *job access,* the problem is that women still lack the same employment opportunities as men. For example, in 2008, men held 86% of architectural and engineering occupations and 73% of computer and mathematical occupations, while 74% of education and library occupations were held by women (U.S. Bureau of the Census, 2008). Ethnic minority women are even less likely than white women to work in high-status, male-dominated occupations. Across all economic sectors, men are more likely than women to hold positions with decision-making authority (Eagly & Sczesny, 2009). In contrast, women are overrepresented in "pink-collar ghetto" occupations, such as secretary and preschool and kindergarten

### Recommended READING

#### The Mismeasure of Woman
by Carol Tavris (Touchstone, 1993)

The title and thesis of this book refer to Protagoras's statement that "Man is the measure of all things." Tavris, a social psychologist, has written this book for the lay audience and uses her natural wit and humor to excellent advantage. She points out the fallacy of using a male-centered standard for evaluating "what is normal" for both men and women. Using research findings, she exposes numerous myths about males and females that are the source of misunderstanding and frustration for many. Tavris is not interested in replacing a male-centered view with a female-dominant view but rather in expanding our view of what it means to be human. She urges people to move away from the tendency to think in "us versus them" terms about gender issues. Instead, she suggests that men and women need to work together and rethink how they need to be to have the kind of relationships and work that are life enhancing.

*Go to the Psychology CourseMate for Weiten at* **www.cengagebrain.com/shop/ISBN/1111186634** *for descriptions of other recommended books.*

teacher (see **Figure 11.11**). Additionally, motherhood can be a liability on the job market. One study found that, there is a bias against mothers (but not fathers) applying for a job, in terms of anticipated competence (Heilman & Okimoto, 2007).

The second aspect of economic discrimination is *differential treatment* on the job. For example, women typically earn lower salaries than men in the same jobs (see **Figure 11.12**). And occupations that are male dominated typically pay more than those that are female dominated (Pratto & Walker, 2004). Further, when women demonstrate leadership qualities such as confidence, ambitiousness, and assertiveness, they are evaluated less favorably than men because this behavior contradicts the female gender stereotype (Eagly & Karau, 2002; Lyness & Heilman, 2006). Thus, they are often penalized for their success (Heilman & Okimoto, 2007). There appears to be a *glass ceiling* that prevents most women and ethnic minorities from being advanced to top-level professional positions (Reid, Miller, & Kerr, 2004). For example, as of February 2005 there were only eight female CEOs of Fortune 500 companies (Inskeep, 2005). One of the reasons for the glass ceiling is the perception by bosses that female subordinates have greater family-work conflict than their male counterparts (Hoobler, Wayne, & Lemmon, 2009). Ironically, men employed in traditionally female fields are promoted more quickly than their female counterparts, a phenomenon dubbed the *glass escalator* (Hultin, 2003; Williams, 1998).

## Aggression Toward Females

Forms of aggression toward girls and women include rape, intimate violence, sexual harassment, sexual abuse, incest, and violent pornography. We've discussed a number of these problems elsewhere (in particular, consult the Application for Chapter 10), so we'll focus here on sexual harassment. ***Sexual harassment* is unwelcome conduct on the basis of gender.** It can include sexual advances, requests for sexual favors, and other verbal or physical harassment of a sexual nature. Sexual harassment has become recognized as a

**Figure 11.11**

**Women in the world of work.** Career opportunities for women have expanded dramatically in recent decades. Nonetheless, women remain underrepresented in many traditionally masculine occupations and overrepresented in many traditionally feminine occupations. (Data from U.S. Bureau of the Census, 2004)

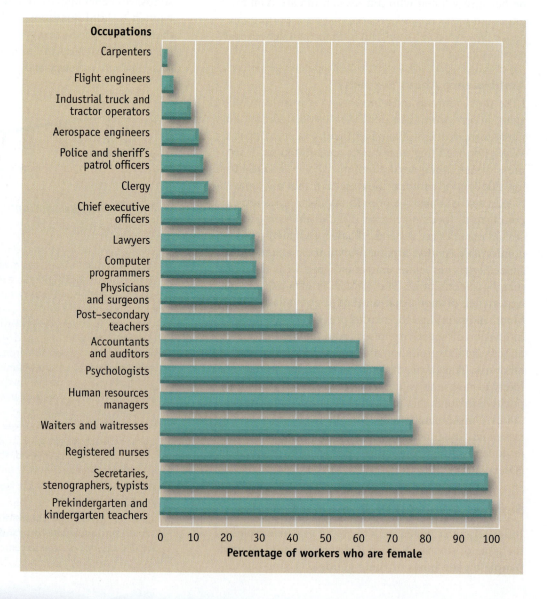

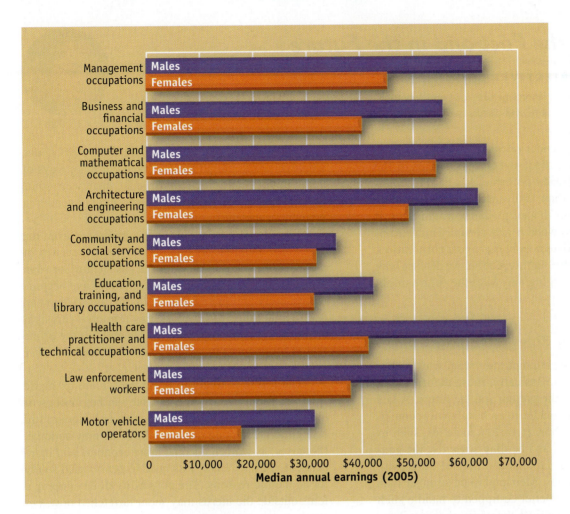

**Figure 11.12**

**The gender gap in annual wages.** Women continue to earn less than men in all occupational categories, as these 2005 data for selected occupations make clear. Many factors can contribute to this gender gap in earned income, but economic discrimination is probably a major consideration. (Data from U.S. Bureau of Labor Statistics, 2005)

**Figure 11.12 chart labels:**

Management occupations — Males / Females
Business and financial occupations — Males / Females
Computer and mathematical occupations — Males / Females
Architecture and engineering occupations — Males / Females
Community and social service occupations — Males / Females
Education, training, and library occupations — Males / Females
Health care practitioner and technical occupations — Males / Females
Law enforcement workers — Males / Females
Motor vehicle operators — Males / Females

x-axis: 0  $10,000  $20,000  $30,000  $40,000  $50,000  $60,000  $70,000

**Median annual earnings (2005)**

widespread problem that occurs not only on the job but also at home (obscene telephone calls), while walking outside (catcalls and whistles), and in medical and psychotherapy settings. It also takes place in schools and colleges (see **Figure 11.13**). Sexual harassment is more about dominance and power than desire. In fact, Berdahl (2007) demonstrated that women in male-dominated organizations were more likely to be harassed than those in female-dominated ones, and women who break traditional gender roles (such as being assertive and showing leadership abilities) in male-dominated organizations are the most likely to be targets.

Betz (2006) distinguishes between two categories of sexual harassment in the workplace. In *quid pro quo harassment* employees are expected to give in to sexual demands in exchange for employment, raises, promotions, and so forth. In *hostile environment harassment* employees are exposed to sexist or sexually oriented comments, cartoons, posters, and so forth. Recent research shows that minority women experience a form of "double jeopardy" when it comes to workplace harassment. When Berdahl and Moore (2006) surveyed employees from five ethnically diverse organizations, they found that women experience more harassment than men, that minorities experience more harassment than whites, and that minority women experience more harassment than

any other group. Given that harassment continues to be a major problem in the workplace and is related to poorer job outcomes (Settles et al., 2006), future researchers will no doubt continue to explore this issue.

| Sexual Harassment in the Schools | |
|---|---|
| **Type of harassment** | **Percentage reporting** |
| Received suggestive gestures, looks, comments, or jokes | 89 |
| Touched, pinched, or grabbed | 83 |
| Leaned over or cornered | 47 |
| Received sexual notes or pictures | 28 |
| Pressured to do something sexual | 27 |
| Forced to do something sexual | 10 |
| Other form of harassment | 7 |

Note: Percentages do not add to 100 because readers could indicate more than one type of harassment.

**Figure 11.13**

**Reported incidence of sexual harassment in the schools.** This figure depicts common forms of sexual harassment in grades 2 through 12 and the percentage of girls reporting them. (Adapted from Stein, Marshall, & Tropp, 1993)

Source: Adapted from Stein, N., Marshall, N. L., & Tropp, L.R. (1993). *Secrets in public: Sexual harassment in our schools*, p. 4. Copyright © 1993 Center for Research on Women at Wellesley College and the NOW Legal Defense and Education Fund.

# Gender in the Past and in the Future

## LEARNING OBJECTIVES

● Explain the basis for traditional gender roles and why they are changing.
● Define gender-role identity, and discuss two alternatives to traditional gender roles.

In Western society, gender roles are in a state of transition. As we have noted, sweeping changes in the female role have already occurred. It's hard to imagine today, but less than 100 years ago, women were not allowed to vote or to manage their own finances. It wasn't that long ago when it was virtually unheard of for a woman to initiate a date, manage a corporation, or run for public office. In this section, we discuss why gender roles are changing and what the future might bring.

## Why Are Gender Roles Changing?

A number of theories attempt to explain why gender roles are in transition. Basically, these theories look at the past to explain the present and the future. A key consideration is that gender roles have always constituted a division of labor. In earlier societies, such as hunting-and-gathering and herding societies, the gender-based division of labor was a natural outgrowth of some simple realities. Men tend to be stronger than women, so they were better equipped to handle such jobs as hunting and farming; therefore, they got those assignments. Women were responsible for nursing young children and so were assigned gathering, home maintenance, and childrearing (Nielsen, 1990). Thus, although people might have worked out other ways of doing things (and some cultures did), there were some basic reasons for dividing labor according to gender in premodern societies.

Traditional gender roles are a carryover from the past. Once traditions are established, they have a way of perpetuating themselves. Over the past century or so in Western society, these divisions of labor have become increasingly antiquated. For example, the widespread use of machines to do work has rendered physical strength relatively unimportant. Therein lies the prime reason for changes in gender roles. *Traditional gender roles no longer make economic sense.*

The future is likely to bring even more dramatic shifts in gender roles. We can see the beginnings of these changes now. For example, although women still bear children, nursing responsibilities are now optional. Moreover, as women become more economically independent, they will have less need to get married solely for economic reasons. The possibility of developing a fetus outside the uterus may seem farfetched now, but some experts predict that it is only a matter of time. If so, both men and women could be "mothers." In light of these and other changes in modern society, it is safe

A division of labor based on gender no longer makes economic sense in our society. Relatively few jobs require great physical strength; the rest call for skills possessed by both men and women.

© Paul Wood/Alamy

## Alternatives to Traditional Gender Roles

*Gender-role identity* **is a person's identification with the qualities regarded as masculine or feminine.** Initially, gender-role identity was conceptualized as either "masculine" or "feminine." All males were expected to develop masculine role identities and females, feminine gender-role identities. Individuals who did not identify with the role expectations for their gender or who identified with the characteristics for the other gender were judged to be few in number and to have psychological problems.

In the 1970s, social scientists began to rethink their ideas about gender-role identity. One assumption that was called into question is that males should be "masculine" and females should be "feminine." For one thing, it appears that the number of people who don't conform to traditional gender-role norms is higher than widely assumed, as is the amount of strain that some people experience trying to conform to conventional roles (Pleck, 1981, 1995). Research suggests that strong identification with traditional gender-role expectations is associated with a variety of negative outcomes. For example, high femininity in females is correlated with low self-esteem (Whitley, 1983) and increased psychological distress (Helgeson, 1994). High masculinity in males has been linked to increased Type A behavior (see Chapter 5), poor health care (Helgeson, 1994), chronic self-destructiveness (Van Volkom, 2008), greater sexual prejudice and homophobia (Barron et al., 2008), and vulnerability to certain types of psychopathology (Evans & Dinning, 1982). Males high in masculinity have a greater likelihood of committing physical and sexual aggression in relationships (Mosher, 1991). Furthermore, relationship satisfaction tends to be lower in heterosexual couples with traditional gender-role identities (Burn & Ward, 2005; Ickes, 1993). Thus, contrary to earlier thinking, the evidence suggests that "masculine" males and "feminine" females may be less well adjusted, on the average, than those who are less traditional.

As people have become aware of the possible costs of conventional gender roles, there has been much debate about moving beyond them. A big question has been: What should we move toward? To date, two ideas have received the most attention: (1) androgyny and (2) gender-role transcendence. Let's examine these options.

### Androgyny

Like masculinity and femininity, androgyny is a type of gender-role identity. *Androgyny* **refers to the coexistence of both masculine and feminine personality traits in a single person.** In other words, an androgynous person is one who scores above average on measures of *both* masculinity and femininity.

To help you fully appreciate the nature of androgyny, we need to briefly review other kinds of gender identity (see **Figure 11.14**). Males who score high on masculinity and low on femininity, and females who score high on femininity and low on masculinity, are said to be *gender-typed*. Males who score high on femininity but low on masculinity, and females who score high on masculinity but low on femininity, are said to be *cross-gender-typed*. Finally, males and females who score low on both masculinity and femininity are characterized as *gender-role undifferentiated*.

Keep in mind that we are referring to individuals' descriptions of themselves in terms of personality traits traditionally associated with each gender (dominance, nurturance, and so on). People sometimes confuse gender-role identity with sexual orientation, but they are not the same. A person can be homosexual, heterosexual, or bisexual (sexual orientation) and be androgynous, gender-typed, cross-gender-typed, or gender-role undifferentiated (gender-role identity).

In groundbreaking research four decades ago, Sandra Bem (1975) challenged the then-prevailing view that males who scored high in masculinity and females who scored high in femininity are better adjusted than "masculine" women and "feminine" men. She argued that traditionally masculine men and feminine women feel compelled to adhere to rigid and narrow gender roles that unnecessarily restrict their behavior. In contrast, androgynous individuals ought to be able to function more

Sandra Bem

*Courtesy of Sandra Bem*

| | Femininity score | |
|---|---|---|
| | **High** | **Low** |
| **Masculinity score — High** | Androgynous males and females | Masculine gender-typed (if male) or cross-gender-typed (if female) |
| **Masculinity score — Low** | Feminine gender-typed (if female) or cross-gender-typed (if male) | Undifferentiated males and females |

**Figure 11.14**

**Possible gender-role identities.** This diagram summarizes the relations between participants' scores on measures of masculinity and femininity and four possible gender identities.

flexibly. She also advanced the idea that androgynous people are psychologically healthier than those who are gender-typed.

How have Bem's ideas played out over time? First, androgynous people do seem more flexible than others. That is, they can be nurturing (feminine) or independent (masculine), depending on the situation (Bem, 1975). In contrast, gender-typed males tend to have difficulty behaving nurturantly, while gender-typed females often have trouble with independence. Also, individuals whose partners are either androgynous or feminine (but not masculine or undifferentiated) report higher relationship satisfaction (Bradbury, Campbell, & Fincham, 1995). This finding holds for cohabiting heterosexuals, as well as for lesbian and gay couples (Kurdek & Schmitt, 1986b). Thus, in these areas, androgyny seems to be advantageous.

Bem's second assertion—that androgynous people are psychologically healthier than gender-typed individuals—requires a more complicated analysis. Since 1976, over a hundred studies have been conducted to try to answer this question. Some early studies *did* find a positive correlation between androgyny and mental health. Ultimately, however, the weight of the evidence did not support Bem's hypothesis that androgyny is especially healthy. In fact, several comprehensive surveys of the research concluded that *masculine* traits (in both males and females) were more strongly associated with psychological health than androgyny (Hyde & Frost, 1993).

One resolution to these contradictory findings might lie in the *type* of masculine and feminine traits an androgynous person adopts. Obviously, there are both positive and negative masculine and feminine traits. Therefore someone who adopts predominantly positive traits for both would be desirably androgynous, whereas someone who adopts predominantly negative traits for both would be undesirably androgynous (Woodhill & Samuels, 2004). In support of differentiating androgyny into categories, Woodhill and Samuels (2003) found that positively androgynous individuals show higher levels of psychological health and well-being than those who were negatively androgynous. However, researchers speculate that, due to changing gender roles, the traits Bem used to categorize gender identities are now outdated. Case in point—in a sample of college students, Auster and Ohm (2000) found that although 18 of the 20 feminine traits still qualified as feminine, only 8 of the 20 masculine traits were still perceived as strictly masculine! These problems with the concept of androgyny and its measurement have led Bem and other psychologists to take a different view of gender roles, as you'll see next.

## Gender-Role Transcendence

As psychologists thought more about androgyny, they realized that the concept had some additional problems. For one thing, the idea that people should have both masculine and feminine traits reinforces the assumption that gender is an integral part of human behavior (Bem, 1983). As such, the androgyny perspective sets up self-fulfilling prophecies. That is, if people use gender-based labels ("masculine" and "feminine") to describe certain human characteristics and behavior, they are likely to associate these traits with one gender or the other. Another criticism of androgyny is that it implies that the solution to gender bias is to change the individual rather than to address the gender inequities in society and its institutions (Matlin, 2004).

Many gender theorists maintain that masculinity and femininity are really only arbitrary labels that we have learned to impose on certain traits through societal conditioning. This assertion is the foundation for the *gender-role transcendence* perspective (Bem, 1983, 1993; Spence, 1983). **The *gender-role transcendence perspective* proposes that to be fully human, people need to move beyond gender roles as a way of organizing their perceptions of themselves and others.** This goal requires that instead of dividing human characteristics into masculine and feminine categories (and then combining them, as the androgyny perspective suggests), we should dispense with the artificially constructed gender categories and labels altogether. How would this work? Instead of the labels "masculine" and "feminine," we would use gender-neutral terms such as "instrumental" and "expressive," respectively, to describe personality traits and behaviors. This "decoupling" of traits and gender could reduce the self-fulfilling prophecy problem.

Given that individuals today have had years of exposure to gender messages, moving toward gender-role transcendence would likely be a gradual process. According to James O'Neil and Jean Egan (1992), such a gender-role journey moves from initial acceptance of traditional gender roles (Stage 1) to a growing ambivalence about gender roles (Stage 2). From there, it evolves to anger about sexism (Stage 3) and then to actions to reduce sexist restrictions (Stage 4). Finally, in Stage 5, people integrate their gender-role beliefs, which enables them to see themselves and the world in less gender-stereotypic ways.

# Understanding Mixed-Gender Communication

## LEARNING OBJECTIVES

- Distinguish between expressive and instrumental styles of communication.
- Describe gender differences in nonverbal communication and speaking styles.
- Explain how the different socialization experiences of males and females might contribute to communication differences.
- Discuss four reasons one should use caution in analyzing theories of mixed-gender communication.

*Answer the following questions "true" or "false."*

___ **1.** Men talk much more than women in mixed-gender groups.

___ **2.** Women are more likely to ask for help than men.

___ **3.** Women are more willing to initiate confrontations in relationships than men.

___ **4.** Men talk about nonpersonal issues with their friends more than women do.

If you answered true to all of these statements, you were correct. They are just some of the observed differences in communication styles between males and females. While not characteristic of all men and women, or of all mixed-gender conversations, these style differences appear to be the source of many misunderstandings between males and females.

When people experience frustrating communication situations in their personal or work relationships, they often attribute them to the other person's quirks or failings. Instead, it seems that some of these frustrating experiences may result from gender differences in communication style. Before we go any further, it is important to remember that scholars who advocate the "gender similarities hypothesis" (see Hyde, 2005) argue that gender differences in many areas including communication are exaggerated and that males and females are similar on most psychological variables. As with many of the gender differences we have discussed in this chapter, differences in communication are often small and inconsistent (MacGeorge et al., 2004). In general, they are a matter of degree, not kind. In other words, it's not a matter of men being from Mars and women from Venus, but more like men are from North Dakota and women are from South Dakota (Dindia, 2006).

## Instrumental and Expressive Styles

Because of the differences in their socialization experiences, men are more likely to use an "instrumental" style of communication and women, an "expressive" style, according to many researchers (Block, 1973; Tannen, 1990). An *instrumental style* focuses on reaching practical goals and finding solutions to problems; an *expressive style* is characterized by being able to express tender emotions easily and being sensitive to the feelings of others. Of course, many individuals use both styles, depending on the situation.

In conflict situations, men's instrumental style means that they are more likely to stay calm and problem oriented and to make more efforts to find compromise solutions to problems. However, an instrumental style can have a darker side. When the instrumental behavior of calmness changes to coldness and unresponsiveness, it becomes negative. Research has shown that this emotional unresponsiveness is characteristic of many men and that it seems to figure importantly in marital dissatisfaction (Larson & Pleck, 1998).

## Nonverbal Communication

Many studies indicate that women are more skilled than men in nonverbal communication—a key component of the expressive style. For example, they are better at reading and sending nonverbal messages (Hall, 1998; Hall & Matsumoto, 2004). And women tend to be better listeners (Miller, Berg, & Archer, 1983). But women engage in some "negative" expressive behaviors as well (Brehm, 1992). For example, during relationship conflicts, women are more likely to (1) display strong negative emotions (Noller, 1985, 1987); (2) use psychologically coercive tactics, such as guilt manipulations, verbal attacks, and power plays (Barnes & Buss, 1985); and (3) reject attempts at reconciliation (Barnes & Buss, 1985). Interestingly, women appear to value online expressive communication (often via social networking sites) more than men (Procopio & Procopio, 2007; Tufekci, 2008).

## Speaking Styles

Most studies have found that women speak more tentatively ("I may be wrong, but") than men (Carli & Bukatko, 2000), especially when discussing masculine topics in mixed-gender groups (Palomares, 2009). One explanation attributes women's greater use of tentative and polite language to lower status; another, to gender-specific socialization (Athenstadt, Haas, & Schwab, 2004). Let's explore some theories about gender socialization specific to language and communication.

## The Clash of Two "Cultures"

According to sociolinguist Deborah Tannen (1990), males and females are typically socialized in different "cultures." That is, males are likely to learn a language of "status and independence," while females learn a language of "connection and intimacy" (p. 42). Tannen likens male/female communications to other "cross-cultural" communications—full of opportunities for misunderstandings to develop. For some hints on how to improve gender-based communication, see **Figure 11.15**.

These differences in communication styles develop in childhood and are fostered by traditional gender stereotypes and the socializing influences of parents, teachers, media, and childhood social interactions—usually

**WEB LINK 11.8  Deborah Tannen's Homepage**

Georgetown University Professor Deborah Tannen has won considerable recognition for her work on communication differences between men and women in diverse settings such as the home and office. Visitors to her homepage will find a complete bibliography of professional and general interest publications.

with same-gender peers. As we noted earlier, boys typically play in larger groups, usually outdoors, and farther away from home than girls (Feiring & Lewis, 1987). Thus, boys are less under the scrutiny of adults and are therefore more likely to engage in activities that encourage exploration and independence. Also, boys' groups are often structured in terms of high- and low-status roles. Boys achieve high status in their groups by engaging in dominant behavior (telling others what to do and enforcing compliance). The games that boys play often result in winners and losers, and boys frequently bid for dominance by interrupting each other,

---

### Hints to Improve Communication

**Hints for men**

1. Notice whether or not you have a tendency to interrupt women. If you do, work on breaking this habit. When you catch yourself interrupting, say, "I'm sorry, I interrupted you. Go ahead with what you were saying."

2. Avoid responding to a woman's questions in monosyllables ("Yep," "Nope," "Uh-huh"). Give her more details about what you did and explain why.

3. Learn the art of conversational give and take. Ask women questions about themselves. And listen carefully when they respond.

4. Don't order women around. For example, don't say, "Get me the newspaper." First, notice whether it might be an inconvenience for her to do something for you. If it isn't, say, "Would you mind giving me the newspaper?" or "Would you please give me the newspaper?"

5. Don't be a space hog. Be more aware of the space you take up when you sit with others (especially women). Watch that you don't make women feel crowded out.

6. Learn to open up about personal issues. Talk about your feelings, interests, hopes, and relationships. Talking about personal things helps others know who you are (and probably helps you clarify your self-perceptions, too).

7. Learn to convey enthusiasm about things in addition to the victories of your favorite sports teams.

8. Don't be afraid to ask for help if you need it.

**Hints for women**

1. When others interrupt you, politely but firmly redirect the conversation back to you. You can say, for example, "Excuse me. I haven't finished my point."

2. Look the person you're talking with directly in the eye.

3. A lower-pitched voice gets more attention and respect than a higher-pitched one, which is associated with little girls. Keeping your abdominal muscles firm as you speak will help keep your voice low.

4. Learn to be comfortable claiming more space (without becoming a space hog). If you want your presence to be noted, don't fold yourself up into an unobtrusive object.

5. Talk more about yourself and your accomplishments. This isn't offensive as long as others are doing the same and the circumstances are appropriate. If the conversation turns to photography and you know a lot about the topic, it's perfectly OK to share your expertise.

6. Make a point of being aware of current events so you'll be knowledgeable about what others are discussing and have an opinion to contribute.

7. Resist the impulse to be overly apologetic. Although many women say "I'm sorry" to convey sympathy or concern (not apology), these words are likely to be interpreted as an apology. Because apologizing puts one in a lower-power position, women who use apologetic words inappropriately put themselves at a disadvantage.

### Figure 11.15

**Hints to improve communication between women and men.** To have productive personal and work relationships in today's world demands that people be knowledgeable about gender and communication styles. Men and women may be able to benefit from the suggestions listed here. (Compiled by the authors based on insights from Tannen, 1990)

calling each other names, boasting to each other about their abilities, and refusing to cooperate with each other (Maccoby, 1998, 2002; Maltz & Borker, 1998).

In contrast, girls usually play in small groups or in pairs, often indoors, and gain high status through popularity—the key to which is intimacy with peers. Many of the games girls play do not have winners or losers. And, while it is true that girls vary in abilities and skills, to call attention to oneself as better than others is frowned upon. Girls are likely to express their wishes as suggestions rather than as demands or orders (Maccoby, 1998, 2002; Maltz & Borker, 1998). Dominance tends to be gained by verbal persuasion rather than by the direct bids for power characteristic of boys' social interactions (Charlesworth & Dzur, 1987). These two cultures shape the functions of speech in different ways. According to Eleanor Maccoby (1990), among boys, "speech serves largely egoistic functions and is used to establish and protect an individual's turf. Among girls, conversation is a more socially binding process" (p. 516).

## Some Caveats

The idea that there are two cultures founded on gender-based communication styles has intuitive appeal because it confirms people's stereotypes and reduces complex issues to simple explanations. But there are some an important caveats here. First, as we have noted, status, power, and gender role differences can lurk behind what seem to be gender differences. Second, many of Tannen's assertions are based on casual observation, and when put to the empirical test, the findings are mixed (Basow & Rubenfeld, 2003; Edwards & Hamilton, 2004; MacGeorge et al., 2004; Michaud & Warner, 1997). Third, there are individual differences in preferred styles: Some women use the "male style" and some men use the "female style." Finally, the social context is a much stronger influence on behavior than gender, which means that many people use either style, depending on the situation. For example, one study found expected gender differences in willingness to initiate negotiations (women were less willing then men), but these differences disappeared when the negotiations were framed in terms of *asking* for something (as opposed to negotiating) (Small et al., 2007).

Therefore, we caution you to avoid reducing *all* communication problems between males and females to gender-based style differences. Many scholars argue that we need to look at gender communication in more complex, less stereotypic ways and that our current way of thinking has far-reaching implications for issues such as expectations for achievement, communication of sexual consent and date rape, and sexual harassment (Cameron, 2007). It is simply not true that men and women come from different planets. In fact, MacGeorge et al. (2004) suggests that the idea of "different cultures is a myth that should be discarded" altogether (p. 143).

### Gender Stereotypes

● Many stereotypes have developed around behavioral differences between the genders, although the distinctions between the male and female stereotypes are less rigid than they used to be. Gender stereotypes may vary depending on ethnicity, and they typically favor males.

### Gender Similarities and Differences

● Some contemporary researchers have adopted the gender similarity hypothesis, emphasizing the fact that males and females are more similar than different on most psychological variables.

● There are no gender differences in general intelligence. When it comes to verbal abilities, gender differences are small, and they generally favor females. Gender differences in mathematical abilities are typically small as well, and they favor males. Males perform much better than females on the spatial ability of mental rotation; however, this skill can be improved through practice.

● Research shows that males typically are somewhat higher in self-esteem, although the findings are complex. Males tend to be more physically aggressive than females, whereas females are higher in relational aggression. Males have more permissive attitudes about casual sex and are more sexually active than females. Males and females are similar in the experience of emotions, but females are more likely to outwardly display emotions. The genders are similar in overall mental health, but they differ in prevalence rates for specific psychological disorders.

● The gender differences that do exist are quite small. Moreover, they are group differences that tell us little about individuals. Nonetheless, some people still adhere to the belief that psychological differences between the genders are substantial. Social role theory and social constructionism provide two explanations for this phenomenon.

### Biological Origins of Gender Differences

● Biological explanations of gender differences include those based on evolution, brain organization, and hormones. Evolutionary psychologists explain gender differences on the basis of their purported adaptive value in ancestral environments. These analyses are speculative and difficult to test empirically.

● Regarding brain organization, some studies suggest that males exhibit more cerebral specialization than females. However, linking this finding to gender differences in cognitive abilities is questionable for a number of reasons.

● Efforts to tie hormone levels to gender differences have also been troubled by interpretive problems. Nonetheless, there probably is some hormonal basis for gender differences in aggression and in some aspects of sexual behavior.

### Environmental Origins of Gender Differences

● The socialization of gender roles appears to take place through the processes of reinforcement and punishment, observational learning, and self-socialization. These processes operate through many social institutions, but parents, peers, schools, and the media are the primary sources of gender-role socialization.

### Gender-Role Expectations

● Five key attributes of the traditional male role include achievement, aggression, autonomy, sexuality, and stoicism. The theme of anti-femininity cuts across these dimensions. Problems associated with the traditional male role include excessive pressure to succeed, difficulty in dealing with emotions, and sexual problems. Homophobia is a particular problem for men.

● Role expectations for females include the marriage mandate, the motherhood mandate, and working outside the home. Among the principal costs of the female role are diminished aspirations, juggling of multiple roles, and ambivalence about sexuality. In addition to these psychological problems, women also face sexist hurdles in the economic domain and may be victims of aggression.

### Gender in the Past and in the Future

● Gender roles have always represented a division of labor. They are changing today, and they seem likely to continue changing because they no longer mesh with economic reality. Consequently, an important question is how to move beyond traditional gender roles. The perspectives of androgyny and gender-role transcendence provide two possible answers to this question.

### Application: Understanding Mixed-Gender Communication

● Because of different socialization experiences, many males and females learn different communication styles. These differences, however, appear to be a matter of degree, not type.

● Women appear to be more skilled at nonverbal communication and tend to use more tentative language. This could be related to gender socialization, including how children use language in play.

● Although the idea of gender-based communication styles has intuitive appeal, the research is mixed. Other factors besides gender play an important role in these differences. In addition, men and women can alter their communication styles to fit the situation. Scholars suggest we explore mixed-gender communication in less stereotypic ways.

| | |
|---|---|
| Aggression p. 343 | Gender schemas p. 349 |
| Androcentrism p. 340 | Gender stereotypes p. 339 |
| Androgyny p. 363 | Hormones p. 347 |
| Cerebral hemispheres p. 346 | Instrumentality p. 339 |
| Corpus callosum p. 347 | Meta-analysis p. 341 |
| Expressiveness p. 339 | Sexism p. 359 |
| Gender p. 339 | Sexual harassment p. 360 |
| Gender-role identity p. 363 | Social constructionism p. 345 |
| Gender-role transcendence perspective p. 364 | Social role theory p. 345 |
| Gender roles p. 348 | Socialization p. 348 |

| | |
|---|---|
| Sandra Bem pp. 363–364 | Joseph Pleck p. 354 |
| Alice Eagly p. 345 | Deborah Tannen |
| Janet Shibley Hyde pp. 339, 341 | pp. 366–367 |

## QUESTIONS

1. Taken as a whole, gender differences in verbal abilities are:
   a. small and favor females.
   b. large and favor females.
   c. nonexistent.
   d. small and favor males.

2. Among the following traits, the largest gender differences are found in:
   a. verbal abilities.
   b. mathematical abilities.
   c. physical aggression.
   d. conformity.

3. Which of the following statements about gender differences is false?
   a. Males have higher self-esteem than females.
   b. Males are more physically aggressive than females.
   c. Males have more permissive attitudes about sex than females.
   d. Women talk more than men.

4. The finding that males exhibit more cerebral specialization than females supports which of the following biologically based explanations for gender differences?
   a. evolutionary theory
   b. brain organization
   c. hormones
   d. social constructionism

5. Four-year-old Rachel seems to pay particular attention to what her mother and her older sister do, and she often imitates them. What is taking place?
   a. sexism
   b. observational learning
   c. operant conditioning
   d. androcentric bias

6. Parents tend to respond negatively to _____ behavior, especially in _____ .
   a. gender appropriate; boys
   b. gender appropriate; girls
   c. gender inappropriate; boys
   d. gender inappropriate; girls

7. Which of the following statements about peer socialization is true?
   a. Peer groups appear to influence gender-role socialization more in boys than girls.
   b. Girls play in smaller groups and boys in larger groups.
   c. High status in boys' groups is achieved by making suggestions to others.
   d. Peers have relatively little impact on gender-role socialization.

8. Which of the following is *not* a problem with the male role?
   a. pressure to succeed
   b. emotional inexpressiveness
   c. sexual problems
   d. androgyny

9. Which of the following is *not* a problem with the female role?
   a. poor nonverbal communication skills
   b. diminished aspirations
   c. juggling multiple roles
   d. ambivalence about sexuality

10. Sara exhibits both masculine and feminine personality traits. According to gender identity theory, she would be classified as _____.
    a. cross-gender-typed
    b. undifferentiated
    c. androcentric
    d. androgynous

## ANSWERS

| | |
|---|---|
| 1. a Page 342 | 6. c Page 349 |
| 2. c Pages 343–344 | 7. b Page 351 |
| 3. d Page 344 | 8. d Pages 354–356 |
| 4. b Pages 346–347 | 9. a Pages 357–359 |
| 5. b Page 349 | 10. d Page 363 |

## Personal Explorations Workbook

Go to the *Personal Explorations Workbook* in the back of your textbook for exercises that can enhance your self-understanding in relation to issues raised in this chapter. **Exercise 11.1** *Self-Assessment:* Personal Attributes Questionnaire (PAQ) **Exercise 11.2** *Self-Reflection:* How Do You Feel About Gender Roles?

## CourseMate

Access an interactive eBook, chapter-specific interactive learning tools, including Personal Explorations, Recommended Readings, Critical Thinking Exercises, flashcards, quizzes, videos and more in your Psychology CourseMate, available at **www.cengagebrain.com/shop/ISBN/1111186634**.

# Development and Expression of Sexuality

Rachel and Marissa, both college seniors and new roommates, headed out to a local club on a Friday night. After a while, they were joined by Luis and Jim, whom they knew a little from one of their classes. As the evening progressed, they all got along well. After a couple of hours, Rachel took Marissa aside and asked if she would drive the car back to their apartment so Rachel could leave with Luis. Marissa agreed and went home. When she woke up the next morning, Marissa realized that Rachel hadn't come home yet. Questions raced through Marissa's mind. How could Rachel have spent the night with a guy she barely even knew? Was it being "prudish" to think that? Did Rachel or Luis have "protection"? Marissa knew she would have been afraid of getting pregnant, or maybe getting a disease of some kind.

As this scenario illustrates, sexuality raises a lot of issues in people's lives. In this chapter we consider sexuality and adjustment. Specifically, we look at the development of sexuality and the interpersonal dynamics of sexual relationships. Then we discuss sexual arousal and the varieties of sexual expression. We also address the important topics of contraception and sexually transmitted diseases. In the Application, we offer some suggestions for enhancing sexual relationships.

# Becoming a Sexual Person

**LEARNING OBJECTIVES**

- Identify four key aspects of sexual identity.
- Clarify how hormones influence sexual differentiation and sexual behavior.
- Discuss how families, peers, schools, religion, and the media shape sexual attitudes and behavior.
- Understand gender differences in sexual socialization and how they affect individuals.

- Summarize the current thinking on the origins of sexual orientation and attitudes toward homosexuality.
- Discuss the process of disclosing one's sexual orientation and the adjustment of lesbians and gay males.

People vary greatly in how they express their sexuality. While some eagerly reveal the intimate details of their sex lives, others can't even utter sexual words without embarrassment. Some people need to turn out the lights before they can have sex; others would like to be on camera with spotlights shining. To understand this diversity, we need to examine developmental influences on human sexual behavior.

Before beginning, we should note that sex research has some unique problems. Given the difficulties in conducting direct observation, sex researchers depend mostly on interviews and questionnaires. And people who are willing to volunteer information tend to be more liberal and more sexually experienced than the general population (Wiederman, 2004). In addition, respondents may shade the truth about their sex lives because of shame, embarrassment, boasting, or wishful thinking. Researchers also have difficulty getting representative samples, so most studies of American sexuality are overrepresented with white, middle-class volunteers. Thus, you need to evaluate the results of sex research with more than the usual caution.

## Key Aspects of Sexual Identity

*Identity* refers to a clear and stable sense of who one is in the larger society. We'll use the term *sexual identity* **to refer to the complex set of personal qualities, self-perceptions, attitudes, values, and preferences that guide one's sexual behavior.** In other words, your sexual identity is your sense of yourself as a sexual person. It includes four key features: sexual orientation, body image, sexual values and ethics, and erotic preferences.

**1.** *Sexual orientation.* Sexual orientation is an individual's preference for emotional and sexual relationships with individuals of one gender or the other. **Heterosexuals** **seek emotional-sexual relationships with members of the other gender.** **Homosexuals** **seek emotional-sexual relationships with members of the same gender.** **Bisexuals** **seek emotional-sexual relationships with members of both genders.** However, sexual orientation is more complicated than these three categories make it appear, and recent research supports the notion of unique subgroups within each category (Worthington & Reynolds, 2009).

In recent years, the terms *gay* and *straight* have become widely used to refer to homosexuals and heterosexuals, respectively. Male homosexuals are called *gay,* whereas female homosexuals prefer to be called *lesbians.* Frequently, the term *LGB* is used to refer, collectively, to lesbians, gay men, and bisexuals. *Transgendered* individuals are those "whose sense of themselves as gendered people is incongruent with the gender they were assigned at birth" (Burdge, 2007). As such, transgendered individuals typically don't adhere to traditional gender roles in terms of physical appearance or sexual behaviors (Crooks & Baur, 2008). The term *transgendered* is different from *transsexual,* which refers to a gender identity disorder in which individuals see themselves as members of the opposite sex and desire a sex change through surgical means (Antoszewski et al., 2007). Because the lesbian, gay male, bisexual, and transgendered communities often have intersecting interests, the term *LGBT* is used to refer to these groups.

**2.** *Body image.* Your body image is how you see yourself physically. Your view of your physical self affects how you feel about yourself in the sexual domain. A positive body image is correlated with greater sexual activity, higher sexual satisfaction, and fewer sexual problems (Nobre & Pinto-Gouveia, 2008; Weaver & Byers, 2006). The relevance of body image for sexual satisfaction holds for both men and women (Holt & Lyness, 2007). While ultra-thinness for women has been a longtime media message, muscular body types for men are getting more promotion (Martins, Tiggeman, & Kirkbride, 2007). The increasing popularity of gym memberships and the recent dramatic increases in facelifts and breast enhancements testifies to the importance of body image to many people (Springen, 2004).

**3.** *Sexual values and ethics.* Sexual values can take the form of absolutism (no sexual activity outside of marriage), relativism (the relationship determines whether sexual activity is appropriate), or hedonism (anything goes) (Richey, Knox, & Zusman, 2009). People are taught that certain expressions of sexuality are "right," while others are "wrong." The nature of these sexual messages are culture-specific and vary depending on gender, race, ethnicity, and socioeconomic status. For example, the sexual double standard encourages sexual experimentation in males, but not females. As a result, while most contemporary college students endorse relativistic sexual values, male students are more hedonistic than female students (Richey et al., 2009). Individuals are faced with the daunting task of sorting through these often-conflicting messages to develop their own sexual values and ethics, and ultimately their values predict their sexual behavior (Balkin et al., 2009).

4. *Erotic preferences.* Within the limits imposed by sexual orientation and values, people still differ in what they find enjoyable. One's erotic preferences encompass one's attitudes about self-stimulation, oral sex, intercourse, and other sexual activities. For instance, a recent study showed that although men and women were equally interested in erotic photos, they differed in terms of their preferences for the sexual activities depicted (Rupp & Wallen, 2009). Such preferences develop through a complex interplay of physiological and psychosocial influences—issues we take up next.

## Recommended READING

### Sex Matters for College Students: FAQ's in Human Sexuality
by Sandra L. Caron (Pearson Prentice Hall, 2007)

This small paperback, in its second edition, is designed around frequently asked questions the author gets in her college sexuality classes. Caron covers a wide range of topics and groups the many questions into sections based on traffic signs. For instance, the "Pass with Care" section addresses issues for which caution is advised: birth control, pregnancy testing, and abortion. The questions under "Traffic Circle Ahead" focus on sexual decisions and address gender roles, sexual orientation, and gender identity issues. "Do Not Enter" deals with questions on sexual assault, sexual abuse, and sexual harassment. The author answers the FAQs as if she were responding to questions in class. Her replies are informative, supportive, and free of jargon. The last two sections are devoted to lists of relevant websites and books, organized by topic.

*Go to the Psychology CourseMate for Weiten at* **www.cengagebrain.com/shop/ISBN/1111186634** *for descriptions of other recommended books.*

## Physiological Influences

Among the various physiological factors involved in sexual behavior, hormones have been of particular interest to researchers.

### Hormones and Sexual Differentiation

During the prenatal period, a number of biological developments result in a fetus that is male or female. Hormones play an important role in this process, which is termed *sexual differentiation.* Around the third month of prenatal development, different hormonal secretions begin to be produced by male and female **gonads—the sex glands.** In males, the testes produce **androgens, the principal class of male sex hormones.** Testosterone is the most important of the androgens. In females, the ovaries produce **estrogens, the principal class of female sex hormones.** Actually, both classes of hormones are present in both genders, but in different proportions. During prenatal development, the differentiation of the genitals depends primarily on the level of testosterone produced—high in males, low in females.

There are instances, though rare, in which sexual differentiation is incomplete and individuals are born with ambiguous genitals, sex organs, or sex chromosomes. These persons, called *intersex individuals* (previously called *hermaphrodites*), typically have both testicular and ovarian tissue (Vilain, 2000). Though their gender is usually difficult to determine at birth, some intersex individuals might not be identified until puberty,

© THOMAS LOHNES/AFP/Getty Images

**After Caster Semnya, a South African athlete who is intersex won the 800-meter world championship, questions were raised about her eligibility to compete as a woman. This controversy brought gender issues to the forefront of athletics.**

and it is often difficult for them to determine their "true" sexual identity (Gough et al., 2008).

At puberty, hormones reassert their influence on sexual development. Adolescents attain reproductive capacity as hormonal changes trigger the maturation of the *primary sex characteristics*, the structures necessary for reproduction (sex organs). Hormonal shifts also regulate the development of *secondary sex characteristics* (physical features that distinguish the genders but are not directly involved in reproduction). In females, more estrogen leads to breast development, widened hips, and more rounded body contours. In males, more androgen results in developing facial hair, a deeper voice, and angular body contours.

In females, the onset of puberty is typically signaled by *menarche—the first occurrence of menstruation.* American girls typically reach menarche between ages 12 and 13, with further sexual maturation continuing until approximately age 16 (Susman, Dorn, & Schiefelbein, 2003). Most girls are sterile for 12 to 18 months following menarche. Nevertheless, pregnancy is a possibility for some girls at this age, so any girl who has begun to menstruate should assume that she could become pregnant.

In males, there is no clear-cut marker of the onset of sexual maturity, although the capacity to ejaculate is used as an index of puberty (the onset of sperm production not being a visible event). *Spermarche,* or the **first ejaculation,** usually occurs through masturbation (Hyde, 1994a). Experts note that ejaculation may not be a valid index of actual maturity, as early ejaculations may contain seminal fluid but not active sperm. The average age of spermarche in American boys is around 13 (Halpern et al., 2000), with complete sexual maturation occurring at about 18 (Susman et al., 2003).

### Hormones and Sexual Behavior

Hormonal fluctuations clearly regulate sex *drive* in many species of animals. Hormones also play a role in human sexuality, but their influence is much more modest. *Androgen* levels appear to be related to sexual motivation in *both* men and women, although the effect is less strong in women (Apperloo et al., 2003; Freeman, Bloom, & McGuire, 2001). High levels of testosterone in men and women correlate with higher rates of sexual activity (Morley & Perry, 2003; van Anders, Hamilton, & Watson, 2007). Curiously, *estrogen* levels among women do not correlate well with sexual interest. In fact, researchers found no hormonal fluctuation differences between women diagnosed with hypoactive (low) sexual desire disorder and those without the diagnosis (Schreiner-Engel et al., 1989). In summary, physiological factors have important effects on sexual development. Their influence on sexual *anatomy,* however, is much greater than their influence on sexual *activity* (Giles, 2008).

## Psychosocial Influences

The principal psychosocial influences on sexual identity are essentially the same as the main sources of gender-role socialization discussed in Chapter 11. Sexual identity is shaped by one's family, peers, schools, and religion, as well as the media.

### Families

Parents and the home environment are significant influences on sexual identity in the early years. Before they reach school age, children usually engage in some sex play and exploration, often under the guise of "playing doctor." They also display curiosity about sexual matters, asking questions such as "Where do babies come from?" Parents who punish innocent, exploratory sex play and who stutter and squirm when kids ask sexual questions convey the idea that sex is "dirty." As a result, children may begin to feel guilty about their sexual urges and curiosity.

Many young people feel dissatisfied with the sexual information they receive from their parents, both in terms of quantity and quality (Rouse-Arnett & Dilworth, 2007). According to a 2003 Gallup Youth Survey, 63% of teenagers (ages 13 to 17) reported that their parents talked to them about sex, while 36% said that their parents mostly left this discussion up to the schools (Mazzuca, 2003). In another national survey of adolescents and young adults (ages 13 to 24), only 37% felt that they learned "a lot" of information about relationships and sexual health from their parents (see **Figure 12.1**).

Parents who are able to talk honestly to their kids about sex tend to be those with open family communication styles and whose own parents talked with them

| Main Sources of Sex Information Among Youth | | | |
|---|---|---|---|
| | Percentage | | |
| Source | Male | Female | Total |
| Friends | 46 | 48 | 47 |
| Sex education classes | 42 | 39 | 40 |
| Boyfriends, girlfriends, partners | 40 | 39 | 39 |
| Media (TV, movies, magazines, the Internet) | 33 | 42 | 38 |
| Parents | 34 | 40 | 37 |
| Doctors, other health care providers | 21 | 50 | 36 |
| Brothers and sisters | 24 | 19 | 22 |

#### Figure 12.1

**Main sources of sex information among youth.** Adolescents and young adults (ages 13 to 24) said they had learned "a lot" from these sources, according to a national survey.

Source: Adapted from Holt, T., Greene, L., & Davis, J. (2003). *National survey of adolescents and young adults: Sexual health knowledge, attitudes, and experience.* Menlo Park, CA: Kaiser Family Foundation, Question 2, p. 97. Henry J. Kaiser Family Foundation.

I don't know what you've been hearing at the playground, but there's no such thing as sex.

David Sipress © 2009

about sex (Fisher, 1990). Adolescents who feel close to their parents and who believe that their parents support them are likely to adopt sexual attitudes similar to their parents' and to limit or delay their sexual activities (Maguen & Armistead, 2006; Sprecher, Christopher, & Cate, 2006). The parents who do not discuss sex with their children are often the same ones who send restrictive sexual messages, especially to their daughters (Kim & Ward, 2007). Parents who make sex a taboo topic reduce their influence on their kids' evolving sexual identity, as the children turn elsewhere for information.

## Peers

As you can see in **Figure 12.1**, friends are a leading source of relationship and sexual health information. Only health care providers are rated higher, and only by females. Adolescents' sexual attitudes and behavior are positively associated with their *perceptions* of their friends' sexual attitudes and behavior (Potard, Courtois, & Rusch, 2008; Sprecher et al., 2006). Unfortunately, peers can be a source of highly misleading information and often champion sexual behavior at odds with parents' views. While researchers acknowledge that the sexual socialization that comes from parents and peers is important for healthy sexual development, sexual education that comes from school-based programs is also significant (Shtarkshall, Santelli, & Hirsch, 2007).

## Schools

Surveys show that the vast majority of parents and other adults support sex education programs in the schools, despite the media attention given to isolated, vocal

protests (Eisenberg et al., 2008; SIECUS, 2004). Also, most teenagers want their schools to offer sex education (McKay & Holoway, 1997). In a 2005 Gallup Poll, 64% of 13- to 17-year-olds indicated that they were taking or had taken a sex education course (Crabtree, 2005).

Researchers who surveyed a nationally representative sample of American public, middle, junior, and senior high schools reported that 90% of schools offered *some* type of sex education (Kaiser Family Foundation, 2004). Among the surveyed schools, 30% offer "abstinence only" programs (no information about contraceptive methods), 47% offer "abstinence plus" programs (information about contraception and sexually transmitted diseases), and 20% offer comprehensive programs (information on such topics as contraception, abortion, sexually transmitted diseases, relationships, sexual orientation, and responsible decision making).

What is the effectiveness of these various programs? Research supports the effectiveness of comprehensive sexuality education (McCave, 2007). "Abstinence only" programs do not deter adolescents from engaging in sex, do not delay first intercourse, and do not reduce the number of sexual partners (U.S. Department of Health and Human Services, 2007). In contrast, comprehensive programs result in a wide range of positive outcomes: increased use of contraception, reduced pregnancies, and reduced high-risk sexual behavior (Kirby, 2001; Schaalma et al., 2004). Also, comprehensive programs do not promote (and may delay) having early sex and do not increase (and may decrease) the number of sexual partners.

## Religion

One's religious background (or lack thereof) can play a major role in the development of sexual identity. Religious teachings and traditions can dictate what is seen as sexually natural or unnatural. Historically, religious institutions have had a lot to say about issues such as

**WEB LINK 12.1   SIECUS (Sexuality Information and Educational Council of the United States)**

This site is produced by one of the oldest organizations in the United States devoted to educating the public about matters of sexuality. It contains an annotated set of web-based links to a variety of topics related to sexuality.

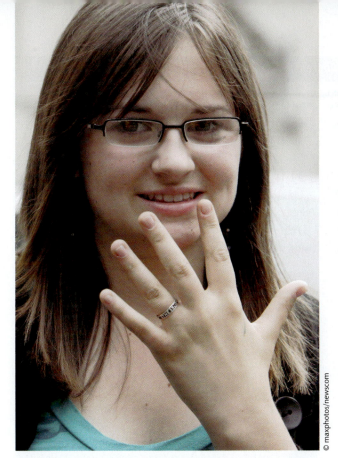

Teens who take abstinence pledges or wear purity rings tend to be just as sexually active as their nonpledging peers.

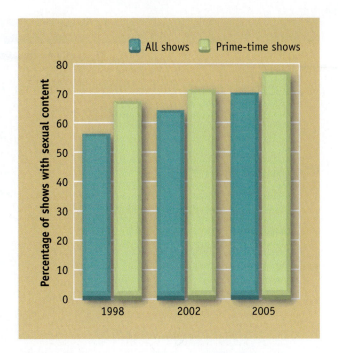

**Figure 12.2**

**Sexual content in television programs continues to increase.** Researchers reviewed a representative sample of more than 1,100 television programs (other than daily newscasts, sports events, and children's shows) in 1998, 2002, and 2005 and identified the proportion of shows that contained sexual content (talk about sex and sexual behaviors). The sexual content in all shows and in prime time shows has increased over these years.

Source: From Kunkel, D., Eyal, K., Finnerty, K., Biely, E., & Donnerstein, E. (2005). *Sex on TV 4, Executive Summary* (#7399), Kaiser Family Foundation, November 2005. Reprinted with permission of the Henry J. Kaiser Family Foundation.

guilt, monogamy, and homosexuality, for example (Francoeur, 2007). Using data from three national surveys, Regnerus (2007) found that the predominant message that teens receive about sex from their religious institutions is "Don't do it until you're married." This message is conveyed through church-based initiatives such as abstinence pledges, chastity vows, and purity rings. This message is largely ineffective, however. Teens who take these pledges tend to be just as sexually active (and less likely to use condoms or other forms of birth control) as their nonpledging peers. On the other hand, they do tend to feel more guilty about it (Rosenbaum, 2009). These findings suggest that although religious teachings might affect sexual attitudes, they do not always influence behavior.

**The Media**

Americans see thousands of sexual encounters a year on television, videos, DVDs, and computers. And the portrayal of sexual content, both in terms of sex talk and behavior, appears to be on the rise (Kunkel et al., 2005b, 2007). As you can see in **Figure 12.2**, the percentage of television shows containing sexual content has been increasing since 1998. When analyzing over 2,000 television programs, Kunkel and his colleagues (2007) found that portrayals of sexual intercourse doubled over a five-year period. They also found that topics related to sexual

risks and responsibilities, though increasing, were still incredibly rare, with such references appearing in only 6% of all sexual scenes. **Figure 12.3** on the next page shows how sexual content is distributed over common television genres. Another study found that 16% of characters involved in sexual intercourse on television are teenagers or young adults (Eyal & Finnerty, 2009). Television portrayals of sexual behavior can influence adolescents' beliefs about typical sexual practices as well as their sexual intentions and behavior (L'Engle, Brown, & Kenneavy, 2006; Taylor, 2005). For adolescents, viewing sexual content is linked to increased sexual activity as well as intentions to engage in sexual behavior in the future (Fisher at al., 2009). At the same time, television can promote responsible sexual behavior and tolerance of homosexuality (Keller & Brown, 2002; Silver, 2002).

Books and magazines are another source of information about sex. Some 20% of adolescents and young adults reported that they had learned "a lot" about relationships and sexual health from magazines (Kaiser Family Foundation, 2003). Regrettably, sexual content in magazines often perpetuates gender stereotypes and sexual myths under the pretense of offering ideas for "improvement" (Johnson, 2007). Although some publications provide accurate and useful information, many

| | Comedy series | Drama series | Movie | News magazine | Soap opera | Talk show | Reality | Total |
|---|---|---|---|---|---|---|---|---|
| **Summary of Sexual Content by Genre** | | | | | | | | |
| Percentage of programs with any sexual content | 73% | 71% | 87% | 53% | 96% | 65% | 28% | 64% |
| *Of programs with any sexual content:* | | | | | | | | |
| Average number of scenes per hour containing sex | 7.8 | 4.6 | 3.7 | 2.3 | 5.1 | 4.0 | 4.5 | 4.4 |
| Number of shows | 166 | 100 | 147 | 32 | 48 | 39 | 63 | 595 |
| Number of hours | 83 | 101 | 321 | 42 | 43 | 39 | 51 | 679 |
| Number of scenes | 648 | 467 | 1182 | 94 | 219 | 153 | 229 | 2992 |
| Percentage of programs with any talk about sex | 71% | 69% | 80% | 52% | 92% | 65% | 27% | 61% |
| *Of programs with any talk about sex:* | | | | | | | | |
| Average number of scenes per hour containing talk | 7.4 | 4.1 | 2.8 | 2.3 | 4.0 | 4.0 | 4.4 | 3.8 |
| Number of shows | 162 | 97 | 134 | 32 | 46 | 39 | 61 | 571 |
| Number of hours | 81 | 98 | 294 | 42 | 41 | 39 | 49 | 643 |
| Number of scenes with talk about sex | 596 | 404 | 827 | 94 | 162 | 153 | 217 | 2453 |
| Percentage of programs with any sexual behavior | 32% | 35% | 74% | 7% | 70% | 0% | 5% | 32% |
| *Of programs with any sexual behavior:* | | | | | | | | |
| Average number of scenes per hour containing behavior | 3.6 | 2.1 | 1.9 | + | 2.6 | 0 | 2.2 | 2.1 |
| Number of shows | 73 | 50 | 125 | 4 | 35 | 0 | 12 | 299 |
| Number of hours | 37 | 51 | 275 | 4 | 33 | 0 | 12 | 411 |
| Number of scenes with sexual behavior | 132 | 106 | 517 | 4 | 85 | 0 | 26 | 870 |
| Total number of shows | 228 | 141 | 168 | 61 | 50 | 60 | 229 | 937 |

**Figure 12.3**

**Sexual content in television programs by genre.** Kunkel and colleagues (2007) examined over 100 hours of television per week for the 2001–2002 television season. They measured both sexual talk (conversations about sex, comments about sexual actions) and sexual behavior (intimate touching, implied sexual intercourse). As you can see, sexual content is common in a variety of television genres.

Source: Adapted from Kunkel, D., Farrar, K. M., Eyal, K., Biely, E., Donnerstein, E., & Rideout, V. (2007). Sexual socialization messages on entertainment television: Comparing content trends 1997–2002. *Media Psychology, 9,* 595–622. Reprinted by permission of the publisher (Taylor & Francis Group, http://www.informaworld.com).

perpetuate myths about sex and miseducate young (and older) readers.

Music lyrics and music videos are additional vehicles of sexual socialization. For example, exposure to music videos has been linked to greater rape acceptance among middle-school males (Kaestle, Halpern, & Brown, 2007). Additionally, teens who listen to music lyrics containing explicit references to sex acts and depicting men as sexually aggressive and women as sex objects are significantly more likely to have sex sooner than teens who listen to music lyrics containing more subtle references to sex (Martino et al., 2006). This study also found that the highest proportion of negative sexual messages occurred in rap and rap-rock music. Rap music videos tend to sexualize female characters more than male ones, and for African American adolescents, exposure to these stereotypes is associated with increases in sexual partners and

negative body image (Conrad, Dixon, & Zhang, 2009; Peterson et al., 2007).

Turning to cyberspace, experts estimate that there were 1.6 billion (23.8% of the total world population) Internet users worldwide in 2009 (Internet World Stats, 2009). Websites with sexually explicit images are extremely popular, especially among males. Parents are understandably alarmed about children having easy access to sexually explicit material online. Among 10- to 17-year-olds, 25% have encountered unwanted pornography, and 20% have been exposed to unwanted sexual solicitations (Finkelhor, Mitchell, & Wolak, 2000). On the up-side, the Internet provides easy and private access to useful information on a variety of sexual topics, including contraceptive methods and resources for the LGBT communities (Ross, 2005; Whitty & Fisher, 2008). The "Living in Today's World" box expands on the issue of sex and the Internet.

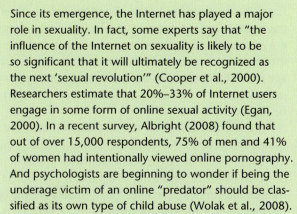

Since its emergence, the Internet has played a major role in sexuality. In fact, some experts say that "the influence of the Internet on sexuality is likely to be so significant that it will ultimately be recognized as the next 'sexual revolution'" (Cooper et al., 2000). Researchers estimate that 20%–33% of Internet users engage in some form of online sexual activity (Egan, 2000). In a recent survey, Albright (2008) found that out of over 15,000 respondents, 75% of men and 41% of women had intentionally viewed online pornography. And psychologists are beginning to wonder if being the underage victim of an online "predator" should be classified as its own type of child abuse (Wolak et al., 2008).

Online sexual activity involves the use of the Internet for any activity (text, audio, or graphics) that involves sexuality (Cooper et al., 2002). These activities are diverse and include using the Internet for information or entertainment, as well as for purchasing sexual materials, searching for sexual partners, and having sexually explicit discussions. Some people use the Internet to engage in forbidden fantasies by masquerading as a member of the other gender (Ross, 2005).

Cybersex, a subcategory of online sexual activity, involves the use of computerized content for sexual stimulation and gratification (Maheu & Subotnik, 2001). People look at erotic pictures (on computers, cell phones, and iPods), engage in sexual chat, and exchange sexually explicit e-mail messages. Some share mutual sexual fantasies while masturbating. In a large online survey, 39% of respondents said that they had engaged in cybersex, although fewer than 3% engaged in it "often" or "all the time" (Cooper et al., 2002). Interestingly, 60% of people in this survey did not believe that cybersex violates a person's marriage vows. Other research disputes these findings (Whitty, 2005), and spouses of individuals who are involved in Internet sexual affairs say that online affairs are as emotionally painful as those offline (Schneider, 2003). Respondents also believe that both emotional and sexual infidelities can develop online (Henline, Lamke, & Howard, 2007).

The large online survey also reported that 25% of respondents had had an in-person meeting for a date or sexual experience with someone whom they had met online (Cooper et al., 2002). More women than men reported engaging in this behavior, as women are more likely to use the Internet to explore online sexual relationships. Because people who make these arrangements are more likely to engage in risky sexual behavior, they expose themselves to potential sexual assault and contracting STDs (McFarlane, Bull, & Reitmeijer, 2000).

Actual cybersex addiction or Internet sex addiction is a specific form of Internet addiction (see Chapter 4). People with this problem engage in online sex so often that it interferes with their personal and work life, they are unable to refrain from the activity (except temporarily), and they deny its negative effects on their lives. This behavior can have serious consequences for addicted individuals and their families (Cooper, 2002). Internet sex addicts may neglect their spouses and children, sow feelings of betrayal in their mates, and destroy their marriages (Schneider, 2003). They can also lose their jobs if they neglect their work or are discovered engaging in cybersex at the office. Amazingly, about 20% of people who engage in online sex use an office computer for this activity, a risky proposition in that many organizations now monitor the online activities of their employees (Cooper, Safir, & Rosenmann, 2006).

Internet technology is always advancing, and with it, new ways to engage in sexual activities. For instance, with the popularity of virtual reality games such as Second Life and other multiplayer role-playing games, users are finding new ways to express their sexuality (Melby, 2008). Because Internet sexuality is an ever-changing phenomenon, mental health professionals are still developing their views about it (Subotnik, 2007). Some see it as just another form of sexual expression. Others are alarmed that Internet sex addiction is a growing problem. To date, research supports both of these perspectives (Cooper et al., 1999; 2002). Online sex does seem to be a normal form of sexual expression for light users (less than 1 hour per week) and moderate users (1 to 10 hours per week). Unfortunately it is quite a different story for high users (11 to 80 hours per week), who make up 8% of all those involved in online sexual activity. These people report significantly more psychological distress and score higher on measures of compulsivity and sensation seeking. They are at high risk for developing psychological problems.

Note that the causal link between sexual behavior and sexual media viewing can go both ways. While those exposed to sex in the media are more sexually active, those who are more sexually active tend to expose themselves to sexual content (Bleakley et al., 2008). Although there are some advantages to sexual content in the media, scientists agree that media depictions of sexuality would have to change dramatically for consumption of sexual media to be considered a healthy part of sexual development (Hust, Brown, & L'Engle, 2008).

To conclude, sexual identities are shaped by a number of intersecting influences. Thus, individuals bring highly diverse expectations to their sexual relationships. As you'll see, this variability can complicate sexual interactions.

## Gender Differences in Sexual Socialization

Letitia Anne Peplau

Courtesy of Letitia Anne Peplau

To what degree are males and females socialized differently about sexual matters? Summarizing the research on gender differences in sexuality, Letitia Anne Peplau (2003; Impett & Peplau, 2006), a major researcher on gender and relationships, concludes that there are five key differences and that all but one of them hold for both gay and straight people:

**1.** Men have more interest in sex than women (they think about and want to have sex more often).

**2.** The connection between sex and intimacy is more important for women than for men (women typically prefer sex in the context of a relationship).

**3.** Aggression is more often linked to sexuality for men than for women (coercive sex is more likely to be initiated by men).

**4.** Women's sexuality is more easily shaped by cultural and situational factors (their sexual attitudes are easier to change, and they are more likely to change their sexual orientation over time).

**5.** Among heterosexual couples, men typically take the lead in initiating sexual intimacy, while women serve as "gatekeepers," determining whether and when a couple engages in sexual activities.

Societal values and gender roles obviously come into play here. American males are encouraged to experiment sexually, to initiate sexual activities, and to enjoy sex without emotional involvement (Kilmartin, 2007). They also get the message to be conquest oriented regarding sex, typically desiring multiple partners (Fenigstein & Preston, 2007). Men are more likely than women to engage in sex activities for purely physical reasons (Meston & Buss, 2007). Thus, men may em-

phasize "sex for fun" in casual relationships and reserve "sex with love" for committed relationships (Oliver & Hyde, 1993).

Females are typically taught to view sex in the context of a loving relationship with one partner (Fenigstein & Preston, 2007; Impett & Peplau, 2006). They learn about romance and the importance of physical attractiveness and catching a mate. Unlike males, they are not encouraged to experiment with sex or to have numerous sexual partners. Whereas social norms encourage males to be sexually active, these norms discourage such behavior in females—sexually active women may be looked on as "easy."

Sexual socialization usually takes longer for females than for males because women usually have more emotional baggage connected with sex than men do. One factor is the *fear of pregnancy*. The media reinforce the gender stereotype that females are the ones responsible for pregnancy (Hust et al., 2008). As a result, concerns about becoming pregnant can inhibit a woman's enthusiasm for sex. Second, females hear *negative messages about sex and men* ("Men only want one thing") from their mothers, siblings, and female peers. They are also aware of rape and incest. Third, women typically develop *negative associations about their genitals and sex* that males don't experience: blood and pain associated with menstruation and fears of penetration. A fourth factor is *sexual guilt.* In a recent national survey, girls associated more shame and guilt with sex than boys did (Cuffee, Hallfors, & Waller, 2007). All these negative associations with sex are combined with the positive rewards of dating and emotional intimacy. Hence, it's no surprise that many women feel ambivalent about sex (Hyde, 2004). These feelings can tilt in the negative direction if early sexual partners are impatient, selfish, or unskilled.

With differing views of sexuality and relationships, males and females can be out of sync with each other—particularly in adolescence and early adulthood. For instance, college men are more likely to believe that oral sex isn't sex, cybersex isn't cheating, and the frequency of intercourse decreases after marriage. College women, on the other hand, are likely to think exactly the opposite (Knox, Zusman, & McNeely, 2008). These gender differences can lead to confusion and mean that communication is essential for mutually satisfying sexual relationships. For both genders, sexual satisfaction is related to relationship satisfaction (Santtila et al., 2008).

Because both members of homosexual couples have been socialized similarly, they are less likely than straight couples to have problems with incompatible expectations. Like heterosexual women, lesbians typically experience emotional attraction to their partners before experiencing sexual feelings (Peplau & Fingerhut, 2007). By contrast, gay men (like heterosexual men) tend to place much more importance on physical appearance and sexual compatibility in selecting partners and to then develop emotional relationships out of sexual ones (Diamond, 2006).

## Sexual Orientation

Gay, straight, or in between? In this section, we'll explore the intriguing and controversial topic of sexual orientation.

### Key Considerations

Most people view heterosexuality and homosexuality as two distinct categories: you're either one or the other. However, many individuals who define themselves as heterosexuals have had homosexual experiences, and vice versa (Kinsey et al., 1948, 1953; Worthington & Reynolds, 2009). Thus, it is more accurate to view heterosexuality and homosexuality as end points on a continuum. Indeed, Alfred Kinsey devised a seven-point scale, shown in **Figure 12.4**, to characterize sexual orientation.

**Alfred Kinsey**

© AP Images/HO

Some researchers argue that even Kinsey's model is too simplistic. For instance, how would you categorize a person who was married for 10 years, has children, is divorced, and is now involved in a committed homosexual relationship? What about a woman who only dates men but who has homosexual fantasies and engages in same-gender sex on the Internet? And what about someone who self-identifies as straight but has had homosexual encounters in the past? Research supports a complex and malleable view of sexual orientation (Diamond, 2003). Savin-Williams (2009) argues that sexual orientation has several components, including sexual attraction (which gender one desires as a sexual partner), romantic attraction (which gender one establishes warm, loving relationships with), sexual behavior (which gender one is sexually involved with), and sexual identity (self-reported orientation). To add to the complexity, these components aren't always consistent with each other and aren't always stable over time.

How many gays and lesbians are there? The answer is, it depends on what question you ask. In the 2000 census, 1.2 million Americans indicated that they were living with a same-sex partner (Hatch, 2009). The overall evidence suggests that about 5%–8% of the population could reasonably be characterized as homosexual (Michaels, 1996). However, as we've seen, there are multiple components to sexual orientation, and estimates of prevalence depend greatly on which component one measures and when.

### Origins

There is no consensus among researchers as to *why* some people are straight and others gay. A number of *environmental explanations* have been suggested as causes of sexual orientation. Freud believed that homosexuality originates from an unresolved Oedipus complex (see Chapter 2). That is, instead of coming to identify with the parent of the same gender, the child continues to identify with the parent of the other gender. Learning theorists assert that homosexuality results from early negative heterosexual encounters or early positive homosexual experiences. Sociologists propose that homosexuality develops because of poor relationships with same-gender peers or because being labeled a homosexual sets up a self-fulfilling prophecy. Surprisingly, a comprehensive review of the causes of sexual orientation found no compelling support for *any* of these explanations of homosexuality (Bell, Weinberg, & Hammersmith, 1981).

Similarly, there is no evidence that parents' sexual orientation is linked to that of their children (Patterson, 2003). That is, heterosexual parents are as likely to produce homosexual (or heterosexual) offspring as homosexual parents are. Children who grow up in gay or lesbian families are predominantly heterosexual (Bailey & Dawood, 1998).

| 0 | 1 | 2 | 3 | 4 | 5 | 6 |
|---|---|---|---|---|---|---|
| Exclusively heterosexual | Predominantly heterosexual only incidentally homosexual | Predominantly heterosexual more than incidentally homosexual | Equally heterosexual and homosexual | Predominantly homosexual more than incidentally heterosexual | Predominantly homosexual only incidentally heterosexual | Exclusively homosexual |

**Figure 12.4**

**Heterosexuality and homosexuality as end points on a continuum.** Kinsey and other sex researchers view heterosexuality and homosexuality as ends of a continuum rather than as all-or-none distinctions. Kinsey created this seven-point scale (from 0 to 6) for describing sexual orientation.

Researchers have found that extremely feminine behavior in young boys and masculine behavior in young girls is correlated with subsequent homosexuality (Bailey, 2003; Bem, 2000). Consistent with this finding, many gay men and some gay women say they can trace their homosexual leanings back to their early childhood (Bailey, 2003). Recently, Rieger and colleagues (2008) asked homosexual and heterosexual adults to supply childhood home videos. When analyzing these videos, Rieger found that prehomosexual children (those that would identify as homosexual in adulthood) were more gender nonconforming than their preheterosexual counterparts. This finding held for both males and females.

Some theorists speculate that *biological factors* are involved in the development of homosexuality. Several lines of research suggest that hormonal secretions during prenatal development may shape sexual development, organize the brain in a lasting manner, and influence subsequent sexual orientation (Byne, 2007; Rahman, 2005). Because of advances in technology that allow researchers to actually map the activity in the brain, we can begin to explore brain differences in sexual orientation. However, it is important to keep in mind that it is difficult to determine whether any brain differences are the cause or the consequence of sexual orientation (Safron et al., 2007).

Genetic factors are also of interest. In an important study, investigators identified gay and bisexual men who had a twin brother or an adopted brother (Bailey & Pillard, 1991). They found that 52% of the participants' identical twins were gay, 22% of their fraternal twins were gay, and only 11% of their adoptive brothers were gay. A companion study of lesbian women with twin or adopted sisters reported a similar pattern of results (Bailey et al., 1993; see **Figure 12.5**). More recent twin studies, with larger and more representative samples, have provided further support for the conclusion that heredity influences sexual orientation, although these studies have yielded smaller estimates of genetic influence (Bailey, Dunne, & Martin, 2000; Kendler et al., 2000). Thus, there may be genetic links to homosexuality.

The bottom line is that it isn't yet clear what determines sexual orientation. Moreover, it appears that complex paradigms are needed to explain male and female homosexuality (Peplau & Garnets, 2000). It is likely that there are a variety of types of homosexuality—and heterosexuality for that matter—that will require a variety of explanations rather than a single account (Hyde & DeLamater, 2003). This issue is exceedingly complex and research is still in its infancy. The most we can conclude is that the explanations must

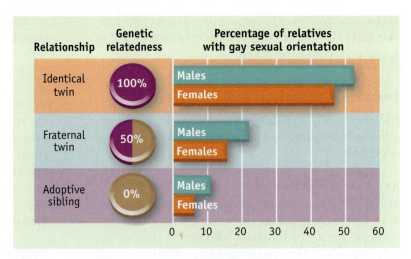

**Figure 12.5**

**Genetics and sexual orientation.** A concordance rate indicates the percentage of twin pairs or other pairs of relatives that exhibit the same characteristic. If relatives who share more genetic relatedness show higher concordance rates than relatives who share less genetic overlap, this evidence suggests a genetic predisposition to the characteristic. Recent studies of both gay men and lesbian women have found higher concordance rates among identical twins than fraternal twins, who, in turn, exhibit more concordance than adoptive siblings. These findings are consistent with the hypothesis that genetic factors influence sexual orientation. If *only* genetic factors were responsible for sexual orientation, the identical twin concordance rates would push 100%; because they are much lower, environmental factors must also play a role. (Data from Bailey & Pillard, 1991; Bailey et. al., 1993)

lie in some complex interaction of biological and environmental factors.

## Attitudes Toward Homosexuality

Gay and lesbian rights have become central in the political arena. The legalization of same-gender marriage in states such as Massachusetts, Connecticut, Vermont, and Iowa and the legal recognition of civil unions and domestic partnerships in other states such as New Jersey and California have set off contentious public debates in the last few years. Fueling the controversy, constitutional amendments banning gay marriage have been introduced in the U.S. Congress and in many state legislatures. Although the public discussion of gay marriage can be divisive, some believe that it has value (Garnets & Kimmel, 2003a). First, it has allowed the gay community to educate straight citizens about the realities and diversity of same-gender couples and their family relationships. Second, it has helped raise the nation's awareness about the facets of discrimination against gays and lesbians. Although many Americans are opposed to gay marriage, they are much more accepting of other issues related to homosexuality (see **Figure 12.6**). Greater acceptance is due, in part, to the increasing visibility of lesbians and gays in society. For instance, homosexual content on television has increased dramatically over the past two decades, including having more openly gay characters (*Ugly Betty*) and individuals (*Ellen*) (Hetsroni, 2007; Schiappa, Gregg, & Hewes, 2006).

| Attitudes Toward Homosexuals | |
|---|---|
| **Poll question*** | **Percent endorsing** |
| **1.** Homosexuals should have equal rights in terms of job opportunities. | 89 |
| **2.** Gay partners should have the same inheritance rights as married couples. | 60 |
| **3.** Gay partners should have the same health insurance and other employee benefits as married couples. | 60 |
| **4.** Gay partners should have the same social security benefits as married couples. | 55 |
| **5.** Gay and lesbian partners should have the same adoption rights as married couples. | 45 |
| **6.** Which of the following do you support for gay couples? | |
| **a.** Marriage rights | 28 |
| **b.** Civil unions | 23 |
| **c.** No legal recognition | 43 |
| **d.** Don't know | 6 |

*Item 1 is based on a May 2–4, 2004 Gallup survey. Items 2–5 are based on a February 5–6, 2004 *Newsweek* survey. Item 6 is based on a May 13–14, 2004 *Newsweek* survey. All surveys are based on randomly selected national samples.

**Figure 12.6**

**Attitudes toward homosexuals.** Americans' attitudes toward gays are highly variable, depending on the specific issue. Women generally have more accepting attitudes than men.

Attitudes about homosexuality are gradually shifting toward greater acceptance of gays. For example, when comedian Ellen DeGeneres first came out of the closet in 1997, there was quite a bit of negative reaction from the general public. Today, however, she has a popular TV talk show and is a judge on *American Idol.*

© 2009 Tony DiMaio/iPhoto/newscom

*Homophobia* **is the intense fear and intolerance of homosexuals.** Because few people with negative attitudes toward homosexuals have the psychopathology that "phobia" implies, some psychologists believe that *sexual prejudice* is a more appropriate term (Herek, 2003, 2009b). The lowest levels of sexual prejudice are associated with individuals who personally know someone who is gay (Herek & Capitanio, 1996; Stotzer, 2009). Higher levels of sexual prejudice are associated with being older, male, less educated, and living in the South or Midwest and in rural areas (Herek & Capitanio, 1996). Sexual prejudice is also correlated with such psychological factors as authoritarianism (see Chapter 6), traditional gender-role attitudes (see Chapter 11), and conservative religious and political beliefs (Altemeyer, 1996; Herek & Capitanio, 1996; Shackelford & Besser, 2007). Unfortunately, negative attitudes sometimes translate into hate crimes. Around a third of gay men and lesbians have been victims of hate crimes (Parrott & Zeichner, 2006). In a recent national survey, 23% of the LGB participants had been threatened with violence, and 49% reported verbal harassment. These percentages were even higher when just considering gay males (35% and 63% respectively; Herek, 2009).

Perhaps we shouldn't be surprised that people's explanations of sexual orientation play a role in their attitudes. Viewing homosexuality as biological or genetic in origin (that is, uncontrollable) is associated with more favorable attitudes than attributing it to choice (Haider-Markel & Joslyn, 2008; Hegarty, 2002). These attitudes often spill over into actions, such as support for public policies and gay rights (Wood & Bartkowski, 2004). Black Americans are more likely that white Americans to endorse choice as an explanation for sexual orientation (Jayaratne et al., 2009) ,which may explain some of the cultural differences in acceptance of homosexuality.

### Disclosing One's Sexual Orientation

Coming to terms with one's sexual identity is complicated and difficult when it must take place in a climate of sexual prejudice. For gays, lesbians, and bisexuals, sexual identity development involves acknowledging, recognizing, and labeling one's sexual orientation, conceptualizing it in positive terms, and disclosing it to others (Garnets & Kimmel, 1991, 2003b). Recent generations are becoming aware of and are disclosing gay, lesbian, or bisexual identities earlier in life (Floyd & Bakeman, 2006).

Because of cultural differences in attitudes toward homosexuality, LGB people of color must contend wit the additional stress of negative reactions in their families and communities (Harper, Jernewall, & Zea, 2004; Iwasaki & Ristock, 2007). The quality of a parent-child relationship prior to disclosure may be the best predictor of how parents will initially react and adjust to their child's coming out (Savin-Williams, 2001). At least half of gay and lesbian teenagers reported that they had lost at least one friend because of their sexual orientation (Ryan & Futterman, 1997). High schools and colleges increasingly support groups for LGBT students. And the Internet offers a wealth of resources for LGBT people (see Web Link 12.2).

In deciding to disclose one's sexual orientation to others, individuals must balance the psychological and social benefits (being honest, having social support) against the costs (losing friends, being fired, falling victim to hate crimes, losing custody of children). A pragmatic solution to this conflict is *rational outness*— being "as open as possible, because it feels healthy to be honest, and as closed as necessary to protect against discrimination" (Bradford & Ryan, 1987, p. 77). People are more likely to disclose their sexual orientation to close heterosexual friends and siblings than to parents, co-workers, or employers.

### Adjustment

The mental health community initially classified homosexuality as a psychological disorder. But researchers demonstrated that view to be a myth; that is, gays and straights are indistinguishable in their general psychological processes and on measures of psychological health (Bell & Weinberg, 1978; Hooker, 1957; Rosen, 1974). As a result of research, changes in public attitudes, and political lobbying, homosexuality was deleted from the official list of psychological disorders in 1973. Since then, research continues to demonstrate that sexual orientation doesn't impair psychological adjustment in gay and straight individuals, couples, and parents (Gonsiorek, 1991; Patterson & Redding, 1996; Peplau &

**WEB LINK 12.2** **Parents, Families, and Friends of Lesbians and Gays**

The mission of this national organization is to promote the health and well-being of gay, lesbian, bisexual, and transgendered people as well as that of their families and friends. The organization is involved in support, education, and advocacy efforts and has more than 500 chapters in every state.

Spaulding, 2003). Similarly, there is no evidence of elevated psychopathology in nonclinical samples of bisexual men and women (Fox, 1996).

Although there is no reliable evidence that homosexual orientation *per se* impairs psychological functioning, exposure to sexual prejudice and discrimination can cause acute distress (Hatzenbuehler, 2009; Meyer, 2003). Some recent studies suggest that gay males and lesbians are at greater risk than their straight peers for anxiety, depression, self-injurious behavior, substance dependence, suicidal ideation, and suicide attempts (Balsam et al., 2005; Cochran, 2001). Fortunately, like their heterosexual counterparts, most LGB individuals are able to cope with this stress and thrive despite adversity (Smith & Gray, 2009).

According to the 2000 U.S. Census, 33% of female same-gender couples and 22% of male same-gender couples are rearing children (see Chapter 10). The children of some couples are their own from previous heterosexual relationships or artificial insemination; other children have been adopted. Studies show that children of gay or lesbian parents are no different than children of heterosexual parents in terms of self-esteem, gender roles, sexual orientation, peer group relationships, school outcomes, or social adjustment (C. J. Patterson, 2003, 2006, 2009; Tasker, 2005). A recent meta-analysis (see Chapter 11) confirmed that children from homosexual and heterosexual parents are equally well adjusted (Crowl, Ahn, & Baker, 2008).

# Interaction in Sexual Relationships

### LEARNING OBJECTIVES

- Identify several approach and several avoidance sexual motives.
- Describe four common barriers in communicating about sex.

People have many different motives for engaging in sexual activity. In all cases, however, communication is critical for healthy sexual relationships. In this section, we'll briefly discuss the interpersonal dynamics of sexual relationships.

## Motives for Engaging in Sex

Sexual motives are numerous and diverse, ranging from purely physical to deeply emotional (Meston & Buss, 2007). One conceptual framework for understanding sexual motives is to classify them as approach and avoidance motives (Cooper, Shapiro, & Powers, 1998; Impett, Peplau, & Gable, 2005). Approach motives focus on obtaining positive outcomes: (1) pursuing one's own sexual pleasure, (2) feeling good about oneself, (3) pleasing one's partner, (4) promoting intimacy in a relationship, and (5) expressing love for one's partner. Avoidance motives center on evading negative outcomes: (1) avoiding relationship conflict, (2) avoiding hurting a partner's feelings, (3) preventing a partner's anger, and (4) preventing a partner from losing interest. Researchers report that sexual encounters based on approach motives are positively associated with personal and relationship well-being. By contrast, sexual interactions based on avoidance motives are negatively associated with relationship satisfaction and are especially detrimental to relationships' continuing (Impett et al., 2005; Katz & Tirone, 2009).

## Communicating About Sex

Because individuals differ in sexual motives, attitudes, and appetites, disagreements about sex are to be expected. Couples have to negotiate whether, how often, and when they will have sex. They also have to decide what kinds of erotic activities will take place and what sexual behavior means to their relationship. This negotiation process may not be explicit, but it's there. Unresolved disparities can be an ongoing source of frustration in a relationship. Still, many people find it difficult to talk with their partner about sex, and inhibited communication is strongly linked to sexual dissatisfaction (Davis et al., 2006). Couples can encounter four common barriers to sexual communication:

1. *Fear of appearing ignorant.* According to a Kinsey Institute/Roper poll, most Americans are woefully ignorant about sex. That is, on an 18-item test of basic sexual knowledge, 55% of adults responded incorrectly to at least half of the questions (Reinisch, 1990). (You can test your own knowledge about some aspects of sex by responding to the questions in **Figure 12.7**.) Because most people feel that they should be experts about sex and know that they are not, they feel ashamed. To hide their ignorance, they avoid talking about sex.

### How Knowledgeable About Sex Are You?

1. Massage oil, petroleum jelly, and body lotions are good lubricants to use with a condom or diaphragm.
   ____ True __✓__ False ____ Don't know

2. Adult male homosexuals have lower than normal levels of male hormones.
   ____ True __✓__ False ____ Don't know

3. A teenage girl or woman can get pregnant during her menstrual period.
   ____ True __✓__ False ____ Don't know

4. Most cases of sexually transmitted diseases occur in people aged 26-50.
   ____ True __✓__ False ____ Don't know

5. In the United States, heterosexually-transmitted HIV infections rarely occur.
   ____ True __✓__ False ____ Don't know

**Scoring:** 1. False. (Oil-based creams, lotions, and jellies can produce microscopic holes in rubber products within 60 seconds of their application.) 2. False. (Research does not support this view.) 3. True. (While the chance of a woman's becoming pregnant during her menstrual period is lower than at other times, pregnancy can occur if she has unprotected sex during her period. Sperm can live for up to 8 days in a woman's reproductive tract, and if the menstrual cycle is irregular, as it is likely to be in adolescence, sperm may still be present in the reproductive tract a week later to fertilize a new egg.) 4. False. (Most cases of sexually transmitted diseases occur in the under-25 age group.) 5. False. (There is currently an upsurge in heterosexually-transmitted HIV infections in the U.S.)

**Figure 12.7**

**How knowledgeable about sex are you?** Check your basic sexual knowledge by answering these five questions. Information about each of the questions is discussed in this chapter.

2. *Concern about partner's response.* Both men and women say they want their partners to tell them what they want sexually (see **Figure 12.8** on the next page). Ironically, neither feels comfortable doing so. People usually hold back because they're afraid of hurting the other's feelings. Or they fear that their partner won't respect and love them if they are truthful. Research shows that more extensive disclosure of sexual likes and dislikes positively predicts sexual and relationship satisfaction in committed relationships (Sprecher et al., 2006). Individuals who keep their preferences to themselves are likely to remain frustrated and unsatisfied.

3. *Conflicting attitudes about sex.* Many people, particularly women, are burdened with the negative sexual messages they learned as children. Also, most individuals have contradictory beliefs about sex ("Sex is 'beautiful'" and "Sex is 'dirty'"), and this dissonance produces psychological conflicts.

4. *Negative early sexual experiences.* Some people have had negative sexual experiences that inhibit their enjoyment of sex. If these experiences are due to ignorant or inconsiderate sexual partners, subsequent

## Figure 12.8

**What men and women want more of during sex.**
Dating and married couples were asked which sexual activities they wanted more of in their relationships. Men and women all agreed that they wanted more instructions from their partners. They also generally agreed that they wanted warmer, more involved sexual relationships and more experimentation. In terms of gender differences, men wanted their partners to take the initiative and to be wilder and sexier; women wanted more emotional reassurance.

Source: From Hatfield, E., & Rapson, R. L. (1997). *Love, sex, and intimacy: Their psychology, biology, and history.* Boston: Allyn & Bacon. Reprinted by permission.

### What Men and Women Want More of During Sex

| Dating couples | |
| --- | --- |
| **Men** | **Women** |
| *Wish their partners would:* | |
| Be more experimental | Talk more lovingly |
| Initiate sex more often | Be more seductive |
| Try more oral-genital sex | Be warmer and more involved |
| Give more instructions | Give more instructions |
| Be warmer and more involved | Be more complimentary |

| Married couples | |
| --- | --- |
| **Men** | **Women** |
| *Wish their partners would:* | |
| Be more seductive | Talk more lovingly |
| Initiate sex more often | Be more seductive |
| Be more experimental | Be more complimentary |
| Be wilder and sexier | Be more experimental |
| Give more instructions | Give more instructions |
| | Be warmer and more involved |

positive sexual interactions will usually resolve the problem over time. If earlier sexual experiences have been traumatic, as in the case of rape or incest, counseling may be required to help a person view sex positively and enjoy it.

A person's sexual self-esteem is a strong predictor of his or her ability to communicate about sex (Oattes & Offman, 2007). To communicate more easily and effectively about sex, you may want to review Chapter 8. Most of the advice on how to improve verbal and nonverbal communication can be applied to sexual relationships. Assertive communication and constructive conflict resolution strategies can keep sexual negotia-tions healthy. A basic rule is to accentuate the positive ("I like it when you . . .") rather than the negative ("I don't like it when you . . .").

# The Human Sexual Response

### LEARNING OBJECTIVES

- Describe the four phases of the human sexual response cycle.
- Discuss gender differences in patterns of orgasm and some reasons for them.

When people engage in sexual activity, exactly how does the body respond? Surprisingly, until William Masters and Virginia Johnson conducted their groundbreaking research in the 1960s, little was known about the physiology of the human sexual response. Masters and Johnson used physiological recording devices to monitor the bodily changes of volunteers engaging in sex. Their observations and interviews with their subjects yielded a detailed description of the human sexual response that won them widespread acclaim.

## The Sexual Response Cycle

Masters and Johnson's (1966, 1970) description of the sexual response cycle is a general one, outlining typical rather than inevitable patterns—people vary considerably. **Figure 12.9** shows how the intensity of sexual arousal changes as women and men progress through the four phases of the sexual response cycle.

## Excitement Phase

During the initial phase of excitement, the level of arousal usually escalates rapidly. In both sexes, muscle tension, respiration rate, heart rate, and blood pressure increase quickly. In males **vasocongestion—engorgement of blood vessels**—produces penile erection, swollen testes, and the movement of the scrotum (the sac containing the testes) closer to the body. In females, vasocongestion leads to a swelling of the clitoris and vaginal lips, vaginal lubrication, and enlargement of the uterus. Most women also experience nipple erection and a swelling of the breasts.

## Plateau Phase

The name given to the "plateau" stage is misleading because physiological arousal does not level off. Instead, it continues to build, but at a much slower pace. In women, further vasocongestion produces a tightening of the lower third of the vagina and a "ballooning" of

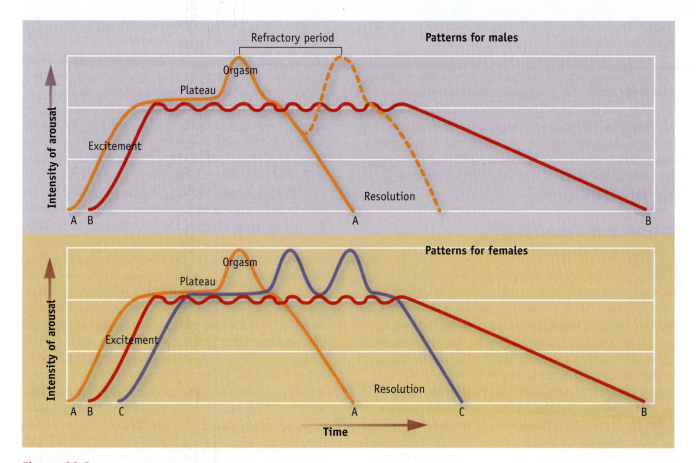

**Figure 12.9**

**The human sexual response cycle.** There are similarities and differences between men and women in patterns of sexual arousal. Pattern A, which culminates in orgasm and resolution, is the most typical sequence for both sexes. Pattern B, which involves sexual arousal without orgasm followed by a slow resolution, is also seen in both genders, but it is more common among women. Pattern C, which involves multiple orgasms, is seen almost exclusively in women, as men go through a refractory period before they are capable of another orgasm. (Based on Masters & Johnson, 1966)

the upper two-thirds, which lifts the uterus and cervix away from the end of the vagina. In men, the head of the penis may swell, and the testicles typically enlarge and move closer to the body. Many men secrete a bit of pre-ejaculatory fluid from the tip of the penis that may contain sperm.

Distractions during the plateau phase can delay or stop movement to the next stage. These include ill-timed interruptions like a telephone ringing or a child's knocking—or not!—on the bedroom door. Equally distracting can be such things as physical discomfort, pain, guilt, frightening thoughts, feelings of insecurity or anger toward one's partner, and anxiety about not having an orgasm.

## Orgasm Phase

*Orgasm* **occurs when sexual arousal reaches its peak intensity and is discharged in a series of muscular contractions that pulsate through the pelvic area.** Heart rate, respiration rate, and blood pressure increase sharply during this exceedingly pleasant spasmodic response. The male orgasm is usually

accompanied by ejaculation of seminal fluid. Some women report that they ejaculate some kind of fluid at orgasm. The prevalence of female ejaculation and the source and nature of the fluid are matters still under debate (Alzate, 1990; Whipple, 2000). The subjective experience of orgasm appears to be essentially the same for men and women, although the relationship between subjective experience and physical response seems to be greater for men than women (Suschinsky, Lalumiere, & Chivers, 2009). That is, there is a higher degree of agreement between a man's physical response (erection) and his self-report of arousal than there is for a woman.

## Resolution Phase

During the resolution phase, the physiological changes produced by sexual arousal subside. If one has not had an orgasm, the reduction in sexual tension may be relatively slow and sometimes unpleasant. After orgasm, men generally experience a *refractory period,* **a time following male orgasm during which males are largely unresponsive to further stimulation.** The refractory period varies from a few minutes to a few hours and increases with age.

Critics note that the Masters and Johnson model focuses entirely on genital changes during sex and ignores cognitive factors. An alternative is the three-stage model of noted sex therapist Helen Singer Kaplan (1979), which begins with desire, followed by excitement and then orgasm. Since people's thoughts and views about sex underlie many sexual problems, it is helpful to keep in mind that the sexual response involves more than just physical factors.

## Gender Differences in Patterns of Orgasm

As a whole, the sexual responses of women and men parallel each other fairly closely. Nonetheless, there are some interesting differences between the genders in their patterns of experiencing orgasm. During *intercourse,* women are less likely than men to reach orgasm (that is, they are more likely to follow pattern B in **Figure 12.9**). According to one survey of American sexual behavior (Laumann et al., 1994), about 29% of women reported that they *always* reached orgasm in their primary sexual relationships, compared to 75% of men (see **Figure 12.10**). However, 62% of partnered women reported that they were very satisfied with the frequency and consistency of their orgasms with their partners (Davis et al., 1996).

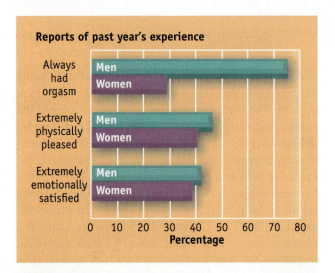

**Figure 12.10**
**Sexual satisfaction with primary partner.** A major survey of American sexual behavior showed large gender differences in the consistency of orgasm, a physical measure of sexual satisfaction. Men's and women's subjective evaluations of physical and emotional sexual satisfaction are much more similar. These data indicate that not everyone who has an orgasm every time has a blissful sex life and that factors other than orgasm contribute to a satisfying sex life.

Source: From Laumann, E. O., Gagnon, J. H., Michael, R. T., & Michaels, S. (1994). *The social organization of sexuality: Sexual practices in the United States.* Chicago: University of Chicago Press. Copyright © 1994 by University of Chicago Press. Reprinted by permission.

In their laboratory, Masters and Johnson found that the men they studied took about 4 minutes to reach a climax with their partners. Women took about 10–20 minutes to reach orgasm with their partners, but they reached orgasm in about 4 minutes when they masturbated. Clearly, then, women are capable of reaching orgasm more quickly than they typically do. Our point here is not that men and women should race each other to the finish line but that physiological factors are not the likely cause of gender differences related to orgasm.

How do we account for these disparities? First, although most women report that they enjoy intercourse, it is not the optimal mode of stimulation for them. This is because intercourse provides rather indirect stimulation to the clitoris, the most sexually sensitive genital area in most women. Thus, more lengthy *foreplay,* including manual or oral stimulation of the clitoris, is usually the key to enhancing women's sexual pleasure. Many men mistakenly assume that women experience the same degree of pleasurable sensations that they do during sexual intercourse. But this is not the case, as the upper two-thirds of the vagina has relatively few nerve endings—a good thing, since the vagina serves as the birth canal. Manual or oral stimulation of the clitoris is typically more effective in producing female orgasm than sexual intercourse alone (Bancroft, 2002b). Unfortunately, many couples are locked into the idea that orgasms should be achieved only through intercourse. Even the word *foreplay* suggests that any other form of sexual stimulation is merely preparation for the "main event." Also, most women associate sex with affection, so they want to hear some tender words during a sexual encounter. Men who verbally express their love and affection usually find their partners more responsive.

Research suggests that lesbians have orgasms more often and more easily in sexual interactions than heterosexual women do (Diamond, 2006; Peplau, Fingerhut, & Beals, 2004). Kinsey (1953) attributed this difference to female partners' knowing more about women's sexuality and how to optimize women's sexual satisfaction than male partners do. Also, female partners are more likely to emphasize the emotional aspects of lovemaking than male partners (Peplau et al., 2004). Taken together, these facts support a socialization-based explanation of gender differences in orgasmic consistency.

Because women reach orgasm through intercourse less consistently than men, they are more likely than men to fake an orgasm. Surveys reveal that more than half of all adult women (straight and lesbian) have faked an orgasm (Elliott & Brantley, 1997). Men (straight and gay) also fake orgasms, but much less frequently. People typically do so to make their partner feel better or to bring sexual activity to an end when they're tired. Frequent faking is not a good idea, because it can become a vicious cycle and undermine communication about sex (Crooks & Bauer, 2008).

# Sexual Expression

**LEARNING OBJECTIVES**

- Discuss fantasy as well as kissing and touching as aspects of sexual expression.
- Describe the prevalence of self-stimulation and attitudes about it.
- Discuss oral and anal sex as forms of sexual expression.
- Discuss intercourse and the preferred sexual activities of gay males and lesbians.

People experience and express sexuality in myriad ways. ***Erogenous zones* are areas of the body that are sexually sensitive or responsive.** The genitals and breasts usually come to mind when people think of erogenous zones, as these areas are particularly sensitive for most people. But it's worth noting that many individuals fail to appreciate the potential that lies in other areas of the body. Virtually any area of the body can function as an erogenous zone. And most long-term couples engage in a variety of sexual practices (see **Figure 12.11**; Kaestle & Halpern, 2007).

Indeed, the ultimate erogenous zone may be the mind. That is, an individual's mental set is extremely important to sexual arousal. Skillful genital stimulation by a partner may have absolutely no impact if a person is not in the mood. Yet fantasy in the absence of any other stimulation can produce great arousal. In this section, we'll consider the most common forms of sexual expression.

## Fantasy

Have you ever fantasized about having sex with someone other than your partner? If so, you've had one of the most commonly reported fantasies. In fact, a study of university students and employees reported that 98% of men and 80% of women had sexual fantasies involving someone other than their current partner (Hicks & Leitenberg, 2001). As you might expect, women's fantasies tend to be more romantic, while men's tend to contain more explicit imagery (Impett & Peplau, 2006). Most sex therapists view sexual fantasies as harmless ways to enhance sexual excitement and achieve orgasm either during masturbation or with a partner.

Dominance and submission fantasies are not uncommon. Research indicates that 31%–57% of women have submission fantasies in which they are forced into sex (Critelli & Bivona, 2008). Still, just because one fantasizes about a particular encounter, such as forced sex, doesn't mean that one really wants to have such an experience. There are several theories behind submission fantasies, including the male rape culture and sexual blame avoidance (Critelli & Bivona, 2008).

## Kissing and Touching

Most two-person sexual activities begin with kissing and mutual caressing. Kissing usually starts at the lips but may be extended to almost any area of the partner's body. In fact, there seems to be something special about kissing as a form of nonverbal communication. Floyd and colleagues (2009) randomly assigned heterosexual partners to either increase their romantic kissing frequency or not. After 6 weeks, they found that those who had increased kissing had lower perceived stress levels and higher relationship satisfaction. These differences were still significant even after the researchers controlled for increased verbal affections and decreased conflict, two factors one might expect with increased romantic kissing.

Men often underestimate the importance of kissing and touching (including clitoral stimulation). It is not

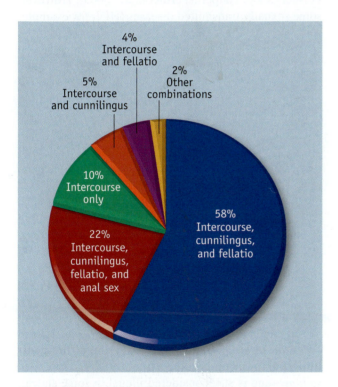

## Figure 12.11

**Percentages of sexual activities for heterosexual couples.** Using data from the National Longitudinal Study of Adolescent Health, Kaestle and Halpern (2007) report the distribution percentages for young heterosexual adults who reported which sexual activities they had engaged in with their current partner (of at least three months). It is clear that young adults engage in a variety of sexual activities.

Source: From Kaestle, C. E., & Halpern, C. T. (2007). What's love got to do with it? Sexual behaviors of opposite-sex couples through emerging adulthood. *Perspectives on Sexual and Reproductive Health, 39*(3), 134–140. Copyright © 2007 by the Guttmacher Institute.

surprising, therefore, that heterosexual women commonly complain that their partners are in too much of a hurry (King, 2005). Partners who seek to learn about each other's preferences and who try to accommodate each other are much more likely to have mutually satisfying sexual experiences than those who don't.

## Self-Stimulation

Masturbation, or the stimulation of one's own genitals, has historically been condemned as immoral because it is nonreproductive. Disapproval and suppression of masturbation were truly intense in the 19th and early 20th centuries, when people believed that the practice was harmful to physical and mental health. Because the term *masturbation* has acquired negative connotations, the preferred terminology is *self-stimulation* or *autoeroticism.*

Kinsey discovered over four decades ago that most people masturbate with no ill effects. Sexologists now recognize that self-stimulation is normal and healthy. In fact, sex therapists often prescribe masturbation to treat both male and female sexual problems (see this Chapter's Application). Nonetheless, nearly half of those who engage in the practice feel guilty about it (Laumann et al., 1994).

Self-stimulation is common in our society: By adulthood, nine out of ten males and eight out of ten females report having masturbated at least once (Atwood & Gagnon, 1987). In a recent national survey, 38% of women and 61% of men reported having engaged in self-stimulation in the past year (Das, 2007). African American males masturbate less than Asian, white, and Hispanic men. Also, masturbation is less common among those with less education (Laumann et al., 1994). Among married couples, 57% of husbands and 37% of wives report engaging in self-stimulation (Laumann et al., 1994). In fact, masturbation in marriage is often associated with a greater degree of marital and sexual satisfaction (Leitenberg, Detzer, & Srebnik, 1993).

Sometimes people, more often women, use vibrators or other "sex toys" for self-stimulation (though these are used during sexual interactions as well). Recent evidence suggests that vibrator use for women is associated with more positive sexual functioning and better sexual health practices (Herbenick et al., 2009). The findings are similar for men who incorporate

---

**WEB LINK 12.4  Kaiser Family Foundation**

This foundation sponsors multiple programs and educational efforts in the United States and South Africa to promote health generally, and its site provides a large set of resources regarding human sexuality.

---

vibrators into foreplay with their partners (Reece at al., 2009). Perhaps self-stimulation leads to greater satisfaction, or perhaps those who are more satisfied are more likely to engage is self-stimulation. The direction of this relationship has yet to be determined.

## Oral and Anal Sex

Oral sex refers to oral stimulation of the genitals. *Cunnilingus* **is oral stimulation of the female genitals;** *fellatio* **is oral stimulation of the penis.** Partners may stimulate each other simultaneously, or one partner may stimulate the other without immediate reciprocation. Oral-genital sex may be one of several activities in a sexual encounter, or it may be the main event. Oral sex is a major source of orgasms for many heterosexual couples, and it plays a central role in homosexual relationships. Both men and women perceive oral sex as less intimate than intercourse (Chambers, 2007).

A positive aspect of oral sex for some people is that it does not result in pregnancy. This fact partly accounts for the finding that younger teens are more likely to engage in oral sex than in intercourse (Cornell & Halpern-Felsher, 2006; Halpern-Felsher et al., 2005). However, some sexually transmitted diseases (HIV, for example) can be contracted through mouth-genital stimulation, especially if there are small cracks in the mouth or if the mouth is exposed to semen (Guest, 2004). And a person with a cold sore can pass along the herpes virus during oral sex or kissing (Carroll, 2007). Unfortunately, data suggest that up to 40% of sexually active teens either don't know that one can become infected with HIV through unprotected oral sex or are unsure about it (Centers for Disease Control, 2009).

Negative attitudes persist about oral sex, particularly among African Americans, Hispanics, religious conservatives, and those with less education (Hunt & Curtis, 2006; Laumann et al., 1994). However, it is a common practice in adolescent sexual experiences and most couples' sexual relationships (Brewster & Tillman, 2008; Kaestle & Halpern, 2007). About 80% of men and 70% of women (both gay and straight) report that they have either given or received oral sex at least once (Laumann et al., 1994).

*Anal intercourse* **involves insertion of the penis into a partner's anus and rectum.** Legally, it is termed *sodomy* (and is still considered illegal in some states). About 25% of men and women report that they have practiced anal sex at least once (Kaestle & Halpern, 2007; Laumann et al., 1994). Anal intercourse is more popular among homosexual male couples than among heterosexual couples. However, even among gay men it ranks behind oral sex and mutual masturbation in prevalence. Anal sex is risky. Gay men who engage in anal sex without a condom (referred to as bareback sex) run a high risk for HIV infection in that rectal tissues are easily torn, facilitating HIV transmission (Bauermeister et al., 2009).

## Intercourse

Vaginal intercourse, known more technically as *coitus,* **involves inserting the penis into the vagina and (typically) pelvic thrusting.** It is the most widely endorsed and widely practiced sexual act in our society. In the American sex survey, 95% of heterosexual respondents said that they had practiced vaginal sex the last time they had sex (Laumann et al., 1994). Frequent intercourse is associated with greater sexual and relationship satisfaction, higher life satisfaction, and better mental health (Brody & Costa, 2009).

Inserting the penis generally requires adequate vaginal lubrication, or intercourse may be difficult and painful for the woman. This is another good reason for couples to spend plenty of time on mutual kissing and touching, since sexual excitement induces vaginal lubrication. In the absence of adequate lubrication, partners may choose to use artificial lubricants.

Couples use a variety of positions in intercourse and may use more than one position in a single encounter. The man-above, or "missionary," position is the most common, but the woman-above, side-by-side, and rear-entry positions are also popular. Each position has its advantages and disadvantages. Although people are fascinated by the relative merits of various positions, specific positions may not be as important as the tempo, depth, and angle of movements in intercourse. As with other aspects of sexual relations, the crucial consideration is that partners talk to each other about their preferences.

What kinds of sexual activities do homosexuals prefer in the absence of coitus (which is, by definition, a heterosexual act)? As is true with heterosexual couples, the preliminary activities of gay and lesbian couples include kissing, hugging, and caressing. Gay men also engage in fellatio, mutual masturbation, and anal intercourse, in that order of prevalence (Lever, 1994). Lesbians engage in cunnilingus, mutual masturbation, and *tribadism* (also known as humping or scissoring), in which partners rub their genitals together so that both receive genital stimulation at the same time.

# *Patterns of Sexual Behavior*

### LEARNING OBJECTIVES

- Describe contemporary sexual health trends.
- Outline the research on sex outside of committed relationships.
- Summarize the findings on sex patterns in dating couples and married couples.
- Compare and contrast sexual behavior in married couples versus committed homosexual couples.
- Discuss the evidence on infidelity in committed relationships.

In this section we consider patterns of sexual behavior, including contemporary sexual health trends. Then we examine how the type of relationship one is in relates to sexual behavior. Finally, we explore the issue of infidelity.

## Sexuality Today

Since the sexual revolution of the 1960s, American sexual attitudes and behaviors have become much more liberal, although this trend has slowed since the 1990s (Christopher & Sprecher, 2000). While heralded by some, the liberal trends have had several serious drawbacks. Two troublesome problems are escalating teenage pregnancy rates and increases in sexually transmitted diseases (Trussell, Brown, & Hogue, 2004). The spread of HIV infection that leads to AIDS remains a special concern. (For a discussion of AIDS, see Chapter 5.) Has public awareness of these problems increased sexual responsibility?

The answer is both yes and no. After a period of decline in teenage birth rates, it appears that some nega-

tive sexual health outcomes are on the rise again. Following decreases from 1991 to 2005, teen birth rates increased in 2006 and 2007 (Centers for Disease Control, 2009). Further, the teen pregnancy rate in the United States remains one of the highest in the world (Trussell et al, 2004; U.S. Department of Health and Human Services, 2002).

Regarding sexually transmitted diseases, rates of genital infections among adolescents remain at high levels. One-fourth of all cases of sexually transmitted diseases occur among teenagers and two-thirds are among people under 25 years of age (Trussell et al., 2004). The good news is that most young people are knowledgeable about HIV and AIDS. Also, between 1991 and 2005, the percentage of high school students who had ever had sexual intercourse decreased, the average number of sex partners decreased, and the incidence of condom use increased, as you can see in **Figure 12.12** on the next page. Unfortunately, these positive patterns do not hold for all teens. An estimated 17,000 young people between the ages of 10 and 14 have an STD.

## Sexual Risk Behavior in High School Students

| Grade | Survey year | Ever had intercourse (%) | Four or more sexual partners in lifetime (%) | Condom use during last sexual intercourse (%) |
|---|---|---|---|---|
| 9 | 1991 | 39 | 13 | 53 |
|  | 2005 | 34 | 9 | 75 |
| 10 | 1991 | 48 | 15 | 46 |
|  | 2005 | 43 | 12 | 65 |
| 11 | 1991 | 62 | 22 | 49 |
|  | 2005 | 51 | 16 | 62 |
| 12 | 1991 | 67 | 25 | 41 |
|  | 2005 | 63 | 21 | 55 |

Note: Percentages are rounded to the nearest whole number.

**Figure 12.12**
**Sexual risk behavior in high school students.** In national surveys over a 14-year period, high school students reported on their sexual behavior: whether they had ever had sexual intercourse, the number of sex partners they had had, and whether they had used a condom during their last intercourse. Between 1991 and 2005, sexual risk behavior declined: Fewer students had sex, fewer had four or more sex partners, and more had used a condom during their last sexual encounter. Still, risky behavior increased as students progressed in school.

Source: From Centers for Disease Control. (2006). Trends in sexual risk behaviors among high school students—United States, 1991–2005. *Morbidity and Mortality Weekly Report, 55*(31), 851–854. (Figure based on data in table on pp. 853–854)

The rates of AIDS among male youth (especially African Americans) and the rates of syphilis for both males and females have increased in recent years (Centers for Disease Control, 2009).

## Sex Outside of Committed Relationships

"Hooking up," a phenomenon that has arisen since the late 1990s, involves two strangers or briefly acquainted people having a single sexual encounter. Hookups don't always involve intercourse (manual stimulation and oral sex are common). According to one study, 78% of college students have had at least one hookup (Paul, McManus, & Hayes, 2000). When looking at hookups that did include sexual intercourse, Eshbaugh and Gute

(2008) found that 36% of sexually active women reported having sex with someone only once and 29% reported having sex with someone they had known less than 24 hours. Further, hookups that included sex were linked to regret for women. Hookups typically result from flirting, drinking, and hanging out, and they typically end when one or both partners reach orgasm, or one person leaves or passes out (Paul, Wenzel, & Harvey, 2008).

It seems that college students wrongly believe that their peers are significantly more comfortable with hooking up than they themselves are (Lambert, Kahn, & Apple, 2003). Researchers speculate that these false perceptions might influence students to override their own comfort level and engage in sexual behavior to be in step with the perceived peer norm. **Figure 12.13** depicts men's and women's comfort level with various hooking-up behaviors. Casual sex is risky: People don't always practice safer sex, and the risk of contracting sexually transmitted diseases increases with multiple partners.

"Friends-with-benefits" refers to friends who engage in sex but who don't label their relationship as romantic. This situation is different from hooking up because participants in a friends-with-benefits relationship anticipate maintaining their friendship (Guerrero & Mongeau, 2008). Surveys indicate that up to 60% of undergraduates have experienced this kind of relationship (Bisson & Levine, 2009). People who engage in a friends-with-benefits arrangement are more likely to be casual daters, to be nonromantics, and to hold more hedonistic sexual values (Puentes, Knoz, & Zusman,

**Figure 12.13**
**Gender differences in comfort level with hooking-up behaviors.** College men and women were asked to rate their comfort level with four hooking-up behaviors. The ratings were made on an 11-point scale (11 = *Very comfortable*; 1 = *Not at all comfortable*). As you can see from the mean ratings shown here, men's comfort levels significantly exceeded women's for all four behaviors.

Source: From Lambert, T.A., Kahn, A. S., & Apple, K. J. (2003). Pluralistic ignorance and hooking up. *The Journal of Sex Research, 40*(2) 129–133. Copyright © 1979 Society for the Scientific Study of Sexuality. Reprinted by permission.

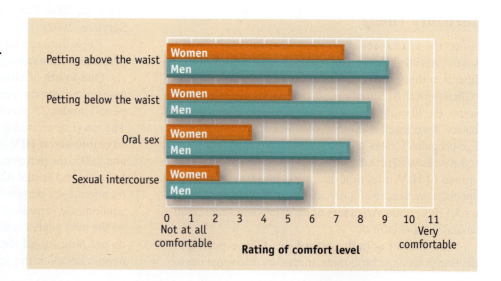

Hooking up with casual acquaintances is not uncommon in today's society. Nonetheless, casual sex can be risky for a variety of reasons.

2008). Obviously, negotiating such relationships can be tricky. Friendships are jeopardized if unreciprocated desires for romantic commitment develop or if one person wants to end the sexual relationship.

## Sex in Committed Relationships

Sex is a key aspect of most committed, romantic relationships. In this section, we examine patterns of sexual activity in dating couples, married couples, and gay couples.

### Sex Between Dating Partners

At some point, couples confront the question of whether or when they should have sex. Some worry that sex might adversely affect the relationship; others

fear that not having sex will cause trouble. Is there evidence to support either view? As it turns out, sexual intimacy is a positive predictor of relationship stability (Sprecher & Cate, 2004). However, gender and sexual and relationship satisfaction are also part of this equation. For men, sexual (but not relationship) satisfaction is significantly correlated with relationship stability; for women, relationship (but not sexual) satisfaction is significantly associated with relationship stability (Sprecher, 2002).

### Marital Sex

Couples' overall marital satisfaction is strongly related to their satisfaction with their sexual relationship (Sprecher et al., 2006). Of course, it is difficult to know whether good sex promotes good marriages or good marriages promote good sex. In all probability, it's a two-way street. Relationship satisfaction is also correlated with satisfaction in other areas of a relationship (fairness in distribution of household labor, for example) (Impett & Peplau, 2006).

Married couples vary greatly in how often they have sex (see **Figure 12.14**). *On the average,* couples in their 20s and 30s engage in sex about two or three times a week. The frequency of sex among married couples tends to decrease as the years pass (Hatfield & Rapson, 2008; Sprecher et al., 2006). Biological changes play some role in this trend, but social factors seem more compelling. Most couples attribute this decline to increasing fatigue from work and childrearing and to growing familiarity with their sexual routine.

As men and women age, sexual arousal tends to build more slowly and orgasms tend to diminish in

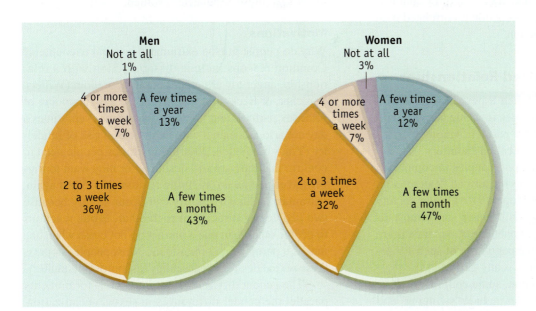

**Figure 12.14**

**Frequency of sex among married men and women.** A well-sampled survey asked Americans, "How often have you had sex in the past 12 months?" Married individuals' responses to the question were wide ranging. The most frequent response was "a few times per month" followed by "2 to 3 times a week."

Source: From Michael, R. T., Gagnon, J. H., Laumann, E. O., & Kolata, G. (1994) *Sex in America: A definitive survey.* Boston: Little, Brown. Copyright © 1994 by CSG Enterprises, Inc. Edward O. Lauman, Robert T. Michael, and Gina Kolata. By permission of Little, Brown and Company, Inc.

frequency and intensity. Males' refractory periods lengthen, and females' vaginal lubrication and elasticity decrease. Nevertheless, older people remain capable of rewarding sexual encounters (Burgess, 2004). In a national survey of individuals ages 40 to 80, 79% of men and 69% of women reported having sex in the previous year (Laumann et al., 2009). In another study of participants 70 years or older, 18% of women and 41% of men were sexually active, with intercourse and masturbation being the most commonly reported sexual activities (Smith et al., 2007). Marrying for love, still being in love, and having income are associated with sexual activity in later adulthood (Papaharitou et al., 2008). Unfortunately, restrictive health-care institutions and professionals often present barriers to sexuality by either explicitly or implicitly discouraging sexual expression by older adults (Bauer, McAuliffe, & Nay, 2007; McAuliffe, Bauer, & Nay, 2007).

## Sex in Homosexual Relationships

What about the frequency of sex among lesbian, gay, and heterosexual couples? Peplau and her colleagues (2004) report three patterns. First, there is a general decline in the frequency of sexual behavior over time. Second, in the early stages of a relationship, gay males engage in sex more frequently than the other types of couples. For example, among couples who had been together for two years or less, 67% of gay men reported having sex three or more times a week, compared to 45% of married couples and 33% of lesbian couples (Blumstein & Schwartz, 1983). Third, lesbian couples have sex less often than other couples.

Like heterosexual women, most lesbians believe that sex and love are intertwined. In contrast (and like straight males), gay men find casual sex more acceptable (Sanders, 2000). Comparative studies find comparable levels of sexual satisfaction in gay, lesbian, and heterosexual couples (Kurdek, 2005). And for both lesbians and gay men, sexual satisfaction is correlated with overall relationship satisfaction.

## Infidelity in Committed Relationships

Sexual infidelity occurs when a person who is in a committed relationship engages in erotic activity with someone other than his or her partner. Among married couples, this behavior is also called "adultery" or "extramarital sex." Infidelity among couples in committed relationships (straight and gay) is termed "extradyadic sex." The vast majority of people (91%) in our society believe that extramarital sex is "always" or "almost always wrong" (Saad, 2007). Nonetheless, Americans are fascinated by infidelity, if the popularity of such TV series as *Desperate Housewives* is any gauge.

Although it's not common, some couples condone extramarital sex. Two examples include "swinging" and "open marriage." Swingers are married couples who agree to exchange partners for sex (Rubin, 2001). In open marriage, now typically called polyamory (Hatch, 2009), both partners agree that it is okay for each to have sex with others (O'Neill & O'Neill, 1972). As we noted, gay male couples are more likely to have open relationships than are lesbian or heterosexual couples.

Precisely what kind of erotic activity qualifies as "cheating" is debatable, especially between men and women. Are you unfaithful if you develop a deep emotional involvement without sex? No doubt many people would say "yes," and research supports the notion that both sexual and emotional infidelity are upsetting (Lishner et al., 2008). Is it "cheating" if a person in a committed relationship uses the Internet for sexual arousal or masturbation? What about exchanging sexually explicit e-mail with someone you've never met face to face? Those are definite issues, and therapists are seeing more couples for problems related to cyber affairs (Cooper & Griffin-Shelley, 2002; Subotnik, 2007).

### Prevalence

Because of the associated stigma and secrecy, accurate estimates of infidelity are difficult to come by. Surveys report that about 25% of married men and about 10% of married women had engaged in an extramarital affair at least once (Laumann et al., 1994; Wiederman, 1997). In one study of over 1300 undergraduates, approximately 20% had engaged in extradyadic oral sex or intercourse without telling their partner (Knox, Vail-Smith, & Zusman, 2008).

As we noted, sexual openness is more common in committed gay male relationships, and the rates of extradyadic sex for this group are higher than for all other groups (Peplau & Fingerhut, 2007). Committed lesbian relationships are much more exclusive, in principle and in practice, than gay male relationships (Peplau & Fingerhut, 2007). Rates of lesbian extradyadic sex are also lower than those for married women.

### Motivations

Why do people pursue extramarital sexual encounters? Common reasons include dissatisfaction with a relationship, anger toward a partner, and boredom (Willets, Sprecher, & Beck, 2004). Having had a high number of prior sex partners and thinking about sex several times a day are also associated with an increased risk of infidelity (Treas & Gieden, 2000). Sometimes people need to confirm that they are still desirable, or they want to trigger the end of an unsatisfying relationship. Then again, extramarital sexual activity can occur simply because two people are attracted to each other. Erotic reactions to people other than one's partner do not cease when one makes a permanent commitment. Most people suppress these sexual desires because they disapprove of adultery.

The gender differences in motivations for infidelity parallel the gender differences in sexual socialization.

Men tend to engage in extradyadic affairs to obtain sexual variety or more frequent sex, while women usually seek an emotional connection (Buunk & Dijkstra, 2006). Low levels of positive communication are associated with infidelity for both genders (Allen at al., 2008). Age is also a factor. People between the ages of 18 and 30 are twice as likely to engage in sex outside a committed relationship than people over 50 (Treas & Giesen, 2000). Too, there is some evidence that insecure attachment styles are positively correlated with infidelity (Buunk & Dijkstra, 2006).

### Impact

The impact of extramarital sexual activity on marriages has not been extensively investigated. Experts speculate that approximately 20% of all divorces are caused by infidelity (Reinisch, 1990). Still, it's hard to know in these cases whether extramarital sex is a symptom of a disintegrating relationship or its cause. When a partner cheats, men tend to react with anger and violence, whereas women tend to show sadness and seek out support from friends (Miller & Maner, 2008). Participants in extramarital affairs, whether or not they are discovered, may experience loss of self-respect, guilt, stress, and complications of sexually transmitted diseases. Occasionally, extramarital affairs can have a positive effect on a marriage if they motivate a couple to resolve relationship problems. Sexual fidelity is positively correlated with relationship satisfaction for lesbian and heterosexual couples, but not for gay male couples (Kurdek, 1991).

# Practical Issues in Sexual Activity

### LEARNING OBJECTIVES

- Identify constraints on effective contraception, and discuss the merits of hormone-based contraceptives and male condoms.
- Describe the various types of STDs, and discuss their prevalence and means of transmission.
- List some suggestions for safer sexual practices.

Regardless of the context of sexual activity, two practical issues are often matters of concern: contraception and sexually transmitted diseases. These topics are more properly in the domain of medicine than of psychology, but birth control and sex-related infections certainly do have their behavioral aspects.

## Contraception

Most people want to control whether and when they will conceive a child, so they need reliable contraception. Despite the availability of effective contraceptive methods, however, many people fail to exercise much control. In the United States, it is estimated that nearly half of pregnancies are unplanned (Finer & Henshaw, 2006).

### Constraints on Effective Contraception

Effective contraception requires that intimate couples negotiate their way through a complex sequence of steps. First, both people must define themselves as sexually active. Second, both must have accurate knowledge about fertility and conception. Third, their chosen method of contraception must be readily accessible. Finally, both must have the motivation and skill to use the method correctly and consistently. Failure to meet even one of these conditions can result in an unintended pregnancy.

Many high school students (23% of girls and 16% of boys) use either withdrawal or no contraception at all (Santelli et al. 2006). These individuals are at high risk for pregnancy and sexually transmitted diseases. In addition, any couples who do not use condoms (even if they use another contraceptive method) can contract sexually transmitted diseases unless both partners have tested negatively for such infections.

MOM - WHAT'S BIRTH CONTROL?

IT'S WHAT THEY SHOULDN'T TEACH YOU IN SCHOOL...

BECAUSE IT'S SOMETHING CHILDREN SHOULD LEARN FROM THEIR PARENTS...

AND THAT'S THE LAST I WANT TO HEAR ABOUT IT!!

© 1986, *The Boston Globe*. Reprinted by permission of The Los Angeles Times Syndicate.

**WEB LINK 12.5  Sexual Health Network**

The health professionals who staff this Connecticut-based site have assembled a comprehensive set of resources related to all aspects of human sexual health, including sexual functioning for persons with physical injuries or disabilities.

Why do some individuals and couples engage in risky sexual behavior? As shown in **Figure 12.15,** researchers have identified various individual, interpersonal, and societal factors (Ayoola, Nettleman, & Brewer, 2007). Once again, conflicting norms about gender and sexual behavior play a role. Men are socialized to be the initiators of sexual activity, but when it comes to birth control, they often rely on women to take charge. It is hard for a woman to maintain an image of sexual naïveté and also be responsible for contraception. Telling her partner that she is "on the pill" or whipping out a condom conveys quite a different image. Unfortunately, a woman's decision to use a condom may be influenced more by concerns about how her partner might perceive her than her perceived susceptibility to infections and attitudes about condom use (Bryan, Aiken, & West, 1999). The mixed messages sent by some sexual education programs ("Use a condom but we can't supply you with one") add to the confusion (Allen, 2007). Finally, alcohol can undermine condom use, although this is not always the case (Cooper, 2006). Some individuals drink as a socially acceptable way to avoid potentially embarrassing discussions about sex.

### Selecting a Contraceptive Method

If a couple is motivated to control their fertility, how should they go about selecting a technique? A rational choice requires accurate knowledge of the effectiveness, benefits, costs, and risks of the various methods. **Figure 12.16** summarizes information on most of the

| Reasons for Unprotected Sex |
| --- |
| **Individual/personal reasons** |
| Side effects of contraceptive method |
| Technical problems using method |
| Method not on hand |
| Forgot |
| Unexpected sex |
| Embarrased to purchase contraceptive |
| **Interpersonal reasons** |
| Partner did not want to use contraception |
| Uncomfortable discussing contraception with partner |
| Fear of partner's reaction |
| Friends don't use/support contraception |
| **Societal reasons** |
| Access to contraception |
| Unanswered questions |
| Incomplete/incorrect information |
| Cost/insurance |
| Unwanted/forced sex |

**Figure 12.15**

**Common reasons why women engage in unprotected sex.** Researchers found that most excuses provided by women for having unprotected sex fall into three categories: individual, interpersonal, or societal.

Source: Adapted from Ayoola, A.B., Nettleman, M., & Brewer, J. (2007). Reasons for unprotected intercourse in adult women. *Journal of Women's Health, 16*(3), 302–310. The publisher for this copyrighted material is Mary Ann Liebert, Inc.

| Contraceptive Methods | | | | |
| --- | --- | --- | --- | --- |
| | Ideal failure rate (%) | Actual failure rate (%) | Advantages | Disadvantages |
| **Hormonal methods** | | | | |
| Birth control pills (combination) | 0.3 | 8 | Highly reliable; coitus-independent; has some health benefits | Side effects; daily use; continual cost; health risks for some women; no protection against STDs |
| Minipill (progestin only) | 0.3 | 8 | Thought to have low risk of side effects; coitus-independent; has some health benefits | Breakthrough bleeding; daily use; continual cost; health risks for some women; no protection against STDs |
| Hormonal injectables (Depo-Provera) | 0.3 | 3 | Highly reliable; coitus independent; no memory or motivation required for use; reduces risk of endometrial and ovarian cancer | Side effects; use may increase risk of certain cancers; continual cost; injection every 3 months; no protection against STDs |

*(continued)*

**Figure 12.16**

**A comparison of widely used contraceptive techniques.** Couples can choose from a variety of contraceptive methods. This chart summarizes the advantages and disadvantages of each method. Note that the typical failure rate is much higher than the ideal failure rate for all methods, because couples do not use contraceptive techniques consistently and correctly. (Based on Carroll, 2007; Crooks & Baur, 2008; Hatcher et al., 2004)

| | Ideal failure rate (%) | Actual failure rate (%) | Advantages | Disadvantages |
|---|---|---|---|---|
| **Contraceptive Methods** *(continued)* | | | | |
| **Hormonal methods** *(continued)* | | | | |
| Hormonal ring (NuvaRing) | 0.3 | 8 | Highly reliable; coitus independent; no memory or motivation required for use; may offer protection against endometrial and ovarian cancer | Side effects; no data on extended use; no protection against STDs |
| Subdermal implants (Implanon) | 0.1 | 0.1 | Highly reliable; coitus independent; no memory or motivation required for use | Side effects; painful removal; possible scarring at site; no protection from STDs |
| Transdermal patch | .03 | 8 | No memory or motivation required to use; coitus-independent; very reliable; has some health benefits | Continual cost; skin irritation for some women; no protection against STDs |
| **Barrier methods** | | | | |
| IUD | 0.6 | 0.8 | No memory or motivation required for use; very reliable; some health benefits | Cramping, bleeding, expulsion; risk of pelvic inflammatory disease; no protection against STDs |
| Diaphragm with spermicidal cream or jelly | 6 | 16 | No major health risks; inexpensive | Aesthetic objections; initial cost |
| Condom (male) | 2 | 15 | Protects against STDs; simple to use; male responsibility; no health risks; no prescriptions required | Unaesthetic to some; requires interruption of sexual activity; continual cost |
| Condom (female) | 5 | 21 | Protects against STDs; reduces post-coital drip; can be used without partner knowledge | Difficult to insert, uncomfortable, can be noisy during intercourse |
| Sponge | 9 | 16 | 24-hour protection; simple to use; no taste or odor; inexpensive; effective with several acts of intercourse | Aesthetic objections; continual cost; no protection against STDs |
| Cervical cap with spermicidal cream or jelly | 9 | 16 | 48-hour protection; no major health risks | May be difficult to insert; may irritate cervix; initial cost |
| Spermicides | 18 | 29 | No major health risks; no prescription required | Unaesthetic to some; must be properly inserted; continual cost; no protection against STDs |
| Fertility awareness (rhythm) | 1–9 | 25 | No cost; acceptable to Catholic church | Requires high motivation and periods of abstinence; unreliable; no protection against STDs |
| **Surgical methods** | | | | |
| Female sterilization (tubal ligation) | 99 | 99 | Effective; permanent; doesn't interfere with sexual activity; reduces risk of ovarian cancer | Side effects associated with surgery; doesn't protect against STDs; expensive; irreversible |
| Male sterilization (vasectomy) | 99 | 99 | Effective; permanent; doesn't interfere with sexual activity | Side effects associated with surgery; doesn't protect agains STDs; expensive; irreversible |
| **Other methods** | | | | |
| Withdrawal | 4 | 27 | No cost or health risks | Reduces sexual pleasure; unreliable; requires high motivation; no protection against STDs |
| No contraception | 85 | 85 | No immediate monetary cost | High risk of pregnancy and STDs |

Note: STDs = Sexually transmitted diseases

methods currently available. The *ideal failure rate* estimates the probability of conception when the technique is used correctly and consistently. The *actual failure rate* is what occurs in the real world, when users' negligence is factored in.

The greater one's knowledge about birth control, the more likely one is to communicate with one's partner before sex (Ryan et al., 2007). Contraception is a joint responsibility. Hence, it's essential for partners to discuss their preferences, to decide what method(s) they are going to use, and to *act* on their decision. Let's look in more detail at two of the most widely used birth control methods in the Western world: hormone-based contraceptives and male condoms.

*Hormone-based contraceptives* contain synthetic forms of estrogen and progesterone (or progesterone only, in the minipill), which inhibit ovulation in women. Types of hormone-based contraceptives include "the pill," hormonal injectables (Depo-Provera), the transdermal patch (worn on the skin), the vaginal ring (inserted once a month), and contraceptive implants. Many couples prefer these birth control options because contraceptive use is not tied to the sex act. Only the interuterine device (IUD) permits a similar degree of sexual spontaneity. But these contraceptives do not protect against sexually transmitted diseases.

Except for Depo-Provera, which may increase the risk of cervical, liver, and/or breast cancers (Carroll, 2007), use of hormone-based contraceptives does not appear to increase a woman's overall risk for cancer (Trussell, 2004). In fact, the likelihood of certain forms of cancer (such as uterine and ovarian cancer) is reduced in women who use low-dosage *oral* contraceptives. These methods do slightly increase the risk of certain cardiovascular disorders, such as heart disease and stroke. Thus, alternative methods of contraception should be considered by women who smoke, are over age 35, have any suspicion of cardiovascular disease, have liver disease, or have breast or uterine cancer.

The *male condom*, a barrier method of contraception, is a sheath worn over the penis during intercourse to collect ejaculated semen. The condom is the only widely available contraceptive device for use by males. A condom slightly reduces a man's sensitivity, but many men see this dulling as a plus because it can make sex last longer. Condoms can be purchased in any drugstore without a prescription. If used correctly, the condom is highly effective in preventing pregnancy (Warner, Hatcher, & Steiner, 2004). It must be placed over the penis after erection but before any contact with the vagina, and space must be left at the tip to collect the ejaculate. The man should withdraw before completely losing his erection and firmly hold the rim of the condom during withdrawal to prevent any semen from spilling into the vagina. Other barrier methods include female condoms (which is inserted into the vagina), diaphragms, and spermicides.

Male condoms are made of polyurethane, latex rubber, or animal membranes ("skin"). Polyurethane condoms are thinner than latex condoms; however, they are more likely to break and to slip off than latex condoms. Using latex condoms definitely reduces the chances of contracting or passing on various sexually transmitted diseases. However, oil-based creams and lotions (petroleum jelly, massage oil, baby oil, and hand and body lotions, for example) should never be used with *latex* condoms (or diaphragms) (Warner et al., 2004). Within 60 seconds, these products can make microscopic holes in the rubber membrane that are large enough to allow passage of HIV and organisms produced by other sexually transmitted diseases. Water-based lubricants such as Astroglide or K-Y Warming Liquid do not cause this problem. Polyurethane condoms are impervious to oils. Skin condoms do *not* offer protection against sexually transmitted diseases.

In closing, we should mention emergency contraception. Women may seek emergency contraception in cases of sexual assault, contraceptive failure, or unprotected sex. Progestin pills (also called Plan B or "morning after" pills) are available from pharmacies without a prescription for women aged 18 and older (younger women must have a prescription) (Alan Guttmacher Institute, 2006). Plan B pills are 95% effective in preventing pregnancy if they are taken within 24 hours after intercourse (75% effective within 72 hours). The drug works like birth control pills, by preventing ovulation or fertilization and implantation of the fertilized egg into the uterine wall ("Condoms—Extra Protection," 2005). If the fertilized egg is already implanted into the wall of the uterus, progestin will not harm it. By contrast, mifepristone (RU 486) is a drug that can induce a miscarriage in the first seven weeks of a pregnancy (Stewart, Ellertson, & Cates, 2004). Prescribed by a physician, mifepristone is typically administered in the form of two pills taken several days apart. Although no substitute for regular birth control, these drugs can be used after unprotected sex and are particularly helpful in cases of rape. They do not, however, provide any protection against sexually transmitted diseases.

## Sexually Transmitted Diseases

A *sexually transmitted disease* (STD) is a disease or infection that is transmitted primarily through sexual contact. When people think of STDs (also referred to as sexually transmitted infections), they typically think of chlamydia and gonorrhea, but these diseases are only the tip of the iceberg. There are actually around 25 sexually transmitted diseases. Some of them—for instance, pubic lice—are minor nuisances that can readily be treated. Others, however, are severe afflictions that are difficult to treat. For instance, if it isn't detected early, syphilis can cause heart failure, blindness, and brain damage, and AIDS is eventually fatal. The principal types of sexually transmitted diseases are listed in **Figure 12.17**, along with their symptoms and modes of transmission. Most of these infections are spread from one person to another through intercourse, oral-genital contact, or anal-genital contact.

### Prevalence and Transmission

No one is immune to sexually transmitted diseases. Even monogamous partners can develop some STDs

## Sexually Transmitted Diseases (STDs)

| STD | Transmission | Symptoms |
| --- | --- | --- |
| Acquired immune deficiency syndrome (AIDS) | The AIDS virus is spread by coitus or anal intercourse. There is a chance the virus may also be spread by oral-genital sex, particularly if semen is swallowed. (AIDS can also be spread by nonsexual means: contaminated blood, contaminated hypodermic needles, and transmission from an infected woman to her baby during pregnancy or childbirth.) | Most people infected with the virus show no immediate symptoms; antibodies usually develop in the blood 2-8 weeks after infection. People with the virus may remain symptom-free for 5 years or more. No cure for the disease has yet been found. Common symptoms include fevers, night sweats, weight loss, chronic fatigue, swollen lymph nodes, diarrhea and/or bloody stools, atypical bruising or bleeding, skin rashes, headache, chronic cough, and a whitish coating on the tongue or throat. |
| Chlamydia infection | The *Chlamydia trichomatis* bacterium is transmitted primarily through sexual contact. It may also be spread by fingers from one body site to another. | In men, chlamydial infection of the urethra may cause a discharge and burning during urination. Chlamydia-caused epididimitis may produce a sense of heaviness in the affected testicle(s), inflammation of the scrotal skin, and painful swelling at the bottom of the testicle. In women, pelvic inflammatory disease caused by chlamydia may disrupt menstrual periods, temperature, and cause abdominal pain, nausea, vomiting, headache, infertility, and ectopic pregnancy. |
| Human papillomavirus (HPV) | Virus is often on genital skin areas not covered by a condom (vulva, scrotum, etc.); virus is spread primarily through penile-vaginal, oral-genital, oral-anal, or genital-anal contact; transmission most often occurs by asymptomatic individuals. | Often asymptomatic; 10% of infections lead to contagious genital warts, which may appear 3 to 8 months after contact with infected person; HPV is associated with various cancers. |
| Gonorrhea ("clap") | The *Neisseria gonorrhoeae* bacterium (gonococcus) is spread through penile-vaginal, oral-genital, or genital-anal contact. | Most common symptoms in men are a cloudy discharge from the penis and burning sensations during urination. If the disease is untreated, complications may include inflammation of the scrotal skin and swelling at the base of the testicle. In women, some green or yellowish discharge is produced, but the disease commonly remains undetected. At a later stage, pelvic inflammatory disease may develop. |
| Herpes | The genital herpes virus (HSV-2) appears to be transmitted primarily by penile-vaginal, oral-genital, or genital-anal contact. The oral herpes virus (HSV-1) is transmitted primarily by kissing, or oral-genital contact. | Small red, painful bumps (papules) appear in the region of the genitals (genital herpes) or mouth (oral herpes). The papules become painful blisters that eventually rupture to form wet, open sores. |
| Pubic lice ("crabs") | *Phthirus pubis,* the pubic louse, is spread easily through body contact or through shared clothing or bedding. | Persistent itching. Lice are visible and may often be located in pubic hair or other body hair. |
| Syphilis | The *Treponema pallidum* bacterium (spirochete) is transmitted from open lesions during penile-vaginal, oral-genital, oral-anal, or genital-anal contact. | *Primary stage:* A painless chancre (sore) appears at the site where the spirochetes entered the body. *Secondary stage:* The chancre disappears and a generalized skin rash develops. *Latent stage:* There may be no observable symptoms. *Tertiary stage:* Heart failure, blindness, mental disturbance, and many other symptoms may occur. Death may result. |
| Trichomoniasis | The protozoan parasite *Trichomonas vaginalis* is passed through genital sexual contact or less frequently by towels, toilet seats, or bathtubs used by an infected person. | In women, white or yellow vaginal discharge with an unpleasant odor; vulva is sore and irritated. Men are usually asymptomatic. |
| Viral hepatitis | The hepatitis B virus may be transmitted by blood, semen, vaginal secretions, and saliva. Manual, oral, or penile stimulation of the anus is strongly associated with the spread of this virus. Hepatitis A seems to be spread primarily via the fecal-oral route. Oral-anal sexual contact is a common mode of sexual transmission for hepatitis A. | Vary from nonexistent to mild, flulike symptoms to an incapacitating illness characterized by high fever, vomiting, and severe abdominal pain. |

**Figure 12.17**

**Overview of common sexually transmitted diseases (STDs).** This chart summarizes the symptoms and modes of transmission of nine STDs. Note that intercourse is not required to transmit all STDs—many can be contracted through oral-genital contact or other forms of physical intimacy. (Adapted from Carroll, 2007; Crooks & Baur, 2008; Hatcher et al., 2004)

(yeast infections, for instance). Health authorities estimate that about 19 million new cases occur in the United States each year (Alan Guttmacher Institute, 2006). The highest incidence of STDs occurs in the under-25 age group (Cates, 2004). About one person in four contracts an STD by age 21 (Feroli & Burstein, 2003).

At the end of 2006, an estimated 1.1 million persons in the United States were living with HIV/AIDS (Centers for Disease Control, 2006). The United States has seen a recent surge of HIV infections stemming from heterosexual transmission (Kaiser Family Foundation, 2006). And an estimated half of all new HIV infections occur in people under age 25. The rate of HIV infections is up among young gay and bisexual men, especially those of color (Kaiser Family Foundation, 2006). Unfortunately, the availability of new drug treatments for HIV seems to have increased risk taking among gay and bisexual men (Peterson & Bakeman, 2006). Although these new drugs are welcome news, they cost over $10,000 per year—well out of the reach of those without health insurance (Freedberg et al., 2001).

AIDS is increasing more rapidly among women than among men, especially among Blacks and Latinas (Kaiser Family Foundation, 2007). Women whose sexual partners have multiple sex partners or who inject drugs are especially at risk. An increasing concern is that a woman's partner may be secretly having sex with other men and may deny that he is gay or bisexual (Kalb & Murr, 2006). This phenomenon, known as being on the "down low," is more common among black and Hispanic than white men, presumably because of cultural differences in attitudes toward homosexuality and bisexuality (Heath & Goggin, 2009; Wolitski et al., 2006). In one study, 22% of men on the down low had recently had both unprotected anal and vaginal sex (Siegel et al., 2008). These men report that they don't use protection because they don't always have condoms available, they enjoy sex more without a condom, and they perceive their females partners as "safe" (Dodge, Jeffries, & Sandfort, 2008). Obviously, this lifestyle has serious implications for unknowing female partners in terms of increasing their risk for HIV infection or any STD (Martinez & Hosek, 2005).

Women suffer more severe long-term consequences of STDs than men, including chronic pelvic pain, infertility, and cervical cancer (Cates, 2004; Centers for Disease Control, 2009). Because of the transmission dynamics of sexual intercourse, they are also more likely to acquire an STD from any single sexual encounter. But women are less likely to seek treatment because more of their STDs are asymptomatic or not perceived to be serious.

Human papillomavirus (HPV) infections cause about half of STDs diagnosed among 15- to 24-year-olds (Alan Guttmacher Institute, 2006). HPV is increasingly common; it's estimated that 50% of sexually active men and women acquire genital HPV infection (Centers for Disease Control, 2007). HPV tends to be more serious for women than men because certain types of HPV can lead to cervical cancer. In 2006, the U.S. Food and Drug Administration approved a vaccine (Gardisil) for use by females aged 9 to 26. It will prevent infection with the types of HPV that lead to cervical cancer.

### Prevention

Abstinence is obviously the best way to avoid acquiring STDs. Of course, for many people this is not an appealing or realistic option. Short of abstinence, the best strategy is to engage in sexual activity only in the context of a long-term relationship, where partners have an opportunity to know each other reasonably well. Casual sex greatly increases the risk for STDs, including HIV.

Along with being judicious about sexual relations, you need to talk openly about safer sexual practices with your partner. But if you don't carry the process one step further and practice what you preach, you remain at risk.

We offer the following suggestions for safer sex (Crooks & Baur, 2008; King, 2005):

● If you are not involved in a sexually exclusive relationship with someone free of disease, always use latex condoms with spermicides. They have a good track record of preventing STDs and offer effective protection against the AIDS virus. (And never use oil-based lubricants with latex condoms; use water-based lubricants instead.)

● If there is any possibility that you or your partner has an STD, abstain from sex, always use condoms, or use other types of sexual expression such as hand-genital stimulation. People can be carriers of sexually transmitted diseases without knowing it. For instance, in its early stages gonorrhea may cause no readily apparent symptoms in women, who may unknowingly transmit the infection to their partners

● Don't have sex with lots of people. You increase your risk of contracting STDs.

● Don't have sex with someone who has had lots of previous partners. People won't always be honest about their sexual history, so it's important to know whether you can trust a prospective partner's word.

● Don't assume that the labels people attach to themselves (heterosexual or homosexual) accurately describe their actual sexual behavior. According to a study based on a nationally representative sample of individuals aged 15 to 44, 6% of males and 11% of females reported that they had had at least one same-gender sexual experience in their lives (Mosher, Chandra, & Jones, 2005). As we discussed previously, many people keep these encounters secret from their partners (Gilbert & Williams, 2007).

- You should consider *any* activity that exposes you to blood (including menstrual blood), semen, vaginal secretions, urine, feces, or saliva as high-risk behavior *unless* you and your partner are in a mutual, sexually exclusive relationship and neither of you is infected.
- Because HIV is easily transmitted through anal intercourse, it's a good idea to avoid this type of sex. Rectal tissues are delicate and easily torn, thus letting the virus pass through the membrane. Always use a condom during anal sex.
- Oral-genital sex may also transmit HIV, particularly if semen is swallowed.
- Wash your genitals with mild soap and warm water before and after sexual contact.
- Urinate shortly after intercourse.
- Watch for sores, rashes, or discharge around the vulva or penis, or elsewhere on your body, especially the mouth. If you have cold sores, avoid kissing or oral sex.

If you have any reason to suspect that you have an STD, find a good health clinic and get tested *as soon as possible*. It's normal to be embarrassed or afraid of getting bad news, but don't delay. Health professionals are in the business of helping people, not judging them. To be really sure, get tested twice. If you have several sexual partners in a year, you should have regular STD checkups. You will have to ask for them, as most doctors and health clinics won't perform them otherwise.

Remember that the symptoms of some STDs disappear as the infection progresses. If your test results are positive, it's essential to get the proper treatment *right away*. Notify your sexual partner(s) so they can be tested immediately, too. And avoid sexual intercourse and oral sex until you and your partner are fully treated and a physician or clinic says you are no longer infectious.

Even with these risks, sexual activity is a normal part of intimate relationships. In the Application, we focus on enhancing sexual satisfaction and treating common sexual problems.

# APPLICATION

# *Enhancing Sexual Relationships*

### LEARNING OBJECTIVES

- List six general suggestions for enhancing sexual relationships.
- Discuss the nature, prevalence, and causes of common sexual dysfunctions.
- Describe the strategies for coping with erectile difficulties, premature ejaculation, orgasmic difficulties, and hypoactive sexual desire.

*Answer the following statements "true" or "false."*

_____ 1. Sexual problems are unusual.

_____ 2. Sexual problems belong to couples rather than individuals.

_____ 3. Sexual problems are highly resistant to treatment.

_____ 4. Sex therapists sometimes recommend masturbation as a treatment for certain types of problems.

The answers are (1) false, (2) true, (3) false, and (4) true. If you missed several of these questions, you are by no means unusual. Misconceptions about sexuality are the norm rather than the exception. Fortunately, there is plenty of useful information on how to improve sexual relationships.

For the sake of simplicity, our advice is directed to heterosexual couples, but much of what we have to say is also relevant to same-gender couples. For advice aimed specifically at same-gender couples, we recommend *Permanent Partners: Building Gay and Lesbian Relationships That Last* by Betty Berzon (2004).

## General Suggestions

Let's begin with some general ideas about how to enhance sexual relationships, drawn from several excellent books on sexuality (Carroll, 2007; Crooks & Baur, 2008; King, 2005). Even if you are satisfied with your sex life, these suggestions may be useful as "preventive medicine."

1. *Pursue adequate sex education.* A surprising number of people are ignorant about the realities of sexual functioning. So the first step in promoting sexual satisfaction is to acquire accurate information about sex. The shelves of most bookstores are bulging with

popular books on sex, but many of them are loaded with inaccuracies. A good bet is to pick up a college textbook on human sexuality. Enrolling in a course on human sexuality is also a good idea. Most colleges offer such courses today.

2. *Review your sexual values system.* Many sexual problems stem from a negative sexual values system that associates sex with immorality. The guilt feelings caused by such an orientation can interfere with sexual functioning. Thus, sex therapists often encourage adults to examine the sources and implications of their sexual values.

3. *Communicate about sex.* As children, people often learn that they shouldn't talk about sex. Many people carry this edict into adulthood and have great difficulty discussing sex, even with their partner. Good communication is essential in a sexual relationship. Many common problems—such as choosing an inconvenient time, too little erotic activity before intercourse, and too little tenderness afterward—are traceable largely to poor communication. Your partner is not a mindreader! You have to share your thoughts and feelings. Remember that both men and women say they want more instructions from their partner (refer back to **Figure 12.8**). If you are unsure about your partner's preferences, ask. And provide candid (but diplomatic) feedback when your partner asks for your reactions.

4. *Avoid goal setting.* Sexual encounters are not tests or races. Sexual experiences are usually best when people relax and enjoy themselves. People get overly concerned about orgasms or about both partners reaching orgasm simultaneously. A grim determination to climax typically makes it harder to do so. This mental set can lead to disruptive habits like *spectatoring,* or stepping outside the sexual act to judge one's performance. It's better to adopt the philosophy that getting there is at least half the fun.

5. *Enjoy your sexual fantasies.* As we noted earlier, the mind is the ultimate erogenous zone. Although Freudian theory originally saw sexual fantasy as an unhealthy by-product of sexual frustration and immaturity, research shows that sexual fantasies are most common among those who have the fewest sexual problems (Leitenberg & Henning, 1995; Renaud & Byers, 2001). Men and women both report that their

sexual fantasies increase their excitement. So don't be afraid to use fantasy to enhance your sexual arousal.

6. *Be selective about sex.* Sexual encounters generally work out better when you have privacy and a relaxed atmosphere, when you are well rested, and when you are enthusiastic. Of course, you can't count on (or insist on) having ideal situations all the time, but you should be aware of the value of being selective. If your heart just isn't in it, it may be wise to wait. Partners often differ about when, where, and how often they like to have sex. Such differences are normal and should not be a source of resentment. Couples simply need to work toward reasonable compromises—through open communication.

## Understanding Sexual Dysfunction

Many people struggle with *sexual dysfunctions— impairments in sexual functioning that cause subjective distress.* **Figure 12.18** shows the prevalence of some of the most common sexual problems (Laumann et al., 1994).

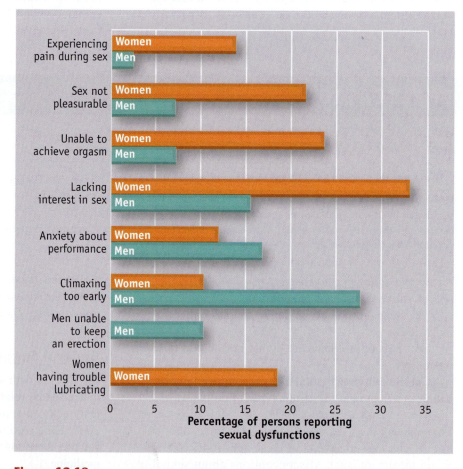

### Figure 12.18

**Sexual dysfunction in normal couples.** This graph shows the prevalence of various sexual dysfunctions during a year in a probability sample of American men and women. The most common problems among men are premature ejaculation and anxiety about performance; in women, they are lack of interest in sex and orgasmic difficulties.

Source: From Laumann, E. O., Gagnon, J. H., Michael, R. T., & Michaels, S. (1994). *The social organization of sexuality: Sexual practices in the United States.* Chicago: University of Chicago Press. Copyright © 1994 by University of Chicago Press. Reprinted by permission.

Physical, psychological, and interpersonal factors can contribute to sexual problems. *Physical factors* include chronic illness, disabilities, some medications, alcohol, and drugs. *Individual psychological factors* include performance anxiety, negative attitudes about sexuality learned during childhood, spectatoring, fears of pregnancy and STDs, life stresses such as unemployment, and prior sexual abuse. *Interpersonal factors* include ineffective communication about sexual matters and unresolved relationship issues that fuel anger and resentment.

People commonly assume that a sexual problem resides in just one partner (physical or individual psychological factors). While this is sometimes the case, most sexual problems emerge out of partners' unique ways of relating to each other (interpersonal factors). Moreover, even in those cases where a problem may lie more with one partner than another, the couple needs to work together for an acceptable solution. In other words, sexual problems belong to couples rather than to individuals.

Now let's examine the symptoms and causes of four common sexual dysfunctions: erectile difficulties, premature ejaculation, orgasmic difficulties, and low sexual desire.

**Erectile difficulties** occur when a man is persistently unable to achieve or maintain an erection adequate for intercourse. The traditional name for this problem is *impotence,* but sex therapists have discarded the term because of its demeaning connotation. A man who has never had an erection sufficient for intercourse is said to have *lifelong erectile difficulties.* A man who has had intercourse in the past but who is currently having problems achieving erections is said to have *acquired erectile difficulties.* The latter problem is more common and easier to overcome.

In a recent international study of 27 countries, nearly half the men surveyed reported having erectile difficulties if a broad criterion (the inability to get an erection adequate for satisfactory sexual performance) is used (Mulhall et al., 2008). In a national survey of adults over the age of 57, 37% of men reported that erectile difficulty was their main sexual problem (Lindau et al., 2007).

Physical factors can play a role in erectile dysfunction. For example, experts estimate that as many as 25% of all cases may be the result of side effects from medication (Miller, 2000). A host of common diseases (such as obesity, diabetes, heart disease, and high blood pressure) can produce erectile problems as a side effect (Mayo Clinic, 2008). Many temporary conditions, such as fatigue, worry about work, an argument with one's partner, a depressed mood, or too much alcohol can cause such incidents. The most common psychological cause of erectile difficulties is anxiety about sexual performance. Anxiety may stem from doubts about virility or conflict about the morality of sexual desires. Interpersonal factors can have an effect if one's partner turns an incident into a major catastrophe. If the man allows himself to get unduly concerned about his sexual response, the seeds of anxiety may be sown.

**Premature ejaculation** occurs when sexual relations are impaired because a man consistently reaches orgasm too quickly. What is "too quickly"? To address this question, researchers asked a random sample of sex therapists from the United States and

Unresolved sexual problems can be a source of tension and frustration in relationships. Physical, psychological, and interpersonal factors can contribute to sexual difficulties.

© Marc Romanelli/The Image Bank/Getty Images

Canada for their expert opinion (Corty & Guardiani, 2008). They found that sustaining intercourse 3 to 13 minutes is not worthy of concern. Obviously, any time estimates, even from "experts," are arbitrary. The critical consideration is the subjective feelings of the partners. If either partner feels that the ejaculation is persistently too fast for sexual gratification, the couple have a problem. Approximately 29% of men repeatedly experience premature ejaculation (Laumann et al, 1994).

What causes this dysfunction? Some men who have a lifelong history of quick ejaculation may have a neurophysiological predisposition to the condition (Metz & Pryor, 2000). Biological causes include hormones, thyroid problems, or inflammation of the prostate (Mayo Clinic, 2009). Psychological causes can include stress, depression, or anger at one's partner. Some therapists believe that early sexual experiences in which a rapid climax was advantageous (or necessary to avoid being discovered) can establish a habit of rapid ejaculation (Mayo Clinic, 2009).

*Orgasmic difficulties* **occur when people experience sexual arousal but have persistent problems in achieving orgasm.** When this problem occurs in men, it is often called *male orgasmic disorder.* The traditional name for this problem in women, *frigidity,* is no longer used because of its derogatory implications. Since this problem is much more common among women, we'll limit our discussion to them. A woman who has never experienced an orgasm through any kind of stimulation is said to have *generalized lifelong orgasmic difficulties.* Women who experience orgasms in some situations or only rarely are said to have *situational orgasmic difficulties.* Although lifelong orgasmic difficulties would seem to be the more severe problem, they are actually more responsive to treatment than situational orgasmic difficulties.

Physical causes of orgasmic difficulties are rare (medications can be a problem). One of the leading psychological causes is a negative attitude toward sex. Women who have been taught that sex is dirty or sinful are likely to approach it with shame and guilt. These feelings can undermine arousal, inhibit sexual expression, and impair orgasmic responsiveness. Arousal may also be inhibited by fear of pregnancy or excessive concern about achieving orgasm.

Some women have orgasmic difficulties because intercourse is too brief. Others fail to experience orgasms because their partners are unconcerned about their needs and preferences. But many couples simply need to explore sexual activities such as manual or oral stimulation of the clitoris that are more effective in producing female orgasm than sexual intercourse alone (Bancroft, 2002b).

*Hypoactive sexual desire,* **or the lack of interest in sexual activity,** seems to be on the rise. Individu-als with this problem rarely initiate sex or tend to avoid sexual activities with their partner (Aubin & Heiman, 2004). It occurs in both men and women, but it is more common among women (see **Figure 12.18**). Many attribute the recent increases in this problem to the fast pace of contemporary life and to couples' heavy workloads both at home and at work. In men, low sexual desire is often related to embarrassment about erectile dysfunction (McCarthy, Bodnar, & Handal, 2004). In women, it is most often associated with relationship difficulties (Aubin & Heiman, 2004). Sometimes the problem arises when a person is trying to sort out his or her sexual orientation. Hypoactive desire tends to increase with age (Clayton & Harsh, 2006). In fact, low desire was the most commonly reported sexual problem for women in a national sample of adults age 57 to 85 (Lindau et al., 2007).

## Coping with Specific Problems

With the advent of modern sex therapy, sexual problems no longer have to be chronic sources of frustration and shame. *Sex therapy* **involves the professional treatment of sexual dysfunctions.** Masters and Johnson reported high success rates for their treatments of specific problems, and there is a consensus that sexual dysfunctions can be overcome with regularity (McCarthy et al., 2004). The advent of medications to treat sexual problems (such as Viagra) has resulted in an increased emphasis on medical and individual treatments over relationship interventions (Aubin & Heiman, 2004; McHugh, 2006). Nonetheless, couple-based treatment approaches definitely have their place and are effective (O'Sullivan, McCrudden, & Tolman, 2006). If you're looking for a sex therapist, be sure to find someone who is qualified to work in this specialized field. One professional credential to look for is that provided by the American Association of Sex Educators, Counselors, and Therapists (AASECT).

**William Masters and Virginia Johnson**

© Bettmann/Corbis

### Erectile Difficulties

Viagra, the much-touted pill for treating erectile disorders, is about 80% effective (Handy, 1998). Still, it is not without its drawbacks—some of them life threatening. Cialis and Levitra are two similar pills that enhance erections over a longer time period (24 to 36 hours) than Viagra. These drugs affect the muscles in the penis, allowing them to relax, which in turn increases the blood flow and results in an erection (Mayo Clinic, 2008). To work effectively, these pills must be incorporated into the couple's lovemaking style (Rosen, 2000). The expectation that a pill alone will solve sexual problems that stem from relationship or psychological issues can set men up for additional sexual dysfunction (McCarthy et al., 2004). There is evidence that exercising and staying physically active help maintain healthy erectile functioning (Janiszewski, Janssen, &Ross, 2009).

To overcome psychologically based erectile difficulties, the key is to decrease the man's performance anxiety. It is a good idea for a couple to discuss the problem openly. The woman should be reassured that the difficulty does not reflect lack of affection by her partner. Obviously, it is crucial for her to be emotionally supportive rather than hostile and demanding.

Masters and Johnson introduced an effective procedure for the treatment of erectile difficulties and other dysfunctions. **Sensate focus is an exercise in which partners take turns pleasuring each other while giving guided verbal feedback and in which certain kinds of stimulation are temporarily forbidden.** One partner stimulates the other, who simply lies back and enjoys it while giving instructions and feedback about what feels good. Initially, the partners are not allowed to touch each other's genitals or to attempt intercourse. This prohibition should free the man from feelings of pressure to perform. Over a number of sessions, the couple gradually includes genital stimulation in their sensate focus, but intercourse is still banned. With the pressure to perform removed, many men spontaneously get erections. Repeated arousals should begin to restore the man's confidence in his sexual response. As his confidence returns, the couple can move on gradually to attempts at intercourse.

## Premature Ejaculation

Men troubled by premature ejaculation range from those who climax almost instantly to those who cannot last the time that their partner requires. In the latter case, simply slowing down the tempo of intercourse may help. Sometimes the problem can be solved indirectly by discarding the traditional assumption that orgasms should come through intercourse. If the female partner enjoys oral or manual stimulation, these techniques can be used to provide her with an orgasm either before or after intercourse. This strategy can reduce the performance pressure for the male partner, and couples may find that intercourse starts to last longer.

For the problem of instant ejaculation, two treatments are very effective: the *stop-start method* (Semans, 1956) and the *squeeze technique* (Masters & Johnson, 1970). With both, the woman brings the man to the verge of orgasm through manual stimulation. Then, she either stops stimulating him (stop-start technique) or squeezes the base or the end of his penis firmly for 3–5 seconds (squeeze technique) until he

calms down. She repeats this procedure three or four times before bringing him to orgasm. These exercises can help a man recognize preorgasmic sensations and teach him that he can delay ejaculation. Medication such as certain antidepressants and topical anesthetic creams may also help (Mayo Clinic, 2009; Renshaw, 2005).

## Orgasmic Difficulties

Negative attitudes and embarrassment about sex are often at the root of women's orgasmic difficulties. Thus, therapeutic discussions are usually geared toward helping nonorgasmic women reduce their ambivalence about sexual expression, become more clear about their sexual needs, and become more assertive about them. Sex therapists often suggest that women who have never had an orgasm try to have one by first using a vibrator and then shifting to masturbation, as the latter more closely approximates stimulation by a partner (Crooks & Baur, 2008). Many women achieve orgasms in intercourse after an initial breakthrough with self-stimulation. To make this transition, it is essential that the woman express her sexual wishes to her partner. Sensate focus is also an effective technique for treating orgasmic difficulties (Heiman & Meston, 1997).

When a woman's orgasmic difficulties stem from not feeling close to her partner, treatment usually focuses on couples' relationship problems more than on sexual functioning per se. Therapists also focus on helping couples improve their communication skills.

## Hypoactive Sexual Desire

Therapists consider reduced sexual desire the most challenging sexual problem to treat (Aubin & Heiman, 2004). This is because the problem usually has multiple causes, which can also be difficult to identify. If the problem is a result of fatigue from overwork, couples may be encouraged to allot more time to personal and relationship needs. Sometimes hypoactive sexual desire reflects relationship problems. Treatment for reduced sexual desire is usually more intensive than that for more specific sexual disorders, and it is usually multifaceted to deal with the multiple aspects of the problem.

Medications can be used for low sexual desire. For instance, some older men take supplemental testosterone to offset the age-related decline in this hormone (Crooks & Baur, 2008). Hormonal therapies are also used for postmenopausal women (Basson, 2008). The medical and financial success of Viagra has encouraged pharmaceutical companies to develop drugs that will boost women's sexual desire (Diamond et al., 2006; Marshall, 2005). Still, drugs will not solve relationship problems. For these, couples therapy is needed. And as we have seen for most problematic issues in this chapter, communication between partners is crucial.

## KEY IDEAS

### Becoming a Sexual Person

● One's sexual identity is made up of sexual orientation, body image, sexual values and ethics, and erotic preferences. Physiological factors such as hormones influence sexual differentiation and anatomy more than they do sexual activity. Psychosocial factors appear to have more impact on sexual behavior. Sexual identity is shaped by families, peers, schools, religion, and the media. Because of differences in sexual socialization, sexuality usually has different meanings for males and females.

● Experts believe that sexual orientation is complex, with multiple components. The determinants of sexual orientation are not yet known but appear to be a complex interaction of biological and environmental factors.

● General attitudes toward homosexuals are negative but appear to be moving in a positive direction. Coming to terms with and disclosing sexual orientation is a complicated process. Recent evidence suggests that homosexuals are at greater risk for depression and suicide attempts than are heterosexuals, a phenomenon linked to their membership in a stigmatized group. Children of homosexual parents do not have increased rates of maladjustment.

### Interaction in Sexual Relationships

● Sexual motives can be grouped into approach and avoidance motives. One's motives for sex are linked to personal and relationship well-being.

● Disparities between partners in sexual interest and erotic preferences lead to disagreements that require negotiation. Effective communication plays an important role in sexual and relationship satisfaction.

### The Human Sexual Response

● The physiology of the human sexual response was described by Masters and Johnson. They divided the sexual response cycle into four phases: excitement, plateau, orgasm, and resolution. For a more complete view of this process, individuals' subjective experiences during sexual encounters also need to be factored in.

● Women reach orgasm in intercourse less consistently than men, usually because foreplay and intercourse are too brief and because of gender differences in sexual socialization.

### Sexual Expression

● Sexual fantasies are normal and are an important aspect of sexual expression. Kissing and touching are important erotic activities, but their importance is often underestimated by heterosexual males. Despite the negative attitudes about masturbation that are traditional in our society, this practice is quite common, even among married people. Oral-genital sex has become a common element in most couples' sexual repertoires.

● Coitus is the most widely practiced sexual act in our society. Sexual activities between gay males include mutual masturbation, fellatio, and, less often, anal intercourse. Lesbians engage in mutual masturbation, cunnilingus, and tribadism.

### Patterns of Sexual Behavior

● American sexual attitudes and behavior have become more liberal over the past 40 years, although this trend slowed in the 1990s. Teen pregnancy rates, which had been declining for some time, appear to be on the rise. STD rates are highest among young people. The incidence of sexually risky behavior among teens has declined in recent years; a pattern that doesn't hold for all teens.

● Hooking up, a phenomenon that has been on the rise since the 1990s, is a common practice for young adults. The casual sex associated with hookups is risky. Many young adults also engage in friends-with-benefits arrangements. These relationships can be tricky to negotiate.

● Satisfaction with the sexual aspect of a relationship is correlated with overall relationship satisfaction in both gay and straight couples. Younger married couples tend to have sex about two or three times a week. This frequency declines with age in both heterosexual and same-gender couples, though sexual activity in late adulthood is common.

● Most Americans strongly disapprove of extramarital sex. Infidelity is less common among married couples and lesbians and more common among gay male couples. People become involved in extradyadic relationships for a variety of reasons.

### Practical Issues in Sexual Activity

● Contraception and sexually transmitted diseases are two practical issues that concern many sexually active individuals. Many people who do not want to conceive a child fail to use contraceptive procedures effectively, if at all. Contraceptive methods differ in effectiveness and have various advantages and disadvantages.

● STDs are increasing in prevalence, especially among those under 25. The danger of contracting STDs is higher among those who have had more sexual partners. In the United States, the rates of HIV infections stemming from heterosexual sex are on the rise, particularly among women. HIV rates are also up among young gay and bisexual men. Using condoms decreases the risk of contracting STDs. Early treatment of STDs is important.

### Application: Enhancing Sexual Relationships

● To enhance their sexual relationships, individuals need to have adequate sex education and positive values about sex. They also need to be able to communicate with their partners about sex and avoid goal setting in sexual encounters. Enjoying sexual fantasies and being selective about sexual encounters are also important.

● Common sexual dysfunctions include erectile difficulties, premature ejaculation, orgasmic difficulties, and hypoactive sexual desire. Treatments for low sexual desire are less effective than those for more specific sexual problems. Sex therapy can be useful.

## KEY TERMS

Anal intercourse   p. 388
Androgens   p. 372
Bisexuals   p. 371
Coitus   p. 389
Cunnilingus   p. 388
Erectile difficulties   p. 401
Erogenous zones   p. 387
Estrogens   p. 372
Fellatio   p. 388
Gonads   p. 372
Heterosexuals   p. 371
Homophobia   p. 381
Homosexuals   p. 371
Hypoactive sexual desire
   p. 402
Menarche   p. 373
Orgasm   p. 385
Orgasmic difficulties   p. 402
Premature ejaculation   p. 401
Refractory period   p. 385
Sensate focus   p. 403
Sex therapy   p. 402
Sexual dysfunction   p. 400
Sexual identity   p. 371
Sexually transmitted disease
   (STD)   p. 396
Spermarche   p. 373
Vasocongestion   p. 384

## KEY PEOPLE

Alfred Kinsey   p. 379
William Masters and Virginia
   Johnson   pp. 384–386,
   402–403

Letitia Anne Peplau
   p. 378

## QUESTIONS

1. Anthony has an "anything goes" attitude about sex. His partner thinks the type of relationship should determine what sexual activities are appropriate. Anthony has _____ sexual values where as his partner has _____ sexual values.
   a. absolute; relativistic
   b. hedonistic; absolute
   c. relativistic; hedonistic
   d. hedonistic; relativistic

2. Which of the following statements about sexual orientation is true?
   a. Heterosexuality and homosexuality are best viewed as two distinct categories.
   b. Sexual orientation is complex and malleable.
   c. Biological factors alone probably determine sexual orientation.
   d. Environmental factors alone probably determine sexual orientation.

3. Stacy is in the initial phase of sexual arousal. Her muscles are tense and her heart rate and blood pressure are elevated. She is in which phase of Masters and Johnson's sexual response cycle?
   a. foreplay
   b. orgasm
   c. excitement
   d. resolution

4. Sexual fantasies:
   a. are signs of abnormality.
   b. are quite normal.
   c. rarely include having sex with someone other than one's partner.
   d. are an excellent indication of what people want to experience in reality.

5. Which of the following characterizes contemporary teen sexual behavior?
   a. After a period of decline, teen birth rates are on the rise.
   b. The teen birth rate has increased since the early 90s and is now in decline.
   c. The teen pregnancy rate has held steady for decades and continues to do so.
   d. The teen pregnancy rate in America is among the lowest in the world.

6. Regarding overall marital satisfaction and sexual satisfaction, research indicates there is:
   a. a strong relationship.
   b. a weak relationship.
   c. no relationship.
   d. a strong relationship, but only in the first year of marriage.

7. Who of the following are most likely to have an "open" relationship?
   a. a heterosexual married couple
   b. a gay male couple
   c. a lesbian couple
   d. all are equally likely

8. Which of the following statements about condoms is true?
   a. It's okay to use oil-based lubricants with latex condoms.
   b. Polyurethane condoms are thicker than latex condoms.
   c. Skin condoms provide protection against STDs.
   d. It's okay to use water-based lubricants with latex condoms.

9. Sexually transmitted diseases:
   a. are all very serious.
   b. always cause symptoms right away.
   c. are most common among people under age 25.
   d. are most common among people between 26 and 40.

10. Which of the following is *not* one of the text's suggestions for enhancing your sexual relationships?
    a. Pursue adequate sex education.
    b. Review your sexual values system.
    c. Communicate about sex.
    d. Set clear goals for each sexual encounter.

## ANSWERS

| | |
|---|---|
| 1. d Pages 371–372 | 6. a Page 391 |
| 2. b Page 379 | 7. b Page 392 |
| 3. c Page 384 | 8. d Page 396 |
| 4. b Page 387 | 9. c Page 398 |
| 5. a Page 389 | 10. d Pages 399–400 |

## Personal Explorations Workbook

Go to the *Personal Explorations Workbook* in the back of your textbook for exercises that can enhance your self-understanding in relation to issues raised in this chapter. **Exercise 12.1** *Self-Assessment:* Sexuality Scale **Exercise 12.2** *Self-Reflection:* How Did You Acquire Your Attitudes About Sex?

## CourseMate

Access an interactive eBook, chapter-specific interactive learning tools, including Personal Explorations, Recommended Readings, Critical Thinking Exercises, flashcards, quizzes, videos and more in your Psychology CourseMate, available at **www.cengagebrain.com/shop/ISBN/1111186634**.

© artparadigm/Getty Images/Photodisc

# Careers and Work

"Love and work . . . work and love, that's all there is." This quote is attributed to Sigmund Freud, whose opinions on love and sex are well known, if sometimes misunderstood. Less well known, however, is the fact that Freud viewed work as another important element in understanding the human condition. Working is a defining characteristic in the lives of many people. Consider this: Do most of the people you know identify themselves by what they do in their careers? Do you introduce yourself by name and your major area of study, which is a way of alluding to your intended profession? When you meet someone new, isn't one of the first things you ask something like, "So, what do you do for a living?" How people reply to this question reveals information not only about their occupation but also about their social status, educational background, lifestyle, personality, interests, and aptitudes. In other words, work plays a pivotal role in adult life, particularly in the United States. According to a Gallup poll, 73% Americans rate work as either "extremely" or "very important" in their life (Moore, 2003). In **Figure 13.1**, you can see that how people view their jobs is strongly correlated with their income. In a very real sense, people are what they do at work. If that observation make sense to you, then it should come as no surprise that being unemployed can have devastating consequences for people's sense of self and well-being.

Because work is such a significant aspect of life, psychologists take a great interest in it. ***Industrial/organizational (I/O) psychology is the study of human behavior in the workplace.*** I/O psychologists strive to increase the dignity and performance of workers and the organizations where they labor (Rucci, 2008). Among other issues, I/O psychologists study worker motivation and satisfaction, job performance, leadership, occupational hazards, personnel selection, and diversity in organizations. A recent concern is how individuals balance work and family life (Borman, Klimoski, & Ilgen, 2003; Greenhaus & Powell, 2006). An imbalance between these two spheres of daily living can lead to what I/O psychologists call work-family conflict (e.g., Lapierre & Allen, 2006).

We begin this chapter by reviewing some important considerations in choosing a career. Then we explore two models of career development and discuss women's career issues. Next, we examine how the workplace and workforce are changing and look at some occupational hazards such as job stress, sexual harassment, and unemployment. Finally, we address the important issues of balancing work, relationships, and leisure. In the Application, we offer some concrete suggestions for enhancing your chances of landing a desirable job.

© Bonnie Kamin/PhotoEdit

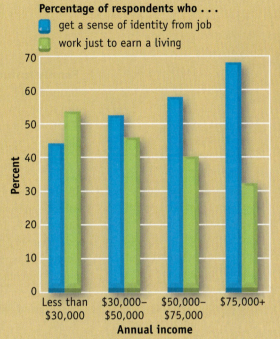

**Percentage of respondents who . . .**
- get a sense of identity from job
- work just to earn a living

Percent (y-axis): 0, 10, 20, 30, 40, 50, 60, 70

Annual income (x-axis): Less than $30,000 | $30,000–$50,000 | $50,000–$75,000 | $75,000+

**Figure 13.1**

**How workers view their jobs.** The way workers view their jobs is strongly related to their income. Those who earn higher salaries are more likely to obtain a sense of identity from their work, whereas those who earn lower salaries typically see their jobs merely as a way to make a living. (Data from Moore, 2001)

# Choosing a Career

## LEARNING OBJECTIVES

- Describe personal and family influences on job choice.
- Cite several helpful sources of career information.
- List some aspects of potential occupations that are important to know about.
- Clarify the role of occupational interest inventories in career decisions.
- Outline five important considerations in choosing an occupation.

One of your biggest decisions in life is choosing a career. Think about it: The average person works at least 8 hours a day, 5 days a week, 50 weeks a year, for 40 to 45 years. Some people work much more and, admittedly, some work considerably less. Still, such a time commitment, really, a life-time commitment—implies that you should both enjoy and be proficient at what you do for a living. Imagine the dissatisfaction, if not drudgery, that people who neither like their careers nor are adept at them feel all the time. Aside from sleeping, most people spend more time working than any other activity. Just consider a typical weekday:

| | |
|---|---|
| Sleep | 6–8 hours |
| Commute to and from work | 1–2 hours |
| Work | 8 hours |
| Prepare and eat meals | 2 hours |
| TV and Internet time | 1–3 hours |
| Other activities | 1–2 hours |

Thus, the importance of your career decision is enormous. It may determine whether you are employed or unemployed, financially secure or insecure, happy or unhappy. Rapidly advancing technology and the increased training and education required to break into most fields make it more important than ever to choose thoughtfully. In theory, what's involved in making a successful career choice is pretty straightforward. First, you need to have a clear grasp of your personal characteristics. Second, you need realistic information about potential careers. From there, it's just a matter of selecting an occupation that is a good match with your personal characteristics. In reality, the process is a lot more complicated than simply finding a match between these two elements. Let's take a closer look.

## Examining Personal Characteristics and Family Influences

People with limited job skills and qualifications (education, training, experience) have limited job options. As a result, they must usually take whatever job is available rather than a job that is well suited for them. In fact, *choosing* a career is a luxury usually afforded to the middle and upper classes. For those who *are* able to select a career, personal qualities and family influences come into play.

### Personal Characteristics

Making career decisions can be scary. Individuals who exhibit *secure attachment* (see Chapter 9) and who have a sense of *self-efficacy* about career-relevant abilities (see Chapter 6) thus find it easier to make career choices (Fouad, 2007; Wolfe & Betz, 2004). What other personal characteristics affect career choice? Although *intelligence* does not necessarily predict occupational success, it does predict the likelihood of entering particular occupations. That's because intelligence is related to academic success—the ticket required to enter certain fields. Professions such as law, medicine, and engineering are open only to those who can meet increasingly selective criteria as they advance from high school to college to graduate education and professional training. The relationship between intelligence and occupational level generally holds well for men, but an ability-achievement gap exists for women, as we noted in Chapter 11.

In many occupations, special talents are more important than general intelligence. *Specific aptitudes* that might make a person well suited for certain occupations include creativity, artistic or musical talent, mechanical ability, clerical skill, mathematical ability, and persuasive talents. A particularly crucial characteristic is *social skills,* since the use of teams to accomplish work tasks is increasingly important in a wide variety of organizations (Kozlowski & Bell, 2003). A worker must be able not only to get along well with peers but also to counsel or supervise them as well. Certainly, social-emotional or interpersonal intelligence, the ability to behave wisely in human relations and to accurately interpret emotions and intentions, is an important part of such social skills (Albrecht, 2009; Goleman, 2007; Kihlstrom & Cantor, 2000; Mayer et al., 2008).

As people travel through life, they acquire a variety of *interests.* Are you intrigued by the business world? the academic world? international affairs? the outdoors? physical sciences? music? athletics? art and culture? human services? hospitality and recreation? The list of potential interests is virtually infinite. Because interests underlie your motivation for work and your

job satisfaction, they should definitely be considered in your career planning.

Finally, it is important to choose an occupation that is compatible with your *personality* (Swanson & D'Achiardi, 2005; Wrzesniewski et al., 1997). We'll examine the relationship between personality types and career choice in a later section.

### Family Influences

Individuals' career choices are strongly influenced by their family background (Whiston & Keller, 2004). That is, the jobs that appeal to people tend to be like those of their parents. For instance, people who grow up in middle-class homes are likely to aspire to high-paying professions in law, medicine, or engineering. On the other hand, individuals from low-income families often lean toward blue-collar jobs in construction work, office work, and food services.

Family background influences career choice for several reasons. For one thing, a key predictor of occupational status is the number of years of education an individual has completed (Arbona, 2005). And, because parents and children often attain similar levels of education, they are likely to have similar jobs. Second, career attainment is related to socioeconomic status. The factors that mediate this relationship are educational aspirations and attainment during the school years (Schoon & Parsons, 2002). This means that parents and teachers can help boost children's career aspirations and opportunities by encouraging them to do well in school. Although socioeconomic status seems to have more influence on career aspirations than ethnicity (Rojewski, 2005), ethnic differences in aspirations are still found. For example, a cross-cultural and multi-ethnic study reported that Chinese and Asian American college students' more often choose investigative (analytical, intellectual, mathematical) occupations, and their career decisions are more influenced by parents than European American college students' decisions are (Tang, 2002).

Finally, parenting practices come into play. Most children from middle-class homes are encouraged to be curious and independent, qualities that are essential to success in many high-status occupations. By contrast, children from lower-status families are often taught to conform and obey. As a result, they may have less opportunity to develop the qualities demanded in high-status jobs. As we noted in Chapter 11, parents' gender-role expectations also influence their children's aspirations and sometimes interact with socioeconomic status and ethnicity.

## Researching Job Characteristics

The second step in selecting an occupation is seeking out information about jobs. Because the sheer number of jobs is overwhelming, you have to narrow the scope of your search before you can start gathering information.

## Sources of Career Information

Once you have selected some jobs that might interest you, the next question is: Where do you get information on them? A helpful place to start is the *Occupational Outlook Handbook,* available in most libraries and on the Internet (see Web Link 13.1). This government document, published every two years by the U.S. Bureau of Labor Statistics, is a comprehensive guide to occupations. It includes job descriptions, education and training requirements, salaries, and employment outlooks for over 800 occupations. In addition, it details numerous career information resources, including those for the military, disabled, women, and minorities. You can also find tips on locating jobs and accepting salary offers in this useful resource.

If you want more detailed information on particular occupations, you can usually get it by doing some online searching. If you're interested in a career in psychology, you can obtain a number of pamphlets or books from the American Psychological Association (APA) or look at a book dedicated to careers in psychology (Kuther & Morgan, 2009; Landrum, 2009). Also, the APA website provides links to other sites describing more than 50 subfields in psychology, many of which provide useful career information. Related professions (social work, school psychology, and so on) also have web pages. You will find the addresses of these pages on Marky Lloyd's Careers in Psychology website (see Web Link 13.2).

## Essential Information About Occupations

When you examine occupational literature and interview people, what kinds of information should you seek? To some extent, the answer depends on your unique interests, values, and needs. However, some things are of concern to virtually anyone. Workers typically give high ratings to good health insurance, retirement plans, limited job stress, and recognition for performing well (Saad, 1999). Some key issues you need to know about include:

- *The nature of the work.* What would your duties and responsibilities be on a day-to-day basis?
- *Working conditions.* Is the work environment pleasant or unpleasant, low key or high pressure?
- *Job entry requirements.* What education and training are required to break into this occupational area?
- *Ongoing training or education.* Will you need to continue learning within or outside the workplace in order to remain proficient at your occupation?
- *Potential earnings.* What are entry-level salaries, and how much can you hope to earn if you're exceptionally successful? What does the average person earn? What are the fringe benefits?
- *Potential status.* What is the social status associated with this occupation? Is it personally satisfactory for you?
- *Opportunities for advancement.* How do you move up in this field? Are there adequate opportunities for promotion and advancement?
- *Intrinsic job satisfaction.* Apart from money and formal fringe benefits, what can you derive in the way of personal satisfaction from this job? Will it allow you to help people, to have fun, to be creative, or to shoulder responsibility?
- *Future outlook.* What is the projected supply and demand for this occupational area?
- *Security.* Is the work apt to be stable or can the job disappear if there is an economic downturn?

By the way, if you're wondering whether your college education will be worth the effort in terms of dollars and cents, the answer is yes. As we'll discuss shortly, the jobs that you can obtain with a college degree typically yield higher pay than those that require less education (Crosby & Moncarz, 2006). Educational attainment alone, however, does not predict who performs well in a given job setting (Hunter & Hunter, 1984). In other words, having a college degree is not as important as the grades you earn during college. Why? Higher grade point averages (GPAs) point to the ability to be trained (Dye & Reck, 1989), which in turn influences subsequent job performance (Roth et al., 1996), salary level (Roth & Clarke, 1998), and frequency of promotions (Cohen, 1984). Still, experts agree that the

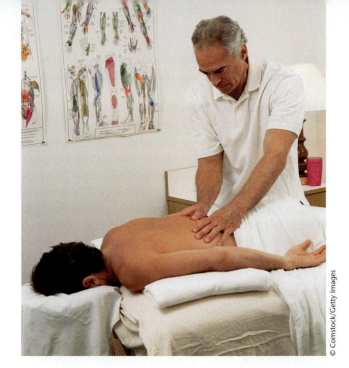

People vary in their preferences for work environments. Some like high-pressure work; others prefer more low-key jobs.

future belongs to those who are better educated (Gordon, 2006).

## Using Psychological Tests for Career Decisions

If you are undecided about an occupation, you might consider taking some tests at your campus counseling center. *Occupational interest inventories* **measure your interests as they relate to various jobs or careers.** Two widely used tests of this type are the Strong Interest Inventory (SII) and the Self-Directed Search (SDS) (Brown, 2007). Another popular interest inventory is the Kuder Career Search with Placement Match (Zytowski & Kuder, 1999).

Occupational interest inventories do not attempt to predict whether you would be successful in various occupations (Aamodt, 2004). Rather, they focus more on the likelihood of job *satisfaction* than job *success*. When you take an occupational interest inventory, you receive many scores indicating how similar your interests are to the typical interests of people in various occupations. For example, a high score on the accountant scale of a test means that your interests are similar to those of the average accountant. This correspondence in interests does not ensure that you would enjoy a career in accounting, but it is a moderately good predictor of job satisfaction (Hansen, 2005; Morris & Campion, 2003).

Interest inventories such as the SII can provide worthwhile food for thought about possible careers. The results may confirm your subjective guesses about your interests and strengthen already-existing occupational preferences. Additionally, the test results may inspire you to investigate career possibilities that you had never thought of before. Unexpected results may stimulate you to rethink your career plans. To do so, you might speak to a vocational counselor, that is, a professional who has expertise matching individuals to particular careers.

Although interest inventories can be helpful in working through career decisions, several cautions are worth noting. First, you may score high on some occupations that you're sure you would hate. Given the sheer number of occupational scales on the tests, this can easily happen by chance. However, you shouldn't dismiss the remainder of the test results just because you're sure that a few specific scores are "wrong." Second, don't let the test make career decisions for you. Some students naively believe that they should pursue whatever occupation yields their highest score. That is not how the tests are meant to be used. They merely provide information for you to consider. Ultimately, you have to think things out for yourself.

Third, you should be aware that most occupational interest inventories have a lingering gender bias. Many of these scales were originally developed 30 to 40 years ago when outright discrimination or more subtle discouragement prevented women from entering many traditionally "male" occupations. Critics assert that interest inventories have helped channel women into gender-typed careers, such as nursing and teaching, while guiding them away from more prestigious "male" occupations, such as medicine and engineering. Undoubtedly, this was true in the past. Recently, progress has been made toward reducing gender bias in occupational tests, although it has not been eliminated (Hansen, 2005). Research suggests that ethnic bias on interest tests is less of a concern than gender bias (Hansen, 2005; Worthington, Flores, & Navarro, 2005). In interpreting interest inventory results, be wary of letting gender stereotypes limit your career options.

## Taking Important Considerations into Account

As you contemplate your career options, here are some important points to keep in mind.

**1.** *You have the potential for success in a variety of occupations.* Career counselors stress that people have multiple potentials (Spokane & Cruza-Guet, 2005). Considering the huge variety of job opportunities, it's foolish to believe that only one career would be right for you. If you expect to find one job that fits you perfectly, you may spend your entire lifetime searching for it.

**2.** *Be cautious about choosing a career solely on the basis of salary.* Because of the tremendous emphasis on material success in America, people are often tempted to choose a career solely on the basis of income or status. However, research suggests that meaning and purpose, rather than money, lead to happiness and well-being (e.g., Diener & Biswas-Diener, 2008; Kasser, 2002). Experts advise against following a strategy aimed at choosing a career based solely on projected earnings (Pollack, 2007). When people ignore personal characteristics in choosing a career, they risk being mismatched. Such job mismatching can result in boredom, frustration, and unhappiness with one's work, and these negative feelings can spill over into other spheres of life.

**3.** *There are limits on your career options.* Entry into a particular occupation is not simply a matter of choosing what you want to do. It's a two-way street. You get to make choices, but you also have to persuade schools and employers to choose you. Your career op-tions will be limited to some extent by factors beyond your control, including fluctuations in the economy and the job market.

**4.** *Career choice is a developmental process that extends throughout life.* Occupational choice involves not a single decision but a series of decisions. Although this process was once believed to extend only from prepuberty to the early 20s, authorities now recognize that the process continues throughout life. Some experts predict that the average person will have ten jobs over the course of his or her working life (Levitt, 2006). Nonetheless, middle-aged people may underestimate the options available to them and therefore miss opportunities to make constructive changes. We want to emphasize that making occupational choices is not limited to youth.

**5.** *Some career decisions are not easily undone.* Although it's never too late to strike out in new career directions, it is important to recognize that many decisions are not readily reversed. Few middle-aged lawyers suddenly decide to attend medical school or become elementary school teachers, for example, but it does happen. Once you invest time, money, and effort in moving along a particular career path, it may not be easy to change paths. And family responsibilities, especially child care and elder care, can make major career changes difficult. This potential problem highlights why it is important to devote careful thought to your occupational choice as soon as you can.

In the next section, we explore in greater detail how personal characteristics are related to career choice and career development.

# *Models of Career Choice and Development*

### LEARNING OBJECTIVES

- Summarize Holland's model of career choice.
- Summarize Super's five-stage model of career development.
- Identify some differences between women's and men's career development.

How do people choose a career? Before interest inventories came along, career counselors routinely asked people to share their likes and dislikes, to identify individuals they admired, and to catalog their hobbies (Reardon et al., 2009). Self-reports and interest tests have their place, but psychologists are interested in more theoretically based approaches aimed at understanding how individuals make career choices and how their careers evolve over time. Theorists have developed several approaches to these issues. Here we examine two influential models.

## Holland's Person-Environment Fit Model

The most influential trait model of career choice is that developed by John Holland (1985, 1996, 1997). According to Holland, career choice is related to an individual's personality characteristics (e.g., values, interests, needs, skills, learning styles, attitudes), which are assumed to be relatively stable over time. In Holland's system, people can be classified into one of six personality types, called *personal orientations*. Similarly, occupations can be classified into six ideal *work environments.* According to Holland, people search for environments that allow them to exercise their abilities and skills, share their attitudes or values with others, and adopt agreeable problems and roles. They flourish when their personality type is matched with a work environment that is congruent with their abilities, interests, and self-beliefs. The term "work environment" should be viewed broadly, not narrowly, as it can be a job or an occupation, a field of study, an educational program, a college or a university, a leisure time activity, or the particular culture found within an organization. In fact, in Holland's view, a work environment can even be construed as a social relationship with another person or persons (Reardon et al., 2009). A good match between one's personality and a work environment typically results in career satisfaction, achievement, and stability. Holland's six personal orientations and their optimal work environments are shown in **Figure 13.2**.

Holland assumes that stability in interests and personality arrives by the time a person turns 21. He has developed several tests to measure the six basic personal orientations in the RIASEC theory (an acronym for the first letter in each of these personality types). One of the tests, the Self-Directed Search (SDS), is self-scoring. Once individuals identify their personality type on the SDS, they can match it with various relevant

Those with a "social" personal orientation in Holland's theory are understanding and want to help others. Teachers typically score high on the "social" orientation.

occupations. Studies have shown the SDS to be a useful career assessment tool (Spokane & Cruza-Guet, 2005).

Obviously, the six personal orientations are ideal types, and no one person will fit perfectly into any one type. In fact, most people are a combination of two or

## Holland's Personal Orientations and Related Work Environments

| Themes | Personal orientations | Work environments |
|---|---|---|
| Realistic | Values concrete and physical tasks. Perceives self as having mechanical skills and lacking social skills. | *Settings:* concrete, physical tasks requiring mechanical skills, persistence, and physical movement<br>*Careers:* machine operator, pilot, draftsperson, engineer |
| Investigative | Wants to solve intellectual, scientific, and mathematical problems. Sees self as analytical, critical, curious, introspective, and methodical. | *Settings:* research laboratory, diagnostic medical case conference, work group of scientists<br>*Careers:* marine biologist, computer programmer, clinical psychologist, architect, dentist |
| Artistic | Prefers unsystematic tasks or artistic projects: painting, writing, or drama. Perceives self as imaginative, expressive, and independent. | *Settings:* theater, concert hall, library, radio or TV studio<br>*Careers:* sculptor, actor, designer, musician, author, editor |
| Social | Prefers educational, helping, and religious careers. Enjoys social involvement, church, music, reading, and dramatics. Is cooperative, friendly, helpful, insightful, persuasive, and responsible. | *Settings:* school and college classrooms, psychiatrist's office, religious meetings, mental institutions, recreational centers<br>*Careers:* counselor, nurse, teacher, social worker, judge, minister, sociologist |
| Enterprising | Values political and economic achievements, supervision, and leadership. Enjoys leadership control, verbal expression, recognition, and power. Perceives self as extraverted, sociable, happy, assertive, popular, and self-confident. | *Settings:* courtroom, political rally, car sales room, real estate firm, advertising company<br>*Careers:* realtor, politician, attorney, salesperson, manager |
| Conventional | Prefers orderly, systematic, concrete tasks with verbal and mathematical data. Sees self as conformist and having clerical and numerical skills. | *Settings:* bank, post office, file room, business office, Internal Revenue office<br>*Careers:* banker, accountant, timekeeper, financial counselor, typist, receptionist |

### Figure 13.2
**Overview of Holland's theory of occupational choice.** According to John Holland (1985), people can be divided into six personality types (personal orientations) that prefer different work environments, as outlined here.

Source: Adapted from Holland, J. L. (1985). *Making occupational choices: A theory of occupational personalities and work environments* (2nd ed.). Englewood Cliffs, NJ: Prentice-Hall. Adapted by permission of Prentice-Hall, Inc.

three types (Holland, 1996). You can take a rough stab at categorizing your own personal orientation by studying **Figure 13.2**. Look at the matching work environments to get some ideas for possible career options.

More research has been conducted on Holland's model than any other theory in vocational psychology—to date, around 1,600 publications have examined it (Ruff, Reardon, & Bertoch, 2008)—and much of this research is supportive (Spokane & Cruza-Guet, 2005). For instance, researchers report that Holland's model describes the career preferences of ethnically diverse male and female college students relatively accurately (Fouad & Mohler, 2004). On the other hand, people with good job-personality matches should be more satisfied with their jobs and likely to remain in these jobs longer than those who are less well matched, but research shows that job-personality fit contributes very little (5%) to job satisfaction (Fouad, 2007).

In contrast to trait models such as Holland's that view occupational choice as a specific event, stage theories view occupational choice as a developmental process. We look at that approach next.

## Super's Developmental Model

A highly influential developmental model of career choice is that outlined by Donald Super (1957, 1985, 1988, 1990). He views occupational development as a process that begins in childhood, unfolds gradually across most of the lifespan, and ends with retirement (Giannantonio & Hurley-Hanson, 2006). Super asserts that the person's *self-concept* is the critical factor in this process. In other words, decisions about work and career commitments reflect people's attempts to express their changing views of themselves. To map these changes, Super breaks the occupational life cycle into five major stages and a variety of substages (see **Figure 13.3**).

**Donald Super**

### Growth Stage

The growth stage occurs during childhood, when youngsters fantasize about exotic jobs they would enjoy. Generally, they imagine themselves as detectives, airplane pilots, and brain surgeons rather than plumbers, salespersons, and bookkeepers. Until near the end of this period, children are largely oblivious to realistic considerations such as the abilities or education required for specific jobs. Naturally, children's aspirations and expectations may vary widely because of their home and educational environments (Cook et al., 1996).

### Exploration Stage

Pressures from parents, teachers, and peers to develop a general career direction begin to intensify during high school. By the end of high school, individuals are

| | Stages of Occupational Development | |
|---|---|---|
| **Stage** | **Approximate ages** | **Key events and transitions** |
| **Growth stage** | **0–14** | **A period of general physical and mental growth** |
| Prevocational substage | 0–3 | No interest or concern with vocations |
| Fantasy substage | 4–10 | Fantasy is basis for vocational thinking |
| Interest substage | 11–12 | Vocational thought is based on individual's likes and dislikes |
| Capacity substage | 13–14 | Ability becomes the basis for vocational thought |
| **Exploration stage** | **15–24** | **General exploration of work** |
| Tentative substage | 15–17 | Needs, interests, capacities, values, and opportunities become bases for tentative occupational decisions |
| Transition substage | 18–21 | Reality increasingly becomes basis for vocational thought and action |
| Trial substage | 22–24 | First trial job is entered after the individual has made an initial vocational commitment |
| **Establishment stage** | **25–44** | **Individual seeks to enter a permanent occupation** |
| Trial substage | 25–30 | Period of some occupational change due to unsatisfactory choices |
| Stabilization substage | 31–44 | Period of stable work in a given occupational field |
| **Maintenance stage** | **45–65** | **Continuation in one's chosen occupation** |
| **Decline stage** | **65·** | **Adaptation to leaving workforce** |
| Deceleration substage | 65–70 | Period of declining vocational activity |
| Retirement substage | 71+ | A cessation of vocational activity |

**Figure 13.3**

**Overview of Super's theory of occupational development.** According to Donald Super, people go through five major stages (and a variety of substages) of occupational development over the lifespan.

Source: Adapted from Zaccaria, J. (1970). *Theories of occupational choice and vocational development.* Boston: Houghton Mifflin. Copyright © 1970 by Time Share Corporation, New Hampshire.

expected to have narrowed a general career direction into a specific one. Young people try to get a real taste of their intended occupation through reading about it or part-time work. During the later part of this stage, youths typically seek full-time work. If their initial work experiences are gratifying, their tentative commitment will be strengthened. However, unrewarding early experiences may motivate individuals to shift to another occupation, where they will continue the exploration process. In effect, it's better to explore a particular career and discover it does not meet one's expectations sooner rather than later. Helwig (2008) found that while parent and teacher support is important, not enough career preparation occurs during the high school years, which means that the subsequent stage in Super's model becomes a very important one.

## Establishment Stage

Vacillation in career commitment continues to be common during the first part of the establishment stage. Once people make gratifying occupational choices, their career commitment is strengthened. With few exceptions, future job moves will take place *within* the preferred occupational area. Having made a commitment, the person now needs to demonstrate the ability to function effectively in the area. To succeed, individuals must use previously acquired skills, learn new skills, and display flexibility in adapting to organizational changes.

## Maintenance Stage

As the years go by, opportunities for further career advancement and occupational mobility decline. However, both formal and informal forms of lifelong learning are often necessary so that workers can keep pace with the ever-changing aspects of their current and future jobs (Pang, Chua, & Chu, 2008). Around their mid-40s, many people cross into the maintenance stage, during which they worry more about *retaining* their achieved status than *improving* it. Although middle-aged employees may need to update their skills to compete with younger workers, their primary goal is to protect the security, power, advantages, and perks that they have attained. With decreased emphasis on career advancement, many people shift energy and attention away from work in favor of family or leisure activities.

## Decline Stage

*Deceleration* involves a decline in work activity in the years prior to retirement. People redirect their energy and attention toward planning for this major transition. Super's original formulation, which was based on research in the 1950s, projected that deceleration ought to begin at around age 65. Since the 1970s, however, the large Baby Boom cohort has created an oversupply of skilled labor and professional talent. This social change has created pressures that promote early retirement. Because of these conditions, deceleration often begins earlier than Super initially indicated. On the other hand, the recent economic recession and accompanying financial worries experienced by people in the United States and around the world may change things yet again. People who have lost their job or retirement savings may be planning a longer time horizon, so that their career deceleration may not begin until closer to age 70.

*Retirement* brings work activity to a halt. People approach this transition with highly varied attitudes. Many individuals look forward to it eagerly. Others approach it with apprehension, unsure about how they will occupy themselves and worried about their financial viability. Still others approach retirement with a combination of hopeful enthusiasm and anxious concern. Although retirement may mean less income, it can also mean more time to spend with friends and on hobbies, travel, and meaningful volunteer or charity work. For some, retirement from a primary career may prompt the launching of a new career.

As a stage theorist, Super deserves credit for recognizing that people follow different patterns in their career development. For example, he identified several patterns for both men and women that do not coincide with the conventional pattern we have described. In support of Super's model, it has been found that career maturity is correlated with self-esteem and self-efficacy (Creed, Prideaux, & Patton, 2005; Kornspan & Etzel, 2001). A more serious problem with Super's theory is that it assumes that people will remain in the same careers all of their working lives. But today's American workers will have many career changes, a reality that is incompatible with the assumptions of long-term models like Super's. The current thinking about career stages or cycles is that they are shorter and recur periodically over the course of a person's career (Greenhaus, 2003). To be useful, stage models must reflect today's workplace realities.

## Women's Career Development

It is currently estimated that 59% of adult women (versus 73% of men) are in the labor force (U.S. Bureau of the Census, 2006b; see also Toossi, 2007). Moreover, the odds that a woman will work outside the home during her adult life are greater than 90% (U.S. Department of Labor, 2003). In the last 50 years, women's employment has positively affected the economy of the U.S., as well as the social and economic lives of families and the women themselves (Sloan Work and Family Research Network , 2009). Although women's labor force participation is approaching that of men's, important gender differences remain when it comes to career choice and development. For one thing, most women still subordinate their career goals to their husband's (Betz,

2005). This is even the case with academically gifted women (Arnold, 1995). If a married man wants or needs to move to another job, his wife typically follows him and takes the best job she can find in the new location. Hence, married women usually have less control over their careers than married men do. Also, the high divorce rate (around 45%) means that many women will have to provide for themselves and their children (Betz, 2006). One study reported that after a divorce, the woman's standard of living drops 27% (Weitzman, 1996). Today's women need to take these factors into account as they consider their career options.

Another gender difference concerns career paths. Men's career paths are usually *continuous,* whereas women's tend to be *discontinuous* (Betz, 1993). In other words, once men start working full-time, they usually continue to work. Women are more likely to interrupt their careers to concentrate on childrearing or family crises (Hynes & Clarkberg, 2005). Because women are having fewer children and are returning to work sooner, the amount of time they are out of the labor force is decreasing. Although labor force discontinuity is a factor in women's lower salaries and status, there is also evidence that women are simply paid less than men (Dey & Hill, 2007; U.S. General Accounting Office, 2003). Women who do not have children usually remain in the labor force and tend to have a pattern of career advancement similar to men's (Blair-Loy & DeHart, 2003).

What about women whose husbands fit the traditional breadwinner model (i.e., he works, she cares for the home and children)? Interestingly, women whose spouses earned incomes in the top and bottom 20% of income levels had the lowest workforce participation rates (Cohany & Sok, 2007). Presumably, women who reside in households where the breadwinner model is still practiced have elected not to work outside the home.

# The Changing World of Work

Before you enter the working world, it's important to get your bearings. In this section we look at several important background issues: contemporary trends in the workplace, the relationship between education and earnings, and diversity in the workforce.

## Workplace Trends

**Work is an activity that produces something of value for others.** For some people, work is just a way to earn a living; for others, work is a way of life. For both types of workers, the nature of work is undergoing dramatic changes. Because such changes can affect your future job prospects, you need to be aware of seven important trends:

1. *Technology is changing the nature of work.* Computers and electronic equipment have dramatically transformed the workplace. From the worker's point of view, these changes have both down sides and up sides. On the negative side, computers automate many jobs that people perform, eliminating jobs. The digital workplace also demands that employees have more education and skills than were previously required (Cetron & Davies, 2003). And workers have to keep upgrading their technology skills, which can be stressful. On the positive side, technological advances allow employees to work at home and to communicate with others in distant offices and while traveling. Working at home while being electronically connected to the office is called *telecommuting,* and approximately 47% of organizations use some form of it (SHRM, 2008). Telecommuting provides psychological as well as obvious practical benefits for workers, including lower levels of work-family life conflict and higher job satisfaction (Gajendran & Harrison,

The growth of technology is significantly changing the nature of work, with both positive and negative effects.

2007; Golden, Veiga, & Simsek, 2006). Another technological "plus" is that computer-driven machines require workers to design, manufacture, sell, and service them.

2. *New work attitudes are required.* Yesterday's workers could usually count on job security. Thus, many could afford a somewhat passive attitude in shaping their careers. But today's workers have job security only as long as they can add value to a company. This situation means that workers must take a more active role in shaping their careers (Smith, 2000). In addition, they must develop a variety of valuable skills, be productive workers, and skillfully market themselves to prospective employers. In the new work environment, the keys to job success are self-direction, self-management, up-to-date knowledge and skills, flexibility, and mobility (Smith, 2000). Conscientious workers, then, would be wise to engage in ongoing self-assessment aimed at improving and expanding their skills.

3. *Lifelong learning is a necessity.* Experts predict that today's jobs are changing so rapidly that in many cases, work skills will become obsolete over a 10- to 15-year period (Lock, 2005a). Thus, lifelong learning and training will become essential for employees. Every year, nearly one-third of American workers take courses to improve their job skills (American Council on Education, 1997). In some cases, retraining occurs on the job; in others, community colleges and technical institutes provide continuing education. Distance learning courses and programs are also available, although you have to watch out for bogus programs (Mariani, 2001). For suggestions on how to evaluate the quality and accreditation claims of distance education programs, see Web Link 13.3. Workers who know "how to learn" will be able to keep pace with the rapidly changing workplace and will be highly valued. Those who cannot may be left behind.

4. *Independent workers are increasing.* Corporations are downsizing and restructuring to cope with the changing economy and to be competitive globally. In doing so, they are slashing thousands of permanent jobs and doling out the work to temporary employees or to workers in other countries, a practice termed *outsourcing*. By reducing the number of regular workers, companies can chop their expenditures on payroll, health insurance, and pension plans, as temporary employees don't typically receive such benefits. A leaner work-

force also enables organizations to respond quickly to fast-changing markets. According to Daniel Pink (2001), one way to survive in this new environment is to become a "free agent" and hire out your skills to one or more organizations on a contract basis. To characterize the "free agent" work pattern, Pink suggests the metaphor of the "LEGO career" instead of the "career ladder." Just as you can build a variety of structures by assembling LEGO blocks, "free agents" assemble and reassemble the building blocks of their work life (values, interests, aptitudes, and skills) in various combinations to match career opportunities that emerge over time. Many professionals thrive on contract work; they have freedom, flexibility, and high incomes. But for those who are short on skills and entrepreneurial spirit, this work can be stressful and risky. About a third of independent employees would prefer to work for someone else than to work for themselves (Bond et al., 2003).

5. *The boundaries between work and home are breaking down.* As already noted, today's technological advances allow people to work at home and stay in touch with the office via high-speed Internet, telephones, and fax machines. Working at home is convenient—workers save time (no commuting) and money (on gas, parking, clothes). Still, family members and friends may interrupt home-workers, necessitating setting rules to protect work time. With the advent of smart phones, expanding wireless networks, and handheld computers, employees can be contacted any time and any place, making some workers feel as though they are on an "electronic leash." Looking at the flip side, the availability of onsite day care in some large companies means that a traditional home function has moved to the office (Drago, 2007). This development is largely a response to increases in the number of single-parent families and **dual-earner households, in which both partners are employed**. Consider this fact: Over 40% of today's workers have children under the age of 18 (O'Toole & Ferry, 2002). Thus, quality onsite day care is a big draw to workers because it allows parents to interact with their children during the day.

6. *The highest job growth will occur in the professional and service occupations.* The United States, like many other industrialized nations, continues to shift from a manufacturing, or "goods-producing," economy to a service-producing one (U.S. Bureau of Labor Statistics, 2006). Whereas the bulk of yesterday's jobs were in manufacturing, construction, agriculture, and mining, the jobs of the next decade will be in the professional (and related technical) occupations and service occupations. Among the professional occupations, jobs in the computer and health care industries are expected to expand dramatically. In psychology, jobs in health, clinical, counseling, and school psychology are expected to show strong growth. In the service occupations, strong job growth should occur

---

**WEB LINK 13.3   DegreeInfo.com**

If you need assistance evaluating distance learning programs, this site can help you. Its purpose is to disseminate accurate information about quality distance-based higher education programs. None of the writers for this site is currently affiliated with any school, although some of them are alumni of regionally accredited distance learning programs.

| "Best Bet" Occupations, 2008–2018 | |
|---|---|
| Biomedical engineers | Physical therapist aides |
| Network systems and data communications analysts | Dental hygienists |
| | Veterinary technologists and technicians |
| Home health aids | Dental assistants |
| Personal and home care aides | Computer software engineers, applications |
| Financial examiners | Medical assistants |
| Medical scientists, except epidemiologists | Physical therapist assistants |
| Physician assistants | Veterinarians |
| Skin care specialists | Self-enrichment education teachers |
| Biochemists and biophysicists | Compliance officers, except agriculture, construction, health and safety, and transportation |
| Athletic trainers | |

**Figure 13.4**

**Fastest growth, high-salary occupations.** According to the Bureau of Labor Statistics (2010), between 2008 and 2018 these 20 occupations will have the largest number of job openings and will provide the highest pay. Median annual salaries range from $85,430 (computer software engineers, applications) to $20,460 (home health aides). (Adapted from *Occupational Outlook Handbook,* 2010–2011).

in education, health services, social services, professional services, and business services. **Figure 13.4** depicts 20 occupations expected to grow the most and pay the most between now and 2018.

**7.** *Job sharing is becoming more common.* Not everyone wants to work a 40-hour week or is able to do so. Having the opportunity to job share—that is, to share one job between two people—may be beneficial. Fewer than 20% of organizations currently provide this option (Burke, 2005). When sharing a job, each person usually works 20 hours per week at separate times. A few hours per week may be conjoined so that each partner can update the other, as well as meet with their supervisor and other workforce members. As you can imagine, job sharing is ideal for people who have small children or other family obligations, are enrolled in degree programs, want to work part time, or are considering gradually winding down their careers.

## Education and Earnings

Although many jobs exist for individuals without a college degree, these jobs usually offer the lowest pay and benefits. In fact, all but one of the 50 highest-paying occupations require a college degree or higher (U.S. Bureau of Labor Statistics, 2004). (The high-paying job that doesn't require a college degree is air traffic controller.) In **Figure 13.5**, you can see that the more you learn, the more you earn. Having a college degree is also associated with more career options, greater opportunities for professional advancement, and lower unemployment (Dohm & Wyatt, 2002). The link between learning and earning holds for both males and females, although, as you can see, men are paid approximately $12,000 to $35,000 more than women with the same educational credentials.

On the other hand, a college diploma is no guarantee of a great job. In fact, many college graduates are underemployed. ***Underemployment* is settling for a job that does not fully utilize one's skills, abilities, and training.** About 18% of college graduates take jobs

that don't usually require a college degree, and experts predict that this situation is unlikely to change in the near future (Lock, 2005a). And while it's true that the jobs you can obtain with a college degree pay more than those requiring less education, the higher-paying jobs go to college graduates with *college-level* reading, writing, and quantitative skills. College graduates without

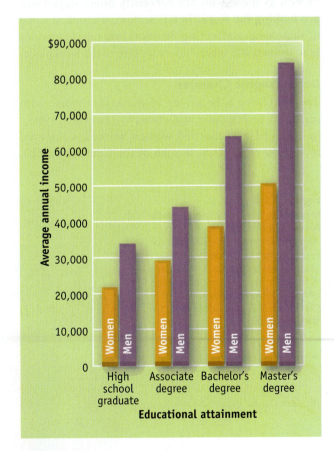

**Figure 13.5**

**Education and income.** This graph shows the average incomes of year-round, full-time workers age 18 and over, by gender and educational attainment. As you can see, the more education people have, the higher their income tends to be. However, at all levels women earn less than men with comparable education. (Data from U.S. Bureau of the Census, 2006b)

these skills more often end up in high-school-level jobs (Pryor & Schaffer, 1997).

Current employers are not very happy with the academic skills of many of their employees. According to a survey by the College Board's National Commission on Writing, a majority of U.S. employers say that about a third of their workers do not meet the writing requirements for their positions (College Entrance Examination Board, 2004). The ability to write clearly, concisely, and well is a skill that any savvy college-graduate should tout to potential employers. As new jobs develop, they will require more education and higher skill levels. International competition and technology are the two driving forces here (U.S. Department of Labor, 2000). Thus, computer literacy is an essential complement to a good basic education. Fortunately, computers are increasingly common in average households, and computer skill development is becoming a routine part of primary and secondary education.

## The Changing Workforce

The *labor force* **consists of all those who are employed as well as those who are currently unemployed but are looking for work.** In this section, we look at some of the changes affecting the workforce and consider how women and other minorities fare in the workplace.

### Demographic Changes

The workforce is becoming increasingly diverse with regard to both gender and ethnicity (Howard, 1995). In 2005, 61% of married women worked, compared to 41% in 1970 (U.S. Bureau of the Census, 2006b).

This percentage-increase holds even for women with very young children. For instance, in 1975 only 33% of women with children under the age of 3 worked outside the home. By 2005, this number had grown to 57% (U.S. Bureau of the Census, 2006b). These changes have implications not only for work and family life but also for men's and women's roles.

The workforce is also becoming more ethnically diversified (see **Figure 13.6**) (U.S. Bureau of Labor Statistics, 2006). High school graduation rates for Asian Americans match those for European Americans, but college graduation rates for Asian Americans exceed those of European Americans. Both high school and college graduation rates of Hispanics and African Americans lag behind those of European Americans, although they have been improving in recent decades (Worthington et al., 2005). Consequently, both groups are at a disadvantage when it comes to competing for the better jobs.

Although gay, lesbian, and bisexual workers have been longstanding participants in the workplace, they are often "closeted" for fear of discrimination. Unfortunately, most of these workers do not have the same legal

**Figure 13.6**

**Increasing diversity in the workforce.** Women and minority group members are entering the workforce in greater numbers than before. This graph projects changes in the share of the labor force by gender and by ethnicity between 1990 and 2010. (Data from U.S. Bureau of Labor Statistics, 2002)

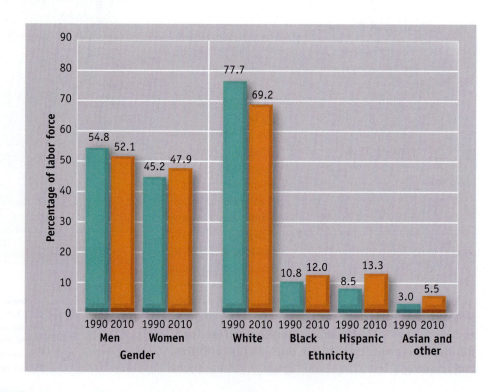

protections against employment discrimination as their heterosexual counterparts (Badgett, 2003); thus, wage gaps can exist because of sexual orientation. One recent study suggests that gay men tend to earn somewhat less than heterosexual men while lesbians may earn somewhat more than heterosexual women (Antecol, Jong, & Steinberger, 2008). Further, disclosing one's sexual orientation may cause a homophobic supervisor to fire, refuse to promote, or reduce the income of a gay or lesbian employee. Regrettably, wage penalties may be associated with disclosing one's sexual orientation (Cushing-Daniels & Tsz-Ying, 2009). Predictably, factors associated with the decision to disclose one's sexual orientation at work include employer policies and perceived gay supportiveness of the employer (Griffith & Hebl, 2002). Research on the effects of sexual orientation disclosure and employment discrimination are scarce. One laboratory study manipulated sexual orientation, gender, and masculinity/femininity while holding bogus résumé qualifications constant (Horvath & Ryan, 2003). Participants rated lesbian and gay male "applicants" less positively than heterosexual male "applicants" (but more positively than heterosexual women). And in a survey of 534 gay and lesbian employees, more heterosexism—showing discriminatory favoritism of heterosexuals over homosexuals—was reported with male supervisors or male work teams, and these effects were stronger for lesbians than for gay men (Ragins, Cornwell, & Miller, 2003).

## Today's Workplace for Women and Minorities

Recent years have seen a dramatic upsurge in the number of females and ethnic minorities in the workplace. Is today's workplace essentially the same for these groups as it is for white males? In many respects, the answer appears to be no. Although job discrimination on the basis of race and gender has been illegal for more than 40 years, women and minority group members continue to face obstacles to occupational success, as evidenced by relatively recent court decisions that found Wal-Mart and Morgan Stanley guilty of sex discrimination. Foremost among these obstacles is *job segregation.* Jobs are simultaneously typed by gender and by race. For example, skycaps are typically African American males and most hotel maids are minority females. Most white women and minority workers tend to be concentrated in jobs where there is little opportunity for advancement or increase in salary (Equal Employment Opportunity Commission, 2007). Also, as we discussed in Chapter 11, workers in female-dominated fields typically earn less than those in male-dominated fields, even when the jobs require similar levels of training, skill, and responsibility.

More women and ethnic minorities are entering higher-status occupations, but they still face discrimination because they are frequently *passed over for promotion* in favor of white men (Whitley & Kite, 2006). This seems to be a problem especially at higher levels of management (Cotter et al., 2001). For example, in 2006, about 16% of corporate officer positions in Fortune 500 companies were held by women and only about 1.5% were held by women of color (Catalyst, 2007). There appears to be a **glass ceiling, or invisible barrier that prevents most women and ethnic minorities from advancing to the highest levels of occupations** (see **Figure 13.7** on the next page). The fact that very few black women are in managerial positions has caused some to term the glass ceiling a "concrete wall" for women of color (U.S. Department of Labor, 1992). Largely because of these reduced opportunities for career advancement, some female corporate managers are quitting their jobs and starting their own firms. In 2002, women owned 28% of nonfarm U.S. businesses (U.S. Small Business Administration, 2006). At the other end of the job spectrum, there seems to be a "sticky floor"

John Browne, the long-time chief executive of British Petroleum and close associate of former British Prime Minister Tony Blair, had little choice but to resign after a judge cleared the way for a newspaper to publish allegations made by a former boyfriend. The exposé of Browne's private life ended his 41-year career at British Petroleum. The stunning demise of Browne's career demonstrates why many gay individuals choose to remain "closeted" in the workplace due to concern about recriminations.

© Peter Macdiarmid/Getty Images

## Figure 13.7

**The glass ceiling for women and minorities.** A longitudinal study looked at the chances of promotion to a managerial position in a sample of more than 26,000 adults over 30 years of career experience. This graph shows that promotion chances increased along with career experience for white men. By contrast, the promotion chances of white women and black men were much lower. As you can see, black women lagged far behind all groups. These trends are consistent with the existence of a glass ceiling for women and minorities.

Source: From Maume, D. J. (2004). Is the glass ceiling a unique form of inequality? *Work and Occupations,* *31*(2), 250–274. Copyright © 2004 by Sage Publications. Reprinted by permission of Sage Publications.

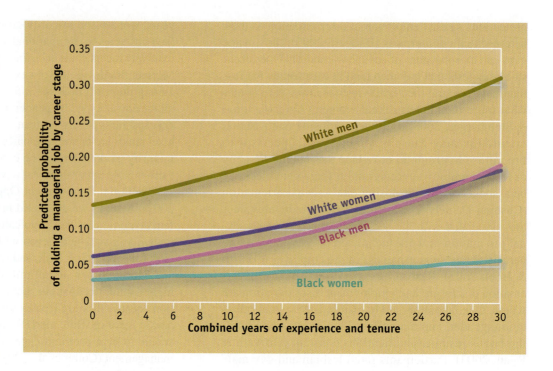

that causes women and minorities to get stuck in low-paying occupations (Brannon, 2005).

When only one woman or minority person is employed in an office, that person becomes a *token*—**or a symbol of all the members of that group.** Tokens are more distinctive or visible than members of the dominant majority. And, as we discussed in Chapter 7, distinctiveness makes a person's actions subject to intense scrutiny, stereotyping, and judgments. Thus, if a white male makes a mistake, it is explained as an *individual* problem. When a token woman or minority person makes a mistake, it is seen as evidence that *all* members of that group are incompetent. Hence, tokens experience a great deal of *performance pressure,* an added source of job stress (Thomas, 2005). Interestingly, if tokens are perceived as being "too successful," they may be labeled "workaholics" or may be accused of trying to "show up" members of the dominant majority. These unfavorable perceptions may be reflected in performance appraisals. The performance of successful white men is less likely to be interpreted in these negative ways.

Another way the world of work is different for women, ethnic, and gay and lesbian minorities is that they have *less access to same-gender or same-group role models and mentors* (Murrell & James, 2001). Finally, *sexual harassment,* a topic we'll take up later, is much more likely to be a problem for working women than for working men. In sum, women and minority individuals must contend with discrimination on the job in a number of forms.

### The Challenges of Change

The increasingly diverse workforce presents challenges to both organizations and workers. These challenges

can occur within the workplace as well as within the community where the workplace and workers reside (Pugh et al., 2008). Important cultural differences exist in managing time and people, in identifying with work, and in making decisions (Thomas, 2005). These differences can contribute to conflict. Not surprisingly, perhaps, members of majority groups (generally white males) do not perceive discrimination as often as the members of minority groups do (Avery, McKay, & Wilson, 2008). Another challenge is that some individuals feel that they are personally paying the price of prejudice in the workplace, and this perception causes resentment. Recognizing the problem, some corporations offer diversity training programs for their employees. Ironically, these programs can make the problem worse if they take a blaming stance toward white males or if they stir up workers' feelings but provide no ongoing support for dealing with them. Thus, it is essential that such programs be carefully designed (Ocon, 2006). The strong support of top management is also critical to their success.

Many who advocate abandoning affirmative action programs that are intended to promote access to jobs for women and minorities argue that these programs promote "reverse discrimination" through the use of unfair hiring and promotion practices. For some, this perception may reflect a sense of *privilege,* an unquestioned assumption that white males should be guaranteed a place in society and that others should compete for the remaining jobs (Jacques, 1997). Some also argue that affirmative action undercuts the role of merit in employment decisions and sets up (supposedly) underprepared workers for failure. Many laboratory studies show that individuals have negative feelings about employees who may have been hired under affirmative action (Crosby et al., 2003). However, studies conducted with actual workers have not found this situation (Taylor, 1995). Regardless, this potential negative effect can be counteracted when workers know that decisions are based on merit as well as on group membership.

To minimize conflict and to maintain worker productivity and satisfaction, companies can provide well-designed diversity programs, and managers can educate themselves about the varied values and needs of their workers (Ocon, 2006). Similarly, both majority and minority employees must be willing to learn to work comfortably with those who come from other backgrounds.

Let's close this section with some good news regarding diversity. A recent survey revealed that 92% of human resources directors connect recruiting diverse employees to their organizations' strategic hiring plans (Koc, 2007). Within the contemporary world of work, diversity is here to stay.

# Coping with Occupational Hazards

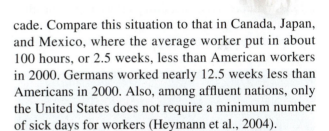

### LEARNING OBJECTIVES

- Recognize some important sources of job stress.
- Summarize the effects of job stress on physical and mental health.
- Describe the prevalence and consequences of sexual harassment.
- Cite some ways that organizations and individuals can reduce sexual harassment.
- Identify some causes and effects of unemployment.

Work can bring people deep satisfaction; indeed, it can promote psychological health and well-being (Blustein, 2008). Yet work can also be a source of frustration and conflict. In this section, we explore three challenges to today's workers: job stress, sexual harassment, and unemployment.

## Job Stress

You saw in Chapter 3 that stress can emerge from any corner of your life. However, many theorists suspect that the workplace is the primary source of stress in modern society. To begin, let's consider this sobering statistic: Over 75% of the workers in the United States claim that their jobs are stressful (Smith, 2003). To put this statistic into context, let's compare the typical stressors experienced by younger adults (ages 17 to 21) and those of older (25+), working adults. As you can see in the left column of **Figure 13.8**, younger people are troubled more by personal stressors, whereas older adults are troubled primarily by work-related stressors (right column). Let's examine the pervasive problem of job stress and see what employers and workers can do about it.

### Sources of Stress on the Job

Between 2001 and 2004, the number of Americans claiming to feel overworked rose from 28% to 44% (Galinsky et al., 2005). Current estimates clock the average full-time workweek at 48 hours; in law and finance, 60-hour weeks are common (Hodge, 2002). According to a United Nations report, the average American worked 1,978 hours in 2000, up from 1,942 hours in 1990 (International Labour Office, 2002). That's an increase of nearly a full week over the previous decade. Compare this situation to that in Canada, Japan, and Mexico, where the average worker put in about 100 hours, or 2.5 weeks, less than American workers in 2000. Germans worked nearly 12.5 weeks less than Americans in 2000. Also, among affluent nations, only the United States does not require a minimum number of sick days for workers (Heymann et al., 2004).

| Common Stressors Found in Younger and Older Adults | |
| --- | --- |
| **Young adults (age 17–21)** | **Older adults (age 25 and beyond)** |
| Graduating from high school | Organizational change |
| Beginning college | Job insecurity (downsizing) |
| Leaving home | Balancing work and family demands |
| Nagging parents | Paying bills |
| Peer pressure | Increasing job demands |
| Taking exams | Dull or unchallenging work |
| Fear of the future | Pay inequity |
| Graduating from college | Attending school while working full time |
| Starting a new job | Job relocation |
| Interviewing for jobs | Planning for retirement |

**Figure 13.8**

**Common stressors found in younger and older adults.** Compare and contrast the typical sources of stress reported by younger and older adults. Do any of these stressors reflect your own experiences? As you can see, as people get older, their stress increasingly comes from work-related issues.

Source: Adapted from Aamodt, M. (2010). *Industrial/organizational psychology: An applied approach.* Belmont, CA: Wadsworth/Cengage. © 2010 Wadsworth, a part of Cengage Learning, Inc. Reproduced by permission. www.cengage.com/permissions.

CATHY

JOB STRESS WEAKENED MY IMMUNE SYSTEM AND MADE ME GET THE FLU!

JOB STRESS DISTORTED MY "FOOD JUDGMENT" AND MADE ME GAIN WEIGHT!

JOB STRESS RUINED MY LOVE LIFE, MY FINANCES AND MY HAIR!

WHATEVER HAPPENED TO THE GOOD OLD DAYS WHEN PEOPLE DEMANDED RAISES?

WE WANT A MEDITATION GARDEN, OFFICE MASSEUR AND FREE JUICE BAR!

In addition to long hours, common job stressors include lack of privacy, high noise levels, unusual hours (such as rotating shifts), the pressure of deadlines, lack of control over one's work, inadequate resources to do a job, and perceived inequities at work (Fairbrother & Warn, 2003). Environmental conditions, such as workplace temperature (e.g., extreme heat in a steel mill, excessive cold in a meat packing plant), can affect physical, cognitive, and perceptual tasks (Pilcher, Nadler, & Busch, 2002). Fears of being downsized, concerns about health care benefits (losing them or paying increasingly higher premiums), and worries about losing pension plans also dog workers in today's economy. Office politics and conflict with supervisors, subordinates, and co-workers also make the list of job stressors. Having to adapt to changing technology and automated offices is another source of work stress. Firefighters, law enforcement officers, and coal miners face frequent threats to their physical safety. High-pressure jobs such as air traffic controller and surgeon demand virtually perfect performance, as errors can have disastrous consequences. Ironically, "underwork" (boring, repetitive tasks) can also be stressful.

Women may experience certain workplace stressors, such as sex discrimination and sexual harassment, at higher rates than men (Betz, 2006; Sulsky & Smith, 2005). African Americans and ethnic minorities must cope with racism and other types of discrimination on the job (Betz, 2006), which means members of minority groups may experience higher levels of stress than nonminorities (Sulsky & Smith, 2005). Discrimination is also a problem for gay and lesbian employees (Badgett, 2003). Workers from lower socioeconomic groups typically work in more dangerous jobs than workers from higher socioeconomic status do.

Why are American workers so stressed out? According to Gwendolyn Keita and Joseph Hurrell (1994), four factors are the culprits:

1. *More workers are employed in service industries.* Workers in these jobs must interact with a variety of individuals on a daily basis. While most customers are civil and easy to deal with, some are decidedly difficult. Nonetheless, even obnoxious and troublesome customers "are always right," so workers have to swallow their frustration and anger, and doing so is stressful.

lapphotos/newscom

**Firefighters obviously face a great deal of stress in their work, but so do people in many other jobs. Work stress is a major issue in a diverse array of occupations.**

Such situations may contribute to residual stress, where strain and tension from work is carried over because workers have a hard time "letting go." Imagine the frustration some workers must feel if their jobs do not allow them to be "right" or to speak candidly to customers.

**2.** *The economy is unpredictable.* In the age of restructuring, downsizing, takeovers, and bankruptcies, even excellent workers aren't assured of keeping their jobs like workers in the past. Change in response to economic pressures often comes in the form of downsizing or restructuring (Robinson & Griffiths, 2005). Thus, the fear of job loss may lurk in the back of workers' minds. People may expend considerable time and emotional energy worrying about various "what if?" scenarios about their future, a future they cannot directly control. Sometimes, even those who get to keep their jobs following corporate upheavals are not spared psychological challenges, as they may develop a "survivor syndrome" (Marks & DeMeuse, 2005).

**3.** *Rapid changes in computer technology tax workers' abilities to keep up.* Computers have taken over some jobs, forcing workers to develop new skills and to do so quickly. In other jobs, the stress comes from rapid and ongoing advances in technology (software as well as hardware) that force workers to keep pace with the changes. Workers may feel that they do not possess the appropriate skills or have the needed resources to complete tasks in allotted timeframes (Bolino & Turnley, 2005).

**4.** *The workplace is becoming more diverse.* As more women and minority group members enter the workplace, individuals from all groups must learn to interact more with people who are unfamiliar to them. Developing these skills takes time and may be stressful.

Taking a broader view, Robert Karasek contends that the two key factors in occupational stress are the *psychological demands* made on a worker and a worker's amount of *decision control* (Karasek, 1979; Karasek & Theorell, 1990). Psychological demands are measured by asking employees questions such as "Is there excessive work?" and "Must you work fast (or hard)?" To measure decision control, employees are asked such questions as "Do you have a lot of say in your job?" and "Do you have freedom to make decisions?" In Karasek's demand-control model, *stress is greatest in jobs characterized by high psychological demands and low decision*

*control.* Based on survey data obtained from workers, he has tentatively mapped out where various jobs fall on these two key dimensions of job stress, as shown in **Figure 13.9**. The jobs thought to be most stressful are those with heavy psychological demands and little control over decisions (see the lower right area of the figure). Considerable research has been conducted on the demand-control model, most of which has been supportive (Sonnentag & Frese, 2003). Still, some criticize the model as being too simplistic (Ippolito et al., 2005).

**Effects of Job Stress**

As with other forms of stress, occupational stress is associated with numerous negative effects. In the work arena itself, job stress has been linked to an increased number of industrial accidents, increased absenteeism, poor job performance, and higher turnover rates (Colligan & Higgins, 2005). Experts estimate that stress-related reductions in workers' productivity may cost American industry hundreds of billions per year. Just under 3% of the workforce is absent on any given workday in the United States, and 13% of all employee absences can be chalked up to the impact of stress (Commerce Clearing House, 2007).

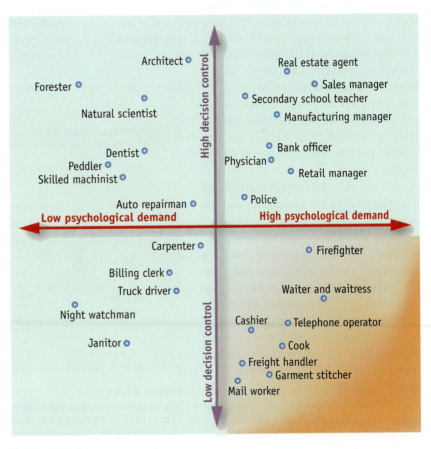

**Figure 13.9**

**Karasek's model of occupational stress as related to specific jobs.** Robert Karasek (1979) theorizes that occupational stress is greatest in jobs characterized by high psychological demands and low decision control. Based on survey data, this chart shows where various familiar jobs fall on these two dimensions. According to Karasek's model, the most stressful jobs are those shown in the shaded area on the lower right.

## Common Signs of Burnout Among Workers

| | |
|---|---|
| Low energy | Negativity and complaining attitude |
| Lessened productivity | |
| Apathy | Increased forgetfulness |
| Routinely late for work | Dread of going to work |
| Limited concentration | Sense of being overwhelmed |
| | Frustration and tension |

**Figure 13.10**

**Common signs of job burnout among workers.** Here are some of the commonly observed symptoms of stress-induced burnout, a physical and psychological condition that is marked by fatigue, pessimism, and a lowered quality of work or job performance. Burnout is most likely to occur when the stress and strain of work is continuous rather than occasional or sporadic.

Source: Adapted from Aamodt, M. (2010). *Industrial/organizational psychology: An applied approach.* Belmont, CA: Wadsworth/Cengage. © 2010 Wadsworth, a part of Cengage Learning, Inc. Reproduced with permission. www.cengage.com/permissions.

When job stress is temporary, as when important deadlines loom, workers usually suffer only minor and brief effects of stress, such as sleeplessness or anxiety. Prolonged high levels of stress are more problematic, as those who work in people-oriented jobs such as human services, education, and health care can attest (Maslach, 2005). As we noted in Chapter 3, prolonged stress can lead to *burnout,* characterized by exhaustion, cynicism, and poor job performance (Maslach, 2005). **Figure 13.10** lists some of the most common signs of burnout among workers. The feelings of listlessness, detachment, and potential for depression among employees with burnout are linked with higher absenteeism rates, greater job turnover, and lowered worker performance (Parker & Kulik, 1995).

Of course, the negative effects of occupational stress extend beyond the workplace. Foremost among these adverse effects are those on employees' *physical health.* Work stress has been related to a variety of physical maladies, including heart disease, high blood pressure, ulcers, arthritis, asthma, and cancer (Thomas, 2005). In a test of Karasek's model of work stress, symptoms of heart disease were more prevalent among Swedish men whose jobs were high in psychological demands and low in decision control (Karasek et al., 1981; see **Figure 13.11**). Job stress can also have a negative impact on workers' *psychological health.* Occupational stress has been related to distress, anxiety, and depression (Blackmore et al., 2007; Melchior et al., 2007; Sonnentag & Frese, 2003).

## Dealing with Job Stress

There are essentially three avenues of attack for dealing with occupational stress (Ivancevich et al., 1990). The first is to intervene at the *individual* level by modifying workers' ways of coping with job stress. The second is to intervene at the *organizational* level by redesigning the work environment itself. The third is to intervene at the *individual-organizational interface* by improving the fit between workers and their companies. Concrete suggestions for coping with stressors, including those found in the workplace, are discussed in Chapter 4.

As already noted, workers from lower socioeconomic groups typically experience more work stress than those from higher-status groups. Ironically, these are the workers who receive less attention through stress management and other programs (Ilgen, 1990). Researchers are beginning to pay more attention to working-class and low-income families (Crosby & Sabattini, 2006). Perhaps their findings will encourage changes in the workplace.

## Sexual Harassment

Sexual harassment burst into the American consciousness in 1991 during the televised confirmation hearings for the nomination of Clarence Thomas as a Justice of the U.S. Supreme Court. Although Justice Thomas survived the confirmation process, many would argue that

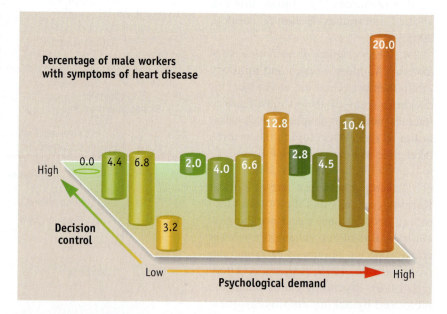

**Figure 13.11**

**Job characteristics in Karasek's model and heart disease prevalence.** Karasek et al. (1981) interviewed 1,621 Swedish men about their work and assessed their cardiovascular health. The vertical bars in this figure show the percentage of the men with symptoms of heart disease as a function of the characteristics of their jobs. The highest incidence of heart disease was found among men who had jobs high in psychological demands and low in decision control, just as Karasek's model of occupational stress predicts.

Source: Redrawn from Karasek, R. A., Baker, D., Marxer, F., Ahlbom, A., & Theorell, T. (1981). Job decision latitude, job demand, and cardiovascular disease: A prospective study of Swedish men. *American Journal of Public Health, 71,* 694–705. Reprinted by permission.

## Sally Forth

his reputation was damaged by Anita Hill's public allegations of sexual harassment (while she was his assistant in the U.S. Department of Education a decade earlier), and so was Hill's. Allegations of sexual harassment also caused serious problems for President Bill Clinton. These highly publicized examples of sexual harassment charges have served as a wake-up call to individuals and companies, as both can be sued for harassment (regulations were instituted in 1980). Although most workers recognize that they need to take the problem of sexual harassment seriously, many people remain relatively naive about what constitutes sexual harassment.

**Sexual harassment occurs when employees are subjected to unwelcome sexually oriented behavior.** According to law, there are two types of sexual harassment. The first is *quid pro quo* (from the Latin expression that translates as "something given or received in exchange for something else"). In the context of sexual harassment, quid pro quo involves making submission to unwanted sexual advances a condition of hiring, advancement (raise, promotion), or not being fired. In other words, the worker's survival on the job depends on agreeing to engage in unwanted sex. The second type of harassment is *hostile environment,* or any type of unwelcome sexual behavior that creates hostile work situations that can inflict psychological harm and interfere with job performance.

Sexual harassment can take a variety of forms: unsolicited and unwelcome flirting, sexual advances, or propositions; insulting comments about an employee's appearance, dress, or anatomy; unappreciated dirty jokes and sexual gestures; intrusive or sexual questions about an employee's personal life; explicit descriptions of the harasser's own sexual experiences; abuse

Highly publicized accusations of sexual harassment have become common in recent years. Here, Andrea Mackris appears with her attorney at a press conference to discuss allegations of sexual harassment lodged against Bill O'Reilly of the Fox News Channel.

of familiarities such as "honey" and "dear"; unnecessary and unwanted physical contact such as touching, hugging, pinching, or kissing; catcalls; exposure of genitals; physical or sexual assault; and rape. As experts have pointed out, sexual harassment is an abuse of power by a person in authority. To determine what legally constitutes sexual harassment, the courts take into account "whether the behavior is motivated by the gender of the victim, whether it is unwelcome, whether it is repetitive, and whether it could lead to negative psychological or organizational outcomes" (Goldberg & Zhang, 2004, p. 823). Same-gender sexual harassment also occurs and is prosecuted according to the same standards applied in cross-sex sexual harassment, although little research has been done on the topic (but see Berkley & Watt, 2006).

### Prevalence and Consequences

Sexual harassment in the workplace is more widespread than most people realize, but the topic is now better understood because of increased research attention (O'Leary-Kelly et al., 2009). A review of 18 studies suggested that approximately 42% of female workers in the United States report having been sexually harassed (Gruber, 1990). A liberal estimate for male workers is 15% (Gutek, 1993). The typical female victim is young, divorced or separated, in a nonsenior position, and in a masculine-stereotyped field (Davidson & Fielden, 1999). A review of studies on women in the military reported rates of sexual harassment ranging from 55% to 79% (Goldzweig, 2006). Women in blue-collar jobs are also at high risk, but sexual harassment also occurs in the professions. For example, in a survey of United Methodist clergywomen, 77% reported that they had experienced sexual harassment—with 41% of these incidents perpetrated by colleagues and other ministers ("Women Clerics," 1990). Sadly, sexual harassment is often associated with other forms of workplace discrimination for blacks and members of other ethnic or minority groups (Rospenda, Richman, & Shannon, 2009).

Experiencing sexual harassment can have negative effects on psychological and physical health (Norton, 2002). Problematic reactions include anger, reduced self-esteem, depression, and anxiety. Victims may also have difficulties in their personal relationships and in sexual adjustment (loss of desire, for example). Increased alcohol consumption, smoking, and dependence on drugs are also reported (Davidson & Fielden, 1999; Rospenda et al., 2008). In addition, sexual harassment can produce fallout on the job: Women who are harassed may be less productive, less satisfied with their jobs, and less committed to their work and employer (Woodzicka & LaFrance, 2005). Women who are sexually harassed also report lower job satisfaction and may withdraw from work as the result of physical and mental health problems. Some of these women are even found to display symptoms of posttraumatic stress disorder (Willness, Steel, & Lee, 2007). Finally, sexual harassment can heighten the incidence of job withdrawal while decreasing job satisfaction and undermining an individual's organizational commitment (Kath et al., 2009).

### Stopping Sexual Harassment

To predict the occurrence of sexual harassment, researchers have developed a two-factor model based on the person (prospective harasser) and the social situation (Pryor, Giedd, & Williams, 1995). According to this model, individuals vary in their proclivity for sexual harassment, and organizational norms regarding the acceptability of sexual harassment also vary. Sexual harassment is most likely to occur when individual proclivity is high and organizational norms are accepting. Thus, it follows that organizations can reduce the incidence of sexual harassment by promoting norms that are intolerant of it.

Acknowledging the prevalence and negative impact of sexual harassment, many organizations have taken steps to educate and protect their workers. Managers are publicly speaking out against sexual harassment, supporting programs designed to increase employees' awareness of the problem, issuing policies expressly forbidding harassment, and implementing formal grievance procedures for handling allegations of harassment.

Responses to sexual harassment may be personal as well as organizational. Researchers have developed a typology of possible responses to this problem (see **Figure 13.12**) and have studied their relative effectiveness (Bowes-Sperry & Tata, 1999; Knapp et al., 1997). Unfortunately, the most frequently used strategy—avoidance/denial—is also the least effective one. Confrontation/negotiation and advocacy seeking are two effective strategies but are infrequently used.

## Unemployment

A major consequence of recent economic upheavals is *displaced workers*—**individuals who are unemployed because their jobs have disappeared.** Between 1999 and 2001, roughly 5 million workers with three or more years of experience were displaced as a result of plant closings, slack or insufficient work, or positions being eliminated (U.S. Bureau of the Census, 2006b). Losing one's job is difficult at best and devastating at worst. Given the high U.S. unemployment rate in late 2009 and early 2010 (over 9%), many Americans have found themselves out of work and worried about their futures. Not only can unemployment cause economic distress, it

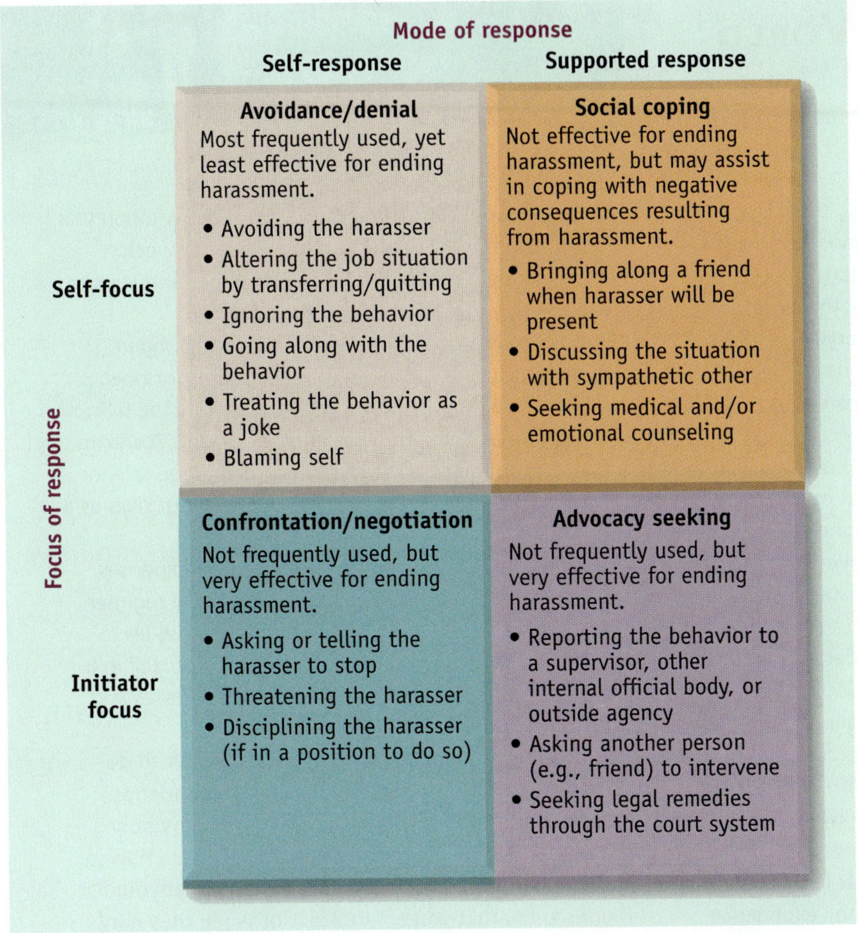
Mode of response
Self-response
Supported response
Focus of response
Self-focus
Initiator focus
Avoidance/denial
Most frequently used, yet least effective for ending harassment.
• Avoiding the harasser
• Altering the job situation by transferring/quitting
• Ignoring the behavior
• Going along with the behavior
• Treating the behavior as a joke
• Blaming self
Social coping
Not effective for ending harassment, but may assist in coping with negative consequences resulting from harassment.
• Bringing along a friend when harasser will be present
• Discussing the situation with sympathetic other
• Seeking medical and/or emotional counseling
Confrontation/negotiation
Not frequently used, but very effective for ending harassment.
• Asking or telling the harasser to stop
• Threatening the harasser
• Disciplining the harasser (if in a position to do so)
Advocacy seeking
Not frequently used, but very effective for ending harassment.
• Reporting the behavior to a supervisor, other internal official body, or outside agency
• Asking another person (e.g., friend) to intervene
• Seeking legal remedies through the court system

**Figure 13.12**

**Effectiveness of responses to sexual harassment.** Responses to sexual harassment can be classified into four categories based on the focus of the response (directed toward self or toward the harasser) and the mode of the response (involving the self or others). Unfortunately, the most frequent reactions turn out to be the least helpful. Effective strategies are available, but they are infrequently used.

Source: From Bowes-Sperry, L., & Tata, J. (1999). A multiperspective framework of sexual harassment. In G. N. Powell (Ed.), *Handbook of gender and work* (pp. 263–280). Thousand Oaks, CA: Sage Publications. Copyright © 1999 by Sage Publications, Inc. Books. Reproduced with permission of Sage Publications, Inc. Books in the formats Textbook and Other book via Copyright Clearance Center.

can also cause health problems and such psychological difficulties as loss of self-esteem, depression, and anxiety (Bobek & Robbins, 2005; McKee-Ryan et al., 2005). A recent meta-analysis found that the rate of psychological problems was more than doubled among unemployed persons compared to those who were working (Paul & Moser, 2009). Also, the rate of attempted and completed suicides increases with unemployment. Gender does not affect the amount of distress experienced as the result of job loss (Kulik, 2000). Even "survivors," those who retain their jobs following a round of layoffs during downsizing, are not immune from psychological distress (Paulsen et al., 2005).

While losing a job at any age is highly stressful, those who are laid off in middle age seem to find the experience most difficult (Breslin & Mustard, 2003). For one thing, they typically have more financial responsibilities than those in other age groups. Second, if other family members aren't able to provide health insurance, the entire family's health and welfare is jeopardized. Third, older workers typically remain out of work for a longer time than younger workers. Thus, economic hardship can be a real possibility and can threaten quality of life for the worker's family. Finally, middle-aged workers have been on the job for a number of years. Because they typically feel highly involved in their work, being cut off from this important source of life satisfaction is painful (Broomhall & Winefield, 1990). Of course, not all middle-aged workers are affected negatively by loss of work (Leana & Feldman, 1991). Individuals who are in their 50s and close to retirement and those who are motivated to try their hand at something

*"The dip in sales seems to coincide with the decision to eliminate the sales staff."*

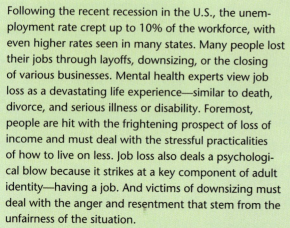

Following the recent recession in the U.S., the unemployment rate crept up to 10% of the workforce, with even higher rates seen in many states. Many people lost their jobs through layoffs, downsizing, or the closing of various businesses. Mental health experts view job loss as a devastating life experience—similar to death, divorce, and serious illness or disability. Foremost, people are hit with the frightening prospect of loss of income and must deal with the stressful practicalities of how to live on less. Job loss also deals a psychological blow because it strikes at a key component of adult identity—having a job. And victims of downsizing must deal with the anger and resentment that stem from the unfairness of the situation.

Understandably, job loss negatively affects mental health (Paul & Moser, 2009) and is associated with decreases in self-confidence, feelings of failure and rejection, and increases in anxiety and depression (Bobek & Robbins, 2005). Unfortunately, job loss also increases the likelihood of marital problems. Being aware of the psychological aspects of job loss can help you cope with the experience. Some experts suggest that individuals' reactions to job loss are similar to what they experience when they confront their own death (Bobek & Robbins, 2005; Lock, 2005b).

For some practical suggestions for coping with job loss, we draw on the advice of career experts Michael Laskoff (2004) and Robert Lock (2005b).

*Apply for unemployment benefits as soon as possible.* The average length of unemployment in 2005 was 18 weeks (U.S. Bureau of the Census, 2006b). Thus you need to look into unemployment benefits, which you may be able to collect for 26 weeks (or longer in some cases). Contact the nearest office of your state's Employment Security Commission or Department of Labor.

*Determine your income and expenses.* Determine precisely your sources of income (unemployment benefits, spouse or partner's income, savings) and how much you can count on per week/month. Itemize your weekly/monthly expenses. Set up a realistic budget and stick to it. Talk with your creditors if you need to.

*Lower your expenses and think of ways to bring in extra income.* Cut out unnecessary expenses for now. Minimize your credit card purchases and pay the bills off every month to avoid building up huge debt. For extra income, consider selling a car, having a garage sale, or putting items up for auction on eBay. Use your skills as a temporary worker.

*Stay healthy.* To save money on medical expenses, eat well-balanced meals, maintain an exercise regimen, and get adequate sleep. Use relaxation techniques to manage your stress (see Chapter 4). Keep yourself in a positive frame of mind by recalling past successes and imagining future ones.

*Reach out for support.* Although it is difficult to do, explain your job situation to your family and friends. You need their support and they need to know how your unemployment will affect them. If you are having relationship problems, consult a counselor. Let your friends know that you are looking for work; they may have job leads.

*Get organized and get going.* Start by setting aside time and space to work on your job search. Then consider your situation. Is your résumé up to date? Can you find the same type of job or do you need to think about other options? Do you need to relocate? Do you need more education or retraining? Some people decide to go into business for themselves, so don't overlook this option. Check out some of the excellent career planning books (see this chapter's recommended reading, *What Color Is Your Parachute?*, for example) and visit relevant websites. Expect to spend 15–25 hours a week on job-searching activities. Spend some time every week on volunteer activities in an area you would like to pursue.

new seem the least affected. In fact, having goals to pursue while searching for work is associated with mental health among older individuals (Niessen, Heinrichs, & Dorr, 2009).

Support from friends and family is essential in coping with unemployment. When a person is out of work for an extended period of time or has little social support, counseling may also be helpful. Some companies offer programs for laid-off workers. These programs typically teach employees how to search for jobs, manage stress, and cultivate social support. In the "Living in Today's World" above, we offer some specific suggestions for coping with unemployment.

# Balancing Work and Other Spheres of Life

- Articulate current perspectives on workaholism.
- Define work-family conflict, and discuss the benefits of multiple roles.
- List several types of leisure activities and summarize their benefits.

A major challenge for individuals today is balancing work, family, and leisure activities in ways that are personally satisfying (APA, 2004; Warr, 2007). We noted earlier that dual-earner families are becoming increasingly common and that the traditional boundaries between family and paid work life are breaking down (Voydanoff, 2005). These two developments are related. Historically, traditional gender roles assigned women's work to the home and men's work outside the home. This division of labor created boundaries between family and work life. With more women entering the workforce, these boundaries have become blurred. The technology-based changes in the workplace are also eroding these distinctions between family and work life (Jackson, 2005). Here we examine three issues related to balancing various life roles.

## Workaholism

Most people cherish their leisure activities and relationships with their families and friends. However, *workaholics* devote nearly all their time and energy to their jobs; for them, work is addictive (Piotrowski & Vodanovich, 2008). They put in lots of overtime, take few vacations, regularly bring work home from the office, and think about work most of the time. They are energetic, intense, and ambitious. In addition to personal factors, situational forces can also promote workaholism (Murphy & Zagorski, 2005). Thus, it is more common where the organizational climate supports imbalances between work and personal life (Burke, 2001).

Although workaholism has received considerable attention in the popular press, empirical research on the topic is relatively limited (Harpaz & Snir, 2003). A survey of 800 senior-level managers reported that nearly one in four considered themselves to be workaholics (Joyner, 1999). Psychologists are divided on the issue of whether workaholism is problematic. Should workaholics be praised for their dedication and encouraged in their single-minded pursuit of fulfillment through work (Burke, 2009)? Or is workaholism a form of addiction (Burke & Fiskenbaum, 2009), a sign that an individual is driven by compulsions he or she cannot control? In support of the former view is evidence that some workaholics tend to be highly satisfied with their jobs and with their lives (Bone-

bright, Clay, & Ankenmann, 2000). They work hard simply because work is the most meaningful activity they know. Yet other evidence suggests that workaholics may have poorer emotional and physical well-being than nonworkaholics (Bonebright et al., 2000; Burke, 2000). How can these conflicting findings be reconciled?

It seems that there are two types of workaholics (Aziz & Zickar, 2006; Spence & Robbins, 1992). One type, the *enthusiastic workaholic*, works for the pure joy of it. Such people derive immense satisfaction from work and generally perform well in highly demanding jobs. These individuals may also qualify as being high in *work engagement*, an emerging positive and fulfilling construct linked to absorption in work (Bakker et al., 2008). The other type, the *nonenthusiastic workaholic*, feels driven to work but reports low job enjoyment. Moreover, these workaholics tend to report lower life satisfaction and less purpose in life than enthusiastic workaholics. Thus, it is not surprising that the nonenthusiastic group is more likely to develop *burnout* (Maslach, 2005).

Both types of workaholics experience an imbalance between work and personal time. Not surprisingly, this situation translates into a high degree of work-family conflict for both groups (Bakker, Demerouti, & Burke, 2009; Bonebright et al., 2000). Moreover, the families of both groups suffer (Robinson, Flowers, & Ng, 2006). A recent study found that students whose parents were workaholics tended to report lower levels of psychological well-being and self acceptance and high numbers of physical health complaints (Chamberlin & Zhang, 2009). So, although enthusiastic workaholics really love their work, their devotion to their jobs has a price, one often paid by their families.

## Work and Family Roles

One of the biggest recent changes in the labor force has been the emergence of dual-earner households, now the dominant family form in the United States (U.S. Bureau of the Census, 2006b). Dual-earner couples are struggling to discover better ways of balancing family life and the demands of work. These changes in work and family life have sparked the interest of researchers in many disciplines, including psychology.

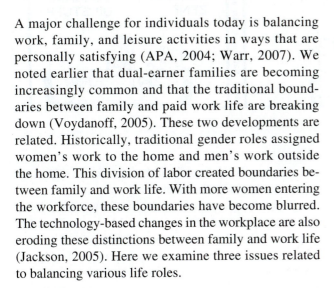

DILBERT

**NO ONE HAS ANY GOOD ADVICE ON HOW I CAN BALANCE MY WORK WITH MY PERSONAL LIFE.**

**YOU DIDN'T ASK ME.**

**I TAKE THE ZEN APPROACH OF HAVING NO FRIENDS AND DOING NO WORK. HENCE, PERFECT BALANCE.**

**WHERE DID YOU GET THAT DEFINITION OF ZEN?**

**I USED TO READ, BUT IT'S FASTER TO MAKE UP STUFF.**

DILBERT © 2005 Scott Adams/Dist. by United Feature Syndicate, Inc.

An important fact of life for dual-earner couples is that they juggle *multiple roles:* spouse or partner and employee. TICKS (two-income couples with kids) add a third role: parent. Thus, today's working parents experience *work-family conflict,* **or the feeling of being pulled in multiple directions by competing demands from the job and the family.** In heterosexual dual-earner families, men are taking on more household chores and child care, but most wives still have greater responsibilities in these areas (Drago, 2007). In gay and lesbian dual-earner households, responsibilities are more evenly divided (Kurdek, 2005; Patterson, 2003). Single parents are especially likely to have work-family conflicts.

Although employers are reducing their contributions to employee benefits such as pension and retirement plans, health care benefits, and the like, they do not seem to be cutting back on flexible work schedules, family leave, and child and elder care support (Bond et al., 2005). A key reason employers are retaining these programs is that they help to recruit and retain employees. Still, the fact is that most employees do not have access to such programs. Some believe that this situation is partly to blame for the downward drift in the percentage of mothers with infant children who are in the labor force (Stone & Lovejoy, 2004). In 1998, the participation rate for this group had reached a high of 59%; by 2005, it had fallen to 56%. According to Ellen Galinsky, president of the Families and Work Institute, "They're not fleeing work—they're fleeing the demanding way of work" (Armour, 2004). Indeed, the more hours women work, the more their marital satisfaction tends to suffer (but keep in mind that this is a correlational relationship and not a causal one). However, it makes sense that longer work hours can spill over into time once reserved for family commitments, thereby introducing strain in family life (Hughes & Parkes, 2007). To gain more control over their lives, some women

are temporarily opting out of the workforce; others are going into business for themselves.

To be fair, some of the decline in women's labor force participation rates can probably be attributed to generational shifts in the views of the optimal balance of work and family roles. As you can see in **Figure 13.13**, more Gen-X employees with children endorse a family-centric view over a work-centric view compared to a comparable group of Boomers. Some suggest that these generational differences are due, in part, to many Gen-Xers seeing their hardworking parents lose their jobs because of downsizing (Families and Work Institute, 2004).

Although today's working parents may feel stressed, researchers find that multiple roles are beneficial for both men's and women's mental, physical, and relationship health, at least in middle-class couples (Barnett, 2005; Barnett & Hyde, 2001). For women, the

| Generational Differences in Work and Family Priorities | | |
|---|---|---|
| | **2002 Ages** | |
| **Relative emphasis on work and family** | **Gen-X (23–37)** | **Boomers (38–57)** |
| Family-centric | 55% | 46% |
| Dual-centric | 33 | 35 |
| Work-centric | 13 | 20 |

**Figure 13.13**

**Generational differences in work and family priorities.** Gen-X parents are significantly more likely than Boomer parents to be family-centric (place more emphasis on family than work), whereas Boomer parents are significantly more likely than Gen-Xers to be work-centric (place greater emphasis on work than family). The fact that both groups have children under 18 living at home suggests that this is a generational, rather than a life cycle, difference.

From Families and Work Institute (2004, October). *Generation and gender in the workplace.* New York: Families and Work Institute.

benefits of multiple roles are attributed primarily to the effects of the employee role. For men, family involvement is important, especially in the area of relationship health. According to Rosalind Barnett and Janet Hyde (2001), a number of factors contribute to the positive outcomes associated with multiple roles, including added income, social support, opportunities to experience success, and buffering. The latter refers to the idea that successes and satisfactions in one role provide a buffer against the negative effects of stress or failure in another role. Of course, there are outside limits to the number of roles and the amount of work that people can take on before they sacrifice the benefits of multiple roles (Barnett & Hyde, 2001). Role overload likely causes psychological distress.

## Leisure and Recreation

Most Americans are putting in 48-hour workweeks, and many work more hours than that. Some workers put in extra hours because their employers mandate it. Others choose to work more hours to maintain their standard of living, because real earning power, especially for low-wage workers, has fallen behind what it was 25 years ago (Joyner, 2001). And when workers arrive home, unpaid family work awaits them. Given the pace of contemporary American life, it's no surprise that almost 60% of Americans say that having leisure time is either "extremely important" or "very important" in their lives, according to a Gallup poll (Moore, 2003).

American workers take an average of 14 days of paid annual vacation. The paid vacation time of American workers lags far behind that of many European workers (see **Figure 13.14**). Moreover, workers in most European Union countries get four weeks of vacation time by law (Roughton, 2001). A generous number of public holidays pushes the average vacation time in the E.U. to about seven weeks!

We define *leisure* **as unpaid activities people choose to engage in because the activities are personally meaningful.** How might we distinguish activities that are meaningful from those that aren't? Although people may lounge in front of the TV set for hours at a time, most would also acknowledge that an important difference exists between this use of time and, say, hiking around a beautiful lake. While one activity merely provides respite from a boring or exhausting day (which you sometimes need), the other can be genuinely revitalizing. Being a couch potato will probably contribute nothing to your state of mind and may even contribute to your feeling apathetic and depressed. On the other hand, participating in activities that are meaningful and fulfilling can contribute to your well-being (Iwasaki et al., 2006).

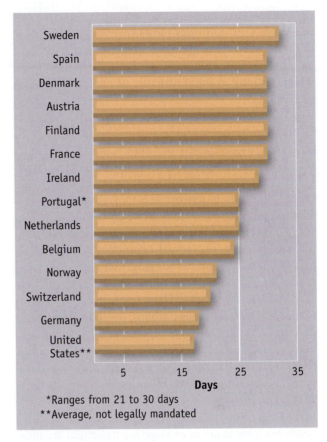

### Figure 13.14

**American and European vacation days.** American workers average 16 paid vacation days a year. Most European workers get considerably longer vacations. Moreover, these are benefits mandated by law.

Source: Adapted from Mischel, L., Bernstein, J., & Schmitt, J., and Economic Policy Institute (2001). *The state of working America 2000–2001.* Ithaca, NY: Cornell University Press. Copyright © 2001 by Cornell University Press. Used by permission of the publisher, Cornell University Press.

## Types of Leisure Activities

The types of leisure activities that people prefer are quite diverse. Popular leisure pursuits include:

● *Hobbies.* Among the most popular hobbies are photography; acting; music (playing and listening); gardening; knitting; drawing; collecting stamps, autographs, and so forth; hiking; camping; fishing; and birdwatching.

● *Reading.* Although fewer individuals read now than in the past, plenty of people still love to curl up with a good book. Books allow readers to escape from daily cares, solve mysteries, travel to real or imaginary places, learn useful information, and find inspiration.

● *Surfing the Internet.* A relatively new entry into the world of leisure, the Internet offers an amazing array of activities: e-mailing friends and relatives, social networking on Facebook, posting on message boards or Twitter, playing multiuser games, and listening to music are just a few options.

● *Travel.* Many choose their destinations spontaneously, but others are more systematic in their travel plans. For example, some individuals want to travel to all the U.S. national parks or every state in the Union. Those who can afford it may travel to other countries—to get a taste of real French cooking or a firsthand look at what remains of ancient Egyptian civilization.

- *Games and puzzles.* Some individuals enjoy playing bridge for relaxation; others like to play board games such as Scrabble or chess. Computerized and video games are highly popular, especially with children and adolescents. For some, the day isn't complete without the daily crossword or Sudoku puzzle.

- *Sports.* Many people like to play team sports such as bowling or softball, enjoying the benefits of both physical exercise and social interaction. Others enjoy individual sports such as jogging, swimming, surfing, ice skating, or skiing.

- *Volunteer activities.* Helping others appeals to individuals in almost all age groups. Moreover, individuals can use their skills to help others in an incredibly diverse array of settings: homeless shelters, hospitals, schools, battered women's shelters, boys' and girls' clubs, and sports teams, for example.

Being aware of the broad range of leisure activities heightens your chances of selecting those that are most meaningful to you.

## Benefits of Leisure Activities

The idea that a satisfying balance of work, relationships, and leisure activities will lead to a more rewarding and healthy life has intuitive appeal. Research generally supports this notion (Hecht & Boies, 2009). In one study of adult males, both job satisfaction and leisure satisfaction were significant predictors of psychological health (Pearson, 1998). Among college students, engaging in various leisure activities to reduce stress was associated with higher levels of perceived stress reduction and coping effectiveness (Iwasaki, 2003). And among older adults, leisure participation is associated with increased happiness, improved physical and cognitive functioning, and greater longevity (Menec, 2003). Also, regular exercise can reduce the effects of stress, improve your mood and self-esteem, and help you shed unwanted pounds, as you learned in Chapter 5. Thus, getting up off the couch is beneficial at any age. To summarize, meaningful work, rewarding family interactions and friendships, and revitalizing leisure pursuits are three components of a fulfilling life. Maintaining a satisfying balance among these three components is a major challenge in contemporary times.

In the upcoming Application, we describe how to conduct a productive job search and offer a few tips for more effective job interviews.

Courtesy of Cade Martin/CDC.gov

Leisure time should be relaxing and personally meaningful; cultivating a garden can be both of those things. Some research suggests that being satisfied with one's job and one's leisure activities is predictive of psychological health.

# Getting Ahead in the Job Game

## LEARNING OBJECTIVES

- Summarize some guidelines for putting together an effective résumé.
- Outline several strategies for landing a job interview.
- Identify some factors that can influence an interviewer's rating of a job candidate.
- List the dos and don'ts of interviewing for jobs.

*Answer the following statements "true" or "false."*

___ 1. The most common and effective job search method is answering classified ads.

___ 2. Your technical qualifications are the main factor in determining the success of your job search.

___ 3. Employment agencies are a good source of leads to high-level professional jobs.

___ 4. Your résumé should be very thorough and include everything you have ever done.

___ 5. It's a good idea to inject some humor into your job interviews to help you and your interviewer relax.

Most career counselors would agree that all these statements are generally false. Although there is no one "tried and true" method for obtaining desirable jobs, experts do have guidelines that can increase your chances of success. Their insights are summarized in this Application. To ensure that you get the best job you can, you'll need to know more details than we can provide here. A good place to start is to read *What Color Is Your Parachute?,* one of the best job search manuals available (see the Recommended Reading box).

Above all else, it is important to conduct a job search that is well organized, thorough, and systematic. Sending out a hastily written résumé to a few randomly selected companies is a waste of effort. An effective job search requires lots of time and careful planning. Thus, it is crucial that you begin your search well in advance of the time when you will need a job.

Of course, no amount of planning and effort can guarantee favorable results in a job search. Luck is definitely a part of the picture. Success may hinge on being in the right place or on meeting the right person at the right time. Also keep in mind that employers are often inundated with applicants who have all of the required training and experience. In fact, the candidate who is ultimately selected may not be the one with the best technical qualifications. Rather, most hiring decisions are made on the basis of subjective impressions gleaned from résumés, telephone conversations, and face-to-face interviews. These impressions are based on perceptions of personality, appearance, social skills, and body language. Knowing this, you can practice certain strategies that may increase the odds in your favor.

No matter what type of job you're looking for, successful searches have certain elements in common. First, you must prepare a résumé. Next, you need to target specific companies or organizations you would like to work for. Then, you must inform these companies of your interest in such a way as to get them interested in you.

## Putting Together a Résumé

No matter what your job search strategy, an excellent résumé is a critical ingredient. The purpose of a résumé is not to get you a job, but to get you an interview. To be effective, your résumé must show that you have at least the minimum technical qualifications for the position, know the standard conventions of the work world, and are a person who is on the fast track to success. Furthermore, it must achieve these goals without being flashy or gimmicky. Especially, it must contain no spelling or grammatical mistakes. Consider these two "fatal flaws" that appeared on cover letters: "I am a *rabid* typist" and "Thank you for your consideration. Hope to hear from you *shorty*"!

Following are a few basic guidelines for a résumé that projects a positive, yet conservative image (Lock, 2005a). For more tips on constructing a résumé, type "how to write a résumé" or "examples of résumés" into your favorite search engine.

1. Use high quality white, ivory, or beige paper for hard copies.

2. Make sure the résumé contains not a single typographical error.

**WEB LINK 13.5** **The Riley Guide: Employment Opportunities and Job Resources on the Internet**

This site, developed by the well-regarded career expert Margaret F. Dikel, complements her excellent book, the *Guide to Internet Job Searching.* Her website contains hundreds of annotated links regarding almost any topic related to employment and careers.

**3.** Keep it short. One side of an 8.5" × 11" sheet of paper will suffice for most college students; do not go over two pages.

**4.** Don't write in full sentences, and avoid using the word *I*. Instead, begin each statement with an "action" word that describes a specific achievement, such as "Supervised a staff of fifteen" or "Handled all customer complaints."

**5.** Avoid giving any personal information that is superfluous to the job. Such information is an unnecessary distraction and may give the reader cause to dislike you and therefore reject your application.

An effective résumé will generally contain the following elements, laid out in an easy-to-read format (**Figure 13.15** shows an attractively prepared résumé):

*Heading.* At the top of the page, give your name, address, phone number, and e-mail address. (By the way, be sure your voice-mail greeting and your e-mail address reflect a "professional" impression.) This is the only section of the résumé that is not given a label. (You do not need to label the document "Résumé.")

*Objective.* State precisely and concisely the kind of position you are seeking, remembering to use action words and to avoid the use of *I*. An example might be "Challenging, creative position in the communication field requiring extensive background in newspaper, radio, and television."

*Education.* List any degrees you've earned, giving major field of study, date, and granting institution for each. You should list the highest degree you received first. If you have a college degree, you don't need to mention your high school diploma. If you have received any *academic* honors or awards, mention them in this section.

**Figure 13.15**

**Example of an attractively formatted résumé.** The physical appearance of a résumé is very important. This example shows what a well-prepared résumé should look like. (Adapted from Lock, 2005b)

---

**TERESA M. MORGAN**

| **Campus Address** | **Permanent Address** |
|---|---|
| 1252 River St., Apt. 808 | 1111 W. Franklin |
| East Lansing, MI 48823 | Jackson, MI 49203 |
| (517)332-6086 | (517)782-0819 |

**OBJECTIVE**
To pursue a career in interior design, or a related field, in which I can utilize my design training. Willing to relocate after June 2010.

**EDUCATION**
Sept. 2008–
June 2010
**Michigan State University,** East Lansing, MI 48825.
Bachelor of Arts–Interior Design, with emphasis in Design Communication and Human Shelter. Courses include Lighting, Computers, Public Relations and History of Art.
(F.I.D.E.R. accredited) 3.0 GPA (4.0 = A).

July 2009–
Aug. 2009
**Michigan State University overseas study,** England and France, Decorative Arts and Architecture. 4.0 GPA (4.0 = A).

Sept. 2006–
June 2008
**Jackson Community College,** Jackson, MI 49201.
Associate's Degree. 3.5 GPA (4.0 = A).

**EMPLOYMENT**
Dec. 2009–
June 2010
**Food Service and Maintenance,** Owen Graduate Center, Michigan State University.
• Prepared and served food.
• Managed upkeep of adjacent Van Hoosen Residence Hall.

Sept. 2008–
June 2009
**Food Service and Maintenance,** McDonel Residence Hall, Michigan State University.
• Served food and cleaned facility.
• Handled general building maintenance.

June 2005–
Dec. 2005
**Waitress,** Charlie Wong's Restaurant, Jackson, MI.
• Served food, dealt with a variety of people on a personal level.
• Additional responsibilities: cashier, hostess, bartender, and employee trainer.

**HONORS AND ACTIVITIES**
• Community College Transfer scholarship from MSU.
• American Society of Interior Design Publicity Chairman; Executive Board, MSU Chapter.
• Sigma Chi Little Sisters.
• Independent European travel, summer 2008.
• Stage manager and performer in plays and musicals.

REFERENCES and PORTFOLIO available upon request.

---

*Experience.* This section should be organized chronologically, beginning with your most recent job and working backward. For each position, give the dates of employment and describe your responsibilities and your accomplishments. Be specific, and make sure your most recent position is the one with the greatest achievements. Don't bother listing trivial attainments. Readers find such material annoying, and it just calls attention to the fact that you don't have more important items to list.

Also, beware of padding your résumé with misrepresentations or outright untruths. One résumé-writing business reported that 43% of 1,000 résumés they received over a six-month period contained one or more "significant inaccuracies" (Cullen, 2007). Be advised that background checking is quite common today. Some firms also conduct such checks at promotion time. And while a padded résumé may help you get an interview, a good interviewer can usually detect a fraud. Thus, the truth is likely to come out—either before or during the interview—and by then the damage has been done. If you are wondering whether to include a questionable entry on your résumé, use the "sniff test" (Theisen, 2002). Could you talk easily with an interviewer about what you claim on your résumé without feeling nervous? If not, delete the information. Again, regarding background checks, remember that information and photographs you post to your blog or personal website or to sites like Facebook and MySpace are available for anyone to see unless you use privacy protections (Chamberlin, 2007).

If you are currently a student or are a recent graduate, your schooling will provide the basis for both your experience and your qualifications. You can get a jump on the competition by gaining experience in the field in which you want to work—through internships or part-time or summer jobs. If this option isn't feasible, do some volunteer work in this area and list it under an "Honors and Activities" section on your résumé.

"Oops! The padding just fell out of your résumé."

## Recommended READING

### What Color Is Your Parachute? 2010 A Practical Manual for Job-Hunters and Career-Changers
by Richard Nelson Bolles (Ten Speed Press, 2010)

Richard Bolles is a clever, creative writer who has put together a landmark book on the process of hunting for a job. "Parachute" was first published in 1970 and has become so successful that it's updated yearly. If you have time to read only one book about getting a job or changing careers, this is the one to choose. Bolles's writing is humorous and opinionated. However, his opinions have merit because he has done his homework. The book is thoroughly researched and documented. The author destroys many of the myths about what does and does not work in seeking jobs. He discusses a variety of practical topics, including where the jobs are, what will get you hired, how to get in to see the boss, whom to see, whom to avoid, and how to start your own business. His discussion of transferable skills is must-reading. Readers will also appreciate helpful hints on using the Internet for career information and job searching. Bolles also has an interesting chapter on integrating work and faith. The book contains a number of useful appendixes, including exercises to help people determine their ideal job and locate a career counselor or coach.

*Go to the Psychology CourseMate for Weiten at* **www.cengagebrain.com/shop/ISBN/1111186634** *for descriptions of other recommended books.*

Technology is changing a number of aspects of the job search process, including the preparation and screening of résumés. Increasingly, companies are likely to electronically scan résumés for key words that match job specifications (Lock, 2005a). Thus, it's helpful to know how to create an electronic résumé in addition to the traditional paper version. You can get this information at your campus Career Services office or at Web Link 13.6. Also, many organizations post formatting instructions on their websites for people who want to submit electronic résumés. The "next big thing" in résumés

**WEB LINK 13.6  CollegeGrad.com**

This site bills itself as "The #1 entryl-level job site." Key sections include "Job Preparation" (explore careers, résumés, and cover letters), "Job Searching" (advice and posting résumés), and "Offers" (salary, negotiating, and new job advice). You can also search for internships here.

may be two- to three- minute video résumés. Because they're new, they're risky. And employers worry that they will provoke lawsuits based on claims of bias because race, gender, and age cues are visible (Cullen, 2007). An alternative is to list links to your website or blog on your résumé—if they are relevant and convey a "professional" impression (Richter, 2007).

## Finding Companies You Want to Work For

Initially, you need to determine what general type of organization will best suit your needs. Do you want to work in a school? a hospital? a small business? a large corporation? a government agency? a human services agency? To select an appropriate work environment, you need an accurate picture of your personal qualities and knowledge of various occupations and their characteristics. Job search manuals like *Parachute* can provide you with helpful exercises in self-exploration. To learn about the characteristics of various occupations, check out relevant websites such as the Occupational Outlook Handbook or visit your Career Services office.

## Landing an Interview

No one is going to hire you without first "checking out the goods." This inspection process typically involves one or more formal interviews. So, how do you get invited for an interview? If you are applying for an advertised vacancy, the traditional approach is to send a résumé with a cover letter to the hiring organization. If your letter and résumé stand out from the crowd, you may be invited for an interview. A good way to increase your chances is to persuade the prospective employer that you are interested enough in the company to have done some research on the organization (Pollak, 2007). By taking the time to learn something about a company, you should be able to make a convincing case about the ways in which your expertise will be particularly useful to the organization.

If you are approaching an organization in the absence of a known opening, your strategy may be somewhat different. You may still opt to send a résumé, along with a more detailed cover letter explaining why you have selected this particular company. Another

**WEB LINK 13.7  CareerRookie.com**
This site is geared to college students seeking internships and part-time or entry-level jobs. Check out the section on internships, where you can search by city, state, or internship category.

option, suggested by Bolles (2007), is to introduce yourself (by phone or in person) directly to the person in charge of hiring and request an interview. You can increase your chances of success by using your network of personal contacts to identify some acquaintance that you and the person in charge have in common. Then, you can use this person's name to facilitate your approach. After you have an interview, you should follow up with a thank-you note and a résumé that will jog the prospective employer's memory about your training and talents.

## Polishing Your Interview Technique

The final, and most crucial, step in the process of securing a job is the face-to-face interview. If you've gotten this far, the employer already knows that you have the necessary training and experience to do the job. Your challenge is to convince the employer that you're the kind of person who would fit well in the organization. Your interviewer will attempt to verify that you have the intangible qualities that will make you a good team player. Even more important, he or she will try to identify any "red flag" behaviors, attitudes, or traits that mark you as an unacceptable risk.

To create the right impression, you must come across as confident, enthusiastic, and ambitious. By the way, a firm (not wishy-washy or bone-crushing) handshake helps create a positive first impression, especially for women (Chaplin et al., 2000). Your demeanor should be somewhat formal and reserved, and you should avoid any attempts at humor—you never know what might offend your interviewer. Above all, never give more information than the interviewer requests, especially negative information. If asked directly what your weaknesses are—a common ploy—respond with a "flaw" that is really a positive, as in "I tend to work too hard at times." And don't interrupt or contradict your interviewer. Finally, don't ever blame or criticize anyone, especially previous employers, even if you feel that the criticism is justified (Lock, 2005b).

Developing an effective interview technique requires practice. Many experts suggest that you never turn down an interview, because you can always benefit from the practice even if you don't want the job. Advance preparation is also crucial. Never go into an interview cold. Find out all you can about the company before you go. Try to anticipate the questions that will be asked and have some answers ready. You can review commonly asked interview questions on websites and in career books (Yate, 2006). In general, you will not be asked simply to reiterate information from your résumé. Remember, it is your personal qualities that are being assessed at this point. A final word of advice: If

© Ariel Skelley/Getty Images/Blend Images

**To be successful on a job interview, candidates need to dress appropriately and convey confidence, enthusiasm, and interest in the job.**

possible, avoid any discussion of salary in an initial interview. The appropriate time for salary negotiation is *after* a firm offer of employment has been extended. By the way, you can scope out salary information for many jobs by visiting Web Link 13.8. And you can find additional tips on interviewing at some of the other Web Links in this chapter.

**WEB LINK 13.8   Salary.com**

This useful site allows you to determine median salaries for numerous occupations at different experience levels and in different geographical areas and compare them to national averages. You can probably get all the information you need for free, but you can also pay (a lot) for a customized salary report.

## KEY IDEAS

### Choosing a Career

● Ideally, people look for jobs that are compatible with their personal characteristics. Thus, individuals need to have a sense of their own abilities, interests, and personality. Family background also influences career choices.

● There are abundant resources for those who want to learn about possible career options. In researching prospective careers, it is important to find out about the nature of the work, working conditions, entry requirements, potential earnings, potential status, opportunities for advancement, intrinsic satisfactions, and the future outlook for jobs.

● Individuals who have trouble making career decisions may find it helpful to take an occupational interest inventory. People have the potential for success in a variety of occupations, and they need to keep this and other considerations in mind as they make career decisions.

### Models of Career Choice and Development

● John Holland's person-environment fit model of career development asserts that people select careers based on their own personality characteristics. Holland's well-supported theory includes six personal orientations and matching work environments.

● Super's stage theory holds that self-concept development is the basis for career choice. According to this model, there are five stages in the occupational life cycle: growth, exploration, establishment, maintenance, and decline. However, the assumption that people will remain in the same career all of their working lives is out of sync with current workplace realities.

● Models of career development in women are still being developed. Women's career paths are often less orderly and predictable than men's because of the need to juggle multiple roles and because many women interrupt their careers to devote time to childrearing.

### The Changing World of Work

● Work is an activity that produces something of value for others. A number of contemporary trends are changing the world of work. Generally, the more education individuals obtain, the higher their salaries will be.

● In the future, more women and minorities will join the labor force. Although women and minorities participate in the workforce at all occupational levels, they tend to be concentrated in lower-paying and lower-status positions. Furthermore, women and minorities face discrimination in a number of areas. Increasing diversity in the workforce presents challenges to both organizations and workers.

### Coping with Occupational Hazards

● Major hazards related to work include job stress, sexual harassment, and unemployment. Stress affects both employers and employees. Interventions to manage stress in the workplace can be made at the individual level, the organizational level, and the individual-organizational interface.

● Victims of sexual harassment often develop physical and psychological symptoms of stress that can lead to decreased work motivation and productivity. Many organizations are educating their workers about this problem. Individuals can also take steps to reduce sexual harassment, although the most popular strategies tend to be the least effective.

● Because of dramatic changes in the economy, unemployment is a problem for both skilled and unskilled workers. Job loss is highly stressful. Middle-aged workers are most distressed by the experience. Unemployed workers who believe that they have been treated unfairly and arbitrarily often feel angry. In coping with unemployment, social support is critical.

### Balancing Work and Other Spheres of Life

● A major challenge for workers today is balancing work, family, and leisure activities in ways that are personally satisfying. Workaholism may be based on positive or negative motives, but it still creates work-family conflict for workaholics and their families.

● As dual-earner families have become the family norm, juggling multiple roles has emerged as a challenge, especially for women. Nonetheless, multiple roles are generally beneficial to mental, physical, and relationship health. Leisure plays an important role in psychological and physical health.

### Application: Getting Ahead in the Job Game

● The essential elements of a successful job search include (1) determining the type of organization that will best suit one's needs, (2) constructing an effective résumé, (3) winning a job interview, and (4) developing an effective interview technique.

● Résumés should be brief and project a positive, yet conservative image. To locate prospective employers, it is good to use a variety of strategies.

● Nonverbal communication skills can be crucial in job interviews. You should try to appear confident and enthusiastic. Try to avoid salary discussions in your initial interview.

## KEY TERMS

Displaced workers   p. 426
Dual-earner households
   p. 416
Glass ceiling   p. 419
Industrial/organizational (I/O)
   psychology   p. 406
Labor force   p. 418
Leisure   p. 431

Occupational interest
   inventories   p. 410
Sexual harassment   p. 425
Token   p. 420
Underemployment   p. 417
Work   p. 415
Work-family conflict   p. 430

## KEY PEOPLE

Richard Nelson Bolles   p. 435
John Holland   pp. 411–413

Robert Karasek   pp. 423–424
Donald Super   pp. 413–414

## QUESTIONS

1. Individuals' career choices are often:
   a. much higher in status than those of their parents.
   b. similar to those of their parents.
   c. much lower in status than those of their parents.
   d. unrelated to their family background.

2. Findings on education and earnings show that:
   a. at all levels of education, men earn more than women.
   b. at all levels of education, women earn more than men.
   c. there are no gender differences in education and earnings.
   d. there is no relationship between education and earnings.

3. Occupational interest inventories are designed to predict:
   a. how successful an individual is likely to be in a job.
   b. how long a person will stay in a career.
   c. how satisfied a person is likely to be in a job.
   d. all of the above.

4. Holland's theory of occupational choice emphasizes:
   a. the role of self-esteem in job choice.
   b. the unfolding of career interests over time.
   c. parental influences and job choice.
   d. matching personality traits and job environments.

5. Which of the following is *not* a work-related trend?
   a. Technology is changing the nature of work.
   b. New work attitudes are required.
   c. Most new jobs will be in the manufacturing sector.
   d. Lifelong learning is a necessity.

6. When there is only one woman or minority person in a workplace setting, that person becomes a symbol of his or her group and is referred to as a:
   a. token.
   b. scapegoat.
   c. sex object.
   d. protected species.

7. Job stress has been found to lead to all but which of the following negative effects?
   a. burnout
   b. bipolar disorder
   c. high blood pressure
   d. anxiety

8. According to law, the two types of sexual harassment are:
   a. quid pro quo and environmental.
   b. legal and illegal.
   c. caveat emptor and confrontational.
   d. industrial and organizational.

9. Compared to European workers, American workers receive:
   a. much less paid vacation time.
   b. about the same amount of paid vacation time.
   c. much more paid vacation time, but less sick leave.
   d. much more paid vacation and more sick leave.

10. Which of the following is a good tip for preparing an effective résumé?
   a. Make your résumé as long as possible.
   b. Use complete sentences.
   c. Keep it short.
   d. Provide a lot of personal information.

## ANSWERS

1. b  Page 408
2. a  Page 417
3. c  Page 410
4. d  Pages 411–413
5. c  Pages 415–417
6. a  Page 420
7. b  Pages 423–424
8. a  Page 425
9. a  Page 431
10. c  Pages 433–436

### Personal Explorations Workbook

Go to the *Personal Explorations Workbook* in the back of your text-book for exercises that can enhance your self-understanding in relation to issues raised in this chapter. **Exercise 13.1** *Self-Assessment:* Assertive Job Hunting Survey **Exercise 13.2** *Self-Reflection:* What Do You Know About the Career That Interests You?

 CourseMate

Access an interactive eBook, chapter-specific interactive learning tools, including Personal Explorations, Recommended Readings, Critical Thinking Exercises, flashcards, quizzes, videos and more in your Psychology CourseMate, available at **www.cengagebrain.com/shop/ISBN/1111186634**.

© Cultura/Alamy

# CHAPTER 14

# *Psychological Disorders*

*"The government of the United States was overthrown more than a year ago! I'm the president of the United States of America and Bob Dylan is vice president!" So said Ed, the author of a prominent book on journalism, who was speaking to a college journalism class, as a guest lecturer. Ed also informed the class that he had killed both John and Robert Kennedy, as well as Charles de Gaulle, the former president of France. He went on to tell the class that all rock music songs were written about him, that he was the greatest karate expert in the universe, and that he had been fighting "space wars" for 2000 years. The students in the class were mystified by Ed's bizarre, disjointed "lecture," but they assumed that he was putting on a show that would eventually lead to a sensible conclusion. However, their perplexed but expectant calm was shattered when Ed pulled a hatchet from the props he had brought with him and hurled the hatchet at the class! Fortunately, he didn't hit anyone, as the hatchet sailed over the students' heads. At that point, the professor for the class realized that Ed's irrational behavior was not a pretense. The professor evacuated the class quickly while Ed continued to rant and rave about his presidential administration, space wars, vampires, his romances with female rock stars, and his personal harem of 38 "chicks." (Adapted from Pearce, 1974)*

Clearly, Ed's behavior was abnormal. Even *he* recognized that when he agreed later to be admitted to a mental hospital, signing himself in as the "President of the United States of America." What causes such abnormal behavior? Does Ed have a mental illness, or does he just behave strangely? What is the basis for judging behavior as normal versus abnormal? How common are such disorders? These are just a few of the questions we address in this chapter as we discuss psychological disorders and their complex causes.

# Abnormal Behavior: Concepts and Controversies

### LEARNING OBJECTIVES

- Describe and evaluate the medical model of abnormal behavior.
- Identify the most commonly used criteria of abnormality.
- Describe the five axes of DSM-IV and controversies surrounding the DSM system.
- Summarize data on the prevalence of various psychological disorders.

Misconceptions about abnormal behavior are common. We therefore need to clear up some preliminary issues before we describe the various types of psychological disorders. In this section, we discuss (1) the medical model of abnormal behavior, (2) the criteria of abnormal behavior, (3) the classification of psychological disorders, and (4) the prevalence of such disorders.

## The Medical Model Applied to Abnormal Behavior

In Ed's case, there's no question that his behavior was abnormal. But does it make sense to view his unusual and irrational behavior as an *illness*? This is a controversial question. **The *medical model* proposes that it is useful to think of abnormal behavior as a disease.** This point of view is the basis for many of the terms used to refer to abnormal behavior, including mental *illness,* psychological *disorder,* and psycho*pathology* (*pathology* refers to manifestations of disease). The medical model gradually became the conventional way of thinking about abnormal behavior during the 19th and 20th centuries, and its influence remains dominant today.

The medical model clearly represented progress over earlier models of abnormal behavior. Prior to the 18th century, most conceptions of abnormal behavior were based on superstition. People who behaved strangely were thought to be possessed by demons, to be witches in league with the devil, or to be victims of God's punishment. Their disorders were "treated" with chants, rituals, exorcisms, and such. If the people's behavior was seen as threatening, they were candidates for chains, dungeons, torture, and death (see **Figure 14.1**).

The rise of the medical model brought improvements in the treatment of those who exhibited abnormal behavior. As victims of an illness, they were viewed with more sympathy and less hatred and fear. Although living conditions in early asylums were often deplorable, gradual progress was made toward more humane care of the mentally ill. It took time, but ineffectual approaches to treatment eventually gave way to scientific investigation of the causes and cures of psychological disorders.

However, in recent decades, some critics have suggested that the medical model may have outlived its usefulness (Boyle, 2007; Kiesler, 1999). A particularly vocal critic has been Thomas Szasz (1974, 1993). He asserts that "strictly speaking, disease or illness can affect only the body; hence there can be no mental illness. . . . Minds can be 'sick' only in the sense that jokes are 'sick' or economies are 'sick'" (1974, p. 267). He further argues that abnormal behavior usually involves a deviation from social norms rather than an illness. He contends that such deviations are "problems in living" rather than medical problems. According to Szasz, the medical model's disease analogy converts moral and social questions about what is acceptable behavior into medical questions.

Some critics are also concerned because medical diagnoses of abnormal behavior pin potentially

**Thomas Szasz**

© David Lees/Corbis

### Figure 14.1

**Historical conceptions of mental illness.** Throughout most of history, psychological disorders were thought to be caused by demonic possession, and the mentally ill were candidates for chains and torture.

derogatory labels on people (Hinshaw, 2007; Overton & Medina, 2008). Being labeled as psychotic, schizophrenic, or mentally ill carries a social stigma that can be difficult to shake. Those characterized as mentally ill are viewed as erratic, dangerous, incompetent, and inferior (Corrigan & Larson, 2008). These stereotypes promote distancing, disdain, prejudice, and rejection. Even after a full recovery, someone who has been labeled mentally ill may have difficulty finding a place to live or getting a job. The stigma of mental illness creates additional difficulties for people who already have more than their share of problems (Hinshaw, 2007). Unfortunately, the stigma associated with psychological disorders appears to be deep-rooted and not easily reduced. In recent decades clear progress has been made in the general public's knowledge and understanding of mental disorders. Moreover, research has increasingly demonstrated that many psychological disorders are at least partly attributable to genetic and physiological factors, making them appear more similar to physical illnesses, which carry far fewer negative connotations. You would think that these trends would lead to a reduction in the stigma associated with mental illness, but research suggests that the stigmatization of mental disorders has increased rather than decreased (Hinshaw & Stier, 2008).

Although critics' analyses of the medical model have some merit, we'll take the position that the disease analogy continues to be useful, although you should keep in mind that it is *only* an analogy. Medical concepts such as *diagnosis, etiology,* and *prognosis* have proven valuable in the treatment and study of abnormality. **Diagnosis involves distinguishing one illness from another. Etiology refers to the apparent causation and developmental history of an illness. A prognosis is a forecast about the probable course of an illness.** These medically based concepts have widely shared meanings that permit clinicians, researchers, and the public to communicate more effectively in their discussions of abnormal behavior.

## Criteria of Abnormal Behavior

If your next-door neighbor scrubs his front porch twice every day and spends virtually all his time cleaning and recleaning his house, is he normal? If your sister-in-law goes to one physician after another seeking treatment

for ailments that appear imaginary, is she psychologically healthy? How are we to judge what's normal and what's abnormal? More important, who's to do the judging?

These are complex questions. In a sense, *all* people make judgments about normality in that they all express opinions about others' (and perhaps their own) mental health. Of course, formal diagnoses of psychological disorders are made by mental health professionals. In making these diagnoses, clinicians rely on a variety of criteria, the foremost of which are the following:

1. *Deviance.* As Szasz has pointed out, people are often said to have a disorder because their behavior deviates from what their society considers acceptable. What constitutes normality varies somewhat from one culture to another, but all cultures have such norms. When people ignore these standards and expectations, they may be labeled mentally ill. For example, *transvestic fetishism* is a sexual disorder in which a man achieves sexual arousal by dressing in women's clothing. This behavior is regarded as disordered because a man who wears a dress, brassiere, and nylons is deviating from our culture's norms. This example illustrates the arbitrary nature of cultural standards regarding normality, as the same overt behavior (cross-gender dressing) is acceptable for women yet deviant for men.

2. *Maladaptive behavior.* In many cases, people are judged to have a psychological disorder because their everyday adaptive behavior is impaired. This is the key criterion in the diagnosis of substance use (drug) disorders. In and of itself, alcohol and drug use is not terribly unusual or deviant. However, when the use of cocaine, for instance, begins to interfere with a person's social or occupational functioning, a substance use disorder exists. In such cases, it is the maladaptive quality of the behavior that makes it disordered.

3. *Personal distress.* Frequently, the diagnosis of a psychological disorder is based on an individual's report of great personal distress. This is usually the criterion met by people who are troubled by depression or anxiety disorders. Depressed people, for instance, may or may not exhibit deviant or maladaptive behavior. Such people are usually labeled as having a disorder when they describe their subjective pain and suffering to friends, relatives, and mental health professionals.

Although two or three criteria may apply in a particular case, people are often viewed as disordered when only one criterion is met. As you may have already noticed, diagnoses of psychological disorders involve *value judgments* about what represents normal or abnormal behavior (Sadler, 2005; Widiger & Sankis, 2000). The criteria of mental illness are not nearly as value-free as the criteria of physical illness. In evaluating physical diseases, people can usually agree that a weak heart or a malfunctioning kidney is pathological, regardless of their personal values. However, judgments about mental illness reflect prevailing cultural values, social trends, and political forces, as well as scientific knowledge (Kutchins & Kirk, 1997; Mechanic, 1999).

Antonyms such as *normal* versus *abnormal* and *mental health* versus *mental illness* imply that people can be divided neatly into two distinct groups: those who are normal and those who are not. In reality, it is often difficult to draw a line that clearly separates normality from abnormality. On occasion, everyone experiences personal distress. Everybody acts in deviant ways once in a while. And everyone displays some maladaptive behavior. People are judged to have psychological disorders only when their behavior becomes *extremely* deviant, maladaptive, or distressing. Thus, normality and abnormality exist on a continuum. It's a matter of degree, not an either-or proposition (see **Figure 14.2**).

## Psychodiagnosis: The Classification of Disorders

Obviously, we cannot lump all psychological disorders together without giving up all hope of understanding them better. A sound taxonomy of mental disorders can facilitate empirical research and enhance communication among scientists and clinicians (First, 2003; Zimmerman & Spitzer, 2009). Hence, a great deal of effort has been invested in devising an elaborate system for classifying psychological disorders.

Guidelines for psychodiagnosis were extremely vague and informal prior to 1952, when the American Psychiatric Association unveiled its *Diagnostic and Statistical Manual of Mental Disorders* (Nathan & Langenbucher, 2003). This classification scheme described about 100 disorders. Revisions intended to improve the system were incorporated into the second edition (DSM-II) published in 1968, but the diagnostic guidelines were still pretty sketchy. However, the

third edition (DSM-III), published in 1980, represented a major advance, as the diagnostic criteria were made much more explicit, concrete, and detailed to facilitate more consistent diagnoses across clinicians (Blacker & Tsuang, 1999). The current, fourth edition (DSM-IV), released in 1994 and revised slightly in 2000, made use of intervening research to refine the criteria introduced in DSM-III. Each revision of the DSM system has expanded the list of disorders covered. The current version describes about three times as many types of psychological disorders as the original DSM (Houts, 2002).

### The Multiaxial System

The publication of DSM-III in 1980 introduced a new multiaxial system of classification, which asks for judgments about individuals on five separate dimensions, or "axes." **Figure 14.3** on the next page provides an overview of the entire system and the five axes. The diagnoses of disorders are made on Axes I and II. Clinicians record most types of disorders on Axis I. They use Axis II to list long-running personality disorders or mental retardation. People may receive diagnoses on both Axes I and II.

The remaining axes are used to record supplemental information. A patient's physical disorders are listed on Axis III (General Medical Conditions). On Axis IV (Psychosocial and Environmental Problems), the clinician makes notations regarding the types of stress experienced by the individual in the past year. On Axis V (Global Assessment of Functioning), estimates are made of the individual's current level of adaptive functioning (in social and occupational behavior, viewed as a whole) and of the individual's highest level of functioning in the past year. Most theorists agree that the multiaxial system is a step in the right direction because it recognizes the importance of information besides a traditional diagnostic label.

Work is currently under way to formulate the next edition (DSM-V) of the diagnostic system (e.g., Banzato, 2004; Spitzer, First, & Wakefield, 2007; Widiger & Simonsen, 2005), which is tentatively scheduled for publication in 2011. Clinical researchers are collecting data, holding conferences, and formulating arguments about whether various syndromes should be added, eliminated, or renamed. Should complicated grief reactions become a standard diagnostic option (Lichtenthal, Cruess, & Prigerson, 2004)? Should the diagnostic system use the term drug *dependence* or drug *addiction* (O'Brien, Volkow, & Li, 2006)? Should pathological gambling be lumped with impulse-control disorders or addictive disorders (Potenza, 2006)? Should night-eating syndrome (regular eating binges after awakening from sleep) be recognized as a disorder

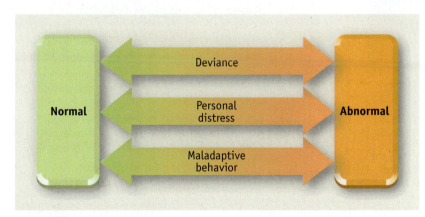

**Figure 14.2**

**Normality and abnormality as a continuum.** No sharp boundary divides normal and abnormal behavior. Behavior is normal or abnormal in degree, depending on the extent to which it is deviant, personally distressing, or maladaptive.

## Axis I
## Clinical Syndromes

1. *Disorders usually first diagnosed in infancy, childhood, or adolescence*
   This category includes disorders that arise before adolescence, such as attention deficit disorders, autism, mental retardation, enuresis, and stuttering.

2. *Organic mental disorders*
   These disorders are temporary or permanent dysfunctions of brain tissue caused by diseases or chemicals. Examples are delirium, dementia, and amnesia.

3. *Substance-related disorders*
   This category refers to the maladaptive use of drugs and alcohol. Mere consumption and recreational use of such substances are not disorders. This category requires a maladaptive pattern of use, as with alcohol abuse and cocaine dependence.

4. *Schizophrenia and other psychotic disorders*
   The schizophrenias are characterized by psychotic symptoms (for example, grossly disorganized behavior, delusions, and hallucinations) and by over 6 months of behavioral deterioration. This category also includes delusional disorder and schizoaffective disorder.

5. *Mood disorders*
   The cardinal feature is emotional disturbance. Patients may, or may not, have psychotic symptoms. These disorders include major depression, bipolar disorder, dysthymic disorder, and cyclothymic disorder.

6. *Anxiety disorders*
   These disorders are characterized by physiological signs of anxiety (for example, palpitations) and subjective feelings of tension, apprehension, or fear. Anxiety may be acute and focused (panic disorder) or continual and diffuse (generalized anxiety disorder).

7. *Somatoform disorders*
   These disorders are dominated by somatic symptoms that resemble physical illnesses. These symptoms cannot be accounted for by organic damage. There must also be strong evidence that these symptoms are produced by psychological factors or conflicts. This category includes somatization, conversion disorder, and hypochondriasis.

8. *Dissociative disorders*
   These disorders all feature a sudden, temporary alteration or dysfunction of memory, consciousness, identity, and behavior, as in dissociative amnesia and multiple personality.

9. *Sexual and gender-identity disorders*
   There are three basic types of disorders in this category: gender identity disorders (discomfort with identity as male or female), paraphilias (preference for unusual acts to achieve sexual arousal), and sexual dysfunctions (impairments in sexual functioning).

## Figure 14.3
**Overview of the DSM diagnostic system.** Published by the American Psychiatric Association, the *Diagnostic and Statistical Manual of Mental Disorders* is the formal classification system used in the diagnosis of psychological disorders. It is a *multiaxial* system, which means that information is recorded on the five axes described here.

Source: Adapted with permission from the *Diagnostic and Statistical Manual of Mental Disorders*, 4th ed. *Text revision*. Copyright © 2000 American Psychiatric Association.

## Axis II
## Personality Disorders

These disorders are patterns of personality traits that are longstanding, maladaptive, and inflexible and involve impaired functioning or subjective distress. Examples include borderline, schizoid, and antisocial personality disorders.

## Axis III
## General Medical Conditions

Physical disorders or conditions are recorded on this axis. Examples include diabetes, arthritis, and hemophilia.

## Axis IV
## Psychosocial and Environmental Problems

Axis IV is for reporting psychosocial and environmental problems that may affect the diagnosis, treatment, and prognosis of mental disorders (Axes I and II). A psychosocial or environmental problem may be a negative life event, an environmental difficulty or deficiency, a familial or other interpersonal stress, an inadequacy of social support or personal resources, or another problem that describes the context in which a person's difficulties have developed.

## Axis V
## Global Assessment of Functioning (GAF) Scale

| Code | Symptoms |
|------|----------|
| 100 | Superior functioning in a wide range of activities |
| 90 | Absent or minimal symptoms, good functioning in all areas |
| 80 | Symptoms transient and expectable reactions to psychosocial stressors |
| 70 | Some mild symptoms or some difficulty in social, occupational, or school functioning, but generally functioning pretty well |
| 60 | Moderate symptoms or difficulty in social, occupational, or school functioning |
| 50 | Serious symptoms or impairment in social, occupational, or school functioning |
| 40 | Some impairment in reality testing or communication or major impairment in family relations, judgment, thinking, or mood |
| 30 | Behavior considerably influenced by delusions or hallucinations, serious impairment in communication or judgment, or inability to function in almost all areas |
| 20 | Some danger of hurting self or others, occasional failure to maintain minimal personal hygiene, or gross impairment in communication |
| 10 | Persistent danger of severely hurting self or others |
| 1 | |

(Stunkard et al., 2009)? Should Internet addiction be added to the official list of disorders (Sandoz, 2004)? Vigorous debates about issues such as these will occupy clinical researchers in their deliberations, and DSM-V may look somewhat different from its predecessors.

## Controversies Surrounding the DSM

Since the publication of the third edition in 1980, the DSM system has become the dominant classification scheme for mental disorders around the world (Blashfield, Keeley, & Burgess, 2009). Nonetheless, the DSM system has garnered its share of criticism. Some critics have questioned the fundamental axiom that the diagnostic system is built on—the assumption that people can reliably be placed in discontinuous (nonoverlapping) diagnostic categories (Helzer et al., 2008; Widiger & Trull, 2007). These critics note that there is enormous overlap among various disorders in symptoms and that people often qualify for more than one diagnosis. These theorists argue that the current *categorical approach* to pathology should be replaced by a *dimensional approach,* which would describe disorders in terms of how people score on a limited number of continuous dimensions, such as the degree to which they exhibit anxiety, depression, agitation, hypochondria, paranoia, and so forth (Kraemer, 2008; Widiger, Livesley, & Clark, 2009). The debate about the merits of the categorical versus dimensional approach is heating up and will be a major bone of contention in future revisions of the DSM system.

Recent editions of the DSM have also sparked controversy by adding everyday problems that are not traditionally thought of as mental illnesses to the diagnostic system. For example, the DSM system includes a *developmental coordination disorder* (basically, extreme clumsiness in children), a *nicotine dependence disorder* (distress derived from quitting smoking), and a *pathological gambling disorder* (difficulty controlling one's gambling). Critics argue that this approach "medicalizes" everyday problems and casts the shadow of pathology on normal behavior (Kirk & Kutchins, 1992; Wakefield, Horwitz, & Schmitz, 2005). In part, everyday problems were added to the diagnostic system so that more people could bill their insurance companies for professional treatment of the conditions (Cooper,

2004; Mayes & Horwitz, 2005). There's merit in making it easier for more people to seek needed professional help. Nonetheless, the pros and cons of including everyday problems in DSM are complicated.

## The Prevalence of Psychological Disorders

How common are psychological disorders? What percentage of the population is afflicted with mental illness? Is it 10%? Perhaps 25%? Could the figure range as high as 40% or 50%? Such estimates fall in the domain of *epidemiology*—**the study of the distribution of mental or physical disorders in a population.** In epidemiology, *prevalence* **refers to the percentage of a population that exhibits a disorder during a specified time period.** In the case of mental disorders, the most interesting data are the estimates of *lifetime prevalence,* the percentage of people having a specific disorder at any time in their lives.

Studies published in the 1980s and early 1990s found psychological disorders in roughly *one-third* of the population (Regier & Kaelber, 1995; Robins, Locke, & Regier, 1991). Subsequent research, which focused on a somewhat younger sample (ages 18–54 instead of over age 18), suggested that about 44% of the adult population will struggle with some sort of psychological disorder at some point in their lives (Kessler & Zhao, 1999; Regier & Burke, 2000). The most recent large-scale epidemiological study estimated the lifetime risk of a psychiatric disorder to be 51% (Kessler et al., 2005a). Obviously, all these figures are *estimates* that depend to some extent on the sampling methods and assessment techniques used (Wakefield, 1999). Some experts believe that recent estimates are implausibly high and that they may trivialize psychiatric diagnoses (Wakefield & Spitzer, 2002).

In any event, the prevalence of psychological disorders is quite a bit higher than most people assume. The data that yielded the 44% estimate of total lifetime prevalence are summarized in **Figure 14.4** on the next page, which shows prevalence estimates for the most common classes of disorders. As you can see, the most common types of psychological disorders are (1) substance (alcohol and drugs) use disorders, (2) anxiety disorders, and (3) mood disorders.

The high prevalence of psychological disorders means that the economic costs of mental illness in modern societies are enormous. The annual cost of treating psychiatric illness in the United States was estimated to be about $150 billion in a 2003 report (New Freedom Commission on Mental Health, 2003). Another study estimated that more than 1.3 billion days of role performance (being able to go to work, function as a homemaker, and so forth) are lost each year in the U.S. to

**WEB LINK 14.2    NAMI: The National Alliance for the Mentally Ill**

Professional and lay evaluators have consistently found NAMI among the most helpful and informative organizations dealing with the entire spectrum of mental disorders, including schizophrenia and depression. The NAMI site offers a rich array of information on specific mental disorders and on how patients and their families can find support.

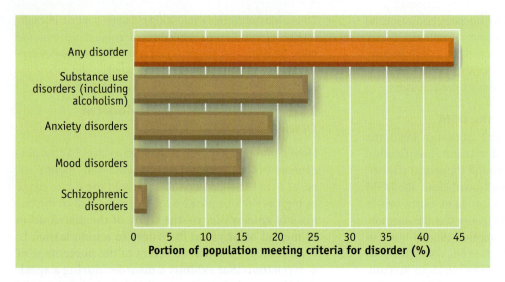

**Figure 14.4**

**Lifetime prevalence of psychological disorders.** The estimated percentage of people who have, at any time in their life, suffered from one of four types of psychological disorders or from a disorder of any kind (top bar) is shown here. Prevalence estimates vary somewhat from one study to the next, depending on the exact methods used in sampling and assessment. The estimates shown here are based on pooling data from Waves 1 and 2 of the Epidemiological Catchment Area studies and the National Comorbidity Study, as summarized by Regier and Burke (2000) and Dew, Bromet, and Switzer (2000). These studies, which collectively evaluated over 28,000 subjects, provide the best data to date on the prevalence of mental illness in the United States.

mental disorders (Merikangas et al., 2007). To put this exorbitant number in perspective, psychological disorders cause about three times as many disability days as cardiovascular diseases and vastly more than cancer. And there is no way to put a price on the extraordinary

anguish suffered by the families of the mentally ill. Thus, the socioeconomic costs of psychological disorders are staggering.

We are now ready to start examining the specific types of psychological disorders. Obviously, we cannot cover all of the diverse disorders listed in DSM-IV. However, we will introduce most of the major categories of disorders to give you an overview of the many forms abnormal behavior takes. In discussing each set of disorders, we begin with brief descriptions of the specific syndromes or subtypes that fall in the category. Then we focus on the *etiology* of the disorders in that category. Although many paths can lead to specific disorders, some are more common than others. We highlight some of the common paths in order to enhance your understanding of the roots of abnormal behavior.

---

**WEB LINK 14.3   National Institute of Mental Health: For the Public**

A wealth of information on psychological disorders is available at this subpage of the U.S. National Institute of Mental Health's massive website. Visitors will find online booklets on generalized anxiety disorder, obsessive-compulsive disorder, panic disorder, depression, bipolar disorder, and so forth. Brief fact sheets, dense technical reports, and many other resources are also available.

---

# Anxiety Disorders

### LEARNING OBJECTIVES

- List and describe four types of anxiety disorders.
- Discuss the contribution of biological factors and conditioning to the etiology of anxiety disorders.
- Explain the contribution of cognitive factors and stress to the etiology of anxiety disorders.

Everyone experiences anxiety from time to time. It is a natural and common reaction to many of life's difficulties. For some people, however, anxiety becomes a chronic problem. These people experience high levels of anxiety with disturbing regularity. *Anxiety disorders*

**are a class of disorders marked by feelings of excessive apprehension and anxiety.** There are four principal types of anxiety disorders: generalized anxiety disorder, phobic disorder, obsessive-compulsive disorder, and panic disorder. They are not mutually exclusive, as many people who develop one anxiety syndrome often suffer from another at some point in their lives (Merikangas & Kalaydjian, 2009).

## Generalized Anxiety Disorder

**The *generalized anxiety disorder* is marked by a chronic high level of anxiety that is not tied to any specific threat.** Generalized anxiety disorder tends to have a gradual onset, has a lifetime prevalence of about 5%, and is seen more frequently in females than males (Brown & Lawrence, 2009). People with this disorder worry constantly about yesterday's mistakes and tomorrow's problems. They worry excessively about minor matters related to family, finances, work, and personal illness. They hope that their worrying will help to ward off negative events (Beidel & Stipelman, 2007), but they nonetheless worry about how much they worry (Barlow et al., 2003). Their anxiety is frequently accompanied by physical symptoms, such as muscle tension, diarrhea, dizziness, faintness, sweating, and heart palpitations.

## Phobic Disorder

In a phobic disorder, an individual's troublesome anxiety has a specific focus. **A *phobic disorder* is marked by a persistent and irrational fear of an object or situation that presents no realistic danger.** Although mild phobias are extremely common, people are said to have a phobic disorder only when their fears seriously interfere with their everyday behavior. Phobic reactions tend to be accompanied by physical symptoms of anxiety, such as trembling and palpitations (Rapee & Barlow, 2001). The following case provides an example of a phobic disorder:

*Hilda is 32 years of age and has a rather unusual fear. She is terrified of snow. She cannot go outside in the snow. She cannot even stand to see snow or hear about it on the weather report. Her phobia severely constricts her day-to-day behavior. Probing in therapy revealed that her phobia was caused by a traumatic experience at age 11. Playing at a ski lodge, she was buried briefly by a small avalanche of snow. She had no recollection of this experience until it was recovered in therapy. (Adapted from Laughlin, 1967, p. 227)*

As Hilda's unusual snow phobia illustrates, people can develop phobic responses to virtually anything. Nonetheless, certain types of phobias are relatively common, as the data in **Figure 14.5** show. Particularly common are acrophobia (fear of heights), claustrophobia (fear of small, enclosed places), brontophobia (fear of storms), hydrophobia (fear of water), and various animal and insect phobias (Antony & McCabe, 2003). People troubled by phobias typically realize that their fears are irrational, but they still are unable to calm themselves when they encounter a phobic object.

## Panic Disorder and Agoraphobia

**A *panic disorder* is characterized by recurrent attacks of overwhelming anxiety that usually occur suddenly and unexpectedly.** These paralyzing attacks are accompanied by physical symptoms of anxiety. After a number of anxiety attacks, victims often become apprehensive, wondering when their next panic attack will occur. Their concern about exhibiting panic in public sometimes escalates to the point where they are afraid to leave home. This creates a condition called *agoraphobia*.

| Common Phobias | | | | |
| --- | --- | --- | --- | --- |
| Category | Percent of all phobias | Gender difference | Typical age of onset | |
| **Agoraphobia** (fear of places of assembly, crowds, open spaces) | 10%–50% | Large majority are women | Early adulthood | |
| **Social phobia** (fear of being observed doing something humiliating) | 10% | Majority are women | Adolescence | |
| **Specific phobias** *Animals* Cats (ailurophobia) Dogs (cynophobia) Insects (insectophobia) Spiders (arachnophobia) Birds (avisophobia) Horses (equinophobia) Snakes (ophidiophobia) Rodents (rodentophobia) | 5%–15% | Vast majority are women | Childhood | |
| *Inanimate objects* Dirt (mysophobia) Storms (brontophobia) Heights (acrophobia) Darkness (nyctophobia) Closed spaces (claustrophobia) | 20% | None | Any age | |
| *Illness-injury (nosophobia)* Death (thanatophobia) Cancer (cancerophobia) Venereal disease (venerophobia) | 15%–25% | None | Middle age | |

**Figure 14.5**
**Common phobias.** Frequently reported phobias are listed here, along with their typical age of onset and information on gender differences in phobias.

Source: From Marks, I. M. (1969). *Fears and phobias.* San Diego: Academic Press. Copyright 1969 by Isaac Marks. Reprinted by permission.

**Agoraphobia** **is a fear of going out to public places** (its literal meaning is "fear of the marketplace or open places"). Because of this fear, some people become prisoners confined to their homes, although many can venture out if accompanied by a trusted companion (Hollander & Simeon, 2008). As its name suggests, agoraphobia has traditionally been viewed as a phobic disorder. However, more recent evidence suggests that agoraphobia is mainly a complication of panic disorder. About two-thirds of people who suffer from panic disorder are female (Taylor, Cox, & Asmundson, 2009). The onset of panic disorder typically occurs during late adolescence or early adulthood (McClure-Tone & Pine, 2009).

## Obsessive-Compulsive Disorder

Obsessions are *thoughts* that repeatedly intrude on one's consciousness in a distressing way. Compulsions are *actions* that one feels forced to carry out. Thus, **an** **obsessive-compulsive disorder (OCD) is marked by persistent, uncontrollable intrusions of unwanted thoughts (obsessions) and urges to engage in sense-less rituals (compulsions).** To illustrate, let's examine the bizarre behavior of a man once reputed to be the wealthiest person in the world:

*The famous industrialist Howard Hughes was obsessed with the possibility of being contaminated by germs. This led him to devise extraordinary rituals to minimize the possibility of such contamination. He would spend hours methodically cleaning a single telephone. He once wrote a three-page memo instructing assistants on exactly how to open cans of fruit for him. The following is just a small portion of the instructions that Hughes provided for a driver who delivered films to his bunga-low. "Get out of the car on the traffic side. Do not at*

**Repetitive handwashing is an example of a common compulsive behavior.**

*any time be on the side of the car between the car and the curb. . . . Carry only one can of film at a time. Step over the gutter opposite the place where the sidewalk dead-ends into the curb from a point as far out into the center of the road as possible. Do not ever walk on the grass at all, also do not step into the gutter at all. Walk to the bungalow keeping as near to the center of the sidewalk as possible." (Adapted from Barlett & Steele, 1979, pp. 227–237)*

Obsessions often center on fear of contamination, inflicting harm on others, suicide, or sexual acts. Compulsions usually involve rituals that temporarily relieve anxiety. Common examples include constant handwashing; repetitive cleaning of things that are already clean; endless rechecking of locks, faucets, and such; and excessive arranging, counting, and hoarding of things (Pato, Eisen, & Phillips, 2003). Specific types of obsessions tend to be associated with specific types of compulsions. For example, obsessions about

**WEB LINK 14.4   Obsessive Compulsive Foundation**

The Obsessive Compulsive Foundation was created to support research, educate the public, and provide help for people suffering from OCD. The site houses news-letters, brochures, and videos on the subject of OCD. Of particular interest are reviews of many books on OCD.

Comedian Howie Mandel has always been very open about the fact that he struggles with obsessive-compulsive disorder.

contamination tend to be paired with cleaning compulsions, and obsessions about symmetry tend to be paired with ordering and arranging compulsions (Hollander & Simeon, 2008). Although many of us can be compulsive at times, full-fledged obsessive-compulsive disorders occur in roughly 2.5% of the population (Turner et al., 2001). The typical age of onset for OCD is late adolescence, with most cases (75%) emerging before the age of 30 (Kessler et al., 2005a). OCD can be a serious disorder, as it is often associated with severe social and occupational impairments (Torres et al., 2006).

## Etiology of Anxiety Disorders

Like most psychological disorders, anxiety disorders develop out of complicated interactions among a variety of factors. Conditioning and learning appear especially important, but biological factors may also contribute to anxiety disorders.

### Biological Factors

Recent studies suggest that there may be a weak to moderate genetic predisposition to anxiety disorders, depending on the specific type of disorder (Fyer, 2009; McMahon & Kassem, 2005). These findings are consistent with the idea that inherited differences in temperament might make some people more vulnerable than others to anxiety disorders. Kagan and his colleagues

(1992) have found that about 15%–20% of infants display an *inhibited temperament,* characterized by shyness, timidity, and wariness, which appears to have a strong genetic basis. Research suggests that this temperament is a risk factor for the development of anxiety disorders (Coles, Schofield, & Pietrefesa, 2006).

One influential theory holds that *anxiety sensitivity* may make people vulnerable to anxiety disorders (McWilliams et al., 2007; Reiss, 1991; Schmidt, Zvolensky, & Maner, 2006). According to this notion, some people are very sensitive to internal physiological symptoms of anxiety and are prone to overreact with fear when they experience these symptoms. Anxiety sensitivity may fuel an inflationary spiral in which anxiety breeds more anxiety, which eventually spins out of control in the form of an anxiety disorder.

Recent evidence suggests that a link may exist between anxiety disorders and neurochemical activity in the brain. **Neurotransmitters are chemicals that carry signals from one neuron to another.** Therapeutic drugs (such as Valium) that reduce excessive anxiety appear to alter activity at synapses for a neurotransmitter called GABA. This finding and other lines of evidence suggest that disturbances in the neural circuits using GABA may play a role in some types of anxiety disorders (Skolnick, 2003). Abnormalities in other neural circuits using the transmitter serotonin have been implicated in panic and obsessive-compulsive disorders (Stein & Hugo, 2004). Thus, scientists are beginning to unravel the neurochemical bases for anxiety disorders.

### Conditioning and Learning

Many anxiety responses may be *acquired through classical conditioning* and *maintained through operant conditioning* (see Chapter 2). According to Mowrer (1947), an originally neutral stimulus (the snow in Hilda's case, for instance) may be paired with a frightening event (the avalanche) so that it becomes a conditioned stimulus eliciting anxiety (see **Figure 14.6** on the next page). Once a fear is acquired through classical conditioning, the person may start avoiding the anxiety-producing stimulus. The avoidance response is *negatively reinforced* because it is followed by a reduction in anxiety. This process involves operant conditioning (also shown in **Figure 14.6**). Thus, separate conditioning processes may create and then sustain specific anxiety responses (Levis, 1989). Consistent with this view, studies find that a substantial portion of people suffering from phobias can identify a traumatic conditioning experience that probably contributed to their anxiety disorder (Antony & McCabe, 2003; Mineka & Zinbarg, 2006).

The tendency to develop phobias of certain types of objects and situations may be explained by Martin Seligman's (1971) concept of *preparedness*. Like many theorists, Seligman believes that classical conditioning creates most phobic responses. *However, he suggests*

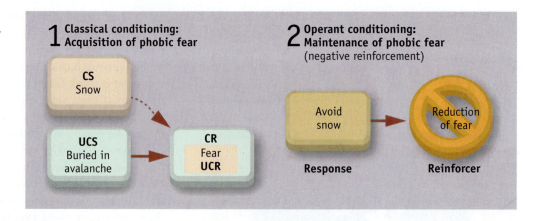

**Figure 14.6**

**Conditioning as an explanation for phobias.**
**(1)** Many phobias appear to be acquired through classical conditioning when a neutral stimulus is paired with an anxiety-arousing stimulus.
**(2)** Once acquired, a phobia may be maintained through operant conditioning, because avoidance of the phobic stimulus leads to a reduction in anxiety, resulting in negative reinforcement.

*that people are biologically prepared by their evolutionary history to acquire some fears much more easily than others.* His theory would explain why people develop phobias of ancient sources of threat (such as snakes, spiders, and heights) much more readily than modern sources of threat (such as electrical outlets, hammers, or hot irons). Arne Öhman and Susan Mineka (2001) have updated the notion of preparedness, which they call an *evolved module for fear learning.* They maintain that this evolved module is automatically activated by stimuli related to survival threats in evolutionary history and relatively resistant to intentional efforts to suppress the resulting fears. Consistent with this view, they have found that phobic stimuli associated with evolutionary threats (snakes, spiders) tend to produce more rapid conditioning of fears and stronger fear responses than modern fear-relevant stimuli, such as guns and knives (Mineka & Öhman, 2002).

### Cognitive Factors

Cognitive theorists maintain that certain styles of thinking make some people particularly vulnerable to anxiety disorders (Craske & Waters, 2005). According to these theorists, some people are prone to suffer from problems with anxiety because they tend to (a) misinterpret harmless situations as threatening, (b) focus excessive attention on perceived threats, and (c) selectively recall information that seems threatening (Beck, 1997; McNally, 1994, 1996). In one intriguing test of the cognitive view, anxious and nonanxious subjects were asked to read 32 sentences that could be interpreted in either a threatening or a nonthreatening manner (Eysenck et al., 1991). For instance, one such sentence was "The doctor examined little Emma's growth," which could mean that the doctor checked her height or the growth of a tumor. As **Figure 14.7** shows, the anxious subjects interpreted

the sentences in a threatening way more often than the nonanxious subjects did. Thus, the cognitive view holds that some people are prone to anxiety disorders because they see threat in every corner of their lives (Aikens & Craske, 2001; Riskind, 2005).

### Stress

Finally, studies have supported the long-held suspicion that anxiety disorders are stress related (Beidel & Stipelman, 2007; Sandin et al., 2004). For instance, Faravelli and Pallanti (1989) found that patients with panic disorder had experienced a dramatic increase in stress in the month prior to the onset of their disorder. In another study, Brown et al. (1998) found an association between stress and the development of social phobia. Thus, there is reason to believe that high stress often helps precipitate the onset of anxiety disorders.

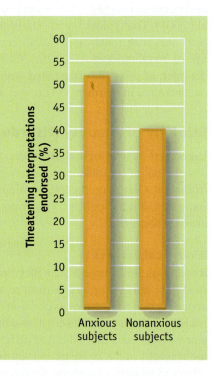

**Figure 14.7**

**Cognitive factors in anxiety disorders.** Eysenck and his colleagues (1991) compared how subjects with anxiety disorders and nonanxious subjects tended to interpret sentences that could be viewed as threatening or nonthreatening. Consistent with cognitive models of anxiety disorders, anxious subjects were more likely to interpret the sentences in a threatening light.

# Somatoform Disorders

## LEARNING OBJECTIVES

- Distinguish among the three types of somatoform disorders.
- Summarize what is known about the causes of somatoform disorders.

Chances are, you have met people who always seem to be complaining about aches, pains, and physical maladies of doubtful authenticity. When physical illness appears *largely* psychological in origin, people are said to suffer from somatoform disorders. **Somatoform disorders are physical ailments that cannot be fully explained by organic conditions and are largely due to psychological factors.** Although their symptoms are more imaginary than real, victims of somatoform disorders are *not* simply faking illness. Deliberate feigning of illness for personal gain is another matter altogether, called *malingering*.

People with somatoform disorders typically seek treatment from physicians practicing neurology, internal medicine, or family medicine, instead of from psychologists or psychiatrists. Making accurate diagnoses of somatoform disorders can be difficult, because the causes of physical ailments are sometimes hard to identify. In some cases, a problem is misdiagnosed as a somatoform disorder when a genuine organic cause for a person's physical symptoms goes undetected despite medical examinations and tests (Yutzy, 2003). Diagnostic ambiguities such as these have led some theorists to argue that the category of somatoform disorders should be eliminated in DSM-V (Mayou et al., 2005), but other theorists have expressed vigorous disagreement (Rief, Henningsen, & Hiller, 2006). In this section, we will look at three specific types of somatoform disorders: somatization disorder, conversion disorder, and hypochondriasis.

## Somatization Disorder

Individuals with somatization disorders are often said to "cling to ill health." **A *somatization disorder* is marked by a history of diverse physical complaints that appear to be psychological in origin.** Somatization disorder occurs mostly in women and often coexists with depression or anxiety disorders (Yutzy & Parish, 2008). Victims report an endless succession of minor physical ailments that seem to wax and wane in response to the stress in their lives (Servan-Schreiber, Kolb, & Tabas, 1999). They usually have a long and complicated history of medical treatment from many doctors. The distinguishing feature of this disorder is the diversity of victims' physical complaints. Over the years, they report a mixed bag of cardiovascular,

gastrointestinal, pulmonary, neurological, and genitourinary symptoms. The unlikely nature of such a mixture of symptoms occurring together often alerts a physician to the possible psychological basis for the patient's problems. However, somatization patients are typically resistant to the suggestion that their symptoms might be the result of psychological distress (Hollifield, 2005).

## Conversion Disorder

***Conversion disorder* is characterized by a significant loss of physical function with no apparent organic basis, usually in a single organ system.** Common symptoms include partial or complete loss of vision, partial or complete loss of hearing, partial paralysis, severe laryngitis or mutism, seizures, vomiting, and loss of feeling or function in limbs, such as that seen in the following case:

*Mildred was a rancher's daughter who lost the use of both of her legs during adolescence. Mildred was at home alone one afternoon when a male relative attempted to assault her. She screamed for help, and her legs gave way as she slipped to the floor. She was found on the floor a few minutes later when her mother returned home. She could not get up, so she was carried to her bed. Her legs buckled when she made subsequent attempts to walk on her own. Due to her illness, she was waited on hand and foot by her family and friends. Neighbors brought her homemade things to eat or to wear. She became the center of attention in the household. (Adapted from Cameron, 1963, pp. 312–313)*

People with conversion disorder are usually troubled by more severe ailments than people with somatization disorder. In some cases of conversion disorder, there are telltale clues about the psychological origins of the illness because the patient's symptoms are not consistent with medical knowledge about their apparent disease. For instance, the loss of feeling in one hand that is seen in "glove anesthesia" is inconsistent with the known facts of neurological organization (see **Figure 14.8** on the next page). Conversion disorders tend to have an acute onset triggered by stress (Kirmayer & Looper, 2007).

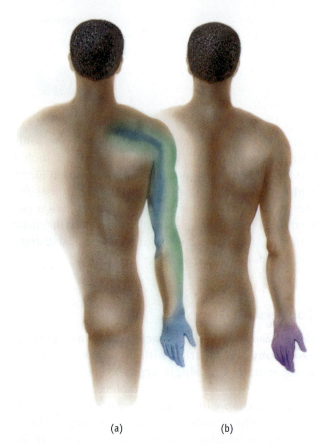

(a)          (b)

**Figure 14.8**
**Glove anesthesia.** In conversion disorders, the physical complaints are sometimes inconsistent with the known facts of physiology. Such is the case in *glove anesthesia*, in which the patient complains of losing feeling in a hand. Given the patterns of nerve distribution in the arm shown in **(a)**, a loss of feeling in the hand exclusively as shown in **(b)** is a physical impossibility, indicating that the patient's problem is psychological in origin.

## Hypochondriasis

*Hypochondriacs* constantly monitor their physical condition, looking for signs of illness. Any tiny alteration from their physical norm leads them to conclude that they have contracted a disease. **Hypochondriasis (more widely known as *hypochondria*) is characterized by excessive preoccupation with health concerns and incessant worry about developing physical illnesses.** The following case illustrates the nature of hypochondria:

*Jeff is a middle-aged man who works as a clerk in a drug store. He spends long hours describing his health problems to anyone who will listen. Jeff is an avid reader of popular magazine articles on medicine. He can tell you all about the latest medical discoveries. He takes all sorts of pills and vitamins to ward off possible illnesses. He's the first to try every new product on the market. Jeff is constantly afflicted by new symptoms of illness. His most recent problems were poor digestion and a heartbeat that he thought was irregular. He frequently goes to physicians who can find nothing wrong*

*with him physically. They tell him that he is healthy. He thinks they use "backward techniques." He suspects that his illness is too rare to be diagnosed successfully. (Adapted from Suinn, 1984, p. 236)*

When hypochondriacs are assured by their physician that they do not have any real illness, they often are skeptical and disbelieving (Starcevic, 2001). As in Jeff's case, they frequently assume that the physician must be incompetent, and they go shopping for another doctor. Hypochondriacs don't subjectively suffer from physical distress as much as they overinterpret every conceivable sign of illness. Hypochondria frequently appears alongside other psychological disorders, especially anxiety disorders and depression (Iezzi, Duckworth, & Adams, 2001). For example, Howard Hughes's obsessive-compulsive disorder was coupled with profound hypochondria.

## Etiology of Somatoform Disorders

Inherited aspects of physiological functioning, such as an elevated sensitivity to bodily sensations, may predispose some people to somatoform disorders (Kirmayer & Looper, 2007), but genetic factors do *not* appear to make much of a contribution to the development of these disorders (Hollifield, 2005). The available evidence suggests that these disorders are largely a function of personality and learning.

### Personality Factors

People with certain types of personality traits seem to be particularly prone to develop somatoform disorders. The prime candidates appear to be people with *histrionic* personality characteristics (Nemiah, 1985; Slavney, 1990). The histrionic personality tends to be self-centered, suggestible, excitable, highly emotional, and overly dramatic. Such people thrive on the attention that they get when they become ill. The personality trait of *neuroticism* also seems to elevate individuals' susceptibility to somatoform disorders (Noyes et al., 2005). Research also suggests that the pathological care-seeking behavior seen in these disorders may be caused by *insecure attachment*

"THE WAY HE MOANS AND GROANS WHEN HE GETS A LITTLE COLD... I CAN'T DECIDE WHETHER HE SHOULD CALL A DOCTOR OR A DRAMA CRITIC."

*styles* (see Chapter 9) that are rooted in early experiences with caregivers (Noyes et al., 2003).

## Cognitive Factors

In recent years, theorists have devoted increased attention to how cognitive peculiarities might contribute to somatoform disorders. For example, Barsky (2001) asserts that some people focus excessive attention on their internal physiological processes and amplify normal bodily sensations into symptoms of distress, which lead them to pursue unnecessary medical treatment. Recent evidence suggests that people with somatoform disorders tend to draw catastrophic conclusions about minor bodily complaints (Bouman & Eifert, 2009). They also seem to apply a faulty standard of good health, equating health with a complete absence of symptoms and discomfort, which is unrealistic (Bouman & Eifert, 2009).

## The Sick Role

Some people grow fond of the role associated with being sick (Hotopf, 2004; Pilowsky, 1993). Their complaints of physical symptoms may be reinforced by indirect benefits derived from their illness (Schwartz, Slater, & Birchler, 1994). One payoff is that becoming ill is a superb way to avoid having to confront life's challenges. Many people with somatoform disorders are avoiding facing up to marital problems, career frustrations, family responsibilities, and the like. After all, when you're sick, others cannot place great demands on you. Another benefit is that physical problems can provide a convenient excuse when people fail, or worry about failing, in endeavors that are critical to their self-esteem (Organista & Miranda, 1991).

Attention from others is another payoff that may reinforce complaints of physical illness. When people become ill, they command the attention of family, friends, co-workers, neighbors, and doctors. The sympathy that illness often brings may strengthen the person's tendency to feel ill. This clearly occurred in Mildred's case of conversion disorder. Her illness paid handsome dividends in terms of attention, consolation, and kindhearted assistance from others.

# Dissociative Disorders

### LEARNING OBJECTIVES

- Distinguish among the three types of dissociative disorders.
- Summarize what is known about the causes of dissociative disorders.

Dissociative disorders are probably the most controversial set of disorders in the diagnostic system, sparking heated debate among normally subdued researchers and clinicians (Simeon & Loewenstein, 2009). *Dissociative disorders* **are a class of disorders in which people lose contact with portions of their consciousness or memory, resulting in disruptions in their sense of identity.** Here we describe three dissociative syndromes—dissociative amnesia, dissociative fugue, and dissociative identity disorder—all of which are relatively uncommon.

## Dissociative Amnesia and Fugue

Dissociative amnesia and fugue are overlapping disorders characterized by serious memory deficits. *Dissociative amnesia* **is a sudden loss of memory for important personal information that is too extensive to be due to normal forgetting.** Memory losses may occur for a single traumatic event (such as an automobile accident or home fire) or for an extended period of time surrounding the event. Cases of amnesia have been observed after people have experienced disasters, accidents, combat stress, physical abuse, and rape, or after they have witnessed the violent death of a parent,

among other things (Arrigo & Pezdek, 1997; Cardeña & Gleaves, 2007). **In** *dissociative fugue,* **people lose their memory for their sense of personal identity.** Having

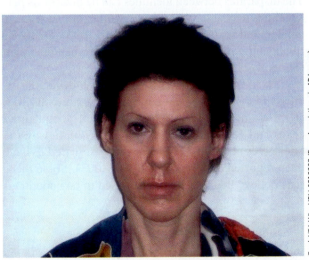

In one recent case of what appears to be dissociative fugue, the woman shown here arrived at a Dublin, Ireland, police station with no identification, reporting that she could not recall any personal details about herself. After appeals to the public for help, the police eventually determined that she was a U.S. citizen from California.

forgotten their name, their family, where they live, and where they work, these people typically wander away from their home area. In spite of this wholesale forgetting, they remember matters unrelated to their identity, such as how to drive a car and how to do math.

## Dissociative Identity Disorder

***Dissociative identity disorder (DID)* involves the coexistence in one person of two or more largely complete, and usually very different, personalities.** The name for this disorder used to be *multiple personality disorder,* which still enjoys informal usage. In dissociative identity disorder, the divergences in behavior go far beyond those that people normally display in adapting to different roles in life. People with "multiple personalities" feel that they have more than one identity. Each personality has his or her own name, memories, traits, and physical mannerisms. Although rare, this "Dr. Jekyll and Mr. Hyde" syndrome is frequently portrayed in novels, movies, and television shows. In popular media portrayals, the syndrome is often mistakenly called *schizophrenia.* As you will see later, schizophrenic disorders are entirely different and do not involve "split personality."

In dissociative identity disorder, the various personalities generally report that they are unaware of each other (Eich et al., 1997), although doubts have been raised about the accuracy of this assertion (Allen & Iacono, 2001). The alternate personalities commonly display traits that are quite foreign to the original personality. For instance, a shy, inhibited person might develop a flamboyant, extraverted alternate personality. Transitions between identities often occur suddenly. The disparities between identities can be bizarre, as personalities may assert that they are different in age, race, gender, and sexual orientation (Kluft, 1996). Dissociative identity disorder is seen more in women than men (Simeon & Loewenstein, 2009).

Starting in the 1970s, there was a dramatic increase in the diagnosis of multiple-personality disorder (Kihlstrom, 2001, 2005). Only 79 well-documented cases had accumulated up through 1970, but by the late-1990s about 40,000 cases were estimated to have been reported (Lilienfeld & Lynn, 2003). Some theorists believe that these disorders used to be underdiagnosed—that is, they often went undetected (Maldonado & Spiegel, 2008). However, other theorists argue that a handful of clinicians have begun overdiagnosing the condition and that some clinicians even *encourage and contribute* to the emergence of DID (McHugh, 1995; Powell & Gee, 1999). Consistent with this view, a survey of all the psychiatrists in Switzerland found that 90% of them had never seen a case of dissociative identity disorder, whereas three of the psychiatrists had each seen more than 20 DID patients (Modestin, 1992). The data from this study suggest that 6 psychiatrists (out of 655 surveyed) accounted for two-thirds of the dissociative identity disorder diagnoses in Switzerland.

## Etiology of Dissociative Disorders

Dissociative amnesia and fugue are usually attributed to excessive stress. However, relatively little is known about why this extreme reaction to stress occurs in a tiny minority of people but not in the vast majority who are subjected to similar stress. Some theorists speculate that certain personality traits—fantasy proneness and a tendency to become intensely absorbed in personal experiences—may make some people more susceptible to dissociative disorders, but adequate evidence is lacking on this line of thought (Kihlstrom, Glisky, & Angiulo, 1994).

The causes of dissociative identity disorder are particularly obscure. Some skeptical theorists, such as Nicholas Spanos (1994, 1996) and others (Gee, Allen, & Powell, 2003; Lilienfeld et al., 1999), believe that people with multiple personalities are engaging in intentional role playing to use mental illness as a face-saving excuse for their personal failings. Spanos also argues that a small minority of therapists help create multiple personalities in their patients by subtly encouraging the emergence of alternate personalities. According to Spanos, dissociative identity disorder is a creation of modern North American culture, much as demonic possession was a creation of early Christianity.

To bolster his argument, he discusses how DID patients' symptom presentations seem to have been influenced by popular media. For example, the typical patient with dissociative identity disorder used to report having two or three personalities, but since the publication of *Sybil* (Schreiber, 1973) and other books describing patients with many personalities, the average number of alternate personalities has climbed to about 15. In a similar vein, a dramatic upsurge occurred in the number of dissociative patients reporting that they were victims of ritual satanic abuse during childhood after the publication of *Michelle Remembers* (Smith & Pazder, 1980), a book about a DID patient who purportedly was tortured by a satanic cult.

In spite of these concerns, many clinicians are convinced that DID is an authentic disorder (Cardeña &

**WEB LINK 14.5   International Society for the Study of Dissociation**

Dissociative disorders, including dissociative identity disorder, are the focus of this organization of research and clinical professionals. In addition to a selective bibliography and a set of treatment guidelines, the site provides links to other professional groups involved in studying and treating dissociation.

Gleaves, 2007; van der Hart & Nijenhuis, 2009). They argue that there is no incentive for either patients or therapists to manufacture cases of multiple personalities, which are often greeted with skepticism and outright hostility. They maintain that most cases of DID are rooted in severe emotional trauma that occurred during childhood (Maldonado & Spiegel, 2008). A substantial majority of people with DID report a history of disturbed home life, beatings and rejection from parents, and sexual abuse (Foote et al., 2006; Van der Hart & Nijenhuis, 2009). However, this abuse typically has not been independently verified (Lilienfeld & Lynn, 2003). Moreover, this link would not be unique to DID, as a history of child abuse elevates the likelihood of *many* disorders, especially among females (MacMillan et al., 2001).

In the final analysis, very little is known about the causes of dissociative identity disorder, which remains a controversial diagnosis (Barry-Walsh, 2005). In one survey of American psychiatrists, only one-quarter of the respondents indicated that they felt there was solid evidence for the scientific validity of the DID diagnosis (Pope et al., 1999). Consistent with this finding, a more recent study found that scientific interest in DID has dwindled since the mid-1990s (Pope et al., 2006).

# Mood Disorders

### LEARNING OBJECTIVES

- Describe the two major mood disorders, and discuss their prevalence.
- Evaluate the degree to which mood disorders elevate the probability of suicide.
- Clarify how genetic and neurochemical factors may be related to the development of mood disorders.

- Discuss how cognitive processes may contribute to mood disorders.
- Outline the role of interpersonal factors and stress in the development of mood disorders.

What might Abraham Lincoln, Leo Tolstoy, Marilyn Monroe, Vincent Van Gogh, Ernest Hemingway, Winston Churchill, Virginia Woolf, Janis Joplin, Irving Berlin, Kurt Cobain, Francis Ford Coppola, Carrie Fisher, Ted Turner, Sting, Mike Wallace, Larry Flynt, Jane Pauley, and Ben Stiller have in common? Yes, they all achieved great prominence, albeit in different ways at different times. But, more pertinent to our interest, they all suffered from severe mood disorders. Although mood disorders can be terribly debilitating, people with mood disorders may still achieve greatness, because such disorders tend to be *episodic*. In other words, emotional disorders often come and go. Thus, episodes of disturbance are interspersed among periods of normality. These episodes of disturbance can vary greatly in length, but they typically last 3 to 12 months (Akiskal, 2005).

Of course, we all have our ups and downs in terms of mood. Life would be dull indeed if emotional tone were constant. Everyone experiences depression occasionally and has other days that bring an emotional high. Such emotional fluctuations are natural, but some people are prone to extreme distortions of mood. ***Mood disorders* are a class of disorders marked by emotional disturbances** **that may spill over to disrupt physical, perceptual, social, and thought processes.**

Mood disorders include two basic types: unipolar and bipolar (see **Figure 14.9** on the next page). People with *unipolar disorders* experience emotional extremes at just one end of the mood continuum—depression. People with *bipolar disorders* experience emotional extremes at both ends of the mood continuum, going through periods of both *depression* and *mania* (excitement and elation).

Mood disorders are common and have afflicted many successful, well-known people, such as Sheryl Crow and Owen Wilson.

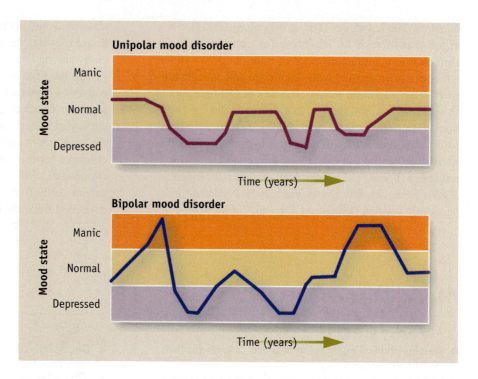

## Figure 14.9

**Episodic patterns in mood disorders.** Episodes of emotional disturbance come and go unpredictably in mood disorders. People with unipolar disorders suffer from bouts of depression only, while people with bipolar disorders experience both manic and depressive episodes. The time between episodes of disturbance varies greatly.

The mood swings in bipolar disorders can be patterned in many ways.

## Major Depressive Disorder

The line between normal and abnormal depression can be difficult to draw (Akiskal, 2009). Ultimately, a subjective judgment is required. Crucial considerations in this judgment include the duration of the depression and its disruptive effects. When depression significantly impairs everyday adaptive behavior for more than a few weeks, there is reason for concern.

In *major depressive disorder* people show persistent feelings of sadness and despair and a loss of interest in previous sources of pleasure. Figure 14.10 summarizes the most common symptoms of depressive disorders and compares them to the symptoms of mania. Negative emotions form the heart of the depressive syndrome, but many other symptoms may appear. Depressed people often give up activities that they used to find enjoyable. For example, a depressed person might quit going bowling or give up a favorite hobby like photography. Reduced appetite and insomnia are common. People with depression often lack energy. They tend to move sluggishly and talk slowly. Anxiety, irritability, and brooding are frequently observed. Self-esteem tends to sink as the depressed person begins to feel worthless. Depression plunges people into feelings of hopelessness, dejection, and boundless guilt. The severity of abnormal depression varies considerably.

The onset of unipolar disorder can occur at any point in the lifespan, but a substantial majority of cases emerge before age 40 (Hammen, 2003). Depression occurs in children and adolescents, as well as adults (Gruenberg & Goldstein, 2003). The vast majority of people who suffer from depression experience more than one episode over the course of their lifetime (Joska & Stein, 2008). The average number of depressive episodes is five to six, and the average length of these episodes is about six months (Akiskal, 2009). Recent evidence suggests that an earlier age of onset is associated with more episodes of depression, more severe

## Figure 14.10

**Common symptoms in manic and depressive episodes.** The emotional, cognitive, and motor symptoms exhibited in manic and depressive illnesses are largely the opposite of each other.

Source: From Sarason, I. G., & Sarason, B. R. (1987). *Abnormal psychology: The problem of maladaptive behavior* (5th ed., p. 283). Englewood Cliffs, NJ: Prentice-Hall. © 1987 Prentice-Hall. Reprinted by permission of Prentice-Hall, Inc.

| Comparison of Manic and Depressive Symptoms | | |
|---|---|---|
| Characteristics | Manic episode | Depressive episode |
| Emotional | Elated, euphoric, very sociable, impatient at any hindrance | Gloomy, hopeless, socially withdrawn, irritable |
| Cognitive | Characterized by racing thoughts, flight of ideas, desire for action, and impulsive behavior; talkative, self-confident; experiencing delusions of grandeur | Characterized by slowness of thought processes, obsessive worrying, inability to make decisions, negative self-image, self-blame, and delusions of guilt and disease |
| Motor | Hyperactive, tireless, requiring less sleep than usual, showing increased sex drive and fluctuating appetite | Less active, tired, experiencing difficulty in sleeping, showing decreased sex drive and decreased appetite |

symptoms, and greater impairment of social and occupational functioning (Zisook et al., 2007).

How common are depressive disorders? Very common. A recent, large-scale study of a nationally representative sample of over 9000 adults found that the lifetime prevalence of depressive disorder was 16.2% (Kessler et al., 2003). That estimate suggests that over 30 million people in the United States have suffered from depression! That said, estimates of the prevalence of depression vary quite a bit from one study to another because of the previously mentioned difficulty in drawing a line between normal dejection and abnormal depression. Hence, researchers using different procedures and cutoff points obtain different estimates.

Researchers also find that the prevalence of depression is about twice as high in women as it is in men (Rihmer & Angst, 2005). The many possible explanations for this gender gap are the subject of considerable debate. The gap does *not* appear to be attributable to differences in genetic makeup (Kessler et al., 2003). A small portion of the disparity may be due to women's elevated vulnerability to depression at certain points in their reproductive life cycle (Kornstein & Sloan, 2006; Nolen-Hoeksema & Hilt, 2009). Obviously, only women have to worry abut the phenomena of postpartum and postmenopausal depression. Susan Nolen-Hoeksema (2001) argues that women experience more depression than men because they are far more likely to be victims of sexual abuse and somewhat more likely to endure poverty, harassment, and role constraints. In other words, she attributes the higher prevalence of depression among women to their experience of greater stress and adversity. Nolen-Hoeksema also believes that women have a greater tendency than men to *ruminate* about setbacks and problems. Evidence suggests that this tendency to dwell on one's difficulties elevates vulnerability to depression, as we will discuss momentarily.

Courtesy of Susan Nolen-Hoeksema

Susan Nolen-Hoeksema

## Bipolar Disorder

*Bipolar disorder* (formerly known as *manic-depressive disorder*) is marked by the experience of both depressed and manic periods. The symptoms seen in manic periods generally are the opposite of those seen in depression (see **Figure 14.10** for a comparison). In a manic episode, a person's mood becomes elevated to the point of euphoria. Self-esteem skyrockets as the person bubbles over with optimism, energy, and extravagant plans. People become hyperactive and may go for days without sleep. They talk rapidly and shift topics wildly as their minds race at breakneck speed. Judgment is often impaired. Some people in manic periods gamble impulsively, spend money frantically, or become sexually reckless. Like depressive disorders, bipolar disorders vary considerably in severity.

You may be thinking that the euphoria in manic episodes sounds appealing. If so, you are not entirely wrong. In their milder forms, manic states can seem attractive. The increases in energy, self-esteem, and optimism can be deceptively seductive. Because of the increase in energy, many bipolar patients report temporary surges of productivity and creativity (Goodwin & Jamison, 2007).

Although manic episodes may have some positive aspects, bipolar disorder ultimately proves to be troublesome for most victims. Manic periods often have a paradoxical negative undertow of uneasiness and irritability (Dilsaver et al., 1999). Moreover, mild manic episodes usually escalate to higher levels that become scary and disturbing. Impaired judgment leads many victims to do things that they greatly regret later, as illustrated in the following case:

*Robert, a dentist, awoke one morning with the idea that he was the most gifted dental surgeon in his tri-state area. He decided that he should try to provide services to as many people as possible, so that more people could benefit from his talents. Thus, he decided to remodel his two-chair dental office, installing 20 booths so that he could simultaneously attend to 20 patients. That same day he drew up plans for this arrangement, telephoned a number of remodelers, and invited bids for the work. Later that day, impatient to get going on*

*"Those? Oh, just a few souvenirs from my bipolar-disorder days."*

© Tom Cheney/The New Yorker Collection/www.cartoonbank.com

*his remodeling, he rolled up his sleeves, got himself a sledgehammer, and began to knock down the walls in his office. Annoyed when that didn't go so well, he smashed his dental tools, washbasins, and X-ray equipment. Later, Robert's wife became concerned about his behavior and summoned two of her adult daughters for assistance. The daughters responded quickly, arriving at the family home with their husbands. In the ensuing discussion, Robert—after bragging about his sexual prowess—made advances toward his daughters. He had to be subdued by their husbands. (Adapted from Kleinmuntz, 1980, p. 309)*

Although not rare, bipolar disorder is much less common than unipolar depression. Bipolar disorder affects about 1%–2.5% of the population (Dubovsky, Davies, & Dubovsky, 2003). Unlike depressive disorder, bipolar disorder is seen equally in men and women (Rihmer & Angst, 2009). As **Figure 14.11** shows, the onset of bipolar disorder is age related, with the age of 25 being the median age of onset (Miklowitz & Johnson, 2007).

## Mood Disorders and Suicide

A tragic, heartbreaking problem associated with mood disorders is suicide, which is the eleventh leading cause of death in the United States, accounting for about 30,000 deaths annually. Official statistics may under-

estimate the scope of the problem, as many suicides are disguised as accidents, either by the suicidal person or by the survivors who try to cover up afterward. Moreeover, experts estimate that suicide attempts may outnumber completed suicides by a ratio of as much as 10 to 1 (Sudak, 2009). Anyone can commit suicide, but some groups are at higher risk than others (Carroll-Ghosh, Victor, & Bourgeois, 2003). Evidence suggests that women *attempt* suicide 3 times more often than men. But men are more likely to actually kill themselves in an attempt, so they *complete* four times as many suicides as women. In regard to age, completed suicides peak in the over-75 age bracket.

With the luxury of hindsight, it is recognized that about 90% of the people who complete suicide suffer from some type of psychological disorder, although in some cases this disorder may not be readily apparent beforehand (Dawkins, Golden, & Fawcett, 2003). As you might expect, suicide rates are highest for people with mood disorders, who account for about 60% of completed suicides (Mann & Currier, 2006). Both bipolar disorder and depression are associated with dramatic elevations in suicide rates. Studies suggest that the lifetime risk of completed suicide is about 15%–20% in people with bipolar disorder and about 10%–15% in those who have grappled with depression (Sudak, 2009), but some experts believe that these estimates are overly high (Joiner et al., 2009). Smaller elevations in suicide rates are seen among people who suffer from schizophrenia, alcoholism, and substance abuse (Mann & Currier, 2006). Unfortunately, there is no foolproof way to prevent suicidal persons from taking their own life, but some useful tips are discussed in the Living in Today's World box on the facing page.

## Etiology of Mood Disorders

We know quite a bit about the etiology of mood disorders, although the puzzle hasn't been assembled completely. There appear to be a number of routes into these disorders, involving intricate interactions between psychological and biological factors.

### Genetic Vulnerability

The evidence strongly suggests that genetic factors influence the likelihood of developing major depression or a bipolar mood disorder (Lohoff & Berrettini, 2009). In studies that assess the impact of heredity on psychological disorders, investigators look at *concordance rates*. **A concordance rate** indicates the

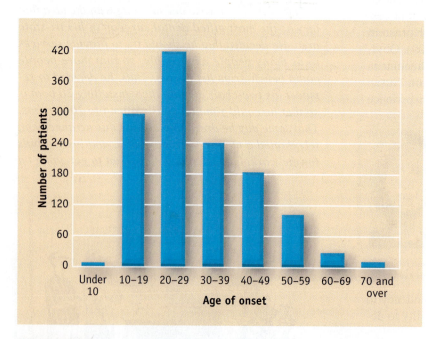

**Figure 14.11**

**Age of onset for bipolar mood disorder.** The onset of bipolar disorder typically occurs in adolescence or early adulthood. The data graphed here, which were combined from ten studies, show the distribution of age of onset for 1,304 bipolar patients. As you can see, bipolar disorder emerges most frequently during the 20s decade.

Source: From Goodwin, F. K., & Jamison, K. R. (1990). *Manic-depressive illness.* New York: Oxford University Press. Copyright © 1990 Oxford University Press, Inc. Used by permission of Oxford University Press, Inc.

## Understanding and Preventing Suicide

Many false beliefs exist regarding the nature of suicidal behavior. Some common myths about suicide include the following (Fremouw, Perczel, & Ellis, 1990; Shneidman, 1985; Suicide Awareness Voices of Education, 2007):

*Myth 1: People who talk about suicide don't actually commit suicide.* Undoubtedly, there are many people who threaten suicide without ever going through with it. Nonetheless, there is no group at higher risk for suicide than those who openly discuss the possibility. Many people who kill themselves have a history of earlier threats that they did not carry out.

*Myth 2: Suicide usually takes place with little or no warning.* The vast majority of suicide attempts are preceded by some kind of warning. These warnings may range from clear threats to vague statements. For example, at dinner with friends the night before he committed suicide, one prominent attorney cut up his American Express card, saying, "I'm not going to need this anymore." The probability of an actual suicide attempt is greatest when a threat is clear, when it includes a detailed plan, and when the plan involves a relatively deadly method.

*Myth 3: People who attempt suicide are fully intent on dying.* It appears that only a small minority of those who attempt suicide definitely want to die. A substantial portion of suicide attempts are made by people who are highly ambivalent about dying! They only want to send out a dramatic distress signal. Thus, they arrange their suicide so that a rescue is relatively likely.

*Myth 4: People who are suicidal remain so forever.* Many people who become suicidal do so for a limited period of time. If they manage to ride through their crisis period, thoughts of suicide may disappear entirely. Apparently, time heals many wounds—if it is given the opportunity.

What can be done to prevent suicides? As Sudak (2005, p. 2449) notes, "It is not possible to prevent all suicides or to totally and absolutely protect a given patient from suicide. What is possible is to reduce the likelihood of suicide." Thus, we will review some general advice that may be useful if you ever have to help someone through a suicidal crisis (American Association of Suicidology, 2007; American Foundation for Suicide Prevention, 2007; Maris, Berman, & Silverman, 2000; Rosenthal, 1988; Shneidman, Farberow, & Litman, 1994).

1. *Take suicidal talk seriously.* When people talk about suicide in vague generalities, it's easy to dismiss it as "idle talk" and let it go. However, people who talk about suicide are a high-risk group and their veiled threats should not be ignored. The first step in suicide prevention is to directly ask such people if they're contemplating suicide.

2. *Provide empathy and social support.* It is important to show the suicidal person that you care. People often contemplate suicide because they see the world around them as indifferent and uncaring. Thus, you must demonstrate to the suicidal person that you are genuinely concerned. Suicide threats are often a last-ditch cry for help. It is therefore imperative that you offer that help.

3. *Identify and clarify the crucial problem.* The suicidal person is often confused and feels lost in a sea of frustration and problems. It is a good idea to try to help sort through this confusion. Encourage the person to try to identify the crucial problem. Once it is isolated, the problem may not seem quite so overwhelming.

4. *Do not promise to keep someone's suicidal ideation secret.* If you really feel like someone's life is in danger, don't agree to keep his or her suicidal plans secret to preserve your friendship.

5. *In an acute crisis, do not leave a suicidal person alone.* Stay with the person until additional help is available. Try to remove any guns, drugs, sharp objects, and so forth that might provide an available means to commit suicide.

6. *Encourage professional consultation.* Most mental health professionals have some experience in dealing with suicidal crises. Many cities have suicide prevention centers with 24-hour hotlines. These centers are staffed with people who have been specially trained to deal with suicidal problems. It is important to try to get a suicidal person to seek professional assistance.

---

**percentage of twin pairs or other pairs of relatives that exhibit the same disorder.** If relatives who share more genetic similarity show higher concordance rates than relatives who share less genetic overlap, this finding supports the genetic hypothesis. Twin studies, which compare identical and fraternal twins (see Chapter 2), suggest that genetic factors *are* involved in mood disorders (Kelsoe, 2009). Concordance rates average around 65%–72% for identical twins but only 14%–19% for fraternal twins, who share less genetic similarity.

Thus, evidence suggests that heredity can create a *predisposition* to mood disorders. Environmental factors probably determine whether this predisposition is converted into an actual disorder. The influence of genetic factors appears to be stronger for bipolar disorders than for unipolar disorders (Kieseppa et al., 2004). Some promising results have been reported in *genetic mapping* studies that have attempted to pinpoint the specific genes that shape vulnerability to mood disorders (Holmans et al., 2007; Levinson, 2009). However, results have been disturbingly inconsistent, and scientists do *not* appear to be on the verge of unraveling the genetic code for mood disorders, which probably depend on subtle variations in constellations of many genes (Kendler, 2005a, 2005b; Merikangas & Risch, 2003).

## Neurochemical and Neuroanatomical Factors

Heredity may influence susceptibility to mood disorders by creating a predisposition toward certain types of neurochemical abnormalities in the brain. Correlations have been found between mood disorders and abnormal levels of two neurotransmitters in the brain: norepinephrine and serotonin (Sher & Mann, 2003), although other neurotransmitter disturbances may also contribute (Dunlop, Garlow, & Nemeroff, 2009). The details remain elusive, but low levels of serotonin appear to be a crucial factor underlying most forms of depression (Johnson et al., 2009). A variety of drug therapies are fairly effective in the treatment of severe mood disorders. Most of these drugs are known to affect the availability (in the brain) of the neurotransmitters that have been related to mood disorders (Dubovsky et al., 2003). Since this effect is unlikely to be a coincidence,

it bolsters the plausibility of the idea that neurochemical changes produce mood disturbances. That said, after 40 years of enormous research effort, the neurochemical bases of mood disorders remain more mysterious than scientists would like (Delgado & Moreno, 2006).

Studies have also found some interesting correlations between mood disorders and a variety of structural abnormalities in the brain (Flores et al., 2004). Perhaps the best documented correlation is the association between depression and *reduced hippocampal volume* (Davidson, Pizzagalli, & Nitschke, 2009; Videbech, 2006). The *hippocampus,* which is known to play a major role in memory (see **Figure 14.12**), tends to be about 8%–10% smaller in depressed subjects than in normal subjects (Videbech & Ravnkilde, 2004).

A fascinating new theory of the biological bases of depression may be able to account for this finding. The springboard for this theory is the recent discovery that the human brain continues to generate new neurons in adulthood, especially in the hippocampal formation (Gage, 2002). This process is called *neurogenesis*. Evidence suggests that depression occurs when major life stress causes neurochemical reactions that suppress neurogenesis, resulting in reduced hippocampal volume (Jacobs, 2004; Warner-Schmidt & Duman, 2006). According to this view, the suppression of neurogenesis is the central cause of depression, and antidepressant drugs that relieve depression do so because they promote neurogenesis (Duman & Monteggia, 2006). A great deal of additional research will be required to fully test this innovative new model of the biological bases of depressive disorders.

### Figure 14.12

**The hippocampus and depression.**
This graphic shows the hippocampus in blue. The photo inset shows a brain dissected to reveal the hippocampus in both the right and left hemispheres. It has long been known that the hippocampus plays a key role in memory, but its possible role in depression has only come to light in recent years. Research suggests that shrinkage of the hippocampal formation due to suppressed neurogenesis may be a key causal factor underlying depressive disorders.

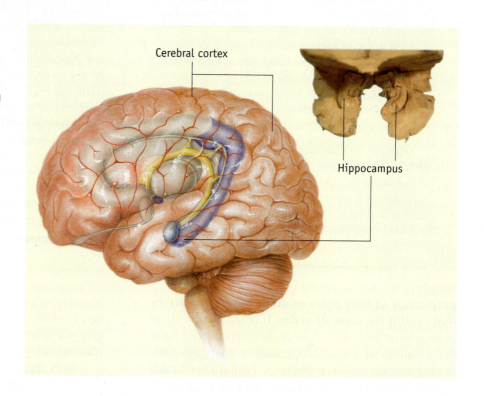

Cerebral cortex

Hippocampus

## Cognitive Factors

A variety of theories emphasize how cognitive factors contribute to depressive disorders (Christensen, Carney, & Segal, 2006). We will discuss Aaron Beck's (1976, 1987, 2008) influential cognitive theory of depression in Chapter 15, where his approach to therapy is described. In this section, we examine Martin Seligman's *learned helplessness model* of depression. Based largely on animal research, Seligman (1974) proposed that depression is caused by *learned helplessness*—passive "giving up" behavior produced by exposure to unavoidable aversive events (such as uncontrollable shock in the laboratory). He originally considered learned helplessness to be a product of conditioning but eventually revised his theory, giving it a cognitive slant. The reformulated theory of learned helplessness postulates that the roots of depression lie in how people explain the setbacks and other negative events that they experience (Abramson, Seligman, & Teasdale, 1978). According to Seligman (1990), people who exhibit a *pessimistic explanatory style* are especially vulnerable to depression. These people tend to attribute their setbacks to their personal flaws instead of situational factors, and they tend to draw global, far-reaching conclusions about their personal inadequacies based on these setbacks.

In accord with cognitive models of depression, Susan Nolen-Hoeksema (1991, 2000) has found that people who *ruminate* about their problems and setbacks have elevated rates of depression and tend to remain depressed longer than those who do not ruminate. People who tend to ruminate repetitively focus their attention on their depressing feelings, thinking constantly about how sad, lethargic, and unmotivated they are. Excessive rumination tends to foster and amplify episodes of depression by increasing negative thinking, impairing problem solving, and undermining social support (Nolen-Hoeksema, Wisco, & Lyubomirsky, 2008). Nolen-Hoeksema believes that women have a greater tendency to ruminate than men and that this disparity may be a major reason that depression is more prevalent in women. Moreover, the effects of rumination are not limited to aggravating depressive disorders. Rumination is also associated with increased anxiety, binge eating, and binge drinking (Nolen-Hoeksema et al., 2008).

In sum, cognitive models of depression maintain that negative thinking is what leads to depression in many people. The principal problem with cognitive theories is their difficulty in separating cause from effect (Feliciano & Areán, 2007). Does negative thinking cause depression? Or does depression cause negative thinking (see **Figure 14.13**)? A *clear* demonstration of a causal link between negative thinking and depression is not possible because it would require manipulating people's explanatory style (which is not easy to change)

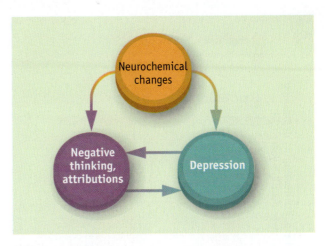

**Figure 14.13**

**Interpreting the correlation between negative thinking and depression.** Cognitive theories of depression assert that consistent patterns of negative thinking cause depression. Although these theories are highly plausible, depression could cause negative thoughts, or both could be caused by a third factor, such as neurochemical changes in the brain.

in sufficient degree to produce full-fledged depressive disorders (which would not be ethical). However, a study by Lauren Alloy and her colleagues (1999) provided impressive evidence consistent with a causal link between negative thinking and vulnerability to depression. They assessed the explanatory style of a sample of first-year college students who were not depressed at the outset of the study. The students were characterized as being at high risk or low risk for depression based on whether they exhibited a negative cognitive style. The follow-up data over the ensuing two and a half years on students who had no prior history of depression showed dramatic differences between the two groups in vulnerability to depression. During this relatively brief period, a major depressive disorder emerged in 17% of the high-risk students in comparison to only 1% of the low-risk students (see **Figure 14.14** on the next page). These findings and other data from the study suggest that negative thinking makes people more vulnerable to depression.

## Interpersonal Roots

Some theorists suggest that inadequate social skills put people on the road to depressive disorders (Ingram, Scott, & Hamill, 2009). According to this notion, depression-prone people lack the social finesse needed to acquire many important kinds of reinforcers, such as good friends, top jobs, and desirable spouses. This paucity of reinforcers could understandably lead to negative emotions and depression (see **Figure 14.15**). Consistent with this theory, researchers have indeed found correlations between poor social skills and depression (Petty, Sachs-Ericsson, & Joiner, 2004).

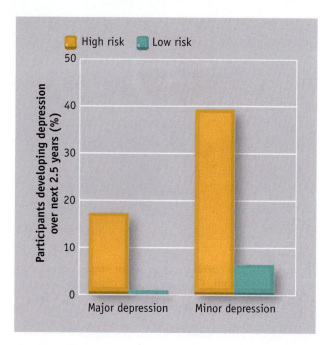

**Figure 14.14**

**Negative thinking and prediction of depression.** Alloy and colleagues (1999) measured the explanatory styles of first-year college students and characterized them as being high risk or low risk for depression. This graph shows the percentage of students who experienced major or minor episodes of depression over the next 2.5 years. As you can see, the high-risk students, who exhibited a negative thinking style, proved to be much more vulnerable to depression.

Another interpersonal factor is that depressed people tend to be depressing (Joiner & Timmons, 2009). Individuals suffering from depression often are irritable and pessimistic. They complain a lot and aren't particularly enjoyable companions. They also alienate people by constantly asking for reassurances about their relationships and their worth (Burns et al., 2006). As a

consequence, depressed people tend to court rejection from those around them (Joiner & Timmons, 2009). This alienation of important sources of social support may contribute to their downward spiral into depression (Joiner & Metalsky, 2001). To compound these problems, evidence indicates that depressed people may gravitate to partners who view them unfavorably and thus reinforce their negative views of themselves (Joiner, 2002). Interestingly, recent evidence suggests that lack of social support may make a larger contribution to depression in women than in men (Kendler, Myers, & Prescott, 2005).

### Precipitating Stress

Mood disorders sometimes appear mysteriously "out of the blue" in people who seem to be leading benign, nonstressful lives. For this reason, experts used to believe that mood disorders are relatively uninfluenced by stress. However, recent advances in the measurement of personal stress have altered this picture. The evidence available today suggests a moderately strong link between stress and the onset of mood disorders (Hammen, 2005; Monroe, Slavich, & Georgiades, 2009). Stress also appears to affect how people with mood disorders respond to treatment and whether they experience a relapse of their disorder (Monroe & Hadjiyannakis, 2002).

Of course, many people endure great stress without getting depressed. The impact of stress varies in part because different people have different degrees of *vulnerability* to mood disorders (Lewinsohn, Joiner, & Rohde, 2001). Variations in vulnerability appear to depend primarily on biological makeup. Similar interactions between stress and vulnerability probably influence the development of many kinds of disorders, including those that are next on our agenda: the schizophrenic disorders.

**Figure 14.15**

**Interpersonal factors in depression.** Interpersonal theories about the etiology of depression emphasize how inadequate social skills may contribute to the development of the disorder. Recent studies suggest that excessive reassurance seeking may play a particularly critical role in the social dynamics promoting depression.

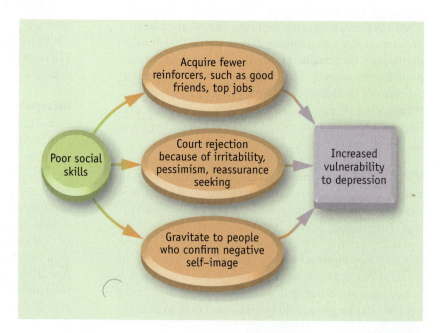

# Schizophrenic Disorders

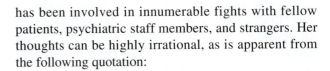

Literally, *schizophrenia* means "split mind." However, when Eugen Bleuler coined the term in 1911, he was referring to the fragmenting of thought processes seen in the disorder—not to a "split personality." Unfortunately, writers in the popular media often assume that the split-mind notion refers to the syndrome in which a person manifests two or more personalities. As you have already learned, this syndrome is actually called *dissociative identity disorder.* Schizophrenia is a much more common, and altogether different, type of disorder.

**Schizophrenic disorders are a class of disorders marked by disturbances in thought that spill over to affect perceptual, social, and emotional processes.** How common is schizophrenia? Prevalence estimates suggest that about 1% of the population may suffer from schizophrenic disorders (Lauriello, Bustillo, & Keith, 2005). That may not sound like much, but it means that in North America alone there may be several million people troubled by schizophrenic disturbances. Moreover, schizophrenia is an extremely costly disorder for society, because it is a severe, debilitating illness that tends to have an early onset and often requires lengthy hospital care (Samnaliev & Clark, 2008). Because of these considerations, the financial impact of schizophrenia is estimated to exceed the costs of all types of cancers combined (Buchanan & Carpenter, 2005).

## General Symptoms

Although there are a number of distinct schizophrenic syndromes, they share some general characteristics that we need to examine before looking at the subtypes. Many of these characteristics are apparent in the following case history (adapted from Sheehan, 1982).

Sylvia was first diagnosed as schizophrenic at age 15. She has been in and out of many types of psychiatric facilities since then. She has never been able to hold a job for any length of time. During severe flare-ups of her disorder, her personal hygiene deteriorates. She rarely washes, wears clothes that neither fit nor match, smears makeup on heavily but randomly, and slops food all over herself. Sylvia occasionally hears voices talking to her. Sylvia tends to be argumentative, aggressive, and emotionally volatile. Over the years, she has been involved in innumerable fights with fellow patients, psychiatric staff members, and strangers. Her thoughts can be highly irrational, as is apparent from the following quotation:

*"Mick Jagger wants to marry me. If I have Mick Jagger, I don't have to covet Geraldo Rivera. Mick Jagger is St. Nicholas and the Maharishi is Santa Claus. I want to form a gospel rock group called the Thorn Oil, but Geraldo wants me to be the music critic on Eyewitness News, so what can I do? Got to listen to my boyfriend. Teddy Kennedy cured me of my ugliness. I'm pregnant with the son of God. I'm going to marry David Berkowitz and get it over with. Creedmoor is the headquarters of the American Nazi Party. They're eating the patients here. Archie Bunker wants me to play his niece on his TV show. I work for Epic Records. I'm Joan of Arc. I'm Florence Nightingale. The door between the ward and the porch is the dividing line between New York and California. Divorce isn't a piece of paper, it's a feeling. Forget about Zip Codes. I need shock treatment." (Sheehan, 1982, pp. 104–105)*

Sylvia's case clearly shows that schizophrenic thinking can be bizarre and that schizophrenia is a brutally serious, psychologically disfiguring disorder. Although no single symptom is inevitably present, the following symptoms are commonly seen in schizophrenia (Lewis, Escalona, & Keith, 2009; Minzenberg, Yoon, & Carter, 2008).

**Irrational thought.** Cognitive deficits and disturbed thought processes are the central, defining feature of schizophrenic disorders (Barch, 2003; Heinrichs, 2005). Various kinds of delusions are common. **Delusions are false beliefs that are maintained even though they clearly are out of touch with reality.** For example, one patient's delusion that he was a tiger (with a deformed body) persisted for 15 years (Kulick, Pope, & Keck, 1990). More typically, affected persons believe that their private thoughts are being broadcast to other people, that thoughts are being injected into their mind against their will, or that their thoughts are being controlled by some external force (Maher, 2001). In *delusions of grandeur,* people maintain that they are extremely famous or important. Sylvia expressed an endless array of grandiose delusions, such as thinking that Mick Jagger wanted to marry her, that she dictated the hobbit stories to Tolkien, and that she was going to win the Nobel Prize for medicine.

In addition to delusions, the schizophrenic person's train of thought deteriorates. Thinking becomes chaotic rather than logical and linear. There is a "loosening of associations" as the schizophrenic shifts topics in disjointed ways. The quotation from Sylvia illustrates this symptom dramatically. The entire passage involves a wild "flight of ideas," but at one point (beginning with the sentence "Creedmoor is the headquarters . . .") she rattles off ten consecutive sentences that have no apparent connection to the preceding sentence.

**Deterioration of adaptive behavior.**    Schizophrenia involves a noticeable deterioration in the quality of one's routine functioning in work, social relations, and personal care. Friends will often make remarks such as "Hal just isn't himself anymore." This deterioration is readily apparent in Sylvia's inability to get along with others or function in the work world. It's also apparent in her neglect of personal hygiene.

**Distorted perception.**    A variety of perceptual distortions may occur in schizophrenia, with the most common being auditory hallucinations, which are reported by about 75% of patients (Combs & Mueser, 2007). ***Hallucinations* are sensory perceptions that occur in the absence of a real external stimulus or that represent gross distortions of perceptual input.** Schizophrenics frequently report that they hear voices of nonexistent or absent people talking to them. Sylvia, for instance, heard messages from Paul McCartney. These voices often provide an insulting running commentary on the person's behavior ("You're an idiot for shaking his hand"). The voices may be argumentative ("You don't need a bath"), and they may issue commands ("Prepare your home for visitors from outer space").

**Disturbed emotion.**    Normal emotional tone can be disrupted in schizophrenia in a variety of ways. Although it may not be an accurate indicator of their underlying emotional experience (Kring, 1999), some victims show little emotional responsiveness, a symptom referred to as "blunted or flat affect." Others show inappropriate emotional responses that don't jell with the situation or with what they are saying. People with schizophrenia may also become emotionally volatile. This pattern was displayed by Sylvia, who often overreacted emotionally in erratic, unpredictable ways.

## *Recommended* **READING**

### *Surviving Schizophrenia: A Manual for Families, Patients, and Providers*
by E. Fuller Torrey (Harper Paperbacks, 2006)

E. Fuller Torrey, a prominent psychiatrist who specializes in the study and treatment of schizophrenia, has written a practical book intended for the lay public. Torrey points out that many myths surrounding schizophrenia have added to the anguish of families who have been victimized by this illness. He explains that schizophrenia is *not* caused by childhood trauma, domineering mothers, or passive fathers. He discusses how genetic vulnerability, flawed brain chemistry, and other factors contribute to the development of schizophrenic disorders. Torrey discusses the treatment of schizophrenia at great length. He also explains the various ways in which the disease can evolve. Some of the best material is found in chapters on what the patient needs and what the family needs. Throughout the book, Torrey writes with clarity, eloquence, and conviction. He is not reluctant to express strong opinions. For instance, in an appendix he lists the ten worst readings on schizophrenia (along with the ten best), and his evaluations are brutal. He characterizes one book as "absurd drivel" and dismisses another by saying, "If a prize were to be given to the book which has produced the most confusion about schizophrenia over the past twenty years, this book would win going away." Scientists and academicians are usually reluctant to express such strong opinions, so Torrey's candor is remarkably refreshing.

*Go to the Psychology CourseMate for Weiten at* **www.cengagebrain.com/shop/ISBN/1111186634** *for descriptions of other recommended books.*

## Subtypes

Four subtypes of schizophrenic disorders are recognized, including a category for people who don't fit neatly into any of the first three categories. The major symptoms of each subtype are as follows (Lewis et al., 2009; Minzenberg et al., 2008).

### Paranoid Type

As its name implies, ***paranoid schizophrenia* is dominated by delusions of persecution, along with delusions of grandeur.** In this common form of schizophrenia, people come to believe that they have many enemies who want to harass and oppress them. They may become suspicious of friends and relatives, or they may attribute the persecution to mysterious, unknown persons. They are convinced that they are being watched and manipulated in malicious ways. To make sense of this persecution, they often develop delusions of grandeur. They believe that they must be enormously important people, often seeing themselves as great inventors or as great religious or political leaders. For example, in the case described at the beginning of the chapter, Ed's belief that he was president of the United States was a delusion of grandeur.

## Catatonic Type

*Catatonic schizophrenia* **is marked by striking motor disturbances, ranging from muscular rigidity to random motor activity.** Some catatonics go into an extreme form of withdrawal known as a catatonic stupor. They may remain virtually motionless and seem oblivious to the environment around them for long periods of time. Others go into a state of catatonic excitement. They become hyperactive and incoherent. Some alternate between these dramatic extremes. The catatonic subtype is not particularly common, and its prevalence seems to be declining.

## Disorganized Type

In *disorganized schizophrenia,* **a particularly severe deterioration of adaptive behavior is seen.** Prominent symptoms include emotional indifference, frequent incoherence, and virtually complete social withdrawal. Aimless babbling and giggling are common. Delusions often center on bodily functions ("My brain is melting out my ears").

## Undifferentiated Type

People who are clearly schizophrenic but who cannot be placed into any of the three previous categories are said to have *undifferentiated schizophrenia,* **which is marked by idiosyncratic mixtures of schizophrenic symptoms.** The undifferentiated subtype is fairly common.

## Positive Versus Negative Symptoms

Many theorists have raised doubts about the value of dividing schizophrenic disorders into these four subtypes (Sanislow & Carson, 2001). Critics note that the catatonic subtype is disappearing and that undifferentiated cases aren't a subtype so much as a hodgepodge of "leftovers." Critics also point out that the classic schizophrenic subtypes do not differ meaningfully in etiology, prognosis, or response to treatment. The absence of such differences casts doubt on the value of the current classification scheme.

Because of such problems, Nancy Andreasen (1990) and others (Carpenter, 1992; McGlashan & Fenton, 1992) have proposed an alternative approach to subtyping. This scheme divides schizophrenic disorders into just two categories based on the predominance of negative versus positive symptoms (see **Figure 14.16**). *Negative symptoms* involve behavioral deficits, such as flattened emotions, social withdrawal, apathy, impaired attention, and poverty of speech. *Positive symptoms* involve behavioral excesses or peculiarities, such as hallucinations, delusions, bizarre behavior, and wild flights of ideas.

Courtesy of Nancy Andreasen, M.D.

**Nancy Andreasen**

Theorists advocating this scheme hoped to find consistent differences between the two subtypes in etiology, prognosis, and response to treatment, and some progress along these lines *has* been made. For example, a predominance of positive symptoms is associated with

| Positive and Negative Symptoms in Schizophrenia ||||
|---|---|---|---|
| **Negative symptoms** | **Percent of patients** | **Positive symptoms** | **Percent of patients** |
| Few friendship relationships | 96 | Delusions of persecution | 81 |
| Few recreational interests | 95 | Auditory hallucinations | 75 |
| Lack of persistence at work or school | 95 | Delusions of being controlled | 46 |
| Impaired grooming or hygiene | 87 | Derailment of thought | 45 |
| Paucity of expressive gestures | 81 | Delusions of grandeur | 39 |
| Social inattentiveness | 78 | Bizarre social, sexual behavior | 33 |
| Emotional nonresponsiveness | 64 | Delusions of thought insertion | 31 |
| Inappropriate emotion | 63 | Aggressive, agitated behavior | 27 |
| Poverty of speech | 53 | Incoherent thought | 23 |

**Figure 14.16**

**Examples of positive and negative symptoms in schizophrenia.** Some theorists believe that schizophrenic disorders should be classified into just two types, depending on whether patients exhibit mostly positive symptoms (behavioral excesses) or negative symptoms (behavioral deficits). The percentages shown here, based on a sample of 111 schizophrenic patients studied by Andreasen (1987), provide an indication of how common each specific symptom is.

better adjustment prior to the onset of schizophrenia and greater responsiveness to treatment (Combs & Mueser, 2007; Galderisi et al., 2002). However, the assumption that patients can be placed into discrete categories based on this scheme now seems untenable. Most patients exhibit both types of symptoms and vary only in the *degree* to which positive or negative symptoms dominate (Black & Andreasen, 1999).

## Course and Outcome

Schizophrenic disorders usually emerge during adolescence or early adulthood, with 75% of cases manifesting by the age of 30 (Perkins, Miller-Anderson, & Lieberman, 2006). Those who develop schizophrenia usually have a long history of peculiar behavior and cognitive and social deficits, although most do not manifest a full-fledged psychological disorder during childhood

(Walker et al., 2004). The emergence of schizophrenia may be sudden, but it usually is insidious and gradual. Once it clearly emerges, the course of schizophrenia is variable, but patients tend to fall into three broad groups. Some patients, presumably those with milder disorders, are treated successfully and enjoy a full recovery. Other patients experience a partial recovery so that they can return to independent living for a time. However, they experience regular relapses and are in and out of treatment facilities for much of the remainder of their lives. Finally, a third group of patients endure chronic illness that sometimes results in permanent hospitalization. Estimates of the percentage of patients falling in each category vary.

Overall, the preponderance of studies have suggested that only about 20% of schizophrenic patients enjoy a full recovery (Perkins et al., 2006; Robinson et al., 2004). However, to some extent, this low recovery

John Nash, the Nobel Prize–winning mathematician whose story was told in the film *A Beautiful Mind,* has struggled with paranoid schizophrenia since 1959.

© Reuters/Corbis

rate may reflect the poor to mediocre quality of mental health care available for severe disorders in the vast majority of countries, including wealthy ones. When comprehensive, well-coordinated, quality care is initiated promptly, higher recovery rates in the vicinity of 50% have been found (Hopper et al., 2007; Liberman & Kopelowicz, 2005). Thus, the outlook for schizophrenia may not need to be as pervasively negative as it has been.

A number of factors are related to the likelihood of recovery from schizophrenic disorders (Cancro & Lehmann, 2000; Liberman et al., 2002). A patient has a relatively *favorable prognosis* when (1) the onset of the disorder has been sudden rather than gradual, (2) the onset has occurred at a later age, (3) the patient's social and work adjustment were relatively good prior to the onset of the disorder, (4) the proportion of negative symptoms is relatively low, (5) the patient's cognitive functioning is relatively preserved, (6) the patient shows good adherence to treatment interventions, and (7) the patient has a relatively healthy, supportive family situation to return to. Many of these predictors are concerned with the etiology of schizophrenic illness, which is the matter we turn to next.

## Etiology of Schizophrenia

Most of us can identify, at least to some extent, with people who suffer from mood disorders, somatoform disorders, and anxiety disorders. You can probably imagine events that might leave you struggling with depression, grappling with anxiety, or worrying about your physical health. But what could possibly have led Ed to believe that he had been fighting space wars and vampires? What could account for Sylvia thinking that she was Joan of Arc, or that she had dictated the hobbit novels to Tolkien? As mystifying as these delusions may seem, you'll see that the etiology of schizophrenic disorders is not all that different from the etiology of other disorders.

### Genetic Vulnerability

Evidence is plentiful that hereditary factors play a role in the development of schizophrenic disorders (Glatt, 2008; Kirov & Owen, 2009). For instance, in twin studies, concordance rates for schizophrenia average around 48% for identical twins, in comparison to about 17% for fraternal twins (Gottesman, 1991, 2001). Studies also indicate that a child born to two schizophrenic parents has about a 46% probability of developing a schizophrenic disorder (as compared to the probability of about 1% for the population as a whole). These and other findings that demonstrate the genetic roots of schizophrenia are summarized in **Figure 14.17**. Overall, the picture is similar to that seen for mood disorders. Several converging lines of evidence indicate that people inherit a genetically transmitted *vulnerability* to schizophrenia (Cornblatt et al., 2009). Although genetic

| Relationship | Genetic relatedness | Concordance rate (%) (lifetime risk) |
|---|---|---|
| Identical twin | 100% | |
| Offspring of two schizophrenic patients | 50% with each parent | |
| Fraternal twin | 50% | |
| Offspring of one schizophrenic patient | 50% | |
| Sibling | 50% | |
| Nephew or niece | 25% | |
| Unrelated person in the general population | 0% | |

**Figure 14.17**

**Genetic vulnerability to schizophrenic disorders.** Relatives of schizophrenic patients have an elevated risk for schizophrenia. This risk is greater among closer relatives. Although environment also plays a role in the etiology of schizophrenia, the concordance rates shown here suggest that there must be a genetic vulnerability to the disorder. These concordance estimates are based on pooled data from 40 studies.

factors may account for more than two-thirds of the variability in susceptibility to schizophrenia, genetic mapping studies have made little progress in identifying the specific genes responsible (Crow, 2007; Walker & Tessner, 2008).

## Neurochemical Factors

Like mood disorders, schizophrenic disorders appear to be accompanied by changes in the activity of one or more neurotransmitters in the brain (Patel, Pinals, Breier, 2003). Excess *dopamine* activity has been implicated as a likely cause of schizophrenia (Javitt & Laruelle, 2006). This hypothesis makes sense because most of the drugs that are useful in the treatment of schizophrenia are known to dampen dopamine activity in the brain (Tamminga & Carlsson, 2003). However, the evidence linking schizophrenia to high dopamine levels is riddled with inconsistencies, complexities, and interpretive problems (Abi-Dargham, 2004). Researchers are currently exploring how interactions between the dopamine, serotonin, and other neurotransmitter systems may contribute to schizophrenia (Patel et al., 2003). New research has also suggested that abnormalities in neural circuits using *glutamate* as a neurotransmitter may play a role in schizophrenic disturbance (Downar & Kapur, 2008).

Recent research has suggested that marijuana use during adolescence may help precipitate schizophrenia in young people who have a genetic vulnerability to the disorder (Compton, Goulding, & Walker, 2007; Degenhardt & Hall, 2006). This unexpected finding has generated considerable debate about whether and how cannabis might contribute to the emergence of schizophrenia (Castle, 2008; DeLisi, 2008). The current thinking is that the key chemical ingredient in marijuana (THC) may amplify neurotransmitter activity in dopamine circuits (Degenhardt & Hall, 2006; Di Forti et al., 2007). The data on this issue are still rather preliminary, and more research will be needed to fully understand the association between marijuana use and schizophrenia.

## Structural Abnormalities in the Brain

For decades, studies have suggested that individuals with schizophrenia exhibit a variety of deficits in attention, perception, and information processing (Belger & Barch, 2009; Keefe & Eesley, 2006). Impairments in working (short-term) memory are especially prominent (Silver et al., 2003). These cognitive deficits suggest that schizophrenic disorders may be caused by neurological defects. Until recent decades, however, this theory was based more on speculation than on actual research. However, advances in brain-imaging technology have yielded mountains of intriguing data since the mid-1980s. Research with various types of

brain scans suggest an association between enlarged brain ventricles (the hollow, fluid-filled cavities in the brain depicted in **Figure 14.18**) and schizophrenic disturbance (Belger & Dichter, 2006; Shenton & Kubicki, 2009). Enlarged ventricles are assumed to reflect either the degeneration or failure to develop of nearby brain tissue. The significance of enlarged ventricles is hotly debated, however. Structural deterioration in the brain could be a contributing *cause* or a *consequence* of schizophrenia.

## The Neurodevelopmental Hypothesis

In recent years, several new lines of evidence have led to the emergence of the *neurodevelopmental hypothesis* of schizophrenia, which posits that schizophrenia is caused in part by various disruptions in the normal maturational processes of the brain before or at birth (Brown, 1999). According to this hypothesis, insults to the brain during sensitive phases of prenatal development or during birth can cause subtle neurological damage that elevates individuals' vulnerability to schizophrenia years later in adolescence and early adulthood (see **Figure 14.19**). What are the sources of these early insults to the brain? Thus far, research has mainly focused on viral infections or malnutrition during prenatal development and obstetrical complications during the birth process.

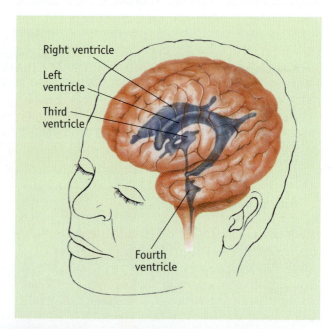

**Figure 14.18**

**Schizophrenia and the ventricles of the brain.** Cerebrospinal fluid (CSF) circulates around the brain and spinal cord. The hollow cavities in the brain filled with CSF are called *ventricles*. The four ventricles in the human brain are depicted here. Studies with modern brain-imaging techniques suggest that an association exists between enlarged ventricles in the brain and the occurrence of schizophrenic disturbance.

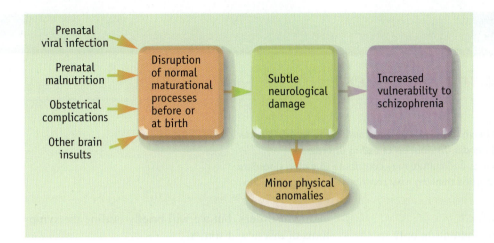

**Figure 14.19**

**The neurodevelopmental hypothesis of schizophrenia.** Research suggests that insults to the brain sustained during prenatal development or at birth may disrupt crucial maturational processes in the brain, resulting in subtle neurological damage that gradually becomes apparent as youngsters develop. This neurological damage is believed to increase both vulnerability to schizophrenia and the incidence of minor physical anomalies.

The evidence on viral infections has been building since Sarnoff Mednick and his colleagues (1988) discovered an elevated incidence of schizophrenia among the children of women who were in their second trimester of prenatal development during a 1957 influenza epidemic in Finland. Several subsequent studies in other locations have also found a link between exposure to influenza during pregnancy and increased prevalence of schizophrenia (Brown et al., 2004). Another study, which investigated the possible impact of prenatal malnutrition, found an elevated incidence of schizophrenia in a cohort of people who were prenatally exposed to a severe famine in 1944–45 because of a Nazi blockade of food deliveries in the Netherlands during World War II (Susser et al., 1996). A follow-up study of some schizophrenic patients exposed to this famine found increased brain abnormalities among the patients, as the neurodevelopmental hypothesis would predict (Hulshoff et al., 2000). Recent research has demonstrated that pregnant women exposed to extreme stress also have more offspring who eventually develop schizophrenic disorders (Malaspina et al., 2008). Other research has shown that schizophrenic patients are more likely than control subjects to have a history of obstetrical complications (Kelly et al., 2004; Murray & Bramon, 2005). Finally, research suggests that minor physical anomalies (slight anatomical defects of the head, hands, feet, and face) that would be consistent with prenatal neurological damage are more common among people with schizophrenia than in other people (McNeil, Cantor-Graae, & Ismail, 2000; Schiffman et al., 2002). Collectively, these diverse studies argue for a relationship between early neurological trauma and a predispostion to schizophrenia (Mednick et al., 1998).

**Expressed Emotion**

Studies of expressed emotion have primarily focused on how this element of family dynamics influences the *course* of schizophrenic illness after the onset of the disorder (Leff & Vaughn, 1985). *Expressed emotion (EE)* reflects the degree to which a relative of a schizophrenic patient displays highly critical or emotionally overinvolved attitudes toward the patient. Audio-taped interviews of relatives' communication are carefully evaluated for critical comments, hostility toward the patient, and excessive emotional involvement (overprotective, overconcerned attitudes) (Hooley, 2004).

Studies show that a family's expressed emotion is a good predictor of the course of a schizophrenic patient's illness (Hooley, 2007). After release from a hospital, patients who return to a family high in expressed emotion show relapse rates two to three times those of patients who return to a family low in expressed emotion (Hooley, 2009). Part of the problem for patients returning to homes high in expressed emotion is that their families are probably sources of stress rather than of social support (Cutting & Docherty, 2000). However, Rosenfarb et al. (1995) caution against placing all the blame on the families high in expressed emotion. They found that patients returning to high-EE homes exhibited more odd and disruptive behavior than patients returning to low-EE homes. Thus, the more critical, negative attitudes experienced by patients in high-EE homes may be caused in part by their own behavior.

**Precipitating Stress**

Many theories of schizophrenia assume that stress plays a role in triggering schizophrenic disorders (Walker & Tessner, 2008). According to this notion, various biological and psychological factors influence individuals' *vulnerability* to schizophrenia. High stress may then serve to precipitate a schizophrenic disorder in someone who is vulnerable. Research indicates that high stress can also trigger relapses in patients who have made progress toward recovery (Walker, Mittal, & Tessner, 2008).

# Understanding Eating Disorders

## LEARNING OBJECTIVES

- Describe the symptoms of anorexia nervosa, bulimia nervosa, and binge-eating disorder.
- Discuss the history, prevalence, and gender distribution of eating disorders.
- Explain how genetic factors, personality, and culture may contribute to eating disorders.
- Clarify how family dynamics and disturbed thinking may contribute to eating disorders.

*Answer the following "true" or "false."*

____ 1. Although they have attracted attention only in recent years, eating disorders have a long history and have always been fairly common.

____ 2. Eating disorders are universal problems found in virtually all cultures.

____ 3. People with anorexia nervosa are much more likely to recognize their eating behavior as pathological than people suffering from bulimia nervosa.

____ 4. The prevalence of eating disorders is twice as high in women as it is in men.

____ 5. The binge-and-purge syndrome seen in bulimia nervosa is not common in anorexia nervosa.

All five of these statements are false, as you will see in this Application. The psychological disorders that we discussed in the main body of the chapter have largely been recognized for centuries and generally are found in one form or another in all cultures and societies. Eating disorders, however, present a sharp contrast to this picture: They have only been recognized in recent decades, and initially they were largely confined to affluent, Westernized cultures (Russell, 1995; Szmukler & Patton, 1995). In spite of these fascinating differences, eating disorders have much in common with traditional forms of pathology.

## Types of Eating Disorders

Although most people don't seem to take eating disorders as seriously as other types of psychological disorders, you will see that they are dangerous and debilitating (Thompson, Roehrig, & Kinder, 2007). No psychological disorder is associated with a greater elevation in mortality (Striegel-Moore & Bulik, 2007). **Eating disorders are severe disturbances in eating behavior characterized by preoccupation with weight and unhealthy efforts to control weight.** The vast majority of cases consist of two sometimes overlapping syndromes: *anorexia nervosa* and *bulimia nervosa*. A third syndrome, called *binge-eating disorder*, is described in the appendix of DSM-IV as a potential new disorder, pending further study. We will devote most of our attention in this Application to the two established

eating disorders, but we will briefly outline the symptoms of this new disorder.

## Anorexia Nervosa

*Anorexia nervosa* **involves intense fear of gaining weight, disturbed body image, refusal to maintain normal weight, and dangerous measures to lose weight.** Two subtypes have been distinguished (Herzog & Delinsky, 2001). In *restricting type anorexia nervosa,* people drastically reduce their intake of food, sometimes literally starving themselves. In *binge-eating/purging type anorexia nervosa,* victims attempt to lose weight by forcing themselves to vomit after meals, by misusing laxatives and diuretics, and by engaging in excessive exercise.

Both types entail a disturbed body image. No matter how frail and emaciated the victims become, they insist that they are too fat. Their morbid fear of obesity means that they are never satisfied with their weight. If they gain a pound or two, they panic. The only thing that makes them happy is to lose more weight. The common result is a relentless decline in body weight—in fact, patients entering treatment for anorexia nervosa are typically 25%–30% below their normal weight (Hsu, 1990). Because of their disturbed body image, people suffering from anorexia generally do *not* appreciate the maladaptive quality of their behavior and rarely seek treatment on their own. They are typically coaxed or coerced into treatment by friends or family members who are alarmed by their appearance.

Anorexia nervosa eventually leads to a cascade of medical problems, including *amenorrhea* (a loss of menstrual cycles in women), gastrointestinal

**WEB LINK 14.8   The Alliance for Eating Disorders Awareness**

This site offers a great deal of information on eating disorders. Visitors can find statistics, suggested readings, information on symptoms and treatments, self-tests, success stories from people who have overcome their eating disorders, and links to other worthwhile websites.

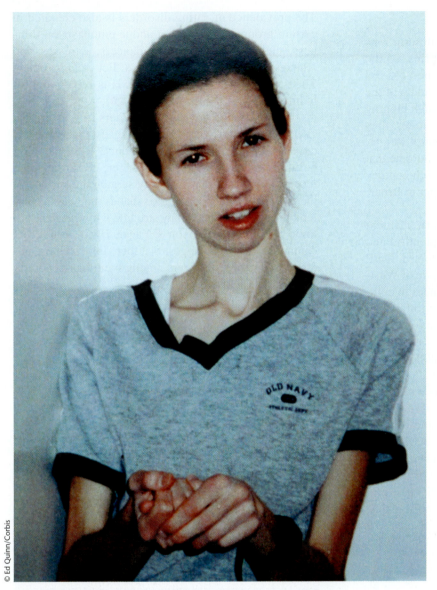

© Ed Quinn/Corbis

Eating disorders have become distressingly common among young women in Western cultures. No matter how frail they become, people suffering from anorexia insist that they are too fat.

about half of recently consumed food, and laxatives and diuretics have negligible impact on caloric intake, so people suffering from bulimia nervosa typically maintain a reasonably normal weight (Beumont, 2002; Kaye et al., 1993).

Medical problems associated with bulimia nervosa include cardiac arrythmias, dental problems, metabolic deficiencies, and gastrointestinal problems (Halmi, 2002, 2008). Bulimia often coexists with other psychological disturbances, including depression, anxiety disorders, and substance abuse (Hudson et al., 2007).

Obviously, bulimia nervosa shares many features with anorexia nervosa, such as a morbid fear of becoming obese, preoccupation with food, and rigid, maladaptive approaches to controlling weight that are grounded in naive all-or-none thinking. The close relationship between the disorders is demonstrated by the fact that many patients who initially develop one syndrome cross over to display the other syndrome (Tozzi et al., 2005). However, the syndromes also differ in crucial ways. First and foremost, bulimia is a less life-threatening condition. Second, although their weight and appearance usually is more "normal" than that seen in anorexia, people with bulimia are much more likely to recognize that their eating behavior is pathological and are more prone to recognize their need for treatment (Striegel-Moore, Silberstein, & Rodin, 1993; Guarda et al., 2007).

problems, low blood pressure, *osteoporosis* (a loss of bone density), and metabolic disturbances that can lead to cardiac arrest or circulatory collapse (Halmi, 2008; Walsh, 2003). Anorexia is a debilitating illness that leads to death in 5%–10% of patients (Steinhausen, 2002).

### Bulimia Nervosa

*Bulimia nervosa* **involves habitually engaging in out-of-control overeating followed by unhealthy compensatory efforts, such as self-induced vomiting, fasting, abuse of laxatives and diuretics, and excessive exercise.** The eating binges are usually carried out in secret and are followed by intense guilt and concern about gaining weight. These feelings motivate ill-advised strategies to undo the effects of the overeating. However, vomiting prevents the absorption of only

### Binge-Eating Disorder

*Binge-eating disorder* **involves distress-inducing eating binges that are not accompanied by the purging, fasting, and excessive exercise seen in bulimia.** Obviously, this syndrome resembles bulimia, but it is a less severe disorder. Still, this disorder creates great distress, as these people tend to be disgusted by their bodies and distraught about their overeating. People with binge-eating disorder are frequently overweight. Their excessive eating is often triggered by stress (Gluck, 2006). Research suggests that this comparatively mild syndrome may be more common than anorexia or bulimia (Hudson et al., 2007). Given the research that has been compiled since DSM-IV was released in 1994, it appears likely that binge-eating disorder will be recognized as an independent disorder in the forthcoming DSM-V (Striegel-Moore & Franko, 2008).

## History and Prevalence

Historians have been able to track down descriptions of anorexia nervosa that date back centuries, so the disorder is not entirely new, but anorexia nervosa did not become a *common* affliction until the middle of the 20th century (Vandereycken, 2002). Although binging and purging have a long history in some cultures, they were not part of a pathological effort to control weight, and bulimia nervosa appears to be a new syndrome that emerged gradually in the middle of the 20th century and was first recognized in the 1970s (Steiger & Bruce, 2009; Vandereycken, 2002).

Both disorders are a product of modern, affluent Western culture, where food is generally plentiful and the desirability of being thin is widely endorsed. Until recently, these problems were not seen outside of Western cultures (Hoek, 2002). However, advances in communication have exported Western culture to farflung corners of the globe, and eating disorders have started showing up in many non-Western societies, especially affluent Asian countries (Becker & Fay, 2006; Lee & Katzman, 2002).

A huge gender gap exists in the likelihood of developing eating disorders. About 90%–95% of individuals who are treated for anorexia nervosa and bulimia nervosa are female (Thompson & Kinder, 2003). This staggering discrepancy appears to be a result of cultural pressures rather than biological factors (Smolak & Murnen, 2001). Western standards of attractiveness emphasize being slender more for females than for males, and women generally experience heavier pressure to be physically attractive than men do (Strahan et al., 2008).

The prevalence of eating disorders is also elevated in certain groups that place an undue emphasis on thinness, such as fashion models, dancers, actresses, and athletes. Eating disorders mostly afflict *young* women. The typical age of onset for anorexia is 14–18, and for bulimia it is 15–21 (see **Figure 14.20**).

How common are eating disorders in Western societies? Studies of young women suggest that about 1% develop anorexia nervosa and about 2%–3% develop bulimia nervosa (Anderson & Yager, 2005). In some respects, these figures may only scratch the surface of the problem. Evidence suggests that as many as 20% of female college students may struggle with transient bulimic symptoms (Anderson & Yager, 2005). And recent community surveys suggest that there may be more undiagnosed eating disorders among men than generally appreciated (Hudson et al., 2007).

## Etiology of Eating Disorders

Like other types of psychological disorders, eating disorders are caused by multiple determinants that work interactively.

### Genetic Vulnerability

The scientific evidence is not nearly as strong or complete for eating disorders as it is for many other types of psychopathology (such as anxiety, mood, and schizophrenic disorders), but some people may inherit a genetic vulnerability to these problems (Slof-Op't Landt et al., 2005). Studies show that relatives of patients with eating disorders have elevated rates of anorexia nervosa

**Figure 14.20**

**Age of onset for anorexia nervosa.** Eating disorders emerge primarily during adolescence, as these data for anorexia nervosa show. This graph depicts how age of onset was distributed in a sample of 166 female patients from Minnesota. As you can see, over half experienced the onset of their illness before the age of 20, with vulnerability clearly peaking between the ages of 15 and 19. (Data from Lucas, et al., 1991)

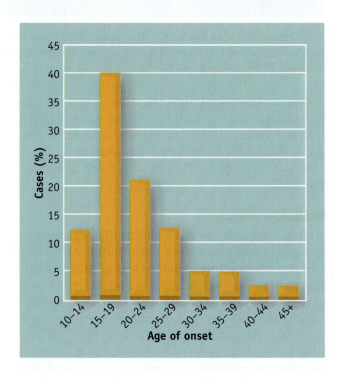

and bulimia nervosa (Bulik, 2004). And studies of female twins report higher concordance rates for identical twins than fraternal twins, suggesting that a genetic predisposition may be at work (Steiger, Bruce, & Israël, 2003).

## Personality Factors

Strober (1995) has suggested that genetic factors may exert their influence indirectly by fostering certain personality traits that make people more vulnerable to eating disorders. Although there are innumerable exceptions, victims of anorexia nervosa tend to be obsessive, rigid, neurotic, and emotionally restrained, whereas victims of bulimia nervosa tend to be impulsive, overly sensitive, and low in self-esteem (Anderluh, Tchanturia & Rabe-Hesketh, 2003; Wonderlich, 2002). Recent research also suggests that perfectionism is a risk factor for anorexia (Steiger & Bruce, 2009).

## Cultural Values

The contribution of cultural values to the increased prevalence of eating disorders can hardly be overestimated (Anderson-Fye & Becker, 2004; Striegel-Moore & Bulik, 2007). In Western society, young women are socialized to believe that they must be attractive and that to be attractive they must be as thin as the actresses and fashion models that dominate the media (Levine & Harrison, 2004). Thanks to this cultural milieu, many young women are dissatisfied with their weight because the societal ideals promoted by the media are unattainable for most of them (Thompson & Stice, 2001).

Unfortunately, in a small portion of these women, the pressure to be thin, in combination with genetic vulnerability, family pathology, and other factors, leads to unhealthy efforts to control weight.

## The Role of the Family

Many theorists emphasize how family dynamics can contribute to the development of anorexia nervosa and bulimia nervosa in young women (Haworth-Hoeppner, 2000). The principal issue appears to be that some mothers contribute to eating disorders simply by endorsing society's message that "you can never be too thin" and by modeling unhealthy dieting behaviors of their own (Francis & Birch, 2005). In conjunction with media pressures, this role modeling leads many daughters to internalize the idea that the thinner you are, the more attractive you are.

## Cognitive Factors

Many theorists emphasize the role of disturbed thinking in the etiology of eating disorders (Williamson et al., 2001). For example, anorexic patients' typical belief that they are fat when they are really wasting away is a dramatic illustration of how thinking goes awry. Patients with eating disorders display rigid, all-or-none thinking and many maladaptive beliefs, such as "I must be thin to be accepted," "If I am not in complete control, I will lose all control," and "If I gain one pound, I'll go on to gain enormous weight." Additional research is needed to determine whether distorted thinking is a *cause* or merely a *symptom* of eating disorders.

## KEY IDEAS

### Abnormal Behavior: Concepts and Controversies

● The medical model views abnormal behavior as a disease. There are some problems with the medical model, but the disease analogy is useful. Three criteria are used in deciding whether people suffer from psychological disorders: deviance, personal distress, and maladaptive behavior. Often, it is difficult to draw a clear line between normality and abnormality.

● DSM-IV is the official psychodiagnostic classification system in the United States, although work has begun on the next edition (DSM-V). This system asks for information about patients on five axes. Some critics have questioned the categorical approach used by the DSM system and the wisdom of labeling everyday problems as mental disorders. Psychological disorders are more common than widely believed, with a lifetime prevalence of roughly 44%. The economic costs of mental illness are enormous.

### Anxiety Disorders

● The anxiety disorders include generalized anxiety disorder, phobic disorder, panic disorder, and obsessive-compulsive disorder (OCD). These disorders have been linked to genetic predisposition, temperament, anxiety sensitivity, and neurochemical abnormalities in the brain.

● Many anxiety responses, especially phobias, may be caused by classical conditioning and maintained by operant conditioning. Cognitive theorists maintain that some people are vulnerable to anxiety disorders because they see threat everywhere. Stress may also contribute to the onset of these disorders.

### Somatoform Disorders

● Somatoform disorders include somatization disorder, conversion disorder, and hypochondriasis. These disorders often emerge in people with highly suggestible, histrionic personalities, who think irrationally about their health. Somatoform disorders may be learned avoidance strategies reinforced by attention and sympathy.

### Dissociative Disorders

● Dissociative disorders include dissociative amnesia, dissociative fugue, and dissociative identity disorder (DID). These disorders appear to be uncommon, although there is some controversy about the prevalence of DID. Stress and childhood trauma may contribute to DID, but overall, the causes of dissociative disorders are not well understood.

### Mood Disorders

● The principal mood disorders are major depressive disorder and bipolar disorder. Mood disorders are associated with an elevated risk for suicide. People vary in their genetic vulnerability to mood disorders, which are accompanied by changes in neurochemical activity in the brain. Reduced hippocampal volume and suppressed neurogenesis may be factors in depression.

● Cognitive models posit that a pessimistic explanatory style, rumination, and other types of negative thinking contribute to depression. Depression is often rooted in interpersonal inadequacies, as people who lack social finesse often have difficulty acquiring life's reinforcers. Mood disorders are sometimes stress related.

### Schizophrenic Disorders

● Schizophrenic disorders are characterized by deterioration of adaptive behavior, irrational thought, distorted perception, and disturbed mood. Schizophrenic disorders are classified as para-

noid, catatonic, disorganized, or undifferentiated. The distinction between positive and negative symptoms has proven useful, but it has not yielded an effective new classification scheme. The prognosis for schizophrenia is poor, as only about 20% of patients enjoy a full recovery.

● Research has linked schizophrenia to genetic vulnerability, changes in neurotransmitter activity, and enlarged ventricles in the brain. The neurodevelopmental hypothesis attributes schizophrenia to disruptions of normal maturational processes in the brain before or at birth. Patients who return to homes high in expressed emotion tend to have elevated relapse rates. Precipitating stress may also contribute to the emergence of schizophrenia.

### Application: Understanding Eating Disorders

● The principal eating disorders are anorexia nervosa and bulimia nervosa. Binge-eating disorder is a new diagnostic syndrome that has been proposed. Anorexia and bulimia are both associated with other psychopathology, and both lead to a cascade of medical problems. Eating disorders appear to be a product of modern, affluent, Westernized culture.

● Females account for 90%–95% of eating disorders. The typical age of onset is roughly 15 to 20. There appears to be a genetic vulnerability to eating disorders, which may be mediated by heritable personality traits. Cultural pressures on young women to be thin clearly help foster eating disorders. Some theorists emphasize how family dynamics and disturbed thinking can contribute to the development of eating disorders.

## KEY TERMS

Agoraphobia   p. 448
Anorexia nervosa   p. 470
Anxiety disorders   p. 446
Binge-eating disorder   p. 471
Bipolar disorder   p. 457
Bulimia nervosa   p. 471
Catatonic schizophrenia
   p. 465
Concordance rate   p. 458
Conversion disorder   p. 451
Delusions   p. 463
Diagnosis   p. 442
Disorganized schizophrenia
   p. 465
Dissociative amnesia   p. 453
Dissociative disorders   p. 453
Dissociative fugue   p. 453
Dissociative identity disorder
   (DID)   p. 454
Eating disorders   p. 470
Epidemiology   p. 445
Etiology   p. 442
Generalized anxiety disorder
   p. 447
Hallucinations   p. 464
Hypochondriasis   p. 452
Major depressive disorder
   p. 456
Manic-depressive disorder
   p. 457
Medical model   p. 441
Mood disorders   p. 455
Multiple-personality disorder
   p. 454
Neurotransmitters   p. 449
Obsessive-compulsive
   disorder (OCD)   p. 448
Panic disorder   p. 447
Paranoid schizophrenia
   p. 464
Phobic disorder   p. 447
Prevalence   p. 445
Prognosis   p. 442
Schizophrenic disorders
   p. 463
Somatization disorder   p. 451
Somatoform disorders
   p. 451
Undifferentiated
   schizophrenia   p. 465

## KEY PEOPLE

Nancy Andreasen
   pp. 465–466
Susan Nolen-Hoeksema
   pp. 457, 461

Martin Seligman
   p. 449–450, 461
Thomas Szasz   p. 441

## QUESTIONS

1. Sergio has just entered treatment for bipolar disorder, and he is informed that most patients respond to drug treatment within a month. This information represents:
   **a.** a prognosis.
   **b.** an etiology.
   **c.** a histology.
   **d.** a concordance.

2. Although Sue always feels high levels of dread, worry, and anxiety, she still meets her daily responsibilities. Sue's behavior:
   **a.** should not be considered abnormal, since her adaptive functioning is not impaired.
   **b.** should not be considered abnormal, since everyone sometimes experiences worry and anxiety.
   **c.** can still be considered abnormal, since she feels great personal distress.
   **d.** both a and b.

3. Recent epidemiological studies have found that the most common types of psychological disorders are:
   **a.** mood disorders and anxiety disorders.
   **b.** anxiety disorders and schizophrenic disorders.
   **c.** substance-use disorders and anxiety disorders.
   **d.** substance-use disorders and somatoform disorders.

4. People who repeatedly perform senseless rituals to overcome their anxiety are said to have a(n):
   **a.** generalized anxiety disorder.
   **b.** manic disorder.
   **c.** obsessive-compulsive disorder.
   **d.** phobic disorder.

5. If a person has a paralyzed arm for which no organic basis can be found, she probably has:
   **a.** a conversion disorder.
   **b.** paralytic hypochondriasis.
   **c.** a dissociative disorder.
   **d.** a schizophrenic disorder.

6. After several months during which he was always gloomy and dejected, Mario has suddenly perked up. He feels elated and energetic and works around the clock on a writing project. He has also started to bet heavily on sporting events over the Internet, which he never did previously. Mario's behavior is consistent with:
   **a.** schizophrenia.
   **b.** obsessive-compulsive disorder.
   **c.** bipolar disorder.
   **d.** dissociative identity disorder.

7. A concordance rate indicates:
   **a.** the percentage of twin pairs or other relatives that exhibit the same disorder.
   **b.** the percentage of people with a given disorder that are currently receiving treatment.

   **c.** the prevalence of a given disorder in the general population.
   **d.** the rate of cure for a given disorder.

8. Which of the following would be a negative symptom of schizophrenia?
   **a.** auditory hallucinations
   **b.** delusions of persecution
   **c.** having virtually no friendships
   **d.** delusions of grandeur

9. Jamaal, who works as a projectionist at the local theater, is convinced that everyone is out to get him. He is sure that his phone is tapped by ruthless enemies. He thinks that most of the people in the theater each night are there to spy on him. Worse yet, he is sure people follow him home from work every night. Jamaal is probably suffering from:
   **a.** paranoid schizophrenia.
   **b.** catatonic schizophrenia.
   **c.** bipolar disorder.
   **d.** dissociative fugue.

10. About _____ % of patients with eating disorders are female.
    **a.** 40
    **b.** 50–60
    **c.** 75
    **d.** 90–95

## ANSWERS

1. a   Page 442
2. c   Page 442
3. c   Pages 445–446
4. c   Page 448
5. a   Pages 451–452
6. c   Pages 456–458
7. a   Pages 458–459
8. c   Pages 465–466
9. a   Pages 464–465
10. d   Page 472

## Personal Explorations Workbook

Go to the *Personal Explorations Workbook* in the back of your textbook for exercises that can enhance your self-understanding in relation to issues raised in this chapter. **Exercise 14.1** *Self-Assessment: Manifest Anxiety Scale* **Exercise 14.2** *Self-Reflection: What Are Your Attitudes on Mental Illness?*

CourseMate

Access an interactive eBook, chapter-specific interactive learning tools, including Personal Explorations, Recommended Readings, Critical Thinking Exercises, flashcards, quizzes, videos and more in your Psychology CourseMate, available at **www.cengagebrain.com/shop/ISBN/1111186634**.

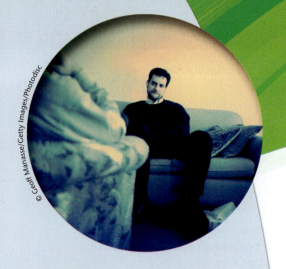

# Psychotherapy

What do you picture when you hear the term *psychotherapy*? If you're like most people, you probably envision a troubled patient lying on a couch in a therapist's office, with the therapist asking penetrating questions and providing sage advice. Typically, people believe that psychotherapy is only for those who are "sick" and that therapists have special powers that allow them to "see through" their clients. It is also widely believed that therapy requires years of deep probing into a client's innermost secrets. Many people further assume that therapists routinely tell their patients how to lead their lives. Like most stereotypes, this picture of psychotherapy is a mixture of fact and fiction, as you'll see in the upcoming pages.

In this chapter, we take a down-to-earth look at the process of *psychotherapy,* using the term in its broadest sense to refer to all the diverse approaches to the treatment of psychological problems. We start by discussing some general questions about the provision of treatment. Who seeks therapy? What kinds of professionals provide treatment? How many types of therapy are there? After considering these general issues, we examine some of the more widely used approaches to treating psychological maladies, analyzing their goals, techniques, and effectiveness. The Application at the end of the chapter focuses on practical issues involved in finding a therapist, in case you ever have to advise someone about seeking help.

# The Elements of the Treatment Process

**LEARNING OBJECTIVES**

- Identify the three major categories of therapy.
- Discuss why people do or do not seek psychotherapy.
- Describe the various types of mental health professionals involved in the provision of therapy.

Today people have a bewildering array of psychotherapy approaches to choose from. In fact, the immense diversity of therapeutic treatments makes defining the concept of *psychotherapy* difficult. After organizing a landmark conference that brought together many of the world's leading authorities on psychotherapy, Jeffrey Zeig (1987) commented, "I do not believe there is any capsule definition of psychotherapy on which the 26 presenters could agree" (p. xix). In lieu of a definition, we can identify a few basic elements that the various approaches to treatment have in common. All psychotherapies involve a helping relationship (the treatment) between a professional with special training (the therapist) and another person in need of help (the client). As we look at each of these three elements, you'll see the diverse nature of modern psychotherapy.

## Treatments: How Many Types Are There?

In their efforts to help people, mental health professionals use many methods of treatment, including discussion, emotional support, persuasion, conditioning procedures, relaxation training, role playing, drug therapy, biofeedback, and group therapy. Some therapists also use a variety of less conventional procedures, such as rebirthing, poetry therapy, and primal therapy. No one knows exactly how many approaches to treatment there are. One expert (Kazdin, 1994) estimates that there may be over 400 distinct types of psychotherapy! Fortunately, we can impose some order on this chaos. As varied as therapists' procedures are, approaches to treatment can be classified into three major categories:

1. *Insight therapies.* Insight therapy is "talk therapy" in the tradition of Freud's psychoanalysis. This is probably the approach to treatment that you envision when you think of psychotherapy. In insight therapies, clients engage in complex verbal interactions with their therapists. The goal in these discussions is to pursue increased insight regarding the nature of the client's difficulties and to sort through possible solutions. Insight therapy can be conducted with an individual or with a group.

2. *Behavior therapies.* Behavior therapies are based on the principles of learning and conditioning, which were introduced in Chapter 2. Instead of emphasizing personal insights, behavior therapists make direct efforts to alter problematic responses (phobic behaviors, for instance) and maladaptive habits (drug use, for instance). Behavior therapists work on changing clients' overt behaviors. They use different procedures for different kinds of problems.

3. *Biomedical therapies.* Biomedical approaches to therapy involve interventions into a person's physiological functioning. The most widely used procedures are drug therapy and electroconvulsive therapy. As the name bio*medical* therapies suggests, these treatments have traditionally been provided only by physicians with a medical degree (usually psychiatrists). This situation is changing, however, as psychologists have been campaigning for prescription privileges (Price, 2008; Welsh, 2003). The chief rationale for this campaign is that many rural areas and underserved populations have inadequate access to psychiatrists (Ax et al., 2008). To date psychologists have obtained prescription authority in two states (New Mexico and Louisiana), and they have made legislative progress toward this goal in many other states (Long, 2005; Munsey, 2008). Although some psychologists have expressed concerns about the wisdom of pursuing the right to prescribe medication, the movement seems to be gathering momentum (Lavoie & Barone, 2006; Stuart & Heiby, 2007).

In this chapter we examine approaches to therapy that fall into each of these three categories. Although different methods are used in each, the three major classes of treatment are not entirely incompatible. For example, a client being seen in insight therapy may also be given medication.

## Clients: Who Seeks Therapy?

In the therapeutic triad (therapists, treatments, clients), the greatest diversity is seen among the clients. According to the 1999 U.S. Surgeon General's report on mental health (U.S. Department of Health and Human Services, 1999), about 15% of the U.S. population use mental health services in a given year. These people bring to therapy the full range of human problems: anxiety, depression, unsatisfactory interpersonal relations, troublesome habits, poor self-control, low self-esteem, marital conflicts, self-doubt, a sense of emptiness, and feelings of personal stagnation. The two most common presenting problems are excessive anxiety and depression (Narrow et al., 1993).

Interestingly, people often hold off for many years before finally seeking treatment for their psychological problems (Kessler, Olfson, & Berglund, 1998). One large-scale study (Wang, Berglund et al., 2005) found that the median delay in seeking treatment was 6 years for bipolar disorder and for drug dependence, 8 years for depression, 9 years for generalized anxiety disorder, and 10 years for panic disorder! **Figure 15.1** summarizes data from the same study on the percentage of people with various disorders who seek treatment within the first year after the onset of the disorder. As you can see, the figures are surprisingly low for most disorders.

A client in treatment does *not* necessarily have an identifiable psychological disorder. Some people seek professional help for everyday problems (career decisions, for instance) or vague feelings of discontent (Strupp, 1996). One surprising finding in recent research has been that only about half of the people who use mental health services in a given year meet the criteria for a full-fledged mental disorder (Kessler et al., 2005b). This finding raised concern that valuable treatment resources might be "misallocated," but a follow-up study found that most of the people seeking treatment without a full-blown disorder *did* have significant mental health issues (Druss et al., 2007). Many had a history of mental illness but were in remission at the time of the study; others were grappling with severe stress. Only about 8% of the people seeking treatment appeared to be relatively free of psychiatric problems.

People vary considerably in their willingness to seek psychotherapy. One study found that even when people perceive a need for professional assistance, only 59% actually seek professional help (Mojtabai, Olfson, & Mechanic, 2002). As you can see in **Figure 15.2**, women are more likely than men to receive treatment, and whites are more likely than blacks or Hispanics to obtain therapy. Treatment is also more likely when people have medical insurance and when they have more education (Olfson et al., 2002; Wang, Lane et al., 2005). *Unfortunately, it appears that many people who need therapy don't receive it* (Kessler et al., 2005b). People who could benefit from therapy do not seek it for a variety of reasons. Lack of health insurance and cost concerns appear to be major barriers to obtaining needed care for many people. According to the Surgeon General's report, the biggest roadblock is the "stigma surrounding the receipt of mental health treatment." Unfortunately, many people equate seeking therapy with admitting personal weakness.

## Therapists: Who Provides Professional Treatment?

Friends and relatives may provide excellent advice about personal problems, but their assistance does not qualify as therapy. Psychotherapy refers to *professional* treatment by someone with special training. However, a common source of confusion about psychotherapy is the variety of "helping professions" available to offer assistance. Psychology and psychiatry are the principal professions involved in psychotherapy, providing the lion's share of mental health care. However, therapy is also provided by social workers, psychiatric nurses, and counselors, as outlined in **Figure 15.3**.

**Figure 15.1**

**Treatment seeking for various disorders.** In a study of the extent to which people seek treatment for psychological disorders, Wang, Berglund et al. (2005) found that only a minority of people promptly pursue treatment for their disorder. The data summarized here show the percentage of people who obtain professional treatment within the first year after the onset of various disorders. The percentages vary depending on the disorder, but all the figures are surprisingly low.

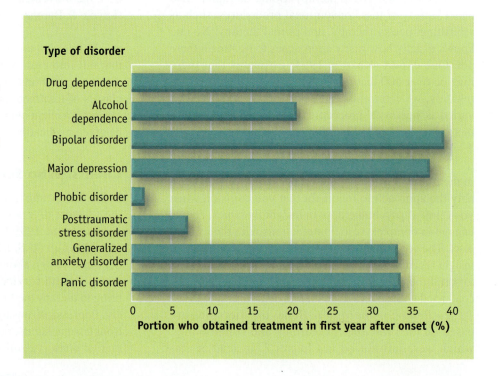

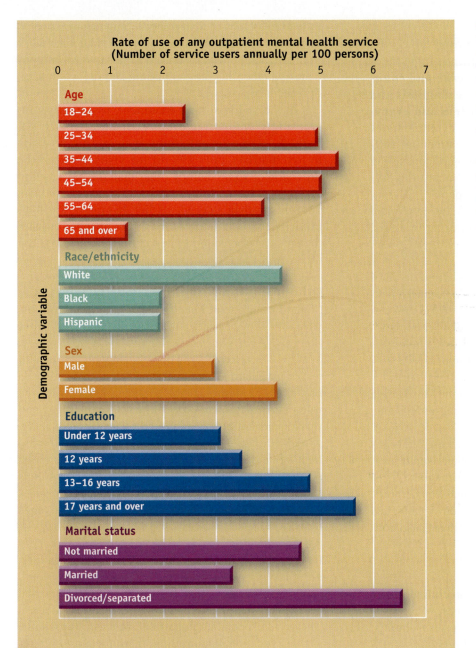

**Figure 15.2**

**Therapy utilization rates.** Olfson and colleagues (2002) gathered data on the use of nonhospital outpatient mental health services in the United States in relation to various demographic variables. In regard to marital status, utilization rates are particularly high among those who are divorced or separated. The use of therapy is greater among those who have more education and, in terms of age, utilization peaks in the 35–44 bracket. Females are more likely to pursue therapy than males are, but utilization rates are extremely low among ethnic minorities.

| Types of Therapists | | | |
|---|---|---|---|
| **Title** | **Degree** | **Years beyond bachelor's degree** | **Typical roles and activities** |
| Clinical or counseling psychologist | Ph.D. Psy.D. Ed.D. | 5–7 | Diagnosis, psychological testing, insight and behavior therapy |
| Psychiatrist | M.D. | 8 | Diagnosis; insight, behavior, and biomedical therapy |
| Social worker | M.S.W. | 2 | Insight and behavior therapy, family therapy, helping patients return to the community |
| Psychiatric nurse | B.S., B.A., M.A. | 0–2 | Inpatient care, insight and behavior therapy |
| Counselor | M.A., M.S. | 2 | Insight and behavior therapy, working primarily with everyday adjustment and marital and career issues |

**Figure 15.3**

**The principal mental health professions.** Psychotherapists come from a variety of professional backgrounds. This chart provides an overview of various types of therapists' education and typical professional activities.

## Psychologists

Two types of psychologists may provide therapy, although the distinction between them is more theoretical than real. *Clinical psychologists* and *counseling psychologists* specialize in the diagnosis and treatment of psychological disorders and everyday behavioral problems. In theory, the training of clinical psychologists emphasizes treatment of full-fledged disorders, whereas the training of counseling psychologists is slanted toward treatment of everyday adjustment problems in normal people. In practice, however, there is great overlap between clinical and counseling psychologists in training, in skills, and in the clientele they serve (Morgan & Cohen, 2008).

Both types of psychologists must earn a doctoral degree (Ph.D., Psy.D., or Ed.D.). A doctorate in psychology requires five to seven years of training beyond a bachelor's degree. The process of gaining admission to a Ph.D. program in clinical psychology is highly competitive (about as competitive as for medical school). Psychologists receive most of their training on university campuses, although they also serve a one- to two-year internship in a clinical setting, such as a hospital.

In providing therapy, psychologists use either insight or behavioral approaches. In comparison to psychiatrists, they are more likely to use behavioral techniques and less likely to use psychoanalytic methods. Clinical and counseling psychologists do psychological testing as well as psychotherapy, and many also conduct research.

## Psychiatrists

*Psychiatrists* are physicians who specialize in the treatment of psychological disorders. Many psychiatrists also treat everyday behavioral problems. However, in comparison to psychologists, psychiatrists devote more time to relatively severe disorders (schizophrenia, mood disorders) and less time to everyday marital, family, job, and school problems. Psychiatrists have an M.D. degree. Their graduate training requires four years of course work in medical school and a four-year apprenticeship in a residency at an approved hospital. Their psychotherapy training occurs during their residency, since the required course work in medical school is essentially the same for all students, whether they are going into surgery, pediatrics, or psychiatry.

In their provision of treatment, psychiatrists increasingly emphasize drugs (Olfson et al., 2002). Indeed, in one recent study of over 14,000 visits to psychiatrists, only 29% of the visits involved the provision of some therapy other than the prescription and management of medications (Mojtabai & Olfson, 2008). Less than a decade earlier that figure was 44% of visits, so psychiatrists clearly are abandoning talk therapies and behavioral interventions in favor of drug treatments.

## Other Mental Health Professionals

Several other mental health professions also provide psychotherapy services. In hospitals and other institutions, *psychiatric social workers* and *psychiatric nurses* often work as part of a treatment team with a psychologist or psychiatrist. Psychiatric nurses, who may have a bachelor's or master's degree in their field, play a large role in hospital inpatient treatment. Psychiatric social workers generally have a master's degree and typically work with patients and their families to ease the patient's integration back into the community. Although social workers have traditionally worked in hospitals and social service agencies, many are licensed as independent, private practitioners who provide a wide range of therapeutic services.

Many kinds of *counselors* also provide therapeutic services. Counselors are usually found working in schools, colleges, and human service agencies (youth centers, geriatric centers, family planning centers, and so forth). Counselors typically have a master's degree. They often specialize in particular types of problems, such as vocational counseling, marital counseling, rehabilitation counseling, and drug counseling. Like social workers, many are licensed as independent, private practitioners who provide diverse services for a diverse clientele.

Although clear differences exist among the helping professions in education and training, their roles in the treatment process overlap considerably. In this chapter, we refer to psychologists or psychiatrists as needed, but otherwise we use the terms *clinician*, *therapist*, and *mental health professional* to refer to psychotherapists of all kinds, regardless of their professional degree.

Now that we have discussed the basic elements in psychotherapy, we can examine specific approaches to treatment in terms of their goals, procedures, and effectiveness. We begin with a few representative insight therapies.

**WEB LINK 15.1  Online Dictionary of Mental Health**

This thematically arranged "dictionary" comprises diverse links involving many forms of psychotherapy, the treatment of psychological disorders, and general issues of mental health. It is sponsored by the Centre for Psychotherapeutic Studies at the University of Sheffield's Medical School in the UK.

# Insight Therapies

## LEARNING OBJECTIVES

- Understand the logic of psychoanalysis, and describe the techniques used to probe the unconscious.
- Explain interpretation, resistance, and transference in psychoanalysis.
- Describe therapeutic climate and process in client-centered therapy.
- Discuss new approaches to insight therapy inspired by positive psychology.

- Describe how group therapy is generally conducted.
- Summarize evidence on the efficacy of insight therapies.
- Clarify the role of common factors in insight therapy.
- Review both sides of the recovered memories controversy.

Many schools of thought exist as to how to do insight therapy. Therapists with different theoretical orientations use different methods to pursue different kinds of insights. What these varied approaches have in common is that *insight therapies* **involve verbal interactions intended to enhance clients' self-knowledge and thus promote healthful changes in personality and behavior.** Although there may be hundreds of insight therapies, the leading eight or ten approaches appear to account for the lion's share of treatment. In this section, we delve into psychoanalysis, client-centered therapy, treatments growing out of positive psychology, and group therapy.

## Psychoanalysis

Sigmund Freud worked as a psychotherapist for almost 50 years in Vienna. Through a painstaking process of trial and error, he developed innovative techniques for the treatment of psychological disorders and distress. His system of *psychoanalysis* came to dominate psychiatry for many decades. Although the dominance of psychoanalysis has eroded in recent decades, a diverse array of psychoanalytic approaches to therapy continue to evolve and remain influential today (Gabbard, 2005; McWilliams & Weinberger, 2003; Ursano, Sonnenberg, & Lazar, 2008).

*Psychoanalysis* **is an insight therapy that emphasizes the recovery of unconscious conflicts, motives, and defenses through techniques such as free association, dream analysis, and transference.**

National Library of Medicine

**Sigmund Freud**

To appreciate the logic of psychoanalysis, we have to look at Freud's thinking about the roots of mental disorders. Freud treated mostly anxiety-dominated disturbances, such as phobic, panic, obsessive-compulsive, and conversion disorders, which were then called *neuroses*. He believed that neurotic problems are caused by unconscious conflicts left over from early childhood. As explained in Chapter 2, he thought that these inner conflicts involve battles among the id, ego, and super-

ego, usually over sexual and aggressive impulses. Freud theorized that people depend on defense mechanisms to avoid confronting these conflicts, which remain hidden in the depths of the unconscious. However, he noted that defensive maneuvers often lead to self-defeating behavior. Furthermore, he asserted that defenses tend to be only partially successful in alleviating anxiety, guilt, and other distressing emotions. With this model in mind, let's take a look at the therapeutic procedures used in psychoanalysis.

### Probing the Unconscious

Given Freud's assumptions, we can see that the logic of psychoanalysis is very simple. The analyst attempts to probe the murky depths of the unconscious to discover the unresolved conflicts causing the client's neurotic behavior. In a sense, the analyst functions as a psychological detective. In this effort to explore the unconscious, he or she relies on two techniques: free association and dream analysis.

In *free association,* **clients spontaneously express their thoughts and feelings exactly as they occur, with as little censorship as possible.** Clients lie on a couch so they will be better able to let their minds drift freely. In free associating, clients expound on anything that comes to mind, regardless of how trivial, silly, or embarrassing it might be. Gradually, most clients begin to let everything pour out without conscious censorship. The analyst studies these free associations for clues about what is going on in the unconscious.

In *dream analysis,* **the therapist interprets the symbolic meaning of the client's dreams.** For Freud, dreams were the "royal road to the unconscious," the most direct means of access to patients' innermost conflicts, wishes, and impulses. Clients are encouraged and trained to remember their dreams, which they describe in therapy. The therapist then analyzes the symbolism in these dreams to interpret their meaning.

To better illustrate these matters, let's look at an actual case treated through psychoanalysis (adapted from Greenson, 1967, pp. 40–41). Mr. N was troubled by an unsatisfactory marriage. He claimed to love his wife, but he preferred sexual relations with prostitutes. Mr. N reported that his parents also endured lifelong marital difficulties. His childhood conflicts about their relationship appeared to be related to his problems. Both dream analysis and free association can be seen in the following description of a session in Mr. N's treatment:

*Mr. N reports a fragment of a dream. All that he can remember is that he is waiting for a red traffic light to change when he feels that someone has bumped into him from behind. . . . The associations led to Mr. N's love of cars, especially sports cars. He loved the sensation, in particular, of whizzing by those fat, old, expensive cars. . . . His father always hinted that he had been a great athlete, but he never substantiated it. . . . Mr. N doubted whether his father could really perform. His father would flirt with a waitress in a cafe or make sexual remarks about women passing by, but he seemed to be showing off. If he were really sexual, he wouldn't resort to that.*

As is characteristic of free association, Mr. N's train of thought meanders about with little direction. Nonetheless, clues about his unconscious conflicts are apparent. What did Mr. N's therapist extract from this session? The therapist saw sexual overtones in the dream fragment, where Mr. N was bumped from behind. The therapist also inferred that Mr. N had a competitive orientation toward his father, based on the free association about whizzing by fat, old, expensive cars. As you can see, analysts must *interpret* their clients' dreams and free associations. This is a critical process throughout psychoanalysis.

## Interpretation

**Interpretation involves the therapist's attempts to explain the inner significance of the client's thoughts, feelings, memories, and behaviors.** Contrary to popular belief, analysts do not interpret everything, and they generally don't try to dazzle clients with startling revelations. Instead, analysts move forward inch by inch, offering interpretations that should be just out of the client's own reach (Samberg & Marcus, 2005). Mr. N's therapist eventually offered the following interpretations to his client:

*I said to Mr. N near the end of the hour that I felt he was struggling with his feelings about his father's sexual life. He seemed to be saying that his father was sexually not a very potent man. . . . He also recalls that he once found a packet of condoms under his father's pillow when he was an adolescent and he thought "My father must be going to prostitutes." I then intervened and pointed out that the condoms under his father's pillow seemed to indicate more obviously that his father used the condoms with his mother, who slept in the same bed.*

© Bruce Ayres/Stone/Getty Images

In psychoanalysis, the therapist encourages the client to reveal thoughts, feelings, dreams, and memories that can then be interpreted in relation to the client's current problems.

*However, Mr. N wanted to believe his wish-fulfilling fantasy: mother doesn't want sex with father and father is not very potent. The patient was silent and the hour ended.*

As you may already have guessed, the therapist has concluded that Mr. N's difficulties are rooted in an Oedipal complex (see Chapter 2). Mr. N has unresolved sexual feelings toward his mother and hostile feelings about his father. These unconscious conflicts, which are rooted in his childhood, are distorting his intimate relations as an adult.

## Resistance

How would you expect Mr. N to respond to his therapist's suggestion that he was in competition with his father for the sexual attention of his mother? Obviously, most clients would have great difficulty accepting such an interpretation. Freud fully expected clients to display some resistance to therapeutic efforts. **Resistance involves largely unconscious defensive maneuvers intended to hinder the progress of therapy.** Resistance is assumed to be an inevitable part of the psychoanalytic process (Samberg & Marcus, 2005). Why do clients try to resist the helping process? Because they don't want to face up to the painful, disturbing conflicts that they

**WEB LINK 15.2  The American Psychoanalytic Association**

The site for this professional organization provides a great deal of useful information about psychoanalytic approaches to treatment. The resources include news releases, background information on psychoanalysis, an engine for literature searches, and a bookstore.

have buried in their unconscious. Although they have sought help, they are reluctant to confront their real problems.

Resistance may take many forms. Patients may show up late for their sessions, merely pretend to engage in free association, or express hostility toward the therapist. For instance, Mr. N's therapist noted that after the session just described, "The next day he began by telling me that he was furious with me." Analysts use a variety of strategies to deal with their clients' resistance. Often, a key consideration is the handling of *transference*, which we consider next.

## Transference

*Transference* **occurs when clients start relating to their therapists in ways that mimic critical relationships in their lives.** Thus, a client might start relating to a therapist as if the therapist were an overprotective mother, rejecting brother, or passive spouse. In a sense, the client *transfers* conflicting feelings about important people onto the therapist. For instance, in his treatment, Mr. N transferred some of the competitive hostility he felt toward his father onto his analyst.

Psychoanalysts often encourage transference so that clients begin to reenact relations with crucial people in the context of therapy. These reenactments can help bring repressed feelings and conflicts to the surface, allowing the client to work through them. The therapist's handling of transference is complicated and difficult because transference may arouse confusing, highly charged emotions in the client.

Undergoing psychoanalysis is not easy. It can be a slow, painful process of self-examination that routinely requires three to five years of hard work. It tends to be a lengthy process because patients need time to gradually work through their problems and genuinely accept unnerving revelations (Williams, 2005). Ultimately, if resistance and transference can be handled effectively, the therapist's interpretations should lead the client to profound insights. For instance, Mr. N eventually admitted, "The old boy is probably right, it does tickle me to imagine that my mother preferred me and I could beat out my father. Later, I wondered whether this had something to do with my own screwed-up sex life with my wife." According to Freud, once clients recognize the unconscious sources of their conflicts, they can resolve these conflicts and discard their neurotic defenses.

Although still available, classical psychoanalysis as done by Freud is not widely practiced anymore (Kay & Kay, 2003). Freud's psychoanalytic method was geared to a particular kind of clientele that he was seeing in Vienna a century ago. As his followers fanned out across Europe and America, many found that it was necessary to adapt psychoanalysis to different cultures, changing times, and new kinds of patients (Karasu, 2005). Thus,

many variations on Freud's original approach to psychoanalysis have developed over the years. These descendants of psychoanalysis are collectively known as *psychodynamic approaches* to therapy.

Today we have a rich variety of psychodynamic approaches to therapy (Magnavita, 2008). Recent reviews of these treatments suggest that interpretation, resistance, and transference continue to play key roles in therapeutic efforts (Hoglend et al., 2008; Luborsky & Barrett, 2006). For example, evidence suggests that the amount of resistance manifested in psychodynamic therapy predicts the outcome of therapy. People who exhibit more resistance are less likely to experience a positive outcome and more likely to drop out of therapy (Luborsky & Barrett, 2006). Recent research also suggests that psychodynamic approaches can be helpful in the treatment of a diverse array of disorders, including depression, anxiety disorders, personality disorders, and substance abuse (Gibbons, Crits-Christoph, & Hearon, 2008; Leichsenring & Rabung, 2008).

## Client-Centered Therapy

You may have heard of people going into therapy to "find themselves" or to "get in touch with their real feelings." These now-popular phrases emerged out of the human potential movement, which was stimulated in part by the work of Carl Rogers (1951, 1986). Taking a humanistic perspective, Rogers devised *client-centered therapy* (also known as *person-centered therapy*) in the 1940s and 1950s.

Courtesy of Carl Rogers Memorial Library

**Carl Rogers**

*Client-centered therapy* **is an insight therapy that emphasizes providing a supportive emotional climate for clients, who play a major role in determining the pace and direction of their therapy.** You may wonder why the troubled, untrained client is put in charge of the pace and direction of the therapy. Rogers (1961) provides a compelling justification:

*It is the client who knows what hurts, what directions to go, what problems are crucial, what experiences have been deeply buried. It began to occur to me that unless I had a need to demonstrate my own cleverness and learning, I would do better to rely upon the client for the direction of movement in the process.* (pp. 11–12)

Rogers's theory about the principal causes of neurotic anxieties is quite different from the Freudian explanation. As discussed in Chapter 2, Rogers maintained that most personal distress is due to inconsistency, or "incongruence," between a person's self-concept and reality (see **Figure 15.4**). According to his theory, incongruence makes people prone to feel threatened by realistic feedback about themselves from others. For example, if you inaccurately viewed yourself as a hardworking, dependable person, you would feel threatened by contradictory feedback from friends or co-workers. According to Rogers, anxiety about such feedback often leads to reliance on defense mechanisms, distortions of reality, and stifled personal growth. Excessive incongruence is thought to be rooted in clients' overdependence on others for approval and acceptance.

Given Rogers's theory, client-centered therapists seek insights that are quite different from the repressed conflicts that psychoanalysts try to track down. Client-centered therapists help clients to realize that they do not have to worry constantly about pleasing others and winning acceptance. They encourage clients to respect their own feelings and values. They help people restructure their self-concept to correspond better to reality. Ultimately, they try to foster self-acceptance and personal growth.

## Therapeutic Climate

In client-centered therapy, the *process* of therapy is not as important as the emotional *climate* in which the therapy takes place. According to Rogers, it is critical for the therapist to provide a warm, supportive, accepting climate in which clients can confront their shortcomings without feeling threatened. The lack of threat should reduce clients' defensive tendencies and thus help them to open up. To create this atmosphere of emotional support, Rogers believed that client-centered therapists must provide three conditions:

1. *Genuineness.* The therapist must be genuine with the client, communicating in an honest and spontaneous manner. The therapist should not be phony or defensive.

2. *Unconditional positive regard.* The therapist must also show complete, nonjudgmental acceptance of the client as a person. The therapist should provide warmth and caring for the client with no strings attached. This mandate does not mean that the therapist has to approve of everything that the client says or does. A therapist can disapprove of a particular behavior while continuing to value the client as a human being.

3. *Empathy.* Finally, the therapist must provide accurate empathy for the client. This means that the therapist must understand the client's world from the client's point of view. Furthermore, the therapist must be articulate enough to communicate this understanding to the client.

Rogers firmly believed that a supportive emotional climate is the major force that promotes healthy changes in therapy. However, some client-centered therapists place more emphasis on the therapeutic process (Rice & Greenberg, 1992).

## Therapeutic Process

In client-centered therapy, the client and therapist work together almost as equals. The therapist provides relatively little guidance and keeps interpretation and advice to a minimum. So, just what does the client-centered therapist do, besides creating a supportive climate? Primarily, the therapist provides feedback to help clients sort out their feelings. The therapist's key task is *clarification.* Client-centered therapists try to function like a human mirror, reflecting statements back to their clients, but with enhanced clarity. They help clients become more aware of their true feelings by highlighting themes that may be obscure in the clients' rambling discourse.

By working with clients to clarify their feelings, client-centered therapists hope to gradually build toward more far-reaching insights. In particular, they try to help clients become more aware of and comfortable about their genuine selves. Obviously, these are ambitious goals. Client-centered therapy resembles

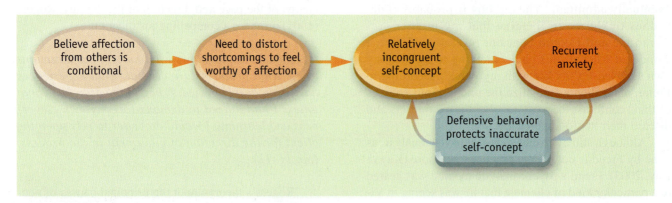

**Figure 15.4**
**Rogers's view of the roots of disorders.** Carl Rogers's theory posits that anxiety and self-defeating behavior are rooted in an incongruent self-concept that makes one prone to recurrent anxiety, which triggers defensive behavior, which fuels more incongruence.

psychoanalysis in that both seek to achieve a major reconstruction of a client's personality.

## Therapies Inspired by Positive Psychology

The growth of the positive psychology movement has begun to inspire new approaches to insight therapy (Duckworth, Steen, & Seligman, 2005; Peterson & Park, 2009). As noted in Chapter 3, *positive psychology* uses theory and research to better understand the positive, adaptive, creative, and fulfilling aspects of human existence. The advocates of *positive psychology* maintain that therapy has historically focused far too heavily on pathology, weakness, and suffering (and how to heal these conditions) rather than health and resilience (Seligman, 2003; Seligman & Csikszentmihalyi, 2000). They argue for increased research on contentment, well-being, human strengths, and positive emotions (see Chapter 16 for an in-depth discussion of positive psychology).

This philosophical approach has led to new therapeutic interventions. For example, *well-being therapy*, developed by Giovanni Fava and colleagues (Fava, 1999; Ruini & Fava, 2004), seeks to enhance clients' self-acceptance, purpose in life, autonomy, and personal growth. It has been used successfully in the treatment of mood disorders and anxiety disorders (Fava et al., 2005).

Another new approach is *positive psychotherapy*, developed by Martin Seligman and colleagues (Seligman, Rashid, & Parks, 2006). Thus far, positive psychotherapy has been used mainly in the treatment of depression. **Positive psychotherapy attempts to get clients to recognize their strengths, appreciate their blessings, savor positive experiences, forgive those who have wronged them, and find meaning in their lives.** Preliminary research suggests that positive psychotherapy can be an effective treatment for depression. For example, in one study positive psychotherapy was compared to treatment as usual (whatever the therapist would normally do) and treatment as usual with medication. The data shown in **Figure 15.5** compare mean depression scores at the end of the study for participants in these three conditions (Seligman et al., 2006). As you can see, the lowest depression scores were observed in the group that received positive psychotherapy. These innovative, new interventions spurred by the positive psychology movement are in their infancy, but the early findings seem promising and it will be interesting to see what the future holds.

## Group Therapy

Although it dates back to the early part of the 20th century, group therapy came of age during World War II

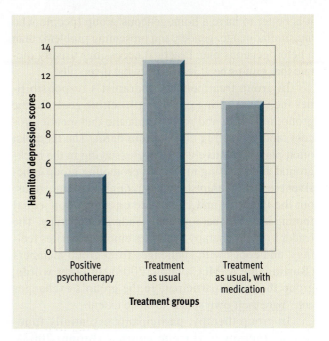

**Figure 15.5**

**Positive psychotherapy for depression.** In a study of the efficacy of positive psychotherapy, it was compared to treatment as usual (clinicians delivered whatever treatment they deemed appropriate) and to treatment as usual combined with antidepressant medication. At the end of 12 weeks of treatment, symptoms of depression were measured with the widely used Hamilton Rating Scale for Depression. The mean depression scores for each group are graphed here. As you can see, the positive psychotherapy group showed less depression than the other two treatment groups, suggesting that positive psychotherapy can be an effective intervention for depression.

Source: Adapted from Seligman, M. E. P., Rashid, T., & Parks, A. C. (2006). Positive psychotherapy. *American Psychologist, 61,* 774–788. Copyright © 2006 by the American Psychological Association.

and its aftermath in the 1950s (Rosenbaum, Lakin, & Roback, 1992). During this period, the expanding demand for therapeutic services forced clinicians to use group techniques (Scheidlinger, 1993). **Group therapy is the simultaneous treatment of several or more clients in a group.** Most major insight therapies have been adapted for use with groups. Because of economic pressures in mental health care, the use of group therapy appears likely to grow in future years (Burlingame & McClendon, 2008). Although group therapy can be conducted in a variety of ways, we can provide a general overview of the process as it usually unfolds (see Alonso, Alonso, & Piper, 2003; Cox, Vinogradov, & Yalom, 2008; Spitz, 2009).

### Participants' Roles

A therapy group typically consists of 4 to 12 people, with 6 to 8 participants regarded as an ideal number (Cox et al., 2008). The therapist usually screens the participants, excluding anyone who seems likely to be disruptive. Some theorists maintain that judicious selection of participants is crucial to effective group treatment (Salvendy, 1993). There is some debate about whether it is better to have a homogeneous group (people who are similar in age, gender, and presenting problem) than a heterogeneous one. Practical necessities usually dictate that groups be at least somewhat diversified.

In group treatment the therapist's responsibilities include selecting participants, setting goals for the group, initiating and maintaining the therapeutic process, and protecting clients from harm. The therapist often plays a relatively subtle role, staying in the background and focusing mainly on promoting group cohesiveness. The therapist always retains a special status, but the therapist and clients are on much more equal footing in group therapy than in individual therapy. The leader in group therapy expresses emotions, shares feelings, and copes with challenges from group members (Burlingame & McClendon, 2008). In other words, group therapists participate in the group's exchanges and "bare their own souls" to some extent.

In group therapy, participants essentially function as therapists for one another (Stone, 2003). Group members describe their problems, trade viewpoints, share experiences, and discuss coping strategies. Most important, they provide acceptance and emotional support for each other. In this supportive atmosphere, group members work at peeling away the social masks that cover their insecurities. Once their problems are exposed, members work at correcting them. As members come to value one another's opinions, they work hard to display healthy changes to win the group's approval.

### Advantages of the Group Experience

Group therapies obviously save time and money, which can be critical in understaffed mental hospitals and other institutional settings (Cox et al., 2008). Therapists in private practice usually charge less for group than individual therapy, making therapy affordable for more people. However, group therapy is *not* just a less costly substitute for individual therapy. For many types of patients and problems, group therapy can be just as effective as individual treatment (Alonso et al., 2003; Knauss, 2005; Stone, 2003). Moreover, group therapy has unique strengths of its own. Irwin Yalom (1995), who has studied group therapy extensively, has described some of these advantages:

1. *In group therapy, participants often come to realize that their misery is not unique.* Clients often enter therapy feeling sorry for themselves. They think that they alone have a burdensome cross to bear. In the group situation, they quickly see that they are not unique. They are reassured to learn that many other people have similar or even worse problems.

2. *Group therapy provides an opportunity for participants to work on their social skills in a safe environment.* Many personal problems essentially involve difficulties in relating effectively to people. Group therapy can provide a workshop for improving interpersonal skills that cannot be matched by individual therapy.

3. *Certain kinds of problems are especially well suited to group treatment.* Specific types of problems and clients respond especially well to the social support that group therapy can provide. Peer self-help groups illustrate this advantage. In peer self-help groups, people who have a problem in common get together regularly to help one another out. The original peer self-help group was Alcoholics Anonymous. Today, similar groups are made up of former psychiatric patients, single parents, drug addicts, and so forth.

Whether treatment is conducted on a group or an individual basis, clients usually invest considerable time, effort, and money in insight therapies. Are they worth the investment? Let's look at the research evidence on the efficacy of insight therapies.

### Evaluating Insight Therapies

Evaluating the effectiveness of any approach to treatment is a complex challenge (Hill & Lambert, 2004; Staines & Cleland, 2007). Evaluating treatment results is especially complicated for insight therapies (Aveline, Strauss, & Stiles, 2005). If you were to undergo insight therapy, how would you judge its effectiveness? By how

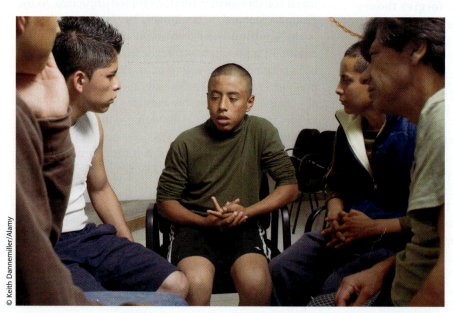

**Group therapies have proven particularly helpful when members share similar problems, such as alcoholism, drug abuse, overeating, or depression.**

you felt? By looking at your behavior? By asking your therapist? By consulting your friends and family? What would you be looking for? Various schools of therapy pursue entirely different goals. And clients' ratings of their progress are likely to be slanted toward a favorable evaluation because they want to justify their effort, their heartache, their expense, and their time. Even evaluations by professional therapists can be highly subjective (Luborsky, Singer, & Luborsky, 1999). Moreover, people enter therapy with diverse problems of varied severity, creating huge confounds in efforts to assess the effectiveness of therapeutic interventions.

Despite these difficulties, thousands of outcome studies have been conducted to evaluate the effectiveness of insight therapy. These studies have examined a broad range of clinical problems and used diverse methods to assess therapeutic outcomes, including scores on psychological tests and ratings by family members, as well as therapists' and clients' ratings. These studies consistently indicate that insight therapy *is* superior to no treatment or to placebo treatment and that the effects of therapy are reasonably durable (Kopta et al., 1999; Lambert & Archer, 2006). And when insight therapies are compared head to head against drug therapies, they usually show roughly equal efficacy (Arkowitz & Lilienfeld, 2007; Pinquart, Duberstein, & Lyness, 2006).

Studies generally find the greatest improvement early in treatment (the first 13–18 weekly sessions), with further gains gradually diminishing over time (Lambert, Bergin, & Garfield, 2004). Overall, about 50% of patients show a clinically meaningful recovery within about 20 sessions, and another 25% of patients achieve this goal after about 45 sessions (Lambert & Ogles, 2004) (see **Figure 15.6**). Of course, these broad

generalizations mask considerable variability in outcome, but the general trends are encouraging.

Although considerable evidence suggests that insight therapy produces positive effects for a sizable majority of clients, there is vigorous debate about the *mechanisms of action* underlying these positive effects (Kazdin, 2007). The advocates of various therapies tend to attribute the benefits of therapy to the particular methods and procedures used by each specific approach to therapy (Chambless & Hollon, 1998). In essence, they argue that different therapies achieve similar benefits through different processes. An alternative view espoused by many theorists is that the diverse approaches to therapy share certain common factors and that it is these common factors that account for much of the improvement experienced by clients (Frank & Frank, 1991). Evidence supporting the common factors view has mounted in recent years (Ahn & Wampold, 2001; Sparks, Duncan, & Miller, 2008).

What are the common denominators that lie at the core of diverse approaches to therapy? Although the models proposed to answer to this question vary considerably, there is some consensus. The most widely cited common factors include (1) the development of a therapeutic alliance with a professional helper, (2) the provision of emotional support and empathic understanding by the therapist, (3) the cultivation of hope and positive expectations in the client, (4) the provision of a rationale for the client's problems and a plausible method for ameliorating them, and (5) the opportunity to express feelings, confront problems, gain new insights, and learn new patterns of behavior (Grencavage & Norcross, 1990; Weinberger, 1995). How important are these common factors in therapy?

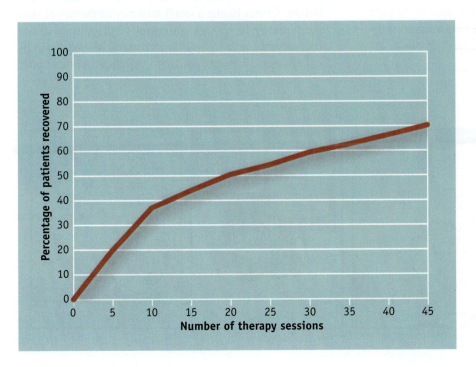

**Figure 15.6**

**Recovery as a function of number of therapy sessions.** Based on a national sample of over 6,000 patients, Lambert, Hansen, and Finch (2001) mapped out the relationship between recovery and the duration of treatment. These data show that about half of the patients had experienced a clinically significant recovery after 20 weekly sessions of therapy. After 45 sessions of therapy, about 70% had recovered.

Source: Adapted from Lambert, M. J., Hansen, N. B., & Finch, A. E. (2001). Patient-focused research: Using patient outcome data to enhance treatment effects. *Journal of Consulting and Clinical Psychology, 69,* 159–172. Copyright © 2001 by the American Psychological Association. Used by permission of the authors.

Some theorists argue that common factors account for virtually *all* of the progress that clients make in therapy (Wampold, 2001). It seems more likely that the benefits of therapy represent the combined effects of common factors and specific procedures (Beutler & Harwood, 2002). Either way, it is clear that common factors play a significant role in insight therapy.

## Therapy and the Recovered Memories Controversy

While debate about the efficacy of insight therapy has simmered for many decades, the 1990s brought an entirely new controversy to rock the psychotherapy profession like never before. This emotionally charged debate was sparked by a spate of reports of people recovering repressed memories of sexual abuse and other childhood trauma through therapy. You've no doubt read or seen media stories about people—including some celebrities—who dredged up long-lost recollections of sexual abuse, typically with the help of their therapists. For example, in 1991 the comedian Roseanne suddenly recalled years of abuse by her parents, and a former Miss America remembered having been sexually assaulted by her father (Wielawski, 1991). Such recovered memories have led to a rash of lawsuits in which adult plaintiffs have sued their parents, teachers, neighbors, pastors, and so forth for alleged child abuse 20 or 30 years earlier. For the most part, these parents, teachers, and neighbors have denied the allegations. Many of them have seemed genuinely baffled by the accusations, which have torn apart some previously happy families (Gudjonsson, 2001; McHugh et al., 2004). In an effort to make sense of the charges, many accused parents have argued that their children's recollections are false memories created inadvertently by well-intentioned therapists through the power of suggestion.

The crux of the debate is that child abuse usually takes place behind closed doors, and in the absence of corroborative evidence, no way exists to reliably distinguish genuine recovered memories from those that are false. A handful of recovered memories have been substantiated by independent witnesses or belated admissions of guilt from the accused (Brewin, 2003, 2007; Shobe & Schooler, 2001). But in the vast majority of cases, the allegations of abuse have been vehemently denied, and independent corroboration has not been available. Recovered recollections of sexual abuse have become so common, a support group has been formed for accused people who feel that they have been victimized by "false memory syndrome."

Psychologists are sharply divided on the issue of recovered memories, leaving the public understandably confused. Many psychologists, especially therapists in clinical practice, accept most recovered memories at face value (Banyard & Williams, 1999; Briere & Conte, 1993; Gleaves & Smith, 2004; Legault & Laurence, 2007). They assert that it is common for patients to bury traumatic incidents in their unconscious (Del Monte, 2000; Wilsnack et al., 2002). Citing evidence that sexual abuse in childhood is far more widespread than most people realize (MacMillan et al., 1997), they argue that most repressed memories of abuse are probably genuine.

In contrast, many other psychologists, especially memory researchers, have expressed skepticism about the recovered memories phenomenon (Kihlstrom, 2004; Loftus, 1998, 2003; McNally, 2004, 2007). They maintain that some suggestible, confused people struggling to understand profound personal problems have been convinced by persuasive therapists that their emotional problems must be the result of abuse that occurred years before. Critics blame a small minority of therapists who presumably have good intentions but operate under the dubious assumption that virtually all psychological problems are attributable to childhood sexual abuse

# DOONESBURY

**Panel 1:** IT'S MANY YEARS AGO... YOU'RE IN YOUR OWN BED... IT'S LATE AT NIGHT...

**Panel 2:** SOMEONE QUIETLY STEPS FROM THE SHADOWS... DO YOU SEE HIM, MARK? / I DO... I SEE HIM IN THE MOONLIGHT!

**Panel 3:** AND WHO IS IT, MARK? WHO'S STANDING BESIDE YOU? / IT'S... IT'S LYNDON JOHNSON!

**Panel 4:** NO, NO, IT'S YOUR FATHER. WHAT'S HE WEARING? / IT'S JOHNSON, I TELL YOU! HE'S COME TO... TO DRAFT ME!

(Lindsay & Read, 1994; Loftus & Davis, 2006; Spanos, 1994). Using hypnosis, dream interpretation, and leading questions, they supposedly prod and probe patients until they inadvertently create the memories of abuse that they are searching for (Thayer & Lynn, 2006).

Psychologists who doubt the authenticity of repressed memories support their analysis by pointing to discredited cases of recovered memories (Brown, Goldstein, & Bjorklund, 2000). For example, with the help of a church counselor, one woman recovered memories of how her minister father repeatedly raped her, got her pregnant, and then aborted the pregnancy with a coathanger. However, subsequent evidence revealed that the woman was still a virgin and that her father had had a vasectomy years before (Brainerd & Reyna, 2005). The skeptics also point to published case histories that clearly involved suggestive questioning and to cases in which patients have recanted recovered memories of sexual abuse after realizing that these memories were implanted by their therapists (Loftus, 1994; Shobe & Schooler, 2001). Those who question recovered memories also point to several lines of carefully controlled laboratory research demonstrating that it is not all that difficult to create "memories" of events that never happened (Lindsay et al., 2004; Loftus & Cahill, 2007; Strange, Clifasefi, & Garry, 2007; Roediger & McDermott, 1995, 2000). Skeptics also note that many repressed memories of abuse have been recovered under the influence of hypnosis, but research indicates that hypnosis tends to increase memory distortions while paradoxically making people feel more confident about their recollections (Mazzoni & Lynn, 2007).

Of course, psychologists who believe in recovered memories have mounted rebuttals to these arguments. For example, Kluft (1999) argues that a recantation of a recovered memory of abuse does not prove that the memory was false. Gleaves (1994) points out that individuals with a history of sexual abuse often vacillate between denying and accepting that the abuse occurred.

Harvey (1999) argues that laboratory demonstrations showing how easy it is to create false memories have involved trivial memory distortions that are a far cry from the vivid, emotionally wrenching recollections of sexual abuse that have generated the recovered memories controversy. Moreover, even if one accepts the assertion that therapists *can* create false memories of abuse in their patients, some critics have noted that virtually no direct evidence exists on how often this occurs and

Tom Rutherford (shown here with his wife, Joyce) received a $1 million settlement in a suit against a church therapist and a Springfield, Missouri, church in a false memory case. Under the church counselor's guidance, the Rutherfords' daughter, Beth, had "recalled" childhood memories of having been raped repeatedly by her minister father, gotten pregnant, and undergone a painful coat-hanger abortion. Her father lost his job and was ostracized. After he later revealed he'd had a vasectomy when Beth was age 4, and a physical exam revealed that at age 23 she was still a virgin, the memories were shown to be false.

that no empirical basis has been found for the claim of an *epidemic* of such cases (Berliner & Briere, 1999; Leavitt, 2001; Wilsnack et al., 2002).

So, what can we conclude about the recovered memories controversy? It seems pretty clear that therapists can unknowingly create false memories in their patients and that a significant portion of recovered memories of abuse are the product of suggestion (Loftus & Davis, 2006; McNally & Geraerts, 2009). But it also seems likely that some cases of recovered memories are authentic (Brewin, 2007; Smith & Gleaves, 2007).

At this point, we don't have adequate data to estimate what proportion of recovered memories of abuse fall in each category. Thus, the matter needs to be addressed with great caution. On the one hand, people should be extremely careful about accepting recovered memories of abuse in the absence of convincing corroboration. On the other hand, recovered memories of abuse cannot be summarily dismissed, and it would be tragic if the repressed memories controversy made people overly skeptical about the all-too-real problem of childhood sexual abuse.

# Behavior Therapies

### LEARNING OBJECTIVES

- Summarize the general approach and principles of behavior therapies.
- Identify the three steps in systematic desensitization, and describe the logic underlying the treatment.
- Describe the use of aversion therapy and social skills training.

- Understand the logic, goals, and techniques of cognitive therapy.
- Assess the evidence on the efficacy of behavior therapies.

Behavior therapy is different from insight therapy in that behavior therapists make no attempt to help clients achieve grand insights about themselves. Why not? Because behavior therapists believe that such insights aren't necessary in order to produce constructive change. Consider a client troubled by compulsive gambling. The behavior therapist doesn't care whether this behavior is rooted in unconscious conflicts or parental rejection. What the client needs is to get rid of the maladaptive behavior. Consequently, the therapist simply designs a program to eliminate the compulsive gambling. The crux of the difference between insight therapy and behavior therapy lies in how each views symptoms. Insight therapists treat pathological symptoms as signs of an underlying problem. In contrast, behavior therapists think that the symptoms *are* the problem. Thus, **behavior therapies involve the application of the principles of learning to direct efforts to change clients' maladaptive behaviors.**

Behaviorism has been an influential school of thought in psychology since the 1920s. But behaviorists devoted little attention to clinical issues until the 1950s, when behavior therapy emerged out of three independent lines of research fostered by B. F. Skinner (1953) and his colleagues in the United States, Hans Eysenck (1959) and his colleagues in Britain, and Joseph Wolpe (1958) and his colleagues in South Africa (Glass &

Arnkoff, 1992). Since then, there has been an explosion of interest in behavioral approaches to psychotherapy.

Behavior therapies are based on two main assumptions (Stanley & Beidel, 2009). *First, it is assumed that behavior is a product of learning.* No matter how self-defeating or pathological a client's behavior might be, the behaviorist believes that it is the result of past conditioning. *Second, it is assumed that what has been learned can be unlearned.* The same learning principles that explain how the maladaptive behavior was acquired can be used to get rid of it. Thus, behavior therapists attempt to change clients' behavior by applying the principles of classical conditioning, operant conditioning, and observational learning.

Behavior therapies are close cousins of the self-modification procedures described in the Chapter 3 Application. Both use the same principles of learning to alter behavior directly. In discussing *self-modification*, we examined some relatively simple procedures that people can apply to themselves to improve everyday self-control. In our discussion of *behavior therapy*, we examine more complex procedures used by mental health professionals in the treatment of more severe problems.

## Systematic Desensitization

Devised by Joseph Wolpe (1958, 1987), systematic desensitization revolutionized psychotherapy by giving therapists their first useful alternative to traditional "talk therapy" (Fishman & Franks, 1992). *Systematic desensitization is a behavior therapy used to reduce clients' anxiety responses through counterconditioning.* The treatment assumes that most anxiety responses are acquired through classical conditioning (as we discussed in Chapter 14). According to this model, a harmless stimulus (for instance, a bridge) may be paired with a frightening event (lightning striking it), so it becomes a conditioned stimulus eliciting anxiety. The goal of systematic desensitization is to weaken the association between the conditioned stimulus (the bridge) and the conditioned response of anxiety (see **Figure 15.7**). Systematic desensitization involves three steps.

Joseph Wolpe

*First, the therapist helps the client build an anxiety hierarchy.* The hierarchy is a list of anxiety-arousing stimuli centering on the specific source of anxiety, such as flying, academic tests, or snakes. The client ranks the stimuli from the least anxiety arousing to the most anxiety arousing. This ordered list of related anxiety-provoking stimuli constitutes the anxiety hierarchy.

An example of an anxiety hierarchy for one woman's fear of heights is shown in **Figure 15.8**.

*The second step involves training the client in deep muscle relaxation.* This second phase may begin during early sessions while the therapist and client are still constructing the anxiety hierarchy. Different therapists use different relaxation training procedures. Whatever procedures are used, the client must learn to engage in deep and thorough relaxation on command from the therapist.

### An Anxiety Hierarchy for Systematic Desensitization

| Degree of fear | |
|---|---|
| 5 | I'm standing on the balcony of the top floor of an apartment tower. |
| 10 | I'm standing on a stepladder in the kitchen to change a light bulb. |
| 15 | I'm walking on a ridge. The edge is hidden by shrubs and treetops. |
| 20 | I'm sitting on the slope of a mountain, looking out over the horizon. |
| 25 | I'm crossing a bridge 6 feet above a creek. The bridge consists of an 18-inch-wide board with a handrail on one side. |
| 30 | I'm riding a ski lift 8 feet above the ground. |
| 35 | I'm crossing a shallow, wide creek on an 18-inch-wide board, 3 feet above water level. |
| 40 | I'm climbing a ladder outside the house to reach a second-story window. |
| 45 | I'm pulling myself up a 30-degree wet, slippery slope on a steel cable. |
| 50 | I'm scrambling up a rock, 8 feet high. |
| 55 | I'm walking 10 feet on a resilient, 18-inch-wide board, which spans an 8-foot-deep gulch. |
| 60 | I'm walking on a wide plateau, 2 feet from the edge of a cliff. |
| 65 | I'm skiing an intermediate hill. The snow is packed. |
| 70 | I'm walking over a railway trestle. |
| 75 | I'm walking on the side of an embankment. The path slopes to the outside. |
| 80 | I'm riding a chair lift 15 feet above the ground. |
| 85 | I'm walking up a long, steep slope. |
| 90 | I'm walking up (or down) a 15-degree slope on a 3-foot-wide trail. On one side of the trail the terrain drops down sharply; on the other side is a steep upward slope. |
| 95 | I'm walking on a 3-foot-wide ridge. The slopes on both sides are long and more than 25 degrees steep. |
| 100 | I'm walking on a 3-foot-wide ridge. The trail slopes on one side. The drop on either side of the trail is more than 25 degrees. |

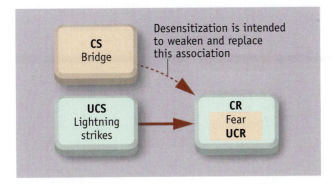

**Figure 15.7**

**The logic underlying systematic desensitization.** Behaviorists argue that many phobic responses are acquired through classical conditioning, as in the example diagrammed here. Systematic desensitization targets the conditioned associations between phobic stimuli and fear responses.

**Figure 15.8**

**Example of an anxiety hierarchy.** Systematic desensitization requires the construction of an anxiety hierarchy like the one shown here, which was developed for a woman with a fear of heights who had a penchant for hiking in the mountains.

*In the third step, the client tries to work through the hierarchy, learning to remain relaxed while imagining each stimulus.* Starting with the least anxiety-arousing stimulus, the client imagines the situation as vividly as possible while relaxing. If the client experiences strong anxiety, he or she drops the imaginary scene and concentrates on relaxation. The client keeps repeating this process until he or she can imagine a scene with little or no anxiety. Once a particular scene is conquered, the client moves on to the next stimulus situation in the anxiety hierarchy. Gradually, over a number of therapy sessions, the client progresses through the hierarchy, unlearning troublesome anxiety responses.

As clients conquer *imagined* phobic stimuli, they may be encouraged to confront the *real* stimuli. Although desensitization to imagined stimuli *can* be effective by itself, contemporary behavior therapists usually follow it up with direct exposures to the real anxiety-arousing stimuli (Emmelkamp, 2004). Indeed, behavioral interventions emphasizing direct exposures to anxiety-arousing situations have become behavior therapists' treatment of choice for phobic and other anxiety disorders (Rachman, 2009). Usually, these real-life confrontations prove harmless, and individuals' anxiety responses decline. Effective exposure treatments for phobias can even be completed in a single session (Ollendick et al., 2009).

According to Wolpe (1958, 1990), the principle at work in systematic desensitization is simple. Anxiety and relaxation are incompatible responses. The trick is to recondition people so that the conditioned stimulus elicits relaxation instead of anxiety. This is *counterconditioning*—an attempt to reverse the process of classical conditioning by associating the crucial stimulus with a new conditioned response. Although Wolpe's explanation of how systematic desensitization works has been questioned, the technique's effectiveness in eliminating specific anxieties has been well documented (Rachman, 2009).

## Aversion Therapy

Aversion therapy is far and away the most controversial of the behavior therapies. It's not something that you would sign up for unless you were pretty desperate. Psychologists usually suggest it only as a treatment of last resort, after other interventions have failed. What's so terrible about aversion therapy? The client has to endure decidedly unpleasant stimuli, such as shocks or drug-induced nausea.

**Aversion therapy is a behavior therapy in which an aversive stimulus is paired with a stimulus that elicits an undesirable response.** For example, alcoholics have had drug-induced nausea paired with their favorite drinks during therapy sessions (Landabaso et al., 1999). By pairing an *emetic drug* (one that causes

vomiting) with alcohol, the therapist hopes to create a conditioned aversion to alcohol (see **Figure 15.9**).

Aversion therapy takes advantage of the automatic nature of responses produced through classical conditioning. Admittedly, alcoholics treated with aversion therapy know that they won't be given an emetic outside of their therapy sessions. However, their reflex response to the stimulus of alcohol may be changed so that they respond to it with nausea and distaste. Obviously, this response should make it much easier to resist the urge to drink.

Aversion therapy is not a widely used technique, and when it is used it is usually only one element in a larger treatment program. Troublesome behaviors treated successfully with aversion therapy have included drug and alcohol abuse, sexual deviance, gambling, shoplifting, stuttering, cigarette smoking, and overeating (Bordnick et al., 2004; Emmelkamp, 1994; Grossman & Ruiz, 2004; Maletzky, 2002).

## Social Skills Training

Many psychological problems grow out of interpersonal difficulties. Behavior therapists point out that humans are not born with social finesse. People acquire their social skills through learning. Unfortunately, some people have not learned how to be friendly, how to make conversation, how to express anger appropriately, and so forth. Social ineptitude can contribute to anxiety, feelings of inferiority, and various kinds of disorders. In light of these findings, therapists are increasingly using social skills training in efforts to improve clients' social abilities. This approach to therapy has yielded promising results in the treatment of social anxiety (Herbert et al., 2005), autism (Scattone, 2007), attention deficit disorder (Monastra, 2008), and schizophrenia (Granholm et al., 2008).

**Social skills training is a behavior therapy designed to improve interpersonal skills that**

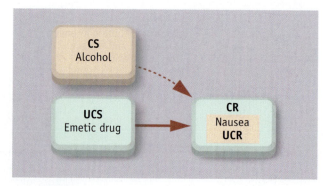

**Figure 15.9**

**Aversion therapy.** Aversion therapy uses classical conditioning to create an aversion to a stimulus that has elicited problematic behavior. For example, in the treatment of drinking problems, alcohol may be paired with a nausea-inducing drug to create a conditioned aversion to alcohol.

emphasizes shaping, modeling, and behavioral rehearsal. This type of behavior therapy can be conducted with individual clients or in groups. Social skills training depends on the principles of operant conditioning and observational learning. The therapist makes use of *modeling* by encouraging clients to watch socially skilled friends and colleagues, so that the clients can acquire responses (eye contact, active listening, and so on) through observation.

In *behavioral rehearsal*, the client tries to practice social techniques in structured role-playing exercises. The therapist provides corrective feedback and uses approval to reinforce progress. Eventually, clients try their newly acquired skills in real-world interactions. Usually, they are given specific homework assignments. *Shaping* is used in that clients are gradually asked to handle more complicated and delicate social situations. For example, a nonassertive client may begin by working on making requests of friends. Only much later will the client be asked to tackle standing up to his or her boss.

## Cognitive-Behavioral Treatments

In Chapter 3 we saw that people's cognitive interpretations of events make all the difference in the world in how well they handle stress. In Chapter 14 we learned that cognitive factors play a key role in the development of depression and other disorders. Citing the importance of findings such as these, behavior therapists started to focus more attention on their clients' cognitions in the 1970s (Arnkoff & Glass, 1992; Hollon & Beck, 2004). *Cognitive-behavioral treatments* **use varied combinations of verbal interventions and behavior modification techniques to help clients change maladaptive patterns of thinking.** Some of these treatments, such as Albert Ellis's (1973) *rational emotive behavior therapy* and Aaron Beck's (1976) *cognitive therapy* emerged

**WEB LINK 15.3   Association for Behavioral and Cognitive Therapies**

The site for this professional organization offers a variety of resources relevant to the general public. The most valuable of these resources are the fact sheets on cognitive-behavioral treatments for over 40 common problems and disorders. These fact sheets explain how cognitive-behavioral interventions can be used in the treatment of alcohol abuse, autism, chronic fatigue, eating disorders, insomnia, phobias, schizophrenia, shyness, and a host of other conditions.

out of an insight therapy tradition, whereas other treatments, such as the systems developed by Donald Meichenbaum (1977) and Michael Mahoney (1974), emerged from the behavioral tradition. Since we covered the main ideas underlying Ellis's approach in our discussion of coping strategies in Chapter 4, we focus on Beck's system of cognitive therapy here (Beck, 1987; Newman & Beck, 2009).

*Cognitive therapy* **uses specific strategies to correct habitual thinking errors that underlie various types of disorders.** Cognitive therapy was originally devised as a treatment for depression, but in recent years it has been applied fruitfully to a wide range of disorders (Wright, Thase, & Beck, 2008; Hollon, Stewart, & Strunk, 2006), and it has proven particularly valuable as a therapy for anxiety disorders (Rachman, 2009). According to cognitive therapists, depression is caused by "errors" in thinking (see **Figure 15.10**). They assert that depression-prone people tend to (1) blame their setbacks on personal inadequacies without considering circumstantial explanations, (2) focus selectively on negative events while ignoring positive ones, (3) make unduly pessimistic projections about the future, and (4) draw negative conclusions about their worth as a person based on insignificant events. For instance, imagine that

| Cognitive Errors That Promote Depression | |
| --- | --- |
| **Cognitive error** | **Description** |
| Overgeneralizing | If it is true in one case, it applies to any case that is even slightly similar. |
| Selective abstraction | The only events that matter are failures, deprivation, and so on. I should measure myself by errors, weaknesses, etc. |
| Excessive responsibility (assuming personal causality) | I am responsible for all bad things, failures, and so on. |
| Assuming temporal causality (predicting without sufficient evidence) | If it has been true in the past, then it is always going to be true. |
| Self-references | I am the center of everyone's attention, especially when it comes to bad performances or personal attributes. |
| "Catastrophizing" | Always think of the worst. It is most likely to happen to you. |
| Dichotomous thinking | Everything is either one extreme or another (black or white; good or bad). |

**Figure 15.10**

**Beck's cognitive theory of depression.** According to Aaron Beck (1976, 1987), depression is caused by certain patterns of negative thinking. This chart lists some of the particularly damaging cognitive errors that can foster depression.

Source: Adapted from Beck, A. T. (1976). *Cognitive therapy and the emotional disorders.* New York: International Universities Press. Copyright © 1976 by International Universities Press, Inc. Adapted by permission of the publisher.

you got a low grade on a minor quiz in a class. If you made the kinds of errors in thinking just described, you might blame the grade on your woeful stupidity, dismiss comments from a classmate that it was an unfair test, gloomily predict that you will surely flunk the course, and conclude that you are not genuine college material.

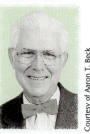

Aaron Beck

The goal of cognitive therapy is to change clients' negative thoughts and maladaptive beliefs (Kellogg & Young, 2008). To begin, clients are taught to detect their automatic negative thoughts, the sorts of self-defeating statements that people are prone to make when analyzing problems. Examples might include "I'm just not smart enough," "No one really likes me," or "It's all my fault." Clients are then trained to subject these automatic thoughts to reality testing. The therapist helps them to see how unrealistically negative the thoughts are.

Cognitive therapy uses a variety of behavioral techniques, including modeling, systematic monitoring of one's behavior, and behavioral rehearsal (Wright, Beck, & Thase, 2003). Clients are given "homework assignments" that focus on changing their overt behaviors. They may be instructed to engage in overt responses on their own, outside of the clinician's office. For example, one shy, insecure young man in cognitive therapy was

told to go to a singles bar and engage three different women in conversations for up to five minutes each (Rush, 1984). He was instructed to record his thoughts before and after each of the conversations. This assignment revealed various maladaptive patterns of thought that gave the young man and his therapist plenty to work on in subsequent sessions.

## Evaluating Behavior Therapies

Behavior therapists have historically placed more emphasis than insight therapists on the importance of measuring therapeutic outcomes. As a result, there is ample research on the effectiveness of behavior therapy (Stanley & Beidel, 2009). How does its effectiveness compare to that of insight therapy? In direct comparisons, the differences between the therapies are usually small. However, these modest differences tend to favor behavioral approaches for certain types of disorders. Of course, behavior therapies are not well suited to the treatment of some types of problems (vague feelings of discontent, for instance). Furthermore, it's misleading to make global statements about the effectiveness of behavior therapies, because they include a variety of procedures designed for different purposes. For example, the value of systematic desensitization for phobias has no bearing on the value of aversion therapy for sexual deviance.

For our purposes, it is sufficient to note that there is favorable evidence on the efficacy of most of the widely used behavioral interventions (Zinbarg & Griffith, 2008). Behavior therapies can make significant contributions to the treatment of depression, anxiety problems, phobias, obsessive-compulsive disorders, sexual dysfunction, schizophrenia, drug-related problems, eating disorders, hyperactivity, autism, and mental retardation (Berkowitz, 2003; Emmelkamp, 2004; Hollon & Dimidjian, 2009).

**WEB LINK 15.4  The Beck Institute of Cognitive Therapy and Research**

This site offers a diverse array of materials relating to Aaron Beck's cognitive therapy. Resources found here include newsletters, a referral system, a bookstore, recommended readings for clients, and questions and answers about cognitive therapy.

# Biomedical Therapies

### LEARNING OBJECTIVES

- Describe the principal drug therapies used in the treatment of psychological disorders, and summarize evidence regarding their efficacy.
- Identify some of the problems associated with drug therapies and drug research.
- Describe ECT, and discuss its efficacy and risks.

In the 1950s, a French surgeon was looking for a drug that would reduce patients' autonomic response to surgical stress. The surgeon noticed that chlorpromazine produced a mild sedation. Based on this observation, Delay and Deniker (1952) decided to give chlorpromazine to hospitalized schizophrenic patients to see

whether it would have a calming effect on them. Their experiment was a dramatic success. Chlorpromazine became the first effective antipsychotic drug—and a revolution in psychiatry had begun. Hundreds of thousands of severely disturbed patients—patients who had appeared doomed to lead the remainder of their lives in mental hospitals—were gradually sent home thanks to the therapeutic effects of antipsychotic drugs (see **Figure 15.11**). Today, biomedical therapies, such as drug treatment, lie at the core of psychiatric practice.

*Biomedical therapies* **are physiological interventions intended to reduce symptoms associated with psychological disorders.** These therapies assume that psychological disorders are caused, at least in part, by biological malfunctions. As we discussed in the previous chapter, this assumption clearly has merit for many disorders, especially the more severe ones. We will discuss two biomedical approaches to psychotherapy: drug therapy and electroconvulsive therapy.

## Treatment with Drugs

*Psychopharmacotherapy* **is the treatment of mental disorders with medication.** We will refer to this kind of treatment more simply as *drug therapy*. Therapeutic drugs for psychological problems fall into four major groups: antianxiety drugs, antipsychotic drugs, antidepressant drugs, and mood stabilizers.

### Antianxiety Drugs

Most of us know someone who pops pills to relieve anxiety. The drugs involved in this common coping strategy are *antianxiety drugs,* **which relieve tension, apprehension, and nervousness.** The most popular of these drugs are Valium and Xanax, which are the trade names (the proprietary names that pharmaceutical companies use in marketing drugs) for diazepam and alprazolam, respectively.

Valium, Xanax, and other drugs in the benzodiazepine family are often called *tranquilizers.* These drugs are routinely prescribed for people with anxiety disorders. They are also given to millions of people who simply suffer from chronic nervous tension. In the

mid-1970s, pharmacists in the United States were filling nearly *100 million* prescriptions each year for Valium and similar antianxiety drugs. Many critics characterized this level of use as excessive (Lickey & Gordon, 1991). However, since the 1990s, benzodiazepine prescriptions have declined noticeably (Raj & Sheehan, 2004).

Antianxiety drugs exert their effects almost immediately. They can be fairly effective in alleviating feelings of anxiety (Dubovsky, 2009). However, their effects are measured in hours, so their impact is relatively short-lived. Common side effects of antianxiety drugs include drowsiness, depression, nausea, and confusion. These drugs also have some potential for abuse, dependency, and overdose, although the prevalence of these problems has been exaggerated (Martinez, Marangell & Martinez, 2008). Another drawback is that patients who have been on antianxiety drugs for a while often experience withdrawal symptoms when their drug treatment is stopped (Raj & Sheehan, 2004).

A newer antianxiety drug called Buspar (buspirone), which does not belong to the benzodiazepine family, appears useful in the treatment of generalized anxiety disorder (Levitt, Schaffer, & Lanctôt, 2009). Unlike Valium, Buspar is slow acting, exerting its effects in one to three weeks, and has fewer sedative side effects (Ninan & Muntasser, 2004).

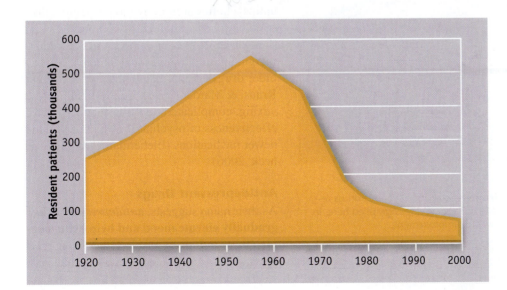

**Figure 15.11**

**The declining inpatient population in mental hospitals.** The number of inpatients in public mental hospitals has declined dramatically since the late 1950s. In part, this drop has been due to "deinstitutionalization"—a philosophy that emphasizes outpatient care whenever possible. However, above all else, this decline was made possible by the development of effective antipsychotic medications.

## Antipsychotic Drugs

Antipsychotic drugs are used primarily in the treatment of schizophrenia. They are also given to people with severe mood disorders who become delusional. The trade names (and generic names) of some prominent drugs in this category are Thorazine (chlorpromazine), Mellaril (thioridazine), and Haldol (haloperidol). *Antipsychotic drugs are used to gradually reduce psychotic symptoms, including hyperactivity, mental confusion, hallucinations, and delusions.*

Studies suggest that antipsychotics reduce psychotic symptoms in about 70% of patients, albeit in varied degrees (Kane, Stroup, & Marder, 2009). When antipsychotic drugs are effective, they work their magic gradually, as shown in **Figure 15.12**. Patients usually begin to respond within one to three weeks, but considerable variability in responsiveness is seen (Emsley, Rabinowitz, & Medori, 2006). Further improvement may occur for several months. Many schizophrenic patients are placed on antipsychotics indefinitely because these drugs can reduce the likelihood of a relapse into an active schizophrenic episode (van Kammen, Hurford, & Marder, 2009).

Antipsychotic drugs undeniably make a major contribution to the treatment of severe mental disorders, but they are not without problems. They have many unpleasant side effects (Dolder, 2008; Wilkaitis, Mulvihill, & Nasrallah, 2004). Drowsiness, constipation, and cotton mouth are common. Patients may also experience tremors, muscular rigidity, and impaired coordination. After being released from a hospital, many schizophrenic patients, supposedly placed on antipsychotics indefinitely, discontinue their drug regimen because of the disagreeable side effects. Unfortunately, after patients stop taking antipsychotic medication, about 70% relapse within a year (van Kammen et al., 2009). In addition to minor side effects, antipsychotics may cause a severe and lasting problem called *tardive dyskinesia,* which is seen in about 20%–30% of patients who receive long-term treatment with traditional antipsychotics (Kane et al., 2009). *Tardive dyskinesia is a neurological disorder marked by chronic tremors and involuntary spastic movements.* Once this debilitating syndrome emerges, there is no cure, although spontaneous remission sometimes occurs after the discontinuation of antipsychotic medication (Pi & Simpson, 2000).

Psychiatrists are currently enthusiastic about a newer class of antipsychotic agents called *atypical or second-generation antipsychotic drugs* (such as clozapine, olanzapine, and quetiapine). These drugs can help some patients who do not respond to conventional antipsychotic medications (Volavka et al., 2002). Moreover, the atypical antipsychotics produce fewer unpleasant side effects and carry less risk for tardive dyskinesia (Correll, Leucht, & Kane, 2004; Lieberman et al., 2003). Of course, like all powerful drugs, they are not without their risks, as they appear to increase patients' vulnerability to diabetes and cardiovascular problems (Meltzer et al., 2002). Although they are much more expensive than traditional, first-generation antipsychotics, the second-generation antipsychotics have become the first line of defense in the treatment of schizophrenia (Marder, Hurford, & van Kammen, 2009). However, recent research has generated some controversy regarding this trend. Studies have found that the newer antipsychotics aren't any more effective than the older ones in reducing symptoms and that the side effects of the newer drugs are only marginally less troublesome than those of the older drugs (Lieberman et al., 2005; Stroup, Kraus, & Marder, 2006). These findings raise vexing, complicated questions about the cost effectiveness of psychiatrists' reliance on the newer medications (Lieberman, 2006; Rosenheck, 2006).

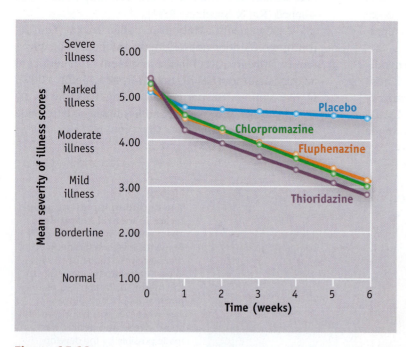

## Figure 15.12

**The time course of antipsychotic drug effects.** Antipsychotic drugs reduce psychotic symptoms gradually, over a span of weeks, as graphed here. In contrast, patients given placebo pills show little improvement.

Source: From Cole, J. O., Goldberg, S. C., & Davis, J. M. (1966). Drugs in the treatment of psychosis. In P. Solomon (Ed.), *Psychiatric drugs.* New York: Grune & Stratton. From data in the NIMH-PSC Collaborative Study I. Reprinted by permission of J. M. Davis.

## Antidepressant Drugs

As their name suggests, *antidepressant drugs gradually elevate mood and help bring people out of a depression.* Reliance on antidepressants has increased dramatically in the last

10 to 15 years, as antidepressants have become the most frequently prescribed class of medication in the United States (Olfson & Marcus, 2009). Prior to 1987, there were two principal types of antidepressants: *tricyclics* (such as Elavil) and *MAO inhibitors* (such as Nardil). These two sets of drugs affect neurochemical activity in different ways and tend to work with different patients. Overall, they are beneficial for about two-thirds of depressed patients (Gitlin, 2002), although only about one-third of treated patients experience a *complete resolution* of their symptoms (Shulman, 2001). The tricyclics have notably fewer problems with side effects and complications than the MAO inhibitors (Potter et al., 2006). Hence, the MAO inhibitors have become a "backup" option that is typically tried only when the tricyclics and other antidepressants have not worked (Kennedy, Holt, & Baker, 2009). Like antipsychotic drugs, antidepressants exert their effects gradually over a period of weeks, but about 60% of improvement tends to occur in the first two weeks (Gitlin, 2009).

Today, psychiatrists are more likely to prescribe a newer class of antidepressants, called *selective serotonin reuptake inhibitors (SSRIs),* which slow the reuptake process at serotonin synapses. The drugs in this class, which include Prozac (fluoxetine), Paxil (paroxetine), and Zoloft (sertraline), yield therapeutic gains similar to the tricyclics in the treatment of depression (Shelton & Lester, 2006) while producing fewer unpleasant or dangerous side effects (Sussman, 2009). SSRIs have also proven valuable in the treatment of obsessive-compulsive disorders, panic disorders, and other anxiety disorders (Mathew, Hoffman, & Charney, 2009; Ravindran & Stein, 2009). However, there is some doubt about how effective the SSRIs (and other antidepressants) are in relieving episodes of depression among patients suffering from bipolar disorder (Berman et al., 2009). Bipolar patients do not seem to respond as well as those who suffer from depression only. And in some cases antidepressants appear to foster a switch back into a manic episode (Altshuler et al., 2006).

A major concern in recent years has been evidence from a number of studies that SSRIs may increase the risk for suicide, primarily among adolescents and young adults (Healy & Whitaker, 2003; Holden, 2004). The challenge of collecting definitive data on this issue is much more daunting than one might guess, in part because suicide rates are already elevated among people who exhibit the disorders for which SSRIs are prescribed (Rihmer, 2003; Wessely & Kerwin, 2004). Some researchers have collected data that suggest that suicide rates have *declined* slightly because of widespread prescription of SSRIs (Baldessarini et al., 2007; Gibbons et al., 2006), while others have found no association between SSRIs and suicide (LaPierre, 2003; Simon et al., 2006).

"I think the dosage needs adjusting. I'm not nearly as happy as the people in the ads."

Overall, however, when antidepressants are compared to placebo treatment, the data suggest that antidepressants lead to a slight elevation in the risk of suicidal behavior, from roughly 2% to 4% (Bridge et al., 2007; Dubicka, Hadley, & Roberts, 2006; Hammad, Laughren, & Racoosin, 2006). Elevated suicide risk appears to be a problem mainly among a small minority of children and adolescents in the first month after starting antidepressants, especially the first nine days (Jick, Kaye, & Jick, 2004). Regulatory warnings from the U.S. Food and Drug Administration (FDA) have led to a decline in the prescription of SSRIs among adolescents (Nemeroff et al., 2007). This trend has prompted concern that increases in suicide may occur among untreated individuals. This concern seems legitimate in that suicide risk clearly peaks in the month prior to people beginning treatment for depression, whether that treatment involves SSRIs or psychotherapy (see **Figure 15.13** on the next page; Simon & Savarino, 2007). This pattern presumably occurs because the escalating agony of depression finally prompts people to seek treatment, but it also suggests that getting treatment with drugs or therapy reduces suicidal risk. In the final analysis, this is a complex issue, but the one thing experts seem to agree on is that adolescents starting on SSRIs should be monitored closely.

The newest class of antidepressants consists of medications that inhibit reuptake at both serotonin and norepinephrine synapses, referred to as SNRIs. Three drugs in this category have been approved for use in the United States (trade names: Effexor, Cymbalta, and Prestiq) (Thase, 2009). Preliminary evidence suggests that these drugs appear to produce slightly stronger antidepressant effects than the SSRIs (Thase & Denko, 2008). However, targeting two neurotransmitter systems also leads to a broader range of side effects, including troublesome elevations in blood pressure (Thase & Sloan, 2006).

## Mood Stabilizers

*Mood stabilizers* **are drugs used to control mood swings in patients with bipolar mood disorders.** For many years, lithium was the only effective drug in this category. Lithium has proven valuable in preventing *future* episodes of both mania and depression in patients with bipolar illness (Post & Altshuler, 2009). Lithium can also be used in efforts to bring patients with bipolar illness out of *current* manic or depressive episodes (Keck & McElroy, 2006), although antipsychotics and antidepressants are also used for these purposes. On the negative side of the ledger, lithium does have some dangerous side effects if its use isn't managed skillfully (Jefferson & Greist, 2009). Lithium levels in the patient's blood must be monitored carefully, because high concentrations can be toxic and even fatal. Kidney and thyroid gland complications are the other major problems associated with lithium therapy.

In recent years a number of alternatives to lithium have been developed. The most popular of these newer mood stabilizers is an anticonvulsant agent called *valproate,* which has become more widely used than lithium in the treatment of bipolar disorders (Thase & Denko, 2008). Valproate appears to be roughly as effective as lithium in efforts to treat current manic episodes and to prevent future affective disturbances (Moseman et al., 2003). The advantage provided by valproate is that it is better tolerated by patients. In some cases, a combination of valproate and lithium may be used in treatment (Post & Altshuler, 2009).

## Evaluating Drug Therapies

Drug therapies can produce clear therapeutic gains for many kinds of patients. What's especially impressive is that they can be effective in severe disorders that otherwise defy therapeutic endeavors. Nonetheless, drug therapies are controversial. Critics of drug therapy have raised a number of issues (Breggin & Cohen, 2007; Greenberg & Fisher, 1997; Healy, 2004; Whitaker, 2002). First, some critics argue that drug therapies often produce superficial curative effects. For example, Valium does not really solve problems with anxiety—it merely provides temporary relief from an unpleasant symptom. Moreover, this temporary relief

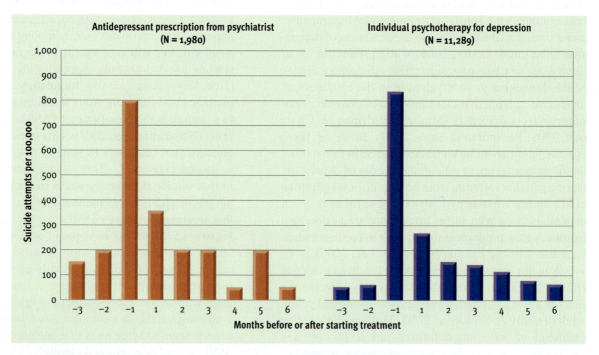

**Figure 15.13**

**Probability of a suicide attempt in relation to the initiation of treatment.** Examining medical records for thousands of patients, Simon and Savarino (2007) were able to gather information on the likelihood of a suicide attempt in the months before and after commencing treatment for depression. They compared patients who were put on an antidepressant medication against those who started in some form of insight or behavioral therapy. The data shown here, for young patients under the age of 25, indicate that suicide risk is highest in the month prior to treatment and next highest in the month after treatment is begun for both groups. These findings suggest that elevated suicide rates are not unique to starting on antidepressants and that getting treatment (whether it is medication or psychotherapy) reduces the risk of suicide.

Source: Adapted from Simon, G. E., & Savarino, J. (2007). Suicide attempts among patients starting depression treatments with medications or psychotherapy. *American Journal of Psychiatry, 164*(7), 1029–1034. Reprinted with permission from the *American Journal of Psychiatry,* copyright 2007. American Psychiatric Association.

may lull patients into complacency about their problem and prevent them from working toward a more lasting solution. Second, critics charge that many drugs are overprescribed and many patients overmedicated. According to these critics, many physicians habitually hand out prescriptions without giving adequate consideration to more complicated and difficult interventions. Critics also argue that there is a tendency in some institutions to overmedicate patients to minimize disruptive behavior. Third, some critics charge that the side effects of therapeutic drugs are worse than the illnesses the drugs are supposed to cure. Citing problems such as tardive dyskinesia, lithium toxicity, and addiction to antianxiety agents, these critics argue that the risks of therapeutic drugs aren't worth the benefits.

Critics maintain that the negative effects of psychiatric drugs are not fully appreciated because the pharmaceutical industry has managed to gain undue influence over the research enterprise as it relates to drug testing (Angell, 2000, 2004; Healy, 2004; Weber, 2006). Today, most researchers who investigate the benefits and risks of medications and write treatment guidelines have lucrative financial arrangements with the pharmaceutical industry, which they often fail to disclose (Bodenheimer, 2000; Choudhry, Stelfox, & Detsky, 2002; Lurie et al., 2006). Their studies are funded by drug companies and they often receive substantial consulting fees. Unfortunately, these financial ties appear to undermine the objectivity required in scientific research, as studies funded by pharmaceutical and other biomedical companies are far more likely to report favorable results than nonprofit-funded studies (Bekelman, Li, & Gross, 2003; Perlis et al., 2005; Rennie & Luft, 2000). Consistent with this finding, when specific antipsychotic drugs are pitted against each other in clinical trials, the sponsoring company's drug is reported to be superior to the other drugs in 90% of studies (Heres et al., 2006). Industry-financed drug trials also tend to be too brief to detect the long-term risks associated with new drugs (O'Brien, 1996), and when unfavorable results emerge, the data are often withheld from publication (Rising, Bacchetti, & Bero, 2008; Turner et al., 2008). Also, research designs are often slanted in a multitude of ways so as to exaggerate the positive effects and minimize the negative effects of the drugs under scrutiny (Carpenter, 2002; Chopra, 2003; Moncrieff, 2001). The conflicts of interest that appear to be pervasive in contemporary drug research raise grave concerns that require attention from researchers, universities, and federal agencies.

Obviously, drug therapies have stirred up some debate. However, this controversy pales in comparison to the furious debates inspired by electroconvulsive (shock) therapy (ECT). ECT is so controversial that the residents of Berkeley, California, voted to outlaw ECT in their city. However, in subsequent lawsuits the courts ruled that scientific questions cannot be settled through a vote, and they overturned the law. What makes ECT so controversial? You'll see in the next section.

### Electroconvulsive Therapy (ECT)

In the 1930s, a Hungarian psychiatrist named Ladislas Meduna speculated that epilepsy and schizophrenia could not coexist in the same body. On the basis of this observation, which turned out to be inaccurate, Meduna theorized that it might be useful to induce epileptic-like seizures in schizophrenic patients. Initially, a drug was used to trigger these seizures. However, by 1938, a pair of Italian psychiatrists (Cerletti & Bini, 1938) demonstrated that it was safer to elicit the seizures with electric shock. Thus, modern electroconvulsive therapy was born.

*Electroconvulsive therapy (ECT) is a biomedical treatment in which electric shock is used to produce a cortical seizure accompanied by convulsions.* In ECT, electrodes are attached to the skull over one or both temporal lobes of the brain (see the photo on the next page). A light anesthesia is induced, and the patient

DILBERT © Scott Adams/Dist. by United Feature Syndicate, Inc.

is given a variety of drugs to minimize the likelihood of complications, such as spinal fractures. An electric current is then applied for about a second. The current should trigger a brief (5–20 seconds) convulsive seizure, during which the patient usually loses consciousness. Patients normally awaken in an hour or two. People typically receive between six and twelve treatments over a period of about a month (Glass, 2001).

The clinical use of ECT peaked in the 1940s and 1950s, before effective drug therapies were widely available. ECT has long been controversial, and its use did decline in the 1960s and 1970s. Nonetheless, there has been a resurgence in the use of ECT, and it is *not* a rare form of therapy. Although only about 8% of psychiatrists administer ECT (Hermann et al., 1998), estimates suggest that about 100,000 people receive ECT treatments each year in the United States (Hermann et al., 1995). Some critics argue that ECT is overused because it is a lucrative procedure that boosts psychiatrists' income while consuming relatively little of their time in comparison to insight therapy (Frank, 1990). Conversely, some advocates argue that ECT is underutilized because the public harbors many misconceptions about its risks and side effects (McDonald et al., 2004). Although ECT was once considered appropriate for a wide range of disorders, in recent decades it

has primarily been recommended for the treatment of depression.

### Effectiveness of ECT

The evidence on the therapeutic efficacy of ECT is open to varied interpretations. Proponents of ECT maintain that it is a remarkably effective treatment for major depression (Prudic, 2009; Rudorfer, Henry, & Sackeim, 2003). Moreover, they note that many patients who do not benefit from antidepressant medication improve in response to ECT (Nobler & Sackeim, 2006). However, opponents of ECT argue that the available studies are flawed and inconclusive and that ECT is probably no more effective than a placebo (Rose et al., 2003). Overall, enough favorable evidence seems to exist to justify *conservative* use of ECT in treating severe mood disorders in patients who have not responded to medication (Carney & Geddes, 2003; Metzger, 1999). Unfortunately, relapse rates after ECT are distressingly high. Over 50% of patients relapse within 6 to 12 months, although relapse rates can be reduced by giving ECT patients antidepressant drugs (Sackeim et al., 2001).

The debate about whether ECT works does *not* make ECT unique among approaches to the treatment of psychological disorders. Controversies exist regarding the effectiveness of most therapies. However, this

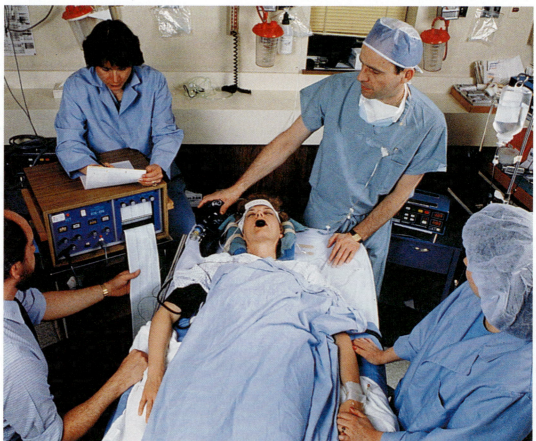

This patient is being prepared for electroconvulsive therapy. The mouthpiece keeps the patient from biting her tongue during the electrically induced seizures.

Given the side effects and risks associated with ECT and drug treatments, scientists are always on the lookout for new methods of treating psychological disorders that might exhibit greater efficacy or produce fewer complications. Some innovative, new approaches to treatment involving stimulation of the brain are being explored with promising results, although they remain highly experimental at this time.

For example, *transcranial magnetic stimulation (TMS)* is a new technique that permits scientists to temporarily enhance or depress activity in a specific area of the brain. In TMS, a magnetic coil mounted on a small paddle is held over specific areas of the head to increase or decrease activity in discrete regions of the cortex (Nahas et al., 2007). Neuroscientists are mostly experimenting with TMS as a treatment for depression. Thus far, treatments delivered to the right and left prefrontal cortex show promise in reducing depressive symptoms (Nobler & Sackeim, 2006; O'Reardon et al., 2007). TMS generally is well tolerated with minimal side effects. But a great deal of additional research will be necessary before the therapeutic value of TMS can be determined.

The other new approach to treatment is *deep brain stimulation (DBS)*, in which a thin electrode is surgically implanted in the brain and connected to an implanted pulse generator so that various electrical currents can be delivered to brain tissue adjacent to the electrode (George, 2003; see **Figure 15.14**). DBS has proven valuable in the treatment of the motor disturbances associated with Parkinson's disease, tardive dyskinesia, and some seizure disorders (Halpern et al., 2007; Wilder et al., 2008). Researchers are currently exploring whether DBS may have value in the treatment of depression or obsessive-compulsive disorder (George et al., 2006; Hardesty & Sackeim, 2007). Obviously,

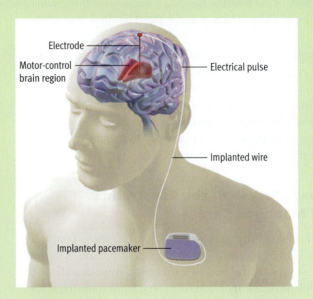

**Figure 15.14**
**Deep brain stimulation.** Deep brain stimulation requires a surgical procedure in which a thin electrode (about the width of a human hair) is inserted into deep areas of the brain. The electrode is connected to a pulse generator implanted under the skin of the chest. The placement of the electrode and the type of current generated depend on what condition is being treated. The electrode shown here was implanted in a motor area of the brain to treat the tremors associated with Parkinson's disease. Researchers are experimenting with other electrode placements in efforts to treat depression and obsessive-compulsive disorder.

Source: Illustration by Brian Christie. Adapted from George, M. S. (2003). Stimulating the brain. *Scientific American, 289*(3), 67–73.

this highly invasive procedure requiring brain surgery will never be a frontline therapy for mental disorders, but scientists hope that it may be valuable for highly treatment-resistant patients who do not benefit from conventional therapies (Kuehn, 2007).

controversy is especially problematic because ECT carries some risks.

### Risks Associated with ECT

Even ECT proponents acknowledge that memory losses, impaired attention, and other cognitive deficits are common short-term side effects of electroconvulsive therapy (Lisanby et al., 2000; Nobler & Sackeim, 2006). However, ECT proponents assert that these deficits are mild and usually disappear within a month or two (Glass, 2001). An American Psychiatric Association

(2001) task force concluded that there is no objective evidence that ECT causes structural damage in the brain or that it has any lasting negative effects on the ability to learn and remember information. In contrast, ECT critics maintain that ECT-induced cognitive deficits are often significant and sometimes permanent (Breggin, 1991; Frank, 1990; Rose et al., 2003), although their evidence seems to be largely anecdotal. Given the concerns about the risks of ECT and the doubts about its efficacy, it appears that the use of ECT will remain controversial for some time to come.

# Current Trends and Issues in Treatment

## LEARNING OBJECTIVES

- Discuss how managed care has affected the provision of therapy.
- Discuss the merits of blending approaches to therapy and the rise of eclecticism.
- Explain why therapy is underutilized by ethnic minorities.

The controversy about ECT is only one of many contentious issues and shifting trends in the world of mental health care. In this section, we discuss the impact of managed care on psychotherapy, the continuing trend toward blending various approaches to therapy, and efforts to respond more effectively to increasing cultural diversity in Western societies.

## Grappling with the Constraints of Managed Care

The 1990s brought a dramatic shift in how people in the United States pay for their health care. Alarmed by skyrocketing health care costs, huge numbers of employers and individuals moved from traditional fee-for-service arrangements to managed care health plans (Hogan & Morrison, 2003; Kiesler, 2000). In the *fee-for-service* system, hospitals, physicians, psychologists, and other providers charged fees for whatever health care services were needed, and most of these fees were reimbursed by private insurance or the government (through Medicaid, Medicare, and other programs). In *managed care systems* people enroll in prepaid plans with small co-payments for services, and the plans agree to provide ongoing health care for a specific sum of money. Managed care usually involves a tradeoff: Consumers pay lower prices for their care, but they give up much of their freedom to choose their providers and to obtain whatever treatments they believe necessary.

The proponents of managed care originally promised individuals and employers that they would be able to hold costs down without having a negative impact on the quality of care by negotiating lower fees from providers, reducing inefficiency, and cracking down on medically unnecessary services. During the 1990s, managed care *was* successful in reducing the acceleration of medical costs in the United States (Drum & Sekel, 2003). However, critics charge that managed care systems have squeezed all the savings they can out of the "fat" that existed in the old system and that they have responded to continued inflation in their costs by rationing care and limiting access to medically *necessary* services (Duckworth & Borus, 1999; Giles & Marafiote, 1998; Sanchez & Turner, 2003).

The possibility that managed care is having a negative effect on the quality of care is a source of concern throughout the health care professions, but the issue is especially sensitive in the area of mental health care (Bursztajn & Brodsky, 2002; Campbell, 2000; Rosenberg & DeMaso, 2008). Critics maintain that mental health care has suffered particularly severe cuts in services because the question of what is "medically necessary" can be more subjective than in other treatment specialties (such as internal medicine or ophthalmology) and because patients who are denied psychotherapy services are relatively unlikely to complain (Duckworth & Borus, 1999). For example, a business executive who is trying to hide his depression or cocaine addiction from his employer will be reluctant to complain to his employer if therapeutic services are denied.

According to critics, the restriction of mental health services sometimes involves outright denial of treatment, but it often takes more subtle forms, such as underdiagnosing conditions, failing to make needed referrals to mental health specialists, and arbitrarily limiting the length of treatment (Bursztajn & Brodsky, 2002; Miller, 1996). Many managed care systems hold down costs by erecting *barriers to access,* such as requiring referrals from primary care physicians who don't have appointments available for weeks or months or authorizing only a few sessions of therapy at a time (Sanchez & Turner, 2003). Another cost-cutting strategy is to reroute patients from highly trained providers, such as psychiatrists and doctoral-level psychologists, to less-well-trained providers, such as masters-level counselors, who may not be adequately prepared to handle serious psychological disorders (Seligman & Levant, 1998).

The extensive utilization review procedures required by managed care have also raised concerns about providers' autonomy and clients' confidentiality (Chambliss, 2000; Plante, 2005). Clinicians who have to "sell" their treatment plans to managed care bureaucrats who may know little about mental health care feel that they have lost control over their professional practice. They also worry that the need to divulge the details of clients' problems to justify treatment may breach the confidentiality of the therapist-client relationship.

Unfortunately, there are no simple solutions to these problems on the horizon. Restraining the burgeoning cost of health care without compromising the quality of care, consumers' freedom of choice, and providers' autonomy is an enormously complex and daunting

## Recommended READING

### Crazy: A Father's Search Through America's Mental Health Madness
by Pete Earley (G. P. Putnam's Sons, 2006)

This book will make you feel outraged. This book will make you cry. Above all else, this book will educate you about how incredibly difficult it can be to get effective mental health care for people troubled by severe disturbances such as schizophrenia and bipolar mood disorder. You will learn that our mental health system sometimes seems insane. The author is a former *Washington Post* investigative reporter who was suddenly drawn into the quagmire of America's mental health system when his son, Mike, developed bipolar disorder at the age of 23. Mike became seriously psychotic—at one point he wrapped aluminum foil around his head so people wouldn't be able to read his thoughts. His behavior became erratic. He crashed his car while trying to drive with his eyes closed, informed strangers at a coffee shop that he had supernatural powers, and broke into a residence where he ignored a wailing burglar alarm and proceeded to pee on the carpet, turn on all the water faucets, thus flooding the home, and give himself a bubble bath—until the police arrived to detain him. In his disoriented state, Earley's son was not willing to voluntarily cooperate with treatment. So, the family repeatedly found themselves in hospital emergency rooms where they were told that their son could not be admitted because—as an adult—he had the right to refuse treatment, even though his judgment obviously was severely impaired.

This frustrating experience was the impetus for Earley's book. It motivated him to conduct a wide-ranging investigation of mental health care in the United States today. His journey took him to mental hospitals, prisons, courts, alternative facilities for the mentally ill, meetings of mental health advocacy groups, and street corners where the homeless mentally ill congregated. He learned that "What was happening to Mike was not an oddity. It was a tiny piece in a bigger story. A major shift had occurred in our country. The mentally ill, who used to be treated in state mental hospitals, were now being arrested. Our nation's jails and prisons were our new asylums" (p. 2).

This book tells two intertwined stories—Earley's personal battle to obtain meaningful treatment for his son and his investigative analysis of modern mental health care. Both stories are compelling, heart-wrenching, and enlightening. And both stories demonstrate that American society is not providing adequate care for a sizable segment of the mentally ill population.

*Go to the Psychology CourseMate for Weiten at* **www.cengagebrain.com/shop/ISBN/1111186634** *for descriptions of other recommended books.*

---

challenge. At this juncture, it is difficult to predict what the future holds. However, it is clear that economic realities have ushered in an era of transition for the treatment of psychological disorders and problems (Huey et al., 2009).

## Blending Approaches to Treatment

In this chapter we have reviewed many approaches to treatment. However, there is no rule that a client must be treated with just one approach. Often, a clinician will use several techniques in working with a client. For example, a depressed person might receive group therapy (an insight therapy), social skills training (a behavior therapy), and antidepressant medication (a biomedical therapy). Multiple approaches are particularly likely when a treatment *team* provides therapy. Studies suggest that combining approaches to treatment has merit (Glass, 2004; Szigethy & Friedman, 2009).

The value of multiple approaches may explain why a significant trend seems to have crept into the field of psychotherapy: a movement away from strong loyalty to individual schools of thought and a corresponding move toward integrating various approaches to therapy (Castonguay et al., 2003; D. Smith, 1999). Most clinicians used to depend exclusively on one system of therapy while rejecting the utility of all others. This era of fragmentation may be drawing to a close. One survey of psychologists' theoretical orientations, which is summarized in **Figure 15.15** (on the next page), found that 36% of the respondents described themselves as *eclectic* in approach (Norcross, Hedges, & Castle, 2002). *Eclecticism* involves drawing ideas from two or more systems of therapy, instead of committing to just one system. Eclectic therapists borrow ideas, insights, and techniques from a variety of sources while tailoring their intervention strategy to the unique needs of each client. Advocates of eclecticism, such as Arnold Lazarus (1992, 1995, 2008), maintain that therapists should ask themselves, "What is the best approach for this specific client, problem, and situation?" and then adjust their strategy accordingly.

## Increasing Multicultural Sensitivity in Treatment

Research on how cultural factors influence the process and outcome of psychotherapy has burgeoned in recent years, motivated in part by the need to improve mental health services for ethnic minority groups in American society (Miranda et al., 2005; Worthington, Soth-McNett, & Moreno, 2007). The data are ambiguous for a couple of ethnic groups, but studies suggest that American minority groups generally underutilize therapeutic services (Bender et al., 2007; Folsom et al., 2007;

**Figure 15.15**

**The leading approaches to therapy among psychologists.** These data, from a survey of 531 psychologists who belong to the American Psychological Association's Division of Psychotherapy, provide some indication of how common an eclectic approach to therapy has become. The findings suggest that the most widely used approaches to therapy are eclectic, psychodynamic, and cognitive-behavioral treatments. (Based on data from Norcross, Hedges, & Castle, 2002)

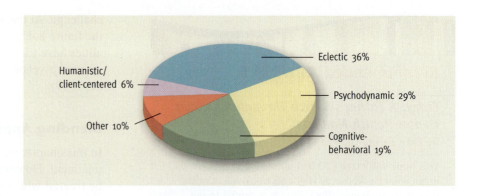

Eclectic 36%

Humanistic/client-centered 6%

Psychodynamic 29%

Other 10%

Cognitive-behavioral 19%

Olfson et al., 2002; Richardson, et al., 2003). Why? A variety of barriers appear to contribute to this problem, including the following (Snowden & Yamada, 2005; U.S. Department of Health and Human Services, 1999; Zane et al., 2004):

1. *Cultural barriers.* In times of psychological distress, some cultural groups are reluctant to turn to formal, professional sources of assistance. Given their socialization, they prefer to rely on informal assistance from family members, the clergy, respected elders, herbalists, acupuncturists, and so forth, who share their cultural heritage. Many members of minority groups have a history of frustrating interactions with American bureaucracies and are distrustful of large, intimidating, foreign institutions, such as hospitals and community mental health centers. For example, research shows that African-American patients tend to trust physicians less than white patients (Armstrong et al., 2007).

2. *Language barriers.* Effective communication is crucial to the provision of psychotherapy, yet most hospitals and mental health agencies are not adequately staffed with therapists who speak the languages used by minority groups in their service areas. The resulting communication problems make it awkward and difficult for many minority group members to explain their problems and obtain the type of help they need.

3. *Institutional barriers.* The vast majority of therapists have been trained almost exclusively in the treatment of middle-class white Americans and are not familiar with the cultural backgrounds and unique characteristics of various ethnic groups. This culture gap often leads to misunderstandings, ill-advised treatment strategies, and reduced rapport. Consistent with this assertion, recent research found that psychiatrists spend less time with black patients than white patients (Olfson, Cherry, & Lewis-Fernandez, 2009). Another study of over 3500 African American participants found that only 27% of their mental health visits resulted in "minimally adequate care" (Neighbors et al., 2007).

Ethnicity aside, those who are poor are less likely than others to gain access to psychotherapy (Smith, 2005). This problem affects ethnic minorities disproportionately because many minority groups suffer from elevated rates of joblessness and poverty. And some critics argue that many middle-class therapists don't feel comfortable with impoverished clients and tend to distance themselves from the poor (Lott, 2002; Smith, 2005). Although this social class bias surely is not limited to therapists, it creates another huge barrier to equal access for those who already have to grapple with countless problems associated with poverty.

What can be done to improve mental health services for American minority groups? Researchers in this area have offered a variety of suggestions (Hong, Garcia, & Soriano, 2000; Miranda et al., 2005; Pedersen, 1994; Yamamoto et al., 1993). Discussions of possible solutions usually begin with the need to recruit and train more ethnic minority therapists. Studies show that ethnic minorities are more likely to go to mental health facilities that are staffed by a higher proportion of people who share their ethnic background (Snowden & Hu, 1996; Sue, Zane, & Young, 1994). Individual therapists have been urged to work harder at building a vigorous *therapeutic alliance* (a strong supportive bond) with their ethnic clients. A strong therapeutic alliance is associated with better therapeutic outcomes regardless of ethnicity, but some studies suggest that it is especially crucial for minority clients (Bender et al., 2007; Comas-Diaz, 2006). Finally, most authorities urge further investigation of how traditional approaches to therapy can be modified and tailored to be more compatible with specific cultural groups' attitudes, values, norms, and traditions (Hwang, 2006). A recent review of 76 studies that examined the effects of culturally adapted interventions found clear evidence that this tailoring process tends to yield positive effects (Griner & Smith, 2006). The benefits are particularly prominent when a treatment is tailored to a single, specific cultural group rather than a mixture of several or more cultural groups.

# Looking for a Therapist

## LEARNING OBJECTIVES

- Discuss where to seek therapy.
- Evaluate the potential importance of a therapist's gender and professional background.
- Assess the evidence on whether therapists' theoretical approaches influence their effectiveness.
- Understand what one should expect from therapy.

*Answer the following "true" or "false."*

___ **1.** Psychotherapy is an art as well as a science.

___ **2.** The type of professional degree that a therapist holds is relatively unimportant.

___ **3.** Psychotherapy can be harmful or damaging to a client.

___ **4.** Psychotherapy does not have to be expensive.

___ **5.** It is a good idea to shop around when choosing a therapist.

All of these statements are true. Do any of them surprise you? If so, you're in good company. Many people know relatively little about the practicalities of selecting a therapist. The task of finding an appropriate therapist is no less complex than shopping for any other major service. Should you see a psychologist or a psychiatrist? Should you opt for individual therapy or group therapy? Should you see a client-centered therapist or a behavior therapist? The unfortunate part of this decision process is that people seeking psychotherapy often feel overwhelmed by personal problems. The last thing they need is to be confronted by yet another complex problem.

Nonetheless, the importance of finding a good therapist cannot be overestimated. Therapy can sometimes have harmful rather than helpful effects. We have already discussed how drug therapies and ECT can sometimes be damaging, but problems are not limited to these interventions. Talking about your problems with a therapist may sound pretty harmless, but studies indicate that insight therapies can also backfire (Lambert & Ogles, 2004; Lilienfeld, 2007). Although a great many talented therapists are available, psychotherapy, like any other profession, has incompetent practitioners as well. Therefore, you should shop for a skilled therapist, just as you would for a good attorney or a good mechanic.

**WEB LINK 15.6  Psych Central**

The work of John Grohol, Psych Central is a source for learning about all aspects of mental health, including psychological disorders and treatment, professional issues, and information for mental health care consumers. Almost 2,000 annotated listings to information sources are offered here.

In this Application, we present some information that should be helpful if you ever have to look for a therapist for yourself or for a friend or family member (based on Beutler, Bongar, & Shurkin, 2001; Bruckner-Gordon, Gangi, & Wallman, 1988; Ehrenberg & Ehrenberg, 1994; Pittman, 1994).

## Where Do You Find Therapeutic Services?

Psychotherapy can be found in a variety of settings. Contrary to general belief, most therapists are not in private practice. Many work in institutional settings such as community mental health centers, hospitals, and human service agencies. The principal sources of therapeutic services are described in **Figure 15.16** on the next page. The exact configuration of therapeutic services available will vary from one community to another. To find out what your community has to offer, it is a good idea to consult your friends, your local phone book, or your local community mental health center.

## Is the Therapist's Profession or Sex Important?

Psychotherapists may be trained in psychology, psychiatry, social work, counseling, psychiatric nursing, or marriage and family therapy. Researchers have *not* found any reliable associations between therapists' professional background and therapeutic efficacy (Beutler et al., 2004), probably because many talented therapists can be found in all of these professions. Thus, the kind of degree that a therapist holds doesn't need to be a crucial consideration in your selection process.

Whether a therapist's sex is important depends on your attitude (Nadelson, Notman, & McCarthy, 2005). If *you* feel that the therapist's sex is important, then for you it is. The therapeutic relationship must be characterized by trust and rapport. Feeling uncomfortable with a therapist of one sex or the other could inhibit the therapeutic process. Hence, you should feel free to look for a male or female therapist if you prefer to do so. This point is probably most relevant to female clients whose troubles may be related to the extensive sexism in our society (Kaplan, 1985). It is entirely reasonable

**Figure 15.16**

**Sources of therapeutic services.** Therapists work in a variety of organizational settings. Foremost among them are the five described here.

| **Principal Sources of Therapeutic Services** | |
| --- | --- |
| **Source** | **Comments** |
| Private practitioners | Self-employed therapists are listed in the Yellow Pages under their professional category, such as psychologists or psychiatrists. Private practitioners tend to be relatively expensive, but they also tend to be highly experienced therapists. |
| Community mental health centers | Community mental health centers have salaried psychologists, psychiatrists, and social workers on staff. The centers provide a variety of services and often have staff available on weekends and at night to deal with emergencies. |
| Hospitals | Several kinds of hospitals provide therapeutic services. There are both public and private mental hospitals that specialize in the care of people with psychological disorders. Many general hospitals have a psychiatric ward, and those that do not will usually have psychiatrists and psychologists on staff and on call. Although hospitals tend to concentrate on inpatient treatment, many provide outpatient therapy as well. |
| Human service agencies | Various social service agencies employ therapists to provide short-term counseling. Depending on your community, you may find agencies that deal with family problems, juvenile problems, drug problems, and so forth. |
| Schools and workplaces | Most high schools and colleges have counseling centers where students can get help with personal problems. Similarly, some large businesses offer in-house counseling to their employees. |

for women to seek a therapist with a feminist perspective if that would make them feel more comfortable.

Speaking of sex, you should be aware that sexual exploitation is an occasional problem in the context of therapy. Studies indicate that a small minority of therapists take advantage of their clients sexually (Pope, Keith-Spiegel, & Tabachnick, 1986). These incidents almost always involve a male therapist making advances to a female client. The available evidence indicates that these sexual liaisons are usually harmful to clients (Gabbard, 1994; Williams, 1992). There are absolutely no situations in which therapist-client sexual relations are an ethical therapeutic practice. If a therapist makes sexual advances, a client should terminate treatment.

### Is Therapy Always Expensive?

Psychotherapy does not have to be prohibitively expensive. Private practitioners tend to be the most expensive, charging between $25 and $140 per (50-minute) hour. These fees may seem high, but they are in line with those of similar professionals, such as dentists and attorneys. Community mental health centers and social service agencies are usually supported by tax dollars. Hence, they can charge lower fees than most therapists in private practice. Many of these organizations use a sliding scale, so that clients are charged according to how much they can afford. Thus, most communities have inexpensive opportunities for psychotherapy. Moreover, many health insurance plans provide at least partial reimbursement for the cost of treatment.

### Is the Therapist's Theoretical Approach Important?

Logically, you might expect that the diverse approaches to therapy ought to vary in effectiveness. For the most part, that is *not* what researchers find, however. After reviewing the evidence, Jerome Frank (1961) and Lester Luborsky and his colleagues (1975) both quote the

**INSIDE WOODY ALLEN**

dodo bird who has just judged a race in *Alice in Wonderland:* "Everybody has won, and *all* must have prizes." Improvement rates for various theoretical orientations usually come out pretty close in most studies (Lambert & Ogles, 2004; Luborsky et al., 2002; Wampold, 2001). In their landmark review of outcome studies, Smith and Glass (1977) estimated the effectiveness of many major approaches to therapy. As **Figure 15.17** shows, the estimates cluster together closely.

However, these findings are a little misleading, as they have been averaged across many types of patients and many types of problems. Most experts seem to think that *for certain types of problems, some approaches to therapy are more effective than others* (Beutler, 2002; Crits-Christoph, 1997; Norcross, 1995). For example, Martin Seligman (1995) asserts that panic disorders respond best to cognitive therapy, that specific phobias are most amenable to treatment with systematic desensitization, and that obsessive-compulsive disorders are best treated with behavior therapy or medication. Thus, for a specific type of problem, a therapist's theoretical approach *may* make a difference.

It is also important to point out that the finding that various approaches to therapy are roughly equal in overall efficacy does not mean that all *therapists* are created equal. Some therapists unquestionably are more effective than others. However, these variations in effectiveness appear to depend on individual therapists' personal skills rather than on their theoretical orientation (Beutler et al., 2004). Good, bad, and mediocre therapists are found within each school of thought. Indeed, the tremendous variation among individual therapists in skills may be one of the main reasons why it is hard to find efficacy differences between theoretical approaches to therapy (Staines, 2008).

The key point is that effective therapy requires skill and creativity. Arnold Lazarus (1989), who devised an approach to treatment called multimodal therapy, emphasizes that therapists "straddle the fence between science and art." Therapy is scientific in that interventions

© Michael Newman/Photo Edit

**Therapy is both a science and an art. It is scientific in that practitioners are guided in their work by a huge body of empirical research. It is an art in that therapists often have to be creative in adapting their treatment procedures to individual patients and their idiosyncrasies.**

are based on extensive theory and empirical research (Forsyth & Strong, 1986). Ultimately, though, each client is a unique human being, and the therapist has to creatively fashion a treatment program that will help that individual.

## What Is Therapy Like?

It is important to have realistic expectations about therapy, or you may be unnecessarily disappointed. Some people expect miracles. They expect to turn their life around quickly with little effort. Others expect their therapist to run their lives for them. These are unrealistic expectations.

Therapy is usually a slow process. Your problems are not likely to melt away quickly. Moreover, therapy is hard work, and your therapist is only a facilitator. Ultimately, *you* have to confront the challenge of changing your behavior, your feelings, or your personality. This process may not be pleasant. You may have to face up to some painful truths about yourself. As Ehrenberg and Ehrenberg (1994) point out, psychotherapy takes time, effort, and courage.

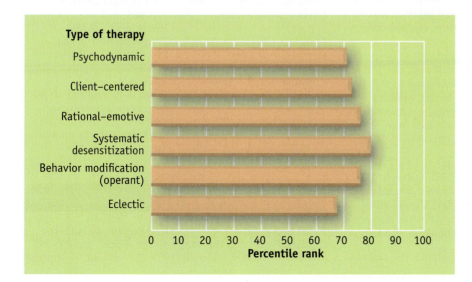

**Percentile rank**

**Figure 15.17**

**Efficacy of various approaches to therapy.** Smith and Glass (1977) reviewed nearly 400 studies in which clients who were treated with a specific type of therapy were compared with a control group made up of people with similar problems who went untreated. The bars indicate the percentile rank (on outcome measures) attained by the average client treated with each type of therapy when compared to control subjects. The higher the percentile, the more effective the therapy was. As you can see, the different approaches were fairly close in their apparent effectiveness.

Source: Adapted from Smith, M. L., & Glass, G. V. (1977). Meta-analysis of psychotherapy outcome series. *American Psychologist, 32,* 752–760. Copyright © 1977 by the American Psychological Association. Adapted by permission of the authors.

### The Elements of the Treatment Process

● Psychotherapy involves three elements: treatments, clients, and therapists. Approaches to treatment are diverse, but they can be grouped into three categories: insight therapies, behavior therapies, and biomedical therapies. People vary considerably in their willingness to seek psychotherapy, and many people who need therapy do not receive it.

● Therapists come from a variety of professional backgrounds. Clinical and counseling psychologists, psychiatrists, social workers, psychiatric nurses, and counselors are the principal providers of therapeutic services.

### Insight Therapies

● Insight therapies involve verbal interactions intended to enhance self-knowledge. In psychoanalysis, free association and dream analysis are used to explore the unconscious. When an analyst's probing hits sensitive areas, resistance can be expected. The transference relationship may be used to overcome this resistance. Classical psychoanalysis is not widely practiced anymore, but Freud's legacy lives on in a rich diversity of modern psychodynamic therapies.

● Rogers pioneered client-centered therapy, which is intended to provide a supportive climate in which clients can restructure their self-concepts. This therapy emphasizes clarification of the client's feelings and self-acceptance. Positive psychotherapy attempts to get clients to recognize their strengths, appreciate their blessings, savor positive experiences, and find meaning in their lives. Most theoretical approaches to insight therapy have been adapted for use with groups. Group therapy has its own unique strengths and is not merely a cheap substitute for individual therapy.

● The weight of the evidence suggests that insight therapies can be effective. The benefits of insight therapies may be due in part to common factors. Repressed memories of childhood sexual abuse recovered through therapy are a new source of controversy in the mental health field. Although many recovered memories of abuse may be the product of suggestion, some probably are authentic.

### Behavior Therapies

● Behavior therapies use the principles of learning in direct efforts to change specific aspects of behavior. Wolpe's systematic desensitization is a treatment for phobias. It involves the construction of an anxiety hierarchy, relaxation training, and step-by-step movement through the hierarchy.

● In aversion therapy, a stimulus associated with an unwanted response is paired with an unpleasant stimulus in an effort to eliminate the maladaptive response. Social skills training can improve clients' interpersonal skills through shaping, modeling, and behavioral rehearsal. Beck's cognitive therapy concentrates on changing the way clients think about events in their lives. Ample evidence shows that behavior therapies are effective.

### Biomedical Therapies

● Biomedical therapies involve physiological interventions for psychological problems. Two examples of biomedical treatments are drug therapy and electroconvulsive therapy. A great variety of disorders are treated with drugs. The principal types of therapeutic drugs are antianxiety drugs, antipsychotic drugs, antidepressant drugs, and mood stabilizers.

● Drug therapies can be effective, but they have their pitfalls. Many drugs produce problematic side effects, and some are overprescribed. Critics are also concerned that the pharmaceutical industry has gained too much influence over drug testing research.

● Electroconvulsive therapy (ECT) is used to trigger a cortical seizure that is believed to have therapeutic value for depression. There is contradictory evidence and heated debate about the effectiveness of ECT and about possible risks associated with its use.

### Current Trends and Issues in Treatment

● Many clinicians and their clients believe that managed care has restricted access to mental health care and undermined its quality. Managed care has also raised concerns about providers' autonomy and clients' confidentiality.

● Combinations of insight, behavioral, and biomedical therapies are often used fruitfully in the treatment of psychological disorders. Many modern therapists are eclectic, using ideas and techniques gleaned from a number of theoretical approaches.

● Because of cultural, language, and access barriers, therapeutic services are underutilized by ethnic minorities in America. The crux of the problem is the failure of institutions to provide culturally sensitive forms of treatment for ethnic minorities.

### Application: Looking for a Therapist

● Therapeutic services are available in many settings, and such services do not have to be expensive. Excellent and mediocre therapists can be found in all of the mental health professions. Thus, therapists' personal skills are more important than their professional degree. In selecting a therapist, it is reasonable to insist on a therapist of one gender or the other.

● The various theoretical approaches to treatment appear to be fairly similar in overall effectiveness. However, for certain types of problems, some approaches to therapy may be more effective than others. Therapy requires time, hard work, and the courage to confront your problems.

Antianxiety drugs  p. 495
Antidepressant drugs  p. 497
Antipsychotic drugs  p. 496
Aversion therapy  p. 492
Behavior therapies  p. 490
Biomedical therapies  p. 495
Client-centered therapy  p. 483
Clinical psychologists  p. 480
Cognitive-behavioral treatments  p. 493
Cognitive therapy  p. 493
Counseling psychologists  p. 480
Dream analysis  p. 481
Electroconvulsive therapy (ECT)  p. 499
Free association  p. 481
Group therapy  p. 485
Insight therapies  p. 481
Interpretation  p. 482
Mood stabilizers  p. 498
Positive psychotherapy  p. 485
Psychiatrists  p. 480
Psychoanalysis  p. 481
Psychopharmacotherapy  p. 495
Resistance  p. 482
Social skills training  p. 492
Systematic desensitization  p. 491
Tardive dyskinesia  p. 496
Transference  p. 483

Aaron Beck  pp. 493–494
Sigmund Freud  pp. 481–483
Carl Rogers  pp. 483–484
Joseph Wolpe  pp. 490–492

# CHAPTER 15 PRACTICE TEST

## QUESTIONS

1. Which of the following approaches to psychotherapy is based on the theories of Sigmund Freud and his followers?
   a. behavior therapies
   b. client-centered therapy
   c. biomedical therapies
   d. psychoanalytic therapy

2. Miriam is seeing a therapist who encourages her to let her mind ramble and say whatever comes up, regardless of how trivial or irrelevant it may seem. The therapist explains that she is interested in probing the depths of Miriam's unconscious mind. This therapist appears to practice _____ and the technique in use is _____.
   a. psychoanalysis; transference
   b. psychoanalysis; free association
   c. cognitive therapy; free association
   d. client-centered therapy; clarification

3. Because Suzanne has an unconscious sexual attraction to her father, she behaves seductively toward her therapist. Suzanne's behavior is most likely a form of:
   a. resistance.
   b. transference.
   c. misinterpretation.
   d. spontaneous remission.

4. Client-centered therapy emphasizes:
   a. interpretation.
   b. probing the unconscious.
   c. clarification.
   d. all of the above.

5. With regard to studies of the efficacy of various treatments, research suggests that:
   a. insight therapy is superior to no treatment or placebo treatment.
   b. individual insight therapy is effective, but group therapy is not.
   c. group therapy is effective, but individual insight therapy rarely works.
   d. insight therapy is effective, but only if patients remain in therapy for at least three years.

6. According to behavior therapists, pathological behaviors:
   a. are signs of an underlying emotional or cognitive problem.
   b. should be viewed as the expression of an unconscious sexual or aggressive conflict.
   c. can be modified directly through the application of established principles of conditioning.
   d. both a and b.

7. A stimulus that elicits an undesirable response is paired with a noxious stimulus in:
   a. systematic desensitization.
   b. cognitive therapy.
   c. aversion therapy.
   d. psychoanalysis.

8. Bryce's psychiatrist has prescribed both Prozac and lithium for him. Bryce's diagnosis is probably:
   a. schizophrenia.
   b. obsessive-compulsive disorder.
   c. bipolar disorder.
   d. dissociative disorder.

9. Drug therapies have been criticized on the grounds that:
   a. they are ineffective in most patients.
   b. they temporarily relieve symptoms without addressing the real problem.
   c. many drugs are overprescribed and many patients are overmedicated.
   d. both b and c.

10. A therapist's theoretical approach is not nearly as important as his or her:
    a. age.
    b. appearance.
    c. personal characteristics and skills.
    d. type of professional training.

## ANSWERS

1. d Page 481
2. b Page 481
3. b Page 483
4. c Page 484
5. a Page 487
6. c Page 490
7. c Page 492
8. c Pages 497–498
9. d Pages 498–499
10. c Pages 506–507

## Personal Explorations Workbook

Go to the *Personal Explorations Workbook* in the back of your textbook for exercises that can enhance your self-understanding in relation to issues raised in this chapter. **Exercise 15.1** *Self-Assessment:* Attitudes Toward Seeking Professional Psychological Help **Exercise 15.2** *Self-Reflection:* Thinking About Therapy

 CourseMate

Access an interactive eBook, chapter-specific interactive learning tools, including Personal Explorations, Recommended Readings, Critical Thinking Exercises, flashcards, quizzes, videos and more in your Psychology CourseMate, available at **www.cengagebrain.com/shop/ISBN/1111186634**.

© Monalyn Gracia/Corbis/photolibrary

# CHAPTER 16

# *Positive Psychology*

On January 15, 2009, a striking event galvanized the American public's attention and imbued people with feelings of joy. The event was unprecedented: A passenger plane made a miraculous landing on the Hudson River in New York City. Minutes before, after taking off from LaGuardia Airport, the pilot reported that a flock of birds had flown into the plane's engines, causing it to quickly lose power and altitude. Such bird strikes are perilous because they usually shut down one of the engines on an aircraft. This strike was much worse because the pilot believed that both engines were affected by the errant fowl. Disaster was imminent, but moments later the pilot executed a near-perfect water landing, and all 155 on board subsequently were rescued from the icy waters. Images of the plane and the rescue of its passengers and crew by air and by boat flashed throughout the news media.

In addition to relief, elation was a common reaction to the plane's miraculous maneuver, which was quickly dubbed the "miracle on the Hudson." The event elevated the spirits of those who witnessed it, heard about it, or watched it on television or the Internet. The pilot, a modest man who claimed that his training served him well, became an instant hero, one whose actions generated a sense of appreciative wonder in observers. What people shared in the aftermath of this event might be called a sense of awe, a state some psychologists refer to as a moral, spiritual, or even an aesthetic emotion (Haidt & Keltner, 2004; Keltner, 2000; Keltner & Haidt, 2003). People who feel elation or a sense of awe report experiencing a warm feeling in their chests, an expansion of their

© Mario Tama/Getty Images

**The miraculous safe landing by US Air 1549 evoked feelings of awe that elevated the spirits of observers around the world.**

hearts, and a strong and sure sense of connection to other people.

Have you ever witnessed an event that touched you deeply and brought you a sense of transcendence—that is, feelings of goodness far beyond normal? Your experience need not have been a public "miracle" such as a disaster avoided. It might have been something as simple as observing a kind deed done selflessly or watching a glorious sunset. The point is that you felt changed for the better by what you witnessed.

This chapter is devoted to exploring the impact of such upbeat phenomena by presenting one of psychology's newest areas of inquiry: positive psychology. To do so, we define this new field and the three areas of research that comprise it. We then discuss representative topics within each area in some detail. Our study of positive psychology concludes by considering the prospects and problems of studying how and why people thrive. This chapter's Application offers a variety of simple exercises you can use to boost your own level of happiness.

# The Scope of Positive Psychology

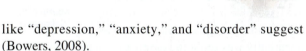

### LEARNING OBJECTIVES

- Define positive psychology, and explain its origins.
- Characterize positive psychology as a counterweight to the historic and dominant negative focus in the discipline.
- Explain why positive psychology can provide a framework for new as well as older research on well-being.
- Identify positive psychology's three lines of inquiry.

You may have seen the popular bumpersticker suggesting that people "Commit Random Acts of Kindness and Senseless Acts of Beauty." If you have seen a car sporting this sentiment, you may well have concluded that the driver or owner is some sort of idealist or wide-eyed optimist. Perhaps the individual is someone who sees the proverbial glass as half-full rather than half-empty. But what if some serious psychological substance underlies the bumpersticker's message? Let's explore how a focus on what's good in life can be good for people.

## Defining Positive Psychology and Its Brief History

*Positive psychology* **is a social and intellectual movement within the discipline of psychology that focuses on human strengths and how people can flourish and be successful** (Gable & Haidt, 2005; Lopez & Snyder, 2009; Peterson, 2006; Snyder & Lopez, 2002, 2007). In part, the emergence of positive psychology was a reaction to the predominant negative focus found in most other areas of the discipline. Stop for a moment and think about your own perceptions of psychology. If you are like most students, you are likely to view psychology as a helping profession more than anything else. Fair enough. But consider how much of that "help" is based primarily on the study of weaknesses and problems—social, emotional, cognitive, and behavioral—that people exhibit (Seligman, 2002). Psychology's language is rooted in the negative, as words

like "depression," "anxiety," and "disorder" suggest (Bowers, 2008).

Until recently, the study of positive qualities and their impact on people's health and well-being occurred entirely outside of the discipline's mainstream. The advocates of positive psychology argue that it provides a needed balance in the discipline of psychology. In other words, instead of always focusing on challenges that need to be overcome, on the damaging effects of stress, or on coping with the hassles of daily life, psychologists should also attend to those conditions that lead to joy, pleasure, and simple gratitude for the experience of living.

This shift in perspective requires more than just donning the equivalent of rose-colored glasses or acting like a "Pollyanna," someone who is encumbered by foolish or even blind optimism. Advocates of positive psychology (including some who actually call themselves "positive psychologists") do not deny that psychological suffering exists; rather, they want to discover how to harness people's strengths, virtues, and other good qualities to help them enhance the lives they lead. In the course of doing so, one of positive psychology's primary aims is to create tools and techniques for promoting well-being and psychological health, which have an impact on individuals, their connections with others, and physical health. A good way to think of positive psychology is as an arm of psychology with potentially beneficial side effects, including the opportunity to prevent mental illness and reduce discontent by cultivating human strengths, such as courage, hope, and resilience (Seligman, 1998).

What led psychologists to consider developing a new subfield, especially one named positive psychology? Admittedly, the name sounds a little faddish, like something you would find in the "pop" psychology section of any bookstore, rather than the serious area of scholarship it aspires to be. As a researchable and teachable topic, positive psychology was only identified and named in 1998. During his year as president of the American Psychological Association (APA), psychologist Martin Seligman developed positive psychology as a counterweight to the discipline's negatively oriented history (Seligman, 1998, 1999). Seligman was well known for his research on learned helplessness, depression, and the acquisition of phobias—downbeat topics that fit comfortably within psychology's traditional emphasis on the negative. So, what prompted his sudden interest in the potential power of people's positive natures? Seligman (2002) reports that an exchange with Nikki, his 5-year-old daughter, piqued his interest and triggered the chain of events that led to the founding of positive psychology. Quite simply, Nikki, told her father that he was (as apparently was often the case) being a grump while the two of them were gardening. Seligman recalled that:

Courtesy of Martin E.P. Seligman

Martin E. P. Seligman

*Nikki . . . was throwing weeds into the air and dancing around. I yelled at her, She walked away, came back, and said . . . "Daddy, do you remember before my fifth birthday? From the time I was three to the time I was five, I was a whiner. I whined every day. When I turned five, I decided not to whine anymore. That was the hardest thing I've ever done. And if I can stop whining, you can stop being such a grouch." (2002, pp. 3–4)*

By speaking some "truth to power," Nikki led Seligman to experience something of an epiphany, a sudden flash of insight into an event. Raising children, for example, is not about telling them what to do (let alone yelling at them); rather, it is really about identifying and nurturing their good qualities and strengths. By extension, Seligman began to think about how the psychology of the past generations could have—*should* have—been about much more than negative, pathological states and human suffering (Selgiman, 2003a, 2003b).

But this is recent history—what about other events in psychology's past that led to present-day positive psychology? Since World War II, for example, psychology has focused on treating an increasing variety of psychological disorders (see Chapter 15). Indeed, clinical psychology was born out of the need to deal with the rise of pathology and psychological maladies linked to

WEB LINK 16.1 The World Database of Happiness

Are people living in one country happier than those in another? How do we know? To explore these and other questions, delve into the World Database of Happiness, which is maintained at Erasmus University, Rotterdam, The Netherlands.

life in the modern world. Progress creates all kinds of stress, strains, and conflict, not just war. Consider the stressors found in daily life—work, money, love (or the lack thereof), family, purpose, and the need to find some meaning in all of them. Since the mid-20th century, the psychological community has responded to these changes and pressures by adhering to a disease model, in which the emphasis is on repairing damage rather than preventing it or, better still, inoculating people in advance against psychological distress (Maddux, 2002).

Seligman and like-minded researchers felt that the time was right to mount a campaign for change so that psychologists and the people they study, treat, and teach would learn to see their lives as fulfilling and flourishing rather than as stress-ridden and dysfunctional (Aspinwall & Staudinger, 2002; Kahneman, Diener, & Schwarz, 1999; Keyes & Haidt, 2003; Seligman & Csikszentmihalyi, 2000). Informal gatherings were held, plans were laid, and then more formal efforts, such as conferences and workshops, were conducted where junior and senior psychologists met to develop a philosophy and identify goals for what became known as positive psychology. Soon after, scholarly articles, books, and even a journal dealing with positive psychology appeared (Linley, 2009). As Seligman and Csikszentmihalyi (2000), another founder of the movement, claimed, "The aim of positive psychology is to begin to catalyze a change in the focus of psychology from preoccupation with only repairing the worst things in life to also building positive qualities" (p. 5).

## Reconsidering Older Research in Light of the New Positive Psychology

Positive psychology represents a turning point, even a change in the zeitgeist, for the discipline of psychology. The term *zeitgeist* refers to a timely intellectual state of mind that many people contribute to and share. The emergence of positive psychology seems to fit this description, but can we really conclude that this subdiscipline just "appeared" once Seligman and other like-minded psychologists began to communicate, organize, and then conceive and publish relevant research?

Probably not, and here's why: Good ideas are often "in the air" before someone begins to study them or before a topical area is formally named. Thus, as an organized effort, the positive psychology movement *is* new, but many of the questions being studied are not; quite a few have been examined by psychologists for decades outside of the discipline's mainstream. A variety of theories, hypotheses, and research results pertaining to beneficial qualities and psychological themes in human experience, for example, have been around since the 1950s and 1960s (e.g., Allport, 1961; Maslow. 1968, 1973; Rogers, 1961). Indeed, the subdiscipline of humanistic psychology has long pursued questions that seem similar to those now asked by positive psychologists (Linley, 2009; Linley & Joseph, 2004; Robbins, 2008). And as many advocates of positive psychology are quick to acknowledge, questions of what constitutes a good life for an individual have been pursued by philosophers since antiquity (Deci & Ryan, 2008; Ryan & Deci, 2001).

To paraphrase Ecclesiastes, "There is nothing new under the sun," but frameworks for understanding existing ideas can change as new findings, theories, and interested scholars begin to coalesce within a research area. As you read the remainder of this chapter, you will notice that older research studies and references are routinely mixed in with newer ones (those appearing after positive psychology's "birth" in 1998). Juxtaposing old with new research should not seem odd, as the questions asked and answers obtained earlier can now fruitfully be examined in light of new data linked to positive psychology's three areas of inquiry.

## Introducing Positive Psychology's Three Lines of Inquiry

As originally conceived, positive psychology pursues three lines of inquiry, which, as shown in **Figure 16.1**, make up the "three legs" on which positive psychology stands (Gillham & Seligman, 1999; Seligman & Czikszentmihalyi, 2000). First, positive psychology is interested in the *positive subjective experiences* people have. Such experiences include good moods, positive

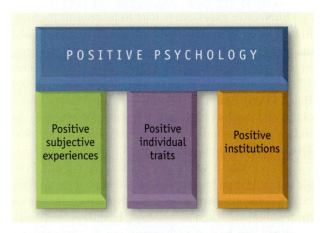

**Figure 16.1**

**The three legs of positive psychology.** Research in positive psychology stands on "three legs" or lines of empirical, scientific inquiry: positive subjective experiences, positive individual traits, and positive institutions.

emotions, happiness, love, and other psychological processes that promote or maintain feelings of well-being in individuals. The second area of concern is *positive individual traits* that enable people to thrive. The traits falling under this heading are often said to be character strengths and virtues and include such qualities as hope, resilience, gratitude, and spirituality. The third line of inquiry focuses on *positive institutions,* or the settings and organizations that gather people together to promote civil discourse and enhance their positive subjective experiences and positive personal traits in a collective way. Positive institutions include close-knit families, quality schools, good work environments, and safe and supportive neighborhoods and communities.

Each of the three areas of inquiry seeks to understand the ways people can flourish in daily life. The next three sections in the chapter review concepts and illustrative research representing each of these areas. We begin with people's private feelings of well-being: positive subjective experiences.

# Positive Subjective Experiences

### LEARNING OBJECTIVES

● Distinguish between moods and emotions, and discuss the benefits of positive moods.
● Understand how the speed and variability of thought are related to mood.
● Describe the broaden-and-build model of positive emotions.

● Explain the flow experience and typical activities that trigger it.
● Outline the advantages of mindfulness over mindlessness.

Some positive psychologists focus on the study of *positive subjective experiences,* **or the positive but private feelings and thoughts people have about themselves and the events in their lives.** The frequency of positive subjective experiences has been linked

to people's success in marriage, friendship, income, and health, among other areas of daily life; such personal accomplishments not only lead to good feelings, they also make people more successful (Lyubomirsky, King, & Diener, 2005).

Subjective experiences tend to be present focused. In fact, a considerable amount of research has examined the most common positive subjective state, happiness, as discussed in detail in Chapter 1 (see also Diener, 1984; Diener & Biswas-Diener, 2008; Gilbert, 2006; Haidt, 2006). Sensual pleasures—pleasant tastes (chocolate) and smells (fresh-baked bread), for example, as well as touch (a friendly pat, a caress)—can trigger positive subjective states in people.

But subjective states are not just in the present. People can reflect on past experiences that conjure up feelings of contentment or satisfaction. Reviewing memories from childhood, such as holidays, birthdays, or family vacations, can be especially gratifying. Events need not be based in the distant past either. An office worker can call up feelings of satisfaction by recalling a successful performance review she received from her boss a month before or by remembering the goal her soccer-playing daughter made during the previous week. Whether you reflect on a distant, recent, or current moment that was pleasant or even happy, you can experience a change in mood from a neutral state to a more positive one.

## Positive Moods

When psychologists talk about moods, such as when someone reports being in a "good mood," they are not usually referring to emotion per se. Emotions are stron-

ger subjective experiences, much more distinct than moods. Moods are more global responses to experience and tend to be more pervasive, lasting much longer than emotions (Morris, 1999). Think about someone you know who is always cheerful and upbeat—that is, she is usually in a good mood. Imagine this friend returning to her parked car only to discover a parking ticket on her windshield. How does she react? She may become angry at herself for forgetting to put change in the meter, but a half-hour later, she has forgotten the costly ticket and returned to her usual smiling and placid self. In other words, she is once again experiencing a relatively good mood.

When people are in a good mood, they anticipate that good things will happen to them; as a consequence, they often make good things happen. In fact, being in a positive mood has several beneficial effects, including making people more agreeable, helpful, less aggressive, and even better decision makers (Isen, 2002; Morris, 1999).

### Positive Moods Can Promote Creative Solutions

We also know that being in a positive mood can enhance people's creativity. Isen and her colleagues, for example, hypothesized that positive mood would promote creative problem solving (Isen, Daubman, & Nowicki, 1987). For 5 minutes, groups of men and women watched either a very funny "blooper" reel or an emotionally neutral film. Afterward, each participant was introduced to the "candle task," a standard measure of creative problem solving (Duncker, 1945). The instructions for the task were roughly as follows.

*On the table [in front of you] are a box of matches, some tacks and string, and two candles. Your task is to figure out how you could mount a candle on the wall so that it could be used as a source of light. You will be given 10 minutes to work on the problem.*

Do you see how to solve the problem quickly and correctly? If you pour out the contents of the box and then tack it to the wall, the box can become a platform (see **Figure 16.2**). The lit candle can then be placed on top of the box. Once you recognize the solution, it seems obvious; yet, many research participants fail to identify the correct solution before the 10 minutes are over.

What was the impact of the mood manipulation (viewing one of the two films) on creativity and solving the candle task? As Isen and colleagues (1987) anticipated, the participants who saw the funny film were more likely to solve the problem correctly in the allotted time than those who watched the neutral film. Related studies support the finding that good moods as well as positive emotions help people to be more creative in their thinking (Fredrikson, 1998; Isen, 1987; 2004; Isen, Daubman, & Nowicki, 1987). One way to think about

*"I don't sing because I am happy. I am happy because I sing."*

**Problem**

**Solution**

**Figure 16.2**

**The Duncker candle task for demonstrating creativity: problem and solution.** Problem solvers are given candles, a box of matches, tacks, and string (left). They are then asked to attach the candle to the wall to provide a light source. The correct solution—tacking the box to the wall so it can serve as a platform to hold the lit candle is shown on the right.

the impact of positive affect (feelings)—whether in the guise of milder moods or stronger emotions—is that it helps people see things in new, unconventional ways.

We have considered how positive mood can lead to particular outcomes, such as creative thinking. What if we reverse the process: Are there qualities associated with thinking that can lead to particular moods, especially positive ones? To answer that, let's take a look at some fascinating new research.

## Positive Moods Are Linked with Quick Thoughts

When was the last time you felt your thoughts racing—that is, they were moving at a faster-than-usual rate? Do you remember the circumstances that led to your quick thinking? Where were you? What were you doing? Most important for present purposes, do you recall how you were feeling? Chances are that if your thoughts were racing along at a brisk pace, you were probably in a good mood.

Pronin and Jacobs (2008) argue that faster thinking generally leads to a more positive mood (see also Pronin, Jacobs, & Wegner, 2008; Pronin & Wegner, 2006). When thoughts are too fast, they can be associated with feelings of *mania*, an abnormally elevated mood. What about slower thoughts? As you may have already surmised, they are often linked with negative moods. And very slow or sluggish thoughts can lead to depressive feelings. Thought speed is one property of a more general concept that Pronin and Jacobs call *mental motion*.

Besides speed of thought, mental motion also involves thought variability (Pronin & Jacobs, 2008). When one's thought is varied—thinking about many

different things, not just one or two—one's mood is usually positive. Repetitive thoughts on the same topic, or what is sometimes referred to as *rumination*, are associated with negative affect. At the positive extreme of thought variation, people can experience mania or even a reverie or dreamlike state. Approaching the negative extreme, however, thoughts can become depressive or anxiety ridden. When quick thoughts and varied thinking meet, people feel elated; when thoughts are plodding and repetitive, however, people experience dejection. Naturally, thought speed and variability can oppose each other—when one is fast (or slow), the other can be varied (or repetitive). The consequences for various possible combinations of mental motion's properties for mood are shown in **Figure 16.3** (note where normal mood lies compared to the predictable deviations surrounding it as thought speed and variability change).

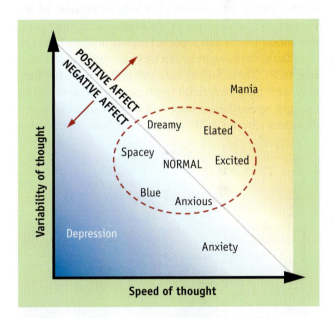

**Figure 16.3**

**Mental motion and mood: The consequences of thought speed and variability for how people may feel.** This diagram illustrates the theorized relationships between the speed and variability of thought and moods. Varied but fast thinking leads to feelings of elation, while slow repetitive thinking causes feelings of dejection. When thought variability and speed oppose each other (one is low while the other is high), people's moods may depend upon which of the two factors is more extreme. The mood states created by these combinations vary apart from their positive or negative valence. For example, repetitive thinking can create feelings of anxiety rather than depression if the thinking is rapid; indeed, anxious states of being are generally linked with more rapid thought than depressive states.

Finally, Pronin and Jacobs (2008) argue that thought speed and variability operate independently of the content of thought. In other words, you might assume that slow thoughts are necessary negative thoughts, but that is not always so. Although emotional problems such as depression and anxiety have been linked to nonrational or dysfunctional thinking (Beck, 1976, 2008), the arguments for mental motion's impact on mood do not require that thoughts have any particular content.

Let's review a simple experiment that illustrates the relationship between basic speed of thought and mood, as well as some of its psychological consequences. Pronin, Jacobs, and Wegner (2008) had a group of college students spend 10 minutes writing down solutions to a hypothetical problem (how to earn one year's private college tuition in a summer). Participants in the *fast thought* group were told to produce "every idea you possibly can," whereas those in the *slow thought* condition were asked to develop "as many good ideas as you can." The findings are summarized in **Figure 16.4**. People in the fast thought group generated more ideas and felt themselves to be thinking at a faster rate compared to the other group (see the left side of **Figure 16.4**). Further, the fast-thought group experienced more positive mood levels and reported higher levels of energy than the slow-thought group (see the right side of **Figure 16.4**). These findings are still preliminary, but they may well have beneficial implications for developing thought–speed-based interventions for treating mood disorders (Pronin & Wegner, 2006). Nonetheless, this

**WEB LINK 16.2   Positive Psychology News Daily**

Want a daily dose of postive psychology? Visit the Positive Psychology News Daily website, which contains up-to-date information on trends in parenting, education, health, exercise, and relationships. New books examining positive psychology are also reviewed here.

novel approach to research introduces a new dimension of study for positive psychology, as well as a new perspective on the power of positive thinking. Let's now turn to the positive subjective states that represent feelings as specific responses—positive emotions.

## Positive Emotions

Whereas moods are low-level feelings that can last for lengthy periods of time ("I was in a grumpy mood all last week"), emotions are stronger but shorter-lived feelings, acute responses to some particular event. As noted in Chapter 3, *emotions* **are powerful, largely uncontrollable feelings, accompanied by physiological changes.** When psychologists speak of emotions, they usually divide them into two categories: positive and negative. *Positive emotions* **consist of pleasant responses to events that promote connections with others, including subjective states such as happiness, joy, euphoria, gratitude, and contentment.** When individuals experience positive emotions, they feel good about

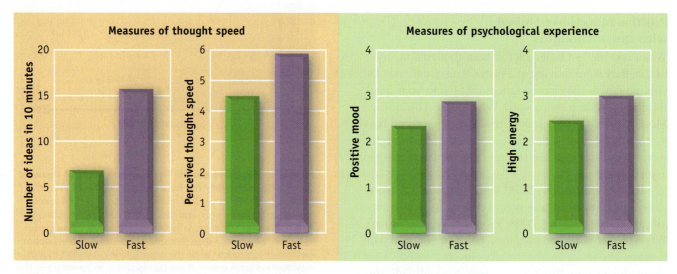

**Figure 16.4**

**Results of the self-generated ideas, speed of thought, and mood experiment.** Participants in the fast-thinking condition of the experiment generated more ideas in the allotted time than did their peers (see the graph on the far left). The crucial results are shown in the two graphs on the right. As you can see, those in the fast-thinking group reported having a more positive mood and higher levels of energy than those in the slow-thinking group.

Source: Adapted from Pronin, E., & Jacobs, E. (2008). Thought speed, mood, and the experience of mental motion. *Perspectives on Psychological Science, 3*, 461–485.

themselves, other people, and often whatever they are doing or thinking about. In contrast, ***negative emotions consist of unpleasant responses to potential threats or dangers, including subjective states like sadness, disgust, anger, guilt, and fear.*** Negative emotions are unpleasant disruptions that, while increasing vigilance, often cause people to turn inward or lead them to be snippy or disagreeable with others. In general, negative emotions draw more attention than positive ones, and this predisposition is likely an evolved process (Froh, 2009). The division of positive and negative emotions is basic, a structural fact of people's normal emotional lives (Watson, 2002; Watson & Tellegen, 1985).

Historically, negative emotions have been studied far more extensively than positive ones. One reason is that negative emotions have evolutionary significance. For example, experiencing negative emotions often alerts people to possible threats. They make people wary, narrowing the focus of attention (Derryberry & Tucker, 1994; Easterbrook, 1959). Second, negative emotions are implicated in the "flight or fight response," which occurs when an organism feels threatened. Negative emotions compel people to act through emotionally linked *specific action tendencies,* or behavioral reactions with survival value. The automatic response—tendency to act—is often to flee from a perceived threat (a mugger, a bully) or to fight off an attacker. Another reason that negative emotions receive so much attention is their sheer quantity; it is estimated that they outnumber positive emotions by about 3 to 1 (Ellsworth & Smith, 1988; Fredrickson, 1998), which may have contributed to the bias among psychologists to study them. (As a quick thought experiment, you might jot down as many positive and negative emotions as you can think of, then compare the totals.) Perhaps this sustained favoritism for negative emotions in the psychological community helped inspire and even launch positive psychology. But what about positive emotions—what value do they have?

Some of the most intriguing answers to this question have come from Barbara Fredrickson, a social and positive psychologist who asserts that positive emotions play particular roles in people's mental and physical lives. Fredrickson (1998, 2001, 2002; Fredrickson & Branigan, 2005) developed the *broaden-and-build model* of positive emotions to explain how they benefit human beings. In contrast to negative emotions, positive ones spawn *nonspecific action tendencies* that nonetheless lead to adaptive responses.

For example, when adults are experiencing positive emotions, they are much more likely to offer aid to people in need, engage others in social interaction, perform some creative activity, or try out some new experience (e.g., Fredrickson, 1998; 2002; see also, for example, Isen, 1987; 2004). Put another way, positive emotions open people up to a variety of new behavioral options.

Courtesy of Jeff Chappell

**Barbara Fredrickson**

At the same time, positive emotions broaden people's cognitive responses by promoting new and beneficial *thought-action tendencies,* in which established ways of positive thinking are associated with particular acts or behaviors. For example, when children are feeling joy, they become more playful and imaginative, often investigating their environments (Fredrickson, 1998; Frijda, 1986). This joyful exploration allows them to learn new things about the world and about themselves.

In one study, Fredrickson and Branigan (2005) demonstrated that the experience of joy did indeed broaden people's thought-action tendencies. After watching one of five emotion-eliciting film clips (joy, contentment, anger, fear, or a neutral condition), a group of research participants wrote down lists of everything they would like to have done at that moment. As shown in **Figure 16.5**, the participants who felt the emotion of either joy or contentment listed significantly more desired possible actions than the individuals in the negative or neutral emotion groups. Being joyful or contented apparently leads people to think of future possible activities they might engage in, whereas being in a negative or even neutral emotional state narrows people's thoughts and reduces the range of possible subsequent actions.

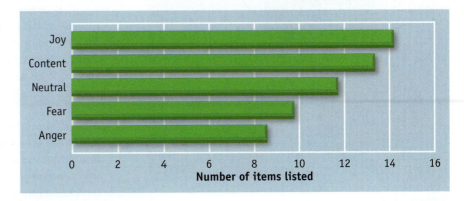

### Figure 16.5

**The broadening effects of positive emotions compared to neutral or negative emotions.** Experiencing an emotional state of joy or contentment led research participants to list a greater number of activities they might like to engage in at that moment than did individuals experiencing a neutral or negative emotional state.

Source: Adapted from Fredrickson, B. L. (2002). Positive emotions. In C. R. Snyder & S. J. Lopez (Eds.), *Handbook of positive psychology* (pp. 120–134). New York: Oxford University Press.

Thus, the broaden-and-build model proposes that positive emotions *broaden* people's outlooks and then *builds on* subsequent learning to develop future emotional and intellectual resources. Positive emotions create "bankable" social, cognitive, and affective resources that can be drawn on with emotional interest in the future. **Figure 16.6** illustrates the broaden-and-build model. Note that Fredrickson postulates that broader thought-action repertoires lead to increased well-being, which in turn triggers more positive emotions leading to happiness and what Fredrickson (2002) refers to as upward spirals of health.

What else do positive emotions accomplish besides broadening thought-action repertoires? Fredrickson (Fredrickson & Joiner, 2002; Fredrickson & Levenson, 1998) also advanced what is known as the ***undoing hypothesis,* which posits that positive emotions aid the mind and the body by recovering a sense of balance and flexibility following an episode of experiencing negative emotion.** When people are stressed, for example, as when a group of students takes an extremely and unexpectedly difficult exam, the presence of positive emotions triggered by the shared experience (e.g., the students meet after the test, discuss it, and share their

anxiety about it) undoes the aftereffects of the stressor more quickly. The students are likely to feel better once they realize they all felt the same way about the exam. They will smile at one another, roll their eyes, possibly even laugh at how absurdly difficult the questions were, leading to positive emotions that effectively wipe out the physiological and biochemical effects caused by the stressful test-taking experience. In addition, the resulting positive emotions reestablish flexible and open thinking after the narrowed perspective caused by the negative (stressful) emotions felt during the tough test.

Many times positive emotions are responses to events—that is, they are caused by good things that happen. We also need to consider the consequences of positive emotions that people intentionally create by pursuing particular activities.

## Flow

Do you ever find yourself so happily or joyfully engaged in a challenging or interesting activity that you "lose yourself" in it? If you are an athlete, for example, you may describe the experience as "being in the zone" when you are playing basketball or tennis (Cooper, 1998; Kimiecik & Stein, 1992). Of course, the activity does not have to be particularly physical, as individuals who play video games routinely report losing all sense of time as they play interactive games. Likewise, surgeons report that the physical and intellectual challenges of doing an operation can place them into a zone for optimal performance. Musicians say the same thing about playing an instrument and performing for others. Psychologist Mihalyi Csikszentmihalyi named this psychological phenomenon "flow." ***Flow* is the state of being in which a person becomes fully involved and engaged in the present time by some interesting, challenging, and intrinsically rewarding activity.**

Csikszentmihalyi recognized the pull of flow experiences in his own life when he played chess or went rock or mountain climbing (Diener & Biswas-Diener, 2008). Csikszentmihalyi refers to flow as an optimal state, one he has studied for close to three decades. To Csikszentmihalyi (1975):

*Flow denotes the holistic sensation present when we act with total involvement. . . . It is the state in which action follows upon action according to an internal logic which seems to need no conscious intervention on our part. We experience it as a unified flowing from one moment to the next, in which we feel in control of our actions, and in which there is little distinction between self and environment; between stimulus and response; or between past, present, and future. (p. 43)*

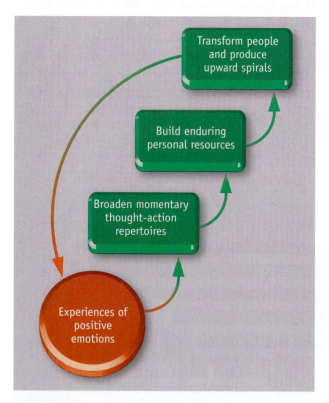

**Figure 16.6**
**The broaden-and-build theory of positive emotions.**
According to Fredrickson (2002), the personal resources people gain during positive emotional states last for some time. This figure illustrates the three hypothesized sequential effects of positive emotions. First, positive emotions broaden people's range of thought-action sequences, which in turn builds personal resources, and culminates by producing upward spirals of positive emotions. The cycle then repeats itself.

**Mihalyi Csikszentmihalyi**

When they enter this "optimal experience," people become less self-aware, lose all track of time, and focus their energies and attention on doing some engaging activity where skill and challenge are in balance.

## Finding Flow

The good news is that everyone is familiar with the flow experience. Virtually anyone can find flow. According to Csikszentmihalyi, flow was originally conceived as a phenomenon falling between the opposite experiences of boredom and anxiety. As shown in **Figure 16.7**, he believes that people experience flow when they find a balanced meaningful place between these poles of experience. He also suggested that flow can be characterized as a balance between a person's current skill level and the challenges of the situation. Indeed, the flow experience is often found at the point where challenges are just manageable. This argument makes sense if you think about it: When the level of challenge in a task is right, people rise to the occasion to meet it. But if the challenge level is too high, then people often begin to feel anxious about what they are doing—worrying about their performance, questioning their own competence and, consequently, not experiencing flow, because they are distracted.

Similarly, if the task in question is monotonous or repetitive, people quickly become bored; it is not possible to achieve the flow state if one is not engaged by what one is doing. Think about a mundane task, such as stuffing envelopes. If you had to do it all day, every day,

you would become fidgety, annoyed, and frustrated, as well as undeniably bored, because the task would be too easy (not to mention tiresome) for you. Once mastered, there would be no challenge in it and nothing new to learn in order to perform it.

Thus, to find flow and develop your creative potential, you must find a challenging activity that matches your skill level. When skills are properly matched to an activity's level of challenge, flow occurs naturally; but it becomes a still more enjoyable experience—a true source of personal happiness—when both the level of challenge and the skills needed are high. This dynamic relationship is shown by the flow model illustrated in **Figure 16.8**. As both the level of challenge and necessary skills increase above some hypothetical midpoint, one enters flow. When levels of both factors are too low, one instead experiences apathy (see the bottom left corner of **Figure 16.8**). Based on varying levels of the respective factors, other possible emotional experiences are shown in **Figure 16.8**. The message is straightforward: Once an activity is chosen and the requisite challenge and skill levels are met, a person can have a flow experience virtually whenever he or she wishes.

A key element of a flow experience is that even if it is initially undertaken for other reasons, it becomes intrinsically rewarding. Thus, a child may be enrolled in a dance class by her parents, who tell her that the exercise will keep her weight down, give her poise, and keep her healthy. But once she begins to enjoy the

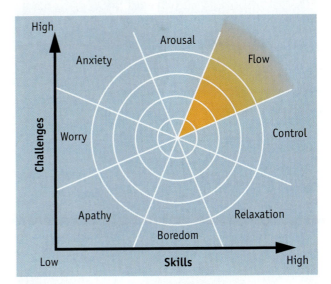

### Figure 16.7

**The original model of the flow state (optimal experience).** In Csikszentmihalyi's early research, he argued that flow is experienced when a person's perceived opportunities for action are in balance with the individual's perceived skills. As conceptualized here, the flow experience falls between anxiety and boredom.

Source: Adapted from Csikszentmihalyi, M. (2000). *Beyond boredom and anxiety.* San Francisco: Jossey-Bass. (Original work published 1975)

### Figure 16.8

**The revised model of the flow state.** According to the revised model, flow is experienced when a person's perceived challenges and skills are above his or her average levels; when they fall below, the individual experiences apathy. The intensity of the experience increases as the distance from the person's average levels of challenge and skills grows greater (illustrated here by the concentric rings).

Source: Adapted from Csikszentmihalyi, M. (1997). *Finding flow.* New York: Basic Books. © 1998 Mihaly Csikszentmihalyi. Reprinted by permission of Basic Books, a member of the Perseus Books Group.

challenge of learning new steps and routines, dancing becomes an activity worth doing for its own sake—her parents' reasons, though still true in one sense, have nothing to do with her reason for dancing. As William Butler Yeats (1997) put it in his 1928 poem *Among School Children:*

*O body swayed to music, O brightening glance,*
*How can we know the dancer from the dance?*

When individiuals experience flow, they have the pleasure of stretching themselves and their talents in new directions. For this reason, flow often occurs when people pursue creative or stimulating work, including aesthetic efforts (art, dance, music, drama, writing), hobbies, or sports, among other possibilities (Nakamura & Csikszentmihalyi, 2002, 2009). Further, anyone in almost any situation can experience flow. Factors such as social class, gender, culture, and age have no influence on its occurrence. Thus, the good news is that a person need only identify a domain and a skill-related activity within it that triggers flow.

Aside from the obvious fact that people find it to be a reinforcing state, why seek flow? For one thing, flow feels good and becomes a source of motivation. Aside from enhancing certain skills, flow provides positive emotions, staves off negative affect, and promotes goal commitment and achievement (Nakamura & Csikszent-mihalyi, 2002; 2009).

If flow feels good and is reinforcing, shouldn't it be most likely to occur when people are having fun? Perhaps, but that all depends on how one defines "fun." For many people, their work is their play. Thus, there may be a somewhat paradoxical side to flow—namely, that people are most likely to experience this absorbing state when they are at work rather than play. Individuals who enjoy their work report being in flow quite often, and, not surprisingly, flow may be linked to job satisfaction (Csikszentmihalyi & LeFevre, 1989). Why does this happen? Presumably because the work done by many people often presents a good balance between challenge and skill. Of course, we need to acknowledge that work is something most everyone does and does quite often when compared to hobbies or recreational sports, for example.

Still, doesn't it strike you as strange that what gives us so much focused, involved, and absorbing pleasure is (for the most part) a necessary, largely economically focused activity rather than an optional one designed exclusively for fun? Of course, many people claim that their work is completely engaging, a form of amusement, and certainly we count individuals who love what they do as truly fortunate. Consider, for example, a person who manages to turn his passion for caving and his interest in ecology into a career—being paid to

© Jeff Greenberg/The Image Works

© Russell Glenister/Corbis

Flow occurs when people are engaged in challenging activities that match their skill levels, such as creating a work of art or reading an exciting novel.

scramble through caverns to study and count bats. We can safely predict that people who truly love their work experience flow states on a regular basis.

Csikszentmihalyi originally began to recognize the force of flow when he was studying the creative processes of artists (Getzels & Csikszentmihalyi, 1976). He noticed that when artists were truly involved in what they were doing, the activity became highly focused and single-minded. The artists ignored their hunger or thirst, whether they were tired, and virtually all other concerns for creature comforts in order to do their creative work. Once a piece of art was complete, however, the artists quickly lost interest in it. The joy was in the doing—the process of creating—and not really in the outcome or product of that process. Most people may not think of the work they do as being creative in an artistic or aesthetic sense, but becoming wrapped up in the moment-to-moment acts of work is similar, and self-imposed time pressures often lead workers to ignore a growling stomach or a dry throat in order to complete what they are doing. The point is that challenges and skill levels may allow people to enjoy what they do in a job, work, or career calling.

Of course, flow is found in all sorts of situations besides work and the workplace. We already mentioned sports (Cosma, 1999). Participating in a religious ritual can lead to flow (Han, 1998), as can teaching (Coleman, 1994), driving a car (Csikszentmihalyi, 1997), reading for pleasure (McQuillan & Conde, 1996), and—surprisingly—cramming for a test (Brinthaupt & Shin, 2001). Boring tasks, such as housework, appear to prevent flow (Csikszentmihalyi, 1997) unless the situation is changed (listening to music while waxing the floor or scrubbing the tub can often do the trick).

### Does Everyone Find Flow?

In one of his studies, Csikszentmihalyi (1997) asked people, "Do you ever get involved in something so deeply that nothing else seems to matter, and you lose track of time?" (p. 33). A similar question was put to you at the opening of this section of the chapter. What do you think most people say? Csikszentmihalyi found that about 20% of respondents in American and European samples said they experienced flow quite frequently, usually several times a day. Very intense flow experiences were felt by a smaller percentage of respondents, however.

Does everyone experience flow-like states? Around 15% of a given sample will report that they have never had such an experience. Positive psychologists may want to address this group by trying to create situations in which flow can be experienced. If you were a positive psychologist, how would you go about instilling flow among students who are part of the minority of folks who have never experienced it? As a student, when, for example, do you experience flow? Helping people to enter flow is arguably a beneficial activity, as those

familiar with flow report that it provides them with good feelings and that they see it as linked to their greater well-being.

## Mindfulness

Active engagement with a challenging and interesting activity—the flow experience—is one way to promote well-being. Surprisingly, there is another, simpler way to do so: by actively and mindfully noticing new things and drawing distinctions among them. Social psychologist Ellen Langer created the term *mindfulness* **to refer to a cultivated perspective in which people are sensitive to context and focused on the present.** People in a state of mindfulness notice novel features and readily attend to them, just as they draw novel distinctions in what they see. According to Langer (2002), to become more mindful people need to (1) resist the impulse to reduce or control the uncertainty found in daily living; (2) become less prone to evaluate themselves, others, and the situations they encounter; and (3) try to override their propensity to perform automatic (sometimes referred to as "stereotyped" or "scripted") behavior. To Langer, mindfulness "is a flexible state of mind—an openness to novelty, a process of actively drawing novel distinctions" (p. 214).

**Ellen J. Langer**

One way to understand the benefits associated with mindfulness in daily life is to compare and contrast it with its problematic counterpart, mindlessness. Langer (1990, 1998) argues that people slip into a state of *mindlessness* **by engaging in rote behavior, performing familiar, scripted actions without much cognition, as if on autopilot** (e.g., Langer, 1990, 1998). In essence, when individuals are mindless, they are not doing much active thinking. Sometimes, of course, mindlessness can be adaptive; it frees up conscious attention and awareness when a task is familiar. Think back to when you learned to drive a car and how you had to pay rapt attention to what you were doing; by comparison, driving is likely to be a veritable breeze now. There is a down side to such mindless adaptation, however; you miss a great deal of information when you behave mindlessly. Sudden changes and novelties that appear in the environment are overlooked, for example, as are fine details. When driving mindlessly, you might miss a stop sign and drive right through it (or you might hit the car that stopped suddenly in front of you because you never saw it slow down). So, there are potential costs when attention and awareness are too free or loose. It's almost as if one is not really "there" to mentally follow what's happening. People are much better off when they take note of new information whatever the context happens to be.

Practically speaking, how can you become more mindful? You can do so by treating the facts you learn as conditional—that is, as linked to one and not necessarily other situations (cultivating a fresh perspective on experiences). Researchers who study mindfulness suggest there is another way: becoming aware of novelty and creating new distinctions by using *meditation,* or the disciplined, continuous, and focused contemplation of some subject or object (see Chapter 4). With regular meditation, people learn to train and direct their attention in nonanalytical and unemotional ways, subsequently becoming more mindful as a result (Langer, 2009; Shapiro & Carlson, 2009; Shapiro, Schwartz, & Santerre, 2002). For example, Kabat-Zinn (1982) used Eastern meditative practices coupled with knowledge of mindfulness research to create a 10-week *mindfulness meditation* program that successfully reduced chronic pain and mood disturbances in a group of 51 patients. In another study, 78 pre-med and medical students were randomly assigned to either a mindfulness meditation condition or a control group (Shapiro, Schwartz, & Bonner, 1998). Compared to the control group, those who learned to meditate were later found to have lower levels of depression and anxiety, as well as increased levels of empathy. These results held up even after the students endured a stressful round of course testing and exams. Later, those individuals in the control group (who were told they were on a waiting list for

the meditation group) received the mindfulness meditation intervention, replicating the results obtained in the original experimental group.

Shapiro, Schwartz, and Santerre (2002) suggest that when people experience moments of mindfulness, some related qualities of this psychological state enter their consciousness. Some of these mindfulness qualities are shown in **Figure 16.9**. Note how well many of these qualities match up with the overall focus and goals of positive psychology. If you were to take up mindfulness meditation, which qualities would you hope to achieve or experience as a result?

If taking up mindfulness meditation does not seem to be a likely course of action for you anytime soon, there is a simpler way for you to increase your attention, reduce your stress, and improve your subjective well-being: Go outside and experience nature. Recent research suggests that spending even a modest amount of time outside in natural surroundings—the forest or woods, a park, perhaps a garden—has restorative effects that make people more cognitively attentive and function better emotionally (Berto, 2005; Hartig et al., 2003; Kaplan, 1995, 2001; Price, 2008b). In one study, for example, 19 undergraduates spent half an hour walking around an arboretum near the University of Michigan's campus, while an equal number of students ambled around downtown Ann Arbor (Berman, Jonides, & Kaplan, 2008, Study 1). When everyone returned to

**Figure 16.9**

**Some qualities associated with mindfulness meditation.** People who learn mindfulness meditation can expect to derive some benefits from the activity. As you can see, the qualities listed here fit well with established themes in positive psychology.

Source: Adapted from Shapiro, S. J., Schwartz, G. E. R., & Santerre, C. (2002). Meditation and positive psychology. In C. R. Snyder & S. J. Lopez (Eds.), *The handbook of positive psychology* (pp. 632–645). New York: Oxford University Press.

| Some Qualities Associated with Mindfulness Meditation | |
|---|---|
| **Quality** | **Description** |
| Nonjudging | Impartial witnessing, observing the present moment by moment without explanation and categorization |
| Acceptance | Open to seeing things as they really are in the present moment with a clear understanding |
| Loving kindness | Being benevolent, compassionate, and forgiving, and demonstrating unconditional love |
| Patience | Allowing things to unfold in their time, bringing patience to oneself, to others, and to the present moment |
| Openness | Seeing things as if for the first time, creating possibility by paying attention to all feedback in the present moment |
| Nonstriving | Non-goal oriented, remaining unattached to outcome or achievement, not forcing things |
| Trust | Trusting the self, as well as one's body, intuitions, and emotions, and that life is unfolding as it is supposed to |
| Gentleness | Having a soft, tender, and considerate quality, but neither passive nor undisciplined |
| Gratitude | The quality of reverence, appreciating and being thankful for the present moment |
| Empathy | The quality of both feeling and understanding the situation of another person in the present time; communicating knowledge of the person's state to the person |
| Generosity | Giving in the present moment within a context of love and compassion, without attachment to gain or thought of return |
| Letting go | Demonstrating nonattachment or holding on to feelings, thoughts, or experiences; letting go does not refer to suppressing these states |

# LIVING IN TODAY'S WORLD
## Savoring, or Deliberately Making Pleasures Last

For most people, the reality of daily life is filled with business and bustling with activities and responsibilities, not to mention the accompanying stressors and demands. How often do people slow down enough to really reflect on what they are doing and experiencing at that moment in time? Why don't people savor more of their daily experiences? And what would be the psychological consequences if they did?

Savoring is a new concept in positive psychology but, as you will see, it has an excellent conceptual fit with the field and its goals. Psychologically, the term *savoring* refers to the power to focus on, value, and even boost the enjoyment of almost any experience, whether great or small (Bryant & Veroff, 2007). To savor is to enjoy subjective states related to some current experience, one rooted in process and not outcome; the journey, if you will, is more important than arriving at the destination. Researchers who study when and how people go about savoring their experiences claim it is an active process. Savoring is more than mere pleasure or the enjoyment of something or some activity. When you savor reading a book or watching a play or film, for example, a reflective quality is involved: Whether reader or viewer, you must attend to and consciously appreciate what is engaging your attention.

What factors affect the intensity of savoring? Bryant and Veroff (2007) suggest several that affect the experience, including the following.

- *Duration.* The more time available for the experience, the greater the chance to savor it. So, you should not try to savor something while doing other things or "on the fly." Dedicated time like that reserved for exercise or socializing should be set aside for enjoying particular pleasures.
- *Stress reduction.* When distracting stress departs (you stop dwelling on all the homework you have to do over the weekend), savoring becomes possible (you can enjoy spending Friday evening with friends).
- *Complexity.* More complex experiences produce greater quality and intensity of savoring. Examining a detailed work of art, such as an intricate painting, can

lead to more sustained delight than perusing a simple drawing. It follows that experts—individuals with deep knowledge in a subject—can experience more complex savoring when encountering a stimulus than can neophytes. Expert coffee, wine, or tea tasters, for instance, are likely to savor particular examples of these beverages more than the rest of us.

- *Balanced self-monitoring.* If you think too much about what you are doing or if you become too self-focused, you can distort your ability to savor an experience.
- *Social connection.* You might believe that savoring is a solitary pursuit. However, research reveals that savoring is that much more pleasurable if you have other people with whom to share the experience. Concerts, for example, are more enjoyable if you attend with a friend. But what about strangers—can you savor an experience with them? Bryant and Veroff (2007) give an example reported by the writer Frances Mayes, author of *Under the Tuscan Sun* (1996), who has long reflected on the special pleasures of her part-time life in Tuscany, Italy. In the following excerpt, she describes happening on several rainbows surrounding a local church:

*Fog completely surrounds the church, and the dome floats above the clouds. Five intersecting rainbows dive and arch around the dome. I almost run off the road. At a curve I stop and get out, wishing everyone were with me. This is staggering. If it were the Middle Ages, I'd claim a miracle. Another car stops and a man dressed in fancy hunting clothes jumps out . . . he, too, looks stunned. We both just stare. As the clouds shift, the rainbows disappear one by one, but the dome still drifts, ready for any sign that might be about to happen. I wave to the hunter. "Auguri" [an Italian expression of good will, best wishes, and good luck] he calls. (pp. 218–219)*

So, take the time to make the time to savor the pleasures you encounter in your life. Research suggests that you will be a happier, more relaxed person if you do.

the lab to complete a battery of stress and short-term memory measures, the researchers found that the individuals who strolled in the arboretum had lower stress levels and heightened attention compared to the control group who ventured downtown. The explanation is that natural environments are much less mentally taxing

than urban settings. Intuitively, individuals know that green and leafy settings are peaceful places that encourage them to relax and renew themselves. In contrast, even medium-sized cities are full of noise and busy distractions made by cars, buses, people, sirens, and the like. A second study found similar (though somewhat

Encountering nature provides restorative benefits, including enhanced attention, lowered stress, and improved emotional function.

weaker) results by having participants look at slides of either nature scenes or cityscapes (Berman, Jonides, & Kaplan, 2008,).

So, when the transcendentalist and author of *Walden* Henry David Thoreau (1817–1862) observed that "in wildness is the preservation of the world," he may well have been speaking of people's mental and emotional worlds. The implications of Berman and colleagues' (2008) results are clear: When you can, you should try to revitalize your heart and mind by enjoying nature and the great outdoors. These findings also have important implications for the design of cities, towns, or any urban public space: It should be done mindfully. Adding natural elements provides benefits besides just beauty (Tennessen & Cimprich, 1995). Not only is the eye entertained, apparently so are the mind and the spirit.

# Positive Individual Traits

**LEARNING OBJECTIVES**

- Explain the concept of positive individual traits.
- Define hope as a future-directed trait.
- Discuss resilience and posttraumatic growth as beneficial qualities.

- Clarify why gratitude is a character strength and positive personal quality.
- Characterize spirituality as a positive trait related to religious behavior.

Positive personal qualities are the character traits that allow individuals to flourish in daily life. Some traits are heavily influenced by genetics (that is, people are born with them, such as extraversion), whereas others are learned through experience (self-discipline can be acquired with training). Still other positive traits can be acquired if a person is willing to put out the effort (for example, by putting in the time necessary to learn a new skill, such as playing the saxophone). This last point is important because it means that beneficial personal qualities that enhance daily life and well-being can be learned (Peterson & Seligman, 2004).

Whereas subjective states account for people's positive feelings, *positive individual traits* are dispositional qualities that account for why some people are happier and psychologically healthier than other people. Traits sway the interpretations people use to find meaning in events, influence their choices, help select goals, and ultimately drive what they do behaviorally. Think about someone you know who gets along well with other people. The fact that you see this person as being highly agreeable or cooperative represents what psychologists call a *trait,* an individual difference that makes your friend stand out from your other acquaintances (see Chapter 2). Another friend of yours might come across as reliable, that is, very organized and high in self-control, someone who takes few risks and works rather deliberately to achieve particular ends.

An important quality of positive traits like these two is the assumption that they can be taught (Peterson & Seligman, 2004). Positive traits can also emerge as a response or reaction to life situations people experience. Here we discuss four examples of positive individual traits: hope, resilience, gratitude, and spirituality.

## Hope: Achieving Future Goals

Just as traits can explain much of what people do in the present, they can also predict how people will act in the future. Positive psychology is keenly interested in positive individual traits that encourage people to anticipate good rather than bad outcomes. Consider *hope,* **which refers to people's expectations that their goals can be achieved in the future** (Snyder, 1994). People become more excited by goals they can actually achieve than those that seem to be out of reach or too much of a challenge. Given its future directedness, hope is related to optimism, which is discussed in Chapters 3 and 6.

The late C. R. Snyder (1994, 2000, 2002), a social and clinical psychologist, argued that these goal-directed expectations have two components: agency and pathways. *Agency* involves a person's judgment that his or her goals can be achieved. For example, a college student may determine whether obtaining a high grade in a required course in her major is possible. In other words, does Sarah expect that she can obtain the desired grade because she possesses the necessary drive or organizational skills? Agency, then, represents one's motivation to seek desired goals. The second component in Snyder's theory, *pathways*, refers to Sarah's beliefs that successful plans can be crafted to reach the goal of a high grade. Pathways represent the realistic roadmap to achieving the goal. Note that a hopeful view would identify several paths to the goal (more hours of study, completing assigned readings in advance, faithfully attending class, doing homework, and so on), not merely one. A person's pathways complement his or her agency by serving as what Snyder (1994) calls "waypower."

Doug Koch/KU University Relations

C. R. ("Rick") Snyder

Snyder and colleagues (1991) developed the Trait Hope Scale to assess both agency and pathways (see **Figure 16.10**). Respondents rate how true each statement on the scale appears to be for them. A summary score of the agency and pathway items indicates a person's degree of hope (scores can range between 8 and 64; see **Figure 16.10**). Separate scales also measure state hope (how a person feels at a single moment in time) (Snyder et al., 1996) and children's hope (Snyder et al.,1997), as well.

Snyder once did a public demonstration of the power of hope on the television show *Good Morning America* (Lopez, 2006a, 2006b). Prior to the start of the show, the host, the weatherman, and a medical reporter completed the Hope Scale. During the live show, Snyder had the three cast members take turns performing the cold pressor test, which involves plunging one's fist into an ice bath of near freezing water and holding it there for as long as possible. (In case you are wondering, this really hurts quite a bit.) While the cast held their right fists in the icy water bath, Snyder described the idea of hope theory and its link to pain tolerance. He explained that a more hopeful person should be able to withstand serious discomfort for longer periods of time than someone with lower levels of the construct. As Snyder expected, the cast members' scores predicted how long each individual could endure keeping a numb hand in the cold, cold water: more hope, greater pain tolerance.

Why should anyone try to be a hopeful person? For several reasons, actually (Snyder, Rand, & Sigmon, 2002). Not surprisingly, hopeful people experience more positive emotions than those who have a more despairing outlook, and, as we have discussed, such emotions can be beneficial for a variety of reasons. Individuals who have hope expect to be better off in the future, just as they believe that they will be better prepared than others to deal with any stressful circumstances that arise. Why might this be the case? Hopeful people are likely to be flexible thinkers, always on the lookout for alternative pathways to attain their goals

## A Measure of Hope as a Trait

Read each item carefully. Using the scale shown below, please select the number that best describes YOU and put that number in the blank provided.

1 Definitely false
2 Mostly false
3 Somewhat false
4 Slightly false
5 Slightly true
6 Somewhat true
7 Mostly true
8 Definitely true

_____ 1. I can think of many ways to get out of a jam.

_____ 2. I energetically pursue my goals.

_____ 3. I feel tired most of the time.

_____ 4. There are lots of ways around any problem.

_____ 5. I am easily downed in an argument.

_____ 6. I can think of many ways to get the things in life that are important to me.

_____ 7. I worry about my health.

_____ 8. Even when others get discouraged, I know I can find a way to solve the problem.

_____ 9. My past experiences have prepared me well for my future.

_____ 10. I've been pretty successful in life.

_____ 11. I usually find myself worrying about something.

_____ 12. I meet the goals I set for myself.

### Figure 16.10

**Snyder's Trait Hope Scale.** According to C. R. Snyder, as a trait, hope has two characteristics: agency and pathways. To determine your agency subscale score, add items 2, 9, 10, and 12; your pathways subscale score is derived by adding items 1, 4, 6, and 8. The total Hope Scale score is the total of the four agency and the four pathway items. A higher total score reflects a greater degree of hope for the future. Scores can range from 8 to 64. In six samples of college students studied by Snyder et al. (1991), the average score was 25.

Source: From Snyder, C. R., Harris, C., Anderson, J. R., Holeran, S. A., Irving, L. M., Sigmon, S. T., Yoshinobu, L., Gibb, J., Langelle, C., & Harney, P. (1991). The will and the ways: Development and validation of an individual-differences measure of hope. *Journal of Personality and Social Psychology, 60,* 570–585.

or to get around obstacles. They are also likely to be buoyed up by the positive social support they receive from those who are drawn to their encouraging, upbeat natures (Snyder, Rand & Sigmon, 2002).

## Resilience: Reacting Well to Life's Challenges

Another important positive trait is *resilience,* **a person's ability to recover and often prosper following some consequential life event.** Such events are often traumatic—an accident, loss, or catastrophe causes an individual to confront and cope with a situation that often psychologically scars others. Resilient people cope with threats, maintaining, recovering, or even improving mental and physical health in the process of doing so (Masten, 2001; Ryff & Singer, 2003).

Resilience research examines a variety of tumultuous events, including how people deal with threats such as natural disasters, war, divorce, alcoholism and mental illness in parents, family violence, the demands of single-parenting, and, of course, the loss of a loved one (Bonanno, 2009; Hetherington, Bridges, & Insabella, 1998; Masten & Reed, 2002; Ryff & Singer, 2003). Note that these threats range from extreme but rare events (war) to those that are tragically commonplace (family problems). Whatever its qualities, the threat is usually so severe and potentially damaging, if not life threatening, that most observers would expect negative rather than positive outcomes. Yet in spite of these traumatic "perfect storms," some people persevere and emerge psychologically resilient.

For example, imagine the future lives of children who are raised in abusive or neglectful households or in communities wracked by poverty, illness, and disease. Individuals born into such environments are said to be at higher risk than others for various mental, physical, social, and economic problems (Masten & Reed, 2002). Would anyone predict that children reared in such settings would eventually thrive and lead productive and happy lives? The surprising reality is that the resilient ones do (e.g., Garmezy, 1991; Masten, Best, & Garmezy, 1990; Masten & Coatsworth, 1998). Interestingly, resilience is not usually recognized by those who have it until they are called on to display it once a trauma occurs. Fortunately, resilience appears to be a relatively common trait among humans, including young children.

In addition to resilience, some people display growth following a trauma such as an accident, a serious illness, or the onset of a disability. ***Posttraumatic growth* refers to enhanced personal strength, realization of what is truly important in life, and increased appreciation for life, friends, and family following trauma.** Posttraumatic growth provides empirical evidence that sometimes personal suffering can pave the way to positive insights (Davis & Nolen-Hoeksema, 2009; Lechner, Tennen, & Affleck, 2009; Tesdeschi & Calhoun, 1995). Whereas resilience can help people rebound to their pretrauma levels, posttraumatic growth implies that people can also psychologically exceed those original levels by displaying enhanced functioning and positive changes. In fact, a surprising number of people actually claim that trauma "was the best thing that ever happened to them" (Park, 1998).

**Figure 16.11** lists a variety of positive changes that are attributed to posttraumatic growth as grounded in the available research (Ryff & Singer, 2003; Tedeschi, Park, & Calhoun, 1998). As you can see, these changes

"He appears to have lost all of his resilience."

can be categorized as being perceptual, relationship-based, or a life priority. Advocates of positive psychology have helped reduce the skepticism associated with claims of posttraumatic growth and related coping strategies. Although it can be difficult to verify documented positive growth, psychologists are now less likely to simply assume such change is due to convenient rationalization, factual distortion, or unfounded self-report (Lechner, Tennen, & Affleck, 2009).

| Aspects of Posttraumatic Growth |
| --- |
| **Perceptual changes** |
| Self is perceived as a survivor and not a victim |
| Increased feelings of personal strength, self-reliance, and self-confidence |
| Enhanced appreciation for life's fragile nature, including one's own |
| **Relationship changes** |
| Increases compassion for and willingness to give to others |
| Closer bonds with family |
| Feelings of closeness with others and greater willingness to disclose emotions |
| **Life priority changes** |
| Reduced concern with possessions, money, and social status |
| Greater willingness to take life easier |
| Enhanced clarity regarding what really matters in life |
| A deeper and more spiritual sense of the meaning of life |

**Figure 16.11**

**Positive changes attributed to posttraumatic growth.** After experiencing a trauma, some people respond by exhibiting positive changes that generally fall into three areas: perceptual changes, relationship changes, and life priority changes. This figure illustrates examples of growth within each area.

Source: Adapted from Baumgardner, S. R., & Crothers, M. K. (2009). *Positive psychology.* Upper Saddle River, NJ: Prentice-Hall. © 2009 Prentice Hall. Reproduced by permission of Pearson Education, Inc.

**WEB LINK 16.3  VIA Institute on Character**

To learn about your own signature character strengths, you may want to complete the Values in Action (VIA) survey available at this site. The survey is a psychometrically sound instrument that is based on 24 personality elements linked to positive behavior and well-being.

## Gratitude: The Power of Being Thankful

One of the most promising positive individual traits that is receiving considerable research attention is gratitude, or being grateful for what you have or others have done for you. **As a human strength, *gratitude* entails recognizing and concentrating on the good things in one's life and being thankful for them.** Gratitude is often considered within a moral context. In fact, being ungrateful—that is, expressing *in*gratitude—is considered to be a vice (Bono, Emmons, & McCullough, 2004). Yet experiencing gratitude (being thankful) and expressing it (thanking someone for being gracious to you) are among the most common ways to experience this beneficial, positive emotion (Bono, Emmons, & McCullough; Emmons & McCullough, 2004).

What are the psychosocial consequences of expressing gratitude? As might be expected, doing so enhances social connections with others: When people do nice things, they appreciate being thanked. More than that, however, expressing gratitude appears to extend the time people feel the positive emotions that are linked to being thankful. Where negative affect tends to linger, positive moods tend to be shorter (Larsen & Prizmic, 2008). Besides benefiting others, conveying gratitude benefits the self, too. Feelings of gratitude make one feel happy, at times joyful, and can be a source of contentment (Bono, Emmons, & McCullough, 2004; Emmons & McCullough, 2004). Experimental research also indicates that focusing on things to be thankful for improves people's moods, triggers coping behaviors, and motivates people to report experiencing health benefits (Emmons & McCullough, 2003). Finally, when gratitude is treated as a personality trait, people who report being more thankful also tend to report higher levels of psychological well-being than less appreciative others (Watkins et al., 2003).

Perhaps the best part of gratitude is that it is so easy to express and, as a virtue, it can be performed almost anytime or anywhere. So, the next time someone does something nice for you, whether great or small, be sure to acknowledge the help or kindness by saying "Thank you" and expressing your appreciation in greater detail. Both you and your recipient will benefit psychologically from your simple act (see the Application section of this chapter for a gratitude-related exercise).

## Spirituality: Seeking a Deeper Meaning

Some people are moved to question whether life has a deeper meaning than is apparent in daily experience. People who have the positive individual trait of spirituality possess a belief that life has transcendent or nonphysical qualities that are worth seeking and exploring (Pargament & Mahoney, 2002; Peterson & Seligman, 2004). Thus, spiritual individuals possess a strong desire to search for the sacred (Pargament, 1997; Pargament & Mahoney, 2009) and usually think of themselves as religious (Zinnebauer & Pargament, 2005; Zinnebauer et al., 1997). Although the terms are often used interchangeably, religion (or religiosity) and spirituality are distinct, albeit overlapping concepts. *Religion* refers primarily to what people do in a religious community (church, synagogue, temple, mosque), whereas *spirituality* refers to the human need for a deeper meaning that often motivates and guides religious behaviors. Religious behaviors are normally bound to the beliefs and rituals of some specific, formal religious institution (Zinnebauer, Pargament, & Scott, 1999).

© Steve Raymer/Getty Images/Asia Images

© Jeff Greenberg/The Image Works

**People engage in religious activities to promote spirituality, which can lead to deeper meaning in daily life.**

2000). Students who are high in school satisfaction tend to have higher grade point averages (GPAs) than other students, as well as fewer reported psychological symptoms and a heightened sense of agency (Huebner & Gillman, 2006). It may come as no surprise that students who are more engaged and performing well academically are also less likely to display adolescent problem behaviors (DeSantis et al., 2006). Thus, school satisfaction appears to be a promising and positive variable for the study of positive academic achievement in schools.

## Positive Families

Although it seems a little odd to say so, families (should) operate like institutions, especially when it comes to cultivating virtues and promoting good behavior. Yet, the structures and dynamics of families have changed dramatically in the past 30 or 40 years (Sheridan & Burt, 2009). Various social and cultural changes, including increased divorce rates and expanded career opportunities for women, among many others, have led to the move away from traditional conceptions of family. Advocates of positive psychology believe that the family, like any institution, should be examined from the perspective of enhancing existing strengths (or developing new ones) rather than emphasizing problems, limitations, deficits, or pathology.

Indeed, a new approach called *family-centered positive psychology (FCPP)* advances the idea that the family is the constant in a child's life, which means that researchers and practitioners should support children's well-being and promote healthy family functioning (Sheridan et al., 2004). To that end, FCPP helps families to identify needs and muster available resources, learn new skills and competencies, build on existing strengths, and strengthen social support. In addition, FCPP presumes that families themselves are better at determining their needs than are professionals (Sheridan & Burt, 2009).

## Virtuous Institutions?

Can positive institutions be like people? That is, can institutions both possess and promote positive virtues? Peterson (2006) notes that qualities that are intrinsically good can be found in everyday institutions like those we discussed in this section, as well as clubs, sports teams, government agencies, and organizations found throughout society. **Figure 16.12** lists the virtues that Peterson suggests make institutions positive contributors to people's lives. As you examine **Figure 16.12**, think about the institutions you come into contact with regularly: How many of them display or enact these virtues?

| The Virtues of Positive Institutions | |
| --- | --- |
| **Virtue** | **Description** |
| *Purpose* | Provides a shared vision of the moral goals promoted by the institution; these goals are routinely remembered and celebrated |
| *Fairness* | Rules exist and are known; rewards and punishments are administered consistently |
| *Humanity* | The institution cares for its members, and vice versa |
| *Safety* | The institution protects its members from threats, dangers, and exploitation |
| *Dignity* | No matter what their status, all members of the institution are treated with respect |

**Figure 16.12**

**Virtues found in positive institutions.** Positive institutions are thought to offer a variety of benefits to the individuals who work within them, as well as to the communities in which they reside. This figure lists some of the basic virtues such institutions provide. Can you think of any others?

Source: Adapted from Peterson, C. (2006). *A primer in positive psychology.* New York: Oxford University Press.

## *Recommended* READING

### *The How of Happiness: A Scientific Approach to Getting the Life You Want*
by Sonja Lyubomirsky (Penguin, 2007)

Some positive psychologists focus on how positive affective states are based on personal circumstances. For example, some people have had more opportunities in life than others—you might call this being in the right place at the right time—which accounts for about 10% of a person's happiness. Other researchers study personality factors, which are not very malleable. Each person has a "set point" that accounts for around 50% of his or her happiness. So, the short answer is that people cannot change their set points or personalities very much. But what can they change? Lyubomirsky focuses on intentional actions, the remaining 40% of the happiness pie. Intentional actions are choices people can make and activities they can pursue. First, she offers helpful guidance on identifying activities that promote happiness but are grounded in your own interests, needs, and values. She then shares empirically corroborated exercises dealing with positive thinking, close social connections, coping with challenges, mindful living, and pursuing goals, among others. The book closes by offering suggestions on sustaining happiness once you acquire it through intentional actions.

*Go to the Psychology CourseMate for Weiten at* **www.cengagebrain.com/shop/ISBN/1111186634** *for descriptions of other recommended books.*

# Positive Psychology: Problems and Prospects

### LEARNING OBJECTIVES

● Identify some criticisms concerning positive psychology.
● Outline some opportunities for positive psychology's future.

Positive psychology has come a relatively long way in a fairly short time. Besides numerous articles and chapters (like this one) touting the benefits of this new approach to psychology, there are now many edited volumes and several textbooks with the title "positive psychology" or some related variation, as well as a few dedicated journals (*Journal of Positive Psychology, Journal of Happiness Studies*). And people who want to learn more about this increasingly active subfield can attend positive psychology conferences, join positive organizations, and even pursue a graduate education in positive psychology. Although positive psychology has not exactly taken the larger discipline of psychology by storm, it has done quite well for being around for only a decade or so.

Still, even positive psychology's creators and staunchest allies have wondered whether it is really here for the long run. Will this new subfield continue to attract interested students and researchers? Is it really more of a fad or psychological fashion than a genuinely new area of empirical inquiry? To paraphrase two of its midwives, Christopher Peterson and Martin Seligman (2003), will it have the evergreen popularity of the Beatles—or suffer the "has-been" fate of Duran Duran?

## Problems

More to the point, positive psychology has not been without critics and skeptics (Lazarus, 2003b; Richardson & Guignon, 2008; Taylor, 2001). For example, the late Richard Lazarus (2003a), a renowned psychologist and stress researcher, wondered whether its message is not only *not* very new but destined to be a fad that will pass, later return, and pass again. Why? Because many important conceptual and empirical issues will likely be left unresolved while new disciplinary fads will appear. Lazarus also questioned whether parsing the discipline of psychology into positive and negative spheres is not only an oversimplification but a way to introduce theoretical as well as practical problems into psychological research. As Lazarus (2003a) humorously but effectively posed it:

*God needs Satan, and vice versa. One would not exist without the other. We need the bad which is part of life, to fully appreciate the good. (p. 94)*

Similarly, as you read this chapter, you might have wondered whether this new area is really all that new.

For example, perhaps positive psychology is little more than the repackaging of "old wine in new bottles." Or, more charitably, perhaps the framework of positive psychology is useful for reorganizing how we think about positive events, thoughts, feelings, and even behaviors, but it might not be the paradigm shift its creators hoped it would be. As partisans on either side of the positive psychology debate will agree, only time will tell whether it has both staying power and ongoing influence in the wider discipline. That being the case, what should we look for, and forward to, if positive psychology is to flourish?

## Prospects

Perhaps the success of positive psychology will be best judged by the research findings and successful applications that emerge in the future. Peterson (2006) offers what may be the most telling indicator of success: Will there be needed balance between the positive and negative aspects of psychology? Perhaps survival of the label "positive psychology" will matter less if this desired and needed balance is achieved. A close second criterion is whether research can address why people don't seek out those qualities of life that make them truly happy. In other words, if research identifies which activities enable people to lead a good life (Dunn & Brody, 2008; Park & Peterson, 2009), will they apply these findings to their own lives? As research evidence and intervention studies appear, it will be exciting to see whether people do indeed change the ways they live (the exercises in this next section of the chapter may provide you with an opportunity to see how easy it is to introduce new, positive routines into you own life).

Linley and colleagues (2006) suggest that positive psychology will have a bright future if the subfield (a) borrows knowledge from overlooked but sympathetic areas of psychology, including humanistic psychology; (b) examines positive phenomena at different levels of analysis, integrating cultural, social, and

---

**WEB LINK 16.5   Positive Psychology Center**

This site, maintained at the University of Pennsylvania, includes a variety of links pertaining to positive psychology. It provides a great deal of information on conferences and educational programs.

● *A "calling"*. The third group view their work as a means for personal fulfillment and social purpose. They see their work as service to themselves as well as to other people. Thus, work becomes a form of community service while providing a sense of personal fulfillment.

Try putting this distinction in more personal terms for yourself: Will you seek work that simply satisfies financial necessity (paying bills, providing security), or do you aspire to work that is personally fulfilling or even that "gives back" to your community? Naturally, there can be some overlap among these three categories, but the truly interesting aspect of people's responses is that when work is seen as a calling, issues such as salary, status, and prestige bear little relation to the reasons that motivate people to select one type of work over another. Under the right conditions, it may well be that no matter how humble, almost any job can be a calling to some individual, which is a very positive state of affairs.

## Positive Schools

Most research on schools and the students' experiences within them has focused on the negative, emphasizing

**WEB LINK 16.4    European Network for Positive Psychology**

Happily, positive psychology is not limited to the United States. Visit the European Network for Positive Psychology (ENPP) to learn about research, events, activities, and various topics concerning positive psychology in Europe. The aim of the ENPP is to attract researchers and practitioners interested in this new area of psychology.

what is wrong with educational efforts (Snyder & Lopez, 2007). Recently, however, some psychologists have begun to focus on what they call school satisfaction, or students' judgments about their holistic school experiences (Huebner et al., 2009). As a psychological construct representing individual differences, school satisfaction is composed of both cognition (what students believe regarding educational experiences) and affect (students' reported frequency of positive and negative emotions in educational settings).

Thus far, a few findings regarding school satisfaction have emerged. First, school satisfaction is a good predictor of student engagement and academic progress as early as kindergarten (Ladd, Buhs, & Seid,

Positive schools promote student satisfaction, which is linked with student engagement and academic progress.

# Positive Institutions

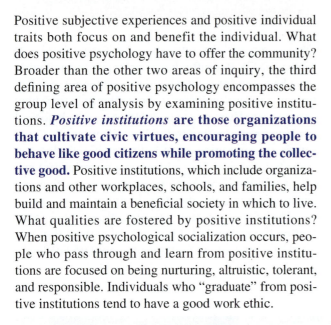

- Characterize the nature of positive institutions.
- Describe the characteristics of positive workplaces, positive schools, and positive families.
- Identify some virtues associated with positive institutions.

Positive subjective experiences and positive individual traits both focus on and benefit the individual. What does positive psychology have to offer the community? Broader than the other two areas of inquiry, the third defining area of positive psychology encompasses the group level of analysis by examining positive institutions. *Positive institutions* **are those organizations that cultivate civic virtues, encouraging people to behave like good citizens while promoting the collective good.** Positive institutions, which include organizations and other workplaces, schools, and families, help build and maintain a beneficial society in which to live. What qualities are fostered by positive institutions? When positive psychological socialization occurs, people who pass through and learn from positive institutions are focused on being nurturing, altruistic, tolerant, and responsible. Individuals who "graduate" from positive institutions tend to have a good work ethic.

## Positive Workplaces

Some positive psychologists are interested in developing and maintaining organizations that provide a pleasant workplace and allow workers to thrive (Cameron, Dutton, & Quinn, 2003; Luthans & Youssef, 2009; Wright, 2003). In fact, a new movement known as *positive organizational behavior (POB)* is dedicated to studying beneficial human strengths and competencies and how they can be advanced, evaluated, and managed as a means to improve worker performance in businesses and organizations (Nelson & Cooper, 2007). Within POB, there is a related emphasis on supporting organizational accomplishments and development of individuals by improving the quality of the relationships formed between co-workers (Dutton & Ragins, 2007; Harter, 2008; Luthans, Youssef, & Avolio, 2007).

A good way to think about the sorts of careers that positive organizations or workplaces spawn is by thinking about the distinction between a job and a calling. While studying people who worked in jobs ranging from clerical to professional, Wrzesniewski et al. (1997) found that workers viewed their chosen occupations in one of three ways.

- *Just a "job."* Money is necessary for survival, so work is done for pay. Individuals with this view often think of themselves as primary providers for their families.
- *A career.* Work satisfies this second group's desire and need to achieve, compete, and acquire status or prestige. Personal pride is clearly at stake here as well.

**Positive workplaces enable employees to thrive and to form beneficial relationships between co-workers.**

Positive psychologists are interested in religion because participating in a religious community appears to enhance well-being (Myers, 2000a, 2000b; Peterson & Seligman, 2004). For example, people who engage in more religiously based activities (attending worship services, doing charity work) are generally mentally and physically healthier than others (Koenig, McCullough, & Larson, 2001). The more religious practice they engage in, the higher the rate of well-being and the lower the rates of alcohol and drug problems, criminal behavior, and other societal ills (Donahue & Benson, 1995; Myers, 1992, 2000a, 2000b). Aside from faith alone, the social connections religious individuals form with others may discourage problematic or risky behaviors (George et al., 2000). Religion probably affects mental and physical health and well-being for a variety of reasons, including the social support from like-minded others (Argyle, 1999; Hill & Pargament, 2003; Myers, 2000a) and the promotion of a healthier lifestyle (Emmons, 1999; Myers, 2000a; Pargament et al., 1998). Religious individuals also tend to have higher levels of optimism, a trait which affects behaviors linked to well-being (Koenig & Cohen, 2002; Sethi & Seligman, 1993).

In contrast to organized religious practice, spirituality encompasses the human need for finding meaning in life and the assumption that such meaning involves something larger than the self or one's own existence (Zinnebauer, Pargament, & Scott, 1999). When psychologists talk about *meaning* in this context, they are referring to the ways in which people experience "perceptions of significance" (Park & Folkman, 1997, p. 116). From this perspective, when people search for or find meaning, they do so in ways that indicate that life is both significant and contains significance for them. Finding such meaning and significance can provide coherence and order to people's experiences (Park & Folkman, 1997; Yalom, 1980). According to Pargament and Mahoney (2009), "to envision, seek, connect, and hold onto, and transform the sacred may be what makes us uniquely human" (p. 616).

Let's consider a particular example of spirituality, one rooted in Eastern religion and philosophy: Buddhism. Buddhism is of interest to some positive psychologists because it offers some intriguing insights concerning the human pursuit of happiness and pleasure (Compton, 2005; Haidt, 2006; Keltner, 2009). To begin, Buddhists emphasize one truth: Life is ever changing. No matter what you do, you and the world around you will change. You, as well as your friends and family, were born; you will all grow old and, in time, die. These sobering changes represent a pure form of truth. Your response to this state of affairs is to attempt to control change by seeking security, finding things that are permanent, and trying to manage your worry (if not despair) by keeping things as stable and predictable as possible.

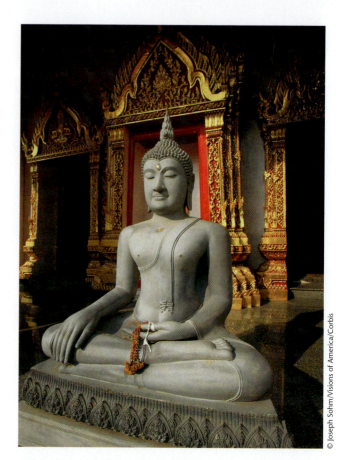

Positive psychologists are interested in Buddhism because it promotes awareness of life's challenges and encourages detachment from them.

The desire for a predictable, safe, and permanent state of affairs is ill-founded; according to Buddhist doctrine, the belief that all will be well if only this state is reached is foolish. Change is inevitable, and still more change will follow. To Buddhists, this truth makes humans "suffer," as does the neverending search for comfort and security. And one will suffer as changes come to pass. In actuality, life is really about seeking illusory security while experiencing inevitable suffering.

The way out of this suffering is to stop trying to control what cannot be controlled by accepting life's changes as routine and absolute. But how can this way of viewing life be achieved? Buddhism advocates embracing and developing two skills: awareness and detachment. Becoming more aware means increasing one's focus on everyday experiences in order to look for and find the sacred in the mundane. At the same time, by becoming "detached" from these experiences, people can release or "let go" of their desire to control what cannot be controlled so that change is allowed to occur in an unhindered fashion. By being both aware and detached, one can become more relaxed and accepting of one's life as it unfolds. Perhaps contentment is possible if people cease their struggles to make things as they wish and instead become conscious of the happiness present in every changing moment.

neuroscience knowledge in the process; and (c) admits that its findings are not neutral—that they prescribe a certain lifestyle (one based on positive subjective experiences, positive individual traits, and positive institutions). These recommendations will not be difficult to follow; in fact, we may assume that many advocates of positive psychology are currently pursuing them. So, the future prospects for positive psychology are—if you will pardon the pun—quite good. It will be exciting to see what developments occur in the next few years.

# Boosting Your Own Happiness

### LEARNING OBJECTIVES

- Explain how counting your blessings and expressions of gratitude can promote happiness.
- Recognize the psychological benefits of sharing a positive story about oneself and sharing good news.

*Answer the following "true" or "false."*

___ **1.** Counting your blessings is a simple way to increase your own happiness.

___ **2.** Writing a sincere thank you note can enhance well-being in you as well as the recipient.

___ **3.** Sharing good things that happen to you with an interested other person (and vice versa) can generate beneficial positive emotions.

If you answered "false" to any or all of these questions because you concluded that the described activities were too simple, there is still more you can learn about the nature of happiness. Enhancing your own well-being and happiness may be easier than you believe. You have spent time reading this chapter and thinking about how positive psychological insights affect and benefit the lives of others. Now it's your turn: How can positive psychology be used to improve your own life? Wouldn't it be nice to smile and laugh more, or to take a little time to appreciate the things that really matter in your life? If you read this chapter carefully, then these are no longer silly or vacuous questions. So, how can positive psychology help you become a happier and psychologically healthier person? This Application contains four simple exercises, each of which can pay some serious psychosocial dividends. All you have to do is give them a try. Good luck.

## Counting Your Blessings for a Week

Some days life seems annoying, if not overwhelming. Often it is not life's big problems that lay one low, but the little ones—the hassles, upsets, and minor disruptions—that get one down. For some people, it's getting stuck in traffic; for others, its never finding an available parking space. Sometimes a person is late to class, forgets a promise, or misses a deadline. A button pops off his shirt or coat. His room is a mess and there's still laundry to be done. The minor is perceived to be major, and suddenly the person feels diminished.

What to do? Several researchers (Emmons & Crumpler, 2000; Emmons & McCullough, 2003; Lyubomirsky, Sheldon, & Schkade, 2005; Seligman et al., 2005) suggest looking on the bright side of your life by counting your blessings—literally. By "blessings," these positive psychologists are referring to the good things that happen to you each day—a warm smile from a stranger, a pleasant lunch with a co-worker, an unexpected contact (perhaps on Facebook) from a long-lost old friend. Your list of good things can also contain grand events like falling in love, starting an exciting new job, or learning that a loved one's health has dramatically improved.

Peterson (2006) offers a few guidelines for keeping a list of good things. First, don't try to list too many things. Three a day is fine—more than that decreases any benefits associated with the exercise. Second, for one week, try to write the list of good things toward the end of the day. Peterson reports that this minimal record keeping is less effective when done too early in the day. Finally, after making your end-of-day list, take a few minutes to jot down reasons that your choices constitute good things for you and your life. By doing so, you will become more mindful about the nature of these good things.

What are the apparent benefits of keeping track of the good things in your life? People who did so for a week were found to have higher levels of happiness and fewer depressive symptoms up to six months after they quit keeping the list (Peterson, 2006). Better still, close to 60% of the original participants maintained their daily lists thereafter on their own and without prompting from the investigators. Follow-up surveys found that the now daily habit encouraged an ongoing sense of well-being and led to enhanced relationships with important others.

## Writing and Delivering a Gratitude Letter

No one writes real letters any more—they text, Tweet, or send e-mail messages. Writing a real letter is a dying art. So, this exercise will not only allow you to revive a dying art, it will afford you a chance to make the recipient of your letter feel good.

Most of us are good at saying thank you to folks who have done something nice for us, but expressing gratitude is tougher. Take a few minutes and think of all the people who have gone out of their way to help you so far in your life. Your parents, siblings, and grandparents are likely candidates, as are some of your teachers or coaches, roommates, close friends, perhaps some neighbors, and select others. Pick one of these people, the one you believe did you the greatest kindness to date. If you have never properly expressed gratitude to that individual, here's your chance.

Write a personal letter to your chosen individual—an e-mail won't do because such messages are usually brief and can seem impersonal—and in the letter explain in clear terms how he or she helped you and why you are so very grateful. Better yet, make your letter more spontaneous by writing it by hand instead of typing it. Make the letter as rich and detailed as possible. In the ideal case, visit the person, hand deliver your letter, and have the individual read it while you are there (Peterson, 2006). If this face-to-face encounter is not possible, you can mail or fax the letter (or e-mail if you absolutely must—but no texting, please!), then later speak to the person by phone.

What will happen once your letter is read? You will move the recipient (possibly to tears), but your expression of gratitude will also gratify him or her. And both of you are likely to feel happy (Seligman et al., 2005). Such letters are more life affirming in the moment than they are life changing in the long run (that is, unless you decide to write a gratitude letter every so often for the foreseeable future!). Still, being grateful is a good thing, as those who feel gratitude turn out to be much happier than those who don't (McCullough et al., 1999; Park, Peterson, & Seligman, 2004).

What about people who are no longer with us, such as loved ones who have died? Is it possible to express gratitude for their kindness to us when they were alive? Yes. If you wish, you can use the above directions as a model for writing a gratitude letter to a departed friend or loved one. You may not be able to directly share the letter with the person, but you are apt to bring up pleasant memories to reflect on as you express your gratitude in words on paper. These memories may allow you to once again have a "conversation" with a person to whom you owe a great deal.

## Sharing a Story Illustrating the Best in You

Do you have any secret moments you are proud of? Perhaps no one saw you do a good deed, but you did it

The expression of sincere gratitude benefits the person being thanked as well as the person doing the thanking.

because it was the right thing to do. Failing to act was not an option for you because you did not want to live with that on your conscience.

Most people avoid blowing their own horns, but they can all remember times when they did things that brought out the best in them. Because people really don't like to brag, they often keep these stories to themselves. Although such modesty is admirable, there may be times when telling others about one's exemplary acts can serve as an example or even a source of inspiration. As you consider this activity, let this be one of these rare times when you disclose an act of private goodness to others.

What are the ground rules? Well, you should be honest and err on the side of modesty (again, no bragging) unless what you did was truly selfless and self-defining. Once you recall your example, be prepared to share it with others, probably members of the class in which you are using this book. You might ask the course instructor if a class could be devoted to having people share their stories with one another. Alternatively, you could write a brief, one-page essay telling your tale. Your essay could then be posted on an online site where only other members of your class could access and read it. Or, copies could be made of everyone's stories and assigned as reading for a future class meeting. This last option lacks the passion and punch of hearing people tell their "personal best" stories, but this is one assignment that is likely to be read by all. If this exercise is not done in the context of your class, you could agree to swap stories with a classmate or two, which is a great way to make new friends as you explore the course material.

One last thing: remember the golden rule of doing unto others. When people listen politely and with interest to your story, be sure to do the same for them (see the next exercise). Once a story is told, respond to it in a friendly and constructive way—try to relate to it. As a student, you are used to being critical, even skeptical, of what you read or hear. Don't be in this instance. Be open to the ideas and experiences of others, just as you want them to be open to what you have to say. What goes around comes around, which is exactly what you want to happen when you are sharing the very best of yourself with others.

## Sharing Good News and Capitalizing with Others

Let's close this chapter's Application section with something easy you can do when exchanging news of the day with your friends and loved ones. The humorist Fran Lebowitz (1982) once wrote that "The opposite of talking isn't listening. The opposite of talking is waiting" (p. 17). Is that how you often treat those who are close to you when they vie for your attention? Do you really listen closely to what they say and respond accordingly, especially when the news they are imparting is good? Or are you not an especially good or responsive listener? Do you focus more on wanting to tell the other person what good thing happened to you rather than celebrating his or her achievement? You of course want friends and loved ones to revel in your good fortune, but unless you do the same for them, you may not get the response you seek—or as we will see—any positive psychosocial benefits.

Positive psychologist Shelly Gable and her colleagues discovered that how people give and respond to good news from others has profound consequences for both the self and others (Gable et al., 2004). Specifically, sharing good news with those close to us can lead to "capitalization" when they respond with sincere interest and enthusiasm to what we say. ***Capitalization refers to telling other people about whatever good things are happening in our own lives.*** The term is admittedly unusual in this context, but one of the word's meanings is to "turn something into an advantage," which is what people do when they share good things with others. How so? Well, others' positive response to sharing creates positive emotions in the sharer, which capitalizes or builds on his or her already good feelings. These feelings of mutual respect, delight, and acknowledgment appear to enhance the qualities of the shared relationship. In short, both parties benefit socially and emotionally when good news is received and responded to in favorable ways.

What happens when people don't respond favorably to the good news of others? (Note that we are not talking about situations that trigger envy for a friend's career success, say, or jealousy at her new romance—we are considering those times when people ignore sharing in some modest, if still happy, event.) Nothing happens: No positive emotions result, so neither self-reported well-being or relationship quality improves. Keep this in mind the next time you are tired at the end of the day and a friend or significant other wants to share some modest successes that occurred since you last talked. Rustling up some smiles and congratulations really won't take much effort on your part, and you are more likely to have the attention repaid to you sometime soon. Better still, you will focus less on your fatigue (always a good thing) and potentially improve your bonds with your pal or partner. Isn't that worth celebrating?

So, from this moment forward, resolve to listen and respect and respond favorably to all the good things that happen to your friends and family. Share your good fortune with them in the hope that they will respond with warmth, interest, and enthusiasm. This simple form of "paying it forward" can benefit everyone.

## KEY IDEAS

### The Scope of Positive Psychology

● Positive psychology is a new area of psychology dedicated to the study of human strengths and how people can flourish in daily life. This subfield emerged as a reaction to the larger discipline's predominant focus on psychological problems. By providing needed balance, positive psychology can encourage people to focus on the positive aspects of daily living.

● Although it is a new area, many of the issues positive psychology explores have been studied outside the mainstream areas of the discipline for some time. Positive psychology provides an organizing framework for older and newer concepts related to well-being and the good life.

● Positive psychology explores three related lines of behavioral research: positive subjective experiences (such as good mood and positive emotions), positive individual traits (including hope, resilience, and gratitude), and positive institutions (such as beneficial work environments, good schools, and solid families).

### Positive Subjective Experiences

● Positive subjective experiences entail the positive but usually private thoughts and feelings people have about their lives. Positive moods are global, longlasting reactions to events, whereas positive emotions are accute, distinct responses that last for shorter periods of time. Positive moods and emotions promote particular thoughts, feelings, and behaviors.

● Fredrickson's broaden-and-build model explains why positive emotions lead to new and beneficial ways of thinking and acting. Whereas negative emotions narrow people's thoughts, positive ones widen people's perspectives, creating future emotional and intellectual resources in the process.

● Flow is a psychological state marked by complete involvement and engagement with interesting, challenging, and intrinsically rewarding activities. Flow occurs when a person's skills are balanced by challenges that are just manageable.

● Mindful behavior is marked by attention and response to novel features of daily experience, whereas mindlessness occurs when individuals engage in familiar or rote actions that require little active thought.

### Positive Individual Traits

● Positive individual traits are qualities of character, some of which are learned while others are inherited. These positive dispositions explain why some people are happier and psychologically healthier than others.

● People who display hope anticipate that their desired goals can be met in the future. According to Snyder, hope consists of agency and pathways. The trait of hope is associated with the experience of positive emotions.

● Resilient people recover their psychological well-being following traumatic experiences better and faster than less-resilient people do. As evidence for such resilience, posttraumatic growth is marked by people's recogntion of what things truly matter, including enhanced appreciation for friends, loved ones, and life in general.

● Gratitude occurs when people are thankful for the good things in their lives, particularly expressing appreciation for what others have done for them.

● As a trait, spirituality refers to people's belief that life has affirming transcendent or nonphysical qualities that warrant their attention.

### Positive Institutions

● Positive institutions are organizations promoting civic virtues that help people act like good citizens who care about the general welfare. Schools and families can fall under this heading as well. Positive institutions promote purpose, fairness, humility, safety, and dignity.

### Positive Psychology: Problems and Prospects

● Some critics argue that positive psychology is nothing more than old or exisiting ideas repackaged in a new, if positive, framework. Positive psychology's defenders counter that this subfield will achieve its goals if the larger discipline becomes more balanced where positive and negative psychological processes are concerned.

### Application: Boosting Your Own Happiness

● Feelings of happiness can be achieved if people count the good things in their lives; express sincere gratitude to someone who helped them in the past; and share stories illustrating their own good actions that benefitted other people.

● There are psychologically beneficial qualities to sharing one's good news with others, as well as enthusiastically listening to positive information other people share.

## KEY TERMS

| | |
|---|---|
| Capitalization  p. 535 | Positive individual traits |
| Emotions  p. 516 |   p. 524 |
| Flow  p. 518 | Positive institutions  p. 529 |
| Gratitude  p. 527 | Positive psychology  p. 511 |
| Hope  p. 524 | Positive subjective |
| Mindlessness  p. 521 |   experiences  p. 513 |
| Mindfulness  p. 521 | Posttraumatic growth  p. 526 |
| Negative emotions  p. 517 | Resilience  p. 525 |
| Positive emotions  p. 516 | Undoing hypothesis  p. 518 |

## KEY PEOPLE

| | |
|---|---|
| Mihalyi Csikszentmihalyi   pp. 518–521 | Ellen J. Langer  pp. 521–522 |
| Barbara Fredrickson   pp. 517–518 | Martin Seligman  p. 512 |
| | C. R. Snyder  pp. 524–525 |

## QUESTIONS

1. As a social and intellectual movement within the larger discipline of psychology, positive psychology is concerned with:
   a. human strengths.
   b. how people can flourish.
   c. creating a balance between the challenges and pleasures of daily life.
   d. all of the above.

2. Of positive psychology's three lines of inquiry, which one deals with psychological processes that promote favorable moods and emotions?
   a. positive subjective experiences
   b. positive individual traits
   c. positive resilience
   d. positive institutions

3. Being placed in a positive mood has been shown to make people:
   a. less alert.
   b. more creative.
   c. more wary.
   d. think slowly.

4. Flow is a state of being in which a person:
   a. perceives a sense of balance and well-being following a negative emotion.
   b. has positive thoughts linked with a broad range of subsequent actions.
   c. is fully engaged in an interesting, challenging, and rewarding activity.
   d. behaves in ways that have survival value.

5. A beneficial change in personal relations following some stressful event, such as developing closer bonds with one's family following a death in the family, is an example of:
   a. postraumatic growth.
   b. capitalization.
   c. hope.
   d. mindfulness.

6. The human need for meaning in daily life is primarily associated with:
   a. hope.
   b. meditation.
   c. postraumatic growth.
   d. spirituality.

7. Which of the following is *not* a virtue found within positive institutions?
   a. dignity
   c. fairness
   b. thrift
   d. humanity

8. Critics and skeptics of positive psychology sometimes argue that:
   a. positive psychological research is unscientific.
   b. positive psychological processes are difficult to demonstrate empirically.
   c. positive psychology's message is not new and may be nothing but a fad.
   d. positive psychology is misguided and that mainstream psychology should focus exclusively on the negative aspects of daily life.

9. As a subfield, positive psychology can anticipate a bright future if:
   a. it admits that its findings are prescriptive rather than neutral.
   b. it borrows results from other areas of the discipline, especially humanistic psychology.
   c. positive data are examined at different levels of analysis.
   d. all of the above occur.

10. Sharing good news about our lives with those we are close to is known as:
    a. capitalization.
    c. resilience.
    b. savoring.
    d. mindfulness.

## ANSWERS

| | |
|---|---|
| 1. d Pages 511–513 | 6. d Pages 527–528 |
| 2. a Page 513 | 7. b Page 531 |
| 3. b Pages 514–515 | 8. c Page 532 |
| 4. c Page 518 | 9. d Page 533 |
| 5. a Page 526 | 10. a Page 535 |

## Personal Explorations Workbook

Go to the *Personal Explorations Workbook* in the back of your textbook for exercises that can enhance your self-understanding in relation to issues raised in this chapter. **Exercise 16.1** *Self-Assessment:* What Is Your Happiness Profile? **Exercise 16.2** *Self-Reflection:* Thinking About How You Construe Happiness

 CourseMate

Access an interactive eBook, chapter-specific interactive learning tools, including Personal Explorations, Recommended Readings, Critical Thinking Exercises, flashcards, quizzes, videos and more in your Psychology CourseMate, available at **www.cengagebrain.com/ shop/ISBN/1111186634**.

# Psychology and Environmental Sustainability: What's Good for the Earth Is Good for Us

## by Britain A. Scott (University of St. Thomas) and Susan M. Koger (Willamette University)

What do pollution, deforestation, species extinctions, and climate change have in common? You might instantly respond, "They're all environmental problems." But is it really the *environment* that has the problems? In fact, what ties all these issues together is their cause: *maladaptive human behavior*. Particularly for the last 150 years, we humans have been behaving in ways that are *unsustainable*, and the effects of our collective actions can no longer be ignored. Humans burn fossil fuels that pollute the air and change the climate, dump wastes into water and soil, overconsume resources (both limited ones, such as oil, and renewable ones, such as wood and seafood), and develop lands that formerly served as habitats for thousands or even millions of other species. If you stop to think about it, these "environmental problems" are really *psychological*. That is, they are caused by destructive behaviors and the underlying thoughts, attitudes, feelings, values, and decisions that lead to these behaviors. Thus, psychologists are increasingly applying their expertise concerning human behavior to understanding and solving these destructive patterns (e.g., Clayton & Myers, 2009; Koger & Scott, 2007; Koger & Winter, 2010). As you will see, psychological insights are critical to the achievement of a ***sustainable world*—one in which human activities and needs are balanced with those of other species and future generations, taking into account ecological as well as social and economic factors** (Schmuck & Schultz, 2002).

Inspired by growing concern about environmental issues among the general public in the "Green Decade" of the 1970s, some psychologists have been conducting research related to environmental issues for several decades. However, because their work does not fit neatly into a particular subdiscipline of the field, it generally receives little attention in psychology courses, although we are trying to change that. You may have heard of ***environmental psychologists*, who study how individuals are affected by, and interact with, their physical environments.** However, the term *environment* in this label does not refer specifically to the natural environment. Only a minority of environmental psychologists study nature-related topics, such as people's cognitive responses to natural settings (Berman, Jonides, & Kaplan, 2008; Kaplan & Kaplan, 1989). Environmental psychologists are more likely to study the effects of noise, crowding, pollution, and urban living on aspects of human behavior. Numerous other researchers grounded in traditional branches of psychology (primarily social, behavioral, and cognitive psychology) have investigated environmentally relevant behaviors such as energy conservation and material consumption. Over the past several years, a new label has emerged that promises to help tie together the work of nature-oriented environmental psychologists and other psychologists who study environmental behaviors. ***Conservation psychology* is the study of the interactive relationships between humans and the rest of nature, with a particular focus on how to enhance conservation of natural resources.** Conservation psychology is viewed as an applied field "that uses psychological principles, theories, or methods to understand and solve issues related to human aspects of conservation" (Saunders, 2003, p. 138).

Environmental problems are really psychological problems; moreover, many of the disorders of adjustment highlighted in this text—anxiety, stress, depres-

**WEB LINK A.1 Teaching Psychology for Sustainability: A Manual of Resources**

The authors of this appendix have also developed a website that serves as a resource for teachers and students in psychology who are interested in how psychological issues intersect with the challenge of achieving sustainability. Links to discussion topics and activities in 13 areas of psychology (such as learning, development, biopsychology, and so forth) can be found here.

sion, interpersonal difficulties—may be exacerbated, if not caused, by the same maladative behavior patterns that degrade the natural environment. That is, many psychological problems may result from humans' unhealthy relationship with nonhuman nature. In the 1990s, holistic thinkers known as *ecopsychologists* began promoting the idea that modern industrialized urban living erodes people's feeling of connectedness to nature, leaving them developmentally deprived and psychologically distressed. As Roszak (1992) put it, "When the Earth hurts, we hurt with it" (p. 308).

Some clinicians are incorporating ecopsychological therapies into their practices to foster mindfulness and a sense of place that may guide people to behave in more environmentally friendly ways (e.g., Buzzell & Chalquist, 2009; Clinebell, 1996; Conn, 1995; White & Heerwagen, 1998). Others promote wilderness experiences as a means of healing and self-expansion (Greenway, 1995; Harper, 1995) and as a catalyst toward more ecologically sustainable lifestyles (Kals & Ittner, 2003). Further, the expanding interdisciplinary field of *environmental health* is highlighting the interconnections between various consumer and industrial practices and adverse human impacts ranging from the neurological (developmental disabilities, Parkinson's disease) to various forms of cancer and reproductive and immune system dysfunction. Some *health psychologists* are thus turning their attention to "environmental" (i.e., toxic chemical) effects on cognitive and emotional development and various aspects of behavior.

In the following sections, we briefly review the current state of understanding about how we humans are negatively affecting the systems on which all species, including humans, rely for our very lives. We illustrate how many of the subdisciplines of psychology can aid in understanding—and hopefully solving—these problems in people's thinking and behavior. We conclude that the health and well-being of humans is inextricably connected with the health of other species and the planet itself. (Note: A more thorough discussion of these issues is available in Koger & Winter, 2010.)

## The Escalating Environmental Crisis

Unless you've been living in a cave without media access, you are at least somewhat familiar with the environmental issues currently con-

fronting humanity. In fact, you may even feel tired of hearing the "gloom and doom" reports concerning melting ice caps and rising sea levels, toxic chemicals in the air and water, overpopulation, dwindling forests, and species losses. It may all seem too depressing, overwhelming, and perhaps even terrifying. Or perhaps it doesn't seem to have much to do with you personally, and you feel powerless to make any difference. Most people quickly tune out the bad news and focus their attention on such concerns as family obligations, work or school, paying bills, or activities with friends. Such a response is understandable and consistent with an evolutionary perspective. Human cognitive and perceptual systems evolved in an environment where any threats to safety were sudden and dramatic, and our ancestors had no need to track gradually worsening problems or assaults that took many years to manifest (Ornstein & Ehrlich, 2000).

As a result, the human species has difficulty responding to slowly developing but potentially calamitous conditions, particularly when the outcomes are likely to occur at distant locations. These characteristics can lead people to discount the danger or take it less seriously than "risks with negative outcomes that occur for sure, now, here, and to us" (Gattig & Hendrickx, 2007, p. 22; see also Leiserowitz, 2007). Consequently, people have a strong tendency to delay action until problems are large scale and readily apparent rather than working to prevent such conditions. Unfortunately, by then it may be too late.

Despite this "hard-wiring" of the brain, the human species is capable of dramatic and rapid cultural evolution, as the pace of the agricultural, industrial, and technological revolutions reveals (Ehrlich & Ehrlich, 2008; Ornstein & Ehrlich, 2000). For example, as undergraduates, the two of us relied on typewriters for writing papers after engaging in library research with massive printed publication indexes and bound volumes of journals. (Can you imagine?) Now the idea of using anything other than high-speed word processing programs and the Internet to conduct research seems horribly inefficient and cumbersome. The human capacity for rapid behavioral change could help people reverse current ecological trends, provided they pay sufficient attention and collectively mobilize into action (Smith et al., 2009).

Let's take, for example, the problem of *global climate change*. If you are among the millions of people who have seen Al Gore's film *An Inconvenient Truth* (2006), you know something about this serious problem. Gases such as carbon dioxide, methane, nitrous oxide, and water vapor trap heat in the atmosphere. The naturally resulting *greenhouse effect* is necessary to stabilize planetary temperatures and maintain a climate suitable for life on this planet. Gas levels vary naturally to some extent, but as you have probably heard, industrialization has created an unprecedented increase in greenhouse gas concentrations (see **Figure A.1**). Simultaneously, forests, which act as the lungs of the Earth by converting carbon dioxide to oxygen, have been rapidly shrinking because of wood extraction, urbanization, and conversion of forests to agricultural land. As a result, carbon dioxide in the atmosphere is at the "highest level in 650,000 years" (Gardner & Prugh, 2008, p. 3) and is clearly correlated with planetary warming patterns (see **Figure A.2**). Although it is not possible to establish causation from these correlational data, the trends suggest that temperatures and associated climatic changes are positively correlated with $CO_2$ levels, and many warming greenhouse gases, including $CO_2$ and methane, will continue to rise if current industrial and social practices do not change.

In its most recent report, the Intergovernmental Panel on Climate Change (IPCC) (2007) predicted that

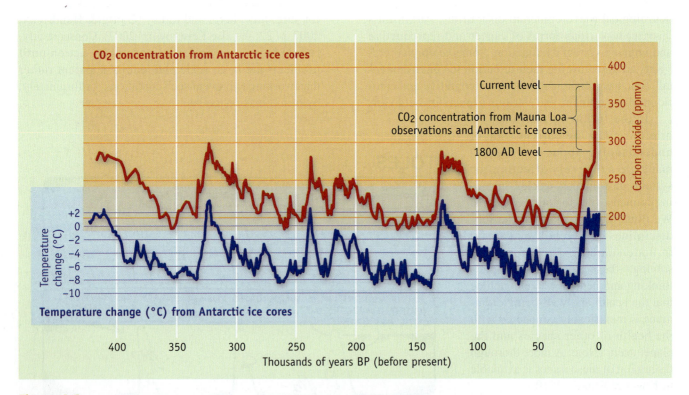

**Figure A.1**

**Long-term trends in atmospheric carbon dioxide concentration and temperature.**
Scientists have sampled ice cores in Antarctica to study fluctuations in atmospheric concentrations of carbon dioxide ($CO_2$), the dominant greenhouse gas. Over the past 400,000 years, there has been a strong correlation between temperature variations and $CO_2$ levels. With the beginning of the Industrial Revolution in the 1800s, $CO_2$ concentrations began a dramatic and unprecedented increase, rising rapidly from 280 ppmv (parts per million by volume) to current levels of 376 ppmv. Note that this represents an increase of 77 ppmv relative to the highest concentrations reached during the course of the preceding 400,000 years (Woods Hole Research Center, 2009). Thus, it is highly unlikely that these recent trends reflect "natural" variability.

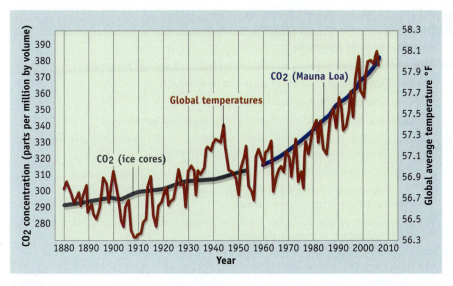

**Figure A.2**
**Trends in global average temperature and carbon dioxide concentration since 1880.** Evidence for a changing climate is also seen in average increases of global temperatures, which are correlated with escalating atmospheric $CO_2$ levels since the beginning of the Industrial Revolution in 1880. $CO_2$ measurements since 1958 are from the Mauna Loa Observatory in Hawaii; earlier data are from ice cores in Antarctica.

the planet could warm as much as 11 degrees Fahrenheit by 2100 (see also NASA Study, 2007). To put that number in perspective, during the last ice age the world was only 9 degrees cooler than it is today. Thus, there is a real possibility of planetary temperature changes of ice age magnitudes within this century. Already, warming trends are evident, based on increased "average air and ocean temperatures, widespread melting of snow and ice, and rising global average sea level" (IPCC, 2007, p. 30; see also Flavin & Engelman, 2009). For example, the years between 1995 and 2006 were eleven of the twelve warmest years since 1850, when recording of global temperatures began. In fact, some scientists think it is far too late to reverse the global warming trends and

that the best we can do is try to minimize the predicted damage.

Climate change can affect *ecosystems,* both directly and indirectly, via flooding, drought, wildfires, insect proliferation, and fragmentation of natural systems. As many as 20%–30% of known plant and animal species are estimated to be at an increased risk of extinction as a result of climate change, threatening the *biodiversity* that is necessary to healthy ecosystems (IPCC, 2007; Lovejoy & Hannah, 2005; Wilson, 2007). Weather events such as typhoons and hurricanes are likely to become more intense, and while it is impossible to directly associate any particular storm with climate change, the devastation wrought by Hurricane Katrina in 2005 exemplifies what is expected. Coastal regions such as those in the United States containing the cities of New York, Boston, and Miami are at particular risk because of rising sea levels, erosion, and flooding. Such hazards will create significant and global *mental health* impacts. The experiences of loss, disruption, and displacement, as well as worry about future consequences, will create profound stress (Few, 2007; Fritze et al., 2008). Consequently, the prevalence and severity of stress disorders will increase, including acute and posttraumatic stress disorder and related problems such as, anxiety, substance abuse, grief, depression, and suicide attempts (Fritze et al, 2008).

Climate change also carries significant *public health* costs. Millions of people are likely to suffer or die from associated malnutrition, disease (including diarrheal, cardiorespiratory, and infectious illnesses), and injury as a result of extreme weather (Blashki, McMichael, & Karoly, 2007; Centers for Disease Control and Prevention, 2009; IPCC, 2007) (see **Figure A.3** on the next page). Densely populated areas, islands, and poor communities are especially vulnerable to the risks of climate change, and such regions are home to nearly half of the planet's population (Gelbspan, 2001).

---

**WEB LINK A.2** **Intergovernmental Panel on Climate Change (IPCC)**

The Intergovernmental Panel on Climate Change (IPCC) is a U.N.-sponsored scientific organization that assesses and disseminates research related to world climate change. The panel was created in 1989 to provide member governments with broad and balanced information about climate change. Its 2007 report was honored with a Nobel Peace Prize. Given the political ramifications of making projections about future climate changes, the report has been controversial in some quarters, and critics have found some flaws, but the Science and Technology Committee of the British House of Commons recently determined that there was no basis for allegations of data misrepresentation. You can draw your own conclusions by visiting the IPCC website, where you will find a wealth of information on their procedures, data, and reports.

---

**WEB LINK A.3** **Global Climate Change**

NASA's Eyes on the Earth offers a quick look at the Planet's "vital signs," including decreases in Arctic sea ice and increases in carbon dioxide, sea level, and global temperatures since 1880. The site also describes the science behind climate change, including causes and anticipated effects.

| Health Outcomes Related to Weather | |
|---|---|
| **Health outcomes** | **Known effects of weather** |
| Heat stress | • Deaths from cardiopulmonary disease increase with high and low temperatures |
| | • Heat-related illness and death increase during heat waves |
| Air-pollution-related mortality and morbidity | • Weather affects air pollutant concentrations |
| | • Weather affects distribution, seasonality, and production of aeroallergens |
| Health impacts of weather disasters | • Floods, landslides, and windstorms cause direct effects (deaths and injuries) and indirect effects (infectious disease, long-term psychological morbidity) |
| | • Droughts are associated with increased risk of disease and malnutrition |
| Mosquito-borne diseases, tick-borne diseases (e.g., malaria, dengue) | • Higher temperatures shorten the development time of pathogens in vectors and increases potential transmission to humans |
| | • Vector species have specific climate conditions (temperature, humidity) necessary to be sufficiently abundant to maintain transmission |
| Undernutrition | • Climate change may decrease food supplies (crop yields, fish stocks) or access to food supplies |
| Water- or food-borne diseases | • Survival of important bacterial pathogens is related to temperature |
| | • Water-borne diseases are most likely to occur in communities with poor water supply and sanitation |
| | • Increases in drought conditions may affect water availability |
| | • Extreme rainfall can affect transport of disease organisms into water supply |

**Figure A.3**
**Health outcomes related to weather.** This list summarizes some of the better-known health effects associated with weather changes.

Source: From Kovats, R. S., Campbell-Lendrum, D. & Matthies, F. (2005). Climate change and human health: Estimating avoidable deaths and disease. *Risk Analysis, 25,* p. 1411.

Thus, the harshest and most chronic consequences will be experienced by the most disadvantaged members of international populations (Agyeman et al., 2007; Fritze et al., 2008). In sum, expected changes in global climate will create extreme stress and related adverse health outcomes (see Chapter 5). The effects on mental health will include both direct (stress-related disorders) and indirect (physical, social, economic, and environmental) consequences.

Global climate change is only one facet of the current environmental crisis, which has been created by an array of interconnected problems. The bottom line is that the Earth has a limited *carrying capacity,* a biological concept describing the maximum number of any specific population that a habitat can support. If the habitat is isolated and the population cannot migrate to a new habitat, the inhabitants must find a sustainable balance with its resource base. If they don't and the population grows too quickly, depleting resources suddenly, the population will crash. In the past, localized crashes in both human and nonhuman populations have occurred in one part of the world without seriously affecting those in another. Today, however, as humans continue to degrade "the great life-supporting systems of the planet's biosphere" (Speth, 1992, p. 27), *global* systems are in crisis and are threatening to "collapse" (Diamond, 2005). Thus, the threat of an ecological

catastrophe on a *planetary level* is looming. The Earth is, essentially, a large island, with no way to borrow resources or dump pollution elsewhere.

## The Psychological Foundation of Environmental Problems

As you were reading the preceding paragraphs, did you feel despair? Anxiety? Irritation? Did you scan the material, thinking to yourself that you already knew it? Did you find yourself growing overwhelmed, angry, or afraid? Did you feel defensive or skeptical? Or did you wonder what any of this has to do with you? These *psychological* reactions are important because they affect how such problems are understood and what people are willing to do about them.

Before someone will change his or her behaviors, that person must recognize which behaviors need changing, know how to change them, and feel that changing them is a worthwhile expenditure of effort. In other words, effort, energy, and motivation are all critical components of behavioral change (e.g., DiClemente, Schlundt, & Gemmell, 2004). A model from the clinical psychology of addiction is applicable here, as many people are addicted to unsustainable consumption patterns. The *Stages of Change Model* describes a five-step process that individuals work through to break a pattern of addiction (see **Figure A.4**). All change requires patience and perseverance because most people relapse (i.e., fall back on old habits).

Many people will not initiate change (such as regarding an addiction) until they experience a personal crisis ("hit bottom"). Comparably, contemporary cultures may not evolve to more sustainable ones without first experiencing and confronting crises that inspire renovation and rebuilding (Beddoe et al., 2009). In that regard, visceral reactions such as fear or worry may be necessary to inspire personal or social action to address risks like climate change (Weber, 2006), although feeling overwhelmed can also block action. Thus, it is important for people to receive specific direction concerning specific actions to take (Bennett, 2008).

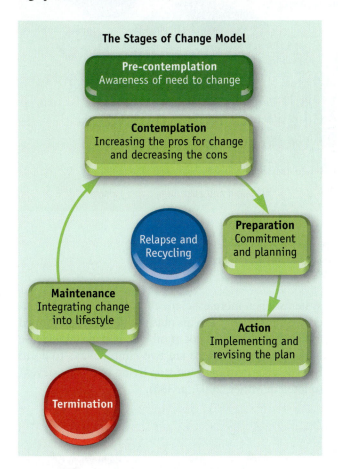

### Figure A.4

**The stages of change model.** According to this model, the difficult behavioral changes required to give up an addiction occur through a series of stages. During the *precontemplation stage*, an addicted individual is not interested in considering change and often denies that there is any problem. Once the person becomes concerned about the issue, the *contemplation stage* involves analyzing the risks and benefits of changing. *Preparation* involves committing to and planning for the change, whereas the *action stage* is reached when specific steps are implemented to overcome one's addiction. If the individual reaches the *maintenance* stage, the new behavior becomes normative. Movement back and forth (relapse and recycling) through the stages is common in this dynamic process.

Source: From DiClemente, C. (2003). *Addiction and change: How addictions develop and addicted people recover.* New York: Guilford, p. 30.

Does environmental destruction actually have anything to do with us as individuals? If you don't have children, you might assume that you are not contributing directly to population growth, and you yourself do not produce industrial wastes or log forests. What, then, is *each person* doing to deplete the carrying capacity of the planet to sustain human life? The most obvious answer lies in individuals' extravagant use and misuse of the world's natural resources.

Human influences on the planet can be estimated by using the *ecological footprint*—a measure of how fast a person (or population) consumes resources and generates waste in comparison to how rapidly nature (the habitat) can absorb the waste and replenish the resources (see **Figure A.5** on next page). People who live in the United States have the largest *ecological footprints*, consuming considerably more resources and generating more waste than any other people on the planet. Unfortunately, the gap between this ecological footprint and the planet's carrying capacity is growing at an alarming pace (see **Figure A.6** on next page). "If everyone in the world had an ecological footprint equivalent to that of the typical North American or Western European, global society would overshoot the planet's biocapacity three to five fold" (Kitzes et al., 2008, p. 468). In other words, if everyone lived like those in the United States do, three or more planets would be needed to support this lifestyle!

People living in the U.S. are by far the biggest users and wasters of the world's commercial energy. Less than 5% of the planet's population live in the U.S., and the country has only about 3% of the planet's oil supply (Kunstler, 2005), yet U.S. residents use a staggering *25%* of the total commercial supply (Energy Information Administration, 2006): 20,802,160 barrels of oil *per day*. The next largest consumer is China, but consider this: China has *four times* the population of the U.S. and uses only one-third of the amount of oil (6,720,000 barrels per day). Each person in the United States uses, on average, more than 30 times the amount of gasoline as the average person in a developing country (World Resources Institute, 2001). This "addiction to oil" is fostering a dangerously unstable international climate. Middle Eastern countries rest on more than 60% of the planet's oil reserves (Kunstler, 2005), inspiring military-based foreign policies that emphasize control and access (e.g., Klare, 2001; Winter & Cava,

**WEB LINK A.4  Global Footprint Network**

The Global Footprint Network is an international think tank working to advance sustainability through the use of the Ecological Footprint, a tool that measures how much nature we have, how much we use, and who uses what. You can estimate your personal ecological footprint here.

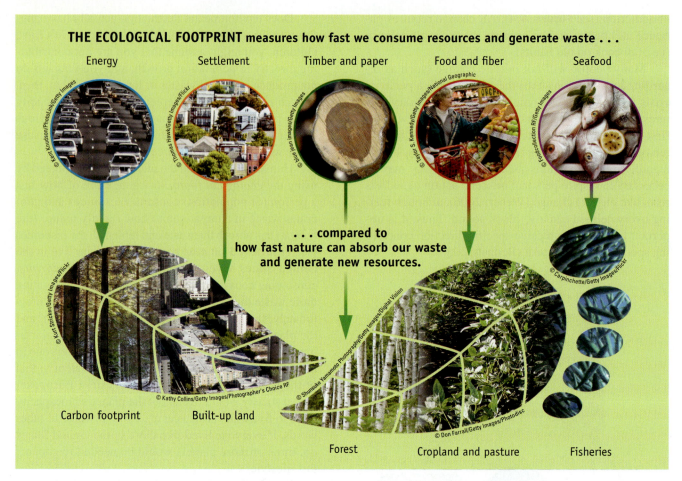

**Figure A.5**

**A graphic overview of the concept of the ecological footprint.** The ecological footprint is a tool used to estimate an individual's, group's, nation's, or the world population's impact on the planet. (Source: Global Footprint Network, http://www.footprintnetwork.org)

2006). Wars over access to resources including oil will likely become more common.

Amazingly, much of this huge expenditure of energy is wasted (Miller, 2007). People in North America waste over 43% of their energy by selecting energy-inefficient automobiles, appliances, and home heating systems when more efficient choices are available. Energy expert Amory Lovins puts it plainly, "If the United States wants to save a lot of oil and money and increase national security, there are two simple ways to do it: Stop driving Petropigs and stop living in energy sieves" (quoted in Miller, 2007, p. 385).

**Figure A.6**

**Trends in the collective ecological footprint of the United States.** This graph shows how the ecological footprint of the United States has io me ncreased dramatically since the 1960s in relation to the (decreasing) carrying capacity that our habitat can support. Carrying capacity, or "biocapacity," varies depending on ecosystem management, agricultural practices (such as fertilizer use and irrigation), ecosystem degradation, and weather. Overall, biocapacity is diminishing as population pressures, changing climates, and urbanization degrade land and other resources. As you can see, the trends are not encouraging.

Source: http://www.footprintnetwork.org/en/index.php/GFN/page/trends/us/. Global Footprint Network 2008 National Footprint Accounts. Reprinted with permission.

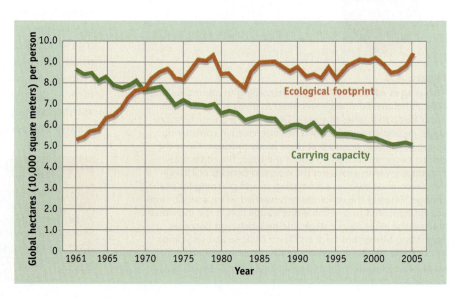

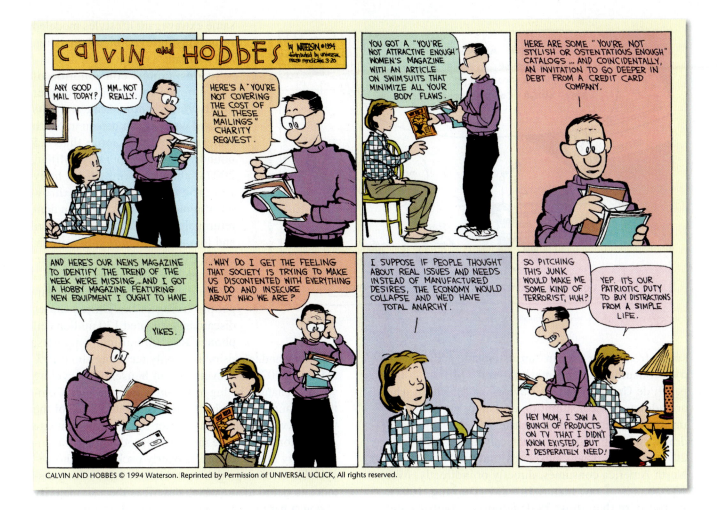

Those living in the U.S. also overuse and abuse water. The toxic chemicals used in industrial production, as well as those used to kill pests like bugs and weeds, clean houses, and even groom and beautify people and pets, are polluting groundwater, lakes, rivers, and oceans. Demand for water from growing populations in arid locations is lowering reservoirs and aquifers. At least one quarter of the groundwater that is currently withdrawn is not being replenished. For example, Las Vegas has doubled in population since 1990. The city gets 90% of its water from the Colorado River, which is currently experiencing the worst drought in recorded history (Hutchinson, 2007). Already more than *one billion* people on the planet do not have safe drinking water. In contrast, people in the developed world pollute and waste gallons of clean water every time they flush the toilet, while half of the population in developing nations lack access to basic sanitation.

The wasteful use of energy and water are two of the primary contributors to the enormous ecological footprint of the U.S. population. Another major factor is diet. Livestock farming produces more greenhouse gases than transportation (Food and Agriculture Organization of the United Nations, 2006), and it has been estimated that it takes 600 gallons of water to produce one hamburger (Kreith, 1991). U.S. citizens eat four times the amount of meat as the average person in a developing country (World Resources Institute, 2001). The per capita annual meat consumption is 275 pounds in the United States, compared to 115 pounds in China and 11.4 in India (Menzel & D'Alusio, 2005). Most people regularly eat food that is out of season or does not grow in their region. This means that their food must travel long distances to get to them. It is typical in the U.S. for food to travel more than 1500 miles from its source to the dinner table (Pirog & Benjamin, 2003). Furthermore, popular convenience foods are subject to energy-intensive processing and are packaged in containers and wrappers that cannot be reused or recycled. Finally, North Americans waste tremendous amounts of food—about 27% of edible food, which comes to over 3,000 pounds *every second* (Kantor et al., 1997). Most of that food ends up in landfills, and as it rots it releases methane, a greenhouse gas that is 20 times more powerful than carbon dioxide at trapping heat in the atmosphere (Environmental Protection Agency, 2006).

Energy, water, and food are not the only things currently consumed in unsustainable ways. *Overconsumption of consumer goods constitutes the biggest drain on the Earth's carrying capacity*. Many people

SELF-DELUSION: AMERICA'S RENEWABLE RESOURCE

same extravagant lifestyles modeled in movies, television, advertising, and tourism.

Conspicuous consumption of convenience foods and consumer goods yields astonishing amounts of solid waste. Each person in North America generates more than 4.5 pounds of garbage per day (Miller, 2007), about 10 times their body weight every year. People throw away approximately 2.5 million non-returnable plastic bottles *every hour* and toss about *25 billion* Styrofoam coffee cups in the garbage each year. Electronic waste, or "e-waste," is growing exponentially. Every year, people living in the United States discard an estimated 130 million cell phones and 100 million computers, monitors, and television sets, only recycling about 10% (Miller, 2007). But even careful household recycling will not change the biggest solid waste problem. Commercial and industrial activities generate 98.5% of the waste. Average citizens sponsor this enormous waste production every time they buy a product that was inefficiently manufactured, is overly packaged, is not recyclable or biodegradable, and has traveled a long distance to get to them (which describes the vast majority of consumer products, including some that are misleadingly labeled "eco-friendly").

Yet, there is good reason to believe that overconsumption is not delivering the "goods." As you read in Chapter 1, empirical studies suggest that it is not how much stuff people own but the quality of their social relations, the creative fulfillment received from work, and their personality and outlook on life that determine how happy they are. In fact, the race to pay for material possessions is likely to detract from these primary ingredients of happiness. Thus, attempting to meet psychological needs through overconsumption jeopardizes not only one's physical habitat but also psychological well-being (Kasser & Kanner, 2004). You have no doubt heard of the 3 R's: Reduce, Reuse, Recycle. But effective solutions to environmental problems must start with *Refusing* to buy things that aren't really necessary and choosing

suffer from *affluenza,* an "unsustainable addiction to overconsumption and materialism" (Miller, 2007, p. 19; de Graaf, Wann, & Naylor, 2005). Those who are addicted to consumption use shopping as a coping strategy similar to overeating, using alcohol and drugs, and surfing the Internet (see Chapter 4). Nearly 20 years ago, it was observed that each person in North America consumes, directly or indirectly, over 100 pounds of raw materials a day (Durning, 1992), vastly more than those in developing countries and even more than people in other developed nations. For example, U.S. residents use "19 times more paper than the average person in a developing country, and most of it becomes trash" (Gardner, 2002, p. 9). Moreover, less than half of the paper used in the United States gets recycled (Miller, 2007). And the things people buy—clothes, electronics, cars, furnishings—are produced from materials that leave a long trail of pollution in many third world countries that is invisible to the U.S. consumer. A pair of pants made of polyester and sold in an American department store may be sewn in a sweatshop in Indonesia, from synthetic material manufactured in Singapore, which comes from oil refined in Mexico. U.S. consumer culture is spreading quickly, so that people in developing countries are aiming for "the good life," hurrying to develop the

**WEB LINK A.5   Affluenza**

Do you suffer from affluenza? Find out at this thought-provoking site that was developed in conjunction with a one-hour show filmed for public television in Oregon. The site includes information on the "diagnosis" and "treatment" of this common condition, as well as an opportunity to order a video of the show.

**WEB LINK A.6   The Story of Stuff**

This site provides a charming, but disturbing, review of how material goods are produced, distributed, and disposed of in ways that are antagonistic to the goal of sustainability.

sustainably produced options for the things that are (Miller, 2007) (see **Figure A.7**).

The field of psychology has much to offer in terms of understanding and solving the problems causing ecological degradation in today's world. Of course, it would be naive to suggest that any one academic discipline will provide the solution to such a complex interplay of issues as those underlying current ecological conditions, and it is clear that interdisciplinary collaborations are urgently needed (Smith et al., 2009). However, psychology has a lot to offer for understanding the roots of environmental problems and the psychological forces maintaining them.

Individuals have the power to make choices that do not exacerbate environmental problems, and *with ability comes responsibility*. Feeling empowered on one level often inspires people to work at a more global level and thus provides hope for more widespread social change. Bringing psychology to speak to the unspoken pessimism most people share about the future on an overcrowded and overburdened planet makes psychological theory personally and intellectually meaningful and provides insight into how to design a sustainable future. Thus, the following sections will explore several subdisciplines within psychology in terms of how they can be applied to understanding and solving environmentally related behavioral problems.

| The UnShopping Card | The UnShopping Card |
|---|---|
| *Do I really need this?* | *Do I really need this?* |
| Is it made of recycled or renewable materials? | Is it overpackaged? |
| Is it recyclable or biodegradable? | How long will it last? |
| Could I borrow, rent or buy it used? | If it breaks, can it be fixed? |
| Is it worth the time I worked to pay for it? | How will I dispose of it? |
|  | What is its environmental cost? |
|  | Is it a fair trade product? |
| Oregon State UNIVERSITY OSU Extension Service | Oregon State UNIVERSITY OSU Extension Service |

**Figure A.7**

**An innovative effort to discourage overconsumption.**
This "UnShopping Card," developed by the Oregon State University Extension Service, was created to help people think more deliberately about their consumption decisions.

## Insights from Psychoanalytic Theory

As you learned in Chapter 2, part of Sigmund Freud's fame lies in the vigorous criticisms and controversies his theories have inspired. Nonetheless, his emphasis on unconscious conflict and ego anxiety and his description of unconscious defenses that people use to ward off emotional discomfort are particularly relevant to environmental issues. Certainly, acknowledging the probable collapse of the planet's ecosystems *should* trigger powerful negative feelings, including despair, bewilderment, grief, anger, and so on. As one bumper sticker puts it, "If you're not outraged, you're not paying attention!" Emotional defenses explain how people can "know" about environmental problems and yet not change their relevant behaviors.

Freud described several *defense mechanisms* that are particularly useful for understanding people's ecologically unfriendly behaviors. For example, *rationalization* is one of the most common defense mechanisms. Thus, people say, "I have to drive because the bus schedule is too inconvenient," even though they know that cars contribute significantly to air pollution and climate change. *Identification* leads to purchasing unnecessary clothing, electronics, and other items that one's peer group or cultural heroes use and promote. When in *denial,* people claim that the anxiety-provoking material doesn't exist, a tendency that can be bolstered by supporting "evidence" from outside sources. For example, conservative think tanks, many funded by industry, have been effective in fostering public denial about the scientific evidence on climate change (Jacques, Dunlap, & Freeman, 2008). Denial about environmental problems includes minimizing their severity, seeing them as irrelevant, and seeing oneself as not responsible (Opotow & Weiss, 2000).

Like denial, *reaction formation* is used to deny a painful feeling but in this case *also* gives intense energy to expressing its opposite. For example, the sneering hostility with which a founder of the anti-environmentalist Wise Use movement describes environmentalists as "pathological fools" (Arnold, 1993, p. 42) who buy into "spiritual crap" (p. 30) makes us wonder about his former role as a Sierra Club official. Finally, *projection* occurs when people perceive in others what they fail to perceive in themselves. One of the authors recalls vehemently grumbling about all the cars on the road during rush hour, only to be reminded by her 3-year-old in the backseat, "But Mommy, you're traffic, too!"

In sum, defenses enable people to make excuses and fail to notice or take responsibility for what they are doing. Consequently, many people ultimately appear apathetic toward fellow human beings, other species, and the future. Yet knowing more about one's personal patterns of defenses may help one to be less habitual in using them. On the other hand, because it takes a lot of patience and time to confront defenses, people may not act soon enough. Psychoanalytic approaches are better at explaining environmentally unfriendly behavior than developing solutions. Fortunately, behavioral theories have more potential for producing meaningful changes in human behavior.

## Insights from Behavioral Psychology

Efforts to bring about immediate changes in behavior are better informed by the theories and techniques of behavioral psychology, which focuses on observable behavior in the present rather than its deeper meanings and underlying motivations. As you may recall from Chapter 2, one of the best-known behavioral psychologists, B. F. Skinner, argued that what people do is a function of the consequences of their behavior: reinforcement strengthens response tendencies, whereas punishment weakens them. Toward the end of his career, Skinner took a particular interest in environmental issues. In an address to the American Psychological Association, he criticized the efforts of environmental activists as inconsistent with operant learning principles in that they focused on inspiring guilt, fear, and shame to motivate greener behaviors instead of helping individuals see the potentially reinforcing consequences of sustainable lifestyles (Skinner, 1987).

Yet many environmentally damaging behaviors continue to be rewarded by social status, convenience, and low costs. For example, gas-guzzling SUVs are very popular, driving is generally more convenient for running errands than biking or using public transit, and gasoline remains relatively cheap for most U.S. citizens. Altering these reinforcement contingencies, such as rewarding bus ridership with tokens redeemable for future trips or movie passes (Everett, Hayward, & Meyers, 1974) or providing *feedback* by praising individuals for reducing the amount of energy they consume (Abrahamse et al., 2005; Lehman & Geller, 2004), can be effective in motivating pro-environmental behaviors. Similarly, *incentives,* such as financial rebates for buying energy-efficient appliances, can motivate such purchases.

Another behavior modification strategy involves altering *antecedent stimuli* to influence behavior (see the Application for Chapter 3). *Prompts* and *social modeling* are examples of strategies involving antecedents that have been used to influence environmentally relevant behaviors. *Prompts* signal particular actions. One example is prominently placing aluminum recycling bins in areas where canned soft drinks are consumed (Lehman & Geller, 2004). Another example would be placing signs over light switches to remind users to turn off the light when they leave a room. Research suggests that the more specific the prompt, the greater its effectiveness. A sign saying "Faculty and students please turn off lights after 5 p.m." is more effective than one reading "Conserve Electricity." Polite prompts are more effective than demanding ones (the word "please" can make a difference), and the closer the prompt is to the point of behavior, the better (a sign over a light switch is more effective than a sign across the room). Thus, polite, salient, and specific reminders can change behavior (Geller, Winett, & Everett, 1982; Lehman & Geller, 2004).

Although providing general information is a technique widely used by environmental groups, distributing slogans, pamphlets, solicitations, or articles is less effective than giving explicit prompts or instructions. For instance, informing maintenance garage managers about specific ways their employees could reduce polluting behaviors at their facility resulted in more positive changes than general information about oil pollution (Daamen et al., 2001). Although common sense suggests the need to educate people about environmental problems, education by itself apparently does little to change behavior. For example, millions of dollars spent on information dissemination resulted in only 2%–3% improvements in energy conservation (Hirst, Berry, & Soderstrom, 1981).

Because attitudes do not necessarily predict people's actions very well, there is little reason to believe that education alone will change what people actually do, a finding supported by many studies (reviewed by Abrahamse et al., 2005; Gardner & Stern, 2002; Lehman & Geller, 2004). On the other hand, *modeling* (Bandura, 1977; see Chapter 2) environmentally friendly behavior can be effective. For instance, in one study participants were exposed to a video showing a person turning down a thermostat, wearing warmer clothes, and using heavy blankets. With this treatment, viewers reduced their energy use by 28% (Winett et al., 1982). Thus, modeling may often work better than simply describing desired behaviors. One of the authors has frequently experienced this phenomenon during walks with friends: when she bends down to pick up litter, her friends do so as well. Modeling may also be effective in addressing some of the most important environmental issues, like overpopulation and overconsumption (Bandura, 2002).

## Insights from Social Psychology

Modeling behavior is one way to communicate *social norms*—informal, unwritten "rules" about what is appropriate or typical behavior in a particular setting. Norms can exert a form of social pressure that may lead to conformity, as described in Chapter 7. Some researchers distinguish between *injunctive norms* (what is expected or approved of) and *descriptive norms* (what most people actually do) (Cialdini, Reno, & Kallgren, 1990). In the case of environmentally responsible behaviors, injunctive and descriptive norms are often inconsistent; that is, most people approve of environmentally responsible behaviors but don't actually engage in them. To test the importance of these two types of norms, researchers conducted a series of field experiments on littering. Our society has injunctive norms against littering, but in some situations the descriptive norm is to litter, resulting in some interesting interactions. For example, in an already littered environment, participants were more likely to litter after witnessing a confederate littering. In a clean environment, however, the participants who saw a confederate littering were less likely to litter than those who saw no littering behavior. In both situations the participants' behavior was influenced by the descriptive norms indicated by both the setting and the confederate's behavior (Cialdini et al., 1990). Cialdini (2003) argued that environmental campaigns emphasizing the various bad behaviors people exhibit may backfire, because they inadvertently draw attention to descriptive norms for anti-environmental behavior.

Norms are just one of the influences that subtly or explicitly motivate and direct behavior in the moment. Certainly, internal factors, such as attitudes and values, influence behavior to some extent. For example, people who appreciate the inherent value of nature and other species (those who hold *biocentric values*) are more likely to engage in pro-environmental behaviors such as sharing resources and taking actions to protect other species, landscapes, and natural resources. In contrast, those with *egocentric* and *materialistic* values

© Dan Sullivan/Alamy

**Good intentions do not necessarily result in good behavior.** Most people endorse environmentally responsible behaviors such as not littering, but depending on the situation, their actual behavior may be quite different. Social psychology can shed light on these disparities between attitudes and behavior.

that emphasize personal wealth and status tend to exhibit fewer environmentally friendly actions (Schultz et al., 2005). Materialistic values have surged over the last few decades. Data collected on incoming college students over a 30-year period (1966–2007) show that they increasingly value materialism above other values, including finding personal meaning, helping others in difficulty, becoming an authority in one's field, and raising a family (Myers, 2010) (see **Figure A.8**). Still, regardless of the individual differences in people's personalities or attitudes, social psychologists know that situation-specific constraints can make it difficult (or costly, inconvenient, or awkward) for people to act on their pro-environmental values (Kollmus & Agyeman, 2002; Staats, 2003). To paraphrase the founder of

**Figure A.8**

**Increasing materialism among college students.** An annual survey of the attitudes and values of first-year college students suggests that materialistic values are on the rise. As you can see, the percentage of students who think that it is crucial to "be very well off financially" has almost doubled since the 1960s.

Source: From Myers, D. G. (2010) *Social psychology.* New York: McGraw Hill, p. 581. Data from surveys of more than 200,000 entering U.S. collegians per year, based on The American Freshman surveys, UCLA, 1966 to 2007.

experimental social psychology, Kurt Lewin, behavior is a function of the person *and* the situation.

Although most of the research on the "person" is conducted by personality psychologists, social psychologists are interested in the *self-concept* as well as *social identity.* How people define themselves relative to others and to the social environment plays a large part in behavior. Inspired by ecopsychological theories, some social psychologists have recently turned their attention to the notion of the *ecologically connected self.* Theoretically, the more one defines and experiences oneself as *part of nature,* the more one should be interested in and attuned to information about the environment and one's impact on it and the more empathy and caring one should exhibit for other living things (Bragg, 1996). Several studies support this idea (e.g., Clayton, 2003; Mayer & Frantz, 2004; Schultz, 2000, 2001). Moreover, the development of an ecologically connected self leads to environmentally appropriate behaviors not out of a sense of self-sacrifice or self-denial, but out of a sense of self-love and common identity. Experiences in nature, particularly during childhood, can foster this positive relationship with nature and other species, as well as pro-environmental behaviors (Chawla, 1988, Kals & Ittner, 2003; Myers, 2007). In contrast, a lack of encounters with unpolluted and undegraded conditions in nature may reduce people's sense of connection and personal responsibility for environmental issues (Kahn, 2007; Pyle, 2002).

A disconnection from nature and egocentric values set the stage for a *social dilemma:* a discrepancy between the interests of oneself and the larger group and the relative short-term and long-term consequences of one's behavior. Many environmental problems result from people acting out of self-interest in the moment, ultimately harming the greater whole. A clear example is commuters' reliance on the convenience of cars rather than using public transit (Joireman, Van Lange, & Van Vugt, 2004), thereby contributing to air pollutants and climate-changing gases, as well as traffic problems. Social dilemmas contribute to environmental degradation in several ways (e.g., Gardner & Stern, 2002; Osbaldiston & Sheldon, 2002; Vlek & Steg, 2007):

● First, in *commons dilemmas* (Hardin, 1968), individuals take more than their fair allotment of a shared resource, such as by careless or excessive water use (Van Vugt, 2001).

● Second, in *public goods dilemmas,* individuals do not contribute their fair share to a pooled resource, such as by voting down a bill that would increase taxes to fund community bus or train services.

● Third, in *risk dilemmas,* acting from self-interest leads to one contributing more than one's share to the hazards suffered by the greater whole. An example would be the homeowner who pours toxic chemicals (paint thinner or cleaning products) down the drain or uses pesticides (insect or weed sprays) on her lawn. These chemicals ultimately contaminate water, air, and soil throughout the community and cause health hazards ranging from headaches and nausea, to attention deficit and learning disabilities, to several forms of cancer (reviewed in Koger & Winter, 2010).

● Fourth, *ecological dilemmas* occur when acting from self-interest upsets the larger balance of things, such as when a landowner fills in a wetland on his property, thereby interfering with waterfowl migration.

In these examples, if not in all environmental problems, rewards to the individual are more immediate and compelling than the delayed costs to the population. The likely result is a damaged biosphere, particularly when the adverse consequences of irresponsible behavior are uncertain and solutions depend on the action of large numbers of people (e.g., Staats, 2003). Individuals tend to cooperate with others in working toward a common goal (such as reducing global emissions) if they are convinced of the high probability that they will be personally and adversely affected if the target goals not be reached. In that regard, many studies have shown that people will forgo immediate, personal reinforcers for longer-term group goals, especially if they identify with the group and feel responsible toward it (Dawes, 1980; Gardner & Stern, 2002; Van Vugt, 2002) and if they perceive the long-term benefits of collective action as relevant to them personally as well as to the larger group (Milinski et al., 2008; Ostrom et al., 2007). Importantly, environmental social dilemmas differ from some other social dilemmas in that they have a temporal dimension (Joireman, 2005; Osbaldiston & Sheldon, 2002). For example, Joireman, Van Lange, and Van Vugt (2004) studied consumers' automobile-related behaviors and found that having a "future orientation" was more predictive of environmentally responsible behavior than having a "prosocial orientation" (which would typically predict taking the selfless route in a social dilemma).

## Insights from Cognitive Psychology

Humans' cognitive and perceptual processes are crucial organizing features of behavior. These mechanisms were shaped by eons of evolution, are modified by personal experiences, and generally function pretty effectively; if they didn't, the species wouldn't have survived for very long. Yet the environments in which perceptual and cognitive systems evolved were very different from those that humans currently encounter. As a result, people tend to focus on threats that are visually noticeable and happening now (smoke pouring out of a smokestack) rather than the many largely invisible or slowly acting dangers, such as climate change or pesticides and other toxins in water and food supplies (Ornstein & Ehrlich, 2000). As Harvard psychologist Daniel Gilbert (2006) put it, "Environmentalists despair that global warming is happening so fast. In fact, it isn't happening fast enough. . . . If climate change had been visited on us by a brutal dictator or an evil empire, the war on warming would be this nation's top priority." Humans apparently respond best to threats that are "PAINful: i.e., Personal, Abrupt, Immoral, and happening Now" (Gilbert, 2008).

Thus, from the perspective of cognitive psychology, environmentally destructive behavior is maintained by cognitive biases. For instance, laypeople assess risks in different terms than professionals do, leading the public to express greater levels of concern about local, immediate threats such as hazardous waste and radiation contamination, compared to experts' greater focus on global, longer-term issues, such as population growth and climate change (Slimak & Dietz, 2006). Thus, although the scientific community has detailed the clear and devastating risks associated with climate change, the public largely maintains a "wait and see" attitude and does not seem to understand the need to drastically and immediately reduce emissions in order to stabilize the climate (Sterman, 2008), although they do report concern about the potential human health risks (Sundblad, Biel, & Gärling, 2007).

Further, the tendency to depend on mental shortcuts called *heuristics* can lead to errors in assessing the relative risks of environmental hazards and in estimating how one's behavior affects the environment. One mental shortcut that may explain people's underestimation of the risk of climate change is the *availability heuristic*. Individuals may have difficulty imagining the risks associated with climate change because of a lack of vivid, personal experiences with melting icecaps and rising sea levels. On the other hand, dramatic environmental hazards, such as oil spills, feature prominently in people's memories and may, therefore, receive more attention and resources than are warranted relative to other less perceptually vivid, but more insidious, hazards (Gardner & Stern, 2002).

Some cognitive biases help people feel good about themselves in spite of their behavior or circumstances. Several of these biases are relevant when considering how people perceive environmental risk and the impact of their own actions. *Comparative optimism* is a heuristic that leads individuals to believe they are less vulnerable than other people to all types of risks, including environmental threats such air and water pollution or nuclear accidents, even though objectively there is no reason to think the risks are any different for one individual versus another (Pahl et al., 2005).

*False consensus* is a cognitive bias that helps people maintain positive self-esteem by convincing themselves that many others engage in the same undesirable behaviors that they do. For example, a water shortage following a tropical storm prompted a temporary shower ban at Princeton University in 1999 and inspired a five-day field study during and after the ban (Benoît & Norton, 2003). The researchers found that students who defied the shower ban overestimated the prevalence of this socially irresponsible behavior in others. In addition, those who showered were seen by others as caring very little about the greater good, whereas those who did not shower were seen as caring very much. However, self-report data suggested that the attitudinal positions of these two groups were much closer together than either group realized (i.e., both groups cared about the larger group's welfare). *False polarization* is the tendency to perceive the views of those on the opposing side of a partisan debate as more extreme than they really are. All of these tendencies distort the perception of one's behavior relative to others' behavior, while they help maintain feelings of safety (comparative optimism), sense of self-esteem (false consensus), and the view of oneself as more reasonable than those who would disagree (false polarization).

Although the use of mental shortcuts is automatic, it is possible to override this tendency when one is sufficiently motivated and not cognitively overloaded by other attentional demands. Humans may be "lazy" thinkers who are prone to biases by default, but they are capable of careful, logical, effortful reasoning. The question is whether "coldly rational" judgments are always superior to emotionally driven ones (Slovic et al., 2004). People's evaluation of the risks and benefits associated with the use of pesticides is based not only on knowledge but also on how they feel about those risks and benefits (Alhakami & Slovic, 1994). This *affect* (emotion-based) *heuristic* also influences judgments of the risks and benefits of nuclear power. For example, after reading a description of nuclear energy that emphasized the risks of this energy source ("Waste is highly radioactive and contaminated with plutonium, a deadly element"), participants not only raised their estimates of the risks of nuclear power (as would be logically expected) but also *lowered* their estimates of the benefits of nuclear power—even though the description had not said anything about benefits. The researchers explained this change in participants' benefit estimates as being due to an overall increase in negative feelings about nuclear power as a result of reading the description of risks (Finucane et al., 2000). In sum, heuristics may sometimes bias people in an anti-environmental direction and sometimes in a pro-environmental direction. The key may be for each person to increase his or her awareness of the potential for errors in thinking. In this way, individuals can become better environmental decision makers.

## Insights from Developmental Psychology

As a discipline, psychology evolved primarily in an urban-industrialized context during the last century. It is probably because of this situation that developmental psychologists have historically overlooked the vital role that nature plays in humans' cognitive, emotional, and social development. Only since the 1990s have some developmental psychologists turned their attention toward topics such as children's relationship with other animals, their understanding of life and ecological systems, their moral reasoning about environmental issues, and the implications of their experiences (or lack thereof) in natural settings.

Developmental psychologists have largely neglected the study of children's relationship with non-human animals, even though animals are a primary focus in children's lives in a variety of forms: as live, stuffed, or imaginary companions; as captive or wild specimens; as zoo attractions; as targets of cruelty; as characters in books and on television; and as roles the children themselves assume. Recently, however, a few developmental psychologists have proposed that in order to fully understand the development of children's perceptual systems, their love relationships and empathy, their play patterns, their fears, and their sense of self, researchers must extend the list of important influences on children to include nonhuman animals—perhaps even putting animals at the top of the list (Melson, 2001, 2003; Myers, 2007).

Experience with animals makes an important contribution to teaching children about the differences

**Experience with animals during childhood can have an impact on people's attitudes about nature in general, not to mention their feelings about the importance of preserving endangered species.**

© Ariel Skelley/CORBIS

© Kevin Fleming/CORBIS

between living and nonliving things. However, learning experiences interact with inherited predispositions. The genetic makeup of the brain enables humans to learn certain concepts more easily than others. For instance, *folkbiology* is a term used to describe how people intuitively perceive, categorize, and think about living things. Research on folkbiology suggests that children recognize a "life force" as something unique to biological phenomena and that they make distinctions between living and nonliving things as well as among plants, animals, and humans (Hatano & Inagaki, 1999; Inagaki & Hatano, 2004). Researchers have also begun to address the questions of whether the acquisition of folkbiological knowledge is a continuous developmental process or a discontinuous one, in which a child's view of the world is replaced by a more sophisticated adult understanding (Coley, Solomon, & Shafto, 2002) and whether the acquisition of folkbiological knowledge occurs in the same way across cultures (e.g., Waxman, 2005). Research on children's folkbiology will not only broaden understanding of cognitive development in general but may also help psychologists to better understand why and how adults' unsustainable behaviors may be influenced by *anthropocentric* (human-centered) thinking and ignorance about ecology.

Children make categorical distinctions between humans, nonhuman animals, plants, and nonliving things, but do they make *moral* distinctions between them? Research suggests the answer is "yes." In several cross-cultural studies, children showed strong moral prohibitions against pollution and associated damage to natural systems, including other species. Their concerns reflected anthropocentric values (harm to humans) as well as biocentric values (reviewed in Kahn, 2003). From the biocentric perspective, natural systems have inherent value and rights and deserve respect comparable to humans. Reasoning that involves seeing the similarities between oneself and natural species such as trees can "evoke feelings of empathy for [an] object that permit it to be regarded as something worthy of moral consideration" (Gebhard, Nevers, & Billmann-Mahecha, 2003, p. 92).

Experiences in nature during childhood help determine whether people recognize themselves to be part of nature, feel connected to it, and understand that protecting nature is key to their own survival and well-being (Gebhard et al., 2003; Kals & Ittner, 2003; Searles, 1960). Activists and ecologists often attribute their environmental concern to early personal experiences in nature, family members who modeled appreciation for nature, or feelings of distress over the destruction of a favorite natural place (Chawla, 1998).

Increasingly, child development experts are becoming convinced that children need outdoor experiences to fully develop their emotional, physical, mental, and social capabilities (e.g., Kahn & Kellert, 2002), a theory that captured the attention of the popular media with the publication of *Last Child in the Woods: Saving Our Children from Nature Deficit Disorder* (Louv, 2005). Although empirical data remain somewhat sparse, some theorists suggest that children need opportunities for spontaneous and independent play or activity in areas that are generally outside human intervention and control (Kellert, 2002; Mergen, 2003; Pyle, 1993). Independent adventure, risk taking, and exploration can foster a sense of mastery, self-sufficiency, and confidence (Derr, 2006). Like adults, children show preferences for natural settings and report that nature offers restoration and relief from stress (e.g., Korpela 2002; Simmons, 1994). Refuges in the form of forts and dens in natural settings are beloved play spaces for many children, primarily because they represent areas under the children's control (Sobel, 2002).

Children's mental health also suffers when deprived of experiences in nature. Children living in rural communities with more "nearby nature" have less psychological distress, including anxiety, depression, and conduct disorders such as bullying than those living in urban areas (Wells & Evans, 2003). Nature encounters can reduce the adverse effects of trauma and childhood distress on children's feelings of global self-worth. Studies have also demonstrated that symptoms of *attention deficit hyperactivity disorders* can be ameliorated by "green activities" such as camping, fishing, soccer, or a simple "walk in the park" (Faber Taylor & Kuo, 2009; Faber Tayler, Kuo, & Sullivan, 2001). Even passive time spent in green settings while relaxing or reading a book outside is negatively correlated with symptoms of attention deficit disorder (Faber Taylor et al., 2001; see also Kuo & Faber Taylor, 2004). While methodological issues may limit some causal inferences (Canu & Gordon, 2005; Kuo & Faber Taylor, 2005), these studies suggest promising research directions and alternative treatment options for the growing problem of attention deficit disorder.

However, many children today experience only degraded and polluted conditions, making identification with nature more difficult (Kahn, 2007; Kals & Ittner, 2003; Pyle, 2002). Further, the average child in the U.S. today spends less than 30 minutes per week engaged in outdoor activities (Hofferth & Curtin, 2005; Hofferth & Sandberg, 2001). More time inside generally means more time in front of a TV or other media sources such as a computer or video game; children are currently spending as many as 6 to 9 hours per day engaged with electronic media (Roberts, Foehr, & Rideout, 2005; Strasburger, 2007). Time with technologies such as television and video games results in less quality time interacting with siblings and parents, less time spent doing homework (as much as an 18% reduction), and less creative play (Vandewater, Bickham, & Lee, 2006), including outdoors. These trends rob children of free time outside and mitigate their understanding of the natural world. Because some investigators have argued that the love of nature and concern about its protection is *only* developed with regular, consistent contact and play outside (Chawla, 1988; Kahn, 2006; Pyle, 2002; Wilson, 1993), children who spend most of their time indoors are less likely to engage in pro-environmental actions.

Perhaps most significant in terms of environmental issues, increased time interacting with media exposes children to an astonishing amount of marketing. The average child sees over 40,000 advertisements on television each year (Linn, 2004). Contemporary advertisers send their messages via television, the Internet, computer games, cell phones, MP3 players, DVDs, virtual world websites, books, and school advertisements (Linn, 2008). This commercialization of childhood constitutes the foundation of the highly destructive consumer culture that depletes resources and degrades the environment (Kasser, 2002; Linn, 2008), in addition to negatively affecting a child's development.

## Insights from Health Psychology

You read in Chapter 3 about the physiology of stress and its associated behavioral and health problems. It turns out that many aspects of contemporary environments that are ecologically unsound are also significant human stressors. Urban noise, traffic, crowding, pollution, and living near toxic industries or waste sites are all associated with increased stress and related symptoms such as anxiety, depression, anger, and aggression/violence (Bell et al., 2001; Hartig et al., 2003; Kuo & Sullivan, 2001; Lima, 2004; Lundberg, 1998), as well as self-reported tension, irritability, distractibility, impaired interpersonal behaviors, and deficits in task performance (Evans & Cohen, 1987; Weil & Rosen, 1997).

Catastrophic events like flooding, hurricanes, windstorms, and wildfires such as those predicted to increase from global climate change are very stressful (Few, 2007; Fritze et al., 2008). The associated loss of loved ones, damage to personal belongings, housing disruption or displacement, and worry about future crises can all cause *posttraumatic stress disorder* (see Chapter 3) and related problems such as grief, depression and suicide attempts, anxiety, and substance abuse (Fritze et al., 2008). For example, mental health services were needed to treat depression, anxiety, and PTSD in approximately 250,000 survivors of Hurricane Katrina in 2005. Yet the storm devastated the infrastructure of Louisiana's Mental Health Office, a system which had only accommodated 40,000 patients prior to the catastrophe (Siegel, 2007).

The manufacture, use, and disposal of tens of thousands of industrial and household chemicals are caus-

**WEB LINK A.8    The Collaborative on Health and the Environment**

The organization that maintains this site works to "advance knowledge and effective action to address growing concerns about the links between human health and environmental factors." The rich resources include access to a searchable database that summarizes research on the links between chemical contaminants and approximately 180 human diseases or conditions.

ing or contributing to increased rates of cancer, developmental disabilities, and reproductive abnormalities, significant stressors in their own right (e.g., Colborn, Dumanoski, & Myers, 1996; Grandjean & Landrigan, 2006; Koger, Schettler, & Weiss, 2005). More than 85,000 chemicals are currently registered with the Environmental Protection Agency, including *pesticides,* which are literally designed to kill (e.g., insects, weeds, and rodents); *flame retardant chemicals;* various *household chemicals* (paint thinners and other solvents, cleaning agents, bleach); and *industrial chemicals;* in addition, certain ingredients in *plastics*, *electronics, cosmetics,* and *air pollution* are all known to be toxic to humans and other animals.

Meanwhile, rapidly accumulating evidence points to a significant role for chemical causes of birth defects; developmental disabilities, including learning and attentional impairments, and autism (Grandjean & Landrigan, 2006; Koger et al., 2005); Parkinson's disease (Landrigan et al., 2005; Stein et al., 2008); various forms of cancer, such as lung, breast, brain, cervical, ovarian, prostate, kidney, as well as leukemia and non-Hodgkin's lymphoma (Bassil et al., 2007; Clapp, Jacobs, & Loechler, 2008; Colborn et al., 1996; vom Saal et al., 2007); and immune system dysfunction (Environmental Protection Agency, 2008). Children are most vulnerable to the effects of chemical toxins at all stages of development—prenatal as well as postnatal, and into adolescence (Rice & Barone, 2000; Stein et al., 2002).

The result is deteriorating health of human beings on physical, mental, emotional, and social levels, as well as degradation of the planet. Thus, the psychology of health and the environment reminds people that they are inherently interconnected with the rest of the biosphere; the health of human bodies is

**WEB LINK A.9    Environmental Working Group**

This nonprofit watchdog organization provides many useful resources (such as "Skin Deep" and "Pots, pans, and plastics: A shopper's guide to food safety") to consumers while simultaneously pushing for national policy change. The website offers recent research-based information on toxic chemicals and ways to avoid them.

In recent years, psychologists have conducted some interesting research on the effects of exposure to natural settings (like the top two photos) versus human-created urban environments (like the bottom two photos). This research indicates that natural environments can decrease individuals' response to stress.

directly related to the health of the planet Earth. The good news is that if individuals perceive a situation or product to be harmful to personal well-being and health, they will be more motivated toward problem solving and engaging in specific behaviors that act to reduce the risks (Homburg & Stolberg, 2006). One innovation in such *problem-focused coping* is reflected in a unique program developed at the Environmental Health Clinic at New York University (see Web Link A.10). Analogous to other university health clinics, "impatients" (people who are tired of waiting for legislative action) make appointments to discuss environmental health concerns, including toxic chemicals and pollution, and receive "prescriptions" for actions: opportunities to engage in local data collection and projects aimed to improve environmental health. The goal is to convert people's anxiety and concern about environmental issues into specific, measurable, and significant actions (Schaffer, 2008).

Perhaps not surprisingly, people strongly prefer healthy, natural settings that include water (lakes, rivers, oceans), plants, trees, and sunlight over urban environments filled with buildings and cars (Kaplan, 2001; Kaplan & Kaplan, 1989; van den Berg et al., 2007). Further, natural environments can alleviate stress by activating the *parasympathetic nervous system* (Chapter 3), providing recovery from sympathetic (fight or flight) arousal by reducing blood pressure and heart rate (Hartig et al., 2003; Laumann, Gärling, & Stormark, 2003). Studies have found that people with views of nature from their workspace reported fewer headaches, greater job satisfaction, and less job stress (Kaplan, 1993; Kaplan & Kaplan, 1989). Viewing natural settings (through a window or on a video) decreased measures of stress, depression, anger, and tension and increased overall happiness and concentration (van den Berg, Koole, & van der Wulp, 2003). Comparably, activities such as gardening, caring for indoor plants, and interacting with non-human animals such as pet dogs can all reduce stress (Frumkin, 2001). Interestingly, restorative experiences in nature can also help motivate environmentally responsible behavior such as recycling (Hartig, Kaiser, & Bowler, 2001).

In addition to stress reduction, nature can provide recovery from prolonged work and concentration

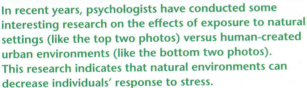

**WEB LINK A.10  Environmental Health Clinic**

This site is hosted by the Environmental Health Clinic at New York University. Patrons of the clinic make appointments to talk about *environmental* health concerns and leave with a prescription—not for medicine, but for *actions* to promote social change that will improve local environmental health. The site features blogs, news, and descriptions of projects being conducted at the clinic.

(Berto, 2005; Hartig & Staats, 2006). You can probably relate to the worn-out feeling that accompanies long-term cognitive effort during midterm and final exams. People can suffer from such fatigue even when the work is enjoyable and thus experience reduced productivity. Attentional fatigue often co-occurs with feelings of stress, but natural, *restorative environments* can mitigate the effects of both (Berman, Jonides, & Kaplan, 2008; Kaplan, 1995; van den Berg et al., 2003). Mental fatigue and other forms of stress can lead people to feel tired, short-tempered, insensitive, and irritable. Thus, to the extent that nature is restorative, it could also help to enhance interpersonal relations and overall life functioning (Herzog & Strevey, 2008).

*Wilderness therapy* programs take advantage of natural, wilderness settings as a backdrop for traditional cognitive-behavioral techniques or integrate wilderness skills and interaction as a part of therapy itself. Wilderness therapy typically involves trips lasting a month or more. Client populations include adolescents struggling with behavioral and emotional problems (e.g., Romi & Kohan, 2004) or women, particularly those who have suffered abuse (Cole, Erdman, & Rothblum, 1994; McBride & Korell, 2005). Because wilderness therapy programs have historically suffered from a lack of consistency in methods, quality, and practitioner credentials, as well as a lack of ethical oversight, some providers banded together in 1997 to form the Outdoor Behavioral Health Industry Council. Outcomes research conducted by members of this organization is beginning to generate some evidence that wilderness therapy can help improve adolescents' self-perceptions, emotional well-being, and social functioning (e.g., Harper et al., 2007; Russell, 2003), but at this point, the lack of consistency in evaluation tools and findings make it difficult to draw firm conclusions about the effectiveness of wilderness therapy and what role the wilderness setting actually plays in its effects.

Overall, it appears that natural environments can contribute to health and well-being, not only for children but also for adults. However, while recognizing the value of restorative environments is important, doing so could also lead to exploitation. Saving natural resources only for the ways in which they can benefit humankind is a limited and anthropocentric view. As Greenway (1995) put it, "Perhaps the clearest evidence of our recovery will be that we do not demand that wilderness heal us. We will have learned to let it be. For a wilderness that must heal us is surely a commodity, just as when we can only look at wilderness as a source of endless wealth" (pp. 134–135).

## What You Can Personally Do

*I am only one. But still I am one.*
*I cannot do everything, but still I can do something;*
*And because I cannot do everything,*
*I will not refuse to do the something that I can do.*
—Quote from Edward Everett Hale (1822–1909), original source unknown.

There are many excellent guides available both online and in print for how to become more environmentally responsible. You can start by taking the online quiz at www.myfootprint.org to determine your own ecological footprint and consider ways to alter your daily life based on your quiz results. You might also consider developing a *behavior modification* project (see the Application for Chapter 3) to address some of your environmentally relevant behaviors.

Six aspects of human lifestyles most significantly and adversely affect the environment (Gardner & Stern, 2008; Miller, 2007): *agriculture, transportation, home energy use, water use, overall resource consumption and waste*, and *toxic chemical production, use, and disposal*. We recommend that you think about these issues and take the following steps toward walking more lightly on the Earth. If you don't feel you can do all of them, select at least a few to get you started on a

more sustainable lifestyle, and then add a new one each month.

## Agriculture

● Reduce your meat consumption by eating *no meat* one day per week, then increase to two days, and so forth.

● Buy locally grown food for at least one month a year, and then try to increase this.

● Buy organically produced food or grow some of your own.

## Transportation

● Walk, bike, carpool, or take mass transit as much as you can.

● If possible, work at home or live near your work or school.

● When you have to drive, note that fuel efficiency can be dramatically increased by reducing your speed, avoiding sudden stops and rapid acceleration, shutting off the engine rather than idling, keeping tires properly inflated, getting regular tune-ups, and turning off your air conditioner.

● Record the distance you drive for one week (baseline), then try to reduce the amount by 10%. Once you accomplish that, try reducing by 15% or more.

● When you purchase a new car, buy a small, fuel-efficient (greater than 35 mpg) model.

## Home energy use

● Turn down the heat by at least a few degrees in winter, and avoid using air conditioning (or turn it up a few degrees).

● Turn off computers, printers, and other appliances when not in use.

● Replace your light bulbs with compact fluorescent bulbs.

● Decrease your energy waste by caulking leaks, adding insulation, and using energy-efficient lights, appliances, and heating/cooling systems.

## Water use

● Always turn off the water while brushing your teeth, and consider turning off the water while soaping up, shampooing, or shaving.

● Take quick showers instead of baths.

● Reuse cups and plates when possible, rather than washing after each use.

● Only run dishwashers and clothes washers with full loads.

● If possible, install water-saving showers and toilets.

● Use the flushing rule: "If it's yellow, let it mellow, if it's brown, flush it down" (urine is sterile).

## Resource Consumption

● The two most important ways to reduce consumption and waste are *Refuse* and *Reuse* (refer to the "Unshopping Card" in **Figure A.7**). Refusing and reusing will save you money, as well as reduce your environmental impact. Recycling is important, but it still requires energy and encourages the production and use of more and more stuff. Keep a list of things you have refused to buy or reused, and try to expand the list each month.

● *Refusing:* Every time you start to buy something, ask yourself whether you really need it, and if you do, whether you can borrow or rent it. If you must buy it, ask yourself if you are purchasing the most eco-friendly version of whatever it is. Note that many products are misleadingly labeled "eco-friendly."

● *Reusing:* Examine your lifestyle and figure out which things you can reuse, such as coffee cups, canvas or other bags for groceries, and your own container for getting food to go and for leftovers when you eat out.

● Buy secondhand items of all kinds whenever possible, and give away, donate to charity, or sell items you no longer need or use, rather than throwing them away.

● Junk mail generates an astonishing amount of waste, utilizes an incredible amount of natural resources, and contributes to climate change. Let organizations know that you don't want to receive their newsletters, catalogs, and solicitations, and be sure to recycle mailings you can't refuse.

## Toxic Chemicals

● Pesticides are designed to kill bugs (insecticides), weeds (herbicides), rodents, and so forth. They are directly toxic to humans as well, producing cancers and developmental disabilities, among other disorders. Don't use any pesticides in your home, lawn, or garden, and educate others about their impacts on human health and neurological function, as well as detrimental effects on biodiversity.

● Avoid chemical cleansers. Baking soda and vinegar are excellent alternatives to many cleaning products; vinegar is also an effective herbicide (weed killer).

● Many plastics, cosmetics, and personal care products contain chemicals that disrupt normal hormone functions (e.g., phthalates and bisphenol A or BPA). Don't buy bottled water; don't reheat or microwave foods in plastic containers; use fewer products with fewer ingredients; and don't trust claims like "dermatologist-tested," "natural," or "organic." Read the ingredient labels and avoid fragrances, dyes, parabens or -paraben, and things you can't pronounce.

● Reduce use of plastics by bringing your own refillable containers, buying in bulk, buying things with minimal packaging, and purchasing products in recyclable and recycled packaging.

● Dispose of household toxic products properly. Many items—paints, pesticides, batteries, and even energy-efficient compact fluorescent light bulbs—contain toxic ingredients. Drop these items off at a local household hazardous waste site.

# Glossary

**acquired immune deficiency syndrome (AIDS)** A disorder in which the immune system is gradually weakened and eventually disabled by the human immunodeficiency virus (HIV).

**aculturation** Changing to adapt to a new culture.

**acute stressors** Threatening events that have a relatively short duration and a clear end point.

**adjustment** The psychological processes through which people manage or cope with the demands and challenges of everyday life.

**affective forecasting** Efforts to predict one's emotional reactions to future events.

**aggression** Any behavior intended to hurt someone, either physically or verbally.

**agoraphobia** A fear of going out to public places.

**alcohol dependence** A chronic, progressive disorder marked by a growing compulsion to drink and impaired control over drinking that eventually interfere with health and social behavior.

**alcoholism** *See* alcohol dependence

**ambient stress** Chronic environmental conditions that, although not urgent, are negatively valued and place adaptive demands on people.

**anal intercourse** The insertion of the penis into a partner's anus and rectum.

**androcentrism** The belief that the male is the norm.

**androgens** The principal class of male sex hormones.

**androgyny** The coexistence of both masculine and feminine personality traits in an individual.

**anorexia nervosa** An eating disorder characterized by intense fear of gaining weight, disturbed body image, refusal to maintain normal weight, and use of dangerous methods to lose weight.

**antecedents** In behavior modification, events that typically precede a target response.

**antianxiety drugs** Drugs that relieve tension, apprehension, and nervousness.

**anticipatory stresses** Upcoming or future events that are perceived to be threatening.

**antidepressant drugs** Drugs that gradually elevate mood and help to bring people out of a depression.

**antipsychotic drugs** Drugs used to gradually reduce psychotic symptoms, including hyperactivity, mental confusion, hallucinations, and delusions.

**anxiety disorders** A class of psychological disorders marked by feelings of excessive apprehension and anxiety.

**approach-approach conflict** A conflict in which a choice must be made between two attractive goals.

**approach-avoidance conflict** A conflict in which a choice must be made about whether to pursue a single goal that has both attractive and unattractive aspects.

**archetypes** Emotionally charged images and thought forms that have universal meaning.

**assertiveness** Acting in one's own best interest by expressing one's feelings and thoughts honestly and directly.

**atherosclerosis** A disease characterized by gradual narrowing of the coronary arteries.

**attachment styles** Typical ways of interacting in close relationships.

**attitudes** Beliefs and feelings about people, objects, and ideas.

**attributions** Inferences that people draw about the causes of events, others' behavior, and their own behavior.

**autonomic nervous system (ANS)** That portion of the peripheral nervous system made up of the nerves that connect to the heart, blood vessels, smooth muscles, and glands.

**aversion therapy** A behavior therapy in which an aversive stimulus is paired with a stimulus that elicits an undesirable response.

**avoidance-avoidance conflict** A conflict in which a choice must be made between two unattractive goals.

**basking in reflected glory** The tendency to enhance one's image by publicly announcing one's association with those who are successful.

**battering** Physical abuse, emotional abuse, and sexual abuse, especially in marriage or relationships.

**behavior** Any overt (observable) response or activity by an organism.

**behavior modification** A systematic approach to changing behavior through the application of the principles of conditioning.

**behavior therapies** The application of the principles of learning to direct efforts to change clients' maladaptive behaviors.

**behavioral contract** A written agreement outlining a promise to adhere to the contingencies of a behavior modification program.

**behaviorism** A theoretical orientation based on the premise that scientific psychology should study observable behavior.

**bereavement** The painful loss of a loved one through death.

**binge-eating disorder** An eating disorder that involves distress-inducing eating binges that are not accompanied by the purging, fasting, and excessive exercise seen in bulimia.

**biomedical therapies** Physiological interventions intended to reduce symptoms associated with psychological disorders.

**biopsychosocial model** The idea that physical illness is caused by a complex interaction of biological, psychological, and sociocultural factors.

**bipolar disorders** Psychological disorders marked by the experience of both depressed and manic periods.

**bisexuals** People who seek emotional-sexual relationships with members of both genders.

**body mass index (BMI)** Weight (in kilograms) divided by height (in meters) squared ($kg/m^2$).

**brainstorming** Generating as many ideas as possible while withholding criticism and evaluation.

**bulimia nervosa** An eating disorder characterized by habitual out-of-control overeating followed by unhealthy compensatory efforts, such as self-induced vomiting, fasting, abuse of laxatives and diuretics, and excessive exercise.

**burnout** Physical, mental, and emotional exhaustion that is attributable to work-related stress.

**bystander effect** The social phenomenon in which individuals are less likely to provide needed help when others are present than when they are alone.

**cancer** Malignant cell growth, which may occur in many organ systems in the body.

**cannabis** The hemp plant from which marijuana, hashish, and THC are derived.

**capitalization** Telling other people about whatever good things are happening in our own lives.

**case study** An in-depth investigation of an individual subject.

**catastrophic thinking** Unrealistic appraisals of stress that exaggerate the magnitude of one's problems.

**catatonic schizophrenia** A type of schizophrenia marked by striking motor disturbances, ranging from muscular rigidity to random motor activity.

**catharsis** The release of emotional tension.

**cerebral hemispheres** The right and left halves of the cerebrum, which is the convoluted outer layer of the brain.

**channel** The medium through which a message reaches the receiver.

**chronic stressors** Threatening events that have a relatively long duration and no readily apparent time limit.

**classical conditioning** A type of learning in which a neutral stimulus acquires the capacity to evoke a response that was originally evoked by another stimulus.

**client-centered therapy** An insight therapy that emphasizes providing a supportive emotional climate for clients, who play a major role in determining the pace and direction of their therapy.

**clinical psychologists** Psychologists who specialize in the diagnosis and treatment of psychological disorders and everyday behavioral problems.

**clinical psychology** The branch of psychology concerned with the diagnosis and treatment of psychological problems and disorders.

**close relationships** Relatively long-lasting relationships in which frequent interactions occur in a variety of settings and in which the impact of the interactions is strong.

**cognitive-behavioral treatments** Therapy approaches that use varied combinations of verbal interventions and behavior modification techniques to help clients change maladaptive patterns of thinking.

**cognitive therapy** An insight therapy that emphasizes recognizing and changing negative thoughts and maladaptive beliefs.

**cohabitation** Living together in a sexually intimate relationship without the legal bonds of marriage.

**coitus** The insertion of the penis into the vagina and (typically) pelvic thrusting.

**collective unconscious** According to Jung, a storehouse of latent memory traces inherited from people's ancestral past that is shared with the entire human race.

**collectivism** Putting group goals ahead of personal goals and defining one's identity in terms of the groups to which one belongs.

**commitment** The decision and intent to maintain a relationship in spite of the difficulties and costs that may arise.

**communication apprehension** The anxiety caused by having to talk with others.

**comparison level** One's standard of what constitutes an acceptable balance of rewards and costs in a relationship.

**comparison level for alternatives** One's estimation of the available outcomes from alternative relationships.

**compensation** A defense mechanism characterized by efforts to overcome imagined or real inferiorities by developing one's abilities.

**compliance** Yielding to social pressure in one's public behavior, even though one's private beliefs have not changed.

**concordance rate** A statistic indicating the percentage of twin pairs or other pairs of relatives that exhibit the same disorder.

**conditioned response (CR)** A learned reaction to a conditioned stimulus that occurs because of previous conditioning.

**conditioned stimulus (CS)** A previously neutral stimulus that has, through conditioning, acquired the capacity to evoke a conditioned response.

**confirmation bias** The tendency to behave toward others in ways that confirm your expectations about them.

**conformity** Yielding to real or imagined social pressure.

**conscious** According to Freud, whatever one is aware of at a particular point in time.

**conservation psychology** The study of the interactive relationships between humans and the rest of nature, with a particular focus on how to enhance conservation of natural resources.

**constructive coping** Efforts to deal with stressful events that are judged to be relatively healthful.

**context** The environment in which communication takes place.

**control group** Subjects in an experiment who do not receive the special treatment given to the experimental group.

**conversion disorder** Psychological disorder characterized by a significant loss of physical function or by other physical symptoms (with no apparent organic basis), usually in a single organ system.

**coping** Active efforts to master, reduce, or tolerate the demands created by stress.

**coronary heart disease** A chronic disease characterized by a reduction in blood flow from the coronary arteries, which supply the heart with blood.

**corpus callosum** The band of fibers connecting the two hemispheres of the brain.

**correlation** The extent to which two variables are related to each other.

**correlation coefficient** A numerical index of the degree of relationship that exists between two variables.

**counseling psychologists** Psychologists who specialize in the treatment of everyday behavioral problems.

**cunnilingus** The oral stimulation of the female genitals.

**date rape** Forced and unwanted intercourse with someone in the context of dating.

**death anxiety** Fear and apprehension about one's own death.

**death system** The collection of rituals and procedures used by a culture to handle death.

**defense mechanisms** Largely unconscious reactions that protect a person from unpleasant emotions such as anxiety and guilt.

**defensive attribution** The tendency to blame victims for their misfortune, so that one feels less likely to be victimized in a similar way.

**defensiveness** An excessive concern with protecting oneself from being hurt.

**delusions** False beliefs that are maintained even though they clearly are out of touch with reality.

**dementia** An abnormal condition marked by multiple cognitive defects that include memory impairment.

**dependent variable** In an experiment, the variable that is thought to be affected by manipulations of the independent variable.

**diagnosis** Distinguishing one illness from another.

**discrimination** Behaving differently, usually unfairly, toward members of a group.

**disorganized schizophrenia** A type of schizophrenia characterized by a particularly severe deterioration of adaptive behavior.

**displaced workers** Individuals who are unemployed because their jobs have disappeared.

**displacement** Diverting emotional feelings (usually anger) from their original source to a substitute target.

**display rules** Norms that govern the appropriate display of emotions.

**dissociative amnesia** A sudden loss of memory for important personal information that is too extensive to be due to normal forgetting.

**dissociative disorders** A class of psychological disorders characterized by loss of contact with portions of one's consciousness or memory, resulting in disruptions in one's sense of identity.

**dissociative fugue** A loss of memory for one's entire past life, along with one's sense of personal identity.

**dissociative identity disorder** Dissociative disorder involving the coexistence in one person of two or more largely complete, and usually very different, personalities. Also called multiple-personality disorder.

**divorce** The legal dissolution of a marriage.

**door-in-the-face technique** Making a very large request that is likely to be turned down to increase the chance that people will agree to a smaller request later.

**downward social comparison** The defensive tendency to compare oneself with someone whose troubles are more serious than one's own.

**dream analysis** A psychotherapeutic technique in which the therapist interprets the symbolic meaning of the client's dreams.

**dual-earner households** Households in which both partners are employed.

**eating disorders** Severe disturbances in eating behavior characterized by preoccupation with weight and unhealthy efforts to control weight.

**ego** According to Freud, the decision-making component of personality that operates according to the reality principle.

**elaboration likelihood model** The idea that an individual's thoughts about a persuasive message (rather than the message itself) determine whether attitude change will occur.

**electroconvulsive therapy (ECT)** A biomedical treatment in which electric shock is used to produce a cortical seizure accompanied by convulsions.

**electronically mediated communication** Interpersonal communication that takes place via technology.

**emotional intelligence** The ability to monitor, assess, express, or regulate one's emotions; the capacity to identify, interpret, and understand others' emotions; and the ability to use this information to guide one's thinking and actions.

**emotions** Powerful, largely uncontrollable feelings, accompanied by physiological changes.

**empiricism** The premise that knowledge should be acquired through observation.

**endocrine system** Glands that secrete chemicals called hormones into the bloodstream.

**endogamy** The tendency of people to marry within their own social group.

**environmental psychologists** Psychologists who study how individuals are affected by, and interact with, their physical environments.

**epidemiology** The study of the distribution of mental or physical disorders in a population.

**erectile difficulties** The male sexual dysfunction characterized by the persistent inability to achieve or maintain an erection adequate for intercourse.

**erogenous zones** Areas of the body that are sexually sensitive or responsive.

**estrogens** The principal class of female sex hormones.

**etiology** The apparent causation and developmental history of an illness.

**evolutionary psychology** A field of psychology that examines behavioral processes in terms of their adaptive value for members of a species over the course of many generations.

**experiment** A research method in which the investigator manipulates an (independent) variable under carefully controlled conditions and observes whether there are changes in a second (dependent) variable as a result.

**experimental group** The subjects in an experiment who receive some special treatment in regard to the independent variable.

**explanatory style** The tendency to use similar causal attributions for a wide variety of events in one's life.

**expressiveness** A style of communication characterized by the ability to express tender emotions easily and to be sensitive to the feelings of others.

**external attributions** Ascribing the causes of behavior to situational demands and environmental constraints.

**extinction** The gradual weakening and disappearance of a conditioned response tendency.

**factor analysis** Technique of analyzing correlations among many variables to identify closely related clusters of variables.

**family life cycle** An orderly sequence of developmental stages that families tend to progress through.

**fellatio** The oral stimulation of the penis.

**fight-or-flight response** A physiological reaction to threat that mobilizes an organism for attacking (fight) or fleeing (flight) an enemy.

**fixation** In Freud's theory, a failure to move forward from one stage to another as expected.

**flow** The state of being in which a person becomes fully involved and engaged in the present time by some interesting, challenging, and intrinsically rewarding activity.

**foot-in-the-door technique** Getting people to agree to a small request to increase the chances that they will agree to a larger request later.

**forgiveness** Counteracting the natural tendencies to seek vengeance or avoid an offender, thereby releasing this person from further liability for his or her transgression.

**free association** A psychotherapeutic technique in which clients spontaneously express their thoughts and feelings exactly as they occur, with as little censorship as possible.

**frustration** The feelings that occur in any situation in which the pursuit of some goal is thwarted.

**fundamental attribution error** The tendency to explain others' behavior as a result of personal rather than situational factors.

**gender** The state of being male or female.

**gender identity** The ability to correctly classify oneself as male or female.

**gender-role identity** A person's identification with the traits regarded as masculine or feminine.

**gender-role transcendence perspective** The idea that to be fully human, people need to move beyond gender roles as a way of organizing the world and of perceiving themselves and others.

**gender roles** Cultural expectations about what is appropriate behavior for each gender.

**gender schemas** Cognitive structures that guide the processing of gender-relevant information.

**gender stereotypes** Widely shared beliefs about males' and females' abilities, personality traits, and social behavior.

**general adaptation syndrome** A model of the body's stress response, consisting of three stages: alarm, resistance, and exhaustion.

**generalized anxiety disorder** A psychological disorder marked by a chronic high level of anxiety that is not tied to any specific threat.

**glass ceiling** An invisible barrier that prevents most women and ethnic minorities from advancing to the highest levels of an occupation.

**gonads** The sex glands.

**gratitude** Recognizing and concentrating on the good things in one's life and being thankful for them.

**group therapy** The simultaneous treatment of several or more clients in a group.

**hallucinations** Sensory perceptions that occur in the absence of a real external stimulus or that represent gross distortions of perceptual input.

**hallucinogens** A diverse group of drugs that have powerful effects on mental and emotional functioning, marked most prominently by distortions in sensory and perceptual experience.

**hardiness** A personality syndrome marked by commitment, challenge, and control that is purportedly associated with strong stress resistance.

**health psychology** The subfield of psychology concerned with the relation of psychosocial factors to the promotion and maintenance of health, and with the causation, prevention, and treatment of illness.

**hedonic adaptation** The phenomenon that occurs when the mental scale that people use to judge the pleasantness and unpleasantness of their experiences shifts so that their neutral point, or baseline for comparison, is changed.

**heritability ratio** An estimate of the proportion of trait variability in a population that is determined by variations in genetic inheritance.

**heterosexism** The assumption that all individuals and relationships are heterosexual.

**heterosexuals** People whose sexual desires and erotic behaviors are directed toward the other gender.

**hierarchy of needs** A systematic arrangement of needs, according to priority, in which basic needs must be met before less basic needs are aroused.

**hindsight bias** The common tendency to mold one's interpretation of the past to fit how events actually turned out.

**homogamy** The tendency of people to marry others who have similar personal characteristics.

**homophobia** The intense fear and intolerance of homosexuality.

**homosexuals** People who seek emotional/sexual relationships with members of the same gender.

**hope** People's expectations that their goals can be achieved in the future.

**hormones** Chemical substances released into the bloodstream by the endocrine glands.

**hostility** A persistent negative attitude marked by cynical, mistrusting thoughts, feelings of anger, and overtly aggressive actions.

**humanism** A theoretical orientation that emphasizes the unique qualities of humans, especially their free will and their potential for personal growth.

**hypoactive sexual desire** Lack of interest in sexual activity.

**hypochondriasis (hypochondria)** Excessive preoccupation with health concerns and incessant worry about developing physical illnesses.

**id** In Freud's theory, the primitive, instinctive component of personality that operates according to the pleasure principle.

**identification** Bolstering self-esteem by forming an imaginary or real alliance with some person or group.

**identity** A relatively clear and stable sense of who one is and what one stands for.

**immune response** The body's defensive reaction to invasion by bacteria, viral agents, or other foreign substances.

**impression management** Usually conscious efforts to influence the way others think of one.

**incongruence** The disparity between one's self-concept and one's actual experience.

**independent variable** In an experiment, a condition or event that an experimenter varies in order to see its impact on another variable.

**individualism** Putting personal goals ahead of group goals and defining one's identity in terms of personal attributes rather than group memberships.

**industrial/organizational (I/O) psychology** The study of human behavior in the workplace.

**informational influence** Pressure to conform that operates when people look to others for how to behave in ambiguous situations.

**ingratiation** Efforts to make oneself likable to others.

**insight therapies** A group of psychotherapies in which verbal interactions are intended to enhance clients' self-knowledge and thus promote healthful changes in personality and behavior.

**instrumentality** A style of communication that focuses on reaching practical goals and finding solutions to problems.

**interdependence theory** See social exchange theory

**internal attributions** Ascribing the causes of behavior to personal dispositions, traits, abilities, and feelings rather than to external events.

**internal conflict** The struggle that occurs when two or more incompatible motivations or behavioral impulses compete for expression.

**Internet addiction** Spending an inordinate amount of time on the Internet and inability to control online use.

**interpersonal communication** An interactional process whereby one person sends a message to another.

**interpersonal conflict** Disagreement among two or more people.

**interpretation** A therapist's attempts to explain the inner significance of the client's thoughts, feelings, memories, and behaviors.

**intimacy** Warmth, closeness, and sharing in a relationship.

**intimate partner violence** Aggression toward those who are in close relationships to the aggressor.

**investments** Things that people contribute to a relationship that they can't get back if the relationship ends.

**kinesics** The study of communication through body movements.

**labor force** All people who are employed as well as those who are currently unemployed but are looking for work.

**learned helplessness** Passive behavior produced by exposure to unavoidable aversive events.

**leisure** Unpaid activities one chooses to engage in because they are personally meaningful.

**life changes** Any noticeable alterations in one's living circumstances that require readjustment.

**listening** A mindful activity and complex process that requires one to select and to organize information, interpret and respond to communications, and recall what one has heard.

**loneliness** The emotional state that occurs when a person has fewer interpersonal relationships than desired or when these relationships are not as satisfying as desired.

**lowball technique** Getting people to commit themselves to an attractive proposition before its hidden costs are revealed.

**major depressive disorder** Psychological disorder characterized by persistent feelings of sadness and despair and a loss of interest in previous sources of pleasure.

**manic-depressive disorder** See bipolar disorder.

**marriage** The legally and socially sanctioned union of sexually intimate adults.

**matching hypothesis** The idea that people of similar levels of physical attractiveness gravitate toward each other.

**medical model** The idea that it is useful to think of abnormal behavior as a disease.

**meditation** A family of mental exercises in which a conscious attempt is made to focus attention in a nonanalytical way.

**menarche** The first occurrence of menstruation.

**mere exposure effect** An increase in positive feelings toward a novel stimulus (such as a person) based on frequent exposure to it.

**message** The information or meaning that is transmitted from one person to another.

**meta-analysis** A statistical technique that evaluates the results of many studies on the same question.

**mindfulness** A cultivated perspective in which people are sensitive to context and focused on the present.

**mindlessness** Engaging in rote behavior, performing familiar, scripted actions without much cognition, as if on autopilot.

**mnemonic devices** Strategies for enhancing memory.

**monogamy** The practice of having only one spouse at a time.

**mood disorders** A class of disorders marked by emotional disturbances that may spill over to disrupt physical, perceptual, social, and thought processes.

**mood stabilizers** Drugs used to control mood swings in patients with bipolar mood disorders.

**mourning** Formal practices of an individual and a community in response to a death.

**multiple-personality disorder** See dissociative identity disorder

**narcissism** The tendency to regard oneself as grandiosely self-important.

**narcotics (opiates)** Drugs derived from opium that are capable of relieving pain.

**naturalistic observation** An approach to research in which the researcher engages in careful observation of behavior without intervening directly with the subjects.

**need for cognition** The tendency to seek out and enjoy effortful thought, problem-solving activities, and in-depth analysis.

**need for self-actualization** The need to fulfill one's potential; the highest need in Maslow's motivational hierarchy.

**negative emotions** Unpleasant responses to potential threats or dangers, including subjective states like sadness, disgust, anger, guilt, and fear.

**negative reinforcement** The strengthening of a response because it is followed by the removal of a (presumably) unpleasant stimulus.

**neuroticism** A broad personality trait associated with chronic anxiety, insecurity, and self-consciousness.

**neurotransmitters** Chemicals that carry signals from one neuron to another.

**noise** Any stimulus that interferes with accurately expressing or understanding a message.

**nonverbal communication** The transmission of meaning from one person to another through means or symbols other than words.

**nonverbal sensitivity** The ability to accurately encode (express) and decode (understand) nonverbal cues.

**normative influence** Pressure to conform that operates when people conform to social norms for fear of negative social consequences.

**nutrition** A collection of processes (mainly food consumption) through which an organism uses the materials (nutrients) required for survival and growth.

**obedience** A form of compliance that occurs when people follow direct commands, usually from someone in a position of authority.

**observational learning** Learning that occurs when an organism's responding is influenced by observing others, who are called models.

**obsessive-compulsive disorder (OCD)** A psychological disorder marked by persistent uncontrollable intrusions of unwanted thoughts (obsessions) and by urges to engage in senseless rituals (compulsions).

**occupational interest inventories** Tests that measure one's interests as they relate to various jobs or careers.

**Oedipal complex** According to Freud, a child's erotically tinged desires for the other-sex parent, accompanied by feelings of hostility toward the same-sex parent.

**operant conditioning** A form of learning in which voluntary responses come to be controlled by their consequences.

**optimism** A general tendency to expect good outcomes.

**orgasm** The release that occurs when sexual arousal reaches its peak intensity and is discharged in a series of muscular contractions that pulsate through the pelvic area.

**orgasmic difficulties** Sexual disorders characterized by an ability to experience sexual arousal but persistent problems in achieving orgasm.

**overcompensation** Making up for frustration in one area by seeking overgratification in another area.

**overlearning** Continued rehearsal of material after one has first appeared to have mastered it.

**overdose** An excessive dose of a drug that can seriously threaten one's life.

**panic disorder** Recurrent attacks of overwhelming anxiety that usually occur suddenly and unexpectedly.

**paralanguage** All vocal cues other than the content of the verbal message itself.

**paranoid schizophrenia** A type of schizophrenia dominated by delusions of persecution, along with delusions of grandeur.

**parental investment theory** The idea that a species' mating patterns depend on what each sex has to invest—in the way of time, energy, and survival risk—to produce and nurture offspring.

**passion** The intense feelings (both positive and negative) experienced in love relationships, including sexual desire.

**person perception** The process of forming impressions of others.

**personal space** A zone of space surrounding a person that is felt to "belong" to that person.

**personality** An individual's unique constellation of consistent behavioral traits.

**personality trait** A durable disposition to behave in a particular way in a variety of situations.

**persuasion** The communication of arguments and information intended to change another person's attitudes.

**phobic disorders** Anxiety disorders marked by a persistent and irrational fear of an object or situation that presents no realistic danger.

**physical dependence** The need to continue to take a drug to avoid withdrawal illness.

**polygamy** Having more than one spouse at one time.

**polygraph** A device that records fluctuations in physiological arousal as a person answers questions.

**positive emotions** Pleasant responses to events that promote connections with others, including subjective states such as happiness, joy, euphoria, gratitude, and contentment.

**positive individual traits** Dispositional qualities that account for why some people are happier and psychologically healthier than other people.

**positive institutions** Those organizations that cultivate civic virtues, encouraging people to behave like good citizens while promoting the collective good.

**positive reinforcement** The strengthening of a response because it is followed by the arrival of a (presumably) pleasant stimulus.

**positive psychology** A social and intellectual movement within the discipline of psychology that focuses on human strengths and how people can flourish and be successful.

**positive psychotherapy** Approach to therapy that attempts to get clients to recognize their strengths, appreciate their blessings, savor positive experiences, forgive those who have wronged them, and find meaning in their lives.

**positive subjective experiences** The positive but private feelings and thoughts people have about themselves and the events in their lives.

**possible selves** One's conceptions about the kind of person one might become in the future.

**posttraumatic growth** Enhanced personal strength, realization of what is truly important in life, and increased appreciation for life, friends, and family following trauma.

**posttraumatic stress disorder (PTSD)** Disturbed behavior that emerges sometime after a major stressful event is over.

**preconscious** According to Freud, material just beneath the surface of awareness that can be easily retrieved.

**prejudice** A negative attitude toward members of a group.

**premature ejaculation** Impaired sexual relations because a man consistently reaches orgasm too quickly.

**pressure** Expectations or demands that one behave in a certain way.

**prevalence** The percentage of a population that exhibits a disorder during a specified time period.

**primacy effect** The fact that initial information tends to carry more weight than subsequent information.

**primary appraisal** An initial evaluation of whether an event is (1) irrelevant to one, (2) relevant, but not threatening, or (3) stressful.

**procrastination** The tendency to delay tackling tasks until the last minute.

**prognosis** A forecast about the probable course of an illness.

**projection** Attributing one's own thoughts, feelings, or motives to another person.

**projective tests** Personality tests that ask subjects to respond to vague, ambiguous stimuli in ways that may reveal the subjects' needs, feelings, and personality traits.

**proxemics** The study of people's use of interpersonal space.

**proximity** Geographic, residential, and other forms of spatial closeness.

**psychiatrists** Physicians who specialize in the treatment of psychological disorders.

**psychoanalysis** An insight therapy that emphasizes the recovery of unconscious conflicts, motives, and defenses through techniques such as free association, dream analysis, and transference.

**psychodynamic theories** All the diverse theories descended from the work of Sigmund Freud that focus on unconscious mental forces.

**psychological dependence** The need to continue to take a drug to satisfy intense mental and emotional craving for it.

**psychological test** A standardized measure of a sample of a person's behavior.

**psychology** The science that studies behavior and the physiological and mental processes that underlie it and the profession that applies the accumulated knowledge of this science to practical problems.

**psychopharmacotherapy** The treatment of mental disorders with medication.

**psychosexual stages** In Freud's theory, developmental periods with a characteristic sexual focus that leave their mark on adult personality.

**psychosomatic diseases** Genuine physical ailments caused in part by psychological factors, especially emotional distress.

**public self** An image presented to others in social interactions.

**punishment** The weakening (decrease in frequency) of a response because it is followed by the arrival of a (presumably) unpleasant stimulus.

**rational-emotive therapy** An approach to therapy that focuses on altering clients' patterns of irrational thinking to reduce maladaptive emotions and behavior.

**rationalization** Creating false but plausible excuses to justify unacceptable behavior.

**reaction formation** Behaving in a way that is exactly the opposite of one's true feelings.

**receiver** The person to whom a message is targeted.

**reciprocal liking** Liking those who show they like you.

**reciprocity principle** The rule that one should pay back in kind what one receives from others.

**reference group** A set of people who are used as a gauge in making social comparisons.

**refractory period** A time after orgasm during which males are unable to experience another orgasm.

**regression** A reversion to immature patterns of behavior.

**relationship maintenance** The actions and activities used to sustain the desired quality of a relationship.

**reliability** The measurement consistency of a test.

**repression** Keeping distressing thoughts and feelings buried in the unconscious.

**resilience** A person's ability to recover and often prosper following some consequential life event.

**resistance** Largely unconscious defensive maneuvers intended to hinder the progress of therapy.

**schizophrenic disorders** A class of disorders marked by disturbances in thought that spill over to affect perceptual, social, and emotional processes.

**secondary appraisal** An evaluation of one's coping resources and options for dealing with stress.

**sedatives** Sleep-inducing drugs that tend to decrease central nervous system and behavioral activity.

**self-actualization** *See* need for self-actualization.

**self-attributions** Inferences that people draw about the causes of their own behavior.

**self-concept** A collection of beliefs about one's basic nature, unique qualities, and typical behavior.

**self-defeating behaviors** Seemingly intentional acts that thwart a person's self-interest.

**self-disclosure** The voluntary act of verbally communicating private information about oneself to another person.

**self-discrepancy** The mismatching of self-perceptions.

**self-efficacy** One's belief about one's ability to perform behaviors that should lead to expected outcomes.

**self-enhancement** The tendency to maintain positive views of oneself.

**self-esteem** One's overall assessment of one's worth as a person; the evaluative component of the self-concept.

**self-fulfilling prophecy** The process whereby expectations about a person cause the person to behave in ways that confirm the expectations.

**self-handicapping** The tendency to sabotage one's performance to provide an excuse for possible failure.

**self-monitoring** The degree to which people attend to and control the impressions they make on others.

**self-regulation** Directing and controlling one's behavior.

**self-report inventories** Personality scales that ask individuals to answer a series of questions about their characteristic behavior.

**self-serving bias** The tendency to attribute one's successes to personal factors and one's failures to situational factors.

**sender** The person who initiates a message.

**sensate focus** A sex-therapy exercise in which partners take turns pleasuring each other with guided verbal feedback while certain kinds of stimulation are temporarily forbidden.

**sensation seeking** A generalized preference for high or low levels of sensory stimulation.

**set-point theory** The idea that there is a natural point of stability in body weight, thought to involve the monitoring of fat cell levels.

**settling-point theory** The idea that weight tends to drift around the level at which the constellation of factors that determine food consumption and energy expenditure achieve an equilibrium.

**sex therapy** The professional treatment of sexual dysfunctions.

**sexism** Discrimination against people on the basis of their sex.

**sexual dysfunction** An impairment in sexual functioning that causes subjective distress.

**sexual harassment** The subjection of individuals to unwelcome sexually oriented behavior.

**sexual identity** The complex of personal qualities, self-perceptions, attitudes, values, and preferences that guide one's sexual behavior.

**sexual orientation** A person's preference for emotional and sexual relationships with individuals of the same gender, the other gender, or either gender.

**sexually transmitted disease (STD)** An illness that is transmitted primarily through sexual contact.

**shaping** Modifying behavior by reinforcing closer and closer approximations of a desired response.

**shyness** Discomfort, inhibition, and excessive caution in interpersonal relations.

**social comparison theory** The idea that people need to compare themselves with others in order to gain insight into their own behavior.

**social constructionism** The assertion that individuals construct their own reality based on societal expectations, conditioning, and self-socialization.

**social exchange theory** The idea that interpersonal relationships are governed by perceptions of the rewards and costs exchanged in interactions.

**social role theory** The assertion that minor gender differences are exaggerated by the different social roles that males and females occupy.

**social skills training** A behavior therapy designed to improve interpersonal skills that emphasizes shaping, modeling, and behavioral rehearsal.

**social support** Aid and succor provided by members of one's social networks.

**socialization** The process by which individuals acquire the norms and roles expected of people in a particular society.

**somatization disorder** A psychological disorder marked by a history of diverse physical complaints that appear to be psychological in origin.

**somatoform disorders** A class of psychological disorders involving physical ailments that have no authentic organic basis but are due solely to psychological factors.

**source** The person who initiates, or sends, a message.

**spermarche** An adolescent male's first ejaculation.

**standardization** The uniform procedures used to administer and score a test.

**stereotypes** Widely held beliefs that people have certain characteristics simply because of their membership in a particular group.

**stimulants** Drugs that tend to increase central nervous system and behavioral activity.

**stress** Any circumstances that threaten or are perceived to threaten one's well-being and thereby tax one's coping abilities.

**subjective well-being** Individuals' personal assessments of their overall happiness or life satisfaction.

**sublimation** Defense mechanism that occurs when unconscious, unacceptable impulses are channeled into socially acceptable, perhaps even admirable, behaviors.

**superego** According to Freud, the moral component of personality that incorporates social standards about what represents right and wrong.

**surveys** Structured questionnaires designed to solicit information about specific aspects of participants' behavior.

**sustainable world** A world in which human activities and needs are balanced with those of other species and future generations, taking into account ecological as well as social and economic factors.

**systematic desensitization** A behavior therapy used to reduce clients' anxiety responses through counterconditioning.

**tardive dyskinesia** A neurological disorder marked by chronic tremors and involuntary spastic movements.

**test norms** Statistics that provide information about where a score on a psychological test ranks in relation to other scores on that test.

**token** A symbol of all the members of a group.

**token economy** A system for doling out symbolic reinforcers that are exchanged later for a variety of genuine reinforcers.

**tolerance** A progressive decrease in responsiveness to a drug with continued use.

**transference** A phenomenon that occurs when clients start relating to their therapist in ways that mimic critical relationships in their lives.

**twin studies** A research method in which researchers assess hereditary influence by comparing the resemblance of identical twins and fraternal twins on a trait.

**Type A personality** A personality style marked by a competitive orientation, impatience and urgency, and anger and hostility.

**Type B personality** A personality style marked by relatively relaxed, patient, easygoing, amicable behavior.

**unconditioned response (UCR)** An unlearned reaction to an unconditioned stimulus that occurs without previous conditioning.

**unconditioned stimulus (UCS)** A stimulus that evokes an unconditioned response without previous conditioning.

**unconscious** According to Freud, thoughts, memories, and desires that are well below the surface of conscious awareness but that nonetheless exert great influence on our behavior.

**underemployment** Settling for a job that does not fully utilize one's skills, abilities, and training.

**undifferentiated schizophrenia** A type of schizophrenia marked by idiosyncratic mixtures of schizophrenic symptoms.

**undoing hypothesis** The idea that positive emotions aid the mind and the body by recovering a sense of balance and flexibility following an episode of experiencing negative emotion.

**unrealistic optimism** Awareness that certain health-related behaviors are dangerous but erroneously viewing those dangers as risks for others rather than oneself.

**validity** The ability of a test to measure what it was designed to measure.

**variables** *See* dependent variable; independent variable.

**vasocongestion** Engorgement of blood vessels.

**work** An activity that produces something of value for others.

**work-family conflict** The feeling of being pulled in multiple directions by competing demands from job and family.

**workforce** *See* labor force.

# References


**Aamodt, M. G.** (2004). *Research in law enforcement selection.* Boca Raton, FL: BrownWalker.

**AAUW Educational Foundation** (1992). *How schools shortchange girls.* Washington, DC: AAUW.

**Abbey, A.** (2009). Alcohol and sexual assault. In H. T. Reis & S. Sprecher (Eds.), *Encyclopedia of human relationships* (Vol. 1). Los Angeles: Sage Reference Publication.

**Abbey, A., Clinton-Sherrod, A. M., McAuslan, P., Zawacki, T., & Buck, P. O.** (2003). The relationship between the quantity of alcohol consumed and the severity of sexual assaults committed by college men. *Journal of Interpersonal Violence, 18*(7), 813–833.

**Abbey, A., McAuslan, P., Zawacki, T., Clinton, A. M., & Buck, P. O.** (2001a). Attitudinal, experimental, and situational predictors of sexual assault perpetration. *Journal of Interpersonal Violence, 16*(8), 784–807.

**Abbey, A., Zawacki, T., Buck, P. O., Clinton, A. M., & McAuslan, P.** (2001b). Alcohol and sexual assault. *Alcohol Research and Health, 25*(1), 43–51.

**Abbey, A., Zawacki, T., Buck, P. O., Clinton, A. M., & McAuslan, P.** (2004). Sexual assault and alcohol consumption: What do we know about their relationship and what types of research are still needed? *Aggression and Violent Behavior, 9*(3), 271–303.

**Abdel-Khalek, A. M.** (2006). Happiness, health, and religiosity: Significant relations. *Mental Health, 9*(1), 85–97.

**Abel, M. H.** (1998). Interaction of humor and gender in moderating relationships between stress and outcomes. *Journal of Psychology, 132,* 267–276.

**Abel, M. H.** (2002). Humor, stress, and coping strategies. *Humor: International Journal of Humor Research, 15*(4), 365–381.

**Abi-Dargham, A.** (2004). Do we still believe in the dopamine hypothesis? New data bring new evidence. *International Journal of Neuropsychopharmacology, 7*(Suppl1), S1–S5.

**Abi-Saleh, B., Iskanadar, S. B., Elgharib, N., & Cohen, M. V.** (2008). C-reactive protein: The harbinger of cardiovascular diseases. *Southern Medical Journal, 101,* 525–533.

**Abma, J. C., & Martinez, G. M.** (2006). Childlessness among older women in the United States: Trends and profiles. *Journal of Marriage and Family, 68,* 1045–1056.

**Aboud, F. E., & Mendelson, M. J.** (1996). Determinants of friendship selection and quality: Developmental perspectives. In W. M. Bukowski, A. F. Newcomb, & W. W. Hartup (Eds.), *The company they keep: Friendship in childhood and adolescence.* Cambridge, UK: Cambridge University Press.

**Abrahamse, W., Steg, L., Vlek, C., & Rothengatter, T.** (2005). A review of intervention studies aimed at household energy conservation. *Journal of Environmental Psychology, 25,* 273–291.

**Abrams, D., Viki, G. T., Masser, B., & Bohner, G.** (2003). Perceptions of stranger acquaintance rape: The role of benevolent and hostile sexism in victim blame and rape proclivity. *Journal of Personality and Social Psychology, 84,* 111–125.

**Abramson, L. Y., Seligman, M. E. P., & Teasdale, J. D.** (1978). Learned helplessness in humans: Critique and reformulation. *Journal of Abnormal Psychology, 87,* 49–74.

**Acevedo, B. P., & Aron, A.** (2009). Does a long-term relationship kill romantic love? *Review of General Psychology 13,* 59–65.

**Ackerman, J. M., Shapiro, J. R., Neuberg, S. L., Kenrick, D. T., Schaller, M., Becker, D. V., et al.** (2006). They all look the same to me (unless they're angry): From out-group homogeneity to out-group heterogeneity. *Psychological Science, 17,* 836–840.

**Ackerman, S., Zuroff, D. C., & Moskowitz, D. S.** (2000). Generativity in midlife and young adults: Links to agency, communion, and subjective well-being. *International Journal of Aging and Human Development, 50*(1), 17–41.

**Acock, A. C., & Demo, D. H.** (1994). *Family diversity and well-being.* Thousand Oaks, CA: Sage.

**Adams, G., Anderson, S. L., & Adonu, J. K.** (2004). The cultural grounding of closeness and intimacy. In D. J. Mashek & A. Aron (Eds.), *Handbook of closeness and intimacy.* Mahwah, NJ: Erlbaum.

**Adams, M., & Coltrane, S.** (2006). Framing divorce reform: Media, morality, and the politics of family. *Family Process, 46,* 17–34.

**Adcock, C. J.** (1965). Thematic Apperception Test. In O. K. Buros (Ed.), *Sixth Mental Measurements Yearbook.* Highland Park, NY: Gryphon Press.

**Addis, M. E., & Mahalik, J. R.** (2003). Men, masculinity, and the contexts of help seeking. *American Psychologist, 58*(1), 5-14.

**Adler, A.** (1917). *Study of organ inferiority and its psychical compensation.* New York: Nervous and Mental Diseases Publishing.

**Adler, A.** (1927). *Practice and theory of individual psychology.* New York: Harcourt, Brace & World.

**Adorno, T. W., Frenkel-Brunswik, E., Levinson, D. J., & Sanford, B. W.** (1950). *The authoritarian personality.* New York: Harper & Row.

**Agarwal, P. K., Karpicke, J. D., Kang, S. H. K., Roediger, H. L., III., & McDermott, K. B.** (2008). Examining the testing effect with open- and closed-book tests. *Applied Cognitive Psychology, 22,* 861–876.

**Agyeman, J., Doppelt, B., Lynn, K., & Hatic, H.** (2007). The climate-justice link: Communicating risk with low-income and minority audiences. In S. C. Moser & L. Dilling (Eds.), *Creating a climate for change: Communicating climate change and facilitating social change* (pp. 119–138). New York, NY: Cambridge University Press.

**Ahern, A. L., Bennett, K. M., & Hetherington, M. M.** (2008). Internalization of the ultra-thin ideal: Positive implicit associations with underweight fashion models are associated with drive for thinness in young women. *Eating Disorders, 16,* 294–307.

**Ahn, H., & Wampold, B. E.** (2001). Where oh where are the specific ingredients? A meta–analysis of component studies in counseling and psychotherapy. *Journal of Counseling Psychology, 48,* 251–257.

**Ahrons, C. R.** (1999). Divorce: An unscheduled family transition. In B. Carter & M. McGoldrick (Eds.), *The expanded family life cycle: Individual, family, and social perspectives* (3rd ed.). Boston: Allyn & Bacon.

**Ahrons, C. R.** (2007). Introduction to the special issue on divorce and its aftermath. *Family Process, 46*(1), 3–6.

**Ai, A. L., Santangelo, L. K., & Cascio, T.** (2006). The traumatic impact of the September 11, 2001, terrorist attacks and the potential protection of optimism. *Journal of Interpersonal Violence, 21,* 689–700.

**Aikawa, A., Fujita, M., & Tanaka, K.** (2007). The relationship between social skills deficits and depression, loneliness, and social anxiety: Rethinking a vulnerability model of social skills deficits. *The Japanese Journal of Social Psychology, 23,* 95–103.

**Aikins, D. E., & Craske, M. G.** (2001). Cognitive theories of generalized anxiety disorder. *Psychiatric Clinics of North America, 24,* 57–74.

**Ainsworth, M. D. S., Blehar, M. C., Waters, E., & Wall, S.** (1978). *Patterns of attachment: A psychological study of the strange situation.* Hillsdale, NJ: Erlbaum.

**Akerstedt, T., Kecklund, G., & Axelsson, J.** (2007). Impaired sleep after bedtime stress and worries. *Biological Psychology, 76*(3), 170–173.

**Akgun, S., & Ciarrochi, J.** (2003). Learned resourcefulness moderates the relationship between academic stress and academic performance. *Educational Psychology, 23*(3), 287-294.

**Akimoto, S. A., & Sanbonmatsu, D. M.** (1999). Differences in self-effacing behavior between European and Japanese Americans: Effect on competence evaluations. *Journal of Cross-Cultural Psychology, 30,* 159–177.

**Akiskal, H. S.** (2005). Mood disorders: Clinical features. In B. J. Sadock & V. A. Sadock (Eds.), *Kaplan & Sadock's comprehensive textbook of psychiatry.* Philadelphia: Lippincott Williams & Wilkins.

**Akiskal, H. S.** (2009). Mood disorders: Clinical features. In B. J. Sadock, V. A. Sadock, & P. Ruiz (Eds.), *Kaplan & Sadock's comprehensive textbook of psychiatry* (pp. 1693–1733). Philadelphia: Lippincott Williams & Wilkins.

**Alan Guttmacher Institute.** (2006). *Plan B decision by FDA a victory for common sense.* Retrieved June 24, 2007 from http://guttmacher.org/media/inthenews/2006/08/27/index.html.

**Alanko, K., Santtila, P., Harlaar, N., Witting, K., Varjonen, M., Jern, P., Johansson, A., von der Pahlen, B., & Sandnabba, N. K.** (2008). The association between childhood gender atypical behavior and adult psychiatric symptoms is moderated by parenting style. *Sex Roles, 58,* 837–847.

**Albarćin, D., Leeper, J., Earl, A., & Durantini, M.** (2008). From brochures to videos to counseling: Exposure to HIV-prevention programs. *AIDS and Behavior, 12,* 354–362.

**Albarraci, D., Johnson, B. T., & Zanna, M. P.** (Eds.). (2005). *Hanbook of attitudes.* Mahwah, NJ: Erlbaum.

**Albert, C. M., Ma, J., Rifai, N., Stampfer, M. J., & Ridker, P. M.** (2002). Prospective study of C-reactive protein, homocysteine, and plasma lipid levels as predictors of sudden cardiac death. *Circulation, 105,* 2595–2599.

**Alberti, R. E., & Emmons, M. L.** (2001). *Your perfect right.* San Luis Obispo, CA: Impact Publishers.

**Albrecht, K.** (2009). *Social intelligence: The new science of success.* New York: Pfeiffer.

**Albright, J. M.** (2008). Sex in America online: An explanation of sex, marital status, and sexual identity in internet sex seeking and its impacts. *Journal of Sex Research, 42,* 175–186.

**Aldwin, C. M.** (2007). *Stress, coping, and development: An integrative perspective.* New York: Guilford.

**Alexander, C. N., Robinson, P., Orme-Johnson, D. W., Schneider, R. H., et al.** (1994). The effects of transcendental meditation compared with other methods of relaxation and meditation in reducing risk factors, morbidity, and mortality. *Homeostasis in Health & Disease, 35,* 243–263.

**Alhakami, A. S. & Slovic, P.** (1994). A psychological study of the inverse relationship between perceived risk and perceived benefit. *Risk Analysis, 14,* 1085–1096.

**Alicke, M. D.** (1985). Global self-evaluation as determined by the desirability and controllability of trait adjectives. *Journal of Personality and Social Psychology, 49*(6), 1621–1630.

**Alicke, M. D., Smith, R. H., & Klotz, J. L.** (1986). Judgments of personal attractiveness: The role of faces and bodies. *Personality and Social Psychology Bulletin, 12,* 381–389.

**Allen, E. S., Rhoades, G. K., Stanley, S. M., Markman, H. J., Williams, T., Melton, J., & Clements, M. L.** (2008). Premarital precursors of marital infidelity. *Family Process, 47,* 243–259.

**Allen, J. J. B., & Iacono, W. G.** (2001). Assessing the validity of amnesia in dissociative identity disorder: A dilemma for the DSM and the courts. *Psychology, Public Policy, and Law, 7,* 311–344.

**Allen, K., Blascovich, J., & Mendes, W. B.** (2002). Cardiovascular reactivity in the presence of pets, friends, and spouses: The truth about cats and dogs. *Psychosomatic Medicine, 64*(5), 727–739.

**Allen, K. R., & Demo, D. H.** (1995). The families of lesbians and gay men: A new frontier in family research. *Journal of Marriage and the Family, 57,* 111–127.

**Allen, L.** (2007). Denying the sexual subject: Schools' regulation of student sexuality. *British Educational Research Journal, 33,* 221–234.

**Allgood, W. P., Risko, V. J., Alvarez, M. C., & Fairbanks, M. M.** (2000). Factors that influence study. In R. F. Flippo & D. C. Caverly (Eds.), *Handbook of college reading and study strategy research.* Mahwah, NJ: Erlbaum.

**Allison, D. B., Fontaine, K. R., Manson, J. E., Stevens, J., & VanItallie, T. B.** (1999). Annual deaths attributable to obesity in the United States. *Journal of the American Medical Association, 282*(16), 1530–1538.

**Allison, D. B., Heshka, S., Neale, M. C., Lykken, D. T., & Heymsfield, S. B.** (1994). A genetic analysis of relative weight among 4,020 twin pairs, with an emphasis on sex effects. *Health Psychology, 13,* 362–365.

**Allman, K.** (2009). Covenant marriage laws in Louisiana: When Louisiana became the first state to enact covenant marriage, supporters expected it to sweep the country and lower the rate of divorce in America. What happened? Retrieved from http://bestofneworleans.com/gyrobase/Content?oid=oid%3A51787

**Alloy, L. B., Abramson, L. Y., Whitehouse, W. G., Hogan, M. E., Tashman, N. A., Steinberg, D. L., Rose, D. T., & Donovan, P.** (1999). Depressogenic cognitive styles: Predictive validity, information processing and personality characteristics, and developmental origins. *Behavioral Research and Therapy, 37,* 503–531.

**Allport, G. W.** (1937). *Personality: A psychological interpretation.* New York: Holt.

**Allport, G. W.** (1961). *Pattern and growth in personality.* New York: Holt, Rinehart & Winston.

**Alonso, A., Alonso, S., & Piper, W.** (2003). Group psychotherapy. In G. Stricker, & T. A. Widiger (Eds.), *Handbook of psychology: Vol. 8. Clinical psychology.* New York: Wiley.

**Altemeyer, B.** (1988a). *Enemies of freedom: Understanding right-wing authoritarianism.* San Francisco: Jossey-Bass.

**Altemeyer, B.** (1988b). The good soldier, marching in step: A psychological explanation of state terror. *Sciences, March/April,* 30–38.

**Altemeyer, B.** (1996). *The authoritarian specter.* Cambridge, MA: Harvard University Press.

**Altemeyer, B.** (1998). The other "authoritarian personality." *Advances in Experimental Social Psychology, 30,* 47–92.

**Altermatt, T. W., & DeWall, C. N.** (2003). Agency and virtue: Dimensions underlying subgroups of women. *Sex Roles, 49,* 631–641.

**Altshuler, L. L., Suppes, T., Black, D. O., Nolen, W. A., Leverich, G., Keck, P. E., Jr., et al.** (2006). Lower switch rate in depressed patients with Bipolar II than Bipolar I disorder treated adjunctively with second-generation antidepressants. *American Journal of Psychiatry, 163,* 313–315.

**Alzate, H.** (1990). Vaginal erogeneity, "female ejaculation," and the "Granfenberg spot." *Archives of Sexual Behavior, 19,* 607–611.

**Amato, P. R.** (1999). Children of divorced parents as young adults. In E. M. Hetheringon (Ed.), *Coping with divorce, single parenting, and remarriage: A risk and resiliency perspective.* Mahwah, NJ: Erlbaum.

**Amato, P. R.** (2001). The consequences of divorce for adults and children. In R. M. Milardo (Ed.), *Understanding families into the new millennium: A decade in review.* Minneapolis, MN: National Council on Family Relations.

**Amato, P. R.** (2003). Reconciling divergent perspectives: Judith Wallerstein, quantitative family research, and children of divorce. *Family Relations: Interdisciplinary Journal of Applied Family Studies, 52*(4), 332–339.

**Amato, P. R.** (2004a). Divorce in social and historical context: Changing scientific perspectives on children and marital dissolution. In M. Coleman & L. H. Ganong (Eds.), *Handbook of contemporary families: Considering the past, contemplating the future.* Thousand Oaks, CA: Sage.

**Amato, P. R.** (2004b). Tension between institutional and individual views of marriage. *Journal of Marriage and Family, 66,* 959–965.

**Amato, P. R.** (2007). Studying marriage and commitment with survey data. In S. L. Hofferth & L. M. Casper (Eds.), *Handbook of measurement issues in family research.* Mahwah, NJ: Erlbaum.

**Amato, P. R., & DeBoer, D. D.** (2001). The transmission of marital instability across generations: Relationship skills or commitment to marriage? *Journal of Marriage and Family, 63,* 1038–1051.

**Amato, P. R., Johnson, D. R., Booth, A., & Rogers, S. J.** (2003). Continuity and change in marital quality between 1980 and 2000. *Journal of Marriage and Family, 65,* 1–22.

**Amato, P. R., & Previti, D.** (2003). People's reasons for divorcing: Gender, social class, the life course, and adjustment. *Journal of Family Issues, 24*(5), 602–626.

**Amato, P. R., & Rogers, S. J.** (1997). A longitudinal study of marital problems and subsequent divorce. *Journal of Marriage and the Family, 59,* 612–624.

**Ambady, N., LaPlante, D., Nguyen, T., Rosenthal, R., Chaumeton, N., & Levinson W.** (2002). Surgeon's tone of voice: A clue to malpractice history. *Surgery, 132,* 5–9.

**American Association of Suicidology.** (2007). *Understanding and helping the suicidal individual.* Retrieved April 12, 2007 from http://www.suicidology.org/associations/1045/files/Understanding.pdf.

**American Council on Education.** (1997). Many college graduates participate in training courses to improve their job skills. *Higher Education and National Affairs, 46*(19), 3.

**American Foundation for Suicide Prevention.** (2007). *When you fear someone may take their own life.* Retrieved April 12, 2007 from http://www.afsp.org/index.cfm?page_id=F2F25092-7E90-9BD4-C4658F1D2B5D19A0.

**American Psychiatric Association.** (1994). *Diagnostic and statistical manual of mental disorders* (4th ed.). Washington, DC: Author.

**American Psychiatric Association Task Force on Electroconvulsive Therapy.** (2001). *The practice of electroconvulsive therapy: Recommendations for treatment* (2nd ed.). Washington, DC: American Psychiatric Association.

**American Psychological Association.** (2004). *Public policy, work, and families: The report of the APA presidential initiative on work and families.* Washington DC: APA.

**American Psychological Association.** (2007, October 24). *Stress a major health problem in the U.S., Warns APA.* Retrieved from http://www.apa.org/news/press/releases/2007/10/stress.aspx

**American Society for Aesthetic Plastic Surgery.** (2008). Surgical and nonsurgical procedures: 12-year Comparison, 1997–2008. Retrieved from http://www.surgy.org.media/statistics

**Ames, S. C., Jones, G. N., Howe, J. T., & Brantley, P. J.** (2001). A prospective study of the impact of stress on quality of life: An investigation of low-income individuals with hypertension. *Annals of Behavioral Medicine, 23*(2), 112–119.

**Anderluh, M. B., Tchanturia, K., & Rabe-Hesketh.** (2003). Childhood obsessive-compulsive personality traits in adult women with eating disorders: Defining a broader eating disorder phenotype. *American Journal of Psychiatry, 160,* 242–247.

**Andersen, B. L., Golden-Kreutz, D. M., & DiLillo, V.** (2001). Cancer. In A. Baum, T. A. Revenson, & J. E. Singer (Eds.), *Handbook of health psychology.* Mahwah, NJ: Erlbaum.

**Andersen, B. L., Kiecolt-Glaser, J. K., & Glaser, R.** (1994). A biobehavioral model of cancer stress and disease course. *American Psychologist, 49,* 389–404.

**Andersen, P., Hecht, M., Hoober, G., & Smallwood, M.** (2002). Nonverbal communication in across cultures. In W. Gudykunst & B. Mody (Eds.), *The handbook of international and intercultural communication* (2nd ed., pp. 89–106). Thousand Oaks, CA: Sage.

**Andersen, S. M., & Chen, S.** (2002). The relational self: An interpersonal social-cognitive theory. *Psychological Review, 109,* 619–645.

**Anderson, A. E., & Yager, J.** (2005). Eating disorders. In B. J. Sadock & V. A. Sadock (Eds.), *Kaplan & Sadock's comprehensive textbook of psychiatry.* Philadelphia: Lippincott Williams & Wilkins.

**Anderson, C. A.** (2004). An update on the effects of playing violent video games. *Journal of Adolescence, 27*(1), 113–122.

**Anderson, C. A., & Bushman, B. J.** (2001). Effects of violent video games on aggressive behavior, aggressive cognition, aggressive affect, physiological arousal, and prosocial behavior: A meta-analytic review of the scientific literature. *Psychological Science, 12,* 353–359.

**Anderson, C. A., & Huesmann, L. R.** (2003). Human aggression: A social-cognitive view. In M. A. Hogg & J. Cooper (Eds.), *The Sage handbook of social psychology.* Thousand Oaks, CA: Sage Publications.

**Anderson, C. A., Miller, R. S., Riger, A. L., Dill, J. C., & Sedikides, C.** (1994). Behavioral and characterological attributional styles as predictors of depression and loneliness: Review, refinement, and test. *Journal of Personality and Social Psychology, 66,* 549–558.

**Anderson, D. A., & Hamilton, M.** (2005). Gender role stereotyping of parents in children's picture books: The invisible father. *Sex Roles, 52*(3–4), 145–151.

**Anderson, K.** (2009, April 6). The end of excess: Is this crisis good for America? *Time.* Retrieved from http://www.time.com/time/nation/article/0,8599,1887728,00.html

**Anderson, K. J.** (1990). Arousal and the inverted-U hypothesis: A critique of Neiss's "reconceptualizing arousal." *Psychological Bulletin, 107,* 96–100.

**Anderson, S. M., Reznik, I., & Manzella, L. M.** (1996). Eliciting facial affect, motivation, and expectancies in transference: Significant-other representations in social relations. *Journal of Personality and Social Psychology, 71,* 1108–1129.

**Anderson, V. L., Levinson, E. M., Barker, W., & Kiewra, K. R.** (1999). The effects of meditation on teacher-perceived occupational stress, state and trait anxiety and burnout. *School Psychology Quarterly, 14,* 3–25.

**Anderson-Fye, E. P., & Becker, A. E.** (2004). Sociocultural aspects of eating disorders. In J. K. Thompson (Ed.), *Handbook of eating disorders and obesity.* New York: Wiley.

**Andreasen, N. C.** (1987). The diagnosis of schizophrenia. *Schizophrenia Bulletin, 13,* 9–22.

**Andreasen, N. C.** (1990). Positive and negative symptoms: Historical and conceptual aspects. In N. C. Andreasen (Ed.), *Modern problems of pharmacopsychiatry: Positive and negative symptoms and syndromes.* Basel: Karger.

**Andresen, J.** (2000). Meditation meets behavioural medicine: The story of experimental research on meditation. *Journal of Consciousness Studies, 7*(11–12), 17–73.

**Andrews, B., & Hejdenberg, J.** (2007). Stress in university students. In G. Fink (Ed.), *Encyclopedia of stress: Vols. 1–4* (2nd ed., pp. 612–614). San Diego, CA: Elsevier Academic Press.

**Angell, M.** (2000). Is academic medicine for sale? *New England Journal of Medicine, 342,* 1516–1518.

**Angell, M.** (2004). *The truth about the drug companies: How they decieve us and what to do about it.* New York: Random House.

**Anson, K., & Ponsford, J.** (2006). Coping and emotional adjustment following traumatic brain injury. *Journal of Head Trauma Rehabilitation, 21,* 248–259.

**Antecol, H., Jong, A., & Steinberger, M.** (2008). The sexual orientation wage gap: The role of occupational sorting and human capital. *Industrial & Labor Relations Review, 61,* 518–543.

**Anthony, I. C., & Bell, J. E.** (2008). The neuropathology of HIV/AIDS. *International Review of Psychiatry, 20*(1), 15–24.

**Antonietti, A., Cocomazzi, D., & Iannello, P.** (2009). Looking at the audience improves music appreciation. *Journal of Nonverbal Behavior, 33,* 89–106.

**Antoniou, A. G.** (2005). Emotional intelligence and transformational leadership. In A. G. Antoniou & C. L. Cooper (Eds.), *Research companion to organizational health psychology.* Northampton, MA: Edward Elgar.

**Antoniou, A. G., & Cooper, C. L.** (2005). *Research companion to organizational health psychology.* Northampton, MA: Edward Elgar.

**Antonucci, T. C., Lansford, J. E., & Ajrouch, K. J.** (2007). Social support. In G. Fink (Ed.), *Encyclopedia of stress: Vols. 1–4* (2nd ed., pp. 539–542). San Diego, CA: Elsevier Academic Press.

**Antony, M. M., & McCabe, R. E.** (2003). Anxiety disorders: Social and specific phobias. In A. Tasman, J. Kay, & J. A. Lieberman (Eds.), *Psychiatry.* New York: Wiley.

**Antoszewski, B., Kasielska, A., Jedrzejczak, M., & Kruk-Jeromin, J.** (2007). Knowledge of and attitude toward transsexualism among college students. *Sexuality and Disability, 25,* 29–35.

**Aono, A.** (2003). The effects of gender and status on interpersonal distance: From the viewpoint of the oppression hypothesis. *The Japanese Journal of Social Psychology, 19,* 51–58.

**Apperloo, M. J. A., Van Der Stege, J. G., Hoek, A., & Weijmar Schultz, W. C. M.** (2003). In the mood for sex: The value of androgens. *Journal of Sex and Marital Therapy, 29*(2), 87–102.

**Aquilino, W. S.** (1997). From adolescent to young adult: A prospective study of parent-child relations during the transition to adulthood. *Journal of Marriage and the Family, 59,* 670–686.

**Aquilino, W. S.** (2009). Empty nest, effects on marriage. In H. T. Reis & S. Sprecher (Eds.), *Encyclopedia of human relationships: Vol. 2* (pp. 523–525). Los Angeles: Sage Reference Publication.

**Arbona, C.** (2005). Promoting the career development and academic achievement of at-risk youth: College access programs. In S. D. Brown & R. W. Lent (Eds.), *Career development and counseling: Putting theory and research to work.* New York: Wiley.

**Archer, J.** (1996). Sex differences in social behavior: Are the social role and evolutionary explanations compatible? *American Psychologist, 51,* 909–917.

**Archer, J.** (2005). Are women or men the more aggressive sex? In S. Fein, G. R. Goethals, & M. J. Sandstrom (Eds.), *Gender and aggression: Interdisciplinary perspectives.* Mahwah, NJ: Erlbaum.

**Arendell, T.** (2000). Conceiving and investigating motherhood: The decade's scholarship. *Journal of Marriage and the Fally, 62*(4), 1192–1207.

**Argyle, M.** (1987). *The psychology of happiness.* London: Metheun.

**Argyle, M.** (1999). Causes and correlates of happiness. In D. Kahneman, E. Diener, & N. Schwarz (Eds.), *Well-being: The foundations of hedonic psychology.* New York: Sage.

**Argyle, M.** (2001). *The psychology of happiness* (2nd ed.). New York: Routledge.

**Argyle, M., & Henderson, M.** (1984). The rules of friendship. *Journal of Social and Personal Relationships, 1,* 211–237.

**Ariely, D., & Wertenbroch, K.** (2002). Procrastination, deadlines, and performance: Self-control by precommitment. *Psychological Science, 13*(3), 219–224.

**Aries, E.** (1998). Gender differences in interaction: A reexamination. In D. J. Canary & K. Dindia (Eds.), *Sex differences and similarities in communication: Critical essays and empirical investigations of sex and gender in interaction.* Mahwah, NJ: Erlbaum.

**Arkowitz, H., & Lilienfeld, S. O.** (2006). Do self-help books help? *Scientific American Mind, 17*(5), 78–79.

**Arkowitz, H., & Lilienfeld, S. O.** (2007). The best medicine? How drugs stack up against talk therapy for the treatment of depression. *Scientific American Mind, 18*(5), 80–83.

**Armbruster, B. B.** (2000). Taking notes from lectures. In R. F. Flippo & D. C. Caverly (Eds.), *Handbook of college reading and study strategy research.* Mahwah, NJ: Erlbaum.

Armor, D. A., Massey, C., & Sackett, A. M. (2008). Prescribed optimism: Is it right to be wrong about the future? *Psychological Science, 19,* 329–331.

Armour, S. (2004, May 4). Some moms quit as offices scrap family-friendliness. *USA Today,* pp. 1A–2A.

Armstrong, K., Ravenell, K. L., McMurphy, S., & Putt, M. (2007). Racial/ethnic differences in physician distrust in the United States. *American Journal of Public Health, 97,* 1283–1289.

Arnaut, G. L. Y. (2006). Sensation seeking, risk taking, and fearlessness. In J. C. Thomas & D. L. Segal (Eds.), *Comprehensive handbook of personality and psychopathology* (Vol 1, pp. 322–344). New York: Wiley.

Arndt, J., Goldenberg, J. L., Greenberg, J., Pyszczynski, T., & Solomon, S. (2000). Death can be hazardous to your health: Adaptive and ironic consequences of defenses against the terror of death. In P. R. Duberstein & J. M. Masling (Eds.), *Psychodynamic perspectives on sickness and health.* Washington, DC: American Psychological Association.

Arnkoff, D. B., & Glass, C. R. (1992). Cognitive therapy and psychotherapy. In D. K. Freedheim (Ed.), *History of psycho-therapy: A century of change.* Washington, DC: American Psychological Association.

Arnold, K. D. (1995). *Lives of promise: What becomes of high school valedictorians.* San Francisco: Jossey-Bass.

Arnold, L. M. (2000). Psychocutaneous disorders. In B. J. Sadock & V. A. Sadock (Eds.), *Kaplan and Sadock's comprehensive textbook of psychiatry* (7th ed.). Philadelphia: Lippincott/Williams & Wilkins.

Arnold, R. (1993). *Ecology wars: Environmentalism as if people mattered.* Bellevue, WA: Meril Press.

Aron, A. (1988). The matching hypothesis reconsidered again: Comment on Kalick and Hamilton. *Journal of Personality and Social Psychology, 54,* 441–446.

Aron, A., Fisher, H., & Strong, G. (2006). Romantic love. In A. L. Vangelisti & D. Perlman (Eds.), *The Cambridge handbook of personal relationships.* New York: Cambridge University Press.

Aron, A., Fisher, H., & Strong, G. (2009). Falling in love. In H. T. Reis & S. Sprecher (Eds.), *Encyclopedia of human relationships: Vol. 2* (pp. 591–595). Los Angeles: Sage Reference Publication.

Aron, A., Norman, C. C., Aron, E. N., McKenna, C., & Heyman, R. E. (2000). Couples' shared participation in novel and arousing activities and experienced relationship quality. *Journal of Personality and Social Psychology, 78,* 273–284.

Aron, A., & Westbay, L. (1996). Dimensions of the prototype of love. *Journal of Personality and Social Psychology, 70,* 535–551.

Aronson, J., Jannone, S., McGlone, M., & Johnson-Campbell, T. (2009). The Obama effect: An experimental test. *Journal of Experimental Social Psychology, 45,* 957–960.

Aronson, J., Lustina, M. J., Good, C., Keough, K., Steele, C. M., & Brown, J. (1999). White men can't do math: Necessary and sufficient factors in stereotype threat. *Journal of Experimental Social Psychology, 35*(1), 29–46.

Aronson, J. M., Cohen, G., & Nail, P. R. (1999). *Cooperation in the classroom: The jigsaw method.* New York: Longman.

Arriaga, P., Esteves, F., Carneiro, P., & Monteiro, M. B. (2006a). Violent computer games and their effects on state hostility and physiological arousal. *Aggressive Behavior, 32,* 358–371.

Arriaga, X. B., Reed, J. T., Goodfriend, W., & Agnew, C. R. (2006b). Relationship perceptions and persistence: Do fluctuations in perceived commitment undermine dating relationships? *Journal of Personality and Social Psychology, 91,* 1045–1065.

Arrigo, J. M., & Pezdek, K. (1997). Self-affirmation theory: An update and appraisal. In E. Harmon-Jones & J. S. Mills (Eds.), *Cognitive dissonance: Progress on a pivotal theory in social psychology.* Washington, DC: American Psychological Association.

Asch, S. E. (1955). Opinions and social pressures. *Scientific American, 193*(5), 31–35.

Asch, S. E. (1956). Studies of independence and conformity: A minority of one against a unanimous majority. *Psychological Monographs, 70* (9, Whole No. 416).

Asher, S., & Paquette, J. A. (2003). Loneliness and peer relations in childhood. *Current Directions in Psychological Science, 12*(3), 75–78.

Ashmore, R. D. (1990). Sex, gender, and the individual. In L. A. Pervin (Ed.), *Handbook of personality.* New York: Guilford Press.

Aspinwall, L. G., Richter, L., & Hoffman R. R., III. (2001). Understanding how optimism works: An examination of optimists' adaptive moderation of belief and behavior. In E. C. Chang (Ed.), *Optimism and pessimism: Implications for theory, research, and practice.* Washington, DC: American Psychological Association.

Aspinwall, L. G., & Staudinger, U. M. (2002). *A psychology of human strengths: Fundamental questions and future directions for a positive psychology.* Washington, DC: American Psychological Association.

Aspinwall, L. G., & Staudinger, U. M. (2003). A psychology of human strengths: Some central issues of an emerging field. In L. G. Aspinwall & U. M. Staudinger (Eds.), *A psychology of human strengths: Fundamental questions and future directions for a positive psychology.* Washington, DC: American Psychological Association.

Aspinwall, L. G., & Taylor, S. E. (1993). Effects of social comparison direction, threat, and self-esteem on affect, evaluation, and expected success. *Journal of Personality and Social Psychology, 64,* 708–722.

Associated Press. (2005, October 22). How many survivors does it take to tell a joke? MSNBC. Retrieved from http://www.msnbc.msn.com/id/9783819/ns/us/us_news-katrina_the_long_road_back/

Athenstaedt, U., Haas, E., & Schwab, S. (2004). Gender role self-concept and gender-typed communication behavior in mixed-sex and same-sex dyads. *Sex Roles, 50*(1/2), 37–52.

Atwood, J. D., & Gagnon, J. H. (1987). Masturbatory behavior in college youth. *Journal of Sex Education and Therapy, 13*(2), 35–42.

Aubin, S., & Heiman, J. R. (2004). Sexual dysfunction from a relationship perspective. In J. H. Harvey, A. Wenzel, & S. Sprecher (Eds.), *The handbook of sexuality in close relationships.* Mahwah, NJ: Lawrence Erlbaum.

Aubrey, J. S., & Harrison, K. (2004). The gender-role content of children's favorite television programs and its links to their gender-related perceptions. *Media Psychology, 6,* 11–146.

Aunola, K., Leskinen, E., Lerkkanen, M., & Nurmi, J. (2004). Developmental dynamics of math performance from preschool to grade 2. *Journal of Educational Psychology, 96,* 699–713.

Auster, C. J., & Ohm, S. C. (2000). Masculinity and femininity in contemporary American society: A reevaluation using the Bem Sex-Role Inventory. *Sex Roles, 43,* 499–528.

Aveline, M., Strauss, B., & Stiles, W. B. (2005). Psychotherapy research. In G. O. Gabbard, J. S. Beck, & J. Holmes (Eds.), *Oxford textbook of psychotherapy.* New York: Oxford University Press.

Avery, D., McKay, P., & Wilson, D. (2008). What are the odds? How demographic similarity affects the prevalence of perceived employment discrimination. *Journal of Applied Psychology, 93*(2), 235–249.

Aviles, F., Earleywine, M., Pollock, V., Stratton, J., & Miller, N. (2005). Alcohol's effect on triggered displaced aggression. *Psychology of Addictive Behaviors, 19,* 108–111.

Ax, R. K., Bigelow, B. J., Harowski, K., Meredith, J. M., Nussbaum, D. & Taylor, R. R. (2008). Prescriptive authority for psychologists and the public sector: Serving underserved health care consumers. *Psychological Services, 5*(2), 184–197.

Ayanian, J. Z., & Cleary, P. D. (1999). Perceived risks of heart disease and cancer among cigarette smokers. *Journal of the American Medical Association, 281*(11), 1019–1021.

Ayar, A. A. (2006). Road Rage: Recognizing a psychological disorder. *Journal of Psychiatry & Law, 34,* 123–143.

Ayoola, A. B., Nettleman, M., & Brewer, J. (2007). Reasons for unprotected intercourse in adult women. *Journal of Women's Health, 16,* 302–310.

Ayres, J. (2005). Performance visualization and behavioral disruption: A clarification. *Communication Reports, 18,* 55–63.

Ayres, J., Hopf, T., & Ayres, D. M. (1994). An examination of whether imaging ability enhances the effectiveness of an intervention designed to reduce speech anxiety. *Communication Education, 43*(3), 252–258.

Aziz, S., & Zickar, M. J. (2006). A cluster analysis investigation of workaholism as a syndrome. *Journal of Occupational Health Psychology , 11*(1), 52–62.

Badgett, M. V. L. (2003). Employment and sexual orientation: Disclosure and discrimination in the workplace. In L. D. Garnets & D. C. Kimmel (Eds.), *Psychological perspectives on lesbian, gay, and bisexual experiences* (2nd ed,). New York: Columbia University Press.

Bailey, J. M. (2003). Biological perspectives on sexual orientation. In L. D. Garnets & D. C. Kimmel (Eds.), *Psychological perspectives on lesbian, gay, and bisexual experiences* (2nd ed.). New York: Columbia University Press.

Bailey, J. M., & Dawood, K. (1998). Behavior genetics, sexual orientation, and the family. In C. J. Patterson & A. R. D'Augelli (Eds.), *Lesbian, gay and bisexual identities in families: Psychological perspectives.* New York: Oxford University Press.

Bailey, J. M., Dunne, M. P., & Martin, N. G. (2000). Genetic and environmental influences on sexual orientation and its correlates in an Australian twin sample. *Journal of Personality and Social Psychology, 78*(3), 524–536.

Bailey, J. M., Kim, P. Y., Hills, A., & Linsenmeier, J. A. W. (1997). Butch, femme, or straight acting? Partner preferences of gay men and lesbians. *Journal of Personality and Social Psychology, 73*(5), 960–973.

Bailey, J. M., & Pillard, R. C. (1991). A genetic study of male sexual orientation. *Archives of General Psychiatry, 48,* 1089–1096.

Bailey, J. M., Pillard, R. C., Neale, M. C., & Agyei, Y. (1993). Heritable factors influence sexual orientation in women. *Archives of General Psychiatry, 50,* 217–223.

Baillargeon, R. H., Zoccolillo, M., Keenan, K., Cote, S., Persusse, D., Wu, H., Boivin, M., & Tremblay, R. E. (2007). Gender differences in physical aggression: A prospective population-based survey of children before and after 2 years of age. *Developmental Psychology, 43,* 13–26.

Baird, B. M., Le, K., & Lucas, R. E. (2006). On the nature of intraindividual personality variability: Reliability, validity, and associations with well-being. *Journal of Personality and Social Psychology, 90,* 521–527.

Baker, F., Ainsworth, S. R., Dye, J. T., Crammer, C., Thun, M. J., Hoffmann, D., Repace, J. L., Henningfield, J. E., Slade, J., Pinney, J., Shanks, T., Burns, D. M., Connolly, G. N., & Shopland, D. R. (2000). Health risks associated with cigar smoking. *Journal of the American Medical Association, 284,* 735–740.

Bakker, A. B., Demerouti, E., & Burke, R. (2009). Workaholism and relationship quality: A spillover-crossover perspective. *Journal of Occupational Health Psychology, 14*(1), 23–33.

Bakker, A. B., Schaufeli, W. B., Leiter, M. P., & Taris, T. W. (2008). Work engagement: An emerging concept in occupational health psychology. *Work & Stress, 22*(3), 187–200.

Baldessarini, R. J., Tondo, L., Strombom, I. M., Dominguez, S., Fawcett, J., Licinio, J., Oquendo, M. A., Tollefson, G. D., Valuck, R. J., & Tohen, M. (2007). Ecological studies of antidepressant treatment and suicidal risks. *Harvard Review of Psychiatry, 15,* 133–145.

Balkin, R. S., Perepiczka, M., Whitely, R., & Kimbrough, S. (2009). The relationship of sexual values and emotional awareness to sexual activity in young adulthood. *Adultspan Journal, 8,* 17–28.

Balsam, K. F., Beauchaine, T. P., Mickey, R. M., & Rothblum, E. D. (2005). Mental health of lesbian, gay, bisexual, and heterosexual siblings: Effects of gender, sexual orientation, and family. *Journal of Abnormal Psychology, 114,* 471–476.

Bancroft, J. (2002a). Biological factors in human sexuality. *The Journal of Sex Research, 39*(1), 15–21.

Bancroft, J. (2002b). The medicalization of female sexual dysfunction: The need for caution. *Archives of Sexual Behavior, 31*(5), 451–455.

Bandura, A. (1977). *Social learning theory.* Englewood Cliffs, NJ: Prentice-Hall.

Bandura, A. (1986). *Social foundations of thought and action: A social-cognitive theory.* Englewood Cliffs, NJ: Prentice-Hall.

Bandura, A. (1993). Perceived self-efficacy in cognitive development and functioning. *Educational Psychologist, 28,* 117–148.

Bandura, A. (1997). *Self-efficacy: The exercise of control.* New York: W. H. Freeman.

Bandura, A. (1999a). A sociocognitive analysis of substance abuse: An agentic perspective. *Psychological Science, 10*(3), 214–217.

Bandura, A. (1999b). Social cognitive theory of personality. In L. A. Pervin & O. P. John (Eds.), *Handbook of personality: Theory and research* (2nd ed.). New York: Guilford Press.

Bandura, A. (2000). Social cognitive theory: An agentic perspective. *Annual Review of Psychology, 52,* 1–26.

Bandura, A. (2002). Environmental sustainability by sociocognitive deceleration of population growth. In P. Schmuck & W. P. Schultz (Eds.), *Psychology of sustainable development* (pp. 209–238). Boston: Kluwer Academic Publishers.

Bandura, A. (2004). Health promotion by social cognitive means. *Health Education & Behavior, 31*(2), 143–164.

Bandura, A. (2006). Toward a psychology of human agency. *Perspectives on Psychological Science, 1,* 164–180.

Bandura, A. (2008). An agentic perspective on positive psychology. In S. J. Lopez (Ed.), *Positive psychology: Exploring the best in people* (pp. 167–196). Westport, CT: Praeger.

Bank, B. J., & Hansford, S. L. (2000). Gender and friendship: Why are men's best same-sex friendships less intimate and supportive? *Personal Relationships, 7*(1), 63–78.

Banse, R., & Scherer, K. R. (1996). Acoustic profiles in vocal emotion expression. *Journal of Personality and Social Psychology, 70*(3), 614636.

Banyard, V. L., & Williams, L. M. (1999). Memories for child sexual abuse and mental health functioning: Findings on a sample of women and implications for future research. In L. M. Williams & V. L. Banyard (Eds.), *Trauma & memory.* Thousand Oaks, CA: Sage.

Banzato, C. E. M. (2004). Classification in psychiatry: The move towards ICD-11 and DSM-V. *Current Opinion in Psychiatry, 17,* 497–501.

Barak, A. (2007). Degree and reciprocity of self-disclosure in online forums. *CyberPsychology and Behavior, 10,* 407–417.

Barak, A., & Buchanan, T. (2004). Internet-based psychological testing and assessment. In R. Krause, G. Stricker & J. Zack (Eds.), *Online counseling: A handbook for mental health professionals.* San Diego: Elsevier Academic Press.

Barak, A., & Gluck-Ofri, O. (2007) Degree and reciprocity of self-disclosure in online forums. *CyberPsychology & Behavior, 10,* 407–417.

Barber, B. K. (1994). Cultural, family, and personal contexts of parent-adolescent conflict. *Journal of Marriage and the Family, 56,* 375–386.

Barber, B. L., & Demo, D. H. (2006). The kids are alright (at least, most of them): Links between divorce and dissolution and child well-being. In M. A. Fine & J. H. Harvey (Eds.), *Handbook of divorce and relationship resolution.* Mahwah, NJ: Erlbaum.

Barch, D. M. (2003). Cognition in schizophrenia: Does working memory work? *Current Directions in Psychological Science, 12*(4), 146–150.

Barden, J., Rucker, D., & Petty, R. E. (2005). "Saying one thing and doing another": Examining the impact of event order on hypocrisy judgments of others. *Personality and Social Psychology Bulletin, 31,* 1463–1474.

Bargh, J. A. (1997). The automaticity of everyday life. In R. S. Wyer Jr.(Ed.), *Advances in social cognition* (Vol. 10). Mahwah, NJ: Erlbaum.

Bargh, J. A. (1999). The cognitive monster: The case against the controllability of automatic stereotype effects. In S. Chaiken & Y. Trope (Eds.), *Dual process theories in social psychology.* New York: Guilford.

Bargh, J. A., Chen, M., & Burrows, L. (1996). Automaticity of social behavior: Direct effects of trait construct and stereotype activation on action. *Journal of Personality and Social Psychology, 71,* 230–244.

Bargh, J. A., & McKenna, K. Y. A. (2004). The Internet and social life. *Annual Review of Psychology, 55,* 573–590.

Bargh, J. A., McKenna, K. Y. A., & Fitzsimons, G. M. (2002). Can you see the real me? Activation and expression of the "true self" on the Internet. *Journal of Social Issues, 58*(1), 33–48.

Barker, E. T., Williams, R. L., & Galambos, N. L. (2006). Daily spillover to and from binge eating in first-year university females. *Eating Disorders: The Journal of Treatment and Prevention, 14,* 229–242.

Barlett, D. L., & Steele, J. B. (1979). *Empire: The life, legend and madness of Howard Hughes.* New York: Norton.

Barlow, D. H., Pincus, D. B., Heinrichs, N., & Choate, M. L. (2003). Anxiety disorders. In G. Stricker & T. A. Widiger (Eds.), *Handbook of psychology: Vol. 8. Clinical psychology.* New York: Wiley.

Barnes, M. L., & Buss, D. M. (1985). Sex differences in the interpersonal behavior of married couples. *Journal of Personality and Social Psychology, 48,* 654–661.

Barnes, V. A., Treiber, F., & Davis, H. (2001). The impact of Transcendental Meditation on cardiovascular function at rest and during acute stress in adolescents with high norspeed in old age. *Current Directions in Psychological Science, 6,* 163–169.

Barnett, H. L., Keel, P. K., & Conoscenti, L. M. (2001). Body type preferences in Asian and Caucasian college students. *Sex Roles, 45* (11–12), 867–878.

Barnett, O. W., & LaViolette, A. D. (1993). *It could happen to anyone: Why battered women stay.* Thousand Oaks, CA: Sage.

Barnett, R. C. (2005). Dual-earner couples: Good/bad for her and/or him? In D. F. Halpern & S. E. Murphy (Eds.), *From work-family balance to work-family interaction: Changing the metaphor.* Mahwah, NJ: Erlbaum.

Barnett, R. C., & Hyde, J. S. (2001). Women, men, work, and family: An expansionist theory. *American Psychologist, 56*(10), 781–796.

Barr-Anderson, D., van den Berg, P., Neumark-Sztainer, D., & Story, M. (2008). Characteristics associated with older adolescents who have a television in their bedrooms. *Pediatrics, 121,* 718–724.

Barrett, L. F., & Bliss-Moreau, E. (2009). She's emotional, he's having a bad day: Attributional explanations for emotion stereotypes. *Emotion, 9*(5), 649–658.

Barron, J. M., Struckman-Johnson, C., Quevillon, R., & Banka, S. R. (2008). Heterosexual men's attitudes toward gay men: A hierarchical model including masculinity, openness, and theoretical explanations. *Psychology of Men & Masculinity, 9,* 154–166.

Barry-Walsh, J. (2005). Dissociative identity disorder. *Australian & New Zealand Journal of Psychiatry, 39*(1–2), 109–110.

Barsky, A. J. (1988). The paradox of health. *New England Journal of Medicine, 318,* 414–418.

Barsky, A. J. (2001). Somatosensory amplification and hypochondriasis. In V. Starcevic & D. R. Lipsitt (Eds.), *Hypochondriasis: Modern perspectives on an ancient malady.* New York: Oxford University Press.

Barsky, A. J., Coeytaux, R. R., Sarnie, M. K., & Cleary, P. D. (1993). Hypochondriacal patients' beliefs about good health. *American Journal of Psychiatry, 150,* 1085–1090.

Bartholomew, K. (1990). Avoidance of intimacy: An attachment perspective. *Journal of Social and Personal Relationships, 7,* 47–178.

Bartholomew, K. (2009). Adult attachment, individual differences. In H. T. Reis & S. Sprecher (Eds.), *Encyclopedia of human relationships: Vol. 1* (pp. 34–39). Los Angeles: Sage Reference Publication.

Bartholomew, K., & Horowitz, L. M. (1991). Attachment styles among young adults: A test of a four-category model. *Journal of Personality and Social Psychology, 61,* 226–244.

Bartholow, B. D., & Heinze, A. (2006). Alcohol and aggression without consumption: Alcohol cues, aggressive thoughts, and hostile perception bias. *Psychological Science, 17,* 30–37.

Bartholow, B. D., Bushman, B. J., & Sestir, M. A. (2006). Chronic violent video game exposure and desensitization to violence: Behavioral and event-related brain potential data. *Journal of Experimental Social Psychology, 42,* 532–539.

Bartone, P., Roland, R., Picano, J., & Williams, T. (2008). Psychological hardiness predicts success in U.S. Army Special Forces candidates. *International Journal of Selections and Assessment, 16*(1), 78–81.

Basow, S. A. (1992). *Gender stereotypes and roles* (3rd ed.). Pacific Grove, CA: Brooks/Cole.

Basow, S. A., & Rubenfeld, K. (2003). "Troubles Talk": Effects of gender and gender-typing. *Sex Roles, 48*(3/4), 183–187.

Bassil, K. L., Vakil, C., Sanborn, M., Cole, D. C., Kaur, J. S., & Kerr, K. J. (2007). Cancer health effects of pesticides: Systematic review. *Canadian Family Physician, 53,* 1704–1711.

Basson, R. (2008). Women's sexual desire and arousal disorders. *Primary Psychiatry, 15*(9), 72–81.

Bauer, M., McAuliffe, L., & Nay, R. (2007) Sexuality, health care and the older person: An overview of the literature. *International Journal of Older People Nursing, 2,* 63–68.

Bauermeister, J. A., Carballo-Dieguez, A., Ventuneac, A., & Bolezal, C. (2009). Assessing motivations to engage in intentional condomless anal intercourse in HIV risk contexts ("bareback sex") among men who have sex with men. *AIDS Education and Prevention, 21,* 156–168.

Baum, A., Perry, N. W., Jr., & Tarbell, S. (2004). The development of psychology as a health science. In R. G. Frank, A. Baum, & J. L. Wallender (Eds.), *Handbook of clinical health psychology* (Vol. 3, pp. 9–28). Washington, DC: American Psychological Association.

Baum, A., Revenson, T. A., & Singer, J. E. E. (2001). *Handbook of health psychology.* Mahwah, NJ: Erlbaum.

Baumbusch, J. L. (2004). Unclaimed treasures: Older women's reflections on lifelong singlehood. *Journal of Women & Aging, 16,* 105–121.

Baumeister, R. F. (1984). Choking under pressure: Self-consciousness and paradoxical effects of incentives on skillful performance. *Journal of Personality and Social Psychology, 46,* 610–620.

Baumeister, R. F. (1989). The optimal margin of illusion. *Journal of Social and Clinical Psychology, 8,* 176–189.

Baumeister, R. F. (1995). Disputing the effects of championship pressures and home audiences. *Journal of Personality and Social Psychology, 68,* 644–648.

Baumeister, R. F. (1997). Esteem threat, self-regulatory breakdown, and emotional distress as factors in self-defeating behavior. *Review of General Psychology, 1,* 145–174.

Baumeister, R. F. (1998). The self. In D. T. Gilbert, S. T. Fiske, & G. Lindzey (Eds.), *The handbook of social psychology.* Boston: Mcgraw-Hill.

Baumeister, R. F. (1999). The nature and structure of the self: An overview. In R. F. Baumeister (Ed.), *The self in social psychology.* Ann Arbor, MI: Edwards Bros.

Baumeister, R. F., & Alquist, J. L. (2009). Is there a downside to good self-control? *Self and Identity, 8*(2–3), 115–130.

Baumeister, R. F., & Bratslavsky, E. (1999). Passion, intimacy, and time: Passionate love as a function of change in intimacy. *Personality and Social Psychology Review, 3*(1), 49–67.

Baumeister, R. F., Bratslavsky, E., Finkenauer, C., & Vohs, K. D. (2001). Bad is stronger than good. *Review of General Psychology, 5*(4), 323–370.

Baumeister, R. F., Bratslavsky, E., Muraven, M., & Tice, D. M. (1998). Ego depletion: Is the active self a limited resource? *Journal of Personality and Social Psychology, 74*(5), 1252–1265.

Baumeister, R. F., Bushman, B. J., & Campbell, W. K. (2000). Self-esteem, narcissism, and aggression: Does violence result from low self-esteem or from threatened egotism? *Current Directions in Psychological Science, 9*(1), 26–29.

Baumeister, R. F., Campbell, J. D., Krueger, J. I., & Vohs, K. D. (2003). Does high self-esteem cause better performance, interpersonal success, happiness, or healthier lifestyles? *Psychological Science in the Public Interest, 4*(1), 1–44.

Baumeister, R. F., Gailliot, M., DeWall, M., & Oaten, M. (2006). Self-regulation and personality: How interventions increase regulatory success, and how depletion moderates the effects of traits on behavior. *Journal of Personality, 74,* 1773–1801.

Baumeister, R. F., & Leary, M. R. (1995). The need to belong: Desire for interpersonal attachments as a fundamental human motivation. *Psychological Bulletin, 117*(3), 497–529.

Baumeister, R. F., Muraven, M., & Tice, D. M. (2000). Ego depletion: A resource model of volition, self regulation, and controlled processing. *Social Cognition, 18*(2), 130–150.

Baumeister, R. F., & Scher, S. J. (1988). Self-defeating behavior patterns among normal individuals: Review and analysis of common self-destructive tendencies. *Psychological Bulletin, 104*(1), 3–22.

Baumeister, R. F., Smart, L., & Boden, J. M. (1996). Relation of threatened egotism to violence and aggression: The dark side of high self-esteem. *Psychological Review, 103,* 5–33.

Baumeister, R. F., & Sommer, K. L. (1997). What do men want? Gender differences and two spheres of belongingness: Comment on Cross and Madson (1997). *Psychological Bulletin, 122*(1), 38–44.

Baumeister, R. F., & Steinhilber, A. (1984). Paradoxical effects of supportive audiences on performance under pressure: The home field disadvantage in sports championships. *Journal of Personality and Social Psychology, 47,* 85–93.

Baumeister, R. F., & Twenge, J. M. (2003). The social self. In T. Millon & M. J. Lerner (Eds.) *Handbook of psychology: Vol. 5. Personality and social psychology.* New York: Wiley.

Baumeister, R. F., & Vohs, K. D. (2003). Self regulation and the executive function of the self. In M.R. Leary & J. P. Tangney (Eds.), *Handbook of Self and Identity.* New York: Guilford.

Baumeister, R. F., & Vohs, K. D. (2007). Self-regulation, ego depletion, and motivation. *Social and Personality Psychology Compass, 1*(1), 115–128.

Baumrind, D. (1964). Some thoughts on the ethics of reading Milgram's "Behavioral study of obedience." *American Psychologist, 19,* 421–423.

Baumrind, D. (1967). Child care practices anteceding three patterns of preschool behavior. *Genetic Psychology Monographs, 75,* 43–88.

Baumrind, D. (1971). Current patterns of parental authority. *Developmental Psychology Monographs, 4* (1, Part 2).

Baumrind, D. (1978). Parental disciplinary patterns and social competence in children. *Youth and Society, 9,* 239–276.

Bavelas, J. B., Coates, L., & Johnson, T. (2002). Listener responses as a collaborative process: The role of gaze. *Journal of Communication, 52*(3), 566–580.

Baxter, L. A. (1988). A dialectical perspective on communication strategies in relationship development. In S. Duck (Ed.), *Handbook of personal relationships.* New York: Wiley.

**Bay-Cheng, L. Y., Zucker, A. N., Stewart, A. J., & Pomerleau, C. S.** (2002). Linking femininity, weight concern, and mental health among Latina, black, and white women. *Psychology of Women Quarterly, 26*(1), 36–45.

**Bay-Hinitz, A. K., Peterson, R. F., & Quilitch, H. R.** (1994). Cooperative games: A way to modify aggressive and cooperative behaviors in young children. *Journal of Applied Behavior Analysis, 27,* 435–446.

**Beall, A. E., Eagly, A. H., & Sternberg, R. J.** (2004). Introduction. In A. H. Eagly, A. E. Beall, & R. J. Sternberg (Eds.), *The psychology of gender.* New York: Guilford Press.

**Beaman, R., Wheldall, K., & Kemp, C.** (2006). Differential teacher attention to boys and girls in the classroom. *Educational Review, 58,* 339–366.

**Beaudry, M., Bousvert, J., Simard, M., Parent, C., & Blais, M.** (2004). Communication: A key component to meeting the challenges of stepfamilies. *Journal of Divorce & Remarriage, 42,* 85–104.

**Beck, A. T.** (1976). *Cognitive therapy and the emotional disorders.* New York: International Universities Press.

**Beck, A. T.** (1987). Cognitive therapy. In J. K. Zeig (Ed.), *The evolution of psychotherapy.* New York: Brunner/Mazel.

**Beck, A. T.** (1991). Cognitive therapy: A 30–year retrospective. *American Psychologist, 46,* 368–375.

**Beck, A. T.** (1997). Cognitive therapy: Reflections. In J. K. Zeig (Ed.), *The evolution of psychotherapy: The third conference* . New York: Brunner/Mazel.

**Beck, A. T.** (2008). The evolution of the cognitive model of depression and its neurobiological correlates. *American Journal of Psychiatry, 165,* 969–977.

**Becker, A., & Fay, K.** (2006). Sociocultural issues and eating disorders. In S. Wonderlich, J. Mitchell, M. de Zwaan, & H. Steiger (Eds.), *Annual review of eating disorders.* Oxon, England: Radcliffe.

**Becker, E.** (1997). *The denial of death.* New York: Free Press.

**Beckman, H., Regier, N., & Young, J.** (2007). Effect of workplace laughter groups on personal efficacy beliefs. *The Journal of Primary Prevention, 28*(2), 167–182.

**Beddoe, R., Costanza, R., Farley, J. U., Garza, E., Kent, J., Kubiszewski, I., Martinez, L., McCowen, T., Murphy, K. I., Myers, N., Ogden, Z., Stapleton, K., & Woodward, J.** (2009). Overcoming systematic roadblocks to sustainability: The evolutionary redesign of worldviews, institutions, and technologies. *Proceedings from the National Academy of Science (PNAS),* 106, 2483–2489.

**Behar, R.** (1991, May 6). The thriving cult of greed and power. *Time,* pp. 50–77.

**Beidel, D. C., & Stipelman, B.** (2007). Anxiety disorders. In M. Hersen, S. M. Turner, & D. C. Beidel (Eds.), *Adult psychopathology and diagnosis.* New York: Wiley.

**Beilock, S. L., Kulp, C. A., Holt, L. E., & Carr, T. H.** (2004). More on the fragility of performance: Choking under pressure in mathematical problem solving. *Journal of Experimental Psychology, 133,* 584–600.

**Beisecker, A. E.** (1990). Patient power in doctor-patient communication: What do we know? *Health Communication, 2,* 105–122.

**Bekelman, J. E., Li, Y., & Gross, C. P.** (2003). Scope and impact of financial conflicts of interests in biomedical research. *Journal of the American Medical Association, 289,* 454–465.

**Belger, A., & Barch, D. M.** (2009). Cognitive neuroscience and neuroimaging in schizophrenia. In D. S. Charney & E. J. Nestler (Eds.), *Neurobiology of mental illness* (pp. 303–320). New York: Oxford University Press.

**Belger, A., & Dichter, G.** (2006). Structural and functional neuroanatomy. In J. A. Liberman, T. S. Stroup, & D. O. Perkins (Eds.), *Textbook of schizophrenia.* Washington, DC: American Psychiatric Publishing.

**Bell, A. P., & Weinberg, M. S.** (1978). *Homosexualities: A study of diversity among men and women.* New York: Simon & Schuster.

**Bell, A. P., Weinberg, M. S., & Hammersmith, K. S.** (1981). *Sexual preference—Its development in men and women.* Bloomington: Indiana University Press.

**Bell, P. A., Greene, T. C., Fisher, J. D., & Baum, A.** (2001). *Environmental psychology* (5th ed.). Fort Worth: Harcourt College Publishers.

**Bell, R. A.** (1991). Gender, friendship network density, and loneliness. *Journal of Social Behavior and Personality, 6,* 45–56.

**Beller, M., & Gafni, N.** (1996). The 1991 international assessment of educational progress in mathematics and sciences: The gender differences perspective. *Journal of Educational Psychology, 88,* 365–377.

**Belmore, S. M.** (1987). Determinants of attention during impression formation. *Journal of Experimental Psychology: Learning, Memory, and Cognition, 13,* 480–489.

**Belsky, J.** (2006). Early child care and early child development: Major findings of the NICHD study of Early Child Care. *European Journal of Developmental Psychology, 3,* 95–110.

**Belsky, J.** (2009). Parenthood, transition to. In H. T. Reis & S. Sprecher (Eds.), *Encyclopedia of human relationships: Vol. 3* (pp. 1204–1207). Los Angeles: Sage Reference Publication.

**Belsky, J., & Kelly, J.** (1994). *The transition to parenthood.* New York: Dell.

**Bem, D. J.** (2000). Exotic becomes erotic: Interpreting the biological correlates of sexual orientation. *Archives of Sexual Behavior, 29*(6), 531–548.

**Bem, S. L.** (1975, September). Androgyny vs. the tight little lives of fluffy women and chesty men. *Psychology Today,* pp. 58–62.

**Bem, S. L.** (1983). Gender schema theory and its implications for child development: Raising gender-aschematic children in a gender-schematic society. *Signs, 8,* 598–616.

**Bem, S. L.** (1993). The lenses of gender: *Transforming the debate on sexual inequality.* New Haven, CT: Yale University Press.

**Benbow, C. P.** (1988). Sex differences in mathematical reasoning ability in intellectually talented preadolescents: Their nature, effects, and possible causes. *Behavioral and Brain Sciences, 11,* 169–232.

**Bender, D. S., Skodol, A. E., Dyck, I. R., Markowitz, J. C., Shea, M. T., Yen, S., et al.** (2007). Ethnicity and mental health treatment utilization by patients with personality disorders. *Journal of Consulting and Clinical Psychology, 75,* 992–999.

**Bender, R., Jockel, K. H., Trautner, C., Spraul, M., & Berger, M.** (1999). Effect of age on excess mortality in obesity. *Journal of the American Medical Association, 281,* 1498–1504.

**Benedict, R.** (1934). *Patterns of culture.* Boston: Houghton Mifflin.

**Benet-Martínez, V., & Oishi, S.** (2008). Culture and personality. In O. P. John, R. W. Robins, & L. A. Pervin (Eds.), *Handbook of personality: Theory and research* (pp. 542–567). New York: Guilford.

**Ben-Ezra, M.** (2004). Trauma in antiquity: 4000 year old post-traumatic reactions? *Stress and Health, 20,* 121–125.

**Bennett, L.** (2008, November 14). Are human beings hard-wired to ignore the threat of catastrophic climate change? *Greater Good, 5*(2), 40–43.

**Benoît, M., & Norton, M. I.** (2003). Perceptions of a fluid consensus: Uniqueness bias, false consensus, false polarization, and pluralistic ignorance in a water conservation crisis. *Personality and Social Psychology Bulletin, 29,* 559–567.

**Benoit, W. L., & Benoit, P. J.** (2008). *Persuasive messages: The process of influence.* Malden, MA: Blackwell Publishing.

**Ben-Porath, Y. S.** (2003). Assessing personality and psychopathology with self-report inventories. In J. R. Graham & J. A. Naglieri (Eds.), *Handbook of psychology: Vol. 10. Assessment psychology.* New York: Wiley.

**Benson, H.** (1975). *The relaxation response* (1st ed.). New York: Morrow.

**Benson, H., & Klipper, M. Z.** (1988). *The relaxation response* (2nd ed.). New York: Avon.

**Berdahl, J. L.** (2007). The sexual harassment of uppity women. *Journal of Applied Psychology, 92,* 425–437.

**Berdahl, J. L., & Moore, C.** (2006). Workplace harassment: Double jeopardy for minority women. *Journal of Applied Psychology, 91,* 426–436.

**Berk, M.** (2007). Should we be targeting exercise as a routine mental health intervention? *Acta Neuropsychiatrica, 19,* 217–218.

**Berkley, R. A., & Watt, A. H.** (2006). Impact of same-sex harassment and gender-role stereotypes on Title VII protection for gay, lesbian, and bisexual employees. *Employee Responsibilities and Rights Journal, 18*(1), 3–19.

**Berkowitz, L.** (1989). Frustration-aggression hypothesis: Examination and reformulation. *Psychological Bulletin, 106,* 59–73.

**Berkowitz, R. I.** (2003). Behavior therapies. In R. E. Hales & S. C. Yudofsky (Eds.), *Textbook of clinical psychiatry.* Washington, DC: American Psychiatric Publishing.

**Berliner, K., Jacob, D., & Schwartzberg, N.** (1999). The single adult and the family life cycle. In B. Carter & M. McGoldrick (Eds.), *The expanded family life cycle: Individual, family, and social perspectives* (3rd ed.). Boston: Allyn & Bacon.

**Berliner, L., & Briere, J.** (1999). Trauma, memory, and clinical practice. In L. M. Williams & V. L. Banyard (Eds.), *Trauma & memory.* Thousand Oaks, CA: Sage.

**Berman, M. G., Jonides, J., & Kaplan, S.** (2008). The cognitive benefits of interacting with nature. *Psychological Science, 19,* 1207–1212.

**Berman, R. M., Sporn, J., Charney, D. S., & Mathew, S. J.** (2009). Principles of the pharmacotherapy of depression. In D. S. Charney & E. J. Nestler (Eds.), *Neurobiology of mental illness* (pp. 491–515). New York: Guilford.

**Bernache-Assollant, I., Lacassagne, M.-F., & Braddock, J. H., II** (2007). Basking in reflected glory and blasting: Differences in identity-management strategies between two groups of highly identified soccer fans. *Journal of Language and Social Psychology, 26*(4), 381–388.

**Bernard, L. C., & Krupat, E.** (1994). *Health psychology: Biopsychosocial factors in health and illness.* Fort Worth, TX: Harcourt Brace.

**Berne, P. H., & Savary, L. M.** (1993). *Building self-esteem in children.* New York: Continuum.

**Berry, D., Sheehan, R., Heschel, R., Knafl, K., Melkus, G., & Grey, M.** (2004). Family-based interventions for childhood obesity: A review. *Journal of Family Nursing, 10,* 429–449.

**Berry, D. S., Pennebaker, J. W., Mueller, J. S., & Hiller, W. S.** (1997). Linguistic bases of social perception. *Personality and Social Psychology Bulletin, 23*(5), 526–537.

**Berry, J. W., & Ataca, B.** (2000). Cultural factors. In G. Fink (Ed.), *Encyclopedia of stress* (Vol. 1). San Diego: Academic Press.

**Berscheid, E., Dion, K., Walster, E., & Walster, G.** (1971). Physical attractiveness and dating choice: A test of the matching hypothesis. *Journal of Personality and Social Psychology, 7,* 173–189.

**Berscheid, E., & Reis, H. T.** (1998). Attraction and close relationships. In D. T. Gilbert, S. T. Fiske, & G. Lindzey (Eds.), *The handbook of social psychology* (Vol. 2). Boston: McGraw-Hill.

**Berscheid, E., Snyder, M., & Omoto, A. M.** (1989). The relationship closeness inventory: Assessing the closeness of interpersonal relationships. *Journal of Personality and Social Psychology, 57,* 792–807.

**Berscheid, E., & Walster, E.** (1978). *Interpersonal attraction.* Reading, MA: Addison-Wesley.

**Bertakis, K. D., Azari, R., Helms, J. L., Callahan, E. J., & Robbins, J. A.** (2000). Gender differences in the utilization of health care services. *Journal of Family Practice, 49*(2), 147–152.

**Berthoud, H., & Morrison, C.** (2008). The brain, appetite, and obesity. *Annual Review of Psychology, 59,* 55–92.

**Berto, R.** (2005). Exposure to restorative environments helps restore attentional capacity. *Journal of Environmental Psychology, 25,* 249–259.

**Berzon, B.** (2004). *Permanent partners: Building gay and lesbian relationships that last.* New York: The Penguin Group.

**Best, D. L., & Thomas, J. J.** (2004). Cultural diversity and cross-cultural perspectives. In A. H. Eagly, A. E. Beall, & R. J. Sternberg (Eds.), *The psychology of gender.* New York: Guilford Press.

**Betz, N. E.** (1993). Women's career development. In F. L. Denmark & M. A. Paludi (Eds.), *Psychology of women: A handbook of issues and theories.* Westport, CT: Greenwood Press.

**Betz, N. E.** (2005). Women's career development. In S. D. Brown & R. W. Lent (Eds.), *Career development and counseling: Putting theory and research to work.* New York: Wiley.

**Betz, N. E.** (2006). Women's career development. In J. Worell & C. D. Goodheart (Eds.), *Handbook of girls' and women's psychological health.* New York: Oxford University Press.

**Betz, N. E., & Klein, K. L.** (1996). Relationships among measures of career self-efficacy, generalized self-efficacy, and global self-esteem. *Journal of Career Assessment, 4*(3), 285–298.

**Beumont, P. J. V.** (2002). Clinical presentation of anorexia nervosa and bulimia nervosa. In C. G. Fairburn & K. D. Brownell (Eds.), *Eating disorders and obesity: A comprehensive handbook.* New York: Guilford.

**Beusterien, K. M., Davis, E. A., Flood, R., Howard, K., & Jordan, J.** (2008). HIV patient insight on adhering to medication: A qualitative analysis. *AIDS Care, 20,* 251–259.

**Beutler, L. E.** (2002). The dodo bird is extinct. *Clinical Psychology: Science & Practice, 9*(1), 30–34.

**Beutler, L. E., Bongar, B., & Shurkin, J. N.** (2001). *A consumers guide to psychotherapy.* New York: Oxford University Press.

**Beutler, L. E., & Harwood, T. M.** (2002). What is and can be attributed to the therapeutic relationship? *Journal of Contemporary Psychotherapy, 32*(1), 25–33.

**Bevans, K., Cerbone, A., & Overstreet, S.** (2008). Relations between recurrent trauma exposure and recent life stress and salivary cortisol among children. *Development and Psychopathology, 20,* 257–272.

**Bhattachary, S., & Powell, J. H.** (2001). Recreational use of 3,4-methylenedioxymethamphetamine (MDMA) or "ecstasy": Evidence for cognitive impairment. *Psychological Medicine, 31*(4), 647–658.

**Bianchi, S., & Casper, L. M.** (2000). American families. *Population Bulletin* (Vol. 55, Chap. 4). Washington, DC: Population Reference Bureau.

**Bianchi, S., Milkie, M. A., Sayer, L. C., & Robinson, J. P.** (2000). Is anyone doing the housework? Trends in the gender division of household labor. *Social Forces, 79*(1), 191–228.

**Bianchi, S., Subaiya, L., & Kahn, J. R.** (1999). The gender gap in the economic well-being of nonresident fathers and custodial mothers. *Demography, 36,* 195–203.

**Biernat, M., & Billings, L. S.** (2001). Standards, expectancies and social comparison. In A. Tesser & N. Schwarz (Eds.), *Blackwell handbook of social psychology: Intraindividual processes.* Malden, MA: Blackwell.

**Biernat, M., & Kobrynowicz, D.** (1997). Gender-and race-based standards of competence: Lower minimum standards but higher ability standards for devalued groups. *Journal of Personality and Social Psychology, 72*(3), 544–557.

**Bin Kassim, M. A., Hanafi, S. R., & Hancock, D. R.** (2008). Test anxiety and its consequences on academic performance among university students. *Advances in Psychology Research, 53,* 75–95.

**Biron, C., Brun, J., Ivers, H., & Cooper, C. L.** (2006). At work but ill: Psychosocial work environment and well-being determinants of presenteeism propensity. *Journal of Public Mental Health, 5,* 26–37.

**Bishop, S. R.** (2002). What do we really know about mindfulness-based stress reduction? *Psychosomatic Medicine, 64*(1), 71–83.

**Bisson, M. A., & Levine, T. R.** (2009). Negotiating a friend with benefits relationship. *Archives of Sexual Behavior, 38,* 66–73.

**Björntorp, P.** (2002). Definition and classification of obesity. In C. G. Fairburn & K. D. Brownell (Eds.), *Eating disorders and obesity: A comprehensive handbook.* New York: Guilford.

**Black, D. W., & Andreasen, N. C.** (1994). Schizophrenia, schizophreniform disorder, and delusional (paranoid) disorder. In R. E. Hales, S. C. Yudofsky, & J. A. Talbott (Eds.), *The American Psychiatric Press textbook of psychiatry* (2nd ed.). Washington, DC: American Psychiatric Press.

**Black, D. W., & Andreasen, N. C.** (1999). Schizophrenia, schizophreniform disorder, and delusional (paranoid) disorders. In R. E. Hales, S. C. Yudofsky, & J. A. Talbott (Eds.), *American Psychiatric Press textbook of psychiatry* (3rd ed.). Washington, DC: American Psychiatric Press.

**Blacker, D., & Tsuang, M. T.** (1999). Classification and DSM-IV. In A. M. Nicholi (Ed.), *The Harvard guide to psychiatry*. Cambridge, MA: Harvard University Press.

**Blacker, L.** (1999). The launching phase of the life cycle. In B. Carter & M. McGoldrick (Eds.), *The expanded family life cycle: Individual, family, and social perspectives* (3rd ed.). Boston: Allyn & Bacon.

**Blackmore, E. R., Stansfield, S. A., Weller, L., Munce, S., Zagorski, B. M., & Stewart, D. E.** (2007). Major depressive episodes and work stress: Results from a national population survey. *American Journal of Public Health, 97,* 2088–2093.

**Blaine, B., & Crocker, J.** (1993). Self-esteem and self-serving biases in reaction to positive and negative events: An integrative review. In R. F. Baumeister (Ed.), *Self-esteem: The puzzle of low self-regard.* New York : Plenum.

**Blair, S. N., Cheng, Y., & Holder, J. S.** (2001). Is physical activity or physical fitness more important in defining health benefits? *Medicine and Science in Sports and Exercise, 33,* S379–S399.

**Blair, S. N., Kohl, H. W., Paffenbarger, R. S., Clark, D. G., Cooper, K. H., & Gibbons, L. W.** (1989). Physical fitness and all-cause mortality: A prospective study of healthy men and women. *Journal of the American Medical Association, 262,* 2395–2401.

**Blair-Loy, M., & DeHart, G.** (2003). Family and careeer trajectories among African American female attorneys. *Journal of Family Issues, 24,* 908–933.

**Blais, J. J., Craig, W. M., Pepler, D., & Connolly, J.** (2008). Adolescents online: The importance of Internet activity choices to salient relationships. *Journal of Youth and Adolescence, 37,* 522–536.

**Blaisure, K. R., & Geasler, M. J.** (2006). Educational interventions for separating and divorcing parents and their children. In M. A. Fine & J. H. Harvey (Eds.), *Handbook of divorce and relationship resolution.* Mahwah, NJ: Erlbaum.

**Blakemore, J. E. O.** (2003). Children's beliefs about violating gender norms: Boys shouldn't look like girls, and girls shouldn't act like boys. *Sex Roles, 48*(9/10), 411–419.

**Blanchard, E. B., & Keefer, L.** (2003). Irritable bowel syndrome. In A. M. Nezu, C. M. Nezu, & P. A. Geller (Eds.), *Handbook of psychology: Vol. 9. Health psychology.* New York: Wiley.

**Blankenship, K. L., & Wegener, D. T.** (2008). Opening the mind to close it: Considering a message in light of important values increases message processing and later resistance to change. *Journal of Personality and Social Psychology, 94*(2), 196–213.

**Blanton, H., Buunk, B. P., Gibbons, F. X., & Kuyper, H.** (1999). When better-than-others compare upward: Choice of comparison and comparative evaluation as independent predictors of academic performance. *Journal of Personality and Social Psychology, 76,* 420–430.

**Blashfield, R. K., Keeley, J. W., & Burgess, D. R.** (2009). Classification. In P. H. Blaney & T. Millon (Eds.), *Oxford textbook of psychopathology* (pp. 35–57). New York: Oxford University Press.

**Blashki, G., McMichael, T., & Karoly, D. J.** (2007). Climate change and primary health care. *Australian Family Physician, 36,* 986–989.

**Blass, T.** (1999). The Milgram paradigm after 35 years: Some things we now know about obedience to authority. *Journal of Applied Social Psychology, 29*(5), 955–978.

**Blass, T.** (2004). *The man who shocked the world: The life and legacy of Stanley Milgram.* New York: Basic Books.

**Blass, T.** (Ed.). (2000). *Obedience to authority: Current perspectives on the Milgram paradigm.* Mahwah, NJ: Erlbaum.

**Blazer, D. G.** (2000). Mood disorders: Epidemiology. In B. J. Sadock & V. A. Sadock (Eds.), *Kaplan and Sadock's Comprehensive textbook of psychiatry* (7th ed., Vol. 1). Philadelphia: Lippincott/Williams & Wilkins.

**Bleakley, A., Hennessy, M., Fishbein, M, & Jordan, A.** (2008). It works both ways: The relationship between exposure to sexual content in the media and adolescent sexual behavior. *Media Psychology, 11,* 443–461.

**Bleier, R.** (1984). *Science and gender: A critique of biology and its theories on women.* New York: Pergamon Press.

**Block, J., & Robbins, R. W.** (1993). A longitudinal study of consistency and change in self-esteem from early adolescence to early adulthood. *Child Development, 64,* 909–923.

**Block, J. H.** (1973). Conceptions of sex role: Some cross-cultural and longitudinal perspectives. *American Psychologist, 28,* 512–526.

**Bloom, P. N., McBride, C. M., & Pollack, K. I.** (2006). Recruiting teen smokers in shopping malls to a smoking cessation program using the foot-in-the-door technique. *Journal of Applied Social Psychology, 36,* 1129–1134.

**Bloor, M. (2005).** Observations of shipboard illness behavior: Work discipline and the sick role in a residential work setting. *Qualitative Health Research, 15*(6), 766–777.

**Blumenthal, J.** (2008). Depression and coronary heart disease: Association and implications for treatment. *Cleveland Clinic Journal of Medicine, 75,* S48–53.

**Blumstein, P., & Schwartz, P.** (1983). *American couples: Money, work, sex.* New York: Morrow.

**Blustein, D. L.** (2008). The role of work in psychological health and well-being: A conceptual, historical, and public policy perspective. *American Psychologist, 63*(4), 228–240.

**Boase, J., & Wellman, B.** (2006). Personal relationships: On and off the internet. In A. L. Vangelisti & D. Perlman (Eds.), *The Cambridge handbook of personal relationships.* New York: Cambridge University Press.

**Bobek, B. L., & Robbins, S. B.** (2005). Counseling for career transition: Career pathing, job loss, and reentry. In S. D. Brown & R. W. Lent (Eds.), *Career development and counseling: Putting theory and research to work.* New York: Wiley.

**Bock, P. K.** (2000). Cultural and personality revisited. *American Behavioral Scientist, 44,* 32–40.

**Bodenhausen, G. V.** (1988). Stereotypic biases in social decision making and memory: Testing process models of stereotype use. *Journal of Personality and Social Psychology, 55,* 726–737.

**Bodenhausen, G. V., & Macrae, C. N.** (1994). Coherence versus ambivalence in cognitive representations of persons. In R. S. Wyer (Ed.), *Advances in social cognition: Associated systems theory: A systematic approach to cognitive representations of persons* (Vol. 7, pp. 149–156). Hillsdale, NJ: Erlbaum.

**Bodenhausen. G. V., Macrae, C. N., & Hugenberg, K.** (2003). Social cognition. In T. Millon, & M. J. Lerner (Eds.) *Handbook of psychology: Vol. 5. Personality and social psychology.* New York: Wiley.

**Bodenheimer, T.** (2000). Uneasy alliance: Clinical investigators and the pharmaceutical industry. *New England Journal of Medicine, 342,*1539–1544.

**Bodenmann, G, Ledermann, T., & Bradbury, T. N.** (2007). Stress, sex, and satisfaction in marriage. *Personal Relationships, 14,* 551–569.

**Boelen, P. A., van den Bout, J., & van den Hout, M. A.** (2003). The role of negative interpretations of grief reactions in emotional problems after bereavement. *Journal of Behavior Therapy and Experimental Psychiatry, 34,* 225–238.

**Boen, F., Van Beselaere, N., & Feys, J.** (2002). Behavioral consequences of fluctuating group success; An Internet study of soccer-team fans. *Journal of Social Psychology, 142,* 769–781.

**Boerner, K., Wortman, C. B., & Bonanno, G. A.** (2005). Resilient or at risk? A 4-year study of older adults who initially showed high or low distress following conjugal loss. *Journal of Gerontology, 60B,* 67–73.

**Bohnert, A. M., Aikins, J. W., & Edidin, J.** (2007). The role of organized activities in facilitating social adaption across the transition to college. *Journal of Adolescent Research, 22,* 189–208.

**Boles, D. B.** (2005). A large-sample study of sex differences in functional cerebral lateralization. *Journal of Clinical and Experimental Neuropsychology, 27,* 759–768.

**Bolger, N.** (1990). Coping as a personality process: A prospective study. *Journal of Personality and Social Psychology, 59,* 525–537.

**Bolger, N., & Amarel, D.** (2007). Effects of social support visibility on adjustment to stress: Experimental evidence. *Journal of Personality and Social Psychology , 92,* 458–475.

**Bolger, N., Zuckerman, A., & Kessler, R. C.** (2000). Invisible support and adjustment to stress. *Journal of Personality and Social Psychology, 79,* 953–961.

**Bolino, M. C., & Turnley, W. H.** (2005). The personal costs of citizenship behavior: The relationship between individual initiative and role overload, job stress, and work-family conflict. *Journal of Applied Psychology, 90*(4), 740–748.

**Bolles, R. N.** (2007). *The 2007 what color is your parachute? A practical manual for job-hunters and career-changers.* Berkeley, CA: Ten Speed Press.

**Bonanno, G. A.** (1998). The concept of "working through" loss: A critical evaluation of the cultural, historical, and empirical evidence. In A. Maercker, M. Schuetzwohl, & Z. Solomon (Eds.), *Posttraumatic stress disorder: Vulnerability and resilience in the life-span.* Göttingen, Germany: Hogrefe and Huber.

**Bonanno, G. A.** (2004). Loss, trauma, and human resilience: Have we underestimated the human capacity to thrive after extremely aversive events? *American Psychologist, 59*(1), 20–28.

**Bonanno, G. A.** (2009). *The other side of sadness: What the new science of bereavement tells us about life after loss.* New York: Basic Books.

**Bonanno, G. A., Galea, S., Bucciarelli, A., & Vlahov, D.** (2006). Psychological resilience after disaster: New York City in the aftermath of the September 11th terrorist attack. *Psychological Science, 17*(3), 181–186.

**Bonanno, G. A., Wortman, C. B., Lehman, D. R., Tweed, R. G., Haring, M., Sonnega, J., Carr, D., & Nesse, R. M.** (2002). Resilience to loss and chronic grief: A prospective study from preloss to 18-months postloss. *Journal of Personality and Social Psychology, 83*(5), 1150–1164.

**Bond, C. F., Jr., & DePaulo, B. M.** (2006). Accuracy of deception judgments. *Personality and Social Psychology Review, 10*(3), 214–234.

**Bond, C. F., Jr., & DePaulo, B. M.** (2008). Individual differences in judging deception: Accuracy and bias. *Psychological Bulletin, 134,* 477–492.

**Bond, J. T., Galinsky, E., Kim, S. S., & Brownfield, E.** (2005). *The 2005 national study of employers.* New York: Families and Work Institute.

**Bond, J. T., Thompson, C., Galinsky, E., & Prottas, D.** (2003). *The 2002 national study of the changing workforce.* New York: Families and Work Institute.

**Bonebright, C. A., Clay, D. L., & Ankenmann, R. D.** (2000). The relationship of workaholism with work-life conflict, life satisfaction, and purpose in life. *Journal of Counseling Psychology, 47,* 469–477.

**Boneva, B., Kraut, R., & Frohlich, D.** (2001). Using e-mail for personal relationships: The difference gender makes. *American Behavioral Scientist, 45,* 530–549.

**Bono, G., Emmons, R. A., & McCullough, M. E.** (2004). Gratitude in practice and the practice of gratitude. In P. A. Linley & S. Joseph (Eds.), *Positive psychology in practice* (pp. 464–484). Hoboken, NJ: Wiley.

Bookwala, J. (2009). Couples in middle age. In H. T. Reis & S. Sprecher (Eds.), *Encyclopedia of human relationships: Vol. 2* (pp. 340–343). Los Angeles: Sage Reference Publication.

Booth, A., & Amato, P. R. (2001). Parental predivorce relations and offspring postdivorce well-being. *Journal of Marriage and Family, 63,* 197–212.

Bordnick, P. S., Elkins, R. L., Orr, T. E., Walters, P., & Thyer, B. A. (2004). Evaluating the relative effectiveness of three aversion therapies designed to reduce craving among cocaine abusers. *Behavioral Interventions, 19*(1), 1–24.

Borman, W. C., Klimoski, R. J., & Ilgen, D. R. (2003). Stability and change in industrial and organizational psychology. In W. C. Borman, D. R. Ilgen, & R. J. Klimoski (Eds.), *Handbook of psychology: Vol. 12. Industrial and organizational psychology.* New York: Wiley.

Bornstein, R. F. (2003). Psychodynamic models of personality. In T. Millon & M. J. Lerner (Eds.), *Handbook of psychology, Vol. 5: Personality and social psychology.* New York: Wiley.

Borys, S., & Perlman, D. (1985). Gender differences in loneliness. *Personality and Social Psychology Bulletin, 11,* 63–74.

Bosson, J. K., Vandello, J. A., Burnaford, R. M., Weaver, J. R., & Wasti, S. A. (2009). Precarious manhood and displays of physical aggression. *Personality and Social Psychology Bulletin, 35,* 623–634.

Boudreaux, E., Carmack, C. L., Scarinci, I. C., & Brantley, P. J. (1998). Predicting smoking stage of change among a sample of low socioeconomic status, primary care outpatients: Replication and extension using decisional balance and self-efficacy theories. *International Journal of Behavioral Medicine, 5*(2), 148–165.

Bouman, T. K. & Eifert, G. H. (2009). Somatoform disorders. In P. H. Blaney & T. Millon (Eds.), *Oxford textbook of psychopathology* (pp. 482–505). New York: Oxford University Press.

Bourhis, J., Allen, M., & Bauman, I. (2006). Communication apprehension: Issues to consider in the classroom. In B. M. Gayle, R. W. Preiss, N. Burrell, & M. Allen (Eds.), *Classroom communication and instructional processes: Advances through meta-analysis* (pp. 211–227). Mahwah, NJ: Erlbaum.

Bower, G. H. (1970). Organizational factors in memory. *Cognitive Psychology, 1,* 18–46.

Bower, S. A., & Bower, G. H. (1991). *Asserting yourself: A practical guide for positive change* (2nd ed.). Reading, MA: Addison-Wesley.

Bower, S. A., & Bower, G. H. (2004). *Asserting yourself: A practical guide for positive change* (updated ed.). Cambridge, MA: Da Capo Press/Perseus.

Bowers, J. W., Metts, S. M., & Duncanson, W. T. (1985). Emotion and interpersonal communication. In M. L. Knapp & G. R. Miller (Eds.), *Handbook of interpersonal communication.* Newbury Park, CA: Sage.

Bowers, K. (2008). Making the most of human strengths. In S. J. Lopez (Ed.), *Positive psychology: Exploring the best in people* (Vol. 1, pp. 23–36). Westport, CT: Praeger.

Bowes-Sperry, L., & Tata, J. (1999). A multiperspective framework of sexual harassment. In G. N. Powell (Ed.), *Handbook of gender and work.* Thousand Oaks, CA: Sage.

Bowins, B. (2004). Psychological defense mechanisms: A new perspective. *American Journal of Psychoanalysis, 64*(1), 1–26.

Bowlby, J. (1980). *Attachment and loss: Vol. 3. Loss: Sadness and depression.* New York: Basic Books.

Boyle, G. J. (2008). Critique of the five-factor model of personality. In G. J. Boyle, G. Matthews, & D. H. Saklofske (Eds.), *The Sage handbook of personality theory and assessment* (pp. 295–312). Los Angeles: Sage.

Boyle, M. (2007). The problem with diagnosis. *The Psychologist, 20,* 290–292.

Bradbury, T. N., Campbell, S. M., & Fincham, F. D. (1995). Longitudinal and behavioral analysis of masculinity and femininity in marriage. *Journal of Personality and Social Psychology, 68*(2), 328–341.

Bradford, J., & Ryan, C. (1987). *National lesbian health care survey: Mental health implications.* Washington, DC: National Lesbian and Gay Health Foundation.

Bragg, E. A. (1996). Towards ecological self: Deep ecology meets constructionist self-theory. *Journal of Environmental Psychology, 16,* 93–108.

Brainerd, C. J., & Reyna, V. F. (2005). *The science of false memory.* New York: Oxford University Press.

Bramlett, M. D., & Mosher, W. D. (2001). *First marriage dissolution, divorce, and remarriage: United States. Advance data from vital and health statistics, No. 323.* Hyattsville, MD: National Center for Health Statistics.

Branaman, T. F., & Gallagher, S. N. (2005). Polygraph testing in sex offender treatment: A review of limitations. *American Journal of Forensic Psychology, 23*(1), 45–64.

Brandes, D., Ben-Schachar, G., Gilboa, A., Bonne, O., Freedman, & S., Shalev, A. Y. (2002). PTSD symptoms and cognitive performance in recent trauma survivors. *Psychiatry Research, 110,* 231–238.

Brannon, L. (2005). *Gender: Psychological perspectives.* Boston: Allyn & Bacon.

Brannon, R. (1976). The male sex role: Our culture's blueprint of manhood, and what it's done for us lately. In D. David & R. Brannon (Eds.), *The forty-nine percent majority.* Reading, MA: Addison-Wesley.

Branscombe, N. R., Wann, D. L., Noel, J. G., & Coleman, J. (1993). In-group or out-group extremity: Importance of the threatened social identity. *Personality and Social Psychology Bulletin, 19,* 381–388.

Bratko, D. & Butkovic, A. (2003). Family study of sensation seeking. *Personality and Individual Differences, 35,* 1559–1570.

Bray, J. H. (2009). Remarriage. In H. T. Reis & S. Sprecher (Eds.), *Encyclopedia of human relationships: Vol. 3* (pp. 1359–1363). Los Angeles: Sage Reference Publication.

Bredt, B. M., Higuera-Alhino, D., Hebert, S. J., McCune, J. M., & Abrams, D. I. (2002). Short-term effects of cannabinoids on immune phenotype and function in HIV-1-infected patients. *Journal of Clinical Pharmacology, 42,* 90S–96S.

Breggin, P. R. (1991). *Toxic psychiatry.* New York: St. Martin's Press.

Breggin, P. R., & Cohen, D. (2007). *Your drug may be your problem: How and why to stop taking psychiatric medications.* New York: Da Capo Lifelong Books.

Brehm, J. W. (1956). Postdecision changes in the desirability of alternatives. *Journal of Abnormal and Social Psychology, 52,* 384–389.

Brehm, J. W. (1966). *A theory of psychological reactance.* New York: Academic Press.

Brehm, S. S. (1992). *Intimate relationships* (2nd ed.). New York: McGraw-Hill.

Brehm, S. S., & Brehm, J. W. (1981). *Psychological reactance.* New York: Academic Press.

Brehm, S. S., Kassin, S. M., & Fein, S. (2002). *Social psychology.* Boston: Houghton Mifflin.

Brennan, K. A., Clark, C. L., & Shaver, P. R. (1998). Self-report measurement of adult attachment: An integrative overview. In J. A. Simpson & W. S. Rholes (Eds.), *Attachment theory and close relationships.* New York: Guilford Press.

Breslin, F. C., & Mustard, C. (2003). Factors influencing the impact of unemployment on mental health among young and older adults in a longitudinal, population-based survey. *Scandinavian Journal of Work, Environment & Health, 29*(1), 5–14.

Brett, J. M. (1980). The effect of job transfer on employees and their families. In C. L. Cooper & R. Payne (Eds.), *Current concerns in occupational stress.* New York: Wiley.

Brewer, M. B. (1999). The psychology of prejudice: Ingroup love or outgroup hate? *Journal of Social Issues, 55,* 429–444.

Brewer, M. B., & Brown, R. J. (1998). Inter-group relations. In D. T. Gilbert, S. T. Fiske, & G. Lindzey (Eds.), *The handbook of social psychology* (4th ed., Vol. 2). New York: McGraw-Hill.

Brewin, C. R. (2003). *Posttraumatic stress disorder: Malady or myth.* New Haven: Yale University Press.

Brewin, C. R. (2007). Autobiographical memory for trauma: Update on four controversies. *Memory, 15,* 227–248.

Brewster, K. L., & Padavic, I. (2000). Change in gender-ideology, 1977–1996: The contributions of intracohort change and population turn-over. *Journal of Marriage and the Family, 62,* 477–487.

Brewster, K. L., & Tillman, K. H. (2008). Who's doing it? Patterns and predictors of youths' oral sexual experiences. *Journal of Adolescent Health Care, 42,* 73–80.

Brewster, M. P. (2002). Domestic violence, theories, research, and practice implications. In A. R. Roberts (Ed.), *Handbook of domestic violence intervention strategies: Policies, programs, and legal remedies.* New York: Oxford University Press.

Brickman, P., Coates, D., & Janoff-Bulman, R. (1978). Lottery winners and accident victims: Is happiness relative? *Journal of Personality and Social Psychology, 36,* 917–927.

Bridge, J. A., Iyengar, S., Salary, C. B., Barbe, R. P., Birmaher, B., Pincus, H. A., et al. (2007). Clinical response and risk for reported suicidal ideation and suicide attempts in pediatric antidepressant treatment: A meta-analysis of randomized controlled trials. *Journal of the American Medical Association, 297,* 1683–1969.

Bridges, K. R., & Roig, M. (1997). Academic procrastination and irrational thinking: A re-examination with

context controlled. *Personality & Individual Differences, 22,* 941–944.

Briere, J., & Conte, J. R. (1993). Self-reported amnesia for abuse in adults molested as children. *Journal of Traumatic Stress, 6,* 21–31.

Brinthaupt, T. M., & Shin, C. M. (2001). The relationship of academic cramming to the flow experience. *College Student Journal, 35,* 457–471.

Brissette, I., Scheier, M. F., & Carver, C. S. (2002). The role of optimism in social network development, coping, and psychological adjustment during a life transition. *Journal of Personality and Social Psychology, 82*(1), 102–111.

Briton, N. J., & Hall, J. A. (1995). Beliefs about female and male nonverbal communication. *Sex Roles, 32*(1-2), 79–90.

Britton, B. K., & Tesser, A. (1991). Effects of time-management practices on college grades. *Journal of Educational Psychology, 83,* 405–410.

Brody, J. E. (1997, November 4). Girls and puberty: The crisis years. *The New York Times,* p. C9.

Brody, L. R. (2000). The socialization of gender differences in emotional expression: Display rules, infant temperament, and differentiation. In A. H. Fischer (Ed.), *Gender and emotion: Social psychological perspectives.* Cambridge, UK: Cambridge University Press.

Brody, L. R., & Hall, J. A. (1993). Gender and emotion. In M. Lewis & J. M. Haviland (Eds.), *Handbook of emotions.* New York: Guilford Press.

Brody, S., & Costa, R. M. (2009). Satisfaction (sexual, life, relationship, and mental health) is associated directly with penile and vaginal intercourse, but inversely with other sexual behavior frequencies. *Journal of Sexual Medicine, 6,* 1947–1954.

Bromage, B. K., & Mayer, R. E. (1986). Quantitative and qualitative effects of repetition on learning from technical text. *Journal of Educational Psychology, 78,* 271–278.

Bromley, M., & Blieszner, R. (1997). Planning for long-term care: Filial behavior and relationship quality of adult children with independent parents. *Family Relations,* 155–162.

Brooks, G. (2010). The crisis of masculinity. In *Beyond the crisis of masculinity: A transtheoretical model for male-friendly therapy* (pp. 13–22). Washington, DC: American Psychological Association.

Broomhall, H. S., & Winefield, A. H. (1990). A comparison of the affective well-being of young and middle-aged unemployed men matched for length of employment. *British Journal of Medical Psychology, 63,* 43–52.

Brown, A. S. (1999). New perspectives on the neurodevelopmental hypothesis of schizophrenia. *Psychiatric Annals, 29*(3), 128–130.

Brown, A. S., Begg, M. D., Gravenstein, S., Schaefer, C. A., Wyatt, R. J., Bresnahan, M., Babulas, V. P., & Susser, E. S. (2004). Serologic evidence of prenatal influenza in the etiology of schizophrenia. *Archives of General Psychiatry, 61*(8), 774–780.

Brown, D. (2007). *Career information, career counseling, and career development.* Boston: Allyn & Bacon.

Brown, E. J., Juster, H. R., Heimberg, R. G., & Winning, C. D. (1998). Stressful life events and personality styles: Relation to impairment and treatment outcome in patients with social phobia. *Journal of Anxiety Disorders, 12*(3), 233–251.

Brown, J. D., & Marshall, M. A. (2006). The three faces of self-esteem. In M. H. Kernis (Ed.), *Self-esteem issues and answers: A sourcebook of current perspectives* (pp. 4–9). New York: Psychology Press.

Brown, J. D., & McGill, K. L. (1989). The cost of good fortune: When positive life events produce negative health consequences. *Journal of Personality and Social Psychology, 57,* 1103–1110.

Brown, L. M., Bradley, M. M., & Lang, P. J. (2006). Affective reactions to pictures of ingroup and outgroup members. *Biological Psychology, 71,* 303–311.

Brown, R., Maras, P., Masser, B., Vivian J., & Hewstone, M. (2001). Life on the ocean wave: Testing some intergroup hypotheses in a naturalistic setting. *Group Processes and Intergroup Relations, 4*(2), 81–97.

Brown, R. D., Goldstein, E., & Bjorklund, D. F. (2000). The history and zeitgeist of the repressed–false memory debate: Scientific and sociological perspectives on suggestibility and childhood memory. In D. F. Bjorklund (Ed.), *False-memory creation in children and adults.* Mahwah, NJ: Erlbaum.

Brown, S., & Booth, A. (1996). Cohabitation versus marriage: A comparison of relationship quality. *Journal of Marriage and the Family,* 668–678.

Brown, S. L., Nesse, R. M., Vinokur, A. D., & Smith, D. M. (2003). Providing social support may be more beneficial than receiving it: Results from a prospective study of mortality. *Psychological Science, 14*(4), 320–327.

**Brown, S. L., Sanchez, L. A., Nock, S. L., & Wright, J. D.** (2006). Links between premarital cohabitation and subsequent marital quality, stability, and divorce: A comparison of covenant versus standard marriages. *Social Science Research, 35,* 454–470.

**Brown, T. A.** (2001). Generalized anxiety disorder and obsessive-compulsive disorder. In T. Millon, P. H. Blaney, & R. D. Davis (Eds.), *Oxford textbook of psychopathology.* New York: Oxford University Press.

**Brown, T. A., & Lawrence, A. E.** (2009). Generalized anxiety disorders and obsessive-compulsive disorder. In P. H. Blaney & T. Millon (Eds.), *Oxford textbook of psychopathology* (pp.146–175). New York: Oxford University Press.

**Brown, T. T., & Dobs, A. S.** (2002). Endocrine effects of marijuana. *Journal of Clinical Pharmacology, 42,* 97S–102S.

**Browne, A.** (1993a). Family violence and homelessness: The relevance of trauma histories in the lives of homeless women. *American Journal of Orthopsychiatry, 63,* 370–384.

**Browne, A.** (1993b). Violence against women by male partners: Prevalence, outcomes, and policy implications. *American Psychologist, 48,* 1077–1087.

**Brownell, K. D.** (1995). Exercise in the treatment of obesity. In K. D. Brownell & C. G. Fairburn (Eds.), *Eating disorders and obesity: A comprehensive handbook.* New York: Guilford Press.

**Brownell, K. D., & Wadden, T. A.** (2000). Obesity. In B. J. Sadock, & V. A. Sadock (Eds.), *Kaplan and Sadock's comprehensive textbook of psychiatry* (7th ed.). Philadelphia: Lippincott/Williams & Wilkins.

**Brubaker, T.** (1990). Families in later life: A burgeoning research area. *Journal of Marriage and the Family, 52,* 959–982.

**Bruckner-Gordon, F., Gangi, B. K., & Wallman, G. U.** (1988). *Making therapy work: Your guide to choosing, using, and ending therapy.* New York: HarperCollins.

**Brummett, B. H., Babyak, M. A., Mark, D. B., Clapp-Channing, N. E., Siegler, I. C., & Barefoot, J. C.** (2004). Prospective study of perceived stress in cardiac patients. *Annual Behavioral Medicine, 27*(1), 22–30.

**Brummett, B. H., Barefoot, J. C., Siegler, I. C., Clapp-Channing, N. E., Lytle, B. L., Bosworth, H. B., Williams, R. B., & Mark, D. B.** (2001). Characteristics of socially isolated patients with coronary artery disease who are at elevated risk for mortality. *Psychosomatic Medicine, 63*(2), 267–272.

**Brunet, P. M., Schmidt, L. A.** (2007). Is shyness context specific? Relation between shyness and online disclosure. *Journal of Research in Personality, 41,* 938–945.

**Bryan, A. D., Aiken, L. S., & West, S. G.** (1999). The impact of males proposing condom use on perceptions of an initial sexual encounter. *Personality and Social Psychology Bulletin, 25*(3), 275–286.

**Bryant, F. B., & Veroff, J.** (2007). *Savoring: A new model of positive experience.* Mahwah, NJ: Erlbaum.

**Bryant, R. A., & Guthrie, R. M.** (2005). Maladaptive appraisals as a risk factor for posttraumatic stress: A study of trainee firefighters. *Psychological Science, 16,* 749–752.

**Bryden, M. P.** (1988). An overview of the dichotic listening procedure and its relation to cerebral organization. In K. Hugdahl (Ed.), *Handbook of dichotic listening.* Chichester, England: Wiley.

**Bryer, K. B.** (1979). The Amish way of death: A study of family support systems. *American Psychologist, 34,* 255–261.

**Buchanan, C. M., & Hughes, J. L.** (2009). Construction of social reality during early adolescence: Can expecting storm and stress increase real or perceived storm and stress? *Journal of Research on Adolescence, 19*(2), 261–285.

**Buchanan, R. W., & Carpenter, W. T.** (2005). Concept of schizophrenia. In B. J. Sadock & V. A. Sadock (Eds.), *Kaplan & Sadock's comprehensive textbook of psychiatry.* Philadelphia: Lippincott Williams & Wilkins.

**Buchanan, T.** (2007). Personality testing on the Internet: What we know, and what we do not. In A. N. Joinson, K. Y. A. McKenna, T. Postmes, & U-D. Reips (Eds.), *The Oxford handbook of Internet psychology.* New York: Oxford University Press.

**Buchanan, T. W., & Tranel, D.** (2008). Stress and emotional memory retrieval: Effects of sex and cortisol response. *Neurobiology of Learning and Memory, 89,* 134–141.

**Buchwald, H., Avidor, Y., Braunwald, E., Jensen, M. D., Pories, W., Fahrbach, K., et al.** (2004). Bariatric surgery: A systematic review and meta-analysis. *Journal of the American Medical Association, 292,* 1724–1737.

**Buckingham, J. T., & Alicke, M. D.** (2002). The influence of individual versus aggregate social comparison and the presence of others on self-evaluations. *Journal of Personality and Social Psychology, 83*(5), 1117–1130.

**Buckman, R.** (2002). Communications and emotions: Skills and effort are key. *British Medical Journal, 325,* 672.

**Buehlman, K. T., Gottman, J. M., & Katz, L. F.** (1992). How a couple views their past predicts their future: Predicting divorce from an oral history interview. *Journal of Family Psychology, 5,* 295–318.

**Bulcroft, R., & Teachman, J.** (2004). Ambiguous constructions: Development of a childless or child-free life course. In M. Coleman, & L. H. Ganong (Eds.), *Handbook of contemporary families: Considering the past, contemplating the future.* Thousand Oaks, CA: Sage.

**Bulik, C. M.** (2004). Genetic and biological risk factors. In J. K. Thompson (Ed.), *Handbook of eating disorders and obesity.* New York: Wiley.

**Bulik, C. M., Tozzi, F., Anderson, C., Mazzeo, S. E., Aggen, S., & Sullivan, P. F.** (2003). The relation between eating disorders and components of perfectionism. *American Journal of Psychiatry, 160,* 366-368.

**Bumpass, L. L., & Acquilino, W. S.** (1995). *A social map of midlife: Family and work over the middle life course.* Madison: University of Wisconsin-Madison Center for Demography and Ecology.

**Bumpass, L. L., & Lu, H. H.** (2000). Trends in cohabitation and implications for children's family contexts in the United States. *Population Studies, 54,* 29–41.

**Bumpass, L. L., Raley, R. K., & Sweet, J.** (1995). The changing character of stepfamilies: Implications of cohabitation and nonmarital childbearing. *Demography, 32,* 425–436.

**Burdge, B. J.** (2007). Bending gender, ending gender: Theoretical foundations for social work practice with the transgender community. *Social Work, 52,* 243–250.

**Bureau of Justice Statistics.** (2006). *Percent distribution of single-offender victimizations, by type of crime and perceived gender offender.* Retrieved from http://bjs.ojp .usdoj.gov/index.cfm?ty=pbdetail&iid=2065

**Burger, J. M.** (1999). The foot-in-the-door compliance procedure: A multiple-process analysis and review. *Personality and Social Psychology Review, 3*(4), 303–325.

**Burger, J. M.** (2000). *Personality* (5th ed.). Belmont, CA: Wadsworth.

**Burger, J. M.** (2004). *Personality* (6th ed.). Belmont, CA: Wadsworth.

**Burger, J. M.** (2008). *Personality* (7th ed.). Belmont, CA: Wadsworth.

**Burger, J. M.** (2009). Replicating Milgram: Would people still obey today? *American Psychologist, 64*(1), 1–11.

**Burger, J. M., & Caldwell, D. F.** (2003). The effects of monetary incentives and labelling on the foot-in-the-door effect: Evidence for a self-perception process. *Basic and Applied Social Psychology, 25*(3), 235–241.

**Burger, J. M., & Cornelius, T.** (2003). Raising the price of agreement: Public commitment and the lowball compliance procedure. *Journal of Applied Social Psychology, 33*(5), 923–934.

**Burger, J. M., & Guadagno, R. E.** (2003). Self-concept clarity and the foot-in-the-door procedure. *Basic and Applied Social Psychology, 25*(1), 79–86.

**Burgess, C., O'Donohoe, A., & Gill, M.** (2000). Agony and ecstasy: A review of MDMA effects and toxicity. *European Psychiatry, 15*(5), 287–294.

**Burgess, E. O.** (2004). Sexuality in midlife and later life couples. In J. H. Harvey & S. Sprecher (Eds.), *The handbook of sexuality in close relationships.* Mahwah, NJ: Lawrence Erlbaum.

**Burgoon, J. K.** (1994). Nonverbal signals. In M. L. Knapp & G. R. Miller (Eds.), *Handbook of interpersonal communication* (2nd ed.). Thousand Oaks, CA: Sage.

**Burhans, K. K., & Dweck, C. S.** (1995). Helplessness in early childhood: The role of contingent worth. *Child Development, 66,* 1719–1738.

**Burke, M. E.** (2005). *2004 reference and background checking survey report.* Alexandria, VA: Society for Human Resource Management.

**Burke, R. J.** (2000). Workaholism in organizations: Psychological and physical well-being. *Stress Medicine, 16*(1), 11–16.

**Burke, R. J.** (2001). Workaholism in organizations: The role of organizational values. *Personnel Review, 30,* 637–645.

**Burke, R. J.** (2009). Working to live or living to work: Should individuals and organizations care? *Journal of Business Ethics, 84*(Suppl2), 167–172.

**Burke, R. J., & Fiskenbaum, L.** (2009). Work motivations, work outcome, and health: Passion versus addiction. *Journal of Business Ethics, 84*(Suppl2), 257–263.

**Burlingame, G. M., & McClendon, D. T.** (2008). Group therapy. In J. L. Lebow (Ed.), *Twenty-first century psychotherapies: Contemporary approaches to theory and practice.* New York: Wiley.

**Burn, S. M., & Ward, A. Z.** (2005). Men's conformity to traditional masculinity and relationship satisfaction. *Psychology of Men and Masculinity, 6,* 254–263.

**Burns, A. B., Brown, J. S., Plant, E. A., Sachs-Ericsson, N., & Joiner, T. E. Jr.** (2006). On the specific depressotypic nature of excessive reassurance-seeking. *Personality and Individual Differences, 40*(1), 135–145.

**Bursztajn, H. J., & Brodsky, A.** (2002). Managed healthcare complications, liability risk, and clinical remedies. *Primary Psychiatry, 9*(4), 37–41.

**Bushman, B. J.** (2002). Does venting anger feed or extinguish the flame? Catharsis, rumination, distraction, anger, and aggressive responding. *Personality and Social Psychology Bulletin, 28,* 724–731.

**Bushman, B. J., & Anderson, C. A.** (2001). Media violence and the American public. *American Psychologist, 56,* 477–489.

**Bushman, B. J., & Baumeister, R. F.** (1998). Threatened egotism, narcissism, self-esteem, and direct and displaced aggression: Does self-love or self-hate lead to violence? *Journal of Personality and Social Psychology, 75*(1), 219–229.

**Bushman, B. J., & Baumeister, R. F.** (2002). Does self-love or self-hate lead to violence? *Journal of Research in Personality, 36*(6), 543–545.

**Bushman, B. J., Baumeister, R. F., Thomaes, S., Ryu, E., Begeer, S., & West, S. G.** (2009). Looking again, and harder, for a link between self-esteem and aggression. *Journal of Personality, 77*(2), 427–446.

**Bushman, B. J., Bonacci, A. M., Pedersen, W. C., Vasquez, E. A., & Miller, N.** (2005). Chewing on it can chew you up: Effects of rumination on triggered displaced aggression. *Journal of Personality and Social Psychology, 88,* 696–983.

**Bushman, B. J., Bonacci, A. M., van Dijk, M., & Baumeister, R. F.** (2003). Narcissism, sexual refusal, and aggression: Testing a narcissistic reactance model of sexual coercion. *Journal of Personality and Social Psychology, 84,* 1027–1040.

**Buss, D. M.** (1988). The evolution of human intrasexual competition: Tactics of mate attraction. *Journal of Personality and Social Psychology, 54,* 616–628.

**Buss, D. M.** (1989). Sex differences in human mate preferences: Evolutionary hypotheses tested in 37 cultures. *Behavioral and Brain Sciences, 12,* 1–14.

**Buss, D. M.** (1991). Evolutionary personality psychology. *Annual Review of Psychology, 42,* 459–491.

**Buss, D. M.** (1994). Mate preferences in 37 cultures. In W. J. Lonner & R. S. Malpass (Eds.), *Psychology and culture.* Boston: Allyn & Bacon.

**Buss, D. M.** (1995). Evolutionary psychology: A new paradigm for psychological science. *Psychological Inquiry, 6,* 1–30.

**Buss, D. M.** (1996). The evolutionary psychology of human social strategies. In E. T. Higgins & A. W. Kruglanski (Eds.), *Social psychology: Handbook of basic principles.*New York: Guilford Press.

**Buss, D. M.** (1997). Evolutionary foundation of personality. In R. Hogan, J. Johnson, & S. Briggs (Eds.), *Handbook of personality psychology.* San Diego: Academic Press.

**Buss, D. M., & Kenrick, D. T.** (1998). Evolutionary social psychology. In D. T. Gilbert, S. T. Fiske, & G. Lindzey (Eds.), *The handbook of social psychology.* New York: McGraw-Hill.

**Buss, D. M., & Schmitt, D. P.** (1993). Sexual strategies theory: A contextual evolutionary analysis of human mating. *Psychological Review, 100,* 204–232.

**Buss, D. M., Shackelford, T. K., Kirkpatrick, L. A., & Larsen, R. J.** (2001). A half century of mate preferences: The cultural evolution of values. *Journal of Marriage and Family, 63,* 491–503.

**Bussey, K., & Bandura, A.** (1984). Influence of gender constancy and social power on sex-linked modeling. *Journal of Personality and Social Psychology, 47,* 1292–1302.

**Bussey, K., & Bandura, A.** (1999). Social cognitive theory of gender development and differentiation. *Psychological Review, 106*(4), 676–713.

**Bussey, K., & Bandura, A.** (2004). Social cognitive theory of gender development and functioning. In A. H. Eagly, A. E. Beall, & R. J. Sternberg (Eds.), *The psychology of gender.* New York: Guilford Press.

**Butler, A. C., Roediger, H. L., III.** (2008). Feedback enhances the positive effects and reduces the negative effects of multiple-choice testing. *Memory & Cognition, 36*(3).

**Butler, E. A., Egloff, B., Wlhelm, F. H., Smith, N. C., Erickson, E. A., & Gross, J. J.** (2003). The social consequences of expressive suppression. *Emotion, 3*(1), 48–67.

**Butler, J. L., & Baumeister, R. F.** (1998). The trouble with friendly faces: Skilled performance with a supportive audience. *Journal of Personality and Social Psychology, 75*(5), 1213–1230.

Butler, R., & Lewis, M. (1982). *Aging and mental health* (3rd ed.). St. Louis: Mosby.

Buunk, A. P., & Dijkstra, P. (2006). Temptation and threat: Extradyadic relations and jealousy. In A. L. Vangelisti & D. Perlman (Eds.), *The Cambridge handbook of personal relationships*. New York: Cambridge University Press.

Buxton, M. N., Arkel, Y., Lagos, J., Deposito, F., Lowenthal, H., & Simring, S. (1981). Stress and platelet aggregation in hemophiliac children and their family members. *Research Communications in Psychology, Psychiatry and Behavior, 6,* 21–48.

Buzzell, L. & Chalquist, C. (2009). *Ecotherapy: Healing with nature in mind.* San Francisco: Sierra Club Books.

Byne, W. (2007). Biology and sexual minority status. In I. L. Meyer & M. E. Northridge (Eds.), *The health of sexual minorities: Public health perspectives on lesbian, gay, bisexual, and transgender populations* (pp. 65–90). New York: Springer Science and Business Media.

Byrm, R. J., & Lenton, R. L. (2001). *Love online: A report on digital dating in Canada.* Retrieved April 30, 2007 from http://www.nelson.com/nelson/harcourt/sociology/newsociety3e/loveonline.pdf.

Byrne, A., & Carr, D. (2005). Caught in the cultural lag: The stigma of singlehood. *Psychological Inquiry, 16,* 84–141.

Byrne, D., & Clore, G. L. (1970). A reinforcement model of evaluative responses. *Personality: An International Journal, 1*(2), 103–128.

Byrne, D., Clore, G. L., & Smeaton, G. (1986). The attraction hypothesis: Do similar attitudes affect anything? *Journal of Personality and Social Psychology, 51,* 1167–1170.

Byrne, R. (2001). *The secret.* New York: Atria Books.

Cabaj, R. P. (2006). Review of barebacking: Psychosocial and public health approaches. *Sexuality Research & Social Policy: A Journal of the NSRC, 3,* 91–93.

Cabral, G. A., & Petit, D. A. D. (1998). Drugs and immunity: Cannabinoids and their role in decreased resistance to infectious disease. *Journal of Neuroimmunology, 83,* 116–123.

Cachelin, F. M., Phinney, J. S., Schug, R. A., & Striegel-Moore, R. H. (2006). Acculturation and eating disorders in a Mexican American community sample. *Psychology of Women Quarterly, 30,* 340–347.

Cacioppo, J. T., & Patrick, W. (2008). *Loneliness.* New York: Norton.

Cacioppo, J. T., Petty, R. E., Feinstein, J., & Jarvis, B. (1996). Individual differences in cognitive motivation: The life and times of people varying in need for cognition. *Psychological Bulletin, 119,* 197–253.

Cadinu, M., Maass, A., Rosablanca, A., & Kiesner, J. (2005). Why do women underperform under stereotype threat? Evidence for the role of negative thinking. *Psychological Science, 16,* 572–578.

Cahn, D. D. (2009). Friendship, conflict and dissolution. In H. T. Reis & S. Sprecher (Eds.), *Encyclopedia of human relationships: Vol. 1* (pp. 703–706). Los Angeles: Sage Reference Publication.

Calasanti, T., & Harrison-Rexrode, J. (2009). Gender roles in relationships. In H. T. Reis & S. Sprecher (Eds.), *Encyclopedia of human relationships: Vol. 1* (pp. 754–757). Los Angeles: Sage Reference Publication.

Cameron, D. (2007). *The myth of Mars and Venus: Do men and women really speak different languages?* Oxford, UK: Oxford University Press.

Cameron, K. S., Dutton, J. E., & Quinn, R. E. (Eds.). (2003). *Positive organizational scholarship: Foundations of a new discipline.* San Francisco: Berrett-Koehler.

Cameron, L., Leventhal, E. A., & Leventhal, H. (1993). Symptom representations and affect as determinants of care seeking in a community-dwelling, adult sample population. *Health Psychology, 12,* 171–179.

Cameron, N. (1963). *Personality development and psychopathology.* Boston: Houghton Mifflin.

Campbell, J. D. (1990). Self-esteem and clarity of the self-concept. *Journal of Personality and Social Psychology, 59,* 538–549.

Campbell, J. D., Assanand, S., & DiPaula, A. (2000). Structural features of the self-concept and adjustment. In A. Tesser, R. B. Felson, & J. M. Suls (Eds.), *Psychological perspectives on self and identity.* Washington, DC: American Psychological Association.

Campbell, J. D., & Lavallee, L. F. (1993). Who am I? The role of self-concept confusion in understanding the behavior of people with low self-esteem. In R. Baumeister (Ed.), *Self-esteem: The puzzle of low self-regard.* New York: Plenum.

Campbell, L., Simpson, J. A., Boldry, J., & Kashy, D. A. (2005). Perceptions of conflict and support in romantic relationships: The role of attachment anxiety. *Journal of Personality and Social Psychology, 88,* 510–531.

Campbell, L. F., & Smith, T. P. (2003). Integrating self-help books into psychotherapy. *Journal of Clinical Psychology, 59*(2), 177–186.

Campbell, R. J. (2000). Managed care. In B. J. Sadock & V. A. Sadock (Eds.), *Kaplan and Sadock's comprehensive textbook of psychiatry* (7th ed., Vol. 2). Philadelphia: Lippincott/Williams & Wilkins.

Campbell, W. K., Sedikides, C., Reeder, G. D., & Elliot A. J. (2000). Among friends? An examination of friendship and the self-serving bias. *British Journal of Social Psychology, 39*(2), 229–239.

Canary, D. J., & Dainton, M. (2006). Maintaining relationships. In A. L. Vangelisti & D. Perlman (Eds.), *The Cambridge handbook of personal relationships.* New York: Cambridge University Press.

Canary, D. J., & Stafford, L. (2001). Equity in the preservation of personal relationships. In J. H. Harvey & A. E. Wenzel (Eds.), *Close romantic relationships: Maintenance and enhancement.* Mahwah, NJ: Erlbaum.

Canary, D. J., Stafford, L., & Semic, B. A. (2002). A panel study of the associations between maintenance strategies and relational characteristics. *Journal of Marriage and Family, 64,* 395–406.

Cancro, R. & Lehmann, H. E. (2000). Schizophrenia: Clinical features. In B. J. Sadock & V. A. Sadock (Eds.), *Kaplan and Sadock's comprehensive textbook of psychiatry* (7th ed., Vol. 1, pp. 1169–1198). Philadelphia: Lippincott/Williams & Wilkins.

Canetto, S. S. (2008). Women and suicidal behavior: A cultural analysis. *American Journal of Orthopsychiatry, 78,* 259–266.

Cann, A., Norman, M. A., Welbourne, J. L., & Calhoun, L. G. (2008). Attachments styles, conflict styles and humour styles: Interrelationships and associations with relationship satisfaction. *European Journal of Personality, 22,* 131–146.

Cannon, W. B. (1929). *Bodily changes in pain, hunger, fear, and rage.* Oxford, England: Appleton.

Cannon, W. B. (1932). *The wisdom of the body.* New York: Norton.

Cantor, J. R., & Venus, P. (1980). The effects of humor on recall of a radio advertisement. *Journal of Broadcasting, 24,* 13–22.

Canu, W., & Gordon, M. (2005). Mother nature as treatment for ADHD: Overstating the benefits of green. *American Journal of Public Health, 95,* 371.

Caprara, G. V., Fida, R., Vecchione, M., Del Bove, G., Vecchio, G. M., Barbaranelli, C., Bandura, A. (2008). Longitudinal analysis of the role of perceived self-efficacy for self-regulated learning in academic continuance and achievement. *Journal of Educational Psychology, 100*(3), 525–534.

Carbonell, D. M., Reinherz, H. Z., & Beardslee, W. R. (2005). Adaptation and coping in childhood and adolescence for those at risk for depression in emerging adulthood. *Child and Adolescent Social Work Journal, 22,* 395–416.

Cardeña, E., & Gleaves, D. H. (2007). Dissociative disorders. In M. Hersen, S. M. Turner, & D. C. Beidel (Eds.), *Adult psychopathology and diagnosis.* New York: Wiley.

Carducci, B. J. (1999). *The pocket guide to making successful small talk.* New Albany, IN: Pocket Guide Publications.

Carey, M. P., & Vanable, P. A. (2003). AIDS/HIV. In A. M. Nezu, C. M. Nezu, & P. A. Geller (Eds.), *Handbook of psychology: Vol. 9. Health psychology.* New York: Wiley.

Carli, L. L., & Bukatko, D. (2000). Gender, communication, and social influence: A developmental perspective. In T. Eckes & H. M. Trautner (Eds.), *The developmental social psychology of gender.* Mahwah, NJ: Erlbaum.

Carlson, E. N., & Furr, R. M. (2009). Evidence of differential meta-accuracy: People understand the different impressions they make. *Psychological Science, 20*(8), 1033–1039.

Carlson, L., Specca, M., Faris, P., & Patel, K. (2007). One year pre-post intervention follow-up of psychological, immune, endocrine, and blood pressure outcomes of mindfulness-based stress reduction (MBSR) in breast cancer and prostate cancer outpatients. *Brain, Behavior, and Immunity, 21*(8), 1038–1049.

Carlson, R. (1997). *Don't sweat the small stuff . . . and it's all small stuff: Simple ways to keep the little things from taking over your life.* New York: Hyperion.

Carnagey, N. L., Anderson, C. A., & Bartholow, B. D. (2007). Media violence and social neuroscience: New questions and new opportunities. *Current Directions in Psychological Science, 16,* 178–182.

Carnelley, K. B., Wortman, C. B., Bolger, N., & Burke, C. T. (2006). The time course of grief reactions to spousal loss: Evidence from a national probability sample. *Journal of Personality and Social Psychology, 91,* 476–492.

Carney, S., & Geddes, J. (2003). Electroconvulsive therapy. *British Medical Journal, 326,* 1343–1344.

Caron, S. L. (2007). *Sex matters for college students: FAQs in human sexuality.* Upper Saddle River, NJ: Prentice Hall.

Carpenter, W. T. (1992). The negative symptom challenge. *Archives of General Psychiatry, 49,* 236–237.

Carpenter, W. T. (2002). From clinical trial to prescription. *Archives of General Psychology, 59,* 282–285.

Carr, V. J. (2000). Stress effects of earthquakes. In G. Fink (Ed.), *Encyclopedia of stress* (Vol. 2). San Diego: Academic Press.

Carrington, P. (1993). Modern forms of meditation. In P. M. Lehrer & R. L. Woolfolk (Eds.), *Principles and practice of stress management* (2nd ed.). New York: Guilford Press.

Carroll, J. L. (2007). *Sexuality now: Embracing diversity.* Belmont, CA: Wadsworth.

Carroll-Ghosh, T., Victor, B. S., & Bourgeois, J. A. (2003). Suicide. In R. E. Hales & S. C. Yudofsky (Eds.), *Textbook of clinical psychiatry.* Washington, DC: American Psychiatric Publishing.

Carson, S. H., & Langer, E. J. (2006). Mindfulness and self-acceptance. *Journal of Rational-Emotive & Cognitive Behavior Therapy, 24,* 29–43.

Carter, B. (1999). Becoming parents: The family with young children. In B. Carter & M. McGoldrick (Eds.), *The expanded family life cycle: Individual, family, and social perspectives* (3rd ed.). Boston: Allyn & Bacon.

Carter, B., & McGoldrick, M. (1988). Overview: The changing family life cycle—A framework for family therapy. In E. A. Carter & M. McGoldrick (Eds.), *The changing family life cycle: A framework for family therapy* (2nd ed.). New York: Gardner Press.

Carter, B., & McGoldrick, M. (1999). Overview: The expanded family life cycle: Individual, family, and social perspectives. In B. Carter & M. McGoldrick (Eds.), *The expanded family life cycle: Individual, family, and social perspectives* (3rd ed.). Boston: Allyn & Bacon.

Carter, R. T., Williams, B., Juby, H. L., & Buckley, T. R. (2005). Racial identity as mediator of the relationship between gender role and conflict and severity of psychological symptoms in Black, Latino, and Asian men. *Sex Roles, 53,* 473–486.

Carter, T. J., & Dunning, D. (2008). Faulty self-assessment: Why evaluating one's own competence is an intrinsically difficult task. *Social and Personality Psychology Compass, 2*(1), 346–360.

Carter-Sowell, A. R., Chen, Z., & Williams, K. D. (2008). Ostracism increases social susceptibility. *Social Influence, 3*(3), 143–153.

Carton, J. S., Kessler, E. A., & Pape, C. L. (1999). Nonverbal decoding skills and relationship well-being in adults. *Journal of Nonverbal Behavior, 23*(1), 91–100.

Carver, C. S. (2007). Stress, coping, and health. In H. S. Friedman & R. C. Silver (Eds.), *Foundations of health psychology.* New York: Oxford University Press.

Carver, C. S., Pozo, C., Harris, S. D., Noriega, V., Scheier, M. F., Robinson, D. S., Ketcham, A. S., Moffat, F. L., Jr., & Clark, K. C. (1993). How coping mediates the effect of optimism on distress: A study of women with early-stage breast cancer. *Journal of Personality and Social Psychology, 65,* 375–390.

Carver, C. S., & Scheier, M. F. (1994). Situational coping and coping dispositions in a stressful transaction. *Journal of Personality and Social Psychology, 66,* 184–195.

Carver, C. S., & Scheier, M. F. (2002). Optimism. In C. R. Snyder & S. J. Lopez (Eds.), *Handbook of positive psychology.* New York: Oxford University Press.

Carver, C. S., & Scheier, M. F. (2005). Optimism. In C. R. Snyder & S. J. Lopez (Eds.), *Foundations of health psychology.* New York: Oxford University Press.

Carver, C. S., Scheier, M. F., & Weintraub, J. K. (1989). Assessing coping strategies: A theoretically based approach. *Journal of Personality and Social Psychology, 56,* 267–283.

Cascio, W. F., & Young, C. E. (2005). Work-family balance: Does the market reward firms that respect it? In D. F. Halpern & S. E. Murphy (Eds.), *From work-family balance to work-family interaction: Changing the metaphor.* Mahwah, NJ: Erlbaum.

Cashdan, E. (1998). Smiles, speech, and body posture: How women and men display sociometric status and power. *Journal of Nonverbal Behavior, 22,* 209–228.

Caspersen, C. J., Bloemberg, B. P., Saris, W. H., Merritt, R. K., & Kromhout, D. (1991). The prevalance of selected physical activities and their relation with coronary heart disease risk factors in elderly men: The Zutphen study, 1985. *American Journal of Epidemiology, 133,* 1078–1092.

**Cassata, D.** (2005, October 16). The decline of American civilization, or at least its manners. *Statesboro Herald,* p. 9A.

**Cassel, R. N.** (2000). Third force psychology and person-centered theory: From ego-status to ego-ideal. *Psychology: A Journal of Human Behavior, 37*(3), 44–48.

**Castle, D.** (2008). Drawing conclusions about cannabis and psychosis. *Psychological Medicine, 38*(3), 459–460.

**Castonguay, L. G., Reid Jr., J. J., Halperin, G. S., & Goldfried, M. R.** (2003). Psychotherapy integration. In G. Stricker, & T. A. Widiger (Eds.), *Handbook of psychology: Vol. 8. Clinical psychology.* New York: Wiley.

**Catalyst.** (2007). *Catalyst releases 2006 census of women in Fortune 500 corporate officer and board positions.* Retrieved on June 5, 2007 from http://www.catalyst.org/pressroom/press_releases/2006_Census_Release.pdf.

**Catania, J. A., Binson, D., Dolcini, M. M., Moskowitz, J. T., & van der Straten, A.** (2001). In A. Baum, T. A. Revenson, & J. E. Singer (Eds.), *Handbook of health psychology.* Mahwah, NJ: Erlbaum.

**Cate, R. M., & Lloyd, S. A.** (1988). Courtship. In S. Duck (Ed.), *Handbook of personal relationships.* New York: Wiley.

**Cates, W., Jr.** (2004). Reproductive tract infections. In R. A. Hatcher, J. Trussell, F. H. Stewart, A. L. Nelson, W. Cates Jr., F. Guest, & D. Kowal (Eds.), *Contraceptive technology.* New York: Ardent Media.

**Cattan, M.** (2009). Loneliness, interventions. In H. T. Reis & S. Sprecher (Eds.), *Encyclopedia of human relationships: Vol. 2* (pp. 993–996). Los Angeles: Sage Reference Publication.

**Cattell, H. E. P. & Mead, A. D.** (2008). The sixteen personality factor questionnaire (16 PF). In G. J. Boyle, G. Matthews, & D. H. Saklofske (Eds.), *The Sage handbook of personality theory and assessment* (Vol. 2, pp. 135–159). Los Angeles: Sage.

**Cattell, R. B.** (1950). *Personality: A systematic, theoretical and factual study.* New York: McGraw-Hill.

**Cattell, R. B.** (1966). *The scientific analysis of personality.* Chicago: Aldine.

**Cattell, R. B.** (1990). Advances in Cattellian personality theory. In L. A. Pervin (Ed.), *Handbook of personality: Theory and research.* New York: Guilford.

**Cattell, R. B., Eber, H. W., & Tatsuoka, M. M.** (1970). *Handbook of the Sixteen Personality Factor Questionnaire* (16PF). Champaign, IL: Institute for Personality and Ability Testing.

**Caverly, D. C., Orlando, V. P., & Mullen, J. L.** (2000). Textbook study reading. In R. F. Flippo & D. C. Caverly (Eds.), *Handbook of college reading and study strategy research.* Mahwah, NJ: Erlbaum.

**Centers for Disease Control.** (2006). Update: Trends in AIDS incidence-United States. *MMWR, 46*(37), 861–867.

**Centers for Disease Control.** (2007a). *A glance at the HIV/AIDS epidemic.* Retrieved June 24, 2007 from http://www.cdc.gov/hiv/resources/factsheets/pdf/at=a-glance.pdf.

**Centers for Disease Control.** (2007b). *Genital HPV.* Retrieved from www.edcp.org/pdf/hpv_fact_sheet.pdf

**Centers for Disease Control.** (2009a). *Oral sex and HIV risk.* Retrieved from http:www.cdc.gov/hiv

**Centers for Disease Control.** (2009b). *Sexual and reproductive health of persons aged 10–24 years-United States, 2002–2007.* Retrieved from http:www.cdc.gov/mmwr/preview/mmwrhtml/ss5806al.htm?s

**Centers for Disease Control and Prevention.** (2009). *Climate change and public health.* Retrieved from http://www.cdc.gov/ClimateChange/policy.htm

**Cepeda, N. J., Pashler, H., Vul, E., Wixted, J. T., & Roher, D.** (2006). Distributed practice in verbal recall tasks: A review and quantitative synthesis. *Psychological Bulletin, 132,* 354–380.

**Cerletti, U., & Bini, L.** (1938). Un nuevo metodo di shockterapie "L'elettro-shock." Boll. Acad. Med. *Roma, 64,* 136–138.

**Cetron, M. J., & Davies, O.** (2003, March–April). Trends shaping the future: Technological, workplace, management, and institutional trends. *The Futurist,* pp. 30–43.

**Chaiken, S.** (1979). Communicator's physical attractiveness and persuasion. *Journal of Personality and Social Psychology, 37,* 1387–1397.

**Chamberlin, C. M., & Zhang, N.** (2009). Workaholism, health, and self-acceptance. *Journal of Counseling & Development, 87*(2), 159–169.

**Chamberlin, J.** (2007, March). Too much information. *GradPSYCH,* pp. 14–16.

**Chambers, W. C.** (2007). Oral sex: Varied behaviors and perceptions in a college population. *Journal of Sex Research, 44,* 28–42.

**Chambless, D. L., & Hollon, S. D.** (1998). Defining empirically supported therapies. *Journal of Consulting & Clinical Psychology, 66*(1), 7–18.

**Chambless, D. L., & Ollendick, T. H.** (2001). Empirically supported psychological interventions: Controversies and evidence. *Annual Review of Psychology, 52,* 685–716.

**Chambliss, C. H.** (2000). *Psychotherapy and managed care: Reconciling research and reality.* Boston, MA: Allyn & Bacon.

**Chan, R. W., Brooks, R. C., Raboy, B., & Patterson, C. J.** (1998). Division of labor among lesbian and heterosexual parents: Associations with children's adjustment. *Journal of Family Psychology, 12,* 402–419.

**Chang, E. C.** (1996). Cultural differences in optimism, pessimism, and coping: Predictors of subsequent adjustment in Asian American and Caucasian American college students. *Journal of Counseling Psychology, 43,* 113–123.

**Chang, R. Y., & Kelly, P. K.** (1993). *Step-by-step problem solving: A practical guide to ensure problems get (and stay) solved.* Irvine, CA: Richard Chang Associates.

**Chaplin, W. F., Phillips, J. B., Brown, J. D., Clanton, N. R., & Stein, J. L.** (2000). Handshaking, gender, personality, and first impressions. *Journal of Personality and Social Psychology, 79*(1), 110–117.

**Charlesworth, W. R., & Dzur, C.** (1987). Gender comparisons of preschoolers' behavior and resource utilization in group problem-solving. *Child Development, 58,* 191–200.

**Chartrand, T., Pinckert, S., & Burger, J. M.** (1999). When manipulation backfires: The effects of time delay and requester on the foot-in-the-door technique. *Journal of Applied Social Psychology, 29*(1), 211–221.

**Chawla, L.** (1988). Children's concern for the natural environment. *Children's Environments Quarterly, 5*(3), 13–20.

**Chawla, L.** (1998). Significant life experiences revisited: A review of research on sources of environmental sensitivity. *Environmental Education Research, 4,* 369–382.

**Chemers, M. M., Hu, L., & Garcia, B. F.** (2001). Academic self-efficacy and first-year college student performance and adjustment. *Journal of Educational Psychology, 93*(1), 55–64.

**Chen E., & Miller, G. E.** (2007). Stress and inflammation in exacerbation of asthma. *Brain, Behavior, and Immunity, 21,* 993–999.

**Chen, G., & Martin, R. A.** (2007). A comparison of humor styles, coping humor, and mental health between Chinese and Canadian university students. *Humor, 20,* 215–234.

**Chen, Y. Y., Gilligan, S., & Coups, E. J.** (2005). Hostility and perceived social support: Interactive effects on cardiovascular reactivity to laboratory stressors. *Annals of Behavioral Medicine, 29,* 37–43.

**Cheng, C.** (2001). Assessing coping flexibility in real-life and laboratory settings: A multimethod approach. *Journal of Personality and Social Psychology, 80*(5), 814–833.

**Cheng, C.** (2003). Cognitive and motivational processes underlying coping flexibility: A dual-process model. *Journal of Personality and Social Psychology, 84,* 425–438.

**Cheng, C., & Cheung, M. W. L.** (2005). Cognitive processes underlying coping flexibility: Differentiation and integration. *Journal of Personality, 73,* 859–886.

**Cherlin, A. J.** (1999). Going to extremes: Family structure, children's well-being, and social science. *Demography, 36,* 421–428.

**Cherlin, A. J.** (2004). The deinstitutionalization of American marriage. *Journal of Marriage and Family, 66,* 848–861.

**Chia, R. C., Moore, J. L., Lam, K. N., Chuang, C. J., & Cheng, B. S.** (1994). Cultural differences in gender role attitudes between Chinese and American students. *Sex Roles, 31,* 23–29.

**Chiappelli, F., & Hodgson, D.** (2000). Immune suppression. In G. Fink (Ed.), *Encyclopedia of stress* (Vol. 2). San Diego: Academic Press.

**Chiappelli, F., & Liu, Q. N.** (2000). Immunity. In G. Fink (Ed.), *Encyclopedia of stress.* San Diego: Academic Press.

**Chick, J.** (1998). Alcohol, health, and the heart: Implications for clinicians. *Alcohol and Alcoholism, 33*(6), 576–591.

**Chick, K. A., Heilman-Houserk, R. A., & Hunter, M. W.** (2002). The impact of child care on gender role development and gender stereotypes. *Early Childhood Education Journal, 29*(3), 149–154.

**Chida, Y., Hamer, M., Wardle, J., & Steptoe, A.** (2008). Do stress-related psychosocial factors contribute to cancer incidence and survival? *Nature Clinical Practice Oncology, 5*(8), 466–475.

**Chiu, C. –Y., Kim, Y. –H., & Wan, W. W. N.** (2008). Personality: Cross-cultural perspectives. In G. J. Boyle, G. Matthews, D. H. Saklofske (Eds.), *The Sage handbook of personality theory and assessment* (pp. 124–144). Los Angeles: Sage.

**Choi, I., Dalal, R., Kim-Prieto, C., & Park, H.** (2003). Culture and judgment of causal relevance. *Journal of Personality and Social Psychology, 84*(1), 46-59.

**Choi, I., Nisbett, R. E., & Norenzayan, A.** (1999). Causal attribution across cultures: Variation and universality. *Psychological Bulletin, 125*(1), 47–63.

**Choice, P., & Lamke, L. K.** (1997). A conceptual approach to understanding abused women's stay/leave decisions. *Journal of Family Issues, 18,* 290–314.

**Chopra, D.** (1993). *Ageless body, timeless mind.* New York: Crown.

**Chopra, S. S.** (2003). Industry funding of clinical trials: Benefit of bias? *JAMA, 290,* 113–114.

**Chou, C., Condron, L., & Belland, J. C.** (2005). A review of the research on Internet addiction. *Educational Psychology Review, 17,* 363–388.

**Choudhry, N. K., Stelfox, H. T., & Detsky, A. S.** (2002). Relationships between authors of clinical practice guidelines and the pharmaceutical industry. *Journal of the American Medical Association, 287*(5), 612–617.

**Christensen, A. J., & Johnson, J. A.** (2002). Patient adherence with medical treatment regimens: An interactive approach. *Current Directions in Psychological Science, 11*(3), 94–97.

**Christensen, B. K., Carney, C. E., & Segal, Z. V.** (2006). Cognitive processing models of depression. In D. J. Stein, D. J. Kupfer, & A. F. Schatzberg (Eds.), *Textbook of mood disorders.* Washington, DC: American Psychiatric Publishing.

**Christoph, R. T., Schoenfeld, G. A., & Tansky, J. W.** (1998). Overcoming barriers to training utilizing technology: The influence of self-efficacy factors on multimedia-based training receptiveness. *Human Resource Development Quarterly, 9*(1), 25–38.

**Christopher, F. S., & Sprecher, S.** (2000). Sexuality in marriage, dating, and other relationships: A decade review. *Journal of Marriage and the Family, 62,* 999–1017.

**Chua, H. F., Leu, J., & Nisbett, R. E.** (2005). Culture and diverging views of social events. *Personality and Social Psychology Bulletin, 31,* 925–934.

**Chun, C., Moos, R. H., & Cronkite, R. C.** (2006). Culture: A fundamental context for the stress and coping paradigm. In P. T. P. Wong & L. C. J. Wong (Eds.), *Handbook of multicultural perspectives on stress and coping.* New York: Springer.

**Cialdini, R. B.** (2001). *Influence: Science and practice* (4th ed.). Boston: Allyn & Bacon.

**Cialdini, R. B.** (2003). Crafting normative messages to protect the environment. *Current Directions in Psychological Science, 12,* 105–109.

**Cialdini, R. B.** (2007). *Influence: Science and practice.* New York: HarperCollins.

**Cialdini, R. B., Borden, R. J., Thorne, A., Walker, M. R., Freeman, S., & Sloan, L. R.** (1976). Basking in reflected glory: Three (football) field studies. *Journal of Personality and Social Psychology, 34,* 366–375.

**Cialdini, R. B., & Goldstein, N. J.** (2004). Social Influence: Compliance and comformity. *Annual Review of Psychology, 55,* 591–621.

**Cialdini, R. B., Reno, R. R., & Kallgren, C. A.** (1990). A focus theory of normative conduct: Recycling the concept of norms to reduce littering in public places. *Journal of Personality and Social Psychology, 58,* 1015–1026.

**Ciarrochi, J., Dean, F. P., & Anderson, S.** (2002). Emotional intelligence moderates the relationship between stress and mental health. *Personality & Individual Differences, 32,* 197–209.

**Ciarrochi, J., & Scott, G.** (2006). The link between emotional competence and well-being: A longitudinal study. *British Journal of Guidance and Counselling, 34,* 231–243.

**Cicirelli, V. G.** (1999). Personality and demographic factors in older adults' fear of death. *Gerontologist, 39*(5), 569–579.

**Cicirelli, V. G.** (2002). *Older adults' views on death.* New York: Springer.

**Clapp, R. W., Jacobs, M. M., & Loechler, E. L.** (2008). Environmental and occupational causes of cancer: New evidence, 2005–2007. *Reviews on Environmental Health, 23,* 1–37.

**Clark, A. J.** (1989). Communication confidence and listening competence: An investigation of the relationships of willingness to communicate, communication apprehension, and receiver apprehension to comprehension of content and emotional meaning in spoken messages. *Communication Education, 38*(3), 237–248.

Clark, D. (2005). *Loving someone gay.* Berkeley, CA: Celestial Arts.

Clark, M. S., & Grote, N. K. (2003). Close relationships. In T. Millon & M. J. Lerner (Eds.) *Handbook of psychology: Vol. 5. Personality and social psychology.* New York: Wiley.

Clark, M. S., & Mills, J. (1993). The difference between communal and exchange relationships: What it is and is not. *Journal of Personality and Social Psychology Bulletin, 19,* 684–691.

Clark, R. (2003). Self-reported racism and social support predict blood pressure reactivity in blacks. *Annals of Behavioral Medicine, 25,* 127–136.

Clarke, V. A., Lovegrove, H., Williams, A., & Machperson, M. (2000). Unrealistic optimism and the health belief model. *Journal of Behavioral Medicine, 23,* 367–376.

Clayton, A. H., & Harsh, V. (2006). Hypoactive sexual desire disorder in women. *Directions in Psychiatry, 26,* 227–233.

Clayton, S. (2003). Environmental identity: A conceptual and an operational definition. In S. Clayton & S. Opotow (Eds.), *Identity and the natural environment* (pp. 4565). Cambridge, MA: MIT Press.

Clayton, S., & Brook, A. (2005). Can psychology help save the world? A model for conservation psychology. *Analyses of Social Issues and Public Policy, 5,* 87–102.

Clayton, S., & Myers, G. (2009). *Conservation psychology: Understanding and promoting human care for nature.* Chichester, West Sussex, UK: Wiley-Blackwell.

Cleek, M. G., & Pearson, T. A. (1985). Perceived causes of divorce: An analysis of interrelationships. *Journal of Marriage and the Family, 47,* 179–183.

Clements, A. M., Rimrodt, S. L., Abel, J. R., Blankner, J. G., Mostofsky, S. H., Pekar, J. J., et al. (2006). Sex differences in cerebral laterality of language and visuospatial processing. *Brain and Language, 98*(2), 150–158.

Clements, M. L., Stanley, S. M., & Markman, H. J. (2004). Before they said "I do": Discriminating among marital outcomes over 13 years. *Journal of Marriage and Family, 66,* 613–626.

Clifford, M., & Walster, E. (1973). The effect of physical attractiveness on teacher expectations. *Sociology of Education, 46,* 248–258.

Clifford, S., Barber, N., & Horne, R. (2008). Understanding different beliefs held by adherers, unintentional nonadherers, and intentional nonadherers: Application of the Necessity-Concerns Framework. *Journal of Psychosomatic Research, 64,* 41–46.

Clinebell, H. (1996). *Ecotherapy: Healing ourselves, healing the earth.* Minneapolis, MN: Augsburg Fortress.

Clow, A. (2001). The physiology of stress. In F. Jones & J. Bright (Eds.), *Stress: Myth, theory and research.* Harlow, England: Pearson Education.

Coates, T. J., & Collins, C. (1998). Preventing HIV infection. *Scientific American, 279*(1), 96–97.

Cochran, S. D. (2001). Emerging issues in research on lesbians' and gay men's mental health: Does sexual orientation really matter? *American Psychologist, 56,* 931–947.

Cohan, C. L., & Kleinbaum, S. (2002). Toward a greater understanding of the cohabitation effect: Premarital cohabitation and marital communication. *Journal of Marriage and Family, 64,* 180–192.

Cohany, S. R., & Sok, E. (2007, February). Trends in labor force participation of married mothers of infants. *Monthly Labor Review,* 9–16.

Cohen, C. E. (1981). Person categories and social perception: Testing some boundaries of the processing effects of prior knowledge. *Journal of Personality and Social Psychology, 40,* 441–452.

Cohen, F., Solomon, S., Maxfield, M. , Pyszczynski, T., & Greenberg, J. (2004). Fatal attraction: The effects of mortality salience on evaluations of charismatic, task-oriented, and relationship-oriented leaders. *Psychological Science, 15,* 846–851.

Cohen, M. J. M., Kunkel, E. S., & Levenson, J. L. (1998). Associations between psychosocial stress and malignancy. In J. R. Hubbard & E. A. Workman (Eds.), *Handbook of stress medicine: An organ system approach.* Boca Raton: CRC Press.

Cohen, P. (1984). College grades and adult achievement. *Research in Higher Education, 20,* 281–293.

Cohen, S. (2005). Keynote presentation at the eighth International Congress of Behavioral Medicine. *International Journal of Behavioral Medicine, 12*(3), 123–131.

Cohen, S., Doyle, W. J., Turner, R., Alper, C. M., & Skoner, D. P. (2003). Sociability and susceptibility to the common cold. *Psychological Science, 14*(5), 389–395.

Cohen, S., Evans, G. W., Krantz, D. S., & Stokols, D. (1980). Physiological, motivational, and cognitive effects of aircraft noise on children: Moving from the laboratory to the field. *American Psychologist, 35,* 231–243.

Cohen, S., Frank, E., Doyle, W. J., Skoner, D. P., Rabin, B. S., & Gwaltney, J. M., Jr. (1998). Types of stressors that increase susceptibility to the common cold in healthy adults. *Health Psychology, 17,* 214–223.

Cohen, S., Kessler, R. C., & Gordon, L. U. (1995). Strategies for measuring stress in studies of psychiatric and physical disorders. In S. Cohen, R. C. Kessler, & L. U. Gordon (Eds.), *Measuring stress: A guide for health and social scientists.* New York: Oxford University Press.

Cohen, S., Lichtenstein, E., Prochaska, J. O., Rossi, J. S., Gritz, E. R., Carr, C. R., Orleans, C. T., Schoenbach, V. J., Biener, L., Abrams, D., DiClemente, C., Curry, S., Marlatt, G. A., Cummings, K. M., Emont, S. L., Giovino, A., & Ossip-Klein, D. (1989). Debunking myths about self-quitting: Evidence from 10 prospective studies of persons who attempt to quit smoking by themselves. *American Psychologist, 44,* 1355–1365.

Colborn, T., Dumanoski, D., & Myers, J. P. (1997). *Our stolen future: Are we threatening our fertility, intelligence, and survival? A scientific detective story.* New York: Plume.

Colder, C. R. (2001). Life stress, physiological and subjective indexes of negative emotionality and coping reasons for drinking: Is there evidence for a self-medication model of alcohol use? *Psychology of Addictive Behaviors, 15*(3), 237–245.

Cole, E., Erdman, E., & Rothblum, E. (Eds.) (1994). *Wilderness therapy for women: The power of adventure.* New York: Haworth Press.

Coleman, L. J. (1994). "Being a teacher": Emotions and optimal experience while teaching gifted children. *Gifted Child Quarterly, 38,* 146–152.

Coleman, M., Ganong, L., & Fine, M. (2001). Reinvestigating remarriage: Another decade of progress. In R. M. Milardo (Ed.), *Understanding families into the new millennium: A decade in review* (pp. 507–526). Minneapolis: National Council on Family Relations.

Coles, M. E., Schofield, C. A., & Pietrefesa, A. S. (2006). Behavioral inhibition and obsessive-compulsive disorder. *Journal of Anxiety Disorders, 20,* 1118–1132.

Coley, J. D., Solomon, G. E. A., & Shafto, P. (2002). The development of folkbiology: A cognitive science perspective on children's understanding of the biological world. In P. H. Kahn, Jr. & S. R. Kellert (Eds.), *Children and nature: Psychological, sociocultural, and evolutionary investigations* (pp. 65–92). Cambridge, MA: MIT Press.

Collaer, M. L., & Hines, M. (1995). Human behavioral sex differences: A role for gonadal hormones during early development? *Psychological Bulletin, 118,* 55–107.

College Entrance Examination Board. (2004). *Writing a Ticket to Work . . . Or a Ticket Out: A Survey of Business Leaders.* Retrieved from www.writingcommission.org/prod_downloads/writingcom/writing-ticket-to-work.pdf

Colley, A., & Todd, Z. (2002). Gender-linked differences in the style and content of e-mails to friends. *Journal of Language and Social Psychology, 21*(4), 380–392.

Colligan, T. W., & Higgins, E. M. (2005). Workplace stress: Etiology and consequences. *Journal of Workplace Behavioral Health, 21*(2), 89–97.

Collins, N. L., & Feeney, B. C. (2004). An attachment theory perspective on closeness and intimacy. In D. J. Mashek & A. Aron (Eds.), *Handbook of closeness and intimacy.* Mahwah, NJ: Erlbaum.

Collins, R. L. (1996). For better or worse: The impact of upward social comparison on self-evaluations. *Psychological Bulletin, 119*(1), 51–69.

Collins, W. A., & Madsen, S. D. (2006). Personal relationships in adolescence and early adulthood. In A. L. Vangelisti & D. Perlman (Eds.), *The Cambridge handbook of personal relationships.* New York: Cambridge University Press.

Coltrane, S. (2001). Marketing the marriage "solution": Misplaced simplicity in the politics of fatherhood. *Sociological Perspectives, 44*(4), 387–418.

Coltrane, S., & Adams, M. (2003). The social construction of the divorce "problem": Morality, child victims, and the politics of gender. *Family Relations: Interdisciplinary Journal of Applied Family Studies, 52*(4), 363–372.

Colvin, C. R., & Block, J. (1994). Do positive illusions foster mental health? An examination of the Taylor and Brown formulation. *Psychological Bulletin, 116,* 3–20.

Colvin, C. R., Block, J., & Funder, D. C. (1995). Overly positive self-evaluations and personality: Negative implications for mental health. *Journal of Personality and Social Psychology, 68,* 1152–1162.

Comas-Diaz, L. (1987). Feminist therapy with mainland Puerto Rican women. *Psychology of Women Quarterly, 11,* 461–474.

Comas-Diaz, L. (2006). Cultural variation in the therapeutic relationship. In C. D. Goodheart, A. E. Kazdin, & R. J. Sternberg (Eds.), *Evidence-based psychotherapy: Where practice and research meet.* Washington, DC: American Psychological Association.

Combs, D. R., & Mueser, K. T. (2007). Schizophrenia. In M. Hersen, S. M. Turner, & D. C. Beidel (Eds.), *Adult psychopathology and diagnosis.* New York: Wiley.

Commerce Clearing House. (2007). *2007 CCH unscheduled absenteeism survey.* Riverwoods, IL: Commerce Clearning House.

Compton, M. T., Goulding, S. M., & Walker, E. F. (2007). Cannabis use, first-episode psychosis, and schizotypy: A summary and synthesis of recent literature. *Current Psychiatry Reviews, 3,* 161–171.

Compton, W. C. (2005). *An introduction to positive psychology.* Belmont, CA: Thompson-Wadsworth.

Consumers Union. (2005, February). Condoms: extra protection. (2005, February). *Consumer Reports,* pp. 34–38.

Condon, J. W., & Crano, W. D. (1988). Inferred evaluation and the relation between attitude similarity and interpersonal attraction. *Journal of Personality and Social Psychology, 54*(5), 789–797.

Conger, R. D. & Donnellan, M. B. (2007). An interactionist perspective on the socioeconomic context of human development. *Annual Review of Psychology, 58,* 175–199.

Conkle, A., & West, C. (2008). Psychology on the road. *The Observer, 21,* 19–23.

Conn, S. (1995). When the earth hurts, who responds? In T. Roszak, M. E. Gomes, & A. D. Kanner (Eds.), *Eco-psychology: Restoring the earth, healing the mind* (pp. 156–171). San Francisco: Sierra Club.

Connor Snibe, A., & Markus, H. R. (2005). You can't always get what you want: Educational attainment, agency, and choice. *Journal of Personality and Social Psychology, 88,* 703–720.

Connor, T. (2004). Methylenedioxymethamphetamine (MDMA, "Ecstasy"): A stressor on the immune system. *Journal of Immunology, 111,* 357–367.

Conrad, K., Dixon, T., & Zhang, Y. (2009). Controversial rap themes, gender portrayals and skin tone distortion: A content analysis of rap music videos. *Journal of Broadcasting & Electronic Media, 53,* 134–156.

Conte, H. R., Weiner, M. B., & Plutchik, R. (1982). Measuring death anxiety: Conceptual, psychometric, and factor-analytic aspects. *Journal of Personality and Social Psychology, 43,* 775–785.

Contrada, R. J., Ashmore, R. D., Gary, M. L., Coups, E., Egeth, J. D., Sewell, A., Ewell, K., Goyal, T. M., & Chasse, V. (2000). Ethnicity-related sources of stress and their effects on well-being. *Current Directions in Psychological Science, 9*(4), 136–139.

Cook, T., Church, M., Ajanaku, S., & Shadish, W. (1996). The development of occupational aspirations and expectations among inner-city boys. *Child Development, 67*(6), 3368–3385.

Coontz, S. (1997, November 17). Divorcing reality. *The Nation,* pp. 21–24.

Coontz, S. (2000). *The way we never were: American families and the nostalgia trap.* New York: Basic Books.

Cooper, A. (1998). *Playing in the zone: Exploring the spiritual dimensions of sports.* Boston: Shambala.

Cooper, A. (2002). *Sex and the Internet.* Philadelphia: Brunner-Routledge.

Cooper, A., Boies, S., Maheu, M., & Greenfield, D. (2000). Sexuality and the Internet: The next sexual revolution. In L. T. Szuchman & F. Muscarella (Eds.), *Psychological perspectives on human sexuality.* New York: Wiley.

Cooper, A., & Griffin-Shelley, E. (2002). A quick tour of online sexuality: Part 1. *Annals of the American Psychotherapy Association, 5*(6), 11–13.

Cooper, A., Morahan-Martin, J., Mathy, R. M., & Maheu, M. (2002). Toward an increased understanding of user demographics in online sexual activities. *Journal of Sex and Marital Therapy, 28,* 105–129.

Cooper, A., Safir, M. P., & Rosenmann, A. (2006). Workplace worries: A preliminary look at online sexual activities at the office-emerging issues for clinicians and employers. *CyberPsychology & Behavior, 9*(1), 22–29.

Cooper, C. L., & Dewe, P. (2004). *Stress: A brief history.* Malden, MA: Blackwell Publishing.

Cooper, C. L., & Dewe, P. (2007). Stress: A brief history from the 1950s to Richard Lazarus. In A. Monat, R. S. Lazarus, & G. Reevy (Eds.), *The Praeger handbook on stress and coping* (pp. 7–32). Westport, CT: Praeger Publishers.

Cooper, D. C., & Waldstein, S. R. (2004). Hostility differentially predicts risk factors in African American and White young adults. *Journal of Psychosomatic Research, 57,* 491–497.

**Cooper, L., & Bright. J.** (2001). Individual differences in reactions to stress. In F. Jones & J. Bright (Eds.), *Stress: Myth, theory and research.* Harlow, England: Pearson Education.

**Cooper, M. L.** (2006). Does drinking promote risky sexual behavior? A complex answer to a simple question. *Current Directions in Psychological Science, 15*(1), 19–23.

**Cooper, M. L., Albino, A. W., Orcutt, H. K., & Williams, N.** (2004). Attachment styles and intrapersonal adjustment: A longitudinal study from adolescence into young adulthood. In W. S. Rholes & J. A. Simpson (Eds.), *Adult attachment: Theory, research, and clinical implications.* New York: Guilford.

**Cooper, M. L., Shapiro, C. M., & Powers, A. M.** (1998). Motivations for sex and risky sexual behavior among adolescents and young adults: A functional perspective. *Journal of Personality and Social Psychology, 75,* 1528–1558.

**Cooper, P. J.** (1995). Eating disorders and their relationship to mood and anxiety disorders. In K. D. Brownell & C. G. Fairburn (Eds.), *Eating disorders and obesity: A comprehensive handbook.* New York: Guilford Press.

**Cooper, R.** (2004), What is wrong with the DSM? *History of Psychiatry, 15*(57, Pt. 1), 005–025.

**Cooper, W. H., & Withey, M. J.** (2009). The strong situation hypothesis. *Personality and Social Psychology Review, 13*(1), 62–72.

**Cope, M. B., Fernández, J. R., & Allilson, D. B.** (2004). Genetic and biological risk factors. In J. K. Thompson (Ed.), *Handbook of eating disorders and obesity.* New York: Wiley.

**Corby, B. C., Hodges, E. V. E., & Perry, D. G.** (2007). Gender identity and adjustment in black, Hispanic, and white preadolescents. *Developmental Psychology, 43,* 261–266.

**Cordova, J. V., Gee, C. B., & Warren, L. Z.** (2005). Emotional skillfulness in marriage: Intimacy as a mediator of the relationship between emotional skillfulness and marital satisfaction. *Journal of Social and Clinical Psychology, 24,* 218–235.

**Cordova, J. V., & Harp, A. G.** (2009). Deteriorating relationships. In H. T. Reis & S. Sprecher (Eds.), *Encyclopedia of human relationships: Vol. 2* (pp. 402–407). Los Angeles: Sage Reference Publication.

**Cornblatt, B. A., Green, M. F., Walker, E. F., & Mittal, V. A.** (2009). Schizophrenia: Etiology and neurocognition. In P. H. Blaney & T. Millon (Eds.), *Oxford textbook of psychopathology* (pp. 298–332). New York: Oxford University Press.

**Cornell, D. G.** (1997). Post hoc explanation is not prediction. *American Psychologist, 52,* 1380.

**Cornell, J. L., & Halpern-Felsher, B. L.** (2006). Adolescents tell us why teens have oral sex. *Journal of Adolescent Health, 38,* 299–301.

**Cornette, M. M., Strauman, T. J., Abramson, L. Y., Busch, & Andrew M.** (2009). Self-discrepancy and suicidal ideation. *Cognition and Emotion, 23*(3), 504–527.

**Correia, I., Vala, J., & Aguiar, P.** (2007). Victim's innocence, social categorization, and the threat to the belief in a just world. *Journal of Experimental Social Psychology, 43,* 31–38.

**Correll, C. U., Leucht, S., & Kane, J. M.** (2004). Lower risk for tardive dyskinesia associated with second-generation antipsychotics: A systematic review of 1-year studies. *American Journal of Psychiatry, 161,* 414–425.

**Corrigan, P. W. & Larson, J. E.** (2008). Stigma. In K. T. Mueser & D. V. Jeste (Eds.), *Clinical handbook of schizophrenia* (pp. 533–540). New York: Guilford.

**Corsica, J. A., & Perri, M. G.** (2003). Obesity. In A. M. Nezu, C. M. Nezu, & P. A. Geller (Eds.), *Handbook of psychology: Vol. 9. Health psychology.* New York: Wiley.

**Corty, E. W., & Guardiani, J. M.** (2008). Canadian and American sex therapists' perceptions of normal and abnormal ejaculatory latencies: How long should intercourse last? *Journal of Sexual Medicine, 5,* 1251–1256.

**Cosma, J. B.** (1999). Flow in teams. *Dissertation Abstracts International.* 60(6-A), 1901.

**Costa, P. T., Jr., & McCrae, R. R.** (1985). *NEO Personality Inventory.* Odessa, FL: Psychological Assessment Resources.

**Costa, P. T., Jr., & McCrae, R. R.** (1992). *Revised NEO Personality Inventory: NEO PI and NEO Five-Factor Inventory (Professional Manual).* Odessa, FL: Psychological Assessment Resources.

**Costa, P. T., Jr., & McCrae, R. R.** (2008). The revised NEO Personality Inventory (NEO-PI-R). In G. J. Boyle, G. Matthews, & D. H. Saklofske (Eds.), *The Sage handbook of personality theory and assessment* (Vol. 2, pp.179–198). Los Angeles: Sage.

**Cotter, D. A., Hermsen, J. M., Ovadia, S., & Vanneman, R.** (2001). The glass ceiling effect. *Social Forces, 80,* 655–682.

**Coursolle, K. M., & Sweeney, M. M.** (2009). Work-family conflict. In H. T. Reis & S. Sprecher (Eds.), *Encyclopedia of human relationships: Vol. 3* (pp. 1691–1694). Los Angeles: Sage Reference Publication.

**Courtenay, W. H.** (2000). Behavioral factors associated with disease, injury, and death among men: Evidence and implications for prevention. *Journal of Men's Studies, 9*(1), 81–142.

**Covey, S. R.** (1989). *The seven habits of highly effective people.* New York: Simon & Schuster.

**Cowan, C. P., & Cowan, P. A.** (1997). Working with couples during stressful transitions. In S. Dreman (Ed.), *The family on the threshold of the 21st century.* Mahwah, NJ: Erlbaum.

**Cowan, C. P., & Cowan, P. A.** (2000). *When partners become parents.* Mahwah, NJ: Erlbaum.

**Cox, M. J., Paley, B., Burchinal, M., & Payne, C. C.** (1999). Marital perceptions and interactions across the transition to parenthood. *Journal of Marriage and the Family, 61,* 611–625.

**Cox, P. D., Vinogradov, S., & Yalom, I. D.** (2008). Group therapy. In R. E. Hales, S. C. Yudofsky, & G. O. Gabbard (Eds.), *The American psychiatric publishing textbook of psychiatry* (pp. 1329–1376). Washington, DC: American Psychiatric Publishing, Inc.

**Coyne, S. M., Archer, J., & Eslea, M.** (2006). "We're not friends anymore! Unless . . .": The frequency and harmfulness of indirect, relational, and social aggression. *Aggressive Behavior, 32,* 294–307.

**Crabtree, S.** (2005). *Teens on sex education: Abstinence-only or safe sex approach?* Retrieved from http://www.gallup.com/poll/15166

**Craik, F. I. M., & Tulving, E.** (1975). Depth of processing and the retention of words in episodic memory. *Journal of Experimental Psychology. General, 104,* 268–294.

**Cramer, P.** (2000). Defense mechanisms in psychology today: Further processes for adaptation. *American Psychologist, 55*(6), 637–646.

**Cramp, F., & Daniel, J.** (2008). Exercise for the management of cancer-related fatigue in adults. *Cochrane Database of Systematic Reviews,* Cochrane AN: CD006145.

**Crano, W. D., & Prislin, R.** (Eds.). (2008). *Attitudes and attitude change.* New York: Psychology Press.

**Craske, M. G., & Waters, A. M.** (2005). Panic disorders, phobias, and generalized anxiety disorder. *Annual Review of Clinical Psychology, 1,* 197–225.

**Creed, F.** (1989). Appendectomy. In G. W. Brown & T. O. Harris (Eds.), *Life events and illness.* New York: Guilford Press.

**Creed, P., Lehmann, K., & Hood, M.** (2009). The relationship between core self-evaluations, employment commitment, and well-being in the unemployed. *Personality and Individual Differences, 47*(4), 310–315.

**Creed, P., Prideaux, L., & Patton, W.** (2005). Antecedents and consequences of career decisional states in adolescence. *Journal of Vocational Behavior, 67,* 397–412.

**Crepaz, N., Hart, T. A., & Marks, G.** (2004). Highly active antiretroviral therapy and sexual risk behavior. *Journal of the American Medical Association, 292*(2), 224–236.

**Crews, F.** (2006). *Follies of the wise: Dissenting essays.* Emeryville, CA: Shoemaker Hoard.

**Crick, N. R., Casas, J. F., & Nelson, D. A.** (2002). Toward a more comprehensive understanding of peer maltreatment: Studies of relational victimization. *Current Directions in Psychological Science, 11*(3), 98–101.

**Crisp, R. J., & Hewstone, M. E.** (2006). *Multiple social categorization: Processes, models, and applications.* New York: Psychology Press.

**Critelli, J. W., & Bivona, J. M.** (2008). Women's erotic rape fantasies: An evaluation of theory and research. *Journal of Sex Research, 45,* 57–70.

**Critelli, J. W., & Ee, J. S.** (1996). Stress and physical illness: Development of an integrative model. In T. W. Miller (Ed.), *Theory and assessment of stressful life events.* Madison, CT: International Universities Press.

**Crits-Christoph, P.** (1997). Limitations of the dodo bird verdict and the role of clinical trials in psychotherapy research: Comment on Wampold, et al. (1997). *Psychological Bulletin, 122,* 216–220.

**Crocker, J., & Luhtanen, R.** (1990). Collective self-esteem and ingroup bias. *Journal of Personality and Social Psychology, 58,* 60–67.

**Crocker, J., & McGraw, K. M.** (1984). What's good for the goose is not good for the gander: Solo status as an obstacle to occupational achievement for males and females. *American Behavioral Scientist, 27,* 357–370.

**Crocker, J., Niiya, Y., & Mischkowski, D.** (2008). Why does writing about important values reduce defensiveness? Self-affirmation and the role of positive other-directed feelings. *Psychological Science, 19*(7), 740–747.

**Crocker, J., & Park, L. E.** (2004). The costly pursuit of self-esteem. *Psychological Bulletin, 130,* 392–414.

**Crohan, S. E.** (1992). Marital happiness and spousal consensus on beliefs about marital conflict: A longitudinal investigation. *Journal of Social and Personal Relationships, 9,* 89–102.

**Croizet, J., Despres, G., Gauzins, M. E., Huguet, P., Leyens, J., & Meot, A.** (2004). Stereotype threat undermines intellectual performance by triggering a disruptive mental load. *Personality and Social Psychology Bulletin, 30,* 721–731.

**Crooks, R., & Baur, K.** (2008). *Our sexuality.* Belmont, CA: Wadsworth.

**Crosby, F. J., & Sabattini, L.** (2006). Family and work balance. In J. Worrell & C. D. Goodheart (Eds.), *Handbook of girls' and women's psychological health.* New York: Oxford University Press.

**Crosby, O., Iyer, A., Clayton, S., & Downing, R. A.** (2003). Affirmative action: Psychological data and the policy debates. *American Psychologist, 58*(1), 93–115.

**Crosby, O., & Moncarz, R.** (2006, Fall). The 2004–14 job outlook for college graduates. *Occupational Outlook Quarterly,* pp. 42–57.

**Cross, P.** (1977). Not can but will college teaching be improved? *New Directions for Higher Education, 17,* 1–15.

**Cross, S. E., & Gore, J. S.** (2003). Cultural models of the self. In M.R. Leary & J. P. Tangney (Eds.), *Handbook of self and identity.* New York: Guilford.

**Cross, S. E., & Madson, L.** (1997). Models of the self: Self-construal and gender. *Psychological Bulletin, 122*(1), 5–37.

**Cross, S. E., & Markus, H.** (1991). Possible selves across the life span. *Human Development, 34*(4), 230–255.

**Cross, S. E., & Markus, H. R.** (1999). The cultural constitution of personality. In L. A. Pervin & O. P. John (Eds.), *Handbook of personality: Theory and research* (2nd ed.). New York: Guilford Press.

**Crouter, A. C., & Bumpus, M. F.** (2001). Linking parents' work stress to children's and adolescents' psychological adjustment. *Current Directions in Psychological Science, 10*(5), 156–159.

**Crouter, A. C., Bumpus, M. F., Maguire, M. C., & McHale, S. M.** (1999). Linking parents' work pressure and adolescents' well-being: Insights into dynamics in dual-earner families. *Developmental Psychology, 35,* 1453–1461.

**Crow, T. J.** (2007). How and why genetic linkage has not solved the problem of psychosis: Review and hypothesis. *American Journal of Psychiatry, 164,* 13–21.

**Crowell, J. A., Treboux, D., & Waters, E.** (2002). Stability of attachment representations: The transition to marriage. *Developmental Psychology, 38,* 467–479.

**Crowl, A., Ahn, S., & Baker, J.** (2008). A meta-analysis of developmental outcomes for children of same-sex and heterosexual parents. *Journal of GLBT Family Studies, 4,* 385–407.

**Crowley, A. E., & Hoyer, W. D.** (1994). An integrative framework for understanding two-sided persuasion. *Journal of Consumer Research, 20,* 561–574.

**Crowley, B. J., Hayslip, B. Jr., & Hobdy, J.** (2003). Psychological hardiness and adjustment to life events in adulthood. *Journal of Adult Development, 10*(4), 237–248.

**Csikszentmihalyi, M.** (1975). Play and intrinsic rewards. *Journal of Humanistic Psychology, 15,* 41–63.

**Csikszentmihalyi, M.** (1997). *Finding flow.* New York: Basic Books.

**Csikszentmihalyi, M., & LeFevre, J.** (1989). Optimal experience in work and leisure. *Journal of Personality and Social Psychology, 56,* 815–822.

**Cuffee, J. J., Hallfors, D. D., & Waller, M. W.** (2007). Racial and gender differences in adolescent sexual attitudes and longitudinal associations with coital debut. *Journal of Adolescent Health Care, 41,* 19–26.

**Cullen, L. T.** (2007, February 22). It's a wrap. You're hired! *Time,* p. 57.

**Cunningham, C. O., & Selwyn, P. A.** (2005). HIV-related medical complications and treatment. In J. H. Lowinson, P. Ruiz, R. B. Millman, & J. G. Langrod (Eds.), *Substance abuse: A comprehensive textbook.* Philadelphia: Lippincott/Williams & Wilkins.

**Cunningham, M.** (2001). The influence of parental attitudes and behaviors on children's attitudes toward gender and household labor in early adulthood. *Journal of Marriage and the Family, 63*(1), 111–122.

**Cunningham, M. R.** (2009a). Physical attractiveness, defining characteristics. In H. T. Reis & S. Sprecher (Eds.), *Encyclopedia of human relationships: Vol. 3* (pp. 1237–1242). Los Angeles: Sage Reference Publication.

Cunningham, M. R. (2009b). Polygamy. In H. T. Reis & S. Sprecher (Eds.), *Encyclopedia of human relationships: Vol. 3* (pp. 1256–1259). Los Angeles: Sage Reference Publication.

Cunningham, M. R., Barbee, A. P., & Pike, C. L. (1990). What do women want? Facialmetric assessment of multiple motives in the perception of male facial physical attractiveness. *Journal of Personality and Social Psychology, 59,* 61–72.

Cunningham, M. R., Druen, P. B., & Barbee, A. P. (1997). Angels, mentors, and friends: Trade-offs among evolutionary, social, and individual variables in physical appearance. In J. A. Simpson & D. T. Kenrick (Eds.), *Evolutionary Social Psychology.* Mahwah, NJ: Erlbaum.

Cunningham, M. R., Roberts, A. R., Barbee, A. P., Druen, P. B., & Wu, C., (1995). "Their ideas of beauty are, on the whole, the same as ours": Consistency and variability in the cross-cultural perception of female physical attractiveness. *Journal of Personality and Social Psychology, 68,* 261–279.

Cupach, W. R. & Spitzberg, B. H. (2008). "Thanks, but no thanks..." The occurrence and management of unwanted relationship pursuit. In S. Sprecher, A. Wenzel, & J. Harvey (Eds.), *Handbook of relationship initiation* (pp. 409–424). New York: Psychology Press.

Curioni, C. C., & Lourenco, P. M. (2005). Long-term weight loss after diet and exercise: A systematic review. *International Journal of Obesity, 29,* 1168–1174.

Curtis, R. C., & Miller, K. (1986). Believing another likes or dislikes you: Behaviors making the beliefs come true. *Journal of Personality and Social Psychology, 51,* 284–290.

Cushing-Daniels, B., & Tsz-Ying, Y. (2009). Wage penalties and sexual orientation: An update using the general social survey. *Contemporary Economic Policy, 27*(2), 164–175.

Cutrona, C. E. (1982). Transition to college: Loneliness and the process of social adjustment. In L. A. Peplau & D. Perlman (Eds.), *Loneliness: A sourcebook of current theory, research, and therapy.* New York: Wiley.

Cutting, L. P., & Docherty, N. M. (2000). Schizophrenia outpatients' perceptions of their parents: Is expressed emotion a factor? *Journal of Abnormal Psychology, 109*(2), 266–272.

Cynkar, A. (2007). A prescription for exercise. *Monitor on Psychology,* 42–43.

Daamen, D. D. L., Staats, H., Wilke, H. A. M., & Engelen, M. (2001). Improving environmental behavior in companies: The effectiveness of tailored versus non-tailored interventions. *Environment and Behavior. 33,* 229–248.

Dabbs, J. M., with Dabbs, M. G. (2000). *Heroes, rogues, and lovers: Testosterone and behavior.* New York: McGraw-Hill.

Daiek, D. B., & Anter, N. M. (2004). *Critical reading for college and beyond.* New York: McGraw Hill.

Dainton, M. (2000). Maintenance behaviors, expectations for maintenance, and satisfaction: Linking comparison levels to relational maintenance strategies. *Journal of Social and Personal Relationships, 17*(6), 827–842.

Dainton, M. (2006). Cat walk conversations: Everyday communication in dating relationships. In J. T. Wood & S. W. Duck (Eds.), *Composing relationships: Communication in everyday life* (pp. 36–45). Belmont, CA: Thompson/Wadsworth.

Dallman, M. F., Bhatnagar, S., & Viau, V. (2000). Hypothalamo-pituitary-adrenal axis. In G. Fink (Ed.), *Encyclopedia of stress* (Vol. 2). San Diego: Academic Press.

D'Amico, M. L. (1998). Internet has become a necessity, U.S. poll shows. *CNNinteractive* [Internet magazine], 1.

Danieli, Y., Engdahl, B., & Schlenger, W. E. (2004). The psychological aftermath of terrorism. In F. M. Moghaddam & A. J. Marsella (Eds.), *Understanding terrorism: Psychological roots, consequences, and interventions.* Washington, DC: American Psychological Association.

Daniels, K., Hartley, R., & Travers, C. J. (2006). Beliefs about stressors alter stressors' impact: Evidence from two experience-sampling studies. *Human Relations, 59,* 1261–1285.

Dantzer, R., & Mormede, P. (1995). Psychoneuroimmunology of stress. In B. E. Leonard & K. Miller (Eds.), *Stress, the immune system and psychiatry.* New York: Wiley.

Das, A. (2007). Masturbation in the United States. *Journal of Sex & Marital Therapy, 33,* 301–317.

Das, E. H. H. J., de Wit, J. B. F., & Stroebe, W. (2003). Fear appeals motivate acceptance of action recommendations: Evidence for a positive bias in the processing of persuasive messages. *Personality and Social Psychology Bulletin, 29*(5), 650–664.

Dasgupta, N. (2009). Mechanisms underlying the malleability of implicit prejudices and stereotypes: The role of automaticity and cognitive control. In T. D. Nelson (Ed.), *Handbook of prejudice, stereotyping, and discrimination* (pp. 267–284). New York: Psychology Press.

David, D. H., & Lyons-Ruth, K. (2005). Differential attachment responses of male and female infants to frightening maternal behavior: Tend or befriend versus fight of flight? *Infant Mental Health Journal, 26*(1), 1–18.

Davidson, M. J., & Fielden, S. (1999). Stress and the working woman. In G. N. Powell (Ed.), *Handbook of gender and work.* Thousand Oaks, CA: Sage.

Davidson, R. J., Pizzagalli, D. A., & Nitschke, J. B. (2009). Representation and regulation of emotion in depression: Perspectives from affective neuroscience. In I. H. Gotlib & C. L. Hammen (Eds.), *Handbook of Depression* (pp. 218–248). New York: The Guilford Press.

Davies, A. P. C., & Shackelford, T. K. (2006). An evolutionary psychological perspective on gender similarities and differences. *American Psychologist, 32,* 640–641.

Davila, J., & Cobb, R. J. (2003). Predicting change in self-reported and interviewer-assessed adult attachment: Tests of the individual difference and life stress models of attachment change. *Personality and Social Psychology Bulletin, 29,* 859–870.

Davila, J., & Kashy, D. (2009). Secure base processes in couples: Daily associations between support experiences and attachment security. *Journal of Family Psychology, 23,* 76–88.

Davila, J., & Sargent, E. (2003). The meaning of life (events) predicts changes in attachment security. *Personality and Social Psychology Bulletin, 29,* 1383–1395.

Davis, C. G., & Nolen-Hoeksema, S. (2009). Making sense of loss, perceiving benefits, and posttraumatic growth. In S. J. Lopez & C. R. Snyder (Eds.), *Oxford handbook of positive psychology* (2nd ed., pp. 641–649). New York: Oxford.

Davis, C. M., Blank, J., Lin, H., & Bonilas, C. (1996). Characteristics of vibrator use among women. *Journal of Sex Research, 33,* 313–320.

Davis, D., Shaver, P. R., Widaman, K. F., Vernon, M. L., Follette, W. C., & Beitz, K. (2006). "I can't get no satisfaction": Insecure attachment, inhibited sexual communication, and sexual dissatisfaction. *Personal Relationships, 13,* 465–483.

Davis, L. L., Frazier, E. C., Williford, R. B., & Newell, J. M. (2006). Long-term pharmacotherapy for post-traumatic stress disorder. *CNS Drugs, 20,* 465–476.

Davis, M. C., Zautra, A. J., Younger, J., Motivala, S. J., Attrep, J., & Irwin, M. R. (2008). Chronic stress and regulation of cellular markers if inflammation in rheumatoid arthritis: Implications for fatigue. *Brain, Behavior, & Immunity, 22,* 24–32.

Davis, M. H., Morris, M. M., & Kraus, L. A. (1998). Relationship-specific and global perceptions of social support: Associations with well-being and attachment. *Journal of Personality and Social Psychology, 74,* 468–481.

Davis, R. A. (2001). A cognitive-behavioral model of pathological Internet use. *Computers in Human Behavior, 17*(2), 187–195.

Dawes, R. M. (1980). Social dilemmas. *Annual Review of Psychology, 31,* 169–193.

Dawkins, K., Golden, R. N., & Fawcett, J. A. (2003). Therapeutic management of the suicidal patient. In A. Tasman, J. Kay, & J. A. Lieberman (Eds.), *Psychiatry.* New York: Wiley.

Dean, L. R., Carroll, J. S., & Yang, C, (2007). Materialism, perceived financial problems, and marital satisfaction. *Family and Consumer Sciences Research Journal, 35,* 260–281.

DeAngelis, T. (2001, December). Are men emotional mummies? *Monitor on Psychology,* pp. 40–41.

DeAngelis, T. (2004). What's to blame for the surge in super-size Americans? *Monitor on Psychology, 35*(1), 46, 62.

Deaux, K., & Hanna, R. (1984). Courtship in the personals column: The influence of gender and sexual orientation. *Sex Roles, 11,* 363–375.

Deaux, K., & Lewis, L. L. (1983). Components of gender stereotypes. *Psychological Documents, 13,* Ms. No. 2583.

Deaux, K., & Lewis, L. L. (1984). Structure of gender stereotypes: Interrelationships among components and gender label. *Journal of Personality and Social Psychology, 46,* 991–1004.

DeCaro, J. A., & Worthman, C. M. (2007). Cultural models, parent behavior, and young child experience in working American families. *Parenting: Science and Practice, 7,* 177–203.

de Calvo, M. P. C., & Reich, D. A. (2009). Detecting perceiver expectancies: The role of perceiver distraction in spontaneously triggering identity negotiation. *Basic and Applied Social Psychology, 31*(2), 174–187.

DeCarvalho, R. J. (1991). *The founders of humanistic psychology.* New York: Praeger.

Deci, E. L., & Ryan, R. M. (2008). Hedonia, eudaimonia, and well-being: An introduction. *Journal of Happiness Studies, 9,* 1–11.

De Cock, K. M., & Janssen, R. S. (2002). An unequal epidemic in an unequal world. *Journal of the American Medical Association, 288*(2), 236–238.

DeFrain, J., & Olson, D. H. (1999). Contemporary family patterns and relationships. In M. B. Sussman, S. K. Steinmetz, & G. W. Peterson (Eds.), *Handbook of marriage and the family.* New York: Plenum Press.

Degenhardt, L., & Hall, W. (2006). Is cannabis use a contributory cause of psychosis? *Canadian Journal of Psychiatry, 51,* 556–565.

de Geus, E., & Neumann, D. L. (2008). Psychophysiological measurement of personality. In G. J. Boyle, G. Matthews, & D. H. Saklofske (Eds.), *The Sage handbook of personality theory and assessment* (Vol. 2, pp. 313–333). Los Angeles: Sage.

de Geus, E., & Stubbe, J. H. (2007). Aerobic exercise and stress reduction. In G. Fink (Ed.), *Encyclopedia of stress: Vols. 1–4* (2nd ed., pp. 73–77). San Diego, CA: Elsevier Academic Press.

de Graaf, J., Wann, D., & Naylor, T. H. (2005). *Affluenza: The all-consuming epidemic.* San Francisco: Berrett-Koehler Publishers.

De Hoog, N., Stroebe, W., & De Wit, J. B. F. (2007). The impact of vulnerability to and severity of a health risk on processing and acceptance of fear-arousing communications: A meta-analysis. *Review of General Psychology, 11*(3), 258–285.

de Jong Gierveld, J., van Tilburg, T., & Dykstra, P. A. (2006). Loneliness and social isolation. In A. L. Vangelisti & D. Perlman (Eds.), *The Cambridge handbook of personal relationships.* New York: Cambridge University Press.

de Kloet, E. R., Joels, M., & Holsboer, F. (2005). Stress and the brain: From adaptation to disease. *Nature Reviews Neuroscience, 6,* 463–474.

Del Monte, M. M. (2000). Retrieved memories of childhood sexual abuse. *British Journal of Medical Psychology, 73,* 1–13.

Delay, J., & Deniker, P. (1952). *Trente-huit cas de psychoses traitees par la cure prolongee et continue de 4560 RP.* Paris: Masson et Cie.

Delgado, P. L., & Moreno, F. A. (2006). Neurochemistry of mood disorders. In D. J. Stein, D. J. Kupfer, & A. F. Schatzberg (Eds.), *Textbook of mood disorders.* Washington, DC: American Psychiatric Publishing.

DeLisi, L. E. (2008). The effect of cannabis on the brain: Can it cause brain anomalies that lead to increased risk for schizophrenia? *Current Opinion in Psychiatry, 21,* 140–150.

DeLongis, A., Folkman, S., & Lazarus, R. S. (1988). The impact of daily stress on health and mood: Psychological and social resources as mediators. *Journal of Personality and Social Psychology, 54,* 486–495.

DeMaris, A., Benson, M. L., Fox, G. L., Hill, T., & Van Wyk, J. (2003). Distal and proximal factors in domestic violence: A test of an integrated model. *Journal of Marriage and Family, 65,* 652–667.

DeMaris, A., & Swinford, S. (1996). Female victims of spousal violence: Factors influencing their level of fearfulness. *Family Relations, 45*(1), 98–106.

Demerouti, E., & Geurts, S. (2004). Towards a typology of work-home interaction. *Community, Work, & Family, 7,* 285–309.

Demir, M., Ozdemir, M., & Weitekamp, L. A. (2007). Looking to happy tomorrows with friends: Best and close friendships as they predict happiness. *Journal of Happiness Studies, 8,* 243–271.

Demir, M., & Weitekamp, L. A. (2006). I am so happy cause today I found my friend! Friendship and personality as predictors of happiness. *Journal of Happiness Studies, 8,* 181–211.

Demo, D. H. (1992). Parent-child relations: Assessing recent changes. *Journal of Marriage and the Family, 54,* 104–117.

Demo, D. H., & Fine, M. A. (2009). Children and divorce. In H. T. Reis & S. Sprecher (Eds.), *Encyclopedia of human relationships: Vol. 2* (pp. 453–458). Los Angeles: Sage Reference Publication.

Denisoff, E., & Endler, N. S. (2000). Life experiences, coping, and weight preoccupation in young adult women. *Canadian Journal of Behavioural Science, 32*(2), 97–103.

Dennerstein, L., Dudley, E., & Guthrie, J. (2002). Empty nest or revolving door? A prospective study of women's quality of life in midlife during the phase of children leaving and re-entering the home. *Psychological Medicine, 32*(3), 545–550.

Dennis, C., & Ross, L. (2005). Relationships among infant sleep patterns, maternal fatigue, and development of depressive symptomatology. *Birth, 32,* 187–193.

Denson, T. F., Aviles, F. E., Pollock, V. E., Earleywine, M., Vasquez, E. A., & Miller, N. (2008). The effects of alcohol and the salience of aggressive cues on triggered displaced aggression. *Aggressive Behavior, 34,* 25–33.

DePaulo, B. M. (1994). Spotting lies: Can humans learn to do better? *Current Directions in Psychological Science, 3(3),* 83–86.

DePaulo, B. M. (2004). The many faces of lies. In A. G. Miller (Ed.), *The social psychology of good and evil* (pp. 303–326). New York: Guilford.

DePaulo, B. M., Ansfield, M. E., Kirkendol, S. E., & Boden, J. M. (2004). Serious lies. *Basic and Applied Social Psychology, 6,* 147–167.

DePaulo, B. M., Charlton, K., Cooper, H., Lindsay, J. J., & Muhlenbruck, L. (1997). The accuracy-confidence correlation in the detection of deception. *Personality and Social Psychology Review, 1(4),* 346–357.

DePaulo, B. M., & Friedman, H. (1998). Nonverbal communication. In D. T. Gilbert, S. T. Fiske, & G. Lindzey (Eds.), *The handbook of social psychology* (Vol. 2). Boston: McGraw-Hill.

DePaulo, B. M., LeMay, C. S., & Epstein, J. A. (1991). Effects of importance of success and expectations for success on effectiveness at deceiving. *Personality and Social Psychology Bulletin, 17,* 14–24.

DePaulo, B. M., Lindsay, J. J., Malone, B. E., Muhlenbruck, L., Charlton, K., & Cooper, H. (2003). Cues to deception. *Psychological Bulletin, 129(1),* 74–118.

DePaulo, B. M., & Morris, W. L. (2005). Singles in society and in science. *Psychological Inquiry, 16,* 57–83.

DePaulo, B. M., & Morris, W. L. (2006). The unrecognized stereotyping and discrimination against singles. *Current Directions in Psychological Science, 15,* 251–254.

DePaulo, B. M., Stone, J., & Lassiter, G. D. (1985). Deceiving and detecting deceit. In B. R. Schlenker (Ed.), *The self and social life.* New York: McGraw-Hill.

De Raad, B. (2009). Structural models of personality. In P. J. Corr & G. Matthews (Eds.), *The Cambridge handbook of personality psychology* (pp. 127–147). New York: Cambridge University Press.

Derlega, V. J., Winstead, B. A., Wong, P. T. P., & Hunter, S. (1985). Gender effects in an initial encounter: A case where men exceed women in disclosure. *Journal of Social and Personal Relationships, 2,* 25–44.

Derr, T. (2006). "Sometimes birds sound like fish": Perspectives on children's place experiences. In C. Spencer & M. Blades (Eds.), *Children and their environments: Learning, using and designing spaces.* (pp. 108–123). New York: Cambridge University Press.

Derryberry, D., & Tucker, D. M. (1994). Motivating the focus of attention. In P. M. Neidenthal & S. Kitayama (Eds.), *The heart's eye: Emotional influences in perception and attention* (pp. 167–196). San Diego, CA: Academic Press.

DeSantis King, A., Huebner, E. S., Suldo, S. M., & Valois, R. F. (2006). An ecological view of school satisfaction in adolescence: Linkages between social support and behavior problems. *Applied Research in Quality of Life, 1,* 279–295.

Desert, M., & Leyens, J. (2006). Social comparisons across cultures I: Gender stereotypes in high and low power distance cultures. In S. Guimond (Ed.), *Social Comparison and Social Psychology: Understanding cognition, intergroup relations, and culture.* New York: Cambridge University Press.

Des Jarlais, D. C., Hagan, H., & Friedman, S. R. (2005). Epidemiology and emerging public heath perspectives. In J. H. Lowinson, P. Ruiz, R. B. Millman, & J. G. Langrod (Eds.), *Substance abuse: A comprehensive textbook.* Philadelphia: Lippincott/Williams & Wilkins.

DeSpelder, L. A., & Strickland, A. L. (1983). *The last dance: Encountering death and dying.* Palo Alto, CA: Mayfield.

Dessler, W. A. (2000). Indigenous societies. In G. Fink (Ed.), *Encyclopedia of stress* (Vol. 1). San Diego: Academic Press.

Deutsch, M., & Gerard, H. B. (1955). A study of normative and informational social influences upon individual judgment. *Journal of Abnormal and Social Psychology, 51,* 629–636.

Devine, P. G. (1989). Stereotypes and prejudice: Their automatic and controlled components. *Journal of Personality and Social Psychology, 56,* 5–18.

Devine, P. G., & Malpass, R. S. (1985). Orienting strategies in differential face recognition. *Personality and Social Psychology Bulletin, 11(1),* 33–40.

de Vries, B. (1996). The understanding of friendship: An adult life course perspective. In C. Magai & S. H. McFadden (Eds), *Handbook of emotion, adult development, and aging.* San Diego, CA: Academic Press.

Dew, J. (2008). Debt change and marital satisfaction change in recently married couples. *Family Relations, 57,* 60–71.

Dew, M. A., Bromet, E. J., & Switzer, G. E. (2000). Epidemiology. In M. Hersen & A. S. Bellack (Eds.), *Psychopathology in adulthood.* Boston: Allyn & Bacon.

DeWall, C. N., Baumeister, R. F., Gailliot, M. T., & Maner, J. K. (2008). Depletion makes the heart grow less helpful: Helping as a function of self-regulatory energy and genetic relatedness. *Personality and Social Psychology Bulletin, 34,* 1653–1662.

DeWall, C. N., Baumeister, R. F., Stillman, T. F., & Gailliot, M. T. (2007). Violence restrained: Effects of self-regulation and its depletion on aggression. *Journal of Experimental Social Psychology, 43,* 62–76.

Dey, J. G., & Hill, C. (2007). *Behind the pay gap.* Washington, DC: American Association of University Women Educational Foundation.

Diamond, J. (2005). *Collapse: How societies choose to fail or survive.* London: Allen Lane.

Diamond, L. E. (2003). Was it a phase? Young women's relinquishment of lesbian/bisexual identities over a 5-year period. *Journal of Personality and Social Psychology, 84,* 352–364.

Diamond, L. E., Earle, D. C., Heiman, J. R., Rosen, R. C., Perelman, M. A., & Harning, R. (2006). An effect on the subjective sexual response in premenopausal women with sexual arousal disorder by Bremelanotide (PT-141), a melanocortin receptor agonist. *Journal of Sexual Medicine, 3,* 628–638.

Diamond, L. M. (2006). The intimate same-sex relationships of sexual minorities. In A. L. Vangelisti & D. Perlman (Eds.), *The Cambridge handbook of personal relationships.* New York: Cambridge University Press.

Diamond, L. M. (2007). "Having a girlfriend without knowing it": Intimate friendships among adolescent sexual-minority women. In K. E. Lovaas & M. M. Jenkins (Eds.), *Sexualities & communication in everyday life* (pp. 107–115). Thousand Oaks, CA: Sage.

Diamond, L. M., & Dubé, E. M. (2002). Friendship and attachment among heterosexual and sexual-minority youths: Does the gender of your friend matter? *Journal of Youth and Adolescence, 31,* 155–166.

Dias-Ferreira, E., Sousa, J. C., Melo, I., Morgado, P., Mesquita, A. R., Cerqueira, J., Costa R. M., & Sousa, N. (2009). Chronic stress causes frontostriatal reorganization and affects decision-making. *Science, 325,* 621–625.

DiBaise, R., & Gunnoe, J. (2004). Gender and culture differences in touching behavior. *Journal of Social Psychology, 144,* 49–62.

Di Chiara, G. (1999). Drug addiction as dopamine-dependent associative learning disorder. *European Journal of Pharmacology, 375,* 13–30.

DiClemente, C. C., Fairhurst, S. K., & Piotrowski, N. A. (1995). Self-efficacy and addictive behaviors. In J. E. Maddux (Ed.), *Self-efficacy, adaptation, and adjustment: Theory, research and application.* New York: Plenum Press.

DiClemente, C. C., Schlundt, D., & Gemmell, L. (2004). Readiness and stages of change in addiction treatment. *The American Journal on Addictions, 13,* 103–119.

Diekman, A. B., & Eagly, A. H. (2000). Stereotypes as dynamic constructs: Women and men of the past, present, and future. *Personality and Social Psychology Bulletin, 26(10),* 1171–1188.

Diekman, A. B., & Murnen, S. K. (2004). Learning to be little women and little men: The inequitable gender equality of nonsexist children's literature. *Sex Roles, 50(5/6),* 373–385.

Diener, E. (1984). Subjective well-being. *Psychological Bulletin, 95,* 542–575.

Diener, E., & Biswas-Diener, R. (2008). *Happiness: Unlocking the mysteries of psychological wealth* London: Wiley-Blackwell.

Diener, E., & Diener, C. (1996). Most people are happy. *Psychological Science, 7,* 181–185.

Diener, E., Gohm, C. L., Suh, E., & Oishi, S. (2000). Similarity of the relations between marital status and subjective well-being across cultures. *Journal of Cross-Cultural Psychology, 31,* 419–436.

Diener, E., Kesebir, P., & Tov, W. (2009). Happiness. In M. R. Leary & R. H. Hoyle (Eds.), *Handbook of individual differences in social behavior* (pp. 147–160). New York: Guilford.

Diener, E., Lucas, R. E., & Scollon, C. N. (2006). Beyond the hedonic treadmill: Revising the adaptation theory of well-being. *American Psychologist, 61,* 305–314.

Diener, E., & Oishi, S. (2005). The nonobvious social psychology of happiness. *Psychological Inquiry, 16(4),* 162–167.

Diener, E., Sandvik, E., Seidlitz, L., & Diener, M. (1993). The relationship between income and subjective well-being: Relative or absolute? *Social Indicators Research, 28,* 195–223.

Diener, E., & Seligman, M. E. P. (2002). Very happy people. *Psychological Science, 13,* 80–83.

Diener, E., & Seligman, M. E. P. (2004). Beyond money: Toward an economy of well-being. *Psychological Science in the Public Interest, 5(1),* 1–31.

Diener, E., Wolsic, B., & Fujita, F. (1995). Physical attractiveness and subjective well-being. *Journal of Personality and Social Psychology, 69,* 120–129.

Di Forti, M., Morrison, P. D., Butt, A., & Murray, R. M. (2007). Cannabis use and psychiatric and cognitive disorders: The chicken or the egg? *Current Opinion in Psychiatry, 20,* 228–234.

Dijkstra, A. F., Verdonk, P., & Lagro-Janssen, A. L. M. (2008). Gender bias in medical textbooks: Examples from coronary heart disease, depression, alcohol abuse and pharmacology. *Medical Education, 42,* 1021–1028.

Dillard, A. J., McCaul, K. D., & Klein, W. M. P. (2006). Unrealistic optimism in smokers: Implications for smoking myth endorsement and self-protective motivation. *Journal of Health Communication, 11,* 93–102.

Dilsaver, S. C., Chen, Y. R., Shoaib, A. M., & Swann, A. C. (1999). Phenomenology of mania: Evidence for distinct depressed, dysphoric, and euphoric presentations. *American Journal of Psychiatry, 156,* 426–430.

Dilworth, J. E. L. (2004). Predictors of negative spill-over from family to work. *Journal of Family Issues, 25,* 241–261.

DiMatteo, M. R. (1997). Health behaviors and care decisions: An overview of professional-patient communication. In D. S. Gochman (Ed.), *Handbook of health behavior research II: Provider determinants.* New York: Plenum Press.

DiMatteo, M. R. (2004). Variations in patients' adherence to medical recommendations: A quantitative review of 50 years of research. *Medical Care, 42(3),* 200–209.

Din, J. N., Newby, D. E., & Flapan, A. D. (2004). Omega 3 fatty acids and cardiovascular disease—fishing for a natural treatment. *British Medical Journal, 328,* 30–35.

Dindia, K. (2006). Men are from North Dakota, women are from South Dakota. In K. Dindia (Ed.), *Sex Differences and similarities in communication* (2nd ed., pp. 3–20). Mahwah, NJ: Lawrence Erlbaum Associates Publishers.

Dindia, K., & Allen, M. (1992). Sex differences in self-disclosure: A meta-analysis. *Psychological Bulletin, 112,* 106–124.

Dinges, D. F., Rogers, N. J., & Baynard, M. D. (2005). Chronic sleep deprivation. In M. H. Kryger, T. Roth, & W. C. Dement (Eds.), *Principles and practice of sleep medicine.* Philadelphia: Elsevier Saunders.

Dion, K. (1973). Young children's stereotyping of facial attractiveness. *Developmental Psychology, 9,* 183–188.

Dion, K. K., Berscheid, E., & Walster, E. (1972). What is beautiful is good. *Journal of Personality and Social Psychology, 24,* 285–290.

Dion, K. K., & Dion, K. L. (1993). Individualistic and collectivistic perspectives on gender and the cultural context of love and intimacy. *Journal of Social Issues, 49,* 53–69.

Dion, K. L. (2003). Prejudice, racism and discrimination. In T. Millon & M. J. Lerner (Eds.), *Handbook of psychology: Vol. 5. Personality and social psychology.* New York: Wiley.

Dishotsky, N. I., Loughman, W. D., Mogar, R. E., & Lipscomb, W. R. (1971). LSD and genetic damage: Is LSD chromosome damaging, carcinogenic, mutagenic, or teratogenic? *Science, 172,* 431–440.

DiTommaso, E., Brannen-McNulty, C., Ross, L., & Burgess, M. (2003). Attachment styles, social skills and loneliness in young adults. *Personality and Individual Differences, 35(2),* 303–312.

Dixon, L., & Browne, K. (2003). The heterogeneity of spouse abuse: A review. *Aggression and Violent Behavior, 8(1),* 107–130.

Dodge, B., Jeffries, W. L., & Sandfort, T. G. M. (2008). Beyond the down low: Sexual risk, protection, and disclosure among at risk Black men who have sex with both men and women (MSMW). *Archive of Sexual Behavior, 37,* 683–696.

Dohm, A., & Wyatt, I. (2002). College at work: Outlook and earnings for college graduates, 2000-10. *Occupational Outlook Quarterly, 46(3),* 3–15.

Dolby, S. K. (2005). *Self-help books: Why Americans keep reading them.* Urbana: University of Illinois Press.

Dolder, C. R. (2008). Side effects of antipsychotics. In K. T. Mueser & D. V. Jeste (Eds.), *Clinical handbook of schizophrenia* (pp. 168–177). New York: Guilford.

Dollard, J., Doob, L. W., Miller, N. E., Mowrer, O. H., & Sears, R. R. (1939). *Frustration and aggression.* New Haven, CT: Yale University Press.

**Donahue, E. M., Robins, R. W., Roberts, B. W., & John, O. P.** (1993). The divided self: Concurrent and longitudinal effects of psychological adjustment and social roles on self-concept differentiation. *Journal of Personality and Social Psychology, 64,* 834–846.

**Donahue, M. J., & Benson, P. L.** (1995). Religion and the well-being of adolescents. *Journal of Social Issues, 51,* 145–160.

**Donovan, R. L., & Jackson, B. L.** (1990). Deciding to divorce: A process guided by social exchange, attachment and cognitive dissonance theories. *Journal of Divorce, 13,* 23–35.

**Dougall, A. L., & Baum, A.** (2000). Three Mile Island, stress effects of. In G. Fink (Ed.), *Encyclopedia of stress* (Vol. 3). San Diego: Academic Press.

**Dougall, A. L., & Baum, A.** (2001). Stress, health, and illness. In A. Baum, T. A. Revenson, & J. E. Singer (Eds.), *Handbook of health psychology*. Mahwah, NJ: Erlbaum.

**Dougherty, J.** (2009, October 22). For some seeking rebirth, Sweat Lodge was end. *The New York Times.* Retrieved from http://www.nytimes.com/2009/10/22/us/22sewat.html?_r-1&scp=5&sq=sweat%20lodge520deaths&st=cse#

**Dougherty, T. W., Turban, D. B., & Callender, J. C.** (1994). Confirming first impressions in the employment interview: A field study of interview behavior. *Journal of Applied Psychology, 79*(5), 659–665.

**Douglass, M. E., & Douglass, D. N.** (1993). *Manage your time, your work, yourself.* New York: American Management Association.

**Dovidio, J. F., Ellyson, S. L., Keating, C. F., Heltman, K., & Brown, C. E.** (1988). The relationship of social power to visual display of dominance between men and women. *Journal of Personality and Social Psychology, 54,* 233–242.

**Dovidio, J. F., & Gaertner, S. L.** (1996). Affirmative action, unintentional racial biases, and intergroup relations. *Journal of Social Issues, 52,* 51–75.

**Dovidio, J. F., & Gaertner, S. L.** (1999). Reducing prejudice: Combating intergroup biases. *Current Directions in Psychological Science, 8,* 101–105.

**Dovidio, J. F., & Gaertner, S. L.** (2004). Aversive racism. In M. P. Zanna (Ed.), *Advances in experimental social psychology*. San Diego: Elsevier.

**Dovidio, J. F., Gaertner, S. L., Esses, V. M., & Brewer, M. B.** (2003). Social conflict, harmony, and integration. In T. Millon & M. J. Lerner (Eds.) *Handbook of psychology: Vol. 5. Personality and social psychology*. New York: Wiley.

**Dovidio, J. F., Gaertner, S. L., & Pearson, A. R.** (2005). On the nature of prejudice: The psychological foundations of hate. In R. J. Sternberg (Ed.), *The psychology of hate*. Washington, DC: American Psychological Association.

**Dovidio, J. F., Gaertner, S. L., Penner, L. A., Pearson, A. R., Norton, W. E.** (2009). Aversive racism—how unconscious bias influences behavior: Implications for legal, employment, and health care contexts. In J. L. Chin (Ed.), *Diversity in mind and in action, Vol. 3: Social justice matters* (pp. 21–35). Santa Barbara, CA: Praeger/ABC-CLIO.

**Downar, J. & Kapur, S.** (2008). Biological theories. In K. T. Mueser & D. V. Jeste (Eds.), *Clinical handbook of schizophrenia* (pp. 25–34). New York: The Guilford Press.

**Downey, L., & van Willigen, M.** (2005). Enviromental stressors: The mental health impacts of living near industrial activity. *Journal of Health and Social Behavior, 46,* 289–305.

**Doyle, J. A.** (1989). *The male experience.* Dubuque, IA: William C. Brown.

**Drago, R. W.** (2007). *Striking a balance: Work, family, life.* Boston: Dollars & Sense.

**Draguns, J. G.** (2009). Personality in cross-cultural perspective. In P. J. Corr & G. Matthews (Eds.), *The Cambridge handbook of personality psychology* (pp. 556–576). New York: Cambridge University Press.

**Dresser, N.** (2005). *Multicultural manners: Essential rules of etiquette for the 21st century.* Hoboken, NJ: Wiley.

**Drew, J.** (2003). The myth of female sexual dysfunction and its medicalization. *Sexualities, Evolution and Gender, 5*(2), 89–96.

**Drigotas, S. M., Rusbult, C. E., Wieselquist, J., & Whitton, S. W.** (1999). Close partner as sculptor of the ideal self: Behavioral affirmation and the Michelangelo phenomenon. *Journal of Personality and Social Psychology, 77*(2), 293–323.

**Driskell, J. E., Willis, R. P., & Copper, C.** (1992). Effect of overlearning on retention. *Journal of Applied Psychology, 77,* 615–622.

**Driver, J., Tabares, A., Shapiro, A. , Nahm, E. Y., & Gottman, J. M.** (2003 ). Interactional patterns in marital success and failure: Gottman laboratory studies. In F. Walsh (Ed.), *Normal family processes: Growing diversity and complexity.* New York: Guilford.

**Driver, J. L., & Gottman, J. M.** (2004). Daily marital interactions and positive affect during marital conflict among newlywed couples. *Family Processes, 43,* 301–314.

**Drum, D. J., & Sekel, A.** (2003). Health care marketplace in the United States. In G. Stricker & T. A. Widiger (Eds.), *Handbook of psychology, Vol. 8. Clinical psychology*. New York: Wiley.

**Druss, B. G., Wang, P. S., Sampson, N. A., Olfson, M., Pincus, H. A., Welss, K. B., et al.** (2007). Understanding mental health treatment in persons without mental diagnoses: Results from the National Comorbidity Survey. *Archives of General Psychiatry, 64,* 1196–1203.

**Dubbert, P. M., King, A. C., Marcus, B. H., & Sallis, J. F.** (2004). Promotion of physical activity through the life span. In J. M. Raczynski & L. C. Leviton (Eds.), *Handbook of clinical health psychology: Vol. 2. Disorders of behavior and health.* Washington, DC: American Psychological Association.

**Dube, M. F., & Green, C. R.** (1982). Methods of collection of smoke for analytical purposes. *Recent Advances in Tobacco Science, 8,* 42–102.

**Dubicka, B., Hadley, S., & Roberts, C.** (2006). Suicidal behaviour in youths with depression treated with new-generation antidepressants—Meta-analysis. *British Journal of Psychiatry, 189,* 393–398.

**Dubovsky, S. L.** (2009). Benzodiazepine receptor agonists and antagonists. In B. J. Sadock, V. A. Sadock, & P. Ruiz (Eds.), *Kaplan & Sadock's comprehensive textbook of psychiatry* (pp. 3044–3055). Philadelphia: Lippincott Williams & Wilkins.

**Dubovsky, S. L., Davies, R., & Dubovsky, A. N.** (2003). Mood disorders. In R. E. Hales, & S. C. Yudofsky (Eds.), *Textbook of clinical psychiatry.* Washington, DC: American Psychiatric Publishing.

**Duck, S. W.** (1982). A topography of relationship disengagement and dissolution. In S. W. Duck (Ed.), *Personal relationship 4: Dissolving personal relationships* (pp. 1–30). London: Academic Press.

**Duck, S. W.** (1994). *Meaningful relationships: Talking, sense, and relating.* Thousand Oaks, CA: Sage.

**Duck, S. W.** (2006). *Human relationships* (4th ed.). London: Sage.

**Duckworth, A. L., Steen, T. A., & Seligman, M. E. P.** (2005). Positive psychology in clinical practice. *Annual Review of Clinical Psychology, 1*(1), 629–651.

**Duckworth, K., & Borus, J. F.** (1999). Population-based psychiatry in the public sector and managed care. In A. M. Nicholi, Jr. (Ed.), *The Harvard guide to psychiatry.* Cambridge, MA: Harvard University Press.

**Duggan, E. S., & Brennan, K. A.** (1994). Social avoidance and its relation to Bartholomew's adult attachment typology. *Journal of Social and Personal Relationships, 11,* 147–153.

**Duman, R. S., & Monteggia, L. M.** (2006). A neurotrophic model for stress–related mood disorders. *Biological Psychiatry, 59,* 1116–1127.

**Dunbar-Jacob, J., & Schlenk, E.** (2001). Patient adherence to treatment regimen. In A. Baum, T. A. Revenson, & J. E. Singer (Eds.), *Handbook of health psychology*. Mahwah, NJ: Erlbaum.

**Duncan, C. P., & Nelson, J. E.** (1985). Effects of humor in a radio advertising experiment. *Journal of Advertising, 14,* 33–40, 64.

**Duncker, K.** (1945). On problem solving. *Psychological Monographs, 58*(5, Whole No. 270).

**Dunkel-Schetter, C., Gurung, R. A. R., Lobel, M., & Wadhwa, P. D.** (2001). Stress processes in pregnancy and birth: Psychological, biological, and sociocultural influences. In A. Baum, T. A. Revenson, & J. E. Singer (Eds.), *Handbook of health psychology*. Mahwah, NJ: Erlbaum.

**Dunkel, C. S., Kelts, D., & Coon, B.** (2006). Possible selves as mechanisms of change in therapy. In C. Dunkel & J. Kerpelman (Eds.), *Possible selves: Theory, research, and applications*. Hauppague, NY: Nova Science Publishers.

**Dunlop, B. W., Garlow, S. J., & Nemeroff, C. B.** The neurochemistry of depressive disorders: Clinical studies. In D. S. Charney & E. J. Nestler (Eds.), *Neurobiology of mental illness* (pp. 435–460). New York: Oxford University Press.

**Dunn, A. L., Trivedi, M. H., & O'Neal, H. A.** (2001). Physical activity dose-response effects on outcomes of depression and anxiety. *Medicine and Science in Sports and Exercise, 33,* S587–S597.

**Dunn, D. S., & Brody, C.** (2008). Defining the good life following acquired physical disability. *Rehabilitation Psychology, 53,* 413–425.

**Dunn, D. S., & Wilson, T. D.** (1990). When the stakes are high: A limit to the illusion-of-control effect. *Social Cognition, 8,* 305–323.

**Dunn, E. W., Wilson, T. D., & Gilbert, D. T.** (2003). Location, location, location: The misprediction of satisfaction in housing lotteries. *Personality and Social Psychology Bulletin, 29,* 1421–1432.

**Dunning, D.** (2006). Strangers to ourselves? *The Psychologist, 19*(10), 600–603.

**Dunning, D., Heath, C., & Suls, J. M.** (2004). Flawed self-assessment: Implications for health, education, and the workplace. *Psychological Science in the Public Interest, 5*(3), 69–106.

**Dunning, D., & Sherman, D. A.** (1997). Stereotypes and tacit inference. *Journal of Personality and Social Psychology, 73*(3), 459–471.

**Durning, A. T.** (1992). *How much is enough? The consumer society and the future of the earth.* New York: Norton.

**Dutton, D. G.** (2007). The complexities of domestic violence. *American Psychologist, 61,* 595–606.

**Dutton, J. E., & Ragins, B. R.** (Eds.). (2007). *Exploring positive relationships at work: Building a theoretical and research foundation.* Mahwah, NJ: Erlbaum.

**Dweck, C. S.** (2007). Is math a gift? Beliefs that put females at risk. In S. J. Ceci & W. M. Williams (Eds.), *Why aren't more women in science?* (pp. 47–56). Washington, DC: American Psychological Association.

**Dye, D. A., & Reck, M.** (1989). College grade point average as a predictor of adult success: A reply. *Public Personnel Management, 18*(2), 239–240.

**Dyer, W. W.** (1976). *Your erroneous zones.* New York: Crowell.

**Dykstra, P. A., & Fokkema, T.** (2007). Social and emotional loneliness among divorced and married men and women: Comparing the deficit and cognitive perspectives. *Basic and Applied Social Psychology, 29,* 1–12.

**Eagly, A. H.** (1987). *Sex differences in social behavior: A social-role interpretation.* Hillsdale, NJ: Erlbaum.

**Eagly, A. H., Ashmore, R. D., Makhijani, M. G., & Longo, L. C.** (1991). What is beautiful is good, but . . . : A meta-analytic review of research on the physical attractiveness stereotype. *Psychology Bulletin, 110,* 107–128.

**Eagly, A. H., & Chaiken, S.** (1998). Attitude structure and function. In D. T. Gilbert, S. T. Fiske, & G. Lindzey (Eds.), *Handbook of social psychology*. New York: McGraw-Hill.

**Eagly, A. H., & Karau, S. J.** (2002). Role congruity theory of prejudice toward female leaders. *Psychological Review, 109*(3), 573–598.

**Eagly, A. H., & Sczesny, S.** (2009). Stereotypes about women, men, and leaders: Have times changed? In M. Barreto, M. K. Ryan, & M. T. Schmitt (Eds.), *The glass ceiling in the 21st century: Understanding barriers to gender equality* (pp. 21–47). Washington, DC: American Psychological Association.

**Eagly, A. H., & Wood, W.** (1999). The origins of sex differences in human behavior: Evolved dispositions versus social roles. *American Psychologist, 54*(6), 408–423.

**Eagly, A. H., Wood, W., & Diekman, A. B.** (2000). Social role theory of sex differences and similarities: A current appraisal. In T. Eckes & H. M. Trautner (Eds.), *The developmental social psychology of gender.* Mahwah, NJ: Erlbaum.

**Eaker, E. D., Sullivan, L. M., Kelly-Hayes, M., D'Agostino, R. B., & Benjamin, E. J.** (2004). Anger and hostility predict the development of atrial fibrillation in men in the Framingham Offspring Study. *Circulation, 109*(10), 1267–1271.

**Earley, P.** (2006). *Crazy: A father's search through America's mental health madness.* New York: G. P. Putnam's Sons.

**Easterbrook, J. A.** (1959). The effect of emotion on cue utilization and the organization of behavior. *Psychological Review, 66,* 183–201.

**Easterlin, B. L., & Cardena, E.** (1999). Cognitive and emotional differences between short- and long-term Vipassana meditators. *Imagination, Cognition and Personality, 18*(1), 68–81.

**Eastwick, P. W., Finkel, E. J.** (2008). The attachment system in fledgling relationships: An activating role for attachment anxiety. *Journal of Personality and Social Psychology, 95,* 628–647.

**Eastwick, P. W., Finkel, E. J., Mochon, D., & Ariely, D.** (2007). Selective versus unselective romantic desire: Not all reciprocity is created equal. *Psychological Science, 18,* 317–319.

**Ebbinghaus, H.** (1885/1964). *Memory: A contribution to experimental psychology.* (H. A. Ruger & E. R. Bussemius, Trans.). New York: Dover. (Original work published 1885)

Ebner, N. C., & Johnson, M. K. (2009). Young and older emotional faces: Are there age group differences in expression identification and memory? *Emotion, 9*, 329–339.

Eccles, J. S. (2001). Achievement. In J. Worrell (Ed.), *Encyclopedia of women and gender.* San Diego: Academic Press.

Eccles, J. S. (2007). Where are all the women? Gender differences in participation in physical science and engineering. In S. J. Ceci & W. M. Williams (Eds.), *Why aren't more women in science?* (pp. 199–210). Washington, DC: American Psychological Association.

Eckert, P., & McConnell-Ginet, S. (2003). *Language and gender.* Cambridge, UK: Cambridge University Press.

Edlin, G., & Golanty, E. (1992). *Health and wellness: A holistic approach.* Boston: Jones and Bartlett.

Edwards, C., Dunham, D. N., Ries, A., & Barnett, J. (2006). Symptoms of traumatic stress and substance use in a non-clinical sample of young adults. *Addictive Behaviors, 31*, 2094–2104.

Edwards, K., & Smith, E. E. (1996). A disconfirmation bias in the evaluation of arguments. *Journal of Personality and Social Psychology, 71*, 5–24.

Edwards, R., & Hamilton, M. A. (2004). You need to understand my gender role: An empirical test of Tannen's model of gender and communication. *Sex Roles, 50*(7/8), 491–504.

Edwards, S. (2006). Physical exercise and psychological well-being. *South Africa Journal of Psychology, 36*, 357–373.

Egan, T. (2000, October 23). Technology sent Wall Street into market for pornography. *New York Times,* pp. 1–20.

Egeci, I. S., & Gençöz, T. (2006). Factors associated with relationship satisfaction: Importance of communication skills. *Contemporary Family Therapy: An International Journal, 28*, 383–391.

Ehrenberg, O., & Ehrenberg, M. (1994). *The psychotherapy maze: A consumer's guide to getting in and out of therapy.* Northvale, NJ: Jason Aronson.

Ehrenreich, H., Rinn, T., Kunert, H. J., Moeller, M. R., Poser, W., Schilling, L., Gigerenzer, G., & Hoehe, M. R. (1999). Specific attentional dysfunction in adults following early start of cannabis use. *Psychopharmacology, 142*, 295–301.

Ehrlich, P. R., & Ehrlich, A. H. (2008). *The dominant animal: Human evolution and the environment.* Washington, DC: Island Press.

Eibl-Eibesfeldt, I. (1975). *Ethology: The biology of behavior.* New York: Holt, Rinehart & Winston.

Eich, E., Macaulay, D., Loewenstein, R. J., & Dihle, P. H. (1997). Memory, amnesia, and dissociative identity disorder. *Psychological Science, 8*, 417–422.

Einstein, G. O., & McDaniel, M. A. (2004). *Memory fitness: A guide for successful aging.* New Haven, CT: Yale University Press.

Eisenberg, M. E., Bernat, D. H., Bearinger, L. H., & Resnick, M. D. (2008). Support for comprehensive sexuality education: Perspectives from parents of school-age youth. *Journal of Adolescent Heath, 42*, 352–359.

Ekman, P. (1972). Universals and cultural differences in facial expressions of emotion. In J. Cole (Ed.), *Nebraska symposium on motivation, 1971.* Lincoln, NE: University of Nebraska Press.

Ekman, P. (1975, September). The universal smile: Face muscles talk every language. *Psychology Today,* pp. 35–39.

Ekman, P. (1994). Strong evidence for universals in facial expressions: A reply to Russell's mistaken critique. *Psychological Bulletin, 115*, 268–287.

Ekman, P. (2009). *Telling lies: Clues to deceit in the marketplace, politics, and marriage* (Rev. ed.). New York: Norton.

Ekman, P., & Friesen, W. V. (1974). Detecting deception from the body or face. *Journal of Personality and Social Psychology, 29*(3), 288–298.

Ekman, P., & Friesen, W. V. (1984). *Unmasking the face.* Palo Alto, CA: Consulting Psychologists Press.

Ekman, P., & O'Sullivan, M. (1991). Who can catch a liar? *American Psychologist, 44*(9), 913–920.

Ekman, P., O'Sullivan, M., & Frank, M. G. (1999). A few can catch a liar. *Psychological Science, 10*(3), 263–266.

Eldridge, K. A. (2009). Conflict patterns. In H. T. Reis & S. Sprecher (Eds.), *Encyclopedia of human relationships: Vol. 1* (pp. 307–310). Los Angeles: Sage Reference Publication.

Elfenbein, H. A., & Ambady, N. (2002). Universals and cultural differences in recognizing emotions of a different cultural group. *Current Directions in Psychological Science, 12*(5), 159–164.

Ellington, L., & Wiebe, D. J. (1999). Neuroticism, symptom presentation, and medical decision making. *Health Psychology, 18*(6), 634–643.

Elliot, A. J., & Church, M. A. (2003). A motivational analysis of defensive pessimism and self-handicapping. *Journal of Personality, 71*, 369–393.

Elliot, L., & Brantley, C. (1997). *Sex on campus.* New York: Random House.

Ellis, A. (1973). *Humanistic psychotherapy: The rational-emotive approach.* New York: Julian Press.

Ellis, A. (1977). *Reason and emotion in psychotherapy.* Seacaucus, NJ: Lyle Stuart.

Ellis, A. (1985). *How to live with and without anger.* New York: Citadel Press.

Ellis, A. (1987). The evolution of rational-emotive therapy (RET) and cognitive behavior therapy (CBT). In J. K. Zeig (Ed.), *The evolution of psychotherapy.* New York: Brunner/Mazel.

Ellis, A. (1989). Rational-emotive therapy. In R. J. Corsini & D. Wedding (Eds.), *Current Psychotherapies.* Itasca, IL: Peacock.

Ellis, A. (1993). The advantages and disadvantages of self-help therapy materials. *Professional Psychology: Research and Practice, 24*, 335–339.

Ellis, A. (1994). *Reason and emotion in psychotherapy.* Seacaucus, NJ: Birch Lane Press.

Ellis, A. (1995). Thinking processes involved in irrational beliefs and their disturbed consequences. *Journal of Cognitive Psychotherapy, 9*, 105–116.

Ellis, A. (1996). How I learned to help clients feel better and get better. *Psychotherapy, 33*, 149–151.

Ellis, A. (2001a). *Feeling better, getting better, staying better: Profound self-help therapy for your emotions.* Atascadero, CA: Impact Publishers.

Ellis, A. (2001b). *Overcoming destructive beliefs, feelings, and behaviors: New directions for Rational Emotive Behavior Therapy.* Amherst, NY: Prometheus Books.

Ellis, A. (2004). Expanding the ABCs of rational emotive behavior therapy. In A. Freeman, M. J. Mahoney, P. Devito, & D. Martin (Eds.), *Cognition and psychotherapy.* New York: Springer Publishing.

Ellis, H. (1898). Autoeroticism: A psychological study. *Alienist and Neurologist, 19*, 260–299.

Ellis, J. (2006, January 28). "IM-speak" struggle for teachers. *Statesboro Herald,* pp. 1A, 14A.

Ellison, N., Heino, R., & Gibbs, J. (2006). Managing impressions online: Self-presentation processes in the online dating environment. *Journal of Computer-Mediated Communication, 11*, 415–441.

Ellsworth, P. C., & Smith, C. A. (1988). Shades of joy: Patterns of appraisal differentiating pleasant emotions. *Cognition and Emotion, 2*, 301–331.

Else-Quest, N. M., Hyde, J. S., & Linn, M. C. (2010). Cross-national patterns of gender differences in mathematics: A meta-analysis. *Psychological Bulletin, 136*, 103–127.

Emanuel, H. M. (1987). Put time on your side. In A. D. Timpe (Ed.), *The management of time.* New York: Facts On File.

Emavardhana, T., & Tori, C. D. (1997). Changes in self-concept, ego defense mechanisms, and religiosity following seven-day Vipassana meditation retreats. *Journal for the Scientific Study of Religion, 36*, 194–206.

Emmelkamp, P. M. G. (1994). Behavior therapy with adults. In A. E. Bergin & S. L. Garfield (Eds.), *Handbook of psychotherapy and behavior change* (4th ed.). New York: Wiley.

Emmelkamp, P. M. G. (2004). In M. J. Lambert (Ed.), *Bergin and Garfield's handbook of psychotherapy and behavior change.* New York: Wiley.

Emmons, R. A. (1999). *The psychology of ultimate concerns: Motivation and spirituality in personality.* New York: Guilford.

Emmons, R. A. (2003). Personal goals, life meaning, and virtue: Wellsprings of a positive life. In C. L. M. Keyes & J. Haidt (Eds.), *Flourishing: Positive psychology and the life well-lived.* Washington, DC: American Psychological Association.

Emmons, R. A., & Crumpler, C. A. (2000). Gratitude as a human strength: Appraising the evidence. *Journal of Social and Clinical Psychology, 19*, 56–69.

Emmons, R. A., & McCullough, M. E. (2003). Counting blessings versus burdens: Experimental studies of gratitude and subjective well-being in daily life. *Journal of Personality and Social Psychology, 84*, 377–389.

Emmons, R. A., & McCullough, M. E. (2004). *The psychology of gratitude.* New York: Oxford.

Emsley, R., Rabinowitz, J., & Medori, R. (2006). Time course for antipsychotic treatment response in first-episode schizophrenia. *American Journal of Psychiatry, 163*, 743–745.

Energy Information Administration. (2006). *International Energy Annual 2006:* Table 1.2: 1.2 World Petroleum Consumption (Thousand Barrels per Day), 1980–2005. Retrieved from http://www.eia.doe.gov/iea/wec.html

Environmental Protection Agency. (2006). *Climate change.* Retrieved from http://epa.gov/climatechange/index.html

Environmental Protection Agency. (2008). *About air toxics.* Retrieved from http://www.epa.gov/ttn/atw/allabout.html

Epel, E. S., Blackburn, E. H., Lin, J., Dhabhar, F. S., Adler, N. E., Morrow, J. D., & Cawthon, R. M. (2004). Accelerated telomere shortening in response to life stress. *Proceedings of the National Academy of Sciences, 101*, 17312–17315.

Epstein, J., & Kinkenberg, W. D. (2001). From Eliza to Internet: A brief history of computerized assessment. *Computers in Human Behavior, 17*, 295–314.

Epstein, M., & Ward, L. M. (2008). "Always use protection": Communication boys receive about sex from parents, peers, and the media. *Journal of Youth and Adolescence, 37*, 113–126.

Epstein, R. (2001). Physiologist Laura. *Psychology Today, 34* (4), 5.

Epstein, R. (2007, February–March). The truth about online dating. *Scientific American Mind, 18,* pp. 28–35.

Equal Employment Opportunity Commission. (2007). *Occupational employment in private industry by race/ethnic group/sex, and by industry, United States, 2005.* Retrieved from http://www.eeoc.gov/stats/jobpat/2005/national.html.

Erdelyi, M. H. (2001). Defense processes can be conscious or unconscious. *American Psychologist, 56*(9), 761–762.

Erikson, E. H. (1963). *Childhood and society.* New York: Norton.

Erikson, E. H. (1968). *Identity: Youth and crisis.* New York: Norton.

Erikson, M. G. (2007). The meaning of the future: Toward a more specific definition of possible selves. *Review of General Psychology, 11*(4), 348–358.

Ernst, C., & Angst, J. (1983). Birth order: Its influence on personality. *Behavioral and Brain Sciences, 10*(1), 55.

Eshbaugh, E. M., & Gute, G. (2008). Hookups and sexual regret among college women. *Journal of Social Psychology, 148*, 77–89.

Esping-Andersen, G. (2007). Sociological explanations of changing income distributions. *American Behavioral Scientist, 50*, 639–658.

Esterling, B. A., Kiecolt-Glaser, J. K., Bodnar, J. D., & Glaser, R. (1994). Chronic stress, social support, and persistent alterations in the natural killer cell response to cytokines in older adults. *Health Psychology, 13*, 291–298.

Esterson, A. (1993). *Seductive mirage: An exploration of the work of Sigmund Freud.* Chicago: Open Court.

Esterson, A. (2001). The mythologizing of psychoanalytic history: Deception and self-deception in Freud's accounts of the seduction theory episode. *History of Psychiatry, 7*, 329–352.

Etaugh, C. (1993). Maternal employment: Effects on children. In J. Frankel (Ed.), *The employed mother and the family context.* New York: Springer.

Evans, G. W. (2001). Environmental stress and health. In A. Baum, T. A. Revenson, & J. E. Singer (Eds.), *Handbook of health psychology.* Mahwah, NJ: Erlbaum.

Evans, G. W., & Cohen, S. (1987). Environmental stress. In D. Stokols & I. Altman (Eds.), *Handbook of environmental psychology* (pp. 571–610). New York: Wiley.

Evans, G. W., Hygge, S., & Bullinger, M. (1995). Chronic noise and psychological stress. *Psychological Science, 6*, 333–338.

Evans, G. W., & Stecker, R. (2004). Motivational consequences of environmental stress. *Journal of Environmental Psychology, 24*(2), 143–165.

Evans, G. W., & Wener, R. E. (2006). Rail commuting duration and passenger stress. *Health Psychology, 25*, 408–412.

Evans, G. W., & Wener, R. E. (2007). Crowding and personal space invasion on the train: Please don't make me sit in the middle. *Journal of Environmental Psychology, 27*, 90–94.

Evans, R. G., & Dinning, W. D. (1982). MMPI correlates of the Bem Sex Role Inventory and Extended Personal Attributes Questionnaire in a male psychiatric sample. *Journal of Clinical Psychology, 38*, 811–815.

Everett, P. B., Hayward, S. C., & Meyers, A. W. (1974). The effects of a token reinforcement procedure on bus ridership. *Journal of Applied Behavior Analysis, 7,* 1–9.

Everson, S. A., Kauhanen, J., Kaplan, G. A., Goldberg, D. E., Julkunen, J., Tuomilehto, J., & Salonen, J. T. (1997). Hostility and increased risk of mortality and acute myocardial infarction: The mediating role of behavioral risk factors. *American Journal of Epidemiology, 146*(2), 142–152.

Exline, J. J., Baumeister, R. F., Bushman, B. J., Campbell, W. K., & Finkel, E. J. (2004). Too proud to let go: Narcissistic entitlement as a barrier to forgiveness. *Journal of Personality and Social Psychology, 87,* 894–912.

Eyal, K, & Finnerty, K. (2009). The portrayal of sexual intercourse on television: How, who, and with what consequence? *Mass Communication & Society, 12,* 143–169.

Eysenck, H. J. (1959). Learning theory and behaviour therapy. *Journal of Mental Science, 195,* 61–75.

Eysenck, H. J. (1967). *The biological basis of personality.* Springfield, IL: Charles C Thomas.

Eysenck, H. J. (1982). *Personality, genetics and behavior: Selected papers.* New York: Praeger.

Eysenck, H. J. (1991). Dimensions of personality: 16, 5, or 3?—Criteria for a taxonomic paradigm. *Personality and Individual Differences, 12,* 773–790.

Eysenck, M. W., Mogg, K., May, J., Richards, A., & Mathews, A. (1991). Bias in interpretation of ambiguous sentences related to threat in anxiety. *Journal of Abnormal Psychology, 100,* 144–150.

Faber Taylor, A., & Kuo, F. E. (2009). Children with attention deficits concentrate better after walk in the park. *Journal of Attention Disorders, 12,* 402–409.

Faber Taylor, A., Kuo, F. E., & Sullivan, W. C. (2001). Coping with ADD: the surprising connection to green play settings. *Environment and Behavior, 33,* 54–77.

Fabes, R. A., Hanish, L. D., & Martin, C.L. (2003). Children at play: The role of peers in understanding the effects of child care. *Child Development, 74,* 1039–1043.

Fabian, G. (2002). Sequential request and organ donation. *Journal of Social Psychology, 22,* 171–178.

Facebook. (2008).Press room, Palo Alto, CA: Facebook. Retrieved from http://www.facebook.com/press/info .php?statistics

Fagot, B. I., & Hagan, R. (1991). Observations of parent reactions to sex-stereotyped behaviors: Age and sex effects. *Child Development, 62,* 617–628.

Fagot, B. I., Hagan, R., Leinbach, M. D., & Kronsberg, S. (1985). Differential reactions to assertive and communicative acts of toddler boys and girls. *Child Development, 56,* 1499–1505.

Fairbrother, K., & Warn, J. (2003). Workplace dimensions, stress, and job satisfaction. *Journal of Managerial Psychology, 18*(1), 8–21.

Falk, P. (1994). The gap between psychological assumptions and empirical research in lesbian-mother child custody cases. In A. E. Gottfried & A. W. Gottfried (Eds.), *Redefining families: Implications for children's development.* New York: Plenum.

Falsetti, S. A., & Ballenger, J. C. (1998). Stress and anxiety disorders. In J. R. Hubbard & E. A. Workman (Eds.), *Handbook of stress medicine: An organ system approach.* New York: CRC Press.

Families and Work Institute. (2004). *Generation and gender in the workplace.* New York: Families and Work Institute.

Fancher, R. E. (1979). *Pioneers of psychology.* New York: Norton.

Fang, C., Miller, S., Bovbjerg, D., Bergman, C., Edelson, M., Rosenblum, N., et al. (2008). Perceived stress is associated with impaired T-cell response to HPV 16 in women with cervical dysplasia. *Annals of Behavioral Medicine, 35*(1), 87–96.

Faravelli, C., & Pallanti, S. (1989). Recent life events and panic disorders. *American Journal of Psychiatry, 146,* 622–626.

Farquhar, J. C., & Wasylkiw, L. (2007). Media images of men: Trends and consequences of body conceptualization. *Psychology of Men & Masculinity, 8*(3), 145–160.

Fassler, D. (2001). *Talking to children about war and terrorism: 20 tips for parents.* Retrieved November 20, 2001 from American Psychiatric Association Web site: http://www.psych.org/disaster/20tipsparents11801.cfm.

Faust, K. A., & McKibben, J. N. (1999). Marital dissolution: Divorce, separation, annulment, and widowhood. In M. B. Sussman, S. K. Steinmetz, & G. W. Peterson (Eds.), *Handbook of marriage and the family.* New York: Plenum Press.

Fausto-Sterling, A. (1992). *Myths of gender: Biological theories about women and men* (2nd ed.). New York: Basic Books.

Fava, G. A. (1999). Well-being therapy: Conceptual and technical issues. *Psychotherapy and Psychosomatics, 68*(4), 171–179.

Fava, G. A., Ruini, C., Rafanelli, C., Finos, L., Salmaso, L., Mangelli, L., et al. (2005). Well-being therapy of generalized anxiety disorder. *Psychotherapy and Psychosomatics, 74*(1), 26–30.

Feder, J., Levant, R. F., & Dean, J. (2007). Boys and violence: A gender-informed analysis. *Professional Psychology: Research and Practice, 38,* 385–391.

Feeney, J. A. (2004). Adult attachment and relationship functioning under stressful conditions: Understanding partners' responses to conflict and challenge. In W. S. Rholes & J. A. Simpson (Eds.), *Adult attachment: Theory, research, and clinical implications.* New York: Guilford.

Feeney, J. A., & Noller, P. (1990). Attachment style as a predictor of adult romantic relationships. *Journal of Personality and Social Psychology, 58,* 281–291.

Feeny, N. C., Stines, L. R., & Foa, E. B. (2007). Posttraumatic stress disorder-clinical. In G. Fink (Ed.), *Encyclopedia of stress: Vols. 1–4* (2nd ed., pp. 135–139). San Diego, CA: Elsevier Academic Press.

Fehr, B. (1996). *Friendship processes.* Thousand Oaks, CA: Sage.

Fehr, B. (2000). The life cycle of friendship. In C. Hendrick & S. S. Hendrick (Eds.), *Close relationships: A sourcebook.* Thousand Oaks, CA: Sage.

Fehr, B. (2004). Intimacy expectations in same-sex friendships: A prototype interaction-pattern model. *Journal of Personality and Social Psychology, 86*(2), 265–284.

Fehr, B. (2008). Friendship formation. In S. Sprecher, A. Wenzel & J. Harvey (Eds.), *Handbook of relationship initiation* (pp. 29–54). New York: Psychology Press.

Fehr, B. (2009). Friendship formation and development. In H. T. Reis & S. Sprecher (Eds.), *Encyclopedia of human relationships: Vol. 1* (pp. 706–710). Los Angeles: Sage Reference Publication.

Fein, S. (1996). Effects of suspicion on attributional thinking and the correspondence bias. *Journal of Personality and Social Psychology, 70,* 1164–1184.

Feingold, A. (1988). Matching for attractiveness in romantic partners and same-sex friends: A meta-analysis and theoretical critique. *Psychological Bulletin, 104,* 226–235.

Feingold, A. (1992a). Gender differences in mate selection preferences: A test of the parental investment model. *Psychological Bulletin, 112,* 125–139.

Feingold, A. (1992b). Good-looking people are not what we think. *Psychological Bulletin, 111,* 304–341.

Feiring, C., & Lewis, M. (1987). The child's social network: Sex differences from three to six years. *Sex Roles, 17,* 621–636.

Feldman, P. J., Cohen, S., Doyle, W. J., Skoner, D. P., & Gwaltney, J. M., Jr. (1999). The impact of personality on the reporting of unfounded symptoms and illness. *Journal of Personality and Social Psychology, 77*(2), 370–378.

Feldman-Barrett, L., & Swim, J. K. (1998). Appraisals of prejudice and discrimination. In J. K. Swim & C. Stangor (Eds.), *Prejudice: The target's perspective.* New York: Academic Press.

Feliciano, L., & Areán, P. A. (2007). Mood disorders: Depressive disorders. In M. Hersen, S. M. Turner, & D. C. Beidel (Eds.), *Adult psychopathology and diagnosis.* New York: Wiley.

Felker, B., & Hubbard, J. R. (1998). Influence of mental stress on the endocrine system. In J. R. Hubbard & E. A. Workman (Eds.), *Handbook of stress medicine: An organ system approach.* New York: CRC Press.

Felmlee, D. H., Sprecher, S., & Bassin, E. (1990). The dissolution of intimate relationships: A hazard model. *Social Psychology Quarterly,* 513–30.

Felson, R. B. (1989). Parents and the reflected appraisal process: A longitudinal analysis. *Journal of Personality and Social Psychology, 56,* 965–971.

Felson, R. B. (1992). Coming to see ourselves: Social sources of self-appraisals. *Advances in Group Processes, 9,* 185–205.

Feng, J., Spence, I., & Pratt, J. (2007). Playing an action video game reduces gender differences in spatial cognition. *Psychological Science, 18,* 850–855.

Fenigstein, A, & Preston, M. (2007). The desired number of sexual partners as a function of gender, sexual risks, and the meaning of "ideal." *Journal of Sex Research, 44,* 89–95.

Fenwick, P. (1987). Meditation and the EEG. In M. A. West (Ed.), *The psychology of meditation.* Oxford: Clarendon Press.

Feroli, K., & Burstein, G. (2003). Adolescent sexually transmitted diseases. *American Journal of Maternal/Child Nursing, 28,* 113–118.

Ferrari, J. R. (1992). Psychometric validation of two adult measures of procrastination: Arousal and avoidance measures. *Journal of Psychopathology & Behavioral Assessment, 14,* 97–100.

Ferrari, J. R. (2001). Getting things done on time: Conquering procrastination. In C. R. Snyder (Ed.), *Coping with stress: Effective people and processes.* New York: Oxford University Press.

Ferrari, J. R., Diaz-Morales, J. F., O'Callaghan, J., Diaz, K., & Argumedo, D. (2007). Frequent behavioral delay tendencies by adults: International prevalence rates of chronic procrastination. *Journal of Cross-Cultural Psychology, 38,* 458–464.

Ferrari, J. R., Johnson, J. L., & McCown, W. G. (1995). *Procrastination and task avoidance: Theory research and treatment.* New York: Plenum Press.

Festinger, L. (1954). A theory of social comparison processes. *Human Relations, 7,* 117–140.

Few, R. (2007). Health and climatic hazards: Framing social research on vulnerability, Response and adaptation. *Global Environmental Change, 17,* 281–295.

Fiatrone, M. A., O'Neill, E. F., Doyle, N., Clements, K. M., Roberts, S. B., Kehayias, J. J., Lipsitz, L. A., & Evans, W. J. (1993). The Boston FICSIT study: The effects of resistance training and nutritional supplementation on physical frailty in the oldest old. *Journal of the American Geriatrics Society, 41,* 333–337.

Fiedler, K., Schmid, J., & Stahl, T. (2002). What is the current truth about polygraph lie detection? *Basic & Applied Social Psychology, 24,* 313–324.

Fifield , J., Mcquillian, J., Armeli, S., Tennen, H., Reisine, S., & Affleck, G. (2004). Chronic strain, daily work stress and pain among workers with rheumatoid arthritis: Does job stress make a bad day worse? *Work and Stress, 18,* 275–291.

Figueredo, A. J., Gladden, P., Vásquez, G., Wolf, P. S. A., & Jones, D. N. (2009). Evolutionary theories of personality. In P. J. Corr & G. Matthews (Eds.), *The Cambridge handbook of personality psychology* (pp. 265–274). New York: Cambridge University Press.

Figueredo, A. J., Sefcek, J. A., Vasquez, G., Brumbach, B. H., King, J. E., & Jacobs, W. J. (2005). Evolutionary personality psychology. In D. M. Buss (Ed.), *The handbook of evolutionary psychology.* New York: Wiley.

Fincham, F. D. (2001). Attributions in close relationships: From Balkanization to integration. In G. J. O. Fletcher, & M. S. Clark (Eds.), *Blackwell handbook of social psychology: Vol. 2. Interpersonal processes.* Oxford: Blackwell.

Fincham, F. D. (2003). Marital conflict: Correlates, structure, and context. *Current Directions in Psychological Science, 12*(1), 23–27.

Fincham, F. D. (2009). Conflict, martial. In H. T. Reis & S. Sprecher (Eds.), *Encyclopedia of human relationships: Vol. 2* (pp. 298–303). Los Angeles: Sage Reference Publication.

Fincham, F. D., & Beach, S. R. H. (2006). Relationship satisfaction. In A. L. Vangelisti & D. Perlman (Eds.), *The Cambridge handbook of personal relationships.* New York: Cambridge University Press.

Finder, A. (2006, June 11). For some, online persona undermines a resume. *New York Times.* Retrieved from http://www.nytimes.com/2006/06/11/us/11recruit.hyml

Fine, R. (1990). *The history of psychoanalysis.* New York: Continuum.

Finer, L. B., & Henshaw, S. K. (2006). Disparities in rates of unintended pregnancy in the United States, 1994 and 2001. *Perspectives on Sexual Reproductive Health, 38,* 90–96.

Finkelhor, D., Mitchell, K., & Wolak, J. (2000). *Online victimization: A report on the nation's youth.* Washington, DC: National Center for Missing and Exploited Children.

Finkelstein, E. A., Ruhm, C. J., & Kosa, K. M. (2005). Economic causes and consequences of obesity. *Annual Review of Public Health, 26,* 239–257.

Finkenauer, C., & Hazam, H. (2000). Disclosure and secrecy in marriage: Do both contribute to marital satisfaction? *Journal of Social and Personal Relationships, 17*(2), 245–263.

Finucane, M. L., Alhakami, A. S., Slovic, P. & Johnson, S. M. (2000). The affect heuristic in judgments of risks and benefits. *Journal of Behavioral Decision Making, 13,* 1–17.

First, M. B. (2003). Psychiatric classification. In A. Tasman, J. Kay, & J. A. Lieberman (Eds.), *Psychiatry.* New York: Wiley.

Fischer, P., Greitemeyer, T., & Pollozek, F. (2006). The unresponsive bystander: Are bystanders more responsive in dangerous emergencies? *European Journal of Social Psychology, 36*, 267–278.

Fischer, R., Ferreira, M. C., Assmar, E., Redford, P., Harb, C., Glazer, S., Cheng, B.-S., Jiang, D.-Y., Wong, C. C., Kumar, N., Kärtner, J., Hofer, J., & Achoui, M. (2009). Individualism-collectivism as descriptive norms: Development of a subjective norm approach to cultural measurement. *Journal of Cross-Cultural Psychology, 40*(2), 187–213.

Fisher, D. A., Hill, D. L., Grube, J. W., Bersamine, M. M., Walker, S., & Gruber, E. L. (2009). Televised sexual content and parental mediation: Influences on adolescent sexuality. *Media Psychology, 12*, 121–147.

Fisher, E. B., Brownson, R. C., Heath, A. C., Luke, D. A., & Sumner II, W. (2004). Cigarette smoking. In J. M. Raczynski & L. C. Leviton (Eds.), *Handbook of clinical health psychology: Vol. 2. Disorders of behavior and health*. Washington, DC: American Psychological Association.

Fisher, S., & Greenberg, R. P. (1996). *Freud scientifically reappraised: Testing the theories and therapy*. New York: Wiley.

Fisher, T. D. (1990). Characteristics of mothers and fathers who talk to their adolescent children about sexuality. *Journals of Psychology & Human Sexuality, 3*, 53–70.

Fishman, D. B., & Franks, C. M. (1992). Evolution and differentiation within behavior therapy: A theoretical epistemological review. In D. K. Freedheim (Ed.), *History of psychotherapy: A century of change*. Washington, DC: American Psychological Association.

Fiske, S. T. (1993). Social cognition and social perception. *Annual Review of Psychology, 44*, 155–194.

Fiske, S. T. (1998). Stereotyping, prejudice, and discrimination. In D. T. Gilbert, S. T. Fiske, & G. Lindzey (Eds.), *The handbook of social psychology*. New York: McGraw-Hill.

Fiske, S. T. (2002). What we know now about bias and intergroup conflict, the problem of the century. *Current Directions in Psychological Science, 11*(4), 123–128.

Fiske, S. T. (2004). *Social beings: A core motives approach to social psychology*. New York: Wiley.

Fiske, S. T., Harris, L. T., & Cuddy, A. J. C. (2004). Why ordinary people torture enemy prisoners. *Science, 36*, 1482–1483.

Fiske, S. T., & Ruscher, J. B. (1993). Negative interdependence and prejudice: Whence the affect? In D. M. Mackie & D. L. Hamilton (Eds.), *Affect, cognition, and stereotyping: Interactive processes in group perception*. New York: Academic.

Fiske, S. T., & Taylor, S. E. (1991). *Social cognition*. New York: McGraw-Hill.

Fitness, J., Fletcher, G., & Overall, N. (2007). Interpersonal attraction and intimate relationships. In M. A. Hogg & J. Cooper (Eds.), *The Sage handbook of social psychology*. Los Angeles: Sage.

Flaks, D. K., Ficher, I., Masterpasqua, M., & Joseph, G. (1995). Lesbians choosing motherhood: A comparative study of lesbians and heterosexual parents and their children. *Developmental Psychology, 31*, 105–114.

Flannery, R. B., Jr. (1999). Psychological trauma and posttraumatic stress disorder: A review. *International Journal of Mental Health, 1*(2), 135–140.

Flavin, C., & Engelman, R. (2009). The perfect storm. In G. Gardner & T. Prugh (Eds.), *2009 state of the world: Into a warming world* (pp. 5–12). Washington, DC: Worldwatch Institute.

Fleeson, W. (2004). Moving personality beyond the person-situation debate: The challenge and the opportunity of within-person variability. *Current Directions in Psychological Science, 13*(2), 83–87.

Fleeson, W., Malanos, A. B., & Achille, N. M. (2002). An intraindividual process approach to the relationship between extraversion and positive affect: Is acting extraverted as "good" as being extraverted? *Journal of Personality and Social Psychology, 83*(6), 1409–1422.

Fletcher, G. J. O., Overall, N. C., & Friesen, M. D. (2006). Social cognition in intimate relationships. In A. L. Vangelisti & D. Perlman (Eds.), *The Cambridge handbook of personal relationships*. New York: Cambridge University Press.

Fletcher, G. J. O., Tither, J. M., O'Loughlin, C., Friesen, M., & Overall, N. (2004). Warm and homely or cold and beautiful? Sex differences in trading off traits in mate selection. *Personality and Social Psychology Bulletin, 30*, 659–672.

Fletcher, G. J. O., & Ward, C. (1988). Attribution theory and processes: A cross-cultural perspective. In M. H. Bond (Ed.), *The cross-cultural challenge to social psychology*. Newbury Park, CA: Sage.

Flett, G. L., Hewitt, P. L., & Martin, T. R. (1995). Dimensions of perfectionism and procrastination. In J. R. Ferrari, J. L. Johnson, & W. G. McCown (Eds.), *Procrastination and task avoidance: Theory, research, and treatment*. New York: Plenum Press.

Flores, B. H., Musselman, D. L., DeBattista, C., Garlow, S. J., Schatzberg, A. F., & Nemeroff, C. B. (2004). Biology of mood disorders. In A. F. Schatzberg & C. B. Nemeroff (Eds.), *Textbook of psychopharmacology*. Washington, DC: American Psychiatric Publishing.

Floyd, F. J., & Bakeman, R. (2006). Coming-out across the life course: Implications of age and historical context. *Archives of Sexual Behavior, 35*, 287–297.

Floyd, K., Boren, J. P., Hannawa, A. F., Hesse, C., McEwan, B., & Veksler, A. E. (2009). Kissing in marital and cohabiting relationships: Effects on blood lipids, stress, and relationship satisfaction. *Western Journal of Communication, 73*, 113–133.

Floyd, M. (2003). Bibliotherapy as an adjunct to psychotherapy for depression in older adults. *Journal of Clinical Psychology, 59*(2), 187–195.

Flynn, F. J. (2005). Having an open mind: The impact of openness to experience on interracial attitudes and impression formation. *Journal of Personality and Social Psychology , 88*, 816–826.

Flynn, F. J., Reagans, R. E., Amanatullah, E. T., & Ames, D. R. (2006). Helping one's way to the top: Self-monitors achieve status by helping others and knowing who helps whom. *Journal of Personality and Social Psychology, 91*, 1123–1137.

Foa, E. B. (1998). Rape and posttraumatic stress disorder. In E. A. Blechman & K. D. Brownell (Eds.), *Behavioral medicine and women: A comprehensive handbook*. New York: Guilford Press.

Foa, E. B., Hembree, E. A., Riggs, D., Rauch, S., & Franklin, M. (2001). *Common reactions to trauma.* Retrieved November 21, 2001 from U.S. Department of Veterans Affairs National Cen-ter for PTSD Web site: http:www.ncptsd.org/facts/disasters/fs_foa_handout.html.

Folkman, S. (1997). Positive psychological states and coping with severe stress. *Social Science and Medicine, 45*, 1207–1221.

Folkman, S. (2008). The case for positive emotions in the stress process. *Anxiety, Stress, Coping, 21*, 3–14.

Folkman, S., & Moskowitz, J. T. (2000). Positive affect and the other side of coping. *American Psychologist, 55*(6), 647–654.

Folkman, S., Moskowitz, J. T., Ozer, E. M., & Park, C. L. (1997). Positive meaningful events and coping in the context of HIV/AIDS. In B. H. Gottlieb (Ed.), *Coping with chronic stress*. New York: Plenum.

Folsom, D. P., Gilmer, T., Barrio, C., Moore, D. J., Bucardo, J., Lindamer, L. A., et al. (2007). A longitudinal study of the use of mental health services by persons with serious mental illness: Do Spanish-speaking Latinos differ from English-speaking Latinos and Caucasians? *American Journal Psychiatry, 164*, 1173–1180.

Food and Agriculture Organization of the United Nations. (2006). Livestock's long shadow: Environmental issues and options. Retrieved from http://www.fao.org/docrep/010/a0701e/a0701e00.HTM

Foote, B., Smolin, Y., Kaplan M., Legatt, M. E., & Lipschitz, D. (2006). Prevalence of dissociative disorders in psychiatric outpatients. *American Journal of Psychiatry, 163*, 623–629.

Foran, H., & O'Leary, K. (2008). Problem drinking, jealousy, and anger control: Variables predicting physical aggression against a partner. *Journal of Family Violence, 23*, 141–148.

Forbes, G. B., Adams-Curtis, L. E., & White, K. B. (2004). First- and second-generation measures of sexism, rape, myths and related beliefs, and hostility toward women: Their interrelationships and associations with college students' experience with dating aggression and sexual coercion. *Violence Against Women, 10*(3), 236–261.

Formicelli, L. (2001, March/April). Baby blues. *Psychology Today*, p. 24.

Forsyth, D. R., & Strong, S. R. (1986). The scientific study of counseling and psychotherapy: A unificationist view. *American Psychologist, 41*, 113–119.

Forsyth, D. R., Lawrence, N. K., Burnette, J. L., & Baumeister, R. F. (2007). Attempting to improve the academic performance of struggling college students by bolstering self-esteem: An intervention that backfired. *Journal of Social and Clinical Psychology, 26*, 447–459.

Fortune, J. L., & Newby-Clark, I. R. (2008). My friend is embarrassing me: Exploring the guilty by association effect. *Journal of Personality and Social Psychology, 95*(6), 1440–1449.

Fouad, N. A. (2007). Work and vocational psychology: Theory, Research, and applications. *Annual Review of Psychology, 58*, 543–564.

Fouad, N. A., & Mohler, C. J. (2004). Cultural validity of Holland's theory and the Strong Interest Inventory for five racial/ethnic groups. *Journal of Career Assessment, 12*, 423–439.

Fouts, G., & Burggraf, K. (1999). Television situation comedies: Female body images and verbal reinforcements. *Sex Roles, 40*(5/6), 473–481.

Fouts, G., & Vaughan, K. (2002). Television situation comedies: Male weight, negative references, and audience reactions. *Sex Roles, 46*(11/12), 439–442.

Fowers, B. J. (2000). *Beyond the myth of marital happiness: How embracing the virtues of loyalty, generosity, justice, and courage can strengthen your relationship*. San Francisco: Jossey-Bass.

Fowers, B. J., Applegate, B., Olson, D. H., & Pomerantz, B. (1994). Marital conventionalization as a measure of marital satisfaction: A confirmatory factor analysis. *Journal of Family Psychology, 8*, 98–103.

Fowers, B. J., Lyons, E., Montel, K. H., & Shaked, N. (2001). Positive illusions about marriage among married and single individuals. *Journal of Family Psychology, 15*(1), 95–109.

Fox, G. L., & Chancey, D. (1998). Sources of economic distress: Individual and family outcomes. *Journal of Family Issues, 19*, 725–749.

Fox, G. L., Bruce, C., & Combs-Orme, T. (2000). Parenting expectations and concerns of fathers and mothers of newborn infants. *Family Relations, 49*(2), 123–131.

Fox, R. (1996). Bisexuality in perspective: A review of theory and research. In B. Firestein (Ed.), *Bisexuality: The psychology and politics of an invisible minority*. Thousand Oaks, CA: Sage.

Fraley, R. C. (2002). Attachment stability from infancy to adulthood: Meta-analysis and dynamic modeling of developmental mechanisms. *Personality and Social Psychology Review, 6*(2), 123–151.

Fraley, R. C., & Brumbaugh, C. C. (2004). A dynamical systems approach to conceptualizing and studying stability and change in attachment security. In W. S. Rholes & J. A. Simpson (Eds.), *Adult attachment: Theory, research, and clinical implications*. New York: The Guilford.

Frame, L. E., Mattson, R. E., & Johnson, M. D. (2009). Predicting success or failure of marital relationships. In H. T. Reis & S. Sprecher (Eds.), *Encyclopedia of human relationships: Vol. 3* (pp. 1275–1279). Los Angeles: Sage Reference Publication.

Francis, L. A., & Birch, L. L. (2005). Maternal influences on daughters' restrained eating behavior. *Health Psychology, 24*, 548–554.

Francoeur, R. T. (2007). Catholic culture and sexual health. In M. S. Tepper & A. F. Owens (Eds.), *Sexual health: Vol 3. Moral and cultural foundations* (pp. 43–77). Westport, CT: Praeger Publishers/Greenwood Publishing Group.

Frank, J. D. (1961). *Persuasion and healing*. Baltimore: John Hopkins University Press.

Frank, J. D., & Frank, J. B. (1991). *Persuasion and healing: A comparison study of psychotherapy*. Baltimore: Johns Hopkins University Press.

Frank, L. R. (1990). Electroshock: Death, brain damage, memory loss, and brainwashing. *The Journal of Mind and Behavior, 11*, 489–512.

Frank, M. G., & Ekman, P. (1997). The ability to detect deceit generalizes different types of high-stake lies. *Journal of Personality and Social Psychology, 72*, 1429–1439.

Frankel, F. H. (1993). Adult reconstruction of childhood events in the multiple personality literature. *American Journal of Psychiatry, 150*, 954–958.

Franzoi, S. L., & Herzog, M. E. (1987). Judging personal attractiveness: What body aspects do we use? *Personality and Social Psychology Bulletin, 13*, 19–33.

Franzoi, S. L., & Kern, K. (2009). Body image, relationship implications. In H. T. Reis & S. Sprecher (Eds.), *Encyclopedia of human relationships: Vol. 1* (pp. 181–183). Los Angeles: Sage Reference Publication.

Frazier, P. A. (2009). Rape. In H. T. Reis & S. Sprecher (Eds.), *Encyclopedia of human relationships: Vol. 3* (pp. 1325–1328). Los Angeles: Sage Reference Publication.

Frazier, P. A., Mortensen, H., & Steward, J. (2005). Coping strategies as mediators of the relations among perceived control and distress in sexual assault survivors. *Journal of Counseling Psychology, 52*, 267–278.

Frederick, S., & Loewenstein, G. (1999). Hedonic adaptation. In D. Kahneman, E. Diener, & N. Schwarz (Eds.), *Well-being: The foundations of hedonic psychology*. New York: Sage.

Fredrickson, B. L. (1998). What good are positive emotions? *Review of General Psychology, 2*, 300–319.

Fredrickson, B. L. (2001). The role of positive emotions in positive psychology: The broaden-and-build theory of positive emotions. *American Psychologist, 56*, 218–226.

Fredrickson, B. L. (2002). Positive emotions. In C. R. Snyder & S. J. Lopez (Eds.), *Handbook of positive psychology* (pp. 120–134). New York: Oxford University Press.

Fredrickson, B. L. (2006). The broaden-and-build theory of positive emotions. In M. Csikszentmihalyi & I. S. Csikszentmihalyi (Eds.), *A life worth living: Contributions to positive psychology*. New York: Oxford University Press.

Fredrickson, B. L., & Branigan, C. (2005). Positive emotions broaden the scope of attention and thought-action repertoires. *Cognition and Emotion, 19,* 313–332.

Fredrickson, B. L., & Joiner, T. (2002). Positive emotions trigger upward spirals toward emotional well-being. *Psychological Science, 13,* 172–175.

Fredrickson, B. L., & Levenson, R. (1998). Positive emotions speed recovery from the cardiovascular sequelae of negative emotions. *Cognition and Emotion, 12,* 191–220.

Fredrickson, B. L., & Losada, M. F. (2005). Positive affect and the complex dynamics of human flourishing. *American Psychologist, 60,* 678–686.

Fredrickson, B. L., Roberts, T., Noll, S. M., Quinn, D. M., & Twenge, J. M. (1998). That swimsuit becomes you: Sex differences in self-objectification, restrained eating, and math performance. *Journal of Personality and Social Psychology , 75,* 269–284.

Fredrickson, B. L., Tugade, M. M., Waugh, C. E., & Larkin, G. R. (2003). What good are positive emotions in crises? A prospective study of resilience and emotions following the terrorist attacks on the United States on September 11th, 2001. *Journal of Personality and Social Psychology, 84*(2), 365–376.

Freedberg, K., Losina, E., Weinstein, M., Paltiel, A., Cohen, C., Seage, G., Craven, D., Zhang, H., Kimmel, A., & Goldie, S. (2001). The cost effectiveness of combination antiretroviral therapy for HIV disease. *New England Journal of Medicine,* 824–831.

Freedman, J. L., & Fraser, S. C. (1966). Compliance without pressure: The foot-in-the-door technique. *Journal of Personality and Social Psychology, 4,* 195–202.

Freeman, D., Aquino, K., & McFerran, B. (2009). Overcoming beneficiary race as an impediment to charitable donations: Social Dominance Orientation, the experience of moral elevation, and donation behavior. *Personality and Social Psychology Bulletin, 35*(1), 72–84.

Freeman, E., Bloom, D., & McGuire, E. (2001). A brief history of testosterone. *Journal of Urology, 165,* 371–373.

Freeman, N. K. (2007). Preschoolers' perceptions of gender appropriate toys and their parents' beliefs about genderized behaviors: Miscommunication, mixed messages, or hidden truths? *Early Childhood Education Journal, 34,* 357–366.

Fremouw, W. J., de Perczel, M., & Ellis, T. E. (1990). *Suicide risk: Assessment and response guidelines.* New York: Pergamon.

French, S. A., Harnack, L., & Jeffrey, R. W. (2000). Fast food restaurant use among women in the Pound of Prevention study: Dietary, behavioral and demographic correlates. *International Journal of Obesity, 24,* 1353–1359.

Freud, S. (1901/1960). *The psychopathology of everyday life* (Standard ed., Vol. 6.) London: Hogarth. (Original work published 1901)

Freud, S. (1910/1957) Leonardo da Vinci: A study in psychosexuality. In J. Strachey (Ed., Trans.), *The standard edition of the complete psychological works of Sigmund Freud* (Vol. 11). London: Hogarth Press. (First German edition, 1910)

Freud, S. (1914/1953). On narcissism: An introduction. In J. Strachey (Ed., Trans.), *The standard edition of the complete psychological works of Sigmund Freud* (Vol. 1). London: Hogarth Press. (original work published 1914)

Freud, S. (1920/1924). *A general introduction to psychoanalysis.* New York: Boni and Liveright. (Original work published 1920)

Freud, S. (1923). *The ego and the id.* In J. Strachey (Ed., Trans.), *The standard edition of the complete psychological works of Sigmund Freud* (Vol. 19). London: Hogarth.

Freud, S. (1935). *A general introduction to psychoanalysis* (J. Rivere, Trans.). New York: Liveright.

Frewen, P. A., Brinker, J., Martin, R. A., & Dozois, D. J. A. (2008). Humor styles and personality-vulnerability to depression. *Humor, 21,* 179–195.

Frey, B. S., & Stutzer, A. (2002). What can economists learn from happiness research? *Journal of Economic Literature, 40,* 402–435.

Fried, S. B., & Schultis, G. A. (1995). *The best self-help and self-awareness books: A topic-by-topic guide to quality information.* Chicago: American Library Association.

Friedan, B. (1964). *The feminine mystique.* New York: Dell.

Friedman, H. S. (1991). *The self-healing personality: Why some people achieve health and others succumb to illness.* New York: Holt.

Friedman, H. S. (2007). Personality, disease, and self-healing. In H. S. Friedman & R. C. Silver (Eds.), *Foundations of health psychology.* New York: Oxford University Press.

Friedman, H. S., & Adler, N. E. (2007). The history and background of health psychology. In H. S. Friedman & R. C. Silver (Eds.), *Foundations of health psychology.* New York: Oxford University Press.

Friedman, H. S., & Silver, R. C. (Eds.). (2007). *Foundations of health psychology.* New York: Oxford University Press.

Friedman, M. (1996). *Type A behavior: Its diagnosis and treatment.* New York: Plenum Press.

Friedman, M., & Rosenman, R. F. (1974). *Type A behavior and your heart.* New York: Knopf.

Friedrich, M. J. (2004). To "E" or not to "E", vitamin E's role in health and disease is the question. *Journal of the American Medical Association, 292*(6), 671–673.

Friedman, M. J. (2006). Posttraumatic stress disorder among military returnees from Afghanistan and Iraq. *American Journal of Psychiatry, 163,* 586-593.

Frieze, I. H., & Ciccocioppo, M. (2009). Gender-role attitudes. In H. T. Reis & S. Sprecher (Eds.), *Encyclopedia of human relationships: Vol. 1* (pp. 751–754). Los Angeles: Sage Reference Publication.

Frijda, N. H. (1986). *The emotions.* Cambridge: Cambridge University Press.

Fritze, J. G., Blashki, G. A., Burke, S. and Wiseman, J. ( 2008). Hope, despair and transformation: Climate change and the promotion of mental health and well-being. *International Journal of Mental Health Systems, 2.*

Froh, J. J. (2009). Positive emotions. In S. J. Lopez (Ed.), *The encyclopedia of positive psychology* (Vol. II, pp. 711–717). Malden, MA: Wiley-Blackwell.

Fromm, E. (1963). *Escape from freedom.* New York: Holt.

Fromm, E. (1981). *Sane society.* New York: Fawcett.

Fruhauf, C. A. (2009). Caregiver role. In H. T. Reis & S. Sprecher (Eds.), *Encyclopedia of human relationships: Vol. 2* (pp. 195–197). Los Angeles: Sage Reference Publication.

Fu, X., & Heaton, T. B. (2008). Racial and educational homogamy: 1980 to 2000. *Sociological Perspectives, 51,* 735–758.

Funder, D. C. (2001). Personality. *Annual Review of Psychology, 52,* 197–221.

Funk, J. L., & Rogge, R. D. (2009). Marital stability, prediction of. In H. T. Reis & S. Sprecher (Eds.), *Encyclopedia of human relationships: Vol. 1* (pp. 1034–1037). Los Angeles: Sage Reference Publication.

Furman, E. (1984). Children's patterns in mourning the death of a loved one. In H. Wass & C. A. Corr (Eds.), *Childhood and death.* Washington, DC: Hemisphere.

Furnham, A., & Cheng, H. (2000). Perceived parental behavior, self-esteem and happiness. *Social Psychiatry and Psychiatric Epidemiology, 35*(10), 463–470.

Furnham, A., & Mak, T. (1999). Sex-role stereotyping in television commercials: A review and comparison of fourteen studies done on five continents over 25 years. *Sex Roles, 41,* 413–437.

Furstenberg, F. F., Jr. (2001). The sociology of adolescence and youth in the 1990s: A critical commentary. In R. M. Milardo (Ed.), *Understanding families into the new millennium: A decade in review.* Minneapolis, MN: National Council on Family Relations.

Furstenberg, F. F., Jr., & Kiernan, K. E. (2001). Delayed parental divorce: How much do children benefit? *Journal of Marriage and Family, 63,* 446–457.

Fyer, A. J. (2009). Anxiety disorders: Genetics. In B. J. Sadock, V. A. Sadock, & P. Ruiz (Eds.), *Kaplan & Sadock's comprehensive textbook of psychiatry* (pp. 1898–1905). Philadelphia: Lippincott Williams & Wilkins.

Gabbard, G. O. (1994). Reconsidering the American Psychological Association's policy on sex with former patients: Is it justifiable? *Professional Psychology: Research and Practice, 25,* 329–335.

Gabbard, G. O. (2005). Major modalities: Psychoanalytic/psychodynamic. In G. O. Gabbard, J. S. Beck, & J. Holmes (Eds.), *Oxford textbook of psychotherapy.* New York: Oxford University Press.

Gable, S. L., & Haidt, J. (2005). What (and why) is positive psychology? *Review of General Psychology, 9,* 103–110.

Gable, S. L., Gonzaga, G. C., & Strachman, A. (2006). Will you be there for me when things go right? Supportive responses to positive event disclosures. *Journal of Personality and Social Psychology, 91,* 904–917.

Gable, S. L., Reis, H. T., Impett, E. A., & Asher, E. R. (2004). What do you do when things go right? The intrapersonal and interpersonal benefits of sharing positive events. *Journal of Personality and Social Psychology, 87,* 228–245.

Gabriel, S., & Gardner, W. L. (1999). Are there "his" and "hers" types of interdependence? The implications of gender differences in collective versus relational interdependence for affect, behavior, and cognition. *Journal of Personality and Social Psychology, 77*(3), 642–655.

Gaertner, S. L., & Dovidio, J. F. (1986). The aversive form of racism. In J. F. Dovidio & S. L. Gaertner (Eds.), *Prejudice, discrimination, and racism: Theory and research.* Orlando, FL: Academic Press.

Gaertner, S. L., & Dovidio, J. F. (2005). Understanding and addressing contemporary racism: From aversive racism to the common ingroup identity model. *Journal of Social Issues, 61,* 615–639.

Gage, F. H. (2002). Neurogenesis in the adult brain. *Journal of Neuroscience, 22,* 612–613.

Gailliot, M. T. (2008). Unlocking the energy dynamics of executive function: Linking executive functioning to brain glycogen. *Perspectives on Psychological Science, 3,* 245–263.

Gailliot, M. T., Baumeister, R. F., DeWall, C. N., Maner, J. K., Plant, E. A., Tice, D. M., Brewer, L. E., & Schmeichel, B. J. (2007). Self-control relies on glucose as a limited energy source: Willpower is more than a metaphor. *Journal of Personality and Social Psychology, 92*(2), 325–336.

Gailliot, M. T., Peruche, B. M., Plant, E. A., & Baumeister, R. F. (2009). Stereotypes and prejudice in the blood: Sucrose drinks reduce prejudice and stereotyping. *Journal of Experimental Social Psychology, 45*(1), 288–290.

Gaines, S. O., Jr. (2009). Interracial and interethnic relationships. In H. T. Reis & S. Sprecher (Eds.), *Encyclopedia of human relationships: Vol. 1* (pp. 905–907). Los Angeles: Sage Reference Publication.

Gajendran, R. S., & Harrison, D. A. (2007). The good, the bad, and the unknown about telecommuting: Meta-analysis of psychological mediators and individual consequences. *Journal of Applied Psychology, 92*(6), 1524–1541.

Galdas, P. M., Cheater, F., & Marshall, P. (2005). Men and health-seeking behavior: Literature review. *Journal of Advanced Nursing, 49,* 616–623.

Galderisi, S., Maj, M., Mucci, A., Cassano, G. B., Invernizzi, G., Rossi, A., Vita, A., Dell'Osso, L., Daneluzzo, E., & Pini, S. (2002). Historical, psychopathological, neurological, and neuropsychological aspects of deficit schizophrenia: A multicenter study. *American Journal of Psychiatry, 159,* 983–990.

Galinsky, E., Bond, J. T., Kim, S. S., Backon, L., Brownfield, E., & Sakai, K. (2005). *Overwork in America.* New York: Families and Work Institute.

Gallup. (2007). *Same-sex marriage: Where Americans stand on the legality of same-sex marriage.* Retrieved from http://www.gallup.com/video/27706/samesex-marriage.aspx?ve

Gambone, J. C., Reiter, R. C., & DiMatteo, M. R. (1994). *The PREPARED provider: A guide for improved patient communication.* Beaverton, OR: Mosybl Great Performance.

Gana, K., Alaphilippe, D., & Bailly, N. (2004). Positive illusions and mental and physical health in later life. *Aging and Mental Health, 8*(1), 58–64.

Ganahl, D. J., Prinsen, T. J., & Netzley, S. B. (2003). A content analysis of prime time commercials: A contextual framework of gender representation. *Sex Roles, 49,* 545–551.

Gangestad, S. W. (1993). Sexual selection and physical attractiveness: Implications for mating dynamics. *Human Nature, 4,* 205–235.

Gangestad, S. W., & Snyder, M. (2000). Self-monitoring appraisal and reappraisal. *Psychological Bulletin, 126*(4), 530–555.

Gantt, W. H. (1975, April 25). Unpublished lecture, Ohio State University. Cited in D. Hothersall (1984), *History of psychology.* New York: Random House.

Gao, G. (2001). Intimacy, passion and commitment in Chinese and U.S. American romantic relationships. *International Journal of Intercultural Relations, 25*(3), 329–342.

Garb, H. N., Florio, C. M., & Grove, W. M. (1998). The validity of the Rorschach and the Minnesota Multiphasic Personality Inventory: Results from meta-analysis. *Psychological Science, 9,* 402–404.

García, F., & Gracia, E. (2009). Is always authoritative parenting the optimal parenting style? Evidence from Spanish families. *Adolescence, 44*(173), 101–131.

Garcia, S. M., & Tor, A. (2009). The N-effect: More competitors, less competition. *Psychological Science, 20*(7), 871–877.

**Gardner, G.** (2002). The challenge for Johannesburg: Creating a more secure world. In C. Flavin, H. French, & G. Gardner (Eds.), *State of the world 2002: A Worldwatch Institute report on progress toward a sustainable society* (pp. 3–23). New York: Norton.

**Gardner, G., & Prugh, T.** (2008). Seeding the sustainable economy. In L. Starke (Ed.), *2008 State of the World: Innovations for a sustainable economy* (pp. 3–17). New York: Norton.

**Gardner, G. T., & Stern, P. C.** (2002). Human reactions to environmental hazards: Perceptual and cognitive processes. In *Environmental problems and human behavior* (2nd ed., pp. 205–252). Boston: Allyn & Bacon.

**Gardner, G. T., & Stern, P. C.** (2008). The short list: The most effective actions U.S. households can take to curb climate change. *Environment, 50(5),* 12–24.

**Garmezy, N.** (1991). Resiliency and vulnerability of adverse developmental outcomes associated with poverty. *American Behavioral Scientist, 34,* 416–430.

**Garnets, L. D., & Kimmel, D. C.** (1991). Lesbian and gay male dimensions in the psychological study of human diversity. In J. D. Goodchilds (Ed.), *Psychological perspectives on human diversity in America.* Washington, DC: American Psychological Association.

**Garnets, L. D., & Kimmel, D. C.** (2003a). Identity development and stigma management. In L. D. Garnets & D. C. Kimmel (Eds.), *Psychological perspectives on lesbian, gay, and bisexual experiences.* New York: Columbia University Press.

**Garnets, L. D., & Kimmel, D. C.** (2003b). Lesbian, gay male, and bisexual dimensions in the psychological study of human diversity. In L. D. Garnets & D. C. Kimmel (Eds.), *Psychological perspectives on lesbian, gay and bisexual experiences.* New York: Columbia University Press.

**Gartrell, N., Banks, A., Hamilton, J., Reed, N., Bishop, H., & Rodas, C.** (1999). The national lesbian family study: Interviews with mothers of toddlers. *American Journal of Orthopsychiatry, 69,* 362–369.

**Gattig, A. & Hendrickx, L.** (2007). Judgmental discounting and environmental risk perception: Dimensional similarities, domain differences, and implications for sustainability. *Journal of Social Issues, 63,* 21–39.

**Gatz, M., & Smyer, M. A.** (2001). Mental health and aging at the outset of the twenty-first century. In J. E. Birren & K. W. Schaie (Eds.), *Handbook of the psychology of aging.* San Diego, CA: Academic Press.

**Gaunt, R.** (2006). Couple similarity and marital satisfaction: Are similar spouses happier? *Journal of Personality, 74,* 1401–1420.

**Gavin, L. E., Black, M. M., Minor, S., Abel, Y., & Bentley, M. E.** (2002). Young, disadvantaged fathers' involvement with their infants: An ecological perspective. *Journal of Adolescent Health, 31,* 266–276.

**Geary, D. C.** (2007). An evolutionary perspective on sex differences in mathematics and the sciences. In S. J. Ceci & W. M. Williams (Eds.), *Why aren't more women in science?* (pp. 173–188). Washington, DC: American Psychological Association.

**Gebhard, U., Nevers, P., & Billmann-Mahecha, E.** (2003). Moralizing trees: Anthropomorphism and identity in children's relationships to nature. In S. Clayton & S. Opotow (Eds.), *Identity and the natural environment: The psychological significance of nature* (pp. 91–111). Cambridge, MA: MIT Press.

**Gecas, V., & Seff, M. A.** (1990). Families and adolescents: A review of the 1980s. *Journal of Marriage and the Family, 52,* 941–958.

**Gee, T., Allen, K., & Powell, R. A.** (2003). Questioning premorbid dissociative symptomatology in dissociative identity disorder. *Professional Psychology: Research & Practice, 34*(1), 114–116.

**Geen, R. G.** (1998). Aggression and antisocial behavior. In D. T. Gilbert, S. T. Fiske, & G. Lindzey (Eds.), *The handbook of social psychology* (4th ed., Vol. 2). Boston: McGraw-Hill.

**Geeraert, N. Y., Yzerbyt, V. Y., Corneille, O., & Wigboldus, D.** (2004). The return of dispositionalism: On the linguistic consequences of dispositional suppression. *Journal of Experimental Social Psychology, 40,* 264–272.

**Gelbspan, R.** (2001 May/June). A modest proposal to stop global warming. *Sierra Magazine,* 62–67.

**Geller, E. S., Winett, R. A., & Everett, P. B.** (1982). *Environmental preservation: New strategies for behavior change.* New York: Pergamon Press.

**Gelles, R. J.** (1996). *The book of David: How preserving families can cost children's lives.* New York: Basic Books.

**Gentile, B., Dolan-Pascoe, B., Grabe, S., & Wells, B. E.** (2009). Gender differences in domain-specific self-esteem: A meta-analysis. *Review of General Psychology, 13,* 34–45.

**Gentile, B., Grabe, S., Dolan-Pascoe, B., Twenge, J. M., Wells, B. E., & Maitino, A.** (2009). Gender differences in domain-specific self-esteem: A meta-analysis. *Review of General Psychology, 13*(1), 34–45.

**George, L. K., Larson, D. B., Koenig, H. G., & McCullough, M. E.** (2000). Spirituality and health: What we know, what we need to know. *Journal of Social and Clinical Psychology, 19,* 102–116.

**George, M. S.** (2003, September). Stimulating the brain. *Scientific American, 289*(3), 66–93.

**George, M. S., Nahas, Z., Bohning, D. E., Kozel, F. A., Anderson, B., Mu, C., et al.** (2006). Vagus nerve stimulation and deep brain stimulation. In D. J. Stein, D. J. Kupfer, & A. F. Schatzberg (Eds.), *Textbook of mood disorders.* Washington, DC: American Psychiatric Publishing.

**Gervey, B., Igou, E. R., & Trope, Y.** (2005). Positive mood and future-oriented self-evaluation. *Motivation and Emotion, 29,* 269–296.

**Getzels, J. W., & Csikszentmihalyi, M.** (1976). *The creative vision.* New York: Wiley.

**Giancola, P. R., Levinson, C. A., Corman, M. D., Godlaski, A. J., Morris, D. H., Philips, J. P., & Holt, J. C. D.** (2009). Men and women, alcohol and aggression. *Experimental and Clinical Psychopharmacology, 17,* 154–164.

**Giannantonio, C., & Hurley-Hanson, A.** (2006). Applying image norms across Super's career development stages. *The Career Development Quarterly, 54*(4), 318–330.

**Giannoglou, G., Chatzizisis, Y., Zamboulis, C., Parcharidis, G., Mikhailidis, D., & Louridas, G.** (2008). Elevated heart rate and atherosclerosis: An overview of the pathogenic mechanisms. *International Journal of Cardiology, 126*(3), 302–312.

**Gibbons, J. L.** (2000). Gender development in cross-cultural perspective. In T. Eckes & H. M. Trautner (Eds.), *The developmental social psychology of gender.* Mahwah, NJ: Erlbaum.

**Gibbons, M. B. C., Crits-Christoph, P., & Hearon, B.** (2008). The empirical status of psychodynamic therapies. *Annual Review of Clinical Psychology, 4,* 93–108.

**Gibbons, R. D., Hur, K., Bhaumik, D. K., & Mann, J. J.** (2006). The relationship between antidepressant prescription rates and rate of early adolescent suicide. *American Journal of Psychiatry, 163,* 1898–1904.

**Gibbs, J. L., Ellison, N. B., & Heino, R. D.** (2006). Self-presentation in online personals: The role of anticipated future interaction, self-disclosure, and perceived success in Internet dating. *Communication Research, 33*(2), 152–177.

**Giddens, A.** (2001). The global revolution in family and personal life. In A. S. Skolnick, & J. H. Skolnick (Eds.), *Families in Transition.* Boston: Allyn & Bacon.

**Gilbert, D. J., & Williams, L.** (2007). Deconstructing the "down low": An ecological perspective on African-American men who have sex with men (MSM). In L. A. See (Ed.), *Human behavior in the social environment from an African-American perspective* (2nd ed., pp. 501–517). New York: Haworth Press.

**Gilbert, D. T.** (2002). Inferential correction. In T. Gilovich, D. W. Griffin, & D. Kahneman (Eds.), *Heuristics and biases: The psychology of intuitive judgment.* New York: Cambridge University Press.

**Gilbert, D. T.** (2006a, July 2). If only gay sex caused global warming. *Los Angeles Times.* Retrieved from http://articles.latimes.com/2006/jul/02/opinion/op-gilbert2

**Gilbert, D. T.** (2006b). *Stumbling on happiness.* New York: Knopf.

**Gilbert, D. T.** (2008). Daniel Gilbert speaks about the psychology of global warming. Retrieved from http://www.youtube.com/watch?v=VTnkT2pcV3s&feature=related

**Gilbert, D. T., Driver-Linn, E., & Wilson, T. D.** (2002). The trouble with Vronsky: Impact bias in the forecasting of future affective states. In L. F. Barrett & P. Salovey (Eds.), *The wisdom in feelings: Psychological processes in emotional intelligence* (pp. 114–143). New York: Guilford.

**Gilbert, D. T., & Malone, P. S.** (1995). The correspondence bias. *Psychological Bulletin, 117,* 21–38.

**Giles, J.** (2008). Sex hormones and sexual desire. *Journal for the Theory of Social Behavior, 38,* 45–66.

**Giles, T. R., & Marafiote, R. A.** (1998). Managed care and the practitioner: A call for unity. *Clinical Psychology: Science & Practice, 5,* 41–50.

**Gilham, J. E., Shatté, A. J., Reivich, K. J., & Seligman, M. E. P.** (2001). Optimism, pessimism, and explanatory style. In E. C. Chang (Ed.), *Optimism & pessimism: Implications for theory, research, and practice.* Washington, DC: American Psychological Association.

**Gill, D. S., Christensen, A., & Fincham, F. D.** (1999). Predicting marital satisfaction from behavior: Do all roads really lead to Rome? *Personal Relationships, 6,* 369–387.

**Gillham, J., & Reivich, K.** (2007). Cultivating optimism in childhood and adolescence. In A. Monat, R. S. Lazarus, & G. Reevy (Eds.), *The Praeger handbook on stress and coping* (pp. 309–326). Westport, CT: Praeger Publishers.

**Gillham, J., & Seligman, M. E. P.** (1999). Footsteps on the road to positive psychology. *Behaviour Research and Therapy, 37,* S163–S173.

**Gilovich, T., Kruger, J., & Medvec, V. H.** (2002). The spotlight effect revisited: Overestimating the manifest variability of our actions and appearance. *Journal of Experimental Social Psychology, 38,* 93–99.

**Gitlin, M.** (2002). Pharmacological treatment of depression. In I. H. Gotlib & C. L. Hammen (Eds.), *Handbook of depression.* New York: Guilford.

**Gitlin, M.** (2009). Pharmacotherapy and other somatic treatments for depression. In I. H. Gotlib & C. L. Hammen (eds.), *Handbook of depression* (pp. 554–585). New York: The Guilford Press.

**Glascock, J.** (2001). Gender roles on prime-time network television: Demograhics and behaviors. *Journal of Broadcasting and Electronic Media, 45*(4), 656–669.

**Glascock, J., & Preston-Schreck, C.** (2004). Gender and racial stereotypes in daily newspaper comics: A time-honored tradition. *Sex Roles, 51,* 423–431.

**Glass, C. R., & Arnkoff, D. B.** (1992). Behavior therapy. In D. K. Freedheim (Ed.), *History of psychotherapy: A century of change.* Washington, DC: American Psychological Association.

**Glass, R. M.** (2001). Electroconvulsive therapy. *Journal of the American Medical Association, 285*(10), 1346–1348.

**Glass, R. M.** (2004). Treatment of adolescents with major depression: Contributions of a major trial. *Journal of the American Medical Association, 292*(7), 861–863.

**Glassman, A., Shapiro, P. A., Ford, D. E., Culpepper, L., Finkel, M. S., Swenson, J. R., Bigger, J. T., Rollman, B. L., & Wise, T. N.** (2003): Cardiovascular health and depression. *Journal of Psychiatric Practice, 9*(6), 409–421.

**Glatt, S. J.** (2008) Genetics. In K. T. Mueser & D. V. Jeste (Eds.), *Clinical handbook of schizophrenia* (pp. 55–64). New York: Guilford.

**Gleason, J. B., & Ely, R.** (2002). Gender differences in language development. In A. McGillicuddy-DeLisi & R. DeLisi (Eds.), *Biology, society, and behavior: The development of sex differences in cognition. Advances in applied developmental psychology, 21.* Westport, CT: Ablex.

**Gleaves, D. H.** (1994). On "the reality of repressed memories." *American Psychologist, 49,* 440–441.

**Gleaves, D. H., Miller, K. J., Williams, T. J., & Summers, S. A.** (2000). Eating disorders: An overview. In K. J. Miller & J. S. Mizes (Eds.), *Comparative treatments for eating disorders.* New York: Springer.

**Gleaves, D. H., & Smith, S. M.** (2004). False and recovered memories in the laboratory and clinic: A review of experimental and clinical evidence. *Clinical Psychology: Science and Practice, 11*(1), 2–28.

**Gluck, M. E.** (2006). Stress response and binge eating disorder. *Appetite, 46*(1), 26–30.

**Gmel, G., & Rehm, J.** (2003). Harmful alcohol use. *Alcohol Research & Health, 27,* 52–62.

**Godfrey, J. R.** (2004). Toward optimal health: The experts discuss therapeutic humor. *Journal of Women's Health, 13,* 474–479.

**Goeders, N. E.** (2004). Stress, motivation, and drug addiction. *Current Directions in Psychological Science, 13*(1), 33–35.

**Goetting, A.** (1986). Parental satisfaction: A review of research. *Journal of Family Issues, 7,* 83–109.

**Goffman, E.** (1959). *The presentation of self in everyday life.* Garden City, NJ: Doubleday.

**Gold, M. S., & Jacobs, W. S.** (2005). Cocaine and crack: Clinical aspects. In J. H. Lowinson, P. Ruiz, R. B. Millman, & J. G. Langrod (Eds.), *Substance abuse: A comprehensive textbook.* Philadelphia: Lippincott/Williams & Wilkins.

**Gold, M. S., Miller, N. S., & Jonas, J. M.** (1992). Cocaine (and crack): Neurobiology. In J. H. Lowinson, P. Ruiz, & R. B. Millman (Eds.), *Substance abuse: A comprehensive textbook* (2nd ed.). Baltimore: Williams & Wilkins.

**Gold, R. (2008).** Unrealistic optimism and event threat. *Psychology, Health, and Medicine, 13,* 193–201.

**Goldberg, A. E., & Perry-Jenkins, M.** (2004). Division of labor and working-class women's well-being across the transition to parenthood. *Journal of Family Psychology, 18*(1), 225–236.

**Goldberg, C., & Zhang, L.** (2004). Simple and joint effects of gender and self-esteem on responses to same-sex sexual harrassment. *Sex Roles, 50*(11/12), 823–833.

**Goldberg, W. A., Prause, J., Lucas-Thompsom, R., & Himsel, A.** (2008). Maternal employment and children's achievement in context: A meta-analysis of four decades of research. *Psychological Bulletin, 134,* 77–108.

**Goldberger, L.** (1993). Sensory deprivation and overload. In L. Goldberger & S. Breznitz (Eds.), *Handbook of stress: Theoretical and clinical aspects* (2nd ed.). New York: Free Press.

**Golden, T. D., Veiga, J. F., & Simsek, Z.** (2006). Telecommuting's differential impact on work-family conflict: Is there no place like home? *Journal of Applied Psychology, 91,* 1340–1350.

**Golding, J. M.** (1996). Sexual assault history and women's reproductive and sexual health. *Psychology of Women Quarterly, 20,* 101–121.

**Goldscheider, F. K., & Goldscheider, C.** (1998). The effects of childhood family structure on leaving and returning home. *Journal of Marriage and the Family, 60,* 745–756.

**Goldsmith, T. D., & Shapira, N. A.** (2006). Problematic Internet use. In E. Hollander & D. J. Stein (Eds.), *Clinical manual of impulse-control disorders.* Washington, DC: American Psychiatric Publishing.

**Goldston, K., & Baillie, A. J.** (2008). Depression and coronary heart disease: A review of the epidemiological evidence, explanatory mechanism and management approaches. *Clinical Psychology Review, 28,* 289–307.

**Goldzweig, C. L., Balekian, T. M., Rolon, C., Yano, E. M., & Shekelle, P. G.** (2006). The state of women veterans' health research: Results of a systematic literature review. *Journal of General Internal Medicine, 21*(Suppl 3), S82–S92.

**Goleman, D.** (2007). *Social intelligence; The new science of human relationships.* New York: Bantam.

**Golombok, S., Perry, B., Burnston, A., Murray, C., Money-Somers, J., Stevens, M., & Golding, J.** (2003). Children with lesbian parents: A community study. *Developmental Psychology, 39,* 20–33.

**Gonsiorek, J. C.** (1991). The empirical basis for the demise of the illness model of homosexuality. In J. Gonsiorek & J. Weinrich (Eds.), *Homosexuality: Research implications for public policy.* Newbury Park, CA: Sage.

**Gonzaga, G. C.** (2009). Similarity in ongoing relationships. In H. T. Reis & S. Sprecher (Eds.), *Encyclopedia of human relationships: Vol. 3* (pp. 1496–1499). Los Angeles: Sage Reference Publication.

**Gonzaga, G. C., Campos, B, & Bradbury, T.** (2007). Similarity, convergence, and relationship satisfaction in dating and married couples. *Journal of Personality and Social Psychology, 93,* 34–48.

**Goodall, K.** (1972, November). Field report: Shapers at work. *Psychology Today,* pp. 53–63, 132–138.

**Goode-Cross, D. T., Good, G. E.** (2008). African American men who have sex with men: Creating safe spaces through relationships. *Psychology of Men & Masculinity, 9,* 221–234.

**Gooden, A. M., & Gooden, M. A.** (2001). Gender representation in notable children's picture books: 1995–1999. *Sex Roles, 45*(1/2), 89–101.

**Goodfriend, W.** (2009). Proximity and attraction. In H. T. Reis & S. Sprecher (Eds.), *Encyclopedia of human relationships: Vol. 3* (pp. 1297–1299). Los Angeles: Sage Reference Publication.

**Goodrick, G. K., Pendleton, V. R., Kimball, K. T., Poston, W. S., Carlos, R., Rebecca, S., & Foreyt, J. P.** (1999). Binge eating severity, self-concept, dieting self-efficacy and social support during treatment of binge eating disorder. *International Journal of Eating Disorders, 26*(3), 295–300.

**Goodwin, F. K. & Jamison, K. R.** (2007). *Manic-depressive illness: Bipolar disorders and recurrent depression.* New York: Oxford University Press.

**Goodwin, R.** (2009). Marriage, historical and cross-cultural trends. In H. T. Reis & S. Sprecher (Eds.), *Encyclopedia of human relationships: Vol. 1* (pp. 1048–1052). Los Angeles: Sage Reference Publication.

**Goodwin, R. D., & Friedman, H. S.** (2006). Health status and the five-factor personality traits in a nationally representative sample. *Journal of Health Psychology, 11,* 643–654.

**Gordon, P. A.** (2003). The decision to remain single: Implications for women across cultures. *Journal of Mental Health Counseling, 25*(1), 33–44.

**Gordon, R. A.** (1996). Impact of ingratiation on judgments and evaluations: A meta-analytic investigation. *Journal of Personality and Social Psychology, 71*(1), 54–70.

**Gordon, R. A.** (2008). Attributional style and athletic performance: Strategic optimism and defensive pessimism. *Psychology of Sport and Exercise, 9*(3), 336–350.

**Gordon, R. M.** (2005). The doom and gloom of divorce research: Comment on Wallerstein and Lewis (2004). *Psychoanalytic Psychology, 22,* 450–451.

**Gordon, V. M.** (2006). *Career advising: An academic advisor's guide.* San Francisco: Jossey-Bass.

**Gosling, S.** (2008). *Snoop: What your stuff says about you.* New York: Basic Books.

**Gottdiener, J. S., Krantz, D. S., & Howell, R. H., Hecht, G. M., Klein, J., Falconer, J. J., & Rozanski, A.** (1994). Induction of silent myocardial ischemia with mental stress testing: Relationship to the triggers of ischemia during daily life activities and to ischemic functional severity. *Journal of the American College of Cardiology, 24,* 1645–1651.

**Gottesman, I. I.** (1991). *Schizophrenia genesis: The origins of madness.* New York: Freeman.

**Gottesman, I. I.** (2001). Psychopathology through a life span–genetic prism. *American Psychologist, 56,* 867–878.

**Gottfried, A. E., & Gottfried, A. W.** (2008). The upside of maternal and dual-earner employment: A focus on positive family adaptations, home environments, and child development in the Fullerton longitudinal study. In A. Marcus-Newhall, D. F. Halpern, & S. J. Tan (Eds.), *The changing realities of work and family* (pp. 25–42). Malden, MA: Wiley-Blackwell.

**Gottman, J. M.** (1993). The roles of conflict engagement, escalation, and avoidance in marital interaction: A longitudinal view of five types of couples. *Journal of Consulting and Clinical Psychology, 61*(1), 6–15.

**Gottman, J. M.** (1994). *What predicts divorce?* Hillsdale, NJ: Erlbaum.

**Gottman, J. M., Coan, J., Carrere, S., & Swanson, C.** (1998). Predicting marital happiness and stability from newlywed interactions. *Journal of Marriage and the Family, 60,* 5–22.

**Gottman, J. M., & Gottman, J. S.** (2008). Gottman method couple therapy. In A. S. Gurman (Ed.), *Clinical handbook of couple therapy* (4th ed., pp. 138–164). New York: Guilford Press.

**Gottman, J. M., Ryan, K. D., Carrére, S., & Erley, A. M.** (2002). Toward a scientifically based marital therapy. In H. Liddle & D. Santisteban (Eds.), *Family psychology: Science-based interventions.* Washington, DC: American Psychological Association.

**Gough, B., Weyman, N., Alderson, J., Butler, G., & Stoner, M.** (2008). "They did not have a word": The parental quest to locate a "true sex" for their intersex children. *Psychology and Health, 23,* 493–507.

**Gourevitch, M. N., & Arnsten, J. H.** (2005). Medical complications of drug use. In J. H. Lowinson, P. Ruiz, R. B. Millman, & J. G. Langrod (Eds.), *Substance abuse: A comprehensive textbook.* Philadelphia: Lippincott/Williams & Wilkins.

**Gouzoulis-Mayfrank, E., Daumann, J., Tuchtenhagen, F., Pelz, S., Becker, S., Kunert, H.-J., Fimm, B., & Sass, H.** (2000). Impaired cognitive performance in drug-free users of recreational ecstasy (MDMA). *Journal of Neurology, Neurosurgery, and Psychiatry, 68*(6), 719–725.

**Gow, A. J., Pattie, A., Whiteman, M. C., Whalley, L. J., & Deary, I. J.** (2007). Social support and successful aging: Investigating the relationships between lifetime cognitive change and life satisfaction. *Journal of Individual Differences, 28,* 103–115.

**Grabe, S., Ward, L. M., & Hyde J. S.** (2008). The role of media in the body image concerns among women: A meta-analysis of experimental and correlational studies. *Psychological Bulletin, 134,* 460–476.

**Graf, M. C., Gaudiano, B. A., & Geller, P. A.** (2008). Written emotional disclosure: A controlled study of the benefits of expressive writing homework in outpatient psychotherapy. *Psychotherapy Research, 18,* 389–399.

**Graham, J. E., Christian, L. M., & Kiecolt-Glaser, J. K.** (2006). Stress, age, and immune function: Toward a lifespan approach. *Journal of Behavioral Medicine, 29,* 389–400.

**Graig, E.** (1993). Stress as a consequence of the urban physical environment. In L. Goldberger & S. Breznitz (Eds.), *Handbook of stress: Theoretical and clinical aspects* (2nd ed.). New York: Free Press.

**Grandjean, P., & Landrigan, P. J.** (2006). Developmental neurotoxicity of industrial chemicals. *Lancet, 368,* 2167–2178.

**Granholm, E., McQuaid, J. R., Link, P. C., Fish, S., Patterson, T., & Jeste, D. V.** (2008). Neuropsychological predictors of functional outcome in cognitive behavioral social skills training for older people with schizophrenia. *Schizophrenia Research, 100,*133–143.

**Grant, I., McDonald, W. I., Patterson, T., & Trimble, M. R.** (1989). Multiple sclerosis. In G. W. Brown & T. O. Harris (Eds.), *Life events and illness.* New York: Guilford Press.

**Grau, R., Salanova, M., & Peiro, J. M.** (2001). Moderator effects of self-efficacy on occupational stress. *Psychology in Spain, 5*(1), 63–74.

**Gray, J.** (1992). *Men are from Mars, women are from Venus: A practical guide for improving communication and getting what you want in your relationship.* New York: HarperCollins.

**Gray-Little, B., & Hafdahl, A. R.** (2000). Factors influencing racial comparisons of self-esteem: A quantitative review. *Psychological Bulletin, 126,* 26–54.

**Graziano, W. G. & Tobin, R. M.** (2009). Agreeableness. In M. R. Leary & R. H. Hoyle (Eds.), *Handbook of individual differences in social behavior* (pp. 46–61). New York: Guilford.

**Grearson, J, & Smith, L.** (2009). The luckiest girls in the world. In T. A. Karis & K. D. Killian, *Intercultural couples: Exploring diversity in intimate relationships* (pp. 71–87). New York: Routledge/Taylor & Francis Group.

**Green, J. D., & Sedikides, C.** (2001). When do self-schemas shape social perception? The role of descriptive ambiguity. *Motivation and Emotion, 25,* 67–83.

**Green, J. D., Sedikides, C., Pinter, B., & Van Tongeren, D. R.** (2009). Two sides to self-protection: Self-improvement strivings and feedback from close relationships eliminate mnemic neglect. *Self and Identity, 8*(2–3), 233–250.

**Green, L. R., Richardson, D. S., Lago, T., & Schatten-Jones, E. C.** (2001). Network correlates of social and emotional loneliness in young and older adults. *Personality and Social Psychology Bulletin, 27*(3), 281–288.

**Greenberg, J. S.** (2002). *Comprehensive stress management: Health and human performance.* New York: McGraw-Hill.

**Greenberg, R. P., & Fisher, S.** (1997). Mood-mending medicines: Probing drug, psychotherapy and placebo solutions. In S. Fisher & R. P. Greenberg (Eds.), *From placebo to panacea: Putting psychiatric drugs to the test.* New York: Wiley.

**Greene, K., Derlega, V., & Mathews, A.** (2006). Self-disclosure in personal relationships. In A. L. Vangelisti & D. Perlman (Eds.), *The Cambridge handbook of personal relationships.* New York: Cambridge University Press.

**Greene, R. L.** (1992). *Human memory: Paradigms and paradoxes.* Hillsdale, NJ: Erlbaum.

**Greenfield, D. N.** (1999). Psychological characteristics of compulsive Internet use: A preliminary analysis. *CyberPsychology and Behavior, 2*(5), 403–412.

**Greenglass, E. R.** (2007). Teaching and stress. In G. Fink (Ed.), *Encyclopedia of stress: Vols. 1–4* (2nd ed., pp. 713–717). San Diego, CA: Elsevier Academic Press.

**Greenhaus, J. H.** (2003). Career dynamics. In W. C. Borman, D. R. Ilgen, & R. J. Klimoski (Eds.), *Handbook of psychology: Vol. 12. Industrial and organizational psychology.* New York: Wiley.

**Greenhaus, J. H., & Powell, G. N.** (2006). When work and family are allies: A theory of work-family enrichment. *Academy of Management Review, 31*(1), 72–92.

**Greenland, P., Knoll, M. D., Stamler, J., Neaton, J. D., Dyer, A. R., Garside, D. B., & Wilson, P. W.** (2003). Major risk factors as antecedents of fatal and nonfatal coronary heart disease events. *Journal of the American Medical Association, 290,* 891–897.

**Greenson, R. R.** (1967). *The technique and practice of psychoanalysis* (Vol. 1). New York: International Universities Press.

**Greenwald, A. G., & Banaji, M. R.** (1995). Implicit social cognition: Attitudes, self-esteem, and stereotypes. *Psychological Review, 102*(1), 4–27.

**Greenway, R.** (1995). The wilderness effect and ecopsychology. In. T. Roszak, M. E. Gomes, & A. D. Kanner (Eds.), *Eco-psychology: Restoring the earth, healing the mind* (pp. 122–135). San Francisco: Sierra Club Books.

**Gregory, R. J., Schwer Canning, S., Lee, T. W., & Wise, J. C.** (2004). Cognitive bibliotherapy for depression: A meta-analysis. *Professional Psychology: Research and Practice, 35*(3), 275–280.

**Greitemeyer, T.** (2006). What do men and women want in a partner? Are educated partners always more desirable? *Journal of Experimental Social Psychology, 43,* 180–194.

**Grencavage, L. M., & Norcross, J. C.** (1990). Where are the commonalities among the therapeutic factors? *Professional Psychology: Research and Practice, 21,* 372–378.

**Griffith, K. H., & Hebl, M. R.** (2002). The disclosure dilemma for gay men and lesbians: "Coming out" at work. *Journal of Applied Psychology, 87*(6), 1191–1199.

**Griner, D., & Smith, T. B.** (2006). Culturally adapted mental health intervention: A meta-analytic review. *Psychotherapy: Theory, Research, Practice, Training, 43,* 531–548.

Grinspoon, L., Bakalar, J. B., & Russo, E. (2005). Marihuana: Clinical aspects. In J. H. Lowinson, P. Ruiz, R. B. Millman, & J. G. Langrod (Eds.), *Substance abuse: A comprehensive textbook*. Philadelphia: Lippincott/Williams & Wilkins.

Grob, C. S., & Poland, R. E. (2005). MDMA. In J. H. Lowinson, P. Ruiz, R. B. Millman, & J. G. Langrod (Eds.), *Substance abuse: A comprehensive textbook*. Philadelphia: Lippincott/Williams & Wilkins.

Groesz, L. M., Levine, M. P., & Murnen, S. K. (2002). The effect of experimental presentation of thin media images on body satisfaction: A meta-analytic review. *International Journal of Eating Disorders, 31*, 1–16.

Gross, J. J. (2001). Emotion regulation in adulthood: Timing is everything. *Current Directions in Psychological Science, 10*, 214–219.

Grossi, G., Perski, A., Evengard, B. , Blomkvist, V., & Orth-Gromer, K. (2003). Physiological correlates of burnout among women. *Journal of Psychosomatic Research, 55*, 309–316.

Grossman, J. B., & Ruiz, P. (2004). Shall we make a leap-of-faith to disulfiram (Antabuse)? *Addictive Disorders & Their Treatment, 3*(3), 129–132.

Groth-Marnat, G. (1997). *Handbook of psychological assessment*. New York: Wiley.

Grothues, C. A., & Marmion, S. L. (2006). Dismantling the myths about intimate violence against women. In P. K. Lundberg-Love & S. L. Marmion (Eds.), *"Intimate" violence against women: When spouses, partners, or lovers attack*. Westport, CT: Praeger Publishers.

Gruber, J. E. (1990). Methodological problems and policy implication in sexual harassment research. *Population Research and Policy Review, 9*, 235–254.

Gruenberg, A. M., & Goldstein, R. D. (2003). Mood disorders: Depression. In A. Tasman, J. Kay, & J. A. Lieberman (Eds.), *Psychiatry*. New York: Wiley.

Grundy, E., & Henretta, J. C. (2006). Between elderly parents and adult children: A new look at the intergenerational care provided by the "sandwich generation." *Ageing & Society, 26*, 707–722.

Grzywacz, J. G., & Butler, A. B. (2007). Work-family balance. In G. Fink (Ed.), *Encyclopedia of stress: Vols. 1–4* (2nd ed., pp. 868–870). San Diego, CA: Elsevier Academic Press.

Grzywacz, J. G., Almeida, D. M., Neupert, S. D., & Ettner, S. L. (2004). Socioeconomic status and health: A micro-level analysis of exposure and vulnerability to daily stressors. *Journal of Health and Social Behavior, 45*, 1–16.

Guarda, A. S., Pinto, A. M., Coughlin, J. W., Hussain, S., Haug, N. A., & Heinberg, L. J. (2007). Perceived coercion and change in perceived need for admission in patients hospitalized for eating disorders. *American Journal of Psychiatry, 164*, 108–114.

Gudjonsson, G. H. (2001). Recovered memories: Effects upon the family and community. In G. M. Davies & T. Dalgleish (Eds.), *Recovered memories: Seeking the middle ground*. Chichester, England: Wiley.

Guéguen, N. (2002). Status, apparel and touch: Their joint effects on compliance to a request. *North American Journal of Psychology, 4*(2), 279–286.

Gueguen, N. (2003). Fundraising on the web: The effect of an electronic door-in-the-face technique on compliance to a request. *CyberPsychology & Behavior, 6*, 189–193.

Guéguen, N., Fischer-Lokou, J., Lefebvre, L., & Lamy, L. (2008). Women's eye contact and men's later interest: Two field experiments. *Perceptual and Motor Skills, 106*(1), 63–66.

Guerrero L. K., & Mongeau P. A. (2008). On becoming "more than friends": The transition from friendship to romantic relationship. In S. Sprecher, A. Wenzel, & J. Harvey (Eds.), *Handbook of Relationship Initiation* (pp. 175–191). New York: Psychology Press.

Guest, F. (2004). HIV/AIDS and reproductive health. In R. A. Hatcher, J. Trussell, F. H. Stewart, A. L. Nelson, W. Cates Jr., F. Guest, & D. Kowal (Eds.), *Contraceptive technology*. New York: Ardent Media.

Gupta, G. R. (1992). Love, arranged marriage, and the Indian social structure. In J. J. Macionis & N. V. Benokraitis (Eds.), *Seeing ourselves: Classic, contemporary and cross-cultural reading in sociology*. Englewood Cliffs, NJ: Prentice-Hall.

Gupta, U., & Singh, P. (1982). Exploratory study of love and liking type of marriages. Indian *Journal of Applied Psychology, 19*, 92–97.

Gur, R. C., & Gur, R. E. (2007). Neural substrates for sex differences in cognition. In S. J. Ceci & W. M. Williams (Eds.), *Why aren't more women in science?* (pp. 189–198). Washington, DC: American Psychological Association.

Gutek, B. A. (1993). Responses to sexual harassment. In S. Oskamp & M. Costanzo (Eds.), *Gender issues in contemporary society*. Newbury Park, CA: Sage.

Haas, L. (1999). Families and work. In M. B. Sussman, S. K. Steinmetz, & G. W. Peterson *Handbook of marriage and the family*. New York: Plenum Press.

Hackam, D. G., & Anand, S. S. (2003). Emerging risk factors for atherosclerotic vascular disease: A critical review of the evidence. *Journal of the American Medical Association, 290*(7), 932–940.

Hackstaff, K. B. (1999). *Marriage in a culture of divorce*. Philadelphia: Temple University Press.

Haden, S. C., Scarpa, A., Jones, R. T., & Ollendick, T. H. (2007). Posttraumatic stress disorder symptoms and injury: The modeling role of perceived social support and coping for young adults. *Personality and Individual Differences, 42*, 1187–1198.

Hadjikhani, N., Hoge, R., Snyder, J., & de Gelder, B. (2008). Pointing with the eyes: The role of gaze in communicating danger. *Brain and Cognition, 68*(1), 1–8.

Hadjistavropoulos, H., Dash, H., Hadjistavropoulos, T., & Sullivan, T. (2007). Recurrent pain among university students: Contributions of self-efficacy and perfectionism to the pain experience. *Personality and Individual Differences, 42*, 1081–1091.

Hafer, C. L. (2000). Do innocent victims threaten the belief in a just world? Evidence from a modified Stroop task. *Journal of Personality and Social Psychology, 79*(2), 165–173.

Hafer, C. L., & Bègue, L. (2005). Experimental research on just-world theory: Problems, developments, and future challenges. *Psychological Bulletin, 131*(1), 128–167.

Hagerty, M. R. (2000). Social comparisons of income in one's community: Evidence from national surveys of income and happiness. *Journal of Personality and Social Psychology, 78*, 746–771.

Haggerty, G., Hilsenroth, M. J., & Vala-Stewart, R. (2009). Attachment and interpersonal distress: Examining the relationship between attachment styles and interpersonal problems in a clinical population. *Clinical Psychology and Psychotherapy, 16*, 1–9.

Haider-Markel, D. P., & Joslyn, M. R. (2008). Beliefs about the origins of homosexuality and support for gay rights: An empirical test of attribution theory. *Public Opinion Quarterly, 72*, 291–310.

Haidt, J. (2006). *The happiness hypothesis: Finding modern truth in ancient wisdom*. New York: Basic Books.

Haidt, J., & Keltner, D. (2004). Appreciation of beauty and excellence (awe, wonder, elevation). In C. Peterson & M. E. P. Seligman (Eds.), *Character strengths and virtues* (pp. 537–551). New York: Oxford University Press.

Hakim, C. (2006). Women, careers, and work-life preferences. *British Journal of Guidance & Counselling, 34*, 279–294.

Hall, D. R. (1996). Marriage as a pure relationship: Exploring the link between premarital cohabitation and divorce in Canada. *Journal of Comparative Family Studies, 27*, 1–12.

Hall, E. T. (1966) *The hidden dimension*. Garden City, NY: Doubleday.

Hall, E. T. (2008). Adumbration as a feature of intercultural communication. In C. D. Mortensen (Ed.), *Communication theory* (2nd ed., pp. 420–432). New Brunswick, NJ: Transaction Publishers.

Hall, J. A. (1984). *Nonverbal sex differences: Communication accuracy and expressive style*. Baltimore: Johns Hopkins University Press.

Hall, J. A. (1990). *Nonverbal sex differences: Communication accuracy and expressive style* (2nd ed.). Baltimore: Johns Hopkins University Press.

Hall, J. A. (1998). How big are nonverbal sex differences? The case of smiling and sensitivity to nonverbal cues. In D. J. Canary & K. Dindia (Eds.), *Sex differences and similarities in communication: Critical essays and empirical investigations of sex and gender in interaction*. Mahwah, NJ: Erlbaum.

Hall, J. A. (2006a). How big are nonverbal sex differences? The case of smiling and nonverbal sensitivity. In K. Dindia & D. Canary (Eds.), *Sex differences and similarities in communication* (pp. 59–81). Mahwah, NJ: Erlbaum.

Hall, J. A. (2006b). Women's and men's nonverbal communication: Similarities, differences, stereotypes, and origins. In V. Manusov & M. L. Patterson (Eds.), *The Sage handbook of nonverbal communication* (pp. 201–218). Thousand Oaks, CA: Sage.

Hall, J. A., Coates, E., & Smith-LeBeau, L. (2005). Nonverbal behavior and the vertical dimension of social relations: A meta-analysis. *Psychological Bulletin, 131*, 898–924.

Hall, J. A., & Matsumoto, D. (2004). Gender differences in judgments of multiple emotions from facial expressions. *Emotion, 4*(2), 201–206.

Hall, J. A., & Veccia, E. M. (1990). More "touching" observations: New insights on men, women, and interpersonal touch. *Journal of Personality and Social Psychology, 59*, 1155–1162.

Hall, J. A., & Veccia, E. M. (1991). Touch asymmetry between the sexes. In C. L. Ridgeway (Ed.), *Gender, interaction, and inequality*. New York: Springer-Verlag.

Halmi, K. A. (2002). Physiology of anorexia nervosa and bulimia nervosa. In C. G. Fairburn & K. D. Brownell (Eds.), *Eating disorders and obesity: A comprehensive handbook*. New York: Guilford.

Halmi, K. A. (2008). Eating disorders: Anorexia nervosa, bulimia nervosa, and obesity. In R. E. Hales, S. C. Yudofsky, & G. O. Gabbard (Eds.), *The American psychiatric publishing textbook of psychiatry* (pp. 971–998). Washington, DC: American Psychiatric Publishing.

Halmi, K. A., Sunday, S. R., Strober, M., Kaplan, A., Woodside, D. B., Fichter, M., Treasure, J., Berrettini, W. H., & Kaye, W. H. (2000). Perfectionism in anorexia nervosa: Variation by clinical subtype, obsessionality, and pathological eating behavior. *American Journal of Psychiatry, 157*, 1799–1805.

Halpern, C., Hurtig, H., Jaggi, J., Grossman, M., Won, M., & Baltuch, G. (2007). Deep brain stimulation in neurologic disorders. *Parkinsonism & Related Disorders, 13*(1), 1–16.

Halpern, C. T., Udry, J. R., Campbell, B., & Suchindran, C. (1999). Effects of body fat on weight concerns, dating, and sexual activity: A longitudinal analysis of black and white adolescent girls. *Developmental Psychology, 35*(3), 721–736.

Halpern, D. F. (1997). Sex differences in intelligence: Implications for education. *American Psychologist, 52*, 1091–1102.

Halpern, D. F. (2000). *Sex differences in cognitive abilities* (3rd ed.). Mahwah, NJ: Erlbaum.

Halpern, D. F. (2004). A cognitive-process taxonomy for sex differences in cognitive abilities. *Current Directions in Psychological Science, 13*(4), 135–139.

Halpern, D. F. (2005). Psychology at the intersection of work and family: Recommendations for employers, working families, and policymakers. *American Psychologist, 60*, 397–409.

Halpern, D. F. (2006). Girls and academic success: Changing patterns of academic achievement. In J. Worrell & C. D. Goodheart (Eds.), *Handbook of girls' and women's psychological health*. New York: Oxford University Press.

Halpern, D. F., Bendow, C. P., Geary, D. C., Gur, R. C., Hyde, J. S. & Gernsbacher, M. A. (2007). The science of sex differences in science and mathematics. *Psychological Science in the Public Interest, 8*, 1–51.

Halpern-Felsher, B. L., Cornell, J. L., Kropp, R. Y., & Tschann, J. M. (2005). Oral versus vaginal sex among adolescents: Perceptions, attitudes, and behavior. *Pediatrics, 115*, 845–851.

Halverson, A. M., Hallahan, M., Hart, A. J., & Rosenthal, R. (1997). Reducing the biasing effects of judges' nonverbal behavior with simplified jury instruction. *Journal of Applied Social Psychology, 82*(4), 590–598.

Hamilton, A. (1999). You've got mail! *Time, 83*.

Hamilton, J. C., Deemer, H. N., & Janata, J. W. (2003). Feeling sad but looking good: Sick role features that lead to favorable interpersonal judgments. *Journal of Social & Clinical Psychology, 22*(3), 253–274.

Hamilton, M. C., Anderson, D., Broaddus, M., & Young, K. (2006), Gender stereotyping and underrepresentation of female characters in 200 popular children's picture books: A twenty-first century update. *Sex Roles, 55*, 757–765.

Hammad, T. A., Laughren, T., & Racoosin, J. (2006). Suicidality in pediatric patients treated with antidepressant drugs. *Archives of General Psychiatry, 63*, 332–339.

Hammen, C. (2003). Mood disorders. In G. Stricker & T. A. Widiger (Eds.), *Handbook of psychology: Vol. 8. Clinical psychology*. New York: Wiley.

Hammen, C. (2005). Stress and depression. *Annual Review of Clinical Psychology, 1*, 293–319.

Hammer, S. M., Saag, M. S., Schechter, M., Montaner, J. S. G., Schooley, R. T., Jacobsen, D. M., et al. (2006). Treatment for adult HIV infection: 2006 recommendations of the international AIDS society-USA panel. *Journal of the American Medical Association, 296*, 827–843.

Hammersley, R., Ditton, J., Smith, I., & Short, E. (1999). Patterns of ecstasy use by drug users. *British Journal of Criminology, 39*(4), 625–647.

Hampson, E., van Anders, S. M., & Mullin, L. I. (2006). A female advantage in the recognition of emotional facial expressions: Test of an evolutionary hypothesis. *Evolution and Human Behavior, 27*, 401–416.

Han, S. (1998). The relationship between life satisfaction and flow in elderly Korean immigrants. In M. Csikszentmihalyi & I. S. Csikszentmihalyi (Eds.), *Optimal experiences: Psychological studies of flow in consciousness* (pp. 138–149). New York: Cambridge University Press

Hancock, D. R. (2001). Effects of test anxiety and evaluative threat on students' achievement and motivation. *Journal of Educational Research, 94*(5), 284–290.

Hancock, P. A., & Ganey, H. C. N. (2003). From the inverted-U to the extended-U: The evolution of a law of psychology. *Journal of Human Performance in Extreme Environment, 7*(1), 5–14.

Handy, B. (1998, May 4). The Viagra craze. *Time,* 50–57.

Hanna, S. L., Suggett, R., & Radtke, D. (2008). *Person to person: Positive relationships don't just happen.* Upper Saddle River, NJ: Pearson/Prentice Hall.

Hansen, J. C. (2005). Assessment of Interests. In S. D. Brown & R. W. Lent (Eds.), *Career development and counseling: Putting theory and research to work.* Hoboken, NJ: Wiley.

Hansen, P. E., Floderus, B., Fredrickson, K., & Johansen, C. B. (2005). Personality traits, health behavior, and risk for cancer: A prospective study of a twin cohort. *Cancer, 103,* 1082–1091.

Happonen, P., Voutilainen, S., & Salonen, J. T. (2004). Coffee drinking is dose dependently related to the risk of acute coronary events in middle-aged men. *Journal of Nutrition, 134*(9), 2381–2386.

Harber, K. D., Zimbardo, P. G., & Boyd, J. N. (2003). Participant self-selection bias as a function of individual differences in time perspective. *Basic and Applied Social Psychology, 25,* 255–264.

Harburg, E., Julius, M., Kactroti, N., Gleiberman, L., & Schork, M. A. (2003). Expressive/suppressive anger-coping responses, gender, and types of mortality: A 17-year follow-up (Tecumseh, Michigan, 1971–1988). *Psychosomatic Medicine, 65,* 588–597.

Hardesty, D. E., & Sackeim, H. A. (2007). Deep brain stimulation in movement and psychiatric disorders. *Biological Psychiatry, 31,* 831–835.

Hardin, E. E., & Lakin, J. L. (2009).The Integrated Self-Discrepancy Index: A valid and reliable measure of self-discrepancies. *Journal of Personality Assessment, 91*(3), 245–253.

Hardin, G. (1968, December). The tragedy of the commons. *Science,* 1243–1248.

Haring, M., Hewitt, P. L., & Flett, G. L. (2003). Perfectionism, coping, and quality of intimate relationships. *Journal of Marriage & Family, 65*(1), 143–158.

Harmsen, P., Rosengren, A., Tsipogianni, A., & Wilhelmsen, L. (1990). Risk factors for stroke in middle-aged men in Goteborg, Sweden. *Stroke, 21,* 23–29.

Harpaz, I., & Snir, R. (2003). Workaholism: Its definition and nature. *Human Relations, 56*(3), 291–319.

Harper, G. W., Jernewall, N., & Zea, M. C. (2004). Giving voice to emerging science and theory for lesbian, gay, and bisexual people of color. *Cultural Diversity and Ethnic Minority Psychology, 10*(3), 187–199.

Harper, N. J., Russell, K. C., Cooley, R., & Cupples, J. (2007). Catherine Freer Wilderness Therapy Expeditions: An exploratory case study of adolescent wilderness therapy, family functioning, and the maintenance of change. *Child & Youth Care Forum, 36,* 111–129.

Harper, S. (1995). The way of wilderness. In T. Roszak, M. E. Gomes, & A. D. Kanner (Eds.), *Ecopsychology: Restoring the Earth, Healing the Mind* (pp. 183–200). San Francisco, CA: Sierra Club Books.

Harrigan, J. A., Lucic, K. S., Kay, D., McLaney, A., & Rosenthal, R. (1991). Effect of expresser role and type of self-touching on observers' perceptions. *Journal of Applied Psychology, 21,* 585–609.

Harris, C. & Wagner, D. (2009, October 23). Business has grown for sweat-lodge guru: Cracks form in motivational mogul's empire. *The Arizona Republic.* Retrieved from http://www.azcentral.com/12news/news/articles/2009/10/23/20091023rayprofile1023-CP.html

Harris, J. B., Schwartz, S. M., & Thompson, B. (2008). Characteristics associated with self-identification as a regular smoker and desire to quit among college students who smoke cigarettes. *Nicotine and Tobacco Research, 10,* 69–76.

Harris, J. R. (2000). Context-specific learning, personality, and birth order. *Current Directions in Psychological Science, 9*(5), 174–177.

Harris, M. B. (1996). Aggressive experiences and aggressiveness: Relationship to ethnicity, gender, and age. *Journal of Applied Social Psychology, 26*(10), 843–870.

Harris, T. (1967). *I'm OK—You're OK.* New York: HarperCollins.

Harrison, J. A., & Wells, R. B. (1991). Bystander effects on male helping behavior: Social comparison and diffusion of responsibility. *Representative Research in Social Psychology, 19*(1), 53–63.

Harrison, K. (2003). Television viewers' ideal body proportions: The case of the curvaceously thin woman. *Sex Roles, 48*(5/6), 255–264.

Harter, J. K. (2008). Employee engagement: How great managing drives performance. In S. J. Lopez (Ed.), *Positive psychology: Exploring the best in people* (Vol. 4, pp. 99–110). Westport, CT: Praeger.

Harter, S. (1998). The development of self-representations. In N. Eisenberg (Ed.), *Handbook of child psychology: Vol. 3. Social, emotional, and personality development.* New York: Wiley.

Harter, S. (2003). The development of self-representations during childhood and adolescence. In M. R. Leary & J. P. Tangney (Eds.), *Handbook of self and identity.* New York: Guilford.

Harter, S. (2006). Developmental and individual difference perspectives on self-esteem. In D. K. Mroczek & T. D. Little (Eds.), *Handbook of personality development.* Mahwah, NJ: Erlbaum.

Hartig, T., Evans, G. W., Jamner, L. D., Davis, D. S., & Gärling, T. (2003). Tracking restoration in natural and urban field settings. *Journal of Environmental Psychology, 23,* 109–123.

Hartig, T., Kaiser, F. G., & Bowler, P. A. (2001). Psychological restoration in nature as a positive motivation for ecological behavior. *Environment and Behavior, 33*(4), 590–607.

Hartig, T., & Staats, H. (2006). The need for psychological restoration as a determinant of environmental preferences. *Journal of Environmental Psychology, 26,* 215–226.

Hartup, W. W., & Stevens, N. (1999). Friendships and adaptation across the life span. *Current Directions in Psychological Science, 8*(3), 76–79.

Harvard Crimson. (2005, January 14). Full transcript: President Summers' remarks at the National Bureau of Economic Research. *Harvard Crimson,* Retrieved April 26, 2007 from http://www.thecrimson.com/article.aspx?ref=505844.

Harvey, J. H., & Omarzu, J. (1997). Minding the close relationship. *Personality and Social Psychology Review, 1*(3), 224–240.

Harvey, J. H., & Pauwels, B. G. (2009). Relationship connection: A redux on the role of minding and the quality of feeling special in the enhancement of closeness. In S. J. Lopez & C. R. Snyder (Eds.), *Oxford handbook of positive psychology* (2nd ed., pp. 385–392). New York: Oxford University Press.

Harvey, J. H., & Wenzel, A. (2006). Theoretical perspectives in the study of close relationships. In A. L. Vangelisti & D. Perlman (Eds.), *The Cambridge handbook of personal relationships.* New York: Cambridge University Press.

Harvey, M. H. (1999). Memory research and clinical practice: A critique of three paradigms and a framework for psychotherapy with trauma survivors. In L. M. Williams, & V. L. Banyard (Eds.), *Trauma & memory.* Thousand Oaks, CA: Sage.

Haskell, W. L., Lee, I., Pate, R. R., Powell, K. E., Blair, S. N., Franklin, B. A., et al. (2007). Physical activity and public health: Updated recommendations from the American College of Sports Medicine and the American Heart Association. *Medical Science Sports Exercise, 39,* 1423–1434.

Hass, D. M., & Stafford, L. (1998). An initial examination of maintenance behaviors in gay and lesbian relationships. *Journal of Social and Personal Relationships, 15*(6), 846–855.

Hass, N. (2006, January 8). In your Facebook.com. *The New York Times,* pp. A4, A30.

Hatano, G., & Inagaki, K. (1999). A developmental perspective on informal biology. In D. L. Medin & S. Atran (Eds.), *Folkbiology* (pp. 321–354). Cambridge, MA: MIT Press.

Hatch, A. (2009). Alternative relationship lifestyles. In H. T. Reis & S. Sprecher (Eds.), *Encyclopedia of human relationships: Vol. 2* (pp. 85–88). Los Angeles: Sage Reference Publication.

Hatcher, R. A., Trussell, J., Stewart, F. H., Nelson, A. L., Cates, W. Jr., Guest, F., & Kowal, D. (2004). *Contraceptive Technology.* New York: Ardent Media.

Hatfield, E., & Rapson, R. L. (1993). *Love, sex, and intimacy: Their psychology, biology, and history.* New York: HarperCollins.

Hatfield, E., & Rapson, R. L. (2008). Passionate love and sexual desire: Multidisciplinary perspectives. In J. P. Forgas & J. Fitness (Eds.), *Social Relationships* (pp. 21–38). New York: Taylor & Francis.

Hatfield, E., & Sprecher, S. (2009). Matching hypothesis. In H. T. Reis & S. Sprecher (Eds.), *Encyclopedia of human relationships: Vol. 2* (pp. 1065–1067). Los Angeles: Sage Reference Publication.

Hatzenbuehler, M. L. (2009). How does sexual minority stigma "get under the skin"? A psychological mediation framework. *Psychological Bulletin, 135,* 707–730.

Havas, S., Dickinson, B. D., & Wilson, M. (2007). The urgent need to reduce sodium consumption. *Journal of the American Medical Association, 298,* 1439–1441.

Hawkins, A. J., Nock, S. L., Wilson, J. C., Sanchez, L., & Wright, J. D. (2002). Attitudes about covenant marriage and divorce: Policy implications from a three state comparison. *Family Relations, 51,* 166–75.

Hawkins, D. N., & Booth, A. (2005). Unhappily ever after: Effects of long-term, low-quality marriages on well-being. *Social Forces, 84,* 451–471.

Hawkley, L. C., & Cacioppo, J. T. (2009). Loneliness. In H. T. Reis & S. Sprecher (Eds.), *Encyclopedia of human relationships: Vol. 2* (pp. 985–990). Los Angeles: Sage Reference Publication.

Haworth-Hoeppner, S. (2000). The critical shapes of body image: The role of culture and family in the production of eating disorders. *Journal of Marriage and the Family, 62,* 212–227.

Hawton, K., & Harriss, L. (2008). The changing gender ratio in occurrence of deliberate self-harm across the life cycle. *Crisis, 29,* 4–10.

Haynes, G. A., & Olson, J. M. (2006). Coping with threats to just-world beliefs: Derogate, blame, or help? *Journal of Applied Social Psychology, 36*(3), 664–682.

Hays, K. F. (1999). *Working it out: Using exercise in psychotherapy.* Washington, DC: American Psychological Association.

Hazan, C., & Shaver, P. (1986). *Parental caregiving style questionnaire.* Unpublished questionnaire.

Hazan, C., & Shaver, P. (1987). Romantic love conceptualized as an attachment process. *Journal of Personality and Social Psychology, 52,* 511–524.

Healy, D. (2004). *Let them eat Prozac: The unhealthy relationship between the pharmaceutical industry and depression.* New York: NYU Press.

Healy, D., & Whitaker, C. (2003). Antidepressants and suicide: Risk-benefit conundrums. *Journal of Psychiatry & Neuroscience, 28*(5), 340–347.

Heath, J., & Goggin, K. (2009). Attitudes towards male homosexuality, bisexuality, and the down low lifestyle: Demographic differences and HIV implications. *Journal of Bisexuality, 9,* 17–31.

Heatherton, T. F., & Polivy, J. (1991). Development and validation of a scale for measuring state self-esteem. *Journal of Personality and Social Psychology, 60,* 895–910.

Heaton, T. B. (2002). Factors contributing to increasing marital stability in the United States. *Journal of Family Issues, 23,* 392–409.

Heaton, T. B., Jacobson, C. K. & Holland, K. (1999). Persistence and change in decisions to remain childless. *Journal of Marriage and the Family, 61,* 531–539.

Hebl, M. R., & Mannix, L. M. (2003). The weight of obesity in evaluating others: A mere proximity effect. *Personality and Social Psychology, 29*(1), 28–38.

Hecht, T., & Boies, K. (2009). Structure and correlates of spillover from nonwork to work: An examination of nonwork activities, well-being, and work outcomes. *Journal of Occupational Health Psychology, 14*(4), 414–426.

Hedges, L. V., & Nowell, A. (1995). Sex differences in mental test scores, variability, and numbers of high-scoring individuals. *Science, 269,* 41–45.

Hegarty, P. (2002). "It's not a choice, it's the way we're built": Symbolic beliefs about sexual orientation in the U.S. and Britain. *Journal of Community & Applied Social Psychology, 12,* 153–166.

Hegarty, P., & Buechel, C. (2006). Androcentric reporting of gender differences in APA journals: 1965–2004. *Review of General Psychology, 10,* 377–389.

Heider, F. (1958). *The psychology of interpersonal relations.* New York: Wiley.

Heilman, M. E., & Okimoto, T. G. (2007). Why are women penalized for success at male tasks? The implied community deficit. *Journal of Applied Psychology, 92,* 81–92.

Heiman, J. R., & Meston, C. M. (1997). Empirically validated treatment for sexual dysfunction. *Annual Review of Sex Research, 8,* 148–194.

Heine, S. J., Buchtel, E. E., & Norenzayan, A. (2008). What do cross-national comparisons of personality traits tell us? The case of conscientiousness. *Psychological Science, 19*(4), 309–313.

Heine, S. J., Kitayama, S., Lehman, D. R., Takata, T., Ide, E., Leung, C., & Matsumoto, H. (2001). Divergent consequences of success and failure in Japan and North America: An investigation of self-improving motivations and malleable selves. *Journal of Personality and Social Psychology, 81,* 599–615.

Heine, S. J., & Renshaw, K. (2002). Interjudge agreement, self-enhancement, and liking: Cross-cultural divergences. *Personality and Social Psychology Bulletin, 28*(5), 578–587.

**Heinrichs, R. W.** (2005). The primacy of cognition in schizophrenia. *American Psychologist, 60,* 229–242.

**Helgeson, V. S.** (1994). Relation of agency and communion to well-being: Evidence and potential explanations. *Psychological Bulletin, 116,* 412–428.

**Helgeson, V. S., & Mickelson, K. D.** (1995). Motives for social comparison. *Personality and Social Psychology Bulletin, 21,* 1200–1209.

**Helgeson, V. S., Reynolds, K. A., & Tomich, P. L.** (2006). A meta-analytic review of benefit finding and growth. *Journal of Consulting and Clinical Psychology, 74,* 797–816.

**Hellström, A., & Tekle, J.** (1994). Person perception through facial photographs: Effects of glasses, hair, and beard on judgments of occupation and personal qualities. *European Journal of Social Psychology, 24*(6), 693–705.

**Helweg-Larsen, M., & Shepperd, J. A.** (2001). Do moderators of the optimistic bias affect personal or target risk estimates? A review of the literature. *Personality & Social Psychology Review, 5*(1), 74–95.

**Helwig, A.** (2008). From childhood to adulthood: A 15-year longitudinal career development study. *Career Development Quarterly, 57*(1), 38–50.

**Helzer, J. E., Wittchen, H., Krueger, R. F., & Kraemer, H. C.** (2008). Dimensional options for DSM-V: The way forward. In J. E. Helzer, H. C. Kraemer, R. F. Krueger, H. Wittchen, P. J. Sirovatka, & D. A. Regier (Eds.), *Dimensional approaches in diagnostic classification: Refining the research agenda for DSM-V* (pp. 115–127). Washington, DC: American Psychiatric Association.

**Hemenover, S. H.** (2003). The good, the bad, and the healthy: Impacts of emotional disclosure of trauma on resilient self-concept and psychological distress. *Personality and Social Psychology Bulletin, 29*(10), 1236–1244.

**Henderson, K. E., & Brownell, K. D.** (2004). The toxic environment and obesity: Contribution and cure. In J. K. Thompson (Ed.), *Handbook of eating disorders and obesity.* New York: Wiley.

**Hendrick, S. S., Hendrick, C., & Adler, N. L.** (1988). Romantic relationships: Love, satisfaction, and staying together. *Journal of Personality and Social Psychology, 54,* 980–988.

**Hendricks N. J., Ortiz, C. W., Sugie, N., & Miller, J.** (2007). Beyond the numbers: Hate crimes and cultural trauma within Arab American immigrant communities. *International Review of Victimology, 14*(1), 95–113.

**Henley, N. M.** (1986). *Body politics: Power, sex, and nonverbal communication* (2nd ed.). New York: Simon & Schuster.

**Henley, N. M., & Freeman, J.** (1995). The sexual politics of interpersonal behavior. In J. Freeman (Ed.), *Women: A feminist perspective* (5th ed.). Mountain View, CA: Mayfield.

**Henline, B. H., Lamke, L. K., & Howard, M. D.** (2007). Exploring perceptions of online infidelity. *Personal Relationships, 14,* 113–128.

**Henman, L. D.** (2001). Humor as a coping mechanism: Lessons from POWs. *Humor, 14,* 83–94.

**Hennessy, D. A., & Wiesenthal, D. L.** (1999). Traffic congestion, driver stress, and driver aggression. *Aggressive Behavior, 25*(6), 409–423.

**Henriksson, M. M., Aro, H. M., Marttunen, M. J., Heikkinen, M. E., Isometsa, E. T., Kuoppasalmi, K. I., & Lonnqvist, J. K.** (1993). Mental disorders and comorbidity of suicide. *American Journal of Psychiatry, 150,* 935–940.

**Henry, R. G., Miller, R. B., & Giarrusso, R.** (2005). Difficulties, disagreements, and disappointments in late-life marriages. *International Journal of Aging and Human Development, 61,* 243–264.

**Heppner, P. P.** (2008). Expanding the conceptualization and measurement of applied problem solving and coping: From stages to dimensions to the almost forgotten cultural context. *American Psychologist,* 805–816.

**Heppner, P. P., & Lee, D.** (2002). Problem-solving appraisal and psychological adjustment. In C. R. Snyder & S. J. Lopez (Eds.), *Handbook of positive psychology.* New York: Oxford University Press.

**Heppner, P. P., & Lee, D.** (2005). Problem-solving appraisal and psychological adjustment. In C. R. Snyder & S. J. Lopez ( Eds.), *Handbook of positive psychology.* New York: Oxford University Press.

**Herbenick, D., Reece, M., Sanders, S., Dodge, B., Ghassemi, A., & Fortenberry, J. D.** (2009). Prevalence and characteristics of vibrator use by women in the United States: Results from a nationally representative study. *Journal of Sexual Medicine, 6,* 1857–1866.

**Herbert, J. D., Gaudiano, B. A., Rheingold, A. A., Myers, V. H., Dalrymple, K., & Nolan, E. M.** (2005). Social skills training augments the effectiveness of cognitive behavioral group therapy for social anxiety disorder. *Behavior Therapy, 36,* 125–138.

**Herek, G. M.** (2000). The psychology of sexual prejudice. *Current Directions in Psychological Science, 9,* 19–22.

**Herek, G. M.** (2002). Gender gaps in public opinion about lesbians and gay men. *Public Opinion Quarterly, 66*(2), 40–66.

**Herek, G. M.** (2003). The psychology of sexual prejudice. In L. D. Garnets & D. C. Kimmel (Eds.), *Psychological perspectives on lesbian, gay, and bisexual experiences.* New York: Columbia University Press.

**Herek, G. M.** (2006). Legal recognition of same-sex relationships in the United States: A social science perspective. *American Psychologist, 61,* 607–621.

**Herek, G. M.** (2009a). Hate crimes and stigma-related experiences among sexual minority adults in the United States: Prevalence estimates from a national probability sample. *Journal of Interpersonal Violence, 24,* 54–74.

**Herek, G. M.** (2009b). Sexual prejudice. In T. D. Nelson (Ed.), *Handbook of prejudice, stereotyping, and discrimination* (pp. 441–467). New York: Psychology Press.

**Herek, G. M., & Capitanio, J.** (1996). "Some of my best friends": Intergroup contact concealable stigma, and heterosexuals' attitudes toward gay men and lesbians. *Personality and Social Psychology Bulletin, 22,* 412–424.

**Herek, G. M., Cogan, J. C., & Gillis, J. R.** (2002). Victim experiences in hate crimes based on sexual orientation. *Journal of Social Issues, 58*(2), 319–339.

**Heres, S., Davis, J., Maino, K., Jetzinger, E., Kissling, W., & Leucht, S.** (2006). Why olanzapine beats risperidone, risperdone beats quetiapine, and quetiapine beats olanzapine: An exploratory analysis of head-to-head comparison studies of second-generation antipsychotics. *American Journal of Psychiatry, 163,* 185–194.

**Hermann, D., Raybeck, D., & Gruneberg, M.** (2002). *Improving memory and study skills: Advances in theory and practice.* Ashland, OH: Hogrefe & Huber.

**Hermann, R. C., Dorwart, R. A., Hoover, C. W., & Brody, J.** (1995). Variation in ECT use in the United States. *American Journal of Psychiatry, 152,* 869–875.

**Hermann, R. C., Ettner, S. L., Dorwart, R. A., Hoover, C. W., & Yeung, E.** (1998). Characteristics of psychiatrists who perform ECT. *American Journal of Psychiatry, 155,* 889–894.

**Hertenstein, M. J., Hansel, C. A., Butts, A. M., & Hile, S. N.** (2009). Smile intensity in photographs predicts divorce later in life. *Motivation and Emotion, 33,* 99–105.

**Hertenstein, M. J., Holmes, R., McCullough, M., & Keltner, D.** (2009). The communication of emotion via touch. *Emotion, 9,* 566–573.

**Herzog, D. B., & Delinski, S. S.** (2001). Classifica-tion of eating disorders. In R. H. Striegel-Moore & L. Smolak (Eds.), *Eating disorders.* Washington, DC: American Psychological Association.

**Herzog, T. R., & Strevey, S. J.** (2008). Contact with nature, sense of humor, and psychological well-being. *Environment and Behavior, 40,* 747–776.

**Hess, N. H., & Hagen, E. H.** (2006). Sex differences in indirect aggression: Psychological evidence from young adults. *Evolution and Human Behavior, 27,* 231–245.

**Hess, U., & Thibault, P.** (2009). Darwin and emotion expression. *American Psychologist, 64,* 120–128.

**Hetherington, E. M.** (1993). An overview of the Virginia longitudinal study of divorce and remarriage with a focus on early adolescence. *Journal of Family Psychology, 7,* 1–18.

**Hetherington, E. M.** (1999). Should we stay together for the sake of the children? In E. M. Hetherington (Ed.), *Coping with divorce, single parenting, and remarriage: A risk and resiliency perspective.* Mahwah, NJ: Erlbaum.

**Hetherington, E. M.** (2003). Intimate pathways: Changing patterns in close personal relationships across time. *Family Relations: Interdisciplinary Journal of Applied Family Studies, 52*(4), 318–331.

**Hetherington, E. M., Bridges, M., & Insabella, G. M.** (1998). What matters? What does not? Five perspectives on the association between marital transitions and children's adjustment. *American Psychologist, 53,* 167–184.

**Hetsroni, A.** (2007). Three decades of sexual content on prime-time network programming: A longitudinal meta-analytic review. *Journal of Communication, 57,* 318–348.

**Hettich, P. I.** (1998). *Learning skills for college and career.* Pacific Grove, CA: Brooks/Cole.

**Hewstone, M.** (1990). The ultimate attribution error? A review of the literature on intergroup causal attribution. *European Journal of Social Psychology, 20,* 311–335.

**Heymann, J., Earle, A., Simmons, S., Breslow, S., & Kuehnhoff, A.** (2004). *The work, family, and equity index: Where does the United States stand globally?* Boston: Harvard School of Public Health.

**Hicks, T. V., & Leitenberg, H.** (2001). Sexual fantasies about one's partner versus someone else: Gender differences in incidence and frequency. *Journal of Sex Research, 38*(1), 43–50.

**Hiedemann, B., Suhomlinova, O., & O'Rand, A. M.** (1998). Economic independence, economic status, and empty nest in midlife marital disruption. *Journal of Marriage and the Family, 60,* 219–231.

**Higgins, E. T.** (1987). Self-discrepancy: A theory relating self and affect. *Psychological Review, 94*(3), 319–340.

**Higgins, E. T.** (1999). When do self-descrepancies have specific relations to emotions? The second-generation question of Tangney, Niedenthal, Covert, and Barlow (1998). *Journal of Personality and Social Psychology, 77*(6), 1313–1317.

**Higgins, E. T., Shah, J., & Friedman, R.** (1997). Emotional responses to goal attainment: Strength of regulatory focus as a moderator. *Journal of Personality and Social Psychology, 72*(3), 515–525.

**Hill, A. J.** (2002). Prevalence and demographics of dieting. In C. G. Fairburn & K. D. Brownell (Eds.), *Eating disorders and obesity: A comprehensive handbook.* New York: Guilford.

**Hill, C. E., & Lambert, M. J.** (2004). Methodological issues in studying psychotherapy processes and outcomes. In M. J. Lambert (Ed.), *Bergin and Garfield's handbook of psychotherapy and behavior change.* New York: Wiley.

**Hill, C. T., Rubin, Z., & Peplau, L. A.** (1976). Breakups before marriage: The end of 103 affairs. *Journal of Social Issues, 32,* 147–168.

**Hill, J. O., & Wyatt, H. R.** (2005). Role of physical activity in preventing and treating obesity. *Journal of Applied Physiology, 99,* 765–770.

**Hill, P. C., & Pargament, K. I.** (2003). Advances in the conceptualization and measurement of religion and spirituality. *American Psychologist, 58,* 64–74.

**Hines, M.** (1982). Prenatal gonadal hormones and sex differences in human behavior. *Psychological Bulletin, 92,* 56–80.

**Hines, M.** (1990). Gonadal hormones and human cognitive development. In J. Balthazart (Ed.), *Hormones, brain and behavior in vertebrates: 1. Sexual differentiation, neuroanatomical aspects, neurotransmitters and neuropeptides.* Basel: Karger.

**Hines, M.** (2004). Androgen, estrogen, and gender: Contributions of the early hormone environment to gender-related behavior. In A. H. Eagly, A. E. Beall, & R. J. Sternberg (Eds.), *The psychology of gender.* New York: Guilford Press.

**Hines, M.** (2007). Do sex differences in cognition cause the shortage of women in science? In S. J. Ceci & W. M. Williams (Eds.), *Why aren't more women in science?* (pp. 101–112).

**Hinshaw, S. P.** (2007). *The mark of shame: Stigma of mental illness and an agenda for change.* New York: Oxford University Press.

**Hinshaw, S. P., & Stier, A.** (2008). Stigma as related to mental disorders. *Annual Review of Clinical Psychology,* 4, 367–393.

**Hipke, K., Wolchik, S. A., & Sandler, I. N.** (2008). Children of divorce. In G. Fink (Ed.), *Encyclopedia of stress: Vols. 1–4.* (2nd ed., pp. 844–848). San Diego, CA: Elsevier Academic Press.

**Hiroto, D. S., & Seligman, M. E. P.** (1975). Generality of learned helplessness in man. *Journal of Personality and Social Psychology, 31,* 311–327.

**Hirsch, J. K., Wolford, K., LaLonde, S. M., Brunk, L., & Parker-Morris, A.** (2009). Optimistic explanatory style as a moderator of the association between negative life events and suicidal ideation. *Crisis, 30,* 48–53.

**Hirst, E., Berry, L., & Soderstrom, J.** (1981). Review of utility home energy audit programs. *Energy, 6,* 621–630.

**Hirt, E. R., Zillman, D., Erikson, G. A., & Kennedy, C.** (1992). Costs and benefits of allegiance: Changes in fans' self-ascribed competence after team victory versus defeat. *Journal of Personality and Social Psychology, 63,* 724–738.

**Hobfoll, S. E., & Vaux, A.** (1993). Social support: Resources and context. In L. Goldberger & S. Breznitz (Eds.), *Handbook of stress: Theoretical and clinical aspects* (2nd ed.). New York: Free Press.

**Hobza, C. L., Walker, K. E., Yakushko, O., & Peugh, J. L.** (2007). What about men? Social comparison and the effects of media images on body and self-esteem. *Psychology of Men & Masculinity, 8,* 161–172.

**Hock, M. F., Deshler, D. D., & Schumaker, J. B.** (2006). Enhancing student motivation through the pursuit of possible selves. In C. Dunkel & J. Kerpelman (Eds.), *Possible selves: Theory, research, and applications.* Hauppague, NY: Nova Science Publishers.

**Hodge, B.** (2002, March). PCs and the healthy office. *Smart Computing,* pp. 64–67.

**Hoek, H. W.** (2002). Distribution of eating disorders. In C. G. Fairburn & K. D. Brownell (Eds.), *Eating disorders* and obesity: A comprehensive handbook. New York: Guilford.

**Hofferth, S. L. & Curtin, S. C.** (2005). Leisure time activities in middle childhood. In K. A. Moore & L. H. Lippman (Eds.), *What do children need to flourish? Conceptualizing and measuring indicators of positive development* (pp. 95–110). New York: Springer.

**Hofferth, S. L. & Sandberg, J. F.** (2001). Changes in American children's time, 1981–1997. In S. Hofferth & T. Owens (Eds.), *Children at the millennium: Where have we come from, where are we going?* (pp. 193–229). New York: Elsevier Science.

**Hoffman, E.** (1994). *The drive for self: Alfred Adler and the founding of individual psychology.* Reading, MA: Addison-Wesley.

**Hoffnung, M.** (2004). Wanting it all: Career, marriage, and motherhood during college-educated women's 20s. *Sex Roles, 50*(9/10), 711–723.

**Hofstede, G.** (1980). *Culture's consequences: International differences in work-related values.* Newbury Park, CA: Sage.

**Hofstede, G.** (1983). Dimensions of national cultures in fifty countries and three regions. In J. Deregowski, S. Dzuirawiec, & R. Annis (Eds.), *Explications in cross-cultural psychology.* Lisse: Swets and Zeitlinger.

**Hogan, B. F., & Linden, W.** (2004). Anger response styles and blood pressure: At least don't ruminate about it! *Annals of Behavioral Medicine, 27,* 38–49.

**Hogan, M. F., & Morrison, A. K.** (2003). Organization and financing of mental health care. In A. Tasman, J. Kay, & J. A. Lieberman (Eds.), *Psychiatry.* New York: Wiley.

**Høglend, P., Bøgwald, K. –P., Amlo, S., Marble, A., Ulberg, R., Sjaastad, M. C., et al.** (2008). Transference interpretations in dynamic psychotherapy: Do they really yield sustained effects? *American Journal of Psychiatry, 165,* 763–771.

**Holahan, C. J., & Moos, R. H.** (1990). Life stressors, resistance factors, and improved psychological functioning: An extension of the stress resistance paradigm. *Journal of Personality and Social Psychology, 58,* 909–917.

**Holahan, C. J., & Moos, R. H.** (1994). Life stressors and mental health: Advances in conceptualizing stress resistance. In W. R. Avison & I. H. Gotlib (Eds.), *Stress and mental health: Contemporary issues and prospects for the future.* New York: Plenum.

**Holahan, C. J., Moos, R. H., Holahan, C. K., Brennan, P. L., & Schutte, K. K.** (2005). Stress generation, avoidance coping and depressive symptoms: A 10-year model. *Journal of Consulting and Clinical Psychology, 73,* 658–666.

**Holden, C.** (2004). FDA weighs suicide risk in children on antidepressants. *Science, 303,* 745.

**Holen, A.** (2007). Posttraumatic stress disorder, delayed. In G. Fink (Ed.), *Encyclopedia of stress: Vols. 1–4* (2nd ed., pp. 150–152). San Diego, CA: Elsevier Academic Press.

**Holland, J.** (1997). *Making vocational choices* (3rd ed.). Odessa, FL: Psychological Assessment Resources.

**Holland, J. C., & Lewis, S.** (1993). Emotions and cancer: What do we really know? In D. Goleman & J. Gurin (Eds.), *Mind/body medicine: How to use your mind for better health.* Yonkers, NY: Consumer Reports Books.

**Holland, J. L.** (1985). *Making vocational choices: A theory of vocational personalities and work environments.* Englewood Cliffs, NJ: Prentice-Hall.

**Holland, J. L.** (1996). Exploring careers with a typology: What we have learned and some new directions. *American Psychologist, 51,* 397–406.

**Holland, R. W., Roeder, U., van Baaren, R. B., Brandt, A. C., & Hannover, B.** (2004). Don't stand so close to me: The effects of self-construal on interpersonal closeness. *Psychological Science, 15,* 237–242.

**Hollander, E. & Simeon, D.** (2008). Anxiety disorders. In R. E. Hales, S. C. Yudofsky, & G. O. Gabbard (Eds.), *The American psychiatric publishing textbook of psychiatry* (pp.505–608). Washington, DC: American Psychiatric Publishing.

**Hollifield, M. A.** (2005). Somatoform disorders. In B. J. Sadock & V. A. Sadock (Eds.), *Kaplan & Sadock's comprehensive textbook of psychiatry.* Philadelphia: Lippincott Williams & Wilkins.

**Hollon, S. D., & Beck, A. T.** (2004). Cognitive and cognitive behavioral therapies. In M. J. Lambert (Ed.), *Bergin and Garfields handbook of psychotherapy and behavior change.* New York: Wiley.

**Hollon, S. D. & Dimidjian, S.** (2009). Cognitive and behavioral treatment of depression. In I. H. Gotlib & C. L. Hammen (eds.), *Handbook of depression* (pp. 586–603). New York: Guilford.

**Hollon, S. D., Stewart, M. O., & Strunk, D.** (2006). Enduring effects for cognitive behavior therapy in the treatment of depression and anxiety. *Annual Review of Psychology, 57,* 285–315.

**Holmans, P., Weissman, M. M., Zubenko, G. S., Scheftner, W. A., Crowe, R. R., DePaulo, J. R., et al.** (2007). Genetics of recurrent early-onset major depression (GenRED): Final genome scan report. *American Journal of Psychiatry, 164,* 248–258.

**Holmes, T. H., & Rahe, R. H.** (1967). The Social Readjustment Rating Scale. *Journal of Psychosomatic Research, 11,* 213–218.

**Holt, A., & Lyness, K. P.** (2007). Body image and sexual satisfaction: Implications for couple therapy. *Journal of Couples & Relationship Therapy, 6*(3), 45–68.

**Homburg, A., & Stolberg, A.** (2006). Explaining pro-environmental behavior with a cognitive theory of stress. *Journal of Environmental Psychology, 26,* 1–14.

**Hong, G. K., Garcia, M., & Soriano, M.** (2000). Responding to the challenge: Preparing mental health professionals for the new millennium. In I. Cuellar & F. A. Paniagua (Eds.), *Handbook of multicultural mental health: Assessment and treatment of diverse populations.* San Diego: Academic Press.

**Honts, C. R., Raskin, D. C., & Kircher, J. C.** (2002). The scientific status of research on polygraph testing. In D. L. Faigman, D. H. Kaye, M. J. Saks, & J. Sanders (Eds.), *Modern scientific evidence: The law and science of expert testimony* (Vol. 2). St. Paul, MN: West Publishing.

**Hoobler, J. M., & Brass, D. J.** (2006). Abusive supervision and family undermining as displaced aggression. *Journal of Applied Psychology, 91,* 1125–1133.

**Hoobler, J. M., Wayne, S. J., & Lemmon, G.** (2009). Bosses' perceptions of family-work conflict and women's promotability: Glass ceiling effects. *Academy of Management Journal, 52,* 939–957.

**Hood, K. E., Draper, P., Crockett, L. J., & Petersen, A. C.** (1987). The ontogeny and phylogeny of sexual differences in development: A biopsychosocial synthesis. In B. Carter (Ed.), *Current conceptions of sex roles and sex typing: Theory and research.* New York: Praeger.

**Hooker, E.** (1957). The adjustment of the male overt homosexual. *Journal of Projective Techniques, 21,* 18–31.

**Hooley, J. M.** (2004). Do psychiatric patients do better clinically if they live with certain kinds of families? *Current Directions in Psychological Science, 13*(5), 202–205.

**Hooley, J. M.** (2007). Expressed emotion and relapse of psychopathology. *Annual Review of Clinical Psychology, 3,* 329–352.

**Hooley, J. M.** (2009). Schizophrenia: Interpersonal functioning. In P. H. Blaney & T. Millon (Eds.), *Oxford textbook of psychopathology* (pp. 333–360). New York: Oxford University Press.

**Hopper, J.** (2001). The symbolic origins of conflict in divorce. *Journal of Marriage and Family, 63,* 430–445.

**Hopper, K., Harrison, G., Janca, A., & Satorius, N.** (2007). *Recovery from schizophrenia: An international perspective—A report from the WHO Collaborative Project, the international study of schizophrenia.* New York: Oxford University Press.

**Horstmann, G.** (2003). What do facial expressions convey: Feeling states, behavioral intentions, or action requests? *Emotion, 3*(2), 150–166.

**Horvath, M., & Ryan, A. M.** (2003). Antecedents and potential moderators of the relationship between attitudes and hiring discrimination on the basis of sexual orientation. *Sex Roles, 48*(3/4), 115–130.

**Horvath, T. L.** (2005). The hardship of obesity: A soft-wired hypothalamus. *Nature Neuroscience, 8,* 561–565.

**Hotopf, M.** (2004). Preventing somatization. *Psychological Medicine, 34,* 195–198.

**Houston, M.** (2004). When black women talk with white women: Why dialogues are difficult. In A. Gonzalez, M. Houston, & V. Chen (Eds.), *Our voices: Essays in culture, ethnicity, and communication* (4th ed., pp. 119–125). Los Angeles: Roxbury.

**Houts, A. C.** (2002). Discovery, invention, and the expansion of the modern *Diagnostic and Statistical Manuals of Mental Disorders.* In L. E. Beutler & M. L. Malik (Eds.), *Rethinking the DSM.* Washington, DC: American Psychological Association.

**Hovanesian, S., Isakov, I., & Cervellione, K. L.** (2009). Defense mechanisms and suicide risk in major depression. *Archives of Suicide Research, 13,* 74–86.

**Hovland, C. I., & Weiss, W.** (1951). The influence of source credibility on communication effectiveness. *Public Opinion Quarterly, 15,* 635–650.

**Howard, A.** (Ed.). (1995). *The changing nature of work.* San Francisco, CA: Jossey-Bass.

**Hoyle, R., Fejfar, M. C., & Miller, J. D.** (2000). Personality and sexual risk taking: A quantitative review. *Journal of Personality, 68,* 1203–1231.

**Hsee, C. K., & Hastie, R.** (2006). Decision and experience: Why don't we choose what makes us happy? *Trends in Cognitive Sciences, 10*(1), 31–37.

**Hsu, L. K. G.** (1990). *Eating disorders.* New York: Guilford Press.

**Hu, F. B., & Willett, W. C.** (2002). Optimal diets for prevention of coronary heart disease. *Journal of the American Medical Association, 288*(20), 2569–2578.

**Hu, Y., Zhang, R., & Li, W.** (2005). Relationships among jealousy, self-esteem and self-efficacy. *Chinese Journal of Clinical Psychology, 13*(2), 165–166, 172.

**Hubbard, J. A., & Coie, J. D.** (1994). Emotional correlates of social competence in children's peer relationships. *Merrill-Palmer Quaterly, 40,* 1–20.

**Hudson, J. I., Hiripi, E., Pope, H. G., & Kessler, R. C.** (2007). The prevelance and correlates of eating disorders in the national comorbidity survey replication. *Biological Psychiatry, 61,* 348–358.

**Huebner, E. S., & Gilman, R.** (2006). Students who like and dislike school. *Applied Research in Quality of Life, 2,* 139–150.

**Huebner, E. S., Gilman, R., Reschly, A. L., & Hall, R.** (2009). Positive schools. In S. J. Lopez & C. R. Snyder (Eds.), *Oxford handbook of positive psychology* (2nd ed., pp. 561–568). New York: Oxford.

**Huesmann, L. R., Moise-Titus, J., Podolski, C.-L., & Eron, L. D.** (2003). Longitudinal relations between children's exposure to TV violence and their aggressive and violent behavior in young adulthood: 1977–1992. *Developmental Psychology, 39,* 201–221.

**Huey, L. Y., Cole, S. Cole, R. F., Daniels, A. S. & Katzelnick, D. J.** (2009). Health care reform. In B. J. Sadock, V. A. Sadock, & P. Ruiz (Eds.), *Kaplan & Sadock's comprehensive textbook of psychiatry* (pp. 4282–4298). Philadelphia: Lippincott Williams & Wilkins.

**Hughes, E., & Parkes, K.** (2007). Work hours and well-being: The roles of work-time control and work-family interference. *Work & Stress, 21*(3), 264–278.

**Hull, J. G., & Young, R. D.** (1983). Self-consciousness, self-esteem, and success-failure as determinants of alcohol consumption in male social drinkers. *Journal of Personality and Social Psychology, 44,* 1097–1109.

**Hull, J. G., Young, R. D. & Jouriles, E.** (1986). Applications of the self-awareness model of alcohol consumption: Predicting patterns of use and abuse. *Journal of Personality and Social Psychology, 51,* 790–796.

**Hulshoff, H. E., Hoek, H. W., Susser, E., Brown, A. S., Dingemans, A., Schnack, H. G., van Haren, N. E. M., Ramos, L. M. P., Gispen-de Wied, C. C., & Kahn, R. S.** (2000). Prenatal exposure to famine and brain morphology in schizophrenia. *American Journal of Psychiatry, 157,* 1170–1172.

**Hultin, M.** (2003). Some take the glass escalator, some hit the glass ceiling? Career consequences of occupational sex segregation. *Work and Occupations, 30*(1), 30–61.

**Hunsley, J., Lee, C. M., & Wood, J. M.** (2003). Controversial and questionable assessment techniques. In S. O. Lilienfeld, S. J. Lynn, & J. M. Lohr (Eds.), *Science and pseudoscience in clinical psychology.* New York: Guilford.

**Hunt, A., & Curtis, B.** (2006). A genealogy of the genital kiss: Oral sex in the twentieth century. *Canadian Journal of Human Sexuality, 15,* 69–84.

**Hunter, E.** (1998). Adolescent attraction to cults. *Adolescence, 33,* 709–714.

**Hunter, J. E., & Hunter, R. F.** (1984). Validity and utility of alternative predictors of job performance. *Psychological Bulletin, 96*(1), 72–98.

**Huntsinger, E. T., & Luecken, L. J.** (2004). Attachment relationships and health behavior: The mediational role of self-esteem. *Psychology & Health, 19,* 515–526.

**Hust, S. J. T., Brown, J. D., & L'Engle, K. L.** (2008). Boys will be boys and girls better be prepared: An analysis of the rare sexual health messages in young adolescents' media. *Mass Communication & Society, 11,* 3–23.

**Huston, A. C., Donnerstein, E., Fairchild, H., Feshbach, N. D., Katz, P. A., Murray, J. P., Rubinstein, E. A., Wilcox, B. L., & Zuckerman, D.** (1992). *Big world, small screen: The role of television in American society.* Lincoln: University of Nebraska Press.

**Huston, T. L., & Melz, H.** (2004). The case for (promoting). *Journal of Marriage and Family, 66,* 943–958.

**Huston, T. L., Niehuis, S., & Smith, S. E.** (2001). The early marital roots of conjugal distress and divorce. *Current Directions in Psychological Science, 10*(4), 116–119.

**Hutchinson, A.** (2007, February). Watering holes: Las Vegas tries to prevent a water shortage. *Popular Mechanics*, p. 20.

**Hwang, W.** (2006). The psychotherapy adaptation and modification framework: Application to Asian Americans. *American Psychologist, 61,* 702–715.

**Hyde, J. S.** (1994a). *Understanding human sexuality* (5th ed.). New York: McGraw-Hill.

**Hyde, J. S.** (1994b). Can meta-analysis make feminist transformations in psychology? *Psychology of Women Quarterly, 18,* 451–462.

**Hyde, J. S.** (1996). Where are the gender differences? Where are the gender similarities? In D.M. Buss & N. M. Malamuth (Eds.), *Sex, power, conflict: Evolutionary and feminist perspectives.* New York: Oxford University Press.

**Hyde, J. S.** (2004). *Half the human experience: The psychology of women.* Boston: Houghton Mifflin.

**Hyde, J. S.** (2005). The gender similarities hypothesis. *American Psychologist, 60,* 581–592.

**Hyde, J. S.** (2007a) Women in science: Gender similarities in abilities and sociocultural forces. In S. J. Ceci & W. M. Williams (Eds.), *Why aren't more women in science?* (pp. 131–146). Washington, DC: American Psychological Association.

**Hyde, J. S.** (2007b). New directions in the study of gender similarities and differences. *Current Directions in Psychological Science, 16,* 259–263.

**Hyde, J. S., & DeLamater, J. D.** (2003). *Understanding human sexuality.* New York: McGraw-Hill.

**Hyde, J. S., Fennema, E., & Lamon, S. J.** (1990). Gender differences in mathematics performance: A meta-analysis. *Psychological Bulletin, 107,* 139–155.

**Hyde, J. S., & Frost, L. A.** (1993). Meta-analysis in the psychology of women. In F. L. Denmark & M. A. Paludi (Eds.), *Psychology of women: A handbook of issue and theories.* Westport, CT: Greenwood Press.

**Hyde, J. S., & Grabe, S.** (2008). Meta-analysis in the psychology of women. In F. L. Denmark & M. A. Paludi (Eds.), *Psychology of Women: A Handbook of Issues and Theories* (2nd ed., pp. 142–173). Westport, CT: Praeger Publishers.

**Hyde, J. S., & Kling, K. C.** (2001). Women, motivation, and achievement. *Psychology of Women Quarterly, 25,* 364–378.

**Hyde, J. S., & Oliver, M. B.** (2000). Gender differences in sexuality: Results from meta-analysis. In C. B. Travis & J. W. White (Eds.), *Sexuality, society, and feminism.* Washington, DC: American Psychological Association.

**Hygge, S., Evans, G. W., & Bullinger, M.** (2002). A prospective study of some effects of aircraft noise on cognitive performance in school children. *Psychological Science, 13*(5), 469–474.

**Hynes, K. H., & Clarkberg, M.** (2005). Women's employment patterns during early parenthood: A group-based trajectory analysis. *Journal of Marriage and Family, 67,* 222–239.

**Iaccino, J. F.** (1996). A further examination of the bizarre imagery mnemonic: Its effectiveness with mixed context and delayed testing. *Perceptual & Motor Skills, 83,* 881–882.

**Iacono, W. G.** (2008). Accuracy of polygraph techniques: Problems using confessions to determine the truth. *Physiology & Behavior, 95*(1–2), 24–26.

**Iacono, W. G.** (2009). Psychophysiological detection of deception and guilty knowledge. In K. S. Douglas, J. L. Skeem, & S. O. Lilienfeld (Eds.), *Psychological science in the courtroom: Consensus and controversy* (pp. 224–241). New York: Guilford.

**Ickes, W.** (1993). Traditional gender roles: Do they make and then break our relationships? *Journal of Social Issues, 3,* 71–85.

**Ickes, W., Patterson, M. L., Rajecki, D. W., & Tanford, S.** (1982). Behavioral and cognitive consequences of reciprocal versus compensatory responses to preinteraction expectancies. *Social Cognition, 1,* 160–190.

**Ickovics, J. R., Thayaparan, B., & Ethier, K. A.** (2001). Women and AIDS: A contextual analysis. In A. Baum, T. A. Revenson, & J. E. Singer (Eds.), *Handbook of health psychology.* Mahwah, NJ: Erlbaum.

**Iezzi, T., Duckworth, M. P., & Adams, H. E.** (2001). Somatoform and factitious disorders. In P. B. Sutker & H. E. Adams (Eds.), *Comprehensive handbook of psychopathology* (3rd ed.). New York: Kluwer Academic/Plenum Publishers.

**Ignatius, E., & Kokkonen, M.** (2007). Factors contributing to verbal self-disclosure. *Nordic Psychology, 59*(4), 362–391.

**Ilgen, D. R.** (1990). Health issues at work: Opportunities for industrial/organization psychology. *American Psychologist, 45,* 252–261.

**Imhoff, R., & Erb, H.-P.** (2009). What motivates nonconformity? Uniqueness seeking blocks majority influence. *Personality and Social Psychology Bulletin, 35*(3), 309–320.

**Impett, E. A., & Peplau, L. A.** (2006). "His" and "her" relationships? A review of the empirical evidence. In A. L. Vangelisti & D. Perlman (Eds.), *The Cambridge handbook of personal relationships.* New York: Cambridge University Press.

**Impett, E. A., Peplau, L. A., & Gable, S. L.** (2005). Approach and avoidance sexual motives: Implications for personal and interpersonal well-being. *Personal Relationships, 12,* 465–482.

**Inagaki, K., & Hatano, G.** (2004). Vitalistic causality in young children's naive biology. *Trends in Cognitive Sciences, 8,* 356–362.

**Infante, J. R., Torres-Avisbal, M., Pinel, P., Vallejo. J. A., Peran, F., Gonzalez, F., Contreras, P., Pacheco, C., Roldan, A., & Latre, J. M.** (2001). Catecholamine levels in practitioners of the transcendental meditation technique. *Physiology & Behavior, 72*(1-2), 141–146.

**Inglehart, R.** (1990). *Culture shift in advanced industrial society.* Princeton, NJ: Princeton University Press.

**Inglehart, R., Foa, R., Peterson, C., & Welzel, C.** (2008). Development, freedom, and rising happiness: A global perspective (1981–2007). *Perspectives on Psychological Science,* 3(4), 264–285.

**Ingoldsby, B. B.** (1995). Mate selection and marriage. In B. B. Ingoldsby & S. Smith (Eds.), *Families in multicultural perspective.* New York: Guilford Press.

**Ingram, R. E., Scott, W. D., & Hamill, S.** (2009). Depression: Social and cognitive aspects. In P. H. Blaney & T. Millon (Eds.), *Oxford textbook of psychopathology* (pp. 230–252). New York: Oxford University Press.

**Innocenti, G. M.** (1994). Some new trends in the study of the corpus callosum. *Behavioral and Brain Research, 64,* 1–8.

**Inskeep, S.** (2005). *Women CEOs still rare among Fortune 500.* Retrieved May 7, 2007 from http://www.npr.org/templates/story/story.php?storyId=4509605.

**Insko, C. A., Smith, R. H., Alicke, M. D., Wade, J., & Taylor, S.** (1985). Conformity and group size: The concern with being right and the concern with being liked. *Personality and Social Psychology Bulletin, 11,* 41–50.

**Intergovernmental Panel on Climate Change.** (2007). *Climate change 2007: Synthesis report.* Retrieved from http://www.ipcc.ch/pdf/assessment-report/ar4/syr/ar4_syr.pdf

**International Labour Office.** (2002). *Key indicators of the labour market, 2001–2002.* Geneva: United Nations International Labour Office.

**Internet World Stats.** (2007). *Internet usage statistics—the big picture.* Retrieved from http://www.internetworldstats.com/stats.htm.

**Internet World Stats.** (2009). Retrieved from http://www.internetworldstats.com/stats.htm

**Ippolito, J., Adler, A. B., Thomas, J. L., Litz, B. T., & Holzl, R.** (2005). Extending and applying the demand-control model: The role of soldier's coping on a peacekeeping deployment. *Journal of Occupational Health Psychology, 10,* 452–464.

**Iribarren, C., Sidney, S., Bild, D. E., Liu, K., Markovitz, J. H., Roseman, J. M., & Matthews, K.** (2000). Association of hostility with coronary artery calcification in young adults: The CARDIA study. *Journal of the American Medical Association, 283*(19), 2546–2551.

**Ironson, G., Wynings, C., Sschneiderman, N., Baum, A., Rodriguez, M., Greenwood, D., Benight, C., Antoni, M., LaPerriere, A., Huang, H. S., Klimas, N., & Fletcher, M. A.** (1997). Post-traumatic stress symptoms, intrusive thoughts, loss, and immune function after Hurricane Andrew. *Psychosomatic Medicine, 59,* 128–141.

**Isen, A. M.** (1987). Positive affect, cognitive processes, and social behavior. In L. Berkowitz (Ed.), *Advances in experimental social psychology* (Vol. 20, pp. 203–253). San Diego, CA: Academic Press.

**Isen, A. M.** (2002). A role for neuropsychology in understanding the facilitating influence of positive affect on social behavior and cognitive processes. In C. R. Snyder & S. J. Lopez (Eds.), *Handbook of positive psychology* (pp. 528–540). New York: Oxford University Press.

**Isen, A. M.** (2004). Some perspectives on positive feelings and emotions: Positive affect facilitates thinking and problem solving. In A. S. R. Manstead, N. Frijda, & A. Fischer (Ed.), *Feelings and emotions: The Amsterdam symposium* (pp. 263–281). New York: Cambridge University Press.

**Isen, A. M., Daubman, K. A., & Nowicki, G. P.** (1987). Positive affect facilitates creative problem solving. *Journal of Personality and Social Psychology, 52,* 1121–1131.

**Isometsa, E. T., Heikkinen, M. E., Marttunen, M. J., Henriksson, M. M., Aro, H. M., & Lonnqvist, J. K.** (1995). The last appointment before suicide: Is suicide intent communicated? *American Journal of Psychiatry, 152,* 919–922.

**Ito, T. A., Chiao, K. W., Devine, P. G., Lorig, T., & Cacioppo, J. T.** (2006). The influence of facial feedback on race bias. *Psychological Science, 17,* 256–261.

**Ivancevich, J. M., Matteson, M. T., Freedman, S. M., & Phillips, J. S.** (1990). Worksite stress management interventions. *American Psychologist, 45,* 252–261.

**Iwao, S.** (1993). *The Japanese woman: Traditional image and changing reality.* New York: Free Press.

**Iwasaki, Y.** (2003). Roles of leisure in coping with stress among university students: A repeated-assessment field study. *Anxiety, Stress & Coping: An International Journal, 16*(1), 31–57.

**Iwasaki, Y., Mackay, K. J., Mactavish, J. B., Ristock, J., & Bartlett, J.** (2006). Voices from the margins: Stress, active living, and leisure as a contributor to coping with stress. *Leisure Sciences, 28,* 163–180.

**Iwasaki, Y., & Ristock, J. L.** (2007). The nature of stress experienced by lesbians and gay men. *Anxiety, Stress, & Coping, 20,* 299–319.

**Izard, C., Fine, S., Schultz, D., Mostow, A., Ackerman, B., & Youngstrom, E.** (2001). Emotion knowledge as a predictor of social behavior and academic competence in children at risk. *Psychological Science, 12*(1), 18–23.

**Izard, C. E.** (1994). Innate and universal facial expressions: Evidence from developmental and cross-cultural research. *Psychological Bulletin, 115,* 288–299.

**Jackson, L. A., & McGill, O. D.** (1996). Body type preferences and body characteristics associated with attractive and unattractive bodies by African Americans and Anglo Americans. *Sex Roles, 35*(5–6), 295–307.

**Jackson, L. A., Hunter, J. E., & Hodge, C. N.** (1995). Physical attractiveness and intellectual competence: A meta-analytic review. *Social Psychology Quarterly, 58,* 108–122.

**Jackson, M.** (2005). The limits of connectivity: Technology and 21st-century life. In D. F. Halpern & S. E. Murphy (Eds.), *From work-family balance to work-family interaction: Changing the metaphor.* Mahwah, NJ: Erlbaum.

**Jackson, T., Fritch, A., Nagasaka, T., & Gunderson, J.** (2002). Towards explaining the association between shyness and loneliness: A path analysis with American college students. *Social Behavior and Personality, 30*(3), 263–270.

**Jacobs, B. L.** (2004). Depression: The brain finally gets into the act. *Current Directions in Psychological Science, 13*(3), 103–106.

**Jacques, P. J., Dunlap, R. E., & Freeman, M.** (2008). The organization of denial: Conservative think tanks and environmental skepticism. *Environmental Politics, 17,* 349–385.

**Jacques, R.** (1997). The unbearable whiteness of being: Reflections of a pale, stale male. In P. Prasad, A. Mills, M. Elmes, & A. Prasad (Eds.), *Managing the organizational melting pot: Dilemmas of workplace diversity.* Thousand Oaks, CA: Sage.

**Jaffe, E.** (2008). Isolating the costs of loneliness. *The Observer, 21*(11), 14–17.

**Jaffe, H. W., Valdiserri, R. O., & De Cock, K. M.** (2007). The reemerging HIV/AIDS epidemic in men who have sex with men. *Journal of the American Medical Association, 298,* 2412–2414.

**Jahoda, M.** (1958). *Current concepts of positive mental health.* New York: Basic Books.

**Jain, S., Shapiro, S. L., Swanick, S., Roesch, S. C., Mills, P. J., Bell, I., & Schwartz, G. E. R.** (2007). A randomized controlled trial of mindfulness meditation versus relaxation training: Effects on distress, positive states of mind, rumination, and distraction. *Annals of Behavioral Medicine, 33,* 11–21.

**Jakicic, J. M., & Gallagher, K. I.** (2002). Physical activity considerations for management of body weight. In D. H. Bessesen, & R. Kushner (Eds.), *Evaluation & Management of Obesity.* Philadelphia: Hanley & Belfus.

**Jakicic, J. M., & Otto, A. D.** (2005). Physical activity considerations for the treatment and prevention of obesity. *American Journal of Clinical Nutrition, 82*(Suppl. 1), 226S–229S.

**Jakupcak, M., Salters, K., Gratz, K. L., & Roemer, L.** (2003). Masculinity and emotionality: An investigation of men's primary and secondary emotional responding. *Sex Roles, 49*(3/4), 111–120.

**James, J. E.** (2004). Critical review of dietary caffeine and blood pressure: A relationship that should be taken more seriously. *Psychosomatic Medicine, 66*(1), 63–71.

**Janis, I. L.** (1958). *Psychological stress.* New York: Wiley.

**Janis, I. L.** (1993). Decision making under stress. In L. Goldberger & S. Breznitz (Eds.), *Handbook of stress: Theoretical and clinical aspects* (2nd ed.). New York: Free Press.

**Janiszewski, P. M., Janssen, I., & Ross, R.** (2009). Abdominal obesity and physical inactivity are associated with erectile dysfunction independent of body mass index. *Journal of Sexual Medicine, 6,* 1990–1998.

**Jankowiak, W. R., & Fischer, E. F.** (1992). A cross-cultural perspective on romantic love. *Ethnology, 31,* 149–155.

Janoff-Bulman, R. (2004). Posttraumatic growth: Three explanatory models. *Psychological Inquiry, 15*(1), 30–34.

Jansz, J. (2000). Masculine identity and restrictive emotionality. In A. H. Fischer (Ed.), *Gender and emotion: Social psychological perspectives*. Cambridge, UK: Cambridge University Press.

Jaroff, L. (1993, November 29). Lies of the mind. *Time*, pp. 52–59.

Javitt, D. C., & Laruelle, M. (2006). Neurochemical theories. In J. A. Liberman, T. S. Stroup, & D. O. Perkins (Eds.), *Textbook of schizophrenia*. Washington, DC: American Psychiatric Publishing.

Jayaratne, T. E., Gelman, S. A., Feldbaum, M., Sheldon, J. P., Petty, E. M., & Kardia, S. L. R. (2009). The perennial debate: Nature, nurture, or choice? Black and white Americans' explanations for individual differences. *Review of General Psychology, 13*, 24–33.

Jefferson, J. W. & Greist, J. H. (2009). Lithium. In B. J. Sadock, V. A. Sadock, & P. Ruiz (Eds.), *Kaplan & Sadock's comprehensive textbook of psychiatry* (pp. 3132–3144). Philadelphia: Lippincott Williams & Wilkins.

Jeffery, R. W. (2001). Public health strategies for obesity treatment and prevention. *American Journal of Health Behavior, 25*(3), 252–259.

Jeffery, R. W., Epstein, L. H., Wilson, G. T., Drewnowski, A., Stunkard, A. J., Wing, R. R., & Hill, D. R. (2000). Long-term maintenance of weight loss: Current status. *Health Psychology, 19*(1), 5–16.

Jeffery, R. W., Kelly, K. M., Rothman, A. J., Sherwood, N. E., & Boutelle, K. N. (2004). The weight-loss experience: A descriptive analysis. *Annals of Behavioral Medicine, 27*, 100–106.

Jeffries, S., & Konnert, C. (2002). Regret and psychological well-being among voluntarily and involuntarily childless women and mothers. *International Journal of Aging and Human Development, 54*, 89–106.

Jemmott, J. B., III, & Magloire, K. (1988). Academic stress, social support, and secretory Immunoglobin A. *Journal of Personality and Social Psychology, 55*, 803–810.

Jeney-Gammon, P., Daugherty, T. K., Finch, A. J., Belter, R. W., & Foster K. Y. (1993). Children's coping styles and report of depressive symptoms following a natural disaster. *Journal of Genetic Psychology, 154*, 259–267.

Jensen-Campbell, L. A., & Graziano, W. G. (2001). Agreeableness as a moderator of interpersonal conflict. *Journal of Personality, 69*, 323–362.

Jepsen, L. K., & Jepsen, C. A. (2002). An empirical analysis of the matching patterns of same-sex and opposite-sex couples. *Demography, 39*, 435–453.

Jex, S. M., Bliese, P. D., Buzzell, S., & Primeau, J. (2001). The impact of self-efficacy on stressor-strain relations: Coping style as an explanatory mechanism. *Journal of Applied Psychology, 86*, 401–409.

Jeynes, W. H. (2006). The impact of parental remarriage on children: A meta-analysis. *Marriage & Family Review, 40*, 75–102.

Jhally, S., & Katz, J. (2001, Winter). Big trouble, little pond. *Umass*, pp. 26–31.

Jick, H., Kaye, J. A., & Jick, S. S. (2004). Antidepressants and the risk of suicidal behaviors. *Journal of the American Medical Association, 292*(3), 338–343.

John, O. P., Naumann, L. P., & Soto, C. J. (2008). Paradigm shift to the integrative big five trait taxonomy: History, measurement, and conceptual issues. In O. P. John, R. W. Robins & L. A. Pervin (Eds.), *Handbook of personality: Theory and research* (pp. 114–158). New York: Guilford.

Johnson, A. J., Haigh, M. M., Becker, J. A. H., Craig, E. A., & Wigley, S. (2008). College students' use of relational management strategies in email in long-distance and geographically close relationships. *Journal of Computer-Mediated Communication, 13*, 381–404.

Johnson, B. A., & Ait-Daoud, N. (2005). Alcohol: Clinical aspects. In J. H. Lowinson, P. Ruiz, R. B. Millman, & J. G. Langrod (Eds.), *Substance abuse: A comprehensive textbook*. Philadelphia: Lippincott/ Williams & Wilkins.

Johnson, I. M., Crowley, J., & Sigler, R. T. (1992). Agency response to domestic violence: Services provided to battered women. In E. C. Viano (Ed.), *Intimate violence: Interdisciplinary perspectives*. Washington, DC: Hemisphere.

Johnson, M. P. (2000). Conflict and control: Images of symmetry and asymmetry in domestic violence. In A. Booth, A. C. Crouter, & M. Clements (Eds.), *Couples in conflict*. Hillsdale, NJ: Erlbaum.

Johnson, M. P., & Ferraro, K. J. (2001). Research on domestic violence in the 1990's: Making distinctions. In R. M. Milardo (Ed.), *Understanding families into the new millennium: A decade in review*. Minneapolis, MN: National Council on Family Relations.

Johnson, S. (2007). Promoting easy sex without genuine intimacy: *Maxim* and *Cosmopolitan* cover lines and cover images. In M. Galician, & D. L. Merskin (Eds.), *Critical thinking about sex, love, and romance in the mass media* (pp. 55–74). Mahwah, NJ: Erlbaum.

Johnson, S. B., & Carlson, D. N. (2004). Medical regimen adherence: Concepts, assessment, and interventions. In J. M. Raczynski, & L. C. Leviton (Eds.), *Handbook of clinical health psychology: Vol. 2. Disorders of behavior and health*. Washington, DC: American Psychological Association.

Johnson, S. L., Joormann, J., Lemoult, J., & Miller, C. (2009). Mood disorders: Biological bases. In P. H. Blaney & T. Millon (Eds.), *Oxford textbook of psychopathology* (pp. 198–229). New York: Oxford University Press.

Johnson, T. W., & Colucci, P. (1999). Lesbians, gay men, and the family life cycle. In B. Carter & M. McGoldrick (Eds.), *The expanded family life cycle: Individual, family, and social perspectives* (3rd ed.). Boston: Allyn & Bacon.

Johnson, W., & Krueger, R. F. (2006). How money buys happiness: Genetic and environmental processes linking finances and life satisfaction. *Journal of Personality and Social Psychology, 90*, 680–691.

Johnston, L. D., O'Malley, P. M., Bachman, J. G., & Schulenberg, J. E. (2007). *Monitoring the future: National survey results on drug use, 1975–2006: Vol. 2. College students and adults ages 19–45* (NIH Publication No. 07–6206). Bethesda, MD: National Institute on Drug Abuse.

Johnston, L. D., O'Malley, P. M., Bachman, J. G., & Schulenberg, J. E. (2008). *Monitoring the future: National results on adolescent drug use: Overview of key findings* (NIH Publication No. 08–6418). Bethesda, MD: National Institute on Drug Abuse.

Joiner, T. E. (2002). Depression in its interpersonal context. In I. H. Gotlib & C. L. Hammen (Eds.), *Handbook of depression*. New York: Guilford.

Joiner, T. E., & Metalsky, G. I. (2001). Excessive reassurance-seeking: Delineating a risk factor involved in the development of depressive symptoms. *Psychological Science, 12*, 371–378.

Joiner, T. E., & Timmons, K. A. (2009). Depression in its interpersonal context. In I. H. Gotlib & C. L. Hammen (Eds.), *Handbook of depression* (pp. 322–339). New York: Guilford.

Joiner, T. E., van Orden, K. A., Witte, T. K., & Rudd, M. D. (2009). *The interpersonal theory of suicide: guidance for working with suicidal patients*. Washington, DC: American Psychological Association.

Joireman, J.A. (2005). Environmental problems as social dilemmas: The temporal dimension. In S. Strathman & J. Joireman (Eds.), *Understanding behavior in the context of time: Theory, research, and application* (pp. 289–304). Mahwah, NJ: Erlbaum.

Joireman, J. A., Van Lange, P. A., & Van Vugt, M. (2004). Who cares about the environmental impact of cars? Those with an eye toward the future. *Environment and Behavior, 36*, 187–206.

Jonah, B. A. (1997). Sensation seeking and risky driving: A review and synthesis of the literature. *Accident Analysis and Prevention. 29*, 651–665.

Jones, C. M., Braithwaite, V. A., & Healy, S. D. (2003). The evolution of sex differences in spatial ability. *Behavioral Neuroscience, 117*, 403–411.

Jones, D. (1995). Sexual selection, physical attractiveness, and facial neotony: Cross-cultural evidence and implications. *Current Anthropology, 36*, 723–748.

Jones, E. E. (1990). *Interpersonal perception*. New York: Freeman.

Jones, E. E., & Davis, K. (1965). From acts to dispositions: The attribution process in person perception. In L. Berkowitz (Ed.), *Advances in experimental social psychology* (Vol. 2). New York: Academic Press.

Jones, F., & Bright, J. (2007). Stress: Health and illness. In A. Monat, R. S. Lazarus, & G. Reevy (Eds.), *The Praeger handbook on stress and coping* (pp. 141–168). Westport, CT: Praeger Publishers.

Jones, F., & Kinman, G. (2001). Approaches to studying stress. In F. Jones & J. Bright (Eds.), *Stress: Myth, theory and research* . Harlow, England: Pearson Education.

Jones, R. A., & Brehm, J. W. (1970). Persuasiveness of one- and two-sided communications as a function of awareness there are two sides. *Journal of Experimental Social Psychology, 6*, 47–56.

Jorgensen, R. S., Johnson, B. T., Kolodziej, M. E., & Schreer, G. E. (1996). Elevated blood pressure and personality: A meta-analytic review. *Psychological Bulletin, 120*, 293–320.

Jorgensen, R. S., & Kolodziej, M. E. (2007). Suppressed anger, evaluative threat, and cardiovascular reactivity: A tripartite profile approach. *International Journal of Psychophysiology, 66*, 102–108.

Joska, J. A. & Stein, D. J. (2008). Mood disorders. In R. E. Hales, S. C. Yudofsky, & G. O. Gabbard (Eds.), *The American psychiatric publishing textbook of psychiatry* (pp. 457–504). Washington, DC: American Psychiatric Publishing.

Joung, I. M. A., Stronks, K., Van De Mheen, H., Van Poppel, F. W. A., Van Der Meer, J. B. W., & Mackenbach, J. P. (1997). The contribution of intermediary factors to marital status differences in self-reported health. *Journal of Marriage and the Family, 59*, 476–490.

Jourard, S. M., & Landsman, T. (1980). *Healthy personality: An approach from the viewpoint of humanistic psychology*. New York: Macmillan.

Joyner, T. (1999, November 14). All-work is American way: Atlanta poll finds 21 percent work 50-plus hours a week. *The Atlanta Journal-Constitution*, pp. R1, R5.

Joyner, T. (2001, May 27). Why can't we enjoy a vacation? Americans getting tired, and it shows at work. *The Atlanta Journal-Constitution*, pp. D1, D3.

Judge, T. A., & Klinger, R. (2008). Job satisfaction: Subjective well-being at work. In M. Eid & R. J. Larsen (Eds.), *The science of subjective well-being* (pp. 393–413). New York: Guilford.

Julien, R. M. (2008). *A primer of drug action* (11th ed.). New York: Worth.

Jung, C. G. (1921). Psychological types. In *Collected Works* (Vol. 6). Princeton, NJ: Princeton University Press.

Jung, C. G. (1933). *Modern man in search of a soul*. New York: Harcourt, Brace & World.

Jussim, L., & Harber, K. D. (2005). Teacher-expectations and self-fulfilling prophecies: Knowns and unknowns, resolved and unresolved controversies. *Personality and Social Psychology Review, 9*, 131–155.

Justman, S. (2005). *Fool's paradise: The unreal world of pop psychology*. Chicago: Ivan R. Dee.

Kabat-Zinn, J. (1982). An outpatient program in behavioral medicine for chronic pain patients based on the practice of mindfulness meditation: Theoretical considerations and preliminary results. *General Hospital Psychiatry, 4*, 33–47.

Kaestle, C. E., & Halpern, C. T. (2007). What's love got to do with it? Sexual behaviors of opposite-sex couples through emerging adulthood. *Perspectives on Sexual and Reproductive Health, 39*, 134–140.

Kaestle, C. E., Halpern, C. T., & Brown J. D. (2007). Music videos, pro wrestling, and acceptance of date rape among middle school males and females: An exploratory analysis. *Journal of Adolescent Health Care, 40*, 185–187.

Kagan, J. (1998). Biology and the child. In W. Damon (Ed.), *Handbook of child psychology* (Vol. 3): *Social, emotional, and personality development*. New York: Wiley.

Kahn, A. S., & Andreoli Mathie, V. (1999). Sexuality, society, and feminism: Psychological perspectives on women. In C. B. Travis & J. W. White (Eds.), *Sexuality, society, and feminism: Psychological perspectives on women*. Washington, DC: American Psychological Association.

Kahn, K., Ho, A. K., Sidanius, J., & Pratto, F. (2009). The space between us and them: Perceptions of status differences. *Group Processes & Intergroup Relations, 12*(5), 591–604.

Kahn, P. H., Jr. (1999). *The human relationship with nature: Development and culture*. Cambridge, MA: MIT Press.

Kahn, P. H., Jr. (2003). The development of environmental moral identity. In S. Clayton & S. Opotow (Eds.), *Identity and the natural environment: The psychological significance of nature* (pp. 113–134). Cambridge, MA: MIT Press.

Kahn, P. H., Jr. (2006). Nature and moral development. In M. Killen, & J. Smetana (Eds.), *Handbook of moral development* (pp. 461–480). Mahwah, NJ: Erlbaum.

Kahn, P. H., Jr. (2007). The child's environmental amnesia—it's ours. *Children, Youth and Environments 17*, 199–207.

Kahn, P. H., Jr., & Kellert, S. R. (2002). *Children and nature: Psychological, sociocultural, and evolutionary investigations*. Cambridge MA: MIT Press.

Kahneman, D. (1999). Objective happiness. In D. Kahneman, E. Diener, & N. Schwarz (Eds.), *Well-being: The foundations of hedonic psychology*. New York: Sage.

Kahneman, D., Diener, E., & Schwarz, N. (Eds.). (1999). *Well-being: The foundations of hedonic psychology*. New York: Russell Sage.

Kahneman, D., Krueger, A. B., Schkade, D., Schwarz, N., & Stone, A. A. (2006). Would you be happier if you were richer? A focusing illusion. *Science, 312*, 1908–1910.

Kaiser, A., Haller, S., Schmitz, S., & Nitsch, C. (2009). On sex/gender related similarities and differences in fMRI language research. *Brain Research Reviews, 61*, 49–59.

**Kaiser Family Foundation, Holt, T., Greene, L., & Davis, J.** (2003). *National Survey of adolescents and young adults: Sexual health knowledge, attitudes, and experiences.* Menlo Park, CA: Henry J. Kaiser Family Foundation.

**Kaiser Family Foundation.** (2004). *Sex education in America: Principals' survey.* Menlo Park, CA: Henry J. Kaiser Family Foundation.

**Kaiser Family Foundation.** (2006). *HIV/AIDS policy fact sheet.* Retrieved June 24, 2007 from http://www.kff.org/hivaids/us.cfm.

**Kalant, H.** (2004). Adverse effects of cannabis on health: An update of the literature since 1966. *Progress in Neuro-Psychopharmocology and Biological Psychiatry, 28,* 849–863.

**Kalant, H., & Kalant, O. J.** (1979). Death in amphetamine users: Causes and rates. In D. E. Smith (Ed.), *Amphetamine use, misuse and abuse.* Boston: G. K. Hall.

**Kalb, C., & Murr, A.** (2006, May 16). Battling a black epidemic. *Newsweek,* pp. 42–48.

**Kalichman, S. C.** (1995). *Understanding AIDS: A guide for mental health professionals.* Washington, DC: American Psychological Association.

**Kalichman, S. C., Eaton, L., Cain, D., Cherry, C., Fuhrel, A., Kaufman, M., & Pope, H.** (2007). Changes in HIV treatment beliefs and sexual risk behaviors among gay and bisexual men, 1997–2005. *Health Psychology, 26,* 650–656.

**Kalichman, S. C., Roffman, R. A., Picciano, J. F., & Bolan, M.** (1998). Risk for HIV infection among bisexual men seeking HIV-prevention services and risks posed to their female partners. *Health Psychology, 17,* 320–327.

**Kalick, S. M., & Hamilton, T. E., III.** (1986). The matching hypothesis reexamined. *Journal of Personality and Social Psychology, 51,* 673–682.

**Kalmijn, M.** (1998). Intermarriage and homogamy: Causes, patterns, trends. *Annual Review of Sociology, 24,* 395–421.

**Kalof, L.** (1999). The effects of gender and music video imagery on sexual attitudes. *The Journal of Social Psychology, 139*(3), 378–385.

**Kals, E., & Ittner, H.** (2003). Children's environmental identity: Indicators and behavioral impacts. In S. Clayton & S. Opotow (Eds.), *Identity and the natural environment: The psychological significance of nature* (pp. 135–157). Cambridge, MA: MIT Press.

**Kamp Dush, C. M., Cohan, C. L., & Amato, P. R.** (2003). The relationship between cohabitation and marital quality and stability: Change across cohorts? *Journal of Marriage and Family, 65,* 539–549.

**Kandell, J. J.** (1998). Internet addiction on campus: The vulnerability of college students. *CyberPsychology and Behavior, 1*(1), 11–17.

**Kane, E. W.** (2000). Racial and ethnic variations in gender-related attitudes. *Annual review of sociology, 26,* 419–439.

**Kane, J. M., Stroup, T. S., & Marder, S. R.** (2009). Schizophrenia: Pharmacological treatment. In B. J. Sadock, V. A. Sadock, & P. Ruiz (Eds.), *Kaplan & Sadock's comprehensive textbook of psychiatry* (pp. 1547–1555). Philadelphia: Lippincott Williams & Wilkins.

**Kane, T. D., Marks, M. A., Zaccaro, S. J., & Blair, V.** (1996). Self-efficacy, personal goals, and wrestlers' self-regulation. *Journal of Sport & Exercise Psychology, 18*(1), 36–48.

**Kanner, A. D., & Soule, R. G.** (2004). Globalization, corporate culture, and freedom. In T. Kasser & A. D. Kanner (Eds.), *Psychology and consumer culture: The struggle for a good life in a materialistic world.* Washington, DC: American Psychological Association.

**Kant, A. K., Schatzkin, A., Graubard, B. I., & Schairer, C.** (2000). A prospective study of diet quality and mortality in women. *Journal of the American Medical Association, 283,* 2109–02115.

**Kantor, L. S., Lipton, K., Manchester, A., & Oliviera, V.** (1997). Estimating and addressing America's food losses. U.S. Department of Agriculture. Retrieved from http://www.ers.usda.gov/Publications/FoodReview/Jan1997/Jan97a.pdf

**Kapinus, C. A., & Johnson, M. P.** (2003). The utility of family life cycle as a theoretical and empirical tool: Commitment and family life-cycle stage. *Journal of Family Issues, 24,* 155–184.

**Kaplan, A. G.** (1985). Female or male therapists for women patients: New formulations. *Psychiatry, 48,* 111–121.

**Kaplan, D. S., Liu, R. X., & Kaplan, H. B.** (2005). School-related stress in early adolescence and academic performance three years later: The conditional influence of self expectation. *Social Psychology of Education, 8,* 3–17.

**Kaplan, H. I.** (1989). History of psychosomatic medicine. In H. I. Kaplan & B. J. Sadock (Eds.), *Comprehensive textbook of psychiatry/V* (Vol. 2) (5th ed.). Baltimore: Williams & Wilkins.

**Kaplan, H. S.** (1979). *Disorders of sexual desire.* New York: Simon & Schuster.

**Kaplan, R.** (1993). The role of nature in the context of the workplace. *Landscape and Urban Planning, 26,* 193–201.

**Kaplan, R.** (2001). The nature of the view from home: Psychological benefits. *Environment and Behavior, 33*(4), 507–542.

**Kaplan, R., & Kaplan, S.** (1989). *The experience of nature: A psychological perspective.* Cambridge, MA: Cambridge University Press.

**Kaplan, S.** (1995). The restorative benefits of nature: Toward an integrative framework. *Journal of Environmental Psychology, 15,* 169–182.

**Kaplan, S.** (2001). Meditation, restoration, and the management of mental fatigue. *Environment and Behavior, 33,* 480–506.

**Karasek, R. A., Jr.** (1979). Job demands, job decision latitude, and mental strain: Implications for job redesign. *Administrative Science Quarterly, 24,* 285–308.

**Karasek, R. A., Jr., Baker, D., Marxer, F., Ahlbom, A., & Theorell, T.** (1981). Job decision latitude, job demands, and cardiovascular disease: A prospective study of Swedish men. *American Journal of Public Health, 71,* 694–705.

**Karasek, R. A., Jr., & Theorell, T.** (1990). *Healthy work: Stress, productivity, and the reconstruction of working life.* New York: Basic Books.

**Karasu, T. B.** (2005). Psychoanalysis and psychoanalytic psychotherapy. In B. J. Sadock & V. A. Sadock (Eds.), *Kaplan and Sadock's comprehensive textbook of psychiatry.* Philadelphia: Lippincott Williams & Wilkins.

**Kardiner, A., & Linton, R.** (1945). *The individual and his society.* New York: Columbia University Press.

**Karlsen, E., Dybdahl, R., & Vitterso, J.** (2006). The possible benefits of difficulty: How stress can increase and decrease subjective well-being. *Scandinavian Journal of Psychology, 47,* 411–417.

**Karpicke, J. D. , & Roediger III, H. L.** (2003).The critical importance of retrieval for learning. *Science,* 319, 966–968.

**Kasser, T.** (2002). *The high prices of materialism.* Cambridge, MA: MIT Press.

**Kasser, T.** (2004). The good life or the goods life? Positive psychology and personal well-being in the culture of consumption. In P. A. Linley & S. Joseph (Eds.), *Positive psychology in practice.* New York: Wiley.

**Kasser, T., & Kanner, A. D.** (2004). *Psychology and consumer culture: The struggle for a good life in a materialistic world.* Washington DC: American Psychological Association.

**Kasser, T., Ryan, R. M., Couchman, C. E., & Sheldon, K. M.** (2004). Materialistic values: Their causes and consequences. In T. Kasser & A. D. Kanner (Eds.), *Psychology and consumer culture: The struggle for a good life in a materialistic world.* Washington, DC: American Psychological Association.

**Kastenbaum, R. J.** (1999). Dying and bereavement. In J. C. Cavanaugh & S. K. Whitbourne (Eds.), *Gerontology: An interdisciplinary perspective.* New York: Oxford University Press.

**Kastenbaum, R. J.** (2001). *Death, society, and human experience* (7th ed.). Boston: Allyn & Bacon.

**Kath, L., Swody, C., Magley, V., Bunk, J., & Gallus, J.** (2009). Cross-level, three-way interactions among work-group climate, gender, and frequency of harassment on morale and withdrawal outcomes of sexual harassment. *Journal of Occupational & Organizational Psychology, 82*(1), 159–182.

**Katigbak, M. S., Church, A. T., Guanzon-Lapena, M. A., Carlota, A. J. & del Pilar, G. H.** (2002). Are indigenous personality dimensions culture specific? Philippine inventories and the five-factor model. *Journal of Personality and Social Psychology, 82,* 89–101.

**Katz, J., & Tirone, V.** (2009). Women's sexual compliance with male dating partners: Associations with investments in ideal womanhood and romantic well–being. *Sex Roles, 60,* 347–356.

**Katz, L. S., & Epstein, S.** (2005). The relation of cancer-prone personality to exceptional recovery from cancer: A preliminary study. *Advances in Mind-Body Medicine, 21,* 6–20.

**Kaufman, G., & Taniguchi, H.** (2006). Gender and marital happiness in later life. *Journal of Family Issues, 27,* 735–757.

**Kaufman, G., & Uhlenberg, P.** (1998). Effects of life course transitions on the quality of relationships between adult children and their parents. *Journal of Marriage & the Family, 60,* 924–938.

**Kavesh, L., & Lavin, C.** (1988). *Tales from the front.* New York: Doubleday.

**Kawachi, I., Colditz, G. A., Stampfer, M. J., Willett, W. C., Manson, J. E., Rosner, B., & et al.** (1994). Smoking cessation and time course of decreased risks of coronary heart disease in middle-aged women. *Archives of Internal Medicine, 154,* 169–175.

**Kay, J., & Kay, R. L.** (2003). Individual psychoanalytic psychotherapy. In A. Tasman, J. Kay, & J. A. Lieberman (Eds.), *Psychiatry.* New York: Wiley.

**Kaye, W. H., Weltzin, T. E., Hsu, L. K. G., McConaha, C. W., & Bolton, B.** (1993). Amount of calories retained after binge eating and vomiting. *American Journal of Psychiatry, 150,* 969–971.

**Kazdin, A.** (2007). Mediators and mechanisms of change in psychotherapy research. *Annual Review of Clinical Psychology, 3,* 1–27.

**Kazdin, A. E.** (1982). History of behavior modification. In A. S. Bellack, M. Hersen, & A. E. Kazdin (Eds.), *International handbook of behavior modification and behavior therapy.* New York: Plenum.

**Kazdin, A. E.** (1994). Methodology, design, and evaluation in psychotherapy research. In A. E. Bergin & S. L. Garfield (Eds.), *Handbook of psychotherapy and behavior change* (4th ed.). New York: Wiley.

**Kazdin, A. E.** (2001). *Behavior modification in applied settings.* Belmont, CA: Wadsworth.

**Keck, P. E., Jr., & McElroy, S. L.** (2006). Lithium and mood stabilizers. In D. J. Stein, D. J. Kupfer, & A. F. Schatzberg (Eds.), *Textbook of mood disorders.* Washington, DC: American Psychiatric Publishing.

**Keefe, F. J., Smith, S. J., Buffington, A. L. H., Gibson, J., Studts, J. L., & Caldwell, D. S.** (2002). Recent advances and future directions in the biopsychosocial assessment and treatment of arthritis. *Journal of Consulting & Clinical Psychology, 70*(3), 640–655.

**Keefe, R. S. E., & Eesley, C. E.** (2006). Neurocognitive impairments. In J. A. Liberman, T. S. Stroup, & D. O. Perkins (Eds.), *Textbook of schizophrenia.* Washington, DC: American Psychiatric Publishing.

**Keesey, R. E.** (1993). Physiological regulation of body energy: Implications for obesity. In A. J. Stunkard & T. A. Wadden (Eds.), *Obesity: Theory and therapy.* New York: Raven Press.

**Keesey, R. E.** (1995). A set-point model of body weight regulation. In K. D. Brownell & C. G. Fairburn (Eds.), *Eating disorders and obesity: A comprehensive handbook.* New York: Guilford Press.

**Kegan, R.** (1994). *In over our heads: The mental demands of modern life.* Cambridge, MA: Harvard University Press.

**Keinan, G.** (1987). Decision making under stress: Scanning of alternatives under controllable and uncontrollable threats. *Journal of Personality and Social Psychology, 52,* 639–644.

**Keita, G. P., & Hurrell, J. J., Jr.** (1994). *Job stress in a changing workforce.* Washington, DC: American Psychological Association.

**Keller, C., Siegrist, M., & Gutscher, H.** (2006). The role of the affect and availability heuristics in risk communication. *Risk Analysis, 26,* 631–639.

**Keller, P. A.** (1999). Converting the unconverted: The effect of inclination and opportunity to discount health-related fear appeals. *Journal of Applied Psychology, 84*(3), 403–415.

**Keller, S. N., & Brown, J. D.** (2002). Media interventions to promote responsible sexual behavior. *The Journal of Sex Research, 39*(1), 67–72.

**Kellert, S. R.** (1997). *Kinship to mastery: Biophilia in human evolution and development.* Washington, DC: Island Press.

**Kellert, S. R.** (2002). Experiencing nature: Affective, cognitive, and evaluative development in children. In P. H. Kahn, Jr. & S. R. Kellert (Eds.), *Children and nature: Psychological, sociocultural, and evolutionary investigations* (pp. 117–151). Cambridge MA: MIT Press.

**Kelley, H. H.** (1950). The warm-cold dimension in first impressions of persons. *Journal of Personality, 18,* 431–439.

**Kelley, H. H.** (1967). Attribution theory in social psychology. In D. Levine (Ed.), *Nebraska Symposium on Motivation* (Vol. 15). Lincoln: University of Nebraska Press.

**Kelley, H. H., & Thibaut, J. W.** (1978). *Interpersonal relations: A theory of interdependence.* New York: Wiley-Interscience.

**Kellogg, J. S., Hopko, D. R., & Ashcraft, M. H.** (1999). The effects of time pressure on arithmetic performance. *Journal of Anxiety Disorders, 13*(6), 591–600.

**Kellogg, S. H., & Young, J. E.** (2008). Cognitive therapy. In J. L. Lebow (Ed.), *Twenty-first century psychotherapies: Contemporary approaches to theory and practice.* New York: Wiley.

**Kelly, B. D., Feeney, L., O'Callaghan, E., Browne, R., Byrne, M., Mulryan, N., Scully, A., Morris, M., Kinsella, A., Takei, N., McNeil, T., Walsh, D., & Larkin, C.** (2004). Obstetric adversity and age at first presentation with schizophrenia: Evidence of a dose-response relationship. *American Journal of Psychiatry, 161,* 920–922.

**Kelly, J. B., & Emery, R. E.** (2003). Children's adjustment following divorce: Risk and resilience perspectives. *Family Relations: Interdisciplinary Journal of Applied Family Studies, 52*(4), 352–362.

**Kelly, K. M., & Schramke, C. J.** (2000). Epilepsy. In G. Fink (Ed.), *Encyclopedia of stress.* San Diego: Academic Press.

**Kelman, H. C., & Hamilton, V. L.** (1989). *Crimes of obedience: Toward a social psychology of authority and responsibility.* New Haven, CT: Yale University Press.

**Kelsoe, J. R.** (2009). Mood disorders: Genetics. In B. J. Sadock, V. A. Sadock, & P. Ruiz (Eds.), *Kaplan & Sadock's comprehensive textbook of psychiatry* (pp. 1653–1663). Philadelphia: Lippincott Williams & Wilkins.

**Keltner, D.** (2000, October). *Laughter, smiling, and the sublime.* Paper presented at the Positive Psychology Summit, Washington, DC.

**Keltner, D.** (2009). *Born to be good: The science of a meaningful life.* New York: Norton.

**Keltner, D., & Haidt, J.** (2003). Approaching awe, a moral, spiritual, and aesthetic emotion. *Cognition and Emotion, 17,* 297–314.

**Kemeny, M. E.** (2003). The psychobiology of stress. *Current Directions in Psychological Science, 12*(4), 124–129.

**Kemeny, M. E.** (2007). Psychoneuroimmunology. In H. S. Friedman & R. C. Silver (Eds.), *Foundations of health psychology.* New York: Oxford University Press.

**Kendall, A. R., Mahue-Giangreco, M., Carpenter, C. L., Ganz, P. A., & Bernstein, L.** (2005). Influence of exercise activity on quality of life in long-term breast cancer survivors. *Quality of Life Research, 14,* 361–371.

**Kendler, K. S.** (2000). Schizophrenia: Genetics. In B. J. Sadock & V. A. Sadock (Eds.), *Kaplan and Sadock's comprehensive textbook of psychiatry* (7th ed.). Philadelphia: Lippincott/Williams & Wilkins.

**Kendler, K. S.** (2005a). "A gene for . . . ?": The nature of gene action in psychiatric disorders. *American Journal of Psychiatry, 162,* 1243–1252.

**Kendler, K. S.** (2005b). Psychiatric genetics: A methodologic critique. *American Journal of Psychiatry, 162,* 3–11.

**Kendler, K. S., Myers, J., & Prescott, C. A.** (2005). Sex differences in the relationship between social support and risk for major depression: A longitudinal study of opposite-sex twin pairs. *American Journal of Psychiatry, 162,* 250–256.

**Kendler, K. S., Thornton, L. M., Gilman, S. E., & Kessler, R. C.** (2000). Sexual orientation in a U.S. national sample of twin and nontwin sibling pairs. *American Journal of Psychiatry, 157*(11), 1843–1846.

**Kenfield, S. A., Stampfer, M. J., Rosner, B. A., & Colditz, G. A.** (2008). Smoking and smoking cessation in relation to mortality in women. *Journal of the American Medical Association, 299,* 2037–2047.

**Kennedy, S.** (2007). Psychological factors and immunity in HIV infections: Stress, coping, social support, and intervention outcomes. In A. Monat, R. S. Lazarus, & G. Reevy (Eds.), *The Praeger handbook on stress and coping* (pp. 199–215). Westport, CT: Praeger Publishers.

**Kennedy, S. H., Holt, A., & Baker, G. B.** (2009). Monoamine oxidase inhibitors. In B. J. Sadock, V. A. Sadock, & P. Ruiz (Eds.), *Kaplan & Sadock's comprehensive textbook of psychiatry* (pp. 3154–3163). Philadelphia: Lippincott Williams & Wilkins.

**Kenrick, D. T., & Trost, M. R.** (1993). The evolutionary perspective. In A. E. Beall & R. J. Sternberg (Eds.), *The psychology of gender.* New York: Guilford Press.

**Kenrick, D. T., Trost, M. R., & Sundie, J. M.** (2004). Sex roles as adaptations: An evolutionary perspective on gender differences and similarities. In A. H. Eagly, A. E. Beall, & R. J. Sternberg (Eds.), *The psychology of gender.* New York: Guilford Press.

**Keogh, E., Bond, F. W., French, C. C., Richards, A., & Davis, R. E.** (2004). Test anxiety, susceptibility to distraction and examination performance. *Anxiety, Stress and Coping: An International Journal, 17*(3), 241–252.

**Kernis, M. H.** (2003a). Optimal self-esteem and authenticity: Separating fantasy from reality. *Psychological Inquiry, 14*(1), 83–89.

**Kernis, M. H.** (2003b). Toward a conceptualization of optimal self-esteem. *Psychological Inquiry, 14*(1), 1–26.

**Kernis, M. H., & Goldman, B. M.** (2003). Stability and variability in self-concept and self-esteem. In M. R. Leary and J. P. Tangney (Eds.), *Handbook of self and identity.* New York: Guilford.

**Kessler, R. C.** (2002). Epidemiology of depression. In I. H. Gotlib, & C. L. Hammen (Eds.), *Handbook of depression.* New York: Guilford.

**Kessler, R. C., Berglund, P., Demler, O., Jin, R., Koretz, D., Merikangas, K. R., Rush, A. J., Walters, E. E., & Wang, P. S.** (2003). The epidemiology of major depressive disorder: Results from the national comorbidity survey replication (NCS-R). *The Journal of the American Medical Association, 289*(23), 3095–3105.

**Kessler, R. C., Berglund, P., Demler, O., Jin, R., & Walters, E. E.** (2005a). Lilfetime prevalence and age-of-onset distributions of DSM-IV disorders in the national comorbidity survey replication. *Archives of General Psychiatry, 62,* 593–602.

**Kessler, R. C., Demier, O., Frank, R. G., Olfson, M., Pincus, H. A., Walters, E. E., Wang, P., Wells, K. B., & Zaslavsky, A. M.** (2005b). Prevalence and treatment of mental disorders. 1990–2003. *New England Journal of Medicine, 352,* 2515–2523.

**Kessler, R. C., Olfson, M., & Berglund, P. A.** (1998). Patterns and predictors of treatment contact after first onset of psychiatric disorders. *American Journal of Psychiatry, 155,* 62–69.

**Kessler, R. C., & Zhao, S.** (1999). The prevalence of mental illness. In A. V. Horvitz & T. L. Scheid (Eds.), *A handbook for the study of mental health: Social contexts, theories, and systems.* New York: Cambridge University Press.

**Keyes, C. L. M., & Haidt, J.** (Eds.). (2003). *Flourishing: Positive psychology and the life well-lived.* Washington, DC: American Psychological Association.

**Keysar, B., & Henly, A. S.** (2002). Speakers' overestimation of their effectiveness. *Psychological Science, 13,* 207–212.

**Khosla, M.** (2006). Positive affect and coping with stress. *Journal of the Indian Academy of Applied Psychology, 32,* 281–288.

**Khot, U. N., Khot, M. B., Bajzer, C. T., Sapp, S. K., Ohman, E. M., Brener, S. J., Ellis, S. G., Lincoff, M. A., & Topol, E. J.** (2003). Prevalence of conventional risk factors in patients with coronary heart disease. *Journal of the American Medical Association, 290,* 898–904.

**Kiecolt-Glaser, J. K., Garner, W., Speicher, C., Penn, G. M., Holliday, J., & Glaser, R.** (1984). Psychosocial modifiers of immunocompetence in medical students. *Psychosomatic Medicine, 46,* 7–14.

**Kiecolt-Glaser, J. K., & Glaser, R.** (1995). Measurement of immune response. In S. Cohen, R. C. Kessler, & L. U. Gordon (Eds.), *Measuring stress: A guide for health and social scientists.* New York: Oxford University Press.

**Kiecolt-Glaser, J. K., & Glaser, R.** (2001). Stress and immunity: Age enhances the risks. *Current Directions in Psychological Science, 10*(1), 18–21.

**Kieffer, K. M., Cronin, C., & Gawet, D. L.** (2006). Test and study worry and emotionality in the prediction of college students' reason for drinking: An exploratory investigation. *Journal of Alcohol and Drug Addiction, 50*(1), 57–81.

**Kierein, N. M., & Gold, M. A.** (2000). Pygmalion in work organizations: A meta-analysis. *Journal of Organizational Behavior, 21*(8), 913–928.

**Kiernan, K.** (2004). Redrawing the boundaries of marriage. *Journal of Marriage and Family, 66,* 980–987.

**Kieseppa, T., Partonen, T., Huakka, J., Kaprio, J., & Lonnqvist, J.** (2004). High concordance of bipolar 1 disorder in a nationwide sample of twins. *American Journal of Psychiatry, 161,* 1814–1821.

**Kiesler, C. A.** (2000). The next wave of change for psychology and mental health services in the health care revolution. *American Psychologist, 55*(5), 481–487.

**Kiesler, D. J.** (1999). *Beyond the disease model of mental disorders.* New York: Praeger.

**Kihlstrom, J., & Cantor, N.** (2000). Social intelligence. In R. J. Sternberg (Ed.), *Handbook of intelligence* (2nd ed., pp. 359–379). Cambridge, UK: Cambridge University Press.

**Kihlstrom, J. F.** (2001). Dissociative disorders. In P. B. Sutker & H. E. Adams (Eds.), *Comprehensive handbook of psychopathology* (3rd ed.). New York: Kluwer Academic/Plenum Publishers.

**Kihlstrom, J. F.** (2004). An unbalanced balancing act: Blocked, recovered, and false memories in the laboratory and clinic. *Clinical Psychology: Science & Practice, 11*(1), 34–41.

**Kihlstrom, J. F.** (2005). Dissociative disorders. *Annual Review of Clinical Psychology, 1,* 227–253.

**Kihlstrom, J. F., Glisky, M. L., & Angiulo, M. J.** (1994). Dissociative tendencies and dissociative disorders. *Journal of Abnormal Psychology, 103,* 117–124.

**Kilby, R. W.** (1993). *The study of human values.* Lanham, MD: University Press of America.

**Kilmartin, C. T.** (2000). *The masculine self* (2nd ed.). Boston: McGraw-Hill.

**Kilmartin, C. T.** (2007). *The masculine self.* Cornwall-on-Hudson, NY: Sloan Publishing.

**Kim, H., & Markus, H. R.** (1999). Deviance or uniqueness, harmony or conformity? A cultural analysis. *Journal of Personality and Social Psychology, 77*(4), 785–800.

**Kim, H. S., Sherman, D. K., & Taylor, S. E.** (2008). Culture and social support. *American Psychologist, 63,* 518–526.

**Kim, H. S., Sherman, D. K., Ko, D., & Taylor, S. E.** (2006). Pursuit of comfort and pursuit of harmony: Culture, relationships, and social support seeking. *Personality and Social Psychology Bulletin, 32,*1595–1607.

**Kim, J., & Gray, K.** (2008). Leave or stay? Battered women's decision after intimate partner violence. *Journal of Interpersonal Violence, 23,* 1465–1482.

**Kim, J. L., & Ward, L. M.** (2007). Silence speaks volumes: Parental sexual communication among Asian American emerging adults. *Journals of Adolescent Research, 22,* 3–31.

**Kimiecik, J. C., & Stein, G. L.** (1992). Examining flow in sports contexts: Conceptual issues and methodological concerns. *Journal of Applied Sport Psychology, 4,* 144–160.

**Kimura, D., & Hampson, E.** (1993). Neural and hormonal mechanisms mediating sex differences in cognition. In P. A. Vernon (Ed.), *Biological approaches to the study of human intelligence.* Norwood, NJ: Ablex.

**King, B. M.** (2005). *Human sexuality today.* Upper Saddle River, NJ: Pearson Prentice Hall.

**King, G. R., & Ellinwood Jr., E. H.** (2005). Amphetamines and other stimulants. In J. H. Lowinson, P. Ruiz, R. B. Millman, & J. G. Langrod (Eds.), *Substance abuse: A comprehensive textbook.* Philadelphia: Lippincott/Williams & Wilkins.

**King, L. A., & Emmons, R. A.** (1990). Conflict over emotional expression: Psychological and physical correlates. *Journal of Personality and Social Psychology, 58,* 864–877.

**King, L. A., & Emmons, R. A.** (1991). Psychological, physical, and interpersonal correlates of emotional expressiveness, conflict and control. *European Journal of Personality, 5,* 131–150.

**King, L. A., King, D. W., Fairbank, J. A., Keane, T. M., & Adams, G. A.** (1998). Resilience-recovery factors in post-traumatic stress disorder among female and male Vietnam veterans: Hardiness, postwar social support, and additional stressful life events. *Journal of Personality and Social Psychology, 74,* 420–434.

**Kinsey, A. C., Pomeroy, W. B., & Martin, C. E.** (1948). *Sexual behavior in the human male.* Philadelphia: Saunders.

**Kinsey, A. C., Pomeroy, W. B., Martin, C. E., & Gebhard, P. H.** (1953). *Sexual behavior in the human female.* Philadelphia: Saunders.

**Kirby, D.** (2001). *Emerging answers: Research findings on programs to reduce teen pregnancy.* Washington, DC: National Campaign to Prevent Teenage Pregnancy.

**Kirk, S. A. & Kutchins, H.** (1992). *The selling of DSM: The rhetoric of science in psychiatry.* New York: Aldine de Gruyter.

**Kirkpatrick, L. A.** (2005). *Attachment, evolution, and the psychology of religion.* New York: Guilford.

**Kirkpatrick, L. A., & Davis, K. E.** (1994). Attachment style, gender, and relationship stability: A longitudinal analysis. *Journal of Personality and Social Psychology, 66,* 502–512.

**Kirkpatrick, L. A., & Hazan, C.** (1994). Attachment styles and close relationships: A four-year prospective study. *Personal Relationships, 1,* 123–142.

**Kirmayer, L. J., & Looper, K. J.** (2007). Somatoform disorders. In M. Hersen, S. M. Turner, & D. C. Beidel (Eds.), *Adult psychopathology and diagnosis.* New York: Wiley.

**Kirov, G. & Owen, M. J.** (2009). Genetics of schizophrenia. In B. J. Sadock, V. A. Sadock, & P. Ruiz (Eds.), *Kaplan & Sadock's comprehensive textbook of psychiatry* (pp. 1462–1474). Philadelphia: Lippincott Williams & Wilkins.

**Kito, M.** (2005). Self-disclosure in romantic relationships and friendships among American and Japanese college students. *Journal of Social Psychology, 145*(2), 127–140.

**Kitzes, J., Wackernagel, M., Loh, J., Peller, A., Goldfinger, S., Cheng, D., & Tea, K.** (2008). Shrink and share: Humanity's present and future ecological footprint. *Philosophical Transactions of the Royal Society of London,* Series B, Biological Sciences, *363,* 467–475.

**Klag, S., & Bradley, G.** (2004). The role of hardiness in stress and illness: An exploration of the effect of negative affectivity and gender. *British Journal of Health Psychology, 9*(2), 137–161.

**Klare, M. T.** (2001). *Resource wars: The new landscape of global conflict.* New York: Holt.

**Klassen, M.** (1987). How to get the most out of your time. In A. D. Timpe (Ed.), *The management of time.* New York: Facts on File.

**Klatsky, A. L.** (2008). Alcohol, wine, and vascular diseases: An abundance of paradoxes. *American Journal of Physiology: Heart and Circulatory Physiology, 63,* 582–583.

**Klein, T. W., Friedman, H., & Specter, S.** (1998). Marijauna, immunity and infection. *Journal of Neuroimmunology, 83,* 102–115.

**Klein, W. M., & Weinstein, N. D.** (1997). Social comparison and unrealistic optimism about personal risk. In B. P. Buunk & F. X. Gibbons (Eds.), *Health, coping, and well-being: Perspectives from social comparison theory* (pp. 25–61). Mahwah, NJ: Erlbaum.

**Kleinke, C. L.** (1986). Gaze and eye contact: A research review. *Psychological Bulletin, 100,* 78–100.

**Kleinke, C. L.** (2007). What does it mean to cope? In A. Monat, R. S. Lazarus, & G. Reevy (Eds.), *The Praeger handbook on stress and coping* (pp. 289–308). Westport, CT: Praeger Publishers.

**Kleinke, C. L., Meeker, F. B., & Staneski, R. A.** (1986). Preference for opening lines: Comparing ratings by men and women. *Sex Roles, 15,* 585–600.

**Kleinmuntz, B.** (1980). *Essentials of abnormal psychology.* San Francisco: Harper & Row.

**Kline, G. H., Pleasant, N. D., Whitton, S. W., & Markman, H. J.** (2006). Understanding couple conflict. In A. L. Vangelisti & D. Perlman (Eds.), *The Cambridge handbook of personal relationships.* New York: Cambridge University Press.

**Kline, P.** (1995). A critical review of the measurement of personality and intelligence. In D. H. Saklofske & M. Zeidner (Eds.), *International handbook of personality and intelligence.* New York: Plenum Press.

**Klinesmith, J., Kasser, T., & McAndrew, F. T.** (2006). Guns, testosterone, and aggression: An experimental test of a mediational hypothesis. *Psychological Science, 17,* 568–571.

**Kling, K. C., Hyde, J. S., Showers, C. J., & Buswell, B. N.** (1999). Gender differences in self-esteem: A meta-analysis. *Psychological Bulletin, 125*(4), 470–500.

**Klohnen, E. C., & Luo, S.** (2003). Interpersonal attraction and personality: What is attractive—self similarity, ideal similarity, complementarity, or attachment security? *Journal of Personality and Social Psychology , 85,* 709–722.

**Klonoff, E. A., & Landrine, H.** (1999). Cross-validation of the schedule of racist events. *Journal of Black Psychology, 25*(2), 231–254.

**Klose, M., & Jacobi, F.** (2004). Can gender differences in the prevalence of mental disorders be explained by sociodemographic factors? *Archives of Women's Mental Health, 7,* 133–148.

**Kluckhohn, C., & Murray, H. A.** (1948). *Personality in nature, society and culture.* New York: Knopf.

**Kluft, R. P.** (1996). Dissociative identity disorder. In L. K. Michelson & W. J. Ray (Eds.), *Handbook of dissociation: Theoretical, empirical, and clinical perspectives.* New York: Plenum.

**Kluft, R. P.** (1999). True lies, false truths, and naturalistic raw data: Applying clinical research findings to the false memory debate. In L. M. Williams & V. L. Banyard (Eds.), *Trauma & memory.* Thousand Oaks, CA: Sage.

**Klumb, P. L., & Baltes, M. M.** (2004). Adverse life events in late life: Their manifestation and management in daily life. *International Journal of Stress Management, 11*(1), 3–20.

**Knapp, C. M., Ciraulo, D. A., & Jaffe, J.** (2005). Opiates: Clinical aspects. In J. H. Lowinson, P. Ruiz, R. B. Millman, & J. G. Langrod (Eds.), *Substance abuse: A comprehensive textbook.* Philadelphia: Lippincott/ Williams & Wilkins.

**Knapp, D. E., Faley, R. H., Ekeberg, W. C., & Dubois, C. L. Z.** (1997). Determinants of target responses to sexual harassment: A conceptual framework. *Academy of Management Review, 22*(3), 687–729.

**Knapp, M. L., & Hall, J. A.** (2006). *Nonverbal communication in human interaction.* Belmont, CA: Thompson/ Wadsworth.

**Knaus, W.** (2000). Procrastination, blame, and change. *Journal of Social Behavior and Personality, 15,* 153–166.

**Knauss, W.** (2005). Group psychotherapy. In G. O. Gabbard, J. S. Beck, & J. Holmes (Eds.), *Oxford textbook of psychotherapy.* New York: Oxford University Press.

**Knickmeyer, N., Sexton, K., & Nishimura, N.** (2002). The impact of same-sex friendships on the well-being of women: A review of the literature. *Women and Therapy, 25*(1), 37–59.

**Knox, D.** (2000). *The divorced dad's survival book: How to stay connected to your kids.* New York: Perseus.

**Knox, D., Vail-Smith, K., & Zusman, M.** (2008). "Men are dogs": Is the stereotype justified? Data on the cheating college male. *College Student Journal, 42,* 1015–1022.

**Knox, D., Zusman, M., & McNeely, A.** (2008). University student beliefs about sex: Men vs. women. *College Student Journal, 42,* 181–185.

**Kobasa, S. C.** (1979). Stressful life events, personality, and health: An inquiry into hardiness. *Journal of Personality and Social Psychology, 37,* 1–11.

**Kobasa, S. C.** (1984, September). How much stress can you survive? *American Health,* pp. 64–77.

**Koc, E. W.** (2007, December). Attracting the recent college graduate: The question of location. *NACE Journal,* pp. 17–20.

**Koenig, H. G., & Cohen, H. J.** (Eds.). (2002). *The link between religion and health: Psychoneuroimmunology and the faith factor.* New York: Oxford University Press.

**Koenig, H. G., McCullough, M. E., & Larson, D. B.** (2001). *Handbook of religion and health.* London: Oxford University Press.

**Koger, S. M. & Scott, B. A.** (2011). Psychology and environmental sustainability: Conservation psychology. In W. Weiten, *Psychology: Themes & variations—Briefer version* (8th ed.). Belmont, CA: Wadsworth/Cengage Learning.

**Koger, S. M., & Scott, B. A.** (2007). Psychology and environmental sustainability: A call for integration. *Teaching of Psychology, 34,* 10–18.

**Koger, S. M., Schettler, T., & Weiss, B.** (2005). Environmental toxicants and developmental disabilities: A challenge for psychologists. *American Psychologist, 60,* 243–255.

**Koger, S. M., & Winter, D. D.** (2010). *The psychology of environmental problems: Psychology for sustainability* (3rd ed.). New York: Taylor & Francis: Psychology Press.

**Kolassa, I., & Elbert, T.** (2007). Structural and functional neuroplasticity in relation to traumatic stress. *Current Directions in Psychological Science, 16,* 321–325.

**Kollmuss, A., & Agyeman, J.** (2002). Mind the gap: Why do people act environmentally and what are the barriers to pro-environmental behaviour? *Environmental Education Research, 8,* 239–260.

**Konrad, A. M.** (2003). Family demands and job attribute preferences: A 4-year longitudinal study of women and men. *Sex Roles, 49*(1–2), 35–46.

**Koopman, C., Classen, C., & Spiegel, D.** (1994). Predictors of posttraumatic stress symptoms among survivors of the Oakland/Berkeley, Calif., firestorm. *American Journal of Psychiatry, 151,* 888–894.

**Koopmans, G. T., & Lamers, L. M.** (2007). Gender and health care utilization: The role of mental distress and help-seeking propensity. *Social Science & Medicine, 64,* 1216–1230.

**Kop, W. J., Gottdiener, J. S., & Krantz, D. S.** (2001). Stress and silent ischemia. In A. Baum, T. A. Revenson, & J. E. Singer (Eds.), *Handbook of health psychology.* Mahwah, NJ: Erlbaum.

**Kopta, S. M., Lueger, R. J., Saunders, S. M., & Howard, K. I.** (1999). Individual psychotherapy outcome and process research: Challenges leading to greater turmoil or a positive transition? *Annual Review of Psychology, 50,* 441–469.

**Koren, D., Arnon, I., & Klein, E.** (1999). Acute stress response and posttraumatic stress disorder in traffic accident victims: A one-year prospective, follow-up study. *American Journal of Psychiatry, 156*(3), 367–373.

**Koriat, A., & Bjork, R. A.** (2005). Illusions of competence in monitoring one's knowledge during study. *Journal of Experimental Psychology: Learning, Memory, and Cognition,* 31, 187–194.

**Kornspan, A. S., & Etzel, E. F.** (2001). The relationship of demographic and psychological variables to career maturity of junior college student-athletes. *Journal of College Student Development,* 42(2), 122–132.

**Kornstein, S. G., & Sloan, D. M. E.** (2006). Depression and gender. In D. J. Stein, D. J. Kupfer, & A. F. Schatzberg (Eds.), *Textbook of mood disorders.* Washington, DC: American Psychiatric Publishing.

**Korpela, K.** (2002). Children's environments. In R. B. Bechtel & A. Churchman (Eds.), *Handbook of environmental psychology* (pp. 363–373). Hoboken, NJ: Wiley.

**Koss, M. P., & Cook, S. I.** (1993). Facing the facts: Date and acquaintance rape are significant problems for women. In R. J. Gelles, & D. R. Losede (Eds.), *Current controversies on family violence.* Thousand Oaks, CA: Sage.

**Koss, M. P., Goodman, L. A., Browne, A., Fitzgerald, L. F., Keita, G. P., & Russo, N. F.** (1994). *No safe haven: Male violence against women at home, at work, and in the community.* Washington, DC: American Psychological Association.

**Kouzma, N. M., & Kennedy, G. A.** (2004). Self-reported sources of stress in senior high school students. *Psychological Reports, 94,* 314–316.

**Kowalski, R. M.** (1993). Inferring sexual interest from behavioral cues: Effects of gender and sexually relevant attitudes. *Sex Roles, 29,* 13–36.

**Kozlowski, L. T., Wilkinson, A., Skinner, W. Kent, C., Franklin, T., & Pope, M.** (1989). Comparing tobacco cigarette dependence with other drug dependences. *Journal of the American Medical Association, 261,* 898–901.

**Kozlowski, S. W. J., & Bell, B. S.** (2003). Work groups and teams in organizations. In W. C. Borman, D. R. Ilgen, & R. J. Klimoski (Eds.), *Handbook of psychology: Vol. 12. Industrial and organizational psychology.* New York: Wiley.

**Kraaij, V., & Garnefski, N.** (2006). The role of intrusion, avoidance, and cognitive coping strategies more then 50 years after war. *Anxiety, Stress, & Coping, 19*(1), 1–14.

**Kraaij, V., Garnefski, N., & Vlietstra, A.** (2008). Cognitive coping and depressive symptoms in definitive infertility: A prospective study. *Journal of Psychosomatic Obstetrics & Gynecology, 29,* 9–16.

**Kraaij, V., Van Der Veek, S., Garnefski, N., Schroevers, M., Witlox, R., & Maes, S.** (2008). Coping, goal adjustment, and psychological well-being in HIV-infected men who have sex with men. *AIDS Patient Care and STDs, 22,* 395–402.

**Kraemer, H. C.** (2008). DSM categories and dimensions in clinical and research contexts. Dimensional approaches in diagnostic classification: Refining the research agenda for DSM-V. In J. E Helzer, H. C. Wittchen, R. F. Krueger, & H. C.Kraemer (Eds.), *Dimensional approaches in diagnostic classification: refining the research agenda for DSM-V* (pp. 5–17). Washington, DC: American Psychiatric Association.

**Kraft, S.** (2009, October 22). Sweat lodge deaths a new test for self-help guru. *LA Times.* Retrieved from http://www.latimes.com/news/nationworld/nation/la-na-guru22-2009oct22,0,6180058.story

**Kramer, P. D.** (2006). *Freud: Inventor of the modern mind.* New York: HarperCollins.

**Krantz, D. S., & McCeny, K. T.** (2002). Effects of psychological and social factors on organic disease: A critical assessment of research on coronary heart disease. *Annual Review of Psychology, 53,* 341–369.

**Krantz, D. S., Sheps, D. S., Carney, R. M., & Natelson, B. H.** (2000). Effects of mental stress in patients with coronary artery disease. *Journal of the American Medical Association, 283*(14), 1800–1802.

**Kreider, R. M.** (2005). *Number, timing, and duration of marriages and divorces: 2001. U.S. Census Bureau, Household Economic Studies.* Washington DC: Department of Commerce.

**Kreith, M.** (1991). Water inputs in California food production. *University of California Agricultural Issues Center.* Retrieved from http://www.sakia.org/cms/fileadmin/content/irrig/general/kreith_1991_water_inputs_in_ca_food_production-excerpt.pdf

**Kring, A. M.** (1999). Emotion in schizophrenia: Old mystery, new understanding. *Current Directions in Psychological Science, 8,* 160–163.

**Kring, A. M., & Gordon, A. H.** (1998). Sex differences in emotion: Expression, experience, and physiology. *Journal of Personality and Social Psychology, 74*(3), 686–703.

**Krueger, J. I., Vohs, K. D., & Baumeister, R. F.** (2009). Is the allure of self-esteem a mirage after all? *American Psychologist, 63,* 64–65.

**Krueger, R. F. & Johnson, W.** (2008). Behavioral genetics and personality: A new look at the integration of nature and nurture. In O. P. John, R. W. Robins, & L. A. Pervin (Eds.), *Handbook of personality: Theory and research* (pp. 287–310). New York: Guilford.

**Krueger, W. C. F.** (1929). The effect of overlearning on retention. *Journal of Experimental Psychology, 12,* 71–78.

**Kruger, J., Galuska, D. A, Serdula, M. K., & Jones, D. A.** (2004). Attempting to lose weight: Specific practices among U. S. adults. *American Journal of Preventive Medicine, 26,* 402-406.

**Krumrei, E, Coit, C., Martin, S., Fogo, W., & Mahoney, A.** (2007). Post-divorce adjustment and social relationships: A meta-analytic review. *Journal of Divorce & Remarriage, 46,* 145–166.

**Krusemark, E. A., Campbell, W. K., & Clementz, B. A.** (2008). Attributions, deception, and event related potentials: An investigation of the self-serving bias. *Psychophysiology, 45*(4), 511–515.

**Kübler-Ross, E.** (1969). *On death and dying.* New York: Macmillan.

**Kübler-Ross, E.** (1970). The dying patient's point of view. In O. G. Brim, Jr., H. E. Freeman, S. Levine, & N. A. Scotch (Eds.), *The dying patient.* New York: Sage.

**Kudo, E.** (2003). Explicit and direct self-serving bias in Japan: Examination of self-serving bias for success and failure. *Journal of Cross-Cultural Psychology, 34,* 511–521.

**Kuehn, B. M.** (2007). Scientists probe deep brain stimulation: Some promise for brain injury, psychiatric illness. *Journal of the American Medical Association, 298,* 2249–2207.

**Kuiper, N., Martin, R, & Olinger, L. J.** (1993). Coping humour, stress, and cognitive appraisals. *Canadian Journal of Behavioural Science, 25,* 81–96.

**Kulick, A. R., Pope, H. G., & Keck, P. E.** (1990). Lycanthropy and self-identification. *Journal of Nervous and Mental Disease, 178,* 134–137.

**Kulik, L.** (2000). Jobless men and women: A comparative analysis of job search intensity, attitudes toward unemployment and related responses. *Journal of Occupational and Behavioral Psychology, 73*(4), 487–500.

**Kunkel, D., Eyal, K., Finnerty, K., Biely, E., & Donnerstein, E.** (2005a). *Sex on TV 4: Executive Summary.* Retrieved June 16, 2007 from http://www.kff.org/entmedia/upload/sex-on-TV-4-Executive-Summary.pdf.

**Kunkel, D., Eyal, K., Finnerty, K., Biely, E., & Donnerstein, E.** (2005b). *Sex on TV 4: Full report.* Retrieved June 16, 2007 from http://www.kff.org/entmedia/upload/sex-on-TV-4-full-report.pdf.

**Kunkel, D., Farrar, K. M., Eyal, K., Biely, E., Donnerstein, E., & Rideout, V.** (2007). Sexual socialization messages on entertainment television: Comparing content trends, 1997–2002. *Media Psychology, 10,* 595–622.

**Kunstler, J. H.** (2005). *The long emergency: Surviving the end of oil, climate change, and other converging catastrophes of the twenty-first century.* New York: Grove Press.

**Kuo, F. E., & Faber Taylor, A.** (2004). A potential natural treatment for attention- deficit/hyperactivity disorder: Evidence from a national study. *American Journal of Public Health, 94,* 1580–1586.

**Kuo, F. E., & Faber Taylor, A.** (2005). Mother nature as treatment for ADHD: Overstating the benefits of green. Kuo and Faber Taylor respond. *American Journal of Public Health, 95,* 371–372.

**Kuo, F. E., & Sullivan, W. C.** (2001). Aggression and violence in the inner city: Effects of environment via mental fatigue. *Environment and Behavior, 33*(4), 543–571.

**Kurdek, L. A.** (1991). Sexuality in homosexual and heterosexual couples. In K. McKinney & S. Sprecher (Eds.), *Sexuality in close relationships.* Hillside, NJ: Erlbaum.

**Kurdek, L. A.** (1994). The nature and correlates of relationship quality in gay, lesbian, and heterosexual cohabiting couples. In B. Greene & G. M. Herek (Eds.), *Lesbian and gay psychology.* Thousand Oaks, CA: Sage.

**Kurdek, L. A.** (1998). Relationship outcomes and their predictors: Longitudinal evidence from heterosexual married, gay cohabiting, and lesbian cohabiting couples. *Journal of Marriage and the Family, 30,* 553–568.

**Kurdek, L. A.** (2004). Gay men and lesbians: The family context. In M. Coleman & L. H. Ganong (Eds.), *Handbook of contemporary families: Considering the past, contemplating the future.* Thousand Oaks, CA: Sage.

**Kurdek, L. A.** (2005). What do we know about gay and lesbian couples? *Current Directions in Psychological Science, 14*(5), 251–254.

**Kurdek, L. A.** (2006). Differences between partners from heterosexual, gay, and lesbian cohabiting couples. *Journal of Marriage and Family, 68,* 509–528.

**Kurdek, L. A., & Schmitt, J. P.** (1986a). Early development of relationship quality in heterosexual married, heterosexual cohabiting, gay, and lesbian couples. *Developmental Psychology, 22,* 305–309.

**Kurdek, L. A., & Schmitt, J. P.** (1986b). Interaction of sex role self-concept with relationship quality and relationship beliefs in married, heterosexual cohabiting, gay, and lesbian couples. *Journal of Personality and Social Psychology, 51,* 365–370.

**Kurman, J.** (2006). Self-enhancement, self-regulation, and self-improvement following failures. *British Journal of Social Psychology, 45*(2), 339–356.

**Kutchins, H., & Kirk, S. A.** (1997). *Making us crazy: DSM—The psychiatric Bible and the creation of mental disorders.* New York: Free Press.

**Kuther, T. L., & Morgan, R. D.** (2009). *Careers in psychology: Opportunities for a changing world.* Belmont, CA: Wadsworth.

**Kuyper, H., & Dijkstra, P.** (2009). Better-than-average effects in secondary education: A 3-year follow-up. *Educational Research and Evaluation, 15*(2), 167–184.

**Ladd, G. W., Buhs, E. S., & Seid, M.** (2000). Children's initial sentiments about kindergarten: Is liking school an antecedent of early classroom participation and achievement? *Merrill-Palmer Quarterly, 46,* 255–278.

**LaFrance, M., Hecht, M. A., & Paluck, E. L.** (2003). The contingent smile: A meta-analysis of sex differences in smiling. *Psychological Bulletin, 129,* 305–334.

**La Greca, A. M.** (2007). Posttraumatic stress disorder in children. In G. Fink (Ed.), *Encyclopedia of stress: Vols. 1–4* (2nd ed., pp. 145–149). San Diego, CA: Elsevier Academic Press.

**Lai, J. C. L.** (2009). Dispositional optimism buffers the impact of daily hassles on mental health in Chinese adolescents. *Personality and Individual Differences, 47,* 247–249.

**Lakein, A.** (1996). *How to get control of your time and your life.* New York: New American Library.

**Lam, C. B., & McBride-Chang, C. A.** (2007). Resilience in young adulthood: The moderating influences of gender-related personality traits and coping flexibility. *Sex Roles, 56* (3–4), 159–172.

**Lam, L. T., & Kirby, S. L.** (2002). Is emotional intelligence an advantage? An exploration of the impact of emotional and general intelligence on individual performance. *Journal of Social Psychology, 142,* 133–143.

**Lambert, A. J., Burroughs, T., & Nguyen, T.** (1999). Perceptions of risk and the buffering hypothesis: The role of just world beliefs and right wing authoritarianism. *Personality and Social Psychology Bulletin, 25,* 643–656.

**Lambert, M. J., & Archer, A.** (2006). Research findings on the effects of psychotherapy and their implications for practice. In C. D. Goodheart, A. E. Kazdin, & R. J. Sternberg (Eds.), *Evidence-based psychotherapy: Where practice and research meet.* Washington, DC: American Psychological Association.

**Lambert, M. J., & Bergin, A. E.** (1994). The effectiveness of psychotherapy. In A. E. Bergin & S. L. Garfield (Eds.), *Handbook of psychotherapy and behavior change* (4th ed.). New York: Wiley.

**Lambert, M. J., Bergin, A. E., & Garfield, S. L.** (2004). Introduction and historical overview. In M. J. Lambert (Ed.), *Bergin and Garfield's handbook of psychotherapy and behavior change.* New York: Wiley.

**Lambert, M. J., & Ogles, B. M.** (2004). The efficacy and effectiveness of psychotherapy. In M. J. Lambert (Ed.), *Bergin and Garfield's handbook of psychotherapy and behavior change.* New York: Wiley.

**Lambert, T. A., Kahn, A. S., & Apple, K. J.** (2003). Pluralistic ignorance and hooking up. *Journal of Sex Research, 40*(2), 129–133.

**Lampe, A., Soellner, W., Krismer, M., Rumpold, G., Kantner-Rumplmair, W., Ogon, M., & Rathner, G.** (1998). The impact of stressful life events on exacerbation of chronic low-back pain. *Journal of Psychosomatic Research, 44*(5), 555–563.

**Landabaso, M. A., Iraurgi, I., Sanz, J., Calle, R., Ruiz de Apodaka, J., Jimenez-Lerma, J. M., & Gutierrez-Fraile, M.** (1999). Naltrexone in the treatment of alcoholism. Two-year follow up results. *European Journal of Psychiatry, 13,* 97–105.

**Landel-Graham, J., Yount, S. E., & Rudnicki, S. R.** (2003). Diabetes mellitus. In A. M. Nezu, C. M. Nezu, & P. A. Geller (Eds.), *Handbook of psychology: Vol. 9. Health psychology.* New York: Wiley.

**Landers, D. M.** (2007). The arousal-performance relationship revisited. In D. Smith & M. Bar-Eli (Eds.), *Essential Readings in Sport and Exercise Psychology* (pp. 211–218). Champaign, IL: Human Kinetics.

**Landrigan, P. J., Sonawane, B., Butler, R. N., Trasande, L., Callan, R., & Droller, D.** (2005). Early environmental origins of neurodegenerative disease in later life. *Environmental Health Perspectives, 113,* 1230–1233.

**Landrine, H., & Klonoff, E. A.** (2001). Cultural diversity and health psychology. In A. Baum, T. A. Revenson, & J. E. Singer (Eds.), *Handbook of health psychology* (pp. 851–891). Mahwah, NJ: Erlbaum.

**Landrum, R. E.** (2009). *Finding jobs with a psychology bachelor's degree: Expert advice for launching your career.* Washington, DC: American Psychological Association.

**Lane S. D., Cherek, D. R., Tcheremissine, O. V., Lieving, L. M., & Pietras, C. J.** (2005). Acute marijuana effects on human risk taking. *Neuropsychopharmocology, 30,* 800–809.

**Lane, J. M., & Addis, M. E.** (2005). Male gender role conflict and patterns of help seeking in Costa Rica and the United States. *Psychology of Men & Masculinity, 6,* 155–168.

**Langbein, L., & Yost, M. A.** (2009). Same-sex marriage and negative externalities. *Social Science Quarterly, 90,* 292–308.

**Langer, E. J.** (1975). The illusion of control. *Journal of Personality and Social Psychology, 32*(2), 311–328.

**Langer, E. J.** (1989). *Mindfulness.* New York: Addison-Wesley.

**Langer, E. J.** (1990). *Mindfulness.* Cambridge, MA: Da Capo Press.

**Langer, E. J.** (1998). *The power of mindful learning.* Cambridge, MA: Da Capo Press.

**Langer, E. J.** (2002). Well-being: Mindfulness versus positive evaluation. In C. R. Snyder & S. J. Lopez (Eds.), *The handbook of positive psychology* (pp. 214–230). New York: Oxford.

**Langer, E. J.** (2009). Mindfulness. In S. J. Lopez (Ed.), *The encyclopedia of positive psychology* (Vol. II, pp. 618–622). Malden, MA: Wiley-Blackwell.

**Langlois, J. H., Kalakanis, L., Rubenstein, A. J., Larson, A., Hallam, M., & Smoot, M.** (2000). Maxims or myths of beauty? A meta-analytic and theoretical review. *Psychological Bulletin, 126*(3), 390–423.

**Lansford, J. E.** (2009). Parental divorce and children's adjustment. *Perspectives on Psychological Science, 4,* 140–152.

**LaPiere, R. T.** (1934). Attitudes vs. actions. *Social Forces, 13,* 230–237.

**Lapierre, L.M. & Allen, T. D.** (2006). Work-supportive family, family-supportive supervision, use of organizational benefits, and problem-focused coping: Implications for work-family conflict and employee well-being. *Journal of Occupational Health Psychology, 11,* 169–181.

**La Pierre, Y. D.** (2003). Suicidality with selective serotonin reuptake inhibitors: Valid claim? *Journal of Psychiatry & Neuroscience, 28*(5), 340–347.

**LaRose, R., & Rifon, N. A.** (2007). Promoting *i*-safety: Effects of privacy warnings and privacy seals on risk assessment and online privacy behavior. *The Journal of Consumer Affairs, 41*(1), 127–149.

**Larsen, R. J., & Prizmic, Z.** (2008). Regulation of emotional well-being: Overcoming the hedonic tredmill. In M. Eid & R. J. Larsen (Eds.), *The science of subjective well-being* (pp. 258–289). New York: Guilford.

**Larson, R., & Pleck, J.** (1998). Hidden feelings: Emotionality in boys and men. In *Gender and motivation* (Vol. 45). Lincoln: University of Nebraska Press.

**Laskoff, M. B.** (2004). *Landing on the right side of your ass: A survival guide for the recently unemployed.* New York: Three Rivers Press.

**Latané, B., & Nida, S. A.** (1981). Ten years of research on group size and helping. *Psychological Bulletin, 89,* 308–324.

**Lauer, J., & Lauer, R.** (1985, June). Marriages made to last. *Psychology Today,* pp. 22–26.

**Laughlin, H.** (1967). *The neuroses.* Washington, DC: Butterworth.

**Laughlin, H.** (1979). *The ego and its defenses.* New York: Aronson.

**Laumann, E. O., Gagnon, J. H., Michael, R. T., & Michaels, S.** (1994). *The social organization of sexuality: Sexual practices in the United States.* Chicago: University of Chicago Press.

**Laumann, E. O., Glasser, D. B., Neves, R. C. S., & Moreira, E. D.** (2009). A population-based survey of sexual activity, sexual problems and associated help-seeking behavior patterns in mature adults in the United States of America. *International Journal of Impotence Research, 21,* 171–178.

**Laumann, K., Gärling, T., & Stormark, K. M.** (2003). Selective attention and heart rate responses to natural and urban environments. *Journal of Environmental Psychology, 23,* 125–134.

**Laurenceau, J., Barrett, L. F., & Rovine, M. J.** (2005). The interpersonal process model of intimacy in marriage: A daily-diary and multilevel modeling approach. *Journal of Family Psychology, 19,* 314–323.

**Laurenceau, J. P., & Kleinman, B. M.** (2006). Intimacy in personal relationships. In A. L. Vangelisti & D. Perlman (Eds.), *The Cambridge handbook of personal relationships.* New York: Cambridge University Press.

**Lauriello, J., Bustillo, J. R., & Keith, S. J.** (2005). Schizophrenia: Scope of the problem. In B. J. Sadock & V. A. Sadock (Eds.), *Kaplan & Sadock's comprehensive textbook of psychiatry.* Philadelphia: Lippincott Williams & Wilkins.

**Lauzen, M. M., & Dozier, D. M.** (2002). You look mahvelous: An examination of gender and appearance comments in the 1999–2000 prime-time season. *Sex Roles, 46*(11/12), 429–437.

**Lavee, Y., & Ben-Ari, A.** (2007). Relationship of dyadic closeness with work-related stress: A daily diary study. *Journal of Marriage and Family, 69,* 1021–1035.

**Lavine, H., Sweeney, D., & Wagner, S. H.** (1999). Depicting women as sex objects in television advertising: Effects on body dissatisfaction. *Personality and Social Psychology Bulletin, 25*(8), 1049–1058.

**Lavoie, K. L. & Barone, S.** (2006). Prescription privileges for psychologists: A comprehensive review and critical analysis of current issues and controversies. *CNS Drugs, 20*(1), 51–66.

**Lawler-Row, K. A., Scott, C. A., Raines, R. L., Edlis-Matityahou, M., & Moore, E. W.** (2007). The varieties of forgiveness experience: Working toward a comprehensive definition of forgiveness. *Journal of Religion and Health, 46,* 233–248.

**Lawrence, E., Rothman, A. D., Cobb, R. J., Rothman, M. T., & Bradbury, T. N.** (2008). Marital satisfaction across the transition to parenthood. *Journal of Family Psychology, 22,* 41–50.

**Lay, C. H.** (1992). Trait procrastination and the perception of person-task characteristics. *Journal of Social Behavior and Personality, 7,* 483–494.

**Lay, C. H.** (1995). Trait procrastination, agitation, dejection, and self-discrepancy. In J. R. Ferrari, J. L. Johnson, & W. G. McCown (Eds.), *Procrastination and task avoidance: Theory, research, and treatment.* New York: Plenum.

**Lay, C. H., Edwards, J. M., Parker, J. D. A., & Endler, N. S.** (1989). An assessment of appraisal anxiety, coping, and procrastination during an examination period. *European Journal of Personality, 3,* 195–208.

**Lazarus, A. A.** (1989). Multimodal therapy. In R. J. Corsini & D. Wedding (Eds.), *Current psychotherapies.* Itasca, IL: F. E. Peacock.

**Lazarus, A. A.** (1992). Multimodal therapy: Technical eclecticism with minimal integration. In J. C. Norcross & M. R. Goldfried (Eds.), *Handbook of psychotherapy integration.* New York: Basic Books.

**Lazarus, A. A.** (1995). Different types of eclecticism and integration: Let's be aware of the dangers. *Journal of Psychotherapy Integration, 5,* 27–39.

**Lazarus, A. A.** (2008). Technical eclecticism and multimodal therapy. In J. L. Lebow (Ed.), *Twenty-first century psychotherapies: Contemporary approaches to theory and practice.* New York: Wiley.

**Lazarus, R. S.** (1991). *Emotion and adaptation.* New York: Oxford.

**Lazarus, R. S.** (1993). Why we should think of stress as a subset of emotion. In L. Goldberger & S. Breznitz (Eds.), *Handbook of stress: Theoretical and clinical aspects* (2nd ed.). New York: Free Press.

**Lazarus, R. S.** (2003a). Does the positive psychology movement have legs? *Psychological Inquiry, 14,* 93–109.

**Lazarus, R. S.** (2003b). The Lazarus manifesto for positive psychology and psychology in general. *Psychological Inquiry, 14,* 173–189.

**Lazarus, R. S.** (2006). Emotions and interpersonal relationships: Toward a person-centered conceptualization of emotions and coping. *Journal of Personality, 71,* 9–46.

**Lazarus, R. S.** (2007). Stress and emotion: A new synthesis. In A. Monat, R. S. Lazarus, & G. Reevy (Eds.), *The Praeger handbook on stress and coping* (pp. 33–52). Westport, CT: Praeger Publishers.

**Lazarus, R. S., & Folkman, S.** (1984). *Stress, appraisal and coping.* New York: Springer.

**Le, B.** (2009). Familiarity principle of attraction. In H. T. Reis & S. Sprecher (Eds.), *Encyclopedia of human relationships: Vol. 1* (pp. 596–597). Los Angeles: Sage Reference Publication.

**Le, B., & Agnew, C. R.** (2003). Commitment and its theorized determinants: A meta-analysis of the investment model. *Personal Relationships, 10*(1), 37–57.

**Leahy, J. M.** (1993). A comparison of depression in women bereaved of a spouse, a child, or a parent. *Omega, 26,* 207–217.

**Leal, S., & Vrij, A.** (2008). Blinking during and after lying. *Journal of Nonverbal Behavior, 32,* pp. 187–194.

**Leana, C. R., & Feldman, D. C.** (1991). Gender differences in responses to unemployment. *Journal of Vocational Behavior, 38,* 65–77.

**Leaper, C. R., Breed, L., Hoffman, L., & Perlman, C. A.** (2002). Variations in the gender-stereotyped content of children's television cartoons across genres. *Journal of Applied Social Psychology, 32,* 1653–1662.

**Leary, M. R.** (2004a). The function of self-esteem in terror management theory and sociometer theory: Comment on Pyszczynski et al. (2004). *Psychological Bulletin, 130*(3), 478–482.

**Leary, M. R.** (2004b). The sociometer, self-esteem, and the regulation of interpersonal behavior. In K. D.Vohs & R. F. Baumeister (Eds.), *Handbook of self-regulation: Research, theory, and applications* (pp. 373–391). New York: Guilford Press.

**Leary, M. R., & Baumeister, R. F.** (2000). The nature and function of self-esteem: Sociometer theory. In M. P. Zanna (Ed.), *Advances in experimental social psychology* (Vol. 32). San Diego, CA: Academic Press.

**Leary, M. R., Tambor, E. S., Terdal, S. K., & Downs, D. L.** (1995). Self-esteem as an interpersonal monitor: The sociometer hypothesis. *Journal of Personality and Social Psychology, 68*(3), 519–530.

**Leavitt, F.** (1995). *Drugs and behavior* (3rd ed.). Thousand Oaks, CA: Sage.

**Leavitt, F.** (2001). Iatrogenic recovered memories: Examining the empirical evidence. *American Journal of Forensic Psychology, 19*(2), 21–32.

**LeBoeuf, M.** (1980, February). Managing time means managing yourself. *Business Horizons,* pp. 41–46.

**Lebowitz, F.** (1982). *Social studies.* New York: Pocket Books.

**Lechner, S. C., Tennen, H., & Affleck G.** (2009). Benefit-finding and growth. In S. J. Lopez & C. R. Snyder (Eds.), *Oxford handbook of positive psychology* (2nd ed., pp. 633–640). New York: Oxford.

**Ledbetter, A. M., Griffin, E., & Sparks, G. G.** (2007). Forecasting "friends forever": A longitudinal investigation of sustained closeness between best friends. *Personal Relationships, 14,* 343–350.

**Lee, F. R.** (2006, March 28). "Big love": Real polygamists look at HBO polygamists and find sex. *New York Times.*

**Lee, G. R.** (1988). Marital satisfaction in later life: The effects of nonmarital roles. *Journal of Marriage and the Family, 50,* 775–783.

**Lee, I.-M., Rexrode, K. M., Cook, N. R., Manson, J. E., & Buring, J. E.** (2001). Physical activity and coronary heart disease in women: Is "no pain, no gain" passé? *Journal of the American Medical Association, 285,* 1447–1454.

**Lee, I.-M., & Skerrett, P. J.** (2001). Physical activity and all-cause mortality. What is the dose-response relation? *Medicine and Science in Sports and Exercise, 33,* S459–S471.

**Lee, S., & Katzman, M. A.** (2002). Cross-cultural perspectives on eating disorders. In C. G. Fairburn & K. D. Brownell (Eds.), *Eating disorders and obesity: A comprehensive handbook.* New York: Guilford.

**Lee, S., & Oyserman, D.** (2009). Expecting to work, fearing homelessness: The possible selves of low-income mothers. *Journal of Applied Social Psychology, 39*(6), 1334–1355.

**Lee, Y. T., & Seligman, M. E. P.** (1997). Are Americans more optimistic than the Chinese? *Personality and Social Psychology Bulletin, 23,* 32–40.

**Lefcourt, H. M.** (2001). The humor solution. In C. R. Snyder (Ed.), *Coping with stress: Effective people and processes.* New York: Oxford University Press.

**Lefcourt, H. M.** (2005). Humor. In C. R. Snyder & S. J. Lopez (Eds.), *Handbook of positive psychology.* New York: Oxford University Press.

**Lefcourt, H. M., Davidson, K., Shepherd, R., Phillips, M., Prkachin, K., & Mills, D.** (1995). Perspective-taking humor: Accounting for stress moderation. *Journal of Social and Clinical Psychology, 14,* 373–391.

**Leff, J., & Vaughn, C.** (1985). *Expressed emotion in families.* New York: Guilford Press.

**Legault, E., & Laurence, J.-R.** (2007). Recovered memories of childhood sexual abuse: Social worker, psychologist, and psychiatrist reports of beliefs, practices, and cases. *Australian Journal of Clinical & Experimental Hypnosis, 35,* 111–133.

**Lehman, P. K., & Geller, E. S.** (2004). Behavior analysis and environmental protection: Accomplishments and potential for more. *Behavior and Social Issues, 13,* 13–32.

**Lehrer, P., Feldman, J., Giardino, N., Song, H., & Schmaling, K.** (2002). Psychological aspects of asthma. *Journal of Consulting & Clinical Psychology, 70*(3), 691–711.

**Lehrer, P. M., & Woolfolk, R. L.** (1984). Are stress reduction techniques interchangeable, or do they have specific effects? A review of the comparative empirical literature. In R. L. Woolfolk & P. M. Lehrer (Eds.), *Principles and practice of stress management.* New York: Guilford Press.

**Lehrer, P. M., & Woolfolk, R. L.** (1993). Specific effects of stress management techniques. In P. M. Lehrer & R. L. Woolfolk (Eds.), *Principles and practice of stress management* (2nd ed.). New York: Guilford Press.

**Leibel, R. L., Rosenbaum, M., & Hirsch, J.** (1995). Changes in energy expenditure resulting from altered body weight. *New England Journal of Medicine, 332,* 621–629.

**Leischsenring, F. & Rabung, S.** (2008). Effectiveness of long-term psychodynamic psychotherapy: A meta-analysis. *Journal of the American Medical Association, 13,* 1551–1565.

**Leiserowitz, A.** (2007). Communicating the risks of global warming: American risk perceptions, affective images, and interpretive communities. In S.C. Moser & L. Dilling (Eds.), *Creating a climate for change: Communicating climate change and facilitating social change* (pp. 44–63). New York: Cambridge University Press.

**Leitenberg, H., Detzer, M. J., & Srebnik, D.** (1993). Gender differences in masturbation and the relation of masturbation experience in preadolescence and/or early adolescence to sexual behavior and sexual adjustment in young adulthood. *Archives of Sexual Behavior, 22,* 87–98.

**Leitenberg, H., & Henning, K.** (1995). Sexual fantasy. *Psychological Bulletin, 117,* 469–496.

**Lemelle, A. J. Jr., & Battle, J.** (2004). Black masculinity matters in attitudes toward gay males. *Journal of Homosexuality, 47,* 39–51.

**Lemieux, R., & Hale, J. L.** (2002). Cross-sectional analysis of intimacy, passion, and commitment: Testing the assumptions of the triangular theory of love. *Psychological Reports, 90,* 1009–1014.

**L'Engle, K. L., Brown, J. D., & Kenneavy, K.** (2006). The mass media are an important context for adolescents' sexual behavior. *Journal of Adolescent Health, 38*(3), 186–192.

**Lengua, L. J., Long, A. C., & Meltzoff, A. N.** (2006). Pre-attack stress-load, appraisals, and coping in children's responses to the 9/11 terrorist attacks. *Journal of Child Psychology and Psychiatry, 47,* 1219–1227.

**Leo, J.** (1987, January 12). Exploring the traits of twins. *Time,* p. 63.

**Leonard, N. H., & Harvey, M.** (2008). Negative perfectionism: Examining negative excessive behavior in the workplace. *Journal of Applied Social Psychology, 38,* 585–610.

**Leondari, A., & Gonida, E. N.** (2008). Adolescents' possible selves, achievement goal orientations, and academic achievement. *Hellenic Journal of Psychology, 5*(2), 179–198.

**Lepore, S. J., Revenson, T. A., Weinberger, S. L., Weston, P., Frisina, P. G., Robertson, R., et al.** (2006). Effects of social stressors on cardiovascular reactivity in black and white women. *Annals of Behavioral Medicine, 31,* 120–127.

**Lerman, H.** (1986). *A mote in Freud's eye: From psychoanalysis to the psychology of women.* New York: Springer.

**Lerner, M. J.** (1980). *The belief in a just world: A fundamental decision.* New York: Plenum.

**Lerner, M. J.** (1998). The two forms of belief in a just world: Some thoughts on why and how people care about justice. In L. Montada & M. J. Lerner (Eds.), *Responses to victimizations and belief in a just world: Critical issues in social justice.* New York: Plenum Press.

**Leslie, L. A., & Letiecq, B. L.** (2004). Marital quality of African American and white partners in interracial couples. *Personal Relationships, 11,* 559–574.

**Letherby, G., & Williams, C.** (1999). Non-motherhood: Ambivalent autobiographies. *Feminist Studies, 25,* 719–728.

**Lett, H. S., Blumenthal, J. A., Babyak, M. A., Sherwood, A., Strauman, T., Robins, C., & Newman, M. F.** (2004). Depression as a risk factor for coronary artery disease: Evidence, mechanisms, and treatment. *Psychosomatic Medicine, 66*(3), 305–315.

**Leung, L.** (2007). Stressful life events, motives for Internet use, and social support among digital kids. *CyberPsychology & Behavior, 10,* 204–214.

**Levant, R. F.** (1996). The new psychology of men. *Professional Psychology: Research and Practice, 27,* 259–265.

**Levant, R. F.** (2003, Fall). Why study boys and men? *Nova Southeastern University Center for Psychological Studies Newsletter,* pp. 12–13.

**Levant, R. F., & Richmond, K.** (2007). A review of research on masculinity ideologies using the Male Role Norms Inventory. *The Journal of Men's Studies, 15,* 130–146.

**Levenson, J. L., McDaniel, J. S., Moran, M. G., & Stoudemire, A.** (1999). Psychological factors affecting medical conditions. In R. E. Hales, S. C. Yudofsky, & J. A. Talbott (Eds.), *Textbook of psychiatry* (3rd ed.). Washington, DC: American Psychiatric Press, Inc.

**Levenson, R. W., Carstensen, L. L., & Gottman, J. M.** (1993). Long-term marriage: Age, gender, and satisfaction. *Psychology and Aging, 8,* 301–313.

**Levenstein, S.** (2002). Psychosocial factors in peptic ulcer and inflammatory bowel disease. *Journal of Consulting & Clinical Psychology, 70*(3), 739–750.

**Leventhal, H., Cameron, L., & Leventhal, E. A.** (2005). Do messages from your body, your friends, your doctor, or the media shape your health behavior? In T. C. Brock & M. C. Green (Eds.), *Persuassion: Psychological insights and perspectives*. Thousand Oaks, CA: Sage.

**Leventhal, H., Musumeci, T., & Leventhal, E.** (2006). Psychological approaches to the connection of health and behavior. *South African Journal of Psychology, 36,* 666–682.

**Lever, J.** (1994, August 24). Sexual revelations. *The Advocate,* 17–24.

**Levin, S., van Laar, C., & Sidanius, J.** (2003). The effects of ingroup and outgroup friendship on ethnic attitudes in college: A longitudinal study. *Group Processes and Intergroup Relations, 6*(1), 76–92.

**Levine, M. P., & Harrison, K.** (2004). Media's role in the perpetuation and prevention of negative body image and disordered eating. In J. K. Thompson (Ed.), *Handbook of eating disorders and obesity*. New York: Wiley.

**LeVine, R. A.** (2001). Culture and personality studies, 1918–1960. *Journal of Personality, 69,* 803–818.

**Levine, R. V., Martinez, T. S., Brase, G., & Sorenson, K.** (1994). Helping in 36 U.S. cities. *Journal of Personality and Social Psychology, 67*(1), 69–82.

**Levine, R. V., Sato, S., Hashimoto, T., & Verma, J.** (1995). Love and marriage in eleven cultures. *Journal of Cross-Cultural Psychology, 26*(5), 554–571.

**Levinson, D. F.** (2009). Genetics of major depression. In I. H. Gotlib & C. L. Hammen (Eds.), *Handbook of Depression* (pp. 165–186). New York: Guilford.

**Levinthal, C. F.** (2008). *Drugs, behavior, and modern society*. Boston: Pearson.

**Levis, D. J.** (1989). The case for a return to a two-factor theory of avoidance: The failure of non-fear interpretations. In S. B. Klein & R. R. Bowrer (Eds.), *Contemporary learning theories: Pavlovian conditioning and the status of traditional learning theory*. Hillsdale, NJ: Erlbaum.

**Levitt, A. J., Schaffer, A., & Lanctôt, K. L.** (2009). Buspirone. In B. J. Sadock, V. A. Sadock, & P. Ruiz (Eds.), *Kaplan & Sadock's comprehensive textbook of psychiatry* (pp. 3060–3064). Philadelphia: Lippincott Williams & Wilkins.

**Levitt, J. G.** (2006). *Your career: How to make it happen.* Mason, OH: South-Western.

**Levy, S. R., Stroessner, S. J., & Dweck, C. S.** (1998). Stereotype formation and endorsement: The role of implicit theories. *Journal of Personality and Social Psychology, 74*(6), 1421–1436.

**Lewandowski, C. A.** (2003). Organizational factors contributing to worker frustration: The precursor to burnout. *Journal of Sociology and Social Welfare, 30*(4), 175–185.

**Lewin, E.** (2004). Does marriage have a future? *Journal of Marriage and Family, 66,* 1000–1006.

**Lewin, K.** (1935). *A dynamic theory of personality*. New York: McGraw-Hill.

**Lewinsohn, P. M., Joiner, T. E. Jr., & Rohde, P.** (2001). Evaluation of cognitive diathesis-stress models in predicting major depressive disorder in adolescents. *Journal of Abnormal Psychology, 110*(2), 203–215.

**Lewis, B. P., & Linder, D. E.** (1997). Thinking about choking? Attentional processes and paradoxical performance. *Personality and Social Psychology Bulletin, 23,* 937–944.

**Lewis, K., Kaufman, J., & Christakis, N.** (2008). The taste for privacy: An analysis of college student privacy settings in an online social network. *Journal of Computer-Mediated Communication, 14,* 79–100.

**Lewis, R. J., Derlega, V. J., Clarke, E. G., & Kuang, J. C.** (2006). Stigma consciousness, social constraints, and lesbian well-being. *Journal of Counseling Psychology, 53,* 48–56.

**Lewis, S., Escalona, P. R., & Keith, S. J.** (2009). Phenomenology of schizophrenia. In B. J. Sadock, V. A. Sadock, & P. Ruiz (Eds.), *Kaplan & Sadock's comprehensive textbook of psychiatry* (pp. 1433–1450). Philadelphia: Lippincott Williams & Wilkins.

**Li, N. P., & Tausczik, Y. R.** (2009). Mate preferences. In H. T. Reis & S. Sprecher (Eds.), *Encyclopedia of human relationships: Vol. 2* (pp. 1070–1075). Los Angeles: Sage Reference Publication.

**Li, S., & Li, Y-M.** (2007). How far is enough? A measure of information privacy in terms of interpersonal distance. *Environment and Behavior, 39,* 317–331.

**Libby, P., Ridker, P. M., & Maseri, A.** (2002). Inflammation and atherosclerosis. *Circulation, 105,* 1135–1143.

**Liberman, R. P., & Kopelowicz, A.** (2005). Recovery from schizophrenia: A concept in search of research. *Psychiatric Services, 56,* 735–742.

**Liberman, R. P., Kopelowicz, A., Ventura, J., & Gutkind, D.** (2002). Operational criteria and factors related to recovery from schizophrenia. *International Review of Psychiatry, 14*(4), 256–272.

**Lichtenthal, W. G., Cruess, D. G., & Prigerson, H. G.** (2004). A case for establishing complicated grief as a distinct mental disorder in DSM-V. *Clinical Psychology Review, 24,* 637–662.

**Lichter, D. T., Batson, C. D., & Brown, J. B.** (2004). Welfare reform and marriage promotion: The marital expectations and desires of single and cohabiting mothers. *Social Service Review, 78*(1), 2–25.

**Lichter, D. T., & Crowley, M. L.** (2004). Welfare reform and child poverty: Effects of maternal employment, marriage, and cohabitation. *Social Science Research, 33,* 385–408.

**Lickey, M. E., & Gordon, B.** (1991). *Medicine and mental illness: The use of drugs in psychiatry.* New York: Freeman.

**Lieberman, J. A.** (2006). Comparative effectiveness of antipsychotic drugs. *Archives of General Psychiatry, 63*(10), 1069–1072.

**Lieberman, J. A., Stoup, T. S., McEvoy, J. P., Swartz, M. S., Rosenheck, R. A., Perkins, D. O., Keefe, R. S. E., Davis, S. M., Davis, C. E., Lebowitz, D. B., Severe, J., Hsiao, J. K., & CATIE Investigators Group.** (2005). Effectiveness of antipsychotic drugs in patients with chronic schizophrenia. *New England Journal of Medicine, 353,* 1209–1223.

**Lieberman, J. A., Tollefson, G., Tohen, M., Green, A. I., Gur, R. E., Kahn, R., McEvoy, J., Perkins, D., Sharma, T., Zipursky, R., Wei, H., Hamer, R. M., & HGDH Study Group.** (2003). Comparative efficacy and safety of atypical and conventional antipsychotic drugs in first-episode psychosis: A randomized double-blind trial of olanzapine versus haloperidol. *American Journal of Psychiatry, 160,* 1396–1404.

**Lieberman, M. D., Gaunt, R., Gilbert, D. T., & Trope, Y.** (2004). Reflection and reflexion: A social cognitive neuroscience approach to attributional inference. In M. P. Zanna (Ed.), *Advances in experimental social psychology* (Vol. 34). San Diego, CA: Academic Press.

**Liebert, R. M., & Liebert, L. L.** (1998). *Liebert & Spiegler's personality strategies and issues.* Pacific Grove: Brooks/Cole.

**Liewer, L., Mains, D., Lykens, K., & René, A.** (2008). Barriers to women's cardiovascular risk knowledge. *Health Care for Women International, 29*(1), 23–38.

**Lilienfeld, S. O.** (2007). Psychological treatments that cause harm. *Perspectives on Psychological Science, 2,* 53–70.

**Lilienfeld, S. O., & Landfield, K.** (2008). Science and pseudoscience in law enforcement: A user-friendly primer. *Criminal Justice and Behavior, 35*(10), 1215–1230.

**Lilienfeld, S. O., & Lynn, S. J.** (2003). Dissociative identity disorder: Multiple personalities, multiple controversies. In S. O. Lilienfeld, S. Lynn, S. Jay, & J. M. Lohr (Eds.), *Science and pseudoscience in clinical psychology*. New York: Guilford Press.

**Lilienfeld, S. O., Lynn, S. J., Kirsch, I., Chaves, J. F., Sarbin, T. R., Ganaway, G. K., & Powell, R. A.** (1999). Dissociative identity disorder and the sociocognitive model: Recalling the lessons of the past. *Psychological Bulletin, 125*(5), 507–523.

**Lilienfeld, S. O., Wood, J. M., & Garb, H. N.** (2000). The scientific status of projective tests. *Psychological Science in the Public Interest, 1*(2), 27–66.

**Lima, M. L.** (2004). On the influence of risk perception on mental health: living near an incinerator. *Journal of Environmental Psychology, 24,* 71–84.

**Lin, Y., & Huang, C.** (2006). The process of transforming daily social interactions to relationship intimacy: A longitudinal study. *Chinese Journal of Psychology, 48*(1), 35–52.

**Lindau, M., Almkvist, O., & Mohammed, A. H.** (2007). Learning and memory, effects of stress on. In G. Fink (Ed.), *Encyclopedia of stress: Vols. 1–4* (2nd ed., pp. 571–576). San Diego, CA: Elsevier Academic Press.

**Lindau, S. T., Schumm, L. P., Laumann, E. O., Levinson, W., O'Muircheartaigh, C. A., & Waite, L. J.** (2007). A study of sexuality and health among older adults in the United States. *The New England Journal of Medicine, 357,* 762–775.

**Linde, J. A., Rothman, A. J., Baldwin, A. S., & Jeffery, R. W.** (2006). The impact of self-efficacy on behavior change and weight change among overweight participants in a weight loss trial. *Health Psychology, 25,* 282–291.

**Lindgren, H. C.** (1969). *The psychology of college success: A dynamic approach.* New York: Wiley.

**Lindsay, D. S., Hagen, L., Read, J. D., Wade, K. A., & Garry, M.** (2004). True photographs and false memories. *Psychological Science, 15*(3), 149–154.

**Lindsay, D. S., & Read, J. D.** (1994). Psychotherapy and memories of childhood sexual abuse: A cognitive perspective. *Applied Cognitive Psychology, 8,* 281–338.

**Linley, P. A.** (2009). Positive psychology (history). In S. J. Lopez (Ed.), *The encyclopedia of positive psychology* (Vol. II, pp. 742–746). Malden, MA: Wiley-Blackwell.

**Linley, P. A., & Joseph, S.** (2004a). Preface. In P. A. Linley & S. Joseph (Eds.), *Positive psychology in practice* (pp. xv–xvi). Hoboken, NJ: Wiley.

**Linley, P. A., & Joseph, S.** (2004b). Positive change following trauma and adversity: A review. *Journal of Traumatic Stress, 17*(1), 11–21.

**Linley, P. A., Joseph, S., Harrington, S., & Wood, A. M.** (2006). Positive psychology: Past, present, and (possible) future. *The Journal of Positive Psychology, 1,* 3–16.

**Linn, S.** (2004). *Consuming kids: The hostile takeover of childhood.* New York & London: New Press.

**Linn, S.** (2008). *Commercializing childhood: The corporate takeover of kids' lives.* (interview by the Multinational Monitor). Retrieved from http://towardfreedom.com/home/content/view/1389/1/

**Linville, P. W., & Jones, E. E.** (1980). Polarized appraisals of outgroup members. *Journal of Personality and Social Psychology, 38,* 689–703.

**Lipkus, I. M., Dalbert, C., & Siegler, I. C.** (1996). The importance of distinguishing the belief in a just world for self versus for others: Implications for psychological well-being. *Personality and Social Psychology Bulletin, 22,* 666–677.

**Lippa, R. A.** (2005). *Gender, nature, and nurture.* Mahwah, NJ: Erlbaum.

**Lippa, R. A.** (2006). The gender reality hypothesis. *American Psychologist, 61,* 639–640.

**Lippa, R. A.** (2007). The preferred traits of mates in a cross-national study of heterosexual and homosexual men and women: An examination of biological and cultural influences. *Archives of Sexual Behavior 36,* 193–208.

**Lisanby, S. H., Maddox, J. H., Prudic, J., Devanand, D. P., & Sackeim, H. A.** (2000). The effects of electroconvulsive therapy on memory of autobiographical and public events. *General Psychiatry, 57,* 581–590.

**Lishner, D. A., Nguyen, S., Stocks, E. L., & Zillmer, E. J.** (2008). Are sexual and emotional infidelity equally upsetting to men and women? Making sense of forced-choice responses. *Evolutionary Psychology, 6,* 667–675.

**Littlefield, M. B.** (2003). Gender role identity and stress in African American women. *Journal of Human Behavior in the Social Environment, 8*(4), 93–104.

**Litzinger, S., & Gordon, K. C.** (2005). Exploring relationships among communication, sexual satisfaction, and marital satisfaction. *Journal of Sex & Marital Therapy, 31,* 409–424.

**Liu, H., & Wang H.** (2009). Relationship between loneliness, friendship quality and peer acceptance in 209 primary school children. *Chinese Mental Health Journal, 23,* 44–47.

**Liverant, G. I., Hofmann, S. G., & Litz, B. T.** (2004). Coping and anxiety in college students after the September 11th terorists attacks. *Anxiety, Stress, & Coping, 17*(2), 127–139.

**Livesay, C., & Duck, S.** (2009). Personal relationships, defining characteristics. In H. T. Reis & S. Sprecher (Eds.), *Encyclopedia of human relationships: Vol. 3* (pp. 1220–1224). Los Angeles: Sage Reference Publication.

**Livesley, W. J., Jang, K. L., & Vernon, P. A.** (2003). Genetic basis of personality structure. In T. Millon, & M. J. Lerner (Eds.), *Handbook of psychology: Vol. 5. Personality and social psychology*. New York: Wiley.

**Llorca, P.** (2008). Monitoring patients to improve physical health and treatment outcome. *European Neuropsychopharmacology, 18,* S140–S145.

**Lock, R. D.** (2005a). *Taking charge of your career direction: Career planning guide, Book 1.* Belmont, CA: Wadsworth.

**Lock, R. D.** (2005b). *Job Search: Career Planning Guide, Book 2.* Belmont, CA: Wadsworth.

**Lockwood, P.** (2002). Could it happen to you? Predicting the impact of downward social comparisons on the self. *Journal of Personality and Social Psychology, 82,* 343–358.

**Loehlin, J. C.** (1992). *Genes and environment in personality development.* Newbury Park, CA: Sage.

**Loewenstein, G., O'Donoghue, T., & Rabin, M.** (2003). Projection bias in predicting future utility. *Quarterly Journal of Economics, 118*(4), 1209–1248.

**Loftus, E. F.** (1994). The repressed memory controversy. *American Psychologist, 49,* 443–445.

**Loftus, E. F.** (1998). Remembering dangerously. In R. A. Baker (Ed.), *Child sexual abuse and false memory syndrome.* Amherst, NY: Prometheus Books.

**Loftus, E. F.** (2003). Make believe memories. *American Psychologist, 58,* 864–873.

**Loftus, E. F., & Cahill, L.** (2007). Memory distortion: From misinformation to rich false memory. In J. S. Nairne (Ed.), *The foundations of remembering: Essays in honor of Henry L. Roediger III.* New York: Psychology Press.

**Loftus, E. F., & Davis, D.** (2006). Recovered memories. *Annual Review of Clinical Psychology, 2,* 469–498.

**Lohoff, F. W. & Berrettini, W. H.** Genetics of mood disorders. In D. S. Charney & E. J. Nestler (Eds.), *Neurobiology of mental illness* (pp. 360–377). New York: Oxford University Press.

**Lohr, J. M., Olatunji, B. O., Baumeister, R. F., & Bushman, B. J.** (2007). The psychology of anger venting and empirically supported alternatives that do no harm. *The Scientific Review of Mental Health Practice, 5,* 53–64.

**Long, J. E., Jr.** (2005). Power to prescribe: The debate over prescription privileges for psychologists and the legal issues implicated. *Law & Psychology, 29,* 243–260.

**Longman, D. G.** (2005). *Class: College learning and study skills.* Belmont, CA: Wadsworth.

**Lonsdale, A. J., & North, A. C.** (2009). Musical taste and ingroup favouritism. *Group Processes & Intergroup Relations, 12*(3), 319–327.

**Lopes, P. N., Brackett, M. A., Nezlek, J. B., Schutz, A., Sellin, I., & Salovey, P.** (2004). Emotional intelligence and social interaction. *Personality and Social Psychology Bulletin, 30*(8), 1018–1034.

**Lopez, S. J.** (2006a, May). *Giving positive psychology away: Ten strategies that promote student engagement.* Invited presentation at the 18th Annual Meeting of the Association for Psychological Science, New York, NY.

**Lopez, S. J.** (2006b). C. R. (Rick) Snyder (1944–2006) [Obituary]. *American Psychologist, 61,* 719.

**Lopez, S. J., & Snyder, C. R.** (Eds.). (2009). *Oxford handbook of positive psychology* (2nd ed.). New York: Oxford.

**Loth, K., van den Berg, P., Eisenberg, M., & Neumark-Sztainer, D.** (2008). Stressful life events and disordered eating behaviors: Findings from Project EAT. *Journal of Adolescent Health,* 43, 514–516.

**Lott, B.** (2002). Cognitive and behavioral distancing from the poor. *American Psychologist,* 57, 100–110.

**Louv, R.** (2005). *Last child in the woods: Saving our children from nature-deficit disorder.* Chapel Hill, NC: Algonquin Books.

**Lovejoy, T. E., & Hannah, L.** (2005). *Climate change and biodiversity.* New Haven, CT: Yale University Press.

**Loving, T. J., Heffner, K. L., & Kiecolt-Glaser, J. K.** (2006). Physiology and interpersonal relationships. In A. L. Vangelisti & D. Perlman (Eds.), *The Cambridge handbook of personal relationships.* New York: Cambridge University Press.

**Lowenstein, G., O' Donoghue, T., & Rabin, M.** (2003). Projection bias in predicting future utility. *Quarterly Journal of Economics, 118,* 1209–1248.

**Lowinson, J. H., Ruiz, P., Millman, R. B., & Langrod, J. G.** (2005). *Substance abuse: A comprehensive textbook.* Philadelphia: Lippincott/Williams & Wilkins.

**Lowry, R., Wechsler, H., Galuska, D. A., Fulton, J. E., & Kann, L.** (2002). Television viewing and its associations with overweight, sedentary lifestyle, and insufficient consumption of fruits and vegetables among US high school students: Differences by race, ethnicity, and gender. *Journal of School Health, 72,* 413–421.

**Lozano, B. E., Stephens, R. S., & Roffman, R. A.** (2006). Abstinence and moderate use goals in the treatment of marijuana dependence. *Addiction, 101,* 1589–1597.

**Lubkin, I. M.** (1990). Illness roles. In I. M. Lubkin (Ed.), *Chronic illness: Impact and interventions* (2nd ed.). Boston: Jones and Bartlett.

**Luborsky, L., & Barrett, M. S.** (2006). The history and empirical status of key psychoanalytic concepts. *Annual Review Clinical Psychology, 2,* 1–19.

**Luborsky, L., Rosenthal, R., Diguer, L., Andrusyna, T. P., Berman, J. S., Levitt, J. T., Seligman, D. A., & Krause, E. D.** (2002). The dodo bird verdict is alive and well—mostly. *Clinical Psychology: Science & Practice, 9,* 2–12.

**Luborsky, L., Singer, B., & Luborsky, L.** (1975). Comparative studies of psychotherapies: Is it true that everyone has won and all must have prizes? *Archives of General Psychiatry, 32,* 995–1008.

**Lucas, A. R., Beard, C. M., O'Fallon, W. M., & Kurland, L. T.** (1991). 50-year trends in the incidence of anorexia nervosa in Rochester, Minn.: A population-based study. *American Journal of Psychiatry, 148,* 917–922.

**Lucas, J. W., & Lovaglia, M. J.** (2005). Self-handicapping: Gender, race, and status. *Current Research in Social Psychology, 10*(16), [electronic journal].

**Lucas, R. E.** (2005). Time does not heal all wounds: A longitudinal study of reaction and adaptation to divorce. *Psychological Science, 16,* 945–950.

**Lucas, R. E.** (2007). Adaptation and the set-point model of subjective well-being: Does happiness change after major life events? *Current Directions in Psychological Science, 16,* 75–79.

**Lucas, R. E.** (2008). Personality and subjective well-being. In M. Eid & R. J. Larsen (Eds.), *The science of subjective well-being* (pp. 171–194). New York: Guilford.

**Lucas, R. E., Clark, A. E., Georgellis, Y., & Diener, E.** (2004). Unemployment alters the set point for life satisfaction. *Psychological Science, 15*(1), 8–13.

**Lucas, R. E., & Diener, E.** (2008). Personality and subjective well-being. In O. P. John, R. W. Robins, & L. A. Pervin (Eds.), *Handbook of personality: Theory and research* (pp. 795–814). New York: Guilford.

**Luhtanen, R., & Crocker, J.** (1992). A collective self-esteem scale: Self-evaluation of one's social identity. *Personality and Social Psychology Bulletin, 18,* 302–318.

**Lulofs, R. S.** (1994). *Conflict: From theory to action.* Scottsdale, AZ: Gorsuch Scarisbuck Publishers.

**Lulofs, R. S., & Cahn, D. D.** (2000). *Conflict: From theory to action* (2nd ed.). Boston: Allyn & Bacon.

**Lumley, M. A., & Provenzano, K. M.** (2003). Stress management through written emotional disclosure improves academic performance among college students with physical symptoms. *Journal of Educational Psychology, 95,* 641–649.

**Lund, O. C. H., Tamnes, C. K., Moestue, C., Buss, D. M., & Vollrath, M.** (2007). Tactics of hierarchy negotiation. *Journal of Research in Personality, 41,* 25–44.

**Lundberg, A.** (1998). Environmental change and human health. In A. Lundberg (Ed.), *The Environment and Mental Health: A Guide for Clinicians* (pp. 5–23). Mahwah, NJ: Erlbaum.

**Lundberg, U.** (2000). Catecholamines. In G. Fink (Ed.), *Encyclopedia of stress* (Vol. 1). San Diego: Academic Press.

**Lundberg, U.** (2007). Workplace stress. In G. Fink (Ed.), *Encyclopedia of stress: Vols. 1–4* (2nd ed., pp. 871–878). San Diego, CA: Elsevier Academic Press.

**Lundberg-Love, P. K., & Wilkerson, D. K.** (2006). Battered women. In P. K. Lundberg-Love & S. L. Marmion (Eds.), *"Intimate" violence against women: When spouses, partners, or lovers attack.* Westport, CT: Praeger.

**Lundeburg, K., Stith, S. M., Penn, C. E., & Ward, D. B.** (2004). A comparison of nonviolent, psychologically violent, and physically violent male college daters. *Journal of Interpersonal Violence, 19*(10), 1191–1200.

**Luo, S., & Klohnen, E. C.** (2005). Assortative mating and marital quality in newlyweds: A couple-centered approach. *Journal of Personality and Social Psychology, 88,* 304–326.

**Lurie, P., Almeida, C. M., Stine, N., Stine, A. R., & Wolfe, S. M.** (2006). Financial conflict of interest disclosure and voting patterns at food and drug administration drug advisory committee meetings. *JAMA, 295,* 1921–1928.

**Luthans, F., & Youssef, C. M.** (2009). Positive workplaces. In S. J. Lopez & C. R. Snyder (Eds.), *Oxford handbook of positive psychology* (2nd ed., pp. 579–588). New York: Oxford University Press.

**Luthans, F., Youssef, C. M., & Avolio, B. J.** (2007). *Psychological capital: Developing the human competitive edge.* Oxford, UK: Oxford University Press.

**Luthar, S. S., & Ziegler, E.** (1991). Vulnerability and competence: A review of research on resiliency in childhood. *Journal of American Orthopsychiatry, 61,* 6–22.

**Lutz, C. J., & Ross, S. R.** (2003). Elaboration versus fragmentation: Distinguishing between self-complexity and self-concept differentiation. *Journal of Social and Clinical Psychology, 22*(5), 537–559.

**Lye, D. N., & Biblarz, T. J.** (1993). The effects of attitudes toward family life and gender roles on marital satisfaction. *Journal of Family Issues, 14,* 157–188.

**Lykken, D.** (1999). *Happiness: The nature and nurture of joy and contentment.* New York: St. Martin's.

**Lykken, D., McGue, M., Tellegen, A., & Bouchard, T. J., Jr.** (1992). Emergenesis: Genetic traits that may not run in families. *American Psychologist, 47*(12), 1565–1577.

**Lykken, D., & Tellegen, A.** (1996). Happiness is a stochastic phenomenon. *Psychological Science, 7,* 186–189.

**Lynch, D. J., McGrady, A., Alvarez, E., & Forman, J.** (2005). Recent life changes and medical utilization in an academic family practice. *Journal of Nervous and Mental Disease, 193,* 633–635.

**Lyness, K. S., & Heilman, M. E.** (2006). When fit is fundamental: Performance evaluations and promotions of upper-level female and male managers. *Journal of Applied Psychology, 91,* 777–785.

**Lynn, D. J., & Vaillant, G. E.** (1998). Anonymity, neutrality, and confidentiality in the actual methods of Sigmund Freud: A review of 43 cases, 1907–1939. *American Journal of Psychiatry, 155,* 163–171.

**Lynn, M., & Shurgot, B. A.** (1984). Responses to lonely hearts advertisements: Effects of reported physical attractiveness, physique, and coloration. *Personality and Social Psychology Bulletin, 10,* 349–357.

**Lytton, H., & Romney, D. M.** (1991). Parents' differential socialization of boys and girls: A meta-analysis. *Psychological Bulletin, 109,* 267–296.

**Lyubomirsky, S., King, L., & Diener, E.** (2005). The benefits of frequent positive affect: Does happiness lead to success? *Psychological Bulletin, 131,* 803–855.

**Lyubomirsky, S., Sheldon, K. M., & Schkade, D.** (2005). Pursuing happiness: The architecture of sustainable change. *Review of General Psychology, 9*(2), 111–131.

**Lyubomirsky, S., Tkach, C., & DiMatteo, R. M.** (2006). What are the differences between happiness and self-esteem? *Social Indicators Research, 78,* 363–404.

**Maatta, S., Nurmi, J., & Stattin, H.** (2007). Achievement orientations, school adjustment, and well-being: A longitudinal study. *Journal of Research on Adolescence, 17,* 789–812.

**Macaskill, A.** (2005). Defining forgiveness: Christian clergy and general population perspectives. *Journal of Personality, 73,* 1237–1265.

**Macaskill, A., Maltby, J. & Day, L.** (2002). Forgiveness of self and others and emotional empathy. *The Journal of Social Psychology, 142,* 663–665.

**Maccoby, E. E.** (1990). Gender and relationships: A developmental account. *American Psychologist, 45,* 513–520.

**Maccoby, E. E.** (1998). *The two sexes: Growing up apart, coming together.* Cambridge, MA: Belknap Press.

**Maccoby, E. E.** (2002). Gender and group processes: A developmental perspective. *Current Direction in Psychological Science, 11*(2), 54–58.

**Maccoby, E. E., & Martin, J. A.** (1983). Socialization in the context of the family: Parent-child interaction. In P. H. Mussen (Series Ed.) & E. M. Hetherington (Vol. Ed.), *Handbook of child psychology: Vol. 4. Socialization, personality, and social development.* New York: Wiley.

**MacDonald, G., Saltzman, J. L., & Leary, M. R.** (2003). Social approval and trait self-esteem. *Journal of Research in Personality, 37*(2), 23–40.

**MacGeorge, E. L., Graves, A. R., Feng, B., Gillihan, S. J., & Burleson, B. R.** (2004). The myth of gender cultures: Similarities outweigh differences in men's and women's provision of and responses to supportive communication. *Sex Roles, 50*(3/4), 143–175.

**Macionis, J. J.** (1997). *Sociology* (6th ed.). Upper Saddle River, NJ: Prentice Hall.

**Mack, A. H., Franklin Jr., J. E., & Frances, R. J.** (2003). Substance use disorders. In R. E. Hales & S. C. Yudofsky (Eds.), *Textbook of clinical psychiatry.* Washington, DC: American Psychiatric Publishing.

**MacKellar, D. A., Valleroy, L. A., Secura, G. M., Behel, S., Bingham, T., Celentano, D. D., Koblin, B. A., LaLota, M., McFarland, W., Shehan, D., Thiede, H., Torian, L. V., & Janssen, R. S., & Young Men's Survey Study Group.** (2005). Unrecognized HIV infection, risk behaviors, and perceptions of risk among young men who have sex with men: Opportunities for advancing HIV prevention in the third decade of HIV/AIDS. *Journal of Acquired Immune Deficiency Syndrome, 38,* 603–614.

**Mackenzie, R. A.** (1997). *The time trap.* New York: AMACOM.

**Mackie, D. M., Worth, L. T., & Asuncion, A. G.** (1990). Processing of persuasive in-group messages. *Journal of Personality and Social Psychology, 58,* 812–822.

**MacMillan, H. L., Fleming, J. E., Streiner, D. L., Lin, E., Boyle, M. H., Jamieson, E., Duku, E. K., Walsh, C. A., Wong, M. Y. Y., & Beardslee, W. R.** (2001). Childhood abuse and lifetime psychopathology in a community sample. *American Journal of Psychiatry, 158,* 1878–1883.

**MacMillian, H. L., Fleming, J. E., Trocme, N., Boyle, M. H., Wong, M., Racine, Y. A., Beardslee, W. R., & Offord, D. R.** (1997). Prevalence of child physical and sexual abuse in the community: Results from the Ontario health supplement. *Journal of the American Medical Association, 278,* 131–135.

**Macmillan, M.** (1991). *Freud evaluated: The completed arc.* Amsterdam: North-Holland.

**Madathil, J., & Benshoff, J. M.** (2008). Importance of marital characteristics and marital satisfaction: A comparison of Asian Indians in arranged marriages and Americans in marriages of choice. *The Family Journal, 16,* 222–230.

**Madden, M., & Lenhart, A.** (2006). *Online dating.* Retrieved April 29, 2007 from http://www.pewinternet.org/pdfs/PIP_Online_Dating.pdf.

**Maddi, S. R.** (2002). The story of hardiness: Twenty years of theorizing, research, and practice. *Consulting Psychology Journal: Practice and Research, 54*(3), 175–185.

**Maddi, S. R.** (2006). Hardiness: The courage to grow from stresses. *Journal of Positive Psychology, 1*(3), 160–168.

**Maddi, S. R.** (2007). The story of hardiness: Twenty years of theorizing, research, and practice. In A. Monat, R. S. Lazarus, & G. Reevy (Eds.), *The Praeger handbook on stress and coping* (pp. 327–340). Westport, CT: Praeger Publishers.

**Maddi, S. R., & Hightower, M.** (1999). Hardiness and optimism as expressed in coping patterns. *Consulting Psychology Journal: Practice and Research, 51*(2), 95–105.

**Maddux, J. E.** (2002). Stopping the "madness." In C. R. Snyder & S. J. Lopez (Eds.), *Handbook of positive psychology* (pp. 13–25). New York: Oxford University Press.

**Maddux, J. E., & Gosselin, J. T.** (2003). Self-efficacy. In M. R. Leary & J. P. Tangney (Eds.), *Handbook of self and identity.* New York: Guilford.

**Madey, S. F., & Rodgers L.** (2009). The effect of attachment and Sternberg's triangular theory of love on relationship satisfaction. *Individual Differences Research, 7,* 76–84.

**Magnavita, J. J.** (2008). Psychoanalytic psychotherapy. In J. L. Lebow (Ed.), *Twenty-first century psychotherapies: Contemporary approaches to theory and practice.* New York: Wiley.

**Maguen, S., & Armistead, L.** (2006). Abstinence among female adolescents: Do parents matter above and beyond the influence of peers? *American Journal of Orthopsychiatry, 76,* 260–264.

**Maher, B. A.** (2001). Delusions. In P. B. Sutker & H. E. Adams (Eds.), *Comprehensive handbook of psychopathology* (3rd ed.). New York: Kluwer Academic/Plenum Publishers.

**Maheu, M., & Subotnik, R.** (2001). *Infidelity and the Internet: Virtual relationships and real betrayal.* New York: Sourcebooks.

**Mahoney, M. J.** (1974). *Cognition and behavior modification.* Cambridge, MA: Ballinger.

**Mahoney, M. J.** (1979). *Self-change: Strategies for solving personal problems.* New York: Norton.

**Maisel, N. C., Gable, S. L., & Strachman, A.** (2008). Responsive behaviors in good times and in bad. *Personal Relationships, 15,* 317–338.

**Maisey, D. S., Vale, E. L. E., Cornelissen, P. L., & Tovee, M. J.** (1999). Characteristics of male attractiveness for women. *Lancet, 353,* 1500.

**Major, B., Barr, L., Zubeck, J., & Babey, S. H.** (1999). Gender and self-esteem: A meta-analysis. In W. B. Swann, Jr., J. H. Langlois, & L. A. Gilbert (Eds.), *Sexism and stereotypes in modern society: The gender science of Janet Taylor Spence.* Washington, DC: American Psychological Association.

**Major, B., Schmidlin, A. M., & Williams, L.** (1990). Gender patterns in social touch: The impact of setting and age. *Journal of Personality and Social Psychology, 58,* 634–643.

**Malaspina, D., Kleinhaus, K. R., Perrin, M. C., Fennig, S., Nahon, D., Friedlander, Y, et al.** (2008). Acute material stress in pregnancy and schizophrenia in offspring: A cohort prospective study. *BMC Psychiatry, 8,* ArtlD 71.

**Maldonado, J. R. & Spiegel, D.** (2008). Dissociative disorders. In R. E. Hales, S. C. Yudofsky, & G. O. Gabbard (Eds.), *The American psychiatric publishing textbook of psychiatry* (pp. 665–710). Washington, DC: American Psychiatric Publishing.

**Maletzky, B. M.** (2002). The paraphilias: Research and treatment. In P. E. Nathan & J. M. Gorman (Eds), *A guide to treatments that work.* London: Oxford University Press.

**Malle, B. F.** (2004). *How the mind explains behavior: Folk explanations, meaning, and social interaction.* Cambridge, MA: MIT Press.

**Malle, B. F.** (2006). *How the mind explains behavior: Folk explanations, meaning, and social interaction.* Cambridge, MA: MIT Press.

**Malle, B. F., & Knobe, J.** (1997). Which behaviors do people explain? A basic actor-observer asymmetry. *Journal of Personality and Social Psychology, 72,* 288–304.

**Mallen, M. J., Day, S. X., & Green, M. A.** (2003). Online versus face-to-face conversations: An examination of relational and discourse variable. *Psychotherapy: Theory, Research, Practice, Training, 40*(1–2), 155–163.

**Maltz, D. N., & Borker, R. A.** (1983). A cultural approach to male-female miscommunication. In J. A. Gumperz (Ed.), *Language and social identity.* New York: Cambridge University Press.

**Mandler, G.** (1993). Thought, memory, and learning: Effects of emotional stress. In L. Goldberger & S. Breznitz (Eds.), *Handbook of stress: Theoretical and clinical aspects* (2nd ed.). New York: Free Press.

**Mann, J. J., & Currier, D.** (2006). Understanding and preventing suicide. In D. J. Stein, D. J. Kupfer, & A. F. Schatzberg (Eds.), *Textbook of mood disorders.* Washington, DC: American Psychiatric Publishing.

**Manning, W. D.** (2004). Children and the stability of cohabiting couples. *Journal of Mariage and Family, 66,* 674–689.

**Manning, W. D., Longmore, M. A., & Giordano, P. C.** (2007). The changing institution of marriage: Adolescents' expectations to cohabit and to marry. *Journal of Marriage and Family, 69,* 559–575.

**Manson, J. E., Skerrett, P. J., Greenland, P., & VanItallie, T. B.** (2004). The escalating pandemics of obesity and sedentary lifestyles: A call to action for clinicians. *Archives of Internal Medicine, 164,* 249–258.

**Manson, J. E., Skerrett, P. J., & Willett, W. C.** (2002). Epidemiology of health risks associated with obesity. In C. G. Fairburn & K. D. Brownell (Eds.), *Eating disorders and obesity: A comprehensive handbook.* New York: Guilford.

**Maracek, J.** (2001). Disorderly constructs: Feminist frameworks for clinical psychology. In R. K. Unger (Ed.), *Handbook of women and gender.* New York: Wiley.

**Marcenes, W. G., & Sheiham, A.** (1992). The relationship between work stress and oral health status. *Social Science and Medicine, 35,* 1511.

**Marcus-Newhall, A., Pedersen, W. C., Carlson, M., & Miller, N.** (2000). Displaced aggression is alive and well: A meta-analytic review. *Journal of Personality and Social Psychology, 78*(4), 670–689.

**Marder, S. R., Hurford, I. M., & van Kammen, D. P.** (2009). Second–generation antipsychotics. In B. J. Sadock, V. A. Sadock, & P. Ruiz (Eds.), *Kaplan & Sadock's comprehensive textbook of psychiatry* (pp. 3206–3240). Philadelphia: Lippincott Williams & Wilkins.

**Margolin, G., & Gordis, E. B.** (2004). Children's exposure to violence in the family and community. *Current Directions in Psychological Science, 13,* 152–155.

**Mariani, M.** (2001, Summer). Distance learning in postsecondary education. *Occupational Outlook Quarterly,* pp. 2–10.

**Maricchiolo, F., Gnisci, A., Bonaiuto, M., & Ficca, G.** (2009). Effects of different types of hand gestures in persuasive speech on receivers' evaluations. *Language and Cognitive Processes, 24*(2), 239–266.

**Maris, R. W., Berman, A. L., & Silverman, M. M.** (2000). *Comprehensive textbook of suicidology.* New York: The Guilford Press.

**Marker, N. F.** (1996). Flying solo at midlife: Gender, marital status, and psychological well-being. *Journal of Marriage and the Family, 58,* 917–932.

**Markey, P. M.** (2000). Bystander intervention in computer-mediated communication. *Computers in Human Behavior, 16*(2), 183–188.

**Markman, A. B., & Maddox, W. T.** (2006). Choking and excelling under pressure. *Psychological Science, 17,* 944–948.

**Marks, M. J., & Fraley, R. C.** (2006). Confirmation bias and the sexual double standard. *Sex Roles, 54,* 19–26.

**Marks, M. L., & De Meuse, K. P.** (2005). Resizing the organization: maximizing the gain while minimizing the pain of layoffs, divestitures, and closings. *Organizational Dynamics, 34*(1), 19–35.

**Marks, N. F., Lambert, J. D., & Choi, H.** (2002). Transitions to caregiving, gender, and psychological well-being: A prospective U. S. national study. *Journal of Marriage and Family, 64,* 657–667.

**Markus, H., & Kitayama, S.** (1991). Culture and the self: Implications for cognition, emotion, and motivation. *Psychological Review, 98,* 224–253.

**Markus, H., & Kitayama, S.** (2004). Models of agency: Sociocultural diversity in the construction of action. In V. Murphy-Berman & J. Berman (Eds.), *Nebraska Symposium on Motivation. Cross-cultural differences in perspectives on the self.* Lincoln: University of Nebraska Press.

**Markus, H., & Nurius, P.** (1986). Possible selves. *American Psychologist, 41,* 954–969.

**Markus, H., & Wurf, E.** (1987). The dynamic self-concept: A social psychological perspective. *Annual Review of Psychology, 38,* 299–337.

**Marsh, A. A., Kozak, M. N., & Ambady, N.** (2007). Accurate identification of fear facial expressions predicts prosocial behavior. *Emotion, 7*(2), 239–251.

**Marshall, L.** (2005, February 25). Sex, romance and a patch. *Statesboro Herald,* p. 6A.

**Marshall, R. D., Bryant, R. A., Amsel, L., Suh, E. J., Cook, J. M., & Neria, Y.** (2007). The psychology of ongoing threat: Relative risk appraisal, the September 11 attacks, and terrorism-related fears. *American Psychologist, 62,* 304–316.

**Martimportugues-Goyenechea, C., & Gomez-Jacinto, L.** (2005). Simultaneous multiple stressors in the environment: Physiological stress reactions, performance, and stress evaluation. *Psychological Reports, 97,* 867–874.

**Martin, A. J., Marsh, H. W., Williamson, A., & Debus, R. L.** (2003). Self-handicapping, defensive pessimism, and goal orientation: A qualitative study of university students. *Journal of Educational Psychology, 95,* 617–628.

**Martin, C. L., & Ruble, D.** (2004). Children's search for gender cues: Cognitive perspectives on gender development. *Current Direction in Psychological Science, 13*(2), 67–70.

**Martin, C. L., Ruble, D., & Szkrybalo, J.** (2002). Cognitive theories of early gender development. *Psychological Bulletin, 128*(6), 903–933.

**Martin, L. R., Friedman, H. S., & Schwartz, J. E.** (2007). Personality and mortality risk across the life span: The importance of conscientiousness as a biopsychosocial attribute. *Health Psychology, 26,* 428–436.

**Martin, R., & Leventhal, H.** (2004). Symptom perception and health care–seeking behavior. In J. M. Raczynski & L. C. Leviton (Eds.), *Handbook of clinical health psychology: Vol. 2. Disorders of behavior and health.* Washington, DC: American Psychological Association.

**Martin, R., Rothrock, N., Leventhal, H., & Leventhal, E.** (2003). Common sense models of illness: Implications for symptom perception and health-related behaviors. In J. Suls & K. A. Wallston (Eds.), *Social psychological foundations of health and illness.* Malden, MA: Blackwell Publishing.

**Martin, R. A.** (1996). The situational humor response questionnaire (SHRQ) and coping humor scale (CHS): A decade of research findings. *Humor: International Journal of Humor Research, 9,* 251–272.

**Martin, R. A.** (2002). Is laughter the best medicine? Humor, laughter, and physical health. *Current Directions in Psychological Science, 11*(6), 216–220.

**Martin, R. A., & Lefcourt, H. M.** (1983). Sense of humor as a moderator of the relation between stressors and moods. *Journal of Personality and Social Psychology, 45,* 1313–1324.

**Martin-Krumm, C. P., Sarrazin, P. G., Peterson, C., & Famose, J.** (2003). Explanatory style and resilience after sports failure. *Personality and Individual Differences, 35*(7), 1685–1695.

**Martinez, E.** (2009, October 27). James Ray gives "laughable" 50 percent refund to Sweat Lodge victim's family. *CBS News,* Retrieved from http://www.cbsnews.com/blogs/2009/08/28/crimesider/entry5271390.shtml

**Martinez, J., & Hosek, S. G.** (2005). An exploration of the down low society: Nongay-identified young African-American men who have sex with men. *Journal of the National Medical Association, 97,* 1103–1112.

**Martinez, M., Marangell, L. B., & Martinez, J. M.** (2008). Psychopharmacology. In R. E. Hales, S. C. Yudofsky, & G. O. Gabbard (Eds.), *The American psychiatric publishing textbook of psychiatry* (pp. 1053–1132). Washington, DC: American Psychiatric Publishing, Inc.

**Martino, S. C., Collins, R. L., Elliott, M. N., Strachman, A., Kanouse, D. E., & Berry, S. H.** (2006). Exposure to degrading versus nondegrading music lyrics and sexual behavior among youth. *Pediatrics, 118,* e430–e441.

**Martins, Y., Tiggemann, M., & Churchett, L.** (2008). The shape of things to come: Gay men's satisfaction with specific body parts. *Psychology of Men & Masculinity, 9,* 248–256.

**Martins, Y., Tiggemann, M., & Kirkbride, A.** (2007). Those speedos become them: The role of self-objectification in gay and heterosexual men's body image. *Personality and Social Psychology Bulletin, 33,* 634–647.

**Marx, D. M., Ko, S. J., & Friedman, R. A.** (2009). The "Obama effect": How a salient role model reduces race-based performance differences. *Journal of Experimental Social Psychology, 45,* 953–956.

**Masheter, C.** (1997). Healthy and unhealthy friendship and hostility between ex-spouses. *Journal of Marriage and the Family, 59,* 463–475.

**Maslach, C.** (2003). Job burnout: New directions in research and intervention. *Current Directions in Psychological Science, 12*(5), 189–192.

**Maslach, C.** (2005). Understanding burnout: Work and family issues. In D. F. Halpern & S. E. Murphy (Eds.), *From work-family balance to work-family interaction: Changing the metaphor.* Mahwah, NJ: Erlbaum.

**Maslach, C., & Leiter, M. P.** (1997). *The truth about burnout.* San Francisco: Jossey-Bass.

**Maslach, C., & Leiter, M. P.** (2000). Burnout. In G. Fink (Ed.), *Encyclopedia of stress* (Vol. 1). San Diego: Academic Press.

**Maslach, C., & Leiter, M. P.** (2007). *Burnout.* In G. Fink (Ed.), *Encyclopedia of stress: Vols. 1–4* (2nd ed., pp. 368–371). San Diego, CA: Elsevier Academic Press.

**Maslow, A. H.** (1968). *Toward a psychology of being.* New York: Van Nostrand.

**Maslow, A. H.** (1970). *Motivation and personality.* New York: Harper & Row.

**Maslow, A. H.** (1973). Self-actualizing people: A study of psychological health. In R. J. Lowry (Ed.), *Dominance, self-esteem, self-actualization: Germinal papers of A. H. Maslow* (pp. 177–201). Monterey, CA: Brooks/Cole. (Original work published 1950)

**Mason, M. A.** (1998). The modern American step-family: Problems and possibilities. In M. A. Mason, A. Skolnick, & S. D. Sugarman (Eds.), *All our families: New policies for a new century.* New York: Oxford University Press.

**Massen, C., & Vaterrodt-Plünnecke, B.** (2006). The role of proactive interference in mnemonic techniques. *Memory, 14,* 189–196.

**Masten, A. S.** (2001). Ordinary magic: Resilience processes in development. *American Psychologist, 56,* 227–238.

**Masten, A. S., Best, K., & Garmezy, N.** (1990). Resilience and development: Contributions from the study of children who overcame adversity. *Development and Psychopathology, 2,* 425–444.

**Masten, A. S., & Coatsworth, J. D.** (1998). The development of competence in favorable and unfavorable environments: Lessons from research on successful children. *American Psychologist, 53,* 205–220.

**Masten, A. S., & Reed, M. J.** (2002). Resilience in development. In C. R. Snyder & S. J. Lopez (Eds.)., *Handbook of positive psychology* (pp. 74–88). New York: Oxford University Press.

**Masters, W. H., & Johnson, V. E.** (1966). *Human sexual response.* Boston: Little, Brown.

**Masters, W. H., & Johnson, V. E.** (1970). *Human sexual inadequacy.* Boston: Little, Brown.

**Masuda, T., & Nisbett, R. E.** (2006). Culture and change blindness. *Cognitive Science, 30,* 381–399.

**Mathes, E. W., & Kozak, G.** (2008). The exchange of physical attractiveness for resource potential and commitment. *Journal of Evolutionary Psychology, 6,* 43–56.

**Mathew, S. J., Hoffman, E. J., Charney, D. S.** (2009). Pharmacotherapy of anxiety disorders. In D. S. Charney & E. J. Nestler (Eds.), *Neurobiology of mental illness* (p. 731). New York: Guilford.

**Mathews, C. A., & Reus, V. I.** (2001). Assortative mating in the affective disorders: A systematic review and meta-analysis. *Comprehensive Psychiatry, 42*(4), 257–262.

**Matlin, M. W.** (2004). *The psychology of women* (5th ed.). Belmont, CA: Wadsworth.

**Matsumoto, D.** (2006). Culture and nonverbal behavior. In V. Manusov & M. L. Patterson (Ed.), *The Sage handbook of nonverbal communication* (pp. 219–235). Thousand Oaks, CA: Sage.

**Matsumoto, D., & Willingham, B.** (2009). Spontaneous facial expressions of emotion of congenitally and non-congenitally blind individuals. *Journal of Personality and Social Psychology, 96*(1), 1–10.

**Mattar, C., Harharahm, L., Su, L., Agarwal, A., Wong, P., & Choolani, M.** (2008). Menopause, hormone therapy and cardiovascular and cerebrovascular disease. *Annals of the Academy of Medicine Singapore, 37*(1), 54–62.

**Matthews, G., Emo, A. K., Funke, G., Zeidner, M., Roberts, R. D., Costa Jr., P. T., & Schulze, R.** (2006). Emotional intelligence, personality, and task-induced stress. *Journal of Experimental Psychology: Applied, 12,* 96–107.

**Maume, D. J., Jr.** (1999). Glass ceilings and glass escalators: Occupational segregation and race and sex differences in managerial promotions. *Work and Occupations, 26*(4), 483–509.

**Maume, D. J., Jr.** (2004). Is the glass ceiling a unique form of inequality? Evidence from a random-effects model of managerial attainment. *Work and Occupation, 31,* 250–274.

**Mayer, F. S., & Frantz, C. M.** (2004). The connectedness to nature scale: A measure of individuals' feeling in community with nature. *Journal of Environmental Psychology, 24,* 503–515.

**Mayer, J. D., Perkins, D. M., Caruso, D. R., & Salovey, P.** (2001). Emotional intelligence and giftedness. *Roeper Review, 23,* 131–137.

**Mayer, J. D., Salovey, P., & Caruso, D. R.** (2002). *Mayer-Salovey-Caruso Emotional Intelligence Test (MSCEIT): User's manual.* Toronto, Canada: Multi-Health Systems.

**Mayer, J. D., Salovey, P. & Caruso, D. R.** (2008). Emotional Intelligence: New ability or eclectic traits, *American Psychologist, 63,* 503–517.

**Mayes, F.** (1996). *Under the Tuscan sun: At home in Italy.* New York: Chronicle Books.

**Mayes, R., & Horwitz, A. V.** (2005). DSM-III and the revolution in the classification of mental illness. *Journal of the History of the Behavioral Sciences,* 41(3), 249–267.

**Mayo Clinic.** (2008). *Erectile dysfunction.* Retrieved from http:/www.mayoclinic.com/health/erectile-dysfunction/DS00162

**Mayo Clinic.** (2009). *Premature ejaculation.* Retrieved from http:/www.mayoclinic.com/health/premature-ejaculation/DS00578

**Mayou, R., Kirmayer, L. J., Simon, G., Kroenke, K., & Sharpe, M.** (2005). Somatoform disorders: Time for a new approach in DSM-V. *American Journal of Psychiatry, 162,* 847–855.

**Mazzoni, G., & Lynn, S. J.** (2007). Using hypnosis in eyewitness memory: Past and current issues. In M. P. Toglia, J. D. Read, D. F. Ross, & R. C. L. Lindsay (Eds.), *Handbook of eyewitness psychology: Volume 1. Memory for events.* Mahwah, NJ: Erlbaum.

**Mazzuca, J.** (2003, March 25). *Open dialogue: Parents talk to teens about sex.* Retrieved January 25, 2005 from http://www.Gallup.Com/Poll/Content/?Ci=8047.

**McAuliffe, L., Bauer, M., & Nay, R.** (2007). Barriers to the expression of sexuality in the older person: The role of the health professional. *International Journal of Older People Nursing, 2,* 69–75.

**McBride, D. L. & Korell, G.** (2005). Wilderness therapy for abused women. *Canadian Journal of Counseling, 39,* 3–14.

**McCarthy, B. W., Bodnar, L. E., & Handal, M.** (2004). Integrating sex therapy and couple therapy. In J. H. Harvey, A. Wenzel, & S. Sprecher (Eds.), *The handbook of sexuality in close relationships.* Mahwah, NJ: Lawrence Erlbaum.

**McCarty, R., & Pacak, K.** (2000). Alarm phase and general adaptation syndrome. In G. Fink (Ed.), *Encyclopedia of stress* (Vol. 1). San Diego: Academic Press.

**McCave, E. L.** (2007). Comprehensive sexuality education vs. abstinence-only sexuality education: The need for evidence-based research and practice. *School Social Work Journal, 32,* 14–28.

**McClernon, F. J., & Gilbert, D. G.** (2007). Smoking and stress. In G. Fink (Ed.), *Encyclopedia of stress: Vols. 1–4* (2nd ed., pp. 515–520). San Diego, CA: Elsevier Academic Press.

**McClure-Tone, E. B. & Pine, D. S.** (2009). Clinical features of the anxiety disorders. In B. J. Sadock, V. A. Sadock, & P. Ruiz (Eds.), *Kaplan & Sadock's comprehensive textbook of psychiatry* (pp. 1844–1555). Philadelphia: Lippincott Williams & Wilkins.

**McCoy, S. K., & Major, B.** (2003). Group identification moderates emotional responses to perceived prejudice. *Personality and Social Psychology Bulletin, 29,* 1005–1017.

**McCrae, R. R.** (1984). Situational determinants of coping responses: Loss, threat and challenge. *Journal of Personality and Social Psychology, 46,* 919–928.

**McCrae, R. R.** (1996). Social consequences of experimental openness. *Psychological Bulletin, 120,* 323–337.

**McCrae, R. R.** (2005). Personality structure. In V. A. Derlega, B. A. Winstead, & W. H. Jones (Eds.), *Personality: Contemporary theory and research.* Belmont, CA: Wadsworth.

**McCrae, R. R., & Costa, P. T., Jr.** (1987). Validation of the five-factor model of personality across instruments and observers. *Journal of Personality and Social Psychology, 52,* 81–90.

**McCrae, R. R., & Costa, P. T., Jr.** (1997). Personality trait structure as a human universal. *American Psychologist, 52,* 509–516.

**McCrae, R. R., & Costa, P. T., Jr.** (1999). A five-factor theory of personality. In L. A. Pervin, & O. P. John (Eds.), *Handbook of personality: Theory and research* (2nd ed.). New York: The Guilford Press.

**McCrae, R. R., & Costa, P. T., Jr.** (2003). *Personality in adulthood: A five-factor theory perspective.* New York: Guilford.

**McCrae, R. R., & Costa, P. T., Jr.** (2004). A contemplated revision of the NEO five-factor inventory. *Personality and Individual Differences, 36,* 587–596.

**McCrae, R. R., & Costa, P. T., Jr.** (2007). Brief versions of the NEO-PI-3. *Journal of Individual Differences, 28,* 116–128.

**McCrae, R. R., & Costa, P. T., Jr.** (2008a). Empirical and theoretical status of the five-factor model of personality traits. In G. J. Boyle, G. Matthews, D. H. Saklofske (Eds.), *The Sage handbook of personality theory and assessment* (pp. 273–294). Los Angeles: Sage.

**McCrae, R. R., & Costa, P. T., Jr.** (2008b). The five-factor theory of personality. In O. P. John, R. W. Robins, & L. A. Pervin (Eds.), *Handbook of personality: Theory and research* (pp. 159–181). New York: Guilford.

**McCrae, R. R., & Sutin, A. R.** (2009). Openness to experience. In M. R. Leary & R. H. Hoyle (Eds.), *Handbook of individual differences in social* behavior (pp. 257–274). New York: Guilford.

**McCrae, R. R., & Terracciano, A.** (2006). National character and personality. *Current Direction in Psychological Science, 15*(4), 156–161.

**McCrae, R. R., Terracciano, A., & 78 members of the Personality Profiles of Cultures Project.** (2005). Universal features of personality traits from the observer's perspective: Data from 50 cultures. *Journal of Personality and Social Psychology, 88,* 547–561.

**McCrea, S. M., Hirt, E. R., Hendrix, K. L., Milner, B. J., Steele, N. L.**(2008). The worker scale: Developing a measure to explain gender differences in behavioral self-handicapping. *Journal of Research in Personality, 42*(4), 949–970.

**McCreary, D. R., & Sadava, S. W.** (1998). Stress, drinking, and the adverse consequences of drinking in two samples of young adults. *Psychology of Addictive Behaviors, 12,* 247–261.

**McCullough, M. E.** (2001). Forgiving. In C. R. Snyder (Ed.), *Coping with stress: Effective people and processes.* New York: Oxford University Press.

**McCullough, M. E., Bellah, C. G., Kilpatrick, S. D., & Johnson, J. L.** (2001). Vengefulness: Relationships with forgiveness, rumination, well-being, and the Big Five. *Personality and Social Psychology Bulletin, 27*(5), 601–610.

**McCullough, M. E., Kilpatrick, S. D., Emmons, R. A., & Larson, D. B.** (1999). Gratitude as moral affect. *Psychological Bulletin, 127,* 249–266.

**McCullough, M. E., & Witvliet, C. V.** (2002). The psychology of forgiveness. In C. R. Synder & S. J. Lopez (Eds.), *Handbook of positive psychology.* New York: Oxford University Press.

**McCullough, M. E., & Witvliet, C. V.** (2005). The psychology of forgiveness. In C. R. Snyder & S. J. Lopez (Eds.), *Handbook of positive psychology.* New York: Oxford University Press.

**McDaniel, E., & Quasha, S.** (2000). The communicative aspects of doing business in Japan. In L. Samovar & R. Porter (Eds.), *Intercultural communication: A reader* (9th ed., pp. 312–324). Belmont, CA: Wadsworth.

**McDaniel, M. A., Waddill, P. J., & Shakesby, P. S.** (1996). Study strategies, interest, and learning from text: The application of material appropriate processing. In D. J. Herrmann, C. McEvoy, C. Hertzog, P. Hertel, & M. K. Johnson (Eds.), *Basic and applied memory research: Theory in context* (Vol. 1). Mahwah, NJ: Erlbaum.

**McDaniel, S. R., & Zuckerman, M.** (2003). The relationship of impulsive sensation seeking and gender to interest and participation in gambling activities. *Personality and Individual Differences, 35,* 1385–1400.

**McDonald, W. M., Thompson, T. R., McCall, W. V., & Zormuski, C. F.** (2004). In A. F. Schatzberg, & C. B. Nemeroff (Eds.), *Textbook of psychopharmacology.* Washington, DC: American Psychiatric Publishing.

**McDougle, L. G.** (1987). Time management: Making every minute count. In A. D. Timpe (Ed.), *The management of time.* New York: Facts on File.

**McEwen, B. S.** (2000). Stress, definitions and concepts of. In G. Fink (Ed.), *Encyclopedia of stress* (Vol. 3). San Diego: Academic Press.

**McEwen, B. S., & Lasley, E. N.** (2002). *The end of stress as we know it.* Washington, DC: Joseph Henry Press.

**McEwen, B. S., & Lasley, E. N.** (2007). Allostatic load: When protection gives way to damage. In A. Monat, R. S. Lazarus, & G. Reevy (Eds.), *The Praeger handbook on stress and coping* (pp. 99–111). Westport, CT: Praeger Publishers.

**McFarlane, M., Bull, S. S., & Rietmeijer, C. A.** (2000). The Internet as a newly emerging risk environment for sexually transmitted diseases. *Journal of the American Medical Association, 284,* 443–446.

**McGee, M.** (2005). *Self-help, Inc.: Makeover culture in American life.* New York: Oxford University Press.

**McGee-Cooper, A., & Trammell, D.** (1994). *Time management for unmanageable people.* New York: Bantam Books.

**McGlashan, T. H., & Fenton, W. S.** (1992). The positive-negative distinction in schizophrenia: Review of natural history validators. *Archives of General Psychiatry, 49,* 63–72.

**McGlashan, T. H., & Hoffman, R. E.** (2000). Schizophrenia: Psychodynamic to neurodynamic theories. In B. J. Sadock & V. A. Sadock (Eds.), *Kaplan and Sadock's comprehensive textbook of psychiatry* (7th ed., Vol. 1). Philadelphia: Lippincott/Williams & Wilkins.

**McGoldrick, M.** (1999). Becoming a couple. In B. Carter & M. McGoldrick (Eds.), *The expanded family life cycle: Individual, family, and social perspectives* (3rd ed.). Boston: Allyn & Bacon.

**McGraw, L. A., & Walker, A. J.** (2004). The more things change, the more they stay the same. In M. Coleman & L. H. Ganong (Eds.), *Handbook of contemporary families: Considering the past, contemplating the future.* Thousand Oaks, CA: Sage.

**McGregor, H. A., Lieberman, J. D., Greenberg, J., Solomon, S., Arndt, J., Simon, L., & Pyszczynski, T.** (1998). Terror management and aggression: Evidence that mortality salience motivates aggression against worldview-threatening others. *Journal of Personality and Social Psychology, 74*(3), 590–605.

**McGuire, W. J., & Padawer-Singer, A.** (1978). Trait salience in the spontaneous self-concept. *Journal of Personality and Social Psychology, 33,* 743–754.

**McHugh, M. C.** (2006). What do women want? A new view of women's sexual problems. *Sex Roles, 54,* 361–369.

**McHugh, P. R.** (1995). Dissociative identity disorder as a socially constructed artifact. *Journal of Practical Psychiatry and Behavioral Health, 1,* 158–166.

**McHugh, P. R., Lief, H. I., Freyd, P. P., & Fetkewicz, J. M.** (2004). From refusal to reconciliation: Family relationships after an accusation based on recovered memories. *Journal of Nervous and Mental Disease, 192,* 525–531.

**McIntyre, K. P., Korn, J. H., & Matsuo, H.** (2008). Sweating the small stuff: How different types of hassles result in the experience of stress. *Stress and Health, 24,* 383–392.

**McKay, A., & Holoway, P.** (1997). Sexual health education: A study of adolescents' opinions, self-perceived needs, and current and preferred sources of information. *Canadian Journal of Human Sexuality, 6,* 29–38.

**McKay, M., Davis, M., & Fanning, P.** (1995). *Messages: The communication skills book.* Oakland, CA: New Harbinger.

**McKay, M., & Fanning, P.** (2000). *Self-esteem* (3rd ed.). Oakland, CA: New Harbinger.

**Mckee-Ryan, F., Song, Z., Wanberg, C. R., & Kinicki, A. J.** (2005). Psychological and physical well-being unemployment: A meta-analytic study. *Journal of Applied Psychology, 90*(1), 53–76.

**McKeever, V. M., & Huff, M. E.** (2003). A diathesis-stress model of posttraumatic stress disorder: Ecological, biological and residual stress pathways. *Review of General Psychology, 7*(3), 237–250.

**McKenna, K. Y. A.** (2009). Internet, attraction on. In H. T. Reis & S. Sprecher (Eds.), *Encyclopedia of human relationships: Vol. 2* (pp. 881–884). Los Angeles: Sage Reference Publication.

**McKenna, K. Y. A., & Bargh, J. A.** (2000). Plan 9 from cyberspace: The implications of the Internet for personality and social psychology. *Personality and Social Psychology Review, 4*(1), 57–75.

**McKenna, K. Y. A., Green, A., & Gleason, M.** (2002). Relationship formation on the Internet: What's the big attraction? *Journal of Social Issues, 58,* 9–31.

**McKenna, M. C., Zevon, M. A., Corn, B., & Rounds, J.** (1999). Psychosocial factors and the development of breast cancer: A meta-analysis. *Health Psychology, 18*(5), 520–531.

**McLean, D. E., & Link, B. G.** (1994). Unraveling complexity: Strategies to refine concepts, measures, and research designs in the study of life events and mental health. In W. R. Avison & I. H. Gotlib (Eds.), *Stress and mental health: Contemporary issues and prospects for the future.* New York: Plenum Press.

**McMahon, F. J., & Kassem, L.** (2005). Anxiety disorders: Genetics. In B. J. Sadock & V. A. Sadock (Eds.), *Kaplan & Sadock's comprehensive textbook of psychiatry.* Philadelphia: Lippincott Williams & Wilkins.

**McManus, P. A., & DiPrete, T.** (2001). Losers and winners: Financial consequences of separation and divorce for men. *American Sociological Review, 66,* 246–268.

**McNally, R., & Breslau, N.** (2008). Does virtual trauma cause posttraumatic stress disorder? *American Psychologist, 63,* 282–283.

**McNally, R. J.** (1994). Cognitive bias in panic disorder. *Current Directions in Psychological Science, 3,* 129–132.

**McNally, R. J.** (1996). *Panic disorder: A critical analysis.* New York: Guilford Press.

**McNally, R. J.** (2004). Is traumatic amnesia nothing but psychiatric folklore? *Cognitive Behaviour Therapy, 33*(2), 97–101.

**McNally, R. J.** (2007). Betrayal trauma theory: A critical appraisal. *Memory, 15,* 280–294.

**McNally, R. J., & Geraerts, E.** (2009). A new solution to the recovered memory debate. *Perspectives on Psychological Science, 4*(2), 126–134.

**McNeil, T. F., Cantor-Graae, E., & Ismail, B.** (2000). Obstetrics complications and congenital malformation in schizophrenia. *Brain Research Reviews, 31,* 166–178.

**McPherson, M., Smith-Lovin, L., & Brashears, M. E.** (2006). Social isolation in America: Changes in core discussion networks over two decades. *American Sociological Review, 71,* 353–375.

**McQuillan, J., & Conde, G.** (1996). The conditions of flow in reading: Two studies of optimal experience. *Reading Psychology: An International Quarterly, 17,* 109–135.

**McWhirter, B. T.** (1990). Loneliness: A review of current literature, with implications for counseling and research. *Journal of Counseling and Development, 68,* 417–422.

**McWhorter, K. T.** (2007). *College reading & study skills.* New York: Pearson Longman.

**McWilliams, L. A., Becker, E. S., Margraf, J., Clara, I. P., & Vriends, N.** (2007). Anxiety disorders specificity of anxiety sensitivity in a community sample of young women. *Personality and Individual Differences, 42,* 345–354.

**McWilliams, N., & Weinberger, J.** (2003). Psychodynamic psychotherapy. In G. Stricker & T. A. Widiger (Eds.), *Handbook of psychology: Vol. 8. Clinical psychology.* New York: Wiley.

**Mead, M.** (1950). *Sex and temperament in three primitive societies.* New York: Mentor Books.

**Mechanic, D.** (1999). Mental health and mental illness. In A. V. Horvitz & T. L. Scheid (Eds.), *A handbook for the study of mental health: Social contexts, theories, and systems.* New York: Cambridge University Press.

**Mednick, S. A., Machon, R. A., Huttunen, M. O., & Bonett, D.** (1988). Adult schizophrenia following prenatal exposure to an influenza epidemic. *Archives of General Psychiatry, 45,* 189–192.

**Mednick, S. A., Watson, J. B., Huttunen, M., Cannon, T. D., Katila, H., Machon, R., Mednick, B., Hollister, M., Parnas, J., Schulsinger, F., Sajaniemi, N., Voldsgaard, P., Pyhala, R., Gutkind, D., & Wang, X.** (1998). A two-hit working model of the etiology of schizophrenia. In M. F. Lenzenweger & R. H. Dworkin (Eds.), *Origins and development of schizophrenia: Advances in experimental psychopathology.* Washington DC: American Psychological Association.

**Medora, N. P., Larson, J. H., Hortacsu, N., & Dave, P.** (2002). Perceived attitudes towards romanticism: A cross-cultural study of American, Asian-Indian, and Turkish young adults. *Journal of Comparative Family Studies, 33*(2), 155–178.

**Meece, J. L., & Scantlebury, K.** (2006). Gender and schooling: Progress and persistent barriers. In J. Worrell & C. D. Goodheart (Eds.), *Handbook of girls' and women's psychological health.* New York: Oxford University Press.

**Mehrabian, A.** (2008). Communication without words. In C. D. Mortensen (Ed.), *Communication theory* (2nd ed., pp. 193–200). New Brunswick, NJ: Transaction Publishers.

**Meichenbaum, D.** (1977). *Cognitive-behavior modification.* New York: Plenum.

**Meichenbaum, D.** (1993). Stress inoculation training: A 20-year update. In P. M. Lehrer & R. L. Woolfolk (Eds.), *Principles and practice of stress management* (2nd ed.). New York: Guilford Press.

**Meijer, A. M., & van den Wittenboer, G. L. H.** (2007). Contribution of infants' sleep and crying to marital relationship of first-time parent couples in the 1st year after childbirth. *Journal of Family Psychology, 21,* 49–57.

**Meissner, C. A., & Brigham, J. C.** (2001). Thirty years of investigating the own-race bias in memory for faces: A meta-analytic review. *Psychology, Public Policy, and Law, 7,* 3–35.

**Melanson, K. J.** (2007). Dietary factors in reducing risk of cardiovascular diseases. *American Journal of Lifestyle Medicine, 1*(1), 24–28.

**Melby, T.** (2007). Open relationships, open lives. *Contemporary Sexuality, 41,* 1–5.

**Melby, T.** (2008). How second life seeps into real life. *Contemporary Sexuality, 42,* 4–6.

**Melchior, M., Caspi, A., Milne, B. J., Danese, A., Poulton, R., & Moffitt, T. E.** (2007). Work stress precipitates depression and anxiety in young working men and women. *Psychological Medicine, 37,* 1119–1129.

**Mellers, B. A., & McGraw, A. P.** (2001). Anticipated emotions as guides to choice. *Current Directions in Psychological Science, 10,* 210–214.

**Mellers, B. A., Richards, V., & Birnbaum, M. H.** (1992). Distributional theories of impression formation. *Organizational Behavior and Human Decision Processes, 51,* 313–343.

**Melson, G. F.** (2001). *Why the wild things are: Animals in the lives of children.* Cambridge, MA: Harvard University Press.

**Melson, G. F.** (2003). Child development and the human-companion animal bond. *American Behavioral Scientist, 47,* 31–39.

**Meltzer, H. Y., Davidson, M., Glassman, A. H., & Vieweg, V. R.** (2002). Assessing cardiovascular risks versus clinical benefits of atypical antipsychotic drug treatment. *Journal of Clinical Psychiatry, 63*(9), 25–29.

**Mendoza-Denton, R., Park, S. H., & O'Connor, A.** (2008). Gender stereotypes as situation-behavior profiles. *Journal of Experimental Social Psychology, 44*(4), 971–982.

**Menec, V. H.** (2003). The relation between everyday activities and successful aging: A 6-year longitudinal study. *Journal of Gerontology, 58,* 74–82.

**Menton, C. M., & Buss, D. M.** (2007). Why humans have sex. *Archives of Sexual Behavior, 36,* 477–507.

**Menzel, P., & D'Alusio, F.** (2005). *Hungry planet: What the world eats.* Napa, CA: Material World Books.

**Mergen, B.** (2003). Review essay: Children and nature in history. *Environmental History, 8*(4).

**Merikangas, K. R., Ames, M., Cui, L., Stang, P. E., Ustun, T. B., Von Korff, M., et al.** (2007). The impact of comorbidity of mental and physical conditions on role disability in the U.S. adult household population. *Archive of General Psychiatry, 64,* 1180–1188.

**Merikangas, K. R., & Kalaydjian, A. E.** (2009). Epidemiology of anxiety disorders. In B. J. Sadock, V. A. Sadock, & P. Ruiz (Eds.), *Kaplan & Sadock's comprehensive textbook of psychiatry* (pp. 1856–1863). Philadelphia: Lippincott Williams & Wilkins.

**Merikangas, K. R., & Risch, N.** (2003). Will the genomics revolution revolutionize psychiatry? *American Journal of Psychiatry, 160,* 625–635.

**Merritt, M. M., Bennett, G. G., Williams, R. B., Sollers, J. J., III, & Thayer, J. F.** (2004). Low educational attainment, John Henryism, and cardiovascular reactivity to and recovery from personally relevant stress. *Psychosomatic Medicine, 66,* 49–55.

**Merton, R.** (1948). The self-fulfilling prophecy. *Antioch Review, 8,* 193–210.

**Mesch, G. S., & Talmund, I.** (2007). Similarity and the quality of online and offline social relationships among adolescents in Israel. *Journal of Research on Adolescence, 17,* 455–466.

**Messineo, M. J.** (2008). Does advertising on Black Entertainment Television portray more positive gender representation compared to broadcast networks? *Sex Roles, 59,* 752–764.

**Meston, C. M., & Buss, D.** (2007). Why humans have sex. *Archives of Sexual Behavior, 36,* 477–507.

**Metz, M. E., & Pryor, J. L.** (2000). Premature ejaculation: A psychological approach for assessment and management. *Journal of Sex and Marital Therapy, 26,* 293–320.

**Metzger, E. D.** (1999). Electroconvulsive therapy. In A. M. Nicholi (Ed.), *The Harvard guide to psychiatry.* Cambridge, MA: Harvard University Press.

**Meyer, I. H.** (2003). Minority stress and mental health in gay men. In L. D. Garnets & D. C. Kimmel (Eds.), *Psychological perspectives on lesbian, gay, and bisexual experiences.* New York: Columbia University Press.

**Meyers, S. A., & Landsberger, S. A.** (2002). Direct and indirect pathways between adult attachment style and marital satisfaction. *Personal Relationships, 9*(2), 159–172.

**Michaels, S.** (1996). The prevalence of homosexuality in the United States. In R. P. Cabaj & T. S. Stein (Eds.), *Textbook of homosexuality and mental health.* Washington, DC: American Psychiatric Press.

**Michaud, S. L., & Warner, R. M.** (1997). Gender differences in self-reported response to troubles talk. *Sex Roles, 37*(7–8), 527–540.

**Mickelson, K. D., Kessler, R. C., & Shaver, P. R.** (1997). Adult attachment in a nationally representative sample. *Journal of Personality and Social Psychology, 73,* 1092–1106.

**Miklowitz, D. J., & Johnson, S. L.** (2007). Bipolar disorders. In M. Hersen, S. M. Turner, & D. C. Beidel (Eds.), *Adult psychopathology and diagnosis.* New York: Wiley.

**Mikulincer, M.** (2006). Attachment, caregiving, and sex within romantic relationships: A behavioral systems perspective. In M. Mikulincer & G. S. Goodman (Eds.), *Dynamics of romantic love: Attachment, caregiving, and sex.* New York: The Guilford Press.

**Mikulincer, M., Florian, V., & Tolmacz, R.** (1990). Attachment styles and fear of personal death: A case study of affect regulation. *Journal of Personality and Social Psychology, 58,* 273–280.

**Mikulincer, M., & Shaver, P. R.** (2003). The attachment behavioral system in adulthood: Activation, psychodynamics, and interpersonal processes. In Mark P. Zanna (Ed.), *Advances in Experimental Social Psychology* (Vol. 35). San Diego: Academic Press.

**Milgram, N., Marshevsky, S., & Sadeh, C.** (1995). Correlates of academic procrastination: Discomfort, task aversiveness, and task capability. *Journal of Psychology, 129,* 145–155.

**Milgram, S.** (1963). Behavioral study of obedience. *Journal of Abnormal and Social Psychology, 67*, 371–378.

**Milgram, S.** (1974). *Obedience to authority.* New York: Harper & Row.

**Milinski, M., Sommerfeld, R. D., Krambeck, H. J., Reed, F. A., & Marotzke, J.** (2008). The collective-risk social dilemma and the prevention of simulated dangerous climate change. *Proceedings of the National Academy of Sciences, 105*, 2291–2294.

**Miller, D. T., & Ross, M.** (1975). Self-serving biases in the attribution of causality: Fact or fiction? *Psychological Bulletin, 82*, 213–225.

**Miller, G. E., & Blackwell, E.** (2006). Turning up the heat: Inflammation as a mechanism linking chronic stress, depression, and heart disease. *Current Directions in Psychological Science, 15*, 269–272.

**Miller, G. P.** (1978). *Life choices: How to make the critical decisions—about your education, career, marriage, family, life style.* New York: Thomas Y. Crowell.

**Miller, G. T.** (2007). *Living in the environment: Principles, connections and solutions* (14th ed.). Belmont, CA: Wadsworth/Thompson Learning.

**Miller, I. J.** (1996). Managed care is harmful to outpatient mental health services: A call for accountability. *Professional Psychology: Research and Practice, 27*, 349–363.

**Miller, J. G.** (1984). Culture and the development of everyday social explanation. *Journal of Personality and Social Psychology, 46*, 961–978.

**Miller, L. C., Berg, J. H., & Archer, R. L.** (1983). Openers: Individuals who elicit intimate self-disclosure. *Journal of Personality and Social Psychology, 44*, 1234–1244.

**Miller, N. E.** (1944). Experimental studies of conflict. In J. McV. Hunt (Ed.), *Personality and the behavior disorders* (Vol. 1). New York: Ronald.

**Miller, N. E.** (1959). Liberalization of basic S-R concepts: Extension to conflict behavior, motivation, and social learning. In S. Koch (Ed.), *Psychology: A study of a science.* (Vol. 2). New York: McGraw-Hill.

**Miller, R. B., Yorgason, J. B., Sandberg, J. G., & White, M. B.** (2003). Problems that couples bring to therapy: A view across the life cycle. *American Journal of Family Therapy, 31*, 395–407.

**Miller, R. S.** (2008). Attending to temptation: The operation (and perils) of attention to alternatives in close relationships. In J. P. Forgas & J. Fitness (Eds.), *Social relationships: Cognitive, affective, and motivational processes* (pp. 321–337). New York: Psychology Press.

**Miller, R. S., Perlman, D., & Brehm, S. S.** (2007). *Intimate relationships.* Boston: McGraw-Hill.

**Miller, S. L., & Maner, J. K.** (2008). Coping with romantic betrayal: Sex differences in responses to partner infidelity. *Evolutionary Psychology, 6*, 413–426.

**Miller, T.** (2000). Diagnostic evaluation of erectile dysfunction. *American Family Physician, 61*, 95–104.

**Miller, T. W.** (2007). Trauma, change, and psychological health in the 21st century. *American Psychologist, 62*, 889–898.

**Millett, K.** (1970). *Sexual politics.* Garden City, NY: Doubleday.

**Millman, R. B., & Beeder, A. B.** (1994). The new psychedelic culture: LSD, ecstasy, "rave" parties and the Grateful Dead. *Psychiatric Annals, 24*(3), 148–150.

**Mills, J., & Clark, M. C.** (2001). Viewing close romantic relationships as communal relationships: Implications for maintenance and enhancement. In J. H. Harvey & A. Wenzel (Eds.), *Close romantic relationships: Maintenance and enhancement.* Mahwah, NJ: Erlbaum.

**Mineka, S., & Öhman, A.** (2002). Phobias and preparedness: The selective, automatic and encapsulated nature of fear. *Biological Psychiatry, 52*, 927–937.

**Mineka, S., & Zinbarg, S.** (2006). A contemporary learning theory perspective on the etiology of anxiety disorders: It's not what you thought it was. *American Psychologist, 61*, 10–26.

**Mino, I., Profit, W. E., & Pierce, C. M.** (2000). Minorities and stress. In G. Fink (Ed.), *Encyclopedia of stress* (Vol. 1). San Diego: Academic Press.

**Minzenberg, M. J., Yoon, J. H., & Carter, C. S.** (2008). Schizophrenia. In R. E. Hales, S. C. Yudofsky, & G. O. Gabbard (Eds.), *The American psychiatric publishing textbook of psychiatry* (pp. 407–456). Washington, DC: American Psychiatric Publishing.

**Miranda, J., Bernal, G., Lau, A., Kohn, L., Hwang, W., & LaFromboise, T.** (2005). State of the science on psychosocial interventions for ethnic minorities. *Annual Review of Clinical Psychology, 1*, 113–142.

**Mischel, W.** (1973). Toward a cognitive social learning conceptualization of personality. *Psychological Review, 80*, 252–283.

**Mischel, W.** (1990). Personality dispositions revisited and revised: A view after three decades. In L. A. Pervin (Ed.), *Handbook of personality: Theory and research.* New York: Guilford Press.

**Mischel, W., & Mischel, H. N.** (1976). A cognitive social learning approach to morality and self-regulation. In T. Lickona (Ed.), *Moral development and behavior: Theory, research and social issues.* New York: Holt, Rinehart & Winston.

**Mischel, W., & Morf, C. C.** (2003). The self as a psychosocial dynamic processing system: A meta-perspective on a century of the self in psychology. In M. R. Leary & J. P. Tangney (Eds.), *Handbook of self and identity.* New York: Guilford.

**Mischel, W., Shoda, Y., & Peake, P. K.** (1988). The nature of adolescent competencies predicted by preschool delay of gratification. *Journal of Personality and Social Psychology, 54*, 687–696.

**Misra, R., & Castillo, L. G.** (2001). Academic stress among college students: Comparison of American and international students. *International Journal of Stress Management, 11*(2), 132–148.

**Mitchell, A. E., Castellani, A. M., Herrington, R. L., Joseph, J. I., Doss, B. D., & Snyder, D. K.** (2008). Predictors of intimacy in couples' discussions of relationship injuries: An observational study. *Journal of Family Psychology, 22*, 21–29.

**Mitchell, B. A.** (2006). *The boomerang age: Transitions to adulthood in families.* New Brunswick, NJ: Aldine Transaction.

**Mitchell, V. F.** (1987). Rx for improving staff effectiveness. In A. D. Timpe (Ed.), *The management of time.* New York: Facts on File.

**Miyamoto, Y., & Kitayama, S.** (2002). Cultural variation in correspondence bias: The critical role of attitude diagnosticity of socially constrained behavior. *Journal of Personality and Social Psychology, 83*(5), 1239–1248.

**Miyamoto, Y., Nisbett, R. E., & Masuda, T.** (2006). Culture and the physical environment: Holistic versus analytic perceptual affordances. *Psychological Science, 17*, 113–119.

**Moak, D. H., & Anton, R. F.** (1999). Alcohol. In B. S. McCrady & E. E. Epstein (Eds.), *Addictions: A comprehensive guidebook.* New York: Oxford University Press.

**Modestin, J.** (1992). Multiple personality disorder in Switzerland. *American Journal of Psychiatry, 149*, 88–92.

**Moe, A., & De Bini, R.** (2004). Studying passages with the loci method: Are subject-generated more effective than experimenter-supplied loci pathways? *Journal of Mental Imagery, 28*(3–4), 75–86.

**Mohren, D. C. L., Swaen, G. M. H., Kant, I., van Schayck, C. P., & Galama, J. M. D.** (2005). Fatigue and job stress as predictors for sickness absence during common infections. *International Journal of Behavioral Medicine, 12*(1), 11–20.

**Mojtabai, R., & Olfson, M.** (2008). National trends in psychotherapy by office-based psychiatrists. *Archives of General Psychiatry, 65*, 962–970.

**Mojtabai, R., Olfson, M., & Mechanic, D.** (2002). Perceived need and help-seeking in adults with mood, anxiety, or substance use disorder. *Archives of General Psychiatry, 59*, 77–84.

**Mokdad, A. H., Marks, J. S., Stroup, D. F., & Gerberding, J. L.** (2004). Actual causes of death in the United States, 2000. *Journal of the American Medical Association, 291*, 1238–1245.

**Molloy, G. J., Perkins-Porras, L., Bhattacharyya, M. R., Strike, P. C., & Steptoe, A.** (2008). Practical support predicts medication adherence and attendance at cardiac rehabilitation following acute coronary syndrome. *Journal of Psychosomatic Research, 65*(6), 581–586.

**Molloy, G. J., Perkins-Porras, L., Strike, P., & Steptoe, A.** (2008). Social networks and partner stress as predictors of adherence to medication, rehabilitation attendance, and quality of life following acute coronary syndrome. *Health Psychology, 27*, 52–58.

**Monastra, V. J.** (2008). Social skills training for children and teens with ADHD: The neuroeducational life skills program. In V. J. Monastra (Ed.), *Unlocking the potential of patients with ADHD: A model for clinical practice.* Washington, DC: American Psychological Association.

**Moncrieff, J.** (2001). Are antidepressants overrated? A review of methodological problems in antidepressant trials. *Journal of Nervous and Mental Disorders, 189*, 288–295.

**Monroe, S. M., & Hadjiyannakis, K.** (2002). The social environment and depression: Focusing on severe life stress. In I. H. Gotlib & C. L. Hammen (Eds.), *Handbook of depression.* New York: Guilford.

**Monroe, S. M., & Kelley, J. M.** (1995). Measurement of stress appraisal. In S. Cohen, R. C. Kessler, & L. U. Gordon (Eds.), *Measuring stress: A guide for health and social scientists.* New York: Oxford University Press.

**Monroe, S. M., & McQuaid, J. R.** (1994). Measuring life stress and assessing its impact on mental health. In W. R. Avison & I. H. Gotlib (Eds.), *Stress and mental health: Contemporary issues and prospects for the future.* New York: Plenum.

**Monroe, S. M., & Reid, M. W.** (2009). Life stress and major depression. *Current Directions in Psychological Science, 18*, 68–72.

**Monroe, S. M., & Slavich, G. M.** (2007). Psychological stressors, overview. In G. Fink (Ed.), *Encyclopedia of stress: Vols. 1–4* (2nd ed., pp. 278–283). San Diego, CA: Elsevier Academic Press.

**Monroe, S. M., Slavich, G. M., & Georgiades, K.** (2009). The social environment and life stress in depression. In I. H. Gotlib & C. L. Hammen (Eds.), *Handbook of depression* (pp. 340–360). New York: Guilford.

**Moore, D. S., & Johnson, S. P.** (2008). Mental rotation in human infants. *Psychological Science, 19*, 1063–1066.

**Moore, D. W.** (2001, August 31). *Most American workers satisfied with their job: One-third would be happier in another job.* [On-line]. The Gallup Organization. Available: www.gallup.com/poll/releases/pr010831.asp. Retrieved 1/19/2002.

**Moore, D. W.** (2003, January 3). *Family, health most important aspects of life.* Retrieved January 20, 2005, from http://www.Gallup.Com/Poll/Content/?Ci=7504.

**Moore, M. K.** (1992). An empirical investigation of the relationship between religiosity and death concern. *Dissertation Abstracts International, 53*, 527.

**Moore, R. C.** (1999). Healing gardens for children. In C. Cooper Marcus and M. Barnes (Eds.), *Healing gardens: Therapeutic benefits and design recommendations* (pp. 323–384). New York: Wiley.

**Moos, R. H., & Billings, A. G.** (1982). Conceptualizing and measuring coping resources and processes. In L. Goldberger & S. Breznitz (Eds.), *Handbook of stress: Theoretical and clinical aspects.* New York: Free Press.

**Moos, R. H., & Schaefer, J. A.** (1993). Coping resources and processes: Current concepts and measures. In L. Goldberger & S. Breznitz (Eds.), *Handbook of stress: Theoretical and clinical aspects* (2nd ed.). New York: Free Press.

**Moradi, B., & Risco, C.** (2006). Perceived discrimination experiences and mental health of Latina/o American persons. *Journal of Counseling Psychology, 53*, 411–421.

**Morahan-Martin, J., & Schumacher, P.** (2000). Incidence and correlates of pathological Internet use among college students. *Computers in Human Behavior, 16*(1), 13–29.

**Morahan-Martin, J., & Schumacher, P.** (2003). Loneliness and social uses of the Internet. *Computers in Human Behavior, 19*(6), 659–671.

**Moray, N.** (1959). Attention in dichotic listening: Affective cues and the influence of instructions. *Quarterly Journal of Experimental Psychology, 11*, 56–60.

**Morell, C.** (2000). Saying no: Women's experiences with reproductive refusal. *Feminism & Psychology, 10*, 313–322.

**Moretti, M. M., & Higgins, E. T.** (1990). Relating self-discrepancy to self-esteem: The contribution of discrepancy beyond actual-self ratings. *Journal of Experimental Social Psychology, 26*, 108–123.

**Morgan, H. J., & Janoff-Bulman, R.** (1994). Victims' responses to traumatic life events: An unjust world or an uncaring world? *Social Justice Research, 7*, 47–68.

**Morgan, M. J.** (2000). Ecstasy (MDMA): A review of its possible persistent psychological effects. *Psychopharmacology, 152*(3), 230–248.

**Morgan, R. D., & Cohen, L. M.** (2008). Clinical and counseling psychology: Can differences be gleaned from printed recruiting materials? *Training and Education in Professional Psychology, 2*(3), 156–164.

**Morgenstern, J.** (2000). *Time management from the inside out.* New York: Holt.

**Morley, J. E., & Perry H. M.** (2003). Androgens and women at the menopause and beyond. *The Journal of Gerontology, 58*(5), 409–416.

**Morris, M. A. & Campion, J. E.** (2003). *New use for an old tool: Vocational interests and outcomes.* Poster presented at the 18th annual meeting of the Society for Industrial and Organizational Psychology, Orlando, FL.

**Morris, M. W., & Peng, K.** (1994). Culture and cause: American and Chinese attributions for social and physical events. *Journal of Personality and Social Psychology, 67*, 949–971.

**Morris, W. L., & DePaulo, B. M.** (2009). Singlehood. In H. T. Reis & S. Sprecher (Eds.), *Encyclopedia of human relationships: Vol. 3* (pp. 1504–1507). Los Angeles: Sage Reference Publication.

**Morris, W. N.** (1999). The mood system. In D. Kahneman, E. Diener, & N. Schwartz (Eds.), *Well-being:*

*The foundations of hedonic psychology* (pp. 169–189). New York: Russell Sage Foundation.

**Morrison, D. R., & Coiro, M. J.** (1999). Parental conflict and marital disruption: Do children benefit when high-conflict marriages are dissolved? *Journal of Marriage and the Family, 61,* 626–637.

**Morrison, T. G., Morrison, M. A., & Hopkins, C.** (2003). Striving for bodily perfection? An exploration of the drive for masculinity in Canadian men. *Psychology of Men and Masculinity, 4*(2), 111–120.

**Morrow, G. D.** (2009). Exchange processes. In H. T. Reis & S. Sprecher (Eds.), *Encyclopedia of human relationships: Vol. 1* (pp. 551–555). Los Angeles: Sage Reference Publication.

**Morry, M. M.** (2007). The attraction-similarity hypothesis among cross-sex friends: Relationship satisfactions, perceived similarities, and self-serving perceptions. *Journal of Social and Personal Relationships, 24,* 117–138.

**Morry, M. M.** (2009). Similarity principle of attraction. In H. T. Reis & S. Sprecher (Eds.), *Encyclopedia of human relationships: Vol. 3* (pp. 1500–1504). Los Angeles: Sage Reference Publication.

**Mortenson, S. T.** (2006). Cultural differences and similarities in seeking support as a response to academic failure: A comparison of American and Chinese college students. *Communication Education, 55*(2), 127–146.

**Moseman, S. E., Freeman, M. P., Misiaszek, J., & Gelenberg, A. J.** (2003). Mood stabilizers. In A. Tasman, J. Kay, & J. A. Lieberman (Eds.), *Psychiatry.* New York: Wiley.

**Mosher, D. L.** (1991). Macho men, machismo, and sexuality. *Annual Review of Sex Research, 2,* 199–248.

**Mosher, W. D., Chandra, A., & Jones, J.** (2005). *Sexual behavior and selected health measures: Men and women 15–44 years of age, United States, 2002.* Hyattsville, MD: National Center for Health Statistics.

**Moskowitz, D. S.** (1994). Cross-situational generality and the interpersonal circumplex. *Journal of Personality and Social Psychology, 66,* 921–933.

**Mowrer, O. H.** (1947). On the dual nature of learning: A reinterpretaton of "conditioning" and "problem-solving." *Harvard Educational Review, 17,* 102–150.

**Moynihan, J. A., & Ader, R.** (1996). Psychoneuroimmunology: Animal models of disease. *Psychosomatic Medicine, 58,* 546–558.

**Mroczek, D. K., & Almeida, D. M.** (2004). The effect of daily stress, personality, and age on daily negative affect. *Journal of Personality, 72,* 355–378.

**Muehlenhard, C. L., & McCoy, M. L.** (1991). Double standard/double bind: The sexual double standard and women's communication about sex. *Psychology of Women Quarterly, 15,* 447–461.

**Mukamal, K. J., Conigrave, K. M., Mittleman, M. A., Camargo, C. A., Stampfer, M. J., Willet, W. C., & Rimm, E. B.** (2003). Roles of drinking pattern and type of alcohol consumed in coronary heart disease in men. *New England Journal of Medicine, 348*(2), 109–118.

**Mulhall, J., King, R., Glina, S., & Hvidsten, K.** (2008). Importance of and satisfaction with sex among men and women worldwide: Results of the Global Better Sex Survey. *Journal of Sexual Medicine, 5,* 788–795.

**Munck, A.** (2000). Corticosteroids and stress. In G. Fink (Ed.), *Encyclopedia of stress* (Vol. 1). San Diego: Academic Press.

**Munsey, C.** (2008). Prescriptive authority in the states: A look at which states allow RxP and which have considered it. *Monitor on Psychology, 39*(2).

**Muris, P.** (2002). Relationships between self-efficacy and symptoms of anxiety disorders and depression in a normal adolescent sample. *Personality and Individual Differences, 32,* 337–348.

**Murison, R., & Milde, A. M.** (2007). Gastrointestinal effects. In G. Fink (Ed.), *Encyclopedia of stress: Vols. 1–4* (2nd ed., pp. 109–114). San Diego, CA: Elsevier Academic Press.

**Murphy, S. E., & Zagorski, D. A.** (2005). Enhancing work-family and work-life interaction: The role of management. In D. F. Halpern & S. E. Murphy (Eds.), *From work-family balance to work-family interaction: Changing the metaphor.* Mahwah, NJ: Erlbaum.

**Murray, C.** (2001). *Family formation.* Washington, DC: American Enterprise Institute.

**Murray, H. A.** (1971). *Thematic Apperception Test.* Cambridge, MA: Harvard University Press.

**Murray, R. M., & Bramon, E.** (2005). Developmental model of schizophrenia. In B. J. Sadock & V. A. Sadock (Eds.), *Kaplan & Sadock's comprehensive textbook of psychiatry.* Philadelphia: Lippincott Williams & Wilkins.

**Murray, S. L., Holmes, J. G., & Griffin, D. W.** (1996). The self-fulfilling nature of positive illusions in romantic relationships: Love is not blind, but prescient. *Journal of Personality and Social Psychology, 71,* 1155–1180.

**Murrell, A. J., Dietz-Uhler, B. L., Dovidio, J. F., Gaertner, S. L., & Drout, E.** (1994). Aversive racism and resistance to affirmative action: Perceptions of justice are not necessarily color blind. *Basic and Applied Social Psychology, 17*(1–2), 71–86.

**Murrell, A. J., & James, E. H.** (2001). Gender and diversity in organizations: Past, present, and future directions. *Sex Roles, 45*(5/6), 243–257.

**Muse, L. A., Harris, S. G., & Field, H. S.** (2003). Has the inverted-U theory of stress and job performance had a fair test? *Human Performance, 16,* 349–364.

**Mussweiler, T., & Rütter, K.** (2003). What are friends for! The use of routine standards in social comparison. *Journal of Personality and Social Psychology, 85,* 467–481.

**Mussweiler, T., Rütter, K., & Epstude, K.** (2004). The man who wasn't there: Subliminal social comparison standards influence self-evaluation. *Journal of Experimental Social Psychology, 40,* 689–696.

**Mussweiler, T., & Strack, F.** (2000). The "relative self": Informational and judgmental consequences of comparative self-evaluation. *Journal of Personality and Social Psychology, 79,* 23–38.

**Myers, D.** (2010). *Social psychology* (10th ed.). New York: McGraw-Hill.

**Myers, D. G.** (1980). *Inflated self: Human illusions and the biblical call to hope.* New York: Seabury Press.

**Myers, D. G.** (1992). *The pursuit of happiness: Who is happy—and why.* New York: Morrow.

**Myers, D. G.** (1999). Close relationships and quality of life. In D. Kahneman, E. Diener, & N. Schwarz (Eds.), *Well-being: The foundations of hedonic psychology.* New York: Sage.

**Myers, D. G.** (2000a). The funds, friends, and faith of happy people. *American Psychologist, 55,* 56–67.

**Myers, D. G.** (2000b). *The American paradox: Spiritual hunger in an age of plenty.* New Haven, CT: Yale University Press.

**Myers, D. G.** (2008). Religion and human flourishing. In M. Eid & R. J. Larsen (Eds.), *The science of subjective well-being* (pp. 323–346). New York: Guilford.

**Myers, D. G., & Diener, E.** (1995). Who is happy? *Psychological Science, 6,* 10–19.

**Myers, D. G., & Diener, E.** (1997). The pursuit of happiness. *Scientific American, Special Issue 7,* 40–43.

**Myers, G.** (2007). *The significance of children and animals: Social development and our connections to other species.* West Lafayette, IN: Purdue University Press.

**Myers, O. E.** (1998). *Children and animals: Social development and our connection to other species.* Boulder, CO: Westview Press.

**Myers, O. E., & Saunders, C. D.** (2002). Animals as links toward developing caring relationships with the natural world. In P. H. Kahn, Jr. & S. R. Kellert (Eds.), *Children and nature: Psychological, sociocultural, and evolutionary investigations* (pp. 153–178). Cambridge, MA: MIT Press.

**Myrtek, M.** (2007). Type A behavior and hostility as independent risk factors for coronary heart disease. In J. Jochen, B. Barde, & A. M. Zeiher (Eds.), *Contributions toward evidence-based psychocardiology: A systematic review of the literature.* Washington, DC: American Psychological Association.

**Nabi, R. L.** (2009). Cosmetic surgery makeover programs and intentions to undergo cosmetic enhancements: A consideration of three models of media effects. *Human Communication Research, 35,* 1–27.

**Nadelson, C. C., Notman, M. T., & McCarthy, M. K.** (2005). Gender issues in psychotherapy. In G. O. Gabbard, J. S. Beck, & J. Holmes (Eds.), *Oxford textbook of psychotherapy.* New York: Oxford University Press.

**Naglieri, J. A., Drasgow, F., Schmit, M., Handler, L., Prifitera, A., Margolis, A., et al.** (2004). Psychological testing on the Internet: New problems, old issues. *American Psychologist, 59,* 150–162.

**Nahas, Z., Kozel, F. A., Molnar, C., Ramsey, D., Holt, R., Ricci, R., et al.** (2007). Methods of administering transcranial magnetic stimulation. In M. S. George & R. H. Belmaker (Eds.), *Transcranial magnetic stimulation in clinical psychiatry* (pp. 39–58). Washington, DC: American Psychiatric Publishing.

**Nakamura, J., & Csikszentmihalyi, M.** (2002). The concept of flow. In C. R. Snyder & S. J. Lopez (Eds.), *Handbook of positive psychology* (pp. 89–105). New York: Oxford.

**Nakamura, J., & Csikszentmihalyi, M.** (2009). Flow theory and research. In S. J. Lopez & C. R. Snyder(Eds.), *Oxford handbook of positive psychology* (2nd ed., pp. 195–206). New York: Oxford.

**Nalwa, K., & Anand, A. P.** (2003). Internet addiction in students: A cause of concern. *CyberPsychology and Behavior, 6*(6), 653–656.

**Nardi, P. M.** (2007). Friendship, sex, and masculinity. In M. Kimmel (Ed.), *The sexual self: The construction of sexual scripts* (pp. 49–57). Nashville, TN: Vanderbilt University Press.

**Narrow, W. E., Rae, D. S., Robins, L. N., & Regier, D. A.** (2002). Revised prevalence based estimates of mental disorders in the United States: Using a clinical significance criterion to reconcile 2 surveys' estimates. *Archives of General Psychology, 59*(2), 115–123.

**Narrow, W. E., Regier, D. A., Rae, D. S., Manderscheid, R. W., & Locke, B. Z.** (1993). Use of services by persons with mental and addictive disorders: Findings from the National Institute of Mental Health Epidemiologic Catchment Area Program. *Archives of General Psychiatry, 50,* 95–107.

**NASA.** (2007, May 9). *NASA study suggests extreme summer warming in the future.* Retrieved from http://www.giss.nasa.gov/research/news/20070509/

**Nathan, P. E., & Langenbucher, J.** (2003). Diagnosis and classification. In G. Stricker & T. A. Widiger (Eds.), *Handbook of psychology: Vol. 8. Clinical psychology.* New York: Wiley.

**National Center for Health Statistics.** (2006). *Chartbook on trends in the health of Americans. Health, United States, 2006.* Hyattsville, MD: Public Health Service.

**Naylor, T. H., Willimon, W. H., & Naylor, M. R.** (1994). *The search for meaning.* Nashville: Abingdon Press.

**Neese, R. M., & Young, E. A.** (2000). Evolutionary origins and functions of the stress response. In G. Fink (Ed.), *Encyclopedia of stress* (Vol. 2). San Diego: Academic Press.

**Neff, L. A.** (2009). Physical attractiveness, role in relationships. In H. T. Reis & S. Sprecher (Eds.), *Encyclopedia of human relationships: Vol. 3* (pp. 1242–1245). Los Angeles: Sage Reference Publication.

**Negy, C., Schwartz, S., & Reig-Ferrer, A.** (2009). Violated expectations and acculturative stress among U.S. Hispanic immigrants. *Cultural Diversity and Ethnic Minority Psychology, 15,* 255–264.

**Neighbors, H. W., Caldwell, C., Williams, D. R., Nesse, R., Taylor, R. J., Bullard, K. M., et al.** (2007). Race, ethnicity, and the use of services for mental disorders: Results from the National Survey of American Life. *Archives of General Psychiatry, 64,* 485–494.

**Neimeyer, R. A., & Van Brunt, D.** (1995). Death anxiety. In H. Wass & R. A. Neimeyer (Eds.), *Dying: Facing the facts* (3rd ed.). Washington, DC: Taylor & Francis.

**Neiss, R.** (1988). Reconceptualizing arousal: Psychobiological states in motor performance. *Psychological Bulletin, 103,* 345–366.

**Neiss, R.** (1990). Ending arousal's reign of error: A reply to Anderson. *Psychological Bulletin, 107,* 101–105.

**Nelson, C., & Demas, G. E.** (2004). Seasonal patterns of stress, disease, and sickness responses. *Current Directions in Psychological Science, 13,* 198–201.

**Nelson, D. L., & Cooper, C. L.** (Eds.). (2007). *Positive organizational behavior.* London: Sage.

**Nelson, E. L., Wenzel, L., Osann, K., Dogan-Ates, A., Chantana, N., Reina-Patton, A., et al.** (2008). Stress, immunity, and cervical cancer: biobehavioral outcomes of a randomized clinical trial. *Clinical Cancer Research, 14,* 2111–2118.

**Nelson, L. D., & Morrison, E. L.** (2005). The symptoms of resource scarcity: Judgment of food and finances influence preferences for potential partners. *Psychological Science, 16,* 167–173.

**Nelson, R. J., Franks, S., & Brose, A.** (2005). The influence of hostility and family history of cardiovascular disease on autonomic activation in response to controllable versus uncontrollable stress, anger imagery reduction, and relaxation therapy. *Journal of Behavioral Medicine, 28,* 213–221.

**Nemeroff, C. B., Kalali, A., Keller, M. B., Charney, D. S., Lenderts, S. E., Cascade, E. F., et al.** (2007). Impact of publicity concerning pediatric suicidality data on physician practice patterns in the United States. *Archives of General Psychiatry, 64,* 466–472.

**Nemiah, J. C.** (1985). Somatoform disorders. In H. I. Kaplan & B. J. Sadock (Eds.), *Comprehensive textbook of psychiatry/IV.* Baltimore: Williams & Wilkins.

**Nettle, D.** (2006). The evolution of personality variation in humans and other animals. *American Psychologist, 61*(6), 622–631.

**Neupert, S. D., Almeida, D. M., Mroczek, D. K., & Spiro, A.** (2006). Daily stressors and memory failures in a naturalistic setting: Findings from the VA normative aging study. *Psychology and Aging, 21,* 424–429.

**New Freedom Commission on Mental Health.** (2003). *Achieving the promise: Transforming mental health care in America.* Rockville, MD: DHHS Pub. No. SMA-03-3831.

**Newcomb, M. D.** (1990). Social support and personal characteristics: A developmental and interactional perspective. *Journal of Social and Clinical Psychology, 9,* 54–68.

**Newcombe, N. S.** (2007). Taking science seriously: Straight thinking about spatial sex differences. In S. J. Ceci & W. M. Williams (Eds.), *Why aren't more women in science?* (pp. 69–78). Washington, DC: American Psychological Association.

**Newman, C. F. & Beck, A. T.** (2009). Cognitive therapy. In B. J. Sadock, V. A. Sadock, & P. Ruiz (Eds.), *Kaplan & Sadock's comprehensive textbook of psychiatry* (pp. 2857–2872). Philadelphia: Lippincott Williams & Wilkins.

**Nezu, A. M., Nezu, C. M., Felgoise, S. H., & Zwick, M. L.** (2003). Psychosocial oncology. In A. M. Nezu, C. M. Nezu, & P. A. Geller (Eds.), *Handbook of psychology: Vol. 9. Health psychology.* New York: Wiley.

**Ng, D. M., & Jeffery, R. W.** (2003). Relationships between perceived stress and health behaviors in a sample of working adults. *Health Psychology, 22,* 638–642.

**Niaura, R., & Abrams, D. B.** (2002). Smoking cessation: Progress, priorities, and prospectus. *Journal of Consulting & Clinical Psychology, 70*(3), 494–509.

**Niaura, R., Todaro, J. F., Stroud, L., Spiro, A., Ward, K. D., & Weiss, S.** (2002). Hostility, the metabolic syndrome, and incident coronary heart disease. *Health Psychology, 21*(16), 588–593.

**NICHD Early Child Care Research Network.** (1997). The effects of infant child care on infant-mother attachment security: Results of the NICHD Study of Early Child Care. *Child Development, 68,* 860–879.

**Nichols, B.** (2006). Violence against women: The extent of the problem. In P. K. Lundberg-Love & S. L. Marmion (Eds.), *"Intimate" violence against women: When spouses, partners, or lovers attack.* Westport, CT: Praeger.

**Nicholson, C.** (2006). Freedom and choice, culture, and class. *APS Observer, 19*(8), 31, 45.

**Nickerson, C., Schwarz, N., Diener, E., & Kahneman, D.** (2003). Zeroing in on the dark side of the American dream: A closer look at the negative consequences of the goal for financial success. *Psychological Science , 14*(6), 531–536.

**Nickerson, R. S.** (1998). Confirmation bias: A ubiquitous phenomenon in many guises. *Review of General Psychology, 2,* 175–220.

**Nie, N. H., & Erbring, L.** (2002). Internet and society: A preliminary report. *IT & Society, 1*(1), 275–283.

**Niederhoffer, K. G., & Pennebaker, J. W.** (2005). Sharing one's story: On the benefits of writing or talking about emotional experience. In C. R. Snyder & S. J. Lopez (Eds.), *Handbook of positive psychology.* New York: Oxford University Press.

**Nielsen, J. M.** (1990). *Sex and gender in society: Perspective on stratification* (2nd ed.). Prospect Heights, IL: Waveland.

**Nielsen Media Research.** (2005). *Nielson reports Americans watch TV at record levels.* Retrieved May 3, 2007 from http://www.nielsenmedia.com.

**Nielsen Media Research.** (2006). *Nielson media research reports television's popularity is still growing.* Retrieved May 3, 2007 from http://www.nielsenmedia.com/nc/portal/site.Public/menuitem.55dc65b4a.

**Niemann, Y. F., Jennings, L., Rozelle, R. M., Baxter, J. C., & Sullivan, E.** (1994). Use of free responses and cluster analysis to determine stereotypes of eight groups. *Personality and Social Psychology Bulletin, 20,* 379–390.

**Niessen, C., Heinrichs, N., & Dorr, S.** (2009). Pursuit and adjustment of goals during unemployment: The role of age. *International Journal of Stress Management, 16*(2), 102–123.

**Ninan, P. T., & Muntasser, S.** (2004). Buspiron and gepirone. In A. F. Schatzberg & C. B. Nemeroff (Eds), *Textbook of psychopharmacology.* Washington, DC: American Psychiatric Publishing.

**Nisbett, R. E., & Miyamoto, Y.** (2005). The influence of culture: Holistic versus analytic perception. *Trends in Cognitive Science, 9,* 467–473.

**Nisbett, R. E., Peng, K., Choi, I., & Norenzayan, A.** (2001). Culture and systems of thought: Holistic versus analytic cognition. *Psychological Review, 108*(2), 291–310.

**Nobler, M. S., & Sackeim, H. A.** (2006). Electroconvulsive therapy and transcranial magnetic stimulation. In D. J. Stein, D. J. Kupfer, & A. F. Schatzberg (Eds.), *Textbook of mood disorders.* Washington, DC: American Psychiatric Publishing.

**Nobre, P., & Pinto-Gouveia, J.** (2008). Cognitive and emotional predictors of female sexual dysfunctions: Preliminary findings. *Journal of Sex & Marital Therapy, 34,* 325–342.

**Nock, S. L.** (1995). A comparison of marriages and cohabitating relationships. *Journal of Family Issues, 13,* 53–76.

**Noftle, E. E., & Robins, R. W.** (2007). Personality predictors of academic outcomes: Big Five correlates of GPA and SAT scores. *Journal of Personality and Social Psychology, 93,* 116–130.

**Nolen-Hoeksema, S.** (1991). Responses to depression and their effects on the duration of depressive episodes. *Journal of Abnormal Psychology, 100,* 569–582.

**Nolen-Hoeksema, S.** (2000). The role of rumination in depressive disorders and mixed anxiety/depressive symptoms. *Journal of Abnormal Psychology, 109*(3), 504–511.

**Nolen-Hoeksema, S.** (2001). Gender differences in depression. *Current Directions in Psychological Science, 10,*173–176.

**Nolen-Hoeksema, S.** (2002). Gender differences in depression. In I. H. Gotlib & C. L. Hammen (Eds.), *Handbook of depression.* New York: Guilford.

**Nolen-Hoeksema, S., & Davis, C. G.** (2005). Positive responses to loss: Perceiving benefits and growth. In C. R. Snyder & S. J. Lopez (Eds.), *Handbook of positive psychology.* New York: Oxford University Press.

**Nolen-Hoeksema, S., & Hilt, L. M.** (2009). Gender differences in depression. In I. H. Gotlib & C. L. Hammen (Eds.), *Handbook of depression* (pp. 386–404). New York: Guilford.

**Nolen-Hoeksema, S., & Keita, G. P.** (2003). Women and depression: An introduction. *Psychology of Women Quarterly, 27,* 89–90.

**Nolen-Hoeksema, S., Wisco, B. E., & Lybomirsky, S.** (2008). Rethinking rumination. *Perspectives on Psychological Science, 3,* 400–424.

**Noller, P.** (1985). Negative communications in marriage. *Journal of Social and Personal Relationships, 2,* 289–301.

**Noller, P.** (1987). Nonverbal communication in marriage. In D. Perlman & S. Duck (Eds.), *Intimate relationships: Development, dynamics, and deterioration.* Newbury Park, CA: Sage.

**Noller, P.** (2009). Abuse and violence in relationships. In H. T. Reis & S. Sprecher (Eds.), *Encyclopedia of human relationships: Vol. 2* (pp. 4–8). Los Angeles: Sage Reference Publication.

**Noller, P., & Fitzpatrick, M. A.** (1990). Marital communication in the eighties. *Journal of Marriage and the Family, 52,* 832–843.

**Noller, P., & Gallois, C.** (1988). Understanding and misunderstanding in marriage: Sex and marital adjustment differences in structured and free interaction. In P. Noller & M. A. Fitzpatrick (Eds.), *Perspectives on marital interaction.* Clevedon, England: Multilingual Matters.

**Nomaguchi, K. M.** (2006). Maternal employment, nonparental care, mother-child interactions and child outcomes during preschool years. *Journal of Marriage and Family, 68,* 1341–1369.

**Nomaguchi, K. M., & Milkie, M. A.** (2003). Costs and rewards of children: The effects of becoming a parent on adults' lives. *Journal of Marriage and Family, 65,* 356–374.

**Norcross, J. C.** (1995). Dispelling the dodo bird verdict and the exclusivity myth in psychotherapy. *Psychotherapy, 32,* 500–504.

**Norcross, J. C., Hedges, M., & Castle, P. H.** (2002). Psychologists conducting psychotherapy in 2001: A study of the Division 29 membership. *Psychotherapy: Theory, Research, Practice, Training, 39,* 97–102.

**Norcross, J. C., Santrock, J. W., Campbell, L. F., Smith, T. P., Sommer, R., & Zuckerman, E. L.** (2003). *Authoritative guide to self-help resources in mental health.* New York: Guilford.

**Norem, J. K.** (1989). Cognitive strategies as personality: Effectiveness, specificity, flexibility, and chance. In D. M. Buss & N. Cantor (Eds.), *Personality psychology: Recent trends and emerging directions.* New York : Springer-Verlag.

**Norem, J. K.** (2001). *The positive power of negative thinking: Using defensive pessimism to manage anxiety and perform at your peak.* New York: Basic Books.

**Norem, J. K.** (2002). Defensive self-deception and social adaptation among optimists. *Journal of Research in Personality, 36,* 549–555.

**Norem, J. K.** (2008). Defensive pessimism, anxiety, and the complexity of evaluating self-regulation. *Social and Personality Psychology Compass, 2*(1), 121–134.

**Norem, J. K., & Smith, S.** (2006). Defensive pessimism: Positive past, anxious present, and pessimistic future. In L. J. Sanna & E. C. Chang (Eds.), *Judgments over time: The interplay of thoughts, feelings, and behaviors.* New York: Oxford University Press.

**Norenzayan, A., Choi, I., & Nisbett, R. E.** (2002). Cultural similarities and differences in social inference: Evidence from behavioral predictions and lay theories of behavior. *Personality and Social Psychology Bulletin, 28,* 109–120.

**Norman, C., & Aron, A.** (2003). Aspects of possible self that predict motivation to achieve or avoid it. *Journal of Experimental Social Psychology, 39,* 500–507.

**North, R. J., & Swann, W. B. Jr.** (2009a). Self-verification 360°: Illuminating the light and dark sides. *Self and Identity, 8*(2–3), 131–146.

**North, R. J., & Swann, W. B. Jr.** (2009b). What's positive about self-verification? In S. J. Lopez & C. R. Snyder (Eds.), *Oxford handbook of positive psychology* (2nd ed., pp. 464–474). New York: Oxford University Press.

**Norton, P. G. W.** (2004, February 1). Low-fat foods helped fuel obesity epidemic. *Family Practice News,* p. 22.

**Norton, S.** (2002). Women exposed: Sexual harrassment and female vulnerability. In L. Diamant & J. Lee (Eds.), *The psychology of sex, gender, and jobs.* Westport, CT: Praeger.

**Norwood, K., & Duck, S.** (2009). Dissolution of relationships, processes. In H. T. Reis & S. Sprecher (Eds.), *Encyclopedia of human relationships: Vol. 2* (pp. 445–449). Los Angeles: Sage Reference Publication.

**Notarius, C., & Markman, H.** (1993). *We can work it out: Making sense of marital conflict.* New York: G. P. Putnam's Sons.

**Novotney, A.** (2009). Yoga as a pratice tool. *Monitor on Psychology, 40*(10), 38–42.

**Nowell, A., & Hedges, L. V.** (1998). Trends in gender differences in academic achievement from 1960–1994: An analysis of differences in mean, variance, and extreme scores. *Sex Roles, 39*(1/2), 21–43.

**Noyes, R. Jr., Stuart, S. P., Lanbehn, D. R., Happel, R., Longley, S. L., Muller, B. A., & Yagla, S. J.** (2003). Test of an interpersonal model of hypochondriasis. *Psychosomatic Medicine, 65,* 292–300.

**Noyes, R. Jr., Watson, D. B., Letuchy, E. M., Longley, S. L., Black, D. W., Carney, C. P., & Doebbeling, B. N.** (2005). Relationship between hypochondriacal concerns and personality dimensions and traits in a military population. *Journal of Nervous and Mental Disease, 193*(2), 110–118.

**Nurnberger, J. I., & Zimmerman, J.** (1970). Applied analysis of human behavior: An alternative to conventional motivational inferences and unconscious determination in therapeutic programming. *Behavior Therapy, 1,* 59–69.

**Oakes, P.** (2001). The root of all evil in intergroup relations? Unearthing the categorization process. In R. Brown & S. L. Gaertner (Eds.), *Blackwell handbook of social psychology: Intergroup processes.* London: Blackwell.

**Oaten, M., & Cheng, K.** (2005). Academic examination stress impairs self-control. *Journal of Social and Clinical Psychology, 24,* 254–279.

**Oaten, M., & Cheng, K.** (2006). Longitudinal gains in self-regulation from regular physical exercise. *British Journal of Health Psychology, 11,* 717–733.

**Oattes, M. K., & Offman, A.** (2007). Global self-esteem and sexual self-esteem as predictors of sexual communication in intimate relationships. *The Canadian Journal of Human Sexuality, 16,* 89–100.

**O'Brien, C. P., Volkow, N., & Li, T.-K.** (2006). What's in a word? Addiction versus dependence in DSM-V. *American Journal of Psychiatry, 163,* 764–765.

**O'Brien, S. J., & Vertinsky, P. A.** (1991). Unfit survivors: Exercise as a resource for aging women. *The Gerontologist, 31,* 347–357.

**O'Brien, B.** (1996). Economic evaluation of pharmaceuticals. *Medical Care, 34,* 99–108.

**O'Callahan, M., Andrews, A. M., & Krantz, D. S.** (2003). Coronary heart disease and hypertension. In A. M. Nezu, C. M. Nezu, & P. A. Geller (Eds.), *Handbook of psychology: Vol. 9. Health psychology.* New York: Wiley.

**Ocon, R.** (2006). *Issues on gender and diversity in management.* Lanham, MD: University Press of America.

**Oesterman, K., Bjoerkqvist, K., Lagerspetz, K. M. J., Kaukiainen, A., Landau, S. F., Fraczek, A., & Caprara, G. V.** (1998). Cross-cultural evidence of female indirect aggression. *Aggressive Behavior, 24*(1), 1–80.

**Oettingen, G., & Gollwitzer, P. M.** (2001). Goal setting and goal striving. In A. Tesser & N. Schwarz. (Eds.), *Blackwell handbook of social psychology: Intraindividual processes.* Malden, MA: Blackwell.

**Ogden, C. L., Carroll, M. D., & Flegal, K. M.** (2008). High body mass index for age among US children and adolescents, 2003–2006. *Journal of the American Medical Association, 299,* 2401–2405.

**O'Hara, M. W.** (2009). Postpartum depression: What we know. *Journal of Clinical Psychology, 65,* 1258–1269.

**Öhman, A., & Mineka, S.** (2001). Fears, phobias, and preparedness: Toward an evolved module of fear and fear learning. *Psychological Review, 108,* 483–522.

**O'Keefe, D.** (2002). *Persuasion: Theory and research* (2nd ed.). Newbury Park, CA: Sage.

**O'Keefe, D. J., & Hale, S. L.** (2001). An odds-ratio based meta-analysis of research on the door-in-the-face influence strategy. *Communication Reports, 14*(1), 31–38.

**O'Leary-Kelly, A. M., Bowes-Sperry, L., Bates, C. A., & Lean, E. R.** (2009). Sexual harassment at work: A decade (plus) of progress. *Journal of Management, 35*(3), 503–536.

**Olff, M., Langeland, W., Draijer, N., & Gersonons, B. P. R.** (2007). Gender differences in posttraumatic stress disorder. *Psychological Bulletin, 133,* 183–204.

**Olfson, M., Cherry, D. K., & Lewis-Fernández, R.** (2009). Racial differences in visit duration of outpatient psychiatric visits. *Archives of General Psychiatry, 66,* 214–221.

**Olfson, M. & Marcus, S. C.** (2009). National patterns in antidepressant medication treatment. *Archives of General Psychiatry, 66,* 848–856.

**Olfson, M., Marcus, S. C., Druss, B. , & Pincus, H. A.** (2002). National trends in the use of outpatient psychotherapy. *American Journal of Psychiatry, 159,* 1914–1920.

**Olfson, M., Shaffer, D., Marcus, S. C., & Greenberg, T.** (2003). Relationship between antidepressant medication treatment and suicide in adolescents. *Archives of General Psychiatry, 60*(10), 978–982.

**Olivardia, R., Pope, H. G., & Phillips, K. A.** (2000). *The Adonis complex: The secret crisis of male body obsession.* New York: Free Press.

**Oliver, M. B., & Hyde, J. S.** (1993). Gender differences in sexuality: A meta-analysis. *Psychological Bulletin, 114,* 29–51.

**Ollendick, T. H., Öst, L. –G., Reuterskiöld, L., Costa, N., Cederlund, R., Sirbu, C., et al.** (2009). One-session treatment of specific phobias in youth: A randomized clinical trial in the United States and Sweden. *Journal of Consulting and Clinical Psychology, 77,* 504–516.

**Omarzu, J.** (2009). Minding the relationship. In H. T. Reis & S. Sprecher (Eds.), *Encyclopedia of human relationships: Vol. 2* (pp. 1107–1108). Los Angeles: Sage Reference Publication.

**Omoto, A. M., & Hawkins, S. A.** (2009). AIDS, effects on relationships. In H. T. Reis & S. Sprecher (Eds.), *Encyclopedia of human relationships: Vol. 2* (pp. 75–77). Los Angeles: Sage Reference Publication.

**Ong, A. D., Bergeman, C. S., Bisconti, T. L., & Wallace, K. A.** (2006). Psychological resilience, positive emotions, and successful adaptation to stress in later life. *Journal of Personality and Social Psychology, 91,* 730–749.

**Ong, A. D., Fuller-Rowell, T., & Burrow, A. L.** (2009). Racial discrimination and the stress process. *Journal of Personality and Social Psychology, 96,* 1259–1271.

**O'Neil, J. M., & Egan, J.** (1992). Men's and women's gender role journeys: A metaphor for healing, transition, and transformation. In B. Wainrib (Ed.), *Gender issues across the life cycle*. New York: Springer.

**O'Neill, N., & O'Neill, G.** (1972). *Open marriage.* New York: Evans.

**Ono, H.** (1998). Husbands' and wives' resources and marital dissolution. *Journal of Marriage and the Family, 60,* 674–689.

**Ono, H.** (2006). Homogamy among the divorced and never married on marital history in recent decades: Evidence from vital statistics data. *Social Science Research, 35,* 356–383.

**Opotow, S., & Weiss, L.** (2000). Denial and the process of moral exclusion in environmental conflict. *Journal of Social Issues, 56,* 475–490.

**Oppliger, P. A.** (2007). Effects of gender stereotyping on socialization. In R. W. Preiss, B. M. Gayle, N. Burrell, M. Allen, & J. Bryant (Eds.), *Mass media effects research: Advances through meta-analysis* (pp. 199–214). Mahwah, NJ: Erlbaum.

**Orbuch, T., & Veroff, J.** (2002). A programmatic review: Building a two-way bridge between social psychology and the early years of marriage. *Journal of Social and Personal Relationships, 19,* 549–568.

**O'Reardon, J. P., Solvason, H. B., Janicak, P. G., Sampson, S., Isenberg, K. E., Nahas, Z., et al.** (2007). Efficacy and safety of transcranial magnetic stimulation in the acute treatment of major depression: A multisite randomized controlled trial. *Biological Psychiatry, 62,* 1208–1216.

**Orenstein, P.** (1994). *School girls: Young women, self-esteem, and the confidence gap.* New York: Doubleday.

**Organista, P. B., & Miranda, J.** (1991). Psychosomatic symptoms in medical outpatients: An investigation of self-handicapping theory. *Health Psychology, 10,* 427–431.

**Ornstein, R., & Ehrlich, P.** (2000). *New world, new mind: Moving toward conscious evolution.* Cambridge, MA: Malor Books, ISHK.

**Orth-Gomer, K., Wamala, S. P., Horsten, M., Schenck-Gustafsson, K., Schneiderman, N., & Mittleman, M. A.** (2000). Marital stress worsens prognosis in women with coronary heart disease: The Stockholm female coronary risk study. *Journal of the American Medical Association, 284*(23), 3008–3014.

**Orth, U., Robins, R. W., Meier, & Laurenz L,** (2009b). Disentangling the effects of low self-esteem and stressful events on depression: Findings from three longitudinal studies. *Journal of Personality and Social Psychology, 97*(2), 307–321.

**Orth, U., Robins, R. W., Trzesniewski, K. H., Maes, J., & Schmitt, M.** (2009a). Low self-esteem is a risk factor for depressive symptoms from young adulthood to old age. *Journal of Abnormal Psychology, 118,* 472–478.

**Osbaldiston, R., & Sheldon, K. M.** (2002). Social dilemmas and sustainability: Promoting peoples' motivation to "cooperate with the future." In P. Schmuck & W. P. Schultz (Eds.), *Psychology of sustainable development* (pp. 37–58). Boston: Kluwer Academic Press.

**Osman, S. L.** (2003). Predicting men's rape perceptions based on the belief that "no" really means "yes." *Journal of Applied Social Psychology, 33*(4), 683–692.

**Osteen, J.** (2009). *Become a better you: 7 keys to improving your life every day.* New York: Free Press.

**Ostrom, E., Burger, J., Field, C. B., Norgaard, R. B., & Policansky, D.** (2007). Revisiting the commons: Local lessons, global challenges. In D. J. Penn & I. Mysterud (Eds.), *Evolutionary perspectives on environmental problems (pp. 129–140).* New Brunswick, NJ: Transaction Publishers.

**O'Sullivan, L. F., McCrudden, M. C., & Tolman, D. L.** (2006). To your sexual health! Incorporating sexuality into the health perspective. In J. Worrell & C. D. Goodheart (Eds.), *Handbook of girls' and women's psychological health.* New York: Oxford University Press.

**O'Toole, R. E., & Ferry, J. L.** (2002). The growing importance of elder care benefits for an aging workforce. *Compensation & Benefits Management, 18*(1), 40–44.

**Ouellette, S. C.** (1993). Inquiries into hardiness. In L. Goldberger & S. Breznitz (Eds.), *Handbook of stress: Theoretical and clinical aspects* (2nd ed.). New York: Free Press.

**Ouellette, S. C., & DiPlacido, J.** (2001). Personality's role in the protection and enhancement of health: Where the research has been, where it is stuck, how it might move. In A. Baum, T. A. Revenson, & J. E. Singer *Handbook of health psychology*. Mahwah, NJ: Erlbaum.

**Overmier, J. B., & Murison, R.** (2005). Trauma and resulting sensitization effects are modulated by psychological factors. *Psychoneuroendocrinology, 30,* 965–973.

**Overstreet, S.** (2000). Exposure to community violence: Defining the problem and understanding the consequences. *Journal of Child and Family Studies, 9,* 7–25.

**Overton, S. L. & Medina, S. L.** (2008). The stigma of mental illness. *Journal of Counseling & Development, 86*(2), 143–151.

**Oyserman, D., Bybee, D., & Terry, K.** (2006). Possible selves and academic outcomes: How and when possible selves impel action. *Journal of Personality and Social Psychology, 91,* 188–204.

**Oyserman, D., Sorensen, N., Reber, R., & Chen, S. X.** (2009). Connecting and separating mind-sets: Culture as situated cognition. *Journal of Personality and Social Psychology, 97*(2), 217–235.

**Ozer, D. J., & Benet-Martínez, V.** (2006). Personality and the prediction of consequential outcomes. *Annual Review of Psychology, 57,* 401–421.

**Ozer, D. J., & Reise, S. P.** (1994). Personality assessment. *Annual Review of Psychology, 45,* 357–388.

**Ozer, E. J., Best, S. R., Lipsey, T. L., & Weiss, D. S.** (2003). Predictors of posttraumatic stress disorder and symptoms in adults: A meta-analysis. *Psychological Bulletin, 129*(1), 52–73.

**Ozer, E. J., & Weiss, D. S. (2004).** Who develops posttraumatic stress disorder? *Current Directions in Psychological Science, 13,* 169–172.

**Ozer, E. M., & Bandura, A.** (1990). Mechanisms governing empowerment effects: A self-efficacy analysis. *Journal of Personality and Social Psychology, 58,* 472–486.

**Padgett, D. A., & Sheridan, J. F.** (2000). Herpesviruses. In G. Fink (Ed.), *Encyclopedia of stress*. San Diego: Academic Press.

**Pahl, S., Etser, J. R., & White, M. P.** (2009). Boundaries of self-positivity: The effect of comparison focus in self-friend comparisons. *The Journal of Social Psychology, 149*(4), 413–424.

**Pahl, S., Harris, P. R., Todd, H. A., & Rutter, D. R.** (2005). Comparative optimism for environmental risks. *Journal of Environmental Psychology, 25,* 1–11.

**Palomares, N. A.** (2009). Women are sort of more tentative than men, aren't they? How men and women use tentative language differently, similarly, and counterstereotypically as a function of gender salience. *Communication Research, 36,* 538–560.

**Pang, M., Chua, B., & Chu, C.** (2008). Learning to stay ahead in an uncertain environment. *International Journal of Human Resource Management, 19*(7), 1383–1394.

**Papaharitou, S., Nakopoulou, E., Kirana, P., Giaglis, G., Moraitou, M., & Hatzichristou, D.** (2008). Factors associated with sexuality in later life: An exploratory study in a group of Greek married older adults. *Archives of Gerontology and Geriatrics, 46,* 191–201.

**Papernow, P. L.** (1993). *Becoming a stepfamily: Patterns of development in remarried families.* San Francisco, CA: Jossey-Bass.

**Papp, L. M., Cummings, E. M., & Schermerhorn, A. C.** (2004). Pathways among marital distress, parental symptomatology, and child adjustment. *Journal of Marriage and Family, 66,* 368–384.

**Pardue, A, & Arrigo, B. A.** (2007). Power, anger, and sadistic rapists: Toward a differentiated model of offender personality. *International Journal of Offender Therapy and Comparative Criminology, 52,* 378–400.

**Pargament, K. I.** (1997). *The psychology of religion and coping: Theory, research and practice.* New York: Guilford.

**Pargament, K. I., & Mahoney, A.** (2002). Spirituality: Discovering and conserving the sacred. In C. R. Snyder & S. J. Lopez (Eds.), *Handbook of positive psychology* (pp. 646–659). New York: Oxford.

**Pargament, K. I., & Mahoney, A.** (2009). Spirituality: The search for the sacred. In S. J. Lopez & C. R. Snyder (Eds.), *Handbook of positive psychology* (2nd ed., pp. 611–619). New York: Oxford.

**Pargament, K. I, Smith, B. W., Koenig, H. G., & Perez, L. M.** (1998). Patterns of positive and negative religious coping with major life stressors. *Journal for the Scientific Study of Religion, 37,* 710–724.

**Park, C. L.** (1998). Implications of posttraumatic growth for individuals. In R. G. Tedeschi, C. L. Park, & L. G. Calhoun (Eds.), *Posttraumatic growth: Positive changes in the aftermath of crisis* (pp. 153–178). Mahwah, NJ: Erlbaum.

**Park, C. L., & Folkman, S.** (1997). Meaning in the context of stress and coping. *Review of General Psychology, 1,* 115–144.

**Park, C. W., & Young, S. M.** (1986). Consumer response to television commercials: The impact of involvement and background music on brand attitude formation. *Journal of Marketing Research, 23* 11–24.

**Park, K.** (2005). Choosing childlessness: Weber's typology of action and motives of the voluntarily childless. *Sociological Inquiry, 75,* 372–402.

**Park, N., & Peterson, C.** (2009). Achieving and sustaining a good life. *Perspectives on Psychological Science, 4,* 422–428.

**Park, N., Peterson, C., & Seligman, M. E. P.** (2004). Strengths of character and well-being. *Journal of Social and Clinical Psychology, 23,* 603–619.

**Parker, P. A., & Kulik, J. A.** (1995). Burnout, self- and supervisor-related job performance and absenteeism among nurses. *Journal of Behavioral Medicine, 18,* 581–599.

**Parker, R.** (2000). Health literacy: A challenge for American patients and their health care providers. *Health Promotion International, 15,* 277–283.

**Parrott, A. C.** (2000). Human research on MDMA (3,4-Methylenedioxymethamphetamine) neurotoxicity: Cognitive and behavioural indices of change. *Neuropsychobiology, 42*(1), 17–24.

**Parrott, D. J., Peterson, J. L., Vincent, W., & Bakeman, R.** (2008). Correlates of anger in response to gay men: Effects of male gender role beliefs, sexual prejudice, and masculine gender role stress. *Psychology of Men & Masculinity, 9,* 167–178.

**Parrott, D. J., & Zeichner, A.** (2006). Effect of psychopathy on physical aggression toward gay and heterosexual men. *Journal of Interpersonal Violence, 21,* 390–410.

**Parsons, T., & Bales, R. F.** (1995). *Family, socialization, and interaction process.* Glencoe, IL: Free Press.

**Pashang, B, & Singh, M.** (2008). Emotional intelligence and use of coping strategies. *Psychological Studies, 53,* 81–82.

**Pasley, K., & Moorefield, B. S.** (2004). Stepfamilies: Changes and challenges. In M. Coleman, & L. H. Ganong (Eds.), *Handbook of contemporary families: Considering the past, contemplating the future.* Thousand Oaks, CA: Sage.

**Pasterski, V. L., Geffner, M. E., Brain, C., Hindmarsh, P., Brook, C., & Hines, M.** (2005). Prenatal hommrones and postnatal socialization by parents as determinants of male-typical toy play in girls with congenital adrenal hyperplasia. *Child Development, 76,* 264–278.

**Pasupathi, M.** (2009). Arranged marriages. In H. T. Reis & S. Sprecher (Eds.), *Encyclopedia of human relationships: Vol. 2* (pp. 113–115). Los Angeles: Sage Reference Publication.

Pasupathi, M., McLean, K. C., & Weeks, T. (2009). To tell or not to tell: Disclosure and the narrative self. *Journal of Personality, 77,* 89–124.

Patel, J. K., Pinals, D. A., & Breier, A. (2003). Schizophrenia and other psychoses. In A. Tasman, J. Kay, & J. A. Lieberman (Eds.), *Psychiatry.* New York: Wiley.

Pato, M. T., Eisen, J. L., & Phillips, K. A. (2003). Obsessive-compulsive disorder. In A. Tasman, J. Kay, & J. A. Lieberman (Eds.), *Psychiatry.* New York: Wiley.

Patterson, C. J. (2001). Family relationships of lesbians and gay men. In R. M. Milardo (Ed.), *Understanding families into the new millennium: A decade in review.* Minneapolis: National Council on Family Relations.

Patterson, C. J. (2003). Children of lesbian and gay parents. In L. D. Garnets & D. C. Kimmel (Eds.), *Psychological perspectives on lesbian, gay, and bisexual experiences.* New York: Columbia University Press.

Patterson, C. J. (2006). Children of lesbian and gay parents. *Current Directions in Psychological Science, 15,* 241–254.

Patterson, C. J. (2009). Lesbian and gay parents and their children: A social science perspective. In D. A. Hope (Ed.), *Contemporary perspectives on lesbian, gay, and bisexual identities* (pp. 141–182). New York: Springer Science and Business Media.

Patterson, C. J., & Redding, R. E. (1996). Lesbian and gay families with children: Implications of social science research for policy. *Journal of Social Issues, 52*(3), 29–50.

Patterson, M. L. (1988). Functions of nonverbal behavior in close relationships. In S. Duck (Ed.), *Handbook of personal relationships: Theory, research, and interventions.* New York: Wiley.

Patterson, M. L. (2009). Nonverbal involvment. In H. T. Reis & S. Sprecher (Eds.), *Encyclopedia of human relationships: Vol. 2* (pp. 1161–1165). Los Angeles: Sage Reference Publication.

Pauker, K., Weisbuch, M., Ambady, N., Sommers, S. R., Adams, R. B., Jr., & Ivcevic, Z. (2009). Not so black and white: Memory for ambiguous group members. *Journal of Personality and Social Psychology, 96*(4), 795–810.

Paul, A. M. (2001). Self-help: Shattering the myths. *Psychology Today, 34*(2), 60.

Paul, E. L., McManus, B., & Hayes, A. (2000). "Hookups": Characteristics and correlates of college students' spontaneous and anonymous sexual experiences. *Journal of Sex Research, 37*(1), 76–88.

Paul, E. L., Wenzel, A., & Harvey J. (2008). Hookups: A facilitator or a barrier to relationship initiation and intimacy development? In S. Sprecher, A. Wenzel, & J. Harvey (Eds.), *Handbook of Relationship Initiation* (pp. 375–388). New York: Psychology Press.

Paul, K. I., & Moser, K. (2009). Unemployment impairs mental health: Meta-analyses. *Journal of Vocational Behavior, 74*(3), 264–282.

Paulhus, D. L. (1991). Measurement and control of response bias. In J. P. Robinson, P. Shaver, & L. S. Wrightsman (Eds.), *Measures of personality and social psychological attitudes.* San Diego: Academic Press.

Paulhus, D. L., Fridhandler, B., & Hayes, S. (1997). Psychological defense: Contemporary theory and research. In R. Hogan, J. Johnson, & S. Briggs (Eds.) *Handbook of personality psychology.* San Diego: Academic Press.

Paulhus, D. L., Trapnell, P. D., & Chen, D. (1999). Birth order effects on personality and achievement within families. *Psychological Science, 10,* 482–488.

Paulsen, N., Callan, V. J., Grice, T. A., Rooney, D., Gallois, C., Jones, E., et al. (2005). Job uncertainty and personal control during downsizing: A comparison of survivors & victims. *Human Relations, 58,* 463–496.

Paunonen, S. V. (2003). Big five factors of personality and replicated predictions of behavior. *Journal of Personality and Social Psychology, 84,* 411–424.

Pavlov, I. P. (1906). The scientific investigation of psychical faculties or processes in the higher animals. *Science, 24,* 613–619.

Paxton, S. J., Norris, M., Wertheim, E. H., Durkin, S. J., & Anderson, J. (2005). Body dissatisfaction, dating, and importance of thinness to attractiveness in adolescent girls. *Sex Roles, 53,* 663–675.

Payne, B. K. (2006). Weapon bias: Split-second decisions and unintended sterotyping. *Current Directions in Psychological Science, 15,* 287–291.

Pearce, L. (1974). Duck! It's the new journalism. *New Times, 2,* 40–41.

Pearson, Q. M. (1998). Job satisfaction, leisure satisfaction, and psychological health. *Career Development Quarterly, 46*(4), 416–426.

Pechacek, T. F., & Babb, S. (2004). Commentary: How acute and reversible are the cardiovascular risks of secondhand smoke? *British Medical Journal, 328,* 980–983.

Pechnick, R. N., & Ungerleider, T. J. (2005). Hallucinogens. In J. H. Lowinson, P. Ruiz, R. B. Millman, & J. G. Langrod (Eds.), *Substance abuse: A comprehensive textbook.* Philadelphia: Lippincott/Williams & Wilkins.

Pedersen, P. (1994). A culture-centered approach to counseling. In W. J. Lonner & R. Malpass (Eds.), *Psychology and culture.* Boston: Allyn & Bacon.

Pedersen, S., Vitaro, F., Barker, E. D., & Borge, A. I. H. (2007). The timing of middle-childhood peer rejection and friendship: Linking early behavior to early-adolescent adjustment. *Child Development, 78,* 1037–1051.

Pedersen, W., & Skrondal, A. (1999). Ecstasy and new patterns of drug use: A normal population study. *Addiction, 94*(11), 1695–1706.

Peirce, R. S., Frone, M. R., Russell, M., & Cooper, M. L. (1996). Financial stress, social support, and alcohol involvement: A longitudinal test of the buffering hypothesis in a general population survey. *Health Psychology, 15,* 38–47.

Peladeau, N., Forget, J., & Gagne, F. (2003). Effect of paced and unpaced practice on skill application and retention: How much is enough? *American Educational Research Journal, 40,* 769–801.

Pelham, W. E., Jr. (2001). ADHD and behavioral modification. *Drug Benefit Trends, 13,* 11–14.

Pennebaker, J. W., Colder, M., & Sharp, L. K. (1990). Accelerating the coping process. *Journal of Personality and Social Psychology, 58,* 528–537.

Peplau, L. A. (1988). Research on homosexual couples: An overview. In J. P. De Cecco (Ed.), *Gay relationships.* New York: Harrington Park Press.

Peplau, L. A. (1991). Lesbian and gay relationships. In J. C. Gonsiorek & J. D. Weinrich (Eds.), *Homosexuality: Research implications for public policy.* Newbury Park, CA: Sage.

Peplau, L. A. (2003). Human sexuality: How do men and women differ? *Current Directions in Psychological Science, 12*(2), 37–40.

Peplau, L. A., & Cochran, S. D. (1990). A relational perspective on homosexuality. In D. P. McWhirter, S. A. Sanders, & J. M. Reinisch (Eds.), *Homosexuality/ heterosexuality: Concepts of sexual orientation.* New York: Oxford University Press.

Peplau, L. A., Fingerhut, A., & Beals, K. P. (2004). Sexuality in the relationships of lesbians and gay men. In J. H. Harvey, A. Wenzel, & S. Sprecher (Eds.), *The handbook of sexuality in close relationships.* Mahwah, NJ: Lawrence Erlbaum.

Peplau, L. A., & Fingerhut, A. W. (2007). The close relationships of lesbians and gay men. *Annual Review of Psychology, 58,* 405–424.

Peplau, L. A., & Garnets, L. D. (2000). A new paradigm for understanding women's sexuality and sexual orientation. *Journal of Social Issues, 56*(2), 329–350.

Peplau, L. A., & Ghavami, N. (2009). Gay, lesbian, and bisexual relationships. In H. T. Reis & S. Sprecher (Eds.), *Encyclopedia of human relationships: Vol. 1* (pp. 746–751). Los Angeles: Sage Reference Publication.

Peplau, L. A., & Gordon, S. L. (1985). Women and men in love: Gender differences in close heterosexual relationships. In V. E. O'Leary, R. K. Unger, & B. S. Wallston (Eds.), *Women, gender, and social psychology.* Hillsdale, NJ: Erlbaum.

Peplau, L. A., Hill, C. T., & Rubin, Z. (1993). Sex role attitudes in dating and marriage: A 15-year follow-up of the Boston couples study. *Journal of Social Issues, 49,* 31–52.

Peplau, L. A., & Spalding, L. R. (2000). The close relationships of lesbians, gay men, and bisexuals. In C. Hendrick & S. S. Hendrick (Eds.), *Close relationships: A sourcebook.* Thousand Oaks, CA: Sage.

Peplau, L. A., & Spalding, L. R. (2003). The close relationships of lesbians, gay men, and bisexuals. In L. D. Garnets & D. C. Kimmel (Eds.), *Psychological perspectives on lesbian, gay, and bisexual experiences.* New York: Columbia University Press.

Pereira, M. A., Kartshov, A. I., Ebbeling, C. B., Van Horn, L., Slattery, M. L., Jacobs, D. R., Jr. et al. (2005). Fast food habits, weight gain, and insulin resistance (the CARDIA Study): 15-year prospective analysis. *Lancet, 365,* 36–42.

Peretti, P. O., & Abplanalp, R. R., Jr. (2004). Chemistry in the college dating process: Structure and function. *Social Behavior and Personality, 32*(2), 147–154.

Perkins, D. O., Miller-Anderson, L., & Lieberman, J. A. (2006). Natural history and predictors of clinical course. In J. A. Lieberman, T. S. Stroup, & D. O. Perkins (Eds.), *Textbook of schizophrenia* (pp. 289–302). Washington, DC: American Psychiatric Publishing.

Perlis, R. H., Perlis, C. S., Wu, Y., Hwang, C., Joseph, M., & Nierenberg, A. A. (2005). Industry sponsorship and financial conflict of interest in the reporting of clinical trials in psychiatry. *American Journal of Psychiatry, 162,* 1957–1960.

Perlman, D. (2007). The best of times, the worst of times: The place of close relationships in psychology and our daily lives. *Canadian Psychology/Psychologie Canadienne, 48,* 7–18.

Perloff, R. M. (1993). *The dynamics of persuasion.* Hillsdale, NJ: Erlbaum.

Perreault, S., & Bourhis, R. Y. (1999). Ethnocentrism, social identification, and discrimination. *Personality and Social Psychology Bulletin, 25*(1), 92–103.

Perrett, D. I., Lee, K. J., Penton-Voak, I., Rowland, D., Yoshikawa, S., Burt, D. M., Henzi, S. P., Castles, D. L., & Akamatsu, S. (1998). Effects of sexual dimorphism on facial attractiveness. *Nature, 394,* 884–887.

Perri, M. G., Anton, S. D., Durning, P. E., Ketterson, T. U., Sydeman, S. J., Berlant, N. E., Kanasky Jr., W. F., Newton Jr., R. L., Llimacher, M. C., & Martin, A. D. (2002). Adherence to exercise prescriptions: Effects of prescribing moderate versus higher levels of intensity and frequency. *Health Psychology, 21*(5), 452–458.

Perry-Jenkins, M., Repetti, R. L., & Crouter, A. C. (2001). Work and family in the 1990s. In R. M. Milardo (Ed.), *Understanding families into the new millennium: A decade in review.* Minneapolis, MN: National Council on Family Relations.

Person, E. S. (1990). The influence of values in psychoanalysis: The case of female psychology. In C. Zanardi (Ed.), *Essential papers in psychoanalysis.* New York: New York University Press.

Pervin, L. A., & John, O. P. (2001). *Personality: Theory and research.* New York: Wiley.

Petersen, J. L., & Hyde, J. S. (2010). A meta-analytic review of research on gender differences in sexuality, 1993–2007. *Psychological Bulletin, 136,* 21–38.

Peterson, C. (2006). *A primer in positive psychology.* New York: Oxford University Press.

Peterson, C., & Bossio, L. M. (2001). Optimism and physical well-being. In E. C. Chang (Ed.), *Optimism and pessimism: Implications for theory, research, and practice.* Washington, DC: American Psychological Association.

Peterson, C., Maier, S. F., & Seligman, M. E. P. (1993). *Learned helplessness: A theory for the age of personal control.* New York: Oxford University Press.

Peterson, C., & Park, N. (2009). Positive psychology. In B. J. Sadock, V. A. Sadock, & P. Ruiz (Eds.), *Kaplan & Sadock's comprehensive textbook of psychiatry* (pp. 2939–2951). Philadelphia: Lippincott Williams & Wilkins.

Peterson, C., Park, N., & Seligman, M. E. P. (2005). Orientations to happiness and life satisfaction: The full life versus the empty life. *Journal of Happiness Studies, 6,* 25–41.

Peterson, C., & Seligman, M. E. P. (2003). Positive organizational studies: Thirteen lessons from positive psychology. In K. S. Cameron, J. E. Dutton, & R. E. Quinn (Eds.), *Positive organizational scholarship: Foundations of a new discipline* (pp. 14–27). San Francisco: Berrett-Koehler.

Peterson, C., & Seligman, M. E. P. (2004). *Character strengths and virtues: A handbook and classification.* New York: Oxford University Press/Washington, DC: American Psychological Association.

Peterson, C., Seligman, M. E. P., & Vaillant, G. E. (1988). Pessimistic explanatory style is a risk factor for physical illness: A thirty-five-year longitudinal study. *Journal of Personality and Social Psychology, 55,* 23–27.

Peterson, C., Seligman, M. E. P., Yurko, K. H., Martin, L. R., & Friedman, H. S. (1998). Castastrophizing and untimely death. *Psychological Science, 9,* 127–130.

Peterson, C., & Steen, T. A. (2009). Optimistic explanatory style. In S. J. Lopez & C. R. Snyder (Eds.), *Oxford handbook of positive psychology* (2nd ed., pp. 313–321). New York: Oxford University Press.

Peterson, C., & Vaidya, R. S. (2001). Explanatory style, expectations, and depressive symptoms. *Personality and Individual Differences, 31,* 1217–1223.

Peterson, J. L., & Bakeman, R. (2006). Impact of beliefs about HIV treatment and peer condom norms on risky sexual behavior among gay and bisexual men. *Journal of Community Psychology, 34*(1), 37–46.

Peterson, S. H., Wingood, G. M., DiClemente, R. J., Davies, S., & Harrington, K. (2007). Images of sexual stereotypes in rap videos and the health of African American female adolescents. *Journal of Women's Health, 16,* 1157–1164.

Petit, J. W., & Joiner, T. E. (2006). *Chronic depression: Interpersonal sources, therapeutic solutions.* Washington, DC: American Psychological Association.

Petras, R., & Petras, K. (1993). *The 776 stupidest things ever said.* New York: Doubleday.

Petrill, S. A. (2005). Behavioral genetics and intelligence. In O. Wilhelm & R. W. Engle (Eds.), *Handbook of understanding and measuring intelligence*. Thousand Oaks, CA: Sage Publications.

Pettigrew, T. F. (2001). The ultimate attribution error: Extending Allport's cognitive analysis of prejudice. In M. A. Hogg & D. Abrams (Eds.), *Intergroup relations: Essential readings*. New York: Psychology Press.

Pettigrew, T. F., & Tropp, L. R. (2000). Does intergroup contact reduce prejudice: Recent meta-analytic findings. In S. Oskamp (Ed.), *Reducing prejudice and discrimination*. Mahwah, NJ: Erlbaum.

Pettigrew, T. F., & Tropp, L. R. (2006). A meta-analytic test of intergroup contact theory. *Journal of Personality and Social Psychology, 90*, 751–783.

Petty, R. E., & Cacioppo, J. T. (1986). The elaboration likelihood model of persuasion. In L. Berkowitz (Ed.), *Advances in experimental social psychology* (Vol. 19). Orlando, FL: Academic Press.

Petty, R. E., & Cacioppo, J. T. (1990). Involvement and persuasion: Tradition versus integration. *Psychological Bulletin, 107*, 367–374.

Petty, R. E., Cacioppo, J. T., Strathman, A. J., Priester, J. R. (2005). To think or not to think: Exploring two routes to persuasion. In T. C. Brock & M. C. Green (Eds.), *Persuasion: Psychological insights and perspectives* (2nd ed., pp. 81–116). Thousand Oaks, CA: Sage Publications.

Petty, R. E., & Fazio, R. H. (Eds.). (2008). *Attitudes: Insights from the new implicit measures*. New York: Psychology Press.

Petty, R. E., Fleming, M. A., Priester, J. R., & Feinstein, A. H. (2001). Individual versus group interest violation: Surprise as a determinant of argument scrutiny and persuasion. *Social Cognition, 19*(4), 418–442.

Petty, R. E., Priester, J. R., & Wegener, D. T. (1994). Cognitive processes in attitude change. In R. S. Wyer & T. K. Srull (Eds.), *Handbook of social cognition* (Vol. 2). Hillsdale, NJ: Erlbaum.

Petty, R. E., & Wegener, D. T. (1998). Attitude change: Multiple roles for persuasion variables. In D. T. Gilbert, S. T. Fiske, & G. Lindzey (Eds.), *The handbook of social psychology* (4th ed., Vol. 1). New York: McGraw-Hill.

Petty, R. E., Wegener, D. T., & Fabrigar, L. R. (1997). Attitudes and attitude change. *Annual Review of Psychology, 48*, 609–647.

Petty, S. C., Sachs-Ericsson, N., & Joiner, T. E., Jr. (2004). Interpersonal functioning deficits: Temporary or stable characteristics of depressed individuals. *Journal of Affective Disorders, 81*(2), 115–122.

Phares, V., Steinberg, A. R., & Thompson, J. K. (2004). Gender differences in peer and parental influences: Body image disturbance, self-worth, and psychological functioning in preadolescent children. *Journal of Youth & Adolescence, 33*, 421–429.

Phillips, W. T., Kiernan, M., & King, A. C. (2001). The effects of physical activity on physical and psychological health. In A. Baum, T. A. Revenson, & J. E. Singer (Eds.), *Handbook of health psychology*. Mahwah, NJ: Erlbaum.

Pi, E. H., & Simpson, G. M. (2001). Medication-induced movement disorders. In B. J. Sadock & V. A. Sadock (Eds.), *Kaplan and Sadock's comprehensive textbook of psychiatry* (7th ed., Vol. 2). Philadelphia: Lippincott/Williams & Wilkins.

Pi-Sunyer, F. X. (2002). Medical complications of obesity in adults. In C. G. Fairburn & K. D. Brownell (Eds.), *Eating disorders and obesity: A comprehensive handbook*. New York: Guilford.

Pietromonaco, P. R., Greenwood, D., & Barrett, L. F. (2004). Conflict in adult close relationships: An attachment perspective. In W. S. Rholes & J. A. Simpson (Eds.), *Adult attachment: Theory, research, and clinical implications*. New York: Guilford.

Piferi, R. L., & Lawler, K. A. (2006). Social support and ambulatory blood pressure: An examination of both receiving and giving. *International Journal of Psychophysiology, 62*, 328–336.

Pilcher, J. J., Nadler, E., & Busch, C. (2002). Effects of hot and cold temperature exposure on performance: A meta-analysis. *Ergonomics, 45*, 682–698.

Pillow, D. R., Zautra, A. J., & Sandler, I. (1996). Major life events and minor stressors: Identifying mediational links in the stress process. *Journal of Personality and Social Psychology, 70*, 381–394.

Pilote, L., Dasgupta, K., Guru, V., Humphries, K. H., McGrath, J., Norris, C., et al. (2007). A comprehensive review of sex-specific issues related to cardiovascular disease. *Canadian Medical Association Journal, 176*(6), S1–S44.

Pilowsky, I. (1993). Aspects of abnormal illness behaviour. *Psychotherapy and Psychosomatics, 60*, 62–74.

Pinel, J. P. J., Assanand, S., & Lehman, D. R. (2000). Hunger, eating, and ill health. *American Psychologist, 55*, 1105–1116.

Pines, A. M. (1993). Burnout. In L. Goldberger & S. Breznitz (Eds.), *Handbook of stress: Theoretical and clinical aspects* (2nd ed.). New York: Free Press.

Pink, D. H. (2001). *Free agent nation: The future of working for yourself*. New York: Warner Business Books.

Pinquart, M. (2003). Loneliness in married, widowed, divorced, and never-married older adults. *Journal of Social and Personal Relationships, 20*(1), 31–53.

Pinquart, M. (2009). Moderating effects of dispositional resilience on associates between hassles and psychological distress. *Journal of Applied Developmental Psychology, 30*, 53–60.

Pinquart, M., Duberstein, P. R., & Lyness, J. M. (2006). Treatments for later-life depressive conditions: A meta-analytic comparison of pharmacotherapy and psychotherapy. *American Journal of Psychiatry, 163*, 1493–1501.

Pinquart, M., & Sorensen, S. (2001). Influences on loneliness in older adults: A meta-analysis. *Basic and Applied Social Psychology, 23*, 245–266.

Piotrowski, C., & Vodanovich, S. J. (2008). The workaholism syndrome: An emerging issue. *Journal of Instructional Psychology, 35*(1), 103–105.

Pipher, M. (1994). *Reviving Ophelia: Saving the selves of adolescent girls*. New York: Ballantine.

Pirog, R., & Benjamin, A. (2003). *Checking the food odometer: Comparing food miles for local versus conventional produce sales to Iowa institutions*. Ames: Leopold Center for Sustainable Agriculture, Iowa State University.

Pitt, R. N., & Borland, E. (2008). Bachelorhood and men's attitudes about gender roles. *The Journal of Men's Studies, 16*, 140–158.

Pittman, F., III. (1994, January/February). A buyer's guide to psychotherapy. *Psychology Today*, pp. 50–53, 74–81.

Piver, S. (2000). *The hard questions: 100 questions to ask before you say "I do."* New York: Jeremy P. Tarcher/Putnam.

Planalp, S., Fitness, J., & Fehr, B. (2006). Emotion in theories of close relationships. In A. L. Vangelisti & D. Perlman (Eds.), *The Cambridge handbook of personal relationships*. New York: Cambridge University Press.

Plante, T. G. (2005). *Contemporary clinical psychology*. New York: Wiley.

Plante, T. G., Caputo, D., & Chizmar, L. (2000). Perceived fitness and responses to laboratory induced stress. *International Journal of Stress Management, 7*(1), 61–73.

Pleck, J. H. (1981). *The myth of masculinity*. Cambridge, MA: MIT Press.

Pleck, J. H. (1995). The gender role strain paradigm: An update. In R. F. Levant & W. S. Pollack (Eds.), *A new psychology of men*. New York: Basic Books.

Plomin, R. (1994). Nature, nurture, and development. In R. J. Sternberg (Ed.), *Encyclopedia of human intelligence*. New York: Macmillan.

Plomin, R., & Caspi, A. (1999). Behavioral genetics and personality. In L. A. Pervin & O. P. John (Eds.), *Handbook of personality: Theory and research* (2nd ed.). New York: Guilford Press.

Plomin, R., DeFries, J. C., McClearn, G. E., & McGuffin, P. (2008). *Behavioral genetics*. New York: Worth.

Plomin, R., & Spinath, F. M. (2004). Intelligence: Genetics, genes, and genomics. *Journal of Personality & Social Psychology, 86*, 112–129.

Plous, S. L., & Zimbardo, P. G. (2004, September 10). How social science can reduce terrorism. *The Chronicle of Higher Education*, pp. B9–B10.

Polivy, J., & Herman, C. P. (2002). Causes of eating disorder. *Annual Review of Psychology, 53*, 187–213.

Pollack, C. E., & Lynch, J. (2009). Health status of people undergoing foreclosure in the Philadelphia region. *American Journal of Public Health, 99*, 1833–1839.

Pollak, L. (2007). *Getting from college to career: 90 things to do before you join the real world*. New York: HarperCollins.

Pope, E., & Shouldice, M. (2001). Drugs and sexual assault: A review. *Trauma Violence and Abuse, 2*(1), 51–55.

Pope, H. G., Barry, S., Bodkin, A., & Hudson, J. I. (2006). Tracking scientific interest in the dissociative disorders: A study of scientific publication output 1984–2003. *Psychotherapy and Psychosomatics, 75*, 19–24.

Pope, H. G., Gruber, A. J., Hudson, J. I., Huestis, M. A., & Yurgelun- Todd, D. (2001). Neuropsychological performance in long-term cannabis users. *Archives of General Psychiatry, 58*, 909–915.

Pope, H. G., Gruber, A. J., & Yurgelun-Todd, D. (2001). Residual neuropsychologic effects of cannabis. *Current Psychiatry Report, 3*, 507–512.

Pope, H. G., Oliva, P. S., Hudson, J. I., Bodkin, J. A., & Gruber, A. J. (1999). Attitudes toward DSM-IV dissociative disorders diagnoses among board-certified American psychiatrists. *American Journal of Psychiatry, 156*(2), 321–323.

Pope, K. S., Keith-Spiegel, P., & Tabachnick, B. G. (1986). Sexual attraction to clients. *American Psychologist, 41*, 147–158.

Popenoe, D. (1993). American family decline, 1960–1990: A review and appraisal. *Journal of Marriage and the Family, 55*, 527–555.

Popenoe, D. (1999). *Life without father: Compelling new evidence that fatherhood and marriage are indispensable for the good of children and society*. Cambridge, MA: Harvard University Press.

Post, R. M. & Altshuler, L. L. (2009). Mood disorders: Treatment of bipolar disorders. In B. J. Sadock, V. A. Sadock, & P. Ruiz (Eds.), *Kaplan & Sadock's comprehensive textbook of psychiatry* (pp. 1743–1812). Philadelphia: Lippincott Williams & Wilkins.

Potard, C., Courtois, R., & Rusch, E. (2008). The influence of peers on risky sexual behaviour during adolescence. *European Journal of Contraception & Reproductive Health Care, 13*, 264–270.

Potenza, M. N. (2006). Should addictive disorders include non–substance-related conditions? *Addiction, 101*(Suppl 1), 142–151.

Potter, W. Z., Padich, R. A., Rudorfer, M. V., & Krishnan, K. R. R. (2006). Tricyclics, tetracyclics, and monoamine oxidase inhibitors. In D. J. Stein, D. J. Kupfer, & A. F. Schatzberg (Eds.), *Textbook of mood disorders*. Washington, DC: American Psychiatric Publishing.

Powell, D. E., & Fine, M. A. (2009). Dissolution of relationships, causes. In H. T. Reis & S. Sprecher (Eds.), *Encyclopedia of human relationships: Vol. 1* (pp. 436–440). Los Angeles: Sage Reference Publication.

Powell, J. L., & Drucker, A. D. (1997). The role of peer conformity in the decision to ride with an intoxicated driver. *Journal of Alcohol and Drug Education, 43*(1), 1–7.

Powell, R. A., & Gee, T. L. (1999). The effects of hypnosis on dissociative identity disorder: A reexamination of the evidence. *Canadian Journal of Psychiatry, 44*, 914–916.

Prati, G., & Pietrantoni, L. (2009). Optimism, social support, and coping strategies as factors contributing to posttraumatic growth: A meta-analysis. *Journal of Loss and Trauma, 1*, 364–388.

Pratkanis, A. R., & Aronson, E. (2000). *Age of propaganda: The everyday use and abuse of persuasion*. New York: Freeman.

Pratt, L. A., Ford, D. E., Crum, R. M., Armenian, H. K., Gallo, J. J., & Eaton, W. W. (1996). Depression, psychotropic medication, and risk of myocardial infarction: Prospective data from the Baltimore ECA follow-up. *Archives of Internal Medicine, 94*, 3123–3129.

Pratto, F., Sidanius, J., Stallworth, L. M., & Malle, B. F. (1994). Social dominance orientation: A personality variable predicting social and political attitudes. *Journal of Personality and Social Psychology, 67*, 741–763.

Pratto, F., & Walker, A. (2004). The bases of gendered power. In A. H. Eagly, A. E. Beall, & R. J. Sternberg (Eds.), *The psychology of gender*. New York: Guilford Press.

Presser, H. B. (2000). Nonstandard work schedules and marital instability. *Journal of Marriage and the Family, 62*, 93–110.

Pressman, S. (1993). *Outrageous betrayal: The real story of Werner Erhard, EST and the Forum*. New York: St. Martin's Press.

Preston, P. (2006). Marijuana use of coping response to psychological strain: Racial, ethnic, and gender differences among young adults. *Deviant Behavior, 27*, 397–421.

Preto, N. G. (1999). Transformation of the family system during adolescence. In B. Carter & M. McGoldrick (Eds.), *The expanded family life cycle: Individual, family, and social perspectives* (3rd ed.). Boston: Allyn & Bacon.

Price, M. (2008a). Div. 55's drive for RxP: The American Society for the Advancement of Pharmacotherapy pushes for prescriptive authority. *Monitor on Psychology, 39*(2).

Price, M. (2008b). Research roundup: Get out of town. *gradPSYCH, 6*(3), 10.

Probst, T. M. & Sears, L. E. (2009) Stress during the financial crisis. *The Society for Occupational Health Psychology Newsletter*, p. 5.

Procopio, C. H., & Procopio, S. T. (2007). Do you know what it means to miss New Orleans? Internet communication, geographic community, and social capital in crisis. *Journal of Applied Communication Research, 35*, 67–87.

Pronin, E., Berger, J., & Moluki, S. (2007). Alone in a crowd of sheep: Asymmetric perceptions of conformity and their roots in an introspection illusion. *Journal of Personality and Social Psychology, 92*, 585–595.

Pronin, E., Fleming, J. J., & Steffel, M. (2008). Value revelations: Disclosure is in the eye of the beholder. *Journal of Personality and Social Psychology, 95,* 795–809.

Pronin, E., & Jacobs, E. (2008). Thought speed, mood, and the experience of mental motion. *Perspectives on Psychological Science, 3,* 461–485.

Pronin, E., Jacobs, E., & Wegner, D. M. (2008). Psychological effects of thought acceleration. *Emotion, 8,* 597–612.

Pronin, E., & Wegner, D. M. (2006). Independent effects of thought speed and thought content on mood. *Psychological Science, 17,* 807–813.

Proulx, C. M., Helms, H. M., & Cheryl, B. (2007). Marital quality and personal well-being: A meta-analysis. *Journal of Marriage and Family, 69,* 576–593.

Prudic, J. (2005). Electroconvulsive therapy. In B. J. Sadock & V. A. Sadock (Eds.), *Kaplan and Sadock's comprehensive textbook of psychiatry.* Philadelphia: Lippincott Williams & Wilkins.

Prudic, J. (2009). Electroconvulsive therapy. In B. J. Sadock, V. A. Sadock, & P. Ruiz (Eds.), *Kaplan & Sadock's comprehensive textbook of psychiatry* (pp. 3285–3300). Philadelphia: Lippincott Williams & Wilkins.

Pryor, F. L., & Schaffer, D. (1997, July). Wages and the university educated: A paradox resolved. *Monthly Labor Review, 3*–14.

Pryor, J. B., Giedd, J. L., & Williams, K. B. (1995). A social psychological model for predicting sexual harassment. *Journal of Social Issues, 51,* 69–84.

Puentes, J., Knox, D., & Zusman, M. E. (2008). Participants in "friends with benefits" relationships. *College Student Journal, 42,* 176–180.

Puetz, T. W., O'Connor, P. J., & Dishman, R. K. (2006). Effects of chronic exercise on feelings of energy and fatigue: A quantitative synthesis. *Psychological Bulletin, 132,* 866–876.

Pugh, S., Dietz, J., Brief, A., & Wiley, J. (2008). Looking inside and out: The impact of employee and community demographic composition on organizational diversity climate. *Journal of Applied Psychology, 93,* 1422–1428.

Putnam, R. D. (1996). The strange disappearance of civic America. *The American Prospect, 24,* 34–46.

Pyle, R. M. (1993). *The thunder tree: Lessons from an urban wildland.* Boston: Houghton Mifflin.

Pyle, R. M. (2002). Eden in a vacant lot: Special places, species and kids in the neighborhood of life. In P. H. Kahn Jr. & S. R. Kellert (Eds.), *Children and nature: Psychological, sociocultural, and evolutionary investigations,* (pp. 305–327). Cambridge MA: MIT Press.

Pyszczynski, T., Greenberg, J., & Goldenberg, J. L. (2003). Freedom versus fear: On the defense, growth, and expansion of the self. In M. R. Leary & J. P. Tangney (Eds.), *Handbook of self and identity.* New York: Guilford.

Pyszczynski, T., Greenberg, J., & Solomon, S. (1999). A dual-process model of defense against conscious and unconscious death-related thoughts: An extension of terror management theory. *Psychological Review, 106*(4), 835–845.

Pyszczynski, T., Greenberg, J., Solomon, S., Arndt, J., & Schimel, J. (2004). Why do people need self-esteem? A theoretical and empirical review. *Psychological Bulletin, 130*(3), 435–468.

Pyszczynski, T., Solomon, S., & Greenberg, J. (2003a). Giving peace a chance. In T. Pyszczynski, S. Solomon, & J. Greenberg (Eds.), *In the wake of 9/11: The psychology of terror.* Washington, DC: American Psychological Association.

Pyszczynski, T., Solomon, S., & Greenberg, J. (2003b). *In the wake of 9/11: The psychology of terror.* Washington, DC: American Psychological Association.

Quick, J. D., Henley, A. B., & Quick J. C. (2004). The balancing act—at work and at home. *Organizational Dynamics, 33,* 426–438.

Quinn, K. A., Macrae, C. N., & Bodenhausen, G. V. (2003). Stereotyping and impression formation: How categorical thinking shapes person perception. In M. A. Hogg & J. Cooper (Eds.), *The Sage handbook of social psychology.* Thousand Oaks, CA: Sage Publications.

Raacke, J., & Bonds-Raacke, J. (2008). Myspace and Facebook: Applying the uses and gratifications theory to exploring friend-networking sites. *CyberPsychology & Behavior 11,* 169–174.

Rachman, S. J. (1992). Behavior therapy. In L. R. Squire (Ed.), *Encyclopedia of learning and memory.* New York: Macmillan.

Rachman, S. J. (2009). Psychological treatment of anxiety: The evolution of behavior therapy and cognitive behavior therapy. *Annual Review of Clinical Psychology, 5,* 97–119.

Ragins, B. R., Cornwell, J. M., & Miller, J. S. (2003). Heterosexism in the workplace: Do race and gender matter? *Group & Organization Management, 28*(1), 45–74.

Ragland, D. R., & Brand, R. J. (1988). Type A behavior and mortality from coronary heart disease. *The New England Journal of Medicine, 318,* 65–69.

Rahe, R. H., & Arthur, R. H. (1978). Life change and illness studies. *Journal of Human Stress, 4,* 3–15.

Rahe, R. H., Veach, T. L., Tolles, R. L., & Murakami, K. (2000). The stress and coping inventory: An educational and research instrument. *Stress Medicine, 16,* 199–208.

Rahim, M. A., & Magner, N. R. (1995). Confirmatory factor analysis of the styles of handling interpersonal conflict: First-order factor model and its invariance across groups. *Journal of Applied Psychology, 80,* 122–132.

Rahman, Q. (2005). Fluctuating asymmetry, second to fourth finger length and human sexual orientation. *Psychoneuroendocrinology, 30,* 382–391.

Raikes, H. A., & Thompson R. A. (2008). Attachment security and parenting quality predict children's problem-solving, attributions, and loneliness with peers. *Attachment & Human Development, 10,* 319–344.

Raj, A., & Sheehan, D. (2004). Benzodiazepines. In A. F. Schatzberg & C. B. Nemeroff (Eds.), *Textbook of psychopharmacology.* Washington, DC: American Psychiatric Publishing.

Raloff, J. (1996). Breakfast trends. *Science News, 150,* 90–91.

Ramadan, N. M. (2000). Migraine. In G. Fink (Ed.), *Encyclopedia of stress.* San Diego: Academic Press.

Ramaekers, J. G., Robbe, H. W. J., & O'Hanlon, J. F. (2000). Marijuana, alcohol and actual driving performance. *Human Psychopharmacology Clinical & Experimental, 15*(7), 551–558.

Ramanathan, S., & Williams, P. (2007). Immediate and delayed emotional consequences of indulgence: The moderating influence of personality type on mixed emotions. *Journal of Consumer Research, 34,* 212–223.

Raphael, B., & Dobson, M. (2000). Effects of public disasters. In G. Fink (Ed.), *Encyclopedia of stress* (Vol. 1). San Diego: Academic Press.

Rassin, E. (2008). Individual differences in susceptibility to conformation bias. *Netherlands Journal of Psychology, 64*(2), 87–93.

Ravindran, L. N. & Stein, M. B. (2009). Anxiety disorders: Somatic treatment. In B. J. Sadock, V. A. Sadock, & P. Ruiz (Eds.), *Kaplan & Sadock's comprehensive textbook of psychiatry* (pp. 1906–1914). Philadelphia: Lippincott Williams & Wilkins.

Ray, G. E., Cohen, R., Secrist, M. E., & Duncan, M. K. (1997). Relating aggressive and victimization behaviors to children's sociometric status and friendships. *Journal of Social and Personal Relationships, 14*(1), 95–108.

Ray, J. A. (1999). *The science of success: How to attract prosperity and create harmonic wealth through proven principles.* Carlsbad, CA: Sun Ark Press.

Ray, J. A. (2005). *Practical spirituality: How to use spiritual power to create tangible results.* Carlsbad, CA: James Ray International.

Read, C. R. (1991). Achievement and career choices: Comparisons of males and females. *Roeper Review, 13* 188–193.

Reardon, R. C., Lenz, J. G., Sampson, J. P., Jr., & Peterson, G. W. (2009). *Career development and planning: A comprehensive approach.* Belmont, CA: Cengage.

Reece, M., Herbenick, D., Sanders, S. A., Dodge, B. Ghassemi, A., & Fortenberry, J. D. (2009). Prevalence and characteristics of vibrator use by men in the United States. *Journal of Sexual Medicine, 6,* 1867–1874.

Reed, G. M., Kemeny, M. E., Taylor, S. E., & Visscher, B. R. (1999). Negative HIV-specific expectancies and AIDS-related bereavement as predictors of symptom onset in asymptomatic HIV-positive gay men. *Health Psychology, 18,* 354–363.

Rees, C. J., & Metcalfe, B. (2003). The faking of personality questionnaire results: Who's kidding whom. *Journal of Managerial Psychology, 18,* 156–165.

Regan, P. C., & Berscheid, E. (1997). Gender differences in characteristics desired in potential sexual and marriage partners. *Journal of Psychology and Human Sexuality, 9*(1), 25–37.

Regier, D. A., & Burke, J. D. (2000). Epidemiology. In B. J. Sadock & V. A. Sadock (Eds.), *Kaplan and Sadock's comprehensive textbook of psychiatry.* Philadelphia: Lippincott/Williams & Wilkins.

Regier, D. A., & Kaelber, C. T. (1995). The epidemiologic catchment area (ECA) program: Studying the prevalence and incidence of psychopathology. In M. T. Tsuang, M. Tohen, & G. E. P. Zahner (Eds.), *Textbook in psychiatric epidemiology.* New York: Wiley.

Regnerus, M. D. (2007). *Forbidden fruit: Sex and religion in the lives of American teenagers.* New York: Oxford Press.

Rehm, L. P., Wagner, A., & Ivens-Tyndal, Co. (2001). Mood disorders: Unipolar and bipolar. In P. B. Sutker & H. E. Adams (Eds.), *Comprehensive handbook of psychopathology* (3rd ed.). New York: Kluwer Academic/Plenum.

Rehman, U. S., & Holtzworth-Munroe, A. (2007). A cross-cultural examination of the relation of marital communication behavior to marital satisfaction. *Journal of Family Psychology, 21,* 759–763.

Reibel, D. K., Greeson, J. M., Brainard, G. C., & Rosenzweig, S. (2001). Mindfulness-based stress reduction and health-related quality of life in a heterogeneous patient population. *General Hospital Psychiatry, 23*(4), 183–192.

Reich, M., Lesur, A., & Perdrizet-Chevallier, C. (2008). Depression, quality of life and breast cancer: A review of the literature. *Breast Cancer Research and Treatment, 110*(1), 9–17.

Reiche, E. M. V., Nunes, S., & Morimoto, H. (2004). Stress, depression, the immune system, and cancer. *The Lancet Oncology, 5,* 617–625.

Reid, M., Miller, W., & Kerr, B. (2004). Sex-based glass ceilings in U. S. state-level bureaucracies, 1987-1997. *Administration and Society, 36,* 377–405.

Reinisch, J. M. (1990). *The Kinsey Institute new report on sex: What you must know to be sexually literate.* New York: St. Martin's.

Reis, H. T. (1998). Gender differences in intimacy and related behaviors: Context and processes. In D. Canary & K. Dindia (Eds.), *Sex and gender in communication: Similarities and differences.* Mahwah, NJ: Erlbaum.

Reis, H. T. (2008). Reinvigorating the concept of situation in social psychology. *Personality and Social Psychology Review, 12*(4), 311–329.

Reis, H. T., & Patrick. B. C. (1996). Attachment and intimacy: Component processes. In E. T. Higgins & A. Kruglanski (Eds.), *Social psychology: Handbook of basic principles.* New York: Guilford.

Reis, H. T., & Shaver, P. (1988). Intimacy as an interpersonal process. In S. W. Duck (Ed.), *Handbook of personal relationships.* New York: Wiley.

Reis, H. T., Snyder, D. K., & Roberts, L. J. (2009). Repairing relationships. In H. T. Reis & S. Sprecher (Eds.), *Encyclopedia of human relationships: Vol. 3* (pp. 1363–1367). Los Angeles: Sage Reference Publication.

Reis, H. T., & Wheeler, L. (1991). Studying social interaction with the Rochester Interaction Record. *Advances in Experimental Social Psychology, 24,* 269–318.

Reis, T. J., Gerrard, M., & Gibbons, F. X. (1993). Social comparison and the pill: Reactions to upward and downward comparison of contraceptive behavior. *Personality and Social Psychology Bulletin, 19,* 13–21.

Reiss, S. (1991). Expectancy model of fear, anxiety and panic. *Clinical Psychology Review, 11,* 141–154.

Reissman, C., Aron, A., & Bergen, M. R. (1993). Shared activities and marital satisfaction: Causal direction and self-expansion versus boredom. *Journal of Social and Personal Relationships, 10,* 243–254.

Renaud, C. A., & Byers, E. S. (2001). Positive and negative sexual cognitions: Subjective experience and relationships to sexual adjustment. *Journal of Sex Research, 38*(3), 252–262.

Rendi, M., Szarbo, A., Szabo, T., Velenczei, A., & Kovacs, A. (2008). Acute psychological benefits of aerobic exercise: A field study into the effects of exercise characteristics. *Psychology, Health & Medicine, 13,* 180–184.

Renner, L. M., & Markward, M. J. (2009). Factors associated with suicidal ideation among women abused in intimate partner relationships. *Smith College Studies in Social Work, 79,* 139–154.

Rennie, D., & Luft, H. S. (2000). Making them transparent, making them credible. *Journal of the American Medical Association, 283,* 2516–2521.

Rennison, C. M., & Welchans, S. (2000). *Intimate partner violence.* Washington, DC: U.S. Department of Justice, Office of Justice Programs, Bureau of Justice Statistics.

Renshaw, D. C. (2005). Premature ejaculation revisited–2005. *Family Journal, 13,* 150–152.

Repetti, R. L., & Wang, S. (2009). Work-family spillover. In H. T. Reis & S. Sprecher (Eds.), *Encyclopedia of human relationships: Vol. 3* (pp. 1694–1697). Los Angeles: Sage Reference Publication.

Repetto, M., & Gold, M. S. (2005). Cocaine and crack: Neurobiology. In J. H. Lowinson, P. Ruiz, R. B. Millman, & J. G. Langrod (Eds.), *Substance abuse: A comprehensive textbook.* Philadelphia: Lippincott/Williams & Wilkins.

**Rhodewalt, F., & Morf, C. C.** (2005). Reflections in troubled waters: Narcissism and the vicissitudes of an interpersonality contextualized self. In A. Tesser, J. V. Wood, & D. A. D. A. Staper (Eds.), *On Building, defending, and regulating the self* (pp. 127–152). New York: Psychology Press.

**Rhodewalt, F., & Peterson, B.** (2009). Narcissism. In M. R. Leary & R. H. Hoyle (Eds.), *Handbook of individual differences in social behavior* (pp. 547–560). New York: Guilford.

**Rhodewalt, F., Tragakis, M. W., & Finnerty, J.** (2006). Narcissism and self-handicapping: Linking self-aggrandizement to behavior. *Journal of Research in Personality, 40,* 573–597.

**Rice D., & Barone, S.** (2000). Critical periods of vulnerability for the developing nervous system: Evidence from humans and animal models. *Environmental Health Perspectives, 108* (Suppl 3), 511–533.

**Rice, J. K., & Else-Quest, N.** (2006). The mixed messages of motherhood. In J. Worrell & C. D. Goodheart (Eds.), *Handbook of girls' and women's psychological health.* New York: Oxford University Press.

**Rice, L. N., & Greenberg, L. S.** (1992). Humanistic approaches to psychotherapy. In D. K. Freedheim (Ed.), *History of psychotherapy: A century of change.* Washington, DC: American Psychological Association.

**Richards, Z., & Hewstone, M.** (2001). Subtyping and subgrouping: Processes for the prevention and promotion of stereotype change. *Personality and Social Psychology Review, 5,* 52–73.

**Richardson, C. R., Kriska, A. M., Lantz, P. M., & Hayword, R. A.** (2004). Physical activity and mortality across cardiovascular disease risk groups. *Medicine and Science in Sports and Exercise, 36*(11), 1923–1929.

**Richardson, F. C., & Guignon, C. B.** (2008). Positive psychology and philosophy of social science. *Theory & Psychology, 18,* 605–627.

**Richardson, J., Anderson, T., Flaherty, J., & Bell, C.** (2003). The quality of mental health care for African Americans. *Culture, Medicine and Psychiatry, 27,* 487–498.

**Richardson, J. G., & Simpson, C. H.** (1982). Children, gender and social structure: An analysis of the contents of letters to Santa Claus. *Child Development, 53* 429–436.

**Richardson, J. T. & Introvigne, M.** (2001). "Brainwashing" theories in European parliamentary and administrative reports on "cults" and "sects." *Journal for the Scientific Study of Religion,* 40 (2), 143–168.

**Richey, E., Knox, D., & Zusman, M.** (2009). Sexual values of 783 undergraduates. *College Student Journal, 43,* 175–180.

**Richmond, V. P., & McCroskey, J. C.** (1995). *Communication: Apprehension, avoidance, and effectiveness* (5th ed.). Boston: Allyn & Bacon.

**Richter, H.** (2007, May 7). Lights, camera, hired! *Newsweek,* p. 65.

**Ricketts, T., & Macaskill, A.** (2003). Gambling as emotion management: Developing a grounded theory of problem gambling. *Addiction Research and Theory, 11,* 383–400.

**Ridge, S. R., & Feeney, J. A.** (1998). Relationship history and relationship attitudes in gay males and lesbians: Attachment style and gender differences. *Australian and New Zealand Journal of Psychiatry, 32*(6), 848–859.

**Ridgeway, C. L., & Bourg, C.** (2004). Gender as status: An expectation states theory approach. In A. H. Eagly, A. E. Beall, & R. J. Sternberg (Eds.), *The psychology of gender.* New York: Guilford Press.

**Ridker, P. M.** (2001). High-sensitivity C-reactive protein: Potential adjunct for global risk assessment in the primary prevention of cardiovascular disease. *Circulation, 103,* 1813–1818.

**Rief, W., Henningsen, P., & Hiller, W.** (2006). Classification of somatoform disorders. *American Journal of Psychiatry, 163,* 746–747.

**Rieger, G., Linsenmeier, J. A. W., Gygax, L., & Bailey, J. M.** (2008). Sexual orientation and childhood gender nonconformity: Evidence from home videos. *Developmental Psychology, 44,* 46–58.

**Riemann, R., Angleitner, A., & Strelau, J.** (1997). Genetic and environmental influences on personality: A study of twins reared together using the self- and peer report NEO-FFI scales. *Journal of Personality, 65,* 449–476.

**Rihmer, Z.** (2003). Do SSRI's increase the risk of suicide among depressives even if they are only taking placebo? *Psychotherapy & Psychosomatics, 72*(6), 357–358.

**Rihmer, Z., & Angst, J.** (2005). Mood disorders: Epidemiology. In B. J. Sadock & V. A. Sadock (Eds.), *Kaplan & Sadock's comprehensive textbook of psychiatry.* Philadelphia: Lippicott Williams & Wilkins.

**Rihmer, Z., & Angst, J.** (2009). Mood disorders: Epidemiology. In B. J. Sadock, V. A. Sadock, & P. Ruiz (Eds.), *Kaplan & Sadock's comprehensive textbook of psychiatry* (pp. 1645–1652). Philadelphia: Lippincott Williams & Wilkins.

**Riis, J., Loewenstein, G., Baron, J., Jepson, C., Fagerlin, A., & Ubel, P. A.** (2005). Ignorance of hedonic adaptation to hemodialysis: A study using ecological momentary assessment. *Journal of Experimental Psychology: General, 134,* 3–9.

**Riley, L. D., & Bowen, C.** (2005). The sandwich generation: Challenges and coping strategies of multigenerational families. *Family Journal: Counseling and Therapy for Couples and Families, 13,* 52–58.

**Rimal R. N.** (2001). Longitudinal influences of knowledge and self-efficacy on exercise behavior: Tests of a mutual reinforcement model. *Journal of Health Psychology, 6,* 31–46.

**Ringström, G., Abrahamsson, H., Strid, H., & Simŕen, M.** (2007). Why do subjects with irritable bowel syndrome seek health care for their symptoms? *Scandinavian Journal of Gastroenterology, 42,* 1194–1203.

**Rising, K., Bacchetti, & Bero, L.** (2008). Reporting bias in drug trials submitted to the Food and Drug Administration: Review of publication and presentation. *PLoS Medicine,* 5(11), e217.

**Riskey, D. R., & Birnbaum, M. H.** (1974). Compensatory effects in moral judgment: Two rights don't make up for a wrong. *Journal of Experimental Psychology, 103,* 171–173.

**Riskind, J. H.** (2005). Cognitive mechanisms in generalized anxiety disorder: A second generation of theoretical perspectives. *Cognitive Therapy & Research, 29*(1), 1–5.

**Riso, L. P., du Toit, P. L., Blandino, J. A., Penna, S., Dacey, S., Duin, J. S., Pacoe, E. M., Grant, M. M., & Ulmer, C. S.** (2003). Cognitive aspects of chronic depression. *Journal of Abnormal Psychology, 112*(1), 72–80.

**Ritskes, R., Ritskes-Hoitinga, M., Stodkilde-Jorgensen, H., Baerentsen, K. , & Hartman, T.** (2003). MRI scanning during Zen meditation: The picture of enlightenment. *Constructivism in the Human Sciences, 8*(1), 85–90.

**Ritz, T., Steptoe, A., DeWilde, S., & Costa, M.** (2000). Emotions and stress increase respiratory resistance in asthma. *Psychosomatic Medicine, 62*(3), 401–412.

**Robbins, B. D.** (2008). What is the good life? Positive psychology and the renaissance of humanistic psychology. *The Humanistic Psychologist, 36,* 96–112.

**Roberts, A. R.** (2002). Myths, facts, and realities regarding battered women and their children: An overview. In A. R. Roberts (Ed.), *Handbook of domestic violence intervention strategies: Policies, programs, and legal remedies.* New York: Oxford University Press.

**Roberts, B. W., Caspi, A., & Moffitt, T.** (2003). Work experiences and personality development in young adulthood. *Journal of Personality and Social Psychology, 84,* 582–593.

**Roberts, B. W., Jackson, J. J., Fayard, J. V., Edmonds, G., & Meints, J.** (2009). Conscientiousness. In M. R. Leary & R. H. Hoyle (Eds.), *Handbook of individual differences in social* behavior (pp. 369–381). New York: Guilford.

**Roberts, B. W., Kuncel, N. R., Shiner, R., Caspi, A., & Goldberg, L. R.** (2007). The power of personality: The comparative validity of personality traits, socioeconomic status, and cognitive ability for predicting important life outcomes. *Perspectives on Psychological Science, 2,* 313–345.

**Roberts, B. W., & Pomerantz, E. M.** (2004). On traits, situations, and their integration: A developmental perspective. *Personality and Social Psychology Review, 8*(4), 402–416.

**Roberts, D. F., Foehr, U. G., & Rideout, V.** (2005). *Generation M: Media in the lives of 8–18 year olds (Publication No. 7251).* Menlo Park, CA: Henry J. Kaiser Family Foundation.

**Roberts, D. F., Foehr, U. G., Rideout, V. J., & Vrodie, M.** (1999). *Kids and media @ the new millennium.* Menlo Park, CA: Kaiser Family Foundation.

**Roberts, L. J., & Krokoff, L. J.** (1990). A time series analysis of withdrawal, hostility, and displeasure in satisfied and dissatisfied marriages. *Journal of Marriage and the Family, 52,* 95–105.

**Roberts, S.** (2006, October 15). It's official: To be married means to be outnumbered. *New York Times.*

**Robertson, J. M., Lin, C., Woodford, J., Danos, K. K., & Hurst, M. A.** (2001). The (un)emotional male: Physiological, verbal and written correlates of expressiveness. *Journal of Men's Studies, 9,* 393–412.

**Robins, L. N., Locke, B. Z., & Regier, D. A.** (1991). An overview of psychiatric disorders in America. In L. N. Robins & D. A. Regier (Eds.), *Psychiatric disorders in America: The epidemiologic catchment area study.* New York: Free Press.

**Robins, R. W., & Trzesniewski, K. H.** (2005). Self-esteem development across the lifespan. *Current Direction in Psychological Science, 14,* 158–162.

**Robinson, B., Frye, E. M., & Bradley, L. J.** (1997). Cult affiliation and disaffiliation: Implications for counseling. *Counseling and Values, 41,* 166–173.

**Robinson, B. E., Flowers, C., & Ng, K.** (2006). The relationship between workaholism and marital disaffection: Husband's perspective. *Family Journal: Counseling and Therapy for Couples and Families, 14,* 213–220.

**Robinson, D. G., Woerner, M. G., McMeniman, M., Mendelowitz, A., & Bilder, R. M.** (2004). Symptomatic and functional recovery from a first episode of schizophrenia or schizoaffective disorder. *American Journal of Psychiatry, 161,* 473–479.

**Robinson, F. P.** (1970). *Effective study* (4th ed.). New York: HarperCollins.

**Robinson, M. D., Johnson, J. T., & Shields, S. A.** (1995). On the advantages of modesty: The benefits of a balanced self-presentation. *Communication Research, 22,* 575–591.

**Robinson, O., & Griffiths, A.** (2005). Coping with the stress of transformational change in a government department. *Journal of Applied Behavioral Science, 41*(2), 203–221.

**Robles, T. F., Glaser, R., & Kiecolt-Glaser, J. K.** (2005). Out of balance: A new look at chronic stress, depression, and immunity. *Current Directions in Psychological Science, 14,* 111–115.

**Rodin, J., Schank, D., & Striegel-Moore, R. H.** (1989). Psychological features of obesity. *Medical Clinics of North America, 73* 47–66.

**Rodrigues, A. E., Hall, J. H., & Fincham, F. D.** (2006). What predicts divorce and relationship dissolution. In M. A. Fine & J. H. Harvey (Eds.), *Handbook of divorce and relationship resolution.* Mahwah, NJ: Erlbaum.

**Roediger, H. L., III, & Karpicke, J. D.** (2006a). Test-enhanced learning: Taking memory tests improves long-term retention. *Psychological Science, 17,* 249–255.

**Roediger, H. L., III, & Karpicke, J. D.** (2006b). The power of testing memory: Basic research and implications for educational practice. *Perspectives on Psychological Science, 1*(3), 181–210.

**Roediger, H. L., III, & McDermott, K. B.** (1995). Creating false memories: Remembering words not presented in lists. *Journal of Experimental Psychology: Learning, Memory, and Cognition, 21,* 803–814.

**Roediger, H. L., III, & McDermott, K. B.** (2000). Tricks of memory. *Current Directions in Psychological Science, 9,* 123–127.

**Rogers, C. J., Colbert, L. H., Greiner, J. W., Perkins, S. N., & Hursting, S. D.** (2008). Physical activity and cancer prevention: Pathways and targets for intervention. *Sports Medicine, 38,* 271–296.

**Rogers, C. R.** (1951). *Client-centered therapy: Its current practice, implications, and theory.* Boston: Houghton Mifflin.

**Rogers, C. R.** (1961). *On becoming a person: A therapist's view of psychotherapy.* Boston: Houghton Mifflin.

**Rogers, C. R.** (1977). *Carl Rogers on personal power.* New York: Delacorte.

**Rogers, C. R.** (1980). *A way of being.* Boston: Houghton Mifflin.

**Rogers, C. R.** (1986). Client-centered therapy. In I. L. Kutash & A. Wolf (Eds.), *Psychotherapist's casebook.* San Francisco: Jossey-Bass.

**Rogers, M. P., Fricchione, G., & Reich, P.** (1999). Psychosomatic medicine and consultation-liaison psychiatry. In A. M. Nicholi (Ed.), *The Harvard guide to psychiatry* (3rd ed.). Cambridge, MA: Harvard University Press.

**Rogers, R. W., & Prentice-Dunn, S.** (1997). Protection motivation theory. In D. Gochman (Ed.), *Handbook of health behavior research* (Vol. 1). New York: Plenum.

**Rogers, S. J., & White, L. K.** (1998). Satisfaction with parenting: The role of marital happiness, family structure, and parents' gender. *Journal of Marriage and the Family, 60,* 293–308.

**Rogge, R. D., Bradbury, T. N., Hahlweg, K., Engl, J., & Thurmaier, F.** (2006). Predicting marital distress and dissolution: Refining the two-factor hypothesis. *Journal of Family Psychology, 20,* 156–159.

**Rohde, P. A., Atzwanger, K., Butovskayad, M., Lampert, A., Mysterud, I., Sanchez-Andres, A., & Sulloway, F. J.** (2003). Perceived parental favoritism, closeness to kin and the rebel of the family: The effects of birth order and sex. *Evolution & Human Behavior, 24,* 261–276.

**Rohner, R. P., & Veneziano, R. A.** (2001). The importance of father love: History and contemporary evidence. *Review of General Psychology, 5*(4), 382–405.

**Rohrer, D., & Taylor, K.** (2006). The effects of overlearning and distributed practice on the retention of mathematics knowledge. *Applied Cognitive Psychology, 20,* 1209–1224.

**Rohrer, D., Taylor, K., Pashler, H., Wixted, J. T., & Capeda, N. J.** (2005). The effect of overlearning on long-term retention. *Applied Cognitive Psychology, 19,* 361–374.

**Rojewski, J. W.** (2005). Occupational aspirations: Constructs, meanings, and application. In S. D. Brown & R. W. Lent (Eds.), *Career development and counseling: Putting theory and research to work.* New York: Wiley.

**Rokach, A.** (2000). Perceived causes of loneliness in adulthood. *Journal of Social Behavior and Personality, 15,* 67–84.

**Rollie, S. S., & Duck, S.** (2006). Divorce and dissolution of romantic relationships. In M. A. Fine & J. H. Harvey (Eds.), *Handbook of divorce and relationship resolution.* Mahwah, NJ: Erlbaum.

**Romi, S., & Kohan, E.** (2004). Wilderness programs: Principles, possibilities and opportunities for intervention with dropout adolescents. *Child & Youth Care Forum, 33,* 115–136.

**Rook, K. S.** (1998). Investigating the positive and negative sides of personal relationships: Through a lens darkly? In B. H. Spitzberg & W. R. Cupach (Eds.), *The dark side of close relationships.* Mahwah, NJ: Lawrence Erlbaum.

**Rook, K. S., & Pietromonaco, P.** (1987). Close relationships: Ties that heal or ties that bind? In W. H. Jones & D. Perlman (Eds.), *Advances in personal relationships.* Greenwich, CT: JAI Press.

**Rose, D., Wykes, T., Leese, M., Bindman, J., & Fleischmann, P.** (2003). Patient's perspectives on electroconvulsive therapy: Systematic review. *British Medical Journal, 326,* 1363–1365.

**Rose, D. P.** (1997). Dietary fatty acids and cancer. *American Journal of Clinical Nutrition, 66*(4), 998S–1003S.

**Rosen, D. H.** (1974). *Lesbianism: A study of female homosexuality.* Springfield, IL: Charles C Thomas.

**Rosen, G. M.** (1993). Self-help or hype? Comments on psychology's failure to advance self-care. *Professional Psychology: Research and Practice, 24,* 340–345.

**Rosen, G. M., Glasgow, R. E., & Moore, T. E.** (2003). Self-help therapy: The science and business of giving psychology away. In S. O. Lilienfeld, S. J. Lynn, & J. M. Lohr (Eds.), *Science and pseudoscience in clinical psychology.* New York: Guilford Press.

**Rosen, R.** (2000). Medical and psychological interventions for erectile dysfunction. In S. Leiblum & R. Rosen (Eds.), *Principles and practice of sex therapy.* New York: Guilford.

**Rosen, R. D.** (1977). *Psychobabble.* New York: Atheneum.

**Rosenbaum, J. E.** (2009). Patient teenagers? A comparison of the sexual behavior of virginity pledgers and matched nonpledgers. *Pediatrics, 123,* 110–120.

**Rosenbaum, M., Lakin, M., & Roback, H. B.** (1992). Psychotherapy in groups. In D. K. Freedheim (Ed.), *History of psychotherapy: A century of change.* Washington, DC: American Psychological Association.

**Rosenberg, E., & DeMaso, D. R.** (2008). A doubtful guest: Managed care and mental health. *Child and Adolescent Psychiatric Clinics of North America, 17,* 53–66.

**Rosenblatt, A., Greenberg, J., Solomon, S., Pyszczynski, T., & Lyon, D.** (1989). Evidence for terror management theory: I. The effects of mortality salience on reactions to those who violate or uphold cultural values. *Journal of Personality and Social Psychology, 57,* 681–690.

**Rosenfarb, I. S., Goldstein, M. J., Mintz, J., & Nuechterlein, K. H.** (1995). Expressed emotion and subclinical psychopathology observable within the transactions between schizophrenic patients and their family members. *Journal of Abnormal Psychology, 104,* 259–267.

**Rosenfeld, L. B., Stewart, S. C., Stinnett, H. J., & Jackson, L. A.** (1999). Preferences for body type and body characteristics associated with attractive and unattractive bodies: Jackson and McGill revisited. *Perceptual and Motor Skills, 89*(2), 459–470.

**Rosenheck, R. A.** (2006). Outcomes, costs, and policy caution. *Archives of General Psychiatry, 63,* 1074–1076.

**Rosenman, R. H.** (1993). Relationships of the Type A behavior pattern with coronary heart disease. In L. Goldberger & S. Breznitz (Eds.), *Handbook of stress: Theoretical and clinical aspects* (2nd ed.). New York: Free Press.

**Rosenthal, H.** (1988). *Not with my life I don't: Preventing suicide and that of others.* Muncie, IN: Accelerated Development.

**Rosenthal, R.** (1985). From unconscious experimenter bias to teacher expectancy effects. In J. B. Dusek, V. C. Hall & W. J. Meyer (Eds.), *Teacher expectancies.* Hillsdale, NJ: Erlbaum.

**Rosenthal, R.** (2002). The Pygmalion effect and its mediating mechanisms. In J. Aronson (Ed.), *Improving academic achievement: Impact of psychological factors on education* (pp. 25–36). San Diego, CA: Academic Press.

**Rosenthal, R.** (2003). Covert communication in laboratories, classrooms, and the truly real world. *Current Directions in Psychological Science, 12*(5), 151–154.

**Rosier, K. B., & Feld, S. L.** (2000). Covenant marriage: A new alternative for traditional families. *Journal of Comparative Family Studies, 31,* 385–394.

**Rospenda, K. M., Fujishiro, K., Shannon, C. A., & Richman, J. A.** (2008). Workplace harassment, stress, and drinking behavior over time: Gender differences in a national sample. *Addictive Behaviors, 33*(7), 964–967.

**Rospenda, K. M., Richman, J. A., Shannon, C. A.** (2009). Prevalence and mental health correlates of harassment and discrimination in the workplace: Results from a national study. *Journal of Interpersonal Violence, 24*(5), 819–843.

**Ross, C. E., & Van Willigen, M.** (1997). Education and the subjective quality of life. *Journal of Health & Social Behavior, 38,* 275–297.

**Ross, L. D.** (1977). The intuitive psychologist and his shortcomings: Distortions in the attribution process. In L. Berkowitz (Ed.), *Advances in experimental social psychology* (Vol. 10). New York: Academic Press.

**Ross, L., & Ward, A.** (1996). Naive realism: Implications for social conflict and misunderstanding. In T. Brown, E. Reed, & E. Turiel (Eds.), *Values and knowledge.* Hillsdale, NJ: Erlbaum.

**Ross, M., & Conway, M.** (1986). Remembering one's own past: The construction of personal histories. In R. M. Sorrentino & E. T. Higgins (Eds.), *Handbook of motivation and cognition: Foundations of social behavior.* New York: Guilford Press.

**Ross, M., & Wilson, A. E.** (2002). It feels like yesterday: Self-esteem, valence of personal past experiences, and judgments of subjective distance. *Journal of Personality and Social Psychology, 82,* 792–803.

**Ross, M. W.** (2005). Typing, doing, and being: Sexuality and the Internet. *Journal of Sex Research, 42,* 342–352.

**Roszak, T.** (1992). *The voice of the earth: An exploration of eco-psychology.* New York: Simon & Schuster.

**Roter, D. L., Hall, J. A., Merisca, R., Nordstrom, B., Cretin, D., & Svarstad, B.** (1998). Effectiveness of interventions to promote patient compliance. *Medical Care, 36,* 1138–1161.

**Roth, P. L., BeVier, C. A., Switzer, F. S., & Schippmann, J. S.** (1996). Meta-analyzing the relationship between grades and job performance. *Journal of Applied Psychology, 81*(5), 548–556.

**Roth, P. L., & Clarke, R. L.** (1998). Meta-analyzing the relationship between grades and salary. *Journal of Vocational Behavior, 53,* 386–400,

**Rotter, J. B.** (1982). *The development and application of social learning theory.* New York: Praeger.

**Roughton, B.** (2001, May 27). In Europe, workers time off adds up. *The Atlanta Journal-Constitution,* pp. D1–D2.

**Rouse-Arnett, M., & Dilworth, J. E. L.** (2007). Early influences on African American women's sexuality. *Journal of Feminist Family Therapy, 18*(3), 39–61.

**Roussi, P., Krikeli, V., Hatzidimitrious, C., & Kourti, I.** (2007). Patterns of coping, flexibility in coping and psychological distress in women diagnosed with breast cancer. *Cognitive Therapy and Research, 31,* 97–109.

**Rowe, D., & van den Oord, E. J. C. G.** (2005). Genetic and environmental influences. In V. A. Derlega, B. A. Winstead, & W. H. Jones (Eds.), *Personality: Contemporary theory and research.* Belmont, CA: Wadsworth.

**Rozanski, A., Blumenthal, J. A., & Kaplan, J.** (1999). Impact of psychological factors on the pathogenesis of cardiovascular disease and implications for therapy. *Circulation, 99*(16), 2192–2197.

**Rozee, P. D., Bateman, P., & Gilmore, T.** (1991). The personal perspective of acquaintance rape prevention: A three-tier approach. In A. Parrot & L. Bechhofer (Eds.), *Acquaintance rape: The hidden crime.* New York: Wiley.

**Rubenstein, C. M., & Shaver, P.** (1982). The experience of loneliness. In L. A. Peplau & D. Perlman (Eds.), *Loneliness: A sourcebook of current theory, research and therapy.* New York: Wiley.

**Rubin, R. H.** (2001). Alternative lifestyles revisited, or whatever happened to swingers, group marriages, and communes? *Journal of Family Issues, 22,* 711–726.

**Rubin, Z., Peplau, L. A., & Hill, C. T.** (1981). Loving and leaving: Sex differences in romantic attachments. *Sex Roles, 7,* 821–835.

**Rucci, A. J.** (2008). I-O psychology's "core purpose": Where science and practice meet. *The Industrial-Organizational Psychologist, 46*(1), 17–34.

**Rudisch, B., & Nemeroff, C. B.** (2003). Epidemiology of comorbid coronary artery disease and depression. *Biological Psychiatry, 54*(3), 227–240.

**Rudorfer, M. V., Henry, M. E., & Sackeim, H. A.** (2003). Electroconvulsive therapy. In A. Tasman, J. Kay, & J. A. Lieberman (Eds.), *Psychiatry.* New York: Wiley.

**Ruff, E. A., Reardon, R. C., & Bertoch, S. C.** (2008, June). Holland's RIASEC theory and applications: Exploring a comprehensive bibliography. *Career Convergence.* Retrieved from TCSLINKTONEWS[5483, ncda.org,layout_details]

**Ruini, C., & Fava, G. A.** (2004). Clinical application of well-being therapy. In P. A. Linley & S. Joseph (Eds.), *Positive psychology in practice.* Hoboken, NJ: Wiley.

**Rupp, H. A., & Wallen, K.** (2009). Sex-specific content preferences for visual sexual stimuli. *Archives of Sexual Behavior, 38,* 417–426.

**Rush, A. J.** (1984). Cognitive therapy. In T. B. Karasu (Ed.), *The psychiatric therapies.* Washington, DC: American Psychiatric Association.

**Russell, G. F. M.** (1995). Anorexia nervosa through time. In G. Szmukler, C. Dare, & J. Treasure (Eds.), *Handbook of eating disorders: Theory, treatment, and research.* New York: Wiley.

**Russell, K. C.** (2003). An assessment of outcomes in outdoor behavioral healthcare treatment. *Child and Youth Care Forum, 32,* 355–381.

**Russo, N. F.** (1979). Overview: Sex roles, fertility, and the motherhood mandate. *Psychology of Women Quarterly, 4,* 7–15.

**Rutledge, T., & Hogan, B. E.** (2002). A quantitative review of prospective evidence linking psychological factors with hypertension development. *Psychosomatic Medicine, 64,* 758–766.

**Rutter, M.** (2007). Gene-environment interdependence. *Developmental Science, 10,* 12–18.

**Ryan, C., & Futterman, D.** (1997). Lesbian and gay youth: Care and counseling. *Adolescent Medicine, 8,* 221.

**Ryan, R. M., & Deci, E. L.** (2001). On happiness and human potentials: A review of research on hedonic and eudaimonic well-being. *Annual Review of Psychology, 52,* 141–166.

**Ryan, S., Franzettta, K., Manlove, J., & Holcombe, E.** (2007). Adolescents' discussions about contraception or STDs with partners before first sex. *Perspectives on Sexual and Reproductive Health, 39,* 149–157.

**Rye, M. S., Folck, C. D., Heim, T. A., Olszewski, B. T., & Traina, E.** (2004). Forgiveness of an ex-spouse: How does it relate to mental health following a divorce? *Journal of Divorce and Remarriage, 41,* 31–51.

**Ryff, C. D., & Singer, B.** (2003). Flourishing under fire: Resilience as a prototype of challenged thriving. In C. L. M. Keyes & J. Haidt (Eds.), *Flourishing: Positive psychology and the life well-lived* (pp. 15–36). Washington, DC: American Psychological Association.

**Saad, L.** (1999, September 3). *American workers generally satisfied, but indicate their jobs leave much to be desired.* Princeton, NJ: Gallup News Service.

**Saad, L.** (2007). *Americans rate the morality of 16 social issues.* Retrieved June 23, 2007 from http://www.galluppoll.com/content/?ci=27757&p=1.

**Saad, L.** (2008). *Americans evenly divided on morality of homosexuality.* Retrieved from http://www.gallup.com/poll/108115/americans-evenly-divided-morality-homosexuality.aspx

**Sabatelli, R. M.** (2009). Social exchange theory. In H. T. Reis & S. Sprecher (Eds.), *Encyclopedia of human relationships: Vol. 3* (pp. 1521–1524). Los Angeles: Sage Reference Publication.

**Sabatelli, R. M., & Ripoll, K.** (2004). Variations in marriage over time: An ecological/exchange perspective. In M. Coleman & L. H. Ganong (Eds.), *Handbook of contemporary families: Considering the past, contemplating the future.* Thousand Oaks, CA: Sage.

**Sackeim, H. A., Haskett, R. F., Mulsant, B. H., Thase, M. E., Mann, J. J., Pettinati, H. M., Greenberg, R. M., Crowe, R. R., Cooper, T. B., & Prudic, J.** (2001). Continuation pharmacotherapy in the prevention of relapse following electroconvulsive therapy: A randomized controlled trial. *Journal of the American Medical Association, 285*(10), 1299–1307.

**Sadker, M., & Sadker, D.** (1994). *Failing at fair-ness: How America's schools cheat girls.* New York: Scribners.

**Sadler, J. Z.** (2005). *Values and psychiatric diagnosis.* New York: Oxford University Press.

**Safron, A., Barch, B., Bailey, J. M., Gitelman, D. R., Parrish, T., & Reber, P.** (2007). Neural correlates of sexual arousal in homosexual and heterosexual men. *Behavioral Neuroscience, 121,* 237–248.

**Sagiv, L., Roccas, S., & Hazan, O.** (2004). Value pathways to well-being: Healthy values, valued goal attainment, and environmental congruence. In P. A. Linley & S. Joseph (Eds.), *Positive psychology in practice*. New York: Wiley.

**Sagrestano, L. M., Heavey, C. L., & Christensen, A.** (2006). Individual differences versus social structural approaches to explaining demand-withdraw and social influence behaviors. In K. Dindia, & D. J. Canary (Eds.), *Sex differences and similarities in communication*. Mahwah, NJ: Erlbaum.

**Saks, A. M.** (2006). Multiple predictions and criteria of job search success. *Journal of Vocational Behavior, 68,* 400–415.

**Salerno, S.** (2005). *Sham: How the self-help movement made America helpless*. New York: Crown Publishers.

**Salganik, M. J., & Watts, D. J.** (2008). Leading the herd astray: An experimental study of self-fulfilling prophecies in an artificial cultural market. *Social Psychology Quarterly, 71*(4), 338–355.

**Salovey, P., & Mayer, J. D.** (1990). Emotional intelligence. *Imagination, Cognition, and Personality, 9,* 185–211.

**Salovey, P., Mayer, J. D., & Caruso, D.** (2002). The positive psychology of emotional intelligence. In C. R. Synder & S. J. Lopez (Eds.), *Handbook of positive psychology*. New York: Oxford University Press.

**Salovey, P., Mayer, J. D., & Caruso, D.** (2005). The positive psychology of emotional intelligence. In C. R. Snyder & S. J. Lopez (Eds.), *Handbook of positive psychology*. New York: Oxford University Press.

**Salvatore, J., & Shelton, J. N.** (2007). Cognitive costs of exposure to racial prejudice. *Psychological Science, 18,* 810–815.

**Salvendy, J. T.** (1993). Selection and preparation of patients and organization of the group. In H. I. Kaplan & B. J. Sadock (Eds.), *Comprehensive group psychotherapy*. Baltimore: Williams & Wilkins.

**Samberg, E., & Marcus, E. R.** (2005). Process, resistance, and interpretation. In E. S. Person, A. M. Cooper, & G. O. Gabbard (Eds.), *Textbook of psychoanalysis*. Washington, DC: American Psychiatric Publishing.

**Samnaliev, M. & Clark, R. E.** (2008) The economics of schizophrenia. In K. T. Mueser & D. V. Jeste (Eds.), *Clinical handbook of schizophrenia* (pp. 507–515). New York: Guilford.

**Samovar, L. A., & Porter, R. E.** (2004). *Communication between cultures* (5th ed.). Belmont, CA: Wadsworth.

**Samovar, L. A., Porter, R. E., & McDaniel, E. R.** (2007). *Communication between cultures* (6th ed.). Belmont, CA: Wadsworth.

**Samovar, L. A., Porter, R. E., & Stefani, L. A.** (1998). *Communication between cultures* (2nd ed.). Belmont, CA: Wadsworth.

**Sampson, R.** (2003). *Acquaintance rape of college students. Problem-oriented guides for police: Problem specific guides series, No. 17.* Washington, DC: U.S. Department of Justice.

**Sanchez, L.** (2009). Covenant marriage. In H. T. Reis & S. Sprecher (Eds.), *Encyclopedia of human relationships: Vol. 2* (pp. 363–365). Los Angeles: Sage Reference Publication.

**Sanchez, L. M., & Turner, S. M.** (2003). Practicing psychology in the era of managed care: Implications for practice and training. *American Psychologist, 58*(2), 116–129.

**Sande, M. A., & Ronald, A.** (2004). Treatment of HIV/AIDS: Do the dilemmas only increase? *Journal of the American Medical Association, 292*(2), 224–236.

**Sanders, G.** (2000). Men together: Working with gay couples in contemporary times. In P. Papp (Ed.), *Couples on the fault line.* New York: Guilford Press.

**Sanderson, C. A. Wallier, J. M., Stockdale, J. E., & Yopyk, D. J. A.** (2008). Who feels discrepant and how does feeling discrepant matter? Examining the presence and consequences of feeling discrepant from personal and social norms related to thinness in American and British high school girls. *Journal of Social and Clinical Psychology, 27,* 995–1020.

**Sandin, B., Chorot, P., Santed, M. A., & Valiente, R. M.** (2004). Differences in negative life events between patients with anxiety disorders, depression and hypochondriasis. *Anxiety, Stress & Coping: An International Journal, 17*(1), 37–47.

**Sandnabba, N. K., & Ahlberg, C.** (1999). Parents' attitudes and expectations about children's cross-gender behavior. *Sex Roles, 40*(3–4), 249–263.

**Sandoz, J.** (2004). Internet addiction. *Annals of the American Psychotherapy Association, 7*(1), 34.

**Sanislow, C. A., & Carson, R. C.** (2001). Schizophrenia: A critical examination. In P. B. Sutker & H. E. Adams (Eds.), *Comprehensive handbook of psychopathology* (3rd ed.). New York: Kluwer Academic/Plenum.

**Santelli, J. S., Morrow, B., Anderson, J. E., & Lindberg, L. D.** (2006). Contraceptive use and pregnancy risk among U. S. high school students, 1991–2003. *Perspectives on Sexual and Reproductive Health, 38*(2), 106–111.

**Santtila, P., Wager, I., Witting, K., Harlaar, N., Jern, P., Johansson, A., Varjonen, M., & Sandnabba, K.** (2008). Discrepancies between sexual desire and sexual activity: Gender differences and associations with relationship satisfaction. *Journal of Sex & Marital Therapy, 34,* 31–44.

**Sanz de Acedo, M. L., & Garcia Ganuza, J. M.** (2003). Improvement of mental rotation in girls and boys. *Sex Roles, 49*(5–6), 277–286.

**Sapolsky, R. M.** (2004). *Why zebras don't get ulcers: The acclaimed guide to stress, stress-related diseases, and coping.* New York: Holt.

**Sarason, I. G., Johnson, J. H., & Siegel, J. M.** (1978). Assessing the impact of life changes: Development of the Life Experiences Survey. *Journal of Consulting and Clinical Psychology, 46,* 932–946.

**Sarason, I. G., Pierce, G. R., & Sarason, B. R.** (1994). General and specific perceptions of social support. In W. R. Avison & I. H. Gotlib (Eds.), *Stress and mental health: Contemporary issues and prospects for the future.* New York: Plenum.

**Sarwer, D. B., Foster, G. D., & Wadden, T. A.** (2004). Treatment of obesity I: Adult obesity. In J. K. Thompson (Ed.), *Handbook of eating disorders and obesity.* New York: Wiley.

**Saunders, C. D.** (2003). The emerging field of conservation psychology. *Human Ecology Review, 10,* 137–149.

**Saunders, C. D., & Myers, O. E.** (Eds.) (2003). Conservation psychology [Special issue]. *Human Ecology Review, 10*(2).

**Savin-Williams, R. C.** (2001). *Mom, dad. I'm gay.* Washington, DC: American Psychological Association.

**Savin-Williams, R. C.** (2009). How many gays are there? It depends. In D. A. Hope (Ed.), *Contemporary perspectives on lesbian, gay, and bisexual identities* (pp. 5–42). New York: Springer Science and Business Media.

**Sawdon, A. M., Cooper, M., & Seabrook, R.** (2007). The relationship between self-discrepancies, eating disorder, and depressive symptoms in women. *European Eating Disorders Review, 15*(3), 207–212.

**Saxena, S., van Ommeren, M., Tang K. C., & Armstrong, T. P.** (2005). Mental health benefits of physical activity. *Journal of Mental Health, 14,* 445–451.

**Sayer, L. C.** (2005). Gender, time, and inequality: Trends in women's and men's paid work, unpaid work, and free time. *Social Forces, 84,* 285–303.

**Sayer, L. C.** (2006). Economic aspects of divorce and relationship dissolution. In M. A. Fine & J. H. Harvey (Eds.), *Handbook of divorce and relationship resolution.* Mahwah, NJ: Erlbaum.

**Sayers, S. L.** (2004). Depression and heart disease: The interrelationship between these two common disorders is complex and requires careful diagnostic and treatment methods. *Psychiatric Annals, 34*(4), 282–288.

**Scanzoni, J.** (2004). Household diversity: The starting point for healthy families in the new century. In M. Coleman & L. H. Ganong (Eds.), *Handbook of contemporary families: Considering the past, contemplating the future.* Thousand Oaks, CA: Sage.

**Scarpa, A., & Haden, S. C.** (2006). Community violence victimization and aggressive behavior: The moderating effects of coping and social support. *Aggressive Behavior, 32,* 502–515.

**Scattone, D.** (2007). Social skills interventions for children with autism. *Psychology in the Schools, 44,* 717–726.

**Schaalma, H. P., Abraham, C., Gillmore, M. R., & Kok, G.** (2004). Sex education as health promotion: What does it take? *Archives of Sexual Behavior, 33,* 259–269.

**Schachner, D. A., Shaver, P. R., & Mikulincer, M.** (2005). Patterns of nonverbal behavior and sensitivity in the context of attachment relations. *Journal of Nonverbal Behavior, 29*(3), 141–169.

**Schachter, S.** (1959). *The psychology of affiliation.* Stanford, CA: Stanford University Press.

**Schachter, S.** (1982). Recidivism and self-cure of smoking and obesity. *American Psychologist, 37,* 436–444.

**Schaffer, A.** (2008, August 11). Prescriptions for health, the environmental kind. *New York Times,* Health section.

**Schaffer, M., Jeglic, E. L., & Stanley, B.** (2008). The relationship between suicidal behavior, ideation, and binge drinking among college students. *Archives of Suicide Research, 12,* 124–132.

**Schaninger, C. M., & Buss, W. C.** (1986). A longitudinal comparison of consumption and finance handling between happily married and divorced couples. *Journal of Marriage and the Family, 48,* 129–136.

**Scheidlinger, S.** (1993). History of group psychotherapy. In H. I. Kaplan & B. J. Sadock (Eds.), *Comprehensive group psychotherapy.* Baltimore: Williams & Wilkins.

**Scheier, M. F., & Carver, C. S.** (1985). Optimism, coping, and health: Assessment and implications of generalized outcome expectancies. *Health Psychology, 4,* 219–247.

**Scheier, M. F., & Carver, C. S.** (2007). Optimism, pessimism, and stress. In G. Fink (Ed.), *Encyclopedia of stress: Vols. 1–4* (2nd ed., pp. 26–29). San Diego, CA: Elsevier Academic Press.

**Scheier, M. F., Carver, C. S., & Bridges, M. W.** (2001). Optimism, pessimism, and psychological well-being. In E. C. Chang (Ed.), *Optimism and pessimism: Implications for theory, research, and practice.* Washington, DC: American Psychological Association.

**Scheier, M. F., Matthews, K. A., Owens, J. F., Magovern, G. J., Sr., Lefebvre, R. C., Abbott, R. A., & Carver, C. S.** (1989). Dispositional optimism and recovery from coronary artery bypass surgery: The beneficial effects on physical and psychological well-being. *Journal of Personality and Social Psychology, 57,* 1024–1040.

**Schiappa, E., Gregg, P. B., & Hewes, D. E.** (2006). Can one TV show make difference? Will & Grace and the parasocial contact hypothesis. *Journal of Homosexuality, 51*(4), 15–37.

**Schiffman, J., Ekstrom, M., LaBrie, J., Schulsinger, F., Sorenson, H., & Mednick, S.** (2002). Minor physical anomalies and schizophrenia spectrum disorders: A prospective investigation. *American Journal of Psychiatry, 159,* 238–243.

**Schilit, W. K.** (1987). Thinking about managing your time. In A. D. Timpe (Ed.), *The management of time.* New York: Facts On File.

**Schimel, J., Simon, L., Greenberg, J., Pyszczynski, T., Solomon, S., Waxmonsky, J., & Arndt, J.** (1999). Stereotypes and terror management: Evidence that mortality salience enhances stereotypic thinking and preferences. *Journal of Personality and Social Psychology, 77*(5), 905–926.

**Schirmer, L. L., & Lopez, F. G.** (2001). Probing the social support and work strain relationship among adult workers: Contributions of adult attachment orientations. *Journal of Vocational Behavior, 59*(1), 17–33.

**Schkade, D. A., & Kahneman, D.** (1998). Does living in California make people happy? A focusing illusion in judgments of life satisfaction. *Psychological Science, 9,* 340–346.

**Schlenger, W. E., Kulka, R. A., Fairbank, J. A., Hough, R. L., et al.** (1992). The prevalence of post-traumatic stress disorder in the Vietnam generation: A multimethod, multisource assessment of psychiatric disorder. *Journal of Traumatic Stress, 5,* 333–363.

**Schlenker, B. R.** (2003). Self-presentation. In M.R. Leary & J. P. Tangney (Eds.), *Handbook of self and identity.* New York: Guilford.

**Schlenker, B. R., & Pontari, B. A.** (2000). The strategic control of information: Impression management and self-presentation in daily life. In A. Tesser, R. B. Felson, & J. M. Suls (Eds.), *Psychological perspectives on self and identity.* Washington, DC: American Psychological Association.

**Schlicht, W., Kanning, M., & Bös, K.** (2007). Psychosocial interventions to influence physical inactivity as a risk factor: Theoretical models and practical evidence. In J. Dordan, B. Bardé, & A. M. Zeiher, (Eds.), *Contributions toward evidence-based psychocardiology: A systematic review of the literature* (pp. 107–123). Washington, DC: American Psychological Association.

**Schmidt, N. B., Zvolensky, M. J., & Maner, J. K.** (2006). Anxiety sensitivity: Prospective prediction of panic attacks and Axis I pathology. *Journal of Psychiatric Research, 40,* 691–699.

**Schmitt, D. P.** (2003). Universal sex differences in the desire for sexual variety: Tests from 52 nations, 6 continents, and 13 islands. *Journal of Personality and Social Psychology, 85*(1), 85–104.

**Schmitt, D. P.** (2008). An evolutionary perspective on mate choice and relationship initiation. In S. Sprecher, A. Wenzel, & J. Harvey (Eds.), *Handbook of relationship initiation* (pp. 55–74). New York: Psychology Press.

**Schmitz, J. M., & DeLaune, K. A.** (2005). Nicotine. In J. H. Lowinson, P. Ruiz, R. B. Millman, & J. G. Langrod (Eds.), *Substance abuse: A comprehensive textbook.* Philadelphia: Lippincott/Williams & Wilkins.

**Schmuck, P., & Schultz, P. W.** (2002). Sustainable development as a challenge for psychology. In P. Schmuck & P. W. Schultz (Eds.), *Psychology of Sustainable Development* (pp. 3–17). Boston: Kluwer Academic Publishers.

**Schneider, D. J.** (2004). *The psychology of stereotyping.* New York: Guilford.

Schneider, J. P. (2003). The impact of compulsive cyber-sex behaviors on the family. *Sexual and Relationship Therapy, 18*(3), 329–354.

Schneider, T. R. (2004). The role of neuroticism on psychological and physiological stress responses. *Journal of Experimental Social Psychology, 40*, 795–804.

Schneider, T. R. (2008). Evaluations of stressful transactions: What's in an appraisal? *Stress and Health, 24*, 151–158.

Schneiderman, N. (2004). Psychosocial, behavioral, and biological aspects of chronic diseases. *Current Directions in Psychological Science, 13*, 247–251.

Schneiders, J., Nicolson, N. A., Berkhof, J., Feron, F. J., van Os, J., & deVries, M. W. (2006). Mood reactivity to daily negative events in early adolescence: Relationship to risk for psychopathology. *Developmental Psychology, 42*, 543–554.

Schnittker, J. (2007). Look (closely) at all the lonely people: Age and the social psychology of social support. *Journal of Aging Health, 19*, 659–682.

Schooler, D., Ward, L. M., Merriwether, A., & Caruthers, A. (2004). Who's that girl: Television's role in the body image development of young white and black women. *Psychology of Women Quarterly, 28*, 38–47.

Schoon, I., & Parsons, S. (2002). Teenage aspirations for future careers and occupational outcomes. *Journal of Vocational Behavior, 60*(2), 262–288.

Schopler, J., & Insko, C. A. (1992). The discontinuity effect in interpersonal and intergroup relations: Generality and mediation. *European Review of Social Psychology, 3*, 121–151.

Schramm, D. G., Marshall, J. P., Harris, V. W., & Lee, T. R. (2005). After "I do": The newlywed transition. *Marriage & Family Review, 38*, 45–67.

Schramm, W. (1955). *The process and effects of mass communication.* Urbana: University of Illinois Press.

Schraw, G., Wadkins, T., & Olafson, L. (2007). Doing the things we do: A grounded theory of academic procrastination. *Journal of Educational Psychology, 99*(1), 12–25.

Schreiber, F. R. (1973). *Sybil.* New York: Warner.

Schreiner-Engel, P., Schiavi, R. C., White, D., & Ghizzani, A. (1989). Low sexual desire in women: The role of reproductive hormones. *Hormones and Behavior, 23*, 221–234.

Schrock, D., & Schwalbe, M. (2009). Men, masculinity, and manhood acts. *Annual Review of Sociology, 35*, 277–259.

Schuckit, M. A. (2000). Alcohol-related disorders. In B. J. Sadock & V. A. Sadock (Eds.), *Kaplan and Sadock's comprehensive textbook of psychiatry* (7th ed.). Philadelphia: Lippincott/Williams & Wilkins.

Schultz, P. W. (2000). Empathizing with nature: The effects of perspective taking on concern for environmental issues. *Journal of Social Issues, 56*, 391–406.

Schultz, P. W. (2001). The structure of environmental concern: Concern for self, other people, and the biosphere. *Journal of Environmental Psychology, 21*, 1–13.

Schultz, P. W., Gouveia, V. V., Cameron, L. D., Tankha, G., Schmuck, P., & Franek, M. (2005). Values and their relationship to environmental concern and conservation behavior. *Journal of Cross-Cultural Psychology, 36*, 457–475.

Schulz, M. S., Pruett, M. K., Kerig, P. K., & Parke, F. D. (Eds., 2010). *Strengthening couple relationships for optimal child development: Lessons from research and intervention.* Washington, DC: American Psychological Association.

Schutte, N. S., Malouff, J. M., Thorsteinsson, E. B., Bhullar, N., & Rooke, S. E. (2007). A meta-analytic investigation of the relationship between emotional intelligence and health. *Personality and Individual Differences, 42*, 921–933.

Schwartz, B. (2004). *The paradox of choice: Why more is less.* New York: Ecco.

Schwartz, J. E., Neale, J., Marco, C., Shiffman, S. S., & Stone, A. A. (1999). Does trait coping exist? A momentary assessment approach to the evaluation of traits. *Journal of Personality and Social Psychology, 77*(2), 360–369.

Schwartz, J. P., Waldo, M., & Higgins, A. J. (2004). Attachment styles: Relationship to masculine gender role conflict in college men. *Psychology of Men & Masculinity, 5*(2), 143–146.

Schwartz, L., Slater, M. A., & Birchler, G. R. (1994). Interpersonal stress and pain behaviors in patients with chronic pain. *Journal of Consulting and Clinical Psychology, 62*, 861–864.

Schwartz, P., & Young, L. (2009). Sexual satisfaction in committed relationships. *Sexuality Research & Social Policy: A Journal of the NSRC, 6*(1), 1–17.

Schwarz, N., & Strack, F. (1999). Reports of subjective well-being: Judgmental processes and their method-ological implications. In D. Kahneman, E. Diener, & N. Schwarz (Eds.), *Well-being: The foundations of hedonic psychology.* New York: Russell Sage Foundation.

Schwarzer, R., & Schulz, U. (2003). Stressful life events. In A. M. Nezu, C. M. Nezu, & P. A. Geller (Eds.), *Handbook of psychology: Vol. 9. Health psychology.* New York: Wiley. Scott, B. A., & Koger, S. M. (2006). *Teaching psychology for sustainability: A manual of resources.* Retrieved from http://www.teachgreenpsych.com/

Scully, J. A., Tosi, H., & Banning, K. (2000). Life event checklists: Revisiting the social readjustment rating scale after 30 years. *Educational & Psychological Measurement, 60*(6), 864–876.

Seabrook, R., Brown, G. D. A., & Solity, J. E. (2005). Distributed and massed practice: From laboratory to classroom. *Applied Cognitive Psychology, 19*(1), 107–122.

Searle, A., & Bennett, P. (2001). Psychological factors and inflammatory bowel disease: A review of a decade of literature. *Psychology, Health and Medicine, 6*(2), 121–135.

Searles, H. F. (1960). *The nonhuman environment in normal development and schizophrenia.* New York: International Universities Press.

Seccombe, K. (2001). Families in poverty in the 1990s: Trends, causes, consequences, and lessons learned. In R. M. Milardo (Ed.), *Understanding families into the new millennium: A decade in review.* Minneapolis: National Council on Family Relations.

Sedikides, C., & Gregg, A. P. (2008). Self-enhancement: Food for thought. *Perspectives on Psychological Science, 3*(2), 102–116.

Sedikides, C., & Strube, M. J. (1997). Self-evaluation: To thine own self be good, to thine own self be sure, to thine own self be true, and to thine own self be better. In M. P. Zanna (Ed.), *Advances in experimental social psychology* (Vol. 29). New York: Academic Press.

See, Y. H. M., Petty, R. E., Evans, L. M. (2009). The impact of perceived message complexity and need for cognition on information processing and attitudes. *Journal of Research in Personality, 43*(5), 880–889.

Segal, M. W. (1974). Alphabet and attraction: An unobtrusive measure of the effect of propinquity in a field setting. *Journal of Personality and Social Psychology, 30*, 654–657.

Segall, A. (1997). Sick role concepts and health behavior. In D. S. Gochman (Ed.), *Handbook of health behavior research I: Personal and social determinants.* New York: Plenum Press.

Segerstrom, S., & Roach, A. R. (2008). On the physical health benefits of self-enhancement. In E. C. Chang (Ed.), *Self-criticism and self-enhancement: Theory, research, and clinical implications* (pp. 37–54). Washington, DC: American Psychological Association.

Segerstrom, S. C. (2007). Stress, energy, and immunity: An ecological view. *Current Directions in Psychological Science, 16*, 326–330.

Segerstrom, S. C., & Miller, G. E. (2004). Psychological stress and the human immune system: A meta-analytic study of 30 years of inquiry. *Psychological Bulletin, 130*, 601–630.

Segerstrom, S. C., Taylor, S. E., Kemeny, M. E., & Fahey, J. L. (1998). Optimism is associated with mood, coping and immune change in response to stress. *Journal of Personality and Social Psychology, 74*, 1646–1655.

Seiter, J. S. (2007). Ingratiation and gratuity: The effect of complimenting customers on tipping behavior in restaurants. *Journal of Applied Social Psychology, 37*(3), 478–485.

Self, D. W. (1998). Neural substrates of drug craving and relapse in drug addiction. *Annals of Medicine, 30*, 379–389.

Selfhout, M., Denissen, J., Branje, S., & Meeus, W. (2009). In the eye of the beholder: Perceived, actual, and peer-rated similarity in personality, communication, and friendship intensity during the acquaintanceship process. *Journal of Personality and Social Psychology, 96*, 1152–1165.

Seligman, M. E. P. (1971). Phobias and preparedness. *Behavior Therapy, 2*, 307–321.

Seligman, M. E. P. (1974). Depression and learned helplessness. In R. J. Friedman & M. M. Katz (Eds.), *The psychology of depression: Contemporary theory and research.* New York: Wiley.

Seligman, M. E. P. (1990). *Learned optimism: How to change your mind and your life.* New York: Pocket Books.

Seligman, M. E. P. (1991). *Learned optimism.* New York: Alfred A. Knopf.

Seligman, M. E. P. (1992). *Helplessness: On depression, development, and death.* New York: Freeman.

Seligman, M. E. P. (1994). *What you can change and what you can't.* New York: Knopf.

Seligman, M. E. P. (1995). The effectiveness of psychotherapy. *American Psychologist, 50*, 965–974.

Seligman, M. E. P. (1998). Positive social science. *APA Monitor Online, 29*(4).

Seligman, M. E. P. (1999). The president's address. *American Psychologist, 54*, 559–562.

Seligman, M. E. P. (2002). Positive psychology, prevention, and positive therapy. In C. R. Snyder & S. J. Lopez (Eds.), *Handbook of positive psychology* (pp. 3–13). New York: Oxford University Press.

Seligman, M. E. P. (2003a). The past and future of positive psychology. In C. L. M. Keyes & J. Haidt (Eds.), *Flourishing: Positive psychology and the life well-lived.* Washington, DC: American Psychological Association.

Seligman, M. E. P. (2003b). *Authentic happiness: Using the new positive psychology to realize your potential for lasting fulfillment.* New York: Free Press.

Seligman, M. E. P., & Csikszentmihalyi, M. (2000). Positive psychology: An introduction. *American Psychologist, 55*(1), 5–14.

Seligman, M. E. P., & Levant, R. F. (1998). Managed care policies rely on inadequate science. *Professional Psychology: Research and Practice, 29*, 211–212.

Seligman, M. E. P., Rashid, T., & Parks, A. C. (2006). Positive psychotherapy. *American Psychologist, 61*, 774–788.

Seligman, M. E. P., Schulman, P., DeRubeis, R. J., & Hollon, S. D. (1999). The prevention of depression and anxiety. *Prevention and Treatment,* http://journals.apa.org/prevention/volume2/pre0020008a.html

Seligman, M. E. P., Schulman, P., & Tryon, A. M. (2007). Group prevention of depression and anxiety symptoms. *Behaviour Research and Therapy, 45*, 1111–1126.

Seligman, M. E. P., Steen, T. A., Park, N., & Peterson, C. (2005). Positive psychology progress: Empirical validation of interventions. *American Psychologist, 60*, 410–421.

Seltzer, J. A. (2001). Families formed outside of marriage. In R. M. Milardo (Ed.), *Understanding families into the new millennium: A decade in review.* Minneapolis: National Council on Family Relations.

Seltzer, J. A. (2004). Cohabitation and family change. In M. Coleman & L. H. Ganong (Eds.), *Handbook of contemporary families: Considering the past, contemplating the future.* Thousand Oaks, CA: Sage.

Selye, H. (1936). A syndrome produced by diverse nocuous agents. *Nature, 138*, 32.

Selye, H. (1956). *The stress of life.* New York: McGraw-Hill.

Selye, H. (1974). *Stress without distress.* New York: Lippincott.

Selye, H. (1982). History and present status of the stress concept. In L. Goldberger & S. Breznitz (Eds.), *Handbook of stress: Theoretical and clinical aspects.* New York: Free Press.

Semans, J. H. (1956). Premature ejaculation: A new approach. *Journal of Southern Medicine, 79*, 353–361.

Senecal, C., Lavoie, K., & Koestner, R. (1997). Trait and situational factors in procrastination: An interactional model. *Journal of Social Behavior and Personality, 12*, 889–903.

Sepahvand, T., Guilani, B., & Zamani, R. (2007). Relationship between attributional styles with stressful life events and general health. *Psychological Research, 9*(3–4), 33–46.

Serido, J., Almeida, D. M., & Wethington, E. (2004). Chronic stressors and daily hassles: Unique and interactive relationships with psychological distress. *Journal of Health and Social Behavior, 45*, 17–33.

Servan-Schreiber, D., Kolb, R., & Tabas, G. (1999). The somatizing patient. *Primary Care, 26*(2), 225–242.

Servin, A., Nordenstrom, A., Larsson, A., & Bohlin, G. (2003). Prenatal androgens and gender-typed behavior: A study of girls with mild and server forms of congenital hyperplasia. *Developmental Psychology, 39*, 440–450.

Sesso, H. D., Buring, J. E., Rifai, N., Blake, G. J., Gaziano, J. M., & Ridker, P. M. (2003). C-reactive protein and the risk of developing hypertension. *Journal of the American Medical Association, 290*(22), 2945–2951.

Seta, J. J., Seta, C. E., & McElroy, T. (2002). Strategies for reducing the stress of negative life experiences: An averaging/summation analysis. *Personality and Social Psychology Bulletin, 28*(11), 1574–1585.

Sethi, S., & Seligman, M. E. P. (1993). Optimism and fundamentalism. *Psychological Science, 4*, 256–259.

Settles, I. H., Cortina, L. M., Malley, J., & Stewart, A. J. (2006). The climate for women in academic science: The good, the bad, and changeable. *Psychology of Women Quarterly, 30*, 47–58.

Shackelford, T. K., & Besser, A. (2007). Predicting attitudes towards homosexuality: Insights from personality psychology. *Individual Differences Research, 5*, 106–114.

**Shaffer, D. R.** (1989). *Developmental psychology: Childhood and adolescence.* Pacific Grove, CA: Brooks/Cole.

**Shah, J., & Higgins, E. T.** (2001). Regulatory concerns and appraisal efficiency: The general impact of promotion and prevention. *Journal of Personality and Social Psychology, 80,* 693–705.

**Shalev, A. Y.** (2001). Posttraumatic stress disorder. *Primary Psychiatry, 8*(10), 41–46.

**Shapira, N., Barak, A., & Gal, I.** (2007). Promoting older adults' well-being through Internet training use. *Aging & Mental Health, 11,* 477–484.

**Shapiro, A. F., Gottman, J. M., & Carrère.** (2000). The baby and marriage: Identifying factors that buffer against decline in marital satisfaction after the first baby arrives. *Journal of Family Psychology, 14*(1), 59–70.

**Shapiro, D. H., Jr.** (1984). Overview: Clinical and physiological comparison of meditation with other self-control strategies. In D. H. Shapiro, Jr. & R. N. Walsh (Eds.), *Meditation: Classic and contemporary perspectives.* New York: Aldine.

**Shapiro, J. R., & Neuberg, S. L.** (2007). From stereotype threat to stereotype threats: Implications of a multi-threat framework causes, moderators, mediators, consequences, and interventions. *Personality & Social Psychology Review, 11,* 107–130.

**Shapiro, S. J., Schwartz, G. E. R., & Santerre, C.** (2002). Meditation and positive psychology. In C. R. Snyder & S. J. Lopez (Eds.), *The handbook of positive psychology* (pp. 632–645). New York: Oxford.

**Shapiro, S. L., Astin, J. A., Bishop, S. R., & Cordova, M.** (2005). Mindfulness-based stress reduction for health care professionals: Results from a randomized trial. *International Journal of Stress Management, 12,* 164–176.

**Shapiro, S. L., & Carlson, L. E.** (2009). *The art and science of mindfulness: Integrating mindfulness into psychology and the helping professions.* Washington, DC: American Psychological Association.

**Shapiro, S. L., Schwartz, G. E. R., & Bonner, G.** (1998). The effects of mindfulness-based stress reduction on medical and pre-medical students. *Journal of Behavioral Medicine, 21,* 581–599.

**Shapiro, S. L., Schwartz, G. E. R., & Santerre, C.** (2002). Meditation and positive psychology. In C. R. Snyder & S. J. Lopez (Eds.), *Handbook of positive psychology.* New York: Oxford University Press.

**Shapiro, S. L., Schwartz, G. E. R., & Santerre, C.** (2005). Meditation and positive psychology. In C. R. Snyder & S. J. Lopez (Eds.), *Handbook of positive psychology.* New York: Oxford University Press.

**Shavelson, R. J., Hubner, J. J., & Stanton, G. C.** (1976). Self-concept: Validation of construct interpretations. *Review of Educational Research, 46,* 407–411.

**Shaver, P. R., & Brennan, K. A.** (1992). Attachment styles and the "Big Five" personality traits: Their connections with each other and with romantic relationship outcomes. *Personality and Social Psychology Bulletin, 18,* 536–545.

**Shaver, P. R., & Hazan, C.** (1993). Adult attachment: Theory and research. In W. Jones & D. Perlman (Eds.), *Advances in personal relationships* (Vol. 4). London: Jessica Kingsley.

**Shaver, P. R., & Mikulincer, M.** (2006). Attachment theory, individual psychodynamics, and relationship functioning. In A. L. Vangelisti & D. Perlman (Eds.), *The Cambridge handbook of personal relationships.* New York: Cambridge University Press.

**Shaver, P. R., & Mikulincer, M.** (2007). Adult attachment strategies and the regulation of emotion. In J. J. Gross (Ed.), *Handbook of emotion regulation* (pp. 446–465). New York: Guilford.

**Shaver, P. R., & Mikulincer, M.** (2008). Augmenting the sense of security in romantic, leader-follower, therapeutic, and group relationships: A relational model of psychological change. In J. P. Forgas & J. Fitness (Eds.) *Social relationships: Cognitive, affective, and motivational processes* (pp. 55–74). New York: Psychology Press.

**Shaver, P. R., Wu, S., & Schwartz, J. C.** (1991). Cross-cultural similarities and differences in emotion and its representation: A prototype approach. In M. S. Clark (Ed.), *Review of personality and social psychology* (Vol. 13). Newbury Park, CA: Sage.

**Shaw, L. H., & Gant, L. M.** (2002). In defense of the Internet: The relationship between Internet communication and depression, loneliness, self-esteem, and perceived social support. *CyberPsychology, 5*(2), 157–171.

**Sheehan, S.** (1982). *Is there no place on earth for me?* Boston: Houghton Mifflin.

**Shelby, R. A., Crespin, T. R., Wells-Di Gregorio, S. M., Siegel, J. E., Taylor, K. L., & Lamdan, R. M.** (2008). Optimism, social support, and adjustment in African American women with breast cancer. *Journal of Behavioral Medicine, 31,* 433–444.

**Sheldon, J. P.** (2004). Gender stereotypes in educational software for young children. *Sex Roles, 51,* 433–444.

**Sheldon, K. M., & Kasser, T.** (2001a). Getting older, getting better? Personal strivings and psychological maturity across the life span. *Developmental Psychology, 37*(4), 491–501.

**Sheldon, K. M., & Kasser, T.** (2001b). Goals, congruence, and positive well-being: New empirical support for humanistic theories. *Journal of Humanistic Psychology, 41*(1), 30–50.

**Shelton, K. H., & Harold, G. T.** (2007). Marital conflict and children's adjustment: The mediating and moderating role of children's coping strategies. *Social Development, 16,* 497–511.

**Shelton, R. C., & Lester, N.** (2006). Selective serotonin reuptake inhibitors and newer antidepressants. In D. J. Stein, D. J. Kupfer, & A. F. Schatzberg (Eds.), *Textbook of mood disorders.* Washington, DC: American Psychiatric Publishing.

**Shenton, M. E. & Kubicki, M.** (2009). Structural brain imaging in schizophrenia. In B. J. Sadock, V. A. Sadock, & P. Ruiz (Eds.), *Kaplan & Sadock's comprehensive textbook of psychiatry* (pp. 1494–1506). Philadelphia: Lippincott Williams & Wilkins.

**Sheperd, J., Malone, W., & Sweeny, K.** (2008). Exploring causes of the self-serving bias. *Social and Personality Psychology Compass, 2*(2), 895–908.

**Shepperd, J. A., & McNulty, J. K.** (2002). The affective consequences of expected and unexpected outcomes. *Psychological Science, 13,* 85–88.

**Sher, L., & Mann, J. J.** (2003). Psychiatric pathophysiology: Mood disorders. In A. Tasman, J. Kay, & J. A. Lieberman (Eds.), *Psychiatry.* New York: Wiley.

**Sher, T. G., & Baucom, D. H.** (1993). Marital communication: Differences among maritally distressed, depressed, and nondistressed-nondepressed couples. *Journal of Family Psychology, 7,* 148–153.

**Sheridan, S. M., & Burt, J. D.** (2009). Family-centered positive psychology. In S. J. Lopez & C. R. Snyder (Eds.), *Oxford handbook of positive psychology* (2nd ed., pp. 551–559). New York: Oxford.

**Sheridan, S. M., Warnes, E., Brown, M., Schemm, A., Cowan, R. J., & Clarke, B. L.** (2004). Family-centered positive psychology: Building on strengths to promote student success. *Psychology in the Schools, 41,* 7–17.

**Sherif, M.** (1936). *The psychology of social norms.* New York: Harper.

**Sherif, M., Harvey, O., White, B., Hood, W., & Sherif, C.** (1961). *Intergroup conflict and cooperation: The Robber's Cave experiment.* Norman: University of Oklahoma, Institute of Group Behavior.

**Shike, M.** (1999). Diet and lifestyle in the prevention of colorectal cancer: An overview. *American Journal of Medicine, 106*(1A), 11S–15S, 50S–51S.

**Shiota, M. N.** (2006). Silver linings and candles in the dark: Differences among positive coping strategies in predicting subjective well-being. *Emotion, 6,* 335–339.

**Shneidman, E. S.** (1985). *At the point of no return.* New York: Wiley.

**Shneidman, E. S., Farberow, N. L., & Litman, R. E.** (1994). *The psychology of suicide: A clinician's guide to evaluation and treatment.* Northvale, NJ: J. Aronson.

**Shobe, K. K., & Schooler, J. W.** (2001). Discovering fact and fiction: Case-based analyses of authentic and fabricated discovered memories of abuse. In G. M. Davies & T. Dalgleish (Eds.), *Recovered memories: Seeking the middle ground.* Chichester, England: Wiley.

**Shoda, Y., Mischel, W., & Peake, P. K.** (1990). Predicting adolescent cognitive and self-regulatory competencies from preschool delay of gratification: Identifying diagnostic conditions. *Developmental Psychology, 26,* 978–986.

**Shook, N. J., & Fazio, R. H.** (2008). Interracial roommate relationships: An experimental field test of the contact hypothesis. *Psychological Science, 19,* 717–723.

**Shors, T. J.** (2004). Learning during stressful times. *Learning and Memory, 11*(2), 137–144.

**Shotland, R. L., & Hunter, B. A.** (1995). Women's "token resistant" and compliant sexual behaviors are related to uncertain sexual intentions and rape. *Personality and Social Psychology Bulletin, 21,* 226–236.

**SHRM** (2008). *2008 Employee benefits: How competitive is your organization?* Alexandria, VA: Society for Human Resource Management.

**Shtarkshall, R. A., Santelli, J. S., & Hirsch, J. S.** (2007). Sex education and sexual socialization: Roles for educators and parents. *Perspectives on Sexual and Reproductive Health, 39,* 116–119.

**Shulman, R. B.** (2001). Response versus remission in the treatment of depression: Understanding residual symptoms. *Primary Psychiatry, 8*(5), 28–30, 34.

**Shuval, J. T.** (1993). Migration and stress. In L. Goldberger & S. Breznitz (Eds.), *Handbook of stress: Theoretical and clinical aspects* (2nd ed.). New York: Free Press.

**Sibley, C. G., & Duckitt, J.** (2008). Personality and prejudice: A meta-analytic and theoretical review. *Personality and Social Psychology Review, 12*(3), 248–279.

**Sidanius, J., & Pratto, P.** (1999). *Social dominance: An intergroup theory of social hierarchy and oppression.* New York: Cambridge University Press.

**Sidanius, J., & Pratto, P.** (2004). Ethnic enclaves and the dynamics of social identity on the college campus: The good, the bad, and the ugly. *Journal of Personality and Social Psychology, 87,* 96–110.

**Siddiqui, R. N., & Pandey, J.** (2003). Coping with environmental stressors by urban slum dwellers. *Enviroment and Behavior, 35,* 589–604.

**Siebert, A.** (1995). *Student success: How to succeed in college and still have time for your friends.* Fort Worth, TX: Harcourt Brace.

**Siebert, A., & Karr, M.** (2003). *The adult student's guide to survival and success.* Portland, OR: Practical Psychology Press.

**SIECUS.** (2004, Fall). *SIECUS Fact Sheet: Public support for comprehensive sexuality education.* Retrieved January 25, 2005 from http://63.73.227.69/Pubs/Fact/Fact0017 .html.

**Siegal, K., Schrimshaw, E. W., Lekas, H., & Parsons, J. T.** (2008). Sexual behaviors of non-gay identified non-disclosing men who have sex with men and women. *Archives of Sexual Behavior, 37,* 720–735.

**Siegel, M.** (2007, August, 28). New Orleans still facing a psychiatric emergency. *The Globe and Mail* (Canada), A17.

**Siegler, I. C., Peterson, B. L., Barefoot, J. C., & Williams, R. B.** (1992). Hostility during late adolescence predicts coronary risk factors at mid-life. *American Journal of Epidemiology, 136*(2), 146–154.

**Siegman, A. W.** (1994). From Type A to hostility to anger: Reflections on the history of coronary-prone behavior. In A. W. Siegman & T. W. Smith (Eds.), *Anger, hostility, and the heart* (pp. 1–21). Hillsdale, NJ: Erlbaum.

**Signorielli, N., & Bacue, A.** (1999). Recognition and respect: A content analysis of prime-time television characters. *Sex Roles, 40*(7/8), 527–544.

**Silke, A.** (2003). *Terrorists, victims, and society: Psychological perspectives on terrrorism and its consequences.* New York: Wiley.

**Silver, H., Feldman, P., Bilker, W., & Gur, R. C.** (2003). Working memory deficit as a core neuropsychological dysfunction in schizophrenia. *American Journal of Psychiatry, 160,* 1809–1816.

**Silver, M.** (2002, June 10). What they're seeing. *U.S. News & World Report,* p. 41.

**Silverman, P. R., & Worden, J. M.** (1992). Children's reactions in the early months after the death of a parent. *American Journal of Orthopsychiatry, 62,* 93–104.

**Silverstein, M., & Ruiz, S.** (2009). Intergenerational relationships in families,. In H. T. Reis & S. Sprecher (Eds.), *Encyclopedia of human relationships: Vol. 1* (pp. 606–610). Los Angeles: Sage Reference Publication.

**Simeon, D. & Loewenstein, R. J.** (2009). Dissociative disorders. In B. J. Sadock, V. A. Sadock, & P. Ruiz (Eds.), *Kaplan & Sadock's comprehensive textbook of psychiatry* (pp. 1965–2026). Philadelphia: Lippincott Williams & Wilkins.

**Simmons, D. A.** (1994). Urban children's preferences for nature: Lessons for environmental education. *Children's Environments, 11,* 194–203.

**Simmons, T., & Dye, J. L.** (2004). What has happened to the median age at first marriage data? Paper presented at the meeting of the American Sociological Association, San Francisco, CA.

**Simmons, T., & O'Connell, M.** (2003). *Married-couple and unmarried-partner households: 2000. U.S. Census Bureau, Census 2000 Special Reports.* Washington, DC: U.S. Department of Commerce.

**Simon, G. E., & Savarino, J.** (2007). Suicide attempts among patients starting depression treatment with medications or psychotherapy. *American Journal of Psychiatry, 164,* 1029–1034.

**Simon, G. E., Savarino, J., Operskalski, B., & Wang, P. S.** (2006). Suicide risk during antidepressant treatment. *American Journal of Psychiatry, 163,* 41–47.

**Simpson, J. A.** (1987). The dissolution of romantic relationships: Factors involved in relationship stability and emotional distress. *Journal of Personality and Social Psychology, 53,* 683–692.

**Simpson, J. R.** (2008). Functional MRI lie detection: Too good to be true? *Journal of the American Academy of Psychiatry and the Law, 36,* 491–498.

**Sinclair, R. C., Mark, M. M., & Clore, G. L.** (1994). Mood-related persuasion depends on (mis)attributions. *Social Cognition, 12,* 309–326.

**Singer, A. R., Cassin, S. E., & Dobson, K. S.** (2005). The role of gender in the career aspirations of professional psychology graduates: Are there more similarities than differences? *Canadian Psychology, 46*(4), 215–222.

**Singer, M. T.** (2003). *Cults in our midst.* San Francisco: Jossey-Bass.

**Singh, D.** (1993). Adaptive significance of female physical attractiveness: Role of waist-to-hip ratio. *Journal of Personality and Social Psychology, 65,* 293–307.

**Singh, D.** (1995). Female judgment of male attractiveness and desirability for relationships: Role of waist-to-hip ratio and financial status. *Journal of Personality and Social Psychology, 69,* 1089–1101.

**Singleton, R, A., Jr., & Vacca, J.** (2007). Interpersonal competition in friendships. *Sex Roles, 57,* 617–627.

**Sirois, F. M., Melia-Gordon, M. L., & Pychyl, T. A.** (2003). "I'll look after my health, later": An investigation of procrastination and health. *Personality and Individual Differences, 35*(5), 1167–1184.

**Skinner, B. F.** (1953). *Science and human behavior.* New York: Macmillan.

**Skinner, B. F.** (1974). *About behaviorism.* New York: Knopf.

**Skinner, B. F.** (1987a). *Upon further reflection.* Englewood Cliffs, NJ: Prentice-Hall.

**Skinner, B. F.** (1987b). Whatever happened to psychology as the science of behavior? *American Psychologist, 42,* 780–786.

**Skinner, B. F.** (1990). Can psychology be a science of mind? *American Psychologist, 45,* 1206–1210.

**Skinner, E. A., Edge, K., Altman, J. , & Sherwood, H.** (2003). Searching for the structure of coping: A review and critique of category systems for classifying ways of coping. *Psychological Bulletin, 129,* 216–269.

**Skinner, N. F.** (2003). Birth order effects in dominance: Failure to support Sulloway's view. *Psychological Reports, 92,* 387–388.

**Skinner, P. H., & Shelton, R. L.** (1985). *Speech, language, and hearing: Normal processes and disorders* (2nd ed.). New York: Wiley.

**Skolnick, P.** (2003). Psychiatric pathophysiology: Anxiety disorders. In A. Tasman, J. Kay, & J. A. Lieberman (Eds.), *Psychiatry.* New York: Wiley.

**Skowronski, J. J., & Carlston, D. E.** (1989). Negativity and extremity biases in impression formation: A review of explanation. *Psychological Review, 105,* 131–142.

**Skowronski, J. J., & Carlston, D. E.** (1992). Caught in the act: When impressions are based on highly diagnostic information behaviours are resistant to contradiction. *European Journal of Social Psychology, 22,* 435–452.

**Slashinki, M. J., Coker, A. L., & Davis, K. E.** (2003). Physical aggression, forced sex, and stalking victimization by a dating partner: An analysis of the National Violence Against Women Survey. *Violence & Victims, 18*(6), 595–617.

**Slaski, M., & Cartwright, S.** (2003). Emotional intelligence training and its implications for stress, health and performance. *Stress and Health: Journal of the International Society for the Investigation of Stress, 19*(4), 233–239.

**Slavney, P. R.** (1990). *Perspectives on hysteria.* Baltimore: John Hopkins University Press.

**Slimak, M. W., & Dietz, T.** (2006). Personal values, beliefs, and ecological risk perception. *Risk Analysis, 26,* 1689–1705.

**Sloan Work and Family Research Network.** (2009). Questions and answers about women in the workforce. *A Sloan Work and Family Research Network Fact Sheet.* Retrieved from http://wfnetwork.bc.edu/statistics.php

**Slof-Op't Landt, M. C. T., van Furth, E. F., Meulenbelt, I., Slagboom, P. E., Bartels, M., Boomsma, D. I., & Bulik, C. M.** (2005). Eating disorders: From twin studies to candidate genes and beyond. *Twin Research and Human Genetics,* 8, 467–482.

**Slonim-Nevo, V., & Al-Krenawi, A.** (2006). Success and failure among polygamous families: The experience of wives, husbands, and children. *Family Process,* 45, 311–330.

**Slosar, J. R.** (2009). *The culture of excess: How America lost self-control and why we need to redefine success.* Santa Barbara, CA: Praeger.

**Slovic, P., Finucane, M. L., Peters, E., & MacGregor, D. G.** (2004). Risk as analysis and risk as feelings: Some thoughts about affect, reason, risk, and rationality. *Risk Analysis, 24,* 311–322.

**Slovic, P., Fischhoff, B., & Lichtenstein, S.** (1982). Facts versus fears: Understanding perceived risk. In D. Kahneman, P. Slovic, & A. Tversky (Eds.), *Judgment under uncertainty: Heuristics and biases.* Cambridge, England: Cambridge University Press.

**Slowinski, J.** (2007). Sexual problems and dysfunctions in men. In A. F. Owens & M. S. Tepper (Eds.), *Sexual Health: Vol. 4. State-of-the-art treatments and research* (pp. 1–14). Westport, CT: Praeger Publishers/Greenwood Publishing Group.

**Small, D. A., Gelfand, M., Babcock, L., & Gettman, H.** (2007). Who goes to the bargaining table? The influence of gender and framing on the initiation of negotiation. *Journal of Personality and Social Psychology, 93,* 600–613.

**Smetana, J. G.** (2009). Parent-adolescent communication. In H. T. Reis & S. Sprecher (Eds.), *Encyclopedia of human relationships: Vol. 3* (pp. 1189–1193). Los Angeles: Sage Reference Publication.

**Smiler, A. P.** (2004). Thirty years after the discovery of gender: Psychological concepts and measures of masculinity. *Sex Roles, 50*(1–2), 15–26.

**Smith, A. K.** (2000, November 6). Charting your own course. *U.S. News & World Report,* 56–60, 62, 64–65.

**Smith, C. A., & Lazarus, R. S.** (1993). Appraisal components, core relational themes, and the emotions. *Cognition and Emotion, 7,* 233–269.

**Smith, D. A.** (1999). The end of theoretical orientations? *Applied & Preventative Psychology, 8,* 269–280.

**Smith, D. M., Langa, K. M., Kabeto, M. U., & Ubel, P. A.** (2005). Health, wealth, and happiness: Financial resources buffer subjective well-being after the onset of a disability. *Psychological Science, 16,* 663–666.

**Smith, E. R., & Collins, E. C.** (2009). Contextualizing person perception: Distributed social cognition. *Psychological Review, 116*(2), 343–364.

**Smith, G. S., Branas, C. C., & Miller, T. R.** (1999). Fatal nontraffic injuries involving alcohol: A meta-analysis. *Annals of Emergency Medicine, 33*(6), 659–668.

**Smith, J. A., McPherson, M., & Smith-Lovin, L.** (2009). Social isolation. In H. T. Reis & S. Sprecher (Eds.), *Encyclopedia of human relationships: Vol. 3* (pp. 1529–1531). Los Angeles: Sage Reference Publication.

**Smith, J. C.** (1975). Meditation and psychotherapy: A review of the literature. *Psychological Bulletin, 32,* 553–564.

**Smith, J. L., Hardy, T., & Arkin, R.** (2009). When practice doesn't make perfect: Effort expenditure as an active behavioral self-handicapping strategy. *Journal of Research in Personality, 43*(1), 95–98.

**Smith, J. W., Positano, S., Stocks, N., & Shearman, D.** (2009). *A new way of thinking about our climate crisis: The rational-comprehensive approach.* Lewiston, NY: Edwin Mellen Press.

**Smith, L.** (2005). Psychotherapy, classism, and the poor: Conspicuous by their absence. *American Psychologist, 60,* 687–696.

**Smith, L. J., Mulhall, J. P., Deveci, S., Monaghan, N., & Reid, M.** (2007). Sex after seventy: A pilot study of sexual function in older persons. *Journal of Sexual Medicine, 4,* 1247–1253.

**Smith, M.** (2003, January). Employee health affects more than the bottom line. *IPMA News,* pp. 8–10.

**Smith, M. L., & Glass, G. V.** (1977). Meta-analysis of psychotherapy outcome studies. *American Psychologist, 32,* 752–760.

**Smith, M. S., & Gray, S. W.** (2009). The courage to challenge: A new measure of hardiness in LGBT adults. *Journal of Gay & Lesbian Social Services, 21,* 73–89.

**Smith, M., & Pazder, L.** (1980). *Michelle remembers.* New York: Pocket Books.

**Smith, P. B., & Bond, M. H.** (1999). *Social psychology across cultures.* Boston: Allyn & Bacon.

**Smith, R. E.** (1989). Effects of coping skills training on generalized self-efficacy and locus of control. *Journal of Personality and Social Psychology, 56,* 228–233.

**Smith, S. M., & Caprariello, P. A.** (2009). Liking. In H. T. Reis & S. Sprecher (Eds.), *Encyclopedia of human relationships: Vol. 2* (pp. 978–982). Los Angeles: Sage Reference Publication.

**Smith, S. M., & Gleaves, D. H.** (2007). Recovered memories. In M. P. Toglia, J. D. Read, D. F. Ross, & R. C. L. Lindsay (Eds.), *Handbook of eyewitness psychology: Volume 1. Memory for events.* Mahwah, NJ: Erlbaum.

**Smith, T. W.** (1999). *The emerging 21st century American family.* University of Chicago: National Opinion Research Center.

**Smith, T. W.** (2003). Hostility and health: Current status of a psychosomatic hypothesis. In P. Salovey & A. J. Rothman (Eds.), *Social psychology of health.* New York: Psychology Press.

**Smith, T. W.** (2006). Personality as risk and resilience in physical health. *Current Directions in Psychological Science, 15,* 227–231.

**Smith, T. W., & Gallo, L. C.** (1999). Hostility and cardiovascular reactivity during marital interaction. *Psychosomatic Medicine, 61,* 436–445.

**Smith, T. W., & Gallo, L. C.** (2001). Personality traits as risk factors for physical illness. In A. Baum, T. A. Revenson, & J. E. Singer (Eds.), *Handbook of health psychology.* Mahwah, NJ: Erlbaum.

**Smith, T. W., Glazer, K., & Ruiz, J. M.** (2004). Hostility, anger, aggressiveness, and coronary heart disease: An interpersonal perspective on personality, emotion, and health. *Journal of Personality, 72,* 1217–1270.

**Smith, T. W., Pope, M. K., Sanders, J. D., Allred, K. D., & O'Keefe, J. L.** (1988). Cynical hostility at home and work: Psychosocial vulnerability across domains. *Journal of Research in Personality, 22,* 525–548.

**Smith, W. P., Compton, W. C., & West, W. B.** (1995). Meditation as an adjunct to a happiness enhancement program. *Journal of Clinical Psychology, 51,* 269–273.

**Smock, P. J.** (2000). Cohabitation in the United States: An appraisal of research themes, findings, and implications. *Annual Review of Sociology, 26,* 1–20.

**Smock, P. J., Manning, W. D., & Gupta, S.** (1999). The effect of marriage and divorce on women's economic well-being. *American Sociological Review, 64,* 794–812.

**Smolak, L.** (2006). Body image. In J. Worrell & C. D. Goodheart (Eds.), *Handbook of girls' and women's psychological health.* New York: Oxford University Press.

**Smolak, L., & Murnen, S. K.** (2001). Gender and eating problems. In R. H. Striegel-Moore & L. Smolak (Eds.), *Eating disorders: Innovative directions in research and practice.* Washington, DC: American Psychological Association.

**Smoot, T. M., Xu, P., Kuppersmith, N. C., Singh, K. P., & Hilserath, P.** (2006). Gastric bypass surgery in the Unites States, 1998–2002. *American Journal of Public Health, 96,* 1187–1189.

**Smyth, J., Litcher, L., Hurewitz, A., & Stone, A.** (2001). Relaxation training and cortisol secretion in adult asthmatics. *Journal of Health Psychology, 6*(2), 217–227.

**Smyth, J. M., & Pennebaker, J. W.** (1999). Sharing one's story: Translating emotional experiences into words as a coping tool. In C. R. Snyder (Ed.), *Coping: The psychology of what works.* New York: Oxford University Press.

**Smyth, J. M., & Pennebaker, J. W.** (2001). What are the health effects of disclosure? In A. Baum, T. A. Revenson, & J. E. Singer (Eds.), *Handbook of health psychology.* Mahwah, NJ: Erlbaum.

**Snell, J. C., & Marsh, M.** (2008). Life cycle loneliness curve. *Psychology and Education: An Interdisciplinary Journal, 45,* 26–28.

**Snowden, L. R., & Hu, T. W.** (1996). Outpatient service use in minority-serving mental health programs. *Administration and Policy in Mental Health, 24,* 149–159.

**Snowden, L. R., & Yamada, A.** (2005). Cultural differences in access to care. *Annual Review of Clinical Psychology, 1,* 143–166.

**Snyder, C. R.** (1994/2000). *The psychology of hope: You can get there from here.* New York: Free Press.

**Snyder, C. R.** (2002). Hope theory: Rainbows of the mind. *Psychological Inquiry, 13,* 249–275.

**Snyder, C. R.** (Ed.). (2000). *Handbook of hope: Theory, measures, and applications.* San Francisco: Academic Press.

**Snyder, C. R., Harris, C., Anderson, J. R., Holeran, S. A., Irving, L. M., Sigmon, S. T., Yoshinobu, L., Gibb, J., Langelle, C., & Harney, P.** (1991). The will and the ways: Development and validation of an individual-differences measure of hope. *Journal of Personality and Social Psychology, 60,* 570–585.

**Snyder, C. R., Hoza, B., Pelham, W. E., Rapoff, M., Ware, L., Danovsky, M., Highberger, L., Rubenstein, H., & Stahl, K. J.** (1997). The development and validation of the Children's Hope Scale. *Journal of Pediatric Psychology, 22,* 399–421.

**Snyder, C. R., & Lopez, S. J.** (2007). *Positive psychology: The scientific and practical exploration of human strengths.* Thousand Oaks, CA: Sage.

**Snyder, C. R., & Lopez, S. J.** (Eds.). (2002). *Handbook of positive psychology.* New York: Oxford University Press.

**Snyder, C. R., Rand, K. L., & Sigmon, D. R.** (2002). Hope theory: A member of the positive psychology family. In C. R. Snyder & S. J. Lopez (Eds.), *Handbook of positive psychology* (pp. 257–276). New York: Oxford.

**Snyder, C. R., Sympson, S. C., Ybasco, F. C., Borders, T. F., Babyak, M. A., & Higgins, R. L.** (1996). Development and validation of the State Hope Scale. *Journal of Personality and Social Psychology, 70,* 321–335.

**Snyder, M.** (1979). Self-monitoring processes. In L. Berkowitz (Ed.), *Advances in experimental social psychology* (Vol. 12). New York: Academic Press.

Snyder, M. (1986). *Public appearances/Private realities: The psychology of self-monitoring.* New York: Freeman.

Snyder, M., & Swann, W. B., Jr. (1978). Hypothesis testing processes in social interaction. *Journal of Personality and Social Psychology, 36*(11), 1202–1212.

Sobel, D. (2002). *Children's special places: Exploring the role of forts, dens, and bush houses in middle childhood* (The Child in the Cities Series). Detroit, MI: Wayne State University Press.

Solberg, E. C., Diener, E., Wirtz, D., Lucas, R. E., & Oishi, S. (2002). Wanting, having, and satisfaction: Examining the role of desire discrepancies in satisfaction with income. *Journal of Personality and Social Psychology, 83*(3), 725–734.

Solms, M. (2004). Freud returns. *Scientific American, 290*(5), 83–88.

Solomon, S., Greenberg, J., & Pyszczynski, T. (2004a). The cultural animal: Twenty years of terror management. In J. Greenberg, S. L. Koole, & T. Pyszczynski (Eds.), *Handbook of experimental existential psychology.* New York: Guilford Press.

Solomon, S., Greenberg, J., & Pyszczynski, T. (2004b). Lethal consumption: Death-denying materialism. In T. Kasser, & A. D. Kanner (Eds.), *Psychology and consumer culture: The struggle for a good life in a materialistic world.* Washington, DC: American Psychological Association.

Solomon, S., Greenberg, J. L., & Pyszczynski, T. A. (1991). A terror management theory of social behavior: The psychological functions of self-esteem and cultural worldviews. In M. Zanna (Ed.), *Advances in experimental social psychology* (Vol. 24). Orlando, FL: Academic Press.

Solomon, S. E., Rothblum, E. D., & Balsam, K. F. (2004). Pioneers in partnership: Lesbian and gay male couples in civil unions compared with those not in civil unions and married heterosexual siblings. *Journal of Family Psychology, 18,* 275–286.

Solowij, N., Stephens, R. S., Roffman, R. A., Babor, T., Kadden, R., Miller, M., Christiansen. K., McRee, B., & Vendetti, J. (2002). Cognitive functioning of long-term heavy cannabis users seeking treatment. *Journal of the American Medical Association, 287,* 1123–1131.

Son Hing, L. S., Bobocel, D. R., & Zanna, M. P. (2007). Authoritarian dynamics and unethical decision making: High social dominance orientation leaders and high right wing authoritarianism followers. *Journal of Personality and Social Psychology, 92,* 67–81.

Son Hing, L. S., Li, W., & Zanna, M. P. (2002). Inducing hypocrisy to reduce prejudicial responses among aversive racists. *Journal of Experimental Social Psychology, 38,* 71–78.

Sonnentag, S., & Frese, M. (2003). Stress in organizations. In W. C. Borman , D. R. Ilgen, & R. J. Klimoski (Eds.), *Handbook of psychology: Vol. 12. Industrial and organizational psychology.* New York: Wiley.

Sonstroem, R. J. (1997). Physical activity and self-esteem. In W. P. Morgan (Ed.), *Physical activity and mental health.* Washington, DC: Taylor & Francis.

South, S. J. (1991). Sociodemographic differentials in mate selection preferences. *Journal of Marriage and the Family, 53,* 928–940.

South, S. J. (1993). Racial and ethnic differences in the desire to marry. *Journal of Marriage and the Family, 55,* 357–370.

South, S. J., Bose, S., & Trent, K. (2004). Anticipating divorce: Spousal agreement, predictive accuracy, and effects on labor supply and fertility. *Journal of Divorce and Remarriage, 40*(3–4), 1–22.

South, S. J., & Lloyd, K. M. (1995). Spousal alternatives and marital dissolution. *American Sociological Review, 60,* 21–35.

Souza, R., Bernatsky, S., Reyes, R., & de Jong, K. (2007). Mental health status of vulnerable tsunami-affected communities: A survey in Aceh Province, Indonesia. *Journal of Traumatic Stress, 20,* 263–269.

Spada, M. M., & Wells, A. (2006). Metacognitions about alcohol use in problem drinkers. *Clinical Psychology & Psychotherapy, 13*(2), 138–143.

Spanos, N. P. (1994). Multiple identity enactments and multiple personality disorder: A sociocognitive perspective. *Psychological Bulletin, 116,* 143–165.

Spanos, N. P. (1996). *Multiple identities and false memories.* Washington, DC: American Psychological Association.

Sparks, J. A., Duncan, B. L., & Miller, S. D. (2008). Common factors in psychotherapy. In J. L. Lebow (Ed.), *Twenty-first century psychotherapies: Contemporary approaches to theory and practice.* New York: Wiley.

Spelke, E. S. (2005). Sex differences in intrinsic aptitude for mathematics and science? *American Psychologist, 60,* 950–958.

Spence, I., Yu, J. J., Feng, J., & Marshman, J. (2009). Women match men when learning a spatial skill. *Journal of Experimental Psychology, 35,* 1097–1103.

Spence, J. T. (1983). Comment on Lubinski, Tellegen, and Butcher's "Masculinity, femininity, and androgyny viewed and assessed as distinct concepts." *Journal of Personality and Social Psychology, 44,* 440–446.

Spence, J. T., & Buckner, C. E. (2000). Instrumental and expressive traits, trait stereotypes, and sexist attitudes. *Psychology of Women Quarterly, 24,* 44–62.

Spence, J. T., & Robbins, A. S. (1992). Workaholism: Definition, measurement, and preliminary results. *Journal of Personality Assessment, 58,* 160–178.

Spencer, P. T. (1990). Exercise as psychotherapy. *Counseling Psychology Quarterly, 3*(3), 291–293.

Spencer, S. J., Steele, C. M., & Quinn, D. M. (1999). Stereotype threat and women's math performance. *Journal of Experimental Social Psychology, 35*(1), 4–28.

Sperry, L. (2006). *Psychological treatment of chronic illness: The biopsychosocial therapy approach.* Washington, DC: American Psychological Association.

Sperry, R. W. (1982). Some effects of disconnecting the cerebral hemispheres. *Science, 217,* 1223–1226, 1250.

Speth, G. (1992). The global environmental challenge. In G. T.Miller (Ed.), *Living in the environment: An introduction to environmental science* (7th ed.). Belmont, CA: Wadsworth.

Spitz, H. I. (2009). Group psychotherapy. In B. J. Sadock, V. A. Sadock, & P. Ruiz (Eds.), *Kaplan & Sadock's comprehensive textbook of psychiatry* (pp. 2832–2856). Philadelphia: Lippincott Williams & Wilkins.

Spitzberg, B. H. (1999). An analysis of empirical estimates of sexual aggression victimization and perpetration. *Violence and Victims, 14*(3), 241–260.

Spitzer, R. L., First, M. B., & Wakefield, J. C. (2007). Saving PTSD from itself in DSM-V. *Journal of Anxiety Disorders, 21,* 233–241.

Spokane, A. R., & Cruza-Guet, M. C. (2005). Holland's theory of vocational personalities in work environments. In S. D. Brown & R. W. Lent (Eds.), *Career development and counseling: Putting theory and research to work.* New York: Wiley.

Sporer, S. L., & Schwandt, B. (2007). Moderators of nonverbal indicators of deception: A meta-analytic synthesis. *Psychology, Public Policy, and Law, 13,* 1–34.

Sprecher, S. (1994). Two sides to the breakup of dating relationships. *Personal Relationships, 1,* 199–222.

Sprecher, S. (2002). Sexual satisfaction in premarital relationships: Associations with satisfaction, love, commitment, and stability. *The Journal of Sex Research, 39*(3), 190–196.

Sprecher, S., & Cate, R. M. (2004). Sexual satisfaction and sexual expression as predictors of relationship satisfaction and stability. In J. H. Harvey, A. Wenzel, & S. Sprecher (Eds.), *The handbook of sexuality and close relationships.* Mahwah, NJ: Lawrence Erlbaum.

Sprecher, S., Christopher, F. S., & Cate, R. (2006). Sexuality in close relationships. In A. L. Vangelisti & D. Perlman (Eds.), *The Cambridge handbook of personal relationships.* New York: Cambridge University Press.

Sprecher, S., & Felmlee, D. (2008). Insider perspectives on attraction. In S. Sprecher, A. Wenzel, & J Harvey (Eds.), *Handbook of relationship initiation* (pp. 297–314). New York: Psychology Press.

Sprecher, S., Sullivan, Q., & Hatfield, E. (1994). Mate selection preferences: Gender differences examined in a national sample. *Journal of Personality and Social Psychology, 66,* 1074–1080.

Springen, K. (2004, November 1). Under the knife. *Newsweek,* pp. 59–60.

Springer, S. P., & Deutsch, G. (1998). *Left brain, right brain.* New York: Freeman.

Staats, H. (2003). Understanding pro-environmental attitudes and behavior: An analysis and review of research based on the theory of planned behavior. In M. Bonnes, T. Lee, & M. Bonaiuto (Eds.), *Psychological theories for environmental issues* (pp. 171–202). Wiltshire, UK: Antony Rowe.

Stack, S., & Eshleman, J. R. (1998). Marital status and happiness: A 17-nation study. *Journal of Marriage and the Family, 60,* 527–536.

Stafford, L., & Canary, D. J. (1991). Maintenance strategies and romantic relationship type, gender and relational characteristics. *Journal of Social and Personal Relationships, 8,* 217–242.

Stafford, L., & Canary, D. J. (2006). Equity and interdependence as predictors of relational maintenance strategies. *The Journal of Family Communication, 6,* 227–254.

Staines, G. L. (2008). The relative efficacy of psychotherapy: Reassessing the methods-based paradigm. *Review of General Psychology, 12*(4), 330–343.

Staines, G. L., & Cleland, C. M. (2007). Bias in meta-analytic estimates of the absolute efficacy of psychotherapy. *Review of General Psychology, 11*(4), 329–347.

Stajkovic, A. D., & Luthans, F. (1998). Self-efficacy and work-related performance: A meta-analysis. *Psychological Bulletin, 124*(2), 240–261.

Stalder, D. R. (2009). Competing roles for the subfactors of need for closure in committing the fundamental attribution error. *Personality and Individual Differences, 47*(7), 701–705.

Stamler, J., Daviglus, M. L., Garside, D. B., Dyer, A. R., Greenland, P., & Neaton, J. D. (2000). Relationship of baseline serum cholesterol levels in 3 large cohorts of younger men to long-term coronary, cardiovascular, and all-cause mortality and to longevity. *Journal of the American Medical Association, 284,* 311–318.

Stanley, M. A. & Beidel, D. C. (2009). Behavior therapy. In B. J. Sadock, V. A. Sadock, & P. Ruiz (Eds.), *Kaplan & Sadock's comprehensive textbook of psychiatry* (pp. 2781–2803). Philadelphia: Lippincott Williams & Wilkins.

Stanley, S. M., & Rhoades, G. K. (2009). Cohabitation. In H. T. Reis & S. Sprecher (Eds.), *Encyclopedia of human relationships: Vol. 2* (pp. 229–231). Los Angeles: Sage Reference Publication.

Stanley, S. M., Whitton, S. W., & Markman, H. J. (2004). Maybe I do? Interpersonal commitment and premarital or nonmarital cohabitation. *Journal of Family Issues, 25,* 496–519.

Stanton, A. L., Lobel, M., Sears, S., & DeLuca, R. S. (2002). Psychosocial aspects of selected issues in women's reproductive health: Current status and future directions. *Journal of Consulting & Clinical Psychology, 70*(3), 751–770.

Starcevic, V. (2001). Clinical features and diagnosis of hypochondriasis. In V. Starcevic & D. R. Lipsitt (Eds.), *Hypochondriasis: Modern perspectives on an ancient malady.* New York: Oxford University Press.

Starker, S. (1990). Self-help books: Ubiquitous agents of health care. *Medical Psychotherapy: An International Journal, 3* 187–194.

Starker, S. (1992). Characteristics of self-help book readers among VA medical outpatients. *Medical Psychotherapy: An International Journal, 5,* 89–93.

Starrels, M. E., Ingersoll-Dayton, B., Dowler, D. W., & Neal, M. B. (1997). The stress of caring for a parent: Effects of the elder's impairment on an employed adult child. *Journal of Marriage and the Family, 59,* 860–872.

Stead, L. F., Perera, R., Bullen, C., Mant, D., & Lancaster, T. (2008). Nicotine replacement therapy for smoking cessation. *Cochrane Database of Systematic Reviews,* Cochrane AN: CD000146.

Steel, P. (2007). The nature of procrastination: A meta-analytic and theoretical review of quintessential self-regulatory failure. *Psychological Bulletin, 133*(1), 65–94.

Steele, C. M. (1988). The psychology of self-affirmation: Sustaining integrity of the self. In L. Berkowitz (Ed.), *Advances in experimental social psychology.* New York: Academic Press.

Steele, C. M. (1992, April). Race and the schooling of black Americans. *The Atlantic Monthly,* 68–78.

Steele, C. M. (1997). A threat in the air: How stereotypes shape intellectual identity and performance. *American Psychologist, 52,* 613–629.

Steele, C. M., & Aronson, J. (1995). Stereotype threat and the intellectual test performance of African Americans. *Journal of Personality and Social Psychology, 69,* 797–811.

Steele, C. M., Spencer, S. J., & Lynch, M. (1993). Self-image resilience and dissonance: The role of affirmational resources. *Journal of Personality and Social Psychology, 64,* 885–896.

Steiger, H., & Bruce, K. R. (2009). Eating disorders. In P. H. Blaney & T. Millon (Eds.), *Oxford textbook of psychopathology* (pp. 431–451). New York: Oxford University Press.

Steiger, H., & Seguin, J. R. (1999). Eating disorders: Anorexia nervosa and bulimia nervosa. In T. Millon, P. H. Blaney, & R. D. Davis (Eds.), *Oxford textbook of psychopathology.* New York: Oxford University Press.

Steiger, H., Bruce, K. R., & Israël, M. (2003). Eating disorders. In G. Stricker & T. A. Widiger (Eds.), *Handbook of psychology: Vol. 8. Clinical psychology.* New York: Wiley.

Steil, J. M. (2009). Dual-earner couples. In H. T. Reis & S. Sprecher (Eds.), *Encyclopedia of human relationships: Vol. 2* (pp. 469–471). Los Angeles: Sage Reference Publication.

Stein, D. J., & Hugo, F. J. (2004). Neuropsychiatric aspects of anxiety disorders. In S. C. Yudofsky & R. E. Hales (Eds.), *Essentials of neuropsychiatry and clinical neurosciences.* Washington, DC: American Psychiatric Publishing.

**Stein, J., Schettler, T., Rohrer, B., & Valenti, M.** (2008). *Environmental threats to healthy aging.* Boston: Physician's for Social Responsibility and Science and Environmental Health Network. Retrieved from http://www.psr.org/site/DocServer/GBPSRSEHN_HealthyAging1017.pdf?docID=5930

**Stein, J., Schettler, T., Wallinga, D., Miller, M. & Valenti, M.** (2002). *In harm's way: Training program for health professionals.* Boston: Physician's for Social Responsibility.

**Stein, M. B., Forde, D. R., Anderson, G., & Walker, J. R.** (1997a). Obsessive-compulsive disorder in the community: An epidemiologic survey with clinical reappraisal. *American Journal of Psychiatry, 154,* 1120–1126.

**Stein, M. B., Walker, J. R., Hazen, A. L., & Forde, D. R.** (1997b). Full and partial posttraumatic stress disorder: Findings from a community survey. *American Journal of Psychiatry, 154,* 1114–1119.

**Stein, N., Marshall, N. L., & Tropp, L. R.** (1993). *Secrets in public: Sexual harassment in our schools.* Wellesley, MA: Center for Research on Women at Wellesley College and the NOW Legal Defense and Education Fund.

**Steinberg, L., & Levine, A.** (1997). *You and your adolescent: A parents' guide for ages 10 to 20.* New York: Harper Perennial.

**Steiner, H., Erickson, S. J., MacLean, P., Medic, S., Plattner, B., & Koopman, C.** (2007). Relationship between defenses, personality, and affect during a stress task in normal adolescents. *Child Psychiatry Human Development, 38,* 107–119.

**Steinhausen, H.** (2002). The outcome of anorexia nervosa in the 20th century. *American Journal of Psychiatry, 159,* 1284–1293.

**Steinmetz, H., Staiger, J. F., Schluag, G., Huang, Y., & Jancke, L.** (1995). Corpus callosum and brain volume in women and men. *Neuroreport, 3,* 1002–1004.

**Stelmack, R. M. & Rammsayer, T. H.** (2008). Psychophysiological and biochemical correlates of personality. In G. J. Boyle, G. Matthews, D. H. Saklofske (Eds.), *The sage handbook of personality theory and assessment* (pp. 33–55). Los Angeles: Sage.

**Stephens, N. M., Markus, H. R., & Townsend, S. S. M.** (2007). Choice as an act of meaning: The case of social class. *Journal of Personality and Social Psychology, 93,* 814–830.

**Stephens, R. S.** (1999). Cannabis and hallucinogens. In B. S. McCrady, & E. E. Epstein (Eds.), *Addictions: A comprehensive guidebook.* New York: Oxford University Press.

**Steptoe, A.** (2007). Control and stress. In G. Fink (Ed.), *Encyclopedia of stress: Vols. 1–4* (2nd ed., pp. 568–573). San Diego, CA: Elsevier Academic Press.

**Sterman, J. D.** (2008). Risk communication on climate: Mental models and mass balance. *Science, 322,* 532–533.

**Sternberg, R. J.** (1986). A triangular theory of love. *Psychological Review, 93* 119–135.

**Sternberg, R. J.** (1988). Triangulating love. In R. J. Sternberg & M. L. Barnes (Eds.), *The psychology of love.* New Haven, CT: Yale University Press.

**Sternberg, R. J.** (2006). A duplex theory of love. In R. J. Sternberg & K. Weis (Eds.), *The New Psychology of Love* (pp. 184–199). New Haven, CT: Yale University Press.

**Sternberg, R. J., Grigorenko, E. L., & Kidd, K. K.** (2005). Intelligence, race, and genetics. *American Psychologist, 60,* 45–69.

**Stevens, D. P., Minnotte, K. L., Mannon, S. E., & Kiger, G.** (2007). Examining the "neglected side of the work-family interface": Antecedents of positive and negative family-to-work spillover. *Journal of Family Issues, 28,* 242–262.

**Stevens, S. B., & Morris, T. L.** (2007). College dating and social anxiety: Using the Internet as a means of connecting to others. *CyberPsychology & Behavior, 10,* 680–688.

**Stewart, F. H., Ellertson, C., & Cates, W. Jr.** (2004). Abortion. In R. A. Hatcher, J. Trussell, F. H. Stewart, A. L. Nelson, W. Cates Jr., F. Guest, & D. Kowal (Eds.), *Contraceptive technology* (18th rev. ed.). New York: Ardent Media.

**Stice, E., Spangler, D., & Agras, W. S.** (2001). Exposure to media-portrayed thin-ideal images adversely affects vulnerable girls: A longitudinal experiment. *Journal of Social and Clinical Psychology, 20,* 270–288.

**Stillion, J. M.** (1995). Death in the lives of adults: Responding to the tolling of the bell. In H. Wass & R. A. Neimeyer (Eds.), *Dying: Facing the facts.* New York: Taylor & Francis.

**Stinson, F. S., Dawson, D. A., Goldstein, R. B., Chou, S. P., Huang, B. F., Smith, S. M., et al.** (2008). Prevalence, correlates, diability, and comorbidity of DSM-IV Narcissistic Personality Disorder: Results from the Wave 2 National Epidemiologic Survey on alcohol and related conditions. *Journal of Clinical Psychiatry, 69,* 1033–1045.

**Stith, S. M., Rosen, K. H., Middleton, K. A., Busch, A. L., Lundeberg, K., & Carlton, R. P.** (2000). The intergenerational transmission of spouse abuse: A meta-analysis. *Journal of Marriage and the Family, 62,* 640–654.

**Stith, S. M., Smith, D. B., Penn, C. E., Ward, D. B., & Tritt, D.** (2004). Intimate partner physical abuse perpetration and victimization risk factors: A meta-analytic review. *Aggression and Violent Behavior, 10,* 65–98.

**Stoll, B. M., Arnaut, G. L., Fromme, D. K., & Felker-Thayer, J. A.** (2005). Adolescents in stepfamilies: A qualitative analysis. *Journal of Divorce & Remarriage, 44,* 177–189.

**Stone, J., & McWhinnie, C.** (2008). Evidence that blatant versus subtle stereotype threat cues impact performance through dual processes. *Journal of Experimental Social Psychology, 44*(2), 445–452.

**Stone, L.** (1977). *The family, sex and marriage in England 1500–1800.* New York: Harper & Row.

**Stone, P., & Lovejoy, M.** (2004, November). Fast-track women and the "choice" to stay home. *Annals of the American Academy of Political and Social Science, 596,* 62–83.

**Stone, W. N.** (2003). Group psychotherapy. In A. Tasman, J. Kay, & J. A. Lieberman (Eds.), *Psychiatry.* New York: Wiley.

**Stoney, C. M.** (2003). Gender and cardiovascular disease: A psychobiological and integrative approach. *Current Directions in Psychological Science, 12*(4), 129–133.

**Stotzer, R. L.** (2009). Straight allies: Supportive attitudes towards lesbians, gay men, and bisexuals in a college sample. *Sex Roles, 60,* 67–80.

**Strahan, E. J., Lafrance, A., Wilson, A. E., Ethier, N., Spencer, S. J., & Zanna, M. P.** (2008). Victoria's dirty secret: How sociocultural norms influence adolescent girls and women. *Personality and Social Psychology Bulletin, 34*(2), 288–301.

**Strange, D., Clifasefi, S., & Garry, M.** (2007). False memories. In M. Garry & H. Hayne (Eds.), *Do justice and let the sky fall: Elizabeth F. Loftus and her contributions to science, law, and academic freedom.* Mahwah, NJ: Erlbaum.

**Strasburger, V. C.** (2007). First do no harm: Why have parents and pediatricians missed the boat on children and media? *Journal of Pediatrics, 151,* 334–336.

**Strauman, T. J., Vookles, J., Berenstein, V., Chaiken, S., & Higgins, E. T.** (1991). Self-discrepancies and vulnerability to body dissatisfaction and disordered eating. *Journal of Personality and Social Psychology, 61,* 946–956.

**Striegel-Moore, R. H., & Bulik, C. M.** (2007). Risk factors for eating disorders. *American Psychologist, 62,* 181–198.

**Striegel-Moore, R. H., & Franko, D. L.** (2008). Should binge eating disorder be included in the DSM-V? A critical review of the state of the evidence. *Annual Review of Clinical Psychology, 4,* 305–324.

**Striegel-Moore, R. H., McMahon, R. P., Biro, F. M., Schreiber, G., Crawford, P. B., & Voorhees, C.** (2001). Exploring the relationship between timing of menarche and eating disorder symptoms in black and white adolescent girls. *International Journal of Eating Disorders, 30*(4), 421–433.

**Striegel-Moore, R. H., Silberstein, L. R., & Rodin, J.** (1993). The social self in bulimia nervosa: Public self-consciousness, social anxiety, and perceived fraudulence. *Journal of Abnormal Psychology, 102,* 297–303.

**Stroebe, K., Lodewijkx, H. F. M., & Spears, R.** (2005). Do unto others as they do unto you: Reciprocity and social identification as determinants of ingroup favoritism. *Personality and Social Psychology Bulletin, 31,* 831–845.

**Stroebe, W., Stroebe, M., Abakoumkin, G., & Schut, H.** (1996). The role of loneliness and social support in adjustment to loss: A test of attachment versus stress theory. *Journal of Personality and Social Psychology, 70*(6), 1241–1249.

**Strong, G., & Harasymchuk, C.** (2009). Boredom in relationships. In H. T. Reis & S. Sprecher (Eds.), *Encyclopedia of human relationships: Vol. 1* (pp. 186–189). Los Angeles: Sage Reference Publication.

**Stroup, T. S., Kraus, J. E., & Marder, S. R.** (2006). Pharmacotherapies. In J. A. Lieberman, T. S. Stroup, & D. O. Perkins (Eds.), *Textbook of schizophrenia.* Washington, DC: American Psychiatric Publishing.

**Strupp, H. H.** (1996). The tripartite model and the *Consumer Reports* study. *American Psychologist, 51,* 1017–1024.

**Stuart, R. B. & Heiby, E. E.** (2007). To prescribe or not to prescribe: Eleven exploratory questions. *The Scientific Review of Mental Health Practice, 5*(1), 4–32.

**Stubbe, J. H., Posthuma, D., Boomsma, D. I., & De Geus, E. J. C.** (2005). Heritability of life satisfaction in adults: A twin-family study. *Psychological Medicine, 35,* 1581–1588.

**Stunkard, A. J., Allison, K. C., Geliebter, A., Lundgren, J. D., Gluck, M. E., O'Reardon, J. P.** (2009). Development of criteria for a diagnosis: Lessons from the night eating syndrome. *Comprehensive Psychiatry, 50*(5), 391–399.

**Stunkard, A. J., Harris, J. R., Pederson, N. L., & McClearn, G. E.** (1990). The body-mass index of twins who have been reared apart. *New England Journal of Medicine, 322,* 1483–1487.

**Stunkard, A. J., Sorensen, T., Hanis, C., Teasdale, T. W., Chakraborty, R., Schull, W. J., & Schulsinger, F.** (1986). An adoption study of human obesity. *New England Journal of Medicine, 314,* 193–198.

**Suarez, E. C.** (2004). C-reactive protein is associated with psychological risk factors of cardiovascular disease in apparently healthy adults. *Psychosomatic Medicine, 66*(5), 684–691.

**Suarez, E. C., Kuhn, C. M., Schanberg, S. M., Williams, R. B., Jr., & Zimmermann, E. A.** (1998). Neuroendocrine, cardiovascular, and emotional responses of hostile men: The role of interpersonal challenge. *Psychosomatic Medicine, 60*(1), 78–88.

**Suarez, E. C., Saab, P. G., Llabre, M. M., Kuhn, C. M., & Zimmerman, E.** (2004). Ethnicity, gender, and age effects on adrenoceptors and physiological responses to emotional stress. *Psychophysiology, 41,* 450–460.

**Suarez-Morales, L., & Lopez, B.** (2009). The impact of acculturative stress and daily hassles on pre-adolescent psychological adjustment: Examining anxiety symptoms. *The Journal of Primary Prevention, 30*(3–4), 335–349.

**Subotnik, R.** (2007). Cyber-infidelity. In P. R. Peluso (Ed.), *Family therapy and counseling* (pp. 169–190). New York: Routledge/Taylor & Francis Group.

**Sudak, H. S.** (2005). Suicide. In B. J. Sadock & V. A. Sadock (Eds.), *Kaplan & Sadock's comprehensive textbook of psychiatry.* Philadelphia: Lippincott Williams & Wilkins.

**Sudak, H. S.** (2009). Suicide. In B. J. Sadock, V. A. Sadock, & P. Ruiz (Eds.), *Kaplan & Sadock's comprehensive textbook of psychiatry* (pp. 2717–2731). Philadelphia: Lippincott Williams & Wilkins.

**Sue, S., Zane, N., & Young, K.** (1994). Research on psychotherapy with culturally diverse populations. In A. E. Bergin & S. L. Garfield (Eds.), *Handbook of psychotherapy and behavior change* (4th ed.). New York: John Wiley.

**Suicide Awareness Voices of Education.** (2007). *Someone you know is suicidal.* Retrieved April 12, 2007 from http://www.save.org/prevention/someone_you_know.html.

**Suinn, R. M.** (1968). Removal of social desirability and response set items from the Manifest Anxiety Scale. *Educational and Psychological Measurement, I 28,* 1189–1192.

**Suinn, R. M.** (1984). *Fundamentals of abnormal psychology.* Chicago: Nelson-Hall.

**Sulloway, F. J.** (1991). Reassessing Freud's case histories: The social construction of psychoanalysis. *ISIS, 82,* 245–275.

**Sulloway, F. J.** (1995). Birth order and evolutionary psychology: A meta-analytic overview. *Psychological Inquiry, 6,* 75–80.

**Sulloway, F. J.** (1996). *Born to rebel: Birth order, family dynamics, and creative lives.* New York: Pantheon Books.

**Sullum, J., Clark, M. M., & King, T. K.** (2000). Predictors of exercise relapse in a college population. *Journal of American College Health, 48,* 175–180.

**Suls, J., & Bunde, J.** (2005). Anger, anxiety, and depression as risk factors for cardiovascular disease: The problems and implications of overlapping affective dispositions. *Psychological Bulletin, 131,* 260–300.

**Suls, J., & Rothman, A.** (2004). Evolution of the biopsychosocial model: Prospects and challenges for health psychology. *Health Psychology, 23*(2), 119–125.

**Sulsky, L., & Smith, C.** (2005). *Work stress.* Belmont, CA: Wadsworth.

**Sulsky, L., & Smith, C.** (2007). Work stress: Macro-level work stressors. In A. Monat, R. S. Lazarus, & G. Reevy (Eds.), *The Praeger handbook on stress and coping* (pp. 53–86). Westport, CT: Praeger Publishers.

**Sum, S., Mathews, R. M., Hughes, I., & Campbell, A.** (2008). Internet use and loneliess in older adults. *CyberPsychology & Behavior, 11,* 208–211.

**Summers, G., & Feldman, N. S.** (1984). Blaming the perpetrator: An attributional analysis of spouse abuse. *Journal of Social and Clinical Psychology, 2,* 339–347.

Sundblad, E. L., Biel, A., & Gärling, T. (2007). Cognitive and affective risk judgments related to climate change. *Journal of Environmental Psychology, 27,* 97–106.

Super, D. E. (1957). *The psychology of careers.* New York: HarperCollins.

Super, D. E. (1985). Career and life development. In D. Brown & L. Brooks (Eds.), *Career choice and development.* San Francisco: Jossey-Bass.

Super, D. E. (1988). Vocational adjustment: Implementing a self-concept. *The Career Development Quarterly, 36,* 351–357.

Super, D. E. (1990). A life-span, life-space approach to career development. In D. Brown & L. Brooks (Eds.), *Career choice and development* (2nd ed., pp. 197–261). San Francisco, CA: Jossey-Bass.

Surra, C. A., Gray, C. R., Boettcher, T. M. J., Cottle, N. R., & West, A. R. (2006). From courtship to universal properties: Research on dating and mate selection, 1950 to 2003. In A. L. Vangelisti & D. Perlman (Eds.), *The Cambridge handbook of personal relationships.* New York: Cambridge University Press.

Suschinsky, K. D., Lalumiere, M. L., & Chivers, M. L. (2009). Sex differences in patterns of genital sexual arousal: Measurement artifacts of true phenomena? *Archives of Sexual Behavior, 38,* 559–574.

Susman, E. J., Dorn, L. D., & Schiefelbein, V. L. (2003). Puberty, sexuality, and health. In R. M. Lerner, M.A. Easterbrooks, & J. Mistry (Eds.), *Handbook of psychology: Vol. 6. Developmental psychology.* New York: Wiley.

Susser, E., Neugebauer, R., Hoek, H. W., Brown, A. S., Lin, S., Labovitz, D., & Gorman, J. M. (1996). Schizophrenia after prenatal famine: Further evidence. *Archives of General Psychiatry, 53,* 25–31.

Sussman, N. (2009). Selective serotonin reuptake inhibitors. In B. J. Sadock, V. A. Sadock, & P. Ruiz (Eds.), *Kaplan & Sadock's comprehensive textbook of psychiatry* (pp. 3190–3205). Philadelphia: Lippincott Williams & Wilkins.

Sutherland, V. J. (2000). Understimulation/boredom. In G. Fink (Ed.), *Encyclopedia of stress* (Vol. 3). San Diego: Academic Press.

Swan, G. E., Hudmon, K. S., & Khroyan, T. V. (2003). Tobacco dependence. In A. M. Nezu, C. M. Nezu , & P. A. Geller (Eds.), *Handbook of psychology: Vol. 9. Health psychology.* New York: Wiley.

Swan, S. C., & Snow, D. L. (2006). The development of a theory of women's use of violence in intimate relationships. *Violence Against Women, 12,* 1026–1045.

Swann, W. B., Jr., Chang-Schneider, C., & McClarty, K. L. (2007). Do people's self–views matter? Self-concept and self-esteem in everyday life. *American Psychologist, 62,* 84–94.

Swann, W. B., Jr., Rentfrow, P. J., & Guinn, J. S. (2003). Self-verification: The search for coherence. In M. R. Leary & J. P. Tangney (Eds.), *Handbook of self and identity.* New York: Guilford.

Swann, W. B., Jr., Stein-Seroussi, A., & McNulty, S. E. (1992). Outcasts in a white-lie society: The enigmatic worlds of people with negative self-conceptions. *Journal of Personality and Social Psychology, 62,* 618–624.

Swanson, J. L., & D'Achiardi, C. (2005). Beyond interests, needs/values, and abilities: Assessing other important career constructs over the life span. In S. D. Brown & R. W. Lent (Eds.), *Career development and counseling: Putting theory and research to work.* New York: Wiley.

Sweeney, M. M., Wang, H., & Videon, T. M. (2009). Reconsidering the association between stepfather families and adolescent well-being. In H. E. Peters & C. M. K. Dush (Eds.), *Marriage and family: Perspectives and complexities* (pp. 177–225). New York: Columbia University Press.

Swim, J. K., Aikin, K. J., Hall, W. S., & Hunter, B. A. (1995). Sexism and racism: Old-fashioned and modern prejudices. *Journal of Personality and Social Psychology, 68,* 199–214.

Swim, J. K., Johnston, K., & Pearson, N. B. (2009). Daily experiences with heterosexism: Relations between heterosexist hassles and psychological well-being. *Journal of Social and Clinical Psychology, 28,* 597–629.

Szasz, T. S. (1974). *The myth of mental illness.* New York: HarperCollins.

Szasz, T. S. (1993). *A lexicon of lunacy: Metaphoric malady, moral responsibility, and psychiatry.* New Brunswick, NJ: Transaction.

Szigethy, E. M. & Friedman, E. S. (2009). Combined psychotherapy and pharmacology. In B. J. Sadock, V. A. Sadock, & P. Ruiz (Eds.), *Kaplan & Sadock's comprehensive textbook of psychiatry* (pp. 2923–2931). Philadelphia: Lippincott Williams & Wilkins.

Szlemko, W. J., Benfield, J. A., Bell, P. A., Deffenbacher, J. L., & Troup, L. (2008). Territorial markings as a predictor of driver aggression and road rage. *Journal of Applied Social Psychology, 38,* 1664–1688.

Szmukler, G. I., & Patton, G. (1995). Sociocultural models of eating disorders. In G. Szmukler, C. Dare, & J. Treasure (Eds.), *Handbook of eating disorders: Theory, treatment and research.* New York: Wiley.

Tajfel, H. (1982). *Social identity and intergroup relations.* London: Cambridge University Press.

Tamir, M. (2009). What do people want to feel and why?: Pleasure and utility in emotion regulation. *Current Directions in Psychological Science, 18,* 101–105.

Tamminga, C. A., & Carlsson, A. (2003). Psychiatric pathophysiology: Schizophrenia. In A. Tasman, J. Kay, & J. A. Lieberman (Eds.), *Psychiatry.* New York: Wiley.

Tang, M. (2002). A comparison of Asian American, Caucasian American, and Chinese college students: An initial report. *Journal of Multicultural Counseling and Development, 30*(2), 124–134.

Tannen, D. (1990). *You just don't understand: Women and men in conversation.* New York: Ballantine.

Tanner, J. M. (1990). *Fetus into man: Physical growth from conception to maturity.* Cambridge, MA: Harvard University Press.

Tardy, C. H., & Dindia, K. (2006). Self-disclosure: Strategic revelation of information in personal and professional relationships. In O. Hargie (Ed.), *The handbook of communication skills* (3rd ed., pp. 229–266). New York: Routledge.

Tashiro, T., Frazier, P., & Berman, M. (2006). Stress-related growth following divorce and relationship dissolution. In M. A. Fine & J. H. Harvey (Eds.), *Handbook of divorce and relationship resolution.* Mahwah, NJ: Erlbaum.

Tasker, F. (2005). Lesbian mothers, gay fathers, and their children: A review. *Journal of Developmental & Behavioral Pediatrics, 26,* 224–240.

Tavris, C. (1982). *Anger: The misunderstood emotion.* New York: Simon & Schuster.

Tavris, C. (1989). *Anger: The misunderstood emotion* (2nd ed.). New York: Simon & Schuster.

Taylor, D. A., & Altman, I. (1987). Communication in interpersonal relationships: Social penetration processes. In M. E. Roloff & G. R. Miller (Eds.), *Interpersonal processes: New directions in communication research.* Newbury Park, CA: Sage.

Taylor, E. (2001). Positive psychology and humanistic psychology: A reply to Seligman. *Journal of Humanistic Psychology, 41,* 13–29.

Taylor, J. A. (1953). A personality scale of manifest anxiety. *Journal of Abnormal Psychology, 48,* 285–290.

Taylor, L. D. (2005). Effects of visual and verbal sexual television content and perceived realism on attitudes and beliefs. *Journal of Sex Research, 42*(2), 130–137.

Taylor, M. C. (1995). White backlash to workplace affirmative action: Peril or myth? *Social Forces, 73,* 1385–1414.

Taylor, S., Cox, B. J., & Asmundson, J. G. (2009). Anxiety disorders: Panic and phobias. In P. H. Blaney & T. Millon (Eds.), *Oxford textbook of psychopathology* (pp. 119–145). New York: Oxford University Press.

Taylor, S. E. (2006). Tend and befriend: Biobehavioral bases of affiliation under stress. *Current Directions in Psychological Science, 15*(6), 273–277.

Taylor, S. E. (2007). Social support. In H. S. Friedman & R. C. Silver (Eds.), *Foundations of health psychology.* New York: Oxford University Press.

Taylor, S. E., & Brown, J. D. (1988). Illusion and well-being: A social psychological perspective on mental health. *Psychological Bulletin, 103,* 193–210.

Taylor, S. E., & Brown, J. D. (1994). Positive illusions and well-being revisited: Separating fact from fiction. *Psychological Bulletin, 116,* 21–27.

Taylor, S. E., Klein, L. C., Lewis, B. P., Gruenewald, T. L., Gurung, R. A. R., & Updegraff, J. A. (2000). Biobehavioral responses to stress in females: Tend-and-befriend, not fight-or-flight. *Psychological Review, 107*(3), 411–429.

Taylor, S. E., Lerner, J. S., Sherman, D. K., Sage, R. M., & McDowell, N. K. (2003). Are self-enhancing cognitions associated with healthy or unhealthy biological profiles? *Journal of Personality and Social Psychology, 85*(4), 605–615.

Taylor, S. E., Sherman, D. K., Kim, H. S., Jarcho, J., Takagi, K., & Dunagan, M. S. (2004). Culture and social support: Who seeks it and why? *Journal of Personality, 87,* 354–362.

Teachman, J. D. (2003). Premarital sex, premarital cohabitation, and the risk of subsequent marital dissolution among women. *Journal of Marriage and Family, 65,* 444–445.

Teachman, J. D. (2008). Complex life course patterns and the risk of divorce in second marriages. *Journal of Marriage and Family, 70,* 294–305.

Teachman, J. D. (2009). Divorce, prevalence and trends. In H. T. Reis & S. Sprecher (Eds.), *Encyclopedia of human relationships: Vol. 2* (pp. 461–464). Los Angeles: Sage Reference Publication.

Teachman, J. D., Tedrow, L. M., & Crowder, K. D. (2001). The changing demography of America's families. In R. M. Milardo (Ed.), *Understanding families into the new millennium: A decade in review.* Minneapolis: National Council on Family Relations.

Teachman, J. D., Tedrow, L., & Hall, M. (2006). The demographic future of divorce and dissolution. In M. A. Fine & J. H. Harvey (Eds.), *Handbook of divorce and relationship resolution.* Mahwah, NJ: Erlbaum.

Tedeschi, R. G., & Calhoun, L. G. (Eds.). (1995). *Trauma and transformation: Growing in the aftermath of suffering.* Thousand Oaks, CA: Sage.

Tedeschi, R. G., & Calhoun, L. G. (1996). The traumatic growth inventory: Measuring the positive legacy of trauma. *Journal of Traumatic Stress, 9,* 455–471.

Tedeschi, R. G., & Calhoun, L. G. (2004). Posttraumatic growth: Conceptual foundations and empirical evidence. *Psychological Inquiry, 15*(1), 1–18.

Tedeschi, R. G., Park, C. L., & Calhoun, L. G. (Eds.). (1998). *Posttraumatic growth: Positive changes in the aftermath of crisis.* Mahwah, NJ: Erlbaum.

Tellegen, A., Lykken, D. T., Bouchard, T. J., Jr., Wilcox, K. J., Segal, N. L., & Rich, S. (1988). Personality similarity in twins reared apart and together. *Journal of Personality and Social Psychology, 54,* 1031–1039.

Tennessen, C. M., & Cimprich, B. (1995). Views to nature: Effects on attention. *Journal of Environmental Psychology, 15,* 77–85.

Tesser, A. (2001). Self-esteem. In A. Tesser & N. Schwarz (Eds.), *Blackwell handbook of social psychology: Intraindividual processes.* Malden, MA: Blackwell.

Tesser, A., Wood, J. V., & Stapel, D. A. (Eds.). (2005). *On building, defending, and regulating the self: A psychological perspective.* New York: Psychology Press.

Testa, M., Vazile-Tamsen, C., & Livingston, J. A. (2004). The role of victim and perpetrator intoxication in sexual assault outcomes. *Journal of Studies on Alcohol, 65,* 320–329.

Tetlie, T., Eik-Nes, N., Palmstierna, T. Nottestad, J. A., & Callaghan, P. (2008). The effect of exercise on psychological & physical health outcomes: Preliminary results from a Norwegian forensic hospital. *Journal of Psychosocial Nursing & Mental Health Services, 46*(7), 39–43.

Tez, M., & Tez, S. (2008). Is cancer an adaptation mechanism to stress? *Cell Biology International, 32*(6), 713.

Thase, M. E. (2009). Selective serotonin-norepinephrine reuptake inhibitors. In B. J. Sadock, V. A. Sadock, & P. Ruiz (Eds.), *Kaplan & Sadock's comprehensive textbook of psychiatry* (pp. 3184–3189). Philadelphia: Lippincott Williams & Wilkins.

Thase, M. E., & Denko, T. (2008). Pharmacotherapy of mood disorders. *Annual Review of Clinical Psychology, 4,* 53–91.

Thase, M. E., & Sloan D. M. E. (2006). Venlafaxine. In A. F. Schatzberg & C. B. Nemeroff (Eds.), *Essentials of clinical psychopharmacology.* Washington, DC: American Psychological Association.

Thayer, A., & Lynn, S. J. (2006). Guided imagery and recovered memory therapy: Considerations and cautions. *Journal of Forensic Psychology Practice, 6,* 63–73.

Thibaut, J. W., & Kelley, H. H. (1959). *The social psychology of groups.* New York: Wiley.

Thobaben, M. (2005). Defense mechanisms and defense levels. *Home Health Care Management & Practice, 17,* 330–332.

Thomas, A. J., Kalaria, R. N., & O'Brien, J. T. (2004). Depression and vascular disease: What is the relationship? *Journal of Affective Disorders, 79*(1–3), 81–95.

Thomas, K. M. (2005). *Diversity dynamics in the workplace.* Belmont, CA: Wadsworth.

Thompkins, C. D., & Rando, R. A. (2003). Gender role conflict and shame in college men. *Psychology of Men and Masculinity, 4*(1), 79–81.

Thompson, B., Coronado, G., Chen, L., Thompson, L. A., Halperin, A., Jaffe, R., et al., (2007). Prevalence and characteristics of smokers at 30 Pacific Northwest colleges and universities. *Nicotine and Tobacco Research, 9,* 429–438.

Thompson, J. K., & Kinder, B. (2003). Easting disorders. In M. Hersen & S. Turner (Eds.), *Handbook of adult psychopathology.* New York: Plenum Press.

Thompson, J. K., Roehrig, M., & Kinder, B. N. (2007). Eating disorders. In M. Hersen, S. M. Turner, & D. C. Beidel (Eds.), *Adult psychopathology and diagnosis.* New York: Wiley.

Thompson, J. K., & Stice, E. (2001). Thin-ideal internalization: Mounting evidence for a new risk factor for body-image disturbance and eating pathology. *Current Directions in Psychological Science, 10*(5), 181–183.

Thompson, T., & Massat, C. R. (2005). Experiences of violence, post-traumatic stress, academic achievement and behavior problems of urban African-American children. *Child and Adolescent Social Work Journal, 22,* 367–393.

Thornton, A., & Young-DeMarco, L. (2001). Four decades of trends in attitudes toward family issues in the United States: The 1960s through the 1990s. *Journal of Marriage and Family, 63,* 1009–1037.

Thune, I., & Furberg, A. (2001). Physical activity and cancer risk: Dose-response and cancer, all sites and site specific. *Medicine and Science in Sports and Exercise, 33*(6), S530–S550.

Tice, D. M., & Baumeister, R. F. (1997). Longitudinal study of procrastination, performance, stress, and health: The cost and benefits of dawdling. *Psychological Science, 8,* 454–458.

Tice, D. M., Baumeister, R. F., Shmueli, D., & Muraven, M. (2007). Restoring the self: Positive affect helps improve self-regulation following ego depletion. *Journal of Experimental Social Psychology, 43*(3), 379–384.

Tice, D. M., Bratslavsky, E., & Baumeister, R. F. (2001). Emotional distress regulation takes precedence over impulse control: If you feel bad, do it! *Journal of Personality and Social Psychology, 80*(1), 53–67.

Tice, D. M., Butler, J. L., Muraven M. B., & Stillwell A. M. (1995). When modesty prevails: Differential favorability of self-presentation to friends and strangers. *Journal of Personality and Social Psychology, 69,* 1120–1138.

Tice, D. M., & Wallace, H. M. (2003). The reflected self: Creating yourself as (you think) others see you. In M. R. Leary & J. P. Tangney (Eds.), *Handbook of self and identity.* New York: Guilford.

Tiggemann, M., Martins, Y., & Kirkbride, A. (2007). Oh to be lean and muscular: Body image ideals in gay and heterosexual men. *Psychology of Men & Masculinity, 8,* 15–24.

Tigner, R. B. (1999). Putting memory research to good use: Hints from cognitive psychology. *College Teaching, 47*(4), 149–151.

Timm, D. A., & Slavin, J. L. (2008). Dietary fiber and the relationship to chronic diseases. *American Journal of Lifestyle Medicine, 2,* 233–240.

Titsworth, B. S., & Kiewra, K. A. (2004). Spoken organizational lecture cues and student notetaking as facilitators of student learning. *Contemporary Educational Psychology, 29,* 447–461.

Tjaden, P., & Thoennes, N. (2000). Prevalence and consequences of male-to-female and female-to-male intimate partner violence as measured by the National Violence Against Women Survey. *Violence Against Women, 6,* 142–161.

Toffler, A. (1970). *Future shock.* New York: Random House.

Toffler, A. (1980). *The third wave.* New York: Bantam Books.

Tolin, D. F., & Foa, E. B. (2006). Sex differences in trauma and posttraumatic stress disorder: A quantitative review of 25 years of research. *Psychological Bulletin, 132,* 959–992.

Tolman, D. L. (2002). *Dilemmas of desire: Teenage girls talk about sexuality.* Cambridge, MA: Harvard University Press.

Tomfohr, L. M., Martin, T. M., & Miller, G. E. (2008). Symptoms of depression and impaired endothelial function in healthy adolescent women. *Journal of Behavioral Medicine, 31,* 137–143.

Toossi, M. (2007, November). Labor force projections to 2016: More workers in their golden years. *Monthly Labor Review,* 33–52.

Torres, A. R., Prince, M. J., Bebbington, P. E., Bhugra, D., Brugha, T. S., Farrell, M., Jenkins, R., Lewis, G., Meltzer, H., & Singleton, N. (2006). Obsessive-compulsive disorder: Prevalence, comorbidity, impact, and help-seeking in the British national psychiatric morbidity survey of 2000. *American Journal of Psychiatry, 163,* 1978–1985.

Torrey, E. F. (1992). *Freudian fraud: The malignant effect of Freud's theory on American thought and culture.* New York: Harper Perennial.

Torrey, E. F. (2006). *Surviving schizophrenia: A manual for families, patients and providers.* New York: Harper Paperbacks.

Toufexis, A. (1990, December 17). Drowsy America. *Time,* pp. 78–85.

Tov, W., & Diener, E. (2007). Culture and subjective well-being. In S. Kitayama & D. Cohen (Eds.), *Handbook of cultural psychology* (pp. 691–713). New York: Guilford.

Tozzi, F., Thornton, L. M., Klump, K. L., Fichter, M. M., Halmi, K. A., Kaplan, A. S., Strober, M., Woodside, D. B., Crow, S., Mitchell, J., Rotondo, A., Mauri, M., Cassano, G., Keel, P., Plotnicov, K. H., Pollice, C., Lilenfeld, L. R., Berrettini, W. H., Bulik, C. M., & Kaye, W. H. (2005). Symptom fluctuation in eating disorders: Correlates of diagnostic crossover. *American Journal of Psychiatry, 162,* 732–740.

Trachtenberg, J. D., & Sande, M. A. (2002). Emerging resistance to nonnucleoside reverse transcriptase inhibitors: A warning and a challenge. *Journal of the American Medical Association, 288*(2), 239–241.

Travis, F. (2001). Autonomic and EEG patterns distinguish transcending from other experiences during Transcendental Meditation practice. *International Journal of Psychophysiology, 42,* 1–9.

Travis, L. A., Bliwise, N. G., Binder, J. L., & Horne-Moyer, H. L. (2001). Changes in clients' attachment style over the course of time-limited dynamic psychotherapy. *Psychotherapy: Theory, Research, Practice, Training, 38*(2), 149–159.

Treas, J., & Gieden, D. (2000). Sexual infidelity among married and cohabiting Americans. *Journal of Marriage and the Family, 62,* 48–60.

Treas, J., & Lawton, L. (1999). Family relations in adulthood. In M. B. Sussman, S. K. Steinmetz, & G. W. Peterson (Eds.), *Handbook of marriage and the family.* New York: Plenum Press.

Triandis, H. C. (1989). Self and social behavior in differing cultural contexts. *Psychological Review, 96,* 269–289.

Triandis, H. C. (1994). *Culture and social behavior.* New York: McGraw-Hill.

Triandis, H. C. (1995). *Individualism and collectivism.* Boulder, CO: Westview.

Triandis, H. C. (2001). Individualism-collectivism and personality. *Journal of Personality, 69*(6), 907–924.

Trope, Y. (1983). Self-assessment in achievement behavior. In J. Suls & A. Greenwald (Eds.), *Psychological perspectives* (Vol. 2). Hillsdale, NJ: Erlbaum.

Trope, Y. (1986). Self-enhancement and self-assessment in achievement behavior. In R. Sorrentino & E. T. Higgins (Eds.), *Handbook of motivation and cognition* (Vol. 2). New York: Guilford Press.

Trope, Y., & Gaunt, R. (2003). Attribution and person perception. In M. A. Hogg & J. Cooper (Eds.), *The Sage handbook of social psychology.* Thousand Oaks, CA: Sage Publications.

Trotter, P. B. (2009). Divorce, effects on adults. In H. T. Reis & S. Sprecher (Eds.), *Encyclopedia of human relationships: Vol. 2* (pp. 458–461). Los Angeles: Sage Reference Publication.

Troy, A. B., Lewis-Smith, J., & Laurenceau, J. (2006). Interracial and intraracial romantic relationships: The search for differences in satisfaction, conflict, and attachment style. *Journal of Social & Personal Relationships, 23,* 65–80.

Trussell, J. (2004). Contraceptive efficacy. In R. A. Hatcher, J. Trussell, F. H. Stewart, A. L. Nelson, W. Cates Jr., F. Guest, & D. Kowal *Contraceptive technology.* New York: Ardent Media.

Trussell, J., Brown, S., & Hogue, C. (2004). Adolescent sexual behavior, pregnancy, and childbearing. In R. A. Hatcher, J. Trussell, F. H. Stewart, A. L. Nelson, W. Cates Jr., F. Guest, & D. Kowal (Eds.), *Contraceptive technology.* New York: Ardent Media.

Trzesniewski, K. H., Donnellan, M. B., & Robins, R. W. (2003). Stability of self-esteem across the life span. *Journal of Personality and Social Psychology, 84*(1), 205–220.

Tsai, M., & Uemera, A. (1988). Asian Americans: The struggles, the conflicts, and the successes. In P. Bronstein & K. Quina (Eds.), *Teaching a psychology of people.* Washington, DC: American Psychological Association.

Tschan, F., Semmer, N. K., Gurtner, A., Bizzari, L., Spychiger, M., Breuer, M., & Marsch, S. U. (2009). Explicit reasoning, confirmation bias, and illusory transactive memory: A simulation study of group medical decision making. *Small Group Research, 40*(3), 271–300.

Tucker, O. N., Szomstein, S., & Rosenthal, R. J. (2007). Nutritional consequences of weight loss surgery. *Medical Clinics of North America, 91,* 499–513.

Tufekci, Z. (2008). Grooming, gossip, Facebook, and Myspace. What can we learn about these sites from those who won't assimilate? *Information, Communication, & Society, 11,* 544–564.

Tugade, M. M., & Fredrickson, B. L. (2004). Resilient individuals use positive emotions to bounce back from negative emotional experiences. *Journal of Personality and Social Psychology, 86*(2), 320–333.

Turner, E. H., Matthews, A. M., Linardos, E., Tell, R. A., & Rosenthal, R. (2008). Selective publication of antidepressant trials and its influence on apparent efficacy. *The New England Journal of Medicine, 358,* 252–260.

Turner, J. C. (1987). *Rediscovering the social group: A self-categorization theory.* Oxford, England: Basil Blackwell.

Turner, J. C., & Reynolds, K. J. (2004). The social identity perspective in intergroup relations: Theories, themes, and controversies. In M. B. Brewer & M. Hewstone (Eds.), *Self and social identity.* Malden, MA: Blackwell.

Turner, J. R., & Wheaton, B. (1995). Checklist measurement of stressful life events. In S. Cohen, R. C. Kessler, & L. U. Gordon (Eds.), *Measuring stress: A guide for health and social scientists.* New York: Oxford University Press.

Turner, S. M., Beidel, D. C., Stanley, M. A., & Heiser, N. (2001). Obsessive-compulsive disorder. In P. B. Sutker & H. E. Adams (Eds.), *Comprehensive textbook of psychiatry* (3rd ed.). New York: Kluwer Academic/Plenum.

Turner-Bowker, D. M. (2001). How can you pull yourself up by your bootstraps if you don't have boots? Work appropriate clothing for women. *Journal of Social Issues, 57,* 311–322.

Twenge, J. M. (2000). The age of anxiety? Birth cohort change in anxiety and neuroticism, 1952–1993. *Journal of Personality and Social Psychology, 79*(6), 1007–1021.

Twenge, J. M., & Campbell W. K. (2003). Isn't it fun to get the respect that we're going to deserve? Narcissism, social rejection, and aggression. *Personality and Social Psychology, 29*(2), 261–272.

Twenge, J. M., & Campbell, W. K. (2009). *The narcissism epidemic: Living in the age of entitlement.* New York: Free Press.

Twenge, J. M., Campbell, W. K., & Foster, C. A. (2003). Parenthood and marital satisfaction: A meta-analytic review. *Journal of Marriage and Family, 65,* 574–83.

Twenge, J. M., Catanese, K. R., & Baumeister, R. F. (2002). Social exclusion causes self-defeating behavior. *Journal of Personality and Social Psychology, 83*(3), 606–615.

Twenge, J. M., & Crocker, J. (2002). Race and self-esteem: Meta-analyses comparing whites, blacks, Hispanics, Asians, and American Indians and comment on Gray-Little and Hafdahl (2000). *Psychological Bulletin, 128*(3), 371–408.

Twenge, J. M., Konrath, S., Foster, J. D., Campbell, W. K., & Bushman, B. J. (2008). Egos inflating over time: A cross-temporal meta-analysis of the Narcissistic Personality Inventory. *Journal of Personality, 76,* 903–917.

Ubel, P. A., Loewenstein, G., Hershey, J., Baron, J., Mohr, T., Asch, D., & Jepson, C. (2001). Do nonpatients underestimate the quality of life associated with chronic health conditions because of a focusing illusion? *Medical Decision Making, 21,* 190–199.

Uchino, B. N., Cacioppo, J. T., & Kiecolt-Glaser, J. K. (1996). The relationship between social support and physiological processes: A review with emphasis on underlying mechanisms and implications for health. *Psychological Bulletin, 119,* 488–531.

Uhlmann, E., & Swanson, J. (2004). Exposure to violent video games increases automatic aggressiveness. *Journal of Adolescence, 27,* 41–52.

Uleman, J. S., Hon, A., Roman, R. J., & Moskowitz, G. B. (1996). Online evidence for spontaneous trait inferences at encoding. *Personality and Psychology Bulletin, 22*(4), 377–394.

Ullman, S. E. (2004). Sexual assault victimization and suicidal behavior in women: A review of the literature. *Aggression and Violent Behavior, 9*(4), 331–351.

Ullman, S. E., Filipas, H. H., Townsend, S. M., & Starzynski, L. L. (2007). Psychosocial correlates of PTSD symptom severity in sexual assault survivors. *Journal of Traumatic Stress, 20,* 821–831.

UNAIDS. (2005). *AIDS epidemic.* Retrieved from http://www.unaids.org/Epi2005/doc/EPIupdate2005_html_en/epi05_03

Unger, R. (2006). Untangling the web: Threat, ideology, and political behavior. In P. R. Kimmel & C. E. Stout (Eds.), *Collateral damage: The psychological consequences of America's war on terrorism.* Westport, CT: Praeger.

Ursano, R. J., Sonnenberg, S. M., & Lazar, S. G. (2008). Psychodynamic psychotherapy. In R. E. Hales, S. C. Yudofsky, & G. O. Gabbard (Eds.), *The American psychiatric publishing textbook of psychiatry* (pp. 1171–1190). Washington, DC: American Psychiatric Publishing.

U.S. Bureau of Labor Statistics. (2004). *Occupational outlook handbook: 2004–2005.* Washington, DC: U.S. Government Printing Office.

U.S. Bureau of Labor Statistics. (2005). *Workers on flexible and shift schedules in 2004 summary.* Retrieved June 4, 2007 from http://www.bls.gov/news.release/flex.nr0.htm.

U.S. Bureau of Labor Statistics. (2006). *Occupational outlook handbook, 2006–2007 edition.* Washington, DC: U.S. Government Printing Office.

U.S. Bureau of Labor Statistics. (2007). *Employment characteristics of families in 2006.* Washington, DC: Department of Labor.

U.S. Bureau of the Census. (2003). *Statistical abstract of the United States: 2003.* Washington, DC: U.S. Government Printing Office.

U.S. Bureau of the Census. (2006–2008). *Percent of married-couple families with both husband and wife in the labor force.* Retrieved from http://factfinder.census.gov/servlet/ThematicMapFramesetServl

U.S. Bureau of the Census. (2006a). *Americans marrying older, living alone more, see households shrinking, Census Bureau reports* (CB06-83). Retrieved May 15, 2007 from http://www.census.gov/Press-Release/www/releases/archives/families_households/006840.html.

U.S. Bureau of the Census. (2006b). *Statistical abstract of the United States: 2007.* Washington, DC: U.S. Government Printing Office.

U.S. Bureau of the Census. (2008). *Occupation by sex and median earnings in the past 12 months (in 2008 inflation-adjusted dollars) for the civilian unemployed population 16 years and over.* Retrieved from http://factfinder.census.gov/servlet/STTable?_bm+y&-geo_id=

U.S. Department of Health and Human Services. (1990). *The health benefits of smoking cessation: A report of the surgeon general.* Washington, DC: U.S. Government Printing Office.

U.S. Department of Health and Human Services. (1995). *Healthy people 2000 review, 1994.* Washington, DC: U.S. Government Printing Office.

U.S. Department of Health and Human Services. (1999). *Mental health: A report of the Surgeon General.* Washington, DC: U.S. Government Printing Office.

U.S. Department of Health and Human Services. (2002, June 10). *Preventing teenage pregnancy.* Retrieved January 30, 2005 from http://www.Hhs.Gov/News/Press/2002pres/Teenpreg.html.

U.S. Department of Health and Human Services. (2004). *The health consequences of smoking: A report of the Surgeon General.* Atlanta, GA: DHHS.

U.S. Department of Health and Human Services. (2007). *Impacts of four Title V, Section 510 abstinence education programs, final report.* Retrieved June 16, 2007 from http://aspe.hhs.gov/hsp/abstinence07/index.htm.

U.S. Department of Justice. (2007). *Criminal offenders statistics.* Retrieved April 22, 2007 from http://www.ojp.usdoj.gov/bjs/crimoff.htm.

U.S. Department of Labor. (1992). *Pipelines of progress: An update on the glass ceiling initiative.* Washington, DC: U.S. Government Printing Office.

U.S. Department of Labor. (2000, Summer). Futurework: Trends and challenges for work in the 21st century. *Occupational Outlook Quarterly,* pp. 31–36.

U.S. Department of Labor. (2003). *Facts on women workers.* Washington, DC: U.S. Government Printing Office.

U.S. Department of Labor. (2007, Summer). Parents and work, 2006. *Occupational Outlook Quarterly,* p. 48.

U.S. General Accounting Office. (2003). *Women's earnings: Work patterns partially explain difference between men's and women's earnings.* Washington, DC: General Accounting Office.

U.S. Small Business Administration. (2006). *Women in business, 2006: A demographic review of women's business ownership.* Retrieved June 4, 2007 from http://www.sba.gov/advo/research/rs280tot.pdf.

Vaillant, G. E. (2000). Adaptive mental mechanisms: Their role in a positive psychology. *American Psychologist, 55*(1), 89–98.

Valkenburg, P. M., & Peter, J. (2007). Preadolescents' and adolescents' online communication and their closeness to friends. *Developmental Psychology, 43,* 267–277.

Vallone, R. P., Ross, L., & Lepper, M. R. (1985). The hostile media phenomenon: Biased perception and perceptions of bias in coverage of the Beirut massacre. *Journal of Personality and Social Psychology, 50,* 482–491.

van Anders, S. M., Hamilton, L. D., & Watson, N. V. (2007). Multiple partners are associated with higher testosterone in North America men and women. *Hormones and Behaviors, 51,* 454–459.

Van Blerkom, D. L. (2006). *College study skills: Becoming a strategic learner.* Belmont, CA: Wadsworth.

Van Boven, L. (2005). Experientialism, materialism, and the pursuit of happiness. *Review of General Psychology, 9*(2), 132–142.

Vandello, J. A., Bosson, J. K., Cohen, D., Burnaford, R. M., & Weaver, J. R. (2008). Precarious manhood. *Journal of Personality and Social Psychology, 95,* 1325–1339.

van den Berg, A. E., Hartig, T., Staats, H. (2007). Preference for nature in urbanized societies: Stress, restoration, and the pursuit of sustainability. *Journal of Social Issues, 63,* 79–96.

van den Berg, A. E., Koole, S. L., & van der Wulp, N. Y. (2003). Environmental preference and restoration: (How) are they related? *Journal of Environmental Psychology, 23,* 135–146.

Vandenberg, S. G. (1987). Sex differences in mental retardation and their implications for sex differences in ability. In J. M. Reinisch, L. A. Rosenblum, & S. A. Sanders (Eds.), *Masculinity/Femininity: Basic perspectives.* New York: Oxford University Press.

Vandereycken, W. (2002). History of anorexia nervosa and bulimia nervosa. In C. G. Fairburn & K. D. Brownell (Eds.), *Eating disorders and obesity.* New York: Guilford Press.

Van der Hart, O. & Nijenhuis, E. R. S. (2009). Dissociative disorders. In P. H. Blaney & T. Millon (Eds.), *Oxford textbook of psychopathology* (pp. 452–481). New York: Oxford University Press.

Vandewater, E. A., Bickham, D. S., Lee, J. H., Cummings, H. M., Wartella, E. A., & Rideout, V. J. (2005). When the television is always on. *American Behavioral Scientist, 48,* 562–577.

Vandewater, E., A., Bickham, D. S., & Lee, J. H. (2006). Time well spent? Relating television use to children's free-time activities. *Pediatrics, 117,* 181–191.

van Griensven, F., Chakkraband, M. L. S., Thienkrua, W., Pengjuntr, W., Cardozo, B. L., Tantipiwatanaskul, P., & et al. (2007). Mental health problems among adults in tsunami-affected areas in Southern Thailand. *JAMA, 296,* 537–548.

van Kammen, D. P., & Marder, S. R. (2005). Serotonin-dopamine antagonists (atypical or second-generation antipsychotics). In B. J. Sadock & V. A. Sadock (Eds.), *Kaplan and Sadock's comprehensive textbook of psychiatry.* Philadelphia: Lippincott Williams & Wilkins.

Van Kammen, D. P., Hurford, I., & Marder, S. R. (2009). First-generation antipsychotics. In B. J. Sadock, V. A. Sadock, & P. Ruiz (Eds.), *Kaplan & Sadock's comprehensive textbook of psychiatry* (pp. 3105–3126). Philadelphia: Lippincott Williams & Wilkins.

van Kesteren, N. M. C., Hospers, H. J., & Kok, G. (2007). Sexual risk behavior among HIV-positive men who have sex with men: A literature review. *Patient Education and Counseling, 65,* 5–20.

Van Volkmon, M. (2008). Attitudes toward cigarette smoking among college students. *College Student Journal, 42,* 294–304.

Van Vugt, M. (2001). Community identification moderating the impact of financial incentives in a natural social dilemma: Water conservation. *Personality and Social Psychology Bulletin, 27,* 1440–1449.

Van Vugt, M. (2002). Central, individual, or collective control? Social dilemma strategies for natural resource management. *American Behavioral Scientist, 45,* 783–800.

Vartanian, L. R., Giant, C. L., & Passino, R. M. (2001). "Ally McBeal vs. Arnold Schwarzenegger": Comparing mass media, interpersonal feedback and gender as predictors of satisfaction with body thinness and masculinity. *Social Behavior and Personality, 29*(7), 711–723.

Vasquez, E. A., Lickel, B., & Hennigan, K. (2009). Gangs, displaced, and group-based aggression. *Aggression and Violent Behavior, 15,* 130–140.

Vazire, S., & Gosling, S. D. (2004). e-Perceptions: Personality impressions based on personal websites. *Journal of Personality and Social Psychology, 87*(1), 123–132.

Vazquez, C., Cervellon, P., Perez-Sales, P., Vidales, D., & Gaborit, M. (2005). Positive emotions in earthquake survivors in El Salvador (2001). *Journal of Anxiety Disorders, 19,* 313–328.

Veenhoven, R. (1993). *Happiness in nations.* Rotterdam, Netherlands: Risbo.

Veenhoven, R. (2008). Healthy happiness: Effects of happiness on physical health and the consequences for preventive care. *Journal of Happiness Studies, 9*(3), 449–469.

Veenstra, M. Y., Lemmens, P. H. H. M., Friesema, I. H. M., Tan, F. E. S., Garrentsen, H. F. L., Knottnerus, J. A., & Zwietering, P. J. (2007). Coping style mediates impact of stress on alcohol use: A prospective population-based study. *Addiction, 102,* 1890–1898.

Veevers, J. E., Gee, E. M., & Wister, A. V. (1996). Homeleaving age norms: Conflict or consensus? *International Journal of Aging and Human Development, 43*(4), 277–295.

Venturello, S., Barzega, G., Maina, G., & Bogetto, F. (2002). Premorbid conditions and precipitating events in early-onset panic disorder. *Comprehensive Psychiatry, 43,* 28–36.

Verderber, K. S., Verderber, R. F., & Berryman-Fink, C. (2007). *Inter-act: Interpersonal communication concepts, skills, and contexts* (11th ed.). New York: Oxford University Press.

Verderber, R. F., & Verderber, K. S. (2004). *Inter-Act: Interpersonal communication concepts, skills, and contexts* (10th ed.). New York: Oxford University Press.

Verderber, R. F., Verderber, K. S., & Berryman-Fink, C. (2008). *Communicate.* Belmont, CA: Wadsworth.

Vernberg, E. M., La Greca, A. M., Silverman, W. K., & Prinstein, M. J. (1996). Prediction of posttraumatic stress symptoms in children after Hurricane Andrew. *Journal of Abnormal Psychology, 105,* 237–248.

Verona, E., & Curtin, J. J. (2006). Gender differences in the negative affective priming of aggressive behavior. *Emotion, 6*(1), 115–124.

Vgontzas, A. N., Bixler, E. O., & Kales, A. K. (2000). Sleep, sleep disorders, and stress. In G. Fink (Ed.), *Encyclopedia of stress* (Vol. 3, p. 449–457). San Diego: Academic Press.

Vidal, M. E., & Petrak, J. (2007). Shame and adult sexual assault: A study with a group of female survivors recruited from an east London population. *Sexual and Relationship Therapy, 22,* 159–171.

Videbech, P. (2006). Hippocampus and unipolar depression. *Directions in Psychiatry, 26*(3), 183–194.

Videbech, P., & Ravnkilde, B. (2004). Hippocampal volume and depression: A meta-analysis of MRI studies. *American Journal of Psychiatry, 161,* 1957–1966.

Viglione, D. J., & Rivera, B. (2003). Assessing personality and psychopathology with projective methods. In J. R. Graham, & J. A. Naglieri (Eds.), *Handbook of psychology: Vol. 10. Assessment psychology.* New York: Wiley.

Vignoles, V. L., Manzi, C., Regalia, C., Jemmolo, S., & Scabini, E. (2008). Identity motives underlying desired and feared possible future selves. *Journal of Personality, 76,* 1165–1200.

Vilain, E. (2000). Genetics of sexual development. *Annual Review of Sex Research, 11,* 1–25.

Vittengl, J. R., & Holt, C. S. (2000). Getting acquainted: The relationship of self-disclosure and social attraction to positive affect. *Journal of Social and Personal Relationships, 17*(1), 53–56.

Vlek, C., & Steg, L. (2007). Human behavior and environmental sustainability: Problems, driving forces, and research topics. *Journal of Social Issues, 63,* 1–19.

Voas, R. B., Roman, T. E., Tippetts, A. S., & Durr-Holden, C. (2006). Drinking status and fatal crashes: Which drinkers contribute most to the problem? *Journal of Studies on Alcohol, 67,* 722–729.

Vohs, K. D., Baumeister, R. F., & Tice, D. M. (2008). Self-regulation: Goals, consumption, choices. In C. P. Haugtvedt, P. M. Herr, & F. R. Kardes (Eds.), *Handbook of consumer psychology* (pp. 349–366). New York: Taylor & Francis Group/Lawrence Erlbaum Associates.

Vohs, K. D., Baumeister, R. F., Schmeichel, B. J., Twenge, J. M., Nelson, N. M., & Tice, D. M. (2008). Making choices impairs subsequent self-control: A limited-resource account of decision making, self-regulation, and active initiative. *Journal of Personality and Social Psychology, 94*(5), 883–898.

Volavka, J., Czobor, P., Sheitman, B., Lindenmayer, J. P., Citrome, L., McEvoy, J. P., Cooper, T. B. , Chakos, M., & Lieberman, J. A. (2002). Clozapine, olanzapine, risperidone, haloperidol in the treatment of patients with chronic schizophrenia and schizoaffective disorder. *American Journal of Psychiatry, 159,* 255–262.

vom Saal, F. S., et al. (2007). Chapel Hill bisphenol A expert panel consensus statement: Integration of mechanisms, effects in animals and potential to impact human health at current levels of exposure. *Reproductive Toxicology, 24,* 131–138.

Von Baeyer, C. L., Sherk, D. L., & Zanna, M. P. (1981). Impression management in the job interview: When the female applicant meets the male (chauvinist) interviewer. *Personality and Social Psychology Bulletin, 7,* 45–51.

Von Drehle, D. (2009, March 9). House of cards: The faces behind foreclosures. *Time.*

Vonk, R. (1993). The negativity effect in trait rating and in open-ended descriptions of persons. *Personality and Social Psychology Bulletin, 19,* 269–278.

Vorauer, J. D., Cameron, J. J., Holmes, J. G., & Pearce, D. G. (2003). Invisible overtures: Fears of rejection and the signal amplification bias. *Journal of Personality and Social Psychology, 84*(4), 793–812.

Voydanoff, P. (2005). Consequences of boundary-spanning demands and resources for work-to-family conflict and perceived stress. *Journal of Occupational Health Psychology, 10,* 491–503.

Voydanoff, P., & Donnelly, B. W. (1999). Multiple roles and psychological distress: The intersection of the paid worker, spouse, and parent roles with the role of the adult child. *Journal of Marriage and the Family, 61,* 725–738.

Voyer, D., & Hou, J. (2006). Type of items and the magnitude of gender differences on the mental rotations test. *Candian Journal of Experimental Psychology, 60*(2), 91–100.

Vrugt, A., & Luyerink, M. (2000). The contribution of bodily posture to gender stereotypical impressions. *Social Behavior and Personality, 28*(1), 91–103.

Wade, C., & Tavris, C. (1990). *Learning to think critically: A handbook to accompany psychology.* New York: HarperCollins.

Waelde, L. C., Uddo, M., Marquett, R., Ropelato, M., Freightman, S., Pardo, A., & Salazar, J. (2008). A pilot study of meditation for mental health workers following Hurricane Katrina. *Journal of Traumatic Stress, 21,* 497–500.

Waggoner, A. S., Smith, E. R., & Collins, E. C. (2009). Person perception by active versus passive perceivers. *Journal of Experimental Social Psychology, 45*(4), 1028–1031.

Wagner, D. M. (1998, Feb 1). Divorce reform: New directions. *Current,* pp. 7–10.

Waite, L. J. (1995). Does marriage matter? *Demography, 32,* 483–507.

Waite, L. J. (2000). Trends in men's and women's well-being in marriage. In L. J. Waite (Ed.), *The ties that bind.* New York: Aldine de Gruyter.

Waite, L. J., & Gallagher, M. (2000). *The case for marriage: Why married people are happier, healthier, and better off financially.* New York: Doubleday.

Wakabayashi, C., & Donato, K. M. (2006). Does caregiving increase poverty among women in later life? Evidence from health and retirement survey. *Journal of Health and Social Behavior, 47,* 258–274.

Wakefield, J. C., Horwitz, A. V., & Schmitz, M. F. (2005). Are we overpathologizing the socially anxious? Social phobia from a harmful dysfunction perspective. *The Canadian Journal of Psychiatry/La Revue canadienne de psychiatrie, 50*(6), 317–319.

Wakefield, J. C., & Spitzer, R. L. (2002). Lowered estimates—but of what? *Archives of General Psychiatry, 59*(2), 129–130.

Wakslak, C. J., & Trope, Y. (2009). Cognitive consequences of affirming the self: The relationship between self-affirmation and object construal. *Journal of Experimental Social Psychology, 45,* 927–932.

Waldrop, D., Lightsey, O. R., Ethington, C. A., Woemmel, C. A., & Coke, A. L. (2001). Self-efficacy, optimism, health competence, and recovery from orthopedic surgery. *Journal of Counseling Psychology, 48,* 233–238.

Walker, E., Kestler, L., Bollini, A., & Hochman, K. M. (2004). Schizophrenia: Etiology and course. *Annual Review of Psychology, 55,* 401–30.

Walker, E., Mittal, V., & Tessner, K. (2008). Stress and the hypothalamic pituitary adrenal axis in the developmental course of schizophrenia. *Annual Review of Clinical Psychology, 4,* 189–216.

Walker, E., & Tessner, K. (2008). Schizophrenia. *Perspectives on Psychological Science, 3,* 30–37.

Walker, K. (1994). Men, women, and friendship: What they say, what they do. *Gender & Society, 8,* 246–265.

Walker, L. S., Claar, R. L., & Garber, J. (2002). Social consequences of children's pain: When do they encourage symptoms of maintenance? *Journal of Pediatric Psychology, 27*(8), 689–698.

Wallace, H. M., Baumeister, R. F., & Vohs, K. D. (2005). Audience support and choking under pressure: A home disadvantage? *Journal of Sports Sciences, 23,* 429–438.

Wallerstein, J. S. (2005). Growing up in the divorced family. *Clinical Social Work Journal, 33,* 401–418.

Wallerstein, J. S., & Blakeslee, S. (1989). *Second chances: Men, women, and children a decade after divorce.* Boston: Houghton Mifflin.

Wallerstein, J. S., & Kelly, J. B. (1980). *Surviving the breakup: How children and parents cope with divorce.* New York: Basic Books.

Wallerstein, J. S., & Lewis, J. M. (2004). The unexpected legacy of divorce: Report of a 25-year study. *Psychoanalytic Psychology, 21,* 353–370.

Wallerstein, J. S., & Lewis, J. M. (2007). Sibling outcomes and disparate parenting and stepparenting after divorce: Report from a 10-year longitudinal study. *Psychoanalytic Psychology, 24,* 445–458.

Wallerstein, J. S., Lewis, J. M., & Blakeslee, S. (2000). *The unexpected legacy of divorce: A 25-year landmark study.* New York: Hyperion.

Wallis, C. (2004, March 22). The case for staying home. *Time,* pp. 51–59.

Walsh, B. T. (2003). Eating disorders. In A. Tasman, J. Kay & J. A. Lieberman (Eds.), *Psychiatry.* New York: Wiley.

Walsh, F. (1999). Families in later life: Challenges and opportunities. In B. Carter & M. McGoldrick (Eds.), *The expanded family life cycle: Individual, family, and social perspectives* (3rd ed.). Boston: Allyn & Bacon.

Walsh, J. K., Dement, W. C., & Dinges, D. F. (2005). Sleep medicine, public safety, and public health. In M. H. Kryger, T. Roth, & W. C. Dement (Eds.), *Principles and practice of sleep medicine.* Philadelphia: Elsevier Saunders.

Wampold, B. E. (2001). *The great psychotherapy debate.* Mahwah, NJ: Erlbaum.

Wang, H., & Amato, P. R. (2000). Predictors of divorce adjustment: Stressors, resources, and definitions. *Journal of Marriage and the Family, 62,* 655–668.

Wang, P. S., Berglund, P., Olfson, M., Pincus, H. A., Wells, K. B., & Kessler, R. C. (2005). Failure and delay in initial treatment contact after first onset of mental disorders in the National Comorbidity Survey Replication. *Archives of General Psychiatry, 62,* 603–613.

Wang, P. S., Lane, M., Olfson, M., Pincus, H. A., Wells, K. B., & Kessler, R. C. (2005). Twelve-month use of mental health services in the United States: Results from the National Comorbidity Survey Replication. *Archives of General Psychiatry, 62,* 629–640.

Ward, A., & Brenner, L. (2006). Accentuate the negative: The positive effects of negative acknowledgement. *Psychological Science, 17,* 959–962.

Ward, C. N., & Lundberg-Love, P. K. (2006). Sexual abuse of women. In P. K. Lundberg-Love & S. L. Marmion (Eds.), *"Intimate" violence against women: When spouses, partners, or lovers attack.* Westport, CT: Praeger.

Ward, L. M., Hansbrough, E., & Walker, E. (2005). Contributions of music video exposure to black adolescents' gender and sexual schemas. *Journal of Adolescent Research, 20,* 143–166.

Wardle, J., & Gibson, E. L. (2007). Diet and stress, non-psychiatric. In G. Fink (Ed.), *Encyclopedia of stress: Vols. 1–4* (2nd ed., pp. 797–805). San Diego, CA: Elsevier Academic Press.

Wareham, J., Boots, D. P., & Chavez, J. M. (2009). A test of social learning and intergenerational transmission among batterers. *Journal of Criminal Justice, 37,* 163–173.

Warner, L., Hatcher, R. A., & Steiner, M. J. (2004). Male condoms. In R. A. Hatcher, J. Trussell, F. H. Stewart, A. L. Nelson, W. Cates Jr., F. Guest, & D. Kowal (Eds.), *Contraceptive technology* (18th rev. ed.). New York: Ardent Media.

Warner-Schmidt, J. L., & Duman, R. S. (2006). Hippocampal neurogenesis: Opposing effects of stress and antidepressant treatment. *Hippocampus, 16,* 239–249.

Warr, P. (1999). Well-being and the workplace. In D. Kahneman, E. Diener, & N. Schwarz (Eds.), *Well-being: The foundations of hedonic psychology.* New York: Sage.

Warr, P. (2007). *Work, happiness, and unhappiness.* Mahwah, NJ: Erlbaum.

Warren, R. (2002). *The purpose driven life: What on Earth am I here for?* Grand Rapids, MI: Zondervan.

Waters, E., Merrick, S., Treboux, D., Crowell, J., & Albersheim, L. (2000). Attachment security in infancy and early adulthood: A twenty-year longitudinal study. *Child Development, 71*(3), 684–689.

Watkins, E. R. (2008). Constructive and unconstructive repetitive thought. *Psychological Bulletin, 134,* 163–206.

Watkins, P. C., Woodward, K., Stone, T., & Russell, L. (2003). Gratitude and happiness: Development of a measure of gratitude and relationships with subjective well-being. *Social Behavior and Personality, 31,* 431–452.

Watkins, P. L., Ward, C. H., & Southard, D. R. (1992). The Type A belief system: Relationship to hostility, social support, and life stress. *Behavioral Medicine, 18,* 27–32.

Watson, D. (2002). Positive affectivity: The disposition to experience pleasurable emotional states. In C. R. Snyder & S. J. Lopez (Eds.), *Handbook of positive psychology* (pp. 106–119). New York: Oxford.

Watson, D., & Clark, L. A. (1997). Extraversion and its positive emotional core. In R. Hogan, J. Johnson, & S. Briggs (Eds.), *Handbook of personality psychology.* San Diego: Academic Press.

Watson, D., Klohnen, E. C., Casillas, A., Nus Simms, E., Haig, J., & Berry, D. S. (2004). Match makers and deal breakers: Analyses of assortative mating in newlywed couples. *Journal of Personality, 72,* 1029–1068.

Watson, D., & Pennebaker, J. W. (1989). Health complaints, stress, and distress: Exploring the central role of negative affectivity. *Psychological Review, 96,* 234–254.

Watson, D., & Tellegen, A. (1985). Toward a consensual structure of mood. *Psychological Bulletin, 98,* 219–235.

Watson, D. L., & Tharp, R. G. (2007). *Self-directed behavior: Self-modification for personal adjustment.* Belmont, CA: Wadsworth.

Watson, J. B. (1913). Psychology as the behaviorist views it. *Psychological Review, 20,* 158–177.

Waxman, S. (2005). Why is the concept "living thing" so elusive? Concepts, languages, and the development of folkbiology. In W. Ahn, R. L. Goldstone, B. C. Love, A. B. Markman, & P. Woolf (Eds.), *Categorization inside and outside the laboratory: Essays in honor of Douglas L. Medin* (pp. 49–67). Washington, DC: American Psychological Association.

Wayment, H. A., & O'Mara, E. M. (2008). The collective and compassionate consequences of downward social comparisons. In H. A. Wayment & J. J. Bauer (Eds.), *Transcending self-interest: Psychological explorations of the quiet ego* (pp. 159–169). Washington, DC: American Psychological Association.

Weaver, A. D., & Byers, E. S. (2006). The relationships among body image, body mass index, exercise, and sexual functioning in heterosexual women. *Psychology of Women Quarterly, 30,* 333–339.

Weaver, M. F., & Schnoll, S. H. (1999). Stimulants: Amphetamines and cocaine. In B. S. McCrady & E. E. Epstein (Eds.), *Addictions: A comprehensive guidebook.* New York: Oxford University Press.

Weber, E. U. (2006). Experience-based and description-based perceptions of long-term risk: why global warming does not scare us (yet). *Climatic Change, 77,* 103–120.

Weber, L. J. (2006). *Profits before people?* Bloomington, IN: Indiana University Press.

Webster, D. M. (1993). Motivated augmentation and reduction of the overattribution bias. *Journal of Personality and Social Psychology, 65,* 261–271.

Webster, D. M., Richter, L., & Kruglanski, A. W. (1996). On leaping to conclusions when feeling tired: Mental fatigue effects on impressional primacy. *Journal of Experimental Social Psychology, 32,* 181–195.

Webster, G. D. (2009). Parental investment theory. In H. T. Reis & S. Sprecher (Eds.), *Encyclopedia of human relationships: Vol. 3* (pp. 1194–1197). Los Angeles: Sage Reference Publication.

Wechsler, H., Kelley, K., Seibring, M., Kuo, M., Rigotti, N.A. (2001). College smoking policies and smoking cessation programs: Results of a survey of college health center directors. *Journal of American College Health, 49*(5), 205–212.

Wechsler, H., Lee, J. E., Kuo, M., Seibring, M., Nelson, T. F., & Lee, H. (2002). Trends in college binge drinking during a period of increased prevention efforts. *Journal of American College Health, 50*(5), 203–217.

Wegener, D. T., & Petty, R. E. (1994). Mood management across affective states: The hedonic contingency hypothesis. *Journal of Personality and Social Psychology, 66,* 1034–1048.

Weil, M. , & Rosen, R. (1997). *Technostress: coping with technology @ work @ home @ play.* New York: Wiley.

Weimer, B. L., Kerns, K. A., & Oldenburg, C. M. (2004). Adolescents' interactions with a best friend: Associations with attachment style. *Journal of Experimental Child Psychology, 88*(1), 102–120.

Weinberger, D. A. (1990). The construct validity of the repressive coping style. In J. L. Singer (Ed.), *Repression and dissociation.* Chicago: University of Chicago Press.

Weinberger, J. (1995). Common factors aren't so common: The common factors dilemma. *Clinical Psychology: Science and Practice, 2,* 45–69, 1915–1933.

Weiner, B. (1986). *An attribution theory of emotion and motivation.* New York: Springer-Verlag.

Weiner, B. (1994). Integrating social and personal theories of achievement striving. *Review of Educational Research, 64,* 557–573.

**Weiner, B.** (2006). *Social motivation, justice, and the moral emotions: An attributional approach.* Mahwah, NJ: Erlbaum.

**Weiner, B.** (Ed). (1974). *Achievement motivation and attribution theory.* Morristown, NJ: General Learning Press.

**Weinfield, N., Sroufe, L. A., & Egeland, B.** (2000). Attachment from early infancy to early adulthood in a high-risk sample: Continuity, discontinuity, and their correlates. *Child Development, 71*(3), 695–702.

**Weinstein, N. D.** (1980). Unrealistic optimism about future life events. *Journal of Personality and Social Psychology, 39,* 806–820.

**Weinstein, N. D.** (1982). Unrealistic optimism about susceptibility to health problems. *Journal of Behavioral Medicine, 5,* 441–460.

**Weinstein, N. D.** (2003). Exploring the links between risk perceptions and preventive health behavior. In J. Suls & K. A. Wallston (Eds.), *Social psychological foundations of health and illness.* Malden, MA: Blackwell Publishing.

**Weinstein, N. D., & Klein, W. M.** (1996). Unrealistic optimism: Present and future. *Journal of Social and Clinical Psychology, 15*(1), 1–8.

**Weinstein, N. D., Slovic, P., & Gibson, G.** (2004). Accuracy and optimism in smokers' beliefs about quitting. *Nicotine & Tobacco Research, 6*(Suppl3), 375–380.

**Weisbuch, M., & Ambady, N.** (2008). Nonconscious routes to building culture: Nonverbal components of socialization. *Journal of Consciousness Studies, 15,* 159–183.

**Weisler, R. H., Barbee, J. G., & Townsend, M. H.** (2007). Mental health and recovery in the Gulf Coast after Hurricanes Katrina and Rita. *JAMA, 296,* 585–588.

**Weiss, A., Bates, T. C., & Luciano, M.** (2008). Happiness is a personal(ity) thing. *Psychological Science, 19,* 205–210.

**Weiss, E. M., Kemmler, G., Deisenhammer, E. A., Fleischhacker, W. W., & Delazer, M.** (2003). Sex differences in cognitive functions. *Personality and Individual Differences, 35,* 863–875.

**Weiss, R.** (1973). *Loneliness: The experience of emotional and social isolation.* Cambridge, MA: MIT Press.

**Weiss, R. S.** (1975). *Marital separation.* New York: Basic Books.

**Weiss, S. E.** (1987), Creating the GM-Toyota joint venture: a case in complex negotiation. *The Columbia Journal of World Business, 22*(2), 23–37.

**Weiten, W.** (1988). Pressure as a form of stress and its relationship to psychological symptomatology. *Journal of Social and Clinical Psychology, 6,* 127–139.

**Weiten, W.** (1998). Pressure, major life events, and psychological symptoms. *Journal of Social Behavior and Personality, 13,* 51–68.

**Weiten, W., Guadagno, R. E., & Beck, C. A.** (1996). Students' perceptions of textbook pedagogical aids. *Teaching of Psychology, 23,* 105–107.

**Weitzman, L.** (1996). The economic consequences of divorce are still unequal: Comment on Peterson. *American Sociological Review, 61,* 537–538.

**Wells, N. M., & Evans, G. W.** (2003). Nearby nature: A buffer of life stress among rural children. *Environment and Behavior, 35,* 311–330.

**Welsh, R. S.** (2003). Prescription priveleges: Pro or con. *Clinical Psychology: Science & Practice, 10,* 371–372.

**Wessely, S., & Kerwin, R.** (2004). Suicide risk and the SSRI's. *Journal of the American Medical Association, 292*(3), 379–381.

**Wesson, D. R., Smith, D. E., Ling, W., & Seymour, R. B.** (2005). Sedatives–hypnotics. In J. H. Lowinson, P. Ruiz, R. B. Millman, & J. G. Langrod (Eds.), *Substance abuse: A comprehensive textbook* . Philadelphia: Lippincott/Williams & Wilkins.

**West, D. S., Harvey-Berino, J., & Raczynski, J. M.** (2004). Behavioral aspects of obesity, dietary intake, and chronic disease. In J. M. Raczynski & L. C. Leviton (Eds.), *Handbook of clinical health psychology: Vol. 2. Disorders of behavior and health.* Washington, DC: American Psychological Association.

**Westefeld, J. S., Maples, M. R., Buford, B., & Taylor, S.** (2001). Gay, lesbian, and bisexual college students: The relationship between sexual orientation and depression, loneliness and suicide. *Journal of College Student Psychotherapy, 15*(3), 71–82.

**Westen, D.** (1998). The scientific legacy of Sigmund Freud: Toward a psychodynamically informed psychological science. *Psychological Bulletin, 124*(3), 333–371.

**Westen, D., Gabbard, G. O., & Ortigo, K. M.** (2008). Psychoanalytic approaches to personality. In O. P. John, R. W. Robins, & L. A. Pervin (Eds.), *Handbook of personality: Theory and research* (pp. 61–113). New York: The Guilford Press.

**Wester, S. R., Vogel, D. L., Wei, M., & McLain, R.** (2006). African American men, gender role conflict, and psychological distress: The role of racial identity. *Journal of Counseling & Development, 84,* 419–429.

**Wheeler, L., & Kim, Y.** (1997). What is beautiful is culturally good: The physical attractiveness stereotype has different content in collectivistic cultures. *Personality and Social Psychology Bulletin, 23,* 795–802.

**Wheeler, L., Koestner, R., & Driver, R.** (1982). Related attributes in the choice of comparison others: It's there, but it isn't all there is. *Journal of Experimental Social Psychology, 18,* 489–500.

**Wheeler, L., & Suls, J.** (2005). Social comparison and self-evaluations of competence. In A. J. Elliot & C. S. Dweck (Eds.), *Handbook of competence and motivation.* New York: Guilford.

**Whelan, C. B.** (2009, October 25). For these "spiritual warriors," the casualties were real. *The Washington Post.* Retrieved from http://www.washigtonpost.com/wp-dyn/content/article/2009/10/23//AR2009102302411.html

**Whipple, B.** (2000). Beyond the G spot. *Scandinavian Journal of Sexology, 3*(2), 35–42.

**Whiston, S. C., & Keller, B. K.** (2004). The influences of the family of origin on career development: A review and analysis. *Counseling Psychologist, 32*(4), 493–568.

**Whitaker, R.** (2002). *Mad in America: Bad science, bad medicine, and the enduring mistreatment of the mentally ill.* New York: Perseus Publishing.

**Whitbourne, S. K.** (1996). *The aging individual: Physical and psychological perspectives.* New York: Springer.

**White, L. K., & Edwards, J. N.** (1990). Emptying the nest and parental well-being: An analysis of national panel data. *American Sociological Review, 55*(2), 235–242.

**White, L. K., & Rogers, S. J.** (1997). Strong support but uneasy relationships: Coresident and adult children's relationships with their parents. *Journal of Marriage and the Family, 59,* 62–76.

**White, L. K., & Rogers, S. J.** (2001). Economic circumstances and family outcomes: A review of the 1990s. In R. M. Milardo (Ed.), *Understanding families into the new millennium: A decade in review.* Minneapolis: National Council on Family Relations.

**White, O. K. Jr., & White, D.** (2005). Polygamy and Mormon identity. *Journal of American Culture, 28,* 165–177.

**White, R., & Heerwagen, J.** (1998). Nature and mental health: Biophilia and biophobia. In A. Lundberg (Ed.), *The environment and mental health: A guide for clinicians* (pp. 175–192). Mahwah, NJ: Erlbaum.

**Whitehead, B. D., & Popenoe, D.** (2001). *The state of our unions: The social health of marriage in America, 2001.* Piscataway, NJ: The National Marriage Project.

**Whitehouse, W. G., Orne, E. C., & Orne, M. T.** (2007). Relaxation techniques. In G. Fink (Ed.), *Encyclopedia of stress: Vols. 1–4* (2nd ed., pp. 345–350). San Diego, CA: Elsevier Academic Press.

**Whiteman, S. D., McHale, S. M., & Crouter, A. C.** (2003). What parents learn from experience: The first child as a first draft? *Journal of Marriage and Family, 65,* 608–621.

**Whitley, B. E.** (1983). Sex role orientation and self-esteem: A critical meta-analytic review. *Journal of Personality and Social Psychology, 44,* 765–778.

**Whitley, B. E.** (2001). Gender-role variables and attitudes toward homosexuality. *Sex Roles, 45,* 691–721.

**Whitley, B. E., & Kite, M. E.** (2006). *The psychology of prejudice and discrimination.* Belmont, CA: Wadsworth.

**Whitton, S. W., Waldinger, R. J., Schulz, M. S., Allen, J. P., Crowell, J. A., & Hauser, S. T.** (2008). Prospective associations from family-of-origin interactions to adult marital interactions and relationship adjustment. *Journal of Family Psychology, 22,* 274–286.

**Whitty, M. T.** (2005). The realness of cybercheating: Men's and women's representations of unfaithful internet relationships. *Social Science Computer Review, 23*(1), 57–67.

**Whitty, M. T.** (2009). Internet dating. In H. T. Reis & S. Sprecher (Eds.), *Encyclopedia of human relationships: Vol. 2* (pp. 886–888). Los Angeles: Sage Reference Publication.

**Whitty, M. T., & Fisher, W. A.** (2008). The sexy side of the Internet: An examination of sexual activities and materials in cyberspace. In A. Barak (Ed.), *Psychological aspects of cyberspace: Theory, research, applications* (pp.185–208). New York: Cambridge University Press.

**Whybrow, P. C.** (2005). *American mania: When more is not enough.* New York: Norton.

**Whybrow, P. C.** (2009, March 13). Dangerously addictive. *The Chronicle of Higher Education,* pp. B11–B13.

**Wickens, C. M., Wiesenthal, D. L., & Rippey, K.** (2005). Motorists' perceptions of aggressive driving: A comparative analysis of Ontario and California drivers. In D. A. Hennessy & D. L. Wiesenthal (Eds.), *Contemporary issues in road user behavior and traffic safety* (pp. 23–36). Hauppage, NY: Nova Science Publishers.

**Wickrama, K. A. S., Lorenz, F. O., Conger, R. D., & Elder, G. H.** (1997). Marital quality and physical illness: A latent growth curve analysis. *Journal of Marriage and Family, 59,* 143–155.

**Widiger, T. A.** (2009). Neuroticism. In M. R. Leary & R. H. Hoyle (Eds.), *Handbook of individual differences in social* behavior (pp. 129–146). New York: The Guilford Press.

**Widiger, T. A., Livesley, W. J., & Clark, L. A.** (2009). An integrative dimensional classification of personality disorder. *Psychological Assessment, 21*(3), 243–255.

**Widiger, T. A., & Sankis, L. M.** (2000). Adult psychopathology: Issues and controversies. *Annual Review of Psychology, 51,* 377–404.

**Widiger, T. A., & Simonsen, E.** (2005). Introduction to the special section: The American psychiatric association's research agenda for the DSM-V. *Journal of Personality Disorders, 19*(2), 103–109.

**Widiger, T. A., & Trull, T. J.** (2007). Plate tectonics in the classification of personality disorder: Shifting to a dimensional model. *American Psychologist, 62*(2), 71–83.

**Wiederman, M. W.** (1993). Evolved gender differences in mate preferences: Evidence from personal advertisements. *Ethology and Sociobiology, 14,* 331–352.

**Wiederman, M. W.** (1997). Extramarital sex: Prevalence and correlates in a national survey. *Journal of Sex Research, 34,* 167–174.

**Wiederman, M. W.** (2004). Methodological issues in studying sexuality in close relationships. In J. H. Harvey, A. Wenzel, & S. Sprecher (Eds.), *The handbook of sexuality in close relationships.* Mahwah, NJ: Lawrence Erlbaum.

**Wielawski, I.** (1991, October 3). *Unlocking the secrets of memory.* Los Angeles Times, p. 1.

**Wierda-Boer, H. H., Gerris, J. R. M., & Vermulst, A. A.** (2009). Managing multiple roles: Personality, stress, and work-family interference in dual-earner couples. *Journal of Individual Differences, 30,* 6–19.

**Wilder, C., Pollo, C., Bloch, J., Burkhard, P. R., & Vingerhoets, F. J. G.** (2008). Long-term outcome of 50 consecutive Parkinson's disease patients treated with subthalamic deep brain stimulation. *Parkinsonism & Related Disorders, 14,* 114–119.

**Wilfong, J. D.** (2006). Computer anxiety and anger: The impact of computer use, computer experience, and self-efficacy beliefs. *Computers in Human Behavior, 22,* 1001–1011.

**Wilgosh, L.** (2001). Enhancing gifts and talents of women and girls. *High Ability Studies, 12*(1), 45–59.

**Wilkaitis, J., Mulvhill, T., & Nasrallah, H. A.** (2004). Classic antipsychotic medications. In A. F. Schatzberg & C. B. Nemeroff (Eds), *Textbook of psychopharmacology.* Washington, DC: American Psychiatric Publishing.

**Willets, M. C., Sprecher, S., & Beck, F. D.** (2004). Overview of sexual practices and attitudes within relationship contexts. In J. H. Harvey, A. Wenzel, & S. Sprecher (Eds.), *The handbook of sexuality in close relationships.* Mahwah, NJ: Lawrence Erlbaum.

**Willett, W. C., & Stampfer, W. J.** (2003). Rebuilding the food pyramid. *Scientific American, 288*(1), 64–71.

**Williams, C. G., Gagne, M., Ryan, R. M., & Deci, E. L.** (2002). Facilitating autonomous motivation for smoking cessation. *Health Psychology, 21,* 40–50.

**Williams, C. L.** (1998). The glass escalator: Hidden advantages for men in the female professions. In M. S. Kimmel & M. A. Messner (Eds.), *Men's lives.* Boston: Allyn & Bacon.

**Williams, D. R., & Mohammed, S. A.** (2007). Racial harassment/discrimination. In G. Fink (Ed.), *Encyclopedia of stress: Vols. 1–4* (2nd ed., pp. 321–326). San Diego, CA: Elsevier Academic Press.

**Williams, J. A., Burns, E. L., & Harmon, E. A.** (2009). Insincere utterances and gaze: Eye contact during sarcastic statements. *Perceptual and Motor Skills, 108*(2), 565–572.

**Williams, J. E., & Best, D. L.** (1982). *Measuring sex stereotypes: A thirty-nation study.* Newbury Park, CA: Sage.

Williams, J. E., & Best, D. L. (1990). *Measuring sex stereotypes: A multination study* (Rev. ed.). Newbury Park, CA: Sage Publications.

Williams, J. E., Paton, C. C., Siegler, I. C., Eigenbrodt, M. L., Neito, F. J., & Tyroler, H. A. (2000). Anger proneness predicts coronary heart disease risk. *Circulation, 101*, 2034–2039.

Williams, J. E., Satterwhite, R. C., & Best, D. L. (1999). Pancultural gender stereotypes revisited: The five-factor model. *Sex Roles, 40*, 513–526.

Williams, J. M. G., Watts, F. N., MacLeod, C., & Mathews, A. (1997). *Cognitive psychology and emotional disorders* (2nd ed.). Chichester, UK: Wiley.

Williams, K. B., Radefeld, P. S., Binning, J. F., & Sudak, J. R. (1993). When job candidates are "hard-" versus "easy-to-get": Effects of candidate availability on employment decisions. *Journal of Applied Social Psychology, 23*(3), 169–198.

Williams, K. E., & Bond, M. J. (2002). The roles of self-efficacy, outcome expectancies and social support in the self-care behaviors of diabetics. *Psychology, Health & Medicine, 7*(2), 127–141.

Williams, M. H. (1992). Exploitation and inference: Mapping the damage from therapist-patient sexual involvement. *American Psychologist, 47*, 412–421.

Williams, N. A., & Deffenbacher, J. L. (1983). Life stress and chronic yeast infections. *Journal of Human Stress, 9*, 26–31.

Williams, P. (2005). What is psychoanalysis? What is a psychoanalyst? In E. S. Person, A. M. Cooper, & G. O. Gabbard (Eds.), *Textbook of psychoanalysis*. Washington, DC: American Psychiatric Publishing.

Williams, R. B. (1989). *The trusting heart: Great news about Type A behavior.* New York: Times Books.

Williams, R. B. (1996). Hostility and the heart. In D. Goleman & J. Gurin (Eds.), *Mind-body medicine: How to use your mind for better health.* Yonkers, NY: Consumer Reports Books.

Williams, R. B. (2001). Hostility (and other psychosocial risk factors): Effects on health and the potential for successful behavioral approaches to prevention and treatment. In A. Baum, T. A. Revenson, & J. E. Singer (Eds.), *Handbook of health psychology.* Mahwah, NJ: Erlbaum.

Williams, R. B., & Williams, V. P. (1993). *Anger kills: Seventeen strategies for controlling the hostility that can harm your health.* New York: Times Books/Random House.

Williams, R. L., & Eggert, A. (2002). Notetaking predictors of test performance. *Teaching of Psychology, 29*, 234–237.

Williams, S. L. (1995). Self-efficacy, anxiety, and phobic disorders. In J. E. Maddux (Ed.), *Self-efficacy, adaptation, and adjustment: Theory, research, and application.* New York: Plenum Press.

Williamson, D. A., Zucker, N. L., Martin, C. K., & Smeets, M. A. M. (2001). Etiology and management of eating disorders. In P. B. Sutker & H. E. Adams (Eds.), *Comprehensive handbook of psychopathology* (3rd ed.). New York: Kluwer Academic/Plenum.

Williamson, I., & Gonzales, M. H. (2007). The subjective experience of forgiveness: Positive construals of the forgiveness experience. *Journal of Social and Clinical Psychology, 26*, 407–446.

Willness, C. R., Steel, P., & Lee, K. (2007). A meta-analysis of antecedents and consequences of workplace sexual harassment. *Personnel Psychology, 60*(1), 127–162.

Wills, T. A. (1986). Stress and coping in early adolescence: Relationships to substance use in urban school samples. *Health Psychology, 5*, 503–529.

Wills, T. A., & Fegan, M. (2001). Social networks and social support. In A. Baum, T. A. Revenson, & J. E. Singer (Eds.), *Handbook of health psychology.* Mahwah, NJ: Erlbaum.

Wills, T. A., & Sandy, J. M. (2001). Comparing favorably: A cognitive approach to coping through comparison with other persons. In C. R. Snyder (Ed.), *Coping with stress: Effective people and processes* (pp. 154–177). New York: Oxford University Press.

Wilmot, W., & Hocker, J. (2006). *Interpersonal conflict* (7th ed.). New York: McGraw-Hill.

Wilsnack, S. C., Wonderlich, S. A., Kristjanson, A. F., Vogeltanz-Holm, N. D., & Wilsnack, R. W. (2002). Self-reports of forgetting and remembering childhood sexual abuse in a nationally representative sample of U.S. women. *Child Abuse and Neglect, 26*(2), 139–147.

Wilson, A. E., & Ross, M. (2000). The frequency of temporal-self and social comparisons in people's personal appraisals. *Journal of Personality and Social Psychology, 78*, 928–942.

Wilson, E. O. (1993). Biophilia and the conservation ethic. In S. R. Kellert & E. O. Wilson (Eds.), *The biophilia hypothesis* (pp. 31–41). Washington, DC: Island Press.

Wilson, E. O. (2007). Foreword. In D. J. Penn & I. Mysterud (Eds.), *Evolutionary perspectives on environmental problems* (pp. xiii–xiv). New Brunswick, NJ: Transaction Publishers.

Wilson, J. P., Drozdek, B., & Turkovic, S. (2006). Posttraumatic shame and guilt. *Trauma, Violence and Abuse, 7*(2), 122–141.

Wilson, T. D. (2002). *Strangers to ourselves: Discovering the adaptive unconscious.* Cambridge: Belknap Press.

Wilson, T. D., & Gilbert, D. T. (2005). Affective forecasting: Knowing what to want. *Current Directions in Psychological Science, 14*, 131–134.

Wilson, T. D., Wheatley, T. P., Meyers, J. M., Gilbert, D. T., & Axsom, D. (2000). Focalism: A source of durability bias in affective forecasting. *Journal of Personality and Social Psychology, 78*, 821–836.

Wilt, J. & Revelle, W. (2009). Extraversion. In M. R. Leary & R. H. Hoyle (Eds.), *Handbook of individual differences in social behavior* (pp. 27–45). New York: Guilford.

Winett, R. A., Hatcher, J. W., Fort, T. R., Leckliter, I. N., Love, S. Q., Riley, A. W., & Fishback, J. F. (1982). The effects of videotape modeling and daily feedback on residential electricity conservation, home temperature and humidity, perceived comfort, and clothing worn: Winter and summer. *Journal of Applied Behavior Analysis, 15*, 381–402.

Wing, J. F., Schutte, N. S., & Byrne, B. (2006). The effect of positive writing on emotional intelligence and life satisfaction. *Journal of Clinical Psychology, 62*, 1291–1302.

Wing, R. R., & Polley, B. A. (2001). Obesity. In A. Baum, T. A. Revenson, & J. E. Singer (Eds.), *Handbook of health psychology.* Mahwah, NJ: Erlbaum.

Winick, C., & Norman, R. L. (2005). Epidemiology. In J. H. Lowinson, P. Ruiz, R. B. Millman, & J. G. Langrod (Eds.), *Substance abuse: A comprehensive textbook.* Philadelphia: Lippincott/Williams & Wilkins.

Winstead, Z. A. (2009). Friendships, sex differences and similarities. In H. T. Reis & S. Sprecher (Eds.), *Encyclopedia of human relationships: Vol. 2* (pp. 713–716). Los Angeles: Sage Reference Publication.

Winter, D. D. (2004). Shopping for sustainability: Psychological solutions to overconsumption. In T. Kasser & A. D. Kanner (Eds.), *Psychology and consumer culture: The struggle for a good life in a materialistic world.* Washington, DC: American Psychological Association.

Winter, D. D., & Cava, M. M. (2006) The psychoecology of armed conflict. *Journal of Social Issues, 62*, 19–40.

Winter, D. D., & Koger, S. M. (2004). *The psychology of environmental problems* (2nd ed.). Mahwah, NJ: Erlbaum.

Wise, D., & Rosqvist, J. (2006). Explanatory style and well-being. In J. C. Thomas, D. L. Segal, & M. Hersen (Eds.), *Comprehensive handbook of personality and psychopathology: Personality and everyday functioning.* Hoboken, NJ: Wiley.

Wissink, I. B., Dekovic, M., & Meijer, A. M. (2006). Parenting behavior, quality of the parent-adolescent functioning in four ethnic groups. *Journal of Early Adolescence, 26*, 133–159.

Wittenbrink, B., & Schwartz, N. (Eds.). (2007). *Implicit measures of attitudes.* New York: Guilford.

Witvliet, C., Ludwig, T. E., & Vander Laan, K. L. (2001). Granting forgiveness or harboring grudges: Implications for emotion, physiology, and health. *Psychological Science, 121*(2), 117–123.

Wolak, J. Finkelhor D., Ybarra, M. L., & Mitchell K. (2008). Online "predators" and their victims: Myths, realities, and implications for prevention and treatment. *American Psychologist, 63*, 111–128.

Wolfe, J. B., & Betz, N. E. (2004). The relationship of attachment variables to career decision-making self-efficacy and fear of commitment. *Career Development Quarterly, 52*, 363–369.

Wolfinger, N. H. (2005). *Understanding the divorce cycle: The children of divorce in their own marriages.* New York: Cambridge University Press.

Wolinsky, F. D. (1988). Sick role legitimation. In D. S. Gochman (Ed.), *Health behavior: Emerging research perspectives.* New York: Plenum Press.

Wolitski, R. J., Henny, K. D., & Lyles, C. M. (2006). Evolution of HIV/AIDS prevention programs—United States, 1981–2006. *Journal of the American Medical Association, 296*, 760–762.

Wolitski, R. J., Jones, K. T., Wasserman, J. L., & Smith, J. C. (2006). Self-identification as "down low" among men who have sex with men (MSM) from 12 US cities. *AIDS and Behavior, 10*, 519–529.

Wolpe, J. (1958). *Psychotherapy by reciprocal inhibition.* Stanford, CA: Stanford University Press.

Wolpe, J. (1987). The promotion of scientific therapy: A long voyage. In J. K. Zeig (Ed.), *The evolution of psychotherapy.* New York: Brunner/Mazel.

Wolpe, J. (1990). *The practice of behavior therapy.* Elmsford, NY: Pergamon.

Women clerics find sexual harassment. (1990, December 1). *Washington Post, C12.*

Wonderlich, S. A. (2002). Personality and eating disorders. In C. G. Fairburn & K. D. Brownell (Eds.), *Eating disorders and obesity: A comprehensive handbook.* New York: Guilford.

Wong, L. A. (2006). *Essential study skills.* Boston: Houghton Mifflin.

Wong, P. T. P. (2006). Existential and humanistic theories. In J. C. Thomas & D. L. Segal (Eds.), *Comprehensive handbook of personality and psychopathology.* New York: Wiley.

Wong, Y. J., & Rochlen, A. B. (2005). Demystifying men's emotional behavior: New directions and implications for counseling and research. *Psychology of Men and Masculinity, 6*(1), 62–72.

Wood, E., Desmarais, S., & Gugula, S. (2002). The impact of parenting experience on gender stereotyped toy play of children. *Sex Roles, 47*(1–2), 39–49.

Wood, J. T. (2006) Chopping the carrots: Creating intimacy moment by moment. In J. T. Wood & S. W. Duck (Eds.), *Composing relationships: Communication in everyday life* (pp. 24–35). Belmont, CA: Thompson/Wadsworth.

Wood, J. T. (2009). Communication, gender differences in. In H. T. Reis & S. Sprecher (Eds.), *Encyclopedia of human relationships: Vol. 2* (pp. 252–256). Los Angeles: Sage Reference Publication.

Wood, J. T. (2010). *Interpersonal communication: Everyday encounters* (6th ed.). Belmont, CA: Wadsworth/Cengage.

Wood, J. V. (1989). Theory and research concerning social comparisons of personal attributes. *Psychological Bulletin, 106*, 231–248.

Wood, J. V., & Wilson, A. E. (2003). How important is social comparison? In M. R. Leary , & J. P. Tangney (Eds.), *Handbook of self and identity.* New York: Guilford.

Wood, M. D., Vinson, D. C., & Sher, K. J. (2001). Alcohol use and misuse. In A. Baum, T. A. Revenson, & J. E. Singer (Eds.), *Handbook of health psychology.* Mahwah, NJ: Erlbaum.

Wood, N., & Cowan, N. (1995). The cocktail party phenomenon revisited: How frequent are attention shifts to one's name in an irrelevant auditory channel? *Journal of Experimental Psychology: Learning, Memory, and Cognition, 21*, 255–260.

Wood, P. B., & Bartkowski, J. P. (2004). Attribution style and public policy attitudes toward gay rights. *Social Science Quarterly, 85*, 58–74.

Wood, R. T. A., & Griffiths, M. D. (2007). A qualitative investigation of problem gambling as an escape-based coping strategy. *Psychology and Psychotherapy: Theory, Research, and Practice, 80*, 107–125.

Wood, W., & Eagly, A. H. (2002). A cross-cultural analysis of the behavior of women and men: Implications for the origins of sex differences. *Psychological Bulletin, 128*(5), 699–727.

Wood, W., & Kallgren, C. A. (1988). Communicator attributes and persuasion: Recipients' access to attitude-relevant information in memory. *Personality and Social Psychology Bulletin, 14*, 172–182.

Wood, W., & Quinn, J. M. (2003). Forewarned and forearmed? Two meta-analytic syntheses of forewarnings of influence appeals. *Psychological Bulletin, 129*(1), 119–138.

Wood, W., Conway, M., Pushkar, D., & Dugas, M. J. (2005). People's perceptions of women's and men's worry about life issues: Worrying about love, accomplishment, or money? *Sex Roles, 53*, 545–551.

Woodhill, B. M., & Samuels, C. A. (2003). Positive and negative androgyny and their relationship with psychological health and well-being. *Sex Roles, 48*, 555–565.

Woodhill, B. M., & Samuels, C. A. (2004). Desirable and undesirable androgyny: A prescription for the twenty-first century. *Journal of Gender Studies, 13*(1), 15–28.

Woods Hole Research Center. (2009). Retrieved from http://whrc.org/

Woodzicka, J. A., & LaFrance, M. (2005). The effects of subtle sexual harassment on women's performance in a job interview. *Sex Roles, 53*, 67–77.

**World Resources Institute.** (2001). *Facts and figures: Environmental data tables, energy and resource use.* Table ERC.5: Resource Consumption. [Data file]. Retrieved from http://www.wri.org/trends/index.html

**Worthen, J. B.** (1997). Resiliency of bizarreness effects under varying conditions of verbal and imaginal elaboration and list composition. *Journal of Mental Imagery, 21,* 167–194.

**Worthington E. L., Jr., Witvliet, C. V. O., Pietrini, P., & Miller, A. J.** (2007). Forgiveness, health, and well-being: A review of evidence for emotional versus decisional forgiveness, dispositional forgivingness, and reduced unforgiveness. *Journal of Behavioral Medicine, 30,* 291–302.

**Worthington, R. L., Flores, L. Y., & Navarro, R. L.** (2005). Career development in context: Research with people of color. In S. D. Brown & R. W. Lent (Eds.), *Career development and counseling: Putting theory and research to work.* New York: Wiley.

**Worthington, R. L., & Reynolds, A. L.** (2009). Within-group differences in sexual orientation and identity. *Journal of Counseling Psychology, 56,* 44–55.

**Worthington, R. L., Soth-McNett, A. M., & Moreno, M. V.** (2007). Multicultural counseling competencies research: A 20-year content analysis. *Journal of Counseling Psychology, 54,* 351–361.

**Wortman, C. B., & Boerner, K.** (2007). Beyond the myths of coping with loss: Assumptions versus scientific evidence. In H. S. Friedman & R. C. Silver (Eds.), *Foundations of health psychology.* New York: Oxford University Press.

**Wortman, C. B., Wolff, K., & Bonanno, G. A.** (2004). Loss of an intimate partner through death. In D. J. Mashek & A. Aron (Eds.), *Handbook of closeness and intimacy.* Mahwah, NJ: Erlbaum.

**Wright, C. E., O'Donnell, K., Brydon, L., Wardle, J., & Steptoe, A.** (2007). Family history of cardiovascular disease is associated with cardiovascular responses to stress in healthy young men and women. *International Journal of Psychophysiology, 63,* 275–282.

**Wright, J. H., Beck, A. T., & Thase, M. E.** (2003). Cognitive therapy. In R. E. Hales & S. C. Yudofsky (Eds.), *Textbook of clinical psychiatry.* Washington, DC: American Psychiatric Publishing.

**Wright, J. H., Thase, M. E., & Beck, A. T.** (2008). Cognitive therapy. In R. E. Hales, S. C. Yudofsky, & G. O. Gabbard (Eds.), *The American psychiatric publishing textbook of psychiatry* (pp. 2111–1256). Washington, DC: American Psychiatric Publishing.

**Wright, P. H.** (2006). Toward an expanded orientation to the comparative study of women's and men's same-sex friendships. In K. Dindia & D. J. Canary (Eds.), *Sex differences and similarities in communication.* Mahwah, NJ: Erlbaum.

**Wright, R. A., & Contrada, R. J.** (1986). Dating selectivity and interpersonal attraction: Toward a better understanding of the "elusive phenomenon." *Journal of Social and Personal Relationships, 3,* 131–148.

**Wright, S. C., & Taylor, D. M.** (2003). The social psychology of cultural diversity: Social stereotyping, prejudice, and discrimination. In M. A. Hogg & J. Cooper (Eds.), *The Sage handbook of social psychology.* Thousand Oaks, CA: Sage Publications.

**Wright, T. A.** (2003). Positive organizational behavior: An idea whose time has truly come. *Journal of Organizational Behavior, 24,* 437–442.

**Wrosch, C., Miller, G. E., & Scheier, M. F.** (2007). Giving up on unattainable goals: Benefits for health? *Personality and Social Psychology Bulletin, 33,* 251–265.

**Wrzesniewski, A., McCauly, C., Rozin, P., & Schwartz, B.** (1997). Jobs, careers, and callings: People's relations to their work. *Journal of Research in Personality, 31,* 21–33.

**Wu, Z., & Hart, R.** (2002). The effects of marital and nonmarital union transition on health. *Journal of Marriage and Family, 64,* 430–432.

**Wynder, E. L., Cohen, L. A., Muscat, J. E., Winters, B., Dwyer, J. T., & Blackburn, G.** (1997). Breast cancer: Weighing the evidence for a promoting role of dietary fat. *Journal of the National Cancer Institute, 89*(11), 766–775.

**Xiaohe, X., & Whyte, M. K.** (1990). Love matches and arranged marriages: A Chinese replication. *Journal of Marriage and the Family, 52,* 709–722.

**Yalom, I. D.** (1980). *Existential psychotherapy.* New York: Basic Books.

**Yalom, I. D.** (1995). *The theory and practice of group psychotherapy* (4th ed.). New York: Basic Books.

**Yamamoto, J., Silva, J. A., Justice, L. R., Chang, C. Y., & Leong, G. B.** (1993). Cross-cultural psychotherapy. In A. C. Gaw (Ed.), *Culture, ethnicity, and mental illness.* Washington, DC: American Psychological Press.

**Yang, H., Liu, T., & Zang, D.** (2000). A study of stressful life events before the onset of hypothyroidism. *Chinese Mental Health Journal, 14*(3), 201–202.

**Yate, M.** (2006). *Knock 'em dead: The ultimate job search guide.* Avon, MA: Adams Media.

**Yeats, W. B.** (1997). *The Yeats reader: A portable compendium of poetry, drama, and prose.* New York: Scribner.

**Yee, N.** (2009). The Proteus effect: Implications of transformed digital self-representation on online and offline behavior. *Communication Research, 36,* 285–312.

**Yee, N., Bailenson, J. N., & Ducheneaut, N.** (2009). The Proteus effect: Implications of transformed digital self-representation on online and offline behavior. *Communication Research, 36*(2), 285–312.

**Yehuda, R.** (2003). Changes in the concept of PTSD and trauma. *Psychiatric Times, 20*(4), 35–40.

**Yehuda, R., & Wong, C. M.** (2007). Acute stress disorder and posttraumatic stress disorder. In G. Fink (Ed.), *Encyclopedia of stress: Vols. 1–4* (2nd ed., pp. 2–6). San Diego, CA: Elsevier Academic Press.

**Yellowlees, P., & Marks, S.** (2007). Problematic Internet use or Internet addiction? *Computers in Human Behavior, 23,* 1447–1453.

**Yi, H., Chen, C. M., & Williams, G. D.** (2006). *Trends in alcohol-related fatal traffic crashes, United States, 1982–2004* (Alcohol Epidemiological Data System, Surveillance Report No. 76). Arlington, VA: National Institute of Alcohol Abuse and Alcoholism.

**Yi, H., Stinson, F. S., Williams, G. D., & Dufour, M. C.** (1999). *Surveillance report #53: Trends in alcohol-related fatal traffic crashes, United States, 1977–1998.* Rockville, MD: National Institute on Alcohol Abuse and Alcoholism.

**Ying, Y., & Han, M.** (2006). The contribution of personality, acculturative stressors, and social affiliation to adjustment: A longitudinal study of Taiwanese students in the United States. *International Journal of Intercultural Relations, 30,* 623–635.

**Yoder, J. D., & Kahn, A. S.** (2003). Making gender comparisons more meaningful: A call for more attention to social context. *Psychology of Women Quarterly, 27,* 281–290.

**Yost, M. R., & Zurbriggen, E. L.** (2006). Gender differences in the enactment of sociosexuality: An examination of implicit social motives, sexual fantasies, coercive sexual attitudes, and aggressive sexual behavior. *Journal of Sex Research, 43,* 163–173.

**Young, J. E.** (1982). Loneliness, depression and cognitive therapy: Theory and application. In L. A. Peplau & D. Perlman (Eds.), *Loneliness: A sourcebook of current theory, research and therapy.* New York: Wiley.

**Young, K. S.** (1998). *Caught in the net: How to recognize the signs of Internet addiction—and a winning strategy for recovery.* New York: Wiley.

**Young, R., & Sweeting, H.** (2004). Adolescent bullying, relationships, psychological well-being, and gender-atypical behavior: A gender diagnosticity approach. *Sex Roles, 50,* 525–537.

**Yuen, C. N., & Lavin, M. J.** (2004). Internet dependence in the collegiate population: The role of shyness. *CyberPsychology & Behavior, 7*(4), 379–383.

**Yutzy, S. H.** (2003). Somatoform disorders. In R. E. Hales & S. C. Yudofsky (Eds.), *Textbook of clinical psychiatry.* Washington, DC: American Psychiatric Publishing.

**Yutzy, S. H. & Parish, B. S.** (2008). Somatoform disorders. In R. E. Hales, S. C. Yudofsky, & G. O. Gabbard (Eds.), *The American psychiatric publishing textbook of psychiatry* (pp. 609–642). Washington, DC: American Psychiatric Publishing.

**Zaalberg, R., Manstead, A. S. R., & Fischer, A, H.** (2004). Relations between emotions, display rules, social motives, and facial behaviour. *Cognition & Emotion, 18,* 183–207.

**Zajonc, R. B.** (1968). Attitudinal effects of mere exposure. *Journal of Personality and Social Psychology, 9,* 1–27.

**Zakzanis, K. K., & Young, D. A.** (2001). Memory impairment in abstinent MDMA ("Ecstasy") users: A longitudinal investigation. *Neurology, 56,* 966–969.

**Zane, N., Hall, G. C. N., Sue, S., Young, K., & Nunez, J.** (2004). Research on psychotherapy with culturally diverse populations. In M. J. Lambert (Ed.), *Bergin and Garfield's handbook of psychotherapy and behavior change.* New York: Wiley.

**Zautra, A. J., & Smith, B. W.** (2001). Depression and reactivity to stress in older women with rheumatoid arthritis and osteoarthritis. *Psychosomatic Medicine, 63*(4), 687–696.

**Zeig, J. K.** (1987). Introduction: The evolution of psychotherapy—Fundamental issues. In J. K. Zeig (Ed.), *The evolution of psychotherapy.* New York: Brunner/Mazel.

**Zemishlany, Z., Aizenberg, D., & Weizman, A.** (2001). Subjective effects of MDMA ("Ecstasy") on human sexual function. *European Psychiatry, 16*(2), 127–130.

**Zhang, L., Amos, C., & McDowell, W. C.** (2008). A comparative study of Internet addiction between the United States and China. *CyberPsychology & Behavior, 11,* 727–729.

**Zhang, Y. B., Harwood, J., & Hummert, M.** (2005). Perceptions of conflict management styles in Chinese intergenerational dyads. *Communication Monographs, 72,* 71–91.

**Zimbardo, P. G.** (1977). *Shyness: What it is, what to do about it.* Reading, MA: Addison-Wesley.

**Zimbardo, P. G.** (1990). *Shyness.* Reading, MA: Addison-Wesley.

**Zimbardo, P. G.** (1992). Cults in everyday life: Dependency and power. *Contemporary Psychology, 37,* 1187–1189.

**Zimbardo, P. G.** (2002). Mind control: Psychological reality or mindless rhetoric. *Cultic Studies Review, 1,* 309–311.

**Zimering, R., Gulliver, S. B., Knight, J., Munroe, J., & Kean, T. M.** (2006). Posttraumatic stress disorder in disaster relief workers following direct and indirect trauma exposure to ground zero. *Journal of Traumatic Stress, 19,* 553–557.

**Zimmerman, B. J.** (1995). Self-efficacy and educational development. In A. Bandura (Ed.), *Self-efficacy in changing societies.* New York: Cambridge University Press.

**Zimmerman, M., & Spitzer, R. L.** (2009). Psychiatric classification. In B. J. Sadock, V. A. Sadock, & P. Ruiz (Eds.), *Kaplan & Sadock's comprehensive textbook of psychiatry* (pp. 1108–1138). Philadelphia: Lippincott Williams & Wilkins.

**Zinbarg, R. E., & Griffith, J. W.** (2008). Behavior therapy. In J. L. Lebow (Ed.), *Twenty-first century psychotherapies: Contemporary approaches to theory and practice.* New York: Wiley.

**Zinnebauer, B. J., & Pargament, K. I.** (2005). Religiousness and spirituality. In R. F. Pargament & C. L. Park (Eds.), *Handbook of the psychology of religion and spirituality* (pp. 21–42). New York: Guilford.

**Zinnebauer, B. J., Pargament, K. I., Cole, B., Rye, M. S., Butter, E. M., Belavich, T. G., et al.** (1997). Religion and spirituality: Unfuzzying the fuzzy. *Journal of the Scientific Study of Religion, 36,* 549–564,

**Zinnebauer, B. J., Pargament, K. I., & Scott, A. B.** (1999). The emerging meanings of religiousness and spirituality: Problems and prospects. *Journal of Personality, 67,* 889–920.

**Zisook, S., Lesser, I., Stewart, J. W., Wisniewski, S. R., Balasubramani, G. K., Fava, M., et al.** (2007). Effect of age at onset on the course of major depressive disorder. *American Journal of Psychiatry, 164,* 1539–1546.

**Zosuls, K. M., Ruble, D. N., Tamis-LeMonda, C. S., Shrout, P. E., Bornstein, M. H., & Greulich, F. K.** (2009). The acquisition of gender labels in infancy: Implications for gender-typed play. *Developmental Psychology, 45,* 688–701.

**Zuckerman, M.** (1971). Dimensions of sensation seeking. *Journal of Consulting and Clinical Psychology, 36,* 45–52.

**Zuckerman, M.** (1979). *Sensation seeking: Beyond the optimal level of arousal.* Hillsdale, NJ: Erlbaum.

**Zuckerman, M.** (1984). Experience and desire: A new format for sensation seeking scales. *Journal of Behavioral Assessment, 6,* 101–114.

**Zuckerman, M.** (1991). *Psychobiology of personality.* New York: Cambridge University Press.

**Zuckerman, M.** (1994). *Behavioral expressions and biosocial bases of sensation seeking.* New York: Cambridge University Press.

**Zuckerman, M.** (1995). Good and bad humors: Biochemical bases of personality and its disorders. *Psychological Science, 6,* 325–332.

**Zuckerman, M.** (1996). The psychobiological model for impulsive unsocialized sensation seeking: A comparative approach. *Neuropsychobiology, 34,* 125–129.

**Zuckerman, M.** (2006). Sensation seeking in entertainment. In J. Bryant & P. Vorderer (Eds.), *Psychology of entertainment* (pp. 367–387). Mahwah, NJ: Erlbaum.

Zuckerman, M. (2007). *Sensation seeking and risky behavior*. Washington, DC: American Psychological Association.

Zuckerman, M. (2008). Personality and sensation seeking. In G. J. Boyle, G. Matthews, D. H. Saklofske (Eds.), *The Sage handbook of personality theory and assessment* (pp. 379–398). Los Angeles: Sage.

Zuckerman, M. (2009). Sensation seeking. In M. R. Leary & R. H. Hoyle (Eds.), *Handbook of individual differences in social* behavior (pp. 455–465). New York: The Guilford Press.

Zuckerman, M., Kieffer, S. C., & Knee, C. R. (1998). Consequences of self-handicapping: Effects of coping, academic performance, and adjustment. *Journal of Personality and Social Psychology, 74*(6), 1619–1628.

Zuckerman, M., & Tsai, F. (2005). Costs of self-handicapping. *Journal of Social Psychology, 73*, 411–442.

Zuo, J., & Tang, S. (2000). Breadwinner status and gender ideologies of men and women regarding family roles. *Sociological Perspectives, 43*(1), 29–43.

Zvonkovic, A. M., Solomon, C. R., Humble, A. M., & Monoogian, M. (2005). Family work and relationships: Lessons from families of men whose jobs require travel. *Family Relations, 54*, 411–422.

Zvonkovic, A. N., Greaves, K. M., Schmiege, C. J., & Hall, L. D. (1996). The marital construction of gender through work and family decisions: A qualitative analysis. *Journal of Marriage and the Family, 58, 1*, 91–100.

Zytowski, D. G., & Kuder, F. (1999). *Kuder career search with person match*. Adel, IA: National Career Assessment Services, Inc.

# Name Index

# Subject Index

diet, health and, 157–160
dieting, 156
direction, search for sense of, 4–8
disasters
  posttraumatic stress disorder following, 90, 92
  probability of, 117
  risk areas for, 73–74
  stress and, 74, 80, 81, 82
discipline, using punishment for, 48
disclosure. *See* self-disclosure
disconfirmation bias, 228
discrimination, 218–220
  employment, 419–420
  against gays and lesbians, 327, 380–381
  gender-based, 358–359
  ingroups and, 224
  modern, 219–220
  subjective perception of, 74
  in workplace, 422
disease(s)
  chronic, 138–139, 147
  contagious, 138–139
  obesity and, 154, 155
  stress and, 146–147
  *see also* illness; sexually transmsitted diseases; specific diseases
disengagement, behavioral, 107
disobedience, to authority, 234
disorganized schizophrenia, 465
displaced workers, 426
displacement, 39, 108
display rules, 248
dissociative amnesia, 453, 454
dissociative disorders, 444, 453–455
dissociative experiences, in posttraumatic stress disorder, 90
dissociative fugue, 453–454
dissociative identity disorder (DID), 454–455
distance, interpersonal, 246, 247
distance education, 416
distinctiveness, personality and, 33
distributed practice, 28
diversity, in workforce, 418–420
diversity training, 420–421
division of labor
  gender roles and, 362
  in marriage, 315
divorce, 320–324
  adjusting to, 322
  causes of, 319
  cohabitation and, 330
  deciding to, 321–322
  effects on children, 322–323, 324
  factors in, 308–309
  financial problems and, 318
  happiness and, 21
  infidelity and, 392
  loneliness and, 297
  predicting likelihood of, 320
  waiting period for, 324
divorce laws, 324
divorce rates, 305, 321, 415
  culture and, 292
  for second marriages, 325
domestic violence, 331–333
door-in-the-face technique, 236, 237
dopamine, 468
double standard, sexual, 212–213, 334, 372
downsizing, 416, 423, 426
downward social comparison, 181, 194
Dr. Laura, 5
Dr. Phil, 4
dream analysis, 42, 481
dream interpretation, 489
drinking, 151–154
drinking water, A-9
drives, basic, 53
driving
  drunk, 153
  marijuana use and, 171
  pleasure of, 521
drug abuse, 167–173
  mortality and, 148
  seeking treatment for, 478
  stress and, 89
drug companies, 499
drug therapy, 477, 480, 494–501
  for anxiety disorders, 449, 495
  effectiveness of, 498–499
  for mood disorders, 460
  for phobic disorders, 497
  for schizophrenia, 494, 496–497
drug use, recreational, 167–173
drugs
  dependence on, 168–169, 170, 478
  effects of, 168, 169
  overdose potential of, 169, 171
  risks of, 168, 169, 170, 171
  tolerance for, 168, 169

drunk driving, 153
DSM-IV, 443, 444
dual-career couples, 316, 416, 429
dying, process of, 134

**E**

e-mail, 243–244, 252, 219
eating
  oral fixation and, 40
  stress-induced, 109, 110
eating disorders, 89, 276–277, 345, 358, 470–473
eating habits, 157–160
eclecticism, in therapy, 503, 504
ecological dilemma, A-14
ecological footprint, A-7–A-8, A-20
ecologically connected self, A-14
economic hardships, 3
economy, unpredictability of, 423
ecopsychology, A-3
ecosystems, A-5
ecstasy, 172–173
education, occupational earnings and, 417–418
educational attainment, happiness and, 20
effectiveness, time management and, 124
Effexor, 497
efficiency
  in person perception, 217
  time management and, 124
ego, 36, 37
ego depletion, 82
ego-depletion model, 197–198
egocentric values, A-13
ejaculation, 385
  premature, 401–402, 403
elaboration likelihood model, 228–229
Elavil, 497
elder care, 430
electroconvulsive therapy (ECT), 499–501
electronically mediated communication, 243–244, 245
emetic drugs, 492
emoticons, 252
emotional arousal, interpretation of, 199
emotional dispositions, marital adjustment and, 309
emotional expression, gender differences in, 344
emotional intelligence, 126
*Emotional Intelligence* (Goleman), 127
emotional loneliness, 296
emotional support, in psychotherapy, 487
emotions
  agitation-related, 179
  appraisal of stress and, 81
  arousal of, 82
  conditioning of, 45–46
  conveyed through touch, 251–252
  defined, 80, 516
  dejection-related, 178
  Ellis's view of, 115–116
  expressing, 126–127
  facial expression of, 15, 247–248
  heart disease and, 144
  masculinity and, 355
  moods and, 514
  negative, 72, 80, 81, 128–129, 144, 517
  nonverbal communication of, 245
  paralanguage and, 252
  physiological indicators of, 254
  positive, 81–82, 118–119, 516–518
  predicting future, 188
  in reaction to trauma, 92
  recognizing, 344
  release of, 108
  in schizophrenic disorders, 464, 465
  suppression of, 127, 144, 355
empathy, 34
  in interpersonal communication, 264
  meditation and, 522
  suicide threats and, 459
  in therapy, 484, 487
empiricism, 12
employee benefits, 430
employees
  job stress and, 421–424
  sexual harassment of, 425
employers
  background checks by, 435
  researching, 436
employment. *See* work
employment opportunities, for women, 359
empty nest, 314
encoding, 241
encouragement, 199
endocrine disorders, 348
endocrine glands, 85, 86, 347
endocrine system, 85
endogamy, 307
energy conservation, A-12
energy consumption, A-7–A-8, A-21
enjoyment, 523

entitlement, 3
  narcissistic, 129
environment
  for communication, 242
  heredity and, 58
  restorative, A-20
  stress in, 73–74, 75
environmental activists, A-12
environmental crisis, A-3–A-6
Environmental Health Clinic, A-19
environmental problems, 2
Environmental Protection Agency, A-18
environmental sustainability, A-2–A-21
Epidemiological Catchment Area, 446
epidemiology, 445
erectile difficulties, 401, 402–403
erogenous zones, 387
erotic preferences, 372
estrogen, 372, 373, 396
ethics, sexual, 371–372
ethnic diversity, in workforce, 418–420
ethnic minorities
  stresses for, 74
  therapeutic services for, 503–504
  in workforce, 418, 419
  *see also* minorities
ethnic stereotypes, 214
etiology, 442
euphoria
  from alcohol, 152
  in bipolar disorder, 457
  from narcotics, 169
  from stimulants, 170
evolutionary perspective
  evaluation of, 346
  on emotions, 517
  on flight-or-flight response, 84
  on gender differences, 346
  on mating patterns, 277–279
  on obesity, 155
  on personality, 58
evolved model for fear learning, 450
exams
  anxiety and, 82
  cramming for, 28
exchange relationships, 282
exchange theory, 281–282
exemplification, 201–202
exercise
  benefits of, 129, 160, 432
  lack of, 155, 160–161
  for weight loss, 157
exercise program, 161–162
exhaustion, emotional, 88–89
exhaustion stage, of general adaptation syndrome, 85
expectations
  happiness and, 23
  hope and, 524
  of perceivers, 211–213, 217
  in person perception, 261
  prejudice and, 223
  self-esteem and, 186, 187
experimental group, 13
experimental research, 12–14
expertise, of source, 226
explanatory style, 192–193, 461
expressed emotion, 469
expressive traits, 276
expressiveness, 339
extinction
  in classical conditioning, 46
  in operant conditioning, 47
extramarital sex, 392–393
extraversion, 33–34, 35, 42, 56, 58
  cancer risk and, 145
  happiness and, 22
*Extreme Makeover*, 276
eye contact, 209, 248–249
  in assertive communication, 267
  when listening, 258

**F**

face, saving, 265
face-to-face communication, 245
Facebook, 244, 293
faces, person perception and, 209
facial expression, 247–248
  emotion and, 15
  of emotion, 344
facial features, desirable, 275
factor analysis, 33, 59
failure
  self-handicapping for, 196
  as source of stress, 75
faith, 528
  happiness and, 20
false consensus, A-15
false memory syndrome, 488

heart attack, 141
heart disease
    alcohol and, 154
    depression and, 144
    diet and, 157, 158
    job stress and, 424
    mortality rates for, 139
    obesity and, 155
    personality and, 140–144
    smoking and, 150
Heaven's Gate cult, 5
hedonic adaptation, 23–24
hedonic treadmill, 23–24
hedonism, 371–372
height, heritability of, 57
helplessness, learned, 106–107, 193, 461
hemispheric specialization, 347
hepatitis, from shared needles, 169
hepatitis B, 397
heredity
    environment and, 58, 346
    happiness and, 22
    homosexuality and, 380
    mood disorders and, 458–460
    in obesity, 155
    personality and, 56–57
heritability ratios, 57, 58
hermaphrodites, 372
heroin, 168, 169
herpes, genital, 397
heterosexism, 284
heterosexuals, 284, 371
heuristics, in judging of environmental hazards, A-15
hierarchy of needs, Maslow's, 53–54
highlighting, in textbooks, 26
highly active antiretroviral therapy, 162
Hill, Anita, 425
hindsight bias, 58
hippocampus, 460
hiring, personality tests in, 67
Hispanic Americans
    divorce rates for, 321
    male role among, 354
    self-esteem in, 189, 190
    stresses for, 74
    in workforce, 418
histrionic personality, 452
Hitler, Adolf, 233
HIV infection, 162 388, 398
    see also AIDS
hobbies, 431
holistic approach, 217
homogamy, 307
homophobia, 327, 356, 381
homosexual relationships, 326–329
    infidelity in, 426–427
    sex in, 392
homosexuality, 379–382
    attitudes toward, 380–381
    causes of, 379–380
    prevalence of, 379
    reaction formation and, 39
homosexuals, 284, 371
    AIDS and, 162, 398
    attitudes toward, 327
    children of, 382
    dating challenges of, 273–274
    friendships and, 283
    loneliness and, 296
    marriage and, 380, 381
    parents of, 382
    sexual activity of, 388
    sexual socialization of, 378–379
    in workforce, 418–429
honesty, in interpersonal communication, 264–265
"hooking up," 390
hope, 524–525
Hope Scale, 525
hopelessness, 179
hopelessness theory, 461
hormone-based contraceptives, 394, 395, 396
hormones, 85, 86, 347
    homosexuality and, 380
    sex, 372–373
    stress and, 73, 74, 129
hostile environment harassment, 361
hostile work environment, 425
hostility
    heart disease and, 142–143
    managing, 128
    narcissism and, 187
household chores, 315–316, 351, 358, 430
How of Happiness, The (Lyubomirsky), 531
Hughes, Howard, 448, 452
human immunodeficiency virus (HIV), 162, 388, 398
human nature, 51, 55
human papillomavirus (PV), 397, 398
human potential movement, 51, 483

humanism, 50
humanistic psychology, 513
humanistic theories
    evaluation of, 54–55
    Maslow's, 52–54
    Rogers', 51–52
humor
    self-defeating, 118
    as stress reducer, 117–119
hunting-and-gathering societies, 346, 362
Hurricane Katrina, 90, 118, A-18
hydrophobia, 447
hypertension, 141
    alcohol and, 154
    caffeine and, 158
    obesity and, 155
    salt and, 157–158
hypnosis, for recovering repressed memories, 489
hypoactive sexual desire, 402, 403
hypochondriasis, 452
hypothalamus, 85, 86
hypothesis, 12, 13

I
id, 36, 37
ideal self, 178–180, 295
identical twins, 57
identification, 39, A-11
identity
    gender-role, 363
    from job, 408
    loss of, 453
    sexual, 371–372
illness
    Big Five traits and, 35
    job stress and, 424
    life changes and, 77
    reactions to, 164–166
    stress and, 85, 91–92
illusion of control, 194
illusions, positive, 113
imitation
    of gender roles, 349
    in observational learning, 49
    see also modeling
immigration, 74
immune functioning
    AIDS and, 162
    marijuana use and, 172
    optimism and, 96
    social support and, 95
    stress and, 86, 145, 146–147
impact bias, 188
Implanon, 395
impotence, 401
impression formation, 209–213
    in job interviews, 436–437
    see also person perception
impression management, 201–202
impressions
    first, 218
    negative, 210, 218
incentives, A-12
income
    education and, 418
    happiness and, 18–19
    job identity and, 408
    marriage and, 318
incongruence, 51, 52, 484
Inconvenient Truth, An, A-4
independent variables, 12–13, 14
independent view of self, 183–184
India, 73, 292
individualism, 190, 258
    assertiveness and, 266
    attribution errors and, 217
    conflict and, 262
    marriage and, 292
    self-concept and, 183–184
    self-serving bias and, 194
    social support and, 121
indulgence, as coping strategy, 108–111
industrial/organizational (I/O) psychology, 406
infants
    attachment styles in, 286–287, 317
    responses to threats of, 84
infectious diseases, 139
inferiority complex, 42, 43
infidelity, 392–393
    Internet sex and, 377
inflammation, heart disease and, 141–142
Influence: Science and Practice (Cialdini), 229, 235
information, retention of, 27
information influence, 232
ingratiation, 201, 202
ingroup advantage, 248
ingroup favoritism, 224
ingroups, 209, 214, 220, 223
injunctive norms, A-12–A-13

inkblots test, 66
insecure attachment, 452–453
insecurity, 309
insight therapies, 477, 481–490
    client-centered, 483–485
    effectiveness of, 486–488, 507
    psychoanalysis, 481–483
insomnia, stress and, 89
instant messaging, 245
institutions, positive, 529–531
instrumentality, 339
intellectualization, 112
intelligence
    emotional, 126
    happiness and, 20
    heritability of, 57
    occupation and, 408
intercourse, sexual, 386, 389
interdependence theory, 281–282
interdependent view of self, 183–184
interest inventories, 410
Intergovernmental Panel on Climate Change (IPCC), A-4
Internet
    close relationships and, 293–295
    communicating via, 243–244, 245
    for overcoming loneliness, 299–300
    personality testing on, 67
    sexual content on, 376, 377
    surfing, 431
Internet addiction, 109–110, 377
interpersonal communication
    barriers to, 261
    defined, 241
    improving, 255–259
    in marriage, 317–319
    methods for improving, 366
    premarital, 309
    problems in, 260–261
    about sex, 383–384
    technology and, 243–244
interpersonal relationships. See close relationships; romantic relationships
interpretation
    in psychoanalysis, 482
interpersonal communication, of aversive events, 106
interruptions, 124
intersex individuals, 372
interviews, job, 436–437
intimacy
    in friendships, 283
    in online communication, 245
    in online dating, 293
    love and, 285
    self-disclosure and, 257
    sex and, 356, 378
intimate violence, 331–335
intimidation, 202
intrauterine device (IUD), 395, 396
intravenous drug use, 162, 163, 169
introducing oneself, 256
introversion, 42, 56
inverted-U hypothesis, 82–83
investments, in relationships, 282
irrational assumptions, 111
irrational thinking, 205, 299, 463
irritability, as response to traumatic events, 92
irritable bowel syndrome, stress and, 145
ischemia, 141, 144

J
Japan, 135, 194, 246, 258
Jim twins, 55
job interviews, 436–437
job loss, 426–428
job performance
    self-efficacy and, 198
    self-esteem and, 186
job satisfaction, 21, 316
    interest inventories and, 410
    leisure satisfaction and, 432
    personality fit and, 411–413
job search, 433–437
job security, 416
job sharing, 417
job skills, 416
job stress, 421–424, A-19
    dealing with, 424
    demand-control model of, 423
    effects of, 423–424
jobs
    information about, 408–409
    positive workplaces and, 529–530
Johnson, Lyndon B., 250
Journal of Happiness Studies, 532
Journal of Positive Psychology, 532
joy, 517, 521
judgments, snap vs. systematic, 210–211, 228
just world, belief in, 217

trichomoniasis, 397
tricyclics, 497
trust
    in friendships, 283
    meditation and, 522
trustworthiness, of source, 226
tsunami, 137
tubal ligation, 395
twin studies, 55, 56–57
    of homosexuality, 380
    of mood disorders, 459
    of obesity, 155
    of schizophrenic disorders, 467
Type A personality, 142
Type B personality, 142

**U**

ultimate attribution error, 223
unconditioned response (UCR), 44, 45, 46
unconditioned stimulus (UCS), 44, 45, 46
unconscious
    Freud's view of, 36, 37, 481
    Jung's view of, 41–42
*Under the Tuscan Sun* (Mayes), 523
underemployment, 417
undifferentiated schizophrenia, 465
undoing, 112
undoing hypothesis, 518
unemployment, 3, 21, 426–428
unipolar disorder, 455, 456
University of Minnesota, 55, 57
upward social comparison, 181
urbanization, 74
U.S. Bureau of Labor Statistics, 409
U.S. Department of Agriculture, 158
U.S. Food and Drug Administration, 497

**V**

vacations, 431
vacillation, 76
vagina, 384–386
validity, of psychological tests, 65
Valium, 170, 449, 495, 498
valproate, 498
values
    self-concept and, 180
    sexual, 371–372, 400
    social, 378
    work-related, 408
variables, 12–13
    clusters of, 33
    correlations between, 14–15
vasectomy, 395

vasocongestion, 384
vengefulness, 128–129
ventricles, of brain, 468
verbal abilities, gender differences in, 342
verbal aggression, 343
verbal attacks, 264
veterans
    Iraq war, 89–90
    Vietnam, 89, 95
Viagra, 402
Vicodin, 169
victims
    blaming of, 217, 333
    of battering, 333
    of date rape, 333–335
    of sexual harassment, 426
Victorian era, 36
video games, 108, 353, A-17
Vienna Psychoanalytic Society, 42
Vietnam veterans, 89, 95
violence
    community, 74
    intimate, 331–335
    in media, 108, 109
violent crimes, 343–344
    on college campuses, 153
viral hepatitis, 397
visual dominance, 249
visualization, 260–261
vitamins, 158, 159
vocal cues, 252
vocalization, 252
vocational psychology, 413
volunteer activities, 432
vomiting, 471
vulnerability, as response to traumatic events, 92

**W**

Wal-Mart, 419
water pollution, A-9
water use, A-21
waypower, 525
wealth, happiness and, 19
weather, extreme, A-5
websites, dating, 293–295
weight loss methods, 156–157
weight problems, 154–157
well-being, subjective, 18–24
well-being therapy, 485
*What Color Is Your Parachute* (Bolles), 433, 434
"what is beautiful is good" stereotype, 214
*Why Marriages Succeed or Fail* (Gottman), 318
*Why Zebras Don't Get Ulcers* (Sapolsky), 87

widowhood, 136
wilderness therapy, A-20
Wilson, Owen, 455
Wise Use movement, A-11
wishful thinking, 113
withdrawal, social, 300
withdrawal illness, 168, 169, 170
withdrawal method, of birth control, 395
withdrawing, from conflict, 263
women
    career development of, 414–415
    careers for, 315, 316, 359
    in workforce, 306, 316, 321, 357, 414–415, 418,
        419–420, 430
Woods, Tiger, 226
words, "loaded," 265
work, 415
    flow state and, 520–521
    from home, 416
    generational differences in, 430
    happiness and, 21
    marriage and, 316, 321
    satisfaction from, 429
    *see also* career choice; jobs; occupation
work-family balance, 79, 316–317, 406
work-family conflict, 429
workaholism, 429
workforce
    demographic changes in, 418–420
    women in, 306, 316, 321, 357, 414–415, 418, 419–420,
        430
working memory, 88
workplace
    harassment in, 361
    hostile, 425
    male bias in, 340
    personality and, 411–413
    positive, 529–530
    sexual harassment in, 424–426
    trends in, 415–417
workweek, 421, 430
World War II, 11
worldviews, cultural, 61–62
writing, about traumatic experiences, 127, 128
writing skills, employment and, 418

**XYZ**

Xanax, 495
yoga, 129
*zeitgeist*, 512
Zen, 129
Zeta-Jones, Catherine, 227
Zoloft, 497

# Personal Explorations Workbook

# Personal Explorations Workbook Contents

# Introduction

In your textbook, *Psychology Applied to Modern Life,* the value of developing an accurate self-concept is emphasized repeatedly. A little self-deception may occasionally be adaptive (see Chapter 4), but most theories of psychological health endorse the importance of forming a realistic picture of one's personal qualities and capabilities. This *Personal Explorations Workbook* contains two types of exercises intended to help you achieve this goal. They are (1) a series of *Self-Assessments,* or self-scoring psychological scales, intended to help you gain insight into your attitudes and personality traits, and (2) a series of *Self-Reflections* intended to help you systematically analyze various aspects of your life in relation to adjustment issues.

How you use these personal exploration exercises will depend, in large part, on your instructor. Some instructors will formally assign some of these exercises and then collect them for individual scrutiny or class discussion. That is why the pages of this workbook are perforated—to make it convenient for those instructors who like to assign the exercises as homework. Other instructors may simply encourage students to complete the exercises that they find intriguing. We believe that, even if the exercises are not assigned, you will find many of them very interesting and we encourage you to complete them on your own. Let's briefly take a closer look at these exercises.

## Self-Assessments

The Self-Assessments are a collection of attitude scales and personality tests that psychologists have used in their research. One Self-Assessment questionnaire has been selected for each chapter in your text. Instructions are provided so that you can administer these scales to yourself and then compute your score. Each Self-Assessment also includes an explanation of what the scale measures followed by a brief review of the research on the scale. These reviews discuss the evidence on the reliability, validity, and behavioral correlates of each scale. The final section of each Self-Assessment provides information which allows you to interpret the meaning of your score. Test norms are supplied to indicate what represents a high, intermediate, or low score on the scale. We hope you may gain some useful insights about yourself by responding to these scales.

However, you should be careful about attributing too much significance to your scores. As explained in Chapter 2 in your text, the results of psychological tests can be misleading, and caution is always in order when interpreting test scores. It is probably best to view your scores as interesting "food for thought" rather than as definitive statements about your personal traits or abilities.

Most of the scales included in this book are self-report inventories. Your scores on such tests are only as accurate as the information that you provide in your responses. Hence, we hasten to emphasize that the Self-Assessments will only be as valuable as you make them by striving to respond honestly. Usually, people taking a scale do not know what the scale measures. The conventional approach is to put some sort of vague or misleading title, such as "Biographical Inventory," at the top of the scale. We have not adhered to this practice because you could easily find out what any scale measures simply by reading ahead a little. Thus, you will be taking each scale with some idea (based on the title) of what the scale measures. Bear in mind, however, that these scales are intended to satisfy your curiosity. There is no reason to try to impress or mislead anyone—including yourself. Your test scores will be accurate and meaningful only if you try very hard to respond in a candid manner.

## Self-Reflections

The Self-Reflections consist of sets of questions designed to make you think about yourself and your personal experiences in relation to specific issues and topics raised in your text. They involve systematic inquiries into how you behave in certain situations, how your behavior has been shaped by past events, how you feel about certain issues, how you might improve yourself in some areas, how you anticipate behaving under certain circumstances in the future, and so forth. There is one Self-Reflection for each of the sixteen chapters in your textbook. The aspects of life probed by these inquiries are, of course, tied to the content of the chapters in your text. You will probably derive the most benefit from them if you read the corresponding text chapter before completing the Self-Reflections.

*Wayne Weiten*
*Dana S. Dunn*
*Elizabeth Yost Hammer*

# References

Ames, S. C., Jones, G. N., Howe, J. T., & Brantley, P. J. (2001). A prospective study of the impact of stress on quality of life: An investigation of low-income individuals with hypertension. *Annals of Behavioral Medicine, 23*(2), 112–119.

Anderson, N. H. (1968). Likableness ratings of 555 personality trait words. *Journal of Personality and Social Psychology, 9,* 272–279.

Arnaut, G. L. Y. (2006). Sensation seeking, risk taking, and fearlessness. In J. C. Thomas & D. L. Segal (Eds.), *Comprehensive handbook of personality and psychopathology, Vol 1: Personality and everyday functioning* (pp. 322–344). New York: Wiley.

Barnes, G. E., & Vulcano, B. A. (1982). Measuring rationality independent of social desirability. *Personality and Individual Differences, 3,* 303–309.

Baumeister, R. F., & Vohs, K. D. (2001). Narcissism as addiction to esteem. *Psychological Inquiry, 12,* 206–210.

Becker, H. A. (1980). The Assertive Job-Hunting Survey. *Measurement and Evaluation in Guidance, 13,* 43–48.

Bringle, R., Roach, S., Andler, C., & Evenbeck, S. (1979). Measuring the intensity of jealous reactions. *Catalogue of Selected Documents in Psychology, 9,* 23–24.

Compton, W. C. (2005). *An introduction to positive psychology.* Belmont, CA: Thompson/Wadsworth.

Corcoran, K., and Fischer, J. (2000). *Measures for clinical practice: A Sourcebook* (Vols. 1 and 2). New York: Free Press.

Denisoff, E., & Endler, N. S. (2000). Life experiences, coping, and weight preoccupation in young adult women. *Canadian Journal of Behavioural Science, 32*(2), 97–103.

Egan, G. (1977). *You and me: The skills of communicating and relating to others.* Pacific Grove, CA: Brooks/Cole.

Ellis, A. (1962). *Reason and emotion in psychotherapy.* Seacaucus, NJ: Lyle Stuart.

Fischer, E. H., & Turner, J. L. (1970). Orientations to seeking professional help: Development and research utility of an attitude scale. *Journal of Consulting and Clinical Psychology, 35,* 82–83.

Ickes, W., &. Barnes, R. D. (1977). The role of sex and self-monitoring in unstructured dyadic interactions. *Journal of Personality and Social Psychology, 35,* 315–330.

Infante, D. A., & Rancer, A. S. (1982). A conceptualization and measure of argumentativeness. *Journal of Personality Assessment, 46,* 72–80.

Kelley, K., Byrne, D., Przybyla, D. P. J., Eberly, C., Eberly, B., Greendlinger, V., Wan, C. K., & Gorsky, J. (1985). Chronic self-destructiveness: Conceptualization, measurement and initial validation of the construct. *Motivation and Emotion, 9,* 135–151.

Malefo, V. (2000). Psycho-social factors and academic performance among African women students at a predominantly white university in South Africa. *South African Journal of Psychology, 30*(4), 40–45.

Miller, L. C., Berg, J. H., & Archer, R. L. (1983). Openers: Individuals who elicit intimate self-disclosure. *Journal of Personality and Social Psychology, 44,* 1234–1244.

Peterson, C. (2006). *A primer in positive psychology.* New York: Oxford University Press.

Peterson, C., Park, N., & Seligman, M. E. P. (2005). Orientations to happiness and life satisfaction: The full life versus the empty life. *Journal of Happiness Studies, 6,* 25–41.

Raskin, R., & Hall, C. S. (1979). A narcissistic personality inventory. *Psychological Reports, 40,* 590.

Raskin, R., & Hall, C. S. (1981). The Narcissistic Personality Inventory: Alternate form reliability and further evidence of construct validity. *Journal of Personality Assessment, 45,* 159–162.

Raskin, R., & Terry, H. (1988). A principal-components analysis of the Narcissistic Personality Inventory and further evidence of its construct validity. *Journal of Personality and Social Psychology, 54,* 890–902.

Rhodewalt, F. & Peterson, B. (2009). Narcissism. In M. R. Leary & R. H. Hoyle (Eds.), *Handbook of individual differences in social behavior* (pp. 547–560). New York: Guilford.

Rhodewalt, F., & Morf, C. C. (2005). Reflections in troubled waters: Narcissism and the vicissitudes of an interpersonality contextualized self. In A. Tesser, J. V. Wood, & D. A. Staper (Eds.), *On Building, defending, and regulating the self* (pp. 127–152). New York: Psychology Press.

Sarason, I. G., Johnson, J. H., & Siegel, J. M. (1978). Assessing the impact of life changes: Development of the Life Experiences Survey. *Journal of Consulting and Clinical Psychology, 46,* 932–946.

Snell, W. E., Jr., & Papini, D. R. (1989). The sexuality scale: An instrument to measure sexual-esteem, sexual-depression, and sexual-preoccupation. *Journal of Sex Research, 26,* 256–263.

Snyder, M. (1974). Self-monitoring of expressive behavior. *Journal of Personality and Social Psychology, 30,* 526–537.

Spence, J. T., & Helmreich, R. L. (1978). *Masculinity and femininity: Their psychological dimensions, correlates, and antecedents.* Austin: University of Texas Press.

Suinn, R. M. (1968). Removal of social desirability and response set items from the Manifest Anxiety Scale. *Educational and Psychological* Measurement, *28,* 1189–1192.

Twenge, J. M., & Campbell, W. K. (2009). *The narcissism epidemic: Living in the age of entitlement.* New York: Free Press.

Twenge, J. M., Konrath, S., Foster, J. D., Campbell, W. K., & Bushman, B. J. (2008). Egos inflating over time: A cross-temporal meta-analysis of the Narcissistic Personality Inventory. *Journal of Personality, 76*(4), 903–917.

U.S. Department of Health and Human Services. (1981). *Health style: A self-test.* Washington, DC: Department of Health and Human Services, Public Health Service, PHS 81–50155.

Watson, D. L., & Friend, R. (1969). Measurement of social-evaluative anxiety. *Journal of Consulting and Clinical Psychology, 33,* 448–457.

Zuckerman, M. (1979). *Sensation seeking: Beyond the optimal level of arousal.* Hillsdale, NJ: Erlbaum.

Zuckerman, M. (1994). *Behavioral expressions and biosocial bases of sensation seeking.* New York: Cambridge University Press.

Zuckerman, M. (2007). *Sensation seeking and risky behavior.* Washington, DC: American Psychological Association.

# Chapter 1 Adjusting to Modern Life

**EXERCISE 1.1** *Self-Assessment:* **Narcissistic Personality Inventory**

## Instructions

Read each pair of statements below and place an "X" by the one that comes closest to describing your feelings and beliefs about yourself. You may feel that neither statement describes you well, but pick the one that comes closest. **Please complete all pairs.**

## The Scale

1. ___A. I have a natural talent for influencing people.
   ___B. I am not good at influencing people.

2. ___A. Modesty doesn't become me.
   ___B. I am essentially a modest person.

3. ___A. I would do almost anything on a dare.
   ___B. I tend to be a fairly cautious person.

4. ___A. When people compliment me I sometimes get embarrassed.
   ___B. I know that I am good because everybody keeps telling me so.

5. ___A. The thought of ruling the world frightens the hell out of me.
   ___B. If I ruled the world it would be a better place.

6. ___A. I can usually talk my way out of anything.
   ___B. I try to accept the consequences of my behavior.

7. ___A. I prefer to blend in with the crowd.
   ___B. I like to be the center of attention.

8. ___A. I will be a success.
   ___B. I am not too concerned about success.

9. ___A. I am no better or worse than most people.
   ___B. I think I am a special person.

10. ___A. I am not sure if I would make a good leader.
    ___B. I see myself as a good leader.

11. ___A. I am assertive.
    ___B. I wish I were more assertive.

12. ___A. I like to have authority over other people.
    ___B. I don't mind following orders.

13. ___A. I find it easy to manipulate people.
    ___B. I don't like it when I find myself manipulating people.

14. ___A. I insist upon getting the respect that is due me.
    ___B. I usually get the respect that I deserve.

15. ___A. I don't particularly like to show off my body.
    ___B. I like to show off my body.

16. ___A. I can read people like a book.
    ___B. People are sometimes hard to understand.

17. ___A. If I feel competent I am willing to take responsibility for making decisions.
    ___B. I like to take responsibility for making decisions.

18. ___A. I just want to be reasonably happy.
    ___B. I want to amount to something in the eyes of the world.

19. ___A. My body is nothing special.
    ___B. I like to look at my body.

20. ___A. I try not to be a show off.
    ___B. I will usually show off if I get the chance.

21. ___A. I always know what I am doing.
    ___B. Sometimes I am not sure of what I am doing.

22. ___A. I sometimes depend on people to get things done.
    ___B. I rarely depend on anyone else to get things done.

23. ___A. Sometimes I tell good stories.
    ___B. Everybody likes to hear my stories.

24. ___A. I expect a great deal from other people.
    ___B. I like to do things for other people.

25. ___A. I will never be satisfied until I get all that I deserve.
    ___B. I take my satisfactions as they come.

26. ___A. Compliments embarrass me.
    ___B. I like to be complimented.

27. ___A. I have a strong will to power.
    ___B. Power for its own sake doesn't interest me.

28. ___A. I don't care about new fads and fashions.
    ___B. I like to start new fads and fashions.

29. ___A. I like to look at myself in the mirror.
    ___B. I am not particularly interested in looking at myself in the mirror.

30. ___A. I really like to be the center of attention.
    ___B. It makes me uncomfortable to be the center of attention.

31. ___A. I can live my life in any way I want to.
    ___B. People can't always live their lives in terms of what they want.

32. ___A. Being an authority doesn't mean that much to me.
    ___B. People always seem to recognize my authority.

33. ___A. I would prefer to be a leader.
    ___B. It makes little difference to me whether I am a leader or not.

34. ___A. I am going to be a great person.
    ___B. I hope I am going to be successful.

35. ___A. People sometimes believe what I tell them.
    ___B. I can make anybody believe anything I want them to.

36. ___A. I am a born leader.
    ___B. Leadership is a quality that takes a long time to develop.

37. ___A. I wish somebody would someday write my biography.
    ___B. I don't like people to pry into my life for any reason.

38. ___A. I get upset when people don't notice how I look when I go out in public.
    ___B. I don't mind blending into the crowd when I go out in public.

39. ___A. I am more capable than other people.
    ___B. There is a lot that I can learn from other people.

40. ___A. I am much like everybody else.
    ___B. I am an extraordinary person.

## Scoring the Scale

The scoring key is reproduced below. You should circle your response of A or B each time it corresponds to the keyed response below. Add up the number of responses you circled. This total is your score on the Narcissistic Personality Inventory. Record your score below.

| | | | | | |
|---|---|---|---|---|---|
| 1. A | 8. A | 15. B | 22. B | 29. A | 36. A |
| 2. A | 9. B | 16. A | 23. B | 30. A | 37. A |
| 3. A | 10. B | 17. B | 24. A | 31. A | 38. A |
| 4. B | 11. A | 18. B | 25. A | 32. B | 39. A |
| 5. B | 12. A | 19. B | 26. B | 33. A | 40. B |
| 6. A | 13. A | 20. B | 27. A | 34. A | |
| 7. B | 14. A | 21. A | 28. B | 35. B | |

**My score** _____

## What the Scale Measures

As noted briefly in Chapter 1, *narcissism* is a personality trait marked by an inflated sense of importance, a need for attention and admiration, a sense of entitlement, and a tendency to exploit others. Those who score high in narcissism tend to exhibit feelings of superiority, although their feelings of self-esteem are actually quite fragile and constantly require validation (Rhodewalt & Morf, 2005). This insecurity creates an insatiable need for expressions of admiration from others that leads to grandiose self-presentations (Rhodewalt & Peterson, 2009). Baumeister and Vohs (2001) compare narcissists' craving for approval and admiration to an addiction. Twenge and Campbell (2009) emphasize narcissists' sense of entitlement—the expectation that everything should revolve around them and that they should receive special favors and treatment. The *Living in Today's World* box in Chapter 2 discusses the trait of narcissism in more detail.

The Narcissistic Personality Inventory (NPI) was developed by Robert Raskin and colleagues (Raskin & Hall, 1979, 1981; Raskin & Terry, 1988) to assess normal levels of narcissism on a continuum. The original 54-item measure was reduced to the current 40-item scale in 1988. The scale has been widely used in research, and there is extensive evidence that it accurately measures what it sets out to measure. As we will discuss in Chapter 2, recent research suggests that scores on the NPI have been rising among recent generations of college students (Twenge et al., 2008).

## Interpreting Your Score

Our norms are based on data from Twenge et al. (2008), which takes into consideration the recent increase in scores on the NPI among college populations. According to data available in Twenge et al (2008), the mean score on the NPI in studies since 2000 has hovered around 17, with a standard deviation of about 7 (the standard deviation is an index of how much variability there tends to be on a measure). Our cutoffs for high and low scores are based on being one-half of a standard deviation above or below the mean of 17. Roughly speaking, that means high scorers fall in the upper 30% on this trait, medium scorers in the middle 40%, and low scorers in the bottom 30%.

*Norms*

| | |
|---|---|
| **High score:** | 20.5–40 |
| **Medium score:** | 13.5–20.5 |
| **Low score:** | 0–13.5 |

# EXERCISE 1.2 *Self-Reflection:* **What Are Your Study Habits Like?**

| | | |
|---|---|---|
| Do you usually complete your class assignments on time? | YES | NO |
| Do you usually find time to prepare adequately for your exams? | YES | NO |
| Do you frequently delay schoolwork until the last minute? | YES | NO |

When do you usually study (mornings, evenings, weekends, etc.)?

| | | |
|---|---|---|
| Do you write out and follow a study schedule? | YES | NO |
| Are your study times planned for when you're likely to be alert? | YES | NO |
| Do you allow time for brief study breaks? | YES | NO |

Where do you usually study (library, kitchen, bedroom, etc.)?

| | | |
|---|---|---|
| Do you have a special place set up for studying and nothing else? | YES | NO |

What types of auditory, visual, and social distractions are present in your study areas?

Can you suggest any changes to reduce distractions in your study areas?

# Chapter 2 Theories of Personality

## EXERCISE 2.1 *Self-Assessment:* **Sensation-Seeking Scale**

### Instructions

Each of the items below contains two choices, A and B. Please indicate in the spaces provided on the left which of the choices most describes your likes or the way you feel. It is important that you respond to all items with only one choice, A or B. In some cases you may find that both choices describe your likes or the way you feel. Please choose the one that better describes your likes or feelings. In some cases you may not like either choice. In these cases mark the choice you dislike least. We are interested only in your likes or feelings, not in how others feel about these things or how one is supposed to feel. There are no right or wrong answers. Be frank and give your honest appraisal of yourself.

### The Scale

_____ 1. A. I would like a job that would require a lot of traveling.

   B. I would prefer a job in one location.

_____ 2. A. I am invigorated by a brisk, cold day.

   B. I can't wait to get indoors on a cold day.

_____ 3. A. I find a certain pleasure in routine kinds of work.

   B. Although it is sometimes necessary, I usually dislike routine kinds of work.

_____ 4. A. I often wish I could be a mountain climber.

   B. I can't understand people who risk their necks climbing mountains.

_____ 5. A. I dislike all body odors.

   B. I like some of the earthy body smells.

_____ 6. A. I get bored seeing the same old faces.

   B. I like the comfortable familiarity of everyday friends.

_____ 7. A. I like to explore a strange city or section of town by myself, even if it means getting lost.

   B. I prefer a guide when I am in a place I don't know well.

_____ 8. A. I find the quickest and easiest route to a place and stick to it.

   B. I sometimes take different routes to a place I often go, just for variety's sake.

_____ 9. A. I would not like to try any drug that might produce strange and dangerous effects on me.

   B. I would like to try some of the new drugs that produce hallucinations.

_____ 10. A. I would prefer living in an ideal society where everyone is safe, secure, and happy.

   B. I would have preferred living in the unsettled days of our history.

_____ 11. A. I sometimes like to do things that are a little frightening.

   B. A sensible person avoids activities that are dangerous.

_____ 12. A. I order dishes with which I am familiar, so as to avoid disappointment and unpleasantness.

   B. I like to try new foods that I have never tasted before.

_____ 13. A. I can't stand riding with a person who likes to speed.

   B. I sometimes like to drive very fast because I find it exciting.

_____ 14. A. If I were a salesperson, I would prefer a straight salary rather than the risk of making little or nothing on a commission basis.

   B. If I were a salesperson, I would prefer working on a commission if I had a chance to make more money than I could on a salary.

_____ 15. A. I would like to take up the sport of water skiing.

   B. I would not like to take up the sport of water skiing.

_____ 16. A. I don't like to argue with people whose beliefs are sharply divergent from mine, since such arguments are never resolved.

   B. I find people who disagree with my beliefs more stimulating than people who agree with me.

_____ 17. A. When I go on a trip, I like to plan my route and time-table fairly carefully.

   B. I would like to take off on a trip with no pre-planned or definite routes or timetables.

_____ 18. A. I enjoy the thrills of watching car races.

   B. I find car races unpleasant.

_____ 19. A. Most people spend entirely too much money on life insurance.

   B. Life insurance is something that no one can afford to be without.

_____ 20. A. I would like to learn to fly an airplane.

   B. I would not like to learn to fly an airplane.

_____ 21. A. I would not like to be hypnotized.

   B. I would like to have the experience of being hypnotized.

_____ 22. A. The most important goal of life is to live it to the fullest and experience as much of it as you can.

   B. The most important goal of life is to find peace and happiness.

_____ 23. A. I would like to try parachute jumping.

B. I would never want to try jumping out of a plane, with or without a parachute.

_____ 24. A. I enter cold water gradually, giving myself time to get used to it.

B. I like to dive or jump right into the ocean or a cold pool.

_____ 25. A. I do not like the irregularity and discord of most modern music.

B. I like to listen to new and unusual kinds of music.

_____ 26. A. I prefer friends who are excitingly unpredictable.

B. I prefer friends who are reliable and predictable.

_____ 27. A. When I go on a vacation, I prefer the comfort of a good room and bed.

B. When I go on a vacation, I would prefer the change of camping out.

_____ 28. A. The essence of good art is in its clarity, symmetry of form, and harmony of colors.

B. I often find beauty in the "clashing" colors and irregular forms of modern paintings.

_____ 29. A. The worst social sin is to be rude.

B. The worst social sin is to be a bore.

_____ 30. A. I look forward to a good night of rest after a long day.

B. I wish I didn't have to waste so much of a day sleeping.

_____ 31. A. I prefer people who are emotionally expressive even if they are a bit unstable.

B. I prefer people who are calm and even-tempered.

_____ 32. A. A good painting should shock or jolt the senses.

B. A good painting should give one a feeling of peace and security.

_____ 33. A. When I feel discouraged, I recover by relaxing and having some soothing diversion.

B. When I feel discouraged, I recover by going out and doing something new and exciting.

_____ 34. A. People who ride motorcycles must have some kind of an unconscious need to hurt themselves.

B. I would like to drive or ride on a motorcycle.

## Scoring the Scale

The scoring key is reproduced below. You should circle your response of A or B each time it corresponds to the keyed response below. Add up the number of responses you circled. This total is your score on the Sensation-Seeking Scale. Record your score below.

| | | | | |
|---|---|---|---|---|
| 1. A | 8. B | 15. A | 22. A | 29. B |
| 2. A | 9. B | 16. B | 23. A | 30. B |
| 3. B | 10. B | 17. B | 24. B | 31. A |
| 4. A | 11. A | 18. A | 25. B | 32. A |
| 5. B | 12. B | 19. A | 26. A | 33. B |
| 6. A | 13. B | 20. A | 27. B | 34. B |
| 7. A | 14. B | 21. B | 28. B | |

**My score** _____

## What the Scale Measures

As its name implies, the Sensation-Seeking Scale (SSS) measures one's need for a high level of stimulation. Sensation seeking involves the active pursuit of experiences that many people would find very stressful. As discussed in the chapter, Marvin Zuckerman (1994, 2007) believes that this thirst for sensation is a highly heritable personality trait that leads people to seek thrills, adventures, and new experiences.

The scale you have just responded to is the second version of the SSS (Zuckerman, 1979), but it shares a great deal of overlap with the current version (Arnaut, 2006). Sensation seeking is distributed along a continuum, and many people fall in the middle. Factor analyses indicate that the personality trait of sensation seeking consists of four related components. When compared to low sensation seekers, those high in sensation seeking display the following four sets of characteristics (Arnaut, 2006; Zuckerman, 1994):

- *Thrill and adventure seeking.* They're more willing to engage in activities that may involve a physical risk. Thus, they're more likely to go mountain climbing, skydiving, surfing, and scuba diving.
- *Experience seeking.* They're more willing to volunteer for unusual experiments or activities that they may know little about. They tend to relish extensive travel, provocative art, wild parties, and unusual friends.
- *Disinhibition.* They are relatively uninhibited. Hence, they are prone to engage in heavy drinking, recreational drug use, gambling, and sexual experimentation.
- *Susceptibility to boredom.* Their chief foe is monotony. They have a low tolerance for routine and repetition, and they quickly and easily become bored.

Test-retest reliabilities are quite respectable and there is ample evidence to support the scale's predictive validity. For example, studies show that high sensation seekers appraise hypothetical situations as less risky than low sensation seekers do and are more willing to volunteer for an experiment in which they will be hypnotized. The scale also shows robust positive correlations with measures of change seeking, novelty seeking, and impulsiveness. Interestingly, SSS scores tend to decline with age.

## Interpreting Your Score

Our norms are based on percentiles reported by Zuckerman and colleagues for a sample of 62 undergraduates. Although males generally tend to score a bit higher than females on the SSS, the differences are small enough to report one set of (averaged) norms. Remember, sensation-seeking scores tend to decline with age. So, if you're not in the modal college student age range (17–23), these norms may be a bit high.

*Norms*

| | |
|---|---|
| **High score:** | 21–34 |
| **Intermediate score:** | 11–20 |
| **Low score:** | 0–10 |

# EXERCISE 2.2  *Self-Reflection:* **Who Are You?**

Below you will find 75 personality trait words taken from an influential list assembled by Anderson (1968). Try to select the 20 traits (20 only!) that describe you best. Check them.

| | | | | |
|---|---|---|---|---|
| sincere | forgetful | truthful | imaginative | outgoing |
| pessimistic | crafty | mature | impolite | dependable |
| open-minded | methodical | skeptical | diligent | persistent |
| suspicious | sly | efficient | prideful | orderly |
| patient | headstrong | resourceful | optimistic | energetic |
| tense | naive | perceptive | considerate | modest |
| cooperative | sloppy | punctual | courteous | smart |
| neat | grouchy | prejudiced | candid | kind |
| logical | ethical | friendly | idealistic | good-humored |
| vain | persuasive | gracious | warm | unselfish |
| sociable | nervous | shy | versatile | cordial |
| scornful | clumsy | short-tempered | courageous | wholesome |
| cheerful | rebellious | compulsive | tactful | generous |
| honest | studious | sarcastic | loyal | boastful |
| reasonable | understanding | respectful | reliable | daring |

Review the 20 traits that you chose. Overall, is it a favorable or unfavorable picture that you have sketched?

Considering Carl Rogers's point that we often distort reality and construct an overly favorable self-concept, do you feel that you were objective?

What characteristics make you unique?

What are your greatest strengths?

What are your greatest weaknesses?

# Chapter 3 Stress and Its Effects

**EXERCISE 3.1** *Self-Assessment:* **The Life Experiences Survey (LES)**

## Instructions

Listed below are a number of events that sometimes bring about change in the lives of those who experience them and that necessitate social readjustment. Examine each event on the list, and if that event has occurred in your life during the past year please indicate the extent to which you viewed the event as having either a positive or negative impact on your life at the time it occurred. That is, circle a number on the appropriate line to indicate the type and extent of impact that the event had. A rating of −3 would indicate an extremely negative impact. A rating of 0 suggests no impact, either positive or negative. A rating of +3 would indicate an extremely positive impact.

## The Scale

| | Extremely negative | Moderately negative | Slightly negative | No impact | Slightly positive | Moderately positive | Extremely positive |
|---|---|---|---|---|---|---|---|
| **Section 1** | | | | | | | |
| 1. Marriage | −3 | −2 | −1 | 0 | +1 | +2 | +3 |
| 2. Detention in jail or comparable institution | −3 | −2 | −1 | 0 | +1 | +2 | +3 |
| 3. Death of spouse | −3 | −2 | −1 | 0 | +1 | +2 | +3 |
| 4. Major change in sleeping habits | −3 | −2 | −1 | 0 | +1 | +2 | +3 |
| 5. Death of a close family member | −3 | −2 | −1 | 0 | +1 | +2 | +3 |
|   a. Mother | −3 | −2 | −1 | 0 | +1 | +2 | +3 |
|   b. Father | −3 | −2 | −1 | 0 | +1 | +2 | +3 |
|   c. Brother | −3 | −2 | −1 | 0 | +1 | +2 | +3 |
|   d. Sister | −3 | −2 | −1 | 0 | +1 | +2 | +3 |
|   e. Grandmother | −3 | −2 | −1 | 0 | +1 | +2 | +3 |
|   f. Grandfather | −3 | −2 | −1 | 0 | +1 | +2 | +3 |
|   g. Other (specify) | −3 | −2 | −1 | 0 | +1 | +2 | +3 |
| 6. Major change in eating habits (much more or much less food intake) | −3 | −2 | −1 | 0 | +1 | +2 | +3 |
| 7. Foreclosure on mortgage or loan | −3 | −2 | −1 | 0 | +1 | +2 | +3 |
| 8. Death of a close friend | −3 | −2 | −1 | 0 | +1 | +2 | +3 |
| 9. Outstanding personal achievement | −3 | −2 | −1 | 0 | +1 | +2 | +3 |
| 10. Minor law violations | −3 | −2 | −1 | 0 | +1 | +2 | +3 |
| 11. Male: Wife/girlfriend's pregnancy | −3 | −2 | −1 | 0 | +1 | +2 | +3 |
| 12. Female: Pregnancy | −3 | −2 | −1 | 0 | +1 | +2 | +3 |
| 13. Changed work situation (different work responsibility, major change in working conditions, working hours, etc.) | −3 | −2 | −1 | 0 | +1 | +2 | +3 |
| 14. New job | −3 | −2 | −1 | 0 | +1 | +2 | +3 |
| 15. Serious illness or injury of close family member: | −3 | −2 | −1 | 0 | +1 | +2 | +3 |
|   a. Mother | −3 | −2 | −1 | 0 | +1 | +2 | +3 |
|   b. Father | −3 | −2 | −1 | 0 | +1 | +2 | +3 |
|   c. Brother | −3 | −2 | −1 | 0 | +1 | +2 | +3 |
|   d. Sister | −3 | −2 | −1 | 0 | +1 | +2 | +3 |
|   e. Grandmother | −3 | −2 | −1 | 0 | +1 | +2 | +3 |
|   f. Grandfather | −3 | −2 | −1 | 0 | +1 | +2 | +3 |

| | | | | | | | |
|---|---|---|---|---|---|---|---|
| g. Spouse | $-3$ | $-2$ | $-1$ | $0$ | $+1$ | $+2$ | $+3$ |
| h. Other (specify) | $-3$ | $-2$ | $-1$ | $0$ | $+1$ | $+2$ | $+3$ |
| **16.** Sexual difficulties | $-3$ | $-2$ | $-1$ | $0$ | $+1$ | $+2$ | $+3$ |
| **17.** Trouble with employer (in danger of losing job, being suspended, being demoted, etc.) | $-3$ | $-2$ | $-1$ | $0$ | $+1$ | $+2$ | $+3$ |
| **18.** Trouble with in-laws | $-3$ | $-2$ | $-1$ | $0$ | $+1$ | $+2$ | $+3$ |
| **19.** Major change in financial status (a lot better off or a lot worse off) | $-3$ | $-2$ | $-1$ | $0$ | $+1$ | $+2$ | $+3$ |
| **20.** Major change in closeness of family members (increased or decreased closeness) | $-3$ | $-2$ | $-1$ | $0$ | $+1$ | $+2$ | $+3$ |
| **21.** Gaining a new family member (through birth, adoption, family member moving in, etc.) | $-3$ | $-2$ | $-1$ | $0$ | $+1$ | $+2$ | $+3$ |
| **22.** Change in residence | $-3$ | $-2$ | $-1$ | $0$ | $+1$ | $+2$ | $+3$ |
| **23.** Marital separation from mate (due to conflict) | $-3$ | $-2$ | $-1$ | $0$ | $+1$ | $+2$ | $+3$ |
| **24.** Major change in church activities (increased or decreased attendance) | $-3$ | $-2$ | $-1$ | $0$ | $+1$ | $+2$ | $+3$ |
| **25.** Marital reconciliation with mate | $-3$ | $-2$ | $-1$ | $0$ | $+1$ | $+2$ | $+3$ |
| **26.** Major change in number of arguments with spouse (a lot more or a lot fewer) | $-3$ | $-2$ | $-1$ | $0$ | $+1$ | $+2$ | $+3$ |
| **27.** Married male: Change in wife's work outside the home (beginning work, ceasing work, changing to a new job, etc.) | $-3$ | $-2$ | $-1$ | $0$ | $+1$ | $+2$ | $+3$ |
| **28.** Married female: Change in husband's work (loss of job, beginning new job, retirement, etc.) | $-3$ | $-2$ | $-1$ | $0$ | $+1$ | $+2$ | $+3$ |
| **29.** Major change in usual type and/or amount of recreation | $-3$ | $-2$ | $-1$ | $0$ | $+1$ | $+2$ | $+3$ |
| **30.** Borrowing for a major purchase (buying a home, business, etc.) | $-3$ | $-2$ | $-1$ | $0$ | $+1$ | $+2$ | $+3$ |
| **31.** Borrowing for a smaller purchase (buying a car or TV, getting school loan, etc.) | $-3$ | $-2$ | $-1$ | $0$ | $+1$ | $+2$ | $+3$ |
| **32.** Being fired from job | $-3$ | $-2$ | $-1$ | $0$ | $+1$ | $+2$ | $+3$ |
| **33.** Male: Wife/girlfriend having an abortion | $-3$ | $-2$ | $-1$ | $0$ | $+1$ | $+2$ | $+3$ |
| **34.** Female: Having an abortion | $-3$ | $-2$ | $-1$ | $0$ | $+1$ | $+2$ | $+3$ |
| **35.** Major personal illness or injury | $-3$ | $-2$ | $-1$ | $0$ | $+1$ | $+2$ | $+3$ |
| **36.** Major change in social activities, e.g., parties, movies, visiting (increased or decreased participation) | $-3$ | $-2$ | $-1$ | $0$ | $+1$ | $+2$ | $+3$ |
| **37.** Major change in living conditions of family (building new home, remodeling, deterioration of home or neighborhood, etc.) | $-3$ | $-2$ | $-1$ | $0$ | $+1$ | $+2$ | $+3$ |
| **38.** Divorce | $-3$ | $-2$ | $-1$ | $0$ | $+1$ | $+2$ | $+3$ |
| **39.** Serious injury or illness of close friend | $-3$ | $-2$ | $-1$ | $0$ | $+1$ | $+2$ | $+3$ |
| **40.** Retirement from work | $-3$ | $-2$ | $-1$ | $0$ | $+1$ | $+2$ | $+3$ |
| **41.** Son or daughter leaving home (due to marriage, college, etc.) | $-3$ | $-2$ | $-1$ | $0$ | $+1$ | $+2$ | $+3$ |
| **42.** End of formal schooling | $-3$ | $-2$ | $-1$ | $0$ | $+1$ | $+2$ | $+3$ |
| **43.** Separation from spouse (due to work, travel, etc.) | $-3$ | $-2$ | $-1$ | $0$ | $+1$ | $+2$ | $+3$ |
| **44.** Engagement | $-3$ | $-2$ | $-1$ | $0$ | $+1$ | $+2$ | $+3$ |
| **45.** Breaking up with boyfriend/girlfriend | $-3$ | $-2$ | $-1$ | $0$ | $+1$ | $+2$ | $+3$ |
| **46.** Leaving home for the first time | $-3$ | $-2$ | $-1$ | $0$ | $+1$ | $+2$ | $+3$ |

| | | | | | | | |
|---|---|---|---|---|---|---|---|
| 47. Reconciliation with boyfriend/girlfriend | −3 | −2 | −1 | 0 | +1 | +2 | +3 |

Other recent experiences that have had an impact on your life. List and rate.

| | | | | | | | |
|---|---|---|---|---|---|---|---|
| 48. ___ | −3 | −2 | −1 | 0 | +1 | +2 | +3 |
| 49. ___ | −3 | −2 | −1 | 0 | +1 | +2 | +3 |
| 50. ___ | −3 | −2 | −1 | 0 | +1 | +2 | +3 |

**Section 2. Students only**

| | | | | | | | |
|---|---|---|---|---|---|---|---|
| 51. Beginning a new school experience at a higher academic level (college, graduate school, professional school) | −3 | −2 | −1 | 0 | +1 | +2 | +3 |
| 52. Changing to a new school at the same academic level (undergraduate, graduate, etc.) | −3 | −2 | −1 | 0 | +1 | +2 | +3 |
| 53. Academic probation | −3 | −2 | −1 | 0 | +1 | +2 | +3 |
| 54. Being dismissed from dormitory or other residence | −3 | −2 | −1 | 0 | +1 | +2 | +3 |
| 55. Failing an important exam | −3 | −2 | −1 | 0 | +1 | +2 | +3 |
| 56. Changing a major | −3 | −2 | −1 | 0 | +1 | +2 | +3 |
| 57. Failing a course | −3 | −2 | −1 | 0 | +1 | +2 | +3 |
| 58. Dropping a course | −3 | −2 | −1 | 0 | +1 | +2 | +3 |
| 59. Joining a fraternity/sorority | −3 | −2 | −1 | 0 | +1 | +2 | +3 |
| 60. Financial problems concerning school (in danger of not having sufficient money to continue) | −3 | −2 | −1 | 0 | +1 | +2 | +3 |

## Scoring the Scale

Arriving at your scores on the LES is very simple. Add up all the positive impact ratings on the right side. The total is your positive change score. Your negative change score is the sum of all of the negative impact ratings that you made on the left side. Adding these two values yields your total change score. Record your scores below.

**My positive change score _____**

**My negative change score _____**

**My total change score _____**

## What the Scale Measures

The Life Experiences Survey (LES), assembled by Irwin Sarason and colleagues (1978), has become a widely used measure of stress in contemporary research (for examples see Ames et al., 2001; Denisoff & Endler, 2000; Malefo, 2000). The LES recognizes that stress involves more than mere change and asks respondents to indicate whether events had a positive or negative impact on them. This strategy helps researchers gain much more insight into which facets of stress are most crucial. The LES also takes into consideration differences among people in their appraisal of stress, by dropping the normative weights and replacing them with personally assigned weightings of the impact of relevant events. The LES allows the respondent to write in personally important events that are not included on the scale. Finally, the LES has an extra section just for students.

## Interpreting Your Score

Approximate norms for all three of the scores are listed below so that you can get some idea of what your score means. Research to date suggests that the negative change score is the crucial one; positive change has not been found to be a good predictor of adaptational outcomes. Thus far, research has shown that negative change scores are related to a variety of negative adaptational outcomes.

There is merit in getting an estimate of how much stress you have experienced lately, but scores on the LES should be interpreted with caution. You need not panic if you add up your negative change score and find that it falls in the "high" category. For one thing, the strength of the association between stress and adaptational problems is modest. Second, stress interacts with many other factors, such as lifestyle, coping skills, social support, hardiness, and genetic inheritance, in influencing one's mental and physical health.

## Norms for LES

| Score change | Negative change | Positive change | Total change |
|---|---|---|---|
| High | 14 and above | 16 and above | 28 and above |
| Medium | 4–13 | 7–15 | 12–27 |
| Low | 0–3 | 0–6 | 0–11 |

## EXERCISE 3.2 *Self-Reflection:* Stress—How Do You Control It?

**1.** Do modern lifestyles create more stress than in the past? How so?

**2.** How do *you* create stress in your own life?

**3.** How could you change the nature of our society to make it less stressful?

**4.** It could be said that some stress comes from leading "out-of-balance" lives. What can people do to "keep it simple"? Furthermore, in what ways can individuals control the stressors they will encounter beforehand?

**5.** How could you change the way in which you interact with your school demands or your work demands to change the amount of stress that you feel?

# Chapter 4 Coping Processes

## EXERCISE 4.1 *Self-Assessment:* Barnes-Vulcano Rationality Test

### Instructions

For each of the following statements, please indicate the degree to which you tend to either agree or disagree with the statement according to the following five-point scale:

| 1 | 2 | 3 | 4 | 5 |
|---|---|---|---|---|
| Agree Strongly | Agree | Neither Agree nor Disagree | Disagree | Disagree Strongly |

### The Scale

_____ 1. I do not need to feel that everyone I meet likes me.

_____ 2. I frequently worry about things over which I have no control.

_____ 3. I find it easy to overcome irrational fears.

_____ 4. I can usually shut off thoughts that are causing me to feel anxious.

_____ 5. Life is a ceaseless battle against irrational worries.

_____ 6. I frequently worry about death.

_____ 7. Crowds make me nervous.

_____ 8. I frequently worry about the state of my health.

_____ 9. I tend to worry about things before they actually happen.

_____ 10. If I were told that someone had a criminal record I would not hire him or her to work for me.

_____ 11. When I make a mistake I feel worthless and inadequate.

_____ 12. When someone is wrong I sure let them know.

_____ 13. When I am frustrated the first thing I do is ask myself whether there is anything I can do to change it now.

_____ 14. Whenever something goes wrong I ask myself, "Why did this have to happen to me?"

_____ 15. Whenever things go wrong I say to myself, "I don't like this, I can't stand it."

_____ 16. I usually find a cure for my own depression when it occurs.

_____ 17. Once I am depressed it takes me a long while to recover.

_____ 18. I feel that when I become depressed or unhappy it is caused by other people or the events that happen.

_____ 19. People have little or no ability to control their sorrows or rid themselves of their negative feelings.

_____ 20. When I become angry I usually control my anger.

_____ 21. I can usually control my appetite for food and alcohol.

_____ 22. The value of a human being is directly proportionate to her/his accomplishments; if s/he is not thoroughly competent and adequate in achieving, s/he might as well curl up and die.

_____ 23. The important part of playing the game is that you succeed.

_____ 24. I feel bad when my achievement level is lower than others'.

_____ 25. I feel that I must succeed at everything I undertake.

_____ 26. When I feel doubts about potential success, I avoid participating and risking the chance of failure.

_____ 27. When I set out to accomplish a task I stick with it to the end.

_____ 28. If I find difficulties in life, I discipline myself to face them.

_____ 29. If I try to do something and encounter problems, I give up easily.

_____ 30. I find it difficult to work at tasks that have a long-range payoff.

_____ 31. I usually like to face my problems head on.

_____ 32. A person never learns from his/her mistakes.

_____ 33. Life is what you make of it.

_____ 34. Unhappy childhoods inevitably lead to problems in adult life.

_____ 35. I try not to brood over past mistakes.

_____ 36. People who are selfish make me mad because they really should not be that way.

_____ 37. If I had to nag someone to get what I wanted I would not think it was worth the trouble.

_____ 38. I frequently find that life is boring.

_____ 39. I often wish that something new and exciting would happen.

_____ 40. I experience life as just the same old thing from day to day.

_____ 41. I often wish life were more stimulating.

_____ 42. I often feel that everything is tiresome and dull.

_____ 43. I wish I could change places with someone who lives an exciting life.

_____ 44. I often wish life were different than it is.

## Scoring the Scale

To score this scale, you must reverse the numbers you entered for 12 of the items. The responses to be reversed are those for items 1, 3, 4, 13, 16, 20, 21, 27, 28, 31, 33, and 35. For each of these items, make the following conversions: If you chose 1, change it to 5. If you chose 2, change it to 4. If you chose 3, leave it unchanged. If you chose 4, change it to 2. If you chose 5, change it to 1.

Now add up the numbers for all 44 items, using the new numbers for the reversed items. This sum, which should fall somewhere between 44 and 220, is your score on the Barnes–Vulcano Rationality Test. Enter it below.

**My score** _____

## What the Scale Measures

Devised by Gordon Barnes and Brent Vulcano (1982), the Barnes–Vulcano Rationality Test (BVRT) measures the degree to which people do or do not subscribe to the irrational assumptions described by Albert Ellis (1962, 1973). As Chapter 4 in your text explains, Ellis believes that troublesome emotions and overreactions to stress are caused by negative self-talk or catastrophic thinking. Such thinking is thought to be derived from irrational assumptions that people hold. The items on the BVRT are based on 10 of the irrational assumptions described by Ellis, such as the idea that one must receive love and affection from certain people, or the idea that one must be thoroughly competent in all endeavors.

The scale is set up so that high scores indicate that one tends to think relatively rationally, whereas low scores indicate that one is prone to the irrational thinking described by Ellis. The BVRT has excellent reliability, and the authors took steps to minimize contamination from social desirability bias. Evidence regarding the test's validity can be gleaned from various correlational analyses. For example, high scores on the BVRT have been found to correlate negatively with measures of neuroticism (–.50), depression (–.55), and fear (–.31), indicating that respondents who score high on the test tend to be less neurotic, depressed, or fearful than those who score lower.

## Interpreting Your Score

Our norms, which are shown below, are based on combined data from two sets of adults studied by Barnes and Vulcano (1982). The first sample consisted of 172 subjects (with a mean age of 22), and the second included 177 subjects (with a mean age of 27).

*Norms*
**High score:** 166–220
**Medium score:** 136–165
**Low score:** 44–135

# EXERCISE 4.2 *Self-Reflection:* Analyzing Coping Strategies

1. You just generally feel "lousy" but are unsure as to what might be causing it. How would you go about figuring out what is wrong? What questions would you ask yourself to ensure that you come to an accurate conclusion?

2. What are some of the phrases that a person might use who is operating in the mode of "learned helplessness"? How could you help individuals tell the difference between something they have control over and something they do not?

3. Rationalization is a mechanism fraught with consequences. List some negative consequences of rationalization in the following areas: school, work, home, and relationships.

4. Discuss the issue of deadlines as they apply to any area of your life. How do you react to deadline pressures? What are some positive and negative coping strategies you have used in dealing with deadlines?

5. How do you explain negative events that occur in your life? What is your explanatory style?

# Chapter 5 Psychology and Physical Health

**EXERCISE 5.1** *Self-Assessment:* **Chronic Self-Destructiveness Scale**

## Instructions

For each of the following statements, indicate the degree to which the statement describes you. Record your responses in the spaces provided by writing in a letter from A to E, using the following scale: **A** expresses *strongest* agreement; **B** expresses moderate *agreement;* **C** indicates that you're *unsure or undecided,* or that it's a toss-up; **D** expresses moderate *disagreement;* **E** expresses *strongest disagreement.*

## The Scale

_____ 1. I like to listen to music with the volume turned up as loud as possible.

_____ 2. Life can be pretty boring.

_____ 3. When I was a kid, I was suspended from school.

_____ 4. I usually eat breakfast.

_____ 5. I do not stay late at school functions when I must get up early.

_____ 6. I use or have used street drugs.

_____ 7. I like to spend my free time "messing around."

_____ 8. As a rule, I do not put off doing chores.

_____ 9. Riding fast in a car is thrilling.

_____ 10. I tend to defy people in authority.

_____ 11. I have a complete physical examination once a year.

_____ 12. I have done dangerous things just for the thrill of it.

_____ 13. I am the kind of person who would stand up on a rollercoaster.

_____ 14. I do not believe in gambling.

_____ 15. I find it necessary to plan my finances and keep a budget.

_____ 16. I let people take advantage of me.

_____ 17. I hate any kind of schedule or routine.

_____ 18. I usually meet deadlines with no trouble.

_____ 19. I am familiar with basic first-aid practices.

_____ 20. Even when I have to get up early, I like to stay up late.

_____ 21. I insist on traveling safely rather than quickly.

_____ 22. I have my car serviced regularly.

_____ 23. People tell me I am disorganized.

_____ 24. It is important to get revenge when someone does you wrong.

_____ 25. Sometimes I don't seem to care what happens to me.

_____ 26. I like to play poker for high stakes.

_____ 27. I smoke over a pack of cigarettes a day.

_____ 28. I have frequently fallen in love with the wrong person.

_____ 29. I just don't know where my money goes.

_____ 30. Wearing a helmet ruins the fun of a motorcycle ride.

_____ 31. I take care to eat a balanced diet.

_____ 32. Lots of laws seem made to be broken.

_____ 33. I am almost always on time.

_____ 34. I like jobs with an element of danger.

_____ 35. I often walk out in the middle of an argument.

_____ 36. Often I don't take very good care of myself.

_____ 37. I rarely put things off.

_____ 38. I speak my mind even when it's not in my best interest.

_____ 39. I usually follow through on projects.

_____ 40. I've made positive contributions to my community.

_____ 41. I make promises that I don't keep.

_____ 42. An occasional fight makes a guy more of a man.

_____ 43. I always do what my doctor or dentist recommends.

_____ 44. I know the various warning signs of cancer.

_____ 45. I usually call a doctor when I'm sure I'm becoming ill.

_____ 46. I maintain an up-to-date address/phone book.

_____ 47. I sometimes forget important appointments I wanted to keep.

_____ 48. I drink two or fewer cups of coffee a day.

_____ 49. It's easy to get a raw deal from life.

_____ 50. I eat too much.

_____ 51. I often skip meals.

_____ 52. I don't usually lock my house or apartment door.

_____ 53. I know who to call in an emergency.

_____ 54. I can drink more alcohol than most of my friends.

_____ 55. The dangers from using contraceptives are greater than the dangers from not using them.

_____ 56. I seem to keep making the same mistakes.

_____ 57. I have my eyes examined at least once a year.

_____ 58. I lose often when I gamble for money.

_____ 59. I leave on an outdoor light when I know I'll be coming home late.

_____ 60. Using contraceptives is too much trouble.

_____ 61. I often use nonprescription medicines (aspirin, laxatives, etc.).

_____ 62. I do things I know will turn out badly.

_____ 63. When I was in high school, I was considered a good student.

_____ 64. I have trouble keeping up with bills and paperwork.

_____ 65. I rarely misplace even small sums of money.

_____ 66. I am frequently late for important things.

_____ 67. I frequently don't do boring things I'm supposed to do.

_____ 68. I feel really good when I'm drinking alcohol.

_____ 69. Sometimes when I don't have anything to drink, I think about how good some booze would taste.

_____ 70. It's really satisfying to inhale a cigarette.

_____ 71. I like to smoke.

_____ 72. I believe that saving money gives a person a real sense of accomplishment.

_____ 73. I like to exercise.

Source: Kelley et al. (1985).

## Scoring the Scale

The scoring instructions are different for males and females. The 73 items you just responded to actually represent two overlapping 52-item scales for each sex.

**Females:** Convert your letter responses to numbers from 1 to 5 (A = 1, B = 2, C = 3, D = 4, E = 5) for items 5, 8, 11, 15, 18, 19, 21, 22, 31, 33, 37, 39, 40, 43, 44, 45, 46, 53, and 63. Convert your responses in the opposite way (A = 5, B = 4, C = 3, D = 2, E = I) for items 1, 2, 6, 7, 9, 10, 12, 16, 17, 20, 23, 24, 25, 26, 28, 29, 30, 32, 36, 38, 41, 47, 49, 54, 56, 58, 60, 61, 62, 64, 66, 67, and 69. You should now have 52 items for which you have a number recorded instead of a letter. Add up these numbers, and the total is your score on the Chronic Self-Destructiveness Scale (CSDS).

**Males:** Convert your letter responses to numbers from 1 to 5 (A = 1, B = 2, C = 3, D = 4, E = 5) for items 4, 14, 18, 21, 22, 39, 40, 45, 48, 53, 57, 59, 63, 65, 72, and 73. Convert your responses in the opposite way (A = 5, B = 4, C = 3, D = 2, E = I) for items 2, 3, 10, 12, 13, 17, 25, 26, 27, 28, 29, 30, 32, 34, 35, 36, 41, 42, 47, 49, 50, 51, 52, 54, 55, 56, 58, 60, 62, 64, 66, 67, 68, 69, 70, and 71. You should now have 52 items for which you have a number recorded instead of a letter. Add up these numbers, and the total is your score on the Chronic Self-Destructiveness Scale (CSDS).

My score _____

## What the Scale Measures

Developed by Kathryn Kelley and associates (Kelley et al., 1985), this scale measures your tendency to behave in a self-destructive manner. Kelley et al. (1985) defined chronic self-destructiveness as a generalized tendency to engage in acts that increase the likelihood of future negative consequences and/or decrease the likelihood of future positive consequences. In other words, chronic self-destructiveness involves behavior that probably will be detrimental to one's well-being in the long run. This self-destructive quality is viewed as an aspect of personality that may underlie a diverse array of counterproductive, often health-impairing habits.

In their initial series of studies, Kelley et al. (1985) administered their scale to twelve groups of undergraduates, a group of businesswomen, and a group of hospital patients. In comparison to people with low scores, high scorers on the CSDS were more likely to (a) report having cheated in classes, (b) have violated traffic laws, (c) have indulged in drug or alcohol abuse meriting treatment, (d) recall a rebellious stage in adolescence, and (e) have postponed important medical tests.

## Interpreting Your Score

Our norms are based on 234 female and 168 male undergraduates studied by Kelley et al. (1985). In light of the age trends mentioned above, these norms may not be appropriate for older students.

*Norms*

| | Females | Males |
|---|---|---|
| **High score:** | 157–260 | 158–260 |
| **Intermediate score:** | 105–156 | 97–157 |
| **Low score:** | 52–104 | 52–96 |

# EXERCISE 5.2 *Self-Reflection:* How Do Your Health Habits Rate?

| | Almost Always | Sometimes | Almost Never |
|---|---|---|---|
| **Eating Habits** | | | |
| 1. I eat a variety of foods each day, such as fruits and vegetables, whole-grain breads and cereals, lean meats, dairy products, dry peas and beans, and nuts and seeds. | 4 | 1 | 0 |
| 2. I limit the amount of fat, saturated fat, and cholesterol I eat (including fat on meats, eggs, butter, cream, shortenings, and organ meats such as liver). | 2 | 1 | 0 |
| 3. I limit the amount of salt I eat by cooking with only small amounts, not adding salt at the table, and avoiding salty snacks. | 2 | 1 | 0 |
| 4. I avoid eating too much sugar (especially frequent snacks of sticky candy or soft drinks). | 2 | 1 | 0 |

*Eating Habits Score:*_____

| | Almost Always | Sometimes | Almost Never |
|---|---|---|---|
| **Exercise/Fitness** | | | |
| 1. I maintain a desired weight, avoiding overweight and underweight. | 3 | 1 | 0 |
| 2. I do vigorous exercises for 15 to 30 minutes at least three times a week (examples include running, swimming, and brisk walking). | 3 | 1 | 0 |
| 3. I do exercises that enhance my muscle tone for 15 to 30 minutes at least three times a week (examples include yoga and calisthenics). | 2 | 1 | 0 |
| 4. I use part of my leisure time participating in individual, family, or team activities that increase my level of fitness (such as gardening, bowling, golf, and baseball). | 2 | 1 | 0 |

*Exercise/Fitness Score:* _____

| | Almost Always | Sometimes | Almost Never |
|---|---|---|---|
| **Alcohol and Drugs** | | | |
| 1. I avoid drinking alcoholic beverages or I drink no more than one or two drinks a day. | 4 | 1 | 0 |
| 2. I avoid using alcohol or other drugs (especially illegal drugs) as a way of handling stressful situations or the problems in my life. | 2 | 1 | 0 |
| 3. I am careful not to drink alcohol when taking certain medicines (for exampie, medicine for sleeping, pain, colds, and allergies). | 2 | 1 | 0 |
| 4. I read and follow the label directions when using prescribed and over-the-counter drugs. | 2 | 1 | 0 |

*Alcohol and Drugs Score:* _____

Source: Adapted from the U.S. Department of Health and Human Services (1981).

## What Your Scores Mean:

| 9–10 | Excellent |
|---|---|
| 6–8 | Good |
| 3–5 | Mediocre |
| 0–2 | Poor |

Do any of your scores surprise you? Why?

# Chapter 6 The Self

## EXERCISE 6.1  *Self-Assessment:* Self-Monitoring Scale

### Instructions

The statements below concern your personal reactions to a number of situations. No two statements are exactly alike, so consider each statement carefully before answering. If a statement is true or mostly true as applied to you, mark T as your answer. If a statement is false or not usually true as applied to you, mark F as your answer. It is important that you answer as frankly and as honestly as you can. Record your responses in the spaces provided on the left.

### The Scale

_____  1. I find it hard to imitate the behavior of other people.

_____  2. My behavior is usually an expression of my true inner feelings, attitudes, and beliefs.

_____  3. At parties and social gatherings, I do not attempt to do or say things that others will like.

_____  4. I can only argue for ideas I already believe.

_____  5. I can make impromptu speeches even on topics about which I have almost no information.

_____  6. I guess I put on a show to impress or entertain people.

_____  7. When I am uncertain how to act in a social situation, I look to the behavior of others for cues.

_____  8. I would probably make a good actor.

_____  9. I rarely need the advice of my friends to choose movies, books, or music.

_____ 10. I sometimes appear to others to be experiencing deeper emotions than I actually am.

_____ 11. I laugh more when I watch a comedy with others than when alone.

_____ 12. In a group of people I am rarely the center of attention.

_____ 13. In different situations and with different people, I often act like very different persons.

_____ 14. I am not particularly good at making other people like me.

_____ 15. Even if I am not enjoying myself, I often pretend to be having a good time.

_____ 16. I'm not always the person I appear to be.

_____ 17. I would not change my opinions (or the way I do things) in order to please someone else or win their favor.

_____ 18. I have considered being an entertainer.

_____ 19. In order to get along and be liked, I tend to be what people expect me to be rather than anything else.

_____ 20. I have never been good at games like charades or improvisational acting.

_____ 21. I have trouble changing my behavior to suit different people and different situations.

_____ 22. At a party, I let others keep the jokes and stories going.

_____ 23. I feel a bit awkward in company and do not show up quite so well as I should.

_____ 24. I can look anyone in the eye and tell a lie with a straight face (if for a right end).

_____ 25. I may deceive people by being friendly when I really dislike them.

Source: Snyder (1974).

### Scoring the Scale

The scoring key is reproduced below. You should circle your response of true or false each time it corresponds to the keyed response below. Add up the number of responses you circle. This total is your score on the Self-Monitoring Scale. Record your score below.

| | | | | |
|---|---|---|---|---|
| 1. False | 6. True | 11. True | 16. True | 21. False |
| 2. False | 7. True | 12. False | 17. False | 22. False |
| 3. False | 8. True | 13. True | 18. True | 23. False |
| 4. False | 9. False | 14. False | 19. True | 24. True |
| 5. True | 10. True | 15. True | 20. False | 25. True |

My Score _____

### What the Scale Measures

Developed by Mark Snyder (1974), the Self-Monitoring (SM) Scale measures the extent to which you consciously use impression management strategies in social interactions. Basically, the scale assesses the degree to which you manipulate the nonverbal signals that you send to others and the degree to which you adjust your behavior to situational demands. Research shows that some people work harder at managing their public images than others do.

In his original study, Snyder (1974) reported very reasonable test-retest reliability (.83 for one month) and, for an initial study, provided ample evidence regarding the scale's validity. In assessing the validity of the scale, he found that in comparison to low SM subjects, high SM subjects were rated by peers as being better at emotional self-control and better at figuring out how to behave appropriately in new social situations. Furthermore, Snyder found that stage actors tended to score higher on the scale than under-graduates, as one would expect. Additionally, Ickes and Barnes (1977) summarize evidence that high SM people are (1) very sensitive to situational cues, (2) particularly skilled at detecting deception on the part of others, and (3) especially insightful about how to influence the emotions of others.

### Interpreting Your Score

Our norms are based on guidelines provided by Ickes and Barnes (1977). The divisions are based on data from 207 undergraduate subjects.

*Norms*

| | |
|---|---|
| **High score:** | 15–22 |
| **Intermediate score:** | 9–14 |
| **Low score:** | 0–8 |

Below you will find a list of 15 traits, each portrayed on a 9-point continuum. Mark with an X where you think you fall on each trait. Try to be candid and accurate; these marks will collectively describe a portion of your self-concept. When you are finished, go back and circle where you *wish* you could be on each dimension. These marks describe your self-ideal. Finally, in the spaces on the right, indicate the size of the discrepancy between self-concept and self-ideal for each trait (subtract one score from the other).

**1.** Decisive                                                Indecisive   _____
9     8     7     6     5     4     3     2     1

**2.** Anxious                                                   Relaxed   _____
9     8     7     6     5     4     3     2     1

**3.** Easily influenced                              Independent thinker   _____
9     8     7     6     5     4     3     2     1

**4.** Very intelligent                               Less intelligent   _____
9     8     7     6     5     4     3     2     1

**5.** In good physical shape                      In poor physical shape   _____
9     8     7     6     5     4     3     2     1

**6.** Undependable                                 Dependable   _____
9     8     7     6     5     4     3     2     1

**7.** Deceitful                                             Honest   _____
9     8     7     6     5     4     3     2     1

**8.** A leader                                        A follower   _____
9     8     7     6     5     4     3     2     1

**9.** Unambitious                                    Ambitious   _____
9     8     7     6     5     4     3     2     1

**10.** Self-confident                                  Insecure   _____
9     8     7     6     5     4     3     2     1

**11.** Conservative                                 Adventurous   _____
9     8     7     6     5     4     3     2     1

**12.** Extraverted                                    Introverted   _____
9     8     7     6   ·  5     4     3     2     1

**13.** Physically attractive                      Physically unattractive   _____
9     8     7     6     5     4     3     2     1

**14.** Lazy                                         Hardworking   _____
9     8     7     6     5     4     3     2     1

**15.** Funny                                  Little sense of humor   _____
9     8     7     6     5     4     3     2     1

Overall, how would you describe the discrepancy between your self-concept and your self-ideal (large, moderate, small, large on a few dimensions)?

How do sizable gaps on any of the traits affect your self-esteem?

Do you feel that any of the gaps exist because you have had others' ideals imposed on you or because you have thoughtlessly accepted others' ideals?

# Chapter 7 Social Thinking and Social Influence

**EXERCISE 7.1** *Self-Assessment:* **Argumentativeness Scale**

## Instructions

This questionnaire contains statements about arguing controversial issues. Indicate how often each statement is true for you personally by placing the appropriate number in the blank to the left of the statement:

| 1 | 2 | 3 | 4 | 5 |
|---|---|---|---|---|
| Almost Never True | Rarely True | Occasionally True | Often True | Almost Always True |

## The Scale

_____ 1. While in an argument, I worry that the person I am arguing with will form a negative impression of me.

_____ 2. Arguing over controversial issues improves my intelligence.

_____ 3. I enjoy avoiding arguments.

_____ 4. I am energetic and enthusiastic when I argue.

_____ 5. Once I finish an argument I promise myself that I will not get into another.

_____ 6. Arguing with a person creates more problems for me than it solves.

_____ 7. I have a pleasant, good feeling when I win a point in an argument.

_____ 8. When I finish arguing with someone I feel nervous and upset.

_____ 9. I enjoy a good argument over a controversial issue.

_____ 10. I get an unpleasant feeling when I realize I am about to get into an argument.

_____ 11. I enjoy defending my point of view on an issue.

_____ 12. I am happy when I keep an argument from happening.

_____ 13. I do not like to miss the opportunity to argue a controversial issue.

_____ 14. I prefer being with people who rarely disagree with me.

_____ 15. I consider an argument an exciting intellectual challenge.

_____ 16. I find myself unable to think of effective points during an argument.

_____ 17. I feel refreshed and satisfied after an argument on a controversial issue.

_____ 18. I have the ability to do well in an argument.

_____ 19. I try to avoid getting into arguments.

_____ 20. I feel excitement when I expect that a conversation I am in is leading to an argument.

Source: Infante & Rancer (1982).

## Scoring the Scale

Add up the numbers that you have recorded for items 1, 3, 5, 6, 8, 10, 12, 14, 16, and 19. This total reflects your tendency to avoid getting into arguments. Next, add up the numbers that you have recorded for items 2, 4, 7, 9, 11, 13, 15, 17, 18, and 20. This total reflects your tendency to approach argumentative situations. Record these subtotals in the spaces below. Subtract your avoidance score from your approach score to arrive at your overall score.

_____  −  _____  =  _____

**Approach score**    **Avoidance score**    **Total score**

## What the Scale Measures

This questionnaire measures an aspect of your social influence behavior. Specifically, it assesses your tendency to argue with others in persuasive efforts. Persons who score high on this scale are not bashful about tackling controversial issues, are willing to attack others verbally to make their points, and are less compliant than the average person. Developed by Infante and Rancer (1982), this scale has high test-retest reliability (.91 for a period of one week). Examinations of the scale's validity show that it correlates well with other measures of communication tendencies and with friends' ratings of subjects' argumentativeness.

## Interpreting Your Score

Our norms are based on the responses of over 800 undergraduate subjects studied by Infante and Rancer (1982).

*Norms*

| | |
|---|---|
| **High score:** | 16 and above |
| **Intermediate score:** | 6 to 15 |
| **Low score:** | 7 and below |

# EXERCISE 7.2 *Self-Reflection:* **Can You Identify Your Prejudicial Stereotypes?**

1. List and briefly describe examples of three prejudicial stereotypes that you hold or have held at one time.

    Example 1:

    Example 2:

    Example 3:

2. Try to identify the sources (family, friends, media, etc.) of each of these stereotypes.

    Example 1:

    Example 2:

    Example 3:

3. For each stereotype, how much actual interaction have you had with the stereotyped group, and has this interaction affected your views?

    Example 1:

    Example 2:

    Example 3:

4. Can you think of any ways in which the fundamental attribution error or defensive attribution has contributed to these stereotypes?

    Fundamental attribution error:

    Defensive attribution:

# Chapter 8 Interpersonal Communication

**EXERCISE 8.1** *Self-Assessment:* **Opener Scale**

## Instructions

For each statement, indicate your degree of agreement or disagreement, using the scale shown below.
Record your responses in the spaces on the left.

4 = I strongly agree
3 = I slightly agree
2 = I am certain
1 = I slightly disagree
0 = I strongly disagree

## The Scale

_____ 1. People frequently tell me about themselves.

_____ 2. I've been told that I'm a good listener.

_____ 3. I'm very accepting of others.

_____ 4. People trust me with their secrets.

_____ 5. I easily get people to "open up."

_____ 6. People feel relaxed around me.

_____ 7. I enjoy listening to people.

_____ 8. I'm sympathetic to people's problems.

_____ 9. I encourage people to tell me how they are feeling.

_____10. I can keep people talking about themselves.

Source: Miller, Berg, & Archer (1983).

## Scoring the Scale

This scale is easy to score! Simply add up the numbers that you have recorded in the spaces on the left. This total is your score on the Opener Scale.

**My Score** _____

## What the Scale Measures

Devised by Lynn Miller, John Berg, and Richard Archer (1983), the Opener Scale is intended to measure your perception of your ability to get others to "open up" around you. In other words, the scale assesses your tendency to elicit intimate self-disclosure from people. The items assess your perceptions of (a) others' reactions to you ("People feel relaxed around me"), (b) your interest in listening ("I enjoy listening to people"), and (c) your interpersonal skills ("I can keep people talking about themselves").

In spite of its brevity, the scale has reasonable test-retest reliability (.69 over a period of six weeks). Correlations with other personality measures were modest, but in the expected directions. For instance, scores on the Opener Scale correlate positively with a measure of empathy and negatively with a measure of shyness. Further evidence for the validity of the scale was obtained in a laboratory study of interactions between same-sex strangers. Subjects who scored high on the scale compared to those who scored low elicited more self-disclosure from people who weren't prone to engage in much disclosure.

## Interpreting Your Score

Our norms are based on the original sample of 740 undergraduates studied by Miller, Berg, and Archer (1983). They found a small but statistically significant difference between males and females.

*Norms*

|  | Females | Males |
|---|---|---|
| **High score:** | 35–40 | 33–40 |
| **Intermediate score:** | 26–34 | 23–32 |
| **Low score:** | 0–25 | 0–22 |

# EXERCISE 8.2  *Self-Reflection:* How Do You Feel About Self-Disclosure?

This exercise is intended to make you think about your self-disclosure behavior. Begin by finishing the incomplete sentences below (adapted from Egan, 1977). Go through the sentences fairly quickly; do not ponder your responses too long. There are no right or wrong answers.

**1.** I dislike people who . . .

**2.** Those who really know me . . .

**3.** When I let someone know something I don't like about myself . . .

**4.** When I'm in a group of strangers . . .

**5.** I envy . . .

**6.** I get hurt when . . .

**7.** I daydream about . . .

**8.** Few people know that I . . .

**9.** One thing I really dislike about myself is . . .

**10.** When I share my values with someone . . .

Based on your responses to the incomplete sentences, do you feel you engage in the right amount of self-disclosure? Too little? Too much?

In general, what prevents you from engaging in self-disclosure?

Are there particular topics on which you find it difficult to be self-disclosing?

Are you the recipient of much self-disclosure from others, or do people have difficulty opening up to you?

# Chapter 9 Friendship and Love

**EXERCISE 9.1** *Self-Assessment:* **Social Avoidance and Distress Scale**

## Instructions

The statements below inquire about your personal reactions to a variety of situations. Consider each statement carefully. Then indicate whether the statement is true or false in regard to your typical behavior. Record your responses (T or F) in the space provided on the left.

## The Scale

_____ 1. I feel relaxed even in unfamiliar social situations.

_____ 2. I try to avoid situations that force me to be very sociable.

_____ 3. It is easy for me to relax when I am with strangers.

_____ 4. I have no particular desire to avoid people.

_____ 5. I often find social occasions upsetting.

_____ 6. I usually feel calm and comfortable at social occasions.

_____ 7. I am usually at ease when talking to someone of the opposite sex.

_____ 8. I try to avoid talking to people unless I know them well.

_____ 9. If the chance comes to meet new people, I often take it.

_____ 10. I often feel nervous or tense in casual get-togethers in which both sexes are present.

_____ 11. I am usually nervous with people unless I know them well.

_____ 12. I usually feel relaxed when I am with a group of people.

_____ 13. I often want to get away from people.

_____ 14. I usually feel uncomfortable when I am in a group of people I don't know.

_____ 15. I usually feel relaxed when I meet someone for the first time.

_____ 16. Being introduced to people makes me tense and nervous.

_____ 17. Even though a room is full of strangers, I may enter it anyway.

_____ 18. I would avoid walking up and joining a large group of people.

_____ 19. When my superiors want to talk with me, I talk willingly.

_____ 20. I often feel on edge when I am with a group of people.

_____ 21. I tend to withdraw from people.

_____ 22. I don't mind talking to people at parties or social gatherings.

_____ 23. I am seldom at ease in a large group of people.

_____ 24. I often think up excuses in order to avoid social engagements.

_____ 25. I sometimes take the responsibility for introducing people to each other.

_____ 26. I try to avoid formal social occasions.

_____ 27. I usually go to whatever social engagements I have.

_____ 28. I find it easy to relax with other people.

Source: Watson & Friend (1969)

## Scoring the Scale

The scoring key is reproduced below. Circle your true or false response each time it corresponds to the keyed response below. Add up the number of responses you circle, and this total is your score on the Social Avoidance and Distress (SAD) Scale. Record your score below.

| | | | |
|---|---|---|---|
| 1. False | 8. True | 15. False | 22. False |
| 2. True | 9. False | 16. True | 23. True |
| 3. False | 10. True | 17. False | 24. True |
| 4. False | 11. True | 18. True | 25. False |
| 5. True | 12. False | 19. False | 26. True |
| 6. False | 13. True | 20. True | 27. False |
| 7. False | 14. True | 21. True | 28. False |

**My Score** _____

## What the Scale Measures

As its name implies, this scale measures avoidance and distress in social interactions. David Watson and Ronald Friend (1969) developed the scale to assess the extent to which individuals experience discomfort, fear, and anxiety in social situations and the extent to which they therefore try to evade many kinds of social encounters. To check the validity of the scale, they used it to predict subjects' social behavior in experimentally contrived situations. As projected, they found that people who scored high on the SAD Scale were less willing than low scorers to participate in a group discussion. The high scorers also reported anticipating more anxiety about their participation in the discussion than the low scorers. Additionally, Watson and Friend found a strong negative correlation ($-.76$) between the SAD and a measure of affiliation drive (the need to seek the company of others).

## Interpreting Your Score

Our norms are based on data collected by Watson and Friend (1969) on over 200 university students.

*Norms*

| | |
|---|---|
| **High score:** | 16–28 |
| **Intermediate score:** | 6–15 |
| **Low score:** | 0–5 |

# EXERCISE 9.2 *Self-Reflection:* How Do You Relate to Friends?

The following questions (adapted from Egan, 1977) are designed to help you think about how you deal with friendships.

**1.** Do you have many friends or very few?

**2.** Whether many or few, do you usually spend a lot of time with your friends?

**3.** What do you like in other people—that is, what makes you choose them as friends?

**4.** Are the people you hang out with like you or different from you? Or are they in some ways like you and in other ways different? How?

**5.** Do you like to control others, to get them to do things your way? Do you let others control you? Do you give in to others much of the time?

**6.** Are there ways in which your friendships are one-sided?

**7.** What would make your friendships more satisfying?

# Chapter 10 Marriage and Intimate Relationships

**EXERCISE 10.1** *Self-Assessment:* **Self-Report Jealousy Scale**

## Instructions

The following scale lists some situations in which you may have been involved, or in which you could be involved. Rate them with regard to how you would feel if you were confronted with the situation by circling a number that corresponds to one of the reactions shown on the right. Do not omit any items.

| 0 | 1 | 2 | 3 | 4 |
|---|---|---|---|---|
| Pleased | Mildly Upset | Upset | Very Upset | Extremely Upset |

## The Scale

_____ 1. Your partner expresses the desire that you both develop other romantic relationships.

_____ 2. Your partner spends increasingly more time at work with a co-employee you feel could be sexually attractive to your partner.

_____ 3. Your partner suddenly shows an interest in going to a party when he or she finds out that someone will be there with whom he or she has been romantically involved previously.

_____ 4. At a party, your partner hugs someone other than you.

_____ 5. You notice your partner repeatedly looking at another.

_____ 6. Your partner spends increasingly more time in outside activities and hobbies in which you are not included.

_____ 7. At a party, your partner kisses someone you do not know.

_____ 8. Your boss, with whom you have had a good working relationship in the past, now seems to be more interested in the work of a co-worker.

_____ 9. Your partner goes to a bar several evenings without you.

_____ 10. Your partner recently received a promotion, and the new position requires a great deal of travel, business dinners, and parties, most of which you are not invited to attend.

_____ 11. At a party, your partner dances with someone you do not know.

_____ 12. You and a co-worker worked very hard on an extremely important project. However, your boss gave your co-worker full credit for it.

_____ 13. Someone flirts with your partner.

_____ 14. At a party, your partner repeatedly kisses someone you do not know.

_____ 15. Your partner has sexual relations with someone else.

_____ 16. Your brother or sister is given more freedom, such as staying up later, or driving the car.

_____ 17. Your partner comments to you on how attractive another person is.

_____ 18. While at a social gathering of a group of friends, your partner spends little time talking to you, but engages the others in animated conversation.

_____ 19. Grandparents visit your family, and they seem to devote most of their attention to a brother or sister instead of you.

_____ 20. Your partner flirts with someone else.

_____ 21. Your brother or sister seems to be receiving more affection and/or attention from your parents.

_____ 22. You have just discovered your partner is having an affair with someone at work.

_____ 23. The person who has been your assistant for a number of years at work decides to take a similar position with someone else.

_____ 24. The group to which you belong appears to be leaving you out of plans, activities, etc.

_____ 25. Your best friend suddenly shows interest in doing things with someone else.

Source: Bringle et at. (1979)

## Scoring the Scale

Give yourself 4 points for every item where your response was "extremely upset," 3 points for every item where your response was "very upset," 2 points for every item where your response was "upset," 1 point for every item where your response was "mildly upset," and 0 for every item where your response was "pleased." In other words, add up the numbers you recorded. This total is your score on the Self-Report Jealousy Scale.

**My Score _____**

## What the Scale Measures

As its name indicates, this scale measures your tendency to get jealous in a variety of situations. It does not measure romantic jealousy exclusively, as ten of the items relate to nonromantic jealousy. Hence, it assesses jealousy in a general way, with a heavy emphasis on romantic relationships.

This scale, which was developed by Bringle, et al. (1979), has adequate test-retest reliability. Correlations with other personality traits have been examined in efforts to demonstrate its validity. People who score high on the scale tend to have low self-esteem, to be anxious, to see the world in negative terms, and to feel they have little control over their lives. These are interesting findings, although more research is needed to better validate this instrument.

## Interpreting Your Score

Our norms are based on the sample of 162 college students studied by Bringle et al. (1979). They may be inappropriate for older, non-traditional college students.

*Norms*

| | |
|---|---|
| **High score:** | 83–100 |
| **Intermediate score:** | 59–82 |
| **Low score:** | 0–58 |

## EXERCISE 10.2 *Self-Reflection:* Thinking Through Your Attitudes About Marriage and Cohabitation

1. Regardless of your current marital status, what are your ideal criteria for selecting a mate?

2. How do you know if you are really ready for marriage?

3. What areas of self-awareness or knowledge of self do you feel you need to explore before you make a long-term commitment to a relationship?

4. In what ways is cohabitation a realistic preparation for marriage, and in what ways is it not?

# Chapter 11 Gender and Behavior

**EXERCISE 11.1** *Self-Assessment:* **Personal Attributes Questionnaire (PAQ)**

## Instructions

The items below inquire about what kind of a person you think you are. Each item consists of a pair of characteristics, with the letters A–E in between. For example:

Not at all artistic      A      B      C      D      E      Very artistic

Each pair describes contradictory characteristics—that is, you cannot be both at the same time, such as very artistic and not at all artistic.

The letters form a scale between the two extremes. You are to enter a letter that describes where you fall on the scale. For example, if you think you have no artistic ability, you would enter A. If you think you are pretty good, you might enter D. If you are only medium, you might enter C, and so forth.

## The Scale

| | | | | | | | |
|---|---|---|---|---|---|---|---|
| _____ | 1. | Not at all aggressive | A | B | C | D | E | Very aggressive |
| _____ | 2. | Not at all independent | A | B | C | D | E | Very independent |
| _____ | 3. | Not at all emotional | A | B | C | D | E | Very emotional |
| _____ | 4. | Very submissive | A | B | C | D | E | Very dominant |
| _____ | 5. | Not at all excitable in a major crisis | A | B | C | D | E | Very excitable in a major crisis |
| _____ | 6. | Very passive | A | B | C | D | E | Very active |
| _____ | 7. | Not at all able to devote self completely to others | A | B | C | D | E | Able to devote self completely to others |
| _____ | 8. | Very rough | A | B | C | D | E | Very gentle |
| _____ | 9. | Not at all helpful to others | A | B | C | D | E | Very helpful to others |
| _____ | 10. | Not at all competitive | A | B | C | D | E | Very competitive |
| _____ | 11. | Very home oriented | A | B | C | D | E | Very worldly |
| _____ | 12. | Not at all kind | A | B | C | D | E | Very kind |
| _____ | 13. | Indifferent to others' approval | A | B | C | D | E | Highly needful of others' approval |
| _____ | 14. | Feelings not easily hurt | A | B | C | D | E | Feelings easily hurt |
| _____ | 15. | Not at all aware of feelings of others | A | B | C | D | E | Very aware of feelings of others |
| _____ | 16. | Can make decisions easily | A | B | C | D | E | Have difficulty making decisions |
| _____ | 17. | Give up very easily | A | B | C | D | E | Never give up easily |
| _____ | 18. | Never cry | A | B | C | D | E | Cry very easily |
| _____ | 19. | Not at all self-confident | A | B | C | D | E | Very self-confident |
| _____ | 20. | Feel very inferior | A | B | C | D | E | Feel very superior |
| _____ | 21. | Not at all understanding of others | A | B | C | D | E | Very understanding of others |
| _____ | 22. | Very cold in relations with others | A | B | C | D | E | Very warm in relations with others |
| _____ | 23. | Very little need for security | A | B | C | D | E | Very strong need for security |
| _____ | 24. | Go to pieces under pressure | A | B | C | D | E | Stand up well under pressure |

Source: Spence & Helmreich (1978)

## Scoring the Scale

The Personal Attributes Questionnaire (PAQ) is made up of three 8-item subscales, but we are only going to compute scores for two of these subscales, so the first step is to eliminate the 8 items from the unused subscale. Put an X in the spaces to the left of the items for the following items: 1, 4, 5, 11, 13, 14, 18, and 23. These items belong to the subscale that we won't be using, and they can be ignored. Of the remaining items, one (item 16) is reverse-scored as follows: If you circled A, enter 4 in the space to the left of the item if you circled B, enter 3; if you circled C, enter 2; if you circled D, enter 1; and if you circled E, enter 0. All the rest of the items are scored in the following manner: A = 0, B = 1, C = 2, D = 3, and E = 4. Based on the responses you circled, enter the appropriate numbers for the remaining items in the spaces to the left of the items.

The next step is to compute your scores on the femininity and masculinity subscales of the PAQ. To compute your score on the *femininity* subscale, add up the numbers next to items 3, 7, 8, 9, 12, 15, 21, and 22, and enter your score in the space below. To compute your score on the *masculinity* subscale, add up the numbers next to items 2, 6, 10, 16, 17, 19, 20, and 24, and enter your score in the space below.

**My score on the femininity subscale** _____

**My score on the masculinity subscale** _____

## What the Scale Measures

Devised by Janet Spence and Robert Helmreich (1978), the PAQ assesses masculinity and femininity in terms of respondents' self-perceived possession of various personality traits that are stereotypically believed to differentiate the sexes. The authors emphasize that the PAQ taps only limited aspects of sex roles: certain self-assertive/instrumental traits traditionally associated with masculinity and certain interpersonal/expressive traits traditionally associated with femininity. Although the PAQ should not be viewed as a global measure of masculinity and femininity, it has been widely used in research to provide a rough classification of subjects in terms of their gender-role identity. As explained in your text, people who score high in both masculinity and femininity are said to be androgynous. People who score high in femininity and low in masculinity are said to be feminine sex-typed. Those who score high in masculinity and low in femininity are characterized as masculine sex-typed, and those who score low on both dimensions are said to be sex-role undifferentiated.

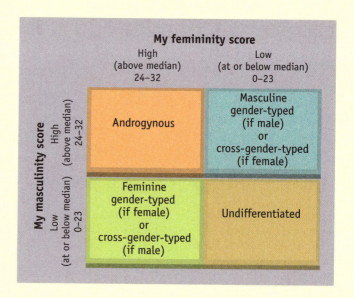

## Interpreting Your Score

You can use the chart here to classify yourself in terms of gender-role identity. Our norms are based on a sample of 715 college students studied by Spence and Helmreich (1978). The cutoffs for "high" scores on the masculinity and femininity subscales are the medians for each scale. Obviously, these are arbitrary cutoffs, and results may be misleading for people who score very close to the median on either scale, as a difference of a point or two could change their classification. Hence, if either of your scores is within a couple of points of the median, you should view your gender-role classification as tentative. Also, keep in mind that the perception of some of these traits has changed over time. As mentioned in your text, some of the traditional masculine traits aren't viewed as strictly masculine today.

**My classification** _____

What percentage of subjects falls into each of the four gender-role categories? The exact breakdown will vary depending on the nature of the sample, but Spence and Helmreich (1978) reported the following distribution for their sample of 715 college students.

| Category | Males | Females |
|---|---|---|
| Androgynous | 25% | 35% |
| Feminine | 8% | 32% |
| Masculine | 44% | 14% |
| Undifferentiated | 23% | 18% |

# EXERCISE 11.2 *Self-Reflection:* How Do You Feel About Gender Roles?

1. Can you recall any experiences that were particularly influential in shaping your attitudes about gender roles? If yes, give a couple of examples.

2. Have you ever engaged in cross-sex-typed behavior? Can you think of a couple of examples? How did people react?

3. Do you ever feel restricted by gender roles? If so, in what ways?

4. Have you ever been a victim of sex discrimination (sexism)? If so, describe the circumstances.

5. How do you think the transition in gender roles has affected you personally?

# Chapter 12 Development and Expression of Sexuality

**EXERCISE 12.1** *Self-Assessment:* **Sexuality Scale**

## Instructions

For the 30 items that follow, indicate the extent of your agreement or disagreement with each statement, using the key shown below. Record your responses in the spaces to the left of the items.

| +2 | +1 | 0 | −1 | −2 |
|----|----|----|----|----|
| Agree | Slightly Agree | Neither Agree nor Disagree | Slightly Disagree | Disagree |

## The Scale

_____ 1. I am a good sexual partner.

_____ 2. I am depressed about the sexual aspects of my life.

_____ 3. I think about sex all the time.

_____ 4. I would rate my sexual skill quite highly.

_____ 5. I feel good about my sexuality.

_____ 6. I think about sex more than anything else.

_____ 7. I am better at sex than most other people.

_____ 8. I am disappointed about the quality of my sex life.

_____ 9. I don't daydream about sexual situations.

_____ 10. I sometimes have doubts about my sexual competence.

_____ 11. Thinking about sex makes me happy.

_____ 12. I tend to be preoccupied with sex.

_____ 13. I am not very confident in sexual encounters.

_____ 14. I derive pleasure and enjoyment from sex.

_____ 15. I'm constantly thinking about having sex.

_____ 16. I think of myself as a very good sexual partner.

_____ 17. I feel down about my sex life.

_____ 18. I think about sex a great deal of the time.

_____ 19. I would rate myself low as a sexual partner.

_____ 20. I feel unhappy about my sexual relationships.

_____ 21. I seldom think about sex.

_____ 22. I am confident about myself as a sexual partner.

_____ 23. I feel pleased with my sex life.

_____ 24. I hardly ever fantasize about having sex.

_____ 25. I am not very confident about myself as a sexual partner.

_____ 26. I feel sad when I think about my sexual experiences.

_____ 27. I probably think about sex less often than most people.

_____ 28. I sometimes doubt my sexual competence.

_____ 29. I am not discouraged about sex.

_____ 30. I don't think about sex very often.

| Sexual Esteem | Sexual Depression | Sexual Preoccupation |
|---------------|-------------------|----------------------|
| 1. _____ | 2. _____ | 3. _____ |
| 4. _____ | 5.R _____ | 6. _____ |
| 7. _____ | 8. _____ | 9.R _____ |
| 10.R _____ | 11.R _____ | 12. _____ |
| 13.R _____ | 14.R _____ | 15. _____ |
| 16. _____ | 17. _____ | 18. _____ |
| 19.R _____ | 20. _____ | 21.R _____ |
| 22. _____ | 23.R _____ | 24. _____ |
| 25.R _____ | 26. _____ | 27.R _____ |
| 28.R _____ | 29.R _____ | 30.R _____ |

**My Scores**

## What the Scale Measures

Developed by William Snell and Dennis Papini (1989), the Sexuality Scale measures three aspects of your sexual identity. The Sexual Esteem subscale measures your tendency to evaluate yourself in a positive way in terms of your capacity to relate sexually to others. The Sexual Depression subscale measures your tendency to feel saddened and discouraged by your ability to relate sexually to others. The Sexual Preoccupation subscale measures your tendency to become absorbed in thoughts about sex on a persistent basis.

Internal reliability is excellent. Thus far, the scale's validity has been examined through factor analysis, which can be used to evaluate the extent of overlap among the subscales. The factor analysis showed that the three subscales do measure independent aspects of one's sexuality.

## Scoring the Scale

To arrive at your scores on the three subscales of this questionnaire, transfer your responses into the spaces provided below. If an item number has an R next to it, this item is reverse-scored, so you should change the + or − sign in front of the number you recorded. After recording your responses, add up the numbers in each column, taking into account the algebraic sign in front of each number. The totals for each column are your scores on the three subscales of the Sexuality Scale. Record your scores at the bottom of each column.

## Interpreting Your Score

Our norms are based on Snell and Papini's (1989) sample of 296 college students drawn from a small university in the Midwest. Significant gender differences were found only on the Sexual Preoccupation subscale, so we report separate norms for males and females only for this subscale.

*Norms*

| | Sexual Esteem Both sexes | Sexual Depression Both sexes | Sexual Preoccupation Males | Females |
|---|---|---|---|---|
| **High score:** | +14 to +20 | +1 to +20 | +8 to +20 | −1 to +20 |
| **Intermediate score:** | 0 to +13 | −12 to 0 | −2 to +7 | −10 to −2 |
| **Low score:** | −20 to −1 | −20 to −13 | −20 to −3 | −20 to −11 |

**EXERCISE 12.2** *Self-Reflection:* **How Did You Acquire Your Attitudes About Sex?**

1. Who do you feel was most important in shaping your attitudes regarding sexual behavior (parents, teachers, peers, early girlfriend or boyfriend, and so forth)?

2. What was the nature of their influence?

3. If the answer to the first question was not your parents, what kind of information did you get at home? Were your parents comfortable talking about sex?

4. In childhood, were you ever made to feel shameful, guilty, or fearful about sex? How?

5. Were your parents open or secretive about their own sex lives?

6. Do you feel comfortable with your sexuality today?

# Chapter 13 Careers and Work

**EXERCISE 13.1** *Self-Assessment:* **Assertive Job-Hunting Survey**

## Instructions

This inventory is designed to provide information about the way in which you look for a job. Picture yourself in each of these job-hunting situations and indicate how likely it is that you would respond in the described manner. If you have never job-hunted before, answer according to how you would try to find a job. Please record your responses in the spaces to the left of the items. Use the following key for your responses:

| 1 | 2 | 3 | 4 | 5 | 6 |
|---|---|---|---|---|---|
| Very Unlikely | Somewhat Unlikely | Slightly Unlikely | Slightly Likely | Somewhat Likely | Very Likely |

## The Scale

_____ 1. When asked to indicate my experiences for a position, I would mention only my paid work experience.

_____ 2. If I heard someone talking about an interesting job opening, I'd be reluctant to ask for more information unless I knew the person.

_____ 3. I would ask an employer who did not have an opening if he knew of other employers who might have job openings.

_____ 4. I downplay my qualifications so that an employer won't think I'm more qualified than I really am.

_____ 5. I would rather use an employment agency to find a job than apply to employers directly.

_____ 6. Before an interview, I would contact an employee of the organization to learn more about that organization.

_____ 7. I hesitate to ask questions when I'm being interviewed for a job.

_____ 8. I avoid contacting potential employers by phone or in person because I feel they are too busy to talk with me.

_____ 9. If an interviewer were very late for my interview, I would leave or arrange for another appointment.

_____ 10. I believe an experienced employment counselor would have a better idea of what jobs I should apply for than I would have.

_____ 11. If a secretary told me that a potential employer was too busy to see me, I would stop trying to contact that employer.

_____ 12. Getting the job I want is largely a matter of luck.

_____ 13. I'd directly contact the person for whom I would be working, rather than the personnel department of an organization.

_____ 14. I am reluctant to ask professors or supervisors to write letters of recommendation for me.

_____ 15. I would not apply for a job unless I had all the qualifications listed on the published job description.

_____ 16. I would ask an employer for a second interview if I felt the first one went poorly.

_____ 17. I am reluctant to contact an organization about employment unless I know there is a job opening.

_____ 18. If I didn't get a job, I would call the employer and ask how I could improve my chances for a similar position.

_____ 19. I feel uncomfortable asking friends for job leads.

_____ 20. With the job market as tight as it is, I had better take whatever job I can get.

_____ 21. If the personnel office refused to refer me for an interview, I would directly contact the person I wanted to work for, if I felt qualified for the position.

_____ 22. I would rather interview with recruiters who come to the college campus than contact employers directly.

_____ 23. If an interviewer says "I'll contact you if there are any openings," I figure there's nothing else I can do.

_____ 24. I'd check out available job openings before deciding what kind of job I'd like to have.

_____ 25. I am reluctant to contact someone I don't know for information about career fields in which I am interested.

Source: Becker (1980).

## Scoring the Scale

To score this scale, you have to begin by reversing your responses on 18 of the items. On these items, convert the response you entered as follows: $1 = 6$, $2 = 5$, $3 = 4$, $4 = 3$, $5 = 2$, and $6 = 1$. The items to be reversed are 1, 2, 4, 5, 7, 8, 10, 11, 12, 14, 15, 17, 19, 20, 22, 23, 24, and 25. After making your reversals, add up the numbers that you have recorded for the 25 items on the scale. This total is your score on the Assertive Job-Hunting Survey.

**My Score** _____

## What the Scale Measures

Developed by Heather Becker, Susan Brown, Pat LaFitte, Mary Jo Magruder, Bob Murff, and Bill Phillips, this scale measures your job-seeking style (Becker, 1980). Some people conduct a job search in a relatively passive way—waiting for jobs to come to them. Others tend to seek jobs in a more vigorous, assertive manner. They act on their environment to procure needed information, obtain helpful contacts, and get their foot in the door at attractive companies. This scale measures your tendency to pursue jobs assertively.

Test-retest reliability for this scale is reasonable (.77 for an interval of two weeks). The scale's validity has been supported by demonstrations that subjects' scores increase as a result of training programs designed to enhance their job-hunting assertiveness. Also, those who have job-hunted before tend to score higher than those who have never job-hunted.

## Interpreting Your Score

Our norms are based on a sample of college students who had applied to a university counseling center for career-planning assistance

*Norms*

| | |
|---|---|
| **High score:** | 117–150 |
| **Intermediate score:** | 95–116 |
| **Low score:** | 0–94 |

Important vocational decisions require information. Your assignment in this exercise is to pick a vocation and research it. You should begin by reading some occupational literature. Then you should interview someone in the field. Use the outline below to summarize your findings.

1. *The nature of the work.* What are the duties and responsibilities on a day-to-day basis?

2. *Working conditions.* Is the working environment pleasant or unpleasant, low-key or high-pressure?

3. *Job entry requirements.* What kind of education and training are required to break into this occupational area?

4. *Potential earnings.* What are entry-level salaries, and how much can you hope to earn if you're exceptionally successful?

5. *Opportunities for advancement.* How do you move up in this field? Are there adequate opportunities for promotion and advancement?

6. *Intrinsic job satisfactions.* What can you derive in the way of personal satisfaction from this job?

7. *Future outlook.* How is supply and demand projected to shape up in the future for this occupational area?

# Chapter 14 Psychological Disorders

**EXERCISE 14.1** *Self-Assessment:* **Manifest Anxiety Scale**

## Instructions

The statements below inquire about your behavior and emotions. Consider each statement carefully. Then indicate whether the statement is generally true or false for you. Record your responses (T or F) in the spaces provided.

## The Scale

_____ 1. I do not tire quickly.

_____ 2. I believe I am no more nervous than most others.

_____ 3. I have very few headaches.

_____ 4. I work under a great deal of tension.

_____ 5. I frequently notice my hand shakes when I try to do something.

_____ 6. I blush no more often than others.

_____ 7. I have diarrhea once a month or more.

_____ 8. I worry quite a bit over possible misfortunes.

_____ 9. I practically never blush.

_____ 10. I am often afraid that I am going to blush.

_____ 11. My hands and feet are usually warm enough.

_____ 12. I sweat very easily even on cool days.

_____ 13. Sometimes when embarrassed, I break out in a sweat that annoys me greatly.

_____ 14. I hardly ever notice my heart pounding, and I am seldom short of breath.

_____ 15. I feel hungry almost all the time.

_____ 16. I am very seldom troubled by constipation.

_____ 17. I have a great deal of stomach trouble.

_____ 18. I have had periods in which I lost sleep over worry.

_____ 19. I am easily embarrassed.

_____ 20. I am more sensitive than most other people.

_____ 21. I frequently find myself worrying about something.

_____ 22. I wish I could be as happy as others seem to be.

_____ 23. I am usually calm and not easily upset.

_____ 24. I feel anxiety about something or someone almost all the time.

_____ 25. I am happy most of the time.

_____ 26. It makes me nervous to have to wait.

_____ 27. Sometimes I become so excited that I find it hard to get to sleep.

_____ 28. I have sometimes felt that difficulties were piling up so high that I could not overcome them.

_____ 29. I must admit that I have at times been worried beyond reason over something that really did not matter.

_____ 30. I have very few fears compared to my friends.

_____ 31. I certainly feel useless at times.

_____ 32. I find it hard to keep my mind on a task or job.

_____ 33. I am unusually self-conscious.

_____ 34. I am inclined to take things hard.

_____ 35. At times I think I am no good at all.

_____ 36. I am certainly lacking in self-confidence.

_____ 37. I sometimes feel that I am about to go to pieces.

_____ 38. I am entirely self-confident.

## Scoring the Scale

The scoring key is reproduced below. You should circle each of your true or false responses that correspond to the keyed responses. Add up the number of responses you circle, and this total is your score on the Manifest Anxiety Scale.

| | | | |
|---|---|---|---|
| **1.** False | **2.** False | **3.** False | **4.** True |
| **5.** True | **6.** False | **7.** True | **8.** True |
| **9.** False | **10.** True | **11.** False | **12.** True |
| **13.** True | **14.** False | **15.** True | **16.** False |
| **17.** True | **18.** True | **19.** True | **20.** True |
| **21.** True | **22.** True | **23.** False | **24.** True |
| **25.** False | **26.** True | **27.** True | **28.** True |
| **29.** True | **30.** False | **31.** True | **32.** True |
| **33.** True | **34.** True | **35.** True | **36.** True |
| **37.** True | **38.** False | | |

**My Score _____**

## What the Scale Measures

You just took a form of the Taylor Manifest Anxiety Scale (1953), as revised by Richard Suinn (1968). Suinn took the original 50-item scale and identified all items for which there was a social desirability bias (11) or a response set (1). He eliminated these 12 items and found that the scale's reliability and validity were not appreciably decreased. Essentially, the scale measures trait anxiety—that is, the tendency to experience anxiety in a wide variety of situations.

Hundreds of studies have been done on the various versions of the Taylor Manifest Anxiety Scale. The validity of the scale has been supported by demonstrations that various groups of psychiatric patients score higher than unselected groups of "normals" and by demonstrations that the scale correlates well with other measures of anxiety. Although the Manifest Anxiety Scale is no longer a "state of the art" measure of anxiety, it is an old classic that is relatively easy to score.

## Interpreting Your Score

Our norms are based on data collected by Suinn (1968) on 89 undergraduates who responded to the scale anonymously.

*Norms*

| | |
|---|---|
| **High score:** | 16–38 |
| **Intermediate score:** | 6–15 |
| **Low score:** | 0–5 |

**1.** List seven adjectives that you associate with people who are diagnosed as mentally ill.

**2.** If you meet someone who was once diagnosed as mentally ill, what are your immediate reactions?

**3.** List some comments about people with psychological disorders that you heard when you were a child.

**4.** Have you had any actual interactions with "mentally ill" people that have supported or contradicted your expectations?

**5.** Do you agree with the idea that psychological disorders should be viewed as an illness or disease? Defend your position.

# Chapter 15 Psychotherapy

**EXERCISE 15.1** *Self-Assessment:* **Attitudes Toward Seeking Professional Psychological Help**

## Instructions
Read each statement carefully and indicate your agreement or disagreement, using the scale below. Please express your frank opinion in responding to each statement, answering as you honestly feel or believe.

0 = Disagreement
1 = Probable disagreement
2 = Probable agreement
3 = Agreement

## The Scale

_____ 1. Although there are clinics for people with mental troubles, I would not have much faith in them.

_____ 2. If a good friend asked my advice about a mental health problem, I might recommend that he see a psychiatrist.

_____ 3. I would feel uneasy going to a psychiatrist because of what some people would think.

_____ 4. A person with a strong character can get over mental conflicts by himself, and would have little need of a psychiatrist.

_____ 5. There are times when I have felt completely lost and would have welcomed professional advice for a personal or emotional problem.

_____ 6. Considering the time and expense involved in psychotherapy, it would have doubtful value for a person like me.

_____ 7. I would willingly confide intimate matters to an appropriate person if I thought it might help me or a member of my family.

_____ 8. I would rather live with certain mental conflicts than go through the ordeal of getting psychiatric treatment.

_____ 9. Emotional difficulties, like many things, tend to work out by themselves.

_____ 10. There are certain problems that should not be discussed outside of one's immediate family.

_____ 11. A person with a serious emotional disturbance would probably feel most secure in a good mental hospital.

_____ 12. If I believed I was having a mental breakdown, my first inclination would be to get professional attention.

_____ 13. Keeping one's mind on a job is a good solution for avoiding personal worries and concerns.

_____ 14. Having been a psychiatric patient is a blot on a person's life.

_____ 15. I would rather be advised by a close friend than by a psychologist, even for an emotional problem.

_____ 16. A person with an emotional problem is not likely to solve it alone; he or she is likely to solve it with professional help.

_____ 17. I resent a person—professionally trained or not—who wants to know about my personal difficulties.

_____ 18. I would want to get psychiatric attention if I was worried or upset for a long period of time.

_____ 19. The idea of talking about problems with a psychologist strikes me as a poor way to get rid of emotional conflicts.

_____ 20. Having been mentally ill carries with it a burden of shame.

_____ 21. There are experiences in my life I would not discuss with anyone.

_____ 22. It is probably best not to know everything about oneself.

_____ 23. If I were experiencing a serious emotional crisis at this point in my life, I would be confident that I could find relief in psychotherapy.

_____ 24. There is something admirable in the attitude of a person who is willing to cope with his conflicts and fears without resorting to professional help.

_____ 25. At some future time I might want to have psychological counseling.

_____ 26. A person should work out his own problems; getting psychological counseling would be a last resort.

_____ 27. Had I received treatment in a mental hospital, I would not feel that it had to be "covered up."

_____ 28. If I thought I needed psychiatric help, I would get it no matter who knew about it.

_____ 29. It is difficult to talk about personal affairs with highly educated people such as doctors, teachers, and clergymen.

## Scoring the Scale
Begin by reversing your response (0 = 3, 1 = 2, 2 = 1, 3 = 0) for items 1, 3, 4, 6, 8, 9, 10, 13, 14, 15, 17, 19, 20, 21, 22, 24, 26, and 29. Then add up the numbers for all 29 items on the scale. This total is your score. Record your score below.

**My Score** _____

## What the Scale Measures
The scale assesses the degree to which you have favorable attitudes toward professional psychotherapy (Fischer & Turner, 1970). As discussed in your text, there are many negative stereotypes about therapy, and many people are reluctant to pursue therapy. This situation is unfortunate, because negative attitudes often prevent people from seeking therapy that could be beneficial to them.

## Interpreting Your Score
Our norms are shown below. The higher your score, the more positive your attitudes about therapy.

*Norms*
**High score:**      64–87
**Medium score:**    50–63
**Low score:**        0–49

**EXERCISE 15.2** *Self-Reflection:* **What Are Your Feelings About Therapy?**

1. What type of therapeutic approach do you think you would respond to best if you were seeking a therapist? In thinking about this question, consider not only theoretical approaches and professions, but whether you would prefer a male versus a female, individual therapy versus group therapy, and so on.

2. What personal traits would you look for in a therapist?

3. Do you have a sense of what your family beliefs are about psychotherapy and its use? If you had to articulate these beliefs in a few sentences, what would you say?

4. Before you read Chapter 15, what did you picture in your mind as happening in a therapy session? How accurate was that picture? What were some of your inaccurate perceptions about therapy?

5. Statistics show that more women seek psychotherapy than men. Why do you think this is so?

# Chapter 16 Positive Psychology

## EXERCISE 16.1 *Self-Assessment:* What Is Your Happiness Profile?

### Instructions

All of the questions below reflect statements that many people would find desirable, but answer only in terms of whether the statement describes how you actually live your life. Please be honest and accurate. Use the following scale to answer the questions:

5 = Very much like me
4 = Mostly like me
3 = Somewhat like me
2 = A little like me
1 = Not like me at all

### The Scale

_____ 1. My life serves a higher purpose.

_____ 2. Life is too short to postpone the pleasures it can provide.

_____ 3. I seek out situations that challenge my skills and abilities.

_____ 4. I keep score at life.

_____ 5. Whether at work or play, I am usually "in a zone" and not conscious of myself.

_____ 6. I am always very absorbed in what I do.

_____ 7. I am rarely distracted by what is going on around me.

_____ 8. I have a responsibility to make the world a better place.

_____ 9. My life has a lasting meaning.

_____10. No matter what I am doing, it is important for me to win.

_____11. In choosing what to do, I always take into account whether it will be pleasurable.

_____12. What I do matters to society.

_____13. I want to accomplish more than other people.

_____14. I agree with this statement: "Life is short—eat dessert first."

_____15. I love to do things that excite my senses.

_____16. I love to compete.

Source: Peterson (2006, pp. 100–103); based on Peterson, Park, & Seligman (2005).

### Scoring the Scale

Your Orientation to Pleasure score is the sum of points for questions 2, 11, 14, and 15; your Orientation to Engagement score is the sum of points for questions 3, 5, 6, and 7; your Orientation to Meaning score is the sum of points for questions 1, 8, 9, and 12; your Orientation to Victory score is the sum of points for questions 4, 10, 13, and 16.

**My Orientation to Pleasure Score** _____

**My Orientation to Engagement Score** _____

**My Orientation to Meaning Score** _____

**My Orientation to Victory Score** _____

### Interpreting Your Scores

The questionnaire measures four possible routes to happiness: through pleasure, through engagement, meaning, and victory. What is the highest score of the four? This is your dominant orientation. And what is the configuration of your scores? That is, are you "high" (> 15) on all four orientations? If so, you are oriented toward a full life and are likely to be highly satisfied. Or are you "low" (< 9) on all four orientations? If so, you may have a more empty life and are likely to be dissatisfied. You might consider doing something different—anything!—in your life. And if you are high on one or two orientations, chances are that you are satisfied with life, although you might seek further opportunities for pursuing your signature way of being happy.

# EXERCISE 16.2 *Self-Reflection:* Thinking About How You Construe Happiness

Imagine that medicine has developed a new "happiness" pill. If you take this pill everyday it will make you feel positive emotions more frequently. There are also no negative side effects, and it is inexpensive to buy. Would you take it? Why or why not?

Imagine that you have found the famous "Aladdin's Lamp" and the genie has granted you three wishes. What would you wish for? Sorry, you can't wish for more wishes.

1.

2.

3.

(a) What do your answers tell you about your idea of happiness or the good life?

(b) Are your answers based on any specific assumptions about human nature or the relationships between people and the societies they live in? What are those assumptions?

Source: Compton (2005), p. 66.